Religious Sites in America

RELIGIOUS SITES IN AMERICA

A DICTIONARY

Mary Ellen Snodgrass

ABC-CLIO

Santa Barbara, California
Denver, Colorado
Oxford, England

Library of Congress Cataloging-in-Publication Data

Snodgrass, Mary Ellen.
   Religious sites in America / Mary Ellen Snodgrass
      p.   cm.
   Includes bibliographical references and index.
      ISBN 1-57607-154-5 (alk. paper)
   1. Sacred space—United States—Encyclopedias. 2. United
States—Religion—Encyclopedias. I. Title.
   BL581.U6 S66 2000
   291.3'5'0973—dc21

                                        00-010425

06 05 04 03 02 01 00   10 9 8 7 6 5 4 3 2 1

ABC-CLIO, Inc.
130 Cremona Drive, P.O. Box 1911
Santa Barbara, California 93116-1911

This book is printed on acid-free paper ∞.

Manufactured in the United States of America

For Gordon and Marion Sperry,
to whom all God's ways are worthy
and all his people dear.

I believe there must be one who is God Himself, like the great sea, and all the rest of us, small gods and men and all, like rivers, we all come to Him in the end.
—Mary Stewart, *The Crystal Cave* (1970)

CONTENTS

Acknowledgments, xi
Preface, xiii
Introduction, xvii

Religious Sites in America

Abbey of Gethsemani, 1

Abhidhyan Yoga Institute, 4

Abyssinian Baptist Church, 5

Acoma Pueblo, 7

Aghor Ashram, 10

Air Force Academy Chapel, 11

All Saints' Chapel, 15

Amana Church Society, 17

Antelope Canyon, 20

Apostolic Church of God, 22

Aryaloka Buddhist Retreat
Center, 23

Ave Maria Grotto, 25

Badger–Two Medicine Area,
29

Bahá'i House of Worship, 30

Baron Hirsch Synagogue, 34

Bethabara Moravian Church,
35

Big Bethel African Methodist
Episcopal Church, 39

Billy Graham Training Center
at the Cove, 41

Black Hills, 44

Boston Avenue Methodist
Church, 48

Brownsville Assembly of God,
50

Bruton Parish Church, 53

Calvary Church, 57

Canyon de Chelly, 59

Cathedral Basilica of St. Louis,
63

Cathedral Basilica of the
Sacred Heart, 67

Cathedral Church of St. John
the Divine, 70

Cathedral of Hope, 73

Cathedral of St. Joseph, 74

Cathedral Rock, 76

Catholic Shrine of the
Immaculate Conception, 78

Center for Dao-Confucianism,
80

Chaco Canyon, 81

Chapel of Massachusetts
Institute of Technology, 84

Chapel of Peace, 86

Chapel of the Prodigal, 88

Charterhouse of the
Transfiguration, 90

Christ Lutheran Church, 93

Christus Gardens, 94

Church of Lukumi Babalu
Aye, 95

Church of Scientology Los
Angeles, 97

Church of the Blessed
Sacrament, 99

Chuska Mountains, 101

Circle Sanctuary Nature
Preserve, 102

Congregation Beth Yeshua, 106

Crater Lake, 108

Crossroads Community
Church of Hyde Park, 111

Crystal Cathedral, 113

Detroit Zen Center, 117

Devils Tower National
Monument, 118

Diana's Grove, 121

Dwight Chapel, 123

Ebenezer Baptist Church, 127

Echo Canyon, 129

Emanuel African Methodist
Episcopal Church, 131

Enchanted Rock, 133

Enola Hill, 135

First Baptist Church of
America, 139

First Church of Christ,
Scientist, 141

First Presbyterian Church, 144

First Unitarian Church of
Philadelphia, 147

French Huguenot Church,
150

Germantown Mennonite
Church, 153

Grotto of the Redemption,
155

Gurdwara Sahib El Sobrante,
157

Harvest Ministries, Inc.®,
159
Hermanos Penitentes, 160
Hindu Temple of Greater
Chicago, 162
Holy Assumption of the Virgin
Mary Church, 165
Holy Cross Abbey, 167
Holy Land USA, 168
Holy Name Monastery, 170
Holy Trinity Chapel of Fort
Ross, 171
Hot Springs Mountain, 175
Islamic Center of America,
179
Jade Buddha Temple, 183
Kahal Kadosh Beth Elohim,
187
Kaho' Olawe, 189
Kannagara Jinja, 193
King's Chapel, 195
Lama Foundation, 197
Lien Hoa Buddhist Temple,
199
The Little Brown Church in
the Vale, 200
Loretto Chapel, 203
Lovely Lane Methodist
Church, 205
Medicine Wheel, 209
Meher Spiritual Center, 211
Memorial Church of Harvard
University, 213
Mepkin Abbey, 215
Methodist Tabernacle, 219
Mission of San Miguel of
Santa Fe, 222
Monastery of Christ in the
Desert, 223
Monastery of the Holy Cross,
225
Mormon Tabernacle, 227
Mosque Maryam, 229
Mount Graham, 232
Mount Shasta, 234
Mount Tabor Retreat Center,
237

Nappanee Missionary Church,
239
National Shrine of the Infant
Jesus of Prague, 240
Native American Church, 244
Old Mission of the Sacred
Heart, 247
Old North Church, 250
Old Swedes Church, 254
Oraibi, 255
Osho Chidvilas, 259
Our Lady of Guadalupe
Trappist Abbey, 261
Painted Rock, 263
Palace of Gold, 264
Pendle Hill, 267
Pentecostals of Alexandria, 270
Pipestone National Monu-
ment, 272
Plum Street Temple, 278
Point Barrow, 279
Prayer Tower, 282
Rainbow Bridge, 287
Ramakrishna-Vivekananda
Center of New York, 289
Riverside Church, 292
Rodef Shalom Congregation,
295
Rothko Chapel, 299
San Juan Bautista Mission, 303
San Juan Capistrano Mission,
304
San Luis Obispo de Tolosa,
307
San Marga Iraivan Temple, 309
Santa Fe Cathedral of St.
Francis of Assisi, 314
El Santuário de Chimayó, 318
Second Baptist Church, 322
Seton Shrine, 323
Shaker Meeting House, Sab-
bathday Lake, Maine, 325
Sisters of Benedict, 329
Sitka National Historical Park,
330
Sixteenth Street Baptist
Church, 333

Sleeping Ute Mountain, 336
Snoqualmie Falls, 339
St. Benedict Center, 342
St. Benedict's Abbey and
Retreat Center, 343
St. Fidelis Church, 346
St. John's Abbey, 348
St. Louis Cathedral, 351
St. Patrick's Cathedral, 355
Subiaco Abbey, 357
Taos Pueblo, 361
Temple Emanu-El, 365
Temple of Eck, 368
Thorncrown Chapel, 370
Touro Synagogue, 373
Tri-County Assembly of God,
376
Trinity Church, 378
Trinity Episcopal Church, 382
Triumph Church and New
Life Christian Fellowship,
384
Tsubaki America Shrine, 386
Unification Church, 389
Universal Peace Buddha Tem-
ple of New York, 391
Ursuline Convent, 393
Voodoo Spiritual Temple,
397
Waldensian Presbyterian
Church, 399
Washington Islamic Mosque
and Cultural Center, 401
Washington National Cathe-
dral, 402
Wat Carolina Buddhajakra
Vanaram, 406
Wat Lao Buddhavong, 408
Wayfarers' Chapel, 409
Wellspring Church and Chris-
tian Center, 412
West Parish Meetinghouse,
413
Yellowstone, 417
Zoroastrian Association of
Metropolitan Washington
(ZAMWI), 421

A Time Line of American Religious Pluralism, 423
Religious Sites by State, 441
Glossary, 445
Bibliography, 457
Index, 491

ACKNOWLEDGMENTS

I am grateful to a host of kind people who have answered my questions, filled in details of sacred sites, made suggestions, and sent photos, news clippings, post cards, and church newsletters.

Brother Richard Aplington
12605 224th Avenue
Bennet Lake, Wisconsin

George J. Badeau III
Director of Visitor Programs
Trinity Church
Boston, Massachusetts

Ethel Baker, Manager
Communications Division
First Church of Christ, Scientist
Boston, Massachusetts

Kathy Ballard
Prayer Tower Visitor Center
Oral Roberts University
Tulsa, Oklahoma

Joanne Barr, Secretary
Bethabara Moravian Church
Winston-Salem, North Carolina

Reverend Koichi Larry Barrish
Kannagara Jinja
Granite Falls, Washington

Sister Joan Barthel
Mt. Tabor Retreat Center
Martin, Kentucky

Bob Bostwick, Press Secretary
Coeur d'Alene Tribe
Plummer, Idaho

Philip Bryant, Pastor
French Huguenot Church
Charleston, South Carolina

Joe Butler, Director of Development
St. Michael's High School
Santa Fe, New Mexico

Mindy Clinard, Director of College
    Communications
Montreat College
Montreat, North Carolina

Brother Patrick Corkrean
Trappist Abbey
Lafayette, Oregon

Brother Mary James Coulter
Charterhouse of the Transfiguration
Arlington, Vermont

Brother Edward
Monastery of the Holy Cross
Chicago, Illinois

Holly Edwards, Church Secretary
First Baptist Church of America
Providence, Rhode Island

Caswell Ellis, Director
Bahá'i House of Worship
Wilmette, Illinois

Timothy Paul Erdel, Assistant Professor
    of Religion and Philosophy
Bethel College
Mishawaka, Indiana

Jo Frost
Church and School of Wicca
Hinton, West Virginia

Monsignor Thomas M. Ginty
Archdiocese of Hartford
Hartford, Connecticut

Yvonne Givens, Secretary
Ebenezer Baptist Church
Atlanta, Georgia

Meish Goldish, writer
Brooklyn, New York

Brother Patrick Hart
Abbey of Gethsemani
Trappist, Kentucky

Monsignor Ken Hedrick, Rector
St. Louis Cathedral
New Orleans, Louisiana

Tanya Homan, Assistant Director
Baha'is of the United States
New York, New York

Marina Ilyin
Holy Trinity Chapel
Jenner, California

Judi A. Joye, Administrative Assistant
International Peace Garden
Dunseith, North Dakota

Herbert Katz
Director of Communications
New York, New York

Bobbi Kelly, Dean's Associate for Outreach
Pendle Hill
Wallingford, Pennsylvania

Peggy Kelly, Supervisor of Chapel Guides
U. S. Air Force Academy Chapel
Colorado Springs, Colorado

Father Louis Kirby, Oblate Director
Holy Cross Abbey
Cañon City, Colorado

Sister Helen Lange
Holy Name Monastery
St. Leo, Florida

Father Thomas Leitner
Saint Benedict Center
Schuyler, Nebraska

Rose Leonhardt, Clerk
Amana Church Society
Middle, Iowa

Carol Anne Marble, Secretary
Triumph Church
Vicksburg, Mississippi

Gay Marks, Librarian
The Shaker Library
New Gloucester, Maine

Helen Matthews, Reference Librarian
Atlanta History Center Library
Atlanta, Georgia

Kathy McKechnie
Martha's Vineyard Campmeeting Association
Oak Bluffs, Massachusetts

Sarah Metzger
The University of the South
Sewanee, Tennessee

Marina Ochoa, Director
Historic Artists Patrimony and Archives
Archdiocese of Santa Fe
Santa Fe, New Mexico

Norma Roberts, Secretary
Emanuel African Methodist Episcopal Church
Charleston, South Carolina

Mary Sabol
Wayfarers' Chapel
Rancho Palos Verdes, California

Brother Ben Salzer, Curator
San Miguel Mission
Albuquerque, New Mexico

Dolores Shaw
Lovely Lane Methodist Church
Baltimore, Maryland

Brother Francis Shaw, O.S.B.
Holy Cross Abbey
Cañon City, Colorado

Shiou Wen Shih
Jade Buddha Temple
Houston, Texas

Sarah C. Smith
Russell Vermontiana Collection
Martha Canfield Memorial Free Library
Arlington, Vermont

Nilima Srikantha
Hinduism Today
Kapaa, Hawaii

Reference Department
Timberland Regional Library
Olympia, Washington

Yukihiko Tsumura
Tsubaki Grand Shrine of America
Stockton, California

Dave Waterman, Manager
Prabhupada's Palace of Gold
Moundsville, West Virginia

Brother Anthony Weber
Abbey of the Genesee
Piffard, New York

In addition, I couldn't have completed this work without Beth Bradshaw of Patrick Beaver Library in Hickory, North Carolina, Mark Schumacher of Jackson Library at the University of North Carolina at Greensboro, and Wanda Rozzelle of the Catawba County Library, my main sources for research, advice, and interlibrary loan.

PREFACE

The plan of *Religious Sites in America* is to present 160 examples of worship groups nationwide as models of individual beliefs and practice as they exist at the beginning of the twenty-first century. I have chosen sites in all fifty states—from elegant churches, temples, and cathedrals to storefront start-ups, nondenominational chapels, retreats, religious tourist attractions, New Age experiments, and shrines to deities that date to petroglyph, rune, medieval chant, Sun Dance, pentagram, firepit, and oral tradition. Although the past permeates tenets and activities, all sites are active religious centers. Each entry contains details of supervision, location and layout, phone and fax, and e-mail and Web site. Text describes the uniqueness, history, sacred architecture, current activities and outreach, and sources of information on each.

Back matter offers an overview of innovations and shifts in worship style. Study aids feature a multifaceted time line of events resulting from American religious pluralism:

- conflicts (Battle of Williamsburg, execution of Quakers, Selma voting rights march, Wounded Knee Massacre, Battle of New Orleans, the Mexican War)
- publishers and publications *(Christian Science Monitor,* "Letter from a Birmingham Jail," *The Final Call, Song of Hiawatha, Summer Service of the Methodists in North America, The Tantrik Path, The Seven Storey Mountain, Witchcraft Today, Ramona,* "Paul Revere's Ride," Beacon Press)
- drama *(Pastorela, From This Day Forward,* "The Glory of Christmas," *Heaven Bound)*
- sermons ("The Last Supper," "I Have a Dream," "Shall the Fundamentalists Win?")

- structures (Old Swedes Church, Medicine Wheel, kivas, Palace of Gold, Jade Buddha Temple, sweat lodges)
- historical events (Captain Cook's voyage to the Sandwich Islands, Fugitive Slave Act, Religious Freedom Act, the Long Walk, purchase of Alaska)
- authors (Helen Hunt Jackson, Ram Dass, Paula Gunn Allen, L. Ron Hubbard, Willa Cather, Henry Wadsworth Longfellow, Ralph Waldo Emerson)
- visionaries (Bahá'u'lláh, Mary Baker Eddy, Wovoka, Meher Baba, Sweet Medicine, Ann Lee, Black Elk, Vivekenanda)
- orators (Greg Laurie, Billy Graham, Malcolm X, Harry Emerson Fosdick, Louis Farrakhan, Adam Clayton Powell, Jr., Timothy Dwight)
- activists (Arvol Looking Horse, Calvin Butts, James R. Weddell, Lillian Wald, Gladdys Muir, Noa Emmett Aluli, Arthur M. Brazier)
- mystics (Eagle Elk, Nanak Dev, John Paul Twitchell, White Buffalo Calf Woman, Meher Baba)
- historical figures (Bernardo Abeyta, Ioann Veniaminov, Popé, George Washington, Lewis and Clark, Olympia Brown, Bhagwan Rajneesh)
- innovators (I. M. Pei, Nampeyo, Sisters of Charity, Quanah Parker, King David Kalahaua, William Billings, Pierre L'Enfant, Oral Roberts, Brigham Young)
- movements (Quaker and Mennonite abolitionism, Promise Keepers, Earth First!, Zoroastrianism, Moonies, Second Great Awakening, Vedanta Society,

totemism, Metropolitan Community
Church)
- native American tribes (Yavapai, Makah,
  Digger Indians, Polynesian aborigines,
  Hopi, Aleut)
- newsmakers (Mark Levy, Fidel Castro,
  Vatican II, "Dynamite Bob" Chambliss,
  W. D. Fard, Dalai Lama)
- national parks and monuments (Crazy
  Horse Monument, Mt. Graham, Pipestone
  National Monument, Zion National
  Forest, Devils Tower, Yellowstone, Mesa
  Verde, Crater Lake).

The glossary offers pronunciations in the h-
based system for unfamiliar religious and architectural terms, e. g., canon, ashram, lauds, binah,
dharma, Sufi, tefillin, chuppah, calumet, hip
roof, and scry. Research aids include a division
of sites by state, extensive bibliography of print
and electronic sources, and a thorough index
with cross-references.

At the outset, I found such wide variance that
I chose to adapt entries to suit the situation.
Controversy colors the ministry of some groups,
in particular, the Voodoo Spiritual Temple in
New Orleans, Wiccan practices of Diana's Grove
in Missouri, same-sex marriages at Harvard's
"Mem Church," obsessive secrecy and restriction
of gender at Vermont's Charterhouse of the
Transfiguration, gay members at Philadelphia's
Germantown Mennonite Church, and a multi-
cultural congregation victimized by neo-Nazi
vandalism at Triumph Church in Vicksburg, Mis-
sissippi. Some entries contain capsule biographies
of leaders—John Wesley, Elizabeth Seton,
Thomas O'Reilly, Thomas Merton, Vivekenanda,
Jean-Baptiste Lamy, Junípero Serra, Bhumibol,
Yukitaka Yamamoto, Pierre Jean de Smet, Isaac
Meyer Wise, Elizabeth Schellenberg, Richard
Allen, Sivaya Subramuniyaswami, Benedict of
Nursia, Peter Valdes, and Robert Schuller. Alongside ministries are the designs and designers of
oustanding landmarks—Robert Mills, Henry
Hobson Richardson, Adah Robinson, E. Fay
Jones, Lloyd Wright, Father Fermín Francisco de
Lasuén, Eero Saarinen, Jean-Baptiste Louis Bour-
geois, Peter Harrison, and Richard Upjohn—as
well as the names of mosaicists, composers, ma-
sons, organ builders, sculptors, pipe makers, call-

ligraphers, and landscapers who have enhanced
sacred places with religious symbolism.

All research bears an element of surprise. For
me, the wealth of worship styles and related issues extended far beyond my expectations. In
addition to the prayer styles of Zen Buddhists,
pluralism of Philadelphia Unitarians, songfests of
the Mormon Tabernacle Choir, revivalism of the
Methodist Tabernacle, and zealotry of Assemblies of God, I encountered

- the whale-centered community of Point
  Barrow, Alaska
- a marriage outreach at the tiny Little
  Brown Church in the Vale in Nashua,
  Iowa
- an annual summer solstice encampment at
  Circle Sanctuary Nature Preserve, Mt.
  Horeb, Wisconsin
- a hiding place for runaway slaves
  under the coffer at Touro Synagogue in
  Newport, Rhode Island
- a silo-shaped campus worship center at
  Massachusetts Institute of Technology
- a series of unity rides that link landmasses
  sacred to plains Indians
- religious tourism at Holy Land USA in
  Bedford, Virginia, and the Ave Maria
  Grotto in Cullman, Alabama
- glossolalia among ecstatic worshippers at
  Louisiana's Pentecostals of Alexandria
- young confirmands studying history
  firsthand at Baltimore's Lovely Lady
  United Methodist Church
- religious, genealogical, and historical
  archives at the Shaker community in
  Sabbathday Lake, Maine
- annual observance of French liturgy at the
  French Huguenot Church of Charleston,
  South Carolina
- a shrine to four dead children at Birmingham's Sixteenth Street Baptist Church
- vegetarian cooking classes at the Jade
  Buddha Temple in Houston, Texas
- a medieval morality play at Big Bethel
  AME Church in Atlanta, Georgia
- a prehistoric navigation school at
  Kaho'Olawe, Hawaii
- a miniature of Japan's Tsubaki Shrine in
  Stockton, California

- outspoken civil rights leadership at Harlem's Abyssinian Baptist Church
- a magical domed Palace of Gold in the hill country of Moundville, West Virginia
- consumption of dirt from a holy well at an Indian-Hispanic shrine in Chimayo, New Mexico
- outdoor drama, *From This Day Forward,* commemorating the flight of Waldensians from Italy to Valdese, North Carolina
- a multiplex worship center at the Air Force Academy in Colorado
- a Buddhist temple in a rain forest in Kapaa, Hawaii
- a clock made of flowers on the Canadian border in Dunseith, North Dakota
- sympathetic news reporting from the *Seattle Times* for the plight of the Snoqualmie of Carnation, Washington
- permaculture classes at the Lama Foundation of San Cristobal, New Mexico
- members at the Detroit Zen Center providing homes for the homeless
- Penina Moise's *Hymns Written for the Use of Hebrew Congregations* at Kahal Kadosh Beth Elohim in Charleston, South Carolina
- singing classes at Gurdwara Sahib El Sobrante in California
- training for ministers and counselors at the Cove in Asheville, North Carolina.

Artistic expression covers a range of styles and forms:

- fresco at Montreat-Anderson's Chapel of the Prodigal
- free noontime organ concerts at the Mormon Tabernacle
- stained glass splendors at the Washington National Cathedral
- rock music and popcorn at Houston's Second Baptist Church
- photo-ops at Arizona's Antelope Canyon
- Greek Orthodox iconography at California's Fort Ross
- a fish-shaped Presbyterian church in Stamford, Connecticut
- ecycled rock at the Grotto of the Redemption in Iowa
- brandy-soaked fruitcake from Our Lady of Guadelupe Trappist Abbey in Lafayette, Oregon.

The finished text offers glimpses of uniquely American worship in Navajo sand painting, Harvest Ministries evangelism, Messianic Judaism in Philadelphia, ki healing at the Kannagara Jinja shrine in Washington state, annual pilgrimages to Idaho's Old Mission, a live passion play enacted by the Hermanos Penitentes, high holy days celebrated live over the Internet, and widespread native American peyotism, perhaps the oldest worship style indigenous to North America. Overall, these expressions of faith define who we are and how we seek the divine.

INTRODUCTION

From whatever ethnic background or family predisposition, people continually search the dark world for paths to light. Patterns of thanksgiving and entreaty vary with the individual, yet derive from a universal longing—to fill the empty spaces within. These yearnings are the stimuli to worship.

Styles of communing with God evolve from the fiber of human experience. From prehistory, aboriginal Americans have venerated the Great Spirit, the animistic creator and protector of humankind. Although European invaders and proselytizers have belittled Indian spirituality, native Americans have continued to retreat into nature's grandeur. To protect their lifeways, they are willing to fight government agencies for the right to venerate in peace and serenity the phenomena of hill and water, horizon and sky. Out of disgust at urban pollution and a need to revive the spirit, non-native city dwellers are emulating the serenitiy of Indian worship by retreating to desert overlooks, silent abbeys, seaside chapels, synagogues, and meditation gardens to commune with the almighty.

For those newcomers to North America who brought a formalized faith and scripture to guide them, the building of churches, temples, abbeys, and shrines resettled the displaced worshipper in a familiar atmosphere of sanctity. For healing and respite, they have propitiated powers that lie outside human control by intoning unique god-names—Allah, Zarathustra, Buddha, Yahweh, Christ, the Goddess, Loa, the tami. When social and political intrusions have disrupted or threatened worship, the faith-driven have pocked history with uprisings, lawsuits, sermons, and outcries in art and press. The willingness of the righteous to protect hallowed turf continues to fuel debate over the right of one group to invade the consecrated ground of another, whether at home or in the training of the next generation.

The demand for freedom to practice faith unmolested has changed little from the country's founding. For all their reformations, schisms, and syncretism, the nation's religious bodies remain strong in heart and mind. Congregants retain the history of their forebears and respect the travails of those who came to the New World in search of liberty—the German Lutherans of Amana, Mennonites, Sephardic Jews, Waldensians, Burmese Buddhists, and Santerians—and the African and Chinese slave laborers whom the greedy uprooted and relocated for profit. Majority faiths, beset by late twentieth-century waves of immigration, are still relearning the basic principles of democracy that shelter minority groups and foster tolerance for prayers in Spanish, female clergy, and full membership for homosexuals. The tensions within religious America continue to force the citizenry, both churched and unchurched, to reevaluate where, when, how, and to what degree the search for God will affect us all.

Aexemplify Saint Benedict's admonition to pray and work. Although the brothers phased out meat products and breads, the current community of seventy-five monks still earns its keep from a mail-order business selling basil pesto, cheese, fudge, and fruitcake, but what brought the abbey lasting fame was the addition of one of its brothers, Thomas Merton.

Abbey of Gethsemani

Father Timothy Kelly, Abbot
3642 Monks Road
Trappist, Kentucky 40051
502-549-3117; 800-549-0912
FAX 502-549-4124
www.monks.org

HISTORY

At the Abbey of Gethsemani, a network of spiritual comrades dedicates its inward journey to praying and loving. Ever since forty-four Trappist monks from the Breton Abbey of Melleray, France, bought a farm retreat from the Sisters of Loretto in Nelson County on December 21, 1848, the Abbey of Gethsemani has flourished. The nation's oldest Trappist monastery, it evolved from log cabins into a sturdy white quadrangle, outbuildings, and dairy constructed on farmland above a creek fifteen miles south of Bardstown, Kentucky. Within eleven years of the abbey's founding, the order spread its outreach to five daughter houses—Holy Spirit, founded in Conyers, Georgia, in 1944; Holy Trinity in Huntsville, Utah, in 1947; Mepkin Abbey in Charleston, South Carolina, in 1949; Genesee in Piffard, New York, in 1951; and the New Abbey Clairvaux in Vina, California, established in 1955.

Before branching out from agriculture, the abbey supported herds of Duroc hogs and beef and Holstein dairy cattle. In the late nineteenth century, monk-farmers earned a reputation for producing and selling quality breads, sausage, country ham, Canadian bacon, cheese, and sweets. Today, the official seal sums up abbey history in four symbols—three bees to denote the beekeeping of the mother house in Melleray and crossed shovel and rake beneath an open Bible to

ARCHITECTURE

On a greensward surrounded by acres of hardwoods, the abbey is a Cistercian-style island of calm and contemplation. The rectangular compound features a four-story, white-walled structure marked at one end by a square tower topped with a pointed roof. On the grounds at the ends of the church and guest house, 270 identical iron crosses in immaculate rows dot the graves in the abbey's walled cemetery. A large concrete cross tops the common grave of twenty brothers who died in the first sixteen years of the order's existence in Kentucky. A secular cemetery features rounded headstones.

The chapel reflects an austere modernism in its pale glass windows in abstract patterns, white walls, gold flooring, and broad dais. At center, the square black altar table holds a white cloth and elements of the Eucharist. To the right of the table, a slender cross rises from a round pedestal. Guests and monks take their places in individual chairs ranged about the altar. Within a wood-paneled choir loft, monks clad in white, cowled cassocks lift their missals and intone the liturgy. A *préau,* or courtyard, at center of the church complex offers walkways, seats, and a small fountain. Designed by Potter and Cox Architects of Louisville, the structure received a Kentucky Society of Architects Honor Award for Design Excellence.

The refectory maintains Benedictine Rule in the designation of places by date of each monk's entrance to the community. Mornings and evenings, residents with faces obscured by hoods serve themselves from the meatless fare on the buffet. At noon, they eat in silence as servers refresh beverages and a lector instructs them medieval style from scripture or religious readings. Outside the formal areas, the men

THOMAS MERTON

One of America's most influential social critics and profound spiritual philosophers, Thomas Merton put the Abbey of Gethsemani on the map after his enlistment in 1941. Born Thomas James Merton on January 31, 1915, in Prades, France, he was the son of two artists, New Zealand painter and church organist Owen Heathcote Merton and Ruth Jenkins, an interior designer from New York. From this idealistic pair, Merton developed a strong esthetic sense. After his mother's death in 1921, he lived with his grandparents until his father achieved success in 1924 and resettled him in France at a Catholic school and at Lycée Ingres in nearby Montauban.

Irregular living arrangements resulted in tuberculosis at age twelve and orphanhood four years later. On income from his grandfather, Merton studied language at Oakham in Strasbourg and edited a literary magazine while preparing for the foreign service. Self-indulgence in youth at Cambridge preceded enrollment at Columbia University at age twenty, when he took up serious inquiry into religion. He completed an M.A. in English literature before entering the priesthood as a Franciscan and adopting the name of Father Louis. With the onset of World War II, he chose the restrictive lifestyle of the Cistercians of the Strict Observance at the Trappist monastery at Gethsemani rather than service in the military.

In 1948, Merton achieved lasting fame for an autobiography, *The Seven Storey Mountain*. After ordination in 1949, he abandoned writing verse and composed a lifelong series of works on contemplation and monasticism, including *The Waters of Siloe* (1949), a history of the Cistercian order, *Praying the Psalms* (1956), *True Solitude* (1969), and *Contemplation in a World of Action* (1971). At the height of his fame, the abbey's vocations rose in number to 279. Because his field of interest widened to pacifism, social issues, racial justice, psychoanalysis, non-Christian spirituality, and Zen Buddhism, he moved from the abbey to a cinder-block hermitage and cultivated a wide friendship and correspondence with leading thinkers of the era. While attending a conference on monasticism and ecumenism, he died of accidental electrocution by a defective fan on December 10, 1968, in Bangkok, Thailand.

In 1963, Father John Loftus, a friend of Thomas Merton's at Bellarmine College, proposed assembling a Merton Collection for scholarly study at the college's W. L. Lyons Brown Library. A year after Merton's death, his will established the Merton Legacy Trust and transferred his private library and manuscripts to the college's Thomas Merton Center, which headquarters the International Thomas Merton Society, founded in 1987. Its aims are these:

- To encourage reading, study, and research into Merton's works
- To promote Merton-centered scholarship, popular writings, publications, and meetings
- To share insight into his unique spiritual journey
- To champion his merit as spiritual theologian and literary figure

Additional centers maintain religious literature in the Merton tradition: the Merton Association at Prades, France; the Thomas Merton Society of Great Britain and Ireland; the Centro Internacional de Studios Misticos (International Center of Mystic Studies) in Avila, Spain; and the International Center for Mobist Studies in Tengzhou City, China.

join in cooking meals in the block-and-stainless-steel kitchen, haul logs from the woods, and cover themselves with net to collect honey from the apiary. Other evidence of monastery chores derives from a horse barn, paint rooms, bakery, cheese and fudge center, storage barn, garage, print shop, dental and photo labs, and tailor and carpentry shops. Beyond the church, chapter room, and refectory lie the brown brick infirmary and scriptorium, both standard features of cloisters since the early Middle Ages. The infirmary offers long-term care for aged and ill brothers in fourteen patient rooms. Other amenities include a hospital chapel, exercise area, day rooms, laundry, and temperature-controlled domiciles for senior brothers. The scriptorium alleviates fatigue with a fireplace, benches, and tables for writing letters and journals and reading periodicals and newspapers.

On a greensward surrounded by acres of hardwoods, the Abbey of Gethsemani in Trappist, Kentucky, is a Cistercian-style island of calm and contemplation. (Courtesy Abbey of Gethsemani)

ACTIVITIES

Today, Thomas Merton's beloved abbey remains dedicated to an austere Trappist rule of cloistering, silence, prayer, restrained friendships, and abstinence from meat. A balanced life calls for manual labor in the 100-acre hayfields, 350 acres of row crops, and 1,400 acres of reforested woodland. Outsiders can access Father Kelly's homilies online and can support the abbey by purchasing pesto, fruitcake topped with California walnuts and Georgia pecans and soaked in Kentucky bourbon, and two kinds of fudge—chocolate bourbon and butter walnut bourbon—which the monks produce to earn their living. A popular favorite, semisoft Port du Salut cheese made from Holstein milk, comes nestled in yellow poplar boxes hand-crafted by Brother Julian Wallace. The abbey bookstore sells titles on Thomas Merton, monasticism, and the Cistercians. A featured work, journalist Dianne Aprile's *The Abbey of Gethsemani: Place of Peace and Paradox* (1998), anthologizes a generous col-

lection of clippings and color photos of monastic life and work and its treasured medieval manuscripts and religious art.

Although the monks perform no ministry or teaching, they are by no means isolated from the world. The brothers support Habitat for Humanity in a three-county area as well as a monastery in a poverty-stricken part of Chile. In the 1990s, after a female driver from United Parcel Service breached the men-only boundary, the brothers normalized relations with female outsiders. They welcomed the first female monk, Sister Catharina Shibuya, from Nasu, Japan, who took up residence for several months to learn English, and received Sister Maricela Garcia from Mexico, who observed a three-year monastic retreat.

To 3,000 laypersons annually, the abbey offers a pleasant guest house of thirty-one rooms, single or double, with private showers, lounge privileges, and meals in the guest dining room, after which they may participate in limited conversation. Women and men book the facilities on alternate weeks. Visitors can choose seclusion from Monday through Friday or over long weekends from Friday until Monday morning to enjoy quiet woodlands and fields or books and tapes from the ample library. Those seeking consultation can speak with a monk or confer with the retreat master. Worship in the chapel seven times a day beginning at 3:15 A.M. for vigils and including the standard breaks for lauds, terce, sext, none, vespers, and compline allows guests to sing, assist with the Eucharist, and pray with the 75 residents. With these prayers, participants perform praise, adoration, thanksgiving, petition, repentance, and resolve—the six purposes of communion with God.

Gethsemani's activities admit outsiders for special occasions. In 1998, the brothers celebrated the Cistercian Jubilee Year with liturgies, public receptions, and a roast honoring Father Kelly's twenty-fifth year as abbot. Spaced out over the year were a July open house, an August luncheon for brothers and their families, a monastic conference in October, an observance of the church dedication anniversary on November 15, a December guest lecture honoring Thomas Merton, and Founders' Day on December 21. Annually at Easter, the monks hold a candlelight procession to a vigil mass, which is open to visitors; on All Souls' Day, the brothers bless the graves of deceased founders and forebears.

> **See also** Mepkin Abbey.
> **Sources:** Aprile 1998; *Biography Resource Center* 1999; Bowker 1997; Cohn-Sherbok 1998; Downey 1997; *Encyclopedia of World Biography* 1998; "Firewatch"; "Great Day for the Monks" 1901; Kelly and Kelly 1992; *New Catholic Encyclopedia* 1967; Sullivan 1967; "A Woman in a Monastery" 1901.

Abhidhyan Yoga Institute

Shri Acharya Abhidhyanananda, Founder
P.O. Box 1414
Nevada City, California 95959-1414
800-737-9642
info@abhidhyan.org
www.abhidhyan.org

The Abhidhyan Yoga Institute in Nevada City, California, is a nonprofit organization offering authentic spiritual teachings inspired by Tantric yoga meditational tradition that dates back 7,000 years. An ancient adjunct to enlightenment, orthodox Tantric yoga survives among few Hindu and Buddhist practitioners. Its purpose is to promote spiritual and personal growth while advancing humanitarian service and education. Through trust in a guru, or initiator, and total immersion in inner resources, each aspirant discovers that purity and harmony of body and mind precedes full spirituality and well-being.

HISTORY

Shri Acharya Abhidhyanananda, formerly known as the Reverend Father Anatole Ruslanov, established the institute to guide initiates into complete knowledge of God. Under the direction of Shri Prabhat Ranjan Sarkarm, a spiritual master at the Tantra yoga spiritual academy in Varanasi, India, Acharya underwent monastic training in traditional and modern methods of religious, personal, and physical growth. After graduating, he continued studying with his mentor to absorb divine energy and transcend cultural limitation and religious dogma. For fifteen years, he has honored Sarkarm's request that he lecture, counsel, and initiate individuals, teach courses and workshops in yoga, and publish a quarterly newsletter, *The Tantrik Path.*

Acharya founded the Abhidhyan Yoga Institute, Inc., in 1991 for the purpose of altruism and life enhancement. He grounds his philosophy on an understanding that humanity is one family and that sanctity dwells in each person. To enlarge the individual's capacity to know God, he trains beginners in abhidhyan yoga, a form of total meditation essential to contemplation. The method relieves the seeker of mundane worries and allows penetration of an absolute—an unfettered godliness in the *atman* (soul) that shakes off *avidya maya* (dark forces) and leads to wealth, happiness, enlightenment, and liberation from worldliness. By banishing the annoyances that trouble and distract, each successful yoga practitioner acquires health, peace of mind, and spirituality for a fuller participation in life.

ACTIVITIES

Acharya provides ongoing teacher training in nonmeditation for nonmeditators. Similar to Vajrayana Buddhist teachings of perfection, the method derives from a mystical form of Mahayana Buddhism known as the "diamond path," a Tibetan philosophy that originated in first-century India. The nonmeditational method incorporates more scripture than the narrowly orthodox Theravadan Buddhism and offers more variety in popular devotional style and method. In contrast, abhidhyan meditation is more complex and requires serious preparation. It facilitates psychotherapy and rehabilitation by calming, balancing body systems, controlling pain, and healing mind, body, and spirit.

Seekers usually recognize an innate longing to escape spiritual emptiness and know the divine. Such longing requires the leadership of a guru to guide, interpret, and direct. To achieve initiation into a deeply soulful state, beginners benefit from insight meditation by focusing on breathing or a mental image and by developing a style suited to personality, body type, and experience. With competent assistance, the seeker reduces intrusive thoughts and divorces the mind from the world's picture of self. Over time and much practice, the resultant relaxation and peace improve human relationships and increase concentration by clarifying reason. The initiate never returns to the former muddled state but retains purification from a constant source—the divinity shining within.

Acharya offers workshops, retreats, and lectures as well as personal consultation and training worldwide. Organizers may schedule an event anywhere by recruiting seven to twenty-five participants, arranging a place, transportation, and accommodations for the guru, providing vegetarian meals, and making a donation to the institute. Participants pay $75 each for a weekend workshop and $150 for a five-day seminar. Each gathering builds a stable foundation for serious study of Tantric yoga as a source of healing, satisfaction, and contentment.

Sources: "Abhidhyan Yoga Institute"; Bowker 1997; *Eerdmans' Handbook to the World's Religions* 1982; Gentz 1973; "Hinduism in America"; Hinnells 1984; McDougall 1998; Smith 1995; "Who is a Hindu?" 1999; *World Religions* 1998.

Abyssinian Baptist Church
Reverend Calvin O. Butts III
132 West 138th Street
New York, New York 10030
212-862-7474

Located at history's crossroads—between Malcolm X and Adam Clayton Powell Jr. Boulevards—the Abyssinian Baptist Church has become an African-American shrine. Billing itself as the "church of the masses," it was at one time the world's largest Protestant church, with 14,000 members. Probably Harlem's oldest, largest, and most active Baptist church, it is the home of a respected liturgical choir and a museum of memorabilia of the Powell family.

Over its history, the church has witnessed the rise of black people in the United States from second-class citizens to full participants in the democratic process. On Sunday morning, tour groups attend morning service to experience the sacred place and the message of one of North America's most prominent religio-political centers. Daily, Harlemites congregate to benefit from a wealth of church programs.

HISTORY
Founded in 1808, Harlem's Abyssinian Baptist Church has served a broad spectrum of social, religious, and political forums. It was the brainchild of eighteen schismatics from Manhattan's First Baptist Church. The black congregation migrated from uptown white society to a black community on Anthony Street. After a sojourn northward on West Fortieth Street, in 1923, trustees founded a permanent home ninety-eight blocks away. In five years, the congregation paid for the impressive Gothic stone structure on West 138th Street.

Integral to the church's success over much of the twentieth century were father and son ministers. While leading the congregation, the Reverend Dr. Adam Clayton Powell, Sr., on staff from 1908 to1937, authored two works of social protest: *Against the Tide* (1938) and *Riots and Ruins* (1945). His son, activist and U.S. Representative Adam Clayton Powell, Jr., remained in the pulpit until the early 1970s during significant political and economic advancement for non-white Americans.

The Abyssinian Baptist Church is probably Harlem's oldest, largest, and most active Baptist Church. Here, Adam Clayton Powell, Jr., demonstrates his skillful, moving delivery. (Bettman/Corbis)

ACTIVITIES

In 1995, the Abyssinian Baptist Church renewed its commitment to the far left when 1,600 locals welcomed Fidel Castro, the president of Cuba, for the United Nations' fiftieth anniversary celebration. He arrived thirty-five years after his first visit to Harlem's Theresa Hotel and a widely condemned address to the United Nations. The enthusiastic crowd buoyed a jubilant mood with chanting and jeers for the Clinton administration and Giuliani mayorship. Pastor Calvin Butts welcomed all seeking global liberation and introduced Castro, who spoke for over an hour comparing Cuban achievements with the squalor of Harlem and targeting capitalism as a failure. Moving directly to world issues, Castro applauded the end of apartheid in South Africa and condemned the arms race and expanded nuclear potential, repression in Nigeria and Angola, and the U.S. blockade of Cuba. Of the Sunday night reception, Castro said, "I had

such a good time that I felt as if I had been in the best of banquets." (Minzesheimer 1995)

Subsequent incidents and issues arousing New York blacks to action called for gatherings at the Abyssinian Baptist Church and moral guidance and protests issuing from the pulpit and members. In August 1998, the Reverend Butts recommended that Americans forgive President Bill Clinton for his sexual improprieties with White House intern Monica Lewinsky. A service honoring Martin Luther King, Jr., in January 1999 prompted an end to suspicion and distrust between blacks and Jews. On February 15, 1999, 1,500 citizens and religious leaders assembled for a rally and prayer to end police brutality as grieving parents returned the body of slain immigrant Amadou Diallo to Guinea, West Africa. Police outraged citizens by shooting the unarmed street peddler on February 4. In March 1999, the Reverend Dr. Butts led boycotts of New York shopping districts to

ADAM CLAYTON POWELL, JR.

One of the nation's charismatic black leaders and an astute forerunner of Dr. Martin Luther King, Jr., Adam Clayton Powell, Jr., rose to youthful greatness at the height of the Great Depression. Native to New Haven, Connecticut, he was born on November 29, 1908, the year his father accepted the pulpit of Harlem's noted church and guided its growth from 1,550 to 14,000 members. His son pursued a scholarly education and earned a B.A. degree from Colgate University, an M.A. in religious education from Columbia University, and a subsequent D.D. from Shaw University.

At age twenty-three, the younger Powell served as church business manager and assistant minister during the worst of hard times. To uplift Harlem's destitute, his father opened soup kitchens. Simultaneously, the young Powell countered the status-quo mentality of mainstream faiths with Bible-based sermons that supported activism presaging the civil disobedience of the 1960s. He organized picket lines and mass demonstrations to end racism at Harlem Hospital and initiated a relief program offering food, clothing, and jobs to the black underclass.

A trusted freedom fighter by his midtwenties, Powell furthered Harlem's campaign for equal rights with rent strikes and crusades against Jim-Crow segregation in restaurants, retail stores, bus lines, utilities, and the 1939 World's Fair. In 1936, he took his father's place as senior pastor of Abyssinian Baptist Church and began an unprecedented climb of the political ladder. From New York City councilman, board member of the Office of Price Administration and Manhattan Civil-ian Defense, and publisher and editor of the weekly newspaper the *People's Voice* during World War II, he advanced to the U.S. Congress in 1945.

For three decades, Powell's articulate oratory influenced committees governing Native-American benefits, pensions for invalids, education and labor, and interior and insular affairs. Among his sweeping public campaigns were lesser-known gestures to rid the Capitol of segregation at the House of Representatives restaurant and press gallery. More dramatic was a scathing denunciation of lynching and of poll taxes and a demand for integration of the U.S. military, housing, employment, and transportation. As a man of color influencing global affairs, he attended the 1955 Bandung Conference of African and Asian nations and urged President Dwight D. Eisenhower to end colonialism in third-world countries.

Near the end of his career, at the beginning of President Lyndon Johnson's Great Society, Powell launched over fifty bills authorizing increased minimum wage, deaf education and vocational training, school lunch, student loans, and aid to public schools and libraries. A slander suit weakened his political clout in 1967. The House Democratic Caucus, smarting at Powell's flight to the Republican Party, divested him of committee chairmanship and ordered the Judiciary Committee to investigate suspected fiscal irregularities. Formally ousted in March, he received a new mandate from his constituency in April. His rocky career ended as it had started, with Powell once more pastoring the Abyssinian Baptist Church *in absentia* from 1971 until his death on April 4, 1972.

protest the unlawful violence police perpetuate against blacks. A follow-up two-hour service of prayers for Diallo, psalms, and preaching in April encouraged Harlemites and guest Mayor Rudolph W. Giuliani to patch up their quarrels with police for the good of society.

Sources: "Abyssinian Baptist Church"; "ACOA at African Church Meeting" 1997; "Adam Clayton Powell, Jr."; Brozan 1999; Cantor 1991; Castro 1995; Low and Clift 1981; Minzesheimer 1995; Newman 1999; "1999–2000 Dissertation Fellowship Grant Abstracts" 1997; Parker 1998; Ploski and Williams 1989; Powell 1967; Pristin 1999; Siegel 1999; Tyner 1995; Wilgoren 1999; Zielbauer 1999.

Acoma Pueblo

P.O. Box 309
Acomita, New Mexico 87034
505-552-6604; 800-747-0181
FAX 505-552-6600

Pueblo Cultural Center
2401 Twelfth Street N.W.
Albuquerque, New Mexico 87192
505-843-7270; 800-766-4405

Acoma, or Ako-Me (People of the White Rock), deserves the name Sky City. Located east of Grants and west of Albuquerque, New Mexico, at

The Acoma Pueblo survives on the crest of a sandstone mesa over three hundred fifty feet above a valley pocked with rocky outcroppings. (North Wind Picture Archives)

an elevation of 7,000 feet, Acoma Pueblo is a seventy-acre National Historic Landmark adjacent to Mount Taylor, an active volcano. Founded at the beginning of the twelfth century, Acoma is one of the oldest continuously inhabited communities in North America. Pueblo is an umbrella term for the Hopi, Keres, Tewa, Tiwa, and Zuñi, all of whom lived in earthen structures and belong to the Western Keresan language group. The Acoman branch occupied three- and four-storied dwellings built from wooden beams supporting layered flat stones. Walls, floors, ceilings, and roofs were plastered with adobe.

The Acoma Pueblo survives on the crest of a sandstone mesa over 350 feet above a valley pocked with rocky outcroppings. Originally, the magnificent location offered both protection from invaders and a link to the sky's canopy above and the desert below. The survival of prehistoric Acoma depended on flocks of turkeys and the irrigation of maize, beans, and squash growing in plots on the valley below at Acomita. Today, husbandry is still a necessity of life, for they lack electricity and conserve rainwater in cisterns.

HISTORY

According to Zuñi-Acoma tradition, thousands of years ago, surface rocks emerged in a fiery explosion that marked the Zuñi-Acoma Trail with natural geological formations. Creation myth dates the pueblo to progenitors who emerged from the underground world. The creator/earth mother, Latiku, founded the religion and organized matrilineal clans, which bear the names of animals and plants. The religious and spiritual leadership fell to the male head of the Antelope clan. As father of benevolent spirits known as kachinas, he summoned their aid through dancing. At these ritual invocations, masked human dancers performed ritual steps and gestures to cure the sick, mark the passing of seasons, and assure rain, fertility, and continuity for the community. Naturally outgoing and accepting of human nature, the kachinas performed humorous gags and offered gifts to children.

The Acoman religion derived from a lifestyle based on harmony with nature. One poet and novelist, James Paytiamo (Flaming Arrow), author of *Flaming Arrow's People* (1932), described how Acoman braves traditionally put on aprons and moccasins, painted their faces and torsos, wrapped yarn about their knees, and stuck eagle feathers in their hair before setting out to hunt deer. In obeisance to nature gods, successful hunters prayed before and after the kill to honor the cycle of life and death.

According to a clearly defined division of labor, men provided meat but left domestic chores to women and girls. In the valley below Acoma Pueblo, female Acoma planted corn in mounds, watered and cultivated it, and shouldered their harvest in conical baskets before climbing ladders to the village. To preserve grain for winter and protect it from vermin, they spread ears of corn on flat roofs to dry in the sun. From sheep acquired from the Spanish, they developed weaving of wool blankets, a trademark of their civilization.

The Acoma have survived a series of adversities, beginning in ancient times with the marooning of one band at Enchanted Mesa, a stepsided promontory where a storm and flood washed out trails to the peak. The people faced their first European invaders in 1540, when conquistador Francisco Vasquez de Coronado led Spanish explorers to the American Southwest. The Spanish left without incident to search for the Seven Cities of Cíbola to plunder fabled riches. Within a half century, some 3,000 people became the slaves of Don Juan de Oñate, a brutal Spanish tyrant and treasure hunter who murdered all who opposed him. With reinforcements from Juan de Zaldivar, Oñate forced his way into the pueblo. The Acoma killed Zaldivar and all but 5 of his men. On January 21, 1599, Zaldivar's brother, Vincente de Zaldivar, led a vengeful force of 70 up a rear entrance to burn and pillage. He murdered 800 residents, enslaved women, and mutilated men and boys by lopping off their feet. The Spanish government condemned Oñate and Zaldivar and stripped them of seniority, but the damage to the Acoma Pueblo was irreparable.

According to Oñate's plan, the Spanish formed the frontier outpost of Nuevo México (New Mexico) and imported Franciscan friars under military guard to evangelize the Zuñi, Hopi, and Acoma. By 1600, the priests had begun proselytizing and baptizing Indians and spread their mission to neighboring areas. The arrival of Father Juan Ramirez, a Roman Catholic missionary, in 1629 and the erection of the church of San Esteven del Rey redirected Acoman piety to Saint Stephen, their patron, who was an early missionary and the first Christian martyr. To recover their independence, the pueblo revolted in 1680, slew 400

Spanish, and ejected the rest, who fled south to Paso del Norte.

The restoration of the Acoman social order lasted until 1692, when Governor Diego de Vargas hired Guadalupe del Paso to subdue the tribe. In seven years, the militia had overcome Pueblo resistance, revived the mission, and established a permanent colony. Reconquest found the Acoma at an ebb of their strength from years of warfare and from dispersal of members to mountain refuges along with the Navajo and Apache. As of 1760, a census numbered only 1,052 villagers, a loss of 65 percent. In 1863, the Acoma recovered sovereignty in tangible form, the Abraham Lincoln Cane, one of the Canes of Authority that acknowledged Indian autonomy and committed the U.S. government to honor aboriginal governments, respect tribal rights, protect natural resources, and enhance native welfare. Unfortunately, such symbolic gestures did little to secure the pueblo. By the 1920s, only some 1,000 inhabitants survived, but their numbers began climbing late in the twentieth century, when there were over 6,000 Pueblo.

New troubles arose in 1987 after Congress established El Malpais National Monument and Conservation Area, a 115,000-acre volcanic wilderness marked by lava flows, cinder cones, pressure ridges, and an underground complex of lava tubes. The 3,400-acre mass that encompasses the Ice Caves and Bandera Volcano contains ancestral Acoman grazing land in a harsh terrain known as the Badlands. Former New Mexico Governor Bruce King requested an exemption of aboriginal lands. The Acoma demanded access to the reservation, assurance of water rights, and, under the American Indian Religious Freedom Act, protection of religious shrines and sacred prehistoric ruins. They received no reply from Senator Pete Domenici, who promoted the monument as a boost to the tourist trade. To the detriment of Native Americans, newly elected Governor Garrey Carruthers endorsed the monument.

Along State Road 117, 100 Acoma organized a demonstration on May 21, 1987. On June 1, the American Indian Religious Freedom Act passed the House unanimously. Domenici offered to negotiate a land exchange, but it failed to protect religious sites. The Acoma went public with their grievance and compared their religious grounds to Jerusalem's Wailing Wall. The loss of seasonal shrines would hinder prayers for rain along a continuum from St. John's, Arizona, across the Zuñi Salt Lake and El Malpais to their pueblo. In protest, the Acoma Tribal Council proposed breaking the heirloom Abraham Lincoln Cane in front of the media in Washington, D.C. President Ronald Reagan rejected all attempts to redraft the El Malpais Monument bill. Despite an appeal by Senator Daniel Inouye, on December 17, 1987, the Senate unanimously approved the monument.

ACTIVITIES

After the Historic Preservation Commission tagged the mission as an endangered building marred by inappropriate plaster repairs, roof leaks, and moisture seepage, which rot timbers and damage artifacts, the Acoma strove to preserve their pueblo apartments while tending local farms and modern homes in the nearby villages of Anzac, Acomita, and McCarty. Annually, devout families resurface the ancient houses and the San Estevan complex, composed of the Franciscan mission church and its adjacent walled cemetery, guarded by symbolic handcrafted heads. To raise funds from tourism, the pueblo offers a visitor's center, museum, tours, and shops. Native artisans sell jewelry and their unique pottery, which art collectors and museum curators prize for its intricate black filigree designs. A noted twentieth-century potter, Santana Antonio, perpetuates the craft by coiling and coloring clay and firing the finished work under a burning pile of animal dung.

The Acoma welcome outsiders to annual festivals and celebrations. The tourist year begins with dancing on the Governor's Feast Day on February 1. On May 1, locals observe the Santa Maria Feast Day in honor of the Virgin Mary. Summer brings the greatest influx of outsiders to San Juan Day on June 23, Saint James's Day and the Corn Dance in July, and the popular Feast of San Estevan and fall Harvest Dance. To accommodate the harvest, over 200 years ago, locals moved the feast from December 26 to September 2. They offer authentic dances, fried bread, and a stew of red and green chiles. Tours of San Estevan del Rey Mission, a valuable

model of colonial Spanish style, focus on its stark dual-towered exterior, forty-foot beams, called *vegas,* and a hand-painted *retablos,* formed from a nine-stage mural of saints that adorns the thick walls above the altar. A religious festival held December 25 through 28 celebrates Christmas Acoma style.

Sources: "Acoma Pueblo"; Bernal; Carmody and Carmody 1993; Champagne 1994; Collins 1991; Heinerman 1989; "History of Acoma"; Kelley and Francis 1994; Kraker 1997, "The Malpais"; "Native American Religious Freedom"; *New Catholic Encyclopedia* 1967; "1997 NHL Endangered List"; Patterson and Snodgrass 1994; Steiger 1974; Strom 1994; Torrez 1998; Walking Turtle 1993.

Aghor Ashram

Sri Sarveshwari Samooh
19348 Carriger Road
Sonoma, California 95476
707-996-8915
www.aghor.org

Aghor Ashram, also known as the Sonoma Yoga Center, is a sacred site and educational source on the Hindu concept of yoga, or enlightenment. Hinduism, which is the religion of 70 percent of India, is an outgrowth of folk religion of the Indus Valley. Formalized through early collections of Vedas, the polytheistic faith evolved from 1400 to 400 B.C. by systematizing ritual and establishing priestly authority.

Since the third century A.D., Hindus have practiced yoga, a practical and intellectual form of exercise and self-control based on Samkhya, one offshoot of ancient Hinduism. For spiritual liberation, the practitioner frees the self from enslavement to earthly concerns, sensuality, and illusions by refocusing on purity and consciousness. By obscuring mental activities, controlling breathing, and withdrawing from materialism, yoga introduces the mind to *samadhi,* an ecstasy or bliss derived from the ultimate reality. Westerners embraced yogic techniques in the twentieth century for their physical and spiritual benefits.

HISTORY

Aghor Ashram derives from the ministry of a venerated holy man, the late Aghoreshwar

Mahaprabhu Bhagwan Ram. Born on September 12, 1937, in Gundi, India, he enjoyed solitude in childhood and entertained himself by singing or sitting in a grove. At age seven, he left home to seek God through meditation and made pilgrimages, beginning with one to the temples of Gaya outside Patna in northeastern India. As a mendicant, he sheltered outdoors, abstained from meat, and subsisted on fruits and vegetables. At a temple in Jagannathpuri on India's east coast, he made a spiritual breakthrough by achieving ecstasy.

At age fifteen, a turning point in his development, the Bhagwan journeyed to the Kashi Vishwanath temple in Banaras and the Kinaram Sthal in Varanasi. His guru initiated him as an *aghor* seeker and wandering *sadhu,* or seeker concentrating on relieving the suffering of the poor and performing miracles. In anticipation of his death in 1992, he visited the United States and blessed Sonoma's ashram. A nurturing site, it welcomes newcomers who seek peace and a clear understanding of spirituality. A monk, Baba Harihar Ramji, resides at the site and, by example, spreads Hindu teachings.

ACTIVITIES

Located in a serene glade, Aghor Ashram is open to all twice daily for prayer and meditation from 6:30 to 7:30 A.M. and 7:30 to 8:15 P.M. On Monday and Wednesday from 5:30 to 7:00 P.M., Tuesday and Thursday from 8:00 to 9:30 A.M., and Saturday from 9:30 to 11:00 A.M., staff holds ongoing meditation classes and offers hatha yoga, a rigorous physical regimen accompanying meditation to arouse dormant energy. The ashram assists seekers in breaking old habits and adhering to purifying principles and guidelines. Serious students further their understanding with an *aghor* mantra and one-on-one guidance. The ashram schedules lectures and discussion following Sunday meditation and publishes Baba Ramji's lectures in a monthly newsletter, the *Sri Sarveshwari Times.*

The ashram supports the Bhagwan's Samooh Relief Fund, a local charitable trust to aid India and other third-world countries. In 1996, the fund provided a mobile clinic for a leprosarium in Varanasi. In 1997, it financed a clinic and elementary school in Madhya Pradesh, India. Currently, the fund supports both the clinic and the school and offers free education to street beggars and scavengers at the town's Little Stars School, a rooftop academy that grew from 18 to 120 pupils. Students arrive by a rickshaw that gathers children from the streets. The school's principal dresses them in clean clothes and offers literacy training. Donors provide school materials, meals, clothing, and pocket money while contributing to a permanent structure still in the planning stages.

Sources: "Aghor Ashram"; *Eerdmans' Handbook to the World's Religions* 1982; Gentz 1973; "Hinduism in America"; Pickford 1999; Smith 1995; "Who is a Hindu?" 1999; *World Religions* 1998.

Air Force Academy Chapel
Chaplain Mark Sahady
U.S. Air Force Academy Chapel
Colorado Springs, Colorado
719-333-3300
FAX 719-333-2856
www.usafa.af.mil/hc

One of North America's prize modern houses of worship, the Air Force Academy Chapel is a symbol of vision and vista. Set in the Rocky Mountain Range, it is actually three religious sites in one. A blend of individualized styles of worship and artistic representations of faith for Protestants, Catholics, and Jews have elevated the structure to one of the mid-twentieth century's grandest architectural feats. Graced by stained glass, needlework, and acoustical precision, the chapel enhances student spirituality, making oneness with God a vital aspect of training for the nation's top military leaders.

HISTORY

Created during the Eisenhower administration, the Air Force Academy received congressional sanction on April 1, 1954. By July 11, 1955, the first class of cadets assembled at a temporary location at Lowry Air Force Base in Denver. Three years later, the institution relocated on a 19,000-acre plot east of the Rampart Range and seven miles north of Colorado Springs. In planning for a chapel, military authorities enlisted input from the General Commission on Chaplains in the Armed Services, the National Jewish Welfare Board, and the Roman Catholic

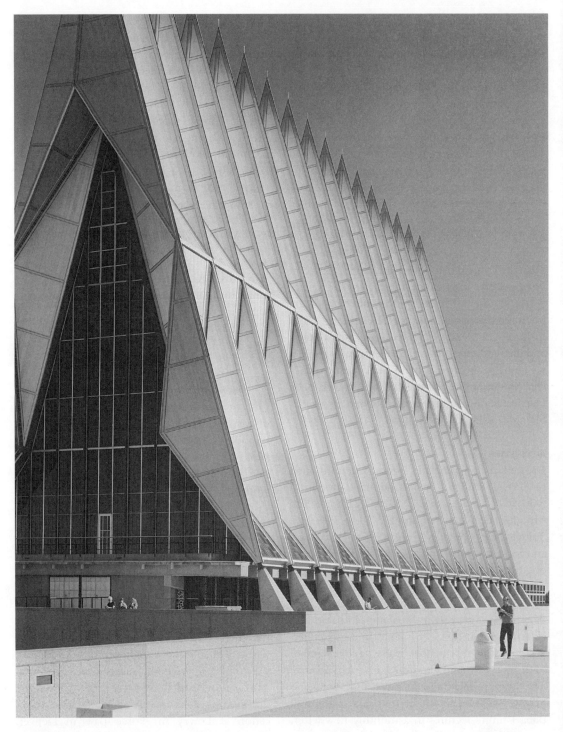

The Air Force Academy Chapel accommodates variety in faith and individual spirituality. (G. E. Kidder Smith/Corbis)

Military Ordinariate. In 1959, contractor Robert E. McKee and associates in Santa Fe, New Mexico, began building, finishing the chapel in 1963.

ARCHITECTURE

An uplifting structural feature of the 4,200-acre campus, the Air Force Academy Chapel crowns the school's architecture and speaks in design the essence of challenge. Over five years of planning and four of construction, campus officials sought a blend of artistry and material to accommodate individuals' spirituality. Its soaring triangular shape connects earth and sky in a union of solid construction and lofty aim. Against the panorama of the Rockies, the structure lifts seventeen aligned spires topping individual denominational chapels for worship, scriptural study, and religious fellowship.

In endorsement of variety in faith, the building is composed of three distinctive chapels under a single roof and offers separate entrances for Protestantism, Catholicism, and Judaism, the nation's predominant faiths. Above parallel flights of steps at the terrace level, the Catholic Chapel, Our Lady of the Skies, opens on a modern narthex featuring baptistery and alcoves walled with marble chips and semiprecious stones mined in Colorado. The sanctuary seats 500 along with 80 choir members. The design adapts concrete beams and columns to support amber and multicolored glass side walls between a gray ceiling and white terrazzo floor. A silvered nickel altar canopy and white Carrara marble sculpture, executed by artist Lumen Martin Winter, impose artistry and grandeur on the interior.

Balanced details contribute to an atmosphere of mystery and worship. Needlepoint kneelers, executed by wives of Air Force officers, edge the communion rail. They present the Christian cross flanked by the symbols of the alpha and omega, the first and last characters of the Greek alphabet. Against mosaic tesserae in blue, turquoise, rose, and gray Venetian glass, the reredos offsets a female figure at left with a guardian angel at right. Over them hovers a dove with outspread wings representing the omnipresence of the Holy Spirit. On the side walls are fourteen modern depictions of the stations of the cross, the path that Christ followed to Calvary.

Each dramatic pose stands out on white marble in high relief against a mosaic background in red and turquoise glass. A small wood crucifix from Jerusalem's Mount of Olives adorns each station in the lower right corner.

The adjacent Jewish Chapel, constructed under the supervision of Frank Greenhaus of New York, accommodates 100 worshippers in a circular space symbolizing the contribution of the Air Force to world peace and the unity of monotheism. Cyprus stanchions and translucent panels of pebble glass dramatize the square foyer. Cushioned walnut armchairs enhance the dignity and comfort of the auditorium. The area reposes in purple-violet light emanating from glass panels on the east and west walls. The foyer flooring of Jerusalem brownstone was a gift from the Israeli Defense Forces. A series of nine paintings on curved wood overlaid in gilt depicts three themes through episodes from scripture—brotherhood in the meeting of Ruth and Boaz, a sermon by Isaiah, and Jacob wrestling with the angel; military might in Solomon at work on Proverbs, Ezekiel's vision, and a chariot of fire poised to take Elijah to heaven; and justice in a verse from Deuteronomy, Solomon's judgment over two women claiming the same child, and Abraham's plea that God save Sodom and Gomorrah. At the west portal, the mezuzah bears the inscription "And God the Almighty Bless Thee."

Ludwig Y. Wolpert of the Jewish Museum in New York City designed the artistic elements. A menorah, or seven-branch candelabrum, lights the wall behind the lectern. The heart of Judaic worship, the Torah, stands in the holy ark. The scroll is a Holocaust relic that remained safe from the Nazis during World War II and resurfaced in 1989 in Czestochowa, Poland. The Ten Commandments in runic script mark the ark's open doors. Surrounding it is a metal circlet of Hebrew letters citing Psalm 139:8—"If I take the wings of the morning, and dwell in the uttermost parts of the sea"—and Proverbs 3:17–18—"Her ways are ways of pleasantness, and all her paths are peace. She is a tree of life to them that lay hold upon her: and happy is everyone that retaineth her." To the right of the ark is a kiddush cup between towering candlesticks. Over all shines the eternal light, suspended from the ceiling within a metal fantasy of the star of David.

An All Faiths Room at the far end of the building, which seats 30, suits the needs of smaller groups. Designed to accommodate all faiths, it continues the mosaic motif of the two chapels and features a tripod lectern, a small electric organ, molded wooden chairs, and an unadorned altar table set before a curtain wall. The staff arranges religious accoutrements to suit the tenets and purpose of each assembly.

On the upper level, aluminum tetrahedrons frame the Protestant Chapel, which seats 1,200 with additional spaces for 120 in the choir loft. Ahead lies a stirring artistic experience. Stained glass braced with cast tracery gentles the convergence of metal ninety-nine feet over terrazzo flooring. The building soars upward from an ample flight of stairs. From twenty-four darker shades of colored glass at the rear of the nave, worshippers experience a suffusion of brighter light from 24,000 pieces of smooth and chipped glass, a symbol of spiritual illumination. Ranks of walnut and mahogany pews convey order. Uprights at the center aisle echo the shape of early airplane propellers; backs replicate the leading edge of supersonic aircraft.

In contrast to the vertical thrust, the altar conveys stability. A curved reredos crafted in multicolored mosaic, also by Lumen Martin Winter, focuses attention on the elements of worship and upward to an elongated metal cross formed of forty-six feet of aluminum suspended above. Slender, yet compelling, it appears to float in air. At dais level, an elegantly simple altar bears an open Bible. Paired flower arrangements, candlesticks, and candelabra above and four travertine marble columns below enhance a fifteen-foot marble slab shaped like a boat symbolizing Christ's selection of fishermen for disciples. To the right, a metal bookrest rises from a sturdy column carved with verses from the Gospel of John declaring, "In the beginning was the word." At left, a slender bronze rail crowns a circular marble pulpit with a reminder from the Gospel of Matthew that "the kingdom of heaven is at hand."

A homey touch brings cadets to earth. Two ranks of arced kneelers, the concept of Mrs. Thomas D. White, wife of the Air Force Chief of Staff, combine the needlepoint of officers' wives worldwide. In religious symbolism colored crimson, gold, blue, and white, the arcs range toward the center. The cover at the far left features the Chi-Rho, an abbreviation of the Greek *Christos*. It is followed in order by five styles of crosses—*alisée paté, barbée, crosslet, bottonnée, quadraté*—and concludes at center with the alpha and omega, a fused symbol of the beginning and end of time. To the right, the order of symbols reverses, moving from alpha and omega through five additional styles of crosses—Canterbury, potent, *pommée, patoncé, commissée*—and concludes with the Chi-Rho.

Above the choir, a classical pipe organ, designed by Walter Holtkamp and constructed by M. P. Möller Organ Company, rises thirty-two feet over the loft. Metallic wing-shaped ranks of pipes echo the cross at the altar in a dramatic rise to right and left with grand pipes at the center. Thrusts of *trompetae* crown the instrument's more than 4,300 pipes and 67 stops.

ACTIVITIES

The Air Force Academy Chapel, under the direction of its chaplains, coordinates formal worship, scriptural study, religious discussion, spiritual retreat, and humanitarian outreach. Cadets are welcome to regular services and holy day and feast day functions and to private counsel from members of the staff. Chapel clergy incorporate the services of cadet assistants as lectors, eucharistic ministers, cantors, ushers, church musicians, and study leaders. To assess student spiritual welfare, three cadet councils—Catholic, Jewish, and Protestant—form a parish advisory board and aid and support religious programs. Participation is voluntary, with annual elections replacing graduating board members. The councils broaden expression of beliefs and represent the academy as delegates to religious conferences and intercollegiate conventions.

The chapel is open Monday through Saturday from 9:00 A.M. to 5:00 P.M. and Sunday from 1:00 to 5:00 P.M. but closed to tours during worship services. Protestant worship is open to the public on Sunday at 9:00 and 11:00 A.M. and open to cadets only on Wednesday night. Weekly devotions are available Monday through Friday from 6:20 to 6:50 A.M. Roman Catholic mass welcomes the public Sunday morning at 9:00 and 11:00 and weekdays at the same time as Protestant devotions. A cadets-only Sunday mass is held at 5:30 P.M. An Orthodox service takes place in the All Faiths Room on Sunday at 10:00 A.M. Jewish worship occurs at 7:00 P.M. on Friday and Muslim worship at 11:30 A.M. on Friday in the new All Faiths Room.

In addition to regular scheduling, the chapel remains in constant use and must be booked months in advance for weddings, receptions, and special occasions and such annual events as the National Day of Prayer, held May 1, and two Protestant candlelight services and a midnight mass on Christmas Eve. In October 1999, Metropolitan Isaiah, an official of the Greek Orthodox Church from Denver, blessed the newly renovated All Faiths Room. Standing in for Archbishop Demetrios, head of the Greek Orthodox Church of America, he initiated open worship at vespers in the Protestant Chapel.

Sources: "Academy Chapel Booked As New Graduates Marry" 1998; "Briefing" 1999; "Chapel, Air Force Academy"; *Encyclopedia Americana* 1999; *Encyclopedia Britannica;* "U.S. Air Force Academy Cadet Chapel"; *World Religions* 1998.

All Faiths Peace Chapel
See Chapel of Peace.

All Saints' Chapel
Chaplain Thomas Ward
Associate Chaplain Annwn Myers
University of the South
731 University Avenue
Sewanee, Tennessee 37375
931-598-1274
FAX 931-598-1645
tward@sewanee.edu

A grand Tennessee landmark, All Saints' Chapel is the geographic and spiritual centerpiece of the University of the South, an Episcopal seminary founded in 1868. Designed in the European tradition of sturdy square towers pierced with arched windows and topped with spires, the sanctuary accommodates daily worship as well as holiday festivals, choral performances, lectures, and leadership seminars that contribute to spiritual growth and continuing education of clergy, lay leaders, and congregations of numerous faiths. The staff's ecumenical outreach typi-

fies the campus reception of followers of the world's religions.

HISTORY AND ARCHITECTURE
The University of the South orients its program toward a balance between godliness and academics. Alumni take pride in the school's twenty-two Rhodes scholars and publication of the *Sewanee Review,* the nation's oldest literary quarterly. Originally, the university worship place, a wood-frame structure built on the south lawn in 1868, was called St. Augustine's Chapel, named for St. Augustine's School in Canterbury, Kent, England. After nine enlargements, as part of the university's golden anniversary, trustees broke ground in 1904 for All Saints' Chapel of Tennessee. New York architect Ralph Adams Cram began work on the edifice on June 25, 1905. His progress faltered in 1907 with the failure of the Bank of Winchester. By 1910, he could offer only a temporary wooden floor and ceiling for interim use.

The university was slow to complete the chapel. Officials began the final stage of construction in 1957 in anticipation of a centennial celebration. The vice-chancellor, Dr. Edward McCrady, provided the plans, which he had drawn in 1937 from a study of Chartres, Notre Dame, and Amiens cathedrals in France and St. Mary the Virgin, the University Church at Oxford University, England. The roofline calls for finials at intervals between each pair of pointed windows. The façade features a large rose window over an ivy-covered lower story, setting off the regular placement of four smaller pointed windows and a central wooden portal. At completion in July 1959, the chapel, which seats 1,400, stretched 35 by 233 feet and reached a height of 51 feet. It followed ancient Christian alignment on an east-west axis and preserved links to the original chapel with narthex pews from the old building.

In medieval Gothic style, the interior reprises the school's first century in four stained-glass narthex windows, the work of J. Wippell and Company, Ltd., of Exeter, England. In twenty-four scenes picturing nineteenth-century chancellors and vice-chancellors, portraits capture the likenesses and personal traits of founders, deans, professors, distinguished alumni, laborers,

A grand Tennessee landmark, All Saints' Chapel is the geographic and spiritual centerpiece of the University of the South, an Episcopal seminary founded in 1868. (Courtesy Office of Communications, Sewanee, The University of the South, Woodrow Blettel)

and benefactors. A rose window uplifts a luminous chalice and vine, symbolizing Christ's unifying body and the spiritual glory of Christianity. Fourteen clerestory windows line the nave with more depictions of Bible stories and church history. The twenty-four aisle windows honor the university's academic disciplines. Three sanctuary windows display the *Te Deum Laudamus* (We Praise Thee, God) in a company of apostles, martyrs, cherubim, seraphim, and church servants worldwide. Windows above the choir characterize Christ's life. In November 1999, the university honored Cecil Woods, founder of the Friends of the Sewanee Summer Music Center, at the dedication of a new window designed by Brenda Welch Belfield.

Smaller worship areas offer more intimate settings for private contemplation, daily offices, weekday communion, and small group assembly. St. Augustine's Chapel extends at the left of the choir. Its two side windows trace church origins from England and Scotland to North America. A rose window combines the symbols

of the apostles. In 1991, women of the diocese of Arkansas stitched needlepoint kneelers.

Music is a focus of All Saints' Chapel. Casavant Frères of Quebec, Canada, completed the three-manual organ in 1962. They designed five divisions of 4,000 pipes, both exposed and enclosed and graced the west wall with a processional trumpet. The addition of the Leonidas Polk Memorial Carillon to the 143-foot Shapard Tower in 1975 augmented the liturgical music program. Installed in 1958 and upgraded in 1991, the instrument harmonizes the voices of fifty-six bells. Artists at the keyboard have included carillonists Marcia de Bary, Jeff Davis, and Laura Hewitt Whipple.

In 1999, the renovation of Quintard and Gorgas halls, remodeling of the campus bookstore, and construction of a restaurant and convenience store refocused student life on the quadrangle and All Saints' Chapel. An adjunct to the campus ministry is a new center for worship, the Chapel of the Apostles at the seminary, slated for completion by August 2000. Designed by

Arkansas architect E. Fay Jones, the 9,500-square-foot building seats 250 worshippers.

ACTIVITIES

As worship site for the campus community, All Saints' Chapel houses daily and Sunday events as well as such university rituals as academic convocations, installation of officers and honor society members, and baccalaureate and commencement ceremonies. To ally themselves with the university mission, students come to the chapel to sign the honor code, a ceremony promoting individual ethics. To promote individual involvement, the staff conducts a variety of services that incorporate student lectors and representatives of the Acolyte Guild and Sacristan Guild. Mission outreach coordinates additional volunteers for Habitat for Humanity and Housing Sewanee, Inc. Pastoral guidance features Methodist and Lutheran faculty members and extends its ministry to St. Mary's Convent and local parishes. A busy calendar lists seminars, quiet days, theological reflection groups, endowed lectureships, and training by visiting bishops, fellows, and scholars. In March 1999, the staff welcomed a notable guest speaker, the Most Reverend and Right Honorable George L. Carey, Archbishop of Canterbury.

A weekly calendar enhances student life with opportunities to explore individual beliefs. Each Sunday evening at 6:30, the campus community gathers for Growing in Grace, which features varied preachers and the music of guitarists, singers, keyboard players, and percussionists. On Monday at 4:00 P.M., Associate Chaplain Annwn Myers leads Gleanings, a religious study for undergraduate women; on Tuesday, the staff offers a catechumenate to introduce newcomers to the Christian faith and to explore religious issues in small-group sessions. A mixed age gathering convenes on Tuesday at 12:15 P.M. for Reading Thomas Merton, a shared reflection on the writings of the influential monk, theologian, social critic, and spiritual master. Centering Prayer, a contemporary form of an ancient way of praying, meets at 4:00 P.M. on Wednesday and Thursday. The chaplain conducts Bible study on Thursday at 12:15 P.M. An ecumenical gathering, the Canterbury Group, meets on Friday at 6:30 P.M. for informal suppers, games, discussion, and movies.

An outstanding feature of chapel worship is the University Choir, directed by Dr. Robert G. Delcamp, university professor of music, organist, and choirmaster. Annually, the 80-member group performs regular liturgy, a monthly traditional choral evensong, holy day services, and concerts and tours, which transport the campus religious program to cathedrals, abbeys, and churches in Great Britain. A seasonal feature for the past forty years, the Christmas Festival of Lessons and Carols, draws a combined attendance of 3,500. The choirmaster bases the blend of carols and anthems on the program sung at King's College Chapel, Cambridge University.

Sources: "All Saints' Chapel"; "Color and Light" 1997; Smith, Huston, 1994; "Welcome to the University of the South"; Williams, Peter W., 1997.

Amana Church Society

1112 Twenty-sixth Avenue
Box 103
Middle Amana, Iowa 52307
319-622-6155
amana@hightruth.com
www.emanna.com

Like many pioneers, the Amana Church Society was a durable nineteenth-century utopian colony of German Lutherans seeking a new start on the American frontier. The current 450 members derive their worship style from the parent group—German pietist immigrants who formed one of the nation's most successful communes. Sustained by a firm belief in God and the Bible, the Amanites worshiped in plain buildings and uplifted group spirit with song, prayer, and cooperative concern. Their organization remained unaltered for nearly ninety years, making the Amana German-language society one of the world's longest-lived mutualistic colonies.

In 1965, for the Amanites' contribution to American history and society, the U.S. Department of the Interior named as a National Historic Landmark the 465 buildings of the Amana complex of seven villages. In 1997, the national landmarks trust listed Amana Colonies among endangered historical buildings. Currently threatened by new construction, unsuitable alteration, deterioration, and local opposition to

Like many pioneer groups, the Amana Church Society was a durable nineteenth-century utopian colony of German Lutherans seeking a new start on the American frontier. (Layne Kennedy/Corbis)

restrictive ordinances, Amana may lose its historical integrity unless maintenance and restoration rescue it from inferior management.

HISTORY AND BELIEFS

The Amana Church Society springs from German Lutherans seeking a revival of the Reformation spirit. They advocated Bible study, pragmatic rather than intellectual Christianity, Christian schools and universities, and the use of constructive preaching rather than criticism to build Christian character. A distant branch of standard Lutheranism, the Amana society dates to 1714, when mystics Johann Friedrich Rock and Eberhard Ludwig Gruber established the Church of True Inspiration near Darmstadt, Germany. In 1716, Johann A. Gruber set down *Twenty-Four Rules of True Godliness,* which guided the Inspirationists into the next century.

The devout venerated the Trinity and anticipated revelation of a divine plan through *Werkzueges* (human instruments or prophets) and in spiritual baptism to obtain forgiveness and salvation. They held communion once every two years. Near the end of the eighteenth century, the group declined. In 1820, the combined efforts of Michael Krausert, organizer and hymnographer Christian Metz, and Alsatian orator and prophet Barbara Heinemann revived the sect under the name of Inspirationists. On January 15 of that year, Heinemann published "Ten Vital Tenets, a Formal Statement of the Re-awakening in the New Community." As their lot improved, the community drew new members to Ysenburg and Armenburg. The influx raised fears outside the church that local jobs in woolen mills and other enterprises were in danger.

Under persecution for refusing to swear oaths or serve in the military, rejecting public-school education for their children, and choosing spiritual baptism rather than physical application of water, Inspirationists suffered scrutiny of their schools, threat to religious freedom, and inflated taxes and rent burdens. Through the writings of member Christian Metz, they clarified their *Glaubensbekentniss* (profession of faith) before the ministry at Darmstadt in April 1839.

Because the ministry issued no ruling, in 1842, the Inspirationists fulfilled a prophecy of resettlement in a foreign land by emigrating to the United States. Led by Metz and Heinemann, they bought land east of Buffalo, New York, and formed a Community of True Inspiration called the Ebenezer Society. On 5,000 acres of the Seneca Indian Reservation, they supported themselves with proceeds from a nursery, greenhouse, and truck farm. In 1859, Amanites incorporated and adopted a constitution and bylaws drawn up by a *Grossebruderrat* (board of trustees).

To maintain rural surroundings and escape the urbanism of Buffalo, 800 of Ebenezer's population of 1,200 moved west over a period of nine years and, in 1864 at the height of the Civil War, regrouped twenty miles from Cedar Rapids, Iowa. On 26,000 acres of farmland and forest on opposite shores of the Iowa River, they founded seven villages—Amana, East Amana, Homestead, High Amana, Middle Amana, South Amana, and West Amana. They chose their group name from scripture—Amana, a mountain range in Lebanon cited in the Song of Solomon 4:8 and meaning "to remain true." As an agricultural trade center, the commune profited from weaving woolens, making wine and barrels, and selling processed meats. Metz led the group until his death in 1867.

Amana village planners grouped shops on the main street and located farm buildings at the outer border of cultivated fields to be near the apiaries, gardens, orchards, and vineyards. The society advocated celibacy but tolerated marriage. Amanite families occupied assigned quarters in large, neatly fenced residences, exercised in strictly segregated groups of men and women, ate in dining halls seating thirty to forty and run by a *Küchebaas* (kitchen overseer), and worked at tasks in fifty-five communal kitchens, breweries, fields, brickyards, sandstone quarries, gristmills, lumber mills, tanneries, cooperages, smithies, and cabinet shops.

Amanites acclimated to lock-step discipline. Inured to hard work, they staffed factories producing woolen blankets, calico, furniture, locks, harnesses, shoes, tinware, and clocks. Six colony agents traveled the country selling their goods. With the proceeds, the society offered free medical care, a *Kinderschule* (day care), and year-round schooling through eighth grade. Beyond minimal education, they apprenticed young men to trades at age fourteen and allowed promising men and women to seek professional careers at public schools and universities or to train as *Hebammen* (midwives) with local doctors. Elders approved betrothals, conducted an annual *Unterredung* (examination) of behavior, and punished infractions. The only private holdings were clothing allowances distributed annually at the rate of $40 for men, $25 for women, and $15 for children.

By 1881, the membership had doubled, but subsequent modernization weakened the fiber of the Amana colonies, bringing interest in Christian Scientism and capitalism along with technological advancements that threatened the agrarian fundamentals. The combined disasters of a fire on August 12, 1923, in the flour and woolen mills and the Great Depression ended the Amanite dream of autonomy. By members' vote, on June 1, 1932, the society forestalled financial collapse with the "Great Change" by opting to dismantle the commune and replace it with two separate structures—the Amana Society, Inc., the formal structure of their business and farming operations, and the Amana Church Society for supervision of worship.

Under reorganization, elders lost most of their governing powers. Members, like most Americans, began dining in intimate family units. They worked for wages and accepted shares of the Amana corporation, a thriving concern that built refrigerators and freezers. Entrepreneurs ventured into new businesses. Villagers in Middle Amana added a high school. Women sought more education. Young members drifted from isolation in the colony's religious communism to the democracy practiced beyond village bounds.

ACTIVITIES

Today, worship style varies from the typical Iowa Protestant church. Eleven weekly services—daily for vespers, plus Wednesday and Saturday matinal services and Sunday morning and evening gatherings—bring people together for *Versammeln* (worship). Elders excuse only the sick and women tending young children. To relieve distraction, elders divide Amanites by gender, with women wearing black caps, shawls, and aprons according to the injunction from Saint Paul in I Corinthians 11:5 that women cover their heads while praying. The added reminder from I Timothy 2:9 that women should adorn their souls, not their bodies, sets the tone for pious females.

At the three-story, steepleless meeting house, congregants enter at a set of steps under a portico leading to the second floor. The unadorned meeting room is painted blue and contains no crucifix or altar. All sing *a cappella* with the aid of *Vorsänger* (song leaders). In place of ministers, congregants follow the direction of thirteen lay elders, devout men and women who sit facing the congregation. Weddings, funerals, and church services involve similar proceedings. Society cemeteries group graves in the order of their deaths to maintain a spirit of equality before God and designate each with identical markers.

Currently, worshippers gather at Middle Amana, the setting for most church society services, which are led by volunteers. The thirteen elders provide a German-language service on Sunday at 8:30 A.M. and English liturgy at 10:00 A.M. When the two congregations combine, they use a larger church. The order of services begins with silent meditation, reflection, and prayer before an opening hymn. After the reading of inspired testimony of recorded events from 1714 to 1883, members kneel facing their pine benches in humble submission to God. One member recites the Apostles' Creed, followed by the presiding elder's prayer. The congregation concludes with the Lord's Prayer. After an elder reads from scripture, members and elders join in reading verses aloud. Commentary precedes the reading of a psalm, a hymn of praise from the *Psalterspiel* (hymnal), closing prayer, and exit proceeding single file by row. Elders extend their service at all times for prayer and personal counseling.

Church activities involve members in community service, East Iowa Bible Camp, leadership training, a fall farm progress show, and benevolences to the Salvation Army and Red Cross for northeast Iowa flood relief. In April 1999, members sold *A Taste of Amana,* a history and cookbook, at the Amana Heritage Museum. Youth raised money for world hunger with a thirty-hour fast. Amanites celebrate Easter with

eggs filled with seeds as symbols of Christ's life. The guild raised funds in May by selling *Obst Küchen* (fruit cookies) and by setting up a quilting frame in the Amana Woolen Mill during Maifest. Congregants joined in the American Cancer Society Relay for Life, in labor for Habitat for Humanity, and in the Cardboard Boat Regatta during the Cedar Rapids Freedom Festival. In June, the society held a Family Dedication Service. From July 19 to July 23, members conducted a vacation Bible school.

The last half of the year for Amanites continues charitable and spiritual activities. In September the church picnic includes an auction of baked goods, crafts, and donated time, with proceeds going to the American Red Cross and Habitat for Humanity. In November, members take Thanksgiving Day as an opportunity for *Bundesschliessung* (covenant renewal), a repledging of life to God. The Community Church Museum in Homestead, open Monday through Saturday from 10:00 A.M. to 5:00 P.M. and Sunday from noon to 5:00 P.M., features church architecture, religious background, and the foundation of the communal society.

Sources: "Amana Church Society Newsletter" 1999; Dimmitt 1998; "*Glaubensbekentniss* or Profession of Faith" 1988; Hennes 1997; "History of Amana Colonies"; Hoppe 1998; "1997 Landmarks at Risk Report" 1997; Searle; Smith 1995; "Towards a Dictionary of Communitarian Societies."

Antelope Canyon

Navajo Parks and Recreation
P.O. Box 4803
Page, Arizona 86040
520-698-3347
FAX 520-698-3360
www.navajoland.com

Outside Page, Arizona, Native Americans connect with the earth mother at Antelope Canyon, a complex corridor of natural slots, narrow defiles, and tortuous natural passageways known as Corkscrew Canyon. During the Jurassic period, the massive underground fissure took shape in the mesa from centuries of subterranean flood waters called turbidity currents. Fueled by gravity, they continue to swirl over a hundred feet

Outside Page, Arizona, Native Americans connect with the earth mother at Antelope Canyon, a complex corridor of natural slots, narrow defiles, and tortuous natural passageways. (Richard Cummins/Corbis)

ways, dark recesses, and colonnades are the residence of the *chindi,* evil spirits who lurk and await opportunities to avenge themselves on their enemies. Strange sobs and moans survive as proof of the *chindis'* earthly sufferings.

The area preserves prehistory in a fragile quarter-mile fissure of soft desert sandstone. Its dramatic sweep of petrified dunes once lay at the bottom of a shallow inland sea. The obscure passage once accommodated pronghorn antelope and nesting birds. According to the Navajo, the ancient Anasazi retreated to the canyon, which offered a natural refuge from harsh weather and enemy attack.

The canyon became a public landmark in 1931 after its discovery by twelve-year-old Sue Tsosie, who was herding sheep from Manson Mesa to Kaibeto. Subsequent Navajo visitors sought its silent halls as a source of reverence and communion with the Great Spirit. Alternatively named Upper Antelope, Wind Cave, and the Crack, it intrigued visitors, hikers, climbers, and artists after photographer Bruce Barnbaum put its spirals and grooves on the map with renowned black-and-white shots of light bouncing from cavern walls. Today, color photography captures the blend of mauve, apricot, crimson, orange, and chocolate tones in the uneven natural union of sand and rock.

down through sinkholes and caves, carving out piers, contouring wave-sided chambers, and sculpting irregular columns on the way to Lake Powell. The eerie quiet and splash of light make the canyon a natural cathedral.

HISTORY

Antelope Canyon is an evocative site because of the shift of light on wind- and water-scoured walls. Varying tone-on-tone over undulating sandstone and rock, the shadowed sweep, pierced by irregular light, produces a natural gallery that the Navajo call Tse'neh'na'eh'diz's-jaa (a place where water paints a picture of itself). According to oral tradition, Antelope Canyon was the birthing chamber from which Mother Earth bore humankind. The striated channel remains intact as a monument to womanhood and to water, a natural force reverenced along with air, fire, and earth. The irregular hall-

ACTIVITIES

Antelope Canyon is part of LeChee Navajo tribal land. It naturally evokes a spontaneous hush and reverence from outsiders who have never experienced light and sound in a slot canyon. Today, the Navajo return to the canyon as a sanctuary for sacred water purification rites. They maintain a gate at the entrance to the narrows and charge admission to tourists, who may explore only when conditions allow. Upper Antelope is less of a challenge than Lower Antelope, which requires entrance by ladder and accommodates inexperienced visitors for only a third of its length. The rugged remainder is so constricted and sharply uneven that it requires ropes and advanced climbing skills.

Erosion is an ongoing process at Antelope Canyon. Without warning, rain can transform the dry wash into a raging river. Because of the danger of falls or flash floods, park officials require tourists to walk the channel with a guide authorized by the John Wesley Powell Memorial Museum in Page, Arizona. Safe navigation requires a flashlight and protection from blustery winds. Officials closed Lower Antelope to the public after a flash flood on August 12, 1997, when unpredictable torrents swept away ten European and two American hikers who ignored a Navajo guide's warning of a thunderstorm. Eleven died amid tons of mud and debris. Recovery required seventy-five volunteers and two search dogs, who retrieved two of the bodies. The surviving adult was seriously buffeted and stripped of clothing before he escaped.

Although the victims violated tribal rules, Albert Hale, president of the Navajo nation, offered his condolences to children orphaned by the disaster. When the canyon reopened February 6, 1998, Navajo guides pressed stronger warnings on the unwary. They installed rescue nets and communications systems and bolted heavy-duty ladders at the entrance to Lower Antelope.

Sources: Cantor, George, 1993; Champagne 1994; "Dogs Aid Search for Flood Victims" 1997; "Eleven Killed in Canyon Flash Flood" 1997; Giese 1996; "Hidden Canyons of the Southwest"; Milne 1995; Milstein 1999; O'Neil 1999; Patterson and Snodgrass 1994; Perry 1998; Steiger 1974; Sutphen 1988; Walking Turtle 1993.

Apostolic Church of God

Bishop Arthur M. Brazier, Pastor
6320 South Dorchester
Chicago, Illinois 60637
773-667-1500
FAX 773-667-4804

In Chicago's decaying Woodlawn community, a megachurch—the Apostolic Church of God— stands firm against the flight of the black middle class to the suburbs. One of sixty black super-churches in the United States, Bishop Arthur M. Brazier's congregation demonstrates the hunger of middle-American black Christians for a different kind of solace from that of black churches of the Reconstruction or civil rights eras. Brazier's answer to many needs is a holistic ministry that keeps God and the Bible at center while ranging beyond rhetoric to deeds that change lives. On its third sanctuary in five years, the huge

congregation is a powerful amalgam—professional role models worshiping alongside the lower class in a symbiosis intended to transform the crumbling inner city through stewardship and self-empowerment. The resulting Christian renaissance has returned Chicago's urban blacks to a more dynamic, less judgmental mind-set.

BELIEFS

One of the ten Churches of God in the United States, the Chicago branch is a part of the Holiness movement begun by John Wesley. In 1903, American Bible Society sales representative A. J. Tomlinson founded the largest sect. He insisted that it have no creed and draw its strength solely from the Bible. The New Testament was the single source of faith and practice and the impetus for three rituals—baptism by immersion, foot washing as a sign of apostolic subservience, and regular observance of the Lord's Supper.

At the founder's death in 1943, his son, Homer Tomlinson, failed to hold a majority. The sect broke into three segments, with one begun in Anderson, Indiana, and another in Cleveland, Tennessee. Today, these variant groups maintain inspirational worship and center their activism on revivalism and missions. Their fundamentalism and legalism links them closely to other charismatic Protestants.

The African-American Church of God, a similar Pentecostal movement, originated at one of the major events of the twentieth century— the Azusa Street Revival in 1906, when William Seymour, father of American Pentecostalism, countenanced glossolalia, or speaking in tongues. In a warehouse setting in downtown Los Angeles, he described the phenomenon of spontaneous, God-driven utterance as a divine gift. His impetus stimulated white and black churches and numerous offshoots, in particular, the Church of the Living God, World Gospel Feast, Fire Baptized Holiness Church of God of the Americas, Dominion of God Incorporated, and Daddy Grace's United House of Prayer.

HISTORY AND ARCHITECTURE

A polished negotiator and likely leader for one of the nation's most spirited, burgeoning black megachurches, the Reverend Arthur Brazier is a nonthreatening freedom fighter. The author of

From Milk to Meat: Primer for Christian Living (1996), he won the 1997 Jesse Owens Humanitarian Award for his unique style of putting faith into action. Professionally, Brazier fills the demands of a massive pastorate that began in 1960 with 100 members. His daily work load encompasses 15,000 mostly middle-class parishioners, whose vehicles overrun four parking lots at two Sunday morning services.

The architecture of the Apostolic Church of God is expansive and inviting. Decked with marble, it features multipurpose rooms and a television studio. In amphitheater style, the seats surround an oversized pulpit. Chairs for 28 line the platform; the choir loft accommodates 125 singers. The 120,000-square-foot edifice offers red upholstered pews and a balcony to seat 3,500 attendees. Worshippers feel free to link arms, sway, reach hands skyward, applaud, sing, and shout "amen."

Congregants typically have compared services and styles of other church homes. They prefer an energetic, inspirational preaching style that uplifts and empowers. To free themselves of the restraints of black urbanism, these seekers have created a new sense of community. They support ministries that reach out to the poor and disadvantaged by rescuing and feeding the homeless and underwriting housing programs. In the view of some members, hope for the black underclass must come from such black altruistic congregations rather than government handouts.

ACTIVITIES

Unlike the traditionally staid churches of the mid-twentieth century, the Apostolic Church of God on South Dorchester meets the demands of worshippers for updated worship and music that surge with fellowship and optimism. Apostolic theology is a complex refinement of old-school conservatism that imposes a light touch on social and political issues. In the pulpit and over radio and television broadcasts, the tone is solacing and pragmatic rather than guilt-laden and moralistic.

Brazier's church has broken out of the mold of the complacent, insular parish to minister to Christians tired of reading about black-on-black violence, drug arrests, broken families, and teen pregnancies and dropouts. Disenchanted with 1960s-style welfare programs and affirmative action, congregants have reengineered their thinking toward black self-sufficiency through faith in God. They embrace a full-time, innovative outreach that schedules a health fair, marriage night out, and programs on single parenting and AIDS education alongside pastor-led Bible-study and prayer meetings.

Beyond parish concerns, Brazier fights what he calls "disinvestment" in local neighborhoods—the slow bleed of people and wealth that has sapped community health for over four decades since the Supreme Court outlawed housing covenants. As a member of Chicago Metropolitan Sponsors, he supports economic endowment projects that end political and social isolation of the underclass—housing and a shopping center in the Kenwood-Oakland section and the upgrading of neighborhood schools to encourage children to finish their education rather than fall into the trap of crime and drugs. In 1995, he coinitiated the Woodlawn Organization, a grassroots protest of the Chicago Transit Authority's attempts to gentrify the Woodlawn area by dismantling the Jackson Park El. In response to his optimism, in 1999, the congregation pledged a half million dollars toward feeding and sheltering the poor in Chicago's dismal South Side.

Sources: Ahlstrom 1972; Baron 1995; Brackett 1997; Crumm 1999; Grossman 1999; Lenz 1998; Moberg 1998; Plotkin; "Reformation Nailed as No. 1" 1999; Smith 1995; Tapia; Washburn 1996; *World Religions* 1998.

Aryaloka Buddhist Retreat Center

Venerable Urgyen Sangharakshita
14 Heartwood Circle
Newmarket, New Hampshire 03857
603-659-5456
FAX 603-659-5456
aryaloka@aol.com
www.fwbo.org

The Aryaloka Buddhist Retreat Center breaks the tradition of celibate monks to welcome uncloistered men and women to an active Buddhist community that divorces itself from Asian ritual.

URGYEN SANGHARAKSHITA

The Venerable Urgyen Sangharakshita, a teacher, poet, and author of forty books, is an experienced minister and reformer of Buddhism. He pioneered a twentieth-century branch of Buddhism that offers modern worshippers a liberal interpretation of age-old ideals and practices. Born Denis Lingwood in South London in 1925, he educated himself in Asian philosophy in boyhood and became a Buddhist at age sixteen. After military service in World War II, he served two decades in India as a monk and scholar with study of major schools of Buddhism and editing of India's Maha Bodhi Society journal. His work with untouchables exemplified a commitment to nurturing humankind. In the Theravadin tradition, his ordination followed initiation and preparation with Tibetan lamas. He has practiced Buddhism for nearly a half century through intensive application of faith to modern social principles.

The Venerable Sangharakshita bases a dynamic ministry on traditional philosophy, teachings, and practice and specializes in meditation, community, and ethical behavior. In England in 1967, he formed the Friends of the Western Buddhist Order, a nonmonastic, nonsectarian global consortium of Buddhist centers, retreats and monasteries, arts centers, educational and wellness programs, and ethical businesses. The movement spread to twenty countries on four continents; its fifty centers list membership at 660 and ordinations at over 1,000. In addition to the New Hampshire retreat, North American Buddhist centers serve San Francisco, Seattle, and Vancouver.

The movement's focus is refuge, the beginning of Buddhist commitment. In addition, it administers benevolences through the Karuna Trust, which supports self-help projects in health, education, and vocational training to alleviate poverty and uplift social welfare in India. In 1977, Sangharakshita defended homosexuals from unjust persecution during a blasphemy trail against the *Gay News of London* and published *Unspeakable: Buddhism and the Gay News,* a bold treatise that refutes the court's attempt to put Christianity ahead of other religions in England. In the late 1990s, he came under media scrutiny for inviting gays and lesbians to seek full involvement in the faith. He declared that his mission to homosexuals counters the exclusion and persecution of gay people by orthodox Christianity, which he characterized as a worldwide tyranny. Now semiretired, he searches for disciples to continue his ministry.

A short drive from Portsmouth, New Hampshire, the pleasant, unassuming compound fights stress by educating newcomers and regular members in relaxation, exercise, and self-study. The founder of a twentieth-century style of Buddhism, Urgyen Sangharakshita, teaches that the key to individual improvement is a blend of calm self-awareness and caring for others.

HISTORY AND ARCHITECTURE

Founded in 1985, Aryaloka Buddhist Retreat Center offers Buddhism without ethnic Asian decor. Located down a shady lane in the New England woods, the complex suits the informality and charm of the pine copse. To meet the needs of a men's monastic community and residential communities for men and women, the center occupies two silver geodesic domes and a barn. The staff finances activities by charging for retreats and classes and by offering bed and breakfast at a daily rate of $15. Preceptors ori-

ent, train, and ordain members in spiritual development and friendship.

A congenial, outgoing institution, the complex consists of a reception room, a shrine, classrooms, and an exercise area for yoga and tai chi. Informal groups convene in an airy open meeting room with picture windows overlooking the New Hampshire countryside. Attendees dress casually and relax in easy chairs and on sofas for conversation and instruction. Outside, paths, gardens, and shrines promote private introspection and meditation. Policy prohibits tobacco, illegal drugs, and firearms; food is vegetarian.

ACTIVITIES

The center is open daily from 9:30 A.M. to 4:00 P.M. and welcomes all comers to weekly classes and discussion groups on Buddhist principles, *sangha* (assembly night) every Tuesday evening, monthly workshops on meditation, a mask-making workshop, and regular weekend retreats. Throughout the year, staff celebrates Buddhist festivals:

- The Buddha's death on Parinvirvana Day, on the full moon in February
- Friends of the Western Buddhist Order Day on April 9
- Celebration of the Buddha's enlightenment on Wesak Day on the full moon in May
- The Buddha's first teaching in Sarnath, India, on Dharmachakra Day on the full moon in July
- Recognition of the spiritual community on Sangha Day on the full moon in November
- Padmasambhava Day on the full moon in September, the recognition of Padmasambhava, the faith's legendary fourth-century B.C. missionary, called Guru Rinpoche (Precious Teacher), who introduced Buddhism to Tibet

The Venerable Sangharakshita conducts retreats lasting from seven to ten days. Course work is available on Sutra or Vedic teachings, the writings of the Venerable Sangharakshita, correct breathing, individual growth, and friendship. The center also coordinates collective *pujas* (pilgrimages). In addition to Web site information, the staff distributes Buddhist books for Windhorse Publications and produces *Dharma Life,* a quarterly magazine, and *Lotus Realm,* a journal for Buddhist women. The year 2000 brought increased activity in commemoration of the center's fifteenth anniversary.

Sources: "Aryaloka Retreat Center"; Bowker 1997; "Buddhist Leader Outed for Gay Relationship" 1999; Bunting 1998; Epstein; "Friends of the Western Buddhist Order," http://balrog.joensuu.fi; "Friends of the Western Buddhist Order," http://www.fwbo.org; "Gay Buddhist Controversy Rocks Western Buddhist Order" 1999; Herbrechtsmeier 1993; Ling 1972; Lorie and Foakes 1997; "Padmasambhava"; "Review: 'Ritual and Devotion in Buddhism'" 1996; "Sangharakshita"; "The Spiritual Test" 1998; "Theravada Buddhism"; Vu.

Ave Maria Grotto

St. Bernard Abbey
1600 St. Bernard Drive S.E.
Cullman, Alabama 35055
256-734-4110
sbabbey@hiway.net
www.sbabbeyprep.org/grotto

The Ave Maria Grotto—a complex of 125 miniatures of churches, shrines, towers, pools and cataracts, glades, and civic buildings of ancient Rome, Palestine, and the United States—began at St. Bernard Abbey as the Little World of Brother Joe, an off-hours work of love. Outside Cullman in northern Alabama, some fifty miles north of Birmingham, the grotto's vernacular architecture bore the name Little Jerusalem because of the designer's focus on the holy city. It quickly became a tourist attraction and destination for pilgrims worldwide. Along the abbey's woodsy hillside, they walk, study and discuss the site, take pictures, and make obeisance to the Virgin Mary at the central display.

HISTORY

St. Bernard Abbey got its start in northern Alabama in 1876 with the arrival of seven monks from St. Vincent's Archabbey in Latrobe, Pennsylvania. After fifteen years, they formed the monastery at a creek east of Cullman and dedicated it September 29, 1891. The monks dedicated themselves to education and the community church and dispatched as many as 103 priests to parishes throughout Alabama, Kentucky, and Mississippi. The abbey gradually added a high school, junior college, and four-year college, which operated from 1956 to1979. During a national downturn in vocations, the number entering holy orders declined to 50 in the 1980s. Since 1981, the monks have established a retreat center in unused classrooms.

The abbey grotto's bejeweled diorama is the design of Brother Joseph Zoettl, a Benedictine monk from Landshut, Bavaria. A small man, he was deformed in childhood by an accident that caused a hump on his back. Because the handicapped were not eligible for ordination at that time, he settled for life as a monk. He arrived at St. Bernard Abbey in 1892, a year after the monastery's founding, as one of its first college students. After a series of assignments as household and kitchen manager in Stonega, Virginia, and Tuscumbia and Cullman, Alabama, in 1910, he took charge of shoveling

The Ave Maria Grotto, a complex of 125 miniatures, began at St. Bernard Abbey as the "Little World of Brother Joe," an off-hours work of love. (Courtesy Ave Maria Grotto)

coal at the monastery furnace and controlling steam production. Beginning in 1912, in his private time, Brother Joseph indulged a fascination with history and achitecture by crafting miniature shrines from scraps of cement and construction debris, stone, seashells, rocks, marbles, paste jewelry, and icons to sell in the abbey souvenir shop.

Because Brother Joseph copied from picture postcards and lacked a comprehensive ground plan for each miniature, he had to guess at the back and sides of each project. For detail work on the petite buildings, he acquired glass, tiles, chandelier prisms, fishermen's floats, and bricolage from around the globe. The assemblage took him more than four decades to gather and sort materials, select buildings to copy, and add such structural minutia as downspouts, finials, clocks, and door knockers. He placed the models on the recreation grounds in shadow-boxed vistas and scenarios, steadily adorning four acres with a majestic architectural collection dubbed a "sermon in stone."

As the display of folk art drew visitors, Father

Patrick O'Neill directed Brother Joseph to move his work to a larger slope—a bluff behind the abbey at a former quarry overlooking Eight Mile Creek. The path begins at the Bethlehem shrine, Jesus' birthplace, and passes the Tower of Thanks, a tiled structure topped with glass balls and cement leaves. Beyond lies a shrine to Saint Peter, the Spanish abbey at Montserrat, two structures from Brother Joseph's hometown, and a Statue of Liberty, by which he honored his adoptive homeland.

Brother Joseph excelled at eclecticism. He added a tribute to World War I-era Red Cross volunteers, Hansel and Gretel's temple of the fairies, and the St. Bernard Abbey. There are mission chapels, Lazarus's tomb, cathedrals, American landmarks, the Brazen Serpent of Moses, a statue of Pope Pius X, and a series of Roman replicas—the Pantheon, the Colosseum, the Temple of Vesta, the Cathedral of the Immaculate Conception, and Roman religious sites, including his masterwork, St. Peter's Basilica. Beyond a depiction of Jerusalem, a grouping to the right features three world shrines—Our Lady of

Fatima in Portugal, Our Lady of Guadalupe in Mexico, and Brother Joe's last project, Our Lady of Lourdes in France, reduced from 230 feet to a 3-foot scale re-creation.

The main tourist attraction, the Ave Maria Grotto for which the site is named, is a 27-foot cube. Inside, artificial stalactites surround statues of Saint Benedict and his sister, Saint Scholastica, kneeling at each side of the Virgin Mary and Christ child. Contemporary images picture veterans of American wars, a Benedictine monastery in Korea, and a replica of Hiroshima's World Peace Church, a monument to the antinuclear accord of nations. They share space with Saint Benedict's tomb at Monte Cassino, St. Martin's Church, the Leaning Tower of Pisa, and the Alamo. The monks dedicated Brother Joseph's grotto on May 17, 1934, but work continued for twenty-four years. In the first thirty years of its fame, it received 60,000 visitors.

Brother Joseph enlarged his project, littering his workbench with recycled bits—a bird cage, pipe stems, cold-cream jars, and reflectors and taillights from bicycles and wrecked cars. In 1957, he celebrated a Diamond Jubilee by accepting the *Baculum Senectutis* (Staff of Venerability) for sixty years of monastic life. At age eighty, he finished his last model, the basilica at Lourdes, France's famed healing center. At his death on October 15, 1961, fellow monks buried him in the abbey cemetery near the grotto gift shop. Brother Joseph's workshop still houses buckets of salvaged junk and jewelry and scrapbooks of postcards, the main source of pictures for projects left undone at his death.

ACTIVITIES

Today, the Ave Maria Grotto is an anomaly among abbeys—a famous hobby attraction constructed on monastery grounds, which are usually known for serenity, prayer, and isolation. An elderly repairman, Leo Schwaiger, Brother Joseph's former assistant, upgrades ornamentation and repaints the replicas, rebuilding the Tower of Babel after a tree demolished it and keeping the Hanging Gardens of Babylon in good repair. At trail's end, he formed wee gates and ramps into a whimsical chipmunk crossing.

The site and picnic grounds are open year-round, except Christmas day, from 7:00 A.M. until sunset and charge an admission fee of $4.50 for adults and $3 for children, which covers the cost of upkeep, graffiti removal, and security. Tour buses bring visitors and students of architecture to admire models of San Juan Capistrano, a Viking tower, the Appius Claudius Aqueduct, Jacob's Well, Mount Tabor, Noah's Ark, the Tower of Babel, and a map of Alabama. They often end their tour with a viewing of Brother Joseph's grave in the abbey cemetery, meditation at the wayside shrine of the "Little Flower," Saint Theresa, and a brief stop at the chapel for prayer.

Sources: "Ave Maria Grotto"; Carter 1996; Chupa 1998; Hargrave 1999; Haring; *New Catholic Encyclopedia* 1967; Rives 1962.

stretch, the Blackfoot pursue their traditional culture and religion through vision quests.

Badger–Two Medicine Area
Floyd Heavy Runner
Blackfoot Brave Dogs Society
P. O. Box 98
Heart Butte, Montana 59448

Montana Wilderness Association
P.O. Box 635
Helena, Montana 59624
406-443-7350
WildMt@aol.com

Edged by the beauties of Glacier Park and Great Bear, Scapegoat, and Bob Marshall wilderness complex, Badger–Two Medicine Area is a wilderness keystone. To the Blackfoot of Montana, home is the Rocky Mountain Front, where the prairie expanse meets vast limestone escarpments covering 128,000 acres, the largest woodland in the contiguous forty-eight states. The 640-square-mile Badger–Two Medicine Area evolved 60 million years ago and was named for the confluence of Badger Creek and the Two Medicine River. Natives call local peaks by aboriginal designations—Morning Star, Poia, Little Plume, Running Crane, Spotted Eagle, Kiyo, Scarface, Elkcalf, Bullshoe, and Curly Bear.

In the estimation of Gloria Flora, supervisor of the Lewis and Clark National Forest, Badger-Two symbolizes the greatness of the North American frontier. An American Serengeti, it hosts a splendid ecosystem—one of the last free-range grizzly habitats and populations of moose and elk, gray wolves, mountain goats, wolverines, and harlequin ducks. It appeals to hikers, fishers, horse packers, campers, hunters, cross-country skiers, snowmobilers, and nature and wilderness enthusiasts. In this same roadless

HISTORY

From prehistory, Badger-Two has been the Blackfoot Jerusalem, an ancestral homeland, and the setting for myths and oral traditions. Immigrant whites jeopardized tribal holdings and, by 1885, exterminated free-roaming bison herds. Weakened by smallpox and the famine of 1895, the Blackfoot Confederacy of Siksika, Kainah, and Piegan tribes signed away ownership, allowing the U.S. government to make the land a public property. In 1896, the unwary Blackfoot misread the treaty, which appeared to promise them worship, lumbering, fishing, and hunting rights in the area in perpetuity. Whites first intruded in 1913, when they created a game preserve for migratory elk herds, followed by additional animal and plant sanctuaries. Simultaneously, the Nature Conservancy and the Boone and Crockett Club set aside large spreads of virgin land.

When multinational oil firms began exploring the Rockies, indigenous people foresaw a struggle similar to that of the Lakota of the Black Hills, the Wintu of Mount Shasta, and the Apache of Mount Graham. The prophecy quickly came true. In 1981, after the Lewis and Clark National Forest and the Bureau of Land Management sold oil and gas leases, Chevron and Belgian Petrofina began preliminary drilling in the thrust belt along Hall Creek and Goat Mountain. Although chances of striking oil or gas were pegged at 0.42 percent, the firms were willing to uproot the Blackfoot and violate the land in the off chance of tapping underground caches ambitiously estimated at 3.6 trillion cubic feet of natural gas.

In 1993, after considerable pressure from local preservationists and environmentalists, Secretary of the Interior Bruce Babbitt withdrew Badger-Two from potential drilling. Two years later, the area came up for wilderness study because its delicate ecosystem lacked protection. It was during this uneasy period that traditional Blackfoot initiated Aamskapi-Pikuni Radio to preserve the Pikuni language, transfer knowledge of elders to the young, strengthen the Blackfoot Confederacy, and promote native music and storytelling among a people who are 80 percent illiterate.

The rush to harvest natural resources began in 1996, when over 100 mining concerns sought claim to a wildlife habitat south of Blackleaf Canyon. The only check on greed is a government moratorium, renewed annually until the area receives more substantial defense. According to John Gatchell, conservation director of the Montana Wilderness Society, the situation is tenuous—a bureaucratic loophole, coupled with a rise in global oil prices, could lead to a shift in sympathies for the Blackfoot wilderness area. Backed by the Native Forest Network, Friends of the Rocky Mountain Front, and thirty-seven other public-spirited groups, Badger-Two awaits a permanent and binding closure of mineral exploration. If the area came under the Northern Rockies Ecosystem Protection Act, guarantors would prevent ecotragedy from deforestation, road building, blasting and industrial noise, pollution from pipeline leaks, and permanent desacralizing of a centuries-old natural sanctuary.

To affirm a tribal consensus, activists moved to ally Christian and traditional Blackfoot. Led by Floyd Heavy Runner, the languishing Brave Dogs Society has given over its role as tribal police to monitor the Pikuni language and sustain a culture threatened by outsiders, notably oil magnates. To legitimize traditional claims, he seeks to renegotiate the treaty of 1896 and remove any ambiguities about preservation of Badger-Two. His activism came at a price—a suspicious car accident that killed his brothers and sister-in-law and ouster from his tribe-owned home and meadows. The next year, his uncle died mysteriously and his daughter's shop burned. Backing for Heavy Runner has come from activist Bob Ekey and William H. Meadows, president of the Wilderness Society, who have targeted fragmentation and despoliation of Badger-Two.

To dramatize the unpredictable future of the wilderness, George Burdeau and Pamela Roberts of Rattlesnake Productions in Bozeman directed and produced a documentary film, *Backbone of the World: The Blackfeet* (1998), detailing the importance of Badger-Two to Blackfoot worship. According to folk tellers, the Indians have always valued the land as theirs from the creator and as the place where cosmic hero Scarface received the gift of the Sun Dance. On sacred ground, they honor victims of the Baker Massacre of January 23, 1869, when the U.S. cavalry from Fort Ellis, under command of Major Eugene M. Baker, slaughtered 173 Blackfoot men, women, and children, who had camped on the Marias River during a smallpox epidemic. Baker tried to cover up an act of genocide as punishment of horse thieves. Lieutenant William B. Pease issued a body count, which General of the Army William T. Sherman denied. Tribal spokeswoman Carol Murray declares that ritual honoring tribal martyrs is a permanent part of Blackfoot culture, not just a temporary observance.

Sources: "Backbone of the World" 1999; "Badger-Two Medicine Area"; Baum 1992; Brown 1970; Dark 1993; Feldman 1965; Fraser 1968; Gibson; Gibson and Hayne; "Group's List of Endangered Wild Lands Focuses on the West" 1998; "The Impact of Proposed Amendments to the American Indian Religious Freedom Act on Other Uses of Public Lands" 1993; Kenworthy 1997; Knudsen 1996; Patterson and Snodgrass 1994; "Protect the Rocky Mountain Front from Mineral Development" 1997.

Bahá'i House of Worship

Caswell Ellis, Director
100 Linden Avenue
Wilmette, Illinois 60091
847-869-9039; 800-22-UNITE
cellis@usnbc.org; how@usbnc.org
www.us.bahai.org

The nation's first Bahá'i temple, the House of Worship in Wilmette north of Chicago, has earned two honorifics—the Mother Temple of the West and Chicago's Taj Mahal. A syncretic faith based on the progression of prophets of Judaism, Christianity, and Islam, Bahá'i contains elements of Hinduism, Unitarianism, and Shi'ite Islam. Free of dogma and sectarianism, the Bahá'i creed stresses equality of all people, a pervasive demand from many religious groups at the beginning of the twenty-first century. The humanism of Bahá'u'llah, the sect's founder, inspired followers to build an unconditionally multicultural temple on the shore of Lake Michigan. Since 1953, it has welcomed all to an assembly fostering unity and peace.

Jean-Baptiste Louis Bourgeois's nine-sided glass and concrete dome design was selected for the Bahá'i House of Worship in Wilmette, Illinois. (Richard Hamilton Smith/Corbis)

HISTORY AND BELIEFS

A Persian sect formed among messianic Shi'ites in the 1850s, the Bahá'is began as a small, powerless group with no money or property and little credibility in an overwhelmingly Muslim land. Through disciples and translations of Bahá'u'llah's writings into 800 languages, the religion has grown to more than 5 million adherents in 233 countries. The first Bahá'i outreach to the United States began in 1893. The faith took root in 1912 with Abdu'l-Bahá's tour of major cities. He spoke at the Universalist Church in Washington, D.C., at Howard University, and before the Bethel Literary Society. In Chicago, he met followers at Lincoln Park and addressed the fourth annual assembly of the National Association for the Advancement of Colored People. By the 1920s, Bahá'is were hosting Race Amity conferences, such as the one in Springfield, Massachusetts, in 1921. That same year, Abdu'l-Bahá died, leaving guardianship of the faith to his grandson, Shoghi Effendi Rabbani.

In the mid-twentieth century, growth of the faith was steady. As of 1930, eighteen books of scripture were available in English. Late in the decade, the Bahá'i national administration headquarters moved to Wilmette, Illinois. Advertising executive Horace Hotchkiss Holley, a native of Torrington, Connecticut, who served thirty-six years on the National Spiritual Assembly of the Bahá'is of the United States and edited *World Unity* magazine and *Bahá'i News,* spearheaded the national drive and representation in Canada, the Middle East, and Central and South America. In 1944, the centennial of Bahá'ism, every state in the union had a Bahá'i office; by 1995, an influx of immigrants and the conversion of Navajo, Sioux, and Inuit raised the number of centers to 7,000 nationwide.

Bahá'is maintain an independent faith symbolized by a nine-pointed star and founded on liberating people from economic, social, religious, and political bondage. Grounded in a belief in monotheism and the oneness of humanity, they proclaim truth as a deterrent to prejudice and superstition. By seeking amity and harmony, they recognize science as a force for bringing peace and order to humankind. Among human rights, they advocate a slate of goals:

- Equal rights and monogamy
- Compulsory education
- Elimination of poverty and extreme wealth
- Abolition of priesthood, intolerance, and slavery
- Withdrawal from partisan politics
- Creation of an international language
- Support of peacekeeping institutions

Bahá'u'llah's balanced value system stresses work, worship, and citizenship. Temples accept no funds from outside sources and make no appeals for money or property.

ARCHITECTURE

After a design competition to produce architectural plans, the national Bahá'i convention met in New York to study four proposals. Three were standard blueprints. A fourth was a plaster model of a temple of light in the form of a nine-sided glass and concrete dome 138 feet high created by French-Canadian amateur designer Jean-Baptiste Louis Bourgeois, who designed Moorish buildings for the 1894 California Midwinter International Exposition in San Francisco's Golden Gate Park. On the advice of New York architect H. Van Buren Magonigle, the planning committee accepted the richly filigreed plan and, in the presence of Abdu'l-Bahá, broke ground May 1, 1912.

Headquartered in Chicago, Bourgeois worked for a decade on refinements to the original blueprint. Building began in 1921 on seven lakeside acres with watertight caissons bored into rock. After a decade of fund-raising, the congregation entered phase two, the support system, implemented by Washington, D.C., sculptor John J. Earley. He advocated cutting shapes in plaster to create molds for a white cement spiked with granules of quartz. In 1930, workers began the third phase, erecting the superstructure—a domed temple in concrete, steel, and 19,500 square feet of glass.

After Bourgeois's death in August 1930, Allen McDaniel supervised construction of the exterior; the interior is the work of Alfred Shaw. The job of applying the cast ornamentation, started in June 1932, took ten years and seven months to

BAHÁ'U'LLAH

Bahá'u'llah, an Iranian prince and religious leader, established the Bahá'i faith, a world religion bent on ending racism. Born Mirza Husayn Ali Nuri in Tehran on November 12, 1817, he grew up in a prestigious household and received no formal education. He followed the custom of marrying multiple wives and fathered two sons and a daughter. When he reached age twenty-seven, Siyyid Ali Muhammad, the Bab, or divine messenger of Allah, identified him as the representative of the Islamic promised one. Renamed Bahá'u'llah (Glory of God), he succeeded as leader of the Babi movement after the Bab was jailed in 1847 and executed by a firing squad three years later. Persecuted and bound with chains under the shah, Bahá'u'llah went to prison in 1852, when he received a revelation that God had chosen him as divine messenger.

Upon his release, Bahá'u'llah was banished to Baghdad, Iraq, and then to the mountains of Kurdistan. For a decade, he and his brother Mirza Yahya inspired scattered disciples. In 1863, the Bahá'u'llah led a small band to Constantinople, where he identified himself as the chosen one and asserted that the world's major religions were losing influence. Virulent forces expelled him to Adrianople in western Turkey, where he claimed to follow a line of prophets that included Abraham, Moses, Zoroaster, Jesus, Muhammad, and Krishna and introduced his mission to Queen Victoria, Tsar Alexander II, Kaiser Wilhelm I, Emperor Napoleon III, Emperor Franz Joseph, Pope Pius IX, and other world leaders. Bahá'u'llah predicted that, as humanity reached maturity, the Bahá'i faith would liberate and equalize all people. To further his aims, he forbade murder, theft, lying, adultery and promiscuity, gambling, alcoholic drinks and drugs, and gossip.

This bold proclamation led to house arrest for Bahá'u'llah and his family in Acre, Palestine, where he codified laws in the *Kitab-i-Aqdas* (Most Holy Book). For a quarter century, he composed religious texts in Persian and Arabic. At the time of his death at age seventy-five on May 29, 1892, the new faith had not yet encircled the globe, but a successor, Abdu'l-Bahá, had assumed the role of divine messenger. The dissemination of Bahá'u'llah's writings, biography, and histories of the faith—*Prayers and Meditations* (1938), *Gleanings from the Writings of Bahá'u'llah* (1939), *The Seven Valleys and the Four Valleys* (1945), *The Proclamation of Bahá'u'llah* (1967), *Epistle to the Son of the Wolf* (1969), *Edward Granville Browne and the Bahá'i Faith* (1970), and *Bahá'u'llah: The King of Glory* (1980)—introduced Bahá'ism to a growing body of worshippers from 2,100 ethnic, racial, and tribal groups.

---

complete. In 1947, workers began interior refinement and seating for 1,200. The final landscaping, started in April 1952, enriched the site with terraced gardens, pathways, groves, and fountains.

The completed temple, dedicated on May 2, 1953, projected a color shift from gray granite steps to a pure white dome ornamented with cast-bronze grillwork and entrance doors. Touches of arabesques, Romanesque arches, and Byzantine shaping contribute to the theme of unity. Within the nine-sided chamber, the temple promotes a prayerful ambience that welcomes all races and religions. Intricate Eastern inlaid flooring, marble skirting, and pietra-dura wall panels anchor deep relief stucco ceilings pierced with stained-glass bays.

Visitors marvel at the blend of old and new—an innovative style grounded in the world's established sacred architecture. The lower level is a functional arrangement of a visitor's center, a bookstore, Foundation Hall, and the Cornerstone Room, a museum of religious artifacts. The rotunda emerges from cast-glass arches alternated with mosaic and gilded cast-bronze grilles soaring skyward to a hemisphere of multihued Tiffany glass. Seating for spectators faces the eastern Mediterranean. Above, the dome displays Arabic script lauding the name of the Almighty, translated "O Glory of the All Glorious."

At present, the Bahá'i House of Worship is the oldest surviving structure in the faith. In 1978, the Department of the Interior listed the temple on the National Register of Historic Places. President Bill Clinton recognized Bahá'i contributions in May 1999 by appointing Dr. Firuz Kazemzadeh, secretary for external affairs of the National Spiritual Assembly of the Bahá'is, to the United States Commission on International Religious Freedom. Annually, the temple's staff greets a quarter million tourists, many of whom know nothing about Bahá'ism, but who depart impressed by its serenity and promise.

ACTIVITIES

Worshippers at the temple read scripture from Bahá'i and other religions and sing *a cappella* hymns. Central to Bahá'i worship is the Nineteen Day Feast, held once every nineteen days as a community gathering. The staff adapts programs to the cultural and social needs of adults and children. At each assembly, worshippers join in devotions, administrative consultation, and fellowship. As a body, they support the Bahá'i Office of the Environment, the association for Bahá'i Studies in Ottawa, the Bahá'i International Health Agency, the Bahá'i Justice Center, and the Chair for World Peace.

The annual calendar begins in January with World Religion Day and the Days of Ha at the end of March. A period of fasting from March 2 to March 20 expands spiritual awareness and reflection as the devout withdraw from material desires. The following day, March 21, is Naw-Ruz, or the Bahá'i New Year's Day to mark the spring equinox. Late spring and summer bring the Festival of Ridvan in late April, Declaration of the Bab on May 23, Ascension of Bahá'u'llah on May 29, Race Unity Day in June, and Martyrdom of the Bab on July 9. The year closes with the Bahá'u'llah's birthday on November 12 and Day of the Covenant on November 26.

Sources: Ahlstrom 1972; *Almanac of Famous People* 1998; Armstrong-Ingram; "The Bahá'i Faith"; "The Bahá'i House of Worship in Wilmette"; *The Bahá'is* 1992; *Biography Resource Center* 1999; Broderick 1958; Cole 1998; *Eerdmans' Handbook to the World's Religions* 1982; Maneck 1994; Oldziey, Smith, and Phillips 1998; Reini 1999; *Religious Leaders of America* 1999; Stockman 1995; "To the Peoples of the World" 1986; "The Vision of Race Unity: America's Most Challenging Issue" 1991.

Baron Hirsch Synagogue

Rabbi Rafael G. Grossman
400 South Yates Road
Memphis, Tennessee 38120
901-683-7485
FAX 901-683-7499
general@baronhirsch.org
www.baronhirsch.org

Baron Hirsch Synagogue, a Tennessee landmark, models the Orthodox Jewish tradition in a southern city. A devout congregation, members support full commitment to religious education and practice. Their methods date to the foundations of Judaism—improving knowledge of liturgy and theology and strengthening families through learning, worship, and wholesome recreation. Countering secularism and the collapse of cultural continuity, the Baron Hirsch congregation maintains a living, substantive response to Jewish law in a world fragmented by change.

HISTORY

Proclaimed a flagship of U.S. Orthodox Judaism, the Baron Hirsch Synagogue, founded over 130 years ago, began with meetings in private homes and on the second floor of a Memphis hotel. In 1912, congregants moved into their first building in the downtown area. In 1950, they erected North America's largest synagogue on Vollintine and Evergreen Streets and experienced rapid growth to over 1,000 members, making them the nation's largest Orthodox Jewish congregation. After launching a satellite synagogue on the former Isaac Hayes estate, trustees determined that city growth into that area mandated a new synagogue. In 1988, they dedicated the new building and campus, a tribute to the vision and dynamism of their current leader, Rabbi Rafael G. Grossman.

For a quarter century, the Baron Hirsch congregation has looked to Rabbi Grossman for leadership, learning, and stability. He is best known for smoothing the transition from the former midtown building to a suburban neighborhood. His contributions to family worship include group counseling, a program for traditional singles, and the creation of Camp Darom, a children's Super Shabbor Program, the South's only Orthodox sleep-away camp. His ongoing contribution is a program of adult education offering twenty classes per week, over 800 pilgrimages to Israel, and the I. E. Hanover Lecture Series by scholars on world Jewry.

Rabbi Grossman has received multiple leadership awards and holds an honorary doctorate in divinity from Yeshiva University. He established the annual Conference on Medical Ethics and chairs the Rabbinical Council International and the board of Religious Zionists of America. His writings include articles for journals, the column "Thinking Aloud" in the *Jewish Press,* and *Binah: The Modern Quest for Torah Understanding* (1993), a six-part series of sermons on scripture.

ARCHITECTURE

The sanctuary of Baron Hirsch Synagogue is a light, inviting space where worshippers separate by gender. In Orthodox tradition, the raised bimah, or dais, at center is the focal point for reading from scripture with an amud, or stand, at the bottom step for the cantor. Collapsible walls allow the staff to enlarge seating for increased attendance on high holy days. For weddings, the bimah separates to allow bride and groom to progress to the chuppah, the ceremonial wedding pavilion. Overhead, the roof opens electronically to allow the union of man and woman to take place under the sky. Stone walls frame the Aron Kodesh (Holy Ark) in token of Jacob's vision of angels ascending a ladder to heaven while he slept on a stone. Artist Milton Angel's stained-glass representation of the Ten Commandments completes the setting. Behind the ark, Kohanic (priestly) washing areas permit purification of the clergy.

Interior appointments link the sanctuary with much of Jewish history. Jerusalem stone suggests the Wailing Wall, the holiest Jewish shrine. Bold colored windows by Canadian glass masters Ron Henig and Jack Grue recount moments in Jewish history and depict the shofar (ram's horn) and menorah (candelabrum), two symbols central to annual ritual. Passage through the tabernacle leads to an assembly hall for group meetings. Memorial Hall features plaques honoring deceased members. Beyond lie the nursery, day-care center, Judaica shop, bridal suite, rabbi's study, offices, and mikvah, a ritual purification pool fed from a rainwater cistern. Additional areas enhancing comfort and access to religious understanding include a youth center, a social hall, kitchens, and the Hanover Library and board room, which houses thousands of books on Judaism.

ACTIVITIES

The synagogue offers daily services and a varied program for nursery-age children and a junior congregation. Dr. Stanley Friedman leads the boys' and men's choirs. A span of programs involves individuals in women's Torah study, men's club, teen Torah, Talmud instruction, Hebrew law, commentary on Jewish perspectives on world affairs and parenting, Passover workshops, conversational Hebrew, and twenty-first-century beliefs. The synagogue calendar schedules a November Chanukah bazaar, occupational therapy, and the Belz/Parker Ascending Artists Concert Series. For relaxation, Cafe Simcha dispenses refreshments and audiovisual materials and features a pool table, periodicals, and a jukebox playing Israeli and religious recordings. Community outreach includes *sukkah* building for celebrating the harvest festival, support for Zionism, and visitation and help for the aged. Annually, the congregation presents the Zachor Award to a person integral in commemorating the Holocaust.

> **Sources:** "Baron Hirsch Synagogue"; *Eerdmans' Handbook to the World's Religions* 1982; Gentz 1973; "Judaism"; Olswanger and Grossman 1996; Smith 1995.

Bethabara Moravian Church

Reverend Donald W. Griffin
2100 Bethabara Road
Winston-Salem, North Carolina 27106
336-924-8789
FAX 336-924-8789
bethabara@alltel.net
www.bethabara.org

The progeny of sturdy Czech-German ancestry, the Bethabara Moravian Church membership is a vibrant, Christ-centered congregation whose ties to the past make it a traditional stronghold of faith in the Carolinas. In the South's tobacco center, the church and its busy calendar restore hope that Christian beliefs and missionary zeal carry weight in the twenty-first century. As in its early days, the seal of the lamb bearing a cross and the motto *Vicit Agnus Noster, Eum Sequamur* (Our lamb has conquered, let us follow him) symbolize a generous expression of Christian outreach and typifies the church's activities.

North Carolina's Moravians are known for Sunnyside Ministries, which assists the needy with food, clothing, and transitional housing, and for promotion of Habitat for Humanity, soup

Candle making at the Bethabara Moravian Church. (Courtesy of Bethabara Moravian Church)

kitchens, and homeless shelters. The church provides a Web site and screen saver, a downloadable rotating twenty-six-point Moravian star, emblem of the Moravian hymn "Morning Star" and a favorite Christmas ornament and porch light in Moravian communities. Visitors to a *Singstunde* (singing hour) of hymn stanzas chosen and arranged to develop a worship theme often leave Winston-Salem with tins of the trademark Moravian sweet, paper-thin sugar cookies uniformly brown with a generous sprinkling of spice, a symbol of the sweetness of God's love.

HISTORY

Proclaiming itself the first Protestant church, Moravianism predates Lutheranism and the Protestant Reformation. The sect began in 1457 with the renewal of the United Brethren, founded in Bohemia and Moravia by the Bohemian martyr John Huss (or Hus), a Catholic priest and theology professor at the University of Prague. He achieved a religious revolution and championed the peasant by proposing that scripture be translated into common dialects. His motivation was reform of Catholicism, an end to the sale of indulgences, and eradication of priestly corruption, issues that resulted in his imprisonment and execution. Rather than recant his great-hearted style of preaching, he chose to be burned at the stake in 1415. The Moravians took a vocal stand against the papacy by breaking with the mother church and, in 1467, by ordaining their own ministers. They also invested in the early printing press and, by 1510, had issued around fifty pious works.

Led by carpenter Christian David, the incipient congregation took refuge in Saxony at Herrnhut (The Lord's Watch), a hamlet on the estate of a wealthy Lutheran pietist, Count Nicholaus Ludwig von Zinzendorf. The theocratic society required an oath of each member and, in seclusion, nurtured a spiritual assembly. Five years later, Moravians formalized their gathering as the Renewed Unitas Fratrum (Unity of Brothers), but never shook off the popular name assigned to them. By 1575, the *Confessio Bohemica* (Bohemian Confession) declared a union with Lutheran Hussites.

The Moravians were frontrunners. They originated hymnals in the common language and, in 1593, became the first Protestant church to publish a modern language Bible based on original Hebrew, Aramaic, and Greek texts. The Kralice (or Kralitz) Bible, a six-volume work printed at the secret printing house at Kralice upon Oslava, features the Old and New Testaments in Czech. When Catholic counter-Reformation troops began confiscating Moravian Bibles and hymnals in 1627 as a means of re-Catholizing dissenters, Moravian housewives baked their copies in loaves of bread. The vital sect unity ended with deliberate scattering and anti-Hussite exile in a diaspora intended to weaken Moravianism. This era saw the rise of Bishop John Amos Comenius (also called Jan Komensky), who preserved and fed the sect's spiritual needs until the "hidden seed" could regroup in more propitious times.

Despite political and religious chaos, for 550 years, Moravians maintained a belief in the necessity of good works as an outward show of faith. Significant to the North American contingent was the location of land where they could freely practice their faith in daily examples of compassion, neighborliness, and worship. Next on their list of priorities was evangelism to blacks and Native Americans. Moravian missionaries succeeded at residing among and Christianizing the Lenape, whom they accepted and loved as brethren. The records of David Zeisberger and John Heckewelder preserved colonial contacts with forest Indians and details of Delaware culture and government, in particular, the Lenape tradition of prophets. Unlike other white visitors among Indians, the Moravians stressed temperance and made no attempt to sell alcohol to natives.

The vigorous, mission-minded sect, headed by Augustus Gottlieb Spangenberg and traveling with John and Charles Wesley, sailed to Georgia in 1735. The simple beginning, which originated in the West Indies in 1732, spread to Pennsylvania in 1740 and "Carolina land" in 1753, when founders established the Bethabara Moravian community. When John Lord Carteret, Earl of Granville, made available a 100,000-acre tract in North Carolina, in 1776, Moravians settled a theocratic commune at Salem, half of the combined city of Winston-Salem. Pastored by Bernard Adam Grube, a missionary to the Lenape, the founding congregation of fifteen brothers traveled overland from the Moravian commune at Bethlehem, Pennsylvania, in balky horse-drawn wagons on a six-week journey ending November 17.

The eleven who settled in North Carolina, including a doctor and a clutch of artisans and skilled laborers, sheltered in an abandoned trapper's hut and began clearing farmland. After the arrival of female members, in 1756, the community erected a log church inside a stockade, where colonists from outlying properties retreated from threat of Indian uprising during the French and Indian War. For a name, the Reverend Grube chose the Hebrew word *Bethabara* (House of Passage) to commemorate the years of dodging persecutors.

Bethabarans shared common stores and even bought slaves in the name of the commune rather than individual ownership. In 1788, members built a stone church, the *Gemainhaus*

(or *Gemein Haus*) (meeting place) that remained in use for 165 years. The whitewashed walls and plain, unadorned windows and interior of the *Saal* (hall) invited each worshipper to commune with God through personal, nondirected experience. In 1971, the congregation inaugurated the present sanctuary and kept *Gemein Haus* for special services, Holy Week (or Passion Week) services, musical programs, and weddings. This modest start evolved into a sturdy commune, the beginning of a southern sect headquarters as well as the forerunner of Salem Academy and Salem College. By 1998, the state's Moravian population approached 40,000, nearly a tenth of communicants nationwide.

BELIEFS AND PRACTICES

The source of Moravian fervor was a rebirth of German pietism, a belief in the intuitive acceptance of divine grace and the formation of a personal faith built on the soul's oneness with Christ. Less dogmatic than more intellectual faiths, Moravianism led its followers to an earnest change of heart and behavior. The outward signs of prayer and daily involvement in religion produced a clean-living society still honored at the historic Old Salem Village, a restoration of colonial life, faith, and arts.

Moravians succeeded through an experiential outreach and through Christian education of their children. Their trademark love feasts originated in imitation of the *agape* (unconditional or unselfish love) of Christ's apostles and their converts, who met and broke bread to celebrate unity and equality. In August 1727, Moravians celebrated the first love feast, a unique sharing of food, singing, and communion that reprises the worship style of early Christians. As described in the book of Acts, the love feast is a communal meal marked by a sweet roll and hot coffee, tea, or chocolate. At the heart of the event is a humility, good-heartedness, and acceptance of all comers seeking Christian uplift and fellowship. Distribution precedes a simple grace:

> Come, Lord Jesus, our guest to be,
> And bless these gifts bestowed by Thee.
> Bless our dear ones everywhere,
> Keep them in Thy loving care.
> Amen.

Central to their communion is the singing of Moravian hymns, which supplant chanting as a rhythmic, vocal expression of spirit. Marked by soft music and prayers for each other, the love feast provides a variant form of communion symbolizing the nurturance of life and spirit. The service may conclude with participants proceeding with uplifted candles into the night.

Another custom unique to colonial Moravians was interment in the *Gottesacker* (God's Acre), a general burying ground where deceased members were buried in the order in which they died. For propriety's sake, married members occupied quadrants apart from unmarried, with men to one side and women in the opposite section. The idea of placing members under a uniform flat white stone in God's family rather than in earthly family plots united and equalized all in a Christian afterlife. This custom gave place to more modern interment, including use of municipal graveyards and columbaria, but Moravians still observe cleaning days when the white stones receive a scrub and polish.

A landmark element of Moravianism was the issuance of daily texts, an ongoing publication of a model prayer, a hymn stanza, and paired devotional texts taken from the Old and New Testaments. The tradition of daily guidance, which Count Zinzendorf pioneered, continues into the twenty-first century with Internet texts called "watchwords," rapidly supplanting print versions. The historic Old Salem district preserves a utopian spirit as it once thrived at Congregation House; gender separation at the Widows House, the Sisters House, and the Single Brothers House (1769), where boys apprenticed in trades; and Home Moravian Church (1771), where Salem's Moravians still worship. The Salem historical site features additional restorations:

- Miksch Tobacco Shop (1771), where Matthew Miksch opened Salem's first private residence and the nation's first tobacconist shop
- Boys School (1794), where young males studied in the education system's first century
- Winkler Bakery (1800), the wood-fired oven that continues to bake Moravian cookies and breads for tourists
- Vierling House and Apothecary (1802), home of the community's physician and general surgeon, Dr. Samuel Benjamin Vierling
- Market-Fire House (1803), a meat market remodeled into a fire station in 1856
- John Vogler House (1819), home and workshop of a silversmith and clockmaker
- Shultz Shoemaker Shop (1827), the area's bootery
- The Salem Tavern, a structure separate from Moravian dormitories and which accommodated overnight visitors but kept them at a distance to avoid worldly contamination of the commune

ACTIVITIES

Today, Bethabara Moravian Church is an up-to-date worship facility consisting of old and new buildings alongside Bethabara Park. The 236 members follow a regular Sunday schedule consisting of 9:45 A.M. Sunday-school assembly followed by Sunday school, worship hour, and a 6:30 P.M. session of Bible study. Sunday-school lessons are posted on the Web along with photos of group activities for adults and children. Worship begins with several passages of scripture, a children's sermon, and an adult sermon. In 1999, Seminar Class Studies in 2000 focused on William F. Fore's *Mythmakers: Gospel, Culture, and the Media* (1990), a challenge for discussion and spiritual growth.

The church bulletin lists prayer concerns by name and details missions in Honduras, hurricane relief to the devastated eastern Carolinas in winter 1999–2000, a day-care center, and annual tithing on the fifth Sunday of the year. On January 27, 2000, the Moravian community celebrated a historic union with the Lutheran church with tours of Old Salem, discussion of historical intersection, a love feast, a band chorale, and an organ prelude. After evening communion at Augsburg Lutheran Church, the eventful day concluded at the Adam's Mark Hotel with a reception.

Standard features of the Christmas season are Moravian love feasts, featuring a darkened sanctuary a-twinkle with lighted tallow and beeswax candles, hand-wicked and molded by church members for Christmas Eve services. The fragrant tan candles symbolize the purity of Christ; their red frill trim reminds believers that Christ was martyred for them. Today, the feast incorporates an uplifting text adapted from Matthew 5:14–16:

> Ye are the light of the world.
> Let your light so shine before men
> that they may see your good works,
> and glorify your father who is in heaven.

Open to people of all faiths, the event is so much a part of local yuletide festivities that the church expands its celebration to accommodate hosts of visitors.

The feast—marked by consumption of hot coffee; spice, lemon, walnut, and chocolate cookies; and cheese straws—has also spread to college campuses and recurs on Great Sabbath (Easter Sunday), Founder's Day, Epiphany Sunday, and Christian Family Sunday. Also traditional at Bethabara are Watch Night on December 31, Veteran's Day celebrations, a Lenten fair, clean-up of sanctuary and grave sites preceding Easter week, handmade palm crosses for Palm Sunday, Holy Week services, a Maundy Thursday communion, a Good Friday Death Hour service and the making of a cross, an Easter Sunday pancake breakfast, annual chicken pie making, and a bazaar of craft items and baked goods.

Sources: Ahlstrom 1972; "Bethabara Moravian Church"; Charles 1999; "Czech Bible of Kralice" 1998; "Delaware (Lenape) Indians"; Fries 1967; Hindmarsh 1999; "Historic Old Salem"; "The Moravian Church," http://cti.itc.virginia.edu, http://www.moravian.org; "Moravian Church Genealogy"; "Moravians, Lutherans Align Faith" 2000; "The Moravian Museum"; Niebuhr (a) 1999; "Old Salem Online"; Pina 1995; Schlosser 1997; Spaugh 1999; "Who Are Moravians?" 1999.

Big Bethel African Methodist Episcopal Church

James L. Davis, Pastor
220 Auburn Avenue, N.E.
Atlanta, Georgia 30303
404-659-0248
FAX 404-233-3060
bigbeth@bellsouth.net
www.bigbethelame.org

In its 153rd year, Atlanta's energetic Big Bethel African Methodist Episcopal Church has shared city triumphs and woes since the third year of the Civil War, when General William Tecumseh Sherman decimated the city, burned the warehouse district, and left citizens destitute. Amid downtown skyscrapers in the Martin Luther King Jr. Historical District, the current sanctuary makes a dramatic statement with its jaunty, conical steeple topped with a double cross and the exclamation "Jesus Saves" in bright neon. The city's oldest and most drama-minded church, Big Bethel remains at the center of religious folk theater with an annual presentation of *Heaven Bound,* an original morality pageant that has contributed to black-white amity during the worst of civil rights turmoil.

HISTORY

Founded in 1847 and built in 1865 on the former Wheat Street, Big Bethel—also known as Old Bethel, Bethel, and the African Methodist Episcopal Tabernacle—was Georgia's first African Methodist Episcopal church. Organized by the Reverend James Lynch and first pastored by the Reverend Joseph Woods, the congregation showed spirit from the beginning. It offered the first classroom to the fledgling Morris Brown College, founded by Big Bethel's second pastor, Bishop Wesley Grimes, in 1881, and now grown to a forty-three-acre campus. Congregants replaced their original sanctuary with a Romanesque Revival building a decade later, which became a community center for political and social gatherings. After it burned in 1920, a day after the insurance policy lapsed, trustees retained the blackened outside walls as the foundation of a new classical auditorium. Part of the burden of debt derived from their installation of a sizeable Möller organ.

Following a decline in membership in the 1950s and 1960s, the church experienced a spiritual rebirth at the Auburn Avenue address revered as Sweet Auburn, the heart of black Atlanta. In 1972, the congregation, led by the Reverend Ruben T. Bussey, acquired a rundown hotel next door, which it turned into Bethel Towers, a 182-unit apartment complex. Targeted for low-income elderly, it earned a portion of its income from welfare funds, which

The congregation rises to sing in the Big Bethel AME Church, Atlanta, Georgia. (Bob Krist/Corbis)

originally covered 35 percent of the rent. During the tenure of the Reverend McKinley Young, a HUD grant for an Auburn Avenue revitalization project in 1980 upgraded Big Bethel with a new roof and new doors and windows.

Since 1981, the church has fostered urban-oriented programs that honor the spirit of denomination founder Richard Allen through service and education to local blacks. For the substance abuser, the staff sponsors a drug hotline and referral service; for the hungry, the Welcome Table began serving 21,000 meals per winter. At Big Bethel's anniversary in 1987, members joined 7,500 African Methodist Episcopal churches in a global celebration of the denomination's 200th year and some 3 million members in the Americas, the Caribbean, and Africa. Other Big Bethelites gathered at the plantation in Dover, Delaware, where Allen was once enslaved, and others sponsored a parade in downtown Atlanta on July 12. Out of oneness with the denomination's national aims, the con-

gregation supports a dozen educational institutions, including Wilberforce University in Ohio and Atlanta's Turner Theological Seminary and Morris Brown College.

ACTIVITIES

Nothing distinguishes Big Bethelites more than the annual all-church pageant, which reprises John Bunyan's Christian allegory *Pilgrim's Progress.* In November 1929, shortly after the stock market crash that spawned the Great Depression, choir member Lula Byrd Jones and chorister Nellie Lindley Davis revitalized the congregation by writing *Heaven Bound,* a fundraising pageant of the soul's earthly journey to the afterlife. Reflecting the morality of medieval religious plays, the annual folk art event merged narrative with folk songs, hymns, and spirituals as twenty pilgrims made their way through enticements and misdirection. The allegorical characters brought Wayward Girl, Pilgrim to Zion, Striver, Widow, Rich Man, Orphans, Determined Soul, Mother's Girl, Preacher, Burden Bearer, Bed-Ridden Soul, Reformed Drunkard, Soldier of the Army of the Lord, and Wayworn Traveler in confrontation with Satan.

As was true of morality plays pantomimed in the Middle Ages, Satan served as the rascally star of the show. The fetching tempter was the creation of director Henry J. Furlow, who carried a pitchfork and wore the stereotypical red shiny devil costume topped with horns. For over forty years, he strutted the aisles and lured the unwary hellward with liquor, flowers, and gambling. One of his most comical quarries is the Hypocrite, a bosomy, coquettish matron, played for decades by Daisy Payne Brown. Decked in rhinestone earrings and red dress, her character expects to waltz into the Promised Land but finds the door slammed in her face.

The soul of the program derives from such up-tempo music as "Rise and Shine," "When We All Get to Heaven," "I'm Going Home," and "I Shall Not Be Moved." The final clash between tempter and Christian warrior, marked by the singing of "Soldier in the Army of the Lord," sets the celestial choir to belting hallelujahs as Satan sinks out of sight. At the Pearly Gates, Saint Peter bears the Lamb's *Book of Life* as the choir salutes the faithful at their eternal rest. A finale of

"All Hail, Immanuel" precedes "Steal Away," "Study War No More," "Couldn't Hear Nobody Pray," "Swing Low, Sweet Chariot," "Down by the Riverside," "Hand Me Down the Silver Trumpet, Gabriel," and the Doxology.

The annual pageant, which opened in February 1930 at the cost of one dime per seat, matured into a citywide festival. With assistance from the 1936 Federal Theatre Project, the setting acquired a cloud bank of beaver board, puffs of smoke from the orchestra pit when hell wins out over godliness, and a cross that lights up when a pilgrim reaches heaven. Gradually, the play gained national acclaim after the choir performed in Atlanta Municipal Auditorium for the 1931 World Ecumenical Conference, at the December 1939 world premiere of the film *Gone with the Wind,* before the 1969 meeting of the American Folklore Society, and with a pops concert series at the Fox Theatre and Chastain Memorial Park. Its text appeared in the December 1963 issue of *Southern Folklore Quarterly* and commentary in cast member Gregory D. Coleman's *We're Heaven Bound!: Portrait of a Black Sacred Drama* (1994). In 1998, during church renovation, director Gregory Coleman had to settle for presenting only selected parts of the play at the Atlanta Civic Center to entertain visitors to the summer Olympic Games.

Drama critics from *Life* and *Time* magazines have lauded the annual production, held the first week of November in an auditorium seating 2,000 for two performances. The *New York Times* called the play "one of Atlanta's most enduring traditions." ("The Choirs of Big Bethel" 1998, 4) The *Atlanta Journal and Constitution* called it "euphoric Brotherhood that would have made the angel Gabriel himself proud." (Buchanan 1971, n.p.) Today, a permanent exhibit at the Atlanta History Center honors the pageant after seven decades and more than 800 performances before a million viewers in venues across Georgia and in Nashville and Chattanooga, Tennessee, and Lake Junaluska, North Carolina. After a long history, it still features Mrs. Esther McDonald, an original cast member, as one of the saints.

Big Bethel maintains a progressive stance among Atlanta churches. In 1982, congregational actors and singers presented James Weldon Johnson's *God's Trombones,* composed of seven sermons in verse, dance, and song. Annually, members contribute to the mid-October Sweet Auburn Heritage Festival, the May Springfest and Garden Show, and the summer curb market. At the beginning of the twenty-first century, the church initiated an annual relighting of the prominent "Jesus Saves" sign, an urban landmark. Trustees intend to restore the sanctuary interior, add a parking deck, and renovate several historic storefronts as part of the ongoing effort to preserve Atlanta's sacred geography.

See also Ebenezer Baptist Church.
Sources: "Atlanta History Center"; "Big Bethel AME Church" 1999; *Big Bethel AME Church: A Century of Progress and Christian Service,* 1968; Buchanan 1971, 1972; "Flocking to Pageant's 'Pearly Gates'" 1985; Harvey 1987; Hatch 1970; "Heaven Bound" 1943; "Heaven Bound: Big Bethel African Methodist Choir"; Helbig 1994; "Historic Church Gets HUD Grant" 1980; Keenan 1988; Lamar 1999; Lyon 1976; "Morris Brown College History"; Perkerson 1937; "Review: 'We're Heaven Bound'" 1995; Sibley 1995; Sugg 1963; "Sweet Auburn" 1999.

Billy Graham Training Center at the Cove

Dr. Billy Graham, Founder
P.O. Box 19223
Asheville, North Carolina 28815
828-298-2092; 800-950-2092
FAX 828-299-0276
www.thecove.org

Deep in the Southern Appalachians amid quiet mountain trails and streams, Billy Graham's religious training center prepares church leaders and pastors for their work. In an invigorating atmosphere established by professional staff, residents retreat from the pressures and burnout common to the clergy to rekindle personal faith, network with other clergy, and develop ministerial talents and skills. The Cove promises empowerment, rich fellowship, and insights into Christian truths. By reacquainting themselves with the original mission, participants enhance their ability to evangelize others.

ARCHITECTURE

Twenty miles from the Graham home in Montreat, North Carolina, the Billy Graham Training

DR. BILLY GRAHAM

The most revered American fundamentalist, evangelist Dr. William Franklin "Billy" Graham survived an era that brought shame and scorn to less principled conservative preachers and crusaders. Born on a dairy farm to strict Presbyterians on November 7, 1918, in Charlotte, North Carolina, he underwent a religious transformation at age sixteen during a sermon by Mordecai F. Ham. After studying at Bob Jones College in Cleveland, Tennessee, and Florida Bible Institute near Tampa, he allied with the fundamentalist Southern Baptists. He graduated from Wheaton College in 1940 and undertook a small Chicago pastorate and a radio broadcast, *Songs in the Night.*

Graham moved steadily away from parish ministry as staff pastor of Youth for Christ, author of *Calling Youth to Christ* (1947), and president of Northwestern Schools in Minneapolis, Minnesota. During a two-week revival campaign in Los Angeles in summer 1949, he honed his trademark charismatic pulpit style. Over half a century of repeat crusades, he gained a reputation for integrity and financial ethics. In 1950, he launched the Billy Graham Evangelistic Association and his popular radio show, *Hour of Decision.* Within a year, he became a full-time evangelist and author of a daily syndicated newspaper column entitled "My Answer."

Graham flourished from a field of innovations that utilized print, electronic, and face-to-face ministry. He and other neoevangelicals initiated *Christianity Today,* a popular journal. In New York City in 1957, he pioneered the televised religious crusade, the beginning of his renown as America's foremost Protestant revivalist. The 1960s were the height of his ministry. In 1960, he convened the first of a series of conferences on world evangelism in Montreux, Switzerland; in 1965, he published the best-selling evangelical treatise *World Aflame,* subsequently translated into Spanish. Two years later, he founded the Billy Graham School of Evangelism. This period of growth paralleled a close consultation with a list of politicians, beginning with Strom Thurmond and including presidents Richard Nixon, Gerald Ford, Jimmy Carter, Ronald Reagan, George Bush, and Bill Clinton.

Still actively crusading in his eighties despite advancing Parkinson's disease, Graham planned a millennial world conference called Amsterdam 2000. The century-end gathering caps a pulpit career in over 185 countries in tents and halls and the grander venues of New York's Central Park, Ottawa's Corel Centre, and Moscow's Olympic Stadium. His World Emergency Fund, founded in 1973, continues to comfort, shelter, and feed victims of famine, war, earthquake, flood, and disease; Operation Christmas Child brings shoeboxes filled with gifts to hundreds of thousands of the world's needy. His School of Evangelism uplifts pastors, ministerial students, and religious workers in five locations—Orlando, Florida; St. Louis, Missouri; Monterey, California; Toronto, Ontario; and Lake Louise, Alberta.

In the 1980s, Graham, his vigor undiminished, led campaigns at a steady pace and, in 1982, preached in the Soviet Union. He produced his most controversial jeremiad, *Approaching Hoofbeats: The Four Horsemen of the Apocalypse* (1983), a melodramatic prophecy of the fate of the unsaved. In a best-selling autobiography, *Just As I Am* (1997), he summarized his calling, ministry, and family life. Other texts, tracts, workbooks, cards, CDs, and cassettes from Grason World Wide Publications detail the religious commitment of Graham, his wife Ruth, and two of their children, Franklin Graham and Anne Graham Lotz, both respected evangelists.

Center at the Cove is situated on 1,500 acres of prime mountain land. Opened in 1987, the complex added the 180-seat Chantlos Memorial Chapel, donated by the Chantlos Foundation in 1989, a conference center in 1991, and the Shepherd's Inn and Pilgrim's Inn in 1992 and 1993. The training center's gray wood exterior, exposed beams and trusses, sharply peaked gables, and stone fascia suit the rugged terrain with a chalet-style informality inspired by the nearby Grove Park Inn and coordinated with the simple granite arches and bridges of the Blue Ridge Parkway. The builder layered the three-story center with educational facilities on the ground floor, offices on the top level, and lobby, assembly halls, and dining room on the main level. The completed 80,000-square-foot complex won a 1995 merit award from the Charlotte Chapter of the American Institute of Architects (AIA).

The Cove is a full-service, year-round conference center offering youth and adults a conference room, dining hall, boardroom, and meeting space equipped with audiovisual aids. The dining hall is a pleasant, family-style area lit by chandeliers in the form of wrought-iron circles suspended on chains. The newly renovated Training Center auditorium accommodates 500 in cushioned seats fitted with flip-up desktops. Although the Cove bans television, radio, and newspapers, the complex bookstore stocks religious works, videos, gifts, music, and apparel and features audio cassettes of seminar speakers. Dogwood Lodge convenes smaller, more intimate groups of up to 100 participants. Overnight guests stay at Shepherd's Inn and Pilgrim's Inn, which accommodate 272 in four-person rooms or five-person suites. The inns extend hospitality in spacious lobbies furnished with raised stone hearths and homey chairs and sofas that invite relaxed conversation and interaction. The porches offer rocking chairs and an unobstructed view of the mountains. Outside, a gray stone gate, raised wood walks, simple wood benches, streams, and graveled paths invite private contemplation of the Appalachian countryside.

The Cove also welcomes children. The Cove Camp, directed by Doug Petty and Hugh Wright, is a complex of eight duplex cabins housing 12 campers each for a full complement of 96 campers plus a combination dining and meeting hall, an amphitheater, two pavilions for sheltered recreation, and a junior Olympic-size swimming pool. Its ten summer programs, led by trained high school and college students, feature youth retreats and ministry opportunities for children ages nine to fifteen. Curriculum stresses Bible study, recreation, singing around the campfire, and a concluding Big Event.

ACTIVITIES

According to executive director Neil Sellers, the Cove is more than a mountain retreat and visitor's center. It equips church workers with a renewed energy and spiritual perspective on the challenges of their task. Of the thousands who register, two-thirds are first-time attendees. Week-long seminars and workshops cover a range of topics: guiding youth, marriage and grandparenting, the singles life, spiritual growth, church management, facing change and adversity, weathering temptation, character building, identifying Christ as the son of God, and establishing convictions to live by. Speakers come from a broad span of backgrounds:

- Kay Arthur, teacher for Precept Ministries
- Richard Bewes, rector of All Souls Church, London, England
- Henry Blackaby, a director of the Southern Baptist Convention
- James Montgomery Boice, senior pastor of Philadelphia's Tenth Presbyterian Church
- Former National Football League player Greg Brezina and his wife, Connie
- Don Carson, research professor of New Testament at Trinity Evangelical Divinity School, Deerfield, Illinois
- Nancy Leigh DeMoss, editor of *Spirit of Revival*
- Tony Evans, president of Urban Alternative, headquartered in Dallas, Texas
- John Guest, pastor of Christ Church, Sewickley, Pennsylvania
- Howard Henricks, professor at Dallas Theological Seminary
- Jay Kesler, president of Taylor University, Upland, Indiana, and former president of Youth for Christ International
- Harvest Christian Fellowship evangelist Greg Laurie
- Laurie Katz McIntyre, author of *Designing Women's Ministries*
- Beth Moore, author of *To Live Is Christ: The Life and Ministry of Paul*
- Elisa Morgan of Mothers of Preschoolers International
- Dick Purnell, founder and director of Single Life Resources
- John Tolson, outreach minister of First Presbyterian Church, Orlando, Florida
- George Sweeting, chancellor of the Moody Bible Institute of Chicago
- Bruce Wilkinson, president of Walk through the Bible Ministries

This all-star cast of evangelical educators teaches one-week seminars on the Bible, four annual marriage seminars, three youth retreats, a parenting seminar, and a missionary medicine series.

The resident staff records events in still photography and videotapes.

Sources: Ahlstrom 1972; "Billy Graham Training Center at the Cove"; *Biography Resource Center* 1999; "The Cove"; "Dr. Billy Graham" 1990; Graham 1999; "Training Center Is Now Graham's Legacy" 1995; Wilson and Ferris 1989.

Black Hills
Crazy Horse Memorial
U.S. 16
Black Hills, South Dakota 57754
605-673-4681

To the plains Indians, the Black Hills are a Promised Land, a source of tribal hope and religious strength. The venerable mountain chain linking southwest South Dakota to Wyoming, the Black Hills—the Lakota revered Paha Sapa (Black Hills) and the Cheyenne Good Mountain—rise 6,000 feet above sea level and encompass 6,000 square miles. The pine-covered summit, Ho-cho-ka, or Harney Peak, looks down on ridges, valleys, plateaus, and the hot curative mineral springs at Evans, Hygeia, Mammoth, and Minnekahta. Dark forests shelter mountain goats, bighorn sheep, elk, deer, antelope, hawks, and eagles. In July 1999, the Lakota blessed a new herd of wild horses that grazed near Interior on the southern border of the Badlands as symbols of the time when freedom was a Native American birthright.

The duality of the Black Hills results from the divergent value systems of whites and Indians. Non-Indian visitors seek recreation at Wind Cave National Park, Homestake Gold Mine, Jewel Cave National Monument, Custer State Park, and Mount Rushmore National Memorial and observe an evolving sacred symbol—the unfinished monument to Crazy Horse, chief of the Oglala Sioux, which stands near Custer, Montana. Nearby, moviemaker Kevin Costner, star of *Dances with Wolves,* has begun building a casino and resort complex on the land his film persona revered as hallowed.

In contrast to outsiders, indigenous Mandan, Arikara, Kiowa, Crow, Sioux, and Cheyenne treasure the Black Hills as the ancient Greeks esteemed Delphi—as a source of mythos and the inviolate citadel of the gods. According to Gilbert Voyat's *Cognitive Development among Sioux Children* (1983), a Sioux legend about Bear describes how he prepares for sleep by thanking Mountains, Pine Tree, Owl, Grass, and Ground for allowing him to rest outdoors and by asking that nature give him a long life. To revive such traditional beliefs and maintain oneness with each other and the earth, members hold annual gatherings, athletic events, conferences, and research projects on their spiritual homeland. Despite despoliation by hunters and herders and the intrusion and litter of tourists, Indians cling to their ancestral worship center and honor its sanctity.

Northeast of Sturgis, South Dakota, lies Sacred Bear Butte, a plains landmark for millennia. The mountain is a laccolith, an emerging monolith of molten magma that pushed through the earth's crust after solidifying underground. A unique site to the Sioux and Cheyenne, it is called Mato Pah in Lakota and Noahvose in Cheyenne. According to Sioux oral tradition, the landmass formed during the female water monster Uncegila's defeat of a great bear. Buried under the rugged mountain, the hibernating bear advanced from fearful enemy to the dream keeper.

The Cheyenne version of Bear Butte's origin echoes the theme of a terrible struggle. After human upheaval and protracted warfare among tribes, the spirits demanded that humanity race around a great circle. The raceway eroded the ground, causing the mountain to emerge at center. In the struggle, Wakinyan—the fierce Thunderbird—unleashed a storm that shattered Uncegila's crimson heart, the mythic description of a volcano. Her bones lie scattered about Mako Sica, the Badlands.

As a source of earth energy and a locus for prayer, introspection, and fasting, Bear Butte is irreplaceable. According to early twentieth-century ethnographer Edward S. Curtis's *Native Families,* Sioux ceremonies honored

> an occasion of thanksgiving, of propitiation, of supplication for divine power. Participation in the dance was entirely voluntary, a mental vow to worship the Mystery in this manner being expressed by a man ardently

A model of Sioux Indian Chief Crazy Horse in front of Thunderhead Mountain in the Black Hills of South Dakota. (Bettmann/Corbis)

desiring the recovery of a sick relative; or surrounded by an enemy with escape apparently impossible; or, it might be, dying of hunger, with helpless children crying for food that he could not supply, since some inscrutable power had swept all game from forest and prairie. (Curtis 1996, 48)

He concluded that worshippers were zealous because they believed they could impress God and stave off future disasters. An unsuccessful religious seeker, Eagle Elk, a warrior under Crazy Horse at the Battle of the Little Bighorn, had to content himself with God's silence. In 1907, after photographing him in warrior's regalia, Edward Curtis commented, "[Eagle Elk] fasted in the Black Hills four days and four nights, but had no vision, and never acquired any fighting medicine." (Curtis, *Chiefs and Warriors,* 1996, 88)

Like Eagle Elk, young seekers continue the tradition of seeking God in solitude. They climb slopes to perform vision quests, held in sweat lodges formed from bent saplings covered with

hides. The subject enters the lodge through the east door and lies naked on the ground in darkness. By maintaining fire over rocks and sprinkling them with water mixed with sage, the devout inhale herbal vapors arising from steaming rocks to cleanse the mind of the present and summon glimpses of the Almighty.

HISTORY

The Black Hills, beloved as Grandmother Earth, the Heart of All That Is, have long been holy. Reverence for the rugged uplands permeated historic, cultural, and ceremonial elements of plains tribes, who lost the herds of wild buffalo vital to an ancient way of life by 1885. After the Sioux migrated from Minnesota around 1650, the Black Hills became a traditional source of wood for tipi poles, furs for trading, meat for family meals, and connection to the divine through ritual, meditation, and prayer. Deeply spiritual Sioux made pilgrimages to the Black Hills to worship their creator, Wakan Tanka (the Great Spirit), and commune with their forebears beyond the thin veil separating earthly life from the afterlife. By propitiating God with drumming, chant, and the annual Sun Dance, the Sioux gained victory over enemies, stronger bodies, and thriving infants who ensured the people's survival.

In the restorative environs of Bear Butte, Sweet Medicine, the prehistoric Cheyenne prophet, lived alone for four years to commune with the God Manitou. Around 1775, Sweet Medicine received a consecrated bundle containing four sacred arrows and moral prohibitions against murder, theft, adultery, and incest. From the creator, he assumed a commission to deliver to his people the four holy commandments and taboos along with an ominous vision of invading Europeans. At the creator's command, he established a council of forty-four chiefs, four each from ten Cheyenne bands and four at-large representatives of the four holy directions. He taught the Sun Dance and the Sacred Arrow Bundle Dance as earthly connections to God.

In 1800, the Sioux expelled the Kiowa from the Dakota hills but had to retake grasslands and hunting grounds repeatedly in the 1840s when pioneers began following the Oregon Trail to the West. In the next decade, the mystic and medicine man Crazy Horse sought communion with the divine in the Black Hills in preparation for his life of service. He experienced a visitation of Wakan Tanka after tracing a gleaming path up the eastern slope to an arrow-shaped cavern. Inside, the Great Spirit imbedded seven message-bearing pebbles into his flesh. As Crazy Horse performed restorative rituals, the stone showered sparks from his body.

By 1861, the Black Hills Mining and Exploration Association had already incorporated to explore for gold, but halted temporarily during the Civil War. Signed at Fort Laramie, Wyoming, the short-lived treaty of 1868 ceded the Black Hills to the Sioux. When white prospectors found gold in August 1874, they attempted to displace the local people, who refused to relinquish ownership. To indigenous tribes, the landmass was more than mineral and timber rights—it unified and restored a dispossessed people.

The Indian awe of holy ground fueled a continuing tug of war between native peoples and European settlers interested in farmland and commercial enrichment through gold mining. In 1872, a federal survey team drew right-of-way maps for the Northern Pacific Railroad, which would traverse Sitting Bull's homeland. Two years later, danger hovered as General George Armstrong Custer, leader of the Washita River massacre in Oklahoma a decade before, halted a Sioux reconnaissance expedition of a thousand soldiers to the Black Hills so he could explore its summit. In his wake came a stream of prospectors eager for Dakota gold.

In vain, federal negotiators sought control of the Black Hills in 1875. Only Red Cloud, chief of the Oglala Sioux, was willing to exchange land for food to prevent his people's starvation. A year later, seizure of Sioux holy grounds and enforced residence of the Sioux on reservations provoked the Battle of the Little Bighorn. As reported by Black Hills native Rain-in-the-Face, an eyewitness among Sioux warriors, the combined 2,000 troops of Sitting Bull and Crazy Horse massacred three battalions of the Seventh U.S. Cavalry, including Custer, his officers, and 1,300 soldiers.

Ownership became the pivotal issue in protracted racial tensions worsened by deceit and greed. In 1877, the Homestake Mining Company headquartered in the Black Hills and outproduced all other mining sites in the Western Hemisphere. That same year, Crazy Horse went to prison for refusing to sell Indian lands and, at age thirty-five, died a martyr, stabbed in the back by a Sioux prison guard. In 1879, Red Cloud signed over the Black Hills to federal agents. In desperation, Cheyenne war chief Dull Knife, a veteran of the Battle of the Little Bighorn, twice attempted to lead his people from imprisonment in Oklahoma and Nebraska to freedom at Red Cloud's reservation in the Black Hills. Within a year, the Dakota Territory entered the Union as North and South Dakota.

In November 1890, the Sioux fell under the revivalism of the Paiute prophet Wovoka, the peace-loving Red Messiah whose Ghost Dance foretold an Indian renaissance, a resurrection of departed friends, and a return of the buffalo and ancestral hunting grounds. When the U.S. government banned the dance, Wovoka's Teton and Yankton Sioux adherents fled to the Bad-

---

THE SUN DANCE

According to John Heinerman's *Spiritual Wisdom of the Native Americans* (1989), the original Sun Dance was a plains ritual safeguarding the tribe for another year by reenacting creation. The dancers built a Sun Dance lodge, which symbolized the cosmos. Worshippers seeking a cure removed their moccasins at the threshold to holiness. At the center cottonwood pole, an emblem of the Milky Way revered as the holy of holies, a log separated participants from spectators. Elders tended the log, where medicine men placed a buffalo head as the source of earthly sustenance. After crowning the pole with an eagle, the Great Spirit's messenger, they performed rites, accessed the power of Wakan Tanka, and communicated personal and tribal requests. After the dance, they abandoned the lodge.

Plains tribes followed varying versions of a long-standing ritual. After pitching tents near the lodge, males readied for the dance by stripping to a ceremonial apron, braids, and otherwise bare torso, legs, and feet. Painted varying colors on the days of the dance and dusted with powdered sage, they blew eagle bone whistles hanging on thongs about their necks. For the remainder of the ritual, they drank no liquids. The rigors of standing up and going without water produced alternative names of "long standing up" and the "Thirst Dance."

Day One At the appearance of the first star, dancers filed into the lodge. After the leader prayed for blessing, dancers rocked and shuffled all night in a vigorous performance while singers repeated sacred songs four times to honor the four directions. A complex pattern performed in a circular court, the ceremony originally required dancers to circle the pole and distribute power to participants.

Day Two Before sunrise the next morning, dancing reverted to solo and paired performances. As the light increased, the corps formed five lines and gestured at the sun before seating themselves for prayer. They rested and then refreshed the painted dots on their skin. At midmorning, singing, dancing, and drumming intensified before the medicine man began blessing and healing the sick.

Day Three At the height of the Sun Dance, celebrants passed sacred pipes, a fundamental worship implement, and healing rituals resumed. To whistling, singing, and drumming, dancers added war whoops and lapsed into sacred visions as they gazed into the sun or at the buffalo head.

Day Four As the medicine man continued blessing and healing, until noon, dancers took turns at the center pole to receive blessing. Dancers' families and those cured by Sun Dance ritual heaped money and goods on a blanket. Before the event ended at sunset, the medicine man poured a gift of water to Mother Earth, then offered drinks to the dancers. The celebration concluded with a feast and social dance.

In 1884, Indian Commissioner Edgar Dewdney began pressing for a halt to the Sun Dance, which was uniting Indians against government interference in their lives and affairs. The actual ban went into effect in 1910, ostensibly to halt self-mutilation. In the early days of the Sun Dance, dancers pierced their flesh with skewers tied to thongs, which attached to the pole or to a buffalo skull. During the lengthy ceremony, rhythmic motions caused them to rip hunks of flesh from their bodies, a sacrificial rigor enacted to benefit the tribe. In 1950, the Sioux revived the midsummer dance. In 1970, factions of the American Indian Movement protested the film *A Man Called Horse* as a degrading mockery of exalted ritual. A year later, an intertribal reenactment of the Sun Dance united John Lame Deer, Leonard Crow Dog, and Wallace Black Elk in a political move to boost Native American activism.

---

lands and chose a site east of the Black Hills at Wounded Knee Creek on Pine Ridge Reservation, South Dakota, where they sang and swayed to pulsing drums. The unification of the plains tribe alarmed whites and spawned genocidal rhetoric in the U.S. Department of the Interior. Late in December, sixteen years of animosity culminated in mass murder when 3,500 troopers of the revitalized Seventh Cavalry slew 250 noncombatants with rifles, lances, and cannon.

SCULPTURE

The Crazy Horse Memorial, the nation's outstanding Native American symbol, began as a tribute to the indomitable Indians of South Dakota. In 1940, sculptor Korczak Ziolkowski accepted an invitation from Chief Henry

Standing Bear to honor his uncle Crazy Horse, military strategist and defender of the Black Hills. Beginning in 1948, artisans, drawing on memories of eyewitnesses, etched on the mountain face the world's largest sculpture—the 600-by 563-foot form of a galloping pony bearing Crazy Horse with arms outstretched toward hallowed lands. The inscription reads, "Where My Dead Lie Buried." In 1962, Bear Butte became a state park; despite a march on Washington by seven Indian nations to retrieve the sacred site, in 1973, it was named a national historic place. After Ziolkowski's death in 1982, his sons worked for the rest of the twentieth century on details of the Crazy Horse Monument.

Congress opened the way to late-twentieth-century claims through the American Indian Religious Freedom Act of 1978. The Lakota and Tsistsista sued for relief and damages against federal authorities who managed the state park. Proponents of native worship lambasted developers and builders of park facilities, parking lots, and campgrounds for promoting tourism and for opening a trail that intersected with the ancestral approach to the summit, disrupted ceremonies, and degraded consecrated ground. Citing First Amendment rights, the Universal Declaration of Human Rights, and the International Covenant on Civil and Political Rights, native claimants proceeded to litigation on grounds that the government restricted access to their sacred geography. They lost in a judgment that favored the state of South Dakota's efforts to accommodate and protect park visitors. Five years later, appeals upheld the judgment.

Near century's end, the National Historic Landmarks commission considered native religious grounds an endangered national site, but protesters like Yankton Dakota activist James R. Weddell continued to reject purchase offers for the Black Hills and denounced what he called a "shameful and bastardly deed." (Weddell) Arvol Looking Horse, nineteenth-generation Keeper of the Sacred Buffalo Calf Pipe, interjected an emotional view by observing that NASA's pictures of the Black Hills reveal the shape of a human heart. The photograph confirmed a Sioux belief that the land is the heart of everything that is. Lakota elder Johnson Holy Rock urged Indians to honor their obligations to their grandfa-

thers, who reverenced the land. Lakota artist Mitchell Zephier concurred with a reminder that the earth is a gift that sustains all life.

> **See also** Devils Tower National Monument, Medicine Wheel.
> **Sources:** Alsberg 1949; "Battle of Wounded Me" 1994; Bellafante 1995; Buchanan 1999; Cantor, George, 1993; Champagne 1994,1998; "The Costner Brothers and the Black Hills"; Cummings 1993; Grinnell 1971; Harrod 1987; Heinerman 1989; Ketchum 1957; *Lakota: Seeking the Great Spirit* 1994; Lehn 1980; Maynor and McLeod 1999; Milne 1995; "Native American Religious Freedom"; "Native Rights Act before Congress" 1992–1993; "1997 NHL Endangered List"; Patterson and Snodgrass 1994; Powell 1969; Rosen 1995; "The Sacred Arrow Renewal"; Skafte 1997; "A Statement from Dr. Arvol Looking Horse"; Steiger 1974; Vogel 1998; Vollers 1996; Waldman 1990; Weddell; Wiget 1996.

Boston Avenue Methodist Church
Dr. Mouzon Biggs, Jr., Senior Minister
1301 South Boston Avenue
Tulsa, Oklahoma
918-583-5181
www.bostonavenueumc.org

During financial boom times in Oklahoma, planners of the Boston Avenue Methodist Church made a promising statement in architecture that American Protestantism still possessed the vigor and vision of earlier eras. Against the skyline of modern Tulsa, the 225-foot tower is an insistent statement of Christianity's presence. In addition to its contribution to art and architecture, the church holds a place among the Department of the Interior's National Historic Landmarks.

HISTORY
The grand Boston Avenue church dates to a small trading-post town, where, in November 1893, the Reverend E. B. Chenoweth settled his wife and son. With seven members, he founded the Methodist Episcopal Church, South, a designation indicating Confederate sympathies three decades after the Civil War. For monthly meetings, the group convened at a Presbyterian mission. By summer 1894, the tiny congregation was content with an American Indian style ramada

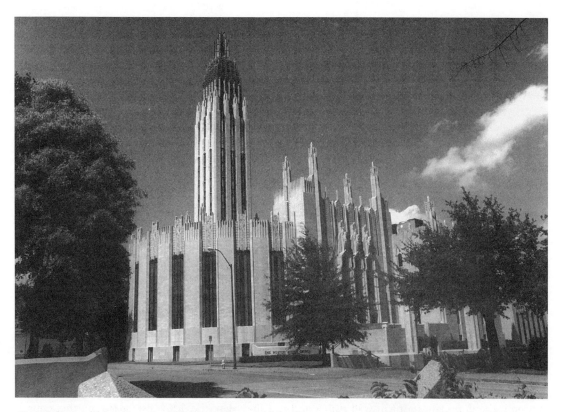

During financial boom times in Oklahoma, planners of the Boston Avenue Methodist Church made a promising statement in architecture that American Protestantism still possessed the vigor and vision of earlier eras. (Courtesy Boston Avenue Methodist Church)

—a brush arbor shading makeshift pews formed by laying wooden planks over railroad ties. When the first frame building was ready for use, the congregation settled into its first permanent church home.

Within seven years, the assembly moved to a brick structure, which sufficed for five more years. In 1906, planners chose the current location—the corner of Fifth Street and Boston Avenue, where they completed an elegant edifice graced with a portico and white columns. Still shackled to slavery's history, they chose the name Boston Avenue Methodist Episcopal Church, South. Building committee chairman C. C. Cole became frustrated at the lack of vision in architectural designs. He gave the task to Quaker artist Adah Robinson, an instructor at the University of Tulsa. Within days, she sketched an art deco structure that broke with the national trend toward Gothic houses of worship.

Planners hired Robinson's student Bruce Goff, of the Rush, Endacott, and Rush architec-

tural firm, to draft blueprints. Another student, Robert Garrison, sculpted appointments in terra cotta. Robinson began supervising construction in 1927. Congregants dedicated their building on June 9, 1929. Within months, they faced the hardships of the stock market crash, but managed to stay solvent over the Great Depression and burn the mortgage in 1946. Additions to the tower in 1963, children's building in 1965, and additional parking space in 1993 rounded out the church complex in its 100th year.

ARCHITECTURE

The Boston Avenue Methodist Church, like medieval stone cathedrals, thrusts heavenward with a bold, fresh gesture of newness and energy. In the words of its creator,

> All appointments have been designed with the hope of creating a place that is honest, harmonious, and spiritualized; that those who may not respond through their reason

and those who may not react through their emotion may at least through visualization be moved to a higher conception of the Presence of Divine Power. ("Boston Avenue Methodist Church")

The building's geometrics offset the fluted linear limestone column of the fifteen-story tower with a round sanctuary. The combination of innovative shape and engaging inner space in the largest cantilevered building west of the Mississippi suggests the optimism and vigor of Oklahoma's pioneer forebears.

In four directions, the building offers entrances, accentuated by sculpted figures from history. Within, angled archways at doors and windows form a unifying motif echoed in the exposed pipes of the 105-rank, 4-manual Möller organ. Behind the choir, a 750,000-piece mosaic channels light beyond the center bronze cross as a symbol of resurrection and new life. The ceiling is a vast medallion centered with an oculus. The tritoma, or torch lily, a common Oklahoma flower, is the dominant motif in wall panels and the ceiling. Another symbol taken from the severe Oklahoma landscape, the coreopsis daisy, replicates the perseverance and ebullience of Christianity.

The tower's four glass shards reflect light to the four directions. Inside, fourteen floors contain areas for religious education and administration; the top floor offers a unique site for prayer. The Great Hall, the long terrazzo hallway east of the sanctuary, houses fellowship as well as Advent and Lenten services. The area features modernistic wall mosaics composed of a half million tiles and mounted in celebration of the church centennial. The north mural features Yahweh, or Adonai, the Old Testament God, revealed to Moses in the burning bush and through Torah scrolls and prophet's staff. On the opposite wall, elements of birth and death grace the New Testament man-God.

ACTIVITIES

As did the founding members, congregants support an active program of Christian worship and education. Sunday-school classes at each age level employ varied learning experiences to nurture Christian faith in prospective and new members as well as those familiar with Methodism. In addition, the staff offers a weekly preschool on one-, two-, three-, or five-day schedules for children ages six months to five years. Children contribute to mission teams and ministry to the handicapped and enjoy enrichment and summer fun at Camp Egan near Tahlequah. Teens respond to similar camp activities and to drama, musical productions, and an annual mission trip to Mexico. Extracurricular classes provide six-week intensive study of the Bible, health issues, financial planning, exercise, travel, genealogy, crafts, and foreign language. Adults direct their faith toward mission opportunities in Neighbor for Neighbor, Habitat for Humanity, Homebound Ministry, Respite Care for full-time caregivers, and volunteer mission trips to Slovakia, Argentina, Nicaragua, Costa Rica, Guatemala, Jamaica, Mexico, and surrounding U.S. states.

The church communicates its mission and outreach through a Web site and a weekly print or electronic newspaper, *Read the Word*. Recent issues describe low-cost space in the church columbarium in a garden adjacent to Bishops' Hall. The niche burial spot is the design of Boston Avenue architect Roger Coffey. The church library, operated by Brenda Haley, offers Sunday morning guidance to readers, who may select from 3,000 titles and 200 videos on world religion and Methodism. Church archivist Martha Jo Bradley organizes 100 titles and realia concerning local city and church history since 1901.

Sources: "Architecture"; "Boston Avenue Methodist Church"; Broderick 1958; "National Landmarks" 1999; "Tulsa Area Libraries"; Williams, Peter W., 1997.

Brownsville Assembly of God

Reverend John A. Kilpatrick
Reverend Steve Hill
Assistant Pastor Richard Crisco
3100 West DeSoto Street
Pensacola, Florida 32505
904-433-3078

A phenomenon in American evangelicalism, the Brownsville Assembly of God Church initiated a one-day revival that burgeoned into the longest charismatic revival of the twentieth century. Worshippers continue to come from a wide span of denominations around the world to sing, pray, rejoice, and join prayer teams to spread a mass appeal known as "refreshing from the Lord." Travel agents book flights for thousands bound for Pensacola, Florida, a military center with a population of 58,000. Others move from out of state to be near the spiritual resurgence. Ministers nationwide request services in their home churches.

Within four years of its founding, the Reverend John A. Kilpatrick's church grew 125 percent—from 2,000 members to 5,000. He declared the response to revivalism a spontaneous presence of the Holy Spirit. In his estimation, the unique Florida revival demonstrates the desperation in worshippers seeking a supportive Pentecostal community.

HISTORY

Pentecostalism is rooted in the Christian feast of Pentecost, a celebration of the descent of the Holy Spirit into the hearts of Christ's disciples. As described in Acts 2, the New Testament Pentecost occurred after the traitor Judas's death while the remaining eleven men shared a meal following the ascension of Christ into heaven. As Paul described the extraordinary event, the diners began to speak in tongues, a manifestation of the Holy Spirit.

The Assembly of God denomination established sixteen "Tenets of Faith," the biblical doctrines that prescribed the sect's constitution and bylaws that outline basic principles. Key Bible passages instructed followers to repent and wipe away sin (Acts 3:19) and to preach to all nations (Luke 24:47). Pentecostal members emulated the scriptural description of speaking in tongues in the presence of the Holy Ghost (Acts 2:4), a physical manifestation that earned them the derision of outsiders and set them apart from less overt congregations.

To cleanse the heart of sin and regenerate the spirit, Pentecostal ministers cling to forceful, energetic evangelism to produce sincere repentance and a lasting change of behavior to ensure life after death among God's elect. Song leaders call for clapping, hand waving, and repetition of key phrases. The final altar call, a standard closure for fundamentalist services, produces involuntary physical signs of a divine presence through uncontrollable tremors, sobs, speaking in tongues, visions, an enveloping haze, and strong currents pulling the convert away from Satan and into the fold of the redeemed. Testimony of miraculous healing, bestial calls, and unruly outbursts are no longer encouraged during Pentecostal worship, which maintains a modicum of order to preserve dignity.

The Brownsville Assembly grew out of Pensacola's First Assembly of God, launched by the E. C. Ward family and 40 founders. Initially called the Full Gospel Tabernacle, the church opened in 1939 at the corner of Y and DeSoto Streets. Its architecture mimicked traditional southern tent revivals—sawdust floors, pole-supported roof, and walls of scrap material. It was 1943 before members built a permanent structure, called Faith Temple. In 1946, they chose Brownsville Assembly of God Church as its name, officially enrolled 60 charter members, and organized a foreign missions program and women's missionary council.

Evangelism fueled local ministry with spirit and commitment. In 1948, the church began a bus ministry and radio outreach over WCOA. By 1956, growth to 200 members called for a larger sanctuary and education building, a minister of music, and education director. To house the minister, planners bought a parsonage and named it Glory House. The program grew with the addition of a men's fellowship, Dorcas women's group, choirs, and youth programs.

The mounting fortunes of Brownsville Assembly of God continued into the 1970s, when planners built a fourth edifice and established Five Flags Christian Academy and Southeastern Bible College Extension Campus. Twenty-one churchmen carried mission fervor to Ecuador, where they built a mission church. In February 1982, the church called John A. Kilpatrick, a native of Columbus, Georgia, who had begun preaching in 1964 at age fourteen. To unify the congregation, he held Sunday prayer meetings called Prayer Banners, which focused on twelve issues: war, family, souls, national leadership, healing, pastors, schools, ministries, peace in Jerusalem, children, catastrophic events, and revival.

In 1991, the church constructed a new sanctuary to seat 2,000 and added the former Brownsville Elementary School property to its campus. That same year, David Yonngi Cho, pastor of the Korean Assemblies of God in Seoul, had a vision of a spiritual tumult in the United States. He claimed that God revealed a huge Pentecostal ingathering in Pensacola, Florida. To force a radical shift in spirituality, the Brownsville congregation pressed for a revival. They hired evangelist Steve Hill, a native of Ankara, Turkey, an adherent of the Reverend Sandy Miller of Trinity Brompton Anglican Church in London, the site of similar spiritual manifestations. For his revival sermon, Hill preached "How to Get the Lord's Attention" and made an altar call for seekers of salvation.

The unprecedented response overwhelmed the church family, who were unprepared for a full-time crusade. Both Brenda Kilpatrick and Lindel Cooley had visited the Toronto Airport Vineyard Church and been anointed with the Toronto Blessing. Their experience offered some clue to the masses of people who flocked to Brownsville. Staunch Pentecostalists declared the phenomenon a sign of the rapture, a religious designation of Christ's return at the end of time to rescue the righteous from doomsday. Hill preferred to think of each site's response as an element of the body of Christ, a term indicating a unified world sanctity. To meet the challenge of revival, Brownsville Assembly of God began constructing an auditorium to seat 5,000, a sure sign of commitment to full-time evangelism.

Beginning on Father's Day, June 18, 1995, the flood of penitents known as the Pensacola Outpouring began demanding the spiritualism of the Reverend John A. Kilpatrick and his fellow evangelist, the Reverend Steve Hill, who extended the original one-hour service to five hours. Hill canceled a trip to Russia to accommodate the influx of suppliants, who came by car and bus. During services held Wednesday through Sunday, the head count quickly rose to 2,500 per night. Into the early morning hours, preaching and singing continued as converts streamed in from bars, honky-tonks, and lower-class neighborhoods to join the mostly upper-middle-class Assembly of God members. Crucial to the atmosphere of renewal were individual crises, emotional trauma, and physical ailments. Director of television ministries Steve White had recorded hundreds of hours of rejoicing and pledges to Christ from people who found new direction for their lives.

ACTIVITIES

Although meetings were reduced to four nights weekly in the second year, attendees continued filling the church's 2,000 seats and overflowed into a separate building to watch services on closed-circuit television screens in the cafeteria. Additional outreach inspired charismatics through the multicity Awake America crusade targeting Chicago, Cincinnati, Minneapolis, Boise, Dallas, Toledo, Anaheim, Houston, and Memphis as a traveling staff of prayer teams, choir singers, local members, and revival supporters followed the outreach minister, the Reverend Michael Brown. Television broadcasts spread the effect to even greater numbers. The revival spawned the Brownsville Revival School of Ministry, Michael Brown's training school for 1,700 preachers and missionaries, and aimed to convert a million people to Pentecostalism by January 1, 2001.

In nightly sessions that parallel early twentieth-century camp meetings and tent revivals, worshippers leap, raise outstretched hands, and shake to contemporary Christian music performed by a choir and soloists under the leadership of music director Lindel Cooley. The *New York Times* dubbed the event a "rock concert in robes." ("The Brownsville Revival") Critics of the mass demonstration accuse the gathering of violating biblical dictates concerning holy worship, promulgating mass hysteria and unsanctified uproar, and appealing for contributions and purchase of books, videos, T-shirts, and religious trinkets. Investigators from the *Pensacola News Journal* pressed for an audit of the millions that the church has gathered into its treasury. The probe forced the revival to collect sales tax.

After acknowledging weaknesses in administration, Hill and Kilpatrick placed their nonprofit ministries—Together in the Harvest and Feast of Fire—under the Reverend Billy Graham's Evangelical Council for Financial Accountability and hired Dallas attorney Stephen Coke to answer questions about nonprofit corporations. To emulate the successful crusades of Dr. Billy Graham, the Brownsville staff requested that local sponsors underwrite the leasing of arenas and pay advertising fees. To produce detailed financial statements on merchandising and on each leg of the city-to-city outreach, the staff also employed an accountant and hired Bob Rogers to shift the crusades' emphasis from collection to ministry.

The Pensacola revival has affected the Florida panhandle by bringing streams of the devout and the curious. To reinforce the appeal, the Brownsville Assembly of God began individualizing services by adding a Tuesday night prayer meeting and a Thursday youth service to evangelize teenagers not yet drawn into illicit behaviors. Hill has claimed that religious renewal in the city and its environs has reduced gang violence, drug addiction, prostitution, and local crime. He predicted that visiting pastors would ignite zeal in their home churches and would ease the doctrinal differences that separate and often antagonize rival denominations.

Sources: Ahlstrom 1972; Allman 1998; "The Brownsville Revival"; Costella 1997; Crann 1996; DeWitt and Grady 1996; Kaczor 1999.

Bruton Parish Church

Herman Hollerith IV, Rector
Duke of Gloucester Street
P.O. Box BP
Williamsburg, Virginia 23187-3520
757-229-2891

Like colonial forebears Thomas Jefferson, George Washington, Richard Henry Lee, George Wythe, Patrick Henry, John Marshall, and George Mason, twenty-first-century congregants of Bruton Parish Church supply the town of Williamsburg with models of Christian faith and mission. Original membership included colonial magistrates and representatives, whom law required to set a good example by attending the state Anglican church. In addition, the church has been the religious anchor to students at the College of William and Mary. Enclosed by the wall that formed the churchyard in 1754, the site remains a favorite haunt of photographers, genealogists, historians, religious tourists, and Episcopalians searching out the religious roots of the United States.

HISTORY

Thirty-nine years before the incorporation of Williamsburg, Bruton Parish Episcopal Church got its start in 1660 as a handsome Flemish-style wood building probably erected on the present site in Old Fields at Middle Plantation. The ten-square-mile parish, named for a town on the River Brue in Somersetshire, England, served the 110 families of Marstown and Middletown. On November 14, 1677, the vestry voted to build a brick structure with land and funds donated by John Page. Near the center of the colonial settlement, Rector Rowland Jones dedicated the new church on January 6, 1684. It served long and well but fell into disrepair by 1710, when planners undertook the design of a third structure.

The present church, built with £200 from the colonial treasury and taxes on liquor and slaves, was roomy enough to accommodate the General Assembly. In 1711, Governor Alexander Spotswood drew the cruciform design 75 by 28 feet with two wings 22 by 19 feet. Construction by carpenter James Morris began on November 17, with John Tyler adding the wings. According to the vestrybook, the delayed completion annoyed the parish, who had to wait until December 2, 1715, to occupy the new sanctuary. It pleased congregants with increased light from rosette windows to the north, south, and east and arched windows on each side. Marble pavers enhanced acoustics. At center, the governor sat on a raised canopied chair opposite the pulpit and sounding board. Parishioners occupied cozy, draft-resistant box pews, with women to the left side of the center aisle and men opposite.

In the ample upper reaches, planners added galleries with exterior entrances. The one assigned to William and Mary students on July 10, 1718, still stands. Extensions in 1744 and 1752 increased the size of the chancel. Near its centennial, the church installed an organ, played by jailer Peter Pelham and pumped by a prisoner, and received from Episcopalians in Jamestown a chalice, paten, and alms basin. The next year, merchant James Tarpley's donation of a bell required a brick belfry, which builders constructed

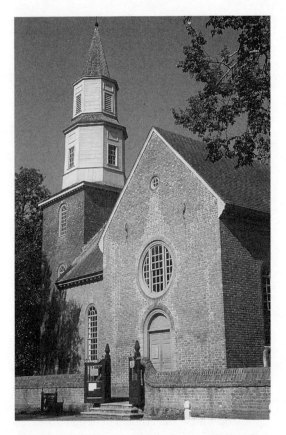

Thirty-nine years before the incorporation of colonial Williamsburg, Virginia, Bruton Parish Episcopal Church got its start in 1660. (Lee Snider/Corbis)

in slightly darker material than the church's salmon-hued brick. Additional honor accrued in 1768 from the under-floor burial of Francis Fauquier, a beloved colonial governor and founder of Williamsburg's Public Hospital.

Bruton Parish Church remained at the center of history, even after the state capital moved to Richmond in 1780. During the Battle of Yorktown in 1781, it appears to have served double duty as a storehouse and dressing station. At the end of England's hold on the colonies, the creation of democracy ended church reliance on taxation as a source of revenue. Repairs and additions funded by the church treasury early in the nineteenth century made the structure easier to heat and access, but robbed it of historical authenticity. In 1840, the town installed a steeple clock. At the Battle of Williamsburg in the second year of the Civil War, Union medical personnel treated soldiers from both

sides in a makeshift sanctuary hospital. Late in the century, the vestry shortened and then removed the original pews and replaced the marble flooring with wood.

In the last 100 years, the rise of religious tourism revived curiosity about the original colonial church. In 1903, for Jamestown's third centennial, Rector W. A. R. Goodwin superintended a renovation and hired New York architect J. Stewart Barney to restore the church to its prefederalist state by reversing the seating arrangement to face east and restoring the governor's pew, wrought-iron weather vane, and wooden gates. In 1937, in the last years of his career, Barney attempted another remodeling, completed by the historic entity known as Colonial Williamsburg. The current baroque pipe organ, made by Samuel Green of London, was the gift of John D. Rockefeller, Jr., who restored the entire city of Colonial Williamsburg in the 1930s.

Growth and development has kept Bruton Parish Church from becoming a museum, the fate of many historic churches. Staff scheduled a "Great Preacher Series" in 1958, a program that substantiated the church's national reputation for excellence. In 1963, planners anticipating growth and new demands purchased additional land for a second Episcopal church to serve Williamsburg. Two decades later, they constructed St. Mary's Chapel for flexbility and added ten Christmas Eve and six Easter Eve and Easter services as well as televised services to accommodate an influx of tourists and outsiders wanting a closer view of the nation's oldest functioning church.

ACTIVITIES

At the height of its enrollment, Bruton Parish encompasses 1,700 members plus college students and visitors. Crowds fill the church's 500 seats for the 11:00 A.M. Sunday service and holidays. Homebound members check out tapes of services from the Hennage Library and keep up with events by reading the *Chronicle*. The church calendar lists 7:30, 9:00, and 11:15 communion and 10:15 Christian education on Sunday morning plus a 5:30 P.M. Holy Eucharist. Additional communion is available at St. Mary's Chapel and area retirement homes on Tuesday morning at

7:00 and at Wren Chapel Wednesday at 6:00 P.M. Wednesday morning Eucharist at 11:00 offers a healing service of anointing and laying on of hands. Lay members hold noonday prayers from the Book of Common Prayer Monday through Saturday for parishioners and guests.

The parish house accommodates church school and such activities as Bible study, vacation Bible school, confirmation class, and family-night gatherings. Informal foyer groups treat oldtimers, new members, singles, and couples to intimate dinners. Men and women of the church hold separate weekly prayer meetings for congregational needs. The parish mentors college students, supports a court advocacy program for children, and responds to local and global needs, including the Jackson-Field Home afghan project, hunger walks, United Thank Offering, and, in September 1999, benevolences to earthquake victims in Turkey. Additional volunteer opportunities include acolytes, guides, library board, altar guild, kitchen guild, historians and archivists of the church and burial ground, Daughters of the King, Youth Lay Readers, Sat-urday Morning Men's Fellowship, and Guild of the Christ Child, which welcomes parents of newborns. The staff also prearranges funeral services and interment in the church yard.

The church supports the arts through a regular program of organ and harpsichord recitals, chamber groups, and visiting choirs, vocalists, and instrumentalists. Church musicians can participate in children's and adults' choirs, Handbell Ringers, and Campana Ringers, led by James S. Darling, organist-choirmaster, and his assistant, JanEl Gortmaker. At the parish house, the Bruton Parish Book and Gift Shop increases funds for ministry through daily sale of religious items and such CDs as *Forward Day by Day* and other musicales featuring organ and choir.

Sources: "Archeology at Colonial Williamsburg"; "Bruton Parish Church," http://www.brutonparish. org/, www.history.org, www.wm.edu; "Bruton Parish Church, Williamsburg, Virginia"; "Bruton Parish Episcopal Church"; Fitch 1973; Ketchum 1957; "Life in the English Colonies"; Williams, Peter W., 1997; Wilson and Ferris 1989.

ism until 1947, when they launched an evangelical outreach and incorporated as the unaffiliated Calvary Presbyterian Church, eventually shortened to its current name. In 1972, the Reverend Rhoads left Valley Forge, Pennsylvania, to assume the pastorate of some 400 Calvary dissenters. By the mid-1980s, a 1,400-seat structure was too small to contain them.

When Charlotte zoning ordinances forced the unwieldy congregation away from the city center in 1985, Calvary Church left the Sardis and Randolph address to relocate on donated acreage at Highway 51 and Rea Road. In an era of phenomenal growth, Rhoads headed the building program. Architect Roe Messner, designer of televangelist Jim Bakker's failed Heritage USA, began a novel project, which called for an outer shell of granite. To save money, planners altered materials to stucco. In December 1989, the Reverend Rhoads and his congregation dedicated a sanctuary that outstripped anything in the area for daring modernity.

Calvary's early years were fiscally unsteady. In 1992, members resorted to a predawn prayer vigil to meet payments on a monstrous mortgage. After Rhoads's abrupt Sunday-morning departure in 1995 to preach for the Billy Graham ministries, stymied Calvaryites tossed about a possible merger with Forest Hill Church. Two years later, planners hired the Reverend Glenn Wagner, a founder of Promise Keepers, a male-centered evangelical campaign similar to Louis Farrakhan's Million Man March. Departing Denver, Colorado, Wagner agreed to lead a staff of 40 plus 180 day-care workers.

Calvary Church

Dr. E. Glenn Wagner, Senior Pastor
5801 Pineville-Matthews Road
Charlotte, North Carolina 28226
704-543-1200
FAX 704-543-1034
bmodzell@calvarychurch.com
www.calvarychurch.com

At the intersection of N.C. Highway 51 and Rea Road in Charlotte, North Carolina, stands Calvary Church, the state's largest sanctuary and an inspiring architectural landmark. It owes its modern pizzazz to former pastor Ross Rhoads, whose modernist dream took shape amid gossip, media furor, and public scorn. Trustees anticipated a burgeoning membership by situating Calvary in the high-growth Metrolina corridor. To date, the evangelical, nondenominational congregation has not been disappointed.

HISTORY

Founded on May 21, 1939, by Frank Graham, the church grew out of the evangelism of Mordecai Ham, the same preacher who started Graham's son, Dr. Billy Graham, on a worldwide revival circuit. The members departed Tenth Avenue Presbyterian Church out of discontent with creeping liberalism and violation of biblical principles. The conservative splinter group named itself the Bible Presbyterian Church and held initial sessions at the old Central High School. In 1941, the congregation, renamed Calvary Presbyterian, found a new home on East Fourth Street near Presbyterian Hospital and then resettled on Sardis and Randolph Roads.

Calvary's metamorphosis was a steady disassociation with the Protestant status quo. Congregants remained within standard Presbyterian-

ARCHITECTURE

A 300,000-square-foot edifice thrusting upward on 1,001 acres, the three-tiered structure, which seats 6,200, is an unusual blend of adobe sand-pink stucco and pointed gray spires pierced by vertical fingers of dark, silvered glass. From the ten-acre parking lot, worshippers take escalators to the upper level, where green carpet anchors the mahogany seating and stage in an expansive quarter-circle auditorium crowned with an overhead cross. Ahead, oversized screens project

Calvary Church owes its modern pizzazz to former pastor Ross Rhoads, whose modernist dream took shape amid gossip, media furor, and public scorn. (Courtesy Calvary Church)

a vivid telecast of stage proceedings. Alongside four clear-glass windows, a stretch of brass pipes reaches to the ceiling. To the right, a chapel replicates the quarter-circle shape. At the rear lie a nursery, classrooms, banquet facilities, the Light Care counseling center, and offices.

A feature of the music ministry is Calvary's 5-manual, 205-rank Möller pipe organ, topped with prominent cornets and millennial trumpets and enhanced with trompeteria, an ancillary rank of brass. Built in Hagerstown, Maryland, the complex is one of the nation's largest instruments. For its dedication, David German, former minister of music, composed "Trumpet Tune," a piece that coordinates the organ's best features. Recordings by Dan Miller at the console are available from the Organ Historical Society or Calvary Church. They include *The Calvary Grand Organ Dedication* (1990), *Christmas Joy* (1990), *Hymns* (1991), and *The Power and The Glory* (1994).

ACTIVITIES

The church's 8 pastors and 220 support personnel oversee a varied program, which reaches out to the elderly, minorities, and the handicapped. Current needs require three Sunday morning

services at 8:00 and 10:30 A.M. and 6:00 P.M. plus Children's Church and Bible classes at 9:15 A.M., Wednesday night electives, children's and youth programs, and a 7:00 P.M. service in the chapel. Programming features modern music and puppetry. The staff boosts attendance by an upbeat ad campaign—"B.Y.O.B.: Bring Your Own Bible." Targeted age and special-interest groups attend Sunday-school classes creatively named Bookworms, Calvary Gold, Coaches' Class, Shepherds' Watch, Agape Singles, Psalms for Life, Living Word, Peculiar People, Commitment 101, Salt and Light, Singles Talk, Life Application, Practical Christian Living, Bridge Builders, Master's Fellowship, Maranatha, Bereans, Joy Class, Prime Time Alive, Upper Room, and Pilgrims in Progress. The weekly calendar accommodates singles klatches, T-ball, soccer, Calvary Academy for the Arts, a 140-voice adult choir, handbell practice, and Charlotte's largest preschool center. Stewardship subsidizes 60 full-time missionaries, the CoMission Program in Petrozavodsk, Russia, street and prison ministries, and the Charlotte Project, which coordinates a volunteer effort in Metrolina's poor neighborhoods. Networking promotes volunteering for Habitat for Humanity and Operation Warm-up, which distributes blankets and clothing throughout pockets of poverty in Appalachia.

Into the twenty-first century, Calvary remains active in varied venues. Its historic presence gained stature from sermons by evangelist Dr. Billy Graham and from Promise Keepers rallies. Thousands have attended Easter and Fourth of July programs. Innovative volunteers augment music, Bible study, and preaching with puppetry, a concert series, Saturday music to a live band, and the Calvary Players, a drama-comedy ensemble with a flair for humor. A Wednesday night elective series offers training in hermeneutics, discussion of spiritual questions, deaf ministry, spiritual warfare boot camp, marriage encounters, divorce recovery, single parenting, and Christian business leadership.

On May 24, 1999, 3,800 well-wishers and members of the congregation celebrated Calvary's sixtieth anniversary with a festival of hymns, prayer, and anthems accompanied by organ, piano, brass choir, and timpani. The festival concluded with a barbecue on the lawn. That same summer, the church joined North Carolina evangelist Franklin Graham's Operation Christmas Child. To provide gifts for needy children and for refugees returning to Kosovo, Calvary members celebrated the Fourth of July by collecting several hundred shoe boxes to fill with toys and surprises. In November 1999, the church made local religious history by hiring a black minister of music, John Leon Lewis, to energize singing and set an example of religious inclusion. In December, he led the orchestra and players in a Christmas pageant, *Heaven's Child,* which featured elaborate costumes and a blend of classical, southern gospel, and contemporary music.

Sources: Aiken; "Charlotte Churches"; Garfield "Hallelujah, Calvary!" 1999, "Preaching Harmony" 1999; Hauser 1999; Laird; McMillan; "Preacher Gets Try-Out at Calvary Church" 1997.

Canyon de Chelly
P.O. Box 588
Chinle, Arizona 86503
520-674-5500

Both psychologist Karl Jung and religion expert Joseph Campbell called Canyon de Chelly (pronounced duh shay') National Monument the earth's most sacred place. The ancient home of the Dinéh, or Navajo, nation, its history began thousands of years before the discovery of the New World. Its prime wonders include the Antelope House, White House, and Mummy Cave. At the 83,840-acre park on Defiance Plateau in Arizona, majestic twin columns of sandstone rise 800 feet from the canyon floor. Alone amid 1,000-foot canyon walls, they are the world's tallest free-standing columns. The rock gave the canyon its name from a mispronunciation of the Navajo word *tsegi,* meaning "standing rock."

BELIEFS
To the Hopi and Navajo, the lithic formation is the home of Tse-che-nako, or Spider Woman, the mythic avenging spinner. When her companion, Speaking Rock, reports misbehavior, Spider Woman sends out a web to ensnare and swallow unruly children. Native dwellers prove their story by pointing to the top of the tower, where light-colored rocks look startlingly like human bones dried white in the desert sun.

To the Navajo, Canyon de Chelly is holy ground. Out of awe for the beginning of time, they call the site the "place where water comes from rock." The water was a necessary intervention of the gods after Coyote started a brush fire and fled rather than put it out. Natives maintain that sacred beings once taught life skills to the first humans, who carved pictographs of antelope, hunters, and shamans known as "holy ones." To rebalance mind and spirit, Navajo sages return to the canyon to perform medicine ceremonies, study the ancient markings on the sandstone precipice at White House Ruins, and cleanse the sacred site of the spirits of climbers and hang gliders killed while trespassing on consecrated ground.

Spider Rock is the emblem of Spider Woman, the wise, all-seeing female creator, who nourished the Navajo in her womb, gave them life on earth, and taught them to weave and inscribe her shape on pottery. Her creative mythos suits a matrilineal culture. The Anasazi-Hopi describe her as a divine mystery associated with regenerative thought, ritual, chant, dance, and song. In creation lore, Spider Woman was the

Both psychologist Karl Jung and religion expert Joseph Campbell called Canyon de Chelly National Monument the earth's most sacred place. (North Wind Picture Archives)

magical earth deity who shared power with Tawa, the sun God. The two deities established earth as the middle ground between the underworld and the sky. Using the first magic song and rhythmic motions, they produced light and life.

As the doer of the pair, Spider Woman shaped Tawa's thoughts into reality, forming fish, birds, and animals. The gods draped the still forms in a fleecy, white woven blanket and called them to life. Next, the two formed human male and female figures. Spider Woman nestled the lifeless figures in her arms and joined Tawa in summoning breath to quicken them. She separated them into tribes and led them through a *sipapu,* the opening between the underworld and earth that lies on Pisisbaiya (the Colorado River).

According to Navajo etiology, Spider Woman intended unique lives for each gender. She assigned homebuilding, gardening, and food preparation to females and taught them to gather webs and suspend them over their infants' cribs to capture stinging night insects. To males, she taught weaponry, weaving, and worship. Central to the male role was kiva construction, the building of consecrated housing for spirits. When Spider Woman completed earthly instruction, she dematerialized. Only the pair of stone towers in Canyon de Chelly remained behind.

HISTORY

Formed from windblown sand amid stratified canyon walls of the Defiance Uplift west of the Chuska Mountains, the double obelisk known as Spider Rock derives from a red monolith shaped 230 million years ago. Basket makers arrived around 350 A.D., followed by potters, Anasazi pueblo builders, and Hopi, who inhabited abandoned pueblos in 1300. Four centuries afterward, the latest arrivals, the Navajo, crossed the Colorado River. They took refuge in caves they dug in cliffs far above the canyon floor, where they were safe from flash floods and attack by enemy tribes or the Mexican government. From their creation myth, they assigned the rock its divine name. As the newcomers prospered, they honored Spider Woman for making them one of the largest and most prosperous tribes.

The nineteenth century ended the canyon's idyllic peace. In 1805, Lieutenant Antonio Narbona, later governor of the New Mexico province, led troops against the entrenched Navajo. An all-day battle killed 115 Navajo. Survivors named their rock fortress Massacre Cave. Shortly before the Civil War, American officials took control of Arizona. They dispatched Colonel Christopher "Kit" Carson to suppress war chief Barboncito and mobilize some 8,000 Navajo and 400 Mescalero Apache on a forced march to Bosque Redondo, New Mexico. The brutal resettlement is known as the Long Walk.

In 1864, Carson's men, aided by Ute trackers, killed sheep herds, destroyed gardens, chopped down 5,000 peach trees, and sealed the canyon entrance to circumvent any hopes of return. On the miserable march, one-fourth perished, some from an epidemic of smallpox. Others died at the hands of their enemies, the Kiowa and Comanche, who resented the intrusion. To end the nightmare, surviving Navajo refused to farm or feed themselves. Acting on petitions from chiefs Barboncito and Manuelito, Government officials relented and sanctioned the Navajo resettlement of Canyon de Chelly.

Although life did not immediately return to normal, native reverence for the canyon and Spider Rock restored faith in the earth's goodness. In 1882, the Smithsonian Institution dispatched a study group led by explorer James Stevenson. In a search for ancient burial chambers, he gave the trident-shaped declivity the name Canyon del Muerto, Spanish for Canyon of the Dead. In 1895, Tewa-Hopi potter Nampeyo revived ancient symbolism in yellow earthen bowls adorned with brown, black, and red designs retrieved from the archological dig at Sityatki on the Hopi Reservation. The Sityatki Revival Movement established five generations of female potters who perpetuate Nampeyo's version of the traditional craft. Architect Jane Colter helped design Lookout Studio on the south rim of the Grand Canyon, where Hopi crafters made traditional wares. To re-create traditional life and worship, she built Hopi House and the Watchtower at Desert View, furnishing it with a sacred kiva room, snake altar, and authentic mural by Fred Kabotie, a Hopi artist who dramatized the arrival of his people across the Colorado River.

In 1931, the canyon became a national monument, a cultural preserve rich in natural beauty.

Famed Maricopa potter Ida Redbird captured the Spider Woman myth in pottery during the mid-1930s. From 1937 to 1940, she instructed the next generation in an arts renaissance known as the Maricopa pottery revival. In the mid-1940s, pictorialist Laura Gilpin began a twenty-year career of preserving the Navajo and Canyon de Chelly on autochrome, platinum, and silver prints, which she published in *The Enduring Navaho* (1968).

ACTIVITIES

Today, Arizona's Native Americans share their sacred trust with the white world. On the Navajo Reservation, a plaque relates how Spider Woman set up the great cosmic loom and taught humanity to weave. Laws protect the delicate ecology of Canyon de Chelly by banning intruders, guarding fragile artifacts, and limiting grazing to native herds. Visitors require a native guide or park ranger to lead them on foot or by Jeep across the canyon floor.

With the help of government agents, the Navajo maintain a community in the canyon of their ancestors. They nourish ties with the past through ceremonies established by the holy ones. These rites teach the current generation essential lessons in ethics, history, responsibility, and ways to strengthen culture, language, and religion. Central to Navajo philosophy is the place of humankind in the universe. Advocating patience and prayer, the elders sing and tell sacred stories, celebrate joyful occasions, and confer blessing on the sick and distressed.

In the hallowed confines of Canyon de Chelly, Spider Woman's ethos thrives as a regenerative force among the Hopi and Navajo, who perpetuate their belief system in loomed goods, pottery, and silversmithy. Through the cleansing and healing method of sand painting, the Hopi *hataali* (singer) combines fine streams of natural earth-toned pigments—turquoise, corn meal, pollen, mudstone, white gypsum, crushed petals, yellow ochre, and pulverized sandstone and charcoal—in hundreds of designs ranging from one to twelve feet in diameter and suited to a particular spiritual or curative need. Against a neutral background, some 1,200 intricate medallions result from supernatural images of stick figures, serpents, birds, plants, rainbows,

clouds, heavenly bodies, and sunrays. These geometric shapes invoke earth's protection through outer colored bands and strength through straight lines and zigzags of black, white, red, and yellow.

When applied by tribal priests, the sand painting is integral to healing. The right geometric pattern corresponds with a particular case to summon wellness and restore harmony. The ailing person sits on the design and rubs colored grains into the flesh to absorbs its force into an unhealthy body. The generation of holy narrative through sand painting may take many hours of work. After a ceremony lasting one to three days, the shaman discards the finished medallion. A medicine man may invoke another form of healing, the *Yei-Bei-Chei* dance, which matches the chanted prayers of a singer to an all-night dance and shaken rattles. Less common is the Fire Dance ritual, a private nine-day ceremony strictly reserved for tribal members.

Native artisans apply religious iconography in dreamcatchers, which they form from crystal, feathers, nuts, and vines into symbolic webs that capture benevolent dreams and allow nightmares to flee through a hole at the center. Healers facilitate physical and spiritual health through music and chants, ritual honor to earth cycles, mystery teachings, and a holy path based on ancient truths. Other forms of art perpetuate ties to Navajo deities:

- The audiotape *Sacred Twins and Spider Woman* (1996) by Navajo rug weaver and storyteller Geri Keams resets such native creation stories as "Creation of First Man, First Woman," "Coyote Brings Fire," and "Snail Carries Water" as an introit to the beauty way ceremony.
- Laguna poet Paula Gunn Allen's *Spider Woman's Granddaughters: Traditional Tales and Contemporary Writing by Native American Women* (1989) anthologizes the mythic tales, memoirs, and short stories of native writers Louise Erdrich, Misha Gallagher, Linda Hogan, Leanne Howe, Vicki Sears, Leslie Marmon Silko, Mary Tall Mountain, and Anna Lee Walters.
- In December 1998, the Colorado History Museum launched an eight-month exhibi-

tion entitled "Spirit of Spider Woman: Tradition and Trade in Navajo Arts," which displayed Navajo weavings, paintings, silverwork, photographs, and demonstrations of native creativity that preserves the traditions of Spider Woman.

Sources: Bierhorst 1994; *Biography Resource Center* 1999; Buchanan 1999; Cantor, George, 1993; "Canyon de Chelly"; "Canyon de Chelly National Monument"; *Contemporary Photographers* 1996; Durham 1967; Feed 1999; Gilpin 1968; Kelley and Francis 1994; Ketchum 1957; Leeming 1992; Loftin 1991; Malinowski 1995; McNamee 1999; McPherson 1992; Milne 1995; "Navajo Rugs"; Patterson and Snodgrass 1994; Sherr and Kazickas 1994; "Spider Rock" 1996; "Spirit of Spider Woman: Tradition and Trade in Navajo Arts"; Steiger 1974; Walking Turtle 1993; Welker 1998.

Cathedral Basilica of St. Louis
4431 Lindell Boulevard
St. Louis, Missouri 63108
314-533-7662
FAX 314-533-2825
www.cathedralstl.org/; www.archstl.org/

A historic congregation energized by the spirit of the frontier, the Cathedral Basilica of St. Louis remains an active, compassionate body committed to Christian stewardship. Its midcontinent splendors ally Missouri Catholics with the artistic and architectural traditions of Istanbul, Bologna, and Rome. Composed of 1,000 members from 825 families, the cathedral offers a sound program of worship, Christian education, and liturgical music to the St. Louis metropolitan area.

HISTORY

St. Louis was a French Catholic city from its birth. The parish grew from the mission of Father Jacques Marquette and companion Louis Joliet, who paddled south of the Missouri River to the Mississippi River's western shore on June 25, 1673. In 1749, authorities organized the first official parish of St. Genevieve in a region served by traders Pierre Laclède-Liguest and Auguste Chouteau, village founder and organizer. It was Laclède-Liguest who reserved a river-view square for a church to serve a city later dubbed the Gateway to the West.

In 1770, local Catholics, led by Father Pierre Gibault, built a log church at Rue de l'Eglise that served until 1776, when Bishop Louis W. DuBourg decreed the erection of a more presentable log edifice. The second church home sufficed until the dedication of a brick building on January 9, 1820. The strong Catholic presence lured talent and energy to the frontier—missionary Pierre De Smet, seminarians Father Felix de Andreis and Father Joseph Rosati, and educator Sister Philippine Duchesne, founder of the region's first free school. Later came the Sisters of Charity of St. Vincent de Paul, who established the first trans-Mississippi hospital, a godsend during the 1833 cholera epidemic.

The surviving cathedral, the third to occupy the site on Second and Walnut Streets and the oldest trans-Mississippi cathedral, was completed in 1834 at the direction of Bishop Joseph Rosati. To minister to the deaf, he invited the Sisters of St. Joseph of Carondelet to open a school in 1836. In 1845, organizers of the Society of St. Vincent de Paul chose the cathedral as the location of their first conference.

At the creation of an archdiocese stretching over much of the Louisiana Purchase from central Illinois to the Rockies, the St. Louis cathedral became the headquarters of Archbishop Peter Richard Kenrick. Two years later, when the *White Cloud* steamed up the river and caught fire, volunteer fire captain Thomas B. Torgee died while saving the cathedral from the resulting city conflagration. Demoted to a parish church, the old cathedral gave place to a newer diocese headquarters, planned in 1903, on Lindell Boulevard at Newstead Avenue. A highly ornamented Byzantine structure, it was the unrealized dream of Archbishop John J. Kain but the building project of Archbishop John J. Glennon, who intended to import Old World culture into the prairie see.

After turning his intent into viable plans, Archbishop Glennon sought American and European architects to submit sketches of a cathedral blending Romanesque, Byzantine, and Renaissance qualities. He chose a man close to home—George D. Barnett of Barnett, Haynes, and Barnett in St. Louis, builder of the Palace of

A historic congregation energized by the spirit of the frontier, the Cathedral Basilica of St. Louis remains an active, compassionate body committed to Christian stewardship. (John William Nagel Photography)

SAINT VINCENT DE PAUL AND LOUISE DE MARILLAC

The fount of Christian charity and personalized community nurse care, Vincent de Paul was a Reformation saint and founder of the order of Lazarists, or Vincentians. A native of Pouy, France, born on April 24, 1581, he studied at the College de Foix of the University of Toulouse and entered the priesthood at age nineteen. In 1605, North African pirates captured him on the way from Marseilles to Toulouse and sold him at a Tunisian slave market. Upon release two years later, he devoted himself to tending the world's most desperate people.

While serving Henry IV as royal chaplain, Father Vincent entered the court of Count Philip de Gondi and served the parish of Châtillon-les-Dombes. In 1617, he formed the Confraternity of Charity, a sisterhood of volunteer public-health nurses, established at the mother house of St. Lazare. Teamed with Louise de Gras, later known as Louise de Marillac, Father Vincent stocked pantries and medical centers, treated the ill, and personally bathed, fed, and solaced the suffering.

The center's attendants, called Sisters of Charity, staffed hospital wards in a ministry that became the first global network of religious nurses.

In 1634, Father Vincent founded *Les Dames de Charité* (Ladies of Charity), a coterie of aristocratic women headquartered at the Hôtel de Dieu, the only hospital to remain in use from the Middle Ages. At his direction, they distributed supplies, medicines, and funds and performed good deeds for slaves, veterans, prisoners, and asylum and workhouse inmates. Another foundation, *La Couche* (The Crib), combated the sale of poor infants into slavery or enforced begging, child prostitution, and thievery. Until his death at age eighty-eight, he involved himself personally in each ministry. In 1737, the Vatican canonized him as Saint Vincent de Paul. In 1833, Frederic Ozanam organized the St. Vincent de Paul Society, which spread to 3,000 chapters on four continents. Pope Leo XIII named Saint Vincent the patron of charities in 1885. Pope Pius XI canonized his partner, Louise de Marillac, on March 11, 1934.

Liberal Arts for the St. Louis World's Fair of 1904. On May 1, 1907, Glennon hosted a groundbreaking of a "great and noble building," which would ally a Byzantine interior with a Romanesque façade. (Faherty 1988, 10)

On November 2, 1916, members of the diocese church surrendered cramped quarters in the cathedral chapel to attend mass observed at a makeshift altar in the unfinished structure. That same year, the staff added a parish school. After consecration on June 29, 1926, the cathedral required nearly three more decades of work until completion. In October 1997, elevation to a minor basilica altered the church name to Cathedral Basilica of St. Louis.

ARCHITECTURE

A grand edifice in Jefferson Memorial Park, St. Louis's new cathedral displays the orderly elegance of a Byzantine masterwork, Constantinople's Sancta Sophia, designed by Anthemius of Tralles and Isidore of Melitus in 532, and of the Cathedral of St. Mark in Venice, Italy. The New World cathedral stands 204 feet by 350 feet.

Prominent are double square towers at each end of the granite façade and in the massive green, ribbed dome, green-tiled roof, cupola, and modest gold Roman cross that rises 227 feet above street level at the crossing. At the portals, three triangular arches point up to the semicircular niche and inset rose window. To right and left, rounded arms of the cruciform shape rise to circular roofing that echoes the striations of the dome. On the Maryland Avenue side, the Cathedral Chapel has served small wedding parties and other church events since its blessing on October 18, 1896. The crypt of All Souls' Chapel holds the remains of the building's patriarchs, Cardinal John J. Glennon and Bishop Joseph Rosati.

Inside the basilica, visitors marvel at *tour de force* mosaic artistry, the world's largest, produced by twenty mosaicists from 1912 to 1988 over 83,000 square feet. The August Wagner Company in Berlin superintended selection of artists, beginning in 1923 with Paul Heuduck, who had adorned Stockholm's city hall. Aided by Emil Frei, stained-glass master, the two set up the Ravenna Mosaic Company to complete the cathedral's decoration, which began with application of red and gold designs to the transept and proceeded to the Arch of Triumph, Arch of Creation, and Doctors of the Church in the north dome. Arno Heuduck completed his father's work, which covers 90 percent of the embellished surfaces.

Heuduck's gilding method involves backing pieces of glass with gold leaf and applying molten glass over the surface. Atop the baldachin that covers the altar and throughout murals and mosaic arches, irregular glass and marble tesserae in 10,000 hues shimmer with light and angled reflection, similar in effect to the primitive Christian surfacing of the tomb of Galla Placidia in Ravenna, Italy. The tiled narthex depicts the life of St. Louis in lush mosaic mural. The center dome and paired minor domes and half domes combine with arches to relate a pictorial narrative of contributors to the Catholic faith from creation to the last judgment, including

- Saint Elizabeth Seton, founder of the Daughters of Charity
- Saint Francis Xavier Cabrini, first U.S. saint
- Saint Isaac Jogues, first U.S. martyr
- Saint John Chrysostom, the medieval orator and patron of preachers
- Saint Philippine Duchesne, activist in the Order of the Sacred Heart

A splendid rose window overlooks the high altar with a Greek cross formed of red at the outer edge and fading to light gold at the center. Surfaces consist of 100 million stone, tile, and glass tesserae under a layer of gold leaf, a testimony to heartland generosity and faith. A cathedral museum displays a detailed background of the artisans who designed and executed the cathedral murals, in particular, John von Wicht, who designed ten panels depicting the life of Saint Louis IX, the cathedral's patron; Aristide Leonori's life of the Virgin Mary in Our Lady's Chapel; and Mary Reardon, who adorned the west transept with a flame-edged scenario of Pentecost.

ACTIVITIES

The Cathedral Basilica of St. Louis is more than a showplace. As diocese headquarters, it coordi-

nates activity composed of liturgical celebration, social outreach committees, music groups, and volunteers. The height of celebrations is Cathedralfête, celebrated in August at the feast day of Saint Louis IX, King of France. The weekly schedule offers twenty-one celebrations of the mass plus a vigil and confession period. Stewardship involves adults and youth in ushering and greeting, hospitality, ministry to the sick and homebound, tutoring, coaching athletics, communications, landscaping, planning and development, finance, health ministry, liturgy, a marriage preparation team, Meals on Wheels, the Parish Council, prolife activism, and the St. Vincent de Paul Society.

In addition to altruism, the Cathedral of St. Louis sponsors a full music program dedicated to enriching the community at the same time it employs individuals in a vital part of parish service. Enhanced visually and aurally by the Kilgen chancel pipe organ, the Cathedral Choir performs for Sunday services and celebrations. Select musicians make up the Cathedral Schola, which performs for special occasions and twice monthly at the Sunday noon mass. The Archdiocesan Choir sings for ordinations, Christmas mass, and election rites. A cantor program trains parish cantors for archdiocesan events.

The church also schedules the youth woodwind quintet and small ensembles for frequent performances. A handbell choir performs monthly for Sunday evening mass. For minimal ticket fees, the St. Louis Cathedral Concerts series presents such world-class performers as the American Boys Choir, Westminster Choir College Handbell Choir, St. Ambrose Chamber Orchestra, Vienna Choir Boys, Chanticleer, Leipzig Chamber Orchestra, Tallis Scholars, Academy of Ancient Music, King's College Choir, Academy of St. Martin in the Fields, Westminster Abbey Choir, and Waverly Consort. The gift shop sells CDs and cassettes of concerts by the Cathedral choirs and organists along with books and postcards detailing church history, architecture, and art. Tours are available Sunday through Friday.

Sources: Alsberg 1949; Baly 1995; Bentley 1993; Broderick 1958; "The Cathedral of St. Louis" 1999; Cohn-Sherbok 1998; "The Diocese of Missouri"; Faherty 1988; Franzwa 1965; Griffin and Griffin 1965; Hallam 1994; McKown 1966; "Muralists

Index"; *New Catholic Encyclopedia* 1967; Ranft 1996; Rigali 1999; Snodgrass 1999, 2000; "St.Vincent de Paul"; Sullivan 1967; "Vincent de Paul and Louise de Marillac, Compassionate Servants and Saints."

Cathedral Basilica of the Sacred Heart
Monsignor Richard F. Groncki, Rector
89 Ridge Street
Newark, New Jersey 07104
973-484-4600
FAX 973-484-4033; 973-483-8253
www.rcan.org

A minor Gothic basilica in Newark, New Jersey, the Cathedral Basilica of the Sacred Heart is a prime example of ecclesiastical art in the Western Hemisphere. The lengthy construction process ended in 1954, when congregants entered the Latin-inscribed bronze doors to a magnificent interior, the spiritual heart of the Newark archdiocese. The structure received its sanction in October 1995 during an official visit by Pope John Paul II. Near century's end, the number of religious tourists rose to 11,000 annually. They come from around the globe to attend services and world-class performances of liturgical music and to admire stunning French Gothic architecture, ranks of elegant lights, and a European artistry that preserves the essence of the Middle Ages.

HISTORY
Catholicism in Newark dates to the 1820s, when the devout attended mass at the family home of Father Daniel Durning. In 1827, Father Gregory B. Pardow, the first resident priest, arrived from New York to build St. John's Church. The basilica dates to 1853, when the Newark diocese designated St. Patrick's Church in Newark as its cathedral. The first bishop, James Roosevelt Bayley, nephew of Mother Elizabeth Seton, added to the state's thirty churches by buying land and commissioning a larger, nobler facility to accommodate a growing community. He also added the Benedictine Fathers to the diocese and founded Seton Hall University in 1856, which he placed in the care of the Sisters of Charity.

The third bishop, Winand Michael Wigger, erected a chapel on an abandoned lot. A wooden structure dedicated in 1891 preceded the cathedral, which the parish launched officially in 1898. Trustees chose the design of Newark architect Jeremiah O'Rourke, who was educated at the Government School of Design in Dublin, Ireland. A slow process produced the outer shell. He based the plan on studies of European cathedrals but created so much dissension that Isaac Ditmars took over the project in 1906 and enclosed the chancel in 1923. By 1927, limestone work concluded in the sanctuary and proceeded up the transepts.

The basilica's first official use was the installation of Archbishop Thomas J. Walsh in 1928, when the edifice consisted of bare rafters and stonework. He committed his tenure to an ambitious plan of action. A focus of his mission was the Mount Carmel Guild, a model approved by Pope Pius XII to link educational, social, and altruistic works under one organization. Among Walsh's goals were rehabilitation of alcohol abusers and training the deaf, blind, and mentally handicapped. His other goal was equally ambitious—overseeing completion of the cathedral.

After Newark advanced to an archdiocese in 1937, Bishop John McNulty collaborated with architect Paul Reilly and Professor Gonippo Raggi to conceive an artistic theme revealing Christ's relationship with the church. Walsh sped the building process, which Archbishop Thomas A. Boland completed in 1953. At a formal ceremony in October 1954, parishioners celebrated the cathedral's opening along with a diocese centennial. Visitors admired the Schantz organ, lacy wood and limestone carvings, and marble floor. The quality of workmanship inspired Newark planners to rehabilitate the city. Around 1975, state and national historic registries designated the basilica a historic site.

ARCHITECTURE
The Cathedral Basilica of the Sacred Heart dominates Newark's skyline on the city's north end. A ten-story edifice rising from brownstone, it extends in cruciform design 365 by 165 feet and seats 2,000. Construction features materials and artistry from the United States and Europe. The builder pierced Rockport green granite walls with 208 stained-glass windows made in

A minor gothic basilica in Newark, New Jersey, the Cathedral Basilica of the Sacred Heart is a prime example of ecclesiastical art in the Western Hemisphere. (Courtesy Archdiocese of Newark, Office of Communications and Public Relations)

Munich, Germany, and capped the whole with a flèche, or arrow-shaped spire, twenty-six stories high. Equal in size to Westminster Abbey in London, the structure features towers set at an angle to the portals and rising higher than those of Notre Dame Cathedral in Paris. Outer embellishments include two similar bell towers made in Florence, Italy, featuring gargoyles projecting from their corners. In the Mary Tower, fourteen bronze bells from Padua, Italy, connect to a keyboard for manual operation. A rose window focuses attention above the pointed arch over the central doors.

Highlighting the floor plan is a narthex unified by the Litany of the Sacred Heart. Columns top polished granite round and octagonal forms. Side aisle panels of white Appalachian oak anchor German stained-glass illustrations of the Mysteries of Faith, which are tinged with gold

and red in the style of France's majestic Chartres Cathedral. The interior shell of Guastavino tile features Botticino marble flooring as the base of a vault ribbed in limestone. The builder purchased raw blocks quarried in Indiana and dispatched them to carvers in Pietrasanta and Rome, Italy, who returned to Newark elongated religious images that enhance the aura of devotion.

The basilica invites the eye with intricacy. To the right of the altar, a mosaic dove adorns the canopied ceiling of Botticino marble, which offsets a filigreed altar, sixteen statues of the doctors of the Church, and a carving of the Virgin Mary, the diocese patroness. Above the altar, a crucifix supports a Christ figure made of Portuguese rose marble with a loincloth of white marble from Carrara, Italy. To each side are the Greek letters alpha and omega, symbolizing the verse in Revelation 21: 6 that characterizes Christ as the beginning and end of all things.

In medieval style, ornate, instructive artistry encircles the sanctuary with Christian history. Screens of Appalachian oak exhibit symbols of the virtues and of Christ, defender of the Church. The narthex screen aligns images of eight canonized popes. Side pillars honor the twelve apostles and the four evangelists, Matthew, Mark, Luke, and John. Corresponding niches capping the choir stalls contain statues of Saint Constantine, the first Christian emperor, and his mother, Saint Helena, who retrieved the true cross from Jerusalem. On the left wall, the carved bishop's chair with a maroon cushioned seat dominates the sanctuary. At the top of the pointed structure, the archbishop's coat of arms establishes his authority. The seat below is the symbolic center of the archdiocese, from which he presides over local rites, major feasts, election of new members, and ordination of deacons, priests, and bishops. To the left, a red and gold tintinnabulum marks the building's rank as a minor basilica.

At left, the Chapel of Our Lady of Lourdes commemorates the visions experienced in 1858 by Bernadette Soubirous, a peasant herder from Lourdes, France. Symbols of the Virgin Mary, who spoke to Bernadette, envelop the chapel. At left is a stained-glass window illustrating the annunciation of the Angel Gabriel to Mary. An inscription near the kneeler records its use by Pope John Paul II when he visited the chapel to pray. Visitors exiting the area can enter the ambulatory, the semicircular walkway that leads around the apse end of the sanctuary past seven additional chapels that honor patron saints of local ethnic groups who emigrated from Asia, South America, Spain, Hungary, Ireland, Italy, Germany, and Poland. The first pictures Saint Patrick, Ireland's apostle, alongside Saints Brigid, Thomas More, Margaret of Scotland, David of Wales, and Columcille. The next, the Chapel of St. Lucy Filipini, commemorates Saints Rocco, Frances X. Cabrini, Januarius, and Anthony of Padua.

An elongated space, the prayerful Lady Chapel, at the center of the walkway, emphasizes Christ's mother as well as Saints Dominic, Catherine Labouré, and Simon Stock. The room, designed for small gatherings and daily mass, features a private entrance, separate organ, and sacristies. Other appointments—the canopied altar, carved table, bronze crucifix decked with onyx and a rose marble corpus—carry out a reverential theme. Behind the altar, a copy of a window in Chartres Cathedral banded in brightly colored glass braid displays a haloed Madonna and child.

Around the remaining half of the ambulatory range the chapels honoring Saint Luke, Saint Boniface, Saint Stanislaus, Saint Anne, and Saint Joseph. The latter, dedicated to Mary's husband, honors the holy family. Dominating the east transept are Saint Paul sculpted in bas-relief and a rose window crafted by Franz Zettler of Munich, Germany. Across the transept at the west window, worshippers can view a complementary rose window. The 149 ranks of organ pipes adorn both the rear gallery and apse. Vividly colored windows in the nave clerestory depict scenarios from Hebrew scripture, hagiography, religious orders, miracles, Christ's passion, and angels, all unified by medieval garb. The chapel crypt features a bronze gate and railings and catacomb chambers below the sanctuary choir.

ACTIVITIES

The Cathedral Basilica of the Sacred Heart is one of Newark's busy religious institutions. In addition to the rector, the Reverend Monsignor Richard F. Groncki, and the archbishop, the Most Reverend Theodore E. McCarrick, a parochial vicar, a deacon, a coordinator of catechetics, a director of music ministries, an auxiliary bishop, a vicar general, and an archbishop's secretary direct events. Mass is available on weekdays at 7:30 A.M. and 5:30 P.M., on Saturday at 6:00 P.M., and twice on Sunday, at 8:45 A.M. and noon. Ministry to Spanish-speaking parishioners includes mass in Spanish on Sunday at 10:00 A.M., Wednesday and first Fridays at 7:00 P.M., and Saturday at 9:00 A.M. Baptism in Spanish is also available the second Sunday of the month.

For all its size and importance, the cathedral extends personal service to each worshipper. The staff offers confession Saturday at 11:30 A.M. and by appointment as well as anointing, communion, and visitation of the sick. A faith-sharing group supports adult initiates. As a benefit to engaged couples, weddings must be arranged one year in advance to allow for pastoral counseling. At the Family Life Center in Maplewood, a weekend program called the Beginning Experience aids widowed, separated, and divorced persons. An Annulment Information Evening led by a canon lawyer from the Tribunal explains guidelines, theology, and requisites for obtaining a church-ordained dissolution of failed marriages. Simultaneously, the archdiocese offers four classes in natural family planning.

A full church calendar schedules memorable worship experiences for parishioners and visitors. For religious tourists, guides provide cathedral tours the first Sunday of the month. Annual Christmas Mass at Midnight and Holy Week services combine the talents of the Cathedral Basilica Choir, cantors, and organists. Special services in fall 1999 expressed concerns of the legal profession, law enforcement, black Catholics, and youth. On October 15, 1999, the staff presented the relics of Saint Thérèse of Lisieux, a cult figure of pious Catholics, and offered religious icons for sale at the Cathedral Shoppe. A one-day bus tour led pilgrims to the National Shrine of the Immaculate Conception in Washington, D.C.

An annual cathedral concert series presents an eight-part program spanning the year. In 1999, the music staff offered a full program: Peter Latona, organist at the Basilica of the National Shrine of the Immaculate Conception; the Dorothy Shaw Handbell Choir of Ft. Worth, Texas, organist Felix Hell of Frankenthal/Pfalz, Germany; and the twenty-ninth Annual Christmas Sing, a family-centered part of the holiday celebration in northern New Jersey. Cathedral music director John J. Miller led the Cathedral Choir, organ, brass, percussion, and audience in traditional songs and presented John Rutter's *Gloria* along with Franz Biebl's "Ave Maria" and Russian classics by Pavel Tschesnokov. The year 2000 began with performances of the New Jersey State Children's Chorus and the New Jersey Chamber Music Society, a Cathedral Choir presentation on the stations of the cross, the Newark Arts High School Advanced Mixed Chorus, and an organ and orchestral performance of Francis Poulenc's Concerto for Organ, Strings, and Timpani, featuring Dr. Ann Labounsky of Duquesne University.

Sources: Broderick 1987; Chevalier and Gheerbrant 1996; Durkin n.d.; Gubernat 1996; "Introduction to Gateway"; James 1999; *New Catholic Encyclopedia* 1967; Smothers 1998; Sullivan 1967.

Cathedral Church of St. John the Divine
Reverend Harry H. Pritchett, Jr., Dean
1047 Amsterdam Avenue
New York, New York 10025
212-316-7540
harrypritchett@juno.com
www.stjohndivine.org

Stretching a tenth of a mile from Amsterdam Avenue to Morningside Drive, New York's Cathedral Church of St. John the Divine is a fine example of Romanesque style and a national landmark. Within the monumental stone walls lie treasures of religious art in stone carving, tapestry, marble sculpture, mosaic, and stained glass. The cathedral aim of ministering to all people suits the city of New York, the home of the Statue of Liberty and scores of immigrants of all faiths, races, and ethnic backgrounds.

HISTORY
The Episcopal cathedral, named for the author of Revelation and incorporated in 1873, was a bold undertaking. In 1887, George Macculoch Miller spied an elevated parcel of thirteen acres along Morningside Drive that would lift a cathedral like an acropolis. Bishop Henry Codman Potter agreed and purchased the acreage from the Leake and Watts Orphan Asylum. Touted as the world's largest Gothic cathedral, the Cathedral Church of St. John the Divine began with the laying of a cornerstone on Saint John's Day, December 27, 1892. The project was problematic, but found a keen supporter in financier J. P. Morgan.

Constructed in French Gothic, the edifice was the work of architects George L. Heinz and C. Grant La Farge, winners of a national design competition, who completed the choir and crossing. Renowned mason Rafael Guastavino and his son, Rafael, Jr., artisans on more than a thousand religious and public institutions, capped the transept with a Catalan tiled dome 162 feet high. In 1911, after the death of Heinz,

The ceremony of the Blessing of the Animals takes place every October at the Cathedral of St. John the Divine, New York City. (Courtesy the Cathedral of St. John the Divine, Mary Bloom 1999)

supervision passed to Ralph Adams Cram of Cram and Ferguson. Guided by Bishop William Thomas Manning, he altered details to accommodate full Gothic style and, in 1916, laid out the entire foundation. Within two years, he surrounded the choir with the seven Chapels of the Tongues, each named for a saint and dedicated to an immigrant population—Scandinavian, German, British, Eastern Christian, French, Italian, and Spanish. In 1921, a model located at Grand Central Station displayed the work at completion and drew supporters from New Yorkers and visitors worldwide.

After installation of the vaulting, the full nave opened on November 30, 1941—nine days before President Franklin Roosevelt responded to Japanese aggressors with a strongly worded declaration to Congress. With the nation's entry into World War II, a thirty-year hiatus ended detailing. The Pearl Harbor Arch preserves an uncompleted task abandoned by a worker who exchanged a work apron and chisel for a uniform and rifle. The return to work in 1972 pressed

into service unemployed, uninitiated laborers in need of training and jobs. In 1979, Bishop Paul Moore imported knowledgeable crafters from England to advance the twin towers. In the late 1980s, English master stonemason Simon Verity, trainer of the stone-yard apprentices, won a competition for the project known as the Portal of Paradise. Aided by French mason Jean-Claude Marchionni, in 1997, Verity sculpted thirty-two stone figures that range from Abraham and Sarah in the Old Testament to Elizabeth and son John the Baptist from the Gospels.

Intended as a symmetrical composition, the Cathedral of St. John the Divine moved into the twenty-first century in an awkward state. In 1998, only two-thirds complete, it entered its fourth construction phase. Although the next two years saw little progress, throngs of visitors delighted in the American History Bay, Sports Bay, Communications Bay, Medicine Bay, and Rose Window. Currently, a Green Tour, dedicated to ecology, supported by the National Religious Partnership for the Environment, focuses on nature. Religious tourists cluster at two favorite sites, the Medicine Wheel and Peace Altar.

Over 350,000 visitors annually make the cathedral a stop on their city tour. Outside, they favor the Biblical Garden, a cruciform path lined with cedars of Lebanon and other vegetation mentioned in the Bible. The charge of organic gardener Jeanne Lane, it is the nation's largest scripturally inspired garden. Nearby, the Hope Rosary, honoring victims of catastrophic illness, displays the country's most varied collection of David Austin roses. A southwest corner nurtures foxgloves, or digitalis, in tribute to artist Keith Haring. Volunteers tend 7,200 spring and summer bulbs in the Kathryn Speicher-Dunham Garden, donated by her husband, Dwight Dunham. Sculptor Greg Wyatt's Peace Fountain on 111th Street centers a sculpture garden featuring thirty bronze figures crafted by children.

ARCHITECTURE

Built on a solid rock foundation some 72 feet deep, the Cathedral Church of St. John the Divine stretches 601 by 330 feet over 121,000 square feet. The outer shell of Mohegan granite from Peekskill, New York, covers a core of Indiana limestone and Wisconsin dolomite surfacing over Maine granite. The only steel framework is the nave ridge. The main characteristic of the cathedral's exterior is an expansive five-portal façade. At center, bronze doors weighing twelve tons reach up 18.5 feet and display dramatic scenes of the Old and New Testaments on twenty-eight panels. Striking human forms balance animals entering Noah's Ark, a pair of elephants, and the wonders of Eden. Framed by twining ivy and topped by dual medallions, the two doors are the last work of sculptor Henry Wilson.

The cathedral's upward reach is a series of small and large spires. Double spires at the west front rise over 266 feet. A conical flèche graces the square transept spire, which towers 452 feet. Inside, a spacious narthex leads to a magnificent nave seating 10,000 spectators. Cram modeled its mystery and loft on Bourges Cathedral, a French see founded around 300 A.D. The crossing displays the Barberini Tapestries designed by Giovanni Francesco Romanelli to order Christ's life in twelve chronological scenes. The arched Byzantine ceiling, filigreed with braided edgings and illuminated by a clerestory, sheds filtered light on the interior space and on chairs placed below in medieval style to seat 2,500 spectators. Multiple arching at the first-floor level rests atop round Corinthian columns. Unique to the semicircular apse design are a series of columns, baptistery, and seven ambulatory chapels. Burial space is open to all in the columbarium of the St. Ansgar's Chapel, designed by Henry Vaughan.

The E. M. Skinner Company designed the first of five organs for the complex and placed the console in a gallery above the south choir stalls. In 1954, Aeolian-Skinner enlarged the original instrument and enhanced its voicing. Located 600 feet from the console, the State Trumpet arises at the west end. An ongoing adopt-a-pipe campaign, launched by Dorothy Papadakos, aims to establish perpetual funding for 8,035 pipes by 2002.

ACTIVITIES

Under the direction of Rita Maria Trucios, the Cathedral Community Cares ministry schedules a full range of services and educational opportunities to involve a broad range of New Yorkers in church life. Annual events include a New Year's peace service, a Lenten supper, a Ukrainian Easter egg decoration, a Palm Sunday processional, an observance of the stations of the cross, an Easter vigil, a blessing of the animals on October 2, Saint Francis Day, Saint Cecilia Day, and the November Holocaust remembrance and Giving of Thanks to the First Peoples. The year climaxes with carols by the Cathedral Choristers and Christmas Eve service.

Cathedral programming offers something for everyone. A Sunday evening feature is the 7:00 Choral Vespers by Candlelight, a liturgical music program combining voices of the cathedral choristers, singers, and chorus. Children's programs range from holiday camps and after-school care to parenting and nursery classes, animal mask making, and music courses. Families enjoy a medieval arts workshop in stone carving, weaving, brass rubbing, illumination, calligraphy, and sculpting. Tourists can join a building or roof tour or shop for such gifts as stone gargoyles, guidebooks, hand-crafted gift items, and organ music celebrating the summer solstice, recorded by Dorothy Papadakos.

Ministry to the community takes numerous forms—a Sunday soup kitchen, an AIDS Outreach Ministry and a National AIDS Memorial Book of Remembrance, a Crisis Intervention and Counseling Center, a clothes closet, a Children's Quest Fund, an Intergenerational Program, the New Hope Shelter for the homeless, and pastoral psychotherapy. The staff assists the bereaved, caregivers for victims of Alzheimer's disease, and women in transition. An educational committee sponsors the Cathedral School, founded in 1901 to serve children from kindergarten through eighth grade. Teachers stress individualized instruction and a balance of the academic basics with classical and modern foreign language, art, music, and physical education.

The arts are a focus of the cathedral calendar. Among the permanent art collection is Keith Haring's triptych *The Life of Christ*. Resident artists include the Ensemble for Early Music, composer Paul Winter, novelist Madeleine L'Engle, the Ralph Lee Mettawee River Company, the Omega and Forces of Nature dance companies, high wire artist Philippe Petit, tambourine virtuoso and dancer Alessandra Belloni, and I Giullari di Piazzi, a musical troupe in the tradition of *commedia del arte*. Touring displays include works by Romare Bearden, Red Grooms, and Merton Simpson and the designs of architects Buckminster Fuller and Santiago Calatrava. Theatrical performances include Molière's *Psyche* by the Ralph Lee Mettawee River Theatre Company. On June 25, 1999, the thirtieth anniversary of the persecution of homosexuals at Stonewall Bar in lower Manhattan, the cathedral sponsored a showing of works by gay and lesbian artists Liz Deschenes, Kevin Larmon, and Donald Moffett.

> Sources: Broderick 1958; Fitch 1973; Hamer 1997; *New Catholic Encyclopedia* 1967; "Newyorkcarver.Com" 1999; "St. John the Divine."

Cathedral Church of St. Peter and St. Paul

See Washington National Cathedral.

Cathedral of Hope

Reverend Michael S. Piazza, Senior Pastor
5910 Cedar Springs Road
P.O. Box 35466
Dallas, Texas 75235
800-501-4673
FAX 214-351-6099
hope@cohmcc.org

The world's largest church focusing on gay and lesbian membership, the Cathedral of Hope is a refuge for Christian homosexuals who have weathered scorn and denunciation at mainstream churches. By meeting justice and faith needs and setting standards for compassionate mission to all people, the Dallas church has initiated a national movement for inclusive worship that draws the handicapped and nonwhite as well as bisexuals, transgendered, gays, and lesbians. Typical of late-twentieth-century evangelism, the pluralistic program taps the energy and flexibility of electronic transmission, which accepts prayer requests and allows marginalized Christians to take part in weekly worship along with local members and become Internet missionaries.

HISTORY

The creation of a church alliance for Christians out of the mainstream began in 1968. The concept derived from Reverend Troy D. Perry, whom the Pentecostal Church of God of Prophecy expelled after he revealed his homosexuality. To minister to fellow outcasts, he founded the Metropolitan Community Church (MCC) of Los Angeles and set up headquarters for the Universal Fellowship of Metropolitan Community Churches in West Hollywood, California. Currently, the sect develops leaders at the Samaritan Institute of Religious Studies in Lewisville, Texas, which enrolls 300 students annually. The much-needed outreach grew rapidly to comprise over 300 congregations in 15 countries, including Dallas, Houston, San Francisco, and Fort Lauderdale in the United States plus churches in Canada, Puerto Rico, Mexico, Chile, Argentina, Europe, Australia, New Zealand, South Africa, Nigeria, parts of Europe, and the Philippines. One of the sect's shining models of inclusion is the Cathedral of Hope.

The Reverend Michael S. Piazza, the church's senior pastor, is a visionary and gay-rights advocate who energizes a full-service, nonjudgmental church home. A veteran pastor in the South, he grew up in Georgia and earned degrees in history and psychology from Valdosta State College and Candler School of Theology before serving pastorates in Texas, Georgia, Oklahoma, and Florida. After eight years of work for the United Methodist Church, in 1981, he established himself as a minister of a Metropolitan Community Church congregation in Atlanta and came to Dallas in 1987, where he and his mate made a home for their two daughters. In the mid-1990s, Piazza published a flurry of useful texts: *Holy Homosexuals: The Truth about Being Gay or Lesbian and Christian* (1994), *Rainbow Family Values* (1996), *Mourning to Morning* (1996), and *Growth or Death* (1996). For his success in meeting the needs of homosexual Christians, in August 1999, *Advocate* magazine honored his contributions to the gay and lesbian movement.

Piazza has made the Cathedral of Hope a spiritual center truly open to all people. The fast-growing congregation of 3,000 attends six weekly services in person or on video plus therapeutic Bible study, weekly Internet devotionals, prayer ministry, counseling services, men's book club, and television broadcasts to thirty-eight cities nationwide. Still under construction, the modernistic 2,500-seat sanctuary is the design of Philip Johnson, architect of St. Basil's Church at St. Thomas University in Houston and the Crystal Cathedral in Garden Grove, California. The project began with the John David Thomas Bell Wall, a national AIDS memorial to be completed in 2000.

ACTIVITIES

Despite bomb threats and derogatory comments, the Cathedral of Hope establishes the warmth of family with traditional Wednesday night suppers and Bible study as well as more innovative programs—a "Music as a Second Language" class, co-op shopping at the local farmer's market, a Crayola Crusade for Maple Lawn Elementary School, aluminum can recycling, free mammograms, massage therapy, and an All Hallows Fest. To draw more members, an infomercial over WGN-TV broadcasts testimo-

nials by members and scenes of worship. Involvement in the nonprofit Montessori School of Park Cities educates the children of gay and lesbian parents with individually paced, hands-on learning. To improve and safeguard health, the staff offers weekly AA and ALANON meetings for teens and adults, support for sex and love addicts, and HIV testing. The bookstore stocks print material on pride and wellness, video and audio cassettes, cards, holiday decorations, and music.

Members express their love to others through a mission trip to El Tamarindo and the San Salvador Orphanage in the Dominican Republic, Thanksgiving and Christmas food baskets for the needy, volunteering as Office Angels and at the Hope Youth Community Center, cleaning and restoring neighborhoods, serving as Carebears to people living with AIDS, supporting the Great American Smokeout, and benefiting the underserved through health clinics. For national members, the church offers programs in spirituality, service, and stewardship. The church database lists lesbian/gay-friendly churches, counseling programs, and chapters of Parents and Friends of Lesbians and Gays (PFLAG).

Sources: "Cathedral of Hope"; Fields 1998; "Gay Congregation Passes $6.2 Million Milestone for New Cathedral" 1998; "Homosexual Denomination Building Cathedral in Texas" 1998; Pederson 1999; "Positive Voices"; "Settlement Clears the Way for Church's Program to Be Televised" 1999; Taylor 1998; Weiss 1999; "Welcome to UFMCC World Center."

Cathedral of St. Joseph

Reverend Monsignor Daniel J. Plocharczyk
140 Farmington Avenue
Hartford, Connecticut 06105-3784
860-249-8431
FAX 860-541-6309
mcs@archdiocese-hartford.org
www.archdiocese-hartford.org

From the stainless-steel cross at top to the granite base, Hartford's Cathedral of St. Joseph offers a spiritual challenge to Roman Catholic members and religious tourists. A sturdy reinforced-concrete block striated with vertical shafts, the U-shaped edifice stands out from other buildings of its era with a startling unity heightened by a multilevel spire. Enhancing artistry as well as a spirit of welcome is a humanistic travertine frieze over Enzo Assenza's bronze entrance doors. In an inviting gesture above the main portal, sculptor Tommaso Peccini's bas-relief of Saint Joseph, patron of the universal church, and surrounding angels equalizes the world's people, from the anonymous seeker to Pope John XXIII.

HISTORY

Subsequent to the founding of the diocese in 1843, the Motherhouse of the Sisters of Mercy, which stands to the left of the cathedral, was the first building on land that Bishop Francis P. McFarland purchased for the diocese. Until 1892, the mother house chapel served the congregation as parish church. Begun in 1877, the first cathedral, a twin-towered, Gothic, brownstone edifice, was the design of architect P. C. Keeley. It suffered weathering and settling until a thorough renovation in 1938 to make it safe for use. After a winter fire engulfed Hartford's cathedral during morning mass on December 31, 1957, bursting windows and consuming timbers and the roof, the cathedral became an ice-encrusted skeleton. The loss cast gloom on the city and the diocese.

Optimistic of the fallen cathedral's rebirth, Archbishop Henry J. O'Brien sought a modern structure to bring the bishop's church at midcentury into a vigorous era. Meanwhile, members used the auditorium of Aetna Life Insurance Company for its three Sunday masses. Revamping the original site, architects Theodore Young and Apollinaire Osadca of Eggers and Higgins, Inc., had the lower church ready for occupancy by Christmas 1960 and finished the entire structure in 1962.

ARCHITECTURE

In comparison to the original cathedral, Hartford's new Cathedral of St. Joseph is taller, heavier, and more provocative. In sculptured stone panels over reinforced concrete, the upper reaches suggest the art deco of Radio City Music Hall and the telescoping spire of the Empire State Building. Builders combed America and Europe for materials, taking Botticino and gray-veined Bianco marble from Italy and glass from France to adorn Alabama limestone, Indiana ve-

neer, and New Hampshire granite. An international touch, the set of twelve bells, required the joint work of an American designer from Cincinnati and a European bronzesmith, who cast them in Holland. Laborers topped their creation with a 25-foot stainless-steel cross, dramatically hoisted into position by gantry.

The luminous interior, stretching 153 by 108 feet, makes a startling break with medieval tradition in its smoothly catenated leaded windows of Betonglas, a faceted colored glass applied by a process developed by Gabriel Loire of Chartres. Designed by an internationally known artist, Jean Barillet of Paris, the twenty-six panels relate a holy narrative, *Saviour in the Gospels*. The captivating rounded apse uplifts a modern statement of faith. For the Institute of Liturgical Art in Rome, Italy, Enzo Assenza worked for a year assembling 1,152 pieces of curved stone and ceramic for the 80- by 40-foot mosaic of Christ in glory, the largest of its kind in the world. A resplendent creation in rose and slate blue, its slashes of golden beams highlight a brilliant masterwork. In balance, a three-legged framework of Arkansas aluminum surmounts the simple marble altar with a corona-shaped baldachin, designed by sculptor Gleb Derujinsky. Flanking the sacristy, six chapels honor medieval saints— Saints Patrick, Anne, and Bernard at left and Saints Brigid, Francis, and Teresa to the right.

Appointments coordinate solidity with graceful iconography, from the altar pieces and polished Venetian terrazzo flooring to each door frame and wall. American walnut pews seat 1,750; similar woodwork panels the cathedral at left. Five aisles separate four ranks of pews and lead to the Madonna Chapel at left and the Blessed Sacrament Chapel at right. The Austin organ, made in Hartford, contains multiple ranks totaling 8,000 pipes that ground Barillet's starkly outlined *Christ the King* window in spare, bright touches of crimson and light gold. Along the sides, square post-and-lintel supports frame parallel aisles. The parade of verticals lifts the eye to a celestial ceiling dotted with huge aluminum stars.

ACTIVITIES

The Cathedral of St. Joseph, as diocese center, offers a full range of religious experiences and services. The staff schedules a Saturday vigil mass at 5:00 P.M. and six Sunday masses at 7:00, 8:00, 9:15, and 11:00 A.M. and twice in the afternoon, at 12:15 and 5:00. Daily mass is available at 6:45 and 7:30 A.M. and 12:10 P.M.; penance is available on Saturday from 9:45 to 11:00 A.M. and 3:00 to 3:45 P.M. Baptisms, weddings, and other family events take place in six small ambulatory chapels and the Lower Church, a first-floor auditorium seating 1,330. Visitors are welcome daily from 9:00 A.M. to 5:00 P.M.

Opportunities for service and witness involve members at many levels of participation. The music program features a cathedral choir, children's choir, and handbell choir. Committees manage altar service, hospitality, evangelism, vocations, stewardship, senior outreach, and social action. Benevolences range from the traditional St. Vincent de Paul Society of Knights of Columbus to a Christmas Giving Tree, a September Pilgrimage Walk, an October Parish Ministry Fair and Food Drive, a Day of Caring volunteer project, and a Help Our Parish Elementary School Collection Sunday. The cathedral school, directed by Principal Thomas Gersz, enrolls students for kindergarten through grade eight in a program of intense academic study, leadership preparedness, and Christian values. In 1999, the cathedral hosted numerous conferences and a weekly concert series featuring organists and vocalists as well as an annual wedding anniversary celebration for parish couples, a lawn festival to benefit the Felician Sisters of Our Lady of the Angels Province, a Hope and Healing support group for victims of breast cancer, a Mercy Day to honor the Sisters of Mercy, and a May Housing Repair Blitz.

Sources: "The Cathedral of St. Joseph" 1962; Kennedy 1962; Mutrux 1982; *New Catholic Encyclopedia* 1967; Smith 1989; Sullivan 1967.

Cathedral Rock
P.O. Box 623
Sedona, Arizona 86339
520-649-3060; 800-350-2693
FAX 520-649-3181
journeys@crossingworlds.com

West of Flagstaff and northwest of the Coconino National Forest and Sedona, Arizona,

Cathedral Rock rises at a mystical center. As sacred geography, it is a national treasure visited and venerated by Native Americans as well as seekers from many cultures and faiths. A site endowed with spiritual energy, the Red Rock country is a desert land enhanced with buttes, canyons, sparse vegetation, and craggy rock spires. Amid artists, balloonists, canoers, hikers, bikers, and photographers, the spiritual seeker absorbs a vivid palette of sensual treats relished by 8 million tourists, who study a night sky unimpeded by light pollution. Along with Wilson Mountain, Coffee Pot Rock, Bell Rock, Chimney Rock, and an ancient medicine wheel at Long Canyon, Cathedral Rock engages the imagination as a consecrated dwelling to the Yavapai-Apache.

HISTORY
Arizona's Red Rock area was home to the Hohokam and Sinagua 10,000 years ago. In 1990, archeologist Jerry Robertson located rock art that had escaped earlier expeditions. Near a spring-fed pool in a hidden canyon of Verde Valley, petroglyphs record the hunt of prehistoric Sinagua dwellers. The proportioned stick figures show humans dressed in feathered headgear and pursuing antelopes. Above Verde Valley River, additional markings denote Sinagua habitation in 100 caves composed of 400 rooms.

The Sinagua's descendents, the Yavapai, members of the Yuman language family, arrived from the Grand Canyon area in the 1500s. They named the land Wipuk, indicating a place at the base of the rocks, which rises 4,500 feet above the Colorado Plateau. The Yavapai took the name of Apache Mohave because they allied with neighboring Apache, from whom they acquired a matrilineal social order, ritual, taboos, and masked dancing. The terrain so entranced the Yavapai that they reserved the canyons as hallowed ground and visited them only for religious observances.

The first historical mention of the Yavapai comes from a conquistador, Antonio de Espejo. In 1582 and 1583, the Spanish treasure hunter followed three Mexicans who had traveled the Southwest decades earlier with Cabeza de Vaca. In search of silver, de Espejo's party crossed the Little Colorado River and pushed west to the

Verde River. He observed the Yavapai, whom his reports numbered at 1,500.

The Yavapai thrived in the Arizona desert and remained until April 23, 1875, when an executive order forced them from the Camp Verde Reserve in a fateful uprooting called the March of Tears. They returned to their homeland near Camp McDowell Military Reservation, which the government ceded to them in 1903. They suffered a severe epidemic of tuberculosis in 1905. Five years later, the greatly diminished tribe received title to Camp Verde and acquired more land at Middle Verde, Prescott, and Clarksdale. They display their history and culture at the Yavapai-Apache Center, about fifty miles south of Flagstaff.

BELIEFS

The native shaman was the first healer, an intuitive student of human nature who took spontaneous events and turned them into ritual to influence crops, hunting, weather, human procreation, tribal solidarity, and union with the earth. The creation of a medicine wheel formed an inclusive, nature-centered ritual that draws all elements of the planet into one figure—the wheel of life, which is constantly in motion. The shaman used the wheel to demonstrate the individual's connectedness to earthly wonders as well as terrifying phenomena. He intended the wheel to dispel doubt and promote joy and understanding. At ritual ceremonies, spontaneous outbursts of dancing, swaying, laughter, clapping, and singing preceded storytelling and mimicry, all parts of the creative response. By acknowledging the cosmic power of the wheel, participants accessed power.

Multiple native stories describe Cathedral Rock and the medicine wheel as spiritual and physical protections of land and people. As emblems of the cycle of the seasons and life, they derive authenticity from the Yavapai creation legend. According to myth, the Goddess Kamalapukwia (First Woman), grandmother of the supernatural, established the matrilineal nation. She arrived on earth by canoe through Montezuma Well, a limestone sinkhole and water source for ancient people northeast of Montezuma Castle National Monument. Because she traveled alone, she brought a sacred stone as protection from unknown elements. Ihija the dove helped her locate the Red Rock country and bore food to sustain her through the first winter on earth.

The founder's story is remarkably human in its dangers and yearnings. Kamalapukwia, her daughter Amjakupooka (Going around the Earth), and grandson Sakarakaamche (Lofty Wanderer) flourished at Red Rock until Sakarakaamche left them. Because she forgot to carry a protective stone, she never returned. Grandmother and grandson settled at Sedona in a cave near the twin towers of Cathedral Rock, where she taught him to gather seeds and berries and to make a bow and arrow for hunting small game. When he longed for a mate, he formed one from clay and created a people known as the Yavapai.

From Sakarakaamche, the Yavapai learned to sing, dance, and pray. Their blended chant and rhythm derives from earth worship, which fosters the growth of medicine plants. The Yavapai fear that abandonment of their ancestral songs, stories, and dance will cause the land to shrivel and die. Out of devotion to tribal lore, they reverence the twin spires of Cathedral Rock as embodiments of the divine creators, Kamalapukwia and Sakarakaamche.

ACTIVITIES

Medicine wheel ritual thrives in astrology guides, modern art, decals, window hangings, and New-Age practice. The wheel has been interpreted as a star guide and observatory. To create a private wheel requires a personal collection of special stones taken close by and the choice of four cardinal stones to represent the elements—earth, air, fire, and water. The collection is a sacred endeavor requiring concentration and reverence. Formation is also a holy act that begins with the demarcation of a center and careful inscription of a circle by the simplest of geometry—swinging a stick on a string. Choice of the four quarters should end with placement of the eastern stone. Filling in the four arcs with four stones each and leaving an equal amount of space between each balances energy as the lesser stones lead to the four directional bases. The placement of four directional stones at center dedicates the space to the Great Spirit.

The uniqueness of the medicine wheel and its application to faith is the multiplicity of meanings it can have on individual lives and needs. Priests may enter the wheel at the southernmost point to display trust and a willingness to change. At this point, a fire ceremony suggests the dynamic element of transformation and rededication. Movement to the west accepts crossing the rainbow bridge from life to death, symbolized by the death arrow.

A constant challenge, the wheel requires regular cleaning and renewing to maintain its sanctity just as the spirit requires a constant attention to renewal. For personal meditation and worship, the individual enters the wheel at the eastern stone after clarifying the mind and ridding it of distraction. The immediate result of the daily walk of the wheel's shamanic path is an introduction to the beauty way, a harmonizing of spirit with earth to steady the individual against external forces, hardships, and difficult decisions. These walks can also celebrate a stage of life that the individual is either entering or leaving, thus readying body and mind for change from youth to adulthood and adulthood to old age. One aspect of the life journey, the medicine wheel suggests an absence of boundaries and a freedom from fear that life ends with death.

In 1999, Sedona and surrounding areas joined in presenting Crossing Worlds, a multicultural experience combining hallowed landscape, myth and legends, history, earth wisdom, rock art, dance, music, and food. Retreats in Sedona, Jerome, Verde Valley, and the Colorado Plateau offered individualized shamanic guidance to inner landscapes through self-discovery. Itineraries promised a symphony of scenery, light, and sound in the contemplation of nature and self. Through fire and drum healing ceremonies, individuals searched for energy, personal longings, joy in the unknown, and an ecstatic appreciation of life. For those seeking shamanic experience, workshops in Sycamore Canyon timed to coincide with the fall equinox introduced the soul journey and the priestly duties of the shaman.

Sources: Cantor 1993; Champagne 1994; "Classes"; "Creating a Medicine Wheel"; "Crossing Worlds" 1999; Giese 1996; Iler 1995; Magdalena 1996; Milne 1995; Milstein 1999; Patterson and Snodgrass 1994; Perry 1998; Sutphen 1988; Walking Turtle 1993; "Yavapai-Apache Web Site."

Catholic Shrine of the Immaculate Conception
48 Martin Luther King Drive S.W.
Atlanta, Georgia 30303
404-521-1866
www.catholicshrineatlanta.org

A source of consolation, education, and charity, the Shrine of the Immaculate Conception is a survivor of war and modern secularism. Now proclaimed Georgia's mother church, it shares the region's most stirring historical moments. At the corner of Central Avenue and Martin Luther King Jr. Drive at the entrance to Underground Atlanta opposite a circular fountain and the Coke Museum, the stately edifice seems impervious to the tinsel delights of a southern metropolis. Its doors open daily to welcome a diverse influx of homeless Atlantans, tourists, students and faculty of Georgia State University, and leaders from government, commerce, and industry.

HISTORY
Begun as a community of Irish Catholics in 1837 at Terminus, incorporated as Marthasville in 1843, a railroad center later renamed Atlanta, Georgia, the church, once called the Catholic Church in Atlanta, came of age with the city. In 1848, the community, led by Father John Barry, built a modest wood structure renamed the Church of the Immaculate Conception. It surprised visitors with an artistic touch, a copy of seventeenth-century painter Bartolomé Esteban Murillo's painting *The Immaculate Conception,* which hangs in Seville's Museo Provincial. A model of Spanish baroque, the canvas poses an enigmatic Virgin Mary in an opaque celestial setting edged with clusters of cherubs.

Civil War brutality altered both the church and the city, which stood in the path of vengeful Union troops. In May 1864, at the height of the conflict, Father Thomas O'Reilly, the only Catholic chaplain, comforted wounded from both sides as well as civilians and slaves. When he learned that General William Tecumseh Sherman intended to level Atlanta, Father O'Reilly made a bold threat: to order Catholics on the Union side to withdraw if the army did not spare the Catholic church and the surrounding four churches—St. Philip's Episcopal, Trinity

Methodist, Second Baptist, and Central Presbyterian. His intervention succeeded in part: the army did not target the area around city hall, but shelling damaged Father O'Reilly's church. In the wake of Yankee bitterness, the city lay smoldering. Sherman stabled horses in St. Philip's, stored provender in Trinity Methodist, cut meat for the troops in Central Presbyterian, and quartered wounded in the remains of the Catholic church. When Father O'Reilly died after an illness, congregants buried their beloved priest in the church crypt; his name survives in the Father Thomas O'Reilly Knights of Columbus.

In the war's aftermath, the homeless sheltered in churches, sleeping in pews and curtaining off living quarters with burlap. Four years into Reconstruction, a planning committee laid the cornerstone for a new church. Until its completion in 1873, the ravaged church reminded locals of Atlanta's suffering. When a new building replaced the ruins, the congregation adopted Immaculate Conception as its name and proclaimed the Blessed Virgin as Patroness of the United States.

Designated a shrine in 1954, the church celebrated its centenary in 1969, and entered the National Register of Historic Places in 1976, the nation's 200th birthday. After an electrical short in the organ produced a spark in 1982, fire destroyed the shrine. The community rebuilt it with a new roof and stained-glass windows, earning a Renovation of the Year Award for their efforts to preserve and restore. Workers exhumed the remains of Father O'Reilly and Father Thomas Francis Cleary, a Georgian educated in Ireland who pastored the church until 1884, when he died suddenly at age thirty-one. In 1988, staff opened the restored crypt to visitors.

ARCHITECTURE

The Catholic Shrine of the Immaculate Conception is a square brick building with an uneven façade. With the gold capitol dome in the background, the larger of two square towers rises over four stories to the left of a new portal, installed in 1988 by Friends of the Shrine. Crowned with four conical spires at the peak, it shadows a shorter version to the right. At center, a Roman cross crowns the peaked front above an arched window composed of four even, pointed arches surmounted by three circular windows.

The interior, softly lighted by twelve elegant chandeliers, features Christian symbols in stained-glass windows along the nave walls and ceiling paintings of the twelve apostles by Georgia artist Henry Barnes. The altar displays two parts of the original altar, which survived the fire, and the original *Pietà* carved in Italy, a dramatic recreation of Christ's body being removed from the cross. Supplying music for services is a Möller pipe organ.

ACTIVITIES

Under the leadership of Father John Murphy and Deacon Bill Payne, Atlanta's shrine church is open daily to visitors and maintains a ministry to the poor, whom it shelters at night from the cold. A neighborhood co-op sets Saint Francis's Table each Saturday morning for over 500 hungry people. Volunteers stock an emergency pantry and conduct home service to AIDS victims. To the parish, the staff offers altar service training, education in the Catholic faith, ministry to gays and lesbians, and an annual arts and crafts festival.

The affairs of a busy city influence the shrine's staff and congregation. During the 1996 Olympic Games, young volunteers from the diocese, led by youth consultant Kathy Wolf and members of the Federation of Catholic Youth Ministers, welcomed visitors to the shrine. As goodwill ambassadors, they staffed greeting tables, directed tours, served at mass, and distributed 10,000 cups of water daily to pedestrians. The Boston archdiocese supplied cups, towels, and tissues. Additional help from Florida teens and 19 New Zealanders made an international humanitarian gesture. A North Carolina contingent placed a tent over the sidewalk water station.

On September 13, 1998, the shrine celebrated a sesquicentennial. Under banners proclaiming "150 Years—People Living Church," an overflow crowd of visitors and congregants found the nave beribboned, strung with bells, and perfumed with incense. The staff praised the collected history of Atlanta Catholics and lauded Irish Catholic pioneers and railroad workers whose faith built and supported the early church. The service honored Father

O'Reilly, the Civil War hero recognized at city hall in 1945 by a memorial plaque. Beneath blue and white helium balloons, 350 parishioners enjoyed a celebratory lunch at the Georgia Depot Train Station, followed by a viewing of photos and memorabilia of church history and the debut of Larry Ruth's historical play *To Build a Church*.

> **Sources:** Anderson 1999; "Archbishop to Lead Pilgrimage to National Shrines" 1998; Broderick 1958; "Immaculate Conception, Atlanta"; Jarvis 1996; *New Catholic Encyclopedia* 1967; Sullivan 1967; Vosburgh 1969.

Center for Dao-Confucianism
Dr. Thomas Hosuck Kang
1318 Randolph Street N.E.
Washington, D.C. 20017
202-526-6818
FAX 202-526-6818
tkang@wam.umd.edu
www.wam.umd.edu/~tkang

A proponent of self-improvement through meditation, Dr. Thomas Hosuck Kang's Center for Dao-Confucianism introduces newcomers to an ancient Asian philosophy. The hallmarks of Daoism are freedom, simplicity, and a mystical contemplation of nature. Confucianism, an early form of utopianism, stresses a unified world order through discipline and respect for authority. Together, Daoism and Confucianism form a living philosophy that favors the contemplative or intellectual who is willing to let learning rule the baser instincts.

HISTORY
Confucius, or K'ung Fu-tsu, is the ceremonial name for Ch'iu Chung-ni, China's legendary wandering scholar-philosopher, who created the nation's first private college. He was born about 551 B.C. in the state of Lu, now known as Shandong province. A tall, imposing figure with modest manners, he came of age during China's feudal period. He was a poor, fatherless youth who sought learning while managing silos and herds for an aristocrat. He married, fathered a daughter and son, and rose to prestige as court minister. In this post, he grew to despise the

---

DR. THOMAS HOSUCK KANG

A native of Milyang, Republic of Korea, Thomas Hosuck Kang, creator of the first Confucian Mission in the West, is a Confucian missionary to the West. He was born November 24, 1918. After years of travel and study in Asia, at age forty, he immigrated to Seattle, Washington. He studied library science at Catholic University of America and completed a doctoral degree in Far Eastern and international studies from American University, and acquired citizenship in 1971. Fluent in English, Korean, Japanese, and Chinese, he has taught elementary and high school in Japan, instructed United Nations Forces officers in Korean, and catalogued Korean and Japanese materials for the East Asia Collection of McKeldin Library at the University of Maryland. At the Library of Congress, he has volunteered as a senior East Asian information specialist.

At the threshold of the twenty-first century, Dr. Kang began teaching Confucianism as a type of humanism, a philosophy grounded in human aims and interests, rather than in deism or theological abstractions. To end war and other forms of violence, he stresses the demands of community, which require peace and cooperation through duty and love. Particulars of his world reform foresee healthy, talented people working at the jobs they do best. On the far end of the continuum, the weak and downtrodden will become wards of the strong. In an ideal Confucian cosmos, no one will hoard or rob others of rights.

---

luxury-loving hereditary aristocrats, who held commoners in contempt.

Confucius left his job around 501 B.C. to reform China. For thirteen years, he traveled Lu, Wei, Ch'en, Ch'u, Ts'ai, and back to Wei and groomed for political posts an estimated 3,000 pupils, both poor youth and the sons of knights. To prepare them, he taught debate, literature, history, mathematics, ritual, music, archery, and horsemanship. He preferred students who thirsted for learning and acquired three outstanding disciples, Jan Ch'iu, Tzu-lu, and a favorite, Yen Hui. By transmitting ancient truths, Confucius hoped to restore the values of an ancient golden age, when people were more concerned with inner goodness than outward appearance. On his mission to the young, he combated bias, arrogance, and selfishness while stressing courtesy, moral and spiritual excellence, benevolence, and proper conduct, particularly toward elders.

Around 483 B.C., Confucius, bereft of his son and favorite pupil, returned to a post in Lu and compiled traditional Chinese wisdom to help students learn to resist evil and attain decorum in all phases of their lives. For the *Book of Songs,* he won the title of Grand Master K'ung. His intent, according to Book XVIII, verse 6, was to establish the *dao* (the way) on earth. He hoped that ethical young readers could influence the state to halt trivial bureaucracy, oppression, torture, and capital punishment. When he died at age seventy, his followers conferred ceremonial honor at the K'unglin cemetery on the Su River in Ch'ufu.

Confucius's disciples Mencius and Hsün-tzu compiled 497 humanistic verses in twenty chapters of a text known as the *Lun-yû* or *Analects.* During periods of suppression, the devout risked execution by hiding the master's sayings from censors. According to the master's overall intent, the greatest human achievements were not money, fame, or power. Rather, he foresaw a utopian haven—a global family free of evil and war and blessed with happiness, goodness, and peace. The keys to these rewards were a respect for truth, integrity, and dignity. Unknown to the master, his teachings took hold in the hearts and minds of followers in China, Korea, Japan, Indochina, and the West. Confucian temples sprang up in all 2,000 of China's counties.

Nearly two and a half millennia after Confucius's journey, his adages continue to influence thought and behavior, not only in Asia, but everywhere Asian philosophy survives. Confucianism's Great Unity leads the seeker along the *dao* toward heaven. By opening each mind to the *dao*-mind, a God-centered consciousness beyond human thinking, and by enhancing and enabling the seeker to find perfection, the analects promote a super consciousness, the internal source of harmony, equilibrium, and God's love and wisdom. Today, Chinese children memorize Confucius's advice in school; civil service tests contain phrases from his text.

ACTIVITIES

At the Center for Dao-Confucianism, Dr. Kang assists beginners in meditation and counsels them in self-healing. He also lectures on *I Ching,* a Confucian text from the twelfth century B.C. that teaches a form of divination and cosmology that unites nature and humankind in a profound but practical symbiosis. In addition, he has published articles on Confucian principles, global religion, and world peace.

Dr. Kang foresees Confucianism launching a new age that will unite East and West on common ground. He intends to establish a world mission of teachers who go out from the center to propagate Confucius's teachings to all people. To that end, the center offers lectures, discussions, and an information and reference service of over 5,000 items in Western languages. Its Web site posts details and introductory essays in Korean.

Sources: Confucius 1992; *Eerdmans' Handbook to the World's Religions* 1982; Fingarette; Kang 1999; *New Catholic Encyclopedia* 1967; Pelikan 1992; Schwartz 1985; Snodgrass 1995; Waley 1986.

Chaco Canyon

Chaco Culture National Historical Park
P.O. Box 220
Nageezi, New Mexico 87037
505-786-7014

Named from the Quechua word for "hunting range," Chaco Canyon was an inviting area to nomadic hunter-gatherers, who settled in northwest New Mexico and built Chetro Ketl, Una Vida, Peñasco Blanco, Hungo Pavi, and Kin Bineola. A valued historic and religious site, the canyon was once the Middle Place, a center of Anasazi civilization, a prehistoric people who lived from 900 to 1300 A.D. Relying on engineering, building, and marketing skills, the "Chaco Phenomenon" grew to a population of 5,000 in 400 settlements on land calculated to feed no more than 2,000. Suddenly, they stopped building around 1130 and dispersed fifty years later, perhaps from a prolonged drought or epidemic. Today, Chaco Culture National Historical Park occupies the southeast wing of Four Corners, the meeting of Utah, Colorado, Arizona, and New Mexico.

At Pueblo Bonito, New Mexico, a D-shaped desert citadel of 1,000 to 1,200 citizens sits at the foot of the northern escarpments, a five-story trading center spread over three acres. (North Wind Picture Archives)

At Pueblo Bonito, a D-shaped desert citadel of 1,000 to 1,200 citizens at the foot of the northern escarpments, a five-story trading center spread over three acres. A political center and architectural wonder built in stone masonry, its urban plan radiated from a central plaza. A complex lifestyle required communal buildings, 800 rooms for living and storing commodities, 32 round kivas, and 400 miles of spacious thoroughfares to an adjacent community at Aztec Ruins, New Mexico, and to the eighty distant villages with whom the Chacoans did business. They thrived on corn traded north from Mexico. Stretches of flood-control canals diverted torrential rain to irrigation ditches to ensure profitable harvests. In an era of plenty, canyon dwellers exported a varied number of items, including turquoise and jet jewelry, Pacific seashells, copper bells, exotic birds, and black-on-white pottery.

BELIEFS

Although the Anasazi left no written records, symbolic art indicates that they regularly at-tended to worship. Their petroglyphs recorded a supernova of 1054 A.D., Halley's Comet, and a solar calendar that marks the summer solstice, and the site perhaps served as an observatory of constellations. According to Navajo oral tradition, the Anasazi holy ones of Chaco Canyon acquired ancestral lands by besting the Great Gambler. The people flourished on their winnings until they neglected worship. For their sin, God sent a whirlwind to blast them out of the canyon.

Ironically, an ancient prediction came true long after the earliest people had vacated their canyon homeland. According to a legend of indeterminate age and source, a cliff in Chaco Canyon would one day collapse on the people and exterminate the village. In the twentieth century, the prophecy came true, but the stones crushed no one as they tumbled harmlessly among empty rooms and roadways.

After the Navajo migrated into New Mexico early in the eighteenth century, they brought their own fables of a many-layered cosmos, the *Yei* (Holy Ones), and formulated religious lore about the all-important blessing way, beauty way, enemy way, night way, and holy way, the structured ceremonies that survive into the twenty-first century. At the Wijiji ruins on former Navajo homelands, tellers recounted a variation on the myth of Spider Woman. One version claims that a nearby Pueblo woman taught the Navajo how to weave their traditional blankets. In another creation story, Changing Woman created corn and molded flakes of dry skin from her body into the Earth-Surface People, an early designation for the Diné, or Navajo.

HISTORY

According to tradition, priests conducted the earliest rituals at the kivas, or underground worship chambers, of Casa Rinconada, Chaco Canyon's 64-foot, keyhole-shaped religious center. Their observations of ritual mimic ancient holy men who tended the sacred fire, painted sacred murals on the walls, and celebrated the emergence of the first people through the *sipapu,* a sand-filled ceremonial hole in the floor that linked earth with the cosmos. In niches in the underground chamber walls, worship leaders stored the first ritual implements—turquoise and shell beads, ceremonial offerings, rattles, and prayer sticks.

Out of reverence for the past, the Pueblo perpetuated Anasazi ritual *kivas.* Before the Snake Dance, they housed and cleansed serpents that the dancers would dust with cornmeal and release to bring favorable weather for crops. The ritual began with dancers clasping live snakes in their mouths and circling the village four times to propitiate deities of the four directions. To mesmerize and subdue the snakes, kilt-clad dancers clutched wands marked with zigzags and fluttered an eagle-feather duster. The reptiles, representing ancestral spirits, slithered away, bearing prayers to the rain gods.

Chaco Canyon lay eerily vacant through centuries. Around 1720, Pueblo and Navajo, descendents of the Kinya'a or Tall House People, migrated into Anasazi stone strongholds, farmed the fallow land, and set their herds to graze. To protect themselves from belligerent tribes, they built fortified stone shelters called *pueblitos* (minipueblos). By 1896, scientists and explorers had begun studying Pueblo Bonito. Two years later, Chama stockman Edward Sargent initiated land wars after he channeled his sheep into the canyon for winter grazing.

To rescue the area from overgrazing and misuse, the parks commission established Chaco Culture National Historical Park in 1907. In the 1920s, the National Geographic Society began excavating Chaco Canyon about the same time that Mary Cabot Wheelwright met Navajo medicine man Hosteen Klah and began recording his tribe's religious practices. Her museum, the House of Navajo Religion—later named the Wheelwright Museum of the American Indian in her honor—opened in Santa Fe in 1937. Preservationists housed a larger cache of artifacts at the Maxwell Museum of Anthropology in Albuquerque. In the last quarter of the twentieth century, study of the Anasazi has turned to the heavens after the Chaco Canyon Research Center produced aerial photography and a land survey. From this archeological database, scientists, using thermal infrared multispectral data, proposed an intense investigation of the vast Anasazi civilization and charts of the roads from trading centers to client peoples on the desert's fringe.

ACTIVITIES

Through drumming and dancing, modern ritual preserves mystic ancestral beliefs in an earth mother who gave birth to humankind. To accommodate mutually exclusive clans, each worship complex may require separate *kivas* for each interrelated group. In stringently guarded privacy, priests perform ceremonies and initiate young men into positions of religious responsibility. Still valued in the Southwest, these rituals are off-limits to most women and outsiders. Only the chosen nonnative guest may witness local men performing *kiva* sacraments.

The park center opens to visitors from 8:00 A.M. to 5:00 P.M. daily and from 8:00 A.M. to 6:00 P.M. during the summer, from Memorial Day through Labor Day. Sites and hiking trails are available from sunrise to sunset. The Wijiji and Kin Klizhin trails are the best choices for biking. Unfortunately for the public and natives, there is structural and environmental evidence that the 100,000 outsiders who visit each year are straining the fragile site, forcing it onto the list of the 100 most endangered monuments.

Sources: Bennett 1975; *Biography Resource Center* 1999; Breeden 1976; Buchanan 1999; Cantor, George, 1993; "Chaco Canyon"; "Chaco Canyon National Historical Park"; "Chaco Culture"; Champagne 1994; Eliade 1987; Gilpin 1968; Ketchum 1957; Linthicum 1999; Milne 1995; Patterson and Snodgrass 1994; Rudoff 1997; Sherr and Kazickas 1994; Steiger 1974; Walking Turtle 1993.

Chapel of Massachusetts Institute of Technology

Chaplain John Wuestneck
Amherst Street
Cambridge, Massachusetts 02139
617-252-1780
chaplain@mit.edu

Sometimes referred to as the Kresge Chapel, Eero Saarinen's starkly solid circular chapel is a welcome retreat. Standing on the west campus of the Massachusetts Institute of Technology (MIT) in Cambridge, it serves a population of students, faculty, and guests. A bold, challenging model of architecture, it bears a distinct, svelte modernism in shape, material, and purpose to suit a multidenominational campus parish. Without windows, steeple, or gabled roof, it arises in silo simplicity from a watery moat as though defying centuries of religious architectural tradition. Saarinen, a daring innovator, intentionally created an atmosphere of mystery and sublimity to channel worshippers' thoughts and prayers to an almighty power.

ARCHITECTURE

With the MIT chapel, Saarinen emulated youthful energy and vision as well as a pervasive human need for quiet and order. By balancing a simple geometric shape with a unique, unexpected entranceway, he maintained a purity of design that departs from the egotism of more

Eero Saarinen's starkly solid circular chapel is a welcome retreat on the west campus of Massachusetts Institute of Technology (MIT) in Cambridge. (Donna Coveney/MIT)

EERO SAARINEN

The son, grandson, and nephew of architects, Eero Saarinen grew up in a family and milieu that encouraged a risk-taking genius. Born August 20, 1910, in Kirkkunummi, Finland, he profited from childhood contact with the atelier of his mother, sculptor Loja Gesellius, and the drafting tools and work of his father, architect Gottlieb Eliel Saarinen. When the family immigrated to Bloomfield Hills, Michigan, in 1923, his father directed the Cranbrook Academy of Art and taught architecture at the University of Michigan.

Following high school, Saarinen studied sculpture in Paris and then apprenticed in furniture design under his father's direction. After advanced training at the Yale School of Architecture and a year with architect Jarl Eklund in Helsinki, he joined the firm of Saarinen, Swanson, and Saarinen and later partnered with his father on the General Motors Technical Center in Warren, Michigan. Eero and his associate, Charles Eames, won furniture competitions sponsored by New York's Museum of Modern Art for a chair molded from plywood. After attaining citizenship months before World War II, he put in three years in Washington, D.C., at the Office of Strategic Services.

In 1948, by mastering the use of metal tubing, plastic foam, and other nonstandard materials for the manufacture of organic home and office furnishings suited to the way people live, Saarinen revolutionized design. He came to the public's attention when *Life* magazine featured his functional, inexpensive plastic and fabric seating. He created fads of the mid-twentieth century with one-piece pedestal furniture and the womb chair, a nestlike receptacle that curled the body into a fetal position.

Saarinen the institutional architect competed with Saarinen the furniture designer for public acclaim. After collaborating with his father on the Smithsonian Institution Art Gallery and laying out the Ann Arbor campus of the University of Michigan, in 1955, he produced two masterworks for the Massachusetts Institute of Technology—the handkerchief-domed Kresge Auditorium and the adjacent cylindrical chapel bearing no formal name. Shortly before his death on September 1, 1961, from a brain tumor, the last creations of his short career—a theater for New York City's Lincoln Center, the Ingalls Hockey Rink at Yale University, U.S. embassies in Oslo and London, Dulles International Airport, the Transworld Airways Terminal at John F. Kennedy International Airport in New York City, St. Louis's catenary Gateway Arch, and Bell Laboratories in Holmdel, New Jersey—elevated him to global prominence.

splendid twentieth-century churches. The red brick presents a textured surface above a circular reflecting pool and varied archways at the base, which reflects shifting waves of light into the nave. The glass and aluminum narthex opens on a 130-seat nave fifty-four feet in diameter and walled with undulating brick walls. The acoustically live interior shimmers with aural and visual drama created by solid walls and controlled natural light from a ceiling oculus above the altar, a stoic polished marble cube.

Saarinen did not work alone. He called on Italian artist Harry Bertoia for an inspired altar sculpture and Theodore Roszak to top the drumlike exterior with an aluminum spire-bell tower. The reredos departs from classic solidity to impose a shaft of harplike strings bearing a shower of glinting bronze confetti. The effect gradually thins out as it approaches the top, where pinholes thread tiny shafts of light. In a parallel thrust, on the flat roof, the spire's clean lines tapering into curving points direct the eye heavenward. The dancing light and graceful forms entrance and soothe spectators. The structure inspired other works of Saarinen's associates, particularly Olav Hammarstrom's Chapel of St. James the Fisherman in Wellfleet, Massachusetts.

ACTIVITIES

Open seven days a week from 7:00 A.M. to 11:00 P.M., the MIT chapel welcomes visitors and worshippers of all faiths for meditation and welcomes musicians to play the organ. The dean's office schedules religious services, which include baptisms, bar mitzvahs, weddings, memorial services, receptions, and funerals. One of its historic services was the funeral of Saarinen. The multipurpose nature of the design allows staff to alter the space to seat 190 by adding folding chairs.

For all its open-ended purpose, the chapel follows a surprisingly normal worship schedule. Protestant students gather weekdays for 6:00 P.M. vespers and on Sunday at 11:00 A.M. for the main weekly service, led by Chaplain John Wuestneck. Students volunteer to read scripture, usher, and perform vocal and instrumental music. A Thursday concert series broadens the outreach of liturgical and classical music.

Sources: *American Decades* 1998; *Biography Resource Center* 1999; Capps; "Harry Bertoia"; Muschamp 1990; Mutrux 1982; Smith 1989.

Chapel of Peace

Brad Bird, Program Director
Rural Route 1, Box 116
Dunseith, North Dakota 58329
701-263-4390; 888-432-6733
FAX 701-263-3169
rob@peacegarden.com
www.peacegarden.com

An unassuming, hallowed site among dark expanses of aspen and birch, Dunseith's Chapel of Peace—also known as the All Faiths Peace Chapel—sits on the dividing line between North Dakota and the Canadian province of Manitoba. The modernistic structure honors the world's largest unfortified common border, which has remained at peace since the War of 1812. Beyond the chapel grounds within rock retaining walls lie six displays featuring terraces, gardens, cascades, flagstone walks, reflecting pools, and fountains. The combined attraction of 140,000 annuals, water birds, native-stone paths, and grazing moose and deer illustrates the natural order of peace.

HISTORY

In 1928, horticulturist Dr. Henry Moore of Islington, Ontario, designed the International Peace Garden as a gesture of good will toward and recognition of the long tradition of mutual accord between Canada and the United States. At the August 1929 session of the National Association of Gardeners of the United States in Toronto, he initiated a three-year fund-raising campaign. Before the end of his quest for donors, in July 1931, he had lined up a site—a free tract in the Turtle Mountains near Boisse-

vain, Manitoba, looking out on prairie wheat fields, lakes, and streams.

Moore made a formal radio announcement on December 25, 1931, that his proposed 2,339-acre garden would combine 888 acres in the United States and 1,451 acres in Canada. Supervised by the Professional Grounds Management Society, it would take shape thirty miles north of the continent's center and equidistant from the Atlantic and Pacific Oceans. The site accesses an intercontinental highway, the Main Street of the Americas, which reaches from Churchill, Manitoba, through the Panama Canal, and south to Cape Horn.

Before 50,000 spectators, Moore presided over the garden's dedication on July 14, 1932. At the center of a large formal garden, a simple fieldstone cairn bears this inscription:

> To God in His Glory,
> We Two Nations
> Dedicate This Garden
> And Pledge Ourselves
> That as Long as Man
> Shall Live, We Will
> Not Take Up Arms
> Against One Another.
> (Gorder 1996)

The marker remains on the international border. In 1934, the Civilian Conservation Corps (CCC) began building roads and carved out foundations for an artificial lake, picnic area and shelters, bridges, and fencing. The lodge, the garden's oldest building, features timber from Manitoba and North Dakota granite. To the right of the entrance, a tablet, which actor Charlton Heston dedicated in 1956, displays the Ten Commandments.

Growth of the project slowed during World War II and then resumed in 1952, when the Order of the Eastern Star of North Dakota and Manitoba met in Milwaukee and resolved to create a worship site and assist with the garden's maintenance. Staff dedicated the Chapel of Peace in 1970. In the 1980s, at the garden's fiftieth anniversary, the National Park Service erected a unity symbol on the Canadian side, the four columns of a 120-foot Peace Tower, which are illuminated by spotlights each night.

In 1996, as a tribute to builders, the National Park Service donated materials for a photographic history of the CCC.

ACTIVITIES

Open year-round from 8:00 A.M. to 9:00 P.M. in warm weather, the garden facilities, maintained by staff from both nations, offer campgrounds, hiking and bike trails, a pavilion, an arboretum, a 500-seat Masonic Auditorium, and a meeting and conference facility. The grounds require four hours for a complete tour. Other events include a crafts program, horticulture classes, greenhouse tours, campfire programs, and environmental education. The site became a popular summer spot for thousands of youth, accommodating the International Music Camp and the Royal Canadian Legion Athletic Camp. On the grounds, campers practice the performing arts and develop athletic skills. Musicians offer an annual free concert. The Peace Garden Cafe makes take-out picnic lunches; a concession and souvenir shop stocks souvenirs, CDs, seeds, and dried flower arrangements.

South of the entry gate lies a functioning eighteen-foot floral clock, built by Bulova and formed of seasonal plants ranged in a circle on a small knoll. A favorite of children, it registers the park's official time. The Dunseith Community Betterment Club sponsors another attraction, Ambassador, the garden's official hot-air balloon. In summer, volunteers pilot it at regional hot-air balloon contests and rallies. At center, the park features the two national flags—the Maple Leaf and the Star-Spangled Banner—and a pond fed by a fountain. In 1999, the staff hosted a National Aeronautical and Space Administration exhibit of moon rocks and astronaut gear. That summer, a red-serge-clad Royal Canadian Mounted Police detail guarded the park in celebration of the site's sixty-seventh year.

At the garden's most hallowed spot, fossil-embellished limestone walls bear fifty-five memorable citations about peace. These thought-provoking words come from the Bible, Sanskrit scriptures, the *Union Prayer Book for Jewish Worship,* Canada's Centennial Prayer, and Vatican II and from the world's notable promoters of peace: Alexander Graham Bell, Tim Bentley, the Buddha, Albert Camus, Winston Churchill, Confucius, Dante, Fyodor Dostoevsky, Sir Francis Drake, Emile Durkheim, Albert Einstein, Dwight D. Eisenhower, Ralph Waldo Emerson, Saint Francis of Assisi, Viktor Frankl, Benjamin Franklin, Mohandas Gandhi, King George VI, Goethe, P. G. Hamerton, Dag Hammarskjold, Admiral Thomas C. Hart, Oliver Wendell Holmes, Douglas Jerrold, John F. Kennedy, Elizabeth Kilbourn, Dr. Martin Luther King, Jr., David E. Lilienthal, Abraham Lincoln, Henry Wadsworth Longfellow, James Russell Lowell, Sir John A. MacDonald, Peter Marshall, Vincent Massey, Reinhold Niebuhr, Richard M. Nixon, Sir William Osler, Louis Pasteur, Sir Alexander Paterson, Lester B. Pearson, Sayda Seybold Pettersen, Franklin D. Roosevelt, John Ruskin, Jean-Paul Sartre, George Bernard Shaw, Robert Louis Stevenson, U Thant, and George Washington. Within the enclosure lie the chapel and bell tower. Situated at the end of the main thoroughfare, the building contains no side windows and no steeple. The two structures are among the site's few permanent structures, which international law prohibits along the border. Various ministers schedule nondenominational services on Sunday at 11:00 A.M. with music from an electric organ.

The chapel's entrance is an unassuming terraced walkway leading beyond tidy beds of annuals to a series of amber windows manufactured in France. Through a low square portal marked "Peace Chapel," the visitor comes upon an unusual interior—four columns centering a round fountain and a reflecting pool. The room seats 150 and hosts weddings, baptisms, anniversaries and receptions. Maintenance is a project of members of the General Grand Chapter Order of the Eastern Star, a men's and women's fraternal organization founded in 1850 by Dr. Rob Morris, Poet Laureate of Masonry, to promote morality and character. The chapel is the object of the group's pilgrimage held the second weekend in August every third year.

Sources: Buchanan 1999; Gorder 1996; "International Peace Garden," http://town.boissevain.mb.ca/, www.whispersonthewind.org/; "Order of the Eastern Star."

Chapel of the Prodigal

William Hurt, President
Ed Bonner, Chaplain
Montreat-Anderson College
Lookout Road
Montreat, North Carolina 28757
828-669-8012; 800-622-6968
bneil@montreat.edu
www.montreat.edu

The Chapel of the Prodigal, a focus of western Carolina fresco art, serves a Presbyterian college, Montreat-Anderson, with a student body of 400. In the 1990s, trustees hired Charlotte architect Richard Henley to unify a chapel and the McGowan Center for Christian Studies at the center of campus. Located near Black Mountain, an arts center of the North Carolina Appalachians, Montreat's chapel adds depth to a campus building conceived to serve students for weekly worship, as a Christian ministry department, and for concerts and recitals.

The chapel opened in October 1998, but its true dedication came two months later with the completion of Ben Long's lifelike chapel fresco. Encased in a pointed arch and entitled *The Return of the Prodigal,* it illustrates the stress on a disjointed family as told in Christ's parable of the Prodigal Son (Luke 15). To artist Ben Long, the grueling work was an essential to decorating hallowed space.

HISTORY

Montreat-Anderson College, under the auspices of the General Assembly of the Presbyterian Church, U.S., developed from Montreat Normal School, a body of eight students who met for classes at the Montreat Hotel in October 1916. Headed by principal Nancy Moorefield, the two-year teacher-training facility recruited students from the synods of Alabama, Georgia, Tennessee, Virginia, and North Carolina. A fire in January 1924 forced the staff to move operations temporarily to Montreat Camp and then, in 1929, to the Alba Hotel on Lake Susan.

By 1933, trustees reorganized the school as Montreat Junior College and the following year as Montreat College. By 1945, the offerings had expanded to a four-year liberal arts curriculum for women. In 1959, the name changed to Montreat-Anderson College to reflect the commitment of its devoted staff head, Dr. R. C. Anderson, and to acknowledge restructuring to a coeducational institution. The student body has remained stable in size and background for four decades. Composed of 50 percent North Carolinians, the alumni include Ruth Graham and Franklin Graham, wife and son of Dr. Billy Graham, America's foremost evangelist.

ACTIVITIES

Traditionally, the coeducational campus has stressed spirituality in its prayer room—replaced in 1985 by a prayer porch—and in the three-story stone bell tower and Gaither Chapel, which seats 400. The auditorium features chestnut pews and woodwork and trusses hewn from 200-year-old timbers. The chapel accommodates student worship, Christian life conferences, performances of the college choir and assembly singers, Wednesday night praise and worship, the Crossroads Spiritual Emphasis Week, and activities of the Student Christian Association. For weddings, the building offers bride's and groom's rooms. The Ruth Bell Graham Prayer Room at the balcony level displays in calligraphy, "Come Unto Me" (Matthew 11:28), which invites individuals for intimate prayer and meditation.

Like other campus worship sites, the chapel doubles as a concert and lecture hall and instructional facility. Groups assemble for vocal recitals and performances on the Allen Renaissance electric organ, built in Macungie, Pennsylvania, and the sixty-one-bell Flemish carillon crafted by Van Bergan Bellfoundries. In 1999, the chapel hosted a segment of the Staley Lecture Series. At the McGowan Center for Christian Studies on the ground floor, the staff of the Christian Ministries Division teaches and holds office hours.

In December 1998, Ben Long completed his fresco for the Chapel of the Prodigal, which is open for tours Tuesday through Sunday from 9:00 A.M. to noon and 1:00 to 4:00 P.M. on Sundays. Positioned above the altar, the fresco features softened lines in tan and cream hues. Docents point out a scene to the rear of the dramatic reunion that introduces a crucifix shape in the scaffolding on which a butcher is dressing meat. In the arched gateway, a woman lifts her hands in joy. Religious groups and individuals

The Chapel of the Prodigal in Montreat, North Carolina, opened in October 1998, but its true dedication came two months later with the completion of Ben Long's lifelike fresco of Christ's parable of the prodigal son. (Courtesy College Communications Department, Montreat College)

BEN LONG

Ben Long is a late-twentieth-century practitioner of fresco, the art of painting by applying fresh plaster to a bare wall. Born in Texas in 1945, he grew up in Statesville, North Carolina. After study at the University of North Carolina in Chapel Hill, he pursued painting at New York City's Art Student's League before journeying to Florence, Italy, at age twenty-five to study under master portrait artist Pietro Annigoni. In seven years, Long mastered tempera, oil, and fresco, a complex structural technique that forms pigmented plaster into the body of the wall itself. The final work cures into a hard, crystalline surface that grows luminous over time.

Long's notable works adorn the NationsBank Corporate Center, TransAmerica Building, and Law Enforcement Center in downtown Charlotte, North Carolina, a city that prizes Long's additions to urban art. His illusionary decoration of domes with iconographic or archetypal images added to his stature as a fresco master. Near the Blue Ridge Parkway, his liturgical scenarios for the apse wall of Holy Trinity Episcopal Church in Glendale Springs, North Carolina, use local models for a rendition of *The Lord's Supper*. At nearby Mary's Episcopal Church in Beaver Creek, he produced the life-size *Mary Great With Child, John The*

Baptist, and *The Mystery of Faith,* a surrealistic glimpse of Jesus' spirit separating from his crucified body.

In 1998, Long joined the faculty of Montreat-Anderson College as the Hamilton Gallery Artist in Residence to teach two courses, anatomy and figure drawing and technique and portraiture. In the 1999 winter semester, he moved operations to a studio in Asheville and began sketching the only extant fresco derived from the parable of the Prodigal Son. During Long's tenure, he applied fresco to a 16- by 17.5-foot space of the chapel altar. Employing five assistants to pat red chalk into perforations in wet lime plaster as an outline, he transferred the scene to the wall from a preliminary full-size storyboard.

Long's medium—lime-resistant minerals dissolved in water—required hand-troweling into place, a tedious process that required chiseling out mistakes and replastering until the images blended into a satisfying whole. His updated family grouping places a troubled mother within a traditionally all-male New Testament exemplum. The finished fresco blends directly into the wall without framing or a border. An air space behind the plaster aids temperature control, which preserves the quality and texture of Long's parable in plaster.

averaging 250 people a week tour the premises to remark on the delicate shadowing and intricate background. They look out from the ground floor and balcony on the theme of forgiveness and atonement, themes aimed at students who have survived rebellion and alienation from family and community.

Sources: "An Artistic Treasure" 1999; "Charlotte's Best"; Cranford 1996; Hogan 1998; Lacour 1999; "Local History and Attractions in Charlotte"; "Montreat College" 1999; "Pietro Annigoni."

Charterhouse of the Transfiguration
Skyline Drive
Mount Equinox
Route 2, Box 2411
Arlington, Vermont 05250
802-362-2550
FAX 802-362-3584

One of the most unusual religious sites, Vermont's Charterhouse of the Transfiguration north of Bennington, chooses total anonymity. Residents are so intensely private that they discourage visits and publicity and strenuously examine all candidates who present themselves for membership. The brotherhood offers only a small glimpse of its piety through external architecture visible from Skyline Drive. Erected in the see of Burlington on Mount Equinox, 3,835 feet above sea level, it is one of twenty-six Carthusian monasteries located in France, Spain, Italy, Portugal, Germany, Switzerland, England, Yugoslavia, Brazil, and the United States.

HISTORY
To accommodate Carthusian piety and withdrawal from materialism, in the late 1950s, Dr. J. G. Davidson, an executive of Union Carbide, donated 7,000 acres to the order at the top of

Equinox Mountain in the Taconic Range in Bennington County. Since 1948, the land had been the site of Wind Swept, his private vacation hideaway. The original twelve brothers occupied twelve cells in a wagon shed until the completion of their monastery, named the Charterhouse of the Transfiguration. The tortuous road is closed during the worst of wintry weather from late October to mid-May, a situation further obscuring local knowledge of monastery activities.

Currently, the charterhouse earns revenue from the inn and restaurant on Equinox Mountain, from leasing land to a utility company that generates power from wind, and from selling hydroelectric power to Green Mountain Power. Also, the brotherhood draws funds from land leased for the Federal Aviation Agency communication station and the University of Vermont ETV station and receives a toll of $6 for each car traveling the 5.2 miles from Skyline Drive to the top of Equinox Mountain. By relying on firewood, hydroelectric power, and wind-power projects and admitting no newspaper or radio or TV news, residents conserve energy and shield themselves from worldliness.

ARCHITECTURE

The charterhouse complex contains a common cloister that shelters a warren of individual hermitages. These private retreats house fifteen monks and priests who devote themselves to the Carthusian vows of poverty, chastity, and obedience. The three strictures placed a philosophical burden on Minnesota-born architect Victor Christ-Janer, designer of New York's Horace Mann School and St. Mary's Abbey in Morristown, New Jersey, who worked out a spare structural expression of self-denial and service to God.

In this remote environment, in 1971, Christ-Janer produced an isolated compound of unrefined granite slabs weighing 7,000 pounds each and quarried in Barrie. At the dedication, the public received a one-time invitation to examine the charterhouse, which Christ-Janer designed to last 900 years. The post-and-lintel styling, one of civilization's earliest architectural styles, dates to Stonehenge, French dolmens, and Druidic rock temples. The architectural method

produced a striking tension between primitivism and enduring strength. In a silent, starkly nonhuman landscape, the complex suggests both prehistoric artistry and a deserted burial ground. The lasting quality of stone on earth symbolizes an integrity of purpose and the return of the body to dust.

The flat-roofed individual cells are two-story efficiency apartments walled in for maximum privacy. No windows open on the outside; long windows facing the south capture solar energy. Each unit is composed of an oratory for recitation of the canonical office, a bookshelf, closets, a bathroom, a dining table and chair, and a cooking area in the upstairs *cubiculum,* the main living quarters. In the adjacent sleeping room, a single bed, desk, and chair complete the upper suite. The sole decoration is a simple crucifix attached to the bedroom wainscoting. Downstairs, one room houses a workshop; the adjacent utility room stores firewood and work supplies for carpentry, gardening, cooking, or woodcutting, according to the subsistence task the prior assigns based on the resident's interest and capability. In the courtyard, each monk may raise vegetables, herbs, and fruit trees.

Attached to the cloister, a third section, the church, holds the brothers who assemble for communal worship. In addition, its chapels allow worshippers to celebrate mass in private. Components contributing to community are the chapter house, library, and refectory. During the noon meal, a monk stands at a lectern alongside a stationary U-shaped table to read aloud from scripture or the patristic writings. After the noon meal on special days, residents gather for informal conversation.

ACTIVITIES

Carthusian service may take one of two forms—as a sequestered monk or as a brother, who tempers solitude with manual labor. According to chapters XII through XIII of the order's statutes, the Carthusian brethren parallel Christ's forty-day withdrawal into the desert by observing a restrictive schedule based on silence, poverty, prayer, penance, and self-denial through fasts and abstinences. From a life of contemplation and devotion comes a perpetual quest for God's love and a study of the inner life.

CARTHUSIANS

The Carthusians got their start in 1085 from Saint Bruno, a scholarly German educator at Rheims cathedral school and supervisor of public education. After his departure from service, he formed a semi-eremitic brotherhood of six companions on the forested Cartusian mountainside twenty-five miles outside Grenoble at Chartreuse. In privacy, the men held vigils, prayed, and fasted. Corruption of the Latin for Cartusian and the French town name produced the English term "Carthusian Charterhouse."

The order spread to Spain, Italy, and Britain, where Henry II established a charterhouse at Witham, Somerset, in 1181. More cells took shape at Sheen, Surrey; Hethorpe, Gloucestershire; Beauvale, Nottinghamshire; Coventry, Warwick-shire; Kingston-upon-Hull, Yorkshire; and London. Each followed the standard plan of inner and outer courtyards, a dormitory for lay brothers, a guest house, and the essentials—a separate house kitchen, pantry, bakery, forge, and carpentry shop. Unlike the Camaldolese and Benedictines, Bruno's brotherhood adhered to a strict asceticism. A parallel Carthusian plan for female eremites served the nuns of Prebyon, France.

Historically, Carthusian postulants are usually males over age twenty and under forty-five who must be physically and psychologically fit for the rigors of asceticism, which requires solitude, manual labor, and study. Monks must be high school graduates educated in the liberal arts and must know the basics of Latin grammar, ecclesiastical vocabulary, and translation. After six to twelve months of service, they may become novices for two years before taking final vows. An alternative membership, called a donate, allows the resident to promise to observe obedience and chastity without giving up personal possessions.

Residents dress in plain white, cowled tunics and confine most daily activities to the inner court, which consists of the chapel, cloister cemetery, and refectory. They maintain garden plots and spend private time in individual exercise yards and workrooms. Spartan cells contain a devotional area, a table and shelf, two chairs, and a sleeping board covered with a blanket. A diet devoid of red meat extends to bread, fruit, vegetables, and herbs except for feast days, when the brothers partake of fish and cheese. Once weekly, the brothers fast on bread, water, and salt. They elect a prior to govern the monastery's family. He appoints a vicar to watch over the monks and a procurator to oversee compliance with rules. The novice masters aid the young and direct vocational retreats.

- The day begins with a bell shortly before midnight calling monks to the chapel for matins, a prayer to the Virgin Mary. At 12:15 A.M., they assemble in the church for matins and lauds.
- Around 2:00 or 3:00 A.M., individuals recite lauds to the Virgin Mary and return to bed.
- At 6:30 A.M., they arise for prime, private prayer offered during the first hour.
- At 7:45 A.M., monks assemble in the church for mass.
- Around 9:15 A.M., they pray privately at terce, the third canonical hour, read and study, and begin the day's manual work.
- At 11:30 A.M., they enjoy ninety minutes for sext, the sixth canonical hour, consisting of the first meal of the day, free time, and a return to church before the afternoon's work period.

- At 2:00 P.M., they begin none, the ninth canonical hour, when they study and read, work, and offer Vespers of Our Lady.
- The work day concludes with evening prayer at the Brother's Chapel at 5:00 P.M. After a return to the cell at 5:30 P.M., the brothers eat supper or fast in their cells, read, pray, enjoy free time, and then go to bed before 8:00 P.M., which is compline, the last canonical hour.

Variances in the schedule are few. On Friday, residents eat only bread and water. Once weekly, the monks assemble for an afternoon walk in the woods or on country lanes; these walks are limited to once a month for brothers. Twice a year, residents take a *speciementum*—a "looking about" in the form of a long hike to Rupert, Vermont. During one of these hikes, they share a picnic lunch. Infrequently, members write letters to their immediate families. No women are admitted beyond the monastery gate; male family members may visit the brothers' cells and stay at the guest house four days out of each year. News of the outside world comes from the prior, who communicates events that the brethren miss because of their withdrawal from the media.

The Charterhouse of the Transfiguration belongs to an association promoting revival of the Latin Gregorian mass. The staff attends a traditional medieval mass each Sunday and holy day at 9:00 A.M. and on weekdays at 7:45 A.M., when residents sing plainsong, partake of Holy Communion, and chant the liturgy in the original Latin and parts of the office in the vernacular. On Sunday, they share chant in the church. These services admit no outsiders. Other interaction with the outside world is limited to rare treks to the village by the porter, Father Tom, who purchases supplies, medicine, and staples not grown in the hermitage garden.

> **Sources:** Andre 1987; "Carthusian Monks and Carthusian Nuns"; "The Carthusian Way of Life" 1987; "The Catholic Encyclopedia" 1997; "Les Chartreuses dans le Monde"; Daley 1990; "Directory of Latin Masses"; Farmer 1992; Joyce 1963; Kelly and Kelly 1992; Mulligan 1980; Mutrux 1982; Snodgrass 2000.

Christ Chapel, Boston
See Old North Church.

Christ Lutheran Church
Reverend D. G. Meyer, Pastor
315 North Shipley Street
Seaford, Delaware 19973
302-629-9755
rstetson@capps-assoc.com
www.capps-assoc.com/church.html

Like many mainstream churches, Seaford's Christ Lutheran Church is a direct descendent of ethnic believers who tried to preserve their homeland faith in a new environment. Although the American Lutherans, Association of Evangelical Lutheran Churches, and Lutheran Church in America merged in 1983, Missouri Lutherans maintain their own synod. A conservative entity, the congregation maintains Old World beliefs and traditions, including a hierarchical and legalistic formality.

BELIEFS

The Lutheran Church Missouri Synod is an outgrowth of American Lutheranism. Followers believe in the trinity—Father, Son, and Holy Spirit—and celebrate the sacraments of baptism, confirmation, communion, and holy matrimony. Doctrinal teachings follow Bible-based writings of Martin Luther, the German monk who launched the sixteenth-century reformation of Catholicism and translated the Vulgate Bible from Latin into German so all church members could bypass priests and read the Bible for themselves. As Lutheranism coalesced into a Protestant denomination, a simple creed summarized the sect: grace alone, scripture alone, faith alone. Fuller explanations exist in the *Lutheran Confessions* and *Luther's Small Catechism*.

Missouri Lutheranism resulted from German immigrants' seeking of a strong, unfettered church like those they left in the old country. The sect began on April 26, 1847, when 22 pastors representing 15 congregations traveled to Chicago by horseback, boat, and stage to discuss issues of faith. Representing the states of Illinois, Indiana, Iowa, Michigan, Missouri, Ohio, and New York, they signed a constitution that established the German Evangelical Lutheran Synod of Missouri, Ohio, and Other States. Their intentions were to start a mission to Native Americans and to other German immigrants. Late in the nineteenth century, home missions supported black southern Lutheran churches and created educational opportunities at black academies in Selma, Alabama, and Greensboro, North Carolina. During the civil rights struggles of the 1960s, a layman, UNC-Greensboro history professor Dr. Richard Bardolph, wrote "Civil Disobedience and the American Constitutional Order," which validated as worthy Christian acts a defiance of segregation and discrimination.

Alterations to the first Missouri Lutheran service began during World War I, when worshippers gave up writing and liturgy in German and adopted English. At the first centennial, the synod shortened its name to the current designation. Fifty years later, the synod numbered 2.6 million members in 6,145 congregations, which included newcomers speaking Spanish, Hmong, Eritrean, Russian, Finnish, Slovak, and Chinese. Seaford's Christ Lutheran Church, organized off Route 20, joined the synod in 1950 and serves Seaford, Blades, and surrounding Delaware and Maryland Communities. The community continues to support Christian education as a focus of the faith.

ACTIVITIES

Christ Lutheran Church offers standard Sunday school at 9:30 A.M. and worship at 11:00 A.M. The pastor serves Holy Communion on the first and third Sunday of the month. Staff and volunteers provide a nursery for small children.

> Sources: Ahlstrom 1972; Bishop and Darton 1987; Buchanan 1999; "Christ Lutheran Church"; Gentz 1973; Parrinder 1971; Smith 1994; Smith 1995; "What Do Lutherans Believe?" 1996; Wilson and Ferris 1989.

Christus Gardens
510 River Road
P.O. Box 587
Gatlinburg, Tennessee 37738
423-436-5155
FAX 423-436-5115
info@christusgardens.com
www.christusgardens.com/

A popular nondenominational religious theme park in the Great Smoky Mountains of Tennessee, Christus Gardens makes real the life of Jesus through life-size scenarios, floral and landscape displays, choral music, dramatic lighting, and narration. The park opened on August 14, 1960, as an alternative vacation and tour site for individuals, families, and groups seeking the sacred during their leisure time. In addition to artistic dioramas, the park features an heirloom Bible and biblical coin collections featuring a first-century shekel, widow's mite, and tribute penny plus original paintings depicting New Testament parables and the face of Jesus carved in a six-ton block of Carrara marble.

HISTORY

The creation of Christus Gardens derives from a plan of Ronald S. Ligon to coordinate the work of domestic and foreign crafters, artists, writers, musicians, landscapers, and laborers. Conceived during a bout with tuberculosis, the idea restored Ligon's despairing spirit and expressed his gratitude for renewed health in a permanent tribute that others could share. To gather material, he traveled 80,000 miles, touring hallowed grounds in Europe, Canada, and the United States. From curators, museum directors, medievalists, and teachers, he learned how to highlight details from biblical history.

At the Deroy Displays in Toronto, Ligon studied the wax figures of period dioramas. The Deroy family helped him plan set construction and background and select the best scenes for dramatization. In London, Gems, Ltd., provided the wax figures; B. J. Simmons, a large-scale wardrobe producer for the films *Ben Hur* and *Quo Vadis,* sewed costumes and headpieces. After Ligon chose Gatlinburg as the park's home, he hired resort designer Tom Windrom of Windrom, Haglund, and Venable in Memphis to create an impressive display of first-century walls and dwellings while preserving dignity and religious significance. To flesh out his park with light and sound, Ligon hired engineers to coordinate audio narration, music, sound, and lighting to establish mood and verisimilitude.

In 1998, the life-size, three-dimensional "Little Town of Bethlehem" display, lighted by expert Mark Pedro, became the most-viewed nativity scene in the world. Its main feature is the holy family—Mary, Joseph, and the Christ child. Designers captured the nativity story from the Gospel of Matthew in visiting magi offering gifts; the story from the Gospel of Luke depicts angels informing shepherds of the arrival of a messiah. Above the scene, the star of Bethlehem lights the montage of events marking Jesus' birth. The staff augmented the biblical focus with seasonal garlands, Christmas trees, and yuletide decorations.

ACTIVITIES

One block from the center of Gatlinburg, Christus Gardens is open year-round. The staff extends a biblical tour amid the changing colors and textures of a terraced landscape and patio garden over the four seasons. Plantings of crown of thorns bushes and orchids enliven spring visits.

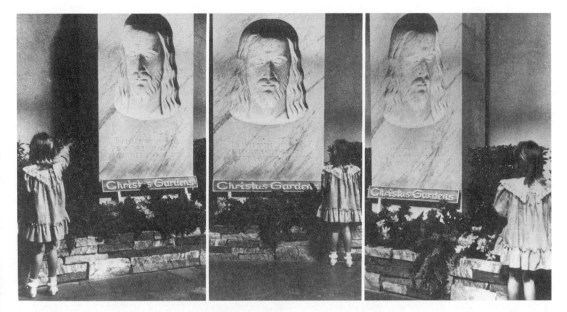

A popular nondenominational religious theme park in the Great Smoky Mountains of Tennessee, Christus Gardens makes real the life of Jesus through life-size scenarios. (Courtesy Christus Gardens)

At Easter, the staff lights a thirty-foot Christ in white beneath the proclamation "He is risen." In fall, the nearby Crockett Mountain adds a show of colored leaves to the display. Before, during, and after the Christmas season, Christus Gardens participates in the Gatlinburg Winterfest with an award-winning light display. The gardens are open to individuals and tour groups from April to October, 8:00 A.M. to 9:00 P.M. and, except for Christmas day, from 9:00 A.M. to 5:00 P.M. during winter months. A gift shop sells gift items, souvenirs, and photos of garden highlights.

Sources: "Christus Gardens"; "Gatlinburg Christmas Manger Light Display Wins Award" 1998; "Visit Bethlehem Now, Then" 1998; Williams, Peter W., 1997.

Church of Lukumi Babalu Aye

Oba Ernesto Pichardo
345 Palm Avenue
Hialeah, Florida 33010
305-887-1901
FAX 305-887-8998

The Church of Lukumi Babalu Aye has broken new ground in American worship by establishing a Santería center, Web site, and legal presence among third-world religions gaining credence in the Western Hemisphere. Predominantly among Hispanics, the Lukumi faith burgeoned in the late twentieth century in Cuba during a loosening of Communist anti-American dogma. In 1959, after dictator Fidel Castro's tyranny forced dissidents to flee Cuba, Santería spread across the Caribbean and North, Central, and South America. It thrives in Latino centers in the United States, notably New York, Miami, and Los Angeles.

HISTORY

Guided by the spirit and divinations of *orisha*, heavenly intermediaries, in 1974, Iyalosha Carmen Pla, Babalosha Raul Rodriguez, Oba Ernesto Pichardo, Babalosha Fernando Pichardo, and Gino Negretti founded the Church of Lukumi Babalu Aye. Four years later, the staff participated in a three-day conference with scholars and Catholic and Lukumi priests and conducted the first ordination at Oyo-Tunji African Village. The staff dedicated itself to academic research from 1979 through 1982 as the organization stabilized. In 1983, it launched the Institute for New World Studies. With funding from the Florida Endowment for the Humanities, the institute organized workshops for law

SANTERÍA

Santería, a traditional Yoruban faith, originated in Nigeria, where the faithful sacrificed goats, chickens, doves, pigeons, and turtles to agricultural gods and offered thanks for a full harvest. Worship incorporates propitiating *orishas,* or guardian deities, and cultivating the folk ways of the Yoruba and Bantu people of Southern Nigeria, Senegal, and the Guinea Coast. Called the Way of the Saints, the faith formalized when slaves pretended to ally with white owners' Catholicism but continued to practice their native religion in private. As a form of code, the Lukumi created a correspondence between Catholic saints and Yoruban deities:

• Saint Lazarus for Babalz Ayi, patron of the sick
• Saint Barbara for Shango, spirit of fire, thunder, and lightning
• Saint Anthony for Eleggua (or Elegba), spirit of roads and gates
• Saint Peter for Oggzn, the war deity
• Our Lady of Mercy for Obatala, the creator and source of spirituality
• Our Lady of Charity for Oshzn, controller of sensuality and money

The syncretism of Yoruban deities with Catholic saints produced the term Santería, a pejorative the Spanish sneered at peasants to ridicule their culture. The faithful preferred La Regla Lucumi (The Order of Lukumi), a more dignified term. In its current form, Santería unites in faith and ritual some 4 million, primarily Latinos in Florida, along the East Coast, and in the Far West. Essential to growth is a late-twentieth-century interest of black people in African faith, which their ancestors lost during the wrenching of blacks from their homeland into slavery.

The Lukumi venerate the supreme God Olorun, the lord of heaven and creator of the universe. They cultivate a relationship with the almighty through lesser guardians called *orishas.* Each *orisha* relates to a number, color, food, dance, gesture, and emblem. The *orisha* require sustenance in the form of praise, prepared dishes, and animal sacrifice. At the core of worship is the ritual slaughter of chickens and other animals and the collection of blood as a gift to the *orisha.* These ceremonies please the deities, and confer luck, purification, and forgiveness of sins. Other facets of worship unite the devout in drumming, ecstatic dance and rhythmic sounds as signs of possession, and veneration of ancestral guides, called Ara Orun or People of Heaven, whom families supplicate in private ceremonies. In lieu of written scripture, priests called *santeras/santeros* study Yoruban oral tradition, dance, songs, and healing methods.

enforcement, medical, and mental-health professionals on Afro-Caribbean religions.

In the mid-1980s, the church began gaining credence. It profited from a local ABC news series on Afro-Cuban worship and a PBS national documentary on Miami, which highlighted Santería. Educators assisted devotees by recognizing the needs of members. The Dade County School Board joined with representatives to study religious exemptions for newly ordained students; Dade Community College initiated courses on Afro-Caribbean religion. Public awareness grew from a presentation for the Florida Folklife Festival, a book, *Oduduwa,* and a Lukumi divination video, *Band on the Hand.* Simultaneously, the church set up a committee to develop a worship and education center and held courses on *bata* drums, divination, and Yoruba history.

In 1987, the Church of Lukumi Babalu Aye celebrated a preopening by implementing educational curriculum. One practitioner, Ernesto Pichardo, riled local critics by admitting that he had sacrificed thousands of animals in the course of worship. Within a year of their move to a church home, Lukumites relocated across from Hialeah City Hall, where vandalism and harassment were constant problems. Controversy mounted concerning the city ban on ritual animal sacrifice. The congregation contested a city prohibition of animal sacrifice and accepted the aid of the American Civil Liberties Union in a widely publicized conflict dubbed the "War of the Chickens." In June 1993, the U.S. Supreme Court overruled two lower court prohibitions of animal killing and declared unanimously that Lukumi ritual sacrifice was both humane and constitu-

The Afro-Caribbean Lukumi religion gained growing acceptance and awareness in America at the end of the twentieth century. (Courtesy of the Church of Lukumi Babalu Aye)

tionally sanctioned under the Bill of Rights. The court required the city to pay $500,000 in church legal fees; Mayor Julio Martinez submitted a symbolic $1 monetary compensation.

Clearing the air of legal problems invigorated the congregation. In 1995, the staff certified forty senior Ifa, Oriate, Iyalosha, and Babalosha priests and priestesses as clergy. A weekly radio program directed to Cuban Lukumi increased ties with the Caribbean. At a new address one block from the old location, staff performed its first marriage and infant-naming ceremonies and established a ministry to federal prisoners. Under the motto "Progress Is Our Religious Mission," the congregation, representing nineteen nationalities, increased its membership 125 percent from 1997 to 1998.

ACTIVITIES

The Church of Lukumi Babalu Aye intends to correct fallacious notions of African faiths. As a central union of clergy and worshippers, the church perpetuates African lineage through a range of services and programs. Its focus is ambitious:

- To maintain organization and character
- To increase longevity of an ancient faith
- To serve members' needs
- To preserve Lukumi ethics and morals

- To educate the congregation, clergy, and public

Central to Lukumi outreach is the establishment of its Hialeah center, where staff can hold sessions and officiate at ancestral worship ceremonies. General activities range from the study of supernatural phenomena and healing to thanksgiving and *bata* drumming. Crucial to a full-service church are performance of baptism and giving of the *ileke,* a protective necklace and also patron *orishas,* marriage, birth rites, ordination, and funeral rites. As an agent of the faith as taught by Ifa, the church certifies ordained members, preserves African culture and tribal order, and fights for religious freedom.

The creation of bilingual Web sites on Afro-Caribbean faith increases awareness of Santería's link to Yoruban oral tradition and Roman Catholicism. The site supports understanding among world religions but, as a means of defining Santería, differentiates between Cuban influence, Brazilian Candomble, and Haitian obeah, or voodoo. Also beneficial to individuals are support of members training for priesthood and a long-distance religious counseling service by phone, fax, or e-mail to Lukumites living far from a worship center.

> **Sources:** Cavendish 1970; "Church of the Lukumi Babalu Aye" 1999; Cohn and Kaplan 1994; Eck 1994; Francione and Charlton; Lewis 1998; Ramirez 2000; "Santeria"; "Santeria, La Regla Lucumi, Lakumi"; Zeinert 1997.

Church of Scientology Los Angeles
4810 West Sunset Boulevard
Los Angeles, California 90027-5910
323-953-3200
info@scientology.net
www.lronhubbard.org; www.scientology.org

New religions typically come under intense scrutiny and criticism from established faiths, especially when a new faith begins to erode a solid base of support for a longstanding religious community. Just as Santeríans, Shakers, Mormons, Seventh-Day Adventists, and Christian Scientists have undergone their initial critique, L. Ron Hubbard and the Church of Scientology

L. RON HUBBARD

L. Ron Hubbard is the unknown element of Scientology. He has written under a list of aliases—Winchester Remington Colt, Frederick Engelhardt, Tom Esterbrook, Michael Keith, Rene Lafayette, Ken Martin, B. A. Northrup, John Seabrook, and Kurt Von Rachen. Born Lafayette Ronald Hubbard in 1911 in Helena, Montana, he developed into a globetrotter, exploring and mapping the Caribbean and Pacific. On his peripatetic adventures, he flew stunt planes, composed music, sailed, made photos, wrote pulp science fiction, and developed methods of rehabilitating drug addicts. In the 1940s, he evolved Dianetics, an amalgamation of Eastern philosophy and modern psychology that he applied to mental health and the eradication of psychological malfunction.

After founding the Church of Scientology in 1954, Hubbard spread his mind-based religion globally and claimed 6 million converts. His first disciples came from university campuses and celebrities, including Lisa Marie Presley, Tom Cruise, Nicole Kidman, John Travolta, Robert Duvall, Kirstie Alley, Sonny Bono, Chick Corea, and Nancy Cartwright, the voice of cartoon figure Bart Simpson. Hubbard maintained research institutes and a demanding lecture schedule that spread his ideas among students and intellectuals. His continued evolution of religious and psychological beliefs resulted in questionable concepts of guilt derived from former lives and the invention of a lie and emotion detector known as an E-meter. To rid people of emotional scarring from events in current and past lives, he charged for auditing their situations and offered rehabilitative courses at exorbitant prices. By the 1970s, he had launched over 600 research groups, missions, and churches

worldwide and sold over 8 million copies of his psychology text *Dianetics: The Modern Science of Mental Health* (1950).

By the early 1980s, Hubbard was weighted down with controversy. Lawsuits filed by former members, convictions for burglary and wiretapping against his wife Mary Sue and ten staff members, and Internal Revenue investigations tarnished his reputation, leaving him open to criticisms of misapplying church revenue and suppressing critics through an internal secret-police system. Unrest among the staff cost him the loyalty of archivist and biographer Gerald Armstrong, who held incriminating documents revealing fraud and misrepresentation in Hubbard's past. Hubbard withdrew from society to his yacht, his residences in England, and a California ranch. In 1982, his son, Ronald DeWolf, announced that Hubbard had either died or lost his sanity. DeWolf petitioned a court to transfer $280 million in church funds to a trusteeship to prevent church officials from stealing his father's estate. The judge rejected DeWolf's claims and declared Hubbard living, sane, and responsible for his own dealings.

Hubbard resurfaced as the author of science fiction novels and topped contemporary sales figures with *Battlefield Earth: A Saga of the Year 3000* (1982). He began a ten-volume series, *Mission Earth*. On January 24, 1986, he died of stroke. Church authorities made the announcement after cremating his remains and scattering the ashes. The church inherited most of his estate. After years of wrangling with the IRS, the Church of Scientology lost its tax-exempt religious status in 1988. In five years, it regained its former status as a bona fide religion.

incurred the wrath of fundamentalist Christians as well as opponents of mind control and tax breaks for pseudoreligions. The founder's mysterious disappearance and death in 1986 left more questions concerning his sincerity and the intent of a church structure that violates the usual assumptions about worship, piety, fund-raising, and missions.

BELIEFS AND ACTIVITIES

Scientologists commit themselves to reforming and uplifting society both locally and world-

wide. Central to their methods are drug rehabilitation, improved literacy, environmental management, establishment of human rights, and compassion for the less fortunate. A popular project is the revitalization of cities through volunteer tutoring in basic skills education for youth and neighborhood programs aimed at bettering the lives of ordinary people of all races and ethnic and religious backgrounds. The Office of Ethnic and Cultural Affairs publishes a syndicated column of guidelines on educational reform and improving self-esteem. Columnists criticize police brutality and government abuse of minorities by exposing discrimination among IRS officials in major U.S. cities. "Lead the Way" antidrug campaigns and conferences apply Hubbard's psychological paradigm to the individual addict.

For general upgrading of health, Scientologists support the Red Cross, the Salvation Army, the Cerebral Palsy Association, the Cystic Fibrosis Foundation, drug-free blood drives, distribution of Toys for Tots to underprivileged children, drives for public television, emergency Food for All programs, Bryan's House for children stricken with AIDS, and Operation Caring to support the elderly. To stop the spread of crime, Scientologists foster a volunteer minister program outlined in Hubbard's *Scientology Handbook* (1976) to save troubled marriages, resolve community conflict, end gang warfare, promote literacy and study skills, and improve business prospects. To improve run-down neighborhoods, Scientologists promote recycling, park cleanup, tree planting, protection of wildlife, and graffiti removal.

> **Sources:** *American Decades* 1998; Atwal 1997; *Biography Resource Center* 1999; Black 1996; "The Church of Scientology"; *Encyclopedia of Occultism and Parapsychology* 1996; *Encyclopedia of World Biography* 1998; Johnson 1984; Mallia 1998; *Religious Leaders of America* 1999; Sappell and Welkos 1990; "Scientology in Your Community"; Zeinert 1997.

Church of the Blessed Sacrament
1945 Northampton Street
Holyoke, Massachusetts 01040
413-532-0713

One of New England's architectural rebels, the Church of the Blessed Sacrament is a model of decentralization. Designed after Vatican II liberalized church dogma, it houses worship in an octagonal structure under a disk-shaped roof, erected during a business and industry boom. The structure suits the tastes and mission of an innovative suburban congregation that separated from a parent church to bring religion closer to home. Central to the move was desire of parents for a phenomenon in American education—the Catholic parochial school, which, by the begin-ning of the twenty-first century, had achieved the most success in battling the decline in student attendance, discipline, and performance.

HISTORY

Holyoke's Church of the Blessed Sacrament dates to 1913 and a strong mandate from 150 Catholic families of the Elmwood section of town who worshiped at Sacred Heart Church. To bring faith closer to home, they left a crowded parish serving five other residential communities and formed a more localized church family. With concurrence from the priest, Father Patrick B. Phelan, the bishop approved the plan to divide the parish. He named Father John Lunny, a native of West Rutland, to pastor the Elmwood congregation, which met temporarily at Metcalf School auditorium and returned to Sacred Heart for sacramental ceremonies.

Blessed Sacrament enjoyed good fortune and steady growth. By 1914, the parish completed its first church home at Northampton and Hitchcock Streets and housed the minister in a newly purchased rectory. In 1923, trustees opened Blessed Sacrament School and enrolled 87 pupils in grades one through three. Continued success emboldened the congregation to house the four nun-schoolteachers in the rectory and move the pastor, Father Michael P. Kavanaugh, to a new rectory. After 1924, the staff added grades to the parochial school to complete grades one through eight. In 1931, Father Kavanaugh recommended the purchase of an estate from the Sisters of Providence.

The land remained untouched until 1951, when Father Daniel E. Hennessey, a spirited builder, laid the foundations for a sanctuary equal to the size and needs of his thriving parish. The design of the new sanctuary sprang from the modernism of Bishop Christopher Waldon of the Springfield diocese. He employed Waltham architect Charles F. Wright to build the round-roofed church, which was finished in 1953 and dedicated on Easter Sunday, with 4,000 attending five masses. An international success, the innovative layout, coupled with the liberalism of Pope John XXIII and Vatican II, sparked a number of innovative churches that broke free of the standard rectangular nave.

VATICAN II

In the last years of the five-year term of Pope John XXIII, the second Vatican Council moved away from the admonitory style of the past council to call for justice and attention to the world's physical and spiritual welfare. The pope's encyclical *Pacem in Terris* (Peace throughout the Lands) expounded a social philosophy that would address the hope of peace. To achieve his ideals, he initiated monumental changes in life and liturgy. Prominent among his revolution were the use of vernacular liturgy and incorporation of lay celebrants. He reached out to rival denominations with gestures of acceptance and tolerance and encouraged reconciliation with Jews. Less than a decade after the Holocaust, the pope made a surprising alteration of previous policy by declaring the church's regret for the results of rampant anti-Semitism.

The pope's articulation of joy in human faith extended to all humankind. In a move to humanize missions, he called for an end to coercive proselytizing. To renew and revitalize the faith, he promoted *Unitatis Redintegratio* (Restoration of Unity), an advancement toward ecumenism, which past popes had repudiated. To free the church from its history of rigidity concerning and prejudice against women, the uneducated, Eastern Orthodox Catholics, and non-Catholics, he called for an embrace of unity for all God's people. His energetic initiative allied professional and lay workers and missionaries in a common goal to witness to God's love.

ARCHITECTURE

Wright's sleek Church Around the World appropriates past architectural success by imitating Charlemagne's eight-sided chapel at Aix-la-Chapelle, which reflects the circular arrangement of the Roman Pantheon. His 850-seat sanctuary features a tan brick and limestone exterior trimmed in cypress and crowned with a smooth circle of concrete. To inject light into the nave, Wright pierced the roof with a skylight. An iron convector system regulates heating and cooling. A rectangular sixty-eight-foot freestanding chimney/bell tower arises to the right of center and features a simple cross attached to the front surface.

Wright combined drama with philosophy in his innovative design. By seating worshippers in white oak pews around the periphery and centering the service on a two-sided cross and three-foot Corpus Christi suspended by a chain over the marble altar, he illustrated the liberating influence of Vatican II, which attempted to modernize Roman Catholicism by shifting emphasis from liturgies from the Middle Ages to contemporary and future styles. Traditional symbolism of the alpha and omega on each side of a golden tabernacle complements the simple integrity of the arrangement, which emulates theater in the round.

Mid-twentieth-century technology enhances the worship experience at the Church of the Blessed Sacrament. The architect flush-lighted sixteen- by four-foot stained-glass windows, which illustrate the Eucharist. He added modern acoustical interiors to the confessionals and provided parents a glassed-in nursery with intercom. A contest determined the remaining designs. A committee selected Peter Paul Abbatte for his marble relief of the holy family, Theodore Barbarossa for an all-saints motif, and Bostonian Ernest E. Morenon to complete the stations of the cross.

ACTIVITIES

The Church of the Blessed Sacrament is open daily from 6:30 A.M. to 8:30 P.M. The staff holds a full schedule of services. The pastor celebrates Sunday mass four times in the morning, at 8:00, 9:15, 10:30, and 11:45. Congregants can attend mass on weekdays at 6:45 A.M. and 5:20 P.M. and on Saturday at 8:00 A.M. or later in the day at 4:00, 5:30, or 7:30. The success of the church education program is measured in part by the seventeen priests who grew up in local youth programs.

A vigorous church program involves the Sisters of St. Joseph, volunteers for the sick and elderly, scouting, and a charismatic prayer group. The parochial school keeps up its program of Christian values and academic preparation. Socials at the parish center invite parishioners and guests to musical variety shows, Irish Nights, Monte Carlo Nites, and Septemberfests. Annually in March since 1951, parishioners join in the city's two-mile Saint Patrick's Day parade, which draws over a quarter million spectators. Festivities include selection of a grand marshal and holiday "colleen," awarding of the Ambassador's Medal, and naming of an outstanding American of Irish descent, beginning with President John F. Kennedy.

Sources: "Blessed Sacrament: The Dream of Its People Remembered" 1988; "Blessed Sacrament School"; Boyle; Mutrux 1982; *New Catholic Encyclopedia* 1967.

Chuska Mountains
Diné CARE
P.O. Box 121
Tsaile, Arizona 86556

10A Town Plaza, Suite 138
Durango, Colorado 81301
303-259-0199
www.cnetco.com/~dinecare/

One of the hallowed sites treasured by Native Americans is the Chuska Mountains, an entrancing outdoor sanctuary. It is a source of sacred plants for Navajo medicine people and holy watering holes and is an offering place where members leave gifts of white shell, abalone, turquoise, and jet. According to Native American tradition, worshippers revere the range's rocks and trees as guardians and kin. Among old-growth ponderosa pines, a respected male deity that tribesman Ervin Redhouse calls "grandfather" trees, individuals pray to the source of life. As development and intrusion by non-Indians threaten the site, Indians fear that the spirits are deserting the area.

BELIEFS
Some seventy miles from the Arizona–New Mexico line near Tsaile, Arizona, the Chuska Mountains lie outside the reservation in a valued landscape bound by four sacred mountains: Sis na'jiin (Blanca Peak), Colorado; Tsoodzil (Mount Taylor), New Mexico; Dook'o'o sliid (San Francisco Peaks), Arizona; and Dibe'Butsaa (La Plata Mountains), Colorado. These spiritual borders encompass an arid red-rock landscape of buttes, domes, cones, reefs, natural arches and canyons, crags, and mesas where divinity dwells. The to-

pography serves as a living narrative, a fable in stone. Chuska is the male entity; Black Mesa is his mate. The balance they epitomize encompasses a universal harmony that gives and sustains life.

The origin of the Diné is found in the writings of ethnographers Washington Matthews, Aileen O'Bryan, Leland Wyman, and Paul Zolbrod. According to oral scripture recounted only in winter, the Navajo emerged from three underworlds through a magic reed. Creation began with the arrival of animals, insects, and masked spirits and proceeded to the arrival from the clouds of 'Altsé Hastiin (First Man) and 'Altsé 'Asdzáá (First Woman). At divine direction, they learned the art of weaving, sang the "Blessing Song," built a sweat house, and lived in a hogan. The sacred mountains inhabited by the Diyinii (Holy People) became the boundaries of their homeland. When evil spirits assaulted humankind, Changing Woman, wife of the sun, and her heroic twin sons, Monster Slayer and Child-Born-of-Water, rescued them.

HISTORY
The Chuska Mountains are a necessary part of tribal identity. For the Navajo to function, they regularly commune with Dinetah (Navajoland), which is vital to tribal welfare. To protect the mountains from desecration and the tribe from further fragmentation, the devout keep secret the sacred landscapes that restore spiritual health and allow them the privacy to perform rituals rooted in nature. At the heart of conflict with non-Indians over sacred geography is the aboriginal culture itself, in which religion and life form a single entity. To preserve an ethnic treasury, the Navajo defend the Chuska Mountains and their rights to history and continuity.

According to Navajo tribesman Earl Tulley, native people must honor the laws of nature. To protect the Chuska Mountains, the tradition-minded protest logging and other forms of commerce on hallowed land. The clash over making money on holy ground pits Anglo against Navajo and Navajo against Navajo over the aims of the Navajo Forest Products Industry (NFPI), a tribal enterprise instigated in 1958 by the tribe and the Bureau of Indian Affairs to bolster the native economy with jobs and income. Because the NFPI has overcut Chuska riparian zones, reduced the Mexican spotted owl population, and destroyed sacred sites, the issue of religious rights has threatened tribal harmony and unanimity.

Natives, led by Navajo Nation president Peterson Zah, fear a loss of balance already inflicted by Peabody Coal Company, which has mined Black Mesa since the 1970s. A Navajo initiative, Diné Citizens Against Ruining Our Environment (Diné CARE), cofounded by whistle-blower Leroy Jackson, opposes further damage from slash roads, dumping, and hazardous waste incineration. In 1991, the coalition demanded an objective environmental impact statement and an accounting of NFPI forestry practice. Following his testimony before the congressional committee on the American Indian Religious Freedom Act, in October 1993, Jackson was found dead in his van of a methadone overdose. Authorities, Jackson's widow, Adella Begaye, and friend Ervin Redhouse suspect opponents murdered him to intimidate Diné CARE members and suppress their activism.

ACTIVITIES

The Navajo value *nahagha'* (ritual) as an ongoing part of their society and an assurance of harmony. Their liturgy includes sixty major rites for blessing, purifying, and curing. During healing ceremonies, they sing and pray to the Holy People as restorers of health and reverence such natural phenomena as wind and corn. In traditional hogans built to the exacting ritual standards of Mother Earth and Father Sky, the Navajo perform daily religious observance of age-old ceremonies, such as the blessing way, the main stalk of their liturgy. To establish blessing, worshippers sing hogan songs that order work and ceremony and guard the home, birthing, weddings, health, property, harvests, and livestock.

The four sacred mountains form a cosmic hogan that shelters Navajoland. These solid symbols make up the life support of the Navajo world and channel heavenly energy to sustain life. As a practical matter, the Chuska Mountains supply essential building material, water, game, grazing land, and medicinal plants. The loss of conifers and the building of roads on sacred ground during the 1980s promoted land erosion

and challenged Navajo existence. To the devout, violation of the earth is a mark of arrogance and disrespect for divine gifts, which the Navajo must treasure and use with reverence and caution.

Sources: "American Natives and the Environment"; Atencio 1994; "Biogeographic Regions of Arizona"; "Black Mesa Area"; "Chuska Mountains"; "Dine CARE"; LaDuke 1994; Lapahie; "Navajoland"; Patterson and Snodgrass 1994; Rudner 1994; "Sacred Mountains As Geographical Markers."

Circle Sanctuary Nature Preserve
PSG, Circle Sanctuary
P.O. Box 219
Mt. Horeb, Wisconsin 53572
608-924-2216
FAX 608-924-5961
circle@mhtc.net
www.circlesanctuary.org

Paganism, the world's earliest form of worship, honors the elemental and primal forces of sun, rain, wind, fire, and earth. In a beneficent outdoor atmosphere, individual nature worshippers assemble to share a mystical communion. Paradoxically, reverence of the earth honors individuality among the devout at the same time that it creates a human unity within creation. A broad-based fellowship, ecospirituality welcomes animism, Celtic tradition, goddess worship, Native American ways, nature mysticism, paganism, pantheism, shamanism, Taoism, astrology, tarot, Nordic runes, and related forms of nature religions.

One of the most respected U.S. pagan groups, the Wiccans of Circle Sanctuary, follows a geocentric calendar:

- Green Sprig Gathering in midsummer
- Fall Equinox around September 23
- Samhain in Late October
- Yule in mid-December
- Candlemas early in February
- Welcome Spring around the spring equinox on March 21
- Earth Day in late April
- Beltane in early May
- Summer Solstice, the crowning festivity honoring June 23, the longest day of the year

At Circle Sanctuary Nature Preserve, paganism, the world's earliest form of worship, honors the elemental and primal forces of sun, rain, wind, fire, and earth. (Courtesy Circle Sanctuary Archive. Photo by Selena Fox)

In celebration of the longest day of the year, Circle Sanctuary holds a Pagan Spirit Gathering, one of the nation's oldest and largest nature spirituality festivals. To accommodate new and returning celebrants, the staff currently rents space at Wisteria Campgrounds, a center for American paganism. Camping in tents and recreational vehicles, celebrants circulate among old friends and form a temporary pagan community bound by respect for each other's traditions and the demands of a daily town meeting.

BELIEFS

Circle Sanctuary encourages paganism through a balanced program of personal growth and planetary well-being based on nature spirituality and a promotion of academic research, interfaith networking, multicultural exchange, and religious tolerance. Their mission calls for dialogue, cooperation, and beneficial networking among individuals. A wider circle of contacts results from publications, correspondence, Web sites, and telephone conversations and through publication of the quarterly *Circle Network News* and

other periodicals. The staff maintains consecrated land as a spiritual nature preserve on which they promote and share rituals, meditations, music, images, and spiritual art.

The work of ministers is an amalgam of counseling, healing, and liturgical services that marry, bless children, honor the dead, sanctify homes and the earth, and observe coming-of-age, croning (celebration of menopause), and other rites of passage. Ministers sponsor spirit gatherings and festivals over the seasonal calendar and hold additional workshops, talks, leadership training, and youth programs. Groups learn and share through Celtic concerts, drumming and storytelling, making altar boxes and Brigid wheels, harvesting sacred herbs, selling crafts, and conducting nature walks. Publication of books, tapes, and spiritual resources broadens their outreach, as does activism for religious freedom through the Lady Liberty League.

HISTORY

Although Wicca stems from a long history of animistic religious practices, the modern form,

Gardinarian Wicca, took shape in 1951 when Englishman Gerald Gardner revived the early coven and published *Witchcraft Today* (1954), a Wiccan handbook. Because of his scholarly approach to knowledge, England repealed its antiwitchcraft law and fostered free practice of sorcery. The law freed Wiccans from fear and the need for secrecy and made Gardner England's most famous witch. He operated a witchcraft museum on the Isle of Man and collected artifacts now owned by Cecil Williamson of Cornwall.

American awareness of Wicca dates to 1979, when Margot Adler wrote *Drawing Down the Moon: Witches, Druids, Goddess-Worshippers, and Other Pagans in America Today* and *The Spiral Dance by Starhawk*. Along with the rise of feminism and environmentalism, the books precipitated a flood of publications and manufactured paraphernalia and the growth in practitioners to over 40,000. Witches such as Leo Martello mitigated the fearful history of witchcraft by broadcasting a simple, nonthreatening definition: that Wicca propitiates and directs nature's power to improve human lives.

Four years before the cult gained acceptance and popularity, psychologist Selena Fox established Circle Sanctuary in Madison, Wisconsin, and joined Jim Alan in the first Sabbat gathering at their home. Within a year, they rented a farm outside Sun Prairie and dedicated a ritual room on the ground floor of the farmhouse before establishing archives, a library, and an outdoor ritual circle. Fox welcomed the public through lectures and a WORT-FM broadcast on paganism, parapsychology, metaphysics, spiritual healing, and consciousness exploration entitled *Circle Magic*. She and Alan expanded to plains states presentations and ritual and formation of the Circle Coven, a unification of Wiccans and pagans in traditional Latvian pagan liturgy. In 1977, Circle Sanctuary published *Circle Magic Songs*, an illustrated miscellany of songs, articles, chants, and illustrations. That same year, the staff initiated a Pan Pagan Festival at an Indiana campground.

Alan and Fox quickly made Wiccan history. In 1978, when Selena Fox advanced to full-time minister, Circle Sanctuary became the Church of Circle Wicca, an incorporated Wiccan sanctuary, by shifting from coven to mainstream church structure supported by ordained ministers, a board of directors, and affiliated covens and practitioners. They issued an audio cassette, *Circle Magick Music*, the first taped album of pagan ritual, and inaugurated a television show, *The Magic Circle Show*, a variety program offering advice on holistic health, inner development, and pagan spirituality.

The emerging faith caught the attention of *American* magazine, which published an article on the 1979 Pan Pagan Festival. After eviction from the Sun Prairie farm, the founders searched for land for permanent headquarters. A PBS documentary and a 1980 interview on the *Today* show introduced Circle Sanctuary as a federally recognized church. Networking of the Pagan Spirit Alliance expanded awareness through a quarterly newspaper for pagans, an International Pagan Spirit Gathering, and a meditation tape, *Magical Journeys*. Resituated outside Black Earth, Wisconsin, the circle offers diversified events at a secluded hill preserve. By 1983, it found a permanent home in southwestern Wisconsin at Mt. Horeb and took the name Circle Sanctuary. Subsequent breakthroughs in pagan worship include a school for priestesses, propagation of sacred herbs, interfaith recognition, an academic network, and victories over prejudicial zoning and the demonizing of witchcraft on commercial television.

Charlene Suggs, editor of *Circle Network News*, recalled her initiation into pagan spirituality and the life-shaping experience of the Summer Solstice festival. She described the pagan community as a long-lost family. In 1997, she cofounded Wisteria, a land-based Wiccan center in southern Ohio, and helped to relocate the summer gathering to a new site to accommodate booths, drummers, and campers. Situated in the heart of 620 rural acres, the improved locale places drummers near the bonfire and provides site services and support for the gathering.

Within the tent city, the Wisteria staff built the first sacred mound, where celebrants sang, chanted, and entwined rich, ancient harmonies. Freed from routine and busy lives, each communed with a magical and sacred space and imagined improving collective selves and the world at large by willing an altered consciousness. Key to their dream was nature's guidance. In an atmosphere of trust and shared customs, individuals sought the divine through altered consciousness and explored their own consciousness and sensory perceptions while assessing their lives and strengthening their understanding of peaceful coexistence.

ACTIVITIES

Begun in 1981, the week-long Summer Solstice festival convenes hundreds of Wiccan practitioners and guests from the United States and other countries for fellowship, communion with nature, and observance of the summer solstice. To assure individual well-being, Circle facilitators staff a twenty-four-hour counseling center and safety/medical center as well as an information booth. Childcare unites small fry in crafts, sandbox play, and frolics at the water sprinkler. Overall, the annual gathering offers personal and cultural enrichment.

According to high priestess Selena Fox, she and seven others began constructing a ceremonial circle at Yule of 1983 following sighting of a light in the north sky at Samhain, a shamanic Wiccan ritual held the previous Halloween. Situated on a natural oak- and birch-sheltered knoll called Ritual Mound, the circle disclosed a sacred gateway to the spirit world. Construction took place in heavy snow. It began with the centering of an altar stone, which builders transported from a stone circle near Sun Prairie, Wisconsin. Gradual addition of smaller stones produced a fire ring, where the group honored the winter solstice.

The circle did its work by drawing others to its sanctity. The next spring and summer, more celebrants added stones to quarter cairns until they had imported several thousand pebbles, rocks, boulders, and crystals along with amulets, coins, fossils, feathers, beads, and shells. The offerings come from hallowed places around the world—masonry from the Berlin Wall, copper from the Statue of Liberty, and a shard from ancient Crete. Contributors accompanied each addition with prayer, meditation, or blessing for earth's well-being.

By fall 1984, the builders had to enlarge and realign the circle to accommodate more people. Before Yule of 1985, celebrants dedicated the circle to the earth mother as a center for planetary healing. They acknowledged seven directions, beginning with north for earth and denoting air at the east, fire at the south, and water at the western point. The point above center stands for the cosmos, below for the planet; the center itself represents the spirit. The circle remained in continuous use for individual rites, quests and vigils, handfastings (ritual betrothals), infant blessing, rites of passage, memorials, Sabbat, the fall equinox, Earth Day, and moon ceremonies. Activities were usually closed to the press.

The all-embracing fire ritual blends ancient and current practice. In the style of Celtic, Teutonic, Baltic, Roman, and Greek pagans, the sacred hearth requires oak wood and the ashes and charred wood from the previous year's bonfire to create continuity with the past. Traditionalists add dried stalks of mugwort, the common name for *Artemisia vulgaris,* which has long been the sacred herb of the solstice ceremony. On opening night, the fire keeping crew kindles a flame as the community sways to the chant. A high point of the kindling is the addition of a pine bough wreath from the previous Yule to commemorate a half turn of the Wheel of the Year.

Coordinators of the festival encircle the embers to cast on dried herbs to bless and strengthen the community. The fire keeper maintains the flame through all weather and may shelter it with a canopy during rain. In the spirit of sharing, celebrants toss on dried flowers, sweet herbs, paper talismans, and spiritual offerings. Others scry (divine) at the fireside and seek spiritual guidance by grounding, a physical contact with earth. Out of respect for holy grounds and spiritual forces, no one throws trash into the fire, which is the source of later rituals, meditation, and healing.

On Solstice Eve, celebrants hold a sacred fire vigil through the night and welcome sunrise on the longest day of the year, a turning point in time. They give thanks, part from the fire on the final morning, and then extinguish the flame in a closing ritual. When the ashes cool, the fire keeper collects them along with charred wood for the next year's flame. Others save bits to bless their own hearths and commemorate a global culture that members carry with them the rest of the year.

Opening day begins with greetings and setting up camp as participants form a week-long pagan town. During initiation, celebrants ignite the sacred fire in the main ceremonial area and keep it burning as a symbol of the sun and festival spirit. New priestesses bless suppliants. Participants mill about informally or attend rituals, workshops, concerts, and programs. In addition to networking, organizers schedule leadership training, youth activities, scholarly presentations, discussions, and bonfire drumming and dancing. The campground marketplace sells food and beverages, apparel, jewelry, ritual tools and drums, pottery, books, and recordings from a wide span of artisans and vendors. A Web site posts the festival brochure.

Pagans, who come together at the sound of the drum to plan the day's activities, scatter to the sacred fire and peripheral bonfires for fireside dancing and drumming. At Wisteria, a large bonfire circle mirrors the main ritual circle. This additional space encompasses ecstatic dancing and nightly drumming. Participants alternate style, speed, and intensity of rhythms; they chant, sing, and rejoice with tambourines, rattles, zills (finger cymbals), flutes, and bells to accompany trance, circle, and ribbon dances.

The reverence for flame serves a variety of worship needs. Fires at workshops and informal gatherings preface shamanic journeys, child blessings, handfasting, coming-of-age rites, rites of passage, women's mysteries, and consecration rites. At the sweat lodge, celebrants warm stones to create sacred heat as part of a vision quest. Elders, shamans, and pipe carriers supervise ritual according to tribal dictates. In each session, a fire keeper feeds the flame and protects the lodge. After a ceremony, the vision seeker may savor the afterglow and reflect on its import to healing and spiritual transformation.

Creative aspects of the festival unite numerous talents. Potters hold clay sculpture workshops, where participants mold divine images and symbols, bowls, pentacles, and altar pieces and fire them in a ritual pit. Amethyst Circle, a drug- and alcohol-free camp, hosts meetings and socials for recovering addicts. On the Town Green commons, embers from the sacred fire kindle the morning fire before each day's meditation, drumming, music, and communal news.

Occasional fireworks and luminarias vary the theme of fire, as do torchlit concerts, storytelling, and performances on the festival stage.

A traditional spectacle, the initial candlelight procession, begins at twilight with celebrants garbed for ritual. Each bears a lighted candle in a lantern or covered holder and proceeds through the grounds to the center for a circling amid flickering lights, which dispel darkness. A merged emblem of individuality and unity, the service connects celebrants to an age-old religious and cultural practice. It ends with ignited sparklers and with wishes and blessings.

In 1997, the festival launched the Seven Circuit Labyrinth, a candle maze formed by floating a thousand votive candles in cups arranged in a labyrinth of a type dating to ancient Crete. Held at twilight, the gracious rite precedes instrumental music and the giving of honor and blessing to the holy space. During the next hours, individuals silently follow the path from the gateway to the center to calm, energize, and transform the spirit. At the core, the most sacred point, they pause before retracing their steps.

Each evening, flame consumes the dark. Members illuminate campsites, the center, and paths with twilight fires. Facilitators welcome the night by lighting tiki torches at roadsides, altars, stages, and ritual sites. Merchants light lamps in their booths; celebrants ignite votive candles, lamps, fire rings, and individual altars and shrines. The camp values fire as a source of warming and cooking food and beverages and as light for private worship, evening activities, singing, and merrymaking. The combined effect links the festival to a time when the hearth was integral to family life.

Sources: Adler 1979; Eck 1994; Fox 1998, 1999; "A History of Circle Sanctuary"; "The History of Wicca"; "International Spirit Gathering"; Niebuhr (b) 1999; Suggs 1999; Zeinert 1997.

Congregation Beth Yeshua
Rabbi David Chernoff
7501 Haverford Avenue
Philadelphia, Pennsylvania 19151
215-477-2706
info@cby.org
www.cby.org

In an era of pluralistic religious movements, the growing messianic drive of American Jews has stirred dissension and hope, depending on the point of view. Greater Philadelphia's Congregation Beth Yeshua—literally, House of Jesus—led an Atlantic coast groundswell of rededication to an anticipated messiah. The faithful identify Jesus of Nazareth as the promised one the prophet Isaiah specified from the house of David in the Torah: "And there shall come forth a rod out of the stem of Jesse, and a Branch shall grow out of his roots." (11:1) In fervent charismatic services, worshippers sway, invoke the Holy Spirit, and sing their faith in a message of imminent salvation in an apocalyptic era.

BELIEFS

Messianic Jews who are experiencing a spiritual renaissance are adding to their traditional faith rather than subtracting from it. They accept the Bible—the Old and New Testament—as infallible and divinely inspired and regard the prophecies of Isaiah, Micah, and Zechariah and three of the Psalms as evidence of the Savior's authenticity. They venerate one God, who manifests himself as Father, Son, and Holy Spirit. In defining Yeshua, they regard as true his conception and virgin birth, pure life, miracles, atoning death, and physical resurrection and ascendence into heaven. They envision him sitting alongside the Father, Yahweh, the same God who spoke to Moses from the burning bush and led the Hebrews out of bondage in Egypt.

The name Yeshua the devout equate with *moshiach* (anointed) and salvation. Most important, messianic Jews anticipate Yeshua's glorious return to rescue sinful humanity and condemn unbelievers. In acknowledgement of their history, Yeshuans maintain practice and unity with Jews. They describe gentiles as grafts on the Jewish olive tree, which grows from one root, much as Isaiah predicted that Jesus would be born of Jesse's root.

HISTORY

Messianic Judaism began late at a peaceful moment in the nineteenth century with the conversion of Joseph Rabinowitz, a Russian Jew who reclaimed Yeshua on the Mount of Olives. Under his leadership, the first Jewish Christian synagogue formed in Kishinev, Moldavia, a historic commercial town near Odessa that suffered tsarist pogroms in April 1903. Mark Levy, an English Jew, bore Rabinowitz's vision to New York City. The move was formalized in April 1915 with the founding of the Hebrew Christian Alliance (HCA). Within a decade, the organization spread globally as the International HCA.

Current American messianic Judaism got its start at the climactic moment in January 1967. Five months before the Six-Day War and the Jews' reclaiming of Jerusalem, Louis Kaplan, a former Assemblies of God evangelist and healer from New York City, predicted that the Jews would restore the sanctity of their capital and reclaim the messiah. After his first prophecy came true, he initiated a Phoenix radio program, *Jewish Voice Broadcasts,* to spread a messianic Jewish faith. By 1978, he had augmented radio with the *Jewish TV Broadcast,* the nation's first messianic Jewish series. Aided by his wife, Chira, he continues his ministry over 125 stations.

Pioneered in Philadelphia by Martin and Yohanna Chernoff, a messianic Jewish circle began meeting in their home in the late 1960s to refresh ancient beliefs in the coming of a savior. Their philosophy directed them away from assimilation into Christian sects toward a renewal of traditional heritage and its unique history and practice. In 1970, Martin Chernoff experienced a vision of a banner lauding messianic Judaism. Inspired, he joined with other believers to draft a creed delineating devotion to Yeshua as the messiah. The statement linked Jewish destiny with a singular vision of the Savior, his lifestyle, followers, holidays, culture, and customs. Based on the sacrifice and earthly return of Jesus, the messianic faith still celebrates the biblical Hanukkah rather than nonscriptural Christmas, Pesach rather than Easter, the Sabbath rather than Sunday.

After 1970, the Chernoffs led a legally incorporated congregation, Beth Messiah, the nation's first indigenous messianic Jewish congregation. Their son Joel embraced the faith and organized a global spiritual ministry. Under his influence, Jews leaped into demonstrative praise and repentance lasting for hours. For the next decade, while Susan Perlman and Moishe Rosen were establishing Jews for Jesus in San Francisco, Joel

Chernoff studied scripture and joined Rick Coghill in forming Lamb, a pop vocal group producing acoustic versions of ancient Jewish music.

In 1989, the barring of messianic Jews from entry into Israel and subsequent confiscation of messianic literature from the mails forced Joel Chernoff from his apolitical stance to activism. He resolved to organize American messianic Jews into a recognized religious force. Among the splinter group's outreach are efforts to supply Israel with physical relief as proof of sincere commitment to Judaism. Chernoff also expresses the repugnance of Jews toward joining repressive Christians, who have historically vilified and tormented Jews as Christ killers.

Rabbi David Chernoff, leader of Congregation Beth Yeshua, worked toward a formal organization of the messianic congregation, which he named the International Alliance of Messianic Congregations and Synagogues. Its 100 member congregations train young Jews at yeshivahs, or Torah schools, and ordain their leaders.

ACTIVITIES

To separate messianic Jews from gentiles, the 400 members of Congregation Beth Yeshua accept their faith as a revival of prophecy that has lain dormant for eighteen centuries. To establish cultural context, they maintain familiar artifacts, focusing on the ark and Torah rather than a crèche or a cross, a symbol of torment that has rallied Christians to the Crusades, Inquisition, pogroms, genocide, and recent acts of anti-Semitic vandalism and terrorism. Instead of assuming the trappings of Christianity, they maintain a strict interpretation of the First Commandment, which prohibits God's people from manufacturing and venerating idols.

Among some 350 messianic groups worldwide, Beth Yeshuans greet Friday night and Saturday morning services with joy and celebration. Adults and children link arms for the traditional hora, a Middle Eastern circle dance. A welcoming committee greets newcomers at the door with traditional tallit (prayer shawl) and kippa or kippot (ritual cap or head-covering). More like Pentecostals than Jews, worshippers belt out Jewish songs tinged with Hebrew and Middle Eastern allusions. Sermons speak of the Christian cross as a tree of sacrifice and recall the mission of Rabbi Shaul, the Jewish Saul who accepted Christ and became the apostle Paul, founder of the Christian church. Temple ministers pray for and support missions in Jerusalem, Haifa, Tel Aviv, and Tiberias. Members popularize the Chassidic Hebrew and English songs performed by Kol Simcha, a singing group that has toured Russia, Europe, and the United States.

In revival services held from October through November 1996, Beth Yeshua's messianic Jews mingled with fundamentalist Christians of many races from 100 churches during four weeks of interchurch evangelism and renewal. Campaigns across the Delaware Valley brought varied devotees together for reconciliation and healing. In Philadelphia, a transdenominational series entitled "30 Days of Gathering Around Jesus" united 2,000 white suburbanites with Pastor Benjamin Smith and 9,000 black members of the Deliverance Evangelistic Church from a gang-riddled residential section at sessions led by charismatic preacher Randy Clark of Vineyard Christian Fellowship in St. Louis. He prefaced the campaign with claims that religion must renew cities because education, government, and the police can't.

In July 1998, 41,000 men assembled in Philadelphia's Veterans Stadium for a rally of Promise Keepers, a Christ-centered ministry begun in 1991 to unite males in a return to godliness and family commitment. Rabbi David Chernoff joined Christian speakers and performers in delivering an inspirational call to atone for sins and renew their lives. He honored Israel's Jubilee, its fiftieth anniversary as a sovereign state, and exhorted messianic Jews to condemn anti-Semitism.

Sources: Cassidy 1996; Cohen 1998; "Congregation Beth Yeshua" 1999; Eliade 1987; Mellskog 1999; "More Than 41,000 Flock to Veterans Stadium" 1998; "Outpouring of Repentence" 1997; "Revival Briefs" 1998; Thomas 1996, 1998.

Crater Lake
Crater Lake National Park
P.O. Box 7
Crater Lake, Oregon 97604
541-594-2211 ext. 402
TDD 541-594-2261

To the Umpqua, Takelma, Molala, and Maklak (or Maqlaq) of Oregon, local legends about Crater Lake parallel geologic history of the destruction of Mount Mazama. (Courtesy National Park Service)

The deepest lake in North America, Crater Lake is a magically crystal-blue ring of water in the Cascade Range of southwestern Oregon. A nearly perfect circle six miles in diameter, it is all that is left of Mount Mazama, a Pleistocene stratovolcanic cluster that once stood 12,000 feet high around 5700 B.C., when it erupted. When the unrestrained molten rock drained into underground fissures, the force of imploding rock left only the base, which formed a caldera, the Spanish term for "kettle." One remnant of the blast, Wizard Island, poked above the lake within a few hundred years of the cataclysm and perches in the sapphire circle like a floating mirage.

The nature-made bowl is valuable for its uniqueness. Its waters are so clear that moss thrives on filtered sunlight as deep as 425 feet. To vacationers, the 250-square-mile park offers a wide choice of activities for the hiker, canoer, photographer, and camper. To the Klamath, a culture adapted to marshes, lakes, and rivers, the lake and its 26-mile shore were once a source of rainbow trout and *wokas* (pond-lily seeds), staples of their diet. In 1923, ethnographer Edward S. Curtis photographed a Klamath chief dressed in deerskin and feathered bonnet in deep contemplation of the lake waters below.

Because the lake has no natural drain, it symbolizes a perfect microcosm. In the Klamath cosmology, the crater is the center of the universe, the source of all being.

BELIEFS

To the Umpqua, Takelma, Molala, and Maklak (or Maqlaq), Crater Lake's aborigines and ancestors of the Klamath, local legends parallel the geologic history of the destruction of Mount Mazama. Along with archeological artifacts, the Maklak version proves that they witnessed the demise of Mount Mazama, the entrance to a lower spirit world. Traumatized, they turned the terrifying event into mythic narrative. In the poetic version, Chief Llao (or Llal) of the Underworld climbed to earth and courted an Indian maiden, the daughter of a chief. Because she rejected his offer of a lasting haven below ground, he threatened to annihilate the tribe with a fire storm. Chief Skell of the Surface World overheard Llao's hard-hearted wooing and intervened. Atop Mount Shasta a hundred miles south in northern California, he squared off against Llao for a decisive duel.

Mythologist Ella E. Clark compiled significant Crater Lake lore about combatants Llao and Skell from four sources: William G. Steel's *The Mountains of Oregon* (1890), William M. Colvig's unpublished manuscript "The Legend of Crater Lake" (1892), Moray L. Applegate's unpublished manuscript "A Legend of Crater Lake" (February 13, 1898), and O. C. Applegate's "The Klamath Legend of La-o" in *Steel Points* (January 1907). The battle consisted of volleys of molten rock, which touched off landslides and shudders deep into the soil. All humankind fled to Klamath Lake except for two tribal sages, who leaped into the fiery pit as an offering to placate the angry God. Skell saw their sacrifice and destroyed Chief Llao's subterranean home, driving him into the earth's core.

In time, the cataclysm evolved into a blessing. When human dwellers returned, they found the mountain gone and the great battleground transformed into a vast hole. After the hole filled with rain, the people named it Lake of Blue Waters, a holy basin in which they purifed their bodies and absorbed the spirit of the nether world. All that remains of Llao is a rock bearing his name. Skell survives in the landmark known as Skell Head.

HISTORY

Crater Lake evidences the extreme pressure at the earth's core, which burst into a shower of flame, ash, dust, and pumice. The cinder produced by an ancient eruption formed cones on the caldera floor, which lies 1,932 feet below the surface. Archeologists have located pumice from the sacred remains of Mount Mazama in caves inhabited by the Maklak. The Klamath were frequent visitors to the lake, perhaps to view its hallowed environs from the safety of Mount Scott or make a pilgrimage to the cave they considered the birthing chamber of humanity. Until the coming of whites, they were the sole stewards of the edenic blue circle. To preserve the lake's sanctity, the Klamath kept its existence a secret.

The white world learned of the unnamed lake on June 12, 1853, when treasure hunters John Wesley Hillman, Henry Klippel, and Isaac Skeeters left Yreka, California, to explore potential gold fields in Oregon. At the top of the encircling mountains, they looked down on the mythic bowl that Skeeters named Deep Blue Lake. Hillman recorded in his journal, "Not until my mule stopped within a few feet of the rim . . . did I look down, and if I had been riding a blind mule I firmly believe I would have ridden over the ledge to death." (Bennett 1975, 310) Without further investigation, the prospectors moved on. Nine years later, Chauncy Nye led a party of Oregon miners to the same region. In the first published account for the Jacksonville, Oregon, *Sentinel,* he described the mystic clear waters, which he dubbed Blue Lake.

Although 50 to 70 feet of snow annually impedes traffic, the establishment of Fort Klamath and subsequent road building returned Crater Lake to public attention. On August 1, 1865, part of a road crew rediscovered the circle of water. Sergeant Orsen Stearns and Captain F. B. Sprague, the first white visitors to walk its shore, proposed the name Lake Majesty. When newsman Jim Sutton brought a study group in June 1969, he crossed the lake by boat. In August, some of his men examined the cinder cone that formed Wizard Island. When Sutton composed an article, he became the first to use the name Crater Lake.

One viewer of the sylvan setting was moved to preserve its purity. In 1870, Ohio-born publisher and activist William Gladstone Steel was intrigued by news stories of the lake and began a long process of conservation, to which he pledged his time and wealth. In 1886, he joined a U.S. geological team of lake surveyors and cartographers and named Llao Rock, Skell Head, and Wizard Island. Captain Clarence Dutton, head of operations, traversed the lake in the *Cleetwood,* a boat equipped with a trailing coil of wire to measure depths. His findings were surprisingly accurate—64 feet over the sonar printout of 1959, which recorded a maximum of 1,932 feet.

Steel's proposed public park was not without opposition. Local herders, timbermen, and miners rejected federal interference. He gained local support by forming the Oregon Alpine Club, a forerunner of John Muir's Sierra Club. In addition, Steel wrote scholarly articles, held mountain-climbing outings, and petitioned Secretary of the Interior Lucius Q. C. Lamar to ask President Grover Cleveland to halt sale of area land to developers and individuals. By 1893, Cleveland made the lake a part of the Cascade Range Forest Reserve, the beginning of permanent rescue from exploitation, grazing, and campfires. On May 22, 1902, President Theodore Roosevelt assured the lake's future as a public property by granting national park status. Crater Lake Lodge began receiving tourists in 1915; Rim Drive, a 33-mile circuit around the lake, opened in 1918.

ACTIVITIES

Protection of hallowed and natural wonders and recreational sites is ongoing. In 1994, forty-four forest fires endangered Crater Lake National Park. Fortunately, the loss was minimal. One of the fires, called the Agee Fire, was so isolated that rangers searched the tree canopy on successive afternoons before concluding that the source of smoke lay on the southwest slope of Crater Peak. The area is so dense that investigation proved them wrong by a mile and a half. The fire was actually devouring hemlock and fir along East Fork Annie Creek, much closer to headquarters on Rim Drive than any of the other fires. It required eight weeks of work to contain and extinguish the blaze. As is the case with spontaneous forest fire, the Agee Fire thinned out saplings to make way for sustained growth of larger trees, more sunlight on undergrowth, and less deadwood to fuel a more devastating wildfire.

Today, people from across the globe come to the Crater Lake volcanic depression to study its exhibits and view many-colored lava walls ranging upward from 500 to 2,000 feet and photograph Wizard Island and its satellite, Phantom Ship. The park offers the hardy a wide choice of sites within the central Sierra Nevadas—the popular Sinnett Memorial Overlook, Castle Crest Wildflower Garden, Pumice Desert, Desert Cone, Red Cone, Timber Crater, and Pinnacles, a bed of spiky pumice deposits eroded by fumaroles, or gas vents. Visitors enjoy the park's natural inhabitants—hawks and owls, grouse and songbirds, deer, bear, and small mammals. Within the circle of pine and fir stands live varied fish, songbirds, mosses, and delicate lupines and monkey flowers. The mystic loveliness of the park's confines retains its hold on Native Americans. Some avoid casual contact with the lake, which

they reserve as a cosmic mystery great enough to swallow an entire mountain.

> **Sources:** Bennett 1975; "Crater Lake National Park"; "Crater Lake National Park History"; "Crater Lake, Oregon"; Curtis 1996; "Klamath Tribes History"; Mack; Milne 1995; "Mount Mazama Volcano and Crater Lake"; "Nature Notes from Crater Lake" 1995; Steiger 1974.

Crazy Horse Memorial
See Black Hills.

Crossroads Community Church of Hyde Park
Brian Tome, Senior Pastor
3322 Erie Avenue
Cincinnati, Ohio 45208
513-871-5480
www.crossroadshp.org/

Part of a growing antiorthodox, antidogma phenomenon of late-twentieth-century religious life, east Cincinnati's Crossroads Community Church is an interdenominational suburban fellowship that has disencumbered itself of excess historical and doctrinal baggage. Members dedicate themselves to the relevance of God to real life. Without steeples, hymnals, organ, or stained glass, the fellowship meets at a community school and holds to a belief that God's people shouldn't have to abandon music, humor, and other things they enjoy.

Originally burdened with contemporary troubles, the congregation has known divorce, single-parent families, religious pluralism, moral relativism, and distrust and has altered its focus from blame to comfort and uplift. Through innovative programming that releases them from legalism and guilt, the start-up church encourages singles and young families to experience a positive faith free of doctrinal hairsplitting. The result is an enthusiastic street-level organization that centers its thought and planning on local tastes and needs.

BELIEFS

The outgrowth of a circle of friends, Crossroads Community Church, like the original followers of Christ, stresses informality and curiosity about God. Services sandwich in up-to-date music among practical messages and opportunities for an authentic relationship with God. Since forming in 1996, the group enumerated its own sectarian beliefs:

- Worship based on the sixty-six books of the Old and New Testament as the inspired, inerrant word of God composed by chosen people and reflecting the background, style, and vocabulary of human writers
- Acceptance of one God, creator and compassionate and loving lord of everything, infinitely perfect, all powerful, all knowing, and eternally existent in the Father, Son, and Holy Spirit, who hears and answers prayer and saves believers from sin and eternal death
- Organization of a church body to reach unbelievers and provide fellowship and outlets for Christians and to observe the ordinances of baptism and communion

In a search for excellence, Crossroads founders expect great things of their church for the benefit of greater Hyde Park. They seek divine will through prayer and trust and extend life-changing evangelism, ministry, forgiveness, and teaching to the unchurched. To update their message, they remain culturally relevant and doctrinally pure and follow a diverse leadership varying in age, sex, ethnic background, and marital status. Programming focuses on small-group relationship as a seedbed of faith and promotes personal holiness through accountability, confession, Bible study, and prayer.

HISTORY

Organized on March 24, 1996, Crossroads Community Church began with informal discussion and Bible study by eight friends in fall 1994. Non-church-going friends reported that they were bored by formal worship, uncomfortable among nosy or judgmental members, and angered by guilt trips and constant demands for money. After consultation with local pastors, the founders met in winter 1994–1995 to explore the possibility of starting an experimental church. Eleven members made the core commitment to the Hyde Park Church plant and spent spring 1995 assessing group talents and personalities.

Before formal organization, trustees completed a vision statement as they relinquished leadership roles at local churches. In May 1995, the pastoral search team began a canvass; five founders attended the Willow Creek Leadership Conference. By June, they elected leaders and directors and published a consensus of vision and strategy. Formal worship began in July with Sunday evening prayers and Wednesday evening council meetings. By August, they could define a permanent ministry. The next month, they accepted Brian Tome as senior pastor and guaranteed a year's salary. In November, after his move from Pittsburgh, he initiated "Seven Habits of Highly Biblical Churches," a study of core values.

Before Easter, without funds from a mother church or denomination, founders pooled a start-up treasury to cover equipment and advertising costs and mailed 17,000 fliers to neighbors. On Founder's Day, March 24, 1996, they welcomed 450 attendees to the church's inaugural 11:00 A.M. service at Clark Montessori School auditorium. Most were young gen-Xers turned off by traditional organized worship sources and styles. They sought validation at sanctuaries that welcomed jeans and sneakers. On subsequent Sundays, attendance ranged from 230 to 350. In May, the core group launched the Inquirer's Class, a four-week session on philosophy aimed at seekers and the unchurched.

Subsequent years have seen a steady list of Crossroads firsts. The first baptism brought 7 people into the Christian faith. In November 1996, the congregaton hired Brian Wells as associate pastor and developer of small groups. The unified body grew to 200 by 1997. In March 1997, the church initiated a day of prayer and week of fasting and added a 9:30 A.M. service to the schedule. Pianist and singer Danyne Sherman joined the staff in July as program director. By January 1998, a fourth staff member, Cyndi King, accepted the ministry to children and families. In February 1998, the calendar called for a third worship service, on Saturday evening at 5:30.

ACTIVITIES

Today, Crossroads Community Church of Hyde Park maintains a four-service outreach—the Saturday service plus Sunday at 9:00, 10:20, and 11:40 A.M. A fifth service, held the second and fourth Thursday evenings at 7:00, offers additional midweek support. Central to congregants' upbeat faith are their high-tech band, popular music and vocals, multimedia programming, and drama. They welcome people with little background in the Bible and vary their outreach to satisfy eclectic tastes.

The church taps the popularity and convenience of electronic communication. It offers unique music on guitarist and band leader Ben Gully's album *One,* which features confessions of faith in such original worship songs as "I Will Sing," "Come Taste," "Beautiful King," "Come Share Your Greatness," "Yours Is the Kingdom," and "How Could I Explain," featuring vocal and piano backup by Danyne Sherman. Messages, history, and staff announcements reach the congregation through a Web site and *Imprint,* a quarterly online newsletter, begun in winter 1997. Among the creative components of success is Kingdom Korner, a weekly games and Bible story center for preschoolers. In 1999, the congregation planned a more open prayer time and a satellite church at Indian Hill.

> **Sources:** "Crossroads Community Church of Hyde Park"; Irwin June 29, 1998, October 17, 1998; Pille 1996; Reeve 1997.

Crystal Cathedral

Dr. Robert Schuller, Senior Pastor
12141 Lewis Street
Garden Grove, California 92840
714-971-4069
Fax 714-750-3836
claudia@crystalcathedral.org; powerpr@pacbell.net

Located off the Santa Ana Freeway in Garden Grove, California, the 10,000-member Crystal Cathedral is a monument to one man's optimistic, people-friendly ministry. Dr. Robert Schuller, a motivational speaker and pastor, oversees a vigorous worship schedule, anchored by two Sunday morning services, an afternoon service in Spanish, and an evening gathering. His outreach draws on a massive pipe organ, a carillon, a 110-voice choir, and an orchestra. Beyond standard worship, the church offers a prayer chapel, memorial gardens, a Walk of Faith, religious statuary featuring Job and the Good Shepherd, annual performances of Christmas and Easter dramas, and *The Hour of Prayer,* a Sunday television broadcast to 30 million listeners on seven continents.

HISTORY

Dr. Robert Harold Schuller, founder of a worldwide ministry, is a native of Alton, Iowa, and graduate of Hope College and Western Theological Seminary. Five years after his ordination as a minister of the Reformed Church in America, he left Ivanhoe Reformed Church in Chicago and, in 1955, came to southern California. He and his wife, organist Arvella DeHaan Schuller, began a campaign at the Orange Drive-in Theater, the first drive-in church. Within six years, he reestablished his congregation at the Arboretum, a sanctuary designed by Richard Neutra. In 1966, Schuller dedicated the Tower of Hope, another Neutra design topped by a cross. The tower contains the 714-NEW-HOPE telephone counseling and suicide prevention service and features a white Vermont marble sculpture of the seated figure of Job, crafted by Dallas Anderson. In four years, Schuller added a Los Angeles television station reaching the Americas, Australia, Asia, Europe, the Middle East, Africa, and the Armed Forces Network and opened a leadership institute open to Protestant and Catholic students.

For the twentieth anniversary, Schuller's Garden Grove Community Church pledged to construct a 207- by 415-foot star-shaped steel and glass sanctuary designed by Philip Johnson and John Burgee as a superstudio to televise congregational worship. The work, a landmark in sacred architecture, opened in September 1980. The white steel frame, the largest in the nation, houses a curtain wall of 10,000 windows, which suggests the name Crystal Cathedral. It has become a California landmark attracting thousands of religious tourists.

Beyond traditional evangelism, Dr. Schuller publishes best-selling self-help and inspiration works, including *The Power of Being Debt Free* (1985) and *If It's Going to Be, It's up to Me* (1997), both available in braille and on tape. His schedule calls for multiple conferences, seminars, workshops, and interchurch rallies. He participates in civic events and addresses baccalaureate and graduation ceremonies. With money donated by J. B. Fuqua, he heads an interdenominational communications school specializing in preaching style and method. His concern for others finds expression in the YMCA, among psychotherapists and counselors, and in the Salvation Army, the Toastmasters, the Rotary Club, and global missions. These interests have earned Schuller Horatio Alger and Freedom Foundation awards, a Clergyman of the Year award, an Excellence for Religion in Media citation, a Humanitarian of the Year award, the Edith Munger Leadership title, the Napoleon Hill Gold Medal literary award, six honorary degrees, the Peacemaker award, and designation as an Outstanding American.

ARCHITECTURE

The multiplex Crystal Cathedral defies stereotypes. Southwest of the Tower of Hope, the lofty cathedral features white concrete columns fractured to resemble marble. A multifaceted 236-foot spire, the Crean Tower, thrusts upward adjacent to a polygonal, 128-foot glass roof. Within the spire, a fifty-two-bell carillon, built by Royal Eijsbouts Bell Foundry in Holland and dedicated in 1990 to the pastor's wife, produces daily calls to worship. At the base stands the Mary Hood Prayer Chapel, composed of thirty-three vertical columns in varied colors of marble to commemorate the years of Jesus' life. Inside, a crystal cross tops the central altar.

Constructed of *rosso alicante* Spanish marble and seating 1,761 people, the chancel requires 16,000 trusses to bear the weight of glass and steel. The clerestory and two 90-foot doors let in air and light. The granite altar and pulpit stand before a 17-foot cross of antique gold leaf. Twelve fountains embellish the center aisle during special services and the opening and closing of weekly worship. East and west balconies, called the Australian and American balconies, seat 806. A third rank of 283 seats are available in the South Balcony, where translators accom-

modate speakers of German, French, Spanish, and Korean. Screens mounted outside allow additional congregants to remain in their cars.

Virgil Fox designed the chancel organ, named for donor Hazel Wright, by melding a 1962 Aeolian-Skinner organ with the 1977 Ruffatti organ from the former sanctuary and thirty-five auxiliary ranks. The main body rises above the stage and triangular choir stall along the glass front in multiple ranks of brass- and silver-toned pipes. Accompanying seven choirs, three bell choirs, instrumental ensembles, and a twenty-piece orchestra, the five-manual console operates fanfare trumpets on the West Balcony and brass bell trumpets on the East Balcony. The South Balcony features a second five-manual console. The total 17,000 pipes form the second largest organ in the world.

ACTIVITIES

The inner workings of the Crystal Cathedral reflect familiar Protestant activities. The 91,000 square feet of floor space accommodates worship, meeting rooms, classes, and civic and church events. The music department accesses a recording and television studio. The Neutra Sanctuary of the former Arboretum is now a banquet hall. Opposite, the granite Walk of Faith leads through the Garden of the Good Shepherd, embellished by Henry Van Wolf's pastoral statue *Christ the Good Shepherd,* a life-size figure, flanked by four sheep and cast in bronze in Munich, Germany.

A focus of the Crystal Cathedral Christmas celebration is *The Glory of Christmas,* a dramatization of Jesus' birth. The musical performance requires lavish costumes and sets and a cast of 200 players, horses, donkeys, sheep, and camels and flying angels. Initiated in 1981, the nativity pageant draws viewers to dazzling special effects. A companion work, *The Glory of Easter,* chronicles the last seven days of Jesus' life. Set in a Jerusalem marketplace, it covers the biblical account of his crucifixion, resurrection, and ascension.

In the shadow of the spire is an intimate garden and open-air mausoleum. A traditional cemetery provides in-ground burial and maintains the Sanctuary of Praise, a columbarium for ash enurnment in stained-glass, marble-tiled, or mosaic niches. The nearby Robert Schuller

Family Life Center, a modern marble and glass edifice fronting on Chapman Avenue, features Dallas Anderson's *Love Without Condemnation,* a bronze statue grouping five full-size human figures. The center offers 145,000 square feet for a Sunday school, conferences, a nursery, and a children's playground; the Crystal Cathedral Academy consists of parochial school training for children from kindergarten through eighth grade. The Family Life Center also headquarters the Hour of Power Television Ministry. The sports program sponsors basketball, volleyball, badminton, and field hockey.

Sources: *American Decades CD-ROM* 1998; *Biography Resource Center* 1999; Calian 1995; Carroll 1993; McGrath 1997; O'Connor 1998; *Religious Leaders of America* 1999; Schuller 1997; "Shelters of the Lord" 1990; Stoddard 1997; Woodward 1997.

Zen, Buddhism's largest school of philosophy, began in Canton, China, when Bodhidharma—a legendary figure whom the Chinese call Ta-mo—formulated Ch'an around 520 A.D. by sitting immobile in a cell for nine years and ultimately losing use of his legs. Blended with Taoism and allied with the martial art of Shao-lin boxing, Ch'an spread to Japan and Korea. Unlike Buddhism, which seeks ultimate reality, Zen stresses the intellect, the source of nirvana, an ideal state of *satori* (enlightenment) that the Buddha obtained and that lies within reach of all minds.

The Zen practitioner requires no cloistering, scriptural studies, vows of obedience to a monastic order, or chanting of the Buddha's name. Each seeker learns from a *roshi,* a teacher who guides the novice toward enlightenment through example and by repetition of *koans,* ancient Chinese adages or brain teasers that have either no correct answer or a surprising answer derived from unusual methods of viewing a problem.

From 618 to 907 A.D., Buddhism flourished in monasteries but incited envy among monks of other faiths. Novices learned to meditate in motion and at rest and to follow a stringent regimen. After Zen Buddhism rose to influence in Japan in 1185, it found favor with rulers, particularly the samurai, or knight, class. For 250 years, Zen practice carried patriotic overtones. Early in the eighteenth century, a monk, Hakuin Ekaku, created original Zen proverbs as complements to discipline and learning. The esthetic rigor of Zen influenced the traditional tea ceremony, art, poetry, and gardening. With a boost from such faith-centered films as *Kundun* (1997) and the activism of film star Richard Gere on behalf of the Dalai Lama, Americans began exploring Buddhism as an alternative to mainstream religion.

Detroit Zen Center

Sahn Bul Sunim, Supervisor
Jo Chim, Director
11464 Mitchell Street
Hamtramck, Michigan 48212
313-366-7738

One of a growing number of Zen Buddhist sites throughout the nation, the Detroit Zen Center of Hamtramck is an oasis of calm. As members kneel for meditation, they relinquish the need to *do* by accepting the demanding task of *being.* Their veneration links them to a direct, pragmatic, and nonmetaphysical faith that suits a secular age. As described by Zen expert Daisetz Teitaro Suzuki in *An Introduction to Zen Buddhism* (1974),

> Zen has no God to worship, no ceremonial rites to observe, no future abode to which the dead are destined, and, last of all, Zen has no soul whose welfare is to be looked after by somebody else and whose immortality is a matter of intense concern. (p. 35)

Unlike the otherworldliness of other faiths, Zen focuses on the allness of the divine, which takes human form in the individual mind and concept of godhood.

Through a series of inward searches and study of cryptic passages of wisdom, each practitioner contemplates daily existence and the reality of the here and now. By stripping away past anguish and removing anxiety over the future, Zen meditation focuses each practitioner on the possibilities of the present. The individual measures Zen's uncomplicated style of spiritual nourishment by undeniable change in attitude, behavior, and well-being.

HISTORY

Hamtramck has long been a Roman Catholic city. Late in the twentieth century, however, the evolving pluralism in greater Detroit, as in other metropolitan areas, had reduced the hold of the majority through incursive minority faiths. Since 1990, a Buddhist monk, Sahn Bul Sunim, has supervised spiritual practice at the Detroit Zen Center, a monastic setting in a 5,000-square-foot structure with an adjacent meditation hall. Directed by Jo Chim, a resident of Grosse Pointe, the center strengthens the individual by forcing a full self-examination. The result is a realistic study of fears and anxiety and an acceptance of responsibility in place of religions requiring blind faith and postponing satisfaction until the afterlife.

In the center's first months, the introduction of a faith from eastern and central Asia stirred the curious. Sunim built on inquiries by teaching a Zen truth—that suffering and life are inseparable. According to doctrine, the individual can move beyond suffering into a state of illumination only by extinguishing the self and the senses. Unlike faiths that cultivate an awareness of sin, heaven, and hell, the Zen state of illumination is an embrace of love and compassion as daily practice rather than distant virtues expounded by the saintly or through an elitist Judeo-Christian theology. As the Dalai Lama described Zen Buddhism, it requires no temples or complicated philosophy because the brain and heart become a temple when the individual learns kindness.

ACTIVITIES

The Detroit Zen Center is an altruistic agency aiding the Hamtramck community. In 1999, staff offered yoga from 5:45 to 7:00 P.M. on Tuesday and Thursday and from 10:30 A.M. to noon on Saturday for $6 per session. The ongoing series of twenty-minute sessions educates new members on the principle of chanting and meditation and leads regular practice of Sun-do, a series of prostrations from a bow at the waist to a squat to a bow to the floor. This humbling posture is a beneficial, all-inclusive learning experience that calms the mind and promotes health and a respect for other people and the universe. Its end goal is a lofty ideal—the eightfold path of right understanding, right action, right livelihood, right mindfulness, right thought, right speech, right effort, and right concentration.

These silent exercises, performed on mats,

make no requirements that individuals convert to Buddhism or give up American-style culture and belief systems. The leader follows each session with questions and answers. Individuals then practice meditation on their own either at regular intervals or when they need to restore peace, self-respect, and a sense of wholeness. According to Sunim, the addition of Sun-do to orthodox Christianity, Islam, or Judaism can improve existing faith by reducing anger and self-destructive habits and offering practitioners room to grow.

A complement to personal development at the Detroit Zen Center is the formation of the members' housing corporation, which they call Our Homes. Beginning in 1992, a core of area Zen practitioners bought and renovated run-down houses through the National Bank of Detroit to sell to low-income, first-time home buyers. Within three years, the outreach offered three homes at a price of $40,000 each.

Sources: Ahlstrom 1972; Bates-Rudd 1997; Gentz 1973; Herbrechtsmeier 1993; Ling 1972; Lorie and Foakes 1997; Palm 1998; "Review: 'Ritual and Devotion in Buddhism'" 1996; Smith 1995; Suzuki 1974; Tanasychuk 1997; *World Religions* 1998.

Devils Tower National Monument
Superintendent's Office
Devils Tower National Monument
P.O. Box 10
Devils Tower, Wyoming 82714
307-467-5283

A mythic focus of the Black Hills, Devils Tower retains a religious significance to the Lakota, Cheyenne, and twenty-three other plains tribes each June 22, the summer solstice. Visitors to northeastern Wyoming come to Crook County to admire, photograph, and sometimes climb the massive gray- and buff-colored monolith, an 865-foot fluted solid that towers 1,253 feet over Belle Fouche River. The flat-top rock is a vertical-sided igneous core, or neck, that may be the remains of a volcanic thrust that occurred 40 to 60 million years ago. The striated magma column may have encountered an impermeable layer of rock and flattened and solidified below ground. Wind, rain, and traffic have excised lay-

A mythic focus of the Black Hills, Devils Tower retains a religious significance to plains tribes during the summer solstice. (Courtesy National Park Service)

ers of rubble along its perimeter, exposing the hallowed landmark.

BELIEFS

A myth common to the Arapaho, Cheyenne, Crow, Kiowa, and Sioux describes the formation of Ursa Major. Devils Tower, which the Lakota call Mato Tipila (Bear's Lodge), is central to the narration. While seven sisters and their brother played together, the boy suddenly fell mute. His body altered grotesquely: his flesh sprouted dense fur and he crawled on all fours, which produced claws. The sisters fled from the boy-turned-bear and begged rescue from Wakan Tanka (the Great Spirit). When they climbed a tree stump, its spirit enfolded them and shot upward farther than a bear could reach. The boy-bear clawed at the trunk, scoring it with spiky paws. Up the tree soared until the seven sisters found safety in the night sky. To this day, they shine benevolently on earth as the Pleiades.

The Lakota version, which omits any sibling violence, tells of another threat to children. When two Sioux lads got lost, they wandered into the territory of Mato, a giant grizzly bear. Like the Kiowa children, they prayed to the Great Spirit for succor. The God shook the earth with a fierce earthquake that boosted the rock tower out of Mato's reach. He continued to claw and snarl at the lofty sides of Bear Rock. When the children called for help, Wanblee the eagle flew down, loaded them on his back, and carried them home.

In a variant by Lame Deer, a hereditary Lakota medicine man and folk teller from Rosebud Reservation, South Dakota, the mountain lay on a flooded plain when water drowned all humanity. One lovely survivor clung to life until the Great Spirit sent his personal messenger. Galeshka, a spotted eagle, who grasped her in his talons and carried her to the end of a protruding rock named Mateo Tipi, or Grizzly Bear Lodge. The two produced twins, who fathered all Lakotas.

HISTORY

From prehistory, the Sioux have honored Devils Tower, which they call He Hota Paha (Gray Horn Butte), particularly in June, a holy month to the local people for some 12,000 years. To westerers pressing across the continental divide, the tower became a majestic trail marker. At the edge of the Black Hills where knolls give way to plains, the tower's mineral surface is home to sage, mosses, and grass and a habitat for chipmunks and birds. Prairie falcons nest in the crevices. At its base rise stretches of ponderosa pine and the burrows of prairie dogs. In 1875, U.S. geological surveyor Colonel Richard Dodge called the rock Devils Tower as a variant of an Indian name, the Bad God's Tower. Native Americans disdain his choice of the Christian personification of evil as a name for their natural sanctuary. Johnson Holy Rock, a Sioux elder from Pine Ridge, South Dakota, remarked that his father often spoke of the rock tower but referred to it as the physical presence of the Great Spirit.

Devils Tower intrigued the white world. The first recorded climb, on July 4, 1893, required a long ladder. At the urging of President Theodore Roosevelt, on September 24, 1906, Congress named the tower the nation's first national monument. The total park, which covers 1,346 acres, draws picnickers, New-Age worshippers, UFO sighters, and athletes, who consider the prismatic shape one of the continent's most challenging climbs. Park history records some 20,000 successful ascents. In 1941, a parachutist chanced a drop to the summit and remained marooned until he could be rescued.

Late in the twentieth century, Devils Tower permeated the arts. In 1969, N. Scott Momaday published a monumental Kiowa memoir, *The Way to Rainy Mountain*. In recounting his people's belief system, he focused on the lithic monument, which he described as one of the "things in nature that engender an awful quiet in the heart of man." (Momaday 1969, 8) He described the awe and dismay of his grandmother, who was a child in 1887, when the last Kiowa Kado (Sun Dance) occurred on the Washita River. Momaday characterized the event as "the essential act of their faith," which cavalry from Fort Sill disrupted in an willful act of deicide. After decades of near anonymity for Devils Rock, in 1978, the movie *Close Encounters of the Third Kind* boosted it to renewed notoriety.

From renewed publicity, the basalt butte began averaging 400,000 visitors a year. To preserve its sanctity, the Gilmette, Wyoming, Climbing Club stripped offensive netting and pitons. Until 1997, 16,000 scaling parties continued their popular crack climbs, with 85 percent voluntarily relinquishing June as a private time for Native Americans to venerate the site. By 1996, June climbs had fallen from 1,294 to 185. On behalf of four climbers, the Bear Lodge Multiple Use Association, and tour guide Andy Petefish, who owns Tower Guides climbing service, and attorney Todd Welch of Mountain States Legal Foundation pressed a lawsuit demanding the separation of church and state in matters of park use. In reply, Dr. Arvol Looking Horse, nineteenth-generation Sioux Keeper of the Sacred Pipe, insisted that nonnatives respect aboriginal worship. On April 2, 1998, Secretary of the Interior Bruce Babbitt expressed his satisfaction that U.S. District Court Judge William Downes had settled the matter.

Despite federal claims, the sanctity of Devils Tower remains in contention. According to the district court decree, the U.S. Park Service has not forced religious observations on visitors by setting aside one month for tribal ritual. Lakota member Elaine Quiver and members of the proenvironmental Sierra Club support the compromise. To assure Indian rights, representative Carol Status and other native spokespersons contest the voluntary thirty-day observance.

Chief among native complaints are the climbers' noise, bolts drilled into the rock face, professional guides' hacking new routes up the steep sides, disturbance of nesting raptors, and litter. More insidious are deliberate destruction of prayer flags and bundles and a pervasive disrespect for an ancient national monument, which Johnson Holy Rock compared to climbing the Washington National Cathedral during a service. Native Americans face protracted animosity from antienvironmental attorney William Perry Pendley of Mountain States Legal Foundation, who has pressed for a court battle.

ACTIVITIES

Open daily, Devils Tower National Monument offers a 1.25-mile hike around the base. For visitors' comfort, the Park Service maintains a campground and welcome center, which is open 8:30 A.M. to 5:00 P.M. April through October. In summer, hours extend to 8:00 A.M. to 7:30 P.M. Park officials host hikes, talks, and campfire programs.

Annually, the Cheyenne River Sioux and twenty other native tribes make a pilgrimage to the tower during June to hold a Sun Dance, the height of the Lakota's seven sacred rituals. The chief purpose of the quest is to drum and retell traditional stories and to honor the summer solstice at a religious site that Looking Horse refers to as "the heart of everything." Lakota scholar Vine Deloria expressed the right of the earth over human greed: "It's not that Indians should have exclusive rights at Devil's Tower. It's that that location is sacred enough so that it should have *time of its own*. And once it has had time of its own, then the people who know how to do ceremonies should come and minister to it. That's so hard to get across to people." (Maynor and McLeod 1999)

> **See also** Black Hills, Medicine Wheel.
> **Sources:** "Battle of Wounded Me" 1994; Bennett 1975; "Black Hills Sight to See—Devils Tower"; Coates 1996; Cummings 1993; "Devils Tower, Wyoming"; Gallagher, *The Power of Place*, 1993; Hamilton 1996; Loftus 1997; Maynor and McLeod 1999; Milne 1995; Momaday 1969; Patterson and Snodgrass 1994; Snodgrass, *Encyclopedia of Frontier Literature*, 1997; Steiger 1974.

Diana's Grove

P.O. Box 159
Salem, Missouri 65560
573-689-2400
info@dianasgrove.com
www.dianasgrove.com

Diana's Grove is a mystical retreat to a simpler time, when communing with nature was a daily celebration of earthly experience and joy. Located in southeastern Missouri between a meadow and Sinking Creek, the 102-acre sanctuary encourages meditation and back-to-the-land solidarity. The key to Diana's Grove's success is its blend of psychology and sanctity. The eclectic environment liberates as it unites participants in community. In evening torchlight, cel-

ebrants embrace an ancient self-knowledge born of relaxation and natural wonder. Each seeks a private vision and truth. Those who find answers to their quandaries dedicate themselves to the pagan Goddess and to magic, the altered state of consciousness that links the seeker with the divine.

HISTORY

Diana's Grove took shape as a religious center after Candlemas 1993 at Starhawk in Chicago, where founders Cynthia Jones and Patricia Storm sought a place to immerse themselves in pagan practice at a ritual space. Storm brought to the partnership her eight years of experience as a psychologist for the state of Illinois before becoming a telephone engineer for Illinois Bell. She made personal discoveries while taking Jones's tarot classes in 1987 and 1988 and became a team teacher in 1989. After additional training in hypnotherapy and alternative psychology, the pair sought a full-time site where they could build a training center.

Envisioning a private retreat, Jones and Storm wanted an isolated piece of land suitable for a Midwest witch camp. After a nine-month search in 1994, they located a grove in the Ozarks. Central to their plans was priestly training to teach leadership through small-group dynamics, magic technique, and ritual.

The grove advanced gradually from a sylvan meadow to a structured camp and mystery school, which doubled and redoubled until it reached an enrollment of 99. To accommodate more needs during the growth process, founders erected hot open-air showers, privies with stained-glass windows, a barn-community center, and rustic cabins. In 1996, the addition of a labyrinth enhanced mystery and pattern. Shared housing is limited; food service is gourmet vegetarian featuring real cream and butter with options of chicken dishes.

BELIEFS

Central to Diana's Grove is a study of astrology and the year's wheel. According to camp beliefs, star study relates earth's story by projecting the cycle of the seasons across the sky. Ancient astral patterns retell the myth of human immersion in nature. Traditional astrological signs, imbued

If, for you, imagining nature is not enough...

Diana's Grove

Diana's Grove is a mystical retreat to a simpler time, when communing with nature was a daily celebration of earthly experience and joy. (Courtesy Diana's Grove)

with seasonal wisdom, indicate intrinsic qualities and urges and offer clues to human behavior. Because the seasons influence lives and choices, the stars invoke an ancient power over humankind and all living things.

Pagans date the astrological new year to December 22, the winter solstice, which opens in the chill sign of Capricorn and instills a need to conserve and perpetuate the clan. Believers observe the quiet of deep winter and power struggles within the social order. Aquarius, the second sign, produces the will to individuate, to escape the smothering inwardness of winter and let out the social animal. Pisces ushers in spring, a time of emergence and shape shifting. As seeds split their coverings, the inner selves quest for resurrection.

A high point in the twelve-month cycle is March 21, the spring equinox, which arrives in Aries. This sign rekindles a will to survive, to push out of confinement into an unpredictable milieu. In pagan tradition, spring is the time for dance, tilling the soil, and walking barefoot to contact earth once more. In Taurus thrives a full appreciation of life in nature, which is once more green and flourishing. Promise reaches fruition in May Day, a sensual celebration. Joy in summer begins in Gemini, a month of travel, enthusiasm, and neighborliness, and climaxes in the sign of Cancer on June 22 with the summer solstice, when earth reaches full bloom.

The return to inward thoughts and needs starts in Virgo as fall brings on the harvest and an end to long days. Autumn is the season of analysis, stocktaking, and organization of resources to last through winter. On September 23, the fall equinox returns with Libra, a merging sign that brings back the nesting urge and the desire to partner. Autumn reaches its depth in Scorpio, a submerging sign that returns thoughts and urges inward to a core mystery. Regenerative power hibernates once more in Sagittarius, the beginning of winter and retreat to the hearth and imagination.

ACTIVITIES

In a setting both drug and alcohol free, celebrants at Diana's Grove enjoy wading in the creek, fire circle programs, drumming, walking the labyrinth, chanting and storytelling, com-

muning with the elements, and a wide selection of seasonal events. From the January mystery school and tarot weekend in February, the calendar branches out to Candlemas, a women's spring equinox, and trance formation. After spring cleaning and the men's magical weekend late in April, the camp moves to a spring mystery school intensive, the forerunner of the springfest family weekend.

Early in June, Diana's Grove offers a session of reclaiming magic and the late-month women's summer weekend. The season expands to lunacy women's week, a tarot intensive, and a fall equinox celebration, followed by initiation, mystery school ordination, rites of passage, autumn communion, a mythic question, and a Samhain retreat in mid to late October. The events culminate in a New Year's Eve celebration.

The serious business of preparing the priest/priestess for officiating at sacred rites also focuses on wonder at natural phenomena, honoring the seasons, dedicating self to the Goddess, and healing. From the one-year study of self, each participant seeks personal growth that empowers, supports, and influences others. The priest becomes a leader and facilitator to serve and cocreate. To enhance the growth process and self-definition, the staff maintains a Web site and provides a monthly correspondence packet and workbook for journal-keeping.

Sources: "Diana's Grove 1999; Eck 1994; "The History of Wicca"; Niebuhr (b) 1999; Snodgrass, *Signs of the Zodiac,* 1997; Suggs 1999; Zeinert 1997.

Dwight Chapel

Reverend Anne Jensen
Yale University
67 High Street
New Haven, Connecticut 06520
203-436-2420

In university tradition dating to the Middle Ages, Yale aims to develop both intellect and spirit. To that end, the faculty provides students, staff, and visitors an inviting sanctuary for meditation and prayer. Dwight Chapel bears the name of Timothy Dwight, a respected educator, preacher, and Christian apologist. Built in a spot of green in 1842, the chapel is the school's first

TIMOTHY DWIGHT

Congregationalist chaplain and psalmodist Timothy Dwight was the grandson of Puritan preacher Jonathan Edwards, the academic founder of the Great Awakening, a spiritual resurgence that democratized American Protestantism. Similarly innovative, Dwight believed that the chapel had as much role in education as the classroom. The son of prestigious parents, he was born on May 14, 1752, in Northampton, Massachusetts, and completed college at age seventeen. Despite an eye disease, he taught at Hopkins Grammar School in New Haven for two years before beginning a career at Yale as a tutor. During the American Revolution, he accepted congressional appointment as chaplain of the Connecticut Continental Brigade in October 1777 and entered a remarkably ambitious phase by pastoring the Congregational Church at Greenfield Hill, Connecticut, managing two farms, serving a term in the Massachusetts Legislature in 1781 and 1782, and founding a progressive coeducational academy.

During Dwight's presidency at Yale from 1795 until his death on January 11, 1817, he modernized the curriculum and taught a senior-level philosophy course in morals. By hiring quality professionals, he combined intellectual and spiritual growth as necessary training of Christian ministers. In addition to promoting liturgical music and collecting 264 hymn texts for the Connecticut Congregational churches, he preached, composed an American epic, *The Conquest of Canaan* (1785), and issued collected sermons in his five-volume masterwork, *Theology Explained and Defended* (1818). Because of Dwight's series on the true word of God, the campus experienced a revival known as the Second Great Awakening, which swept New England at the end of the eighteenth century. As a result, twenty-six students established the Moral Society of Yale College to discourage profanity, immorality, and intemperance.

HISTORY

By 1821, Yale University separated sanctity from learning by creating a separate department of divinity. In keeping with Dwight's philosophy, faculty still required daily chapel attendance and Sunday services, which featured the singing of hymns and anthems. Constructed as a library in 1841, Dwight Chapel, located in the Dwight Center for Social Justice and Community Service, has maintained holy endeavors as a valuable addition to the Old Campus. Chapel programs continue Timothy Dwight's intent to channel spirituality into academic thought on ethical issues.

The chapel design was the work of Mount Carmel architect Henry Austin, creator of an Egyptian gateway at New Haven's Oak Grove Cemetery. He chose the floor plan from a sketch of London's St. Katherine's Hospital. Architect John Russell Pope proposed that Philadelphia architect Charles Klauder alter the layout to suit worship rather than books. The ivy-covered façade and walls feature slender, diamond-paned windows and rounded domes atop the twin towers, which are a community landmark.

ACTIVITIES

Dwight Chapel, which seats 300, offers multidenominational services year-round. It remains open daily from 9:00 A.M. to 5:00 P.M. and schedules Holy Eucharist for Sunday, Monday, and Wednesday through Friday. In addition to regular meetings of Alcoholics Anonymous, the building has housed assemblies on parents weekend and hosts question-and-answer sessions on Sunday afternoon and the New Haven Zen Center, which meets on Monday evening. On January 23, 1999, the chapel was the site of a Concert for Peace with the People of Iraq, sponsored by Magee Fellowship. Later in 1999, the chapel staff welcomed Father Roy Bourgeois, founder of the School of the Americas, for a lecture entitled "The U. S.'s Promotion of Oppression in Latin America."

Dwight Chapel's varied programs include a performance of the Yale Collegium Musicum; Wednesday meetings of the Baptist Student Union; candlelight prayer meetings; a fall open house; pastoral counseling to AIDS patients; a benefit concert to aid victims of the Chernobyl

neo-Gothic structure. Like many campus religious sites, it combines the sanctity of communion and meditations on the stations of the cross with campus and community outreach, current programs of music, and challenging lectures on world issues.

disaster; the 1999 spring concert of the Yale International Singers, who performed exotic folk songs from America, Ghana, India, Ireland, Japan, and Kenya; and such solo musicians as harpist Andrew Lawrence-King and organists Ellen Espenschied, Christopher Pankratz, and Ken Cowan. In 1997, Yale Collegium Musicum chose the chapel for a performance of Reinhard Keiser's rarely heard *St. Mark Passion*.

The Yale Russian Chorus, specializing in Russian and Eastern European music of the twelfth through twentieth centuries often performs at Dwight Chapel and chose it in 1999 as the location for a forty-fifth anniversary concert. On March 19 and 20, 1996, the chorus, directed by Igor Kipnis, recorded a CD, *Chants and Carols,* performed in the chapel. The varied program ranged from Sergei Rachmaninov's "Virgin Mother of God, Rejoice" and Peter Ilyich Tchaikovsky's "Holy God" to the liturgical works of Kedros, Diletsky, Turankov, Kovalevsky, and Alexander Glazunov. In April 1999, director Mark Bailey led the chorus in a program of Russian folk and liturgical music.

Sources: Bauer 1998; *Biography Resource Center* 1999; "Calendar of Events" 1999; "A Digital Archive of American Architecture"; *Encyclopedia of World Biography* 1998; "Institute of Sacred Music"; Mutrux 1982; "Newcomer's Guide to New Haven Churches"; Pappis; "Yale through the Seasons"; "Yale University."

Ebenezer Baptist Church

Pastor Joseph L. Roberts, Jr.
407 Auburn Avenue
Atlanta, Georgia 30312
404-688-7263
ebenezer@ebenezer.org
www.ebenezer.org

Made famous by the Reverend Martin Luther King, Sr., and his son, martyred freedom fighter Dr. Martin Luther King, Jr., the original Ebenezer Baptist Church, cradle of the civil rights movement, is a historic Atlanta landmark. The U.S. Department of the Interior has listed it on the National Register of Historic Places and staffs it with National Park Service rangers. The building is part of the Martin Luther King National Historic Site along with the house where Dr. King was born, his grave, and sixty-four other buildings of Sweet Auburn, the middle-class neighborhood in which he grew up. Tourism rose to 100,000 daily during the 1996 Olympic Games and reached an annual total of 4.5 million. Over 400 worshippers visit the church each Sunday; thousands join daily free tour groups, led by volunteer docents. In addition, organizers of conferences and forums choose the historic church as an appropriate and inspiring setting for meetings.

HISTORY

Ebenezer Baptist Church dates to 1886, during the post–Civil War Reconstruction. From the original eight founders, Reverend John A. Parker, the first pastor, built a stable congregation and led fifty members at a small structure on Airline Street. In 1894, Reverend Alfred Daniel Williams, Dr. King's grandfather, took the pastorate and envigorated the church program by increasing membership by 30 percent. He instilled hope for equality by urging blacks to support African American businesses and institutions as a means of developing the southern economic base.

Known as Mount Pleasant Baptist Church, the church's first sanctuary, erected on McGruder Street, remained in service until 1898, when the congregation purchased the Old Fifth Street Baptist Church at Bell and Gilmer Streets. During a period of construction from 1912 to 1914, congregants made do at a storefront at 444 Edgewood Avenue. The familiar Ebenezer Baptist sanctuary, a red-brick, rectangular structure marked with stained-glass windows, opened for basement services for eight years until completion of a 750-seat chancel in 1922. In addition to religious meetings, the church hosted black leaders, who plotted strategies to end segregation. The Reverend Martin Luther King, Sr., was an associate minister from 1927 to 1930. In 1931, he replaced Reverend Williams as senior pastor.

The ministry of Dr. Martin Luther King, Jr., enlarged the church outlook to ecumenical and international humanitarian concerns. He was ordained on February 25, 1948, and maintained the family's ties with Ebenezer Baptist during campaigns for human rights. At the end of a civil rights campaign in Montgomery, Alabama, in 1960, he joined his father's pastorate at Ebenezer as copastor and directed the Southern Christian Leadership Conference (SCLC), a pressure group seeking the social, economic, and political betterment of minorities. While in these leadership positions, he led a march on Washington in 1963 and, two years later, a voting rights march in Selma and Montgomery. He remained on staff until a lone gunman shot and killed him in 1968. His funeral, held at the church on April 9, was an international focus during heightened racial confrontations. Thousands filed by his casket during all-night viewing before its burial in Southview Cemetery.

The death of Dr. King did not end Ebenezer's vision. When the Reverend Alfred Daniel Williams King joined the pastorate, he modernized worship order, established benevolences,

Made famous by the Reverend Martin Luther King, Sr., and his son, martyred freedom fighter Dr. Martin Luther King, Jr., the original Ebenezer Baptist Church, cradle of the civil rights movement, is a historic Atlanta landmark. (Flip Schulke/Corbis)

and initiated a television ministry. In 1971, Dr. Otis Moss extended this dynamic period with formation of the Ebenezer Credit Union and additional community activism. The tenure of Dr. Joseph L. Roberts, Jr., has continued an era of growth with an increase in budget, the creation of an early Sunday morning service and an Adult Rehabilitation Center and the employment of the first female associate pastor, the Reverend Sharon G. Austin.

ARCHITECTURE

Honoraria for Dr. Martin Luther King, Jr., have made Ebenezer Baptist Church a southern shrine. A block from the sanctuary, the Center for Non-Violent Social Change, founded by his widow, Coretta Scott King, houses the crypt where his remains were reinterred in a memorial tomb in 1977. A bronze statue entitled *Behold* depicts a stylized black male holding an infant. Nearby are the Community Center Plaza and a museum of Dr. King's life and work. The King family tradition lives on in a son and namesake, whom the congregation appointed in 1997 to direct the SCLC. The original sanctuary will become a museum managed by the National Park Service.

In 1999, Ebenezer Baptist's former sanctuary gave place to a new structure, the New Horizon Sanctuary, which stresses African heritage and commitment to nonviolent social change. The new edifice was the design of Ivenue Love-Stanley and William J. Stanley III, a husband-and-wife team. Ivenue was the first black female architect and the youngest black architect in the Southeast. Both graduated from the Georgia Institute of Technology and base their urban-centered work in Atlanta, for which they designed the Southwest Regional Library, Ida Prather YWCA, Delta West End Redevelopment, and professional office of physician Calvin W. McLarin.

Accommodating 1,800 in oak pews plus a 150-member choir, the new sanctuary is three times the size of the older building. Its copper roof and brick shell emulate the simplicity of a thatch-roofed African hut. The fan-shaped nave centers on a dais holding the pulpit and the choir. Stained-glass windows interpret the advancement of black Americans alongside images of Jesus. Quiet niches encourage individual reflection.

ACTIVITIES

The 1,600 members of Ebenezer Baptist Church maintain an outreach to the poor of the Sweet Auburn neighborhood that surrounds it. In addition to holding standard services, the congregation feeds 300 homeless each Sunday morning and offers subway cards for job seekers and transportation for senior citizens. In service to some 14,000 needy, the membership operates a child and adult day-care center, a food closet, legal and psychological service, a homeless shelter, and after-school tutoring. To stabilize and support families, the church extends scholarships, assistance to teen mothers, respite for caretakers of the handicapped and elderly, emergency utility assistance, eviction prevention, employment counseling, aid to children whose parents are in prison, and parenting classes. Trustees also envision a medical clinic, boys' school, and food cooperative for the church community center.

See also Big Bethel African Methodist Episcopal Church.
Sources: "Atlanta Lucky but Wary" 1996; *Biographical Resource Center* 1999; Cantor 1991; Copeland 1999, "Ebenezer Baptist Church"; "Ebenezer Baptist Prepares for a Big Move" 1998; "Former King Congregation Moves" 1999; Grossman 1993; Low and Clift 1981; "Martin Luther King, Jr., National Historic Site"; Travis 1991; Williams, Peter W., 1997.

Echo Canyon
Zion National Park
78 East 100 South, Highway 89
Kanab, Utah 84741
435-644-5033; 800-733-5263
kanetrav@xpressweb.com
www.americanparknetwork.com

A revered site since prehistory, the fifteen-mile-long Echo Canyon, a fossil-rich labyrinth carved out by the Virgin River, was home to the Basket Makers and Anasazi. Their animism demanded awe and respect for the unique beauty of rust-red domes, cliffs, and valleys. The area teemed with mule deer, mountain lions, rabbits,

A revered site since prehistory, the 15-mile Echo Canyon, a fossil-rich labyrinth carved out by the Virgin River, was home to the Basket Makers and Anasazi. (David Muench/Corbis)

and squirrels. In addition to wild tufts of datura, columbine, shooting star, monkey flower, and the white evening primrose, the terrain offered semiarid cactus, cottonwood, willow, box elder, juniper, yucca, ash, fir, and pine. When these early pueblo dwellers departed, the peaceable Paiute, or Digger Indians, migrated to the Great Basin around 1200 A.D. and survived on ample sources of seeds, roots, berries, rabbits, and birds until the Ute and Navajo forced them farther west into California.

BELIEFS

The Paiute were respecters of dreams and protective animal spirits. According to oral tradition, Coyote's wife sent him south from their home in Canada to find the Great Basin, a place where the sun touched the earth. Along the way, against his wife's orders, he opened a sealed water jug and spilled the contents—human figures

who evolved into various tribes. The last pair of brothers he kept to sire the people of the Great Basin, where they became the ancestors of two amicable nations, the Paiute and Shoshone.

Another earth myth accounts for the rugged terrain occupied by the Northern Paiute. When two gods, Shinob and Kusav, got into a bow-shooting match, Shinob overshot the mark and set an arrow skittering out of control over the earth. Before the missile came to rest, it had gouged out ravines and canyons, valleys and cliffs, and irregular streams and riverbeds.

In naming Echo Canyon's bowl-shaped crater, the Paiute honored their wolf God. Like the nurturing land itself, he was a benevolent deity equipped with power over evil. They saw him battling predators in the I-oo-goon, or Narrows, a cul-de-sac at the end of the canyon. Out of fear of these match-ups between good and evil, people avoided this area by night. A less fearful spot, Weeping Rock, was a refreshing crag where subterranean waters forced streamlets through porous rock and over the escarpment in tear-size drops. The constant flow reminded the Paiute of Stone Woman, the sad earth mother who wept for her lost children.

HISTORY

The Paiute chose a sensible name for Echo Canyon, which they called Mukuntuweap (Straight Canyon). Some Paiute were still living in Utah when the Mormons left Missouri in 1847 to journey west from winter quarters to explore the best route to the Valley of the Great Salt Lake. From Fort Bridger, they westered in search of the route followed by the Donner-Reed party and, on the grueling leg from Wyoming across the Wasatch Range, discovered the narrow pass at Echo Canyon. In the 1850s and 1860s, the Mormons sought arable land on which to grow cotton as a major crop after it became scarce during the Civil War. In "Utah's Dixie," they founded the cities of Grafton, Rockville, and Springdale.

In 1858, expeditioner Nephi Johnson explored Echo Canyon. Exhilarated and awed by its majesty and sanctity, he and his company named it Zion Canyon for God's heavenly kingdom and returned two years later to settle. Three years after, farmer Isaac Behunin chose the canyon floor to graze his flocks and grow tobacco, vegetables, grain, and fruit. For surrounding landmarks, the Mormons chose holy names—Angels Landing, the monolithic Great White Throne, the Temple of Sinawava, West Temple, the Watchman, Cathedral Mountain, the Altar of Sacrifice, Sentinel Mountain, and the Three Patriarchs—Abraham, Isaac, and Jacob. In 1909, Congress proclaimed the 147,035-acre area the Mukuntuweap National Monument and then altered the name a decade later to Zion National Park. With the addition of Kolob Canyon in 1956, the park totaled 229 square miles. The National Park Service has marked the advance of the Latter Day Saints as Mormon Pioneer National Historic Trail.

ACTIVITIES

The park is a popular Southwest vacation site. In addition to providing a visitor center, it stocks maps and guidebooks in the park bookshop. Park rangers assist newcomers with suggestions about the scenic drive along Angels Landing, overlooks to photograph, swimming in Emerald Pools, strolling along the Virgin River, and the safest trails for hiking. They point out the tunnel, old bridge road, and Grafton, the ghost-town setting for the film *Butch Cassidy and the Sundance Kid*.

Echo Canyon remains a historic boulevard of the way west. It saw the coming of the Donner Party, Pony Express, Overland Stage, Transcontinental Railroad, and forty-niners on the way to the California gold fields. Reenactments of the Mormon Trail pass through Echo Canyon on the way to Henefer. Throngs greet arriving wagons with emotional cries as they honor the founders of Utah's Mormon enclave. On September 18, 1996, President Bill Clinton authorized the preservation of the Grand Staircase-Escalante National Monument, including the Kaiparowits Plateau, proposed during the administration of President Franklin D. Roosevelt. This 1.7-million-acre parcel of wild country became the first addition of a historic preserve to southeast Utah in sixty years. In addition to parts of two national parks, two state parks, and recreational areas, the land preserves sites revered by the Paiute and Mormons.

Sources: "A Brand New National Monument"; "Creation Myths from around the World"; "How the Canyons Were Made"; Kimball; Milne 1995; "The Paiute Story of Creation"; Patterson and Snodgrass 1994; Steiger 1974; "Wagon Train Now in Henefer After Passing through Echo Canyon" 1997; Waldman 1990; Wharton 1996.

Emanuel African Methodist Episcopal Church
110 Calhoun Street
Charleston, South Carolina
843-722-2561

Built at Boundary Street, the demarcation of black society by Charleston's tight caste system, Emanuel African Methodist Episcopal Church was one of many congregations awaiting the signal of Abraham Lincoln's Emancipation Proclamation, which he issued in 1862 to take effect January 1, 1863. Liberation swelled the number of Charleston's worshippers to map out the future of a church rid of bondage. Following the model of Bishop Richard Allen of the Philadelphia see, Charleston's first AME church evolved into a powerful stabilizing agent among free South Carolina blacks.

HISTORY

Established in 1791, the Emanuel African Methodist Episcopal Church formed the Free African Society, a prayer band of slaves and free blacks. Planners modeled the association after a similar band, the Bethel African Methodist Episcopal Church, which Richard Allen, a manumitted layman, founded in Philadelphia in 1787. Charleston's black religious society, later known as Bethel Circuit, gathered on Amherst and Hanover Streets and maintained a burying ground. The society moved closer to being a formalized denomination after a Charleston native, Morris Brown, traveled in secret to Philadelphia in 1791 to seek ordination in the Free African Society. His purpose was a step toward emancipation—he and his followers were tired of creeping into the balconies of white churches to worship like voyeurs. He returned from Philadelphia to organize the Negro Methodists. Within months, Emanuel Church membership reached 1,000.

To provide a permanent church home, Emanuel's members purchased a lot and erected a simple building in 1818. Four years later, the church was the meeting place of freedom fighter Denmark Vesey, whose plans to liberate slaves reached the ears of white authorities. The arrest and hanging of Vesey resulted in the departure of Morris Brown, the burning of Emanuel Church by angry whites, and suppression of congregational activities.

Emanuel Church revived on May 16, 1865, when Bishop Daniel Alexander Payne, also a Charleston native, met with members at Zion Presbyterian Church. The Reverend James Lynch proposed a governing system and called New York preacher Richard H. Cain to Emanuel's pulpit. The congregation, the South's largest AME church, voted on an open-door policy that admitted everyone but slaveholders. They chose the motto "God our father, Christ our redeemer, man our brother." (Lilly 1966, 53) In 1867, an offshoot of the Emanuel congregation formed the Morris Brown AME Church, which built a separate structure on Morris Street. In 1880, a second splinter group disagreed with traditionalists who chose to repair Emanuel Church and formed Mount Zion AME Church on Glebe Street.

ARCHITECTURE

Emanuel is an imposing structure. The façade rises from a double stairway and lower door at street level to a triple portal topped by pointed windows set in stained glass. Above, a simple Latin cross made of thirteen inset bricks pierces white stucco. A circle and second cross top the pointed eave. The element that gives the church presence is a massive square tower to the left, which passes from a second street-level door through three stories to a proportional steeple. Slim buttresses along the tower and sides frame a series of stained-glass windows.

Inside, an airy open space accommodates seating in three ranks of pews. Along the sides, square columns support a double gallery and connect to a gently curved ceiling. A two-tiered glass chandelier lights the interior. The apse parallels the front doors with a trio of pointed arches. The left and right arches contain dramatic images of the crucifixion and resurrection of Christ. The central arch is another grouping of three arches—two smaller arched windows and a four-petaled flower surmounting them—all in stained glass.

ACTIVITIES

Emanuel African Methodist Episcopal Church serves 1,600 with two Sunday morning worship services, a Monday Bible-study group, and a Thursday evening service. The choir presents seasonal concerts. A vigorous part of Charleston culture and history, the church assists the Charleston Interfaith Crisis Ministry. On May 23, 1998, for the Piccolo Spoleto festival, the staff hosted the program "Music of the Old South: Choraliers." On October 1 that same year, during the Moja Arts Festival, a celebration of African American and Caribbean art, Emanuel hosted the Choraliers Music Club. As a gesture to the past, the church preserves its link to Denmark Vesey with a plaque. According to Frances T. Mack and Lee Bennett, elderly members of the church's history committee, reflections of history fill in years of concealment of the church's role in the fight for freedom.

Sources: Ahlstrom 1972; Jacoby 1999; Lilly 1966; Low and Clift 1981; Ploski and Williams 1989; Wilson and Ferris 1989.

Enchanted Rock
Enchanted Rock State Natural Area
16710 Ranch Road 965
Route 4, Box 170
Fredericksburg, Texas 78624
915-247-3903

Enchanted Rock, Texas's geologic center, is the holy mountain of the state's hill country. To Native Americans, the rock offers a satisfying communion with the earth mother. The allure of the spot fills the writings of Ira Kennedy, publisher of a local journal, *The Enchanted Rock,* which relates tribal tales of seekers praying and offering gifts to the Great Spirit. The shamans, or "rock people," who interpret spiritual needs and demands carry the title of "wisdom keepers." Almost matter-of-factly, they accept the great granite bulge as an entrance to the afterworld. For 11,000 years, native dwellers have gathered on the pink dome to celebrate the seasons. Paleolithic dwellers of the ancient campground dropped flakes of flint from newly chipped spear points and left behind stone manos with which they ground berries and grains for meals.

In *Land of the Spotted Eagle* (1978), author Luther Standing Bear, a Lakota chief, accounts for the sanctity of Enchanted Rock. To Lakota elders, being near the soil allows them to return to nature and contact earth's mothering power. With bare feet brushing the rock's surface, they feel reassured, much as birds relax their wings when their feet reach a solid perch. Just as the Lakota build tipis on the ground and mold altars of soil, they accept earth as the final resting place of living creatures and plants. By sitting or reclining on the rock, they can ponder the mystery of existence and show respect for the source of all being.

HISTORY
In a 1,643-acre Texas state park sixty miles northwest of San Antonio and seventeen miles northeast of Fredericksburg in Gillespie County, Enchanted Rock is the main attraction. The second largest batholith, or mass of intruded rock, in the nation after Stone Mountain, Georgia, it rises 425 feet above the plain and 1,825 feet above sea level. The complex formation of the Proterozoic era 10,000 years ago resulted from subterranaean force pushing molten rock to the surface into an igneous ridge known as the Town Mountain Granite Suite of the Proterozoic Llano Uplift. The huge rock bubble, or magmatic exfoliation dome, is naturally pink and coarse grained. Its porphyritic granite consists predominantly of feldspar and glittering quartz blended with black biotite crystals and hornblende, a complex silicate. Irregular dark streaks and sparkles result from mineral additives—titanite, zircon, magnetite, fluorite, allanite, and pyrite, commonly known as fool's gold.

Boulders like Enchanted Rock hold a significant place in Texas history. The first record of events on the dome date to European explorers. In 1723, when the Spanish began colonizing Texas, they reconnoitered the rocks north and northwest of San Antonio. On the San Saba River, they set up a presidio and established a mission before mining on Honey Creek near the Llano River. In the mid-nineteenth century, John O. Meusebach, protector of German newcomers, immigrated to Texas primarily to study Enchanted Rock and locate precious ores. In May 1846, he founded the village of Fredericksburg and sought peace with local Comanche. Since 1882, quarriers have carved out high-quality building blocks, which form part of the Texas Capitol and other regional structures.

In terms of esthetic beauty, the granite bulge creates a spectacular landscape. Below its weathered lichens, grasses, and cacti, live deer, raccoons, skunks, wild turkeys, rabbits, armadillos, lizards, and rattlesnakes. In 1970, the Department of the Interior named the rock a National Natural Landmark. To maintain and protect it from daily foot traffic, the Texas Parks and Wildlife Department and Texas Nature Conservancy bought the rock and, in 1983, added it to the National Register of Historic Places.

Enchanted Rock, Texas's geologic center, is a holy mountain of the state's hill country. (Courtesy Enchanted Rock State Natural Area)

BELIEFS

The aboriginal understanding of Enchanted Rock varies widely in interpretation. Apache sages value the mysterious stirrings of Enchanted Rock and urge the younger generation to listen and learn from the enduring mountain. According to Tonkawa oral tradition, since the beginning of the tenth century, ancient tribes inhabiting central Texas speared mammoth and shot arrows into herds of bison. The Tonkawa, who arrived in 8,000 B.C., developed an abiding respect for their forebears and believed that ancestral spirits departed earth as wolves and owls. They explained the rock's ghost fires as remnants of past visitations and interpreted strange creaking sounds as cries of restless spirits, who could kill trespassers.

Another story explains why visitors report ghostly council fires and piteous groans at the base of Enchanted Rock. To end internal squabbling that threatened tribal unity, a chief summoned his people to the dome. While members stoked flames at the circle fires below, the chief's daughter ascended the rock. At the summit, she appeared to be pushed from safe footing. Her instant death from the fall implies a sacrifice as though the Great Spirit demanded a gift to assure the tribe's reunion.

A less mythic event was the escape of a Spanish conquistador, who fled his Tonkawa captors and hid in the Enchanted Rock complex. His captors evolved a legend about the rock's swallowing a pale-skinned man and reissuing him as an Indian. The Tonkawa declared that the changeling joined the mass of native spirits in weaving enchantment at the rock.

ACTIVITIES

Today, medicine men traverse the rugged terrain to experience its power, interact with spirits, and perform rituals. Through sparse clumps of mesquite, oak, persimmon, agarita, white brush, prickly pear, and grama grass, worshippers and hikers walk the winding creek and climb to a vantage point above crevices, caverns, and granite slabs. Cradled in boulders, after sunset, they sit in pale moonlight on cooling ledges to hear strange creaks of contracting granite and observe a reddish luminosity.

Visitors enjoy hiking the designated four-mile trail or the short ascent to the summit of Enchanted Rock, which is open daily. Many come to backpack, camp, climb, picnic, photograph birds and rocks, and gaze at constellations in the clear night sky. In the floodplain below, naturalists study elm, pecan, hackberry, black hickory, buttonbush, Indiangrass, bluestem, and soapberry. Botanists collect seed from Texas bluebonnets, Indian paintbrush, yellow coreopsis daisies, bladderpods, and bellflowers. In addition to a park store and visitor center, the facility provides wading sites, restrooms with showers, tent pads, fire rings, and a pavilion. Park authorities patrol wildlife and geological formations and protect Indian and historic artifacts.

Sources: "Enchanted Rock Archives"; "Enchanted Rock State Natural Area"; "Images from Enchanted Rock State Natural Area"; Kennedy 1998; Milne 1995; Patterson and Snodgrass 1994; Steiger 1974; "The Tonkawa Indians"; Waldman 1990.

Enola Hill
Sacred Earth Coalition
9317 S.E. Stanley Avenue
Portland, Oregon 97222-4236

Among beleaguered Native American sacred lands are the greenswards, teeming trout streams, and spiritual environs of Enola Hill, forty-five miles east of Portland, Oregon. Mid-nineteenth-century pioneer Elsie Creighton chose the name from "alone" spelled backward. A 3,200-foot elevation east of Rhododendron, it juts out of Zig Zag Mountain south of Mount Hood. Aborigines call Mount Hood Wy'East, which is the most active of the region's volcanoes. When flowing water eroded soft underrock, it left hardened lava ridges atop former streambeds. During this formative era, lava displaced rivers from their canyons. By the Ice Age, the peak had reached its greatest height of 12,000 feet. In the 1800s, the volcano erupted steam, magma, and ash. In 1907, it sent rocky embers into the White River Glacier. Currently, Mount Hood's southern depression, between Crater Rock and Steel Cliff, vents underground steam and a pungent sulfur odor.

The prominent peak of Mount Hood draws some 10,000 hikers per year up well-developed trails to a slumbering crater ringed with eleven glaciers. Along the way, they view wildflowers in the alpine meadows, photograph dozens of cataracts, and explore the 1,000-foot Zig Zag Canyon. Snowshoers exult in blue skies and smooth slopes. Naturalists prefer Douglas fir and hemlock, huckleberry and Oregon grape, rhododendron, lupine, Indian paintbrush, beargrass, penstemon, aster and pasque flower, avalanche lily, and salal, a heath shrub that the Kwakiutl prize for its thumb-size berries. Animal species range from hummingbird and bald eagle to pika, marmot, black bear, mountain lion, and elk.

Enola, according to U.S. Senator Ron Wyden, is a national treasure. A diminished population of coho salmon of the Lower Columbia still spawn in local waters; cougars rove its precipices. In 1989, rare spotted owls nested in the area. As described by oral tradition, the hill hosted Indians during hunts for food and medicinal plants and sheltered vision quests and water rituals. In the estimation of Dr. David French, former professor of anthropology at Reed College, the hill, like Mecca to Muslims, is a land of pilgrimages wrapped in a sacred aura. In May 1988, a citizens' task force appointed by the U.S. Forest Service informed Zig Zag District Ranger Donna Lamb that the area deserves protection.

Less popular than the Black Hills and Devils Tower, but no less beautiful than Crater Lake and Mount Shasta, Enola Hill holds divine and cultural significance to Indians of Wy'East yet merits little respect from government agencies set up to preserve native heritage. According to the Sacred Earth Coalition, Friends of Enola Hill, and elders of the Umatilla, Warm Springs, and Nez Perce, traditional practitioners hold prior claim under the Treaty of 1855, the First Amendment, and the American Indian Religious Freedom Act. Ray Olney, vice chair of the Yakima tribal council, countered U.S. Forest Service environmental and ethnographic assessments with testimony concerning the many miles elders travel to seek spiritual solace and bury their dead on Enola Hill.

BELIEFS
Ella E. Clark, a Pacific Northwest mythologist, compiled a substantive collection of lore from

Washington and Oregon tribes. From Grant Bushnell's "The Chief's Shadow," published in the January 1903 edition of *Oregon Teacher's Monthly,* she derived "The Chief's Face on Mount Hood," a creation myth linking the land's formation with indigenous peoples. The story describes a bold chief who protected his people from volcanic eruptions, which resulted from anger of evil spirits deep in Mount Hood's peaks. He climbed the peak and tossed boulders into the crater, which the spirits hurled into the sky. The combat between the chief and evil spirits caused such mayhem below that the people fled. In despair, the chief sank into the lava flow. When his people returned to their homeland, they thrived on the green meadows and looked up to Mount Hood's northern slope to see their great chief's profile and scalp lock.

HISTORY

The claims of northwest Indians to sanctuary on religious grounds are less clear than those for other native hallowed sites. Warm Springs elder Sylvia Walulatuma of Simnasho, Oregon, described the locale as a place where her children encountered spirit animals who entered their souls and remained with them for life. Susana Santos, of the Tygh River Band, helped found the Sacred Earth Coalition to protect indigenous people's rediscovery of the sacred land and water from Mount Hood. In 1990, the Confederated Tribes of the Umatilla Indian Reservation legitimized the area's traditional cultural values, particularly the Cayuse way of life. Walter Speedis, Cascades Klickitat elder and Senior Cultural Assistant to the Yakima Indian Nation, testified in 1992 that the pristine beauty of Enola Hill compelled him to remain a part of the land to seek spiritual affirmation.

To substantiate such claims, the U.S. Forest Service hired anthropologist Robert Winthrop of Ashland, Oregon. Winthrop reported that the area is a traditional cultural property deserving nomination to the National Register of Historic Places. A second Forest Service anthropologist, Beth Walton, seconded by coworker Doug Jones, rebutted Winthrop's advice on grounds that there is insufficient evidence that Indians have traditionally used the land for worship. She cited a Cherokee, Les McConnell, who supported her

contention that native claims to religiosity are nonspecific. In response, Michael P. Jones, director of the Friends of Enola Hill and cultural and natural resource consultant for the Cascade Geographic Society in nearby Rhododendron, repudiated Forest Service evidence as lies.

Strong testimony failed to protect Enola Hill from commercialism. Despite the testimony of Richard Moe, president of the National Trust for Historic Preservation, that Enola Hill is severely threatened and merits inclusion among protected properties, despite the Clackamas County Board of Commissioners' recognition of the hill's rich pioneer and Indian history, in 1995, the U.S. Forest Service awarded to loggers the cutting rights to 4.8 million board feet of old-growth evergreens and deciduous trees within 158 acres. His justification was the Salvage Logging Rider on environmental protection laws, which countenanced clear-cutting in forests throughout the Pacific Northwest. The decision ignored warnings from forest pathologist Thomas Lawson that intruders will spread laminated root rot, undermining forest health.

As early as 1992, protesters from Earth First! took positions along the trail to stop sacrilege against Enola Hill. Earth Firsters mobilized against an attitude they considered cultural arrogance. They brought drummers, waved banners proclaiming ecocide, formed a human blockade, smoked a peace pipe, and organized a prayer circle composed of Warm Springs Indians. On April 5, 1996, Indians issued a formal claim describing Enola Hill as a feature of the Mount Hood National Forest and a revered cultural and spiritual stronghold of Indians of the Mid-Columbia River Basin and Willamette River Basin. They declared that the 1855 treaties reserved hunting, fishing, and gathering rights to their accustomed places. The Yakima, Umatilla, and Cayuse embrace the land as a source of food, pure water, and medicines for fundamental religious purposes. The Affiliated Tribes of the Northwest Indians affirmed in 1990 that Enola Hill has been sacred since prehistory. Signers declared that the U.S. Forest Service deliberately disregarded experts and pursued illegal logging. Joe Keating of Witness against Lawless Logging claimed that President Bill Clinton met with 200 Indian leaders at the White House on

April 29, 1994, and promised to protect native rights to practice the aboriginal faith and to cancel the timber sale.

Near the century's end, the furor rose. Because the logging sites infringed on sacred Native American geography, in April 1996, *60 Minutes* aired an investigative report on the desecration of Enola Hill. Rip Lone Wolf, a 62-year-old Nez Perce tribesman and spokesman for Native Americans for Enola Hill, spoke before 700 people at an April rally and vowed to carry on the fight. A ten-day injunction inconvenienced clear-cutters, but did not stop the project. Members of the Warm Springs, Umatilla, and Yakima held a weekend protest rally, but could not derail a federal appeals court order upholding Judge Michael Hogan's sanction of logging.

Lumberjacks for Hannell Lumber claimed that they advanced on ancient stands of trees as gently as is possible in their business. During selective airlifting performed in 1996 by Columbia Helicopters Inc. of Aurora, Oregon, Hannell avoided road building and clear-cutting by harvesting via the Boeing Chinook, which can hoist fourteen tons. Still, protesters reclined among downed trees to stall operations. One daredevil grasped the skyhook that dangled from the Chinook until heliloggers pried his hands free. As work progressed, authorities arrested thirty-eight protesters.

ACTIVITIES

Individuals continue to reverence Enola Hill for its divine inspiration, but conceal from whites and the press exact locations of shrines and cemeteries. Rip Lone Wolf has pledged himself to fight loggers in court and, in 1995, appeared as complainant in the lawsuit tried in the Ninth Circuit Court. A devout holy man, he reveres the trees as temples and the source of native spiritual power. He directed his 14-year-old son's vision quest among 350-year-old Douglas firs at ceremonial sites that honor the natural world.

To justify his insistence that the land is sacred, Lone Wolf built a sweat lodge on posted land and received a citation for camping without a permit. U.S. Representative Ron Wyden petitioned the Forest Service to respect the lodge, but Lone Wolf returned to find it in pieces. Forest Service spokeswoman Gayle Aschenbrener claimed that agents destroyed the lodge because they thought it was the work of vandals. Lone Wolf rescinded his earlier vow of silence and agreed to identify sacred sites if the revelation would shift public opinion against encroachment.

Artists, too, have their say about the desecration of native sites. After a year's work, in summer 1998, the Sacred Land Film Project—directed by Toby McLeod, coproduced by Malinda Maynor, an instructor in American Indian studies at San Francisco State University, and aided by the Seventh Generation Fund of Arcata, California—hurried to film *In the Light of Reverence*. The two-hour documentary delineates sacred geography and the plight of Native Americans trying to preserve a vanishing spiritual landscape.

Sources: Brock 1996; Clark 1953; Dark 1993; "Enola Hill Timber Sale" 1996; "Environmental Movement Fights Clinton's Ecology Double-Talk" 1997; "The Impact of Proposed Amendments to the American Indian Religious Freedom Act on Other Uses of Public Lands"; "Letters" 1996; Lewis, David Rich, 1995; Maynor and McLeod 1999; Mazza 1995; "Mt. Hood Wilderness"; "Native Americans for Enola vs. the United States Forest Service" 1995; "Seventh Generation Fund—Threatened Sacred Sites"; Taylor 1996; Thompson 1996.

First Baptist Church of America
Holly Edwards, Church Secretary
75 North Main Street
Providence, Rhode Island 02903
401-454-3418

The highlight of architectural history in Providence, Rhode Island, the First Baptist Church of America predates the republic and symbolizes the state's dedication to personal and religious freedom. In New England's highest steeple built in the nineteenth century, inscriptions on the 2.25-ton bronze bell claim the site as Rhode Island's first church and the nation's first Baptist church. Designed by Joseph Brown and built by James Sumner, the church introduced to the New England colonies the individualistic Italian-English style of Scotsman Sir James Gibbs.

HISTORY

A commanding presence in the colonies and a monument to freedom of speech, Providence's American Baptist community dates to 1639 and Rhode Island's founder, Roger Williams. He was a Puritan dissenter and separatist from the Church of England eventually banished from Salem. An advocate of "soul liberty," his term for religious freedom, Williams bought land from the Narragansett and settled an area appropriately named Providence. (Smith 1989, 146) His intent was both spiritual and altruistic:

> And I . . . having a Sence of Gods merciful!
> Providence unto me in my distresse, called
> the place providence; I desired that it might
> be a shelter for persons distressed for Con-
> science. (church pamphlet)

The experiment was successful. In 1700, local Baptists completed their first church home and replaced it by 1726 with an upgrade. They were fortunate to have benefactor Nicholas Brown, a wealthy Baptist whose family generously aided the congregation and who, in 1771, established Rhode Island College, later named Brown in his honor.

In 1775, the current building, the third to follow Roger Williams's original building, began serving 118 members, who tired of meeting in homes or outdoors. Led by the Reverend James Manning, they planned the structure as a combination worship center–meeting house and as an auditorium for holding Brown University's commencement. Local merchant Joseph Brown, an amateur architect and altruist, rejected the styles of churches he toured in Boston and turned to sketches of St. Martin-in-the-Fields in Sir James Gibbs's *Book of Architecture*. By adding a Doric porch from Marybone Chapel and a Palladian window to the façade, he created a trend.

History helped shape the work schedule. After the Boston Tea Party, when Parliament closed the harbor to trade, ships' carpenters found themselves unemployed. With these skilled woodworkers, supervisor James Sumner organized construction of the 185-foot steeple from the bottom up without scaffolding by hoisting each segment with a windlass. The finished tower begins with the clock module and rises to an arched belvedere and on to two windowed stories and the crowning spire. The shipbuilders produced so sturdy a steeple that it withstood two mighty windstorms in 1815 and 1938. The original ton-and-a-quarter bell, cast in London, bore a four-line inscription that began, "For freedom of conscience the town was first planted" and concluded joyfully that no Anglican law prohibited it from designating itself a "church" or from having a steeple or bell. (Broderick 1958, 8)

ARCHITECTURE

A sizeable church situated on 1.25 acre of prime land, First Baptist Church of Providence is a square, eighty feet on a side, and seats 1,400. The two-story structure balances the loft and elegance of the spire with a classic portico, double pairs of Tuscan columns, and symmetrical arched

JAMES GIBBS

A student of Italian baroque and Sir Christopher Wren's churches, architect James Gibbs influenced American public buildings through published drawings that provided a floor plan for Providence's First Baptist Church. Born in December 1682 in Footdeesmire outside Aberdeen, Scotland, he grew up in a privileged environment, traveled Europe, and studied architecture in Rome with Carlo Fontana. He began work drawing plans for English aristocrats. At age twenty-seven, he came under the mentorship of Edward Harley, Earl of Oxford, who named him the surveyor for fifty London churches. While serving the commission, Gibbs designed his first public edifice, St. Mary-le-Strand, which he completed in 1717.

After building a wing of Burlington House, Piccadilly, in 1715, Gibbs fell into disfavor during a political shift and spent most of his time erecting private homes for members of the Tory party. He gained a second public commission in 1720 to build St. Martin-in-the-Fields, one of London's most treasured houses of worship. After moving on to build the Senate House at Cambridge and structures at King's College, he completed three temples, Oxford's Radcliffe Library, and a column bearing the statue of Lord Cobham and published *Book of Architecture* (1728) and *Rules for Drawing the Several Parts of Architecture* (1732).

The highlight of architectural history in Providence, Rhode Island, the First Baptist Church of America predates the republic and symbolizes the state's dedication to personal and religious freedom. (Courtesy The First Baptist Church of America)

windows. Central to the beauty of the second-floor interior are ten slender Ionic columns rising from the nave to support galleries at each side and attach to arches of the vaulted ceiling. In its early days, the balcony seated slaves, freedmen, and Indians.

In the gallery wall, the clerestory augments light from the two-tiered crystal chandelier, built in Waterford, Ireland, in 1792, which hangs over the center rank of boxed pews. Behind the pulpit, two shuttered arched windows and central baptistery surmount a pair of handsomely ornate doors. The whole retains its original design, thanks to restoration in 1958 by architect Joseph Brown. The funds came from John D. Rockefeller, Jr., a First Baptist Sunday-school instructor while he attended Brown University.

ACTIVITIES

Still an urban sanctuary, the First Baptist Church of Providence remains in service, offering traditional Sunday morning worship at 11:00. Tours are available daily from 10:00 A.M. to early afternoon; a walking tour of Benefit Street puts the property in context of other religious sites. In addition to serving Brown University as its commencement site, the church hosts a spirited Advent season. In 1999, staff scheduled Brown University's performance of *Carmina de Christi Nativitate atque Lectiones Sacres et Profanas* (Christmas Carols and Lessons Sacred and Secular) and the hanging of the greens and joined the Providence Intown Churches Association for a Christmas celebration that engaged the Beavertail Opera Companies for a presentation of Gian Carlo Menotti's seasonal opera *Amahl and the Night Visitors.*

Other activities kept First Baptist's trustees occupied from the 1990s into the twenty-first century. In 1995, former minister Kate Penfield, executive director of the American Baptist Ministers Council, anthologized eleven addresses by

Baptists in *Into a New Day: Exploring a Baptist Journey of Division, Diversity, and Dialogue,* a rhetorical account of the separation of the Northern and Southern Baptists. The volume derives from a strategic conference held at Providence First Baptist in August 1995 to survey the sect's past and determine its future. In preparation for a historical festival, the congregation voted to replace the organ, which was removed from the nave early in 2000 to prepare the sanctuary for a new organ.

> **Sources:** *Biography Resource Center* 1999; Broderick 1958; *Encyclopedia of World Biography* 1998; "First Baptist Church, Providence, Rhode Island"; *Historic World Leaders* 1994; Mutrux 1982; Sinnott 1963; Smith 1989; Williams, Peter W., 1997.

First Church of Christ, Scientist
Gary A. Jones, Manager
175 Huntington Avenue
Boston, Massachusetts 02115
800-450-8950; 617-450-2000
infoline@compub.org
www.tfccs.com/GV/jc/jc.html

The only American woman to found a religion, Mary Baker Eddy, originator of the concept of Christian science and metaphysical healing, knew pain for most of her early life. (North Wind Picture Archives)

At home in the sophisticated Boston Back Bay milieu is the First Church of Christ, Scientist, the sect's world headquarters for a vast publishing industry and 2,200 branch churches in sixty countries. The complex makes economical use of nineteen acres. A 1,000-seat Renaissance-Byzantine sanctuary, erected in 1894, is the heart of the religious outreach. Constructed of New Hampshire granite by architect Franklin Welch, it displays the original educational purpose of churches with stained-glass windows. The domed extension, completed by architect Charles Brigham in 1906, increased capacity by 3,000. The organ, one of the world's largest, is a 13,595-pipe instrument built by the Aeolian-Skinner Company of Boston.

BELIEFS
Through a lifelong study of the relationship between mind and health, Mary Baker Eddy forged a science from the teachings of Christ and Saint Paul. From her own experience with pain, she acquired a vivid realization of God as an all-encompassing and loving spirit and looked to the Bible for revelation and emotional support. By denying materialism, she intensified an awareness of an ineffable presence and concluded that Christianity professed a faulty belief—that God ended physical suffering only in the afterlife. By characterizing supernatural healing as an outgrowth of a divine order, she restructured the nature and purpose of prayer from petition to affirmation of power. The purpose of oneness with God, she avowed, was to cast off sin and the mind's misperceptions of illness as God's will.

Unlike mainstream Christians, Eddy denied Christ's deity but valued him as an example of earthly goodness. She interpreted his resurrection as proof of a workable science that overcomes human limitations. Her understanding of self-healing was a lengthy process of regeneration through rigorous self-study, Bible reading, and prayer. She concluded that, to achieve health, the individual required a litany of old-school Calvinist virtues—repentence, humility, self-denial, perseverence, and patience.

MARY BAKER EDDY

The only American woman to found a religion, Mary Baker Eddy, originator of the concept of Christian science and metaphysical healing, knew pain most of her early life. A natural intellectual and idealist, she grew up in a Puritan household and sought oneness with God in childhood. Born on July 16, 1821, in Bow, New Hampshire, because of a chronic spinal infirmity, she received a sketchy education. She rose above physical complaints and concentrated on heavenly voices that taught her forbearance and kindness.

After marriage to builder George Washington Glover in 1843, Eddy lived in Charleston, South Carolina. She detested the state of black-white relations in the South and, to the dismay of in-laws, openly protested slavery. At her husband's sudden death in 1844, she freed his slaves and returned home before delivery of a son, George, Jr. The birth worsened her illness. A second blow to her confidence was the capture of her second husband, dentist Daniel Patterson, during the Civil War.

Eddy's understanding of faith healing derived from friendship with faith healer and hypnotist Phineas Parkhurst Quimby, who advised good thoughts in place of bad. Her relapse after his death brought Eddy new despair. She plunged into a three-year immersion in the New Testament. After suffering through medical examinations, homeopathy, hydropathy, hypnotism, and quackery, she determined that Christians could heal themselves through prayer and guided interpretation of scripture. When she managed to heal her own ailments, she applied the experience to religion and organized practice founded on faith in Christ's regeneration.

Eddy earned a place in American religion and philosophy with a major publication—the Christian Science textbook, *Science and Health with Key to the Scriptures* (1875). After marriage to Asa Gilbert Eddy, she and fifteen followers chartered Boston's First Church of Christ, Scientist, in 1879. To direct Christian education away from widespread liberalism, she founded and taught at Massachusetts Metaphysical College for eight years. Beginning in 1895, she administered the sect's outreach from the mother church. In 1908, she earned international renown for founding the *Christian Science Monitor*, a current-events journal respected for objective reporting. For equalizing women's role in faith, in 1995, Eddy was inducted into the National Women's Hall of Fame.

Eddy's text *Science and Health with Key to the Scriptures* guides seekers in applying God's earthly power to daily needs. She advocates compliance with public-health regulations and observance of laws governing immunization and quarantine. Members accept dental and optometric intervention, employ nurse care, accept rest cures at sanitaria, and seek the aid of midwives and obstetricians for childbirth. For all other health needs, the devout call on full-time Christian Science practitioners, men and women registered in the *Christian Science Journal* as authorized healers and counselors.

HISTORY

After abandoning a frame church building in Oconto, Wisconsin, in 1892, Mary Baker Eddy set her sights on an appropriate mother church and commissioned a Romanesque building in Boston on October 19, 1893. In preparation for dedication in 1894, she organized church hier-archy and published *The Manual of the Mother Church* (1895) to guide its democratic government, administration, and expansion. The church returned worship to the style of the initial followers of Christ and to a healing presence that Christians once invoked. Christian Scientists adopted her altered understanding of faith despite condemnation of Protestant clergy, hostility from neighbors, and ridicule in the popular press. Congregants required no liturgy, prayer book, sacraments, pastors, or missionaries; instead, they disseminated the tenets of spiritual healing through health practitioners and a substantial publishing house.

Before Eddy's death on December 3, 1910, the church stabilized, took hold worldwide, and spread the concept of spiritual healing. Although church officials set up a five-member board of directors, the immediate effect of her loss was a protracted period of power struggle, schism, and litigation between Annie C. Bill in England and

Mrs. A. E. Stetson in New York. At the height of the sect's popularity, headquarters remained in Boston until the construction of Pleasant View Home in Concord, New Hampshire, in 1927.

Midcentury shifts in American experience brought new challenges to Christian Science. To reinvigorate a declining membership and enroll more converts, the church expanded in 1950 and, in the 1980s, broadened its services to include television and the Internet. Purists feared that these updated missions would divert attention from spiritual healing and thus secularize Christian Science. Court cases in the 1990s clashed with the separation of church and state by charging parents with neglecting conventional medical therapy for their children.

ARCHITECTURE

Boston's First Church of Christ, Scientist, stands apart from a five-story curved education building, twenty-eight-story office complex, colonnade, circular fountain and pool, and 600-car underground parking facility. A dynamic physical presence in a major city, the original church home echoes the Renaissance splendors of St. Mark's Piazza in Venice but replaces the opulent materials of past eras with Pei's hallmark, reinforced concrete. Surrounding it are manicured trees and lawn on each side of a wide entranceway to give the whole a sense of composure amid city bustle. Inside, the main auditorium expands in domed splendor. Classic archways and square pillars highlight seating on the main floor and in parallel balconies. Another arch frames a massive organ that serves as a reredos to a railed pulpit elevated from the pews.

Pei's partner, Araldo Cassutta, laid out the grounds for the center in 1970, when the firm designed the Sunday-school buildings, office, and colonnade. Central to the effect is a 670-foot reflecting pool in front of the mother church. Attendants maintain formal beds of red begonia, yellow marigold, orange columbine, and silvery dusty miller around the fountain and along the linden tree arcade that parallels Huntington Avenue. The garden, a favorite with strollers and children, is open daily.

ACTIVITIES

The Boston Christian Science center holds Sun-

IEOH MING PEI

An urban innovator and the organizer of the Christian Science Center, modernist I. M. Pei, like Mary Baker Eddy, sought a genuine redirection of prevailing principles. Born April 26, 1917, in Guangzhou, China, he grew up during unstable times that required his family to flee to Hong Kong. He studied under missionaries at St. John's Middle School before taking passage to the United States at age seventeen to enroll in engineering at the Massachusetts Institute of Technology. In 1943, he aided the National Defense Research Committee in developing protocols for destroying buildings. While completing a master's degree at Harvard University Graduate School in 1945, he joined the staff of the department of architecture. In 1948, he left teaching to direct urban construction for the firm of Webb and Knapp and then opened his own office in 1955.

Pei's early career displays a verve and substance unique to his style. After triumphing with the National Center for Atmospheric Research in Boulder, Colorado, and Dallas City Hall, he completed the expansion of the Christian Science Center in 1975. The complex became a valuable complement to Boston's evolving urbanism. He introduced glass curtain walls and upgraded precast concrete with finish details that polished humble material into a marblelike sheen. Later works—the East Wing of the National Gallery of Art in Washington, D.C., Boston's John F. Kennedy Library, New York's Javits Convention Center, and La Pyramide du Louvre in Paris—assured his place among the world's great builders. In 1982, he returned to Hong Kong to design a headquarters for the Bank of China, Asia's tallest building, and the Fragrant Hill Hotel in Beijing. Culminating a career filled with prizes and honors was the Medal of Liberty, conferred by President Ronald Reagan in 1986.

---

day and Wednesday evening testimony meetings in the main sanctuary. Sunday school, held at 10:45 A.M. for participants under age twenty, coordinates discussion about God, prayer, healing, and moral and spiritual law. Simultaneously, adults gather for a prayerful service and return at 7:30 P.M.; the Wednesday service is also at 7:30 P.M.

The Sunday lesson-sermon, delivered by two elected readers, derives from the *Christian Science Quarterly.* In addition, the congregation sings from the *Christian Science Hymnal,* repeats the Lord's Prayer, and prays silently. The Wednesday service begins with Bible passages and readings from *Science and Health with Key to the Scriptures* and culminates with voluntary testimony of healing and insight gained from study and experience. The facility is open Monday through Saturday from 10:00 A.M. to 3:30 P.M. and on Sunday from noon until 3:30 P.M.

In addition to structured teaching, the church sponsors Christian Science reading rooms, quiet nooks and lounges for exploring the Bible and Mary Baker Eddy's writings. Staff maintains these neighborhood centers as sources of material on health, personal growth, and spiritual discovery. Visitors may read on the premises or purchase church publications, which are available in French, Norwegian, Swedish, Danish, Dutch, Spanish, Portuguese, Italian, Indonesian, Japanese, Greek, and braille. The church also sponsors centers on college and university campuses worldwide, where visitors attend lectures and share perceptions of Christian healing.

> **Sources:** *American Decades* 1998; *Biography Resource Center* 1999; Broderick 1958; Carpenter and Carpenter 1985; *Contemporary Heroes and Heroines* 1998; Dakin 1990; *Encyclopedia of World Biography* 1998; "The First Church of Christ, Scientist" 1999; Melton 1992; Mutrux 1982; *New Catholic Encyclopedia* 1967; *Notable Asian Americans* 1995; Powell 1950; Rice 1982; Sherr and Kazickas 1994; Singer and Lalich 1995; Smaus 1966; Smith 1989; Snodgrass 1993; Zeinert 1997; Zweig 1990.

First Presbyterian Church
Mary M. Thies
R. Blair Moffett
David R. Van Dyke, copastors
1101 Bedford Street
Stamford, Connecticut 06905
203-324-9522
www.fishchurch.org

Recapturing the the symbolism of ICHTHUS, the Christian acronym of the Greek word for "fish," First Presbyterian Church has dubbed itself the Fish Church. Just northeast of Stamford's commercial center, the sparkling nontraditional shape leaves open to interpretation its architectural and theological purpose. To some eyes, the bright shape suggests the myriad possibilities of the future in a vibrant, ethnically diverse congregation. To others, the open-sided form represents a work in progress and a people who, like Jonah in the whale, await a transformation and reemergence into a needy world.

HISTORY
Stamford's First Presbyterian Church got its start in the New England tradition—in a functional wood building on Broad Street. Begun in 1854, the church celebrated its first centennial by opting to move to Bedford Street and rebuild on ten acres purchased in the early 1940s. To tie the past with the future, planners preserved for the new building sixteen stained-glass windows representing post-Reformation churches of Europe.

In response to a forward-thinking congregation, in 1956, the building committee opted for modernism in a spatially challenging façade and towering carillon and chose as its designer a mid-twentieth-century star—Wallace Kirkman Harrison of Harrison and Abramovitz in New York City. The selection acknowledged the creativity he applied to buildings for Corning Glass, Time-Life, Exxon, Celanese, McGraw-Hill, and Albany's Empire State Plaza and his domination of the New York skyline in major contributions, notably, Rockefeller Center, the United Nations Headquarters, the Metropolitan Opera House, the World Trade Towers, and Lincoln Center.

Other talents contributed to the functional beauty of First Presbyterian. For assistance with the nave walls, Harrison turned to Gabriel Loire, Chartres glass master, who arranged French Betonglas—inch-thick, jewel-cut glass—set in concrete for the giant fish's outer skin. A local architect, Willis Mills of Sherwood, Smith, and Mills, completed the complex with offices, a lounge, and an education center. A fan-shaped fellowship hall seats 250 for stage presentations, dining, and lectures. Mills also constructed a chapel seating 75 for weddings, funerals, church-school classes, and small assemblies. Embellishing the interior is a triangular window by New Haven artist Matthew Wysocki displaying five

Recapturing the symbolism of ICHTHUS, the Christian acronym of the Greek word for "fish," First Presbyterian Church has dubbed itself the "Fish Church." (Courtesy The First Presbyterian Church)

emblems—God's hands, plants, a bird, stars, and Christ's crown of thorns.

In 1991, the congregation enhanced the music program by purchasing a Visser-Rowland four-manual organ, composed of 74 ranks, 51 stops, and 4,026 pipes. Surface pipes ally polished tin and copper trumpets and façade pipes. Complementing the metalwork, the console casing, built of Honduras mahogany, gleams with maple sunbursts.

ARCHITECTURE

A one-of-a-kind free form, Stamford's First Presbyterian Church imposes angles and planes on faceted stained glass, lead, slate, limestone, sand, and gravel to create a multidimensional spiritual impression. For strength, Deluca Construction Company pleated the outer shell of 152 precast, reinforced-concrete panels into a symbolic shape 234 feet long and 60 feet high. Harrison completed the church in March 1958, presenting the drama of Christ's crucifixion on the north side of the nave and of the resurrec-

tion on the opposite side. To the rear of the narthex, the windows depict Christian themes of peace, sacrifice, and sharing.

The ribbed fish shape takes form in structural steel and 22,000 panes of glass that glitter like rainbow-hued fish scales. The unique profile and site plan links the congregation to the original body of energetic Christians. In uncertain company, they silently signaled their allegiance to Christ by drawing the stark outline of the fish, which stood for the name and titles of Christ in Greek, "Iesous Christos Theou Uios Soter" (Jesus Christ, Son of God, Savior). As a symbol of faith and communal support, the fish reminded early Christians that Christ's apostles were fishermen, whom he promised to make "fishers of men" (Mark 1:17).

In medieval style, First Presbyterian is an architectural lesson in history and faith. Along the outside, a stone wall along Bedford Street aligns tablets chronologically from 1641 to 1975 to recall events, institutions, and individuals in Stamford history. The Memorial Walk from Fellowship Hall to the front portal contains over 100 stones that former pastor Dr. George Stewart gathered worldwide to trace Christian history. Each represents a spiritual giant of the Judeo-Christian tradition from Abraham to the present. Built alongside the sanctuary in 1967, a 260-foot freestanding bell tower, the Walter N. McGuire Memorial Carillon, supports 56 bells in a reinforced concrete frame. Some were gifts to the church in 1947 from the Nestle Company of Switzerland.

Within, the polyhedral worship center gives the impression of a sturdy, columnless space platform bathed in prismatic glints. A narrow nave grounds two glass walls that incline toward a steeply pitched groin. Shaped like the upturned keel of a Galilean fishing vessel, it shelters worshippers in an atmosphere both exhilarating and comforting. Pews of African mahogany seat 670. The rear balcony holds an additional 50 spectators; the chancel choir accommodates 50 singers. At the center of the altar, upward angles guide the eye to an unadorned cross standing 32 feet high and displaying wood veneer from England's Canterbury Cathedral, which was decimated by bombers during the Blitz of World War II. To the left, an inverted roof tops the pulpit. Unassuming futuristic chandeliers focus light on the double rank of pews.

ACTIVITIES

In token of commitment as a servant congregation, First Presbyterian aims to be more than an architectural landmark. Staff holds regular Sunday worship at 10:30 A.M., which concludes with a coffee hour and carillon recital, and welcomes visitors daily from 9:00 A.M. to 4:00 P.M. On March 1, 1998, to benefit the New Covenant House of Hospitality, the church hosted its seventh annual Soup Kitchen Cantata. The concert featured Metropolitan Opera star Betty Jones, the Union Baptist Men's Chorus, and the Fairfield University Chamber Singers in a varied program of spirituals and gospel, arias, ensembles, and a musical tribute to George Gershwin.

The annual calendar carries the congregation through the major religious seasons:

- Wreath-making at Advent
- A Christmas brunch and organ and brass concert and a Christmas Eve pageant and living crêche, 9:00 P.M. lessons and carols, and an 11:00 P.M. candlelight service with communion
- Two Easter services featuring the New York Brass
- A church picnic on the lawn at Pentecost
- A series of musicales on the green Thursday evenings in July, combining carillon music and a jazz concert
- October's Scottish Sunday, celebrating ethnic heritage with pipers and a blessing of the tartans
- Thanksgiving worship with the New York Brass

First Presbyterian balances programs for adults with a regular Sunday Babyfold and classes for children and youth, incorporating music and activities with Bible instruction keyed to the sermon text. In addition, staff provides a nursery school that supports Christian values for children three to five years of age and a summer learning community, which welcomes visitors. A youth ministry offers an eight-week confirmation class and retreat for teens plus an integrated experience of fellowship, mission, prayer, study, and fun. Adult education ranges from Bible study to seminars, workshops, and retreats.

The music program augments worship with an adult choir and a handbell choir, a carillon guild, and children's classes in reading music, playing hand chimes and rhythm games, identifying orchestral instruments, and sight and ear training. A CD, *The People Respond . . . Amen,* recorded at the church by Marilyn Keiser, features Dan Locklair's "Rubrics, A Liturgical Suite for Organ," Leo Sowerby's "Requiescat in Pace," Alec Wyton's "Fanfare" and "A Wedding Blessing," John Ferguson's "Prelude on 'Unser Herrscher,'" Herbert Howells's "Rhapsody in D-flat," Felix Mendelssohn-Bartholdy's "Sonata in A, Opus 65 #3," Maurice Duruflé's "Fugue sur le thème du carillon des heures de la Cathédral de Soissons," and Louise Vierne's "Allegro Vivace" and "Finale" from Symphony No. 1 in D.

Sources: *Biography Resource Center* 1999; "First Presbyterian Church, Stamford, Connecticut"; "The Kidder Smith Images Project"; Mutrux 1982; Smith 1989; "Soup Kitchen Cantata" 1998.

First Unitarian Church of Philadelphia
Reverend Doctor Holly Horn
Reverend Benjamin Maucere, copastors
2125 Chestnut Street
Philadelphia, Pennsylvania 19103
215-563-3980
FAX 215-563-4209
FirstUU@libertynet.org
www.firstuu-philly.org

A revolution in worship, the First Unitarian Church of Philadelphia has celebrated over 300 years of liberal thought and service to humanity. Its history incorporates the thoughts and deeds of great men and women devoted to religious freedom against a backdrop of grim, unforgiving New England puritanism. Church architecture, both past and present, derives from Robert Mills and Frank Furness, two of America's foremost urban designers. The resilience of New England Unitarianism thrives into the twenty-first century in over 1,200 Unitarian Universalist fellowships nationwide.

HISTORY
Unitarianism resulted from Council of Nicaea of 325 A.D., when the early Christian church adopted the dogma of the Trinity. The majority of the resulting schism branded as heretics all believers in the unity of God. Formal Unitarianism dates to the Protestant Reformation in Europe, when an anti-Catholic, anti-Trinitarian movement launched the concept of a single God.

In rejecting the orthodox Catholic view of the Trinity, many encountered persecution. One, Spanish physician and theologian Michael Servetus, author of *On The Errors of the Trinity* (1551), died at the stake in Geneva in 1553 after John Calvin's court condemned him for refuting dogma on Christ's divinity and infant baptism. Forerunners of formal Unitarianism Laelius Socinus, Faustus Socinus, and Franz David organized like-minded worshippers in Poland and Transylvania. By emphasizing Jesus' teachings over his evolved cult, the strands of Socinianism and evangelical rationalism spread to Holland and Germany. John Biddle and Stephen Nye fostered these beliefs in England among intellectual giants—Isaac Newton, John Locke, Charles Darwin, and Joseph Priestley.

In the United States, Unitarianism took root in New England in defiance of the Puritan heritage, a stern belief system that limited a free society. A rebel individualist, John Murray, organized American Universalism in 1770 and established a congregation at Gloucester, Massachusetts. The movement flourished among congregants at the Episcopal King's Chapel in Boston. In 1785, James Freeman's adherents revised the Book of Common Prayer by eradicating mention of the Trinity.

Under the influence of scientist Joseph Priestley, who fled a firebombing that consumed his home and threatened his family, Unitarians formalized their sect. Led by English adherents, the first twenty-one members to adopt the name Unitarian organized on August 21, 1796, on Lombard Street in Philadelphia, which was then the nation's capital. Because of its rational approach to faith, Priestley's New World Unitarianism enticed enlightened followers, notably, Thomas Jefferson, George Washington, Thomas Paine, John Adams, and Benjamin Franklin, who had attended London's first Unitarian fellowship, led by Anglican pastor Theophilus Lindsey in 1774.

The nineteenth century witnessed less amiable relations between old-school Christians and the new liberal faith. In 1805, the Reverend Henry Ware demonstrated enlightened Unitarianism as Hollis professor of divinity at Harvard. In reaction, in 1808 Congregationalists launched a theological seminary at Andover, Massachusetts. Eight years later, Harvard riposted by founding the first nonsectarian seminary. By 1820, the claims and counterclaims of Congregationalists and Unitarians came before the Massachusetts supreme court, which upheld the rights of schismatics to formalize minority beliefs.

Unitarianism acquired its oratorical champion in William Ellery Channing, who ordained Jared Sparks in Baltimore in 1819. Six years later, Unitarian churches chose Channing's writings as the foundation of the American Unitarian Association, a society dedicated to the dissemination of pure Christianity. New England's transcendentalists, a philosophical group drawn to the liberal beliefs of Unitarians, swelled the numbers of the growing sect.

ROBERT MILLS

By 1814, Philadelphia acquired its first Unitarian church, designed by Robert Mills, the nation's first Native American architect and popularizer of the American Greek Revival. Born August 12, 1781, in Charleston, South Carolina, he completed a degree at Charleston College and, at age nineteen, apprenticed to builder James Hoban. Mentored by Thomas Jefferson, Mills studied architecture at Monticello and toured construction along the eastern seaboard. Still in his twenties, Mills joined the staff of Benjamin H. Latrobe, architect of the Capitol, and designed Philadelphia's Sansom Street Church, America's first domed house of worship.

In private practice by 1808, Mills worked at row housing before building the Unitarian church, which the Reverend William Christie dedicated in 1814. Subsequent works include additions to Independence Hall, a New Jersey prison, residences throughout the South, and the Upper Ferry Bridge, which contained the longest arch in the world. In Baltimore, he supervised the city waterworks, designed churches and public buildings, and issued a tract on transportation, *Treatise on Inland Navigation* (1820). In South Carolina, he planned Columbia's State Hospital for the Insane and Charleston's fireproof Record Building and issued a statistical handbook and state atlas.

In the last phase of his career, Mills lived in Washington, D.C., and published a lighthouse guide and a handbook to the Capitol. As architect of public buildings, he helped set a dignified tone with the Greek stylistic details of the Treasury Building, U.S. Patent Office, and city post office. In 1848, he began construction of the Washington Monument, completed in 1884 as his most famous endeavor.

This romantic movement produced pulpit orator and essayist Ralph Waldo Emerson, who held the post of senior pastor of the Second Church of Boston from 1829 to 1832. In a dramatic move, he resigned over a doctrinal dispute. Still grieving for his wife, who had died the previous year, he grew restive with established Anglican doctrine and doubted the origins of the sacraments. In "The Last Supper," a farewell sermon delivered September 9, 1832,

he rejected the divisive nature of communion and abandoned the ministry because he could no longer deem communion a sacral act. Six years later, he addressed Harvard Divinity School on the religious shift older Unitarians would soon witness in the next generation of believers.

In the backlash against Calvinism and Puritanism, creeds varied greatly from established church dogmas. Because of Ellery Channing's attempt to blend Hinduism with Christianity and Theodore Parker's syncretic sympathies and support of humanism, conservative elements fought rampant liberalism. At the center of the feud, Frederic Henry Hedge, a Harvard professor of church history, coined the term "ecumenism" to embrace all forms of Christianity. Additional humanizing agents in American Unitarianism derive from the stirrings of feminism. Prominent among nineteenth-century Unitarian women were the nation's first female minister, Olympia Brown, ordained in 1863; social activist Jane Addams; abolitionist Julia Ward Howe; nurse advocate and reformer Dorothea Dix; philosopher Margaret Fuller; Clara Barton, reformer and founder of the American Red Cross; and women's-rights activist Susan B. Anthony.

ARCHITECTURE

For three centuries, the First Unitarian Church, the oldest Unitarian fellowship in the Western Hemisphere, has supported individual spiritual enrichment and religious pluralism in Philadelphia, the city of brotherly love. From the beginning, its humanistic concepts flourished in philosophy and architecture. Mills's original octagonal structure, seating 300, deliberately violated the Christian tradition of a cross-shaped sanctuary by suggesting a multifaceted world order bound into unity and harmony.

The choice was fortuitous. During the energetic twenty-year pastorate of the Reverend William Henry Furness, a fervid abolitionist, the congregation quickly doubled. It outgrew the original floor plan and called for an expansion in 1828 to seat 700. By the Reconstruction era, the membership stabilized as Philadelphians embraced the end of servitude in the South. The Parish House opened in 1884. The following year, congregants laid the cornerstone of a new church on Chestnut Street, which they dedicated in 1886. Patterned after the Greek cross, it derives its innovation from architect Frank Furness, the pastor's son and daring planner of the Emlen Physick estate on Cape May, the Pennsylvania Academy of Fine Arts, the Provident Life and Trust building, and the Baltimore-Ohio Railroad Depot. A decorated Civil War veteran and holder of the Congressional Medal of Honor, he earned renown for blending neoclassical and Gothic Revival elements into a highly romantic, whimsically Victorian style. Influenced by English art critic John Ruskin, Furness introduced private clients and American cities to European chic.

Furness's use of Gothic stone carving and ironwork linked First Unitarian Church to the great cathedrals of Europe. He enhanced the impact with rough masonry, fish-scaled roof vents, carved stone ferns, and dominant wood and iron trusses decked with leaf shapes. The building outpaced period artistry from the combined talents of John La Farge and Louis Comfort Tiffany. La Farge, a painter and foremost decorator of American churches and residences in the pre-Raphaelite style, applied techniques he perfected for the murals of Boston's Trinity Church, Harvard University's *Battle Window,* and domestic decor for Cornelius Vanderbilt. Tiffany, an interior designer and painter, produced shimmering, bright-toned glasswork heightened by direct injection of dyes into molten Favrile glass.

BELIEFS

To ally non-Christians, Christians, and nontheists, Unitarians joined Universalists as Unitarian Universalists (UU) in 1961. This loosely structured entity supports monotheism through a dogma-free faith that champions the individual conscience, maintains inherent human worth and goodness, foresees an afterlife for all people, and promotes intellectual freedom, equity, justice, and ethics. Unitarians avoid the emotion found in evangelicalism in favor of reason and science. Each congregation functions as helpmeet of the individual. Fellowships adhere to the principles of democracy, cooperation, spiritual growth, tolerance, respect for world religions and scriptures, and open membership. Congregants vary from antifundamentalists,

Wiccans, animists, and Native Americans to agnostics, secular humanists, Jews, Buddhists, Hindus, and mystics.

Church ministry, which rejects proselytizing and missions, strives for civil rights and the search for truth. Unitarians oppose fascism and violence and seek justice, fairness, and world peace. Members seek spiritual renewal and respect all forms of direct experience with transcendent mystery. They honor the transforming power of love and disdain idolatry.

Church teachings are earth centered, harmonious, and pluralistic. Through mutual trust and support, members value ennobling, enriching experience and an expanded view of humanity. Because of their open-mindedness, they have a larger percentage of female clergy and a stronger support from gay members than do traditional Christians. The UU church program varies with the individual congregation's interests. Among the wide span of activities are blessing of gay unions, protection of animals and the environment, and support of Buddhist, neopagan, and Christian fellowships. Through Beacon House Publishing, established in Boston in 1902, Unitarians disseminate books, pamphlets, and a liberalized church hymnal that anthologizes world praise anthems and seasonal and holiday songs from many faiths.

ACTIVITIES

The First Unitarian Church of Philadelphia holds regular Sunday services at 11:00 A.M. and provides Children's Chapel and childcare for young ones. Free parking is available at the nearby College of Physicians on Twenty-first and Ludlow Streets. Services project words and deeds of prophetic men and women, the pluralistic wisdom of world scripture, humanist teaching, and spiritual messages of earth-centered traditions. An inviting array of special programs orients new members, explores the individual spiritual path, and coordinates spirituality retreats, holiday pageants, orchestra and concert dinners, and responsible parenting. Frequent lunch and dinner meetings and architectural tours acquaint guests and newcomers with the church's background and members. Community efforts apply members' energies to rehabilitating homes of the poor, elderly, and disabled in north and west Philadelphia and supporting Seder ser-vices for Jews, feminist Bible interpretation, reli-gious education for young adults and children, the Harper Furness Racial Justice group, literacy training, Christmas in April, and a weekly cam-pus outreach to the University of Pennsylvania. Web site verse and the monthly NOTcoffee-House Poetry reading in Griffin Hall showcase amateur musicians and writers. A Women's Book Club promotes literary discussions; a 1999 Can-didates' Forum studied potential mayors and their views on homelessness and housing.

> **Sources:** *American Decades* 1998; "Architect Frank Furness"; *Biography Resource Center* 1999; Buchanan 1999; Emerson 1832; *Encyclopedia of World Biography* 1998; *New Catholic Encyclopedia* 1967; "NOTcoffee-House Poetry and Performance Series"; *Singing the Living Tradition* 1993; "Unitarian Universalist Association"; "Welcome to the First Unitarian Church of Philadelphia"; "What Is Unitarian Universalism?"; Wilson 1998.

Fort Ross Chapel
See Holy Trinity Chapel of Fort Ross.

French Huguenot Church
Philip Bryant, Pastor
136 Church Street
Charleston, South Carolina 29401
843-722-4385

Huguenot Society of South Carolina
138 Logan Street
Charleston, South Carolina 29401-1941
843-723-3235
FAX 843-853-8476
huguenot@cchat.com

Dubbed the second Notre Dame des Victoires of Paris, Charleston's French Huguenot Church on historic Church Street preserves in little the majesty of medieval Gothic. Founded by dis-senters, it is the nation's only church employing the original Huguenot liturgy in French at an annual celebration. The architectural combina-tion of Gothic details with the simple esthetic of low-church Protestantism endows the sanctuary with a grace and appeal that preserves tradition dating to the Reformation.

The first assembly of fifteen Huguenot fami-lies and their pastor, Philip Trouillard, arrived at Oyster Point, Charles Town, in April 1680 aboard the *Richmond*. They immediately estab-lished a worship center. The original church, deeded May 5, 1687, was deliberately destroyed in the great fire of June 13, 1796, to halt the blaze. During this period, a three-story brick and stucco house at 134 Church Street served as the rectory.

The church's replacement flourished from 1800 to 1844 under Presbyterian government. Liturgy of the early nineteenth century was al-tered from French to English in 1828. The structure gave place to the present edifice on May 11, 1845. Designed by Edward B. White, architect of Grace Episcopal Church, the build-ing was the city's first model of Gothic Revival. After the earthquake of August 31, 1886, New York philanthropist Charles Lanier funded restoration.

ARCHITECTURE
The simple front portal, set in a pointed arch, parallels restrained arched windows at each side and above. The crowning ornament on each arch recurs at the top of the roof and coordi-nates with paired spires that bolster the façade and echo six spire-topped columns on each of the side walls. The paneled narthex honors illus-trious Huguenots. An entrance inscription of Isaiah 55:6 reminds, "Seek ye the Lord while He may be found." On departure, congregants read from James 1:22, "Be ye doers of the Word, and not hearers only."

Within, worshippers take seats to right and left of the center aisle. The austerity of the steeply arched ceiling and simple glass windows suits a pragmatism associated with French im-migrants. The apse end of the church preserves a stately raredos below exposed organ pipes. Overhead, a two-tiered circular chandelier hangs at the center of the roofline.

Detail work distinguishes the church. In ad-dition to a modern Allen organ, the staff main-tains an 1820 Henry Erben tracker organ, which artisans restored in 1998 in Concord, North Carolina. The walls display memorial marble stones, which are of interest to French groups and religious tourists who make up 15,000 an-

FRENCH HUGUENOTS

Centered in Strasbourg, Alsace, Huguenots worshiped within a swirl of religious and political controversy in sixteenth- and seventeenth-century France. By 1550, their beliefs influenced a quarter of French Christians. By professing the beliefs of John Calvin, a French exile in Geneva, Switzerland, as explained in his treatise *Institutes of the Christian Religion* (1541), they came under strong Catholic interdiction. In derision of the Swiss leader Hugues Besançon (or Bezanson), they were dubbed Huguenots, a name that later served the sect in place of Reformed Church, their first designation. Enmity against the growing body of worshippers arose from the envious Guise family, who forced Francis II and his successor, Charles IX, to increase persecution in a conflict later named the French Wars of Religion.

Civil conflict erupted on August 24, 1572, when the queen mother, Catherine de Médicis, incited the Saint Bartholomew's Day Massacre, a rampage that cost the lives of 70,000 Huguenots. A rocky period of religious power struggle forced Henry III to issue the Edict of Nantes in 1598, allowing the minority sect freedom of worship in 100 communities in the south and southeast. This republic-within-a-monarchy lasted until the rule of Louis XIII, whose minister, Cardinal Armand Richelieu, crushed Huguenot worship sites and, in 1628, captured La Rochelle. In 1680, a series of *dragonnades* quartered troops in Huguenot households to force conversions. Liberty eroded further in 1685, when Louis XIV revoked the Edict of Nantes. The repeal of religious freedom remained in effect until the French Revolution in 1789. By then, only a handful of Huguenots still lived in France.

The unsettled religious situation forced nearly 300,000 French Huguenots out of the country to Britain, Prussia, Holland, Switzerland, and North America. The De Lancey, Jay, Legaré, Maury, Petigru, and Revere families settled in Massachusetts, New York, Virginia, and South Carolina. Their skill at crafts and textiles made them valued artisans wherever they settled and cost the French the leadership of the Industrial Revolution.

nual visitors. These monuments, begun as a money-raising effort during the depression of 1903, honor George and Martha Washington, Alexander Hamilton, poets Sidney Lanier and Henry Wadsworth Longfellow, and Robert E. Lee. A plaque names Huguenot soldiers who died in the Civil War. Outside, the church maintains a burying ground, which dates to 1687 and still offers plots for sale.

ACTIVITIES

One of the nation's few surviving Huguenot churches, the French Huguenot Church is a popular shrine and monument to survivors of persecution. The order of service preserves historical liturgy in translation, drawing from the churches of Neufchatel and Vallangin with additions from the Protestant Episcopal Church. Congregants sing from a self-published hymnal, which contains songs from the original Huguenot psalter. They begin each service with Psalm 68, which opens with "Let God arise, let his enemies be scattered," an entreaty that persecuted Huguenots once chanted in their travail. Scheduling calls for monthly open communion to all comers, a weekly prayer circle requesting healing, a handbell choir, and a Monday women's Bible-study class.

For all its ties to the past, the church has weathered the religious vicissitudes of the late twentieth century. In 1982, membership hovered at 25, but a resilient spirit drew others to a simple, nonjudgmental Christian message. In a recent interview, Pastor Philip Bryant characterized the current body of 300 families as a refuge, a safety valve for disgruntled members of other churches who retreat to the Huguenot church until things work out. A down-to-earth clergyman, he offers realistic marital counseling, sympathizes with marginalized Christians, rides a motorcycle to hospital and home visits, and often digs graves for deceased members and friends.

The unaffiliated church maintains a prominent role in missions and Charleston arts, particularly the Festival of Churches. On June 1, 1999, Julia Harlow performed an organ recital at the church as part of Piccolo Spoleto, Charleston's local spring arts festival. At Advent 1999, staff arranged a harp performance and an organ concert free to the public for the price of canned goods, which they donated to the homeless. In spring 2000, the church's annual French liturgy was the subject of a television documentary filmed by a French company interested in Huguenots in America. In addition, planners project a medical mission to the needy of Columbia, South Carolina.

Sources: Hirsch 1998; "The Huguenot Church"; "The Huguenot Society of South Carolina"; Jacoby 1999; Lilly 1966; *New Catholic Encyclopedia* 1967; Williams, Peter W., 1997.

Germantown Mennonite Church

Richard Lichty, Pastor
21 West Washington Lane
Philadelphia, Pennsylvania 19144
215-843-5599
gtownmenno@juno.com

In the spirit of the agrarian immigrants who founded it, Germantown's Mennonite church is a modest worship site. Located in a historic district in northwest Philadelphia, it offers conservative but graciously nonjudgmental Christian fare. The congregation is a body of plain people but less austere than their more conservative Amish kin. In keeping with the unwritten *ordnung* (rules) of simplicity, they reflect modesty, humility, and a rejection of pride in manner and dress.

Germantown projects an outward meekness tempered by an inner respect for scripture. In Christlike tradition, worshippers have offered a refuge to homosexual Christians for over a decade. The acceptance and acknowledgment of all people opened the church to criticism in 1997, when the sect's ruling body censured reception of gays. For the congregation's unconditional extension of fellowship and support to all people, it earned the condemnation of Mennonite authorities and the admiration of families and supporters of homosexuals who had previously found no sanctuary to bid them welcome.

HISTORY

Mennonites, relatives of the Anabaptists, derive from a sixteenth-century movement. They vary in lifestyle and practice from the plainness of the Amish and Hutterites to urban worship communities that wrestle with late-twentieth-century issues. The original Anabaptists broke with reformer Martin Luther for accepting the Catholic ritual of infant baptism. In 1525, Conrad Grebel and other members in Zurich, Switzerland, rebelled from the official church in a public "anabaptism," or rebaptism. Their schism prefaced generations of persecution and martyrdom for refusing to swear oaths, comply with a military draft, or follow a state religion. They took the name Mennonites after the baptism of Menno Simons, a converted Dutch Catholic priest, in 1536.

The first to flee to the New World were thirteen families from Krefeld, Germany, who sailed aboard the *Concord* in 1683 and rebuilt their lives in Germantown, Pennsylvania. Germantown Mennonite Church, the nation's oldest active congregation, began in 1690. More Mennonites moved from Prussia, Poland, Switzerland, Holland, and Russia to the prairie states and Canada. Their religious conference promised to strengthen Christian evangelism and education and to stabilize member support. Throughout the twentieth century, adherents read the Bible as God's inspired word and maintained Christ as the focus of worship and life.

From the beginning, Mennonites avowed the rights of the individual conscience, discipleship of the Christian believer, and practice of nonresistance, love, and sanctity. Their everyday appearance historically is quiet; their demeanor is hospitable, compassionate, and helpful. Their ranks have produced Kansas visiting nurse Frieda Kaufman as well as social reformers and conscientious objectors. A public stand against slavery and violence produced notable abolitionists Abram op de Graeff, Derick op de Graeff, Garret Henderich, and Francis Daniel Pastorius, who signed the Germantown Mennonite Resolution against Slavery, the nation's first abolitionist document, in 1688. In 1725, the congregation hosted North America's Mennonite conference. In the 1730s, educator Christopher Dock opened a summer school.

Into the twenty-first century, Mennonites live their faith in such quiet displays of discipleship as prayer walks for the homeless. Volunteers earned international respect for supporting victims of natural disasters and war. In 1997,

153

Located within a historic district in northwest Philadelphia, Germantown Mennonite Church offers conservative but graciously non-judgmental Christian fare. (Courtesy Germantown Mennonite Historic Trust)

Germantown Mennonite Church entered a national controversy over the question of membership of gays and lesbians united in committed relationships. The Philadelphia congregation is composed of 10 to15 percent gay, lesbian, and bisexual members. The option to accept homosexuals in full participation defied Mennonite principle, established in 1987, to admit only celibate gays to membership.

Because of this inclusion of all people despite their sexual preference, on October 14, the Franconia Mennonite Conference voted 178 to 40 by mail ballot to expel the church and strip the Reverend Richard Lichty of his clerical credentials. Moderator Donella Clemens personally escorted Ken White, a gay Germantown church member, to the door in a gesture of formal ejection from the Mennonite Church and body of Christ and publicly castigated the Reverend Lichty. The vote for ouster, drawn from 52 member churches, took effect on January 1, 1998. Ramifications soon spread to churches in Indiana, Kansas, Minnesota, and Iowa. During an unprecedented incident of shunning by fellow Christians, Germantown congregants valued the support of other bold Mennonites, notably the First Mennonite Church of San Francisco.

ARCHITECTURE

The Germantown cemetery, established in 1708, and the stone meeting house, built in 1770 to replace a log meeting house, are Philadelphia landmarks open Tuesday through Saturday for tours. In 1908, trustees added to the meeting house; in 1952, they restored the church interior to colonial simplicity. Guides point out wooden trusses supporting a double gabled front and roof topped with shingles. The wooden communion table and a pew from the original log church remain in use. The doors function on the original wrought-iron hardware—box lock, strap hinges, top and bottom bolts. The plain interior features plastered ceilings and wainscoted walls and sixteen colonial wooden benches with severe horizontal back rests and book racks. Lighting in ranks of twelve fixtures paralleling a central aisle augments natural light from six double-hung shuttered windows.

Similarly straightforward and unadorned, the congregation has committed its members to an urban ministry to the racially and economically oppressed. Staff has made the historic building more accessible to the handicapped by building a ramp to the first floor and by raising funds for an elevator to the second floor and for renovations to the assembly hall to accommodate community activities. Members share their facility with the Germantown Women's Education Project, a literacy and job-training program for neighborhood women.

Sources: "A Brief History of Mennonites"; "Congregations under Censure" 1999; Engelbrecht 1997; Gentz 1973; Leahy 1997; Linscheid 1998; "The Mennonite Church and Homosexuality"; "Mennonite Church Expelled for Accepting Gays" 1997; "North American Scene" 1998; Smith 1995; Williams, Peter W., 1997.

Gethsemane Abbey
See Abbey of Gethsemani.

Grotto of the Redemption
Deacon Gerald Streit, Director
P.O. Box 376
West Bend, Iowa 50597
515-887-2371
FAX 515-887-2372
grotto@ncn.net
www.nw-cybermall.com/grotto.htm

The Grotto of the Redemption, a tourist attraction in West Bend, northwest of Fort Dodge, Iowa, is a model of organic American folk architecture. The work of Father Paul Dobberstein, an immigrant from Rosenfeld, Germany, the shrine honors the Virgin Mary and the life of Jesus with the world's largest grotto and lapidary collection—over 100 carloads of minerals and petrification, interspersed with statuary, art glass, rubies, emeralds, sapphires, and pearls and set in and around carved white Carrara marble from the Apennines in Italy. Still under construction, the nine-stage sacred scenes, towers, and mosaic walls grow with the imagination of its most recently appointed builder.

Over 100,000 visitors view the grotto annually and walk the stations of the cross. Their ad-

miration and donations are a testimony to the hallowed nature and purpose of the Iowa grotto. Late in the twentieth century, a film crew arrived in the area for production of *The Straight Story* (1998), starring Sissy Spacek and Richard Farnsworth and directed by Mary Sweeney. Deacon Gerald Streit, director of the grotto, overheard a crewman declaring that, on a visit to West Bend, the grotto confirmed his faith.

HISTORY
While pastoring his parish, Father Dobberstein began the grotto in 1912. The impetus for the project was a serious bout with pneumonia that he survived while still at the Seminary of St. Francis outside Milwaukee, Wisconsin. After his ordination, he served a year as chaplain of the Sisters of Mount Carmel in Dubuque before his assignment in 1898 to the lush farm community of West Bend. While pastoring Sts. Peter and Paul Catholic Church, he honored a sickbed vow to honor his protector, the Virgin Mary. As a beginning, he purchased a swampy parcel of land, which parishioners helped to drain and improve with a pond.

In 1901, Father Dobberstein prepared the site and planted birches, short-lived trees that did not survive to the project's completion. He crafted the first part of the display in 1912 but issued no formal statement of purpose until 1936, when he linked the grotto to a European tradition dating to the early Middle Ages. For years, he stockpiled materials for a glorious shrine dedicated to his rescuer. Until his death from stroke in 1954, he amassed ornamental rock shards, mineral ore, fossils, petrified wood, coral, shells, quartz, calcite, and gemstones from various parts of the globe. He scrutinized each piece, which he cleaned, identified, and sorted before placement in the rambling diorama.

After forty-two years of labor by Father Dobberstein and Matthew Szerensce, a skilled assistant laborer, the grotto was the size of a city block and reached forty feet upward by a winding stone stair. Dobberstein took pride in the multihued labyrinth, which cost him several painful injuries, and lectured on geology and lapidary. Father Louis Greving, his cobuilder for eight years and ultimate replacement, installed an electric hoist and a sound system to broadcast

The Grotto of the Redemption, a tourist attraction in West Bend, northwest of Fort Dodge, Iowa, is a model of organic American folk architecture. (Courtesy Grotto of the Redemption)

a script urging visitors to activate their faith. He added to the original vernacular architecture until his retirement in 1994, when Deacon Gerald Streit took the post of grotto director to maintain and protect it, repair damage from a 1996 ice storm, and plan an addition representing Pentecost.

ACTIVITIES

The Grotto of the Redemption, which Father Dobberstein willed to the diocese, is a dynamic force in human faith for its narration in stone of the story of Christian redemption. The plan, which Father Dobberstein never committed to paper, begins with the Garden of Eden and the Tree of Life and includes the Ten Commandments, a manger scene, the Nazareth home of the holy family, symbolism of the Trinity, a Christmas chapel, and Christ's suffering in Gethsemane, formed from Carrara marble and Venetian mosaic. Visitors enjoy a grassy swale, picnic area, and campground accommodating eighty vehicles. Individuals can visit Father Dobberstein's grave a half-mile west of the grotto.

The body of work, open daily year-round, falls into nine segments that summarize the life of Christ, which viewers may study during hourly tours in warm months from June 1 to October 15. Each tour returns to the Rock Display Studio for a geological lecture identifying materials. School groups identify polished agate, Russian alexandrite in green and red, amber, amethyst from the Andes, tan barite and green beryl, red-spotted bloodstone and crimson carbuncle, clear carnelian, waxy chalcedony, glassy chrysoberyl, olive topaz, apple-green chrysoprase, delicate-hued coral, flint, local geodes, gypsum, hematite laced with mica, jacinth, Asian jade, matte-black jet, prized lapis lazuli, lodestone, malachite, milky moonstone, onyx, brassy pyrite, quartz, scoria from the Badlands of South Dakota, fibrous serpentine, smaragdite, conical stalactites and stalagmites from Carlsbad and the Ozarks, and turquoise. Of historical interest is rock from Antarctica, which the Reverend William Menster, chaplain of Admiral Richard Byrd's expedition, retrieved in 1930. An evening light show offers an alternative to daylight visits.

To cover expenses, parish women operate a cafeteria-style restaurant for the convenience of pilgrims. A souvenir stand sells postcards, religious medals, slides, audio cassettes, brochures, a biography of the "Grotto Father," and a video and pictorial history on the grotto. From 10:00 A.M. to 5:00 P.M., the Reverend Greving conducts hourly tours or group tours by appointment. The site remains lighted until 11:00 P.M. The staff charges no fee but suggests a donation of $5 per adult. On weekends, visitors may attend Saturday mass at 5:00 P.M. and Sunday mass at 7:00 and 9:00 A.M. Special events include prayer at the stations of the cross on Good Friday from noon to 1:00 P.M., an Easter sunrise service at 7:00 A.M., and a living rosary on August 15. Other prayers and celebrations of the mass are available on request.

Sources: Buehner 1998; "Grotto of the Redemption" 1999; "Grotto of the Redemption," http://www.roadsideamerica.com; Isay 1998; Niles 1995; "North Iowa Attractions."

Gurdwara Sahib El Sobrante
Baldev Singh, Head Priest
3550 Hill Crest Road
El Sobrante, California 94803
510-223-9987
www.angelfire.com/ak/satguru/

The Gurdwara Sahib El Sobrante, also known as the Sikh Center of San Francisco Bay Area, espouses the Sikh tenets of equality and service to God. Situated twenty-five miles north of the

---

SIKHISM

Sikhism (literally, discipleship) is a monotheistic religion that allies Vaisnava Hinduism with the Sufi mysticism of Islam. The father of this syncretic faith, Guru Nanak Dev ji, experienced a call from God and established the *bhakti* (devotional) tradition in the Punjab in the late 1400s. Traveling to Tamil, Basra, Baghdad, and Sri Lanka, he studied with Asian sages of many beliefs. At the end of his wanderings, he settled in Kartarpur to teach Hindu and Muslim peasants about the all-powerful and ever-present God. To perpetuate the faith, he proclaimed himself God's bard and servant and set up a system of guruship to guide future seekers to truth.

From Nanak's time to 1708, ten gurus, or teachers, maintained his beginnings. The fifth guru, Arjan Mal, who lived from 1563 to 1606, carried early Sikhism to a height of unity and aspiration. In addition to building Hari Mandir, the golden temple in Amritsar, India, he composed the *Adi Granth,* the first book of Sikh scripture, which anthologizes sayings of the saints. His death at the hands of Muslim aggressors established his martyrdom to the Sikh faith.

Sikhism spread to Delhi, the Haryana state, and pockets of worshippers in other parts of India. Dispersion carried the faith east to Malaysia and Singapore and west to Africa, Great Britain, and North America. Crucial to Sikh worship is the repetition of the divine name *Sanskrit nama,* the singing of anthems, prayer, and meditation supervised by a guru. The belief system espouses justice, decency, and human equality and opposes excessive ceremonies, infanticide, *suttee* (ritual immolation of widows), and the caste system that places Hindus under the control of Brahmins, India's elite class.

Sikhs follow the Hindu concept of a cycle of birth, death, and reincarnation and a belief in karma, the determination of an individual life based on actions in a previous existence. They accept *khalsa,* a belief in a chosen race of soldier-saints who live abstemiously, devote themselves to prayer, serve humankind, and fight for righteousness. Historically, *khalsa* has produced a class of sturdy, morally upright warriors. Sikh numerology favors the number five. The faith prohibits idolatry and the artistic representation of God. Worship involves obeisance, offerings, processions, and recitation of scripture.

Essential to each Sikh enclave is the guru, who helps followers understand reality, rid themselves of pride and selfishness, and attain *moksha* (or *moksa*), a release from the endless cycle of reincarnation. After parents dedicate and name a child at the temple, the young Sikh begins learning ritual and scripture and undergoes initiation at puberty through baptism. Physically, the male sikh leaves the hair and beard uncut and wears a ritual comb and metal bracelet, traditional underwear, and a dagger. During a Sikh wedding, the couple walks four times around the holy book to the chant of wedding hymns extolling duty and obligation. The same type of chanting accompanies preparation of a body for cremation. Mourners inter the ashes in the sacred Ganges River or whatever river is nearby.

city in the hills of El Sobrante Valley, it has served the bay area Sikh community since the late 1970s. Before its foundation, local Sikhs conducted ritual at home before moving into Langar Hall, a traditional communal dining room that fostered fellowship and provided food for the hungry. An increase in Asian immigration led to a demand for a Sikh temple to house ceremonies, social occasions, and weddings. In the late 1980s, the congregation began constructing a temple to accommodate 800 people.

Upon its completion in 1993, Gurdwara Sahib displayed an exoticism that contrasts with the verdant California backcountry. Its traditional onion dome, colonnades, and symmetrical arched windows link the site with India's great Sikh architecture. The main hall offers open, unobstructed space for worshippers to hear speakers and join in celebrations and communal meals. A feature that attracts visitors is the spacious deck on the northeast wing of the second floor overlooking the valley and San Pablo Bay.

ACTIVITIES

Gurdwara Sahib El Sobrante holds daily services from 5:15 to 6:45 A.M. and from 6:30 to 7:30 P.M. An additional late-night Sunday session begins at 10:30 P.M. and lasts until 2:30 Monday morning. The Wednesday evening service includes the traditional communal meal, which is open to visitors. For four years, the temple, with the aid of Bhai Satinderpal Singh ji, Dr. Janmeja Singh ji, and Bibi Amarjit Kaur ji, has hosted the Guru Andad Dev Khalsa School to introduce young Sikhs to the ideals of the faith and promote international academic competitions. In addition, the staff offers *kirtan,* or praise singing, classes and musical training on the harmonium.

The temple has involved itself in special events. A recycling project aims to reduce trash and conserve resources in the Sikh community. Congregants support Amritras Radio, which broadcasts sacred music and lectures. The program is the only one of its type in the San Francisco Bay area.

Sources: *Eerdmans' Handbook to the World's Religions* 1982; "Kirtan and Katha"; "Online Kirtan"; Smith 1995; "Welcome to El Sobrante Gurdwara Sahib" 1999; *World Religions* 1998.

H

Harvard Memorial Church
See Memorial Church of Harvard University

Harvest Ministries, Inc.®
Greg Laurie, Pastor
6115 Arlington Avenue
Riverside, California 92504
P.O. Box 4424
Riverside, California 92514
909-687-6902; 800-821-3300
www.harvest.org

In the style of Billy Graham's crusade, evangelist Greg Laurie's itinerant Harvest Ministries makes holy space of whatever auditorium or stadium it happens to occupy. His nonprofit corporation, governed by a ten-member board of directors, is a sect-free and church-free national pulpit. Whether in Seattle, Anaheim, Philadelphia, or Hickory, North Carolina, his ninety minutes of emotional preaching, country ballads, and hard rock treat fundamentalists and nonbelievers to a phenomenon of American evangelism. The appeal to teens and gen-Xers is an intentional crossover from traditional middle-class, middle-aged revival-goers to the population who will determine the fate of Christianity in the twenty-first century. Over a nine-year period in the 1990s, Harvest Crusades hosted 2.1 million attendees from 3,000 churches in sixteen cities nationwide to present the Christian gospel in English, Spanish, Japanese, Arabic, Korean, Vietnamese, and signing for the deaf.

HISTORY

As senior pastor of Harvest Christian Fellowship of Riverside, California, in the declining years of Billy Graham's ministry, Greg Laurie is a viable contender for the title of America's top preacher. He first experienced Christian witness at age nineteen, when he led 30 people in Bible study. The thrill spurred him on to larger audiences. From a run-down church in 1974, he drew crowds that required the building of a new auditorium, completed in 1979. In 1982, after a series of appearances in parks and stadiums, he restyled Calvary Chapel Riverside into a traveling entity called Harvest Christian Fellowship. At a summer revival in the rented Pacific Amphitheater in Costa Mesa, he was pleased to find 90,000 people eager for preaching at the first Harvest Crusade.

Since 1990, Laurie's following has avoided intrusive doctrines by maintaining a nontraditional, nonchurch environment. More important to his philosophy is the expression of Christianity in terms that modern hearers can receive and apply to their lives. Basing ministry on biblical themes, he joined a mentor, Chuck Smith, a Jesus Movement pastor of Calvary Chapel in Costa Mesa, for a strong foray against spiritual malaise. From California, Laurie moved his staff to Oregon, Washington, Arizona, New Mexico, Hawaii, Colorado, New York, Pennsylvania, and Florida and became a regular speaker at the Billy Graham Training Center at the Cove, in Asheville, North Carolina, and the Billy Graham School of Evangelism.

From southern California, where Laurie lives with his wife, Cathe Laurie, and two sons, Greg Laurie conducts an invigorated campaign to spread basic Christian tenets. Today, his church, California's third largest and one of America's eight largest assemblies, consists of 15,000 members. He channels a consuming passion for soul-saving into the theme *A New Beginning,* a program available live and over global radio and television broadcasts over Inspirational Life Digital Television Network, on audio cassettes, and in Internet "cyberwitness," aimed at a quarter million annually in Macedonia, Brazil, the Czech Republic, Argentina, New Zealand, India, and Japan.

Evangelist Greg Laurie's itinerant Harvest Ministries makes holy space of whatever auditorium or stadium it happens to occupy. (Courtesy Harvest Christian Fellowship)

Laurie's cachet derives from service as a director of the Billy Graham Evangelistic Association and Samaritan's Purse and conferred doctor's degrees from Biola and Azusa Pacific Universities. He has augmented pulpit work with a flurry of publications—*God's Design for Christian Dating* (1983), *On Fire* (1993), *The Great Compromise* (1994), *The New Believer's Growth Book* (1994), *Life, Any Questions?* (1995), *Every Day with Jesus* (1996), *The God of the Second Chance: Experiencing Forgiveness* (1997), *Passion for God* (1998), *How to Live Forever* (1999), *The Upside Down Church* (1999), and *Discipleship: The Next Step in Following Jesus* (1999). After a quarter century of preaching, he aimed a campaign at Australia in 2000.

ACTIVITIES

A baby boomer who surfs and rides a Harley-Davidson and speaks to the average person, Lau-

rie echoes real people's concerns—timeless humanistic questions about the meaning of existence, death, and the end of all life on earth. His examples, drawn from newpaper headlines and the lives of athletes and media stars, attach significance to such pervasive, everyday concerns as divorce, mixed marriages, and the decline of traditional faith. Harvest programming incorporates such modern musicians and groups as the Katinas, Audio Adrenaline, Big Tent Revival, the Richie Furay Band, Small Town Poets, Supertones, and hip-hoppers called Cross Movement plus the Harvest Crusade Band and Harvest Gospel Choir.

At the October 1999 crusade in Hickory, North Carolina, a three-day event drawing 20,000, Laurie augmented preaching with an ingathering of nonperishable foods for the area's needy. For local appeal, he called on NASCAR racer Dale Jarrett for personal witness and organized 50 counselors from the Harvest staff to aid local counselors advising new and rejuvenated Christians. The emotional appeal—enlivened with big-screen video to the overflow crowd and the parking lot—brought a standing ovation from some 7,000.

Sources: Braswell 1999; "Harvest Online"; "History of Harvest Christian Fellowship and the Calvary Chapel Movement"; Jones 1999; Niebuhr and Goodstein 1999; Rooke 1999.

Hermanos Penitentes
Truchas, New Mexico 87578
505-758-0062; 505-758-5440

New Mexico's Hermanos Penitentes (Penitent Brothers) are a complex by-product of folk interpretation of the life of Christ. As described by George Johnson in the preface to his book *Fire in the Mind* (1995), Truchas's Morada Centro (Central Structure) in northern New Mexico on the road linking Taos and Santa Fe is a humble adobe assembly hall topped with a steeple formed of corrugated plastic. Located high in the Sangre de Cristo (Blood of Christ) Mountains, the entrance looks down on the Rio Grande Valley. Like members of the Native American Church, only those duly elected to the underground society of Hermanos Penitentes enter

the building for a unique form of worship ranging from processional chant to self-inflicted punishment as a form of atonement for sin.

HISTORY

The fabled Penitentes, originally called La
Fraternidad Piadosa de Nuestro Padre Jesus
Nazareno (Pious Fraternity of Our Father Jesus
the Nazarene), stem from Mediterranean
Catholic fraternities, such as the Misericordia, a
masked band of Italian laymen who established
an ambulance and first-aid service in Florence,
Italy, in 1244. Similarly devoted to village service, the Penitentes are a Catholic male lay society that emulates an isolated Spanish lay sect of
the Third Order of Saint Francis and cultivates a
personal and physical experience with the divine. To this end, the society lives a double life.
Outwardly, members, known as Los Hermanos
(The Brothers or Brotherhood), are a folk social
welfare network that performs benevolent acts
for the needy in the community. Out of the
public eye, they carry out intense, dignified devotions and a secret masochism.

The traditional acts of atonement consisted
of tying off blood flow to the limbs and march-
ing barefoot and stripped to the waist but with
covered heads. Followed by lantern-carrying
compañeros (escorts), they traversed a path strewn
with cactus strips. At intervals, flagellants raised
their arms to scourge themselves in imitation of
Christ's sufferings. For a *disciplina* (whip), they
held both hands on braided strips of yucca, or
amole, leaves. According to one source, the
members tested novices by forcing them to
wash members' feet, beg pardon for offenses, and
accept punishment in the form of lashes on
their bare backs. Those accepted into brotherhood received a token of religious passion—a
cross sketched below their shoulder blades with
sharpened flint.

A major political, social, and religious event
among mountain communities, this Hispanic
version of a first-century Palestinian drama was
a unifying factor among the illiterate working
class. It preserved Indian-Hispanic identity and
faith after the arrival of white settlers jeopardized an autonomous majority. After the Spanish
recalled priests from the Southwest, the Penitentes filled the gap left in Christian practice

with a unique, independent faith that united
isolated villages with social structure. They
served neighbors in time of natural disaster and
provided the young with models of piety, obedience, and respect for tradition. To the good of
the culture, the brothers preserved liturgy and
hymns and kept alive the mountain dialect and
its mythos.

The autonomy of the Penitentes ended with
appointment of a French aristocrat, Bishop Jean
Baptiste Lamy, to the southwestern see. He began systematically obliterating Hispanic customs
in 1847 and excommunicated the Penitentes as
a bizarre offshoot of Christian worship that deliberately mortified the flesh. In 1856, Lamy issued a set of regulations to control the brotherhood and halt its excesses.

When Catholicism resumed its formal organization in New Mexico, the brothers professed
loyalty to the church, both in parish activity and
private ritual. Because the church's concerted
extermination process began replacing Penitentes chapters with orthodoxy, the brothers
concealed their identity and the time and place
of gatherings. They separated themselves from
the prying eyes and thrill-seeking of tourists,
artists, and reporters, who sensationalized their
customs as an arcane subversion of orthodox
Roman Catholicism. One unidentified brother
alleged that the Penitentes deliberately cultivated the myth of self-torture to scare off intruders. Another source claims that the sacred
fraternity generated a parallel sisterhood of Pen-
itentas, who built their own *moradas* for private
ceremony.

In 1946, Don Miguel Archibeque organized
El Concilio Supremo Arzobispal (The Supreme
Council of the Archbishop) to legitimize village
chapters with the church. Although Archbishop
Edwin V. Byrne sanctioned and commended Los
Hermanos for their faith on January 28, 1947,
membership declined over the next two
decades. In 1969, the remaining two brothers
deeded the *morada* to a local museum as a model
of folk church architecture. According to one
Hermano, the brotherhood has abandoned strict
secrecy but continues to protect the anonymity
of other *moradas*. In the decline of Roman
Catholicism, village *moradas* have begun to
flourish once more. In the absence of a strong

orthodox faith, the brothers' Easter procession survives as a commemoration of Christ's passion and death and as a ritual form of spirituality and prayerful penance. Since 1981, the A. R. Mitchell Memorial Museum of Western Art has collected artistic re-creations of penitent worship and *moradas* as models of Hispanic religious folk art.

ACTIVITIES

Today, the Penitentes perpetuate their zealotry and even made a public procession to El Sanctuario de Chimayó in early summer 1999. Each *morada* maintains its own hierarchy of some twelve positions. The *hermano mayor* (brother superior) supervises the group's functions. Membership requires testimony of morality and Christian devotion and may reach 100 per village by enrolling every male citizen. A chapter may appoint a *maestro de los novicios* (teacher of the initiates), an *enfermo* (nurse) to succor the sick, and a *rezador* (liturgist), who reads scripture, orations, and prayers from the chapter handbook. Some groups name a secretary, treasurer, chaplain, sergeant-at-arms, singer, and *pitero* (flute player).

In Truchas at the oldest, largest, and most significant of Penitentes worship sites on the continent, the brotherhood practices a folk interpretation of scripture that dates to the early 1800s. In one voice, they chant the mournful medieval liturgy of Holy Week. The male-centered worship phenomenon reaches an emotional and spiritual peak at the end of Lent during Holy Week. Typically, they complete society business on Good Friday and then move to a nearby *campo santo* (holy plain) to reenact Christ's trudge toward Calvary. For this passion play, each brother takes a dramatic role, with one honored brother playing Cristo (Christ) and carrying a full-size wooden *madero* (cross) to the place of crucifixion.

The ritual bears the elements of a medieval morality play. On the route, brothers sing hymns and cry *Pecado* (I have sinned) as they drag *el carro de la muerte* (the wagon of death), which transports a chalky-white death figure. He aims an arrow in a stretched bowstring as a reminder of the sinister omnipresence of death. This symbolic pantomime is strictly playacting, despite fiction and film insistence that the brothers actually torment a member on a cross.

Sources: "Biography of Guadalupe Lupita Gallego" 1938; Boon 1911; Gillespie 1994; Gould 1995; Henderson 1998; Jamison; Johnson, George, 1995; Johnson 1997; "Kit Carson Historic Museums"; Lewis, Roger, 1995; Loomis 1965; Louden-Sundahl 1998; Pulido 1999; Thompson 1998; Ulibarri 1994.

Hindu Temple of Greater Chicago

Sri Tirupatiah Tella, President
10915 Lemont Road
Lemont, Illinois 60439
630-972-0300
FAX 630-972-9111
www.ramatemple.org

Above the Des Plaines River valley, the Hindu Temple of Greater Chicago testifies to the swell of immigration to the United States from Asia in the 1960s. Seeking better lives through education and professional careers, these new Americans contributed energy and vision to the Great Lakes religious community. To import the familiarity of native customs and beliefs, they focused on families in need of activities and worship in the Hindu tradition. Worshippers chose to transmit culture and tradition through a new temple performing ritual that dates to 6000 B.C.

HISTORY

In 1977, Sri Tirupatiah Tella, president of the Telugu Association of Greater Chicago, joined other seekers of a religious home. Meeting in Oak Park for weeks, committees studied needs before forming the Hindu Temple of Greater Chicago, a broad-based nonprofit organization intended to serve Hindus of all backgrounds. By 1978, contributors had elected officials of a governing body, naming Sri Vidyasagar Dharmapuri the first president. Plans called for a place of worship, a venue for cultural and fine-arts activities, religious and language schools, and a library. The consensus was to serve Sri Rama, the redeemer, along with Sita Devi, Sri Lakshmana, Hanuman, and Lord Vinayaka as chief divinities.

After surveying thirty likely locations in the Greater Chicago area, trustees chose a sylvan bluff and waterfalls on 17.6 acres in Lemont, Illinois, with easy access to I-55. In 1980, Sri Manoharlal Rathi led a membership campaign and raised funds with a dance recital by Hema Rajagopalan, the leading exponent of Bharatanatyam, an esoteric dance. The successful dance-drama enactment of the epic *Ramayana* raised nearly $35,000. By August 8, the temple committee had the funds to pay cash for the land.

In 1981, Indian and American architects sketched a master plan to satisfy regional Hindu tastes. In December, trustees appointed as chief Indian architect Sri Sthapathi Ganapathi, the retired principal of the College of Temple Architecture near Madras, India, and builder of the Sri Siva Vishnu Temple in Lanham, Maryland. In anticipation of questions, from May 29 to 31, 1982, the board displayed the temple-complex model at the Second Convention of Asian Indians in America at Chicago's Palmer House.

The congregation hired a leader in Gurudeva Sivaya Subramaniya Swami, who arrived from Hawaii on November 3, 1982. Pleased by the enthusiasm of Chicago Hindus, he moved to the area and lived at the residence of P. Rajagopalan in Lombard, where he began worship ceremonies on November 19. On January 12, 1983, the temple installed a statue of Lord Vinayaka and moved temporary worship services to Downers Grove, where 400 devotees celebrated Rama's birth at the Ramanavami and attended Upanayanams, Annamuhurtha, Satyanarayana Puja, and Harikatha services. In addition, they enjoyed a Nadaswaram concert by Namagiri Pettai Krishnan and an amateur theatrical program, Kalidasa's *Abhignana Shakuntalam*.

The temple opened on January 25, 1985. Skilled Indian artisans known as *silpis* continued Indianizing the exterior with ornamentation left incomplete at the temple's dedication. Congregants welcomed *veena* (lute) artist Suma Sudhindra, vocalist Jyothi Ramachandra, and Lata Mangeshkar, the nightingale of India. That summer, members' children enjoyed a Hindu Heritage Youth Camp and, in 1986, began regular Sunday school for primary grades on alternate weeks and monthly teen meetings. That same year, the temple, led by Sri Krishna P. Reddy, celebrated the Kumbhabhishekam (installation of deities) of Sri Rama Temple from June 27 to July 6. In 1987, congregants increased attendance

with the observance of Diwali, the New Year and autumn light festival. In 1988, the arrival of the marble likeness of Durga Devi, an incarnation of a many-faceted Goddess, attracted more Hindus to the temple. The establishment of a youth branch, In the Wings, preceded celebration of Mother's Day, Father's Day, and Youth Nite.

Local Hindus drew up architectural sketches and purchased land for a community center and expansion of the existing temple, bringing property holdings to 22 acres.

With adequate land, they could attend to details: linking parts of the complex, replacing marble tiles with granite, constructing a main gate in the shape of Ramabana (Rama's bow), and upgrading parking lots, water, and sewer. Planners also added eight apartments to a residential complex for priests and repaired damage to the Bluff Road entrance incurred during the 1996 flood. With the completion of much preliminary work and the reduction of loans from $2.5 million to $400,000, the temple reached completion.

ARCHITECTURE AND WORSHIP

Sri Sthapathi Ganapathi and master artisans and sculptors from India constructed a two-part temple complex composed of the Rama temple and Ganesha-Shiva-Durga temple blending ancient and modern design. The former follows the specifications set up in the Chola dynasty of the tenth century. An eighty-foot *gopuram* (tower) symbolizes Hindu spirit. On the lower level, a spacious hall accommodates staging of cultural events. The smaller Ganesha-Shiva-Durga temple follows the architectural style of the Kalinga dynasty of the first century B.C.

The temple altar fosters a serene atmosphere by displaying sacred statuary, which turns thoughts from worldly matters to God. These symbolic forms are used to awaken the spirit and help seekers visualize a shapeless, formless deity. Ritual and ceremony channel devotions to God and enhance self-realization or union with the divine. Central to the Hindu pantheon is Shree (Lord) Rama, one incarnation of Lord Vishnu, the preserver. As described in the *Ramayana,* he was a prince who fought a fourteen-year battle against demon forces. He models the ideal king, parent, spouse, sibling, child, and friend. At his right sits his wife Sita and brother Lakshmana. The pair accompanied Lord Rama to the forest during his long years of combat.

Another divine pair are Shree Krishna, incarnation of Lord Vishnu, and his companion Radha. Lord Krishna taught the various paths to *moksha* (salvation), which appear in the Bhagavad Gita, the essence of Hindu scripture. In the scriptures, Lord Krishna promised to protect the pious, stamp out evildoers, and establish righteousness by returning to earth millennium after millennium. Additional figures symbolize right thinking and sanctity:

- Shree Venkateshwara, a third incarnation of Lord Vishnu, preserver of the universe, accompanies two mates, the earth mother Bhoodevi and Shridevi, Goddess of beauty.
- An ardent devotee of Lord Rama, Hanuman, also called Anjaneya, personifies obedience and devotion to the supreme deity. As depicted in the *Ramayana,* his life demonstrates attainment of salvation through *bhakti* (devotion). Hanuman, also called the monkeyman, illustrates that the body is valueless to a worshipper seeking salvation through dedication to God.
- The fortune Goddess Mahalakshmi, Lord Vishnu's mate, bestows prosperity. She often appears seated on a lotus flower, a representation of purity.
- Shree Parvati, Lord Shiva's mate and the universal mother, represents the peaceful form of *shakti* (energy).
- Shree Ganesha, son of Lord Shiva and the Goddess Parvati, protects living beings from obstacles. His elephant head signifies infinite wisdom, which he gained through his large ears. The mouse at his feet represents ego, which can nibble away at the human will. Because Ganesha is blessed, Hindus begin their ceremonies by invoking him.
- Shree Shiva the redeemer, symbolized by the Shivalingam, joins Vishnu and Brahma in forming Hinduism's holy trinity. Shiva's task is to dispel the old and prepare the individual for reincarnation during a perpetual cycle of life, death, and rebirth.

- Shree Durga, Goddess of shakti, protects all from evil. She also takes the form of Mata (mother), Amba, and Kali.
- Shree Kartikeya, also known as Kumaraswamy, was incarnated by a divine spark from Lord Shiva. The celestial women known as Krithikas reared him. He offers worshippers prosperity and protection from evil.

ACTIVITIES

The temple serves the Hindus of greater Chicago with a full calendar of events. In a congenial atmosphere, staff supports spiritual advancement for a diverse Hindu population. Daily worship—the *puja* (adoration) and *archana* (ritual prayers) beginning with praise of the deities and ending with Aarti (a ceremonial conclusion), Charanamrit (holy water), and Prasad (blessed sweets)—along with festivals, cultural programs, children's education, youth activities and humanitarian missions attest to the temple's spirituality. Among its ministries are a bone-marrow donor drive, walkathon benefit for disabled children, and grandparents' day. The addition of meditation and yoga classes broadens the temple's appeal to more than 13,000 Hindu families in the greater Chicago area.

To assure the future of the Hindu community, the temple youth group, In the Wings, unites over 300 students from ages eight to twenty-five. By helping the young cope with cross-cultural conflict, In the Wings maintains intergenerational communication. Programmers schedule youth forums, cooperative peer projects, socials and retreats, an annual Youth Night, education and athletic games during a two-day Youthfest, and distribution of a bimonthly newsletter, *Wings of Time.*

For young adults, the temple offers Akshaya, taken from the Sanskrit for "perennial," a program that steers individuals toward full commitment to Hindu religion and culture and its adaptation to life in the United States. Akshaya helps members understand Hindu philosophy, scripture, tradition, and customs and builds leadership. During monthly meetings on the fourth Sunday at 11:30 A.M., members participate in *puja,* hear temple priests explain ritual, attend guest lectures, discuss religious matters, and share a meal. Sessions are interactive, informative, and entertaining.

Sources: *Eerdmans' Handbook to the World's Religions* 1982; "Hindu Temple in Illinois"; "Hindu Temple of Greater Chicago"; "Hinduism in America"; Sharma 1987; "Sri Siva Vishnu Temple" 1997; "Who is a Hindu?" 1999; *World Religions* 1998.

Holy Assumption of the Virgin Mary Church

Reverend Michael Trefon, Priest-in-Charge
1106 Mission Road
Kenai, Alaska 99611
907-283-0922
www.oca.org

A visual and spiritual link to Alaska's Russian pioneers, the Holy Assumption of the Virgin Mary Church is both a landmark and a promise. Located in south-central Alaska and surrounded by the natural beauty of Cook Inlet, two mountain ranges, and three active volcanoes—Mount Redoubt, Mount Spurr, and Mount Iliamna—the church, along with its chapel, rectory, and burying ground, represents a sacred presence that has invigorated Kenai since 1841. For Kenaitze Indians, the church has served as educational, religious, administrative, and judicial center. For its value to architecture, culture, and history, the U.S. Secretary of the Interior proclaimed the church a National Historic Landmark in 1970, making it one of the state's twenty buildings on the list. A bicentennial celebration and designation of Kenai as a 1991 All-America City boosted pride in the church and encouraged congregants to protect it from the elements and rejuvenate its sanctity.

HISTORY

Russian Orthodoxy was the first nonnative religion to take root on the Kenai Peninsula. At the village of Skitok, the Dena'ina Athabascan, the peninsula's aborigines, first sighted European colonists in the late 1700s, about the time that Captain James Cook explored Cook Inlet in a misguided quest for the Northwest Passage. When Russian fur traders followed to harvest sea otter pelts, in August 1791, they built Redoubt Nikolaevsk, later called Fort St.

Nicholas, overlooking the Kenai River near the bluff where the church now stands. In 1841, the Russian American Company initiated religious observances until a permanent pastor took over.

In 1845, Father Igumen Nikolai Militov founded Kenai parish and kept journals on frontier events. Within four years, parishioners had constructed a church; over the first decade, Father Nikolai baptized 1,432 Kenaitze. In 1867, the year the United States purchased Alaska from Russia for $7.2 million, Makary Ivanov served the church as its second priest. The parish house, erected in 1887, became the oldest building in the Cook Inlet area.

With a grant of $400 from the Holy Synod of St. Petersburg, the current Holy Assumption of the Virgin Mary Church took shape in 1895 on 13.47 acres of the Russian Mission Reserve. An enduring model of Russo-Alaskan culture, it helped to assimilate the Kenaitze Indians, who formed the majority of the population. In 1906, parishioners, led by Father John Bortnovsky, added a log chapel and shrine to honor Father Nikolai and Makary Ivanov. Through the first half of the century, Father Paul Shadura extended church influence by erecting chapels in Tyonek and Seldovia. St. Herman's Seminary added to the Kenai religious community with the cataloguing of anthropologist Lydia Black, an expert in Alaskan ethnic history, who, in 1998, began rescuing early Russian documents from neglect.

ARCHITECTURE

Alaska's oldest Russian Orthodox church, Holy Assumption of the Virgin Mary Church, is a strikingly appealing wood-frame structure built in *pskov* (ship) style. Flanked by tall trees, it features clapboard siding and a two-story hexagonal bell tower with a crown-shaped hexagonal cupola topped by a three-bar Orthodox cross. A white picket fence and wide gate admit worshippers to a small porch and double door. Above, dentate molding sets the building apart from stores and residences. Inside, traditional icons, religious artifacts, and historic objects connect to the past, but remain in use as worshippers follow the liturgy and Orthodox worship style of their forebears.

A visual and spiritual link to Alaska's Russian pioneers, the Holy Assumption of the Virgin Mary Church is both a landmark and a promise. (Courtesy Holy Assumption of the Virgin Mary Church)

In 1997, the National Historic Landmarks commission declared the fragile wooden church an endangered historic site. Lack of funds for conservation and environmental control is jeopardizing maintenance and repairs. A thorough remodeling in 1978 based on architectural sketches of the 1880s upgraded the body of the sanctuary. Workers added insulation and a new foundation plus replacement portals and mechanical and electrical systems, but ornamentation and artifacts require additional preservation and security systems. Deterioration from mildew and weathering to the turret and steeple has compromised the original glass windows and buckled the foundation.

ACTIVITIES

In an atmosphere of historic preservation, the Reverend Michael Trefon maintains a full schedule of events for the here and now. On Saturday, he offers confessions following 6:00 P.M. vespers; Sunday liturgy at 10:00 A.M. precedes Sunday school for children. Additional activities center on Brotherhood and Sisterhood, which welcome all to a coffee hour at Fort Kenay the first Sunday of the month. The church bookstore stocks religious texts, icons, crosses, ritual *lampadas* (lanterns), Russian dolls and boxes, holiday cards by liturgical watercolorist Dorothy Hook, an anthology of native Kenaitze cookery, and a video, *Heaven on Earth: Orthodox Treasures of Siberia and North America,* a production of the Anchorage Museum of History and Art. The text describes the antique Bible of Father Igumen Nikolai, Kenai's pioneer priest, and Gregori Petukhov's icons of the archangels Gabriel and Michael, all sacred items from the Kenai church.

> **Sources:** "About Kenai"; Ahlstrom 1972; Behr 1998; Buchanan 1999; "Damaged Kodiak Archives Open Window for Ex-professor" 1998; "History of Kenai"; "Holy Assumption of the Virgin Mary Church" 1999; Little 1998, 1999; "1997 Landmarks at Risk Report" 1997.

Holy Cross Abbey

Kenneth C. Hein, Abbot
P.O. Box 1510
Cañon City, Colorado 81215-1510
719-275-8631

br.francis@juno.com
www.holycrossabbey.org

Located fifty miles northwest of Pueblo, Colorado, Holy Cross Abbey is a Roman Catholic monastery of the American Cassinese Congregation, a union of Benedictines known as the Black Fathers for their black habits and separate cowls. Their complex is an elegant Tudor Gothic edifice that houses thirty monks. The imposing light brick chapel façade, marked by a sturdy square tower and offset bell tower, sits among conifers and deciduous trees in a pleasant 200-acre setting. Within the old world charm of the cloister and hall, the monks have created a sensible symbiosis by extending facilities to educational and benevolent agencies.

HISTORY

Holy Cross Abbey attributes its establishment to priests from St. Vincent's Archabbey and College, founded in 1846 by Father Boniface Wimmer of Bavaria in Latrobe, Pennsylvania. These pioneers settled in an area that once served the Ute as a campground and frontier poet Joaquin Miller as a judgeship. Upon the priests' arrival in 1886, they settled in Breckenridge for two years before moving to Boulder, then Pueblo, and then Cañon City in 1924. Within a year, the community became an official monastery and elected an abbot.

The monastery welcomed applicant males between twenty and fifty-five years of age of good physical, mental, and spiritual health who regularly practiced the Catholic faith and had no incumbent responsibilities for parents or family members. Selection required that potential monks fit a rigorous set of personal qualities—that they

- Have no debts
- Live with others in the Rocky Mountain altitudes
- Be stable and useful
- Be chaste and free of addictions
- Desire to serve others

After six months of postulancy, regular chores and duties, and morning classes in the Rule of Saint Benedict, spirituality, liturgy, Psalms, and music theory, they progressed to a one-year novitiate, monthly examinations, and classes in monastic history, the Rule of Saint Benedict, scripture, and vows. The last stage before full membership, a three-year juniorite, required temporary vows, weekly classes with the junior master, and assigned jobs.

Built in 1926, the complex housed the monks in its private cloister, which is composed of offices, parlors, guest rooms, permanent residences, reading and recreation areas, utility rooms, and a library of 20,000 volumes. The monks offer the chapel to visitors for prayer and meditation. The altarpiece and canopy are the work of Father Michael Jankowski, a woodcrafter who also carved the holy-water font. The highlight of the chapel is a hand-carved crucifix from Oberammergau, Germany, a gift to Abbot Leonard Schwinn in 1961. Additional appointments include a stained-glass window, given by the Simon P. Smith family, and a Rodgers Cambridge 730 organ, donated in 1992 by the Sacred Heart of Mary Parish in Boulder, Colorado, in gratitude for the monks' service to parishioners. In 1993, the abbey staff adorned the choir loft with computer-generated shields of the seven sacraments—baptism, confirmation, Eucharist, reconciliation, holy orders, matrimony, and last rites. At center hangs the red and silver abbey coat of arms. Carved statues depict the Sacred Heart of Jesus and Our Lady of Montserrat, patroness of a Benedictine monastery in Spain.

In addition to caring for the cloister and chapel, residents farm 137 acres of grass hay, alfalfa, and corn and board horses and graze cattle as a means of self-support. Until 1985, the abbey ran Holy Cross Boys' School, a college-preparatory academy, but suspended operations after costs exceeded demand. The complex, which the U.S. Department of the Interior listed on the National Register of Historic Places in 1983, maintains a museum in the community center to display Native American artifacts, a Toben Hawken rifle from frontier days, and a monastic collection.

ACTIVITIES

In the Benedictine tradition of service and hospitality, Holy Cross Abbey welcomes male and female oblates and individuals on private retreat. Because of the advanced age of the brothers, the staff is unable to offer guided retreats. The chapel is open daily for prayer and meditation. The former high school currently provides rental space. Sheeby Hall, St. Joseph's Hall, and St. Mary's Hall accommodate Pueblo Community College; the music building and Stansbeck Hall enhance the curriculum of Garden Park High School. The Cañon City Recreation Department headquarters in Abbot Alcuin Hall and Abbot Ernest Fieldhouse. Ullathorne Hall is dedicated to hospital and prison ministries, addiction recovery, the Red Cross, and the United Way.

As a brotherhood, the monks chant Gregory style and pray in the chapel at the south end of the complex at 6:00, 7:00, and 11:45 A.M. and in the evening at 5:30 and 7:30, the official end of their day. They dine together in a subdued environment and work at monastery upkeep, farming, beekeeping, livestock breeding, crafts, and rental property, which sustain their order. As chaplains and pastors in the community, they aid the local hospital, St. Scholastica Academy, St. Joseph's Manor, St. Benedict's Parish, and the Colorado State Veterans' Home in Florence.

Unlike the stereotypical closed monastic community, the abbey is typically active. It announces seasons of the Christian calendar with colorful banners. During Advent and Lent, the brothers anticipate Easter with purple. From Easter to Christmas, they hoist white banners with fleurs-de-lis. In addition to soccer games and car shows, in April 1999, they sponsored the Cañon Car Club Fun Run. Visitors may tour the abbey daily from 8:30 A.M. to 5:00 P.M.

Sources: Alsberg 1949; "Holy Cross Abbey" 1999; Loeffler 1996; *New Catholic Encyclopedia* 1967; Sullivan 1967.

Holy Land USA

Richard Dooley, General Manager
1060 Jericho Road
Bedford, Virginia 24523
540-586-2823
www.holyland.pleasevisit.com

One of the more relaxing hallowed sites in America is Holy Land USA, a 250-acre replica

One of the more relaxing hallowed sites in America is Holy Land USA in Bedford, Virginia, a 250-acre replica of biblical geography in Israel, Syria, and Jordan. (Courtesy Holy Land USA)

of biblical geography in Israel, Syria, and Jordan. The nondenominational re-creation of Jesus' life, journeys, and deeds offers an unusual option—a sacred vacation or day trip to a religious theme park. Supported solely by contributions, the tour is Bible based and suitable for adults and children.

HISTORY

Bedford's Holy Land is an unusual undertaking. In 1972, investor Robert Johnson purchased the promising acreage with the intent of renting its structures and farming the rest. In walking the land, he recognized a greater potential—the possibility of a religious theme park. His first idea was to build a model nation of Israel as a spiritual exhibit. His son added a second possibility, a nature sanctuary. The two men worked at a blend of their ideas and opened part of the permanent exhibit in 1973. The elder Johnson maintained enthusiasm for the park until his death in 1999. Currently owned by the Bible Center Chapel, a nondenominational ministry,

the park is an ongoing project devoted to religious tourism.

ACTIVITIES

A natural outdoor attraction open all year from 8:00 A.M. to 5:00 P.M., Holy Land USA extends opportunities to walk, study, discuss, and photograph in an outdoor sanctuary. Without fee, visitors can hike the entire three-mile trail, beginning in Bethlehem and covering the Judean hill country and Shepherds Field, where staff maintains donkeys and flocks of sheep and goats. The tour continues down Jericho Road past the baptismal pool in the Jordan Valley and through Nain to Galilee. At Nazareth, a model of Joseph's carpentry shop, grotto home, and Mary's well present the lifestyle and work of the holy family. For a nominal fee, visitors can take a farm wagon or bus tour of familiar Bible geography—Cana, the Sea of Galilee, Capernaum, Samaria, and Jerusalem, site of the Dome of the Rock on Mount Moriah. Elements central to Jesus' final days cover the Upper Room, the Synagogue, the three crosses on Mount Calvary, and the empty tomb donated by Joseph of Arimathea.

More recent events take tourists to Qumran, where a shepherd located the Dead Sea Scrolls, and to Mount Tabor, site of the Basilica of the Transfiguration. The town of Bethany, the setting of Lazarus's resurrection from the dead, precedes Emmaus and the Mount of Olives, where Jesus ascended into heaven. At a bookroom/gift shop, park staff sells devotional materials, Bibles, books, and eastern Mediterranean items. The site provides guided and unguided group tours for up to fifty people and offers a weekday discount for senior citizens. Visitors may schedule baptisms and communions and can participate in a Christmas Eve service of music or drama held annually in the Bethlehem Barn at 7:00 P.M. and an Easter sunrise service led by a selected pastor or speaker at the Garden Tomb at 7:00 A.M.

Sources: "Holy Land USA," *New Catholic Encyclopedia* 1967; Williams, Peter W., 1997.

Holy Name Monastery

Mary Clare Neuhofer, Prioress
33201 State Road 52
P.O. Box 2450
St. Leo, Florida 33574-2450
352-588-8320
FAX 352-588-8319
holyname@saintleo.edu
http://monet.saintleo.edu/holyname/

Located in orange groves and sandy hills five miles northeast of Tampa, the sisterhood of Holy Name Monastery pursues a lifelong promise of obedience, devotion, and stability. In a modern three-story building overlooking Lake Jovita and graced with green lawns, palm trees, and colorful coastal perennials, the sisters go about their tasks as teachers and counselors and welcome outsiders to a nurturing climate of love and understanding. Whether working in the print shop, solacing alcoholics or abused women and children, or tending the garden, the nuns maintain a commitment to caring.

HISTORY

The first Benedictine nuns in the United States arrived from Eichstatt, Bavaria, in 1852. From

their convent in St. Marys, Pennsylvania, on February 23, 1889, five nuns led by the Reverend Mother Dolorosa Scanlan traveled to the Florida panhandle, part of the Savannah diocese. They built a three-story country daughter house, Holy Name Convent and Academy, to educate children in San Antonio, Florida. Dedicated to classroom work and counseling, the St. Leo sisterhood operated an academy from 1889 to 1964 and St. Benedict's Preparatory School for Boys from 1929 to 1959. Some of their number staffed local public and parochial schools as well as mission schools in Florida, Louisiana, and Texas and taught weekend religion classes in small parishes.

The Benedictine Sisters of Florida of the Federation of St. Scholastica are a cenobitic community devoted to prayer, service, Holy Communion, the Liturgy of the Hours, and the *Lectio Divina* (Divine Office). They follow the example of their fifth-century founder, Saint Benedict, and his twin sister, Saint Scholastica. They accept single, practicing Catholic women aged twenty and above holding college degrees or equivalent work after high school. Entrants must be in good physical and mental health and free of financial and family obligations. Additional requirements are familiarity with the community, a two- to six-week stay at the monastery, and staff approval. Newcomers pass through five stages of belonging: affiliation through visits, a one- to two-year postulancy to learn the religious life, a one- to two-year novitiate to study charism and vows, a three- to six-year scholastic residency in ministry and studies, and finally full profession.

ACTIVITIES

At the beginning of the twenty-first century, Prioress Mary Clare Neuhofer led the multicultural sisterhood of thirty nuns aged thirty to ninety in teaching and in the values contained in the Rule of Saint Benedict. According to their publication *The Benedictine Tide,* the order's ministries range from the Gold Seal award-winning Montessori school, Holy Name Academy Child Care Center, and St. Leo College to individual counseling and spiritual direction. The sisters' outreach includes traditional Benedictine hospitality expressed through retreats and benevolence to the poor, the sick, the elderly,

Located in orange groves and sandy hills five miles northeast of Tampa, the sisterhood of Holy Name Monastery pursues a lifelong promise of obedience, conversion of life, and stability. (Courtesy Holy Name Monastery)

and migrants. Male and female oblates make a lifelong promise to assist the nuns by bonding with the monastic community and living by standards of prayer, devotion, and religious practice. In addition, Marmion Center hosts a dining and reception area for weddings, anniversaries, jubilees, concerts, Lenten suppers, and holiday banquets.

Current programs schedule periods of private or directed withdrawal for men and women to walk in the garden, write journals, read, pray, reflect, and rest as a form of spiritual revival or respite from alcohol abuse. For groups and organizations, the staff leads discernment retreats, days of reflection, and weekends studying the shared life and monastic experience. Residents serve the community, aid the academy and local schools, assist at St. Leo College, and minister to the parish. As part of individual rejuvenation, guests share leisure, prayers, and meals with the sisters, enjoy walks in the vegetable and herb gardens and among the fruit trees, and worship in the chapel.

Sources: Doyle 1948; "Holy Name Monastery" 1998; Nelson 1999; *New Catholic Encyclopedia* 1967; "The Order of St. Benedict"; "St. Benedict Observes 'Year of the Spirit'" 1997; Theisen 1999.

Holy Trinity Chapel of Fort Ross

Right Reverend Tikhon
19005 Coast Highway One
Jenner, California 95450
707-847-3437
FAX 707-847-3601
fria@mcn.org
www.oca.org/OCA/pim/oca-we-ftrhtc.html

A relic of a failed Russian enterprise on the West Coast, the restored Holy Trinity Chapel of Fort Ross, the first Russian Orthodox sanctuary erected south of Alaska, remains in service to Orthodox Catholics of California. The land around Fort Ross originally belonged to some 1,500 Kashaya Pomo, who built Metini village to profit from the harbor-based sea salt trade, forage, and surrounding woods. The area, which lay south of Spanish usurpers of the San Francisco Bay area, developed into a multiethnic community of several hundred Kashaya laborers, eighty Aleut hunters, and twenty-five Russian soldiers and administrators of the Russian American Trading Company, who monopolized the coastal fur trade. Located on Highway One in Sonoma County eleven miles north of Jenner at the mouth of the Russian River, the chapel is

A relic of a failed Russian enterprise on the West Coast, the restored Holy Trinity Chapel at Fort Ross, California, the first Russian Orthodox sanctuary erected south of Alaska, remains in service to Orthodox Catholics of California. (Daniel F. Murley)

an active sacred site, a goal of Russian and Russian-American pilgrims, and the favorite religious tourist spot at the historical settlement.

BELIEFS

Like the Armenian, Coptic, Greek, and Syrian offshoots, the Russian Orthodox faith is an autonomous sect under patriarchal authority since the conversion of Valdimir I of Russia in 988. The devout, independent of Roman Catholicism, acknowledge the Roman pope as Christendom's chief bishop but one devoid of universal supremacy. Priests administer seven sacraments, or mysteries:

- Baptism by triple immersion and annointing with chrism (oil), usually within months after birth
- Chrismation, or confirmation, for children seeking full membership in the church
- Eucharist, or Holy Communion, celebrated four or five times annually following confession
- Holy matrimony

- Holy orders for people wishing to devote themselves to a religious life
- Penance for sins
- Extreme unction, the anointing and forgiveness of the dying

A significant part of Russian Orthodox worship involves veneration of icons, which are pictures of saints or sacred events, and celebration of saints and Theotokos (Mary, the mother of God), through liturgy and prayer. Followers exclude the Roman Catholic doctrine of Mary's assumption into heaven and the punishment of sins in purgatory. The traditional language of Russian Orthodox Catholicism is Church Slavonic, introduced in the late ninth century by Saints Cyril and Methodius, missionary brothers from Thessalonica, Greece, who translated scripture, Christian literature, and liturgy by means of a Slavonic alphabet that they devised.

HISTORY

Russian involvement in the New World began early in the seventeenth century, when fur trappers sought unharvested territory rich in sable. The more adventuresome moved from Siberia's Lena River in 1628 to the Sea of Okhotsk bordering Mongolia in 1639. With service of the Trans-Siberian Railroad at Inkutcsh in 1650, the tea and fur trade expanded seaward to the Pacific Northwest. Tsar Peter the Great furthered colonialism by dispatching a Danish navigator, Captain Vitus Bering, to broaden Russian commerce to the continents to the east. His voyage to Alaska with Captain Alexia Chirikov in 1741 preceded the construction of outposts among indigenous peoples of the Aleutian Islands.

In search of sea otter, Russian adventurers pushed south as far as California's Farallon Islands to plunder natural otter habitats. Under Tsar Paul I, the Russian American Company organized in 1799 as a semiofficial government-sponsored corporation regulating the fur trade and other commercial enterprise in Alaska and the Pacific Northwest. Led by Alexia Baranov, the firm pressed southwest into the Sandwich Islands and due south to a stout redwood stockade at Fort Ross, where a native of Tot'ma, Ivan Kuskov, built the first house.

The Russians, primarily citizens of Vologda, 330 miles east of Leningrad, left hunting to Kodiak islanders, who manned bidarkas (kayaks) and aimed their darts with atlatls toward abundant sea life. Enriched by stores of pelts, settlers cut redwood, Bishop pine, and Douglas fir, framed two blockhouses, and raised livestock and grain to feed Russians and natives at Alaskan outposts. The fort's shops branched out into manufacture of utensils, farm implements, furniture, and clothing. As the number of settlers increased and entrepreneurs muscled into the Spanish trade zone, authorities supplied homes for Russians, Creoles, and Native Americans—Chugach, Hawaiian, Tlingit, Tanaina, Kodiak, Aleut, Yakut, Pomo, Kashaya, and Miwok. The fort carpenters constructed Holy Trinity Chapel in 1824 with donations by the officers and crew of the frigate *Kreiser* (alternatively given as the cruiser *Apollo*). Although it was never consecrated and had no permanent priest, the chapel flourished under the lay ministry of Fedor Svin'in, a company official.

From July to October 1836, Father Ioann (John) Veniaminov—canonized in 1977 as Saint Innocent of Alaska, the pioneer Russian-American priest to the Aleut and creator of the Aleutian alphabet—kept a journal of Fort Ross activities. Entries covered shipbuilders in Rumiatsev harbor, twenty-five houses, Aleutian yurts, a store, and three satellite farms. In the first ten days of his visit, he offered religious instruction, baptized Indians, administered the sacraments, and blessed marriages.

Of the chapel and its worshippers, Father Ioann made a detailed inventory by gender, race, and national origin:

> Fort Ross contains 260 people: 154 male and 106 female. There are 120 Russians, 51 Creoles, 50 Kodiak Aleuts, and 39 baptized Indians. The chapel is constructed of wooden boards, as are almost all of the local houses. It has a small belfry and is rather plain; its entire interior decoration consists of two icons of silver rizas [engraved metal shields]. The chapel at Fort Ross receives almost no income from its members or from those Russians who are occasional visitors. (Hague)

The success of the Russian colony he described foundered in the 1830s for a number of reasons, notably failed crops, depletion of the sea otter, expansion of Latino-American holdings to the east, and limited Russian interest in pioneering. In 1841, the company sold the fort to John Sutter.

The fort passed to George W. Call in 1873, becoming the 15,000-acre Call Ranch, which used the harbor to export lumber, dairy products, vegetables, and fruit. In 1903, the California Historical Landmarks Committee purchased the three-acre Fort Ross complex. After severe earthquake damage to the foundation on April 18 three years later, the chapel walls collapsed. The California Department of Parks and Recreation hired Carlos Call and a team of local carpenters to restore the stockade, barracks, and chapel, which survived with its roof and cupola intact. To preserve architectural integrity, builders replaced crushed walls with the original Russian-cut planks and timbers from the officers' quarters. In 1914, the federal government altered the blended communitiy by remanding the Kashaya to a nearby reservation.

ARCHITECTURE

The twin-domed chapel, the nation's first Orthodox church, is a national landmark and a favorite wedding site. Built according to prevailing Russian Orthodox style, it is simple and unadorned except for a raised platform and three icons on the east wall. Its front bell tower is a six-sided box topped with a steep roof and three-bar Orthodox Russian cross. In 1939, a carpenter followed a priest's hand-drawn plan for the cross, but mistakenly mounted it upside down. It remained upended until worshippers wrote Governor B. L. Olson in 1941 to right it. Down the roofline, a much shorter second tower, circular and pierced by round windows on each side, stands over the altar.

Below a steep plank roof, light enters the sanctuary through sashed windows, four on a side. Visitors enter over a porch and through a wooden door to a vestibule leading to the sanctuary door. Because there are no seats in a traditional Russian Orthodox chapel, priests and attendees stand to celebrate the Slavonic liturgy. There is no iconostasis (icon screen). Instead, in keeping with the chapel's original arrangement, three small icons are suspended over the altar behind a six-cupped brass chandelier, a gift from Commandant Peter Kostromitinov in the 1830s, which hangs at the circular opening below the cupola. In front of the altar, worshippers anchor lighted candles in two traditional sand tables during worship services.

The chapel fell victim to an earthquake and arson in 1970. Following old photos and models of Russian churches, restorers rebuilt it once more with redwood timber cut in the nearby forests and preserved its original bell, forged in St. Petersburg, Russia. Recast from original metal, the bell bears the inscription "Cast in the St. Petersburg Foundry of Master Craftsman Mikhail Makharovich Stukolkin." The chapel received its first Russian-American pilgrims from the Eastern Orthodox Church Society of San Francisco on July 3, 1925. The next morning, the Reverend V. Sakovich held services. In recent times, the chapel welcomes 150,000 visitors annually.

ACTIVITIES

Holy Trinity Chapel receives daily visitors for prayer and meditation from 10:00 A.M. to 5:00 P.M. Since the 1990s, improved U.S. relations with Russia encouraged an influx of religious leaders, church historians, scholars, politicians, and genealogists. Another spurt of visitation marked the 1997 bicentennial of the birth of Saint Innocent. In July 1998 and 1999, the Slavyanka Men's Slavic Chorus performed morning and afternoon programs of liturgical music and projected another visit for July 28, 2000. The chapel is also the site of an annual pilgrimage of clergy of the Orthodox Church of America and holds services at 10:00 A.M. on the Fourth of July to celebrate liturgy, led by the Very Reverend Archimandrite Nikolai Soraich, chancellor of the Diocese of the West and rector of St. Paul Church in Las Vegas, Nevada. A fuller day of worship and remembrance is Memorial Day. After 10:00 A.M. liturgy, worshippers walk on foot the mile and a half across the ravine to the cemetery to view a historic pyramidal mausoleum and cross-topped graves. The celebration typically features authentic period costumes and ends with a steak feast.

Through the Fort Ross Interpretive Association, around 1,000 visitors annually participate in the late July pageant Living History Day, which features Russian dishes, carpentry, wool spinning, Russian music, and tours of the palisade, cemetery, and chapel. The association displays artifacts and research information at the library and archives, staffs a bookstore at the visitor center, and finances programs for adults and children. Hikers, campers, and picnickers explore the park, bird sanctuary, orchard, redwood groves, canyons, cove, and ridges, which look out on the Pacific. For young children, the Fort Ross Environmental Living Program places volunteers in historical roles to relive past events. The Fort Ross Global Village project links schoolchildren from California, Russia, and Alaska for an Internet study of area archaeology and history. Stewards of Salvianka and seal- and whale-watching societies sponsor an annual celebration of the gray whale during its coastal migration off Bodega Head.

Sources: Buchanan 1999; *Eerdmans' Handbook to the World's Religions* 1982; "First Pilgrimage to Fort Ross"; "Fort Ross State Historical Park"; Gentz 1973; Hague; "Holy Trinity Chapel" 1999; Istomin 1992; Kalani, Rudy, and Sperry 1998; LeBaron

1999; "The Life of St. Innocent of Alaska"; Monroe 1984; *New Catholic Encyclopedia* 1967; Norbert 1997, 1999; Parish; Parkman 1997; Smith 1995; "State Will Restore Old Greek Chapel" 1915; "Stockade and Chapel at Fort Ross"; "Two Hundredth Anniversary of Russian-American Company"; Williams, Peter W., 1997.

Holy Trinity Episcopal Church

See Old Swedes Church.

Hot Springs Mountain

Superintendent
Hot Springs National Park, Arkansas
P.O. Box 1860
Hot Springs, Arkansas 71902-1860
501-624-3383 ext. 640

A site hallowed by Native Americans of the Mississippi Valley, Hot Springs Mountain, in Garland County, Arkansas, fifty-two miles southwest of Little Rock, lies within the 1,000-square-mile Hot Springs National Park. At black rock formations spewing boiling streams, tribes were so awed by the presence of the Great Spirit that they maintained neutrality in the presence of enemies while communing with supernatural powers. Stretched out in the hot mud of the Valley of Vapors, the sick of numerous tribes soothed their aching bodies in peace and knelt at rivulets to sip effervescent waters charged with carbonic acid.

HISTORY

A unique source of medicinal waters and ceremonial stones, Hot Springs National Park is a rare geological spot. Over 4,000 years, the curative blend of lime and other minerals dissolved and permeated underground seepage before pulsing upward through faults or fissures at forty-seven natural basins on the western rim of Hot Springs Mountain. Beneath forest and meadow, the ground is rich in sparkly mica, soft stone suited to carving, and chert, or novaculite, a grainy, flintlike quartz that Native Americans prized for its hardness and keen edge. The earliest weapon- and toolmakers fashioned arrowheads and tomahawks from it. Most adults carried chert pieces in buckskin pouches or on lanyards suspended about the neck to use as cutting tools, whetstones, and fire starters.

The Caddo of Red River, Louisiana, and the Tunica-Biloxi, who inhabited the Mississippi Delta in the sixteenth century, settled near Hot Springs Mountain, deep in the Ouachita Mountain Range. Tunica medicine men revered the springs for curative reasons. They identified the clear crystal rocks as earth's healing stones and led victims of paralysis, skin and digestive ailments, headache, rheumatism, neuritis, and arthritis to the thermal springs to inhale beneficial vapors. Imbued with the breath of the Great Spirit, the mountains became a health spa; its surface springs produced a million gallons of mineral water daily, which geothermal energy maintained at a precise temperature of 143°F.

According to myth, the dragon Mogmothon inflicted natural disaster, illness, and starvation on the region's inhabitants. Out of mutual need, local tribes conferred and prayed together. The Great Spirit answered their calls by confining Mogmothon in a cavern, where he writhed and raged, causing earth tremors and fierce storms. The Great Spirit countered the beast's anger by unleashing curative waters. Out of gratitude for deliverance, the Indians reverenced Hot Springs as a sanctuary for all life and determined to live in harmony with the earth and each other.

When the Spanish conquistador Hernando de Soto traveled southwest from Tennessee and arrived at the springs on September 16, 1541, he searched for gold among the Natchez and Tunica. He may have observed the native reverence for the natural source of refreshment and healing. In the eighteenth century, the French touted the location as a hydrotherapeutic wonder worker. In 1804, President Thomas Jefferson named William Dunbar and Dr. George Hunter to head a surveying expedition of the area above the Ouachita River. In December, the explorers reported huts and a log cabin left by trappers and settlers taking the cure. Within four years, cartographers had mapped the area as a link to the Natchez Trace, the 500-mile route that parallels the Mississippi River from Tennessee to Mississippi. The U.S. Corps of Engineers analyzed the water to determine its mineral content.

Hot Springs quickly became a fashionable site to imbibe mineral waters and soak in hot

At Hot Springs Mountain, Arkansas, tribes were so awed by the presence of the Great Spirit that they maintained neutrality in the presence of enemies while communing with supernatural powers. (David Muench / Corbis)

pools. In 1807, trapper Manuel Prudhomme, a former Louisiana planter, followed Natchitoches to the spot and established a settlement. After two developers, Isaac Cates and John Perciful, advertised the therapeutic powers of the springs, Cates constructed a wooden bunk that channeled the flow; Perciful rented cabins to visitors seeking cures. Pioneers built a village and set up an inn and bathing facilities. According to naturalist Thomas Nuttall's 1817 report on Hot Springs therapy, a chill stream blended with the bubbling hot mineral water to cool the flow to bath temperature.

In 1832, under the direction of President Andrew Jackson, Congress specified the region's 5,840 acres as a federal reserve, the nation's first health and recreation resort. The U.S. Department of the Interior designated it a national park in 1921. The city of Hot Springs became the only U.S. city to contain most of a national park inside city limits. In 1941, citizens initiated a pageant called "Saga of the Waters," an Independence Day festival that reviewed historical and cultural data from Indian times to the mid-twentieth century.

ACTIVITIES

The Buckstaff Bathhouse welcomes visitors for a traditional soak as therapy for varied ailments. Like the early Caddo and Tunica-Biloxi, millions of tourists continue to drink the healing waters, store them in containers, and soothe their aching joints in the naturally heated pools at Hot Springs Rehabilitation Center and other area medical facilities. A museum and visitor center in the former Fordyce Bathhouse stocks artifacts and information on native religious practices.

Hot Springs National Park is open daily from 9:00 A.M. to 5:00 P.M., except for New Year's Day, Thanksgiving, and December 25. Along Hot Springs, North, Sugar Loaf, and West Mountains and at Gulpha Gorge Campground, visitors hike, ride horseback, and enjoy wildlife. At Catherine, Hamilton, and Ouachita Lakes, they relax, swim, and fish. At sunrise on Easter on Hot Springs Mountain, local ministers hold annual services reverencing Christ's resurrection.

Sources: "All US Tribes"; Cantor, George, 1993; Champagne 1994; Hall 1941; "Hot Springs National Park"; Milne 1995; Patterson and Snodgrass 1994; Scully 1966; Steiger 1974; Swanton, 1969; "Tunica County, Mississippi"; Waldman 1990.

Islamic Center of America
Imam Hassan Qazwini
15571 Joy Road
Detroit, Michigan 48228
313-582-7442
FAX 313- 582-0988
info@icofa.com; imamqazwini@icofa.com

At the forefront of a surge in Islamic conversion, the Islamic Center of America is a buoyant metropolitan religious community of 10,000 members influencing the Great Lakes region, nation, and world. Located west of Greenfield, the center welcomes 350 worshippers, 80 percent of whom are Lebanese immigrants. Principal Dahlia M. Afr heads an academy that educates 350 elementary school children. The center's dynamic leader, Imam Hassan Qazwini, continues the work begun by his predecessor, founder Mohamad Jawad Chirri, while serving as spokesman for current events and answering questions involving Islam. His mandate comes from God: "It is Allah that giveth you want or plenty, and to Him shall be your return." (Qur'an II:245)

HISTORY
Greater Detroit has had a permanent Islamic community since the 1920s, when Muslim immigrants found work in automotives. Shortly after World War II, a small devout circle of newcomers, primarily from Lebanon and Syria, gathered for prayer and discussion in homes and storefronts. Wearied of makeshift quarters, in the 1950s, they scraped together savings and took out loans to pay for a permanent dwelling, the Islamic Center of America, to which Jordan's King Hussein donated $7,500.

To stabilize the religious community, the founders hired a Lebanese scholar, the late Imam Mohamad Jawad Chirri, a graduate of Iraq's religious institute of Najaf. A learned man and peacemaker between warring Islamic factions, he was a renowned historian and author of *Inquiries about Islam, The Faith of Islam, The Five Daily Prayers, The Brother of Prophet Mohammad,* and *Imam Hussein, Leader of the Martyrs.* After he immigrated to Dearborn, Michigan, in 1949, he hosted a weekly program, *Islam in Focus,* on Detroit's WNIC Radio. His philosophies and dynamism stirred jealousies that forced him temporarily to live in Michigan City, Indiana. Still, under his leadership, for four years, the movement succeeded in unifying area families and providing Qur'an-based education for their children.

To return Imam Chirri to Michigan, the Detroit Islamic Center Foundation Society courted him with zeal and financial backing. After gaining fluency in English, he accepted their offer and relocated in Detroit. The planning committee envisioned a strong ethical and monetary commitment to assure the community's longevity. With help from professional fundraisers, in 1961, 200 families built a permanent headquarters for Shi'ite Muslims—a practical rectanglar structure crowned with the traditional dome. To the left stands the minaret, a round column topped by a railing and conic roof. In addition to prayer facilities, in 1997, the congregation completed a 17,000-square-foot Islamic K–8 school complex, the Muslim American Youth Academy, composed of ten classrooms, a computer lab, a cafeteria, a gymnasium, and offices to serve 450 students.

The center's success is measured in part by the demand for six or seven services each holy day to accommodate worshippers, made up of successful professionals and business leaders. In December 1998, members broke ground for a new Islamic Center of America at the same time that new mosques were going up in Dearborn, Detroit, and Port Huron and Canton, Hamtramck, and Rochester Hills were expanding their facilities. Imam Abdullah El-Amin, executive director of the 33-member Council of

At the forefront of a surge in Islamic conversion, the Islamic Center of America in Detroit is a buoyant metropolitan religious community influencing the Great Lakes region, the nation, and the world. (Courtesy Islamic Center of America)

Islamic Organizations of Michigan, attributes the boom to a burgeoning interest in Islamic worship and religious education among metro-Detroit's 150,000 Muslims. Projected for completion late in 2001 or early 2002, the finished center will take shape near the academy on a ten-acre parcel on Ford Road in Dearborn. The finished plan is a drawing by David Donnellon of Donnellon, Swarthout and Associates and the work of the Sorenson Gross Construction Company, Inc. Upon completion, it will be the largest mosque in North America and an object of pride to the congregation.

An artist's sketch projects a pleasantly symmetrical building, low-slung and capped by a massive dome and two smaller domes flanking the entrance. Corner domes and paired minarets in traditional style to each side of the main dome create a sense of grace and prayerful guardianship. Worship space is designed to welcome 1,000–1,700 in the men's prayer area and 300 in the upstairs women's prayer room. Integral to worship are ablution areas for cleansing hands and storing shoes. A kitchen, a banquet hall for 950 diners, and a 700-seat auditorium equipped with audio and video resources for lectures, conferences, school plays, award ceremonies, and graduations will boost

the center's ministry to 3,000 families from Wayne, Oakland, and Macomb. The complex will include imam chambers, a community center seating 950, an infant room and play area, offices, a boardroom, an elevator, and a 2,000-square-foot library. The expanded school will offer thirteen classrooms, a science lab, a staff lounge, and a gym.

ACTIVITIES

Islamic worship is low-key and devoid of the heavily structured ritual and liturgy found in Catholic and Jewish worship centers. On Thursday evening, the mosque holds congregational prayer at 7:00 P.M., followed by the traditional Du'a Kumail (or Kumayl), a profession of faith composed of a heartfelt invocation to Allah and summary of his goodness. To assure a strong new generation of devout, Imam Qazwini provides Islamic Insights for young members. The evening concludes with refreshments.

On Friday, the mosque hosts the high holy Juma'a, or noontime prayer. Saturday Arabic School at MAYA on Ford Road introduces youth to reading and writing the traditional Qu'ranic language. On Sunday morning at 11:00 A.M., Imam Qazwini lectures before the 12:30 P.M. congregational prayer. In November

IMAM SAYYID HASSAN QAZWINI

A proponent of logic as a component of faith, the gentle Imam Sayyid Hassan Qazwini is a mainstay of Detroit's Islamic Center of America. A native of Kerbala, Iraq, he grew up in a prestigious religious family. In 1992, he graduated from the Islamic Seminary in Qom and began studying law, jurisprudence, and Qur'anic analysis. Influencing his education were scholars Ayatollah Waheed Khorasani, Ayatollah Jawad Tabrizi of Iran, and Ayat Muntazari. Within months, he immigrated to Los Angeles, where he directed the Azzahra Islamic Center of Orange County.

Fluent in English, Arabic, and Farsi, Imam Qazwini is a speaker, author, and renowned professor of religion. He founded *Annebras* (The Eternal Light), an Islamic journal, and published *Meditation in Sahehain* and *The Prophet Mohammad: The Ethical Prospect.* In 1997, he settled his family in Detroit and joined the staff of the Islamic Center of America, where he followed the scriptural injunction to "turn thy face in the direction of the Sacred Mosque; that is indeed the truth from thy Lord. And Allah is not unmindful of what ye do." (Qur'an II:148–149) Today, he leads prayer toward Qibla, the orientation toward Mecca's shrine, the Kaaba, the Islamic holy of holies, and delivers scholarly sermons that draw on world religious principle and practice, science, current events, and tradition from the past 1,400 years.

1998, Imam Qazwini motivated newcomers with an open house. The event was part of a series of receptions from other U.S. mosques for newcomers interested in learning more about Islam.

Sources: Bullard March 8, 1999, June 28, 1999; "Islamic Center of America" 1999; Krodel 1999; Moses 1998; Robertson 1999; "Shi'ites Under Attack"; Singer and Bates-Rudd 1998; Smith 1958; Whitall 1998; *World Religions* 1998.

ened the internal relations of fellow Buddhist organizations and practitioners.

As a gesture to interfaith organizations, in the fall of 1991, officers from the American Buddhist Congress formed a statewide association to enrich Buddhism in Texas. The next year, the reverends Phap Nhan, Hung-I Shih, K. Nanda, and Huyen Viet founded the Texas Buddhist Council, which elected officers in July 1993 at a celebration in Houston. With council backing, the Jade Buddha Temple, completed in 1989, grew to be one of the state's largest Buddhist institutions.

Open daily from 10:00 A.M. to 5:00 P.M., the center features a central lotus pond at front centered with a statue of Kwan-Yin, the all-powerful lord of mercy, healer, and savior. The tranquil waters entice visitors to view pastel blooms and bright orange carp. Immediately behind the pond, the complex consists of a Grand Hall to the right, Kwan-Yin Hall at center with garden and cafeteria, and living quarters, meeting rooms, library, and childcare center to the left. In the Youth Activity Center on the west end of the campus, the Bodhi Chinese School, founded in 1992, carries out the Buddha's intent to uplift through education.

Jade Buddha Temple
Venerable Jan Hai
6969 Westbranch Drive
Houston, Texas 77072
281-498-1616
FAX 281-498-8133
tba@jadebuddha.org
www.jadebuddha.org

On 2.5 acres in southwest Houston stands the Jade Buddha Temple, a religious and education center accommodating over 1,000 members from various Buddhist traditions. In compliance with the Texas Buddhist Association, the temple promotes basic injunctions of the Buddha:

- To practice loving kindness, compassion, joy, and serenity daily for the benefit of all
- To maintain calm through meditation
- To cultivate wisdom for a clear understanding of humanity and the universe

In general, the temple strives to preserve and nurture cosmic order, to unify Buddhists, and to disseminate the teachings of the Buddha to the American mainstream.

HISTORY AND ARCHITECTURE
Founded in 1979, the Jade Buddha Temple was the vision of lay members led by the venerables Wing Sing, Jan Hai, and Hung-I Shih. During the 1980s, Southeast Asian refugees and some 20,000 Chinese-Americans increased interest in Asian religion. These families established Buddhism as a religious force in Texas. Meditation groups and temples amplified a sense of community and shared vision for Texas Buddhists. An exchange of monks and teachers strength-

ACTIVITIES
The Jade Buddha Temple invites people of all religious affiliations to enrich themselves through worship, song, classes, and special events. Staff accommodates individuals who need transportation and childcare. Temple assemblies and activities fill the calendar. Since 1990, the 35-voice Bodhi Choir, directed by Ann Chan, has performed Buddhist hymns and art songs at special events and concerts. Other annual events begin with a traditional Chinese New Year and extend through birthday ceremonies for Kwan-Yin Boddhisattva and Amitabha Buddha, a Vesak Ceremony honoring Sakyamuni Buddha's birthday, and a Ullambana Festival commemorating the dead.

Education is a mainstay at the Jade Buddha Temple. The staff teaches vegetarian cooking and both walking and sitting meditation, which

The Jade Buddha Temple, a religious and education center in Texas. (Courtesy of Jade Buddha Temple)

focuses on breathing and concentration through repetition of standard phrases. Each Sunday morning from 9:00 to 10:00, the staff offers meditation classes free to the public and holds four-day meditation retreats in English at Houston's Margratt Retreat Center and a similar schedule of classes in Chinese at the temple. The purpose of these meditation symposia is to nurture health and inner strength, distinguish life essentials, and refine character.

Through the Texas Buddhist Association, the temple supports a number of charities: worldwide emergency disaster relief, food and clothing donations and physical examinations for the poor, a school supply pantry, aid to disabled children at Richmond State School, promotion of organ donation, visits to nursing homes, and the Chinese American Relief Association. In February 1998, the temple opened the Texas Buddhist College, which holds evening and weekend classes in Chinese only. The temple library, located on the south end, is open to the public on Tuesday and Thursday mornings and afternoons and on weekends. It stocks Tripitaka, the Sutras, Vinaya, Abhidharma, and other contemporary

Chinese and English Buddhist texts, studies of Buddhism, personal experiences, children's books, and audiovisual resources in English and Chinese.

The temple devotes much of its effort to youth and offers resources to Rice, Houston, and Texas Universities and St. John's School. Through private donations, the Bodhi scholarship funds education for 12 students. Essential to the temple's ministry is the Bodhi Chinese School, where a staff of 20 teachers instructs two semesters in the traditional characters of the Chinese language and introduces culture to K–12 grades. Divided among twenty-two classes are 300 students in fourteen academic levels. In addition, the school teaches kung-fu, violin, chess, Chinese calligraphy, folk dance, crafts, Buddhist study, and children's Sutra reading.

The Jade Buddha Temple congregation supports a cultural and religious ministry enabled by simultaneous translation through earphones to include non-Chinese-speaking attendees. Members Jan Hai, Chen Hwa, Hung-I, Sherry Glover, and Frank Glover lecture on Buddhist philosophy and history. A teen group enjoys

JAN HAI

A pioneer Buddhist missionary in the Western Hemisphere, the Venerable Jan Hai is a scholarly force for peace and for the dissemination of *Dharma*, an Asian concept of cosmic order. Born in the Chiang Shu Province of China in 1931, he began studying at the Lung Chang Temple at Bao Hua Mountain at age nine under the Venerable Chuo and continued his education at the Buddhist School of Tien Ning Temple. At age eighteen, he joined the Youth Cadets in Taiwan and studied for a decade at the Mi Le School under the Venerable Chi Han.

At age twenty, Jan Hai sought more enlightenment in Thailand by learning the Thai and Balinese languages. In addition to joining the Hinayana monks, he enrolled at Juralongon Buddhist College for an eight-year concentration on types of meditation. His research covered analysis of Hinayana Buddhist texts and concluded with advanced graduate work at the Tokyo Buddhist College and a thesis entitled "An Analysis of the Dhammapada."

Concerned with the absence of an American Buddhism, Jan Hai came to the Da Jueh Temple in 1972. Six years later, he and the Venerable Wing Sing established the Texas Buddhist Association and built the Buddha Light Temple. After overcoming illness brought on by exhaustion, with the aid of the Venerable Hung-I Shih, abbot of the Light Temple, Jan Hai completed a scholarly evaluation of Hinayana Buddhism and issued *The History of Hinayana Buddhism* (1975) as well as translations of *The Language of Truth* and *The Illustrated Biography of Buddha's Life.*

ment. Editor Simon Young of the bimonthly Chinese magazine *Buddha's Light* publishes articles and essays by lay members and monks; the *Sporadical,* a bimonthly English newsletter, summarizes temple activities.

In 1999, the temple celebrated the twentieth anniversary of the Texas Buddhist Association. On April 3, members hosted a concert of 100 voices—the Bodhi Choir, Ran Deng women's chorus, and Guan Zi Zai mixed chorus—for Celebration of Life with a Musical Evening, a performance of six Buddhist hymns at Cullen Performance Hall at the University of Houston. Four of the hymns—"Praise of the Sakyamuni Buddha," "Incense Anthem Lu Hsiang," "The Ten Grand Vows of Boddhisatva Pu-Hsian," and "The Texas Buddhist Association Anthem"—are compositions of Eddy Xiao, the previous conductor of the Bodhi choir. The annual fund-raising bazaar and donation drive concluded the year.

Into the twenty-first century, the temple enlivened its programs with dharma talks and discussion in Chinese and English, assemblies, guest speakers, Buddhism classes, Great Compassion Mantra and Amita Buddha chanting, a Life Release of captive animals into the wild, and readings from scripture. In addition to education, the staff offers a lamp festival, Sunday Chinese-style vegetarian lunches, picnics, and family camping. An annual February carnival, May Interfaith Ministry Friendship Program, and September open house advanced the temple's outreach to other area religions. The staff performs Buddhist weddings for members and the public.

Sources: Eck 1994; Epstein "Comments on Buddhism"; Epstein 1985; Glover 1997; Grimes 1996; Holmes 2000; Huang 1997; "Jade Buddhist Temple"; Kaye and Schmidt 1999; Klein 1999; Ling 1972; "Mid-American Buddhist Association" 1999; "Official Response of the Japanese Church to the Lineamenta" 1997; Vu, *World Religions* 1998; Young 1999.

leisure activities that instill Buddhism in daily life. The youth summer camp develops more thoroughly a single theme, such as cherishing the moment, loving kindness, and the environ-

Kahal Kadosh Beth Elohim
Rabbi Anthony David Holz
Myles Glick, President
90 Hasell Street
Charleston, South Carolina 29401
843-723-1090
FAX 843-723-0537
kkbe@awod.com

A product of colonial religious freedom, Kahal Kadosh Beth Elohim is a pacesetter deriving energy from past and present. Temple members, who chose a name translating to English as "Holy Congregational House of God," led the movement toward American Reformed Judaism. The nation's first reform congregation and the oldest U.S. temple in continuous use, it displays Charleston's reputation as a haven of religious dissent and innovation. In 1980, the U.S. Department of the Interior added the synagogue to the list of National Historic Landmarks.

HISTORY

Organized in 1749, Kahal Kadosh Beth Elohim united Sephardic Jewish pioneers in the nation's fourth oldest Jewish congregation after New York, Newport, and Savannah. Among its founders were Moses Lindo, the colonies' first indigo cultivator, and Joseph Levy, veteran of the Cherokee War of 1760–1761 and possibly North America's first Jewish military officer. A fallen hero among the two dozen Jews serving in the American Revolution, Francis Salvador, elected to the South Carolina Provincial Congresses of 1775 and 1776, was one of the first Jewish-American legislators. He became the first Jew to die for the American cause when Indians scalped and murdered him on August 1, 1776.

Until members of Beth Elohim built a perma-

nent temple in 1775, they worshiped in homes. Integral to area families was Coming Street Cemetery, the South's oldest Jewish burial ground, with graves dating to 1762. Among congregation innovations were the Hebrew Orphan Society, the temple parochial school, and the Hebrew Benevolent Society, the nation's oldest Jewish charity. A blind poet and hymnographer, Penina Moise, author of *Hymns Written for the Use of Hebrew Congregations* (1856), superintended the Sunday school, which Sally Lopez established. Esteemed members included a steamship magnate, a gas utilities founder, members of the Supreme Court, and the surgeon general and quartermaster general of the Confederate Army.

In 1797, the congregation commissioned a stately Georgian synagogue on Hasell Street. Dedicated in 1799, it served them until the great Charleston fire of April 28, 1838. During this period of growth, the temple became the birthplace of U.S. reform Judaism. In 1824, forty-seven members formalized liberal beliefs by requesting an abridged Sephardic Orthodox liturgy and the delivery of sermons and prayers in English. Because the synod denied their request, Charleston progressives withdrew from the parent sect and formed the Reformed Society of Israelites. Influenced by the Hamburg Reform congregation, they instituted principles still in use.

In 1840, the current facility took shape on the original site. Henry Erben fitted a tracker pipe organ in the rear balcony, an innovation in instrumental music. Traditionalists opposed the use of organ music and unsuccessfully pressed their complaint in court. In anger at violations of tradition, they withdrew to form Shearit Israel, a synogogue on Wentworth Street, but failed to halt trends toward modernization. The two factions remained apart until a reunion in 1866.

Dedicated in 1841, Beth Elohim synagogue enjoyed a quarter century of advancement before South Carolina seceded from the Union. The threat of Sherman's army near the end of the Civil War forced the congregation to dispatch their organ, ornamented scrolls of Jewish law, and chandeliers to Columbia, South Carolina, but the items did not survive Union marauders. Both

A product of colonial religious freedom, Kahal Kadosh Beth Elohim in Charleston, South Carolina, is a pacesetter deriving energy from past and present. (Photo by Louis Schwarz. Courtesy of K.K.B.E. Archives)

Shearit Israel and Beth Elohim suffered structural damage from shelling, a permanent disfiguration that the Reverend Isaac Leeser mourned in 1866 in his newspaper, the *Occident*.

During Reconstruction, the synagogue aided Charleston's recovery with leadership and social and economic ministry. In 1873, it was a founding body of the Union of American Hebrew Congregations. In 1879, the planning committee rearranged seating from a pulpit-centered plan to place the reader before the ark and space family pews in double rows and side rows ranging from the center of the room. The railings of the old platform surrounded the reading table of the new pulpit.

The organ required frequent upgrading. In 1865, Henry Erben installed a replacement instrument encased in a black-walnut console. In 1886, staff commissioned renovation of the organ, which is inscribed with a verse from the poet David, "Praise Him with stringed instruments and organs" (Psalms 150:4). The alterations served until 1914, when the congregation purchased an instrument from the Austin Organ

Company but preserved and revoiced ranks of pipes from former installations. It remained in use for seventy-six years, when deterioration forced them to choose a new model, this time from Ontko and Young. A subsequent upgrading of the organ in 1995 restored up-to-date musical performance to the auditorium.

ARCHITECTURE

Inside a wrought-iron fence and ornamental gate, the Greek Revival synagogue is a downtown Charleston architectural treasure. Designed by C. L. Warner and constructed by member David Lopez, at the front entrance, it proclaims on a marble tablet the Sh'ma: "Hear, O Israel, the Lord our God is the Sole Eternal Being" (Deuteronomy 6:4). The foyer preserves the stone foundation from the parent church. The interior features an ark of Santo Domingan mahogany and silver Torah ornaments. Stained-glass windows inset with religious symbols replace original glass destroyed in the earthquake of August 1886.

Alongside the temple is the Pearlstine Tabernacle, erected in 1950 for a bicentennial celebration. Murals by William Halsey honor Beth Elohim's founders and patriots; a pair of iron statues created by Willard Hirsch depict biblical prophets. The tabernacle houses a religious school, a social hall, and the Mildred Bernstein kitchen. In the H. Sydney and Len Heyman Building behind the temple, the congregation maintains an archive and museum alongside the library, rabbi's study, and administrative offices. Among temple keepsakes are records from 1800, photos of past presidents and presiding rabbis, the cash book of Isaac Harby's academy, photos and documents of congregants, prayer books, and Solomon N. Carvalho's painting of the interior of the 1792 synagogue. The museum is open weekdays from 9:00 A.M. to 4:00 P.M. Additional holdings are on display at the Robert Smalls Library of the College of Charleston.

ACTIVITIES

With pride in its establishment of U.S. Reform Judaism, Kahal Kadosh Beth Elohim serves religious needs of families and individuals through lifelong education, communal worship and ritual, acts of loving kindness, and an ongoing quest for justice and peace. To attain these lofty aims, the staff heads activities and committees to suit its members. In addition to a sisterhood, brotherhood, and temple youth groups, members involve themselves in hospitality through potluck dinners and dinner dances, the Raisin Library and fine arts, and a membership committee, which publishes a temple photo directory. Some choose work in a religious school enrolling 100 students, social action through the Community Relations Committee, the Judaica shop, temple tours weekdays from 10:00 A.M. to noon, and the volunteer choir. Groups provide Shiva meals for bereaved families, maintain burial records, post a temple Web site, and oversee cemeteries, building and grounds maintenance and repairs, publicity, house services, membership, caring for residents of hospitals and nursing homes, office volunteerism, strategic planning, and the liturgy and music of temple ritual.

At the regular Shabbat service and social hour on Friday evening at 8:15 and the Saturday service at 11:00 A.M., the Participation Committee honors members by recruiting volunteers and seating them on the bimah to recite blessings and kiddush and to partipate in Oneg Shabbat, the after-worship social hour. In addition, the staff, led by Rabbi Anthony David Holz and Rabbi Emeritus William A. Rosenthall, schedules discussions, films, and musical presentations and provides a monthly Family Torah Service that welcomes children. Holy days include Rosh Hashanah, Yom Kippur service and breakfast, Sukkot, Simchat Torah, Chanukah, Purim, Passover Seder, Selichot, Shabbat Shuvah, and Shavuot. Yom Hashoah commemorates the Holocaust; Yom Ha-atzma-ut honors Israel Independence Day.

Temple activities involve members in the greater Charleston community. The Reform Jewish Outreach counsels on interfaith dating and welcomes interfaith couples, Jews by Choice, and unaffiliated Jews. The educational outreach organizes Sunday brunch and scholar-in-residence lectures sponsored by the College of Charleston Jewish Studies Department, an annual temple block party with St. Mary's Catholic Church, and an annual temple retreat. The religious school, held on Sunday from 9:30 A.M. to 11:30 A.M., educates children from kindergarten through confirmation. Hebrew classes, which develop Jewish identity and further cultural awareness, meet Sunday from 11:30 A.M. to 1:15 P.M. The curriculum centers on holidays, customs, Jewish history, and Reformed Jewish thought. The temple issues a newletter, *Chai Lights,* and the Jewish Residents Telephone Book free to Jewish households throughout the South Carolina low country.

Sources: Jacoby 1999; "Kahal Kadosh Beth Elohim"; Lilly 1966; Sarna and Golden 1999; "The Story of Kahal Kadosh Beth Elohim"; Williams, Peter W., 1997; *World Religions* 1998.

Kaho'Olawe

Burt Lum
Kaho'Olawe Island Reserve Commission
P.O. Box 152
Honolulu, Hawaii 96810
808-586-0761
blum@brouhaha.net
www.kahoolawe.org

On Kaho'Olawe, the smallest of Hawaii's eight major land masses, the 10.85 by 6.6-mile island has become the state's cause célèbre. A denuded, windswept barren once called the Island of Death, the volcanic island was once a significant *wahe pana* (religious site) green with lush savanna and twisted wiliwili trees. According to ancient chants, 1,000 years ago, it was known as Kohemalamalama 'o Kanaloa—the hallowed site of whale watches, strong ocean currents, sightings of star clusters, burials of chiefs and priests, petroglyphs, and tributes to the gods.

Because it carried the name of the God Kanaloa, the entire 48 square miles is holy. A revered ancestor, Ai'ai, a builder of *ko'a* (fishing shrines), erected the island's first altar overlooking Honokoa Bay on the northwestern shore. He placed the erect, elongated *akua* (sacred stone) at the center before offering the first catch of the day. To native Hawaiians, the right to religious freedom on this spiritual mound has become a central issue in their demands for sovereignty.

In the last quarter of the twentieth century, the Protect Kaho'Olawe 'Ohana (Family), led by activist George Helm and mentored by traditionalist folk sayer Charlie Maxwell and healer Harry Kunihi Mitchell, demanded that the U.S. Navy cease pelting the land with bombs and grant visitation rights to worshippers of indigenous gods. After military officials began removing ordnance from the surface, they turned over safe zones to natives to manage as a Hawaiian cultural reserve and center teaching traditional Hawaiian hula, beliefs, chants, and practices. The shift from militarism to preservation gladdens Hawaiians longing to save the shreds of a former culture inundated with Eurocentrism.

BELIEFS

Once known as the Southern Beacon, Kaho'Olawe was a holy habitation for a pantheon of nature gods born of Papa and Wakea, personifications of earth and sky, brought to shore by East Polynesian adventurers. To ward off famine, disease, rebellion, and war, chiefs honored a supreme triad—Kane, the organizer; Ku, the architect and builder; and Lono, the executor of elements. According to creation myths in King David Kalakaua's *The Legends and Myths of Hawaii,* originally compiled in 1888, Lono provided the white clay from which the first human head was made. He was heaven's intellectual, a

reciter of epic verse, and battler of the winds and waters. In his canoe, he faced down the angry sea and returned to earth to carry out human contests of skill and grit. He returned to heaven to settle a rebellion and lived there to old age.

In Hawaiian tradition, offerings of fish, shellfish, seashells, and coral at more than sixty island shrines to Lono, a compassionate God of peace and prosperity, assured a full harvest. When twentieth-century natives reclaimed Kaho'Olawe from the military, they petitioned Lono to green up the shell-pocked land and restore native species and animals. To symbolize resettlement, leaders constructed a *hale,* the traditional Hawaiian house, and vowed to reinstitute seasonal rites and respect for natural elements, which form the body of Lono.

HISTORY

From its first inhabitation around 400 A.D., Kaho'Olawe was a religious center for 150 part-time residents in semipermanent huts near sacred springs. On Moa'ulanui, petroglyphs on rock faces depict aboriginal runners or dancers, animals, and complex symbols. Island poets led chants honoring the islands' birth and genealogy of the *ali'i* (chiefs). At a stone slab on the island's highest summit, Moa'ulaiki, 1,444 feet above sea level, the *kahunas* (priests) studied astronomy. From 1150 to 1400, seasoned sea pilots trained the next generation of navigators to interpret the currents of 'Alalakeiki Channel, trade winds, cloud formations, and constellations to make safe voyages to and from Kahiki, the old name for Tahiti or for Polynesia in general. An armchair-shaped rock earned the name Navigator's Chair for its command of the summit. By 1600, islanders inhabited the land, an honored gathering place for priests.

For a millennium, several hundred Hawaiians spanning fifty generations valued the island's waters for fishing and built shrines at favored sea lookouts. At the center of the island's southern shore, in 1913, archeologist John F. G. Stokes identified a shrine at Kamohio Bay. It was a propitious setting. The altar at the water's edge was also a sheltered retreat where overhanging cliffs formed a shallow cave. Stone steps led into a vestibule and four platforms, which builders faced with sea-worn rock. The popularity of the

The entire 48 square miles of Kaho'Olawe island, the smallest of Hawaii's eight major land masses, is holy. (Need photo credit)

niche as a pre-1800 workshop for carving wood, shell, and tortoise fishhooks was obvious to excavators, who catalogued coral knives, files, gourd vessels, firesticks, human and fish bones, charcoal, bundle offerings, and kapa (or tapa) (bark cloth) along with figurines of echinoderm, sandalwood, and stone. All reside in the Bernice Pauahi Bishop Museum. Remains left at the shrine disappeared in a rockslide or fell to scavengers who looted it in 1990.

In the basalt deposits at Pu'u Moiwi, a knoll south of the island's center, people worked the island chain's second largest quarry of stone for the *koi* (adz), the chief woodworking tool in Hawaiian culture. These aborigines celebrated their craft through prayer at a workshop shrine. In the nineteenth century, they suffered their worst decimation from European diseases—measles, scarlet fever, pneumonia, tuberculosis—and either died out or relocated to other islands.

To preserve their religion, they hid their sacred statuary and practiced their faith in strict seclusion from intrusive Christian missionaries. In 1826, the island was used as a prison. After the government leased the land to private interests in 1858, stockmen introduced goats, sheep, and cattle that gradually reduced the soil-stabilizing Hawaiian cotton and sweet grass by overgrazing.

From 1880 to 1920, attempts to revive agrarianism proved too late to halt depletion. In 1920, the U.S. military chose the desolate spot for ordnance training and an artillery range. After the Japanese bombing of Pearl Harbor in 1941, the military took over the entire island as a target zone, reducing the center to hardpan with strafing, torpedoes, and troop maneuvers. Violence to the land decimated petroglyphs, artifacts, fragile reefs, and coastal waters. Erosion washed nearly 2 million tons of topsoil into valley bottoms, burying artifacts. In 1965, the navy simulated an atomic blast with 500 tons of TNT that blew a fifty-meter crater in the surface. Alarmed, native Hawaiians pressed for the land's return under a decade-old promise of President Dwight D. Eisenhower to relinquish the island when it was no longer useful.

Through acts of protest, illegal occupation, and civil disobedience, a coterie of reclaimers including elders Barbara Hanchett, Lani Kapuni, Clara Ku, Mary Lee, Rose Wainui, and Emma DeFries brought the issue to public attention and began repatriating Kaho'Olawe. Natives made their first legal visit in 1976. Within twenty years, 5,000 had come to worship and restore the home of Hawaii's primeval gods. In an attempted occupation, on March 7, 1977, two leading activists—George Helm and Kimo Mitchell—appear to have drowned off the island's coast.

Pressure in the right places saved Kaho'Olawe. In 1981, to protect 540 hallowed sites, the National Register of Historic Places added the island to its list. Nine years later, President George Bush ended military target practice and appointed a commission to study the best way of returning the island to citizen control. Native botanist Rene Sylva urged the removal of the alien tamarisk and the growing of naupaka and hau trees and subsistence plants long valued for food and healing.

In 1994, two years after worshippers left the traditional gift of coral at Mua Ha'i Kapuna to heal the island, official reclamation began. Signs of health appear in the frolics of spinner dolphins, integrity of reefs, and growing populations of monk seals and green sea turtles, which nest on the island's western shores. In Nelson Foster's pictorial tribute, *Kaho'olawe: Na Leo o Kanaloa* (1995), photographed from 1992 to 1994, Dr. Noa Emmett Aluli explained the importance of the island to well-being,

We begin to look after our *kupuna* [elders] the way they looked after us when we were young. What we've seen and felt and learned on Kaho'olawe filters into our lives in many ways.

He connected picking up fallen stone to "picking ourselves up as a people." (Foster 1995, xiv) The act of reviving consecrated ground has

become an "extended-family process" by which participants learn patience, respect, and camaraderie and give back to the land.

In August 1998, supporters held an eighteen-hour vigil at the Iolani Palace honoring activists martyred during the quarter century of protests. As an act of good faith, the government guaranteed removal of debris, toxic waste, and unexploded ordnance plus reforestation and creation of a liveable habitat by 2004. Named the Kaho'Olawe Island Reserve, the land and ocean for two miles beyond its shores fell under state regulation. Legislators imposed a controversial ban on fishing and diving to save schools of onaga and ehu and fostered scientific inquiry, indigenous plants and traditions, and reconsecration of temples and shrines.

ACTIVITIES

Since 1982, native Hawaiians have celebrated Makahiki, the November to February harvest season. Central to the agricultural deity Lono, the three-month ritual begins with the first sighting of the *makali'i,* the constellation Pleiades, which marks winter rains. The season closes with purification in December and January, a standard Polynesian thanksgiving for fertility and bounty. In a peaceful period, the devout allow the land to rest and absorb nurturing rains in anticipation of a new agricultural cycle. At one with nature, they abandon war and foster good will through feasting, debate, and athletic contests.

At the call of the pu shell, rituals begin at the base of a sixteen-foot monolith carved like a skull at the top and draped in tapa, fern fronds, and feather streamers. *Kupuna,* or elders, bear it about the island, halting at each plot to accept tributes. After this solemn obeisance, worshippers dismantle icons until the next year. To close the Makahiki season, *kahunas,* or priests, fill a *wa'a'auhau* (ceremonial canoe) with offerings of pork and taro wrapped in ti leaves and push it out to sea to return Lono to his ancestral land.

Late-twentieth-century reclamation of Kaho'Olawe focuses on rededication and thanks for abundance and for cloud cover and rain. Adoration of Lono results in greater abundance and in the resumption of ancestral religion and identity. In 1987, stewards of the island began negotiating with the U.S. Navy. In safe zones,

they built *lele* (altars, or offering platforms) at select spots to hold *ho'okupu* (offerings) to Lono.

- They chose Hakioawa Bay, a gulch on the
  northeast coast, for its *heiau* (temple, or
  family chapel), the *hale o papa* (women's
  temple), a temple to the Goddess Papa, and
  the *hale mua* (men's temple, or fish shrine);
  thatched a *hale halawai* (gathering place)
  out of pandanus leaves and floored it with
  water-worn pebbles; and erected and dedicated a *pa hula* (dance platform), dedicated
  to Iaka, patron Goddess of the hula.
- At Moa'ula on the island summit, they
  looked out on the islands of Hawai'i,
  Maui, Moloka'i, and Lana'i from a vantage
  point valued as a navigational and astronomical observatory, where the bell-stone
  of an ancient temple summoned worshippers.
- A third blessed site, Kealaikahiki, the channel separating the island and Maui, is the
  pathway to Kahiki. There, a Polynesian ancestor lived until he paddled back to
  Tahiti. The spot was the traditional em-
  barkation point of subsequent migrations
  to the homeland.
- At the northwestern tip above Hakioawa,
  in 1992, restorers constructed a platform
  dedicated to the memory of ancestors.
  Formed of stones in a rectangle edged
  with fronds, it honors natives who loved
  and revered the island.

With the restoration of Kaho'Olawe, worshippers intend to line up annually behind the
banner carrier and progress into the valley of
Hakioawa to present once more the ten traditional offerings of black coconut, lama wood,
'awa (a bitter beverage made from kava), meat of
black pigs wrapped in ki leaves, red fish, bread-
fruit, sweet potato, banana, and gourds of fresh
water. These ritual gestures reaffirm Hawaiian
society and its dependence on the land and waters. The procession invites all to participate,
wear traditional garb, prepare dishes for the
God, make offerings at the temple, chant, carry
the holy icon and island banners, and drum.
Central to the resurrection of sanctity is a reac-
quaintance with the *ka po'e kahiko* (people of

old). By reinstating the seasonal spirit of rain,
growth, peace, and renewal, they intend to
nourish the land by watering island plants, controlling weeds and erosion, planting windbreaks,
repairing stoneworks, supplying fire pits, moni-
toring the well, and rebuilding island sanctity.

Sources: Eck 1994; Enomoto 1997; Foster 1995;
Gomes 1997; "Hawaiian Sacred Sites and Power
Spots" 1999; Hurley 1997; "Interview with Charlie
Maxwell" 1996; "Kaho'Olawe Mahakiki Overview,"
Kalakaua 1972; King; Kubota May 23, 1997, July 3,
1997; McAllister 1973; Miller and Snodgrass 1998;
Omandam 1998; Torres, *World Religions* 1998.

Kannagara Jinja

Reverend Koichi Larry Barrish
17720 Crooked Mile Road
Granite Falls, Washington 98252
360-691-6389
FAX 360-691-6389
Kannagara@prodigy.net
www.kannagara.org

Kannagara Jinja is a Shinto temple introducing
Northwestern Americans to Japanese traditional
religion. The dream of the Reverend Doctor
Yukitaka Yamamoto, the *jinja* (shrine) carries to
a new location the traditions of the 2,000-year-
old Tsubaki Grand Shrine, the parent *jinja,* in
Mie, Japan, and the Tsubaki American Shrine in
Stockton, California. Located in the western
end of Washington state, the shrine occupies a
serene woodsy spot suited to its message of contentment and reverence for ancestry.

HISTORY

Kannagara Jinja is a licensed *kami* (spirit) shrine
led by Guji (chief priest) Koichi Larry Barrish,
the only American Shinto priest and eighth-
generation headmaster of Ideta Ryu Budokan
school of Aiki-jutsu, who has practiced esoteric
Shinto and aikido for a quarter century. The
shrine sanctifies a space dedicated to a venerable *kami,* Sarutahiko No OhKami, Japan's primal deity of guidance, optimism, and protection.
The shrine also extols the God's wife, Ame No
Uzume No Mikoto, deity of divine movement,
marriage, and meditation, and Ama No Murakumo Kukisamuhara Ryu O Haya Takemusu
OhKami, a controller of energy.

Kannagara Jinja in Great Falls, Washington, is a Shinto temple introducing Northwestern Americans to Japanese traditional religion. (Courtesy Kannagara Jinja)

Visitors arrive at the *torii,* or entrance gate, proceed down the *sando,* or approach pathway, that leads to the purification font. The shrine's interior offers a place for removing shoes before entering the worship area. Worshippers sit or kneel on mats. Prayers are in Japanese, which a printed text translates into English. The staff conducts regular and festival worship as well as weddings, prayer requests, baby dedication, groundbreaking, and ongoing classes in aikido, Japanese martial arts. The chief priest counsels people on personal dilemmas, difficult decisions, and life changes. For the deceased, he holds memorial services and may offer a commemorative plaque for family members to place in a home shrine. There is a set fee for ceremonies. Attendees may place free-will offerings in a money box before or after a service.

ACTIVITIES

On an eight-acre riverside site, the staff offers a full range of Shinto purification ceremonies to harmonize devotees with nature. The chief priest personally tends the shrine and offers daily *misogi* (water purification). The result of ritual cleansing is *kansha* (thankfulness) and the balance of heart identified by five qualities:

- *Akaki Kokoro*—purity and cheer
- *Kiyoki Kokoro*—clarity and brilliance
- *Makoto Kokoro*—sincerity
- *Naoki Kokoro*—straightforward simplicity
- *Tadashiki Kokoro*—pursuit of justice

Associate priests train newcomers in *Misogi Shu Ho* (purification) and *Chinkon Gyo Ho,* Shinto-style meditation, along with guidance in ki healing and a macrobiotic diet stressing cooked grains and Japanese vegetables—miso, sesame seeds, sea vegetables, and *tsukemono* (pickles). Macrobiotic foods reflect the seasons and ecology as well as individual activity, occupation, physical makeup, previous eating patterns, personal tastes, and social environment

The Reverend Barrish ended the millennium with advances in interfaith cooperation. In June 1999, he copresented a Shinto workshop at the General Assembly of the Unitarian Universalist Association in Salt Lake City, Utah. In late July, he sent a portable shrine to the Congress of International Association for Religious Freedom in Vancouver, British Columbia, and, in August, joined the Reverend Doctor Yamamoto in conducting a Shinto seminar. Scheduled for November was a trip of shrine members to the Tsubaki Grand Shrine in Japan.

The Reverend Barrish's work is in a formative stage that includes remodeling of the hall, begun in October 1999. He initiates lay priests and has trained Anne Evans as Canada's first licensed Shinto priest and founder of a private branch shrine in the Gulf Islands. In the planning stages at the Granite Falls shrine is a Shinto learning center. The staff has purchased twenty-five acres adjacent to the shrine and intends to build guest houses. Staff projects adult classes in meditation, purification ritual, and macrobiotic cooking.

> **Sources:** "Center for Shinto Studies and Japanese Culture" 1998; Eck 1994; *Eerdmans' Handbook to the World's Religions* 1982; "Kannagara Jinja" 1998; "Seattle Aikido History" 1998; Sonoda; Tsumuro 1988; *World Religions* 1998; Yamamoto 1999.

King's Chapel
64 Beacon Street
Boston, Massachusetts 02109
617-227-2155

Near Boston's Old South Church stands a paradigm of stern, granite-faced American pragmatism—King's Chapel, the first U.S. Unitarian church. A compact entity among taller, more imposing buildings, the church gave new life to New England's first Anglican sanctuary, a boxy wood structure founded in 1688 to serve the two-year-old parish. The edifice was completed the next year and more than doubled in size in 1710.

America's first major stone edifice, the current King's Chapel is the design of America's first architect, Peter Harrison, who prepared the site in 1748 by encasing an older wooden church in granite and systematically tossing discarded wood beams and siding out the window as he replaced them. He completed the job in August 1753. The sumptuous interior makes an architectural statement about the upstart Congregationalist and staid old Anglican tories, who obviously intended to look down their noses at religious newcomers.

A focus of the Boston Freedom Trail tour is the King's Chapel Burying Ground, Boston's first cemetery. Open during daylight in the city's historic district, the cemetery is listed with the National Register of Historic Places. Established in 1630 by Puritan colonists, it was a municipal burial place open to the public and maintained by the village. Intricate headstones preserve the somber Puritan outlook. A favorite of tourists is Rebecca Gerrish's slate monument featuring a dancing skeleton and an angel lifting an hourglass in one hand. Between them, a candle represents the fragility and brevity of human life.

Period symbolism dominates the other plots. One, dedicated to Joseph Tapping, bears carved scrollwork and a winged skull, an hourglass, two spinning wheels, and the Latin injunction *Memento Mori* (Remember to Die). A skeleton struggles to extinguish a candle while Father Time yanks the bony arm as if to allow a few more moments of life. In similar fashion, Elizabeth Pain's marker displays a coat of arms, a winged skull and hourglass, and greenery edging the stone. Less ominous is Rosanna Black's monument, which shows two cherubs bending their wings toward each other over a crown. Prominent residents of the cemetery include John Winthrop, first governor of the Massachusetts Bay Colony; *Mayflower* passenger Mary Chilton; patriot William Dawes; Hezekiah Usher, the colonies' first printer and publisher; distinguished minister John Cotton; and Elizabeth Pain, Nathaniel Hawthorne's model for Hester Prynne, protagonist of *The Scarlet Letter* (1850).

Boston's King's Chapel developed into a philosophical battleground when Unitarianism took hold in Massachusetts. Proponents founded the first parish at the Episcopal King's Chapel. In 1785, James Freeman directed the revision of the Book of Common Prayer to exclude references to the Trinity. In 1805, the vigorous congregation influenced the election of the Reverend Henry Ware, a Unitarian, as Harvard professor of divinity. The break with Congregationalism so outraged opponents that they instituted a seminary at Andover in 1808, the first major American theological training center for ministers. By 1816, Harvard had moved farther from sectarianism by opening the nation's first unaffiliated graduate divinity school.

ARCHITECTURE
Seating 700, King's Chapel is an elegant sanctuary built of Quincy granite to reflect the gravity and means of a well-to-do congregation. Harrison built the basis of a steeple, but inadequate finances prevented its completion. For maximum dignity at a bargain price, the portico sheltering

PETER HARRISON

Lauded by architectural historian William Pierson as the epitome of the gentleman-architect, Peter Harrison was the unlikely blend of sea captain, merchant, and colonial builder. A native of York, England, he was born June 14, 1716, and grew up in a Quaker household before going to sea. At age twenty-one, he sailed to Newport, Rhode Island, and languished in a Louisburg, Nova Scotia, guardhouse after the French navy captured his cargo vessel. On gaining release, he mapped the area for the English military. In 1746, he made Newport home for himself and his bride. He partnered with his brother Joseph to deal in wine, rum, molasses, and mahogany and rose to the post of customs collector, a suitable sinecure for his last years.

Harrison departed from trade to architecture when he built a home for Governor Shirley in Roxbury, Massachusetts. After completing Newport's Redwood Library, he began work on King's Chapel. At the invitation of Rector Henry Caner, he drew the plans based on those of Palladio, Gibbs, and Langley and donated the work to the congregation. Later in his full career, in addition to private homes, he planned the Touro Synagogue; the Newport Brick Market; Christ Church, Cambridge; and possibly St. Michael's Church in Charleston, South Carolina. Because of his staunch loyalty to the English king, at Harrison's death in 1775, mobs ransacked his office and destroyed his papers, library, and architectural blueprints.

the portal stands on Ionic columns built of wood and painted to resemble stone. Inside the uncompromising exterior, a grandly proportioned Georgian nave modeled on London's St. Martin-in-the-Field Church encompasses a center aisle separating two ranks of box pews. Paired two-story Corinthian columns at the side aisles support galleries and connect to gracefully arched bays to create a lively overhead interest.

The church claims noteworthy appointments, including vestments and silver donated by Queen Anne and King George III. After the bell cracked in 1814, colonial silversmith and engraver Paul Revere recast it two years later at a foundry in Canton and labeled it his sweetest creation. At center, a three-tiered chandelier illuminates the interior. At left, the lectern, the oldest American pulpit in uninterrupted use, is a slender pedestal shape. The lectern's mass and the ornamented staircase and roof anchor the sunlit apse windows to liturgical purpose. Four plaques display the Ten Commandments, Lord's Prayer, and Apostles' Creed, the standard lessons for colonial Christians. Grouped in two niches beside the sanctuary are four busts of the first four Unitarian pastors. An impressive organ, the first church organ in the United States, placed the church in an honored position among music lovers.

ACTIVITIES

King's Chapel continues to serve Boston Unitarians with regular Sunday and Wednesday services and monthly communion. When not in use for weddings, funerals, receptions, or church gatherings, it is open to visitors Monday, Friday, and Saturday from 10:00 A.M. to 2:00 P.M. and Sunday from 1:00 to 3:00 P.M. or for guided tours free of charge by appointment.

Music remains a focus of King's Chapel. All comers are invited to join in hymn sings at noon on Wednesday. A free King's Chapel Concert Series, conducted by Daniel Pinkham, performs three annual choral and orchestral programs of sacred music in diverse styles. In 1996, a public sing followed *The Sacred Harp* (1844) tradition after a popular American songbook anthologized by B. F. White and E. J. King. The program commemorated the 250th birthday of America's first native-born musician, William Billings, a tanner-turned-composer of the liturgical round "When Jesus Wept" (1768). He taught hymns and anthems to King's Chapel and other Boston congregations and collected original liturgical music in *The New England Psalm Singer* (1770), *The Singing Master's Assistant* (1778), *The Suffolk Harmony* (1786), and *The Continental Harmony* (1794).

Sources: *Biography Resource Center* 1999; *Encyclopedia of World Biography* 1998; Fixler 1996; Mutrux 1982; Rose 1963; "Sacred Harp Singing"; Sinnott 1963; Smith 1989.

L

Lama Foundation

Ram Dass, Guru
Box 140
San Cristobal, New Mexico 87564
505-586-1269; Taos Office: 505-758-8622
lama@newmex.com

Set on a 105-acre parcel of the Rocky Mountains of New Mexico overlooking the Rio Grande Valley, the Lama Foundation is a self-sustaining spiritual community and education center deeply influenced by the writings of American Hindu guru Ram Dass. The aim of the complex is to awaken consciousness through the integration of body, mind, and spirit. In Hindu tradition, the foundation unifies singing, chanting, meditating, and other religious methods to produce a oneness of multiple holy paths. By unifying diverse spiritual traditions, the staff promotes inclusion and harmony. By extension, the promotion of healthy attitudes toward the web of life encourages sensible use of land and respect for the health of the planet.

HISTORY

For over three decades, the Lama Foundation has allied human seekers with nature by channeling energy at a nurturing and hallowed environment. Located 8,600 feet in the Sangre de Cristo Mountains, twenty miles north of Taos, the institute profits from natural panoramas, clean air and invigorating terrain, prayer and ritual in the Truth Room, self-support through gardening and livestock breeding, and an open-minded staff. The foundation's aim is to generate a profound change of heart, both personal and collective, through retreat and hermitage. Central to foundation philosophy is *Be Here Now* (1971), the best-selling introduction to

Hinduism composed by Ram Dass. He evolved an ongoing understanding of volunteerism, which he outlined in *Compassion in Action: Setting Out on the Path of Service* (1991), written in conjunction with his follower Mirabai Bush. Dass also publishes taped guides, videos, and study aids to Hindu practice.

The foundation suffered a major setback on May 5, 1996, when the 7,000-acre Hondo forest fire destroyed most of ten year-round residences, twelve rooms of the Intensive Studies Center, the office, and the cottage industry and charred massive ponderosa pines. An immediate canvass of supporters requested builders, trailers, tents, tipis, computers, tools, solar components, and shop equipment. Nine days later, seventy-five people arrived to clear away debris and aid the seven residents in returning to life on the land. Permaculture specialist Tim Murphy surveyed the damage and determined that a new road had protected the land from total destruction.

To finance renewal, staff set up the Lama Foundation Fire Relief Fund at a Santa Fe bank, canceled some summer events, rescheduled a Sufist pilgrimage, and continued plans for the May 19 opening day with Dances of Universal Peace in the Main Dome. Rebuilding followed a comprehensive plan to unify structures with the environment. The Land Restoration Team planted 6,000 seedlings, predominantly hardy ponderosa pines, followed by plantings of quick-growing willows and cottonwoods. By the next season, the aspen grove was reviving and the appearance of Gamble's oaks and snowberries heartened the community with the promise of new growth. Builders added three solar showers, Robert La Porte's unique Eco-Nest teacher's house, and dormitories.

ACTIVITIES

The Lama Community continues its tradition of spiritual uplift through numerous ingatherings of guests, residents, and creative talents. At the foundation's core is the community school of practical spirituality, which teaches mindfulness, spiritual discipline and practice, communication skills, *seva* (selfless service to the community),

RAM DASS

Ram Dass has had a significant impact on Hinduism and its acceptance in the United States. Born Richard Alpert in 1933, he was the scion of a wealthy, prestigious family. His father was president of the New York, New Haven, and Hartford Railroad and founder of Brandeis University. After completing a psychology degree from Wesleyan University and a doctorate from Stanford, Alpert taught at Harvard University for five years and and conducted research on LSD with Timothy Leary, Aldous Huxley, and Allen Ginsberg. After Alpert's dismissal in 1963, he worked through a private foundation and traveled in India, where he studied under Hindu guru Neem Karoli Baba.

Renamed Ram Dass (Servant of God), in 1968, he mastered Hinduism, Kharma yoga, and Sufism. In 1974, he offered lectures and workshops through the Hanuman Foundation, which undertook the Prison-Ashram Project to foster spirituality in inmates and the Living Dying Project, which supported the terminally ill. As cofounder of the Seva Foundation, he traveled widely to relieve suffering, provide healthcare to Native Americans, restore Asian agrarianism, and eradicate blindness in India and Nepal.

In February 19, 1997, Dass suffered a massive cerebral hemorrhage, which left him partially paralyzed and aphasic. After four months' recuperation, he returned to his home in San Anselmo, California, in late May to undertake rehabilitation, acupuncture, and hyperbaric oxygen therapy and chose as his meditation mantra "patience, persistence, acceptance." His rapid improvement allowed more freedom of movement, clearer communication, and travel to New Mexico, Hawaii, and Michigan. In 1998, he returned to writing a treatise, *Conscious Aging*. In summer 1999, he initiated a series of speaking engagements by delivering two sermons at the First Church of Religious Science in Oakland.

and wildflowers in the meadows and the new Maqbara hermitage and Community Center, designed by Vishu Magee. Individuals staying from three to seven days experienced stimulus from healing bodywork, gardening and silk-screen printing, lectures, meditation, rigorous hatha yoga, Shabbat celebration, and minisessions in Hindu philosophy, particularly *seva*. In large tent dormitories housing six to eight people, participants experienced sanctity through community.

In June 1999, the Lama Foundation, *Last Straw* Journal, and Permaculture Drylands Institute cosponsored a week-long Natural Building Permaculture Convergence. Among the skills participants learned were sustainable timber harvesting and preparation, framing and joining, straw bale construction, adobe construction, dry stone wall construction, eco-village design, watershed management, maintenance of renewable energy systems, and ecosystem regeneration. The purpose of the consortium was to rebuild the Lama Foundation and create a community through networking and collaborative construction. The foundation demonstrated natural building at the Taos Fair, held June 13, 1999, at Kit Carson Park and scheduled educational activities, music, food, hikes, and fun.

Additional opportunities for sanctity and oneness with the divine introduce newcomers to world religious practices outside mainstream American custom. The Gathering of the Dervish Healing Order, a Sufi exercise in spiritual healing, offers breathwork, dance, a sweat lodge, a spiritual walk, body prayer, meditation, qi gong, the Japanese Tea Ceremony, and discussion of the renewal of body, heart, and soul. Another seminar, Spirit and Sustainability for the Twenty-first Century, revives interest in universal patterns of nature and archetypal sources of creativity and transformation, especially holotropic breathing, mythology, dreamwork, and shamanic journey.

Visiting specialists offer additional training in Vipassana meditation. In September 1999, the foundation reunited former residents for Gay and Lesbian Spirituality. For guests needing childcare, staff offers a children's program and Children's Camp. The foundation charges fees for seminars and, since the 1970s, has supported itself through Flag Mountain Cottage Indus-

stewardship, balance, healing, ecumenism, and the life circle. The staff enrolls needy students through a scholarship fund and augments coursework with short-term enrichment. At a day of appreciation on the mountain, guests shared a vegetarian lunch and viewed the greening trees

tries, which publishes books and tapes and produces meditation cushions, notecards, Tibetan postcards, stamps, T-shirts, and silk-screened prayer flags.

Sources: Clevenger 1998; Cobb 1998; Cross 1998; Geroy 1998; "Lama Foundation"; "The Lama Foundation Fire"; Lattin 1997; MacDonald 1998; "More about Ram Dass"; "Ram Dass"; Sharples 1998; *World Religions* 1998.

Lien Hoa Buddhist Temple

Venerable Bhante Siyabalagoda Ananda, priest
1211 North Wilson Street
Olympia, Washington
360-352-7109
FAX 360-570-0247

Located in southwest Olympia on South Sound near Bigelow Lake, the Lien Hoa Buddhist Temple has enjoyed its first decade of success as a much-needed cultural and religious center in a blend of Asian traditions. The staff welcomes all Buddhist denominations and bases its outreach on the Buddha's teachings that the past and future are irrelevant. According to scripture, the best way to live is to examine the present to determine how to secure stability and freedom. The temple's emphasis is on responsibility for personal actions to improve earthly existence.

HISTORY

Since the 1920s, Vietnam has expressed unique culture and principles that foreign intervention continually threatens. During the perpetual battleground wrought in midcentury by the rise of communism and by opposition from European and American interests, traditional worship gave place to four religions. Prominent were Buddhism and Roman Catholicism, with its parochial schools that introduced the French language to young Vietnamese. A third sect, the mystical Cao Dai, impressed peasants by allying the teachings of the Buddha, Lao Tse, Moses, and Christ along with traditional ancestor cults, vegetarianism, and a new awareness of women's rights. The fourth religious group, the Hoa Hao, is a neo-Buddhist sect initiated by the evangelist Huynh Phu So. Primarily among peasants of southern Vietnam, the cult advocated love of parents and country and respect for Buddhism.

According to Hoang Nguyen, the temple's chairman, these variant religions influenced the Southeast Asian refugees and immigrants who settled in North America after 1975 at the close of the Vietnam War. For fourteen years, a temple in Seattle was the only source of Buddhist nurturance for newcomers to a wide geographic area. In response to the diverse backgrounds of Washington's Asian population, six Vietnamese Buddhists of greater Olympia met January 1, 1989, to form the Buddhist Association of Olympia and Neighboring Communities. To meet the religious and ceremonial needs of the group, the association met weekly at the Olympia Center for services and held fund-raisers to pay for a temple.

The following year, the group purchased a Korean church and remodeled it into the Lien Hoa Buddhist Temple, decked with red and yellow ornamental globes suspended from the ceiling, flowering trees, and photos and candles honoring the dead. At center sits the image of the Buddha behind a table decked with candles, bowls of fruit, and imposing urns exuding incense. In this holy space, around 300 jubilant members celebrated Tet, their first traditional Vietnamese New Year, with a motorcade, visits with friends, dragon dances, firecrackers, puppets, martial arts demonstrations and contests, a fair with food and games, and line dances. The holiday is the traditional renewal—a paying of debts, cleaning house, and setting affairs in order. According to temple officer Son Tran, Tet is a time to

> remember the good things of the last year, and wish good things for the new year. . . . It's also a time to pay respect to parents, friends, and ancestors—and anyone that helps you in life. It's time for the community and the family to be together in harmony. (Rainville 1994)

The holiday, which falls between January 20 and February 20, has become the temple's annual crowning event, now led by the Venerable Bhante Siyabalagoda Ananda, the resident priest from Sri Lanka, and attended by 700 worshippers. In Ananda's words, he leads the congregation in a search for success and happiness by answering the recurrent human question "What should you do as a parent, as a husband, as a wife, as children, as a worker?" (Coffins 1999, 23) His answers relieve the stress of Asian families adapting to a loosely disciplined American society that frees children from traditional parental control.

ACTIVITIES

Weekly, the temple offers Sunday services from noon to 4:00 P.M. and a monthly Sunday gathering from 10:00 A.M. to 4:00 P.M. In addition to regular services, weekly meditation, Sunday school for children, and New Year's festivals, the temple hosts the Buddhist Association of Olympia and Neighboring Communities and a local chapter of the Vietnamese Buddhist Youth Association in the United States. The latter group's aim is to educate young members in all aspects of Buddhist teachings and to promote Vietnamese cultural awareness. This grounding in religion and culture enhances lives and undergirds the individual, the family, and citizenship. To promote understanding, the group supports exchanges with neighboring cities and states through performances of the Lien Hoa Lion Dance Group and the Lien Hoa Performing Arts Group at colleges, universities, and associations.

The temple staff strives to keep membership from becoming ingrown. In August 1991, the congregation supported the fifth annual conference of the U.S. Vietnamese Buddhist Congregation. In September 1992, members honored the founding of the Unified Vietnamese Buddhist Congregation in the U.S.A. The 1997 temple calendar scheduled recognition day in June and four annual retreats: April in Portland, July in Seattle, an August retreat in San Diego, and an October session in Seattle. In addition, the staff sponsored women's gatherings, a friendship camp in Vancouver, British Columbia, leadership training in Spokane, holidays shared with the local Chinese Fellowship, and a cultural exchange that took the Lien Hoa traditional dance group to South Puget Sound Community College and Pacific Lutheran University.

Sources: Coffins 1999; *Eerdmans' Handbook to the World's Religions* 1982; "It's Not Just Another Boring Religion" 1999; Lamm 1997; MacDonald 1992; Rainville 1994; Sawyer 1978; Smith 1995; "Who Are Lien-Hoa?" 1997; *World Religions* 1998.

Little Brown Church in the Vale

Bob and Linda Myren, Co-Pastors
2730 Cheyenne Ave.
Nashua, Iowa 50658
515-435-2027

Set in a pine glade, the Little Brown Church in the Vale, after years of neglect, has had a rebirth. Its 80 members, two ministers, and 60,000 annual visitors cherish the shaded spot as did hospitable, peace-loving Iowans in the Civil War era. At the beginning of the twenty-first century, some 600 couples choose this famous rural shrine each year for weddings, which number around 70,000 to date. Brides and grooms conclude vows and prayers with a joint pull on the bell rope, an Iowa tradition. Other couples come to recommit themselves to their union or to have children baptized.

HISTORY

The prairie town of Bradford, county seat of Chickasaw County in north central Iowa, was an appealing stopping place for the Lutheran, Amanan, Catholic, and Congregationalist westerers arriving from New England and points east. They traveled upriver from St. Louis, Missouri, to likely farms in the Midwest to establish orchards, grow corn and small grains, and raise livestock. The first, Truman Merritt, arrived in 1848 to inviting land at the confluence of the Cedar and Little Cedar Rivers. The town acquired a sawmill, doctor, newspaper, and stops on two stagecoach routes. The Puritan-Congregational congregation—5 members led by the Reverend Ozias Littlefield—began meeting in 1855. Within a year, Bradford, the first town, grew to 500 citizens.

Tired of assembling in a log house, a lawyer's office, a schoolhouse, a hotel dining room, and abandoned stores, in 1859, the citizens of Bradford determined to build a Congregational church. S. F. Eastman served as treasurer, often upping the week's collection from his pocket. The arrival of the Reverend John Keep Nutting put legs on church plans. With fifteen acres of virgin land donated by Mr. and Mrs. Joseph Bird, members were ready to begin work. Frugal and unpretentious, they chose limestone for the foundation and local red oak for construc-

Each year, some 600 couples choose for weddings the Little Brown Church in the Vale, a famous rural shrine in Nashua, Iowa. (Courtesy Little Brown Church)

tion. The exigencies of the Civil War and scarcity of cash slowed completion until families began donating trees, milling, and labor. A check for $140 from the Sunday-school class of Dr. John Todd in Pittsfield, Massachusetts, paid for hardware, finished lumber, lighting, and furnishing.

Into his wartime miracle church, the unnamed builder cut an arched double door, shaped the ceiling with a gently curved molding, and spaced pews down the center, with short rows to each side. At center, the pulpit stood before a pointed arched recess. He lit the interior with hanging kerosene landerns. In lieu of more expensive white paint, he covered the walls with Ohio mineral paint, a wood preservative that came in only one homely shade of brown. In the steeple, he placed a donated bell, cast at McNeely Bell Foundry in Troy, New York. Locals took such pride in the new bell that they rang it the entire time it was transported from Dubuque. By the time the church stood ready for occupancy on December 19, 1864, it had cost nothing from the limited treasury.

In the last three days of 1864, at the depths of the war, congregants dedicated their building with a hymn sing, a rural gathering where songs by soloists and congregation precede a church picnic, sometimes called "dinner on the grounds." The church, which seats 140, preserved a communal form of worship that had shored up the spirits of pioneers and rural farmers from the time of the nation's founding. In 1870, the church purchased a pump organ, which is still in use. On the top riser of the three steps, the staff inscribed a line by early-twentieth-century poet Samuel Foss, who proposed a populist ideal: "Let me live by the side of the road and be a friend to all." Because of the popularity and suitability of Dr. William Pitts's hymn, the congregation adopted as their official name the Little Brown Church in the Vale.

Because the railroad passed through Iowa at Nashua and a miller relocated his flour mill at New Hampton, Bradford village never grew beyond a modest burg. The church closed in 1888; its yard grew wild. The remnants of congregants met for church services at a local school. In the early 1900s, the congregation underwent a resurgence of spirit. Led by the Society for the Preservation of the Little Brown Church, they repaired and painted the building, which thrummed with life by March 1914, when the Reverend B. W. Burleigh launched a two-week revival. At a 1916 reunion, Reverend John Nutting spoke and Dr. Pitts sang his hymn.

A second serendipity altered the little church's fortunes. While touring Canada and the United States on the Chautauqua circuit in the 1920s and 1930s, four itinerant Iowa farm boys from Charles City—Asa, Lester, William, and Tom—known as the Weatherwax Brothers Quartet discovered "The Church in the Wildwood" and made it their theme song. It became a country and gospel favorite of such singers as the Mormon Tabernacle Choir and Tennessee Ernie Ford, who performed it on his family television program, *The Tennessee Ernie Ford Show*. The song turned Nashua's church into a popular attraction.

ACTIVITIES

Today, pastoral couple Bob and Linda Myren share the pulpit and lead standard Sunday school at 9:00 A.M. and worship at 10:30 in the Congregational tradition. Weekly, they sponsor youth gatherings, choir practice, men's and women's fellowship, Bible study, and a prayer chain and host bus tours and photographers looking for the modest grace of Christianity in the past. Daily, the church door is open to all who seek a quiet spot for prayer and meditation. On Sunday afternoons, the pastors perform baptisms for a fee of $25. To finance future upgrades to the roof and walkway, the staff sells postcards, cookbooks, coin purses, church banks, suncatchers, and hymn collections by the honor system. For tours, they suggest a donation of $1 per person.

From Monday through Saturday, the Myrens perform the weddings of people who choose an uncluttered setting and small gathering to hear the exchange of vows. A busy Saturday in summer or on holidays may host a dozen weddings. Basic Christian text is the norm, but the Myrens often officiate alongside a rabbi or priest for a Jewish or Catholic service and have also joined a signer to unite a deaf couple. When children of former marriages attend, the Myrens include a vow from each child to honor the new stepparent.

"THE LITTLE BROWN CHURCH IN THE VALE"

The gospel hymn "The Little Brown Church in the Vale" is a nostalgic holdover from simpler times and uncomplicated faith. According to tradition, in 1857 (1860 in some versions), composer William Savage Pitts, a New York-born music teacher then age twenty-seven, was taking the stage from McGregor, Wisconsin, where he taught public school, to Fredericksburg, Iowa, to visit his fiancée. When the coach stopped at Bradford, he decided to walk down Cedar Street to a lush grove near the Cedar River. He was unaware that the land had been donated for the Bradford Congregational Church.

Pitts formed a mental picture of a small church that stayed with him. Some days afterward, he composed "The Church in the Wildwood," a poem and music about the imaginary church. Its lyrics and refrain were infectious:

There's a church in the valley by the wildwood,
No lovelier spot in the dale;
No place is so dear to my childhood,
As the little brown church in the vale.
Refrain:
Come to the church in the wildwood,
Oh, come to the church in the dale,
No spot is so dear to my childhood,
As the little brown church in the vale.

In 1862, when Dr. Pitts was teaching music at Bradford Academy, he was astonished to see carpenters framing a small church and painting it brown like the one in his vision. He offered his vocal students to sing for the church dedication and performed the hymn as a solo. In 1865, H. M. Higgins, a Chicago publisher, paid Pitts $25 for the song. He applied the money to tuition at Rush Medical College. In 1868, Pitts returned to Fredericksburg to practice medicine and remained an Iowa doctor until 1906.

The church staff takes the worry of planning from the family by offering a half hour's rental plus dressing rooms, flowers, taped organ marches, and bell ringing. To assure privacy, they lock the front door to prevent tourists from interrupting the sacrament. Total cost for the nuptial package is $120. An extra $20 adds a rose unity service, a live solo, or an organ accompaniment. There is no charge for the idyllic photo opportunity at a weeping willow, where couples pose among neatly groomed green fronds. The women's fellowship is available to serve sandwiches and relishes and the traditional wedding cake for an unfussy basement reception. In summer, some families choose a reception picnic at the church shelter across the street. The truly nostalgic pair may opt to depart in a horse-drawn carriage.

On Saturday, July 31, 1999, the Little Brown Church held its forty-seventh annual Wedding Reunion and Pastor's Reception. Set in a tent large enough to accommodate couples of past weddings, the gala offered cake and punch along with fellowship and a sharing of wedding pictures. On Sunday morning, the staff hosted a continental breakfast, followed by a hymn sing. At the 10:30 worship service, members dedicated a newly renovated bell tower and an enlarged porch and witnessed a wedding renewal service. A picnic hosted by the Women's Fellowship preceded a group photo session featuring couples celebrating over fifty years of marriage. The day concluded with a lawn polka to the music of Dan's Band, music by the Real Review Singers, and the celebration of a century of worship and fellowship.

> **Sources:** Broderick 1958; "History of 'The Little Brown Church in the Vale'"; "The Little Brown Church" 1996; "The Little Brown Church in the Vale" 1997; Myren n.d.; Reynolds 1996; "There's a Church in the Valley by the Wildwood."

Loretto Chapel

207 Old Santa Fe Trail
Santa Fe, New Mexico 87501
505-984-7923
lorettoc@concentric.net

Against the backdrop of the Sandia, Sangre de Cristo, Jemez, and Manzano Mountains, the Loretto Chapel preserves the ideals of the early Hispanic culture that settled Mexico and the American Southwest. Its building materials reflect desert resources—sandstone for walls and porous volcanic stone for the ceiling, both transported by local wagoneers. The stained-glass panels, bordered in braid and capped with an ornate arch, arrived from DuBois Studios in Paris in 1876. More recent embellishment includes a Gothic altar, frescos, and stations of the cross. Parish duties ended long ago, but the chapel retains a religiosity that gentles the city bustle of Santa Fe.

HISTORY

The chapel bears the name of the sisters of Loretto, pioneer teaching nuns of the Order of Loretto. On an invitation from Archbishop Jean-Baptiste Lamy, who arrived from France to the New Mexico Territory in 1850, the nuns traveled from the diocese of Louisville, Kentucky, to St. Louis by paddle steamer and overland by covered wagon and arrived in September 1852. Cholera struck their group, killing Mother Superior Matilda, but the survivors—the new superior, Mother Magdalen, and sisters Catherine, Hilaria, and Roberta—regrouped and finished the journey.

To serve a community composed mostly of Native Americans and Hispanics, the sisters founded Loretto Academy of Our Lady of Light for young ladies in 1853. The first trans-Mississippi edifice in Gothic Revival style, the Loretto Chapel is contemporary with Santa Fe's St. Francis Cathedral and mirrors Viollet-le-Duc's stylish touches on the cathedral of Clermont-Ferrand near Lamy's home in Auvergne, France. Originally, the chapel stood between the Loretto Academy and the Convent of Our Lady of Light. Today, only the chapel survives on a busy street near a popular hotel.

ARCHITECTURE

To serve students, the chapel, also called the Chapel of Our Lady of Light, took shape twenty years after the convent, from 1873 to 1878. The structure, which echoes the local stone and detailing of the St. Francis Cathedral, was designed by the same father and son French architects, named Antoine and Projectus Moulay (or Molny) of Volvic in Auvergne. The team hired French and Italian masons to execute precise plans. Modeled on Louis XVI's private chapel, Sainte Chapelle, in Paris, France, the Loretto Chapel is a simple twenty-five- by seventy-five-

Against the backdrop of the Sandia, Sangre de Cristo, Jemez, and Manzano Mountains, the Loretto Chapel in Santa Fe preserves the ideals of the early Hispanic culture that settled Mexico and the American Southwest. (Courtesy of Loretto Chapel)

foot structure eighty-five feet high that opens with a double door on the west end. The sanctuary houses ten and a half rows of pews flanking a central aisle, a side entry to the colonnade, and a railing separating the priest from the congregation. At the east end, an altar stands before the one-story sacristy. At the right rear is a unique circular stair rising to the choir loft, which is sparsely lighted by a rose window.

The famous Loretto staircase teases the imagination. According to legend, the structure stood incomplete after John Lamy, nephew of the archbishop, shot the architect for seducing Lamy's wife. The architect died without leaving his plans for linking the nave with the balcony. For the first time, the sisters realized that there was no access to the loft. When local carpenters admitted defeat, the sisters determined to reach the upper level by ladder.

The sisters maintain that Saint Joseph solved the puzzle for them. A gray-haired itinerant carpenter, who arrived on a donkey in 1877, built an access to the choir loft. Adherents to the story identify the carpenter as Jesus' father, Joseph, the Nazarene carpenter of the Gospels, to whom the Sisters of Loretto prayed for assistance with fervid novenas. The unidentified artisan ordered no wood. He set to work with a saw, a hammer, a T-square, and tubs to soak precisely cut segments of wood. After six months' work, he left without payment.

The miraculous stairs are composed of thirty-three steps, one for each year of Christ's life. The carpenter pegged them within parallel spirals with wooden dowels. The finished stair contains neither nails nor identifiable supports. Risers between the wooden treads contain nine splices on the outside and seven on the inside. The fittings supply a springiness to foot traffic. The backing, a mixture of lime plaster and horsehair, resembles light wood. Forestry analysts have not identified the source of the sturdy wood, which is not typically American. They tentatively classify it as a fir or yellow pine. The completed stair makes two 360-degree turns without a central support.

The sisters dedicated the chapel on April 25, 1878. They added a delicate wood railing and simple banisters in 1880. In 1971, a family purchased the chapel, which was deconsecrated. Although it is no longer flanked by the Loretto Academy and the Convent of Our Lady of Light, it retains a singular hallowed allure that draws religious tourists and seekers to pray and meditate.

See also Mission of San Miguel of Santa Fe, Santa Fe Cathedral of St. Francis of Assisi.

Sources: Albach 1965; Beresky 1991; Florian 1960; "Loretto Chapel"; Morgan 1994; "Santa Fe" 1997; Sheppard 1994; Spritzer 1994; "St. Joseph's Staircase."

Lovely Lane Methodist Church
Reverend Nancy Nedwell, Pastor
2200 St. Paul Street
Baltimore, Maryland 21218-5897
410-889-1512; 800-368-2520
nanwell@erols.com; johnowen3@aol.com
www.gbgm-umc.org/lovelylaneumc

From a pejorative to the name of a uniquely American denomination, Methodism has incorporated fervor, piety, and simplified worship style into the national fabric. The origin of organized Methodism began at Lovely Lane Church, a Baltimore historical site later named a national landmark.

Methodism found strong support in the Northeast, especially after John Wesley dispatched two ministers ordained in the new faith and supplied them with news of England's religious climate. In 1738, the Wesley brothers led a renewal of the Church of England. By midcentury, news of their ebullient faith, known as Methodism, spread to North America. On both sides of the Atlantic, it took shape as a decentralized lay movement, led by Robert Strawbridge in Maryland and Virginia, Philip Embury and Barbara Heck in New York, and Captain Thomas Webb in Philadelphia.

Sixty of the nation's eighty-one American Methodist lay ministers convened on December 24, 1784, at Lovely Lane Meeting House in Baltimore, organized the Methodist Episcopal Church, and appointed Thomas Coke and Francis Asbury as superintendents. The gathering appears to have included two black ministers, Harry Hosier and Richard Allen. Since that date, Lovely Lane Church has been known as

JOHN WESLEY

Hymnographer and exemplary evangelist John Wesley, author of "Hark the Herald Angels Sing" and "Christ the Lord Is Risen Today," evolved from a proponent of Anglicanism to the founder of a new and vigorous sect. In 1736, he began his work in Savannah, Georgia, as a colonial religious leader and converter of Indians. His brother Charles also began a New World career as secretary of Indian affairs for General Oglethorpe and Anglican faith leader at Fort Frederica on St. Simons Island. While residing with Moravians, John began formulating his notions of a more liberal Protestantism, although he had no intention of forming a new sect.

After Charles returned to England in poor health, John Wesley took over his ministry and became a preacher and spiritual adviser to the entire English colony, a task that interfered with his hopes of converting indigenous people from animism to Christianity. In 1737, discouraged by the overwhelming size of his parish, he returned to England but left behind a flourishing movement called Methodism. He strengthened the fundamental plan with lay preachers, in particular, Francis Asbury, a devoted Wesleyan who became the sect's general superintendent and supporter of camp-meeting revivals.

Even though the Wesleys refused to support the American Revolution, at the end of the war for independence, John realized the necessity of curtailing his tory prejudice. He remained the sect's prime mover and managed it long distance through a circuit system that would infuse Christian life with love and celebration rather than the dogma and authoritarianism that burdened Anglicanism. From the Moravians, he imported annual love feasts and watch nights and an overriding concern for the laboring class. He dispatched Thomas Coke to oversee Asbury's work and to distribute Wesley's prayer book, *The Sunday Service of the Methodists in North America* (1784), which incorporates the revision of the Church of England's *Thirty-Nine Articles of Religion*.

Hymnographer and exemplary evangelist John Wesley evolved from a proponent of Anglicanism to the founder of Methodism, a new and vigorous sect. (North Wind Picture Archives)

the mother of American Methodism. In subsequent fine-tuning of the faith, the general conference established the nation's oldest and the world's largest religious publisher—Methodist Publishing House, founded in Nashville, Tennessee, in 1789. To maintain grassroots support, they promoted revivalism and the camp meeting, one of the nation's unique innovations in worship.

ACTIVITIES

Today, Lovely Lane, Methodism's mother church, rises above the limitations of a small urban facility by celebrating an evangelical vision and a commitment to liturgy, learning, and life through a revitalized congregation. The church calendar schedules standard Sunday morning worship at 11:00 A.M. for nearly 100 members. The 1885 Hilburn-Roosevelt organ, which was remodeled by the Austin Organ Company in 1930, provides music for the choir and congregation. Members serve an Easter brunch, Thanksgiving dinner, and Christmas brunch and decorate the sanctuary at Advent with two symbolic Chrismon trees and 100 poinsettias donated by well-wishers nationwide.

Staff tackles the ongoing task of restoring the building from water damage while strengthening traditions and broadening missions to the city of Baltimore. Weekdays, from 8:30 to 10:00 A.M., 1,000 people line up at the church feeding station, called Manna House, operated by director Esther Reaves, three paid assistants, and church volunteers. Located five blocks from the sanctuary, Baltimore's oldest soup kitchen admits 20 to 25 diners at a time and serves food donated by area churches and the Baltimore Hebrew Congregation. Pastor Nedwell coordinates donations of texts, encyclopedias, and thesauruses to two public schools and reads to classes each week. Two nearby Roman Catholic schools train students at the church gymmasium. In support of history and the arts, on Monday and Wednesday evening, the church hosts proponents of English country dance, contra dance, and square dance. Daily, the church secretary, Dolores Shaw, doubles as a tour guide to 28,000 annual visitors, which include around 4,000 confirmation classes from Methodist churches along the Atlantic seaboard who come to Lovely Lane to study the history of Methodism.

See also Methodist Tabernacle.
Sources: "John Wesley"; "Lovely Lane United Methodist Church"; *New Catholic Encyclopedia* 1967; "United Methodist Church"; Williams, Peter W., 1997.

Medicine Wheel

Forest Supervisor
Bighorn National Forest
1969 South Sheridan Avenue
Sheridan, Wyoming 82801
307-672-0751

On a windy plateau summit of 10,000-foot Medicine Mountain, Medicine Wheel, Wyoming, is one of the world's most famous circular rock configurations existing from prehistory. Among the Bighorn Mountains, a segment of the Rockies in northern Wyoming that rises to 5,000 feet above the Bighorn Basin, its white-gray rocks form a prayer shrine, a unique blend of art and sacrament. The circle suits its surroundings—a dramatic uplift composed of granite, sandstone, and limestone dotted with yellow, purple, and white wildflowers. A part of the Bighorn Forest Reservation, it extends nearly 70 feet in diameter and 245 feet in circumference and consists of twenty-eight spokes marking the lunar calendar and radiating from the 12-foot-wide hub.

Medicine Wheel is an obviously hand-laid pattern composed of rocks that a team of workers could lift and place without tools or wheelbarrows. Of interest to archeologists and astronomers is the implementation of the wheel as a huge permanent calendar and observation point capable of calculating the summer solstice. Tracks left by travois of plains Indians attest to the importance of the site to pilgrims. Rock cairns at the finials of six spokes probably served these prehistoric visitors as shelters or altars.

HISTORY

Located near Lovell in north central Wyoming, Medicine Wheel is one of multiple examples of circular stone paths that archaeoastronomers study for astronomical alignments with the equinoxes. The Bighorn Medicine Wheel points to sunrise at the summer solstice and toward Aldebaran, Rigel, and Sirius, the Dog Star, three prominent points of light at dawn in midsummer. The central cairn appears to have been arranged 7,000 years ago. The wheel may have evolved in several segments, beginning around 1600 B.C. and continuing to 1500 B.C. The alignment with celestial season indicators may have marked periods of sun worship.

In the mid-1990s, Native American demands for preservation of sacred sites spurred new interest in the wheel, which the U.S. Department of the Interior proclaimed the Medicine Wheel National Historic Landmark. Authorities established an interpretive program at Bighorn National Forest to assist more than 50,000 annual visitors in appreciating the cosmic nature of the wheel and to respect medicine bundles and prayer sticks attached to the fence that protects it. Park rangers guard the area's privacy when worship leaders of the Arapahoe, Blackfoot, Cheyenne, Crow, Salish, Shoshone, and Sioux hold late-night sacred ceremonies but question the right of Native Americans to alter the design by moving rocks. In one incident, the Northern Cheyenne held a formal blessing ritual to replace a rock removed by a tourist in the 1960s. After regretting the act, to complete the circle once more, the anonymous rock thief mailed the rock to the park.

BELIEFS

More than any other Native American concept, the medicine wheel expresses the omnipresence of divinity in Indian worship. Unlike churches, synagogues, chapels, and cathedrals of white culture, the hallowed circle symbolizes the sanctity of all places, both on earth and in the human heart. The great hoop is a visible symbol of sacred space and of the power that can heal and transform. It separates into four quadrants or directions, suggesting four cosmic elements of earth, air, fire, and water. Each possesses individuality, expressed through sacred colors, objects, and life phases:

	North	South	East	West
Animals	buffalo, birds	mouse, badger	buffalo, dolphin, whale	eagle, hawk
Colors	white	green	black	yellow
Elements	earth	fire	water	air
Seasons	winter	summer	spring	fall
Life phases	ancestral wisdom, illumination	trust, change, strength, youth	introspection, death, idealism, new start	learning, self-knowledge, fulfillment
Aims	pure thoughts	kind hearts	understanding	redemption

At the center lies the life core, from which springs the tree of life, an emblem of eternity. The four directions apply also to the four aspects of human life—physical, mental, emotional, and spiritual. When the four reach a balance, the wheel turns on its axis and the individual attains contentment and productivity.

A universal emblem, the wheel marks the beliefs of people worldwide, for all honor the revolutions of heavenly bodies and the return of the seasons. As ancient psychology, the sacred circle maps a human landscape, with humankind at the center. To maintain harmony among all living elements, the wheel compels the individual to respect the interlinkage of the sky, the earth, plants, and animals. To apply the wheel to healing, the seeker must pursue wholeness and balance by altering destructive habits and attitudes and by harnessing the power within the noosphere, or human consciousness as it impacts nature. By extension, humankind must serve earth by following the same path to reassert an earthly balance and protect the environment from pollution and people from disease and destruction.

ACTIVITIES

The mystical essence of Medicine Wheel is a source of rejuvenation among Native Americans currently reacquainting themselves with tradition. Cheyenne elder Bill Tall Bull, his tribe's Cultural Chairman and an appointee to the Advisory Council for Historic Preservation, supports the Medicine Wheel Alliance and Medicine Wheel Coalition, which ally with the Forest Service to maintain the site's dignity and sanctity. He advocates that rangers observe all of Medicine Mountain as a consecrated stronghold. A 1993 native consortium, the Medicine Wheel Coalition, directed by Jerry Flute, demanded that rangers block traffic to limit tourist

access to the site, where visitation rose from 12,000 to 70,000 between 1990 and 1993. Park authorities compromised by limiting tourists and closing the circle during high holy days of the summer solstice but extending a thoroughfare to cattle ranchers and loggers.

In 1995, Dr. Arvol Looking Horse, nineteenth-generation Sioux Keeper of the Sacred Pipe, a sacred gift from White Buffalo Calf Woman, reasserted a belief that Wakan Tanka, the Great Spirit, created all nature. Looking Horse stressed that Paha Sapa, the sacred Black Hills in South Dakota, provides native worshippers with spiritual power and identity and with stories of how humankind was born from Wind Cave and how the faithful gained understanding through star knowledge. Looking Horse retold the story of a great flood that cleansed Mother Earth and of Pipestone, Minnesota, repository of the blood of ancestors. He extolled the hallowed rituals taught by White Buffalo Calf Woman, who helped Indians to live balanced lives. He cited Black Elk's suffering after the massacre at Wounded Knee destroyed the sacred hoop on December 29, 1890, when cavalry destroyed a village and brutally strafed its people and ponies with a Gatling gun. A century later, as Native Americans strove to heal from frontier-era genocide, they anticipated the return of the white buffalo calf.

Preparation for a unity ceremony began with a series of intertribal processions on horseback. In 1992, the Wopila Ride was a thanksgiving to spirits for safe passage for participants. From 1993 to 1995, there were three annual Canadian and American Unity Rides to reunite relatives and prepare for the 1996 event. Unity Ride 1993, the first in 112 years to unite the Sioux, covered 400 miles from Medicine Rock at the Standing Rock Sioux Reservation, North Dakota, to Birdtail Dakota Reserve in Manitoba. After the birth of a white female buffalo calf in August 1994, Looking Horse concluded that the world was ready for a new attempt at peace and harmony. Unity Ride 1994 doubled the length from Rosebud Sioux Reservation, South Dakota, to Pheasant Rump Nakota Reserve, Saskatchewan. This sacred company combined participants from the Arikara, Chippewa, Hidatsa, Mandan, and Ojibway. Unity Ride 1995 stopped at fifteen reservations on a 450-mile trek from Pheasant Rump to Wahpeton Dakota Reserve in Prince Alberta, Saskatchewan.

These ceremonial pilgrimages perpetuated the Chief Sitting Bull and Chief Bigfoot Memorial Rides and the Wiping of Tears/Mending the Sacred Hoop Ride, which began in 1986, seven generations after the Wounded Knee massacre. The procession preserved the prophetic dreams of holy Sioux like Black Elk, who recognized that the coming of whites to the plains was the end of an era of aboriginal dominance and of a native dream of unity. To Looking Horse and his party, the time had come to fulfill the prophecies of past medicine men and to restore life's sacred circle.

On May 3, 1996, to unite all people in prayer for earth, the Sioux organized a fifty-day Unity Ride through sacred natural landforms. The procession began at Wahpeton Dakota Reserve and moved south through Chief Sitting Bull's campsite at Wood Mountain, Saskatchewan, to the Bighorn Medicine Wheel. From there, it continued west to Grey Buffalo Horn Butte (Devils Tower), Wyoming, arriving on June 20. The world prayer day began on June 21, preceding the summer solstice, when Looking Horse led a delegation of indigenous peoples to the Indian holy land—the Black Hills—to pray for world peace for all beings. As a preface to the new millennium, the groups sought a solution to hunger, violence, and toxic waste and a new commitment of earth's caretakers.

See also Black Hills, Devils Tower National Monument.

Sources: Albanese 1990; "Apache Survival Coalition" 1996; Baum 1992; Cantor, George, 1993; Champagne 1994; "Classes"; "Creating a Medicine Wheel"; "Crossing Worlds" 1999; Giese 1996; Iler 1995; Lakota: Seeking the Great Spirit 1994; Magdalena 1996; McCullen 1992; Milne 1995; Milstein 1993, 1999; "Native Rights Act before Congress" 1992–1993; Patterson and Snodgrass 1994; Steiger 1974; "Unity Ride" 1996; Walking Turtle 1993.

Meher Spiritual Center
10200 U.S. Highway 17 North
Myrtle Beach, South Carolina 29572
873-272-8793; 843-272-5777
MeherGate@aol.com

An island of serenity in the tourist swirl of Myrtle Beach, the Meher Spiritual Center is a nondenominational retreat from commercialism and pleasure-seeking. The religious aspect of the site is loosely structured. In unadorned cabins set in the thick woods of Briarcliffe Acres on South Carolina's Waccamaw Neck, the complex offers the wisdom of the neo-Sufi mystic Meher Baba along with a divine presence found in quiet lakes, hiking trails, a library, and a habitat for alligators, bald eagles, river otters, bobcats, mink, black bears, and white-tailed deer. Center rules require visitors to wear shoes, swim only with partners, carry a flashlight at night, avoid drugs and alcohol, refrain from hunting and fishing, and turn in at 11:30 P.M. In 1998, the center accommodated 12,000 seekers, who fled electronic and technological distractions to rest, reflect, and refresh themselves in a sacred atmosphere.

HISTORY
In 1952, Elizabeth Chapin Patterson established the center as a Western dissemination point of Meher Baba's spiritualism. Born Merwan Sheriar Irani on February 25, 1894, at Poona, in west-central India, he was the second son of a Zoroastrian (or Parsi) family. He attended Christian High School and Deccan College, where he came under the influence of Muslim mystic Hazrat Babajan. To corroborate Meher's belief that he was an avatar of God, he traveled and studied with five masters. The third, Upasni Maharaj, achieved unity with the divine by withdrawing to a cave for a year. In his late teens, Meher followed a similar period of retreat with the assistance of a friend, Sayyed Saheb, and then began a ministry at age nineteen.

Meher Baba set out to inform humanity of the redemptive power of God's love. At his ashram near Bombay, Sayyed and other followers proclaimed him the Divine Beloved, a new incarnation of God on earth. They altered his name from Irani to Meher Baba, meaning Compassionate Father. He referred to himself as "the ancient one" and father of the human family, whom he sought to unite.

Over his ministry, Meher Baba has used various methods of expressing God-centeredness. He chose to become a hermitic model of godliness by imitating the patterns set by Zoroaster,

Abraham, Rama, Krishna, Jesus, the Buddha, and Muhammed. An energetic friend maker, Meher Baba shared funny stories, sang, and played the drums. Under the pseudonym Huma (Phoenix), he wrote *ghazals,* or stanzas, in the style of the medieval Sufist poet Rumi. Bhau Kalchuri anthologized the holy man's verses in *Meher Sarod.*

To reach the suffering, in 1924, Meher Baba founded Meherabad, an altruistic colony in Ahmednagar, India, composed of a receiving home, hospital, and school. Twelve years into his mission, he retreated into a lifelong silence and communicated through gesture and an alphabet board, on which he composed speeches and numerous books, including *God Speaks, Discourses, The Everything and Nothing, Mastery of Consciousness, God to Man and Man to God, The Path of Love,* and *Life at Its Best.* In 1931, he sailed to London with Mohandas Gandhi and became his spiritual adviser. During the 1940s, Meher Baba traveled India to succor lepers and mental patients, whom he aided at temporary ashrams.

Oblivious to mockers, the holy one focused on his task. At his death on January 31, 1969, a prepared tomb in Ahmednagar became a shrine to pilgrims, who followed his motto of "mastery in servitude." His centers flourished at the Avatar Meher Baba Trust in Ahmednagar, India; Meher Mount in Ojai, California; the Meher Baba Bhopal Centre in Nagar, Bhopal; and Avatar's Abode Trust in Nambour, Queensland, Australia. Additional centers sprang up: Meher Baba Information Office in Berkeley, California; Meher Baha House in New York City; Avatar Meher Baba Center of Southern California in Los Angeles; Meher Baba Association in London; Meher Baba Kilden in Oslo, Norway; and Meherana in Mariposa County, California. Web sites carry original speeches, sayings, poems, and reminiscences of his disciples and friends.

BELIEFS

Meher Baba formulated an unstructured faith in God's love that avoids dogma and legalism. His central message followed humane injunctions:

- To be remade by love, followers should divest themselves of learning, let go of the past and present, and renounce selfishness, violence, and greed.

- To escape the illusion of earthly life, take refuge in reality, joy, and service.
- To strip away desire and longing, focus on the divine.
- To become God, make others divine.
- To be worthy of love, let the vision of God control all thoughts, words, and deeds.

He disseminated these precepts through his publishing house, Sheriar Press Book Division, and through MANifestation, Inc., which issued his biography.

Meher Baba intended to spread his mission to the West. He requested that Elizabeth Patterson and disciple Princess Norina Matchabelli find a locale surrounded by water, untouched land, fertile soil, and a favorable climate. After rejecting sites in California, Patterson chose the South Carolina coast as an appealing terminus for religious pilgrimages. On half of a 1,000-acre parcel at Myrtle Beach Farms, donated by her father, Simeon Chapin, she established Meher's retreat on seven freshwater lakes. His stipulation of its transfer to the ministry required that Chapin give from the heart and that the land serve a nonprofit religious organization and never be sold for profit.

Meher Baba brought disciples to open Patterson's center in 1952, when he planted a young holly tree as a token of the site's focus on ecology. He returned in 1956 and 1958 for respites at his Western home. On the last visit, eleven years before his death, he established a nonprofit religious corporation, run by a board of directors. In 1971, disciple Marshall Hay, a tolerant, gentle man, became the center director. He supervises 15 staff members and 150 volunteers. His philosophy maintains that all living things deserve to live, an appropriate viewpoint for an idyllic camp set in the Atlantic coast sandhills.

ACTIVITIES

The center, a designated state wildlife sanctuary, is open weekdays for three hours in the afternoon and six hours on weekends and holidays. For the spiritual benefit of daily visitors and a maximum of 72 overnight guests, it features 200 types of plants and 100 species of birds and animals, including 44 indigenous mammals. Visitors desiring to stay on the premises apply for a reservation at least three months in advance. The center's un-air-conditioned cabins, some with kitchens, suit the pleasant arbor and unspoiled shore of Long Lake, where Meher Baba himself once walked and communed with disciples.

For the convenience of residents, the Meher Spiritual Center provides a meeting room, a meditation cabin, and two communal kitchens. During stays ranging from one to fourteen days, visitors wishing to replenish their spirits and achieve wholehearted humanity converse with other seekers, read and meditate, walk the nature trails, and row across the lake. The library offers photos and writings of Meher Baba. Evening films, slide shows, and lectures by disciples—called "Baba-lovers"—inspire questions about the ministry of love and readings from the "Baba Das," a collection of disciples' reflections, anecdotes, and testimonials.

Sources: *Biography Resource Center* 1999; "Meher Baba"; "Meher Baba Spiritual Center"; "Meher Baba Web Sites"; *Religious Leaders of America* 1999; Rothacker 1999; Solibakke; *World Religions* 1998.

Memorial Church of Harvard University
Peter John Gomes, Senior Pastor
Harvard Yard
Cambridge, Massachusetts 02138
617-495-5508
memchurch@camail1.harvard.edu
www.memorialchurch.harvard.edu

Dubbed "Mem Church" by students, Harvard's Memorial Church has witnessed its share of commencements, weddings, and funerals. An integral part of campus and community at the university, the staff offers thought-provoking sermons, guest lectures, and musical events throughout the year and broadcasts live over Harvard WHRB Radio. Pulpit philosophy has set a standard of fairness and hospitality toward female and nonwhite clergy and respect for religious philosophies that span the globe. Currently, the Reverend Peter J. Gomes, Plummer Professor of Christian morals and Pusey Minister, has challenged closed attitudes toward homosexuals by offering same-sex marriages.

HISTORY

Harvard University, founded as a training ground for New World ministers, derives from a Puritan past. Into the early twentieth century, America's religious underpinnings influenced the growth of Harvard Yard and the elegant structure and traditional white spire of Memorial Church, a nondenominational sacred house operated in the Protestant tradition. It was the design of Coolidge, Shepley, Bulfinch and Abbott, who chose modified colonial style to coordinate with campus buildings. Subdued ornamentation, clear-glass windows, granite steps, and Doric columns produce a serene, unified appearance balanced by a 197-foot tower, steeple, and weather vane in the shape of a medieval battle pennant. A link to England is a stone on the west porch from St. Saviour's Church, Southwark, where John Harvard was baptized in 1607.

Through the arched entrance facing Thayer Hall, the interior expresses the church's modest grace and dignity. From the oak-paneled Pusey meeting room, a maximum of 1,200 worshippers sit in four ranks of white-cushioned pews edged in mahogany. Overhead, carved capitals edging the colonnades connect to a vaulted ceiling. A series of Christian symbols—ram, lion, bull, eagle, man, dove, lamb, and pelican—link the artistry to scripture. A brass clock capped with an eagle adorns the gallery. The oak pulpit and lectern perpetuate New England style, which dominates the choir screen, stalls, and Appleton Chapel, named for Harvard's original church, built in 1858. Charles B. Fisk built the four-manual Isham organ, installed in 1967.

Completed on Armistice Day in 1932 as a memorial to Harvard alumni killed in World War I, Memorial Church and Memorial Room derive their names from inscriptions to the dead of World War I. The practice of honoring war heroes continued in World War II, the Korean War, and the Vietnam War. Names appear by class, faculty, and graduate school. On the floor, the university seal in bronze reads "*Veritas: Christo et Ecclesiae*" (Truth: Through Christ and the Church). Wall figures of *Columbia* (Dove) and *Alma Mater* (Foster Mother) in Tennessee marble are the work of an alumnus, sculptor Joseph Arthur Coletti; a third statue, *The Sacrifice,* is the design of Malvina Hoffman, sculptor

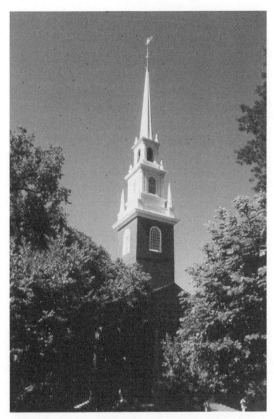

Dubbed "Mem Church" by students, Harvard's Memorial Church is an integral part of campus and community life. (Courtesy Communications Officer, The Memorial Church of Harvard University)

for the Ramakrishna-Vivekananda Center of New York Center. Commencement exercises take place in Tercentenary Theatre, the open sward that links the church and Widener Library. The 2.5-ton college bell, donated by President James Russell Lowell, bears the inscription "In Memory of Voices That Are Hushed." It summons students to class, daily prayer, and Sunday services and tolls the deaths of faculty members.

Through a broad ecumenical program of worship, service, and teaching, Memorial Church is a catalyst for thought and debate on current issues. The structure complements a respected ministry to students and faculty. Over time, it has served as the meeting place for Radcliffe College, as the first university day-care center, and for a Learning in Retirement program. It welcomes world religious leaders and guests the stature of Dr. Billy Graham, the Very

Reverend Derek Watson of Salisbury Cathedral, Nelson Mandela, Harvey Cox, Tallis Scholars, the Berlin Chamber Choir, and the Kuumba gospel singers.

In 1974, the Reverend Peter Gomes began pastoring Memorial Church. Born on May 22, 1942, in Boston, he is a first-generation American born to Cape Verdean immigrant Peter Lobo Gomes and Orissa Josephine White. Gomes grew up in Plymouth in the American Baptist tradition and began preaching in prepuberty. With a history degree from Bates College and B.D. from Harvard, he taught at Tuskegee Institute before joining the staff of Memorial Church as assistant minister and tutor at the divinity school. He has issued strong liberal interpretations of the Bible in *The Good Book: Reading the Bible with Mind and Heart* (1996), which calls for Christians to halt the persecution and marginalization of women and gays.

ACTIVITIES

Memorial Church schedules Sunday school in the Buttrick Room and 11:00 A.M. Sunday worship in the sanctuary plus a candlelit compline from 10:00 to 10:20 P.M. in Appleton Chapel. The annual calendar coordinates fall and spring choir concerts, an annual Martin Luther King Day, a Christmas carol service, and a 5:00 P.M. Christmas Eve service of Holy Communion and a church pageant. The pastor continues the tradition of an 8:45 A.M. prayer Monday through Saturday in Appleton Chapel, begun when the university was founded in 1636. The service features the Morning Choir, a group of eighteen singers selected from the Harvard University choir, directed by organist and choirmaster Murray Forbes Somerville.

Additional gatherings range from occasional Sunday brunches and a Wednesday tea from 5:00 to 6:00 P.M. at Sparks House to ecumenical and adult forums, graduate student fellowship in the Sperry Room, and youth-group outings and projects. The Harvard-Radcliffe Organ Society oversees an annual organ recital series. Staff maintains a Web site and issues a brochure, *Religious Life at Harvard,* four hardbound anthologies of the Reverend Peter Gomes's Sunday sermons over the last four years of his three decades as Memorial Church pastor, and recordings of the eighty-fifth annual carol service, performances by the Harvard University Choir, and organ compositions by John Knowles Paine, the university's first organist and choirmaster.

On June 4, 1998, the city of Cambridge joined with Memorial Church in a unison ringing of bells from Lowell House, Harvard Business School, Christ Church Cambridge, Andover Hall, Church of the New Jerusalem, First Church Congregational, First Parish Unitarian Universalist, St. Paul Roman Catholic Church, St. Peter's Roman Catholic Church, University Lutheran Church, Holy Trinity Armenian Apostolic Church, North Prospect United Church of Christ, First Baptist Church, St. Anthony's Church, and Harvard Divinity School to celebrate the university's 347th commencement exercises. Bells of varying pitches chimed and tolled from 11:45 A.M. until noon after the sheriff of Middlesex County adjourned the assembly. The bell serenade commemorated the utilitarian ringing of bells at the university since 1643.

A momentous offering of Memorial Church followed a study of same-sex marriage in the 1990s. After a year's debate, in 1997, the Board of Ministry recommended unanimously that Memorial Church offer religious ceremonies of commitment between members of the same sex who are students, alumni, officers, instructors, or employees of the university. The Reverend Peter Gomes, the church's gay chaplain, stated publicly his delight in being able to offer the church's hospitality to all members of the university. The board based its decision on longstanding principles of nondiscrimination and in its intentions to follow the prophet Isaiah in providing a "house of prayer for all people." The uproar that followed launched a series of candlelight prayer vigils and protests of Concerned Christians, who unsuccessfully demanded Gomes's ouster. The church continues its campus ministry with baptisms, weddings, funerals, ordination dinners, and memorial and commitment services.

Sources: "Bells Ring Out for Commencement" 1998; "Bells to Ring on Commencement Day" 1998; "Beloved Community of Memory and Hope" 1998–1999; "Billy Graham's Illness Forces Him to Postpone Harvard Events" 1999; *Biography Resource Center* 1999; "The Good Book" 1996; "Landmarks at Harvard"; "The Last Word" 1999; McGrath 1998; "Memorial Church;" "Memorial Church Welcomes Gay Commitment Rites" 1997; *Religious Leaders of America* 1999; Rogers 1992; "Same-Sex Ceremonies to Be Available to University Members at Memorial Church" 1997; Webster 1997.

Mepkin Abbey
Father Aelred Hagan, Director of Novices
1098 Mepkin Abbey Road
Moncks Corner, South Carolina 29461
843-761-8509
FAX 803-761-6719
www.mepkinabbey.org

A quiet contemplative-monastic community in South Carolina's low country for over a half century, Mepkin Abbey is a Cistercian, or Trappist, monastery devoted to enriching the church and human life with the gift of God's spirit. Thirty-five miles north of Charleston, the abbey occupies 3,000 acres of bamboo-edged riverfront property on the Cooper River, one of two major waterways that converge near the coast. Its grounds offer variety in wetlands, pine woods, and massive live oaks decked in Spanish moss. Spring wisteria, azaleas, camellias, and sasanquas give place to colorful summer borders of Carolina jasmine, elephant ears, palmettos, agaves, and Cherokee roses. A half-mile, tree-shaded boulevard thrusts past deer browsing the lawn and skirts the tidal marshes, where blue herons pause on one leg and water moccasins and alligators flourish. The night air echoes with cicadas and peepers, the invisible singers of placid marshes. In the enveloping beauty of Mepkin's grounds, the order lives at peace and communes with the mystery of the divine.

HISTORY AND BELIEFS
Emulating the Christian communitiy of Jesus' twelve apostles, the Cistercians—formally known as the Order of Cistercians of the Strict Observance (O.C.S.O.)—created a unique monastic order during a revival of the simple, gospel-centered life. The founders—Saint Alberic, Saint Robert of Molesme, and Saint Stephen Harding—chose a suitable retreat at Cîteaux, France, in 1098. Armand-Jean le Bouthillier de Rancé reformed the order in

A quiet contemplative-monastic community in South Carolina's low country for over a half century, Mepkin Abbey captures the spirit of St. Benedict of Nursia, father of Western monasticism. (Courtesy of Mepkin Abbey)

1664, when it took the name Trappist or Trappist Cistercians from the Abbey of La Trappe, France. Each Trappist enclave modeled faith and charity to the outside world and measured spirituality in humility, discipline and order, vigilant prayer, silence and solitude, sacred reading, work, and unceasing praise.

Disruption of the religious mission began during the French Revolution, when Trappists either disbanded or sought refuge beyond the borders of France. In 1794, Master Augustin de Lestrange led twenty-one monks of La Trappe to La Val Sainte, Switzerland, where they reformed the order under a stricter rule. Protected by Pope Pius VI, the brothers dispatched monks to Italy, Spain, Belgium, and England and drew recruits to a revived interest in discipline. In 1796, the order extended its rule to the first Trappistine convent at Saint-Branchier. Unsettled conditions forced the monks across Europe during Napoleon's reign and back to France in 1815.

During a fertile period, Trappists expanded to twenty-three sites. The order reached the United States in 1803 when Dom Urban Guillet's monks arrived in Baltimore, Maryland, in search of a refuge. The brothers settled temporarily at Pigeon Hill outside Hanover, Pennsylvania, and then moved west to Casey Creek, Kentucky. One band occupied a site in New York City later chosen for St. Patrick's Cathedral. Farther north, Father Vincent de Paul Merle founded Petit Clairvaux at Big Tracadie near Halifax in Canada. In 1848, the Abbey of Melleray spawned the Abbey of Our Lady of Gethsemani, which took shape in Bardstown, Kentucky.

An offshoot of Gethsemani, Mepkin Abbey formed in 1949 on a former plantation established in South Carolina in 1681. Settlers cultivated 600 acres in rice, the prize low-country crop and star of its cuisine. Rice cultivation ended early in the twentieth century after hurricanes hurled salt water into the fields. From 1762 to 1792, the land belonged to statesman Henry Laurens, president of the Continental Congress, who developed a successful method of cultivating and harvesting rice that remained in practice for a century. Publisher Henry R. Luce and his wife, Republican Congresswoman Clare Boothe Luce, bought the land in 1936 and commissioned landscape designer Loutrel Briggs to establish Mepkin Gardens along a winding waterway. Influenced by Trappist author Thomas Merton, Clare Luce donated a portion of the land to Gethsemani Abbey in 1949. Her intent was to provide the atmosphere of solitude essential to Cistercians, who follow Christ's paschal mystery by seeking open spaces and welcoming the presence and power of the Holy Spirit.

Under the name the Monastery of the Immaculate Heart of Mary, the retreat was the creation of Bishop Emmett Michael Walsh of Charleston, who staffed the donated property with twenty-nine founding monks from Gethsemani on November 14. The brothers found a heavy stand of timber surrounding a two-story house, a gardener's cottage, and several guest cottages. The intensity of tidewater humidity, heat, seasonal storms, and insects plagued the new owners. To assure their success, in 1950, the mother house sent seven monks, called the Seven Gifts of the Holy Spirit, to assist the community until it was assured of independence. Three years later, a third wave brought eleven more brothers to bolster the abbey.

1950 was a year of firsts at Mepkin Abbey. The first addition took place on February 26, when Brother Laurence Hoevel made his profession. On June 3, the company celebrated a first mass at the provisional church. The following year, two brothers were ordained as deacons and, four months later, to the priesthood. As of 1955, Mepkin was an official Trappist Cistercian abbey. Dom James Fox, abbot of Gethsemani, dispatched Father Anthony Chassagne, a Californian from the diocese of Monterey-Fresno and trained at the Gregory University in Rome, as Mepkin's initial abbot. He received blessing at the Cathedral of St. John the Baptist in Charleston on December 15, 1955, and retained the title of abbot until his death in 1974. During his tenure, he served as professor of theology and *censor librorum* (examiner of publications); in retirement from official duties, he retreated to the humble labors that all brothers perform.

From the beginning, Mepkin Abbey established its own style. In *The Silent Life* (1960),

---

SAINT BENEDICT THE GREAT

The Cistercian order derived from the spirit of Saint Benedict of Nursia, father of Western monasticism. He and his twin, Saint Scholastica, were born about 480 in Nursia (or Norcia), Italy, and dedicated their religious careers to monasticism. After training in Rome, Benedict retreated to a cave in the Sabine Hills of Subiaco for three years. From this ascetic beginning, he evolved twelve colonies. At age thirty-five, after he fought off a would-be assassin, he reassessed the mission and moved his disciples to an abandoned pagan fort at Monte Cassino near Naples. Called *abba* (father), he built his followers a house from the stones of ancient buildings. The order dedicated itself to Christ, supported and governed activities according to the simple tradition of *ora et labora* (pray and work), and followed the single watchword *pax* (peace). At Benedict's command, the brothers loved and respected each member, bore human weaknesses with patience, and extended charity to all.

A skilled administrator, Benedict rejected excesses of self-denial and physical punishment. He replaced exhibitionism with poverty, purity, and obedience. His monks adhered to daily recitation, study, teaching, and labor, primarily the copying of religious manuscripts. He succeeded at firm discipline and practical organization and formalized the system in *Regula Monachorum* (Rules for Monks) (ca. 515), the foundation of a moderate monasticism free of the extremism and exotic self-denial that Benedict abhorred. His sensible monastic model influenced the medieval era and remained viable into the modern age. Monte Cassino's order and hospital thrived until Lombards overran it in 575. In 1964, Pope Paul VI named Benedict the Great Europe's patron saint.

Thomas Merton described the site as peaceful and unhurried. Although devout members suffered some upheaval after the Second Vatican Council called into question the holiness of their purpose, Father Anthony affirmed abbey policy during the difficult 1960s and 1970s and secured the brotherhood into the last quarter of the twentieth century. Father Aidan Carr, who was elected the second abbot, continued in Father

Anthony's tradition of prudent adminstration, counseling, and preaching and redirected emphasis to hospitality.

At century's end, Mepkin managed a series of advancements and losses. In its fifteenth year, the brotherhood buried the first deceased member on abbey grounds. After a three-year recovery period from the devastation of the chicken and wood industries wrought by Hurricane Hugo, in 1992, under the leadership of Abbot Francis Kline, Mepkin accepted sponsorship and material support of an order of Trappistine nuns at the monastery of Esperanza (Hope) in Esmeraldas, Ecuador, a mission supported by Father Anthony in his last months.

ARCHITECTURE

On June 15, 1999, the order broke ground for a new Mepkin Abbey Church designed by Theodore Butler and built by Frank Kacmarcik. Standing at the center of the complex, the worship center expresses the Cistercian style with an altar at center and unadorned wooden choir stalls lining the narrow chancel. Inside glass doors, a red tiled floor balances the geometric crossing of exposed yellow pine beams down the nave. The open, airy space between stark white walls enhances accoustics and the tones of the Zimmer electronic pipe organ, installed in 1994.

On March 22, 1993, the abbey opened Ecumenical Chapel and celebrated a first mass on Palm Sunday. David B. Thompson, Bishop of Charleston, inaugurated the abbey church on November 14. The following year, trustees added the Tower of the Seven Spirits, a fifty-foot bell tower formed of steel, laced in a herringbone pattern of copper louvers, and surmounted with a copper cap. Inside, the bells—cast in Holland and named John, Maria, Bernard, and Irene—manifest the craftsmanship of the Verdin Company of Cincinnati as they call brothers to daily prayer. Expanded holdings include dormitories, a kitchen and refectory, office buildings, a library and scriptorium (reading room), an infirmary, a visitors center, a music building, and retreat facilities.

ACTIVITIES

An amalgam of many cultures, races, and language groups, the thirty residents of Mepkin

Abbey retain the unity, vigor, commitment, and devotion of Benedictine forebears. Central to abbey discipline is the reception of God through *lectio divina* (sacred reading), which impels each brother to serious contemplation of holy scripture as well as of nature, sacred relics, stained glass, icons, and architecture. A constant of monasticism is the ascetic *hororarium* (routine) established in the Middle Ages. At the forefront is prayer, which calls the monks seven times a day to sing or recite psalms—at 3:20 A.M. vigils, 5:30 A.M. lauds (morning), terce at 8:15 to end the grand silence, sext (midday), none at 12:50 P.M. after the noon meal, vespers at 6:00 P.M., and compline (end of day) at 7:35 P.M. The statelier moments occur at morning lauds and evening vespers. More formal prayers ennoble the religious calendar at religious feasts and holy days.

More mundane matters conform to the outlook of the ascetic individual. With little fuss, each satisfies the need for meals and drink in moderation as did the founding Benedictines, who withdrew from the Roman Empire to celebrate God in lone, spare places around the Mediterranean rim. To empty themselves of worldliness and absorb God's presence, Mepkin's brothers choose abstinence, fasting, and nighttime vigils as exercises in discipline.

Mepkin Abbey became self-supporting by selling eggs, compost and compost tea, lumber, handwritten copies of the Grail psalter, cookbooks and religious books, audio and video tapes, and cinnamon buns. As the monks' confidence grew in agriculture and commerce, they constructed twelve houses to hold 38,000 Leghorn hens and grading sheds for a thriving egg business, barns and a milk processor for a herd of Jerseys, a sawmill to produce timber and pulpwood, a water tank, and a machine shop and tool and equipment sheds to accommodate cultivation of 200 acres. They maintain Mepkin's Nancy Bryan Luce Gardens, which are open free of charge from 8:30 A.M. to 4:30 P.M. year-round to tourists. An irrigation system supports its flowers plus fields of soybeans, wheat, and corn, azaleas and camellias, cattle, hogs, and poultry. Wise husbandry has brought profit from sale of composted chicken litter and white pine shavings, packaged under the logo *Earth Healer.*

Visitors are a constant at the abbey. They often arrive for a brief visit and prayer at noon or meditate in the church, which is always open. Prayer services are open to guests, who may sit in the monastic choir. Those requiring extended periods of quiet or spiritual counsel reserve one of two rooms in the Reception Center. For pilgrims or couples on retreat, guest houses are available for one- to six-night stays of up to nine visitors. Accommodations provide simple necessities—a bed and linens, desk, reading chair, private bath, and dining room adjacent to the refectory. The brothers serve vegetarian meals and expect guests to maintain silence and heed the communal reading during the noon meal. Up to three male guests at a time choose a renewable sabbatical residency up to thirty days.

A vital part of the religious community of greater Charleston, Mepkin Abbey is a favorite haven. Father Kline, a Juilliard graduate, has performed Bach organ recitals for assemblies. In 1998, the monastery joined the priests of the diocese of Charleston for the Sacred Chrism Mass and invited Duke University's Self-Knowledge Symposium to spend time with the brothers and live the Benedictine life. In 1999, the brothers introduced a lecture and concert series with a performance of Friedrich Handel's *Messiah*. Later in the year, they hosted a segment of the University of South Carolina's Hall Lectureship in New Testament and Early Christianity series and enhanced the region's annual May–June Spoleto festival with a tour of the grounds and performance of Bach's solo cantatas. The end of the century brought the abbey's golden anniversary, which coincided with the retirement of the Right Reverend Timothy Kelly, abbot of Gethsemani, the mother house. In March 2000, the monks scheduled a Lenten study series on the life of Saint Francis de Sales, a performance of Bach's *St. John Passion* by the Charleston Vocal Arts Ensemble and the orchestra and choir, and a self-knowledge symposium for students from Duke University, the University of North Carolina at Chapel Hill, and North Carolina State University.

See also Abbey of Gethsemani.

Sources: Cantor, Norman F., 1993; "Clare Booth Luce"; Cohn-Sherbok 1998; Cunningham 1998; Dolan 1968; Downey 1997; Hastings 1951; "History of the Cistercian Order"; Hodges 1999; Hollister 1994; Holmes 1988; Hughes, B.; Jamieson and Sewall 1949; Lopez 1967; McMorrough 1997–1998; "Mepkin Abbey"; *New Catholic Encyclopedia* 1967; Raby 1953; Snodgrass 1999; "Trappist."

Methodist Tabernacle

Kathy McKechnie
Martha's Vineyard Campmeeting Association
P.O. Box 1176
Oak Bluffs, Massachusetts 02557-1176
508-693-0525

Amid multicolored gingerbread cottages built in nineteenth-century carpenter's Gothic stands the Methodist Tabernacle. The functional gazebo-shaped assembly hall takes its name from the revered Old Testament hall that housed the ark, as directed by Yahweh in Exodus 27:9. Built in the unpretentious style of Methodist founder John Wesley, the tabernacle was treasured in the Martha's Vineyard area for summer hymn sings with a nineteenth-century revivalist flair. Balanced with after-hours hikes, beach walks, croquet matches, sailing, fishing, cookouts, and huckleberry picking, the Methodist Tabernacle worship style suited the religious needs of its day.

HISTORY

The 2,000-seat Methodist Tabernacle is an unpretentious but historic spiritual center in southeastern Massachusetts. The area has a long history of group instruction, beginning with the first Indian school and advancing to Parson Joseph Thaxter's Thaxter Academy at Edgartown. Local revivals centered first on Falmouth and Sandwich before moving to an island copse known as Vineyard Haven. In the 1830s, the worship phenomenon sprang up spontaneously in the town of Cottage City and relocated to Oak Bluffs in 1907. During soft summer nights, the tabernacle's beachy ambience enhanced an informal, family-centered Christian experience composed of singing and Bible-based evangelism frequently quickened with shouts of hallelujah and joyous amens.

According to Henry Franklin Norton's informative *History of Martha's Vineyard* (1823), the tabernacle's forerunner, Wesleyan Grove tenting grounds, opened in a sheep pasture on August

REVIVALISM

American revivalism, an emotional stimulus to repentance and acceptance of Christianity, springs from the English Methodism of English evangelists Charles and John Wesley, who served from 1736 to 1737 as missionaries to Indians in the Georgia colony. A form of religious instruction and moral admonition, revivalism dates to itinerant preacher George Whitefield and the homegrown colonial theology of Jonathan Edwards, the era's renowned preacher. The combination sparked the Great Awakening, a compelling crusade to revive moribund faith among New Englanders. A sequel, called the Second Awakening, sparked religious soul-searching among Presbyterians in the nineteenth century and spread to Baptists and Methodists. Disseminators were circuit riders and camp meetings, a frontier phenomenon that wedded an all-day social to preaching and group baptism.

Championed by Bishop Francis Asbury, the first camp meetings took place in Kentucky, Tennessee, and Ohio among Methodists and Presbyterians and moved east to New England. Organizers pioneered the movable camp, which they erected in open space and removed with the aid of teams of volunteers. By midcentury, transient camp meetings evolved into unassuming permanent wood

fixtures. They catered to families and served as a social and emotional outlet. To make use of daylight and fair weather and the annual school hiatus, ministers and congregations usually scheduled week-long gatherings for July through early fall. Families and their animals sheltered in groves and lived in tents and branch huts. Skilled preachers manipulated emotions by concentrating on individual sins, particularly drunkenness. The more emotional version of revivalism caused new converts to collapse, jerk and twitch, and bark, babble, or sing.

The giant of frontier revivalism, evangelist Dwight Lyman Moody of Northfield, Massachusetts, rejuvenated the movement in the early 1870s. By reconciling urbanism with old-time religion, he carried the high drama of rural hymn singing, fellowship, and pulpit oratory to Brooklyn, Philadelphia, New York, and St. Louis. He closed each session by urging new converts to join a church, no matter what kind. In the second half of the twentieth century, the style and format developed into slick soul-saving campaigns carried on radio. End-of-the-era evangelism intensified from the preaching of Billy Sunday and Dr. Billy Graham, who refined the outdoor meetings with televised crusades worldwide.

24, 1835. Several times per day, the Reverend Jeremiah Pease of Edgartown addressed a body of worshippers already numbering in the hundreds. Amid a working-class atmosphere that combined spiritual renewal with a refreshing, low-cost family vacation, participants arrived on oxcarts or arrived by boat with cushions, folding chairs, and picnic baskets. They pitched nine communal tents in a semicircle at the grove's outer edge and spread mounds of straw purchased at area stables. Eventually, communal tents gave place to family tents, which staff authorized only to sober Christians. The annual return of families led to wooden shelters designed to emulate tents.

Architecture had the look of makeshift hammering and sawing of the plainest sort. For a pulpit, which they designated the "preacher's stand," workers knocked together a two-story, slant-roofed shed of recycled boards and driftwood. To reach the lectern, the speaker climbed a short

ladder leading to the unpaneled side. Open-air seating consisted of split tree trunks perched on pegs driven in with a mallet. Some of the congregation chose to sit on the ground, stretch their legs in a brief stroll, or lean against trees. At mealtime, they shared picnic baskets in a folksy holiday atmosphere. To meet sanitation needs, organizers dug a new well in 1849, a peak year when 53 Methodist ministers attended and preached round-robin style from August 20 to 25.

The experiment in fresh air evangelism succeeded, bringing back regulars each summer along with their relatives and friends. Norton claims that the campground became "the most fully-attended meetings of their kind in this country." (Norton 1923, Part IV) Articles in *New York Times* and *Harper's* brought newcomers. In 1851, there were around 3,500 attendees and 100 tents, requiring the Committee on Order to police the gathering and prohibit peddling. In 1858, a second well supplied more water for some 10,000 people and 300 horses; the next year, an office building stored baggage and tents, delivered mail, and housed the campground manager and his family. By 1860, attendance mounted to 12,000 and 500 tents. Steamers from New York, Providence, Boston, and Portland, Maine, brought first-timers just learning of the experiment. They swelled attendance to its height in 1869, when the seasonal head count passed 30,000. That year began a tradition known as the Grand Illumination, a display of Japanese lanterns and fireworks.

Within a decade, Cottage City had grown to a permanent campground edged with a picket fence to prohibit nonreligious activities. Around the grove, speculators under the name of Oak Bluffs Land and Wharf Company built a summer resort that echoed the campground's homeyness and targeted strait-laced Christians as opposed to rowdy, alcohol-swilling summer drifters. Their selectivity nurtured a middle-class colony of shopkeepers, blacksmiths, carpenters, and artisans. In addition to 1,000 cottages, the village spawned boarding houses, a bakery and shops, a lumber yard, and horse cars and trolleys to ferry crowds to the campground. In 1874, a week after the opening of a steam railroad, President Ulysses S. Grant and his wife, Julia Dent Grant, led a party of dignitaries to the tabernacle.

On April 24, 1879, the tabernacle's administrators selected Boston architect S. S. Woodcock to design an assembly hall. They hired John Hoyt and George Dwight of Springfield, Massachusetts, to build a permanent structure 100 feet high and 130 feet in diameter. To save on bids ranging up to $15,000, trustees abandoned wood and chose wrought-iron supports and metal siding, which cost around $7,125 to build and lessened the danger of fire. Supplies from the Phoenix Iron Company in Phoenixville, Pennsylvania, arrived in June 1879. Hicks and Son of Boston installed the roof. On July 16, seven weeks after the groundbreaking, the structure opened for services. A ring of single-story, 11- by 16-foot cottages completed the revival village and enhanced the island atmosphere of simplicity and cozy friendliness. In 1926, the staff hoisted the first cross to the summit. The latest cross, first lighted in 1969, was a gift from islander Gordon MacGillvray.

ARCHITECTURE

The tabernacle is a model of nineteenth-century prefabrication. The move to the all-metal structure combined fresh air and the ease of a beach pavilion with the jubilance and camaraderie of an 1890s tent revival and camp meeting. Its broad-eaved design is disarmingly artless and well suited to all-day gospel sessions. Below a layered roof and a sign proclaiming, "1835— Martha's Vineyard Camp Meeting Association Tabernacle Erected 1879," a half-round window surmounts the broad entrance. At the summit of the corrugated roof, an octagonal cupola rests on a louver-sided tower with an eight-gore dome and sturdy cross guyed into place with wire.

Inside, a series of modest multibranched, wrought-iron columns support the roof. The design augments sound by projecting an orator's least nuance. Two stories above the open sides and dirt floor, stained glass in a double clerestory provides both natural light and ventilation for the close-packed assemblies. Ranks of right-angled, gray wooden benches surround a stage that accommodates musical groups and a piano alongside the main pulpit. Additional worship space at Trinity Church and Grace Chapel outside the main circle offered varied services to extend the camp meeting season.

ACTIVITIES

Still in operation 165 years after its inception, the Methodist Tabernacle survives in the heart of a more urban, more sophisticated Oak Bluffs. The pavilion is open daily to visitors. In addition, groups engage the facility for weddings, receptions, and memorial services. Sunday services begin at 9:30 A.M. through July and August. The staff welcomes all comers to inspirational preaching as well as cottage tours and such charitable efforts as the Haiti Fish Farm benefit performance. The traditional Wednesday evening community sings collect goodwill offerings to support restoration and maintenance; children's projects earn additional amounts from street singing and the sale of lemonade and jewelry. By late summer 1999, the community had raised $925,000.

The tabernacle doubles as a civic auditorium for high school graduations, patriotic programs, art and craft shows, auctions, lectures, and popular music concerts. Among the famous who have used the tabernacle are actors Patricia Neal and Merv Griffin, comedian Mark Russell, newsman Walter Cronkite, and performers Judy Collins, B. B. King, Arlo Guthrie, and the Boston Pops Esplanade Orchestra. In November 1998, the Massachusetts Foundation for the Humanities financed a history of the campground. Produced by filmmaker Daniel Jones of Brookline, Massachusetts, and the Center for Independent Documentary, the finished half-hour video, *Birth of the Vacation* (1999), traces the Wesleyan Grove religious experience from family worship to leisure community.

> **See also** Lovely Lane Methodist Church.
> **Sources:** Ahlstrom 1972; Goeringer 1998; Mutrux 1982; Norton 1923; "Oak Bluffs"; "Oak Bluffs Town Government" 1999; Perk 1999; Sigelman 1998; Smith 1989.

Mission of San Miguel of Santa Fe
Ben Sulzer, Curator
401 East de Vargas Street and
Old Santa Fe Trail
Santa Fe, New Mexico 87501
505-983-3974

A testament to the practicality and devotion of Spanish settlers, the San Miguel Mission was an evangelical outreach to the area's Pueblo. Worshippers once came to services at the call of America's oldest bell, the 780-pound San José Bell, cast in Spain in 1356, hauled by oxcart from Mexico City, and hoisted into place in 1854. The mission interior, marked by thick walls and high windows, features the Franciscan missionaries' deer- and buffalo-skin paintings, which illustrate Bible stories and hagiography. One example, the Segesser hide painting, portrays Pueblo joining the Spaniards in 1720 to battle the French and Pawnee. Carved in the choir loft timber is an authentic inscription naming the church's presiding officer: *El Señor Marquez de la Penuela Hizo esta fabrica Alferes Rl Dn Agn flos Vergara su criado Ano de 1710* (The Marques de la Penuela constructed this building with the aid of Alferes Real Don Agustin Flores Vergara, his servant, in the year 1710).

In the adjacent St. Michael's College, Christian brethren educated local children. The col-

lege survived as St. Michael's High School until 1947, when diocese authorities converted it to the College of Santa Fe. The historical complex includes the Loretto Chapel (or Our Lady of Light Chapel) and the oldest house in the United States, built on East de Vargas Street in 1740 of puddled adobe.

HISTORY

Erected over an abandoned pueblo dating to 1100, San Miguel Mission, dedicated to San Miguel Arcángel (the Archangel Saint Michael), was the work of Father Alonso de Benavides. Begun in 1610, it took shape in 1612 in view of corn and wheat fields and the Acequia Madre (Mother Watercourse), which irrigated crops. The structure, the nation's oldest mission church, is contemporary with the Palace of the Governors. It originally served its builders, the 700 Tlaxcala (or Tlascalteca) slave laborers and their families, whom Spanish settlers imported from Mexico and housed in the Barrio de Analco, the oldest Hispanic neighborhood in North America.

In June 1628, Governo Sotelo upbraided territorial troopers for failing to rise when he arrived for mass and claimed that deference to him superceded sacred liturgy. For his arrogance, he was called before the Court of the Inquisition of La Cañada. Twelve years later, the friars redesignated the chapel as a hermitage, to serve special masses, pilgrims, and suppliants of Saint Michael. Next door, they constructed a short-lived infirmary, which the spiteful Governor Luis de Rosas destroyed during a political confrontation over state and religious authority shortly before his assassination in 1641.

In the August 1680 revolt against *encomenderos* (tax collectors), the Indian shaman named Popé of San Juan Pueblo ousted Spanish rulers and priests for having him flogged and charged with sorcery. His insurgents burned the mission's records, roof, and interior, slaughtered 21 Franciscan churchmen without warning, besieged haciendas, and murdered nearly 400 Spanish inhabitants. Thirty years after the revolt, General Don Diego de Vargas slew many Indians and reconquered New Mexico.

To assure a long service, postrevolt planners added stone buttresses and remodeled the tower and façade. Slowly and at considerable cost, they rebuilt and reroofed the Hermita de San Miguel (St. Michael Hermitage) fortress style over the old foundations as a temporary military presidio against Indian attack. The new governor, the Marquis de Peñuela, provided 2,000 adobe bricks; the friars solicited additional funds. To commemorate the completion in 1710, builders carved end braces to support the Peñuela beam, which records the date and governor's name. Over a half century, the mission returned to its original purpose. At the time of the nation's founding in 1776, Brother Atanacio described a front-door embellishment—a modest arch supporting a bell.

The church developed piecemeal from decades of repair, replacement, and expansion. Builders imposed a railing dividing brothers and their students from neighbors and soldiers and finished the façade with a cross-topped square tower over the narthex. The sanctuary interior features an artistic reredos executed and signed by José Antonio Ortiz in 1798. It displays a seventeenth-century *santo,* or carving, of Saint Michael, the chapel's patron, and six canvases, four in oval frames, painted in Mexico in 1710. An ungainly tri-story tower with a monstrous bell, pagoda roof, and railed galleries replaced the arch and smaller bell in 1830. The imposing superstructure did not survive a storm on March 16, 1872.

Over the nearby Santa Fe Trail, settlers traveled from Franklin, Missouri, to the Southwest from 1821 to 1880. With the influx of newcomers, in 1859, the De La Salle Christian Brothers began using the chapel for St. Michael's College student assemblies. Brother Hilarion made repairs and laid the original puncheon floor over dirt in 1862. Archbishop Lamy donated a harmonium in 1879. In 1881, the brothers purchased the church and adjacent residence for $3,000. Their illustrative buffalo-hide paintings of Saint John the Baptist and the crucifixion adorn the walls as teaching art. The single façade, refurbished reredos, and repaired tower date to 1887; stone buttresses shored up ancient adobe walls the next year.

By the end of the nineteenth century, San Miguel Chapel was drawing a stream of religious tourists, who required tour guides when the chapel was unoccupied. Their interest brought in donations that paid for an oak floor in 1927. In 1955, restorers remodeled the interior in Spanish colonial style. After the boys' school relocated in 1967, the brotherhood maintained historical features.

ACTIVITIES
Today, the chapel, America's oldest active Christian worship center, is owned by the De La Salle Brothers and is operated as a wayside church for the convenience of visitors to the city. The sanctuary is open daily for tours, private devotions, confession, and Sunday mass at 5:00 P.M. but, unlike parish churches, offers no facilities for confession, weddings, or baptisms. A six-minute audio recounts the building's history and describes the internal structure, artwork, and ornate wooden carving. A gift shop stocks souvenirs, a mission history, and religious mementos.

See also Loretto Chapel.

Sources: Beresky 1991; Bustamante 1993; Marlowe 1998; "Mission of San Miguel of Santa Fe"; Morgan 1994; "New Mexico State Timeline"; "Santa Fe" 1997; Sheppard 1994; Spritzer 1994.

Monastery of Christ in the Desert
Brother André, Guestmaster
P.O. Box 270
Abiquiu, New Mexico 87510
505-470-4515 (answering service)
Broandre@aol.com
www.technet.nm.org/pax.html; www:christ-desert.org

Among sturdy piñon trees 6,500 feet above sea level stands the Monastery of Christ in the Desert, a stately Benedictine retreat in Chama Canyon near Abiquiu, a village seventy-five miles northwest of Santa Fe, New Mexico. Beneath circling hawks and restless surges of wind, the flat-roofed retreat enjoys a peace accomplished through abandonment of modern devices. Apart from the jangled society outside its confines, the complex offers serenity to all comers based on the philosophy of *metanoia,* a Greek term meaning inner revolution—an abandonment of ease and privilege and an embrace of work, contemplation, and prayer. Among the

Like Benedictine retreats of Europe, the Monastery of Christ in the Desert introduces outsiders to glimpses of reclusive life. (Courtesy the Monastery of Christ in the Desert)

community's twenty-four monks, up to fifteen guests at a time arrive from many lands to pray, keep vigils, fast, read, perform benevolent work, maintain buildings, and converse when necessary in English. Trappist monk and author Thomas Merton visited in 1968 and extolled the sweep of sky, clear air, and red cliffs.

For a minimal charge of $30 per day, pilgrims enjoy two or more days of vegetarian meals and simple accommodation in one of the five single and four double rooms, which provide baths with heated water. Outside the assembly area and chapel, lighting derives from kerosene lanterns or flashlights. Guests help the monks with hoeing, clerking in the gift shop, sweeping the chapel, and dishwashing. The red stucco compound's seventeen eight- by ten-foot cells are heated by wood stoves. Furnishings are limited to a desk and chair, a bench, a futon, a cupboard, and two oil lamps. Embellishments are limited to a modest cross carved from twigs and centered with a dried cactus flower.

HISTORY

Like Benedictine retreats of Europe, the Monastery of Christ in the Desert introduces outsiders to glimpses of reclusive life. Father Aelred Wall, a Benedictine monk, established the Monastery of Christ in the Desert in June 1964 as an outgrowth of Mount Saviour Monastery, a Benedictine abbey in New York state. The site offers maximum withdrawal from urban life in the midst of government-protected wilderness. The nonclerical community had its beginning as the hermitage of Father Aelred, who traveled to La Soledad south of the Rio Grande in 1973 to find peace and to revive the Rule of Saint Benedict. Within a year, other monks joined the community. Shortly before his death in 1984, Father Aelred formally chartered the Monastery of Christ in the Desert. In 1985, Francisco Cumberland expanded the monks' ministry with an independent sister monastery, Monasterio de Nuestra Senora de la Soledad (Monastery of Our Lady of Solitude) near San Miguel de Allende, Mexico.

After the arrival of Father Ezequiel Bas Luna and Brother Fernando Hool Salazar in 1987, the community took on new purpose. By 1990, the staff had erected a complex to house twenty monks and held religious services in Father Aelred's chapel. Additional dependents—St. Mary and All the Saints in Xalapa, Mexico, and Holy Cross Monastery in Chicago, Illinois—draw strength from the primary house. In 1996, the compound became an autonomous abbey, where residents farm, craft, and perform computer work. Brothers earn their living by weaving clothing, wall hangings, vestments, and rugs. One paints icons and retablos; another quilts and hooks rugs.

The original buildings, crafted in 1964 by Japanese American woodworker/architect George Nakashima, blend cedar and pine with the juniper and piñon indigenous to the area. The attractive chapel, built of adobe, wood, stone, and glass, opens on Mesa Alta, a rock landmark painted by American landscape artist Georgia O'Keeffe, who lived at nearby Ghost Ranch. Its steeple bears the vertical Hispanic lines and simple cutout for the bell. The cross above is a stark juncture of two straight wood pieces. Moorish doors enclose worshippers early and late for meditation, prayer, and praise. The nave, lit by candles and natural light from clerestory windows, has no need of the trickle of electric power from the monks' solar panels, which also fuel the compound water pump. The gift shop, Zarza y Cruz (Bush and Cross), takes its name from the burning bush that Moses saw in the desert and from the Christian cross.

ACTIVITIES

A Sunday and feast day schedule calls the monks at vigils for 4:00 A.M. prayers. Guests assemble at lauds at dawn and terce at midmorning, followed by the Eucharist at 9:15 A.M. The prayer schedule continues with sext and an optional light meal at noon, a main meal at 4:00 P.M., and vespers and benediction at 5:30 P.M. The last prayer session, compline, is private and silent. A daily regimen incorporates reading and work along with the prayer, daily Eucharist, and meal schedule. In the absence of musical instruments, hymn and response singing at chapel is *a capella*. Liturgical music is a mix of ancient and modern verses, some composed by the brothers themselves.

A bell calls residents and guests to the refectory for joint meals, which may be accompanied by music or spiritual reading. Times of common prayer are posted. The abbot does not mingle with guests. The area north of the church and residence are restricted; the refectory and library are open only at stated times. Smoking, pets, radios, headsets, and musical instruments are forbidden. Adventurers hike through cactus and follow the stations of the cross marked along the incline of a nearby rock formation. At the summit, sojourners enjoy the vista alongside a cairn that anchors a cross in view of the valley below.

Sources: Dowling; Fry 1982; Kelleher 1996; "Monasterio de la Nuestra Senora Soledad"; "The Monastery of Christ in the Desert"; "The Monastery Sustainability Project"; *New Catholic Encyclopedia* 1967; "Sacred Sites of Northern New Mexico"; Spritzer 1994.

Monastery of the Holy Cross
3111 South Aberdeen Street
Chicago, Illinois 60608-6503
773-927-7424
FAX 773-927-5734
porter@chicagomonk.org
www.chicagomonk.org

A unique urban brotherhood witnessing to hospitality and spiritual uplift in Chicago, the Monastery of the Holy Cross is a rarity—an abbey built in the medieval tradition, but situated in the least restful part of the city. An affiliate of the Monastery of Christ in the Desert in Abiquiu, New Mexico, it is located south of the downtown loop in the Bridgeport section. Within minutes of buses and the elevated train, it offers an oasis of prayer and silence where commuters, neighbors, and passersby can find and celebrate God. Like their forebear, Saint Benedict of Nursia, the monks follow a lifestyle of obedience, stability, and devotion and follow the Benedictine motto *pax* (peace) by witnessing to God's presence in the city.

Founded in 1988 in Minnesota and established in July 1991 in the Chicago Archdiocese of Chicago by Joseph Cardinal Bernardin, the

A unique urban brotherhood in Chicago, the Monastery of the Holy Cross is a rarity—an abbey built in the medieval tradition, but situated in the least restful part of the city. (Courtesy the Monastery of the Holy Cross)

Monastery of the Holy Cross is a relative newcomer among the nation's long-lived abbeys. The choice of a metropolitan setting is a deliberate intersection with the technological and social demands of urbanism that typically alienate and overwhelm neighborhoods. In a leased church, the small uncloistered community makes its home; the monks worship off-campus at a parish church. In an upgrade of the classical tradition of manuscript copying, they operate the Roman Catholic Web Ring and earn wages in computer outsourcing for churches, data-service firms, university libraries, and law offices. The service is limited to the amount of work monks can perform without compromising a life of prayer and spiritual commitment.

ACTIVITIES

In the ancient monastic tradition, the monastery dedicates its mission to praise, evangelism, spirituality, and uplift to area laity and clergy. The monks have initiated an oblate program to support seekers on their spiritual quest. They host men and women on retreat for stays of hours, a day, or longer. The four-person guest area, St. Joseph's

Loft, is a quiet place free of televisions and telephones and equipped with a full bath, a kitchenette, and commons. For $35 a day room and board, guests can contemplate difficulties in their lives or seek direction for new ventures. Each may choose to dine in solitude or take meals with the monks in the monastery refectory. The brothers celebrate the Eucharist daily and chant the divine office regularly—at 5:30 and 7:00 A.M. and 12:30, 5:00, 6:00, and 6:30 P.M., followed by silent meditation after vespers.

In its tenth year, the monastery welcomed thirteen musicians, readers, and speakers in a series of musical programs from March to December. The schedule began with the local Schola of St. Peter's in the Loop for a Lenten concert and continued through the spring and summer with the A Cappella Touring Quartet of the Institute for Eastern Orthodox Studies in Houston, an Easter lecture by Sister Dianne Bergant, two readings by the Schola Cantorum for Pentecost and Corpus Christi Day, a harp concert by the Reverend Robert Hutmacher, Dr. Bernard McGinn's lecture on monasticism and mysticism, and Dr. Francis-Noel Thomas's introduction to the iconography of Jan van Eyck. The anniversary series concluded with fall lectures by the Reverend Joel Rippinger and Dr. Aurelie Hagstrom, a pre-Thanksgiving lecture by Dr. Peter Dombowski on Saint Mary of Egypt, and a string and vocal performance of the monks celebrating the Feast of Our Lady of Guadalupe, led by Brother Peter Funk.

The monastery's activities suit urban needs. In July 1999, the monks ran a garage sale to raise funds for flood relief to the Sacred Heart Parish in East Grand Forks, Minnesota, and hosted a rummage sale for the Nicaragua Medical Alliance, which supplies ultrasound and dental equipment, drugs, and vitamins to Central America. In May 2000, the monastery led a twelve-day Great Jubilee Pilgrimage to Rome and Constantinople. The gift shop offers icons, crafts, toiletries, incense, mugs, CDs, cards and books, gift baskets, and fancy foods from monasteries nationwide. Eight times a year, the monks withdraw for Desert Day, a Sunday to Tuesday retreat for recollection.

See also Monastery of Christ in the Desert.
Sources: "Artist Takes Creations to a Higher

Level" 1997; "Home in the City" 1993; "In
Search of Serenity" 1997; "Latin Chant Is New
Wave"1996; "Schola Cantorum of St. Peter the
Apostle"; "Silence in the City"; "Updating
Monastic Tradition" 1995.

Mormon Tabernacle

Temple Square
Salt Lake City, Utah 84150
800-453-3860 ext. 2205; 801-240-3171
FAX 801-240-4886
taborgan@ldschurch.org

*Within a well-groomed park and promenade in Salt
Lake City, the turtle-back Mormon Tabernacle, one of
the West's most admired buildings, seats 8,000 people
under an oval roof in an acoustically thrilling setting.
(Courtesy Public Communications Department, The
Church of Jesus Christ of Latter-Day Saints, Salt
Lake City, Utah)*

At the center of an urban complex of high-rises,
hotels, and restaurants, the Salt Lake City business district bears little resemblance to its prairie
origins as the mecca and self-sustaining colony
of Mormons. Amid a stream of visitors, the "City
of the Saints" is a paradox—a revered American
showplace and headquarters of the most persecuted religious group in American history.
Against a stream of malignment, gossip, and bad
publicity, the city has acquired the panache of a
world-class metropolis despite its reputation for
strict morality that bans alcohol, tobacco, gambling, and prostitution. To entrepreneurship, the
Mormon enclave has contributed a sense of divine mission and guidance, unity, lay stewardship,
and implementation of faith in economic life. Its
contributions to worship and culture derive primarily from the admirable program of music and
culture from the Mormon Tabernacle, an ex-
traordinarily versatile assembly hall that directs
quality programs to homes worldwide.

HISTORY

The trade metropolis of Salt Lake City began as
an agrarian society founded on July 24, 1847, after Brigham Young led 148 Mormon refugees to
the Wasatch Mountains to escape lethal vigilantism and murder in Missouri and Illinois. In
1838, Missouri governor Lillburn W. Boggs had
launched an extermination drive against local
Mormons, whom he labeled enemies of the
state. On October 30, a raid of the state militia
on men, women, and children in a Mormon
community at Haun's Mill outside Far West resulted in 17 dead and 12 wounded. The attack
ended Mormon plans for settlement in Missouri

and centered their hopes on a barren stretch
near Utah's Great Salt Lake.

Originally designated as Great Salt Lake City,
the village followed the plan of the idealized city
of Zion as determined by martyred prophet
Joseph Smith. Before developing the center into
a grid of ten-acre blocks and wide tree-lined
streets, on July 28, 1847, Young thrust his cane
into the ground to designate the temple block,
the worship and global administrative center for
all Latter-Day Saints. Proclaimed a new Jerusalem
and city of saints, it drew converts from the Atlantic Coast and Europe to the provisional state
of Deseret. The Treaty of Guadalupe Hidalgo in
1848 brought Utah into U.S. sovereignty as a territory with Salt Lake City as its capital from 1856
to 1896. With the creation of the state of Utah,
the city became a state capital.

GEORGE DONALD HARRISON

No single item connected the non-Mormon world to Salt Lake City like its magnificent pipe organ. The accompaniment to the Mormon Tabernacle Choir has become the centerpiece of radio and television broadcasts of Christmas Eve services, an annual concert series, and a lengthy discography of LPs, tapes, videos, and CDs of sacred, patriotic, folk, and traditional American music. The organ builder, George Donald Harrison, was born in Huddersfield, Yorkshire, on April 21, 1889. He received keyboard training in childhood and established a career as an engineer. At age twenty-three, he gained certification from the Chartered Institute of Patent Agents and worked with his father before becoming a patent attorney for organ builders Henry Willis and Sons. After a hitch in the army, he assisted Willis in designing and voicing instruments and earned promotion to company director.

In 1927, Harrison supervised the technical side of tonal and mechanical design with Aeolian-Skinner Organ Company of Boston. During the Great Depression, a loss of sales gave him more time to tune and harmonize each new project. His reputation for meticulous work gave him influence over major installations of the world's most complex organs. By age fifty-one, he rose to president and treasurer of the company. In addition to organs at New York's Riverside Church and Cathedral of St. John the Divine and Boston's Christian Science mother church, in 1948, he designed and installed the Salt Lake City instrument.

Utah's development was not without conflict. Even though Mormons believed their city a haven from religious persecution, they fought against federal troops in the Mormon War and struggled to gain respectability for a sect ridiculed and reviled worldwide for instituting polygamy. The success of the University of Utah, the connection of the Union Pacific Railroad with Utah's rail line in Ogden, and copper, silver, zinc, coal, iron, and lead mining promoted commerce and began smoothing the rough edges of a frontier town immersed in world trade.

Music was a spirit builder along the trail that led the pioneers west and bolstered them during the establishment of their homeland. In 1867, after fourteen years of labor, city fathers opened a grand performance hall, the Mormon Tabernacle. Built by volunteer labor, the edifice required grueling journeys by ox team from the granite quarry twenty miles northeast to deliver foundation stones one by one. The tabernacle was the first of a five-building complex at Temple Square that includes two visitor centers and an assembly hall. Forty years of labor culminated in the Mormon Temple, a six-tower worship center completed on April 6, 1893, and glorified by a landmark, sculptor Cyrus E. Dalin's golden Angel Moroni. Welsh director John Parry formally organized the world famous 350-voice Mormon Tabernacle Choir, which first performed on August 22, 1847. In 1849, the group welcomed 85 Welsh converts to their number.

Two tabernacles have served the Mormon's singers as base of operations. The first, erected in 1851, offered the music of a small Australian organ that Joseph Ridges installed in 1857. On September 1, 1865, the Latter-Day Saints began building the present facility. At the suggestion of Brigham Young, William H. Folsom, architect of the Salt Lake Theater and the Manti Temple, and bridge engineer Henry Grow designed and constructed the tabernacle. It employs architect Ithiel Town's lattice-truss arch system, a dowel and wedge support frame adapted from a bridge that spans a river west of Salt Lake City.

The tabernacle opened in 1867 with a 700-pipe organ built by Joseph H. Ridges and Niels Johnson. Truman O. Angell made changes in the interior to enhance acoustics and, in 1870, added a 30- by 390-foot gallery atop 72 columns and seating 2,000 spectators. The choir, led by London-born director George Careless and organist Joseph J. Daynes, emerged as a defining characteristic of Mormon worship. In 1880, under director Ebeneezer Beesely, the choir initiated tours to neighboring towns.

Near the twentieth century, the Mormon Tabernacle shucked off its mystique as a prairie utopia and entered the American mainstream. In 1895, the Reverend Anna Howard Shaw, a frontier orator and suffragist, gained permission to address worshippers. Before a gathering of stern Mormon bishops, she delivered a rattling sermon directed at the emancipation of women nationwide through the vote, which Utah had granted in 1870. During the tenure of director Evan Stephens, the congregation built the present choir loft on the west end to seat 600 singers, who achieved status as religious musicians. The Kimball Organ Company enlarged and upgraded the instrument in 1901; a second refurbishment by the Austin Company in 1915 carried services to midcentury, when George Donald Harrison designed the Aeolian-Skinner organ that shaped the choir's style and ministry.

ARCHITECTURE

Within a well-groomed park and promenade, the turtle-back Mormon Tabernacle, one of the West's most admired buildings, seats 8,000 people under an oval roof in an acoustically thrilling setting. Grounded on 44 sandstone pillars 3 feet thick and ranging from 14 to 20 feet high, the massive structure stretches 250 by 150 feet. The hemispheric ceiling, a unique sounding board, is a double shell of wood separated by 9 feet of open space supported by a trusswork of latticed timbers held together with wooden dowels. The finished roof stretches unsupported across 170 feet. In 1900, workers covered the original wood-shingled roof with an aluminum covering.

At center stands the American Classic style organ, a versatile instrument featuring 10,700 individually voiced pipes in 206 ranks. The pipes range in size from pencil length to 30 by 3 feet. Three full-time and two associate organists accompany choirs for religious services. Two professional technicians maintain the organ for daily half-hour 2:00 P.M. organ recitals, which the staff offers free to the public. For their pleasant informality, these noontime respites draw pedestrians, office workers, tourists, and regulars.

ACTIVITIES

Salt Lake City's tabernacle is a stake, or diocese center of worship, culture, entertainment, and recreation. According to Mormon philosophy, the building is a unifying agent of the family, a magnet of civic and religious life among Latter-Day Saints. Tabernacle staff schedules large assemblies and sermons, including the sect's general conferences. Tourists vie for seats at concerts of the Mormon Tabernacle Choir and attend Thursday evening rehearsals. Performances by

the Utah Symphony Orchestra, Utah Opera Company, and Salt Lake Oratorio Society round out a full calendar of fine music.

Late-twentieth-century performances have displayed the breadth of the tabernacle musicians' expertise. As part of the American Guild of Organists centennial, on April 14, 1996, the staff invited performers to the world's largest organ recital. From January 14 to 17, 1999, an American Classic Organ Symposium honored the tabernacle instrument's golden anniversary with recitals, lectures, discussions, tours, and a Sunday morning edition of the weekly *Music and the Spoken Word,* a live radio and television broadcast of song and inspirational messages. Begun in 1962, it reaches 1,500 stations worldwide.

Away from home, the Mormon Tabernacle Choir competed at Chicago's 1893 Columbian Exposition and performed for the first worldwide televised satellite broadcast, the November 24, 1963, memorial services for John F. Kennedy; the 1984 summer Olympics in Los Angeles; the American Bicentennial on July 4, 1976, in Washington, D.C.; the bicentennial of the American Constitution in 1987 at Philadelphia's Constitution Hall; and in Washington, D.C., and New York City at the 1995 fiftieth anniversary of the end of World War II. In addition, tabernacle singers have sung from Mount Rushmore, at Carnegie Hall, and in the 1952 film *Cinerama* and graced inaugurations of presidents Lyndon B. Johnson, Richard Nixon, Ronald Reagan, and George Bush.

Sources: Alsberg 1949; Ambrosino 1997; Broderick 1958; Florin 1969; Josephson 1999; Lewis 1998; Loofbourow 1964; Miller, Roger L.; "The Mormon Tabernacle Organs"; Ritter, "Mormons' Property," 1999; "Sacrament in the Mormon Tabernacle" 1871; "Temple Square."

Mosque Maryam
Louis Farrakhan, Minister
7351 South Stoney Island Avenue
Chicago, Illinois 60649
312-324-7619
www.noi.org/main.html

An agency for the empowerment of black people, Mosque Maryam stands in service to the be-

LOUIS FARRAKHAN

One of the most incendiary civil-rights activists and black religious leaders of the late twentieth century, Louis Farrakhan followed the failed visionary Malcolm X as the shepherd of the ascetic Nation of Islam. Born Louis Eugene Walcott in New York City in 1933, he came of age in the Roxbury section of Boston. After dropping out of college at age twenty, he married Betsy Ross and began a nightclub career as a guitarist and calypso singer. In 1955, he joined the Nation of Islam as a disciple of schismatist Malcolm X, became Minister Louis X, and altered his name to Louis Haleem Abdul Farrakhan. His wife took the name Khadijah after a desert entrepreneur who became the first wife and first convert of the prophet Muhammad. When black gunmen gunned down Malcolm X while he was delivering a speech on February 21, 1965, Farrakhan took his place as leader of the Harlem mosque.

After choosing radical black nationalism over the appeasement recommended by Wallace D. Muhammad, Farrakhan left the movement in 1977 and formed a separate Nation of Islam dedicated to strict personal accountability and economic self-sufficiency. In October 1985, he packed New York City's Madison Square Garden for a speech advocating pride, atonement, and self-reliance. He launched a self-help initiative called POWER, an acronym for People Organized and Working for Economic Rebirth, and opened the Salaam Restaurant in Chicago's slum district.

Today, only Farrakhan's 200,000 members use the name Nation of Islam. In 1991, he began radiation therapy for prostate cancer, which brought on severe fatigue and anemia. In April 1999, he recovered from surgery at Howard University Hospital while his lieutenant, Leonard Muhammad, took charge of denominational matters. Claiming a positive prognosis, Farrakhan planned a thirty-five- to forty-city tour to initiate another Million Man March in October 2000 despite news reports in the *Washington Post* that he is sicker than he admits. Although young rappers champion him and African Methodist Episcopalians formed a tentative alliance with the Nation of Islam to fight drugs and crime, Farrakhan lost stature in the media for anti-Semitism, threats against journalists, and virulent antiwhite hatred. His caustic rhetoric cost him the support of Jesse Jackson and reduced his body of disciples to a tenth the original number.

liefs and ideals of the Nation of Islam (NOI), a black separatist organization that mistrusts white America for its long history of discrimination and oppression. The internal struggles over philosophy and turf and the assassination of Malcolm X have weakened the original ideals of black nationalism and a separate territory for blacks. In the past decade, the mosque owes its survival to the vision and direction of a controversial leader, Louis Farrakhan.

BELIEFS

An inclusive, politically radical pressure group, Black Muslims bear little resemblance to orthodox followers of Islam. Black Muslims believe in one God and follow his teachings in the Qur'an. They follow Allah's prophets and expect his judgment and the resurrection of the righteous. For maximum liberation of blacks, they require separation of black and white societies, demand reparations for past oppression, and reject partic-

ipation in war. Members respect and protect women and the person of W. Fard Muhammad (or Wali Fard), to whom Allah appeared in 1930. It was Fard who established the Nation of Islam in Detroit in 1931.

According to Fard's followers' tenets, derived from Elijah Muhammad's speech "What Do the Muslims Want?," the aim of the original Nation of Islam is to attain the desires that date back to disgruntled American slaves: complete freedom, equal justice under the law, equality of opportunity, full employment and membership in society, freedom for Muslim prisoners, an end to police brutality and genocide, exemption from taxation, separate but equal schools led by black teachers, and an end to miscegenation, poverty, disease, hopelessness, and crime. A unique element of these beliefs is a demand for a separate black-owned state. In 1990, Farrakhan discarded plans for a separate black state in North America and turned the

Nation of Islam's hopes toward sub-Saharan Africa.

HISTORY AND ARCHITECTURE

Mosque Maryam has passed from leader to leader as the Black Muslims attempt to stabilize their following under tenets that will lead to a black renaissance. In 1972, Elijah Muhammad opened the Black Muslim Temple #2 in a former Greek Orthodox church, a stately structure surrounded by a wrought-iron fence and marked by multiple flat-roofed gables and four rectangular columns at the top of a sweeping stairway. Muhammad made the mosque and school the headquarters and national center of the Nation of Islam. At his death three years later, his son, Imam Wallace D. Muhammad, took charge and liberalized the Nation of Islam under the name of American Muslim Mission, which dropped racism to follow traditional Arabic Islam.

In 1977, Louis Farrakhan made a symbolic gesture by purchasing the Chicago mosque and the mansion of Elijah Muhammad. To return the faithful to the NOI's original beliefs, he rededicated the temple and revived the more conservative teachings of Elijah Muhammad. To express the sanctity of a place where worshippers are reborn in service to God, the temple took its current name in 1988 after Mary, Jesus' mother. In the dome, the Arabic words for "Allah is the Greatest" center an expanse lighted by a clerestory and surrounded by "There is no God but Allah." Around the dome appears "Al-Nur" (The Light), a favorite passage of the Qur'an from Surah 24:35–40. Adjacent to the sanctuary is Muhammad University of Islam, a coeducational K–12 academy.

Farrakhan advanced his own patriarchal philosophy and condemned homosexuality. He reinitiated the savings program of $10 per month begun in 1964 by Elijah Muhammad to fight hunger, unemployment, and inadequate housing. NOI members purchased 1,556 acres of farmland at Bronwood in Terrell County, Georgia, in December 1994. Named Muhammad Farms, it is part of a 4,500-acre farm once owned by the NOI until the 1970s. Staff has begun annual plantings and preservation of vegetables as the beginning of a general program of black self-sufficiency.

ACTIVITIES

Mosque Maryam communicates to members and interested parties through an online Afrocentric newspaper, the *Final Call,* online sale of books and tapes, an online self-directed study of the Qur'an, and sermons on radio and television covering gender issues, racism, American morality, and differences between Arab Americans and Black Muslims. The congregation supports the Nation of Islam Student Association [NOISA], which influences youth at forty U.S. college campuses and through affiliates throughout North America, South Africa, and Ghana.

Mosque Maryam is the setting for many of Farrakhan's speeches and media events, such as a special Jumu'ah prayer service on February 26, 1999. Larger crowds meet at McCormick Convention Center. During his sabbatical, his son hosted the annual Savior's Day in remembrance of Elijah Muhammad's birthday and welcomed the departed imam's son, W. D. Muhammad. On October 16, 1995, at the Mall in Washington, D.C., Farrakhan led a million black males in the first Holy Day of Atonement and Reconciliation, the largest audience ever commanded by a black speaker. Commonly known as the Million Man March, the gathering launched a campaign for responsibility toward self and family to counter drugs, gang violence, and unemployment. Among Farrakhan's challenges were a demand for more voter registration, the adoption of black children, a decrease in black-on-black crime, and an increase in service to the black community.

Farrakhan's Day of Atonement in mid-October 1997 asked blacks to observe the second anniversary of the Million Man March by abstaining from work and school to demonstrate the value of blacks to the nation. On the fourth anniversary in 1999, members began fasting at sunset October 15. At dawn the next day, families gathered to pray and read from the Qur'an about atonement and responsibility. At the mosque, they reconciled differences with fellow NOI congregants. NOI ministers and other leaders met with street-gang leaders to encourage peace and nonviolence. An evening gathering at the mosque concluded the two-day celebration.

Sources: Ahlstrom 1972; *American Decades* 1998; *Biography Resource Center* 1999; *Contemporary Black*

Biography 1999; "Evolution of a Nation"; Farrakhan; "Farrakhan Addresses Philadelphia Rally on Racial Healing" 1997; Harris and Strausas 1999; Hinnells 1984; "Imam W. D. Muhammad Joins Farrakhan Followers at Saviours' Day" 1999; Kelly 1997; "Louis Farrakhan"; Marable 1998; Muhammad 1998; Murray 1997; "The Nation of Islam"; "Nation of Islam Leader Minister Louis Farrakhan Takes Four-Month Sabbatical for Health Reasons" 1999; Noel 1999; "Woman's Civil Rights Lawsuit against Nation of Islam Is Thrown Out" 1999; *World Religions* 1998.

Mount Graham

Apache Survival Coalition
Ola Cassadore Davis
P.O. Box 1237
San Carlos, Arizona 85550
520-475-2543
FAX 520-475-2543

Robert Witzeman, M.D.
4619 East Arcadia Lane
Phoenix, Arizona 85018
602-840-0052
FAX 602-840-3001

The highest peak of the Pinaleno Mountains, southeastern Arizona's Mount Graham stands 10,720 feet, lifting its top above the Sonoran desert and a swirl of controversy over preservation and use of its 200,000-acre sacred geography. A segment of the Coronado National Forest still covered in virgin greenery, since 1869, the mountain has belonged to the San Carlos Apache Reservation. In 1871, Mormon settlers gained access yet maintained the sanctity of the land. It took twentieth-century greed to jeopardize the traditional spiritual landscape and required the leadership of people like Ola Davis, an elderly activist of the Apache Survival Coalition, to bring the matter of sacred space to public attention.

HISTORY

From prehistory, Dzil Nchaa Si An, the Apache's sacred mountain, has affirmed the faith of the San Carlos Apache. Isolated from the Mogollon Rim around 9,000 B.C., it was the home of mammoths. Around 1889 A.D., the red squirrel

claimed a habitat in the canyons where loggers removed prime timber. In 1894, Dr. J. A. Allen, curator of birds and mammals at the American Museum of Natural History, proclaimed a new red squirrel subspecies, *Tamiasciurus hudsonicus grahamensis,* found exclusively in the spruce and fir of the Pinaleno range. In addition, the mountain possesses nine trout streams and eighteen indigenous varieties of plants, insects, and animals found nowhere else.

From the 1930s, Apache nurses'-aid-turned-dissident Ola Cassadore Davis began frequenting Mount Graham with her father, a medicine man. He sang and prayed on the slopes, introduced her to tribal burial grounds on the summit, and gathered herbs and plants for traditional ceremonies. Ola's grandmother remembered visits from Geronimo, who revered Mount Graham. The sanctity of the place received its first threat from technology in midcentury, when homebuilding occurred simultaneously with the disappearance of the red squirrel. In the 1970s, biologists located at least four red squirrels about the time of the waning of timber harvesting. By 1976, the recovered red squirrel appeared on lists of endangered species, but federal lists did not target the squirrel for preservation until eleven years later.

The heart of controversy over Mount Graham began in 1981, when the Smithsonian Astrophysical Observatory and the University of Arizona tested Mount Graham among 280 possible sites for a new binocular telescope, the world's largest. In 1988, the university chose a 150-acre complex on Mount Graham for its low light pollution and formally announced plans for seven telescopes. U.S. Fish and Wildlife Service biologists warned that construction threatened the red squirrel's survival but sanctioned the erection of three telescopes on Emerald Peak. Government preferment of the telescope made it the first peacetime U.S. project exempted from the Endangered Species Act and the National Environmental Policy Act.

Dave Foreman, founder of Earth First!, was quick to condemn the sky-watching project; but, two months later, Congress exempted the university from environmental protection laws and okayed the building project. In April 1989, an unidentified "scope buster" confessed to the Arizona *Republic* that he axed a power pole to

The highest peak of the Pinaleno Mountains, southeastern Arizona's Mount Graham rises above the Sonoran desert and a swirl of controversy over preservation and use of its 200,000-acre sacred geography. (David Muench/Corbis)

retaliate for damage to Kitt Peak and that he was prepared to apply similar civil disobedience to save Mount Graham. That summer, the Sierra Club filed a lawsuit to halt the observatory. In 1990, university scientist Conrad Istock received a death threat if the project exterminated the red squirrel.

Protest moved into the courts in 1991, when the Apache Survival Coalition filed a federal lawsuit against the Forest Service to block construction as a violation of the American Indian Religious Freedom Act of 1978. Because of controversy and new information about high winds, the university sidestepped the Apache by changing the site of its planned telescope to East Emerald Peak, about 1,500 feet east of the original plot and beyond the congressionally designated 8.6-acre cluster. The U.S. Fish and Wildlife

Service and Forest Service sanctioned the modified plan in 1993. Father George Coyne, director of the Vatican Observatory in Tucson, further denigrated land-based faith and oral tradition by demanding material artifacts and/or shrines as proof that the land is truly hallowed. The university, led by president Manuel Pacheco, offered emoluments to the Apache—$90,000 worth of language classes, high-school equivalency courses, livestock management assistance, and a cultural museum—an act capable of dividing the tribe and creating ambivalence, thus weakening native opposition.

The university's offers preceded additional questionable acts. On December 7, 1993, its agents toppled 250 old-growth trees on their chosen site, a violation that angered Audubon Society president Charles J. Babbitt. Apache protester Diana Valenzuela disrupted dedication of the site for two hours by tying herself to a home-made timber tripod; others blocked the road by chaining themselves to cattle guards and gates while members of the American Indian Movement drummed a menacing cadence. Although former Apache councilman Buck Kitcheyan blessed the project, a year later, consensus in the academic realm wavered after the University of Toronto withdrew from partnership. In 1994, twenty-one environmental groups sued the University of Arizona over its destructive intent; fifty European astronomers petitioned the university to respect the holiness of Mount Graham.

Throughout bitter strife, the San Carlos Apache remained neutral, even though some of the members protested decimation of ground consecrated since prehistory. Chief among native concerns were access to herbs and water for ritual, desecration of holy land, and less than candid treatment of indigenous peoples concerning due process. Tribal Chairman Ned Anderson called for study of the telescope's impact on traditional religious practice and beliefs but received no formal reply. The environmental coalition won its first major victory on July 28, 1994, when U.S. District Court Judge Alfredo Marquez sided with protesters and against the university. Gradually, universities in Pennsylvania, Michigan, and Ohio drifted away from the project.

In summer 1997, an unexpected event altered public opinion about religious rights after the detention of Apache activist Wendsler Mosie for trespassing by praying on Mount Graham. He stated a belief that the mountain is sacred and has been for centuries. Interference with worshippers is, therefore, an obstruction of Native American religious practice and a violation of religious freedoms. Backed by medicine man Harold Kenton, Ola Cassadore Davis, and the Apache Survival Coalition, native spiritual leaders proclaimed Mount Graham a central religious site and opposed the telescope project as interference with their locus of prayer and meditation and a traditional Apache burying ground. Chris Peters of the Pohlik-Lah/Karuk characterized development as an act of physical and cultural genocide and charged that "the U.S. government has contracted with corporate America to destroy a sacred place." (Maynor and McLeod 1999, n.p.)

Spurred to action, Bob Witzeman, conservation chairman of the Phoenix-based Maricopa Audubon Society, submitted a petition to the United States Congress to spare Mount Graham from technological intruders. He considered Native Americans ill used and the environment compromised by the university's grandiose and self-serving building project. Under provision of the American Indian Religious Freedom Act, he called exclusion of the site from existing environmental laws unjustified and declared the cavalier attitude of authorities an insult to the San Carlos Apache and their love of the earth mother. Ola Davis contributed her support with a reminder that the style and nature of prayer on the site is private and not open to outsiders' interpretation or evaluation.

Sources: Abel 1996; "Battle of Wounded Me" 1994; Baum 1992; Cuevas 1991; Cummings 1993; "Discovery Park" 1999; Dougherty 1995; Jones 1995; Lampis 1999; Maynor and McLeod 1999; McGowan 1993; "The Mount Graham Case" 1999; "Mount Graham Time Line" 1995; "Native Rights Act before Congress" 1992–1993; Rambler 1997; Walsh 2000.

Mount Shasta

Steve Lewis
P.O. Box 649
Mt. Shasta, California 96067
http://vulcan.wr.usgs.gov/home.html

Mount Shasta Ranger District
204 West Alma
Mt. Shasta, California 96067
916-926-4511

At the juncture of the Klamath and Cascade Mountains and the Sierra Nevadas, the double peaks of Mount Shasta soar 14,162 feet into a massive scenic and religious landmark. A beautifully proportioned extinct stratovolcano, Mount Shasta harbors glaciers that feed the McCloud, Sacramento, and Shasta Rivers. Located forty miles south of the Oregon border in the Cascade Range and the Shasta-Trinity National Forest, the mountain is a traditional holy ground to the Karuk, Klamath, Modoc, Shasta, Umpqua, and Wintun of the mid-Pacific coast. From ancient times, the mountain has represented the power and majesty of creation and terrorized the superstitious with steamy vents, acidic hot springs, and fearful rumblings, which prefaced eruptions around 1300 and in 1786 and farther back at 600-year intervals since 2500 B.C. Vocal proponents such as Mark Franco of the San Carlos Apache, Chris Peters of the Poh-lik-Lah/Karuk, and Floyd Buckskin of the Achumawi treasure the slopes for their spirituality, healing plants and springs, and mystic sounds of native chants carried in the winds.

BELIEFS

Native reverence for Mount Shasta has a long oral history. In the Karuk version, a chief commanded his tribe to pile up dirt so he could climb it and view the Pacific Ocean. The people obeyed by carrying buckets of earth to one spot and heaping up Mount Shasta. They dug so much soil that they had enough left to toss into the plains, forming the hill country below. A Modoc creation myth—which mythologist Ella E. Clark draws from Hubert Howe Bancroft's *The Native Races* (1883) and Joaquin Miller's *Unwritten History: Life amongst the Modocs* (1874)—tells of a chief of the upper regions who wearied of heaven. To escape the cold clime, he opened a slit in the sky and poured down enough snow to make Mount Shasta. When the cold surface softened, he sculpted paths, streambeds, animals, and plants. The mountain so pleased him that he established his family's lodge on its slopes and built a big fire. His offspring founded earth's Indian tribes.

Other mythic accounts add a tinge of dread. According to native activist Ellen Furlong Crispen of the Cow Creek Umpqua, Tamanous (the Great Spirit), creator of Indians, forbade them to venture onto the volcano. He warned the Calapooia, Klamath, and Umpqua of an undisclosed evil. To this version, the Shasta add an embellishment about Thumb Rock, which extends from the eastern jut of Red Banks. A willful Indian maiden ignored her father's warning and climbed the forbidden mountain. When she froze to death, her icy thumb protruded from the slope. The story conveys a warning obeyed by aboriginal Californians, who admired Mount Shasta from the safety of the plain below. A trickster tale adds the antics of Coyote, who

tried to quell a nest of yellow jackets by stopping up the hole in the mountain. When pressure built up, the mountain exploded and radiated enough heat to cook Coyote's supper of salmon.

HISTORY

Over 100,000 years, Mount Shasta arose in a series of overlapping cones of lava, basalt and silicate rock, ash, and mud, which shroud an older cone formed around 280,000 B.C. Twin peaks formed around 8,000 to 7,000 B.C. In 1788, Pacific coast and Australasian explorer Jean-Francois La Pérouse recorded the exact date of the 1786 eruption. The Spanish explored in 1808, the Russians in 1812. Mountain men, lured by teeming game, began streaming into the Shasta area in the 1820s. The first European to explore Mount Shasta was Peter Skene Ogden, a member of the 1824–1825 Hudson Bay Company trapping expedition to northern Utah. In 1827, he named the mountain for the Shasta Indians. The Sutter's Mill gold rush brought an influx of miners in the late 1840s. In September 1854, Captain E. D. Pearce climbed the slopes and returned in October with a party of nine for a second survey.

When panners discovered gold in the Salmon and Klamath Rivers, the Shasta and Modoc fell victim to drifters and fortune hunters who uprooted and murdered indigenous people they deemed a hindrance to white settlement. Removal of the Modoc to Oregon's Klamath Reservation produced ill feeling. Because game became scarce, Chief Kintpuash, known as Captain Jack, led rebels to the lava beds of Tule Lake and countered a cavalry attack on January 17, 1873. He remained at large until June, when government agents apprehended him and sentenced him to hang. At his death on October 3, grave robbers stole his remains and exhibited them on a carnival tour. The Bureau of Indian Affairs banished Captain Jack's survivors to the Oklahoma Territory. In 1909, fifty-one returned to the Pacific reservation.

In 1888, Mount Shasta acquired an eloquent defender in John Muir, father of the Sierra Club, who proposed that the land remain fresh and unspoiled like Yosemite as part of the National Park System. Congressman John E. Raker was guiding a protective bill in 1914 when Mount Lassen erupted. National attention turned from Mount Shasta, leaving its fate in limbo. Under protection of the U.S. Forest Service, directed by Gifford Pinchot, it maintained its forests until the post–World War II housing boom, when business interests pressed for timber rights in national preserves. The prospect of shared revenues altered state thinking on virgin timber as loggers rushed to harvest prime stands of trees.

ACTIVITIES

Today, Mount Shasta is a variety vacationland. Some 15,000 climbers and 100,000 adventurers annually enjoy skiing, camping, rappelling, photography, and bird-watching. Northeast of the mountain, they visit the metal figures of Living Memorial Sculpture Garden, a tribute to peace. As did their ancestors, native worshippers seek the mountain's peaceful sanctuary and gather in Pluto Caves and Panther Meadows, a mile-long stretch leading to Panther Spring, a holy site and the source for Panther Creek. Priests lead a ritual world renewal through sharing of first fruits, blessing a new fire, and preventing disease and calamity. They share the sanctity of Mount Shasta with a variety of vibration kinesiologists, herbalists and holistic healers, channelers, spiritualists, mystics, and millennialists who find answers to mysteries of the universe in the rugged slopes, lava cliffs, waterfalls, and healing springs. In 1979, author Andrew Weissner declared to the Congressional Lands Subcommittee that Mount Shasta has a spiritual value and unique soul. In 1984, his counsel led to declaration of the area as part of the National Wilderness Preservation System.

Near the end of the twentieth century, to halt clear-cutting of Mount Shasta's black forests of pine, fir, and juniper, local people protected the mountain by petitioning government officials to name it a National Historic Landmark, free from development and road building. In 1993, the Wintun, aided by the Cultural Conservancy, forced the U.S. Forest Service to study Panther Meadows as a sacred medicine site for nomination to the National Register of Historic Places. Their action delayed development of a forest service ski resort.

In a historic decision, in 1998, Lynn Sprague of the U.S. Forest Service halted Carl Martin's plans for a complex calling for a ski resort, a golf course, condos, a shopping center, and an RV park by declaring the land sacred from prehistory. Finding in favor of activist Michelle Berditschevsky, forest supervisor Sharon Heywood, the Sierra Club, the Audubon Society, the Save Mount Shasta coalition, and medicine man Charlie Thom and Gloria Gomes of the Wintun tribe, Sprague revoked Martin's permit on July 28, 1998. She noted that the Karuk revere the mountain as the creator's home and a source of healing plants and materials for baskets; the Pit River tribe believe that the creator will return to earth on the slopes when the mountain's snows melt and the world is rejuvenated. The Shasta continue a long heritage of honoring the place where the creator rested after molding the world. Shasta spokeswoman Mary Carpelan compared the locale to the Garden of Eden and declared it no place for a theme park. Caleen Sisk-Franco of the Wintun warned, "When you take Mount Shasta, you're taking the heart of the whole creation—what holds the world up." (Maynor and McLeod 1999, n.p.)

The victory for Mount Shasta brought hope to native groups hanging on to decimated and devalued holy places worldwide. Berditschevsky summarized the shift in public attitude to a microcosm of end-of-century issues involving stewardship and reverence for earth, reemergence of indigenous life ways, and reverence for the interconnected life web. As sacred sites on a par with Mount Fuji and the Himalayas, the Mount Shasta summit and Panther Meadows are eligible for inclusion in the National Register of Historic Places.

Sources: Abbott; Allen 1966; "Battle of Wounded Me" 1994; "Chronology of California History"; Clark 1953; Collins 1991; Crispen 1999; Cummings 1993; Davie 1996; Freeman 1997; "The Impact of Proposed Amendments to the American Indian Religious Freedom Act on Other Uses of Public Lands"; Mathes 1998; Maynor and McLeod 1999; McKee 1854; Miller, Joaquin, 1998; Milne 1995; "Mount Shasta Eruptive History"; "Mt. Shasta Ski Area Becomes Past History" 1998; "Native Rights Act before Congress" 1992–1993; "Sims Flat History Trail"; Snodgrass, *Encyclopedia of Frontier Literature,* 1997; Steele 1997; Steiger 1974; Waldman 1990; Walker 1998.

Mount Tabor Retreat Center

Sister Joan Barthel
150 Mt. Tabor Road
Martin, Kentucky 41649
606-886-9624
mtabor150@hotmail.com
www.geocities.com/athens/9871

On a mountainside between Prestonsburg and Martin in southeastern Kentucky, the Benedictine sisters of the Dwelling Place Monastery maintain a modest respite—the Mount Tabor Retreat Center. As a contemplative, uncloistered monastic community of women, the sisterhood devotes itself to serving others. Under the Rule of Saint Benedict, they share a reverent, hospitable life with oblates, volunteers, and visitors. The modest monastery fosters interfaith dialogue and respects all people's beliefs.

As was true of isolated sisterhoods of the Middle Ages and Renaissance, the success of the retreat center has been serendipitous. The sisters describe themselves as risk takers and good listeners who share sanctity as their major gift to troubled people. Rooted in godliness, they teach, counsel, tend the sick, welcome guests, and minister to the parish and retreats.

HISTORY AND ARCHITECTURE

A daughter house of the Benedictine Monastery at Ferdinand, Indiana, the Mount Tabor Benedictines came to the Appalachians in 1979 to found a house of prayer. Their impetus was the Appalachian Bishops' pastoral letter, *This Land Is Home to Me* (1979), which declared:

> Appalachia makes us think of people who live in the hills, who love nature's freedom and beauty, who are alive with song and poetry. But many of these people are also poor and suffer oppression. ("Catholic Committee of Appalachia")

To maintain a mission to the mountain poor, the sisters have taken up residence in the community. They live in a pleasant wood-frame building fronted by a modest arch and four-column porch surrounded by a low flagstone wall. They maintain Mountain Christian Academy, a private Christian school, and offer classes for the mentally handicapped, ministry to the parish, and a small retreat center.

The center, known as the Transfiguration Oratory, is an octagonal wood structure that functions like a sundial. Encircled with windows, it admits light over 360 degrees at the same time that it admits a stirring view of the mountains. On the second floor, a library houses books and journals on spiritual and biblical topics plus a collection of videos of retreat directors and speakers. Individuals and groups from all faiths can arrange assemblies, faculty or staff orientation, mother-daughter retreats, spiritual direction, and school and volunteer groups who want to experience a women's monastic community. The staff helps groups with secretarial duties and summer camps and teaches library skills. The cost for retreats is $25 per day, including three meals. Those who can't afford tuition and board pay only what they are able.

Outdoors, a free-form Benedictine cross by Jared J. Bradley of the University of Kentucky combines ornamental iron in an expressive symbol of faith. The four-piece swirl departs from the standard straight arms to balance earth with sky in an imploring gesture toward heaven. Nearby, the center maintains a meditative nature walk over the Way of the Cross. The tranquil, meandering path blends rocks and trees for an experience in events of Christ's life and death. Beyond the community is Glenwood Hermitage, a small cabin with a private kitchen beyond the monastery garden. A visitor seeking solitude can pray, read, or write without interruption. The sisters keep chickens and a vegetable garden.

ACTIVITIES

The sisterhood supervises oblates, voluntary or lay residents of a monastic community living under modified rule to join in the religious experience or stewardship. Membership is open to any volunteer, married or single, without dependent children. The staff requires a year dedicated to learning before an individual becomes a lifetime oblate. Newcomers to the community share morning and evening prayer, meals, indoor and outdoor duties, hospitality to guests, and ministry under the Benedictine rule. After a three- to six-month probation, each oblate un-

On a mountainside between Prestonsburg and Martin in southeastern Kentucky, Benedictine sisters maintain a modest respite, the Mount Tabor Retreat Center, a contemplative uncloistered monastic community. (Courtesy Mount Tabor Benedictines)

dergoes evaluation every six to twelve weeks and subsquently every six months.

Projects and involvement vary with the gifts of the individual. Under the direction of Sub-prioress Eileen Schepers, the sisters support St. Luke's parish in stocking an emergency food pantry and used-clothing store, particularly items for infants. Sister Kathleen Weigand directs the St. Vincent Mission in David, Kentucky, a ministry of the Brother of Charity in Philadel-phia. Begun in the 1960s, the mission sells mountain crafts at the David Craft Center, stocks a used-clothing store and food pantry, and collects a scholarship fund for needy students. The Christmas Store offers appliances, cloth-ings, shoes, tools, toys, and other gift suggestions to low-income shoppers.

Other evidence of creative stewardship en-hances the work of the sisters among local fami-lies. In May 1999, Sister Judy Yunker proposed a local farmers' market to offer fruits and vegetables to enhance a healthy diet in the area. The Martin city council agreed and opened a co-op outlet the first and third Saturdays of August and Sep-tember. A more difficult challenge is the need for public transportations for the poor in Appalachia. The sisters have proposed a fund to help families repair their cars and have begun gathering other suggestions to aid disadvantaged people who have no way to get to work or appointments.

Sources: "Catholic Committee of Appalachia"; "The Dwelling Place" 1997; Gabriel 1998; *New Catholic Encyclopedia* 1967; "Transportation Dilemma" 1999.

N

Nappanee Missionary Church
Dave Engbrecht, Senior Pastor
70417 State Road 19
P.O. Box 110
Nappanee, Indiana 46550
219-773-7773
FAX 219-773-2727
nmc1@nmc1.org
www.nmc1.org/

Nappanee Missionary Church is a typical evangelical paradox—a Christian assemblage limited in funds and outward show but grand in its zeal to disseminate the New Testament promise of eternal life worldwide. In the first-century missionary tradition of Paul and Silas, Nappanee runs on a pervasive idealism. Rather than glory in a showplace sanctuary or stained-glass windows, members exult in the number of babies dedicated, converts baptized, ministries launched, and mortgages burned. The group's goal is mission in the biblical sense—a generous sharing of the gospel through prayer, commitment, and teamwork. With fervor, the congregation flaunts a visionary motto: "Our greatest days are just ahead!"

HISTORY

The activism of American mission churches parallels the enthusiasm and resourcefulness of the nation itself. Beginning in the mid-nineteenth century, a diverse, optimistic surge in outreach catapulted congregations into a global undertaking. Their prime objective was the spread of Christianity and proselytization of groups the devout deemed "lost," particularly Native Americans and the peoples of China and sub-Saharan Africa. The certainty of fundamentalists that their crusade is the only road to the afterlife

promised in the New Testament spurred them to grandiose campaigns to convert huge geographic areas, including large cities in the United States, and targeted populations, particularly Mormons.

In the midst of overeager expansionism, the Nappanee Missionary Church got its start in the late 1870s from Daniel Brenneman, a local preacher. A hazy history omits details of its modest beginning until the tremendous growth years in the last decades of the twentieth century, when fundamentalism experienced a new boom and self-confidence following the sexual revolution and a decline in mainstream church attendance. The church relocated in July 1981 after a two-year construction campaign. Within four years, the congregation doubled the size of the sanctuary; three years later, members added the Family Life Center. A Youth Ministry Center dedicated to "Building a Generation of Champions," a Worship Center, and a worldwide mission campaign highlighted the 1990s, when membership rose to 2,000 and targeted home and foreign mission fields rose to 15.

ACTIVITIES

Led by Dave Engbrecht, senior pastor, and five associate pastors, the Nappanee Missionary Church maintains a full schedule. Sunday worship at 8:15 and 10:45 A.M., Small Church and Kids' Kingdom at 9:30 A.M., and evening Gospel Hour at 7:00 P.M. begin the week, followed midweek with Family Night on Wednesday at 7:00 P.M. Services are available over WFRN, WLRX, and WLNB radio on eleven frequencies. The church holds summer baptismal services at Wagner's Pond, which conclude with music, fellowship, and food. Additional activities unite groups by age and gender for prairie camp, coffee break Bible study on Tuesday morning, Wednesday night practice of the Worship Choir, and weekly ladies' and men's prayer breakfasts on Friday morning. Interest groups range from quilting to aerobics.

In 1999, the staff chose as the annual theme "Building Godly Families," a response to domestic disintegration, through mentoring couples, bolstering spirituality in children and youth, and pastoral teaching through family-centered sermons. On Father's Day, staff sponsored a showing of Billy Graham's film *A Vow to Cherish*. For preschoolers, the Learning Center, a child-pleasing space featuring walls painted with jungle and barnyard animal motifs, houses a structured two-hour Sunday school featuring toys, books, puzzles, and guided conversation. Similar to those in Christian kindergartens, lessons center on the Bible and human-interest stories that apply biblical truths along with memory verses, music, and activity sheets. Annually, the center offers Halloween alternative programs and vacation Bible school. A special outreach targets special-needs children. The youth ministry prepares the most studious for the Missionary Church Bible Quiz championship, which the church team won in 1981.

The Nappanee congregation supports missionaries in the United States, Ecuador, Peru, Venezuela, Bolivia, Jamaica, Puerto Rico, Kenya, Mali, India, Nepal, Kosovo, Romania, Russia, and Hungary. At home, the staff initiated a ministers-at-risk program, renewed partnerships with mission churches, and held a homecoming reunion. Children collected funds to buy copies of a Bible picture book, *Leading Little Ones to God,* to send to Romania.

To sustain the Life Trac Ministry, the congregation broadcasts on closed-circuit television to Greencroft Retirement Center in Goshen, Indiana, distributes audio cassettes of services, and airs a weekly half-hour radio program entitled *Fanning the Flame.* Each segment begins with interactive conversation between pastors and advances to a sermon. Popular series include "Developing a Well-Ordered Heart," "Confronting the Spirit of the Age," and "The Ten Commandments." The first recordings, made reel-to-reel in the sanctuary balcony in 1986, now take shape in a modern, climate-controlled studio featuring audio software and computerized video. Producer Andrew Patton is planning nationwide distribution through linkage to other Missionary Churches and exploring cable television outlets.

Local ministries take pastoral teams to Atlanta's Campus Crusade and the Southside Missionary Church as well as the Keller Park church in South Bend, Crystal Valley in Middlebury, New

Hope in Valparaiso, Southside in Mishawaka, and Tree of Life in Gary and additional outreaches to Warsaw, Plymouth, and the Meadows community. Thirty members carry lay ministries to two nursing homes, dispatch a birth team to visit the families of newborns, offer taxi service to patients undergoing chemotherapy and radiation treatment, and help single parents plan a course of study. In September 1999, the church sent members to the North Central District Women's Retreat, planned a Christmas shopping trip, and hosted the African Children's Choir.

Sources: Ahlstrom 1972; "Annual Report" 1998; "Nappanee Missionary Church"; "WFRN Ministry Links."

Nation of Islam
See Mosque Maryam.

National Cathedral
See Washington National Cathedral.

National Shrine of the Infant Jesus of Prague
Father Adrian Vorderlandwehr
St. Wenceslaus Church
304 Jim Thorpe Boulevard
P.O. Box 488
Prague, Oklahoma 74864-0488
405-567-3080; 405-567-3404

After three centuries of veneration in Prague, the *Infant Jesus of Prague* lost its safe altar in Europe when the Iron Curtain closed off Czechoslovakia from the free world in February 1948. The famous figurine found a home among free people in the American Midwest at St. Wenceslaus Church in Prague, Oklahoma, where it resides on a golden throne behind the main altar. Since that time, the sacred figurine has received the visits and prayers of pilgrims worldwide and binds the devout in holy fraternity.

HISTORY
The *Infant Jesus of Prague* is a nineteen-inch sacred statue formed out of cloth and wax-covered wood. The faithful have crowned it with gold and posed it in a yard-high silver case.

The babe epitomizes the divine infancy of Jesus Christ. His priestly pluviale, or ceremonial cloak, covers a white undershirt, white linen rocheta, or surplice, and silk tunic; he raises his right hand in a papal benediction. To express the gift of God's son to humankind, in his left hand, the Christ Child holds a golden globe surmounted by a cross.

The figurine and its broad pedestal were a commission of Spain's royal family. In 1556, the Countess Maria Manriquez de Lara, wife of Czech Nobleman Vojtech of Pernstejn, presented the statue to her daughter, Princess Polyxena, to accompany her to a new country upon her marriage to Count Vratislav Lubkovice (or Lobkowitz) in Prague. In widowhood in 1628, Polyxena Lubkovice devoted her life to piety and charity. Out of pity for the Discalced Carmelite Fathers at the Church of Our Lady of Victory, who lost support after their founder, Emperor Ferdinand II, moved to Vienna, she gave them the treasured statue, which became a favorite of novices.

The figure stood at the altar, where Cyrillus a Matre Dei (Brother Cyril of the Mother of God) championed it in twice daily devotions and composed beautiful novenas to it. Because King Gustavus Adolphus of Sweden invaded and ravaged Czechoslovakia in 1630, the Carmelites abandoned their monastery and fled to Munich, Germany, where their community languished. When anti-Catholic looters ransacked the Prague sanctuary, they broke the Christ figure's fingers and tossed the maimed wax figurine behind the high altar. After the Carmelites reclaimed the monastery seven years later, Brother Cyril, who had been ordained Father Cyril, retrieved the holy figure from the trash and replaced it on the altar of the oratory in 1637 at the Feast of Pentecost. He heard a voice promising "Have pity on me and I will have pity on you. Give me my hands and I will give you peace. The more you honor me, the more I will bless you!" (Ball 1994, n.p.)

The statue suffered a precarious history. Cyril acquired donations from a rich nobleman and had an artist replace the badly buffeted figure, which was believed to have interceded in the illness of one of the monks. On the first day of its veneration, a candle flame damaged the second model. Cyril heard the statue order him to set it aside. A wealthy man passed it, noticed its sad state, and paid for repairs. An artisan restored the figure, which again spoke to Father Cyril and was believed to have aided the priory during an epidemic.

The statue rose in prominence. In 1641, a benefactor paid for an altar to the Blessed Trinity and commissioned a gilded tabernacle to house the statue. The next year, a baroness built a chapel for the statue, which the monks dedicated on the feast of the Most Holy Name of Jesus in 1644. The day has remained the statue's principal feast day. In 1648, the bishop of Prague approved the figure's veneration. The Martinic family sponsored a procession in 1651 from the Church of Our Lady Victorious to all the churches in Prague. In 1655, the Archbishop of Prague in solemn ceremony crowned the statue with a tiara presented by Bernard Ignac of Martinic, the supreme burgrave of the Czech kingdom. After a miraculous cure of a nobleman's daughter, in 1788, the family presented the statue two jeweled rings and a wig of blond or possibly white human hair. When worshippers regularly revered the figure, the religious community thrived and the infant's fame spread from Bohemia throughout Europe and the Americas.

Since a cholera epidemic of 1713, throughout the canonical year, the devout have clothed the statue in appropriate liturgical robes and cloaks to manifest his beneficence. In 1741, the statue moved to its current shrine, which drew pilgrims from around the world. Pope Leo XIII affirmed the Sodality of the Infant of Prague in 1896 and granted indulgences to its devotion.

Dressing the infant became the work of the devout, who assembled a wardrobe of seventy changes from seamstresses around the world. Empress Maria Theresa and Emperor Ferdinand donated an outfit suited to Thanksgiving. The honor of changing the garments belongs to the nuns from St. Joseph's Church in the Mala Strana sector of Prague, who place fresh garments over a silver sheath that protects the bottom half of the wax surface. On changing day, the dressers touch medals, pictures, and rosaries to the statue and distribute them to Catholics worldwide. The figure's original robes remain on display in a museum.

THE MORE YOU
HONOR ME

THE MORE I WILL
BLESS YOU

NATIONAL SHRINE

After three centuries of veneration in Prague, the Infant Jesus of Prague lost its safe altar in Europe and found a home among free people in the American Midwest at St. Wenceslaus Church in Prague, Oklahoma. (Courtesy National Shrine of the Infant Jesus of Prague)

The Catholics of Prague, Oklahoma, established a church in 1899. In June 1909, Bishop Theophile Meerschaert dedicated a new church under the patronage of Saint Wenceslaus, the Czech patron. In March 1913, Pope Pius X granted an exclusive privilege to the Confraternity of the National Shrine of the Infant Jesus of Prague to display the sacred figurine. In 1947, the Prague congregation received a copy of the *Infant Jesus of Prague* during a medical crisis in the family of Father George V. Johnson. The figurine has blessed members ever since. In 1949, the shrine received a new designation as the National Shrine of the Infant Jesus of Prague.

The purpose of the shrine is to promote devotion to the boyish statue for pious meditation and contemplation of Jesus' life. The figure protects innocence and guards the faithful from worldly corruption. Members of the Confraternity of the Infant Jesus of Prague wear a special medal and recite three times daily a prayer and call, "Divine Infant Jesus, bless me." Members receive mention in the shrine's masses and devotions, gain plenary indulgence on obtaining membership and again at their death, and acquire partial indulgence on preparing children to receive penance and the Eucharist.

ARCHITECTURE

Northeast of Oklahoma City on Highway 99, the modern shrine combines the humble materials and boxy shape of Southwestern mission architecture with the bold thrust and monochromatics of modernism. A monument to the shrine at the entrance combines a rose marble base and a circle depicting the Western Hemisphere. To the right, the blank wall ties adjacent structures into a pleasing whole. A white marble figure of the Infant Jesus of Prague tops the circle. In the Meditation Garden, a brick wall encloses a courtyard and enhances the restrained grace of a statue of the Virgin Mary holding the infant Jesus. To each side, miniature angels kneel in prayer.

The mix of structures of varying height gives the impression of a religious compound. To the left, a blank wall fronts a square four-story tower alongside the shrine basilica. Beneath a two-story portico and austere brown cross, the portal opens on the chapel beneath a stained-glass window of the Infant Jesus and alongside a sec-

ond glass window of St. Wenceslaus preserved from the former sanctuary. These and six other windows are the work of the Nobis Studios of North Canton, Ohio. They honor the Czech Republic, the survival of the statue, petitions to the figurine, and establishment of the New World shrine. At the altar, the little king himself stands on a pedestal alongside models of his parents, Mary and Joseph, and before the papal and American flags. A hand-carved altar screen depicts the twelve mysteries of Christ's infancy and childhood.

Beyond the sanctuary lies the baptismal chapel, with its carving of the Sacred Heart, relics of the Holy Cross and manger of Bethlehem, and cabinets containing the figurine's festal garments, chaplets, and crosses. Pictures of Maria de Lara and her daughter Polyxena adorn the entryway.

ACTIVITIES

Today, the figure of the Little King of Prague, which survived perilous times, assists those in difficulty. Throughout Christendom, replicas of the Infant of Prague perpetuate his devotion at shrines, churches, and homes in Europe, the Americas, the Philippines, China, and Vietnam. The U.S. shrine, at Prague, Oklahoma, forty miles east of Oklahoma City, receives thousands of pilgrims and regular members of the confraternity daily from 7:00 A.M. to 7:00 P.M. An association publishes a monthly newsletter and accepts petitions to the Infant Jesus. Donations maintain the shrine and support a mission to Santiago Atitlán, Guatemala.

In honor of the figurine, the staff holds twelve regular novenas at the shrine at 1:00 P.M. as well as the prayers of the chaplet, litany of the Divine Infant, blessing of children and the sick, and benediction of the sacrament. Visitors celebrate weekday mass at 8:30 A.M., a Sunday vigil at 6:00 P.M., and Sunday mass at 7:30 and 11:00 A.M. The Eucharist is available on Friday at noon. Pilgrimage Sunday falls between the seventeenth and twenty-fifth day of the month and concludes at 1:00 P.M. with lunch in Pilgrim Hall. The gift shop, open Monday through Friday from 9:00 A.M. to 4:30 P.M., sells copies of the statue as well as crucifixes, medals, Bibles, baby gifts, and children's books.

Recent activities, such as a prayer chain, teen angel meetings, and visits to nursing homes, epitomize the importance of the shrine to area Catholics. Many Czech visitors came for the May 1, 1999, Kolache Festival at City Park, where they enjoyed kolaches and klobasy, entertainments at a beer garden, a costume contest and parade, arts and crafts, a carnival, a polka street dance, and the crowning of the prince and princess. In October, the women's altar society served an annual meal for the Knights of Columbus and Catholic Daughters. The parish joined with members of the United Methodist Church on November 18 for a community Thanksgiving service. At the November 21 service, the sick came for anointing. On January 2, 2000, the parish took part in a Jubilee Mass uniting Oklahoma Catholics.

Sources: Ball 1994, Hastings 1951; "History of the Church Maria and St. Antony of Padua—Infant Jesus of Prague"; *New Catholic Encyclopedia* 1967; "Prayers to God the Son"; Raymond; "Shrine of the Infant of Prague."

Native American Church

c/o Walter Echohawk Religious
  Freedom Campaign
Native American Rights Fund
1506 Broadway
Boulder, Colorado 80302

Virtually out of sight of most people, the Native American Church is the spiritual focus of a quarter million Indians. Unlike other religious sites, it is a pan-Indian moveable feast with no fixed sanctuary beyond the hearts of the faithful. At the core of sacrament is peyote, a hallucinogenic cactus that is the heart of much Native American creation lore, such as the Apache story of the Dream People.

Despite the church's importance to indigenous people, white society tends to relegate peyote to indulgence and decadence, outside the realm of legal sacraments. Some critics interpret the spiritual phenomenon as a bizarre form of drug abuse or New-Age extremism. In defense of peyotism, Ted Strong of the Yakima nation declared the herb as the source of "four powers—love, hope, charity, and faith." (Smith and

Snake 1996, 41) Such polarized positions on the peyote faith are often the result of a racial boundary derived from ethnocentrism and disgust at unfamiliar rituals at odds with mainstream religion.

BELIEFS

According to Native American Church leader Reuben Snake, a Winnebago from Nebraska, native worship is eternal and always available for strength and solace. This sense of permanence derives from creation, when the first humans experienced nature's sights, sounds, smells, and textures. The magnitude of creation so filled prehistoric beings that they concluded that Grandmother Earth was a gift from a wondrous creator God. To live up to the honor of a vibrant land, they pledged to put the creator first in their lives and attune themselves to the harmony and rhythms of nature.

To refresh belief in God's generosity, Snake followed a daily ritual that he learned in boyhood from his grandparents. After rising from sleep, his family stood quietly outside their dwelling before sunrise. As the sun appeared at the horizon, they lifted their hands to the creator in thanks for another day. In anticipation of fault, they acknowledged weakness and begged forgiveness before disturbing earth's harmony in search of food, shelter, and clothing.

Snake stressed that peyote is the sacred herb or medicine that strengthens the faith of native animists. According to legend, peyote is the most powerful of the creator's plants because it bears God's love and compassion. Thus, worshippers sit humbly on the ground in a circle around a sacred fire to consume peyote. This ritual act puts the physical loving force of God inside the human body and radiates outward an abundance of tenderness, joy, love, and respect.

HISTORY

A cultural unifier among Native Americans, sacramental consumption of peyote dates into prehistory, when seekers on a vision quest entered a period of solitude. One ancient cache located in a Texas cave dates to 5000 B.C., making peyotism at least 7,000 years old. The pan-Indian belief derived from the pre-Columbian culture of the Aztec, Huichol, and Mexica of the Rio

Grande valley. Amid the despair caused by diminishing buffalo herds in the 1850s, it spread across the Rio Grande valley to tribes of the Great Basin. In the 1890s, medicine men like John Wilson of the Caddo and Quanah Parker of the Comanche formalized peyote ceremonies to aid Indians during the hardships of their displacement and loss of land to whites. The practice of peyotism reached pueblo and plains tribes around 1919 and became the belief system of 75 percent of the Shoshone. Early devotees made an annual hunt for sacred buttons, a source of life consumed only for ritual and ceremonial purposes. Later, seekers traded with *peyoteros,* harvester-dealers who sold dried buttons by mail or in person.

Peyote ceremonies have evolved among plains Indians as formal worship circles conducted in tipis, hogans, or houses designated as sacramental centers. The syncretism of peyotism with facets of Christian worship has lent a legitimacy among seekers who need the approval of the white world. The umbrella group that sanctioned peyote consumption was the Firstborn Church of Christ, forerunner of the Native American Church, which incorporated in Oklahoma in October 1918. The implications of an organized church was an intentional cover to dissuade European-American proselytizers from labeling Indian worship as savage or uncivilized. Unaltered by white evangelism, by 1970, the Native American Church became the largest and most influential Indian religious body.

An ungovernable church structure split into four large divisions: the Native American Church of North America, Native American Church of Navajoland, Native American Church of Oklahoma, and Native American Church of South Dakota. Chapters formed around trained clergy. Services require the guidance of a road chief, who supervises navigation of the peyote road, a metaphor for a lifestyle in harmony with nature. Among the beliefs of members are clean and ethical living, loyalty to family, and abstinence from alcohol.

Peyote has frequently run afoul of antidrug laws, which forbid consumption by non-Indians. Also unlawful is the collection of peyote by unlicensed individuals. A Montana judge upheld a 1923 antipeyote ordinance in 1926 and ruled that consumption for religious ritual did not justify eating a dangerous controlled substance. A more favorable judgment in California in 1962 concerning a raid on peyote-based worship in Needles resulted in a sanctioning of the drug for legitimate religious ritual. One peyotist, Johnny White Cloud, took peyote with him to Vietnam and depended on it during paratroop and scuba diving maneuvers. In his words, "The medicine took me over there and it brought me back." (Smith and Snake 1996, 553)

Despite the long history of peyotism, near the end of the twentieth century, confusion prevailed. In 1990, the U.S. Supreme Court ruled against the free exercise of religion in *Employment Division v. Smith.* The case involved two Indians, Alfred Smith and Galen Black, working in an Oregon drug-treatment program. Authorities fired them and denied them unemployment benefits in punishment for sacramental use of peyote in the Native American Church. Exonerated by the Oregon Court of Appeals, the two saw the judgment overturned by the Supreme Court, which ruled that peyote carried religious diversity from a right to a luxury. Outraged, Native Americans launched a congressional bill, the American Indian Religious Freedom Act of 1993.

Still unclear, the legality of the use of peyote by members of the Native American Church finally reached resolution on October 6, 1994, when, at the urging of Reuben Snake, President Bill Clinton signed a law legitimizing use of the substance as part of traditional Indian worship services. Abraham Spotted Elk, president of Wyoming's Native American Church, declared the legislation a boon to Indians, who can pray and worship openly without fear. However, in spring 1995, news reports of a peyote shortage due to depletion of native cactus threatened the very source of peyotism.

ACTIVITIES

The peyote religion is both extremely personal and uniquely Native American in its revival of shamanic experience. Unlike mainstream faiths, it has no administrative center, church buildings, or ordained clergy. Its veneration of peyote expresses a belief that nature is a living entity that can rid Indian worshippers of soul-deadening white philosophy and confer blessing and strength through a hallowed act. Blended with facets of Christian fundamentalism, it currently unites Indians of all tribes in worship, celebration of weddings and births, baptisms, memorial services, and acknowledgement of graduations and service in the armed forces.

As peyotism is practiced at the Taos Pueblo, believers in peyote's supernatural power assemble at night to eat cactus buttons and pray. They also may steep peyote in a tea. Celebrants use a water drum to begin a male-centered prayer meeting and absorb its vibrations like earth's reassuring heartbeat. The hallucinogen instills psychic change furthering fellowship and a sense of racial solidarity. The ritual Cedar Man cleanses his hands with sage and sprinkles incense in the fire to purify the atmosphere and warm the peyote. Amid smoking of tobacco, drinking water, singing, and drumming, the practitioners of peyotism continue until dawn, when Water Woman, a female appointee, and her fellow servers pour water and offer a ritual breakfast of corn, beef, and fruit to renew life.

The segregation of women does not exclude their use of peyote. Patricia Mousetrail Russell, a Southern Cheyenne, says she joined in peyote worship in childhood under the guidance of her grandfather. According to a Lakota mother, Loretta Afraid-of-Bear Cook, the sacred herb is an essential to parturient women. When labor begins, ingestion of peyote calms and centers their minds on the birthing process. In Cook's experience, the drug deepened bonding with her child and made her a more responsible parent. Truman Daily, an Otoe-Missouri Indian, stated that his mother ate peyote before he was born and immediately served him peyote tea to envelope him in peyotism from the first moments of life. Eva Gap reported a similar sacramental use of peyote when her grandmother was dying. The old woman ate peyote while her family prayed. She chose a holy death to return to the earth mother, just as she had begun.

Sources: Ahlstrom 1972; Anderson 1996; Biskupic 1993; Carmody and Carmody 1993; Champagne 1998; Collins 1991; Cuevas 1991; Heinerman 1989; Kelley and Francis 1994; McGowan 1993; "Native American Religion"; "Peyote Bill Signed" 1994; "The Peyote Religion"; "Peyote Shortage Strikes Native American Church" 1995; Smith and Snake 1996; Steiger 1974.

Old Mission of the Sacred Heart
Old Mission State Park
P.O. Box 30
Cataldo, Idaho 83810
208-682-3814

Bob Bostwick, Press Secretary
Coeur d'Alene Tribe
850 A Street
P.O. Box 408
Plummer, Idaho 83851
208-686-1800
bostwick@nidlink.com

The oldest building in Idaho, Old Mission of the Sacred Heart, like other Native American religious sites, functions as both a park and a shrine of the Coeur d'Alene, a Salishan or Shuswap people who originated near Vancouver. Located a mile east of Cataldo between Montana and Washington within the historic 120-mile-long Silver Valley, the 18-acre campus lies in Coeur d'Alene heartland along a complex of sacred waterways. From these waters come trout and salmon for sustenance and water for therapeutic sweat baths, a healing and spiritually transforming ritual dating to antiquity.

Situated in the Idaho panhandle along the Oregon Trail, the Old Mission borders land that prospectors once searched for gold. Today, the mission is the site of an annual pilgrimage that attests to the Jesuit spirit of assimilation and acceptance. Because the missionaries who first encountered these isolated villagers were open to the local lifestyle, they made fast friends and quickly acclimated the Coeur d'Alene to Roman Catholicism, which has remained the predominant native faith for over one and a half centuries.

HISTORY

The coming of Catholicism was not a surprise to the Coeur d'Alene. In 1782, a shaman of the Upper Spokane, Yureerachen (Circling Raven), had a vision of the arrival of the Black Robes, the native name for Jesuit missionaries. After the death of his small son from small-pox, the grieving father undertook a ritual four-day fast in the wild that brought him a puzzling message from the creator. He saw in the future a new people—white men, dressed in black, marked with crossed sticks on their belts, and carrying a sacred book. Because the coming of these pale-skinned strangers preceded a dramatic upheaval in Indian life, Circling Raven kept the vision to himself. In 1790, following a volcanic eruption that terrorized the tribe, he divulged that they would not die of falling "dry snow," their term for ash. He explained his vision in terms of the great change that awaited them.

After the Iroquois began working for the French as employees of the Hudson Bay Company, they settled in the northern Rockies among the Flathead, or Salish, of Montana. The newcomers bore encouraging news of the medicine and power of missionary Black Robes. In native terms, a band of Jesuits prayed to a powerful God and understood the mysterious diseases brought by Europeans that devastated indigenous people. In 1831, the Flathead of Bitter Root Valley, mindful of Circling Raven's prophecy, eagerly dispatched the first of four delegations to St. Louis to learn about the European religion and about combating disease.

At Council Bluffs, Iowa, in 1840, two devout church messengers—Ignace La Mousse and Peter Gaucher—encountered a Jesuit evangelist, Father Pierre Jean de Smet, from Termonde, Belgium, who sought assignment among the Flathead. A peacemaker and teacher, Father de Smet received welcome from Circling Raven's grand-daughter and some 1,600 others, who had already set up a tent for him. In anticipation of fulfilling prophecy, they circulated a calumet as a gesture of friendship and hospitality. He met with Chief Twisted Earth, a grandson of Circling Raven and adherent of the old man's vision. On

July 29, 1841, at Henry's Lake, at what is now the western terminus of Yellowstone Park, Father de Smet celebrated Idaho's first mass with the territory's first Catholics.

To encourage donations for the mission project, Father de Smet wrote letters about a peaceful arrival among a willing tribe of converts. He described how they occupied a beautiful valley rich in pine and camas roots, a staple in the Indian diet. To achieve his mission, he began baptizing and educating the Flathead and Pend d'Oreille and, on September 24, 1841, established St. Mary's Mission near Missoula, Montana. Among his early accomplishments was the translation into native tongues of the Lord's Prayer, Hail Mary, Ten Commandments, and Acts of Faith, Hope, Charity, and Contrition, which he taught to converts.

De Smet's assistants, Father Nicholas Point and Brother Charles Huet, a carpenter, planned a village complex featuring public fields and roads. First, they founded the Sacred Heart Mission, a bark structure later named De Smet Mission. They set up mission headquarters at the site and entrusted local religion for the 100 Christian families to the Reverend Joseph Joset, vice-provincial of the Missions of the Northwest and a valued peacemaker during the Indian War of 1858. Father Point preserved the mission's activities in a watercolor picturing the baptism of an Indian, the first picture of a Spokane. The old man had struggled over twenty miles on snowshoes to receive the sacrament. Within a decade, the Coeur d'Alene had developed from having a low standard of living to prosperity from their mastery of agriculture, herding of milk cows and beef cattle, and woodcutting.

ARCHITECTURE

The original log church at Mission Point on the St. Joe River, built in 1842, failed to survive annual flooding. In 1847, Father de Smet planned a new mission for a grassy knoll above the South Fork of the Coeur d'Alene River as part of a mission chain over the Northwest. The building, a massive undertaking that 300 Indians constructed between 1848 and 1853, was the design of Father Antonio Ravalli of Ferrara, Italy, a physician and jack of all trades. It arose from sheer wilderness and startled unsuspecting prospectors and pioneers with its ornate mission façade, burst of rays surrounding the Greek monogram IHS, and six Doric columns supporting the porch roof. A soldier and road builder, John Mullan, proclaimed it "a Saint Bernard in the Coeur d'Alene Mountains." (Florin 1969, 104)

Beloved by natives as their "House of the Great Spirit," the church lies alongside a parish house, trail, and cemetery. Its foot-thick adobe walls, composed of straw and river mud, extend ninety by forty feet and forty feet high. Native workers, male and female, ferried rocks and pine logs to the site by handcart, where finishers applied a broad ax for planing and shaping. Willow withes lashed the steep roof to the walls and uprights. Hand-carved wooden pegs attach doors, joists, beams, and fittings, including Ravalli's statuary and carvings at each side of the altar.

Split logs formed steps leading to the porch. Inside, Father Ravalli's carvings of the Virgin Mary and Saint John the Evangelist top pillars at the entrance. To suit native tastes, he supplied an open, pewless room, where people preferred to squat on the timber floor to hear Bible stories. He built three altars and covered the walls with flowered cloth. For decoration, he mounted a sacred heart at the center beneath a semidomed apse. Alternative versions of the mission's history state that he either created or imported European depictions of heaven, hell, and the fourteen stations of the cross as adornment of the side altars. His assistant, Brother Huybrechts, carved seventeen panels and placed them in the ceiling himself. By the time of its dedication in 1852, the finished church astounded the local people with its grandeur.

By 1865, Father de Smet had completed nine missions when Father Joseph Cataldo arrived in Idaho. In 1867, Cataldo began evangelizing the Nez Perce at Lapwai. He established a church for whites, St. Stanislaus, in Lewiston and built the first Catholic church for the Nez Perce at Arrow Beach. To broaden the education system, he opened a school for whites and Indians at the mission run by the Sisters of St. Joseph and followed with Gonzaga College in Spokane, Washington, so students would have a thorough preparation.

Despite natural and political crises, the mission project prospered. Weeptes Sumpq'in, or

Eagle Shirt, chief of the Siminekem and a convert to Catholicism, donated land for St. Joseph's Mission at Slickpoo at the confluence of the Snake and Clearwater Rivers. In 1877, the U.S. government resettled the Coeur d'Alene to the south, away from their homeland and the beloved Old Mission and cemetery. The complex remained dear to them; however, after the tribe ceded its lands to whites, buildings collapsed from disuse. In 1930, the Knights of Columbus of Idaho completed restoration with a new roof and split-log steps, supports for the portico, an upgraded foundation, and a repaired façade. In 1962, the U.S. Department of the Interior listed the mission as one of a few National Historic Landmarks in Idaho.

ACTIVITIES

Since 1975, the mission building has come under administration of the National Park Service. Park staff maintains picnic grounds, tours, a visitor center, and a museum exhibit on the history of the Coeur d'Alene. The environs are a popular wedding spot and provide 1,000 miles of trails for hiking, mountain cycling, snowmobiling, and Nordic skiing. Unfortunately, the pristine waters that greeted pioneers long ago gave place to milky runoff from over 100 silver, zinc, and cadmium mines that have produced more than $5 billion worth of ore since 1884. During two world wars, the area reached maximum productivity while providing raw material for the manufacture of tanks and artillery. These boom sites continue to pour toxic residue into the Coeur d'Alene River and its tributaries.

To preserve the area's bounty, natives have begun protesting the metallic tailings that cloud local waters. They have hired their own biologists and chemists to assess damage from decades of ill treatment to Silver Valley. In conjunction with the federal Department of the Interior, Department of Agriculture, and Environmental Protection Agency, Indians are forcing the state of Idaho to cleanse the watershed. The current estimate of sediment thirty feet thick at the bottom of the lake and river indicates lead and zinc levels as high as 50,000 parts per million, 1,000 times the government's accepted level of heavy-metal contamination. Scientists declare the metals hazardous to wood ducks, swans, and Canadian geese and suspect that some humans living near the watershed have lost their ability to reproduce.

Native lawsuits to reclaim Lake Coeur d'Alene and protect the watershed forced one of the nation's largest clean-up projects to sustain a fragile ecosystem. According to tribe liaison Henry SiJohn, pollution has caused anomie by the uprooting of an indigenous people and destruction of their culture and lifestyle. Tribe biologist Phil Cernera belittles the small commitment of the four remaining mining companies and the state of Idaho to battle a massive lead problem. Local natives insist that the Natural Resource Damage Assessment turn over management to the Coeur d'Alene, who have a clean record of using and protecting natural resources.

The Coeur d'Alene maintain the Old Mission of the Sacred Heart and its adjacent cemetery as an integral part of their culture. In late spring, the sanctuary is the site of annual graduation exercises of Our Lady of Victory School. Each year on August 15, the Coeur d'Alene hold a reunion and renewal ceremony at the Old Mission by celebrating the Feast of the Assumption. The day begins with a 60-mile pilgrimage by land and river from the reservation at Palmer, Idaho. In 1999, at the Coming of the Black Robes pageant, thirty marchers followed the bearers of the eagle staff and crucifix and a contingent of Catholic priests. Participants camped, took part in an outdoor Mass of the Angels, performed a ritual thanksgiving dance before the Eucharist, prayed in sign language, and observed a blessing at the old cemetery. Native emcee Cliff SiJohn invited all 1,000 guests to a free meal of traditional frybread, corn, salmon, and smoked meat of three deer and an elk.

The annual pilgrimage affirms Catholic and native beliefs. In the words of Rose Goddard, "Indians celebrate both the religion they come from and the newer spirituality." (Shireman 1999) Participants wear traditional regalia for an afternoon powwow that includes drumming, singing, dancing, and storytelling. At the 1999 observance, Father Thomas Connolly dressed in beaded gloves and moccasins to join the tribal dance. He praised mutual acculturation, which brought Christianity to Indians and whites a new appreciation of family and the environment. Tribal chairman Ernie Stensgar reminded worshippers of their reliance on the creator and the sacred ground of the mission, where tribal heroes are buried. In tribute he declared, "This is the heart of Coeur d'Alene." (Shireman 1999)

Sources: Alsberg 1949; Anderson, Hilda, 1999; Barbato; Buchanan 1999; Cantor, George, 1993; Champagne 1994; "Chronological History of Idaho"; Cody 1930; "Coeur d'Alene Indians"; "Diocese of Boise"; Fanselow; Florin 1969; "Fur Traders and Missionaries"; Hayes 1996; "Idaho Indian Reservations"; *New Catholic Encyclopedia* 1967; "Nez Perce National Historical Park"; "Old Mission State Park" 1996; Patterson and Snodgrass 1994; Ruby and Brown 1970; Shireman 1999; Sullivan 1967; "Summer Listings" 1996; Titone 1997; Wakley 1998; Waldman 1990.

Old North Church
193 Salem Street
Boston, Massachusetts 02113-1198
617-523-6676
www.oldnorth.com

Immortalized in Henry Wadsworth Longfellow's patriotic poem "Paul Revere's Ride" (1863), Boston's Christ Church is forever identified as Old North Church. The term was loosely applied to the city's northernmost house of worship, but the name stopped changing hands after construction of Christ Chapel. Proportioned, elegant, and much beloved and photographed as a tourist attraction, it is a functioning Episcopal church and the city's oldest sanctuary. Its location at North End facing the confluence of the Charles and Mystic Rivers and Boston Harbor links it with Constitution Wharf, Old Ironsides's berth, Faneuil Hall, and streets that Massachusetts patriots once walked.

HISTORY
Established near the graves of the activist Mathers—Cotton, Increase, and Samuel—Christ Church influenced New England and American history. Having evolved from Boston's original Meeting House, the first Anglican congregation moved to the north end of town after outgrowing the original quarters at King's Chapel, built on Boston Common in 1686. Thus, Christ Church became the first Anglican church home in the colonial city.

Boston's tallest church spire tops the historic Old North Church. (Courtesy of Old North Church)

Staff looked to their sacred mission while involving themselves in city planning. Choosing an Essex County pasture alongside Copp's Hill Burying Ground and near Central, King's Chapel, and Granary cemeteries and the busy wharf area, they built on an ideal location. Before Dr. Timothy Cutler's new pastorate took shape, the Reverend Samuel Myles, rector of King's Chapel, laid the church cornerstone on April 15, 1723. Book dealer and cabinetmaker William Price, a gentleman-amateur architect, appears to have adapted the 71- by 51-foot floor plan from drawings of St. Andrew's by the Wardrobe Church in Blackfriars, London, drafted by Christopher Wren, England's foremost church architect of the 1660s. The projecting tower was the design of American architect Charles Bulfinch, who planned the Massachusetts State House.

Most of the materials came from the colonies. Draymen hauled timbers from York, Maine, for the square, fluted columns, which support each bay of the galleries. Boosting spirits among Ebenezer Clough's work crew was one free beer each as part of a day's wages. At the center of the nave ceiling, they hoisted brass chandeliers that Captain William Maxwell donated in 1724 to light the center aisles. Decked with a dove of peace, each bore twelve candles, which ushers lit for morning and evening services. The unusually tall box pews sheltered worshipers from drafts. Additional heat from portable foot warmers made two-hour services more comfortable.

On December 29, 1723, standing at the pedestal pulpit, Dr. Cutler preached Old North Church's first sermon. The church sold seating to individuals and families for their personal use and decoration. Parishioners donated an octagon-faced clock, which remains in service on the rear gallery wall below the organ stall and polished organ pipes. In 1746, privateer captain Thomas James Gruchy offered four polychrome cherubs hoisting trumpets, which flank the organ. Carved in Belgium, the statues arrived aboard the *Queen of Hungary* as part of Gruchy's share of cargo pirated from a ship bound for a Catholic convent in Canada during the French and Indian War. In 1759, the church replaced its secondhand organ with a new instrument built by Thomas Johnston.

Central to church and United States history is the 197-foot wood spire above the brick steeple, Boston's tallest. Completed in 1740, the 24-square-foot tower stood empty until church wardens John Hannmock, Robert Temple, Robert Jenkins, and John Gould solicited funds to add eight bells. Cast in 1744 by Abel Rudhall at a foundry in Gloucester, England, they bore name, date, and citations honoring local donors and the Church of England. One inscription proclaims, "The first ring cast for the British empire in North America, 1744." (Broderick 1958, 10) The finished octet hung in the ringing room a year later and could be heard across the Charles River at Harvard University. On September 13, 1757, John Childs, a Boston inventor, used the belfry as a command post for three test runs of his flying machine. The events drew such interest that selectmen banned future exhibitions, which distracted townsfolk from their work.

Although the steeple has required two replacements and numerous repairs, the site holds a place in colonial legend for its use in warning

DR. TIMOTHY CUTLER

Founded during a rocky period for denominational allegiance, Christ Church owes its formation to Dr. Timothy Cutler, an orator, logician, geographer, and Episcopal minister from Charlestown, Massachusetts. Born May 31, 1684, to Martha Wiswall and anchorsmith John Cutler, he came from strong tory stock. He completed college training at Harvard at age seventeen and, at age twenty-five, assumed the pastorate of the Congregational church of Stratford, Connecticut. Under the influence of John Checkley, he converted to Episcopalianism. A decade later, he accepted a call as rector of Yale College, where he succeeded his father-in-law, the Reverend Samuel Andrew.

Cutler thrived in a job that allowed him to cut a grand figure. The rectorship suffered from dissent in 1722 as Congregationalists sought entrance into the Church of England. College trustees voted to suspend his appointment until church elders could determine doctrinal matters concerning the Saybrooke Confession of Faith. Cutler concealed his allegiance until he had assurance of a pulpit in the established church. After ordination in London in 1723, he completed doctor of divinity degrees from Oxford and Cambridge.

Somewhat overeducated for parish work, Cutler retained an English priggishness and offered no sympathy to dissenters. He returned to Massachusetts to accept the pastorate of Christ Church, which was in its formative stage. Declared one of New England's prominent clergy, he demanded a position on Harvard's governing board as a teaching elder but lost his case in court. He remained at the Christ Church post until his death on August 17, 1765. Cutler published no writings and left only four sermons as evidence of his life's work

the local Sons of Liberty of advancing Redcoats. Since age fifteen, Paul Revere, Jr., a Congregationalist whose family lived at North Square, two blocks away, had been a founding member of the bell ringers' society and was involved in the spread of rebellion as far away as New York and Philadelphia. Longfellow enhanced Revere's historic prerevolution signal with a galloping dramatic monologue:

He said to his friend, "If the British march
By land or sea from the town to-night,
Hang a lantern aloft in the belfry arch
Of the North Church tower as a signal
     light,—
One if by land, and two if by sea;
And I on the opposite shore will be,
Ready to ride and spread the alarm
Through every Middlesex village and farm,
For the country folk to be up and to arm."

According to the poet, on the night of April 18, 1775, Revere climbed the familiar ladder, gazed out on the serene streets below, and then secured two lanterns as a signal to patriots to prepare for invasion.

The truth is less romantic. Revere, a forty-year-old veteran of the French and Indian War, was a courier for the Massachusetts Committee of Correspondence. He arranged with Dr. Joseph Warren to signal the advance of General Thomas Gage and 700 British regulars from Boston up the Charles River to Cambridge. Protected by vestryman Pulling, Robert Newman, the sexton, climbed the ladder to hang two lanterns to betoken invasion by water. In an instant, he doused the light and climbed out a window to elude the British watch.

Revere, who silently rowed around the British man-of-war *Somerset* and across to Charlestown, saddled a borrowed Narragansett pacer at 10:00 P.M. for the two-hour gallop to the Hancock-Clarke House thriteen miles away in Lexington. His mission was crucial—to warn Samuel Adams and John Hancock of an imminent landing at Long Wharf and to prevent the duo's arrest for treason. At 1:00 A.M., Revere and two backup messengers set out for the second leg of their ride. Although a British cavalry patrol apprehended Revere, his companion, William "Billy" Dawes, escaped and completed the mission. Revere later gained his freedom and twice crossed the Mystic River to continue spreading the alarm to colonists living along the road to Concord.

The event prefaced the Redcoats' march on Lexington Green the next day to seize the colonial arsenal, dispensary, and pantry. Because of the patriots' preparation, Captain John Parker's 77 minutemen greeted the invaders with a spontaneous rifle volley. In poetic terms, the day's engagement was the "shot heard round the world," the onset of the American Revolution, but it preceded hard times and a chancy six-year struggle. During the siege of Boston, the British fired on seventeenth-century tombstones for target practice and commandeered the church spire as an observation post of battle and supply lines. At war's end, Old North Church returned to patriot hands and, on October 19, 1781, rang out with joy Lord Charles Cornwallis's surrender at Yorktown. In 1878, patriots erected a tablet to Revere on the church façade.

ARCHITECTURE

In two and a half centuries, Old North Church has changed with the times without losing its unique architecture. Built Georgian style during a period of prosperity in 1725, the structure is one of the earliest stone churches in Essex County. It required 513,654 bricks formed in a double English Bond pattern at the nearby kilns of Medford, Massachusetts. The walls are six inches thick. The designer capped the door with a fan and embellished the spire with a gilded codfish. The edifice also houses twenty-five pieces of sacramental silver crafted by William Jones and Paul Revere, both noted silversmiths and engravers. In 1815, the congregation acquired unusual ornamentation at the apse end that remains on view: James Penniman's painting of Jesus at the Last Supper and copies of the Ten Commandments, Lord's Prayer, and Apostles' Creed.

The interior is distinctive for its Georgian simplicity and dignity. The chancel separates into four rows with three aisles dividing some fifty box pews, although the sale of family pews ended in 1912. A plaque on the left wall of the sanctuary notes a visit from hymnographer Charles Wesley in 1736; another, Major Robert Pitcairn's plaque on the right wall over his tomb in the crypt, cites the British marine major who led Redcoats at the Battle of Bunker Hill and for whom the penal island of Pitcairn is named. In the rear gallery, the adult choir occupies pews designed for 150. For day services, large clear-paned windows let in natural light; evening services retain the softness of candlelight, which flickers from wall sconces.

In 1989, renovators removing brick from the tower discovered the original steeple window where Newman hung his lanterns. Within a rounded arch, the structure displays the dignity and colonial beauty of the times. The congregation honored its past with the Third Lantern, which President Gerald R. Ford lit on April 18, 1975, to commemorate the fight for freedom. Altar rail kneelers, which the Massachusetts Chapter of the American Needlepoint Guild designed and stitched in 1989, soften the sturdy interior with pictures and phrases reflecting church history. In 1990, A. David Moore restored the organ, which he placed in the original cabinet, built in 1759.

External features that reflect ties with the nation's founding include a bust of George Washington, the first public memorial to the nation's first president, now located over the vestry door. The eight steeple bells, restored in 1894 and 1975 and still rung by hand, announced the Boston Bicentennial and began a regular schedule of service. Located next door in the former Chapel of St. Francis, which was built to serve Waldensian Italian immigrants, the museum and gift shop display church documents and the massive Vinegar Bible, which King George II donated in 1733. The book earned its nickname for a printing error that misnamed "The Parable of the Vineyard" as "The Parable of the Vinegar." In the 1970s, the congregation honored the Waldensian presence in Boston with a chapel garden.

Additional plantings soften the brick structure. Within the church complex lies the Eighteenth Century Garden, which replaced brick residences the church razed after World War II to expand the church grounds. Adjacent to the Clough House, Boston's oldest brick residence built in 1712, trustees renovated terraces and brick walls in the late 1950s. Plantings of the antique White Rose of York, licorice-flavored angelica, night-scented dame's rocket, tall-stalked Siberian iris and foxglove, filigreed love-in-a-mist, pincushion flowers, climbing sweet pea, and other perennial seeds and shrubs produced a living glimpse of period style. Since 1995, volunteer gardeners have maintained the project. On the north side, the cloistered Washington Memorial Garden welcomes people following Boston's Freedom Trail. The Beacon Hill Garden Club tends the beds and secures its commemorative plaques. On the shady side, the Third Lantern Garden presents pedestrians with a memorial fountain and access to a columbarium, which houses cremated parishioners near thirty-seven colonial gravesites beneath the church.

ACTIVITIES

The congregation of Old North Church takes seriously its religious mission to the neighborhood and its historical significance as an official National Historic Landmark. It has participated in celebrations of the city's founding and the American Revolution and in a lantern-lighting on the annual April 18 Patriot's Day, when the chosen lighter bears two symbolic lanterns down the aisle and into the steeple. Commemorating the church's past, the Fellowship of the Lantern Light contributes to church preservation and receives notice of special events, news, and issues of the *Old North Steeple.*

Planning sessions center church energies on balancing worship and tourism into 2001. With local donations, a matching grant from the Massachusetts Historical Commission, and funds from the Children of the American Revolution, a national patriotic youth organization, members intend to paint and install new lights in the steeple, regild the Shem Drowne weathervane, and reclaim structures on Salem Street as a three-story education center and office. Vital to the capital project is the restoration of 1850s appointments and a new entrance from the Washington Courtyard.

The church invites religious tourists to pray and meditate from 9:00 A.M. to 6:00 P.M. daily. A full schedule offers three Sunday services, a Wednesday morning service, and staff to baptize, marry, and make emergency calls. On Sundays and festive occasions, a professional choir performs in tandem with instrumental specialists in medieval and modern music. To accommodate visitors seeking to park in the crowded tourist center, the church provides validated parking on Sunday from 8:00 A.M. to 1:00 P.M. The gift shop stocks pewter memorabilia, books, woodcuts, flags, and other items of religious and historical significance.

Sources: *Biography Resource Center* 1999; Broderick 1958; Buchanan 1999; Burns 1997; "The Catholic Encyclopedia" 1997; "Christ Chapel/Old North Church"; Ehrlich and Carruth 1982; *Encyclopedia of World Biography* 1998; Hoss 1999; Johnson and Malone 1930; Ketchum 1957; Longfellow; Mutrux 1982; "Old North Church"; Rose 1963; Sinnott 1963; Smith 1989; Williams, Peter W., 1997; Williams 1999.

Old Swedes Church

Reverend Anne Bonnyman, Rector
606 Church Street
Wilmington, Delaware 19801
302-652-5629
www.oldswedes.org/index.htm

One of the nation's longest-lived Protestant churches, Old Swedes Church of Wilmington, Delaware, has been in constant service since 1698. A testament to the faith of Swedish Lutherans, it came under the jurisdiction of the Protestant Episcopal Church in 1791. Congregants identify the original church, called Helga Trefaldighet Kyrcka, as the nation's oldest in constant use—home to colonizers of New Sweden, the Dutch of New Amstel, the English in New Castle County, and the American citizens of Delaware.

HISTORY

Aboard the *Kalmar Nyckel*, Swedish colonists arrived in the New World on May 28, 1638. After negotiating with Lenni Lenape tribe members, they founded a burying ground, marked with carved wood, slate, sandstone, and fieldstone, and erected Fort Christina on the Christina River, named in honor of the Swedish queen. The nation's first Swedish Lutheran minister, the Reverend Reorus Torkillus, arrived in 1640.

In 1647, the Swedes, led by the Reverend Lars Lock, founded Tranhook (Crane Hook) Church on the riverbank. In 1655, Swedish pioneers surrendered to Dutch invaders who rejected their attempt to build a Lutheran church. The structure sufficed until 1698, when parishioners of Pastor Ericus Bjork erected Old Swedes Church adjacent to the original cemetery. The church, supported by the Swedish Missionary Society, earned some notoriety as temporary quarters for the Redcoats after the Battle of the Brandywine in 1777.

Except for regular burials in the cemetery—including those of a secretary of state, an ambassador, a mayor, a ship captain, a scoutmaster, a war hero, a doctor, a senator, and an Episcopal bishop—the site remained unchanged for sixty years, when the congregation added a stone fence and iron gate at the Seventh Street entrance. By the 1850s, they constructed adjacent residences for the vicar and sexton at Seventh and Church Streets and an archway leading to the graveyard. In 1893, the property acquired a parish house, which survived the razing of the older manses and arch in 1947. The members celebrated a year-long tricentennial in 1999 with a June 7 Eucharist, a commemorative granite table on May 28, and holiday veneration of Sankta Lucia and decoration of a Swedish Christmas tree at the Hendrickson House on December 12.

ARCHITECTURE

As do many churches surviving from colonial times, Old Swedes, in its thirty- by sixty-foot frame, blends authentic details such as Swedish brick, oyster shell bricolage, and a Delaware blue granite foundation with modern upgrades. The black-walnut pulpit, the nation's oldest church pulpit, and the accompanying canopy were the work of Philadelphia cabinetmaker Joseph Harrison. Above the sounding board, a hand-carved dove betokens the affection of a modern Swedish congregation. A black-walnut altar, the church's third, is a modern addition. Woodworkers completed the enclosed raised pews in 1899 using patterns of original furnishings, which protected worshippers from drafts. In Old World style, occupants separated at the center aisle, with men sitting at the right and women at the left.

The upper and lower reaches gained additional light from small panes of clear glass, replaced by stained-glass memorial windows late in the nineteenth century. Above the sanctuary, a central brass chandelier was a gift from an Irish abbey church in the mid-1960s. It illuminates the bricks below, set in a herringbone pattern, where the original congregation may have placed a Christmas tree to prevent fire. Later, trustees installed a stove to augment warmth from bricks and pocket stones, which were heated and wrapped before the attendee left home. A church chest, dating from 1713, stored documents, valuables, and the church treasury and required two keys to open it. Heavy metal fittings exemplify the need for security. The south door locked with a key; other doors fastened with wooden bars.

Steps from the south porch and gate lead to a balcony, added in 1774. Around it hang portraits of the first pastor, the Reverend Pastor Bjork, and his two immediate successors. Music for the sanctuary issues from a sixteen-rank neo-classical pipe organ built by the Austin Company of Hartford, Connecticut, in 1965. Rooms lining the sanctuary fill in gaps between brick buttresses, which the practical Swedes turned into usable space. The prim, square bell tower dates to 1802, when church trustees removed the thirty-five-pound bell from a walnut limb and placed it in more dignified surroundings.

The twentieth century brought additional changes and losses. In 1958, the congregation moved the Andrew Hendrickson House, home of a Swedish farmer and his wife and eight children, from Chester, Pennsylvania, to the church site for restoration and use as church offices and a small museum. One exhibit displays a scale model of the ship *Kalmar Nyckel,* a gift of citizens of Kalmar, Sweden. In 1963, the U.S. Department of the Interior declared the church a National Historic Landmark. In recent years, loss of original trees to disease has marred the European *allée* planting that once adorned and shaded the cemetery. The Old Swedes Foundation is undertaking a replanting project with trees indigenous to the original colony.

ACTIVITIES

Old Swedes, currently known as Holy Trinity Episcopal Church, offers services on Sunday at 9:30 A.M. (10:00 A.M. in July and August). For a fee of $2 per person or $75 per bus, guides direct tours Monday through Saturday from 10:00 A.M. to 4:00 P.M. The gift shop features handmade Swedish ornaments, crafts, dolls, linens, and books. The church honors the tradition of Saint Lucia, a mythic figure, named from the Latin *lux* (light), who walked abroad with can-

dles in her hair on the winter solstice, around December 22, the darkest evening of the year. She symbolizes love, compassion, and light. The Swedish festival of Sankta Lucia, brought from Syracusa, Sicily, by Mediterranean sailors, reanimates Lucia's goodness and purity with a family tradition. To announce the Christmas season, the eldest daughter dresses in a white gown and red sash at dawn and leads her siblings to their parents by candlelight to serve them all coffee, ginger cookies, and *lusse*-bread.

Additional commemorative events hosted by the Delaware Swedish Colonial Society maintain ties with the past by promoting culture and preserving archival material. On March 29, members lay a wreath at the rocks at Fort Christina Park, where the *Kalmar Nyckel* first reached the New World, and host a luncheon, annual meeting, and election of officers. In June, they celebrate Midsommarfest with music, food, dancing, and the raising of a flowered pole in honor of summer. In fall, the society holds a smörgåsbord seminar, discussion, and lecture or film on a topic of historical interest. Annually around December 13, members gather once more at Old Swedes Church to welcome Lucia, bringer of light.

> **Sources:** Ahlstrom 1972; "American Swedish Historical Museum"; Bishop and Darton 1987; Blow 1967; Buchanan 1999; "Delaware Swedish Colonial Society"; "Kalmar Nyckel"; "Old Swedes Church."

Oraibi

Hopi Tribe's Office of Public Relations:
Box 123
Kykotsmovi, Arizona 86039
520-734-2441 ext. 190 or 191

A living Hopi community, Oraibi, also called Old Oraibi, preserves a centuries-old religious tradition. Located in Navajo County in northeastern Arizona, at an elevation of 6,500 feet, Oraibi Pueblo sits within the 1,840,000-acre Navajo reservation and serves the narrow Third Mesa of the Hopi Indian Reservation as an unofficial capital. Lower Oraibi occupies the base of Black Mesa and encompasses a native elementary school and trading post.

BELIEFS

The Hopituh, or "Peaceful Ones," observed a tradition picturing the underworld as a haven. Before creation, it was a huge sea, where the Hurung Whuti (a pair of goddesses)—one to the east and the other to the west—lived in round underground chambers similar to the Hopi kiva. They owned all beauty, consisting of turquoise, coral, and seashells. The sun wore one goddess's gray fox hide at dawn, then put on a yellow skin as morning grew light. At nightfall, the sun jostled the western goddess's turtle-shell rattle before climbing down the sky ladder.

This duo of goddesses proposed a stretch of dry land. Overhead, the eastern deity slid over the rainbow to the west to confer with the western goddess about creating life. From common clay, the two goddesses formed a wren and sang the life-giving songs that would make it fly. They dispatched it across earth to search for living beings before constructing more fowl and four-footed animals. The eastern goddess fashioned male and female humans, dressed them in cloth, and gave them life and a language so they could talk to each other. The western goddess made a new set of people to inhabit the west.

Just as the goddesses do, the Hopi, offspring of the first people, treasure the beauty of turquoise, coral, and seashells to remind them of their origin. They look to the San Francisco Mountains as the dwelling place of divinity. In honor of the spot on earth from which their ancestors emerged, they make sacred pilgrimages to the world's *sipapu,* the egress from the Hopi underworld, in a canyon at the confluence of the Little Colorado and the Colorado Rivers.

The early people's guardian, Masaw, offered the Fire Clan and the Bear Clan four sacred tablets that instructed them to journey into the world. Dividing into subclans called the Coyotes and the Parrots, they migrated south. Their kachinas (benevolent spirits) led them back north to Palatkwapi (Red House) in Central America, helped them build earth homes, and taught them about history and nature. When evil invaders forced them to flee, the clans followed the kachinas' instructions and settled in the San Francisco Mountains southeast of Flagstaff, Arizona. They dwelt in safety and peace and used their pahos (prayer sticks) to communicate with the kachinas, who disappeared forever from sight. To preserve in their memories the sacred beings' appearance, the Hopi made masks and costumes of each spirit. The marriage of a comely maiden and Coyote Boy produced Oraibi's Coyote Clan.

In another version, the cosmos was a dark, lifeless barren. In the lowest zone lived a miserable people. Two brothers pushed their way through the underworld cave and planted seeds. They sprouted a cornstalk that shot up into the air. The brothers and their followers joined Coyote, Locust, Spider, Swallow, and Vulture and emerged into the uppermost world, where they found fire to light the way. The people formed a disk to light the sky and a spider blanket, which became the moon. Across the night sky, Coyote sprinkled stars from a jar. Vulture fanned the ground to make wrinkles that grew into mountains. The older brother left to establish white people; his younger sibling became the father of the Hopi.

The Hopi evolved rituals for all phases of life, beginning with the birth of babies and the ceremonial burial of the afterbirth. Ritual taboo delineated the lifestyle of unmarried girls, who ground black corn and stoked outdoor ovens with dry cedar to bake *piki,* a thin blue cornbread circle that is the staple of their diet. Their male counterparts hunted rabbits and small game. Wooing involved the young boy's theft of the girl's virginity. Among her lovers, she was free to choose a favorite.

Before nuptials, the bride ground corn to prove she was a suitable wife. In an early-morning ritual, the family celebrated the couple's union by rinsing the couple's hair in a communal water jar. Husband and wife preserved their wedding outfits, in which they were buried. Family members arranged the dead in a sitting position, dusted them with corn meal, placed feathers in the navel, and honored the soul as it made its way back to the netherworld.

Beginning at the winter solstice around December 22, the clan calendar followed an agrarian cycle that nurtured fertility. Priests performed specific ceremonies to assure good weather. To bless the ground, worshippers painted faces on prayer sticks and inserted them in the furrows to ensure bounty. To propitiate the 350 different kachinas, kiva groups retained each deity's mask and costume in an underground chamber. During annual holidays, members danced the spirits' steps and imitated their gestures. To teach the next generation to respect kachinas, parents carved spirit dolls from cottonwood roots and posted the images in their homes as reminders of the gods' injunctions.

HISTORY

In use from A.D. 1125, the Oraibi complex is one of the oldest occupied settlements in the United States. Its founders, who were the ancient Anasazi, may have followed the supernova of the Crab Nebula in 1054 for their trek north, as indicated by cosmic rock art. Newcomers chose an elevated spot easily defended from invasion and built stone pueblos in remote canyons. The evolving Hohokam, Hopi, Pueblo, and Navajo tapped underground aquifers and irrigated garden plots of corn, beans, melons, gourds, and squash, which they cultivated with a primitive digging stick. In pre-Columbian times, one matrilinear society became the largest Hopi enclave, with a population of around 14,000 Uto-Aztecan speakers.

After early contact with Francisco Vasquez de Coronado and his Spanish conquistadors, the Hopi began losing their highly structured social order. They saw their first European after guiding Pedro de Továr, Coronado's scout, to the Grand Canyon in 1540, when the Spaniards enslaved them. Around 1598, the Hopi agreed to serve the Spanish king. European contacts taught them herding and burro and horse breeding. From 1629 to 1680, Franciscan friars operated the San Francisco Mission but had limited success in proselytizing the Hopi, who retreated to kivas for private traditional worship. Because the Spanish forced them to pull huge poles for construction of their church, the Hopi referred to it as a slave church.

Heavy-handed Catholic authorities battled paganism by closing kivas and halting kachina dances. A murderous revolt in 1680 temporarily restored traditional religion to the Hopi, who obliterated the mission church. By 1692, the military had conquered the Pueblo for the last time. Governor de Vargas sweetened the reconquest with gifts of herd animals and horses. Only the Hopi of Oraibi refused his bribes.

Into the nineteenth century, the Hopi suffered a three-pronged attack—a series of raids by hostile Apaches, Navajos, and Utes, extensive drought, and decimating epidemics of smallpox, which rapidly reduced the indigenous population. The greatest change came in 1850 with the Treaty of Guadalupe Hidalgo and the creation of the Territory of New Mexico. At the time, Indian agents signed a pact with the Hopi promising to respect their culture and religion and to protect them from marauding Navajos, but change continued to roll over the fragile culture. With the arrival of the railroad and creation of the state of Arizona, government control subsumed their autonomy. In 1874, a mission school encouraged Indians to accept European languages.

The issue of land ownership kept whites and the Hopi from reaching an understanding. President Chester A. Arthur's administration carved out a 2.4-million-acre reservation in 1882. In 1891 Senator Henry Dawes proposed a land allotment similar to that of the Cherokee Strip in Oklahoma, but he failed to reckon with the communal nature of Hopi philosophy, which holds the land in common as a gift from the gods. The era erupted in a turbulent battle between traditional Hopi ways and the few who broke with the past and accepted land, schools, modern medicine, and government direction. Desecration of hallowed sites by Mormon missionaries weakened the already tattered Hopi social and religious fabric. In 1894, government agents arrested the staunchest rebels and confined them to Alcatraz, a desolate island prison in San Francisco Bay.

A defining moment for Oraibi came about in 1906 after the loss of an appeaser of whites, Chief Lololoma, in 1902 and the succession of his nephew Tewaquaptewa, also an appeaser. For four years, tempers boiled between Hopis who were friendly to whites and the hostiles, conservatives who rejected white education, religion, and values in favor of aboriginal ways. The rivalry reached critical mass in September 1906 at the Snake Dance, when the two sides threatened a civil war. Youkioma staved off military intervention by a game of strength—drawing a line in the sand and inviting liberals to push the hostiles to the other side. When the friendlies won the communal shoving match, Youkioma's splinter group departed and founded the Hotevilla Pueblo six miles northwest of Oraibi. After serving a year at Alcatraz, he continued to lobby for native autonomy and journeyed to the White House to discuss issues with President William Howard Taft. In the Hopi view, the schism was deliberate, a necessary division that the old ones had prophesied for the preservation of tradition.

ACTIVITIES

As Youkioma asserted, religion is a binding force in pueblo lifestyle. The Hopi begin training children in the sacred way in the first years of life. As they view their purpose, the only assurance that humankind can survive in nature is through observance of the sacred way—perpetuation of the sacred creation song, prayer, and meditation. As proponents of the Great Spirit's command, the Hopi envision themselves as the caretakers of life, which can thrive only by altering the current pattern of pollution and technological self-destruction.

The Hopi still venerate Prophecy Rock, a desert stronghold of spirituality that pictures the god Taiowa holding a bow and a thread. The stone's images of corn and an aged man symbolize the core of their philosophy, that change must not violate the Hopi essentials of peace and balance. These complex pictographs predict that uncontrolled alteration to nature will cause a terrible backlash of earthquake, flood, volcanic disturbance, hail, drought, and famine. In 1955, Dan Katchongvu, also called White Cloud above Horizon, carried a message to a congressional hearing that the Hopi were anticipating the arrival of a messiah. New-Age philosophy respects this tradition as proof that human life on earth is reaching its conclusion.

The Hopi observe self-strengthening and purification rites through kiva worship. Impersonators take the roles of chiefs, guards, disciplinarians, runners, hunters, birds, animals, and insects. Before climbing from the underground chambers, bare-chested dancers begin with prayer at the altar and offerings of cornmeal, tobacco, and feathered prayer sticks. They stamp around the *sipapu* and then hold drumming and kachina dances for observers in the plaza.

- Worship begins a liturgical cycle in November, when the Hopi hold sixteen days of praise and thanksgiving for creation, health, and village welfare. Priests and men dressed in embroidered kilts chant the history of the earth. At the fire ceremony and Wuwuchim (the Initiation Dance of the new year) on the eve of the new moon, elders initiate young men into full citizenship.
- The first kachina appears at the winter solstice in December to represent the first man and serve as intermediary between the Hopi and the gods. Priests honor the occasion by blessing prayer feathers. They once used only eagle feathers but have voluntarily supplemented with turkey feathers to protect the endangered eagle population.
- In February, after the January kiva dances, the Powamu (Bean Dance) purifies and initiates young Hopi into tribal societies. Tall masked spirits threaten children who misbehave and spank the naughtiest.
- The Hopi mark spring months with the March Anktioni and Soyohim (Plaza Dances) in April and May.
- The end of the kachina year occurs in July with the Niman (Home Dance), a second sixteen-day ceremony that ends the half-year's masked ceremonies.
- August brings the Snake Dance and Flute Dance in alternate years. Social dancing from 10:00 A.M. to 6:00 P.M. gives the young a chance to visit. For the Butterfly Dance, men wear velvet ribbon shirts and embroidered kilts and may engage in competition with dancers from neighboring Hopi villages.
- In September, the women's society holds a Marau (Basket Dance) to celebrate the harvest and commemorate a time when men were gone for long stretches, leaving the women in charge of village welfare and spiritual life. As the costumed women move about, they toss small gifts from their baskets to spectators.
- The Hopi close the year in October with Oaqole (another Basket Dance), which anticipates the return of the kachinas for an-

other six months on earth to cure illness, bring rain, and mark the passing of the agricultural year.

An unusual feature of Hopi worship is the function of the *koshare,* a society of holy clowns who perform a two-day ceremony. A satiric force, these fun-loving tricksters use humiliation and ridicule to remind villagers of their behavior codes. They gobble food, steal shoes and garments, parody the pompous, and gather groups to perform beneficial work. As punishment for their foolery, the owl kachina tosses small stones to symbolize pricks of conscience. The whipper kachinas warn the *koshare* to mend their ways and administer lashes with yucca whips, followed by a jovially redemptive baptism. The overall effect of these antics is a lighthearted reminder of shortcomings and limitations. To preserve the sanctity of their pranksters, the Hopi refuse to answer the questions of outsiders, prohibit alcohol and drugs, and ban photography, recording, or sketching of the interaction between clowns and spectators.

Sources: Brinkley-Rogers 1995; Buchanan 1999; Cantor, George, 1993; Champagne 1998; Church 1995; Curtis, *Native Family,* 1996; "The Hopi"; "The Hopi Prophecy Rock"; James 1974; Loftin 1991; Milne 1995; Patterson and Snodgrass 1994; Smith 1989; Steiger 1974; Waldman 1990; Walking Turtle 1993; Waters 1963.

Osho Chidvilas

Kailash Sozzani, President
8111 East Broadway, No. 466
Tucson, Arizona 85710
800-777-7743; 520-282-3953
FAX 520-282-4053
http://osho.com/homepage.htm

Widely reviled as a body of mindless cultists and free spirits, Osho began as the Rajneesh Foundation, the creation of the Bhagwan Shree Rajneesh. Its influence and parameters were never clear. In 1983, an article in the *Rajneesh Times* claimed a following of 350,000 initiates; the *Oregonian* challenged the figure and estimated enlistment at 60,000. Whatever their number, the Bhagwan's commune of monks consisted mostly white, college-educated males with some background in Judaism, Catholicism, or Protestantism. They revered his name, even after police, customs officers, and tax officials found multiple irregularities in his handling of funds and entry to the United States. At his death, the faithful continued to follow the teachings of the unique guru who had introduced them to Osho.

HISTORY

Osho or Rajneeshism reached a peak membership of 200,000 at 600 centers worldwide. The Bhagwan's disciples observed common Asian worship forms—meditation, chanting a mantra—along with harsh physical exertion, naturism, and free love as a means of overcoming inhibitions and attaining enlightenment. They took new names beginning with Ma for women and Swami for men and adopted a uniform of red robes and *mala* (strings of rosary beads) centered with a photo of their guru. Parents of followers and religious and civic leaders hounded the group to halt alleged mind control of minors, who cut ties with home and family. The media ridiculed the Bhagwan's sumptuous lifestyle, particularly his collection of Rolls Royces. Devout Hindus took offense at Osho's exuberant devotees, who did not take the traditional vows renouncing sex, wealth, and family and who defamed the traditional sacred title of *sannya* (monk) by behaving wildly, selling drugs, contracting venereal diseases, and practicing prostitution to earn money for their sojourn at the ashram. Following a monk's rudeness to an Indian woman, authorities in India reexamined the ashram's tax-free status and discovered irregularities in accounts totaling $80 million. Charity commissioners fined the ashram $4 million in back taxes.

In some 100 books in Hindi and another 100 in English, the Bhagwan collected his teachings, which reduced earthly life to monism, a belief that God and matter are one. Staff issued his works in German, Japanese, Dutch, Italian, French, Spanish, and Portuguese. His successor, Swami Prem Jayesh, a former Canadian realtor named Michael William O'Byrne, superintends around 20 meditation centers and communes. Some disciples, whom he called *neosannyasins* (beginning monks), train at the Bhagwan's Humaniversity, a center of humanism founded in Holland in 1978.

BHAGWAN SHREE RAJNEESH

Rajneeshism, later called Osho, was the creation of Rajneesh Chandra Mohan. Born on December 31, 1931, in Kutchwara, India, he grew up in the Jain faith and studied at the Gunj School in Gadwara and at Jabalpur University. At age twenty-one, he received enlightenment. After completing an M.A. in philosophy at the University of Saugar and, under the title of Acharya (Professor), he taught for nine years at the University of Jabalpur while leading a group of disciples. At age thirty-five, he gave up teaching for religious work and lecturing. His series of talks on sex as an introduction to meditation and enlightenment enticed adventuresome American and European initiates.

As guru of an ashram in Bombay, India, Rajneesh took the title Bhagwan (Lord). He encountered American students eager to break ties with traditional faiths to adopt a guilt-free, sex-oriented religion. Because of conservative opposition to his philosophy, in 1974, he resettled his followers ninety miles southwest of Bombay in Poona. There, some 50,000 North American followers sought enlightenment from a syncretism of Christianity, Greek philosophy, Hinduism, humanism, Jainism, psychology, Taoism, and Zen Buddhism. In 1979, he declared that Rajneeshism was capable of rescuing humankind from destruction.

Under a cloud of rumor, Rajneesh suddenly retired from teaching, entered a period of silence, and wrote full time. In 1981, he left India and moved to his new Rajneesh Foundation in the United States. He and his staff settled in Montclair, New Jersey, in headquarters managed by disciple Ma Anand Sheela, formerly known as Sheela Ambalal Patel. He established a cult following on Rajneeshpuram (Essence of Rajneesh), a ranch outside Antelope, Oregon. The enclave dismayed townspeople by creating a voting majority among his followers, who quickly grew from 500 in 1982 to 4,000 in 1985. Staff amassed $120 million to construct an ashram complex composed of a meditation center, an airfield, a hotel, a shopping mall, and a casino.

After charges of fire-bombing a city office and murder, the cult departed in October 1985. The Bhagwan broke with Sheela, whom he accused of attempted poisoning and eavesdropping. At the airport in Charlotte, North Carolina, U.S. Immigration and Naturalization agents arrested him and questioned him about convenient marriages arranged between Indian cultists and Americans to obtain U.S. residency. His punishment amounted to a $400,000 fine for visa fraud, a ten-year suspended prison sentence, and deportation from the United States for a minimum of five years. He roamed the globe and found no welcome in twenty-one countries. Reestablished in Poona in 1986, Rajneesh renamed himself Osho and resumed teaching. In 1988, his foundation held a convention of American devotees. Afflicted with asthma, diabetes, and joint pain for over a decade, he died suddenly in 1990.

ACTIVITIES

Founded in 1977, Osho is a multinational outreach headquartered at Osho Viha Meditation Center, Mill Valley, California, and sponsoring twenty meditation centers worldwide. Headed by President Kailash Sozzani, staff at Osho Chidvilas in Tucson, Arizona, teach the philosophies of Jesus, the Buddha, Tantra, western mystics, and Zen. Unlike Hindu Tantric yoga masters, the Bhagwan linked unrestrained sexual release with higher consciousness. His disciples foster an intense form of concentration beginning with rapid breathing to relieve stress and emotional blocks followed by release of emotional energy and a shout of "Hoo," which boosts the energy level and charges the body's sexual centers. The dynamic preparation ends with quiet and meditation.

At the Deepta Meditation Center (formerly known as the Chidvilas Rajneesh Meditation Center), staff conducts research, sponsors meditation retreats, and maintains a Web site and lending library of 500 books. Publications include the free annual *Meditation Catalog,* the quarterly *Osho Times International,* and the bimonthly *OSHO Chidvilas—Flowering of Consciousness,* which distributes music, books, talks on audio cassettes, and videos. In 1999, the center organized a Bravo America Meditation Tour. Also available are tarot readings in English and Spanish.

Sources: "Bhagwan Shree Rajneesh—Guru in the Western Wild" 1985; *Biography Resource Center*

1999; Grafstein 1984; "The Humaniversity"; Latkin 1994; Latkin et al. 1987; Mano 1989; "Osho"; "Osho: Never Born, Never Died"; Palmer 1988; Stern 1991.

Our Lady of Guadalupe Trappist Abbey

Abbot Peter McCarthy
P.O. Box 97
Lafayette, Oregon 97127
503-852-0105; 800-294-0105
bakery@trappistabbey.org
www.trappistabbey.org

In the sylvan hill country of Yamhill County, the Trappist Abbey, formally known as Our Lady of Guadalupe, is home to an elderly brotherhood whose average age is sixty-eight. In simplicity, prayer, and self-denial, they follow a daily round of meditation, worship, and work to sustain the abbey. An hour southwest of Portland, the rhythm of monastic life sends them to appointed tasks on 1,300 acres renewing spiritual vitality in weary visitors, harvesting hardwood, binding books, tending the grounds, hoeing winter squash, and baking cakes.

HISTORY

The Trappist brother- and sisterhood, derived from the Cistercians of the Strict Observance, began in 1664 with the founding of an abbey in La Trappe, France. Under the discipline of abbot Armond-Jean le Bouthillier de Rancé, the original community lived a formidable daily trio of directives—prayer, work, and silence—but gave up severe Lenten fasts that undermined health. The French Revolution uprooted the monks and nuns, who, in 1790, sheltered in Switzerland. In 1815, they repatriated the order in France.

Essentially nonassertive, nonviolent Trappist teachings reached Nova Scotia and the United States in 1803 with the arrival of Dom Urban Guillet in Baltimore. The first successful abbey took shape in 1848 in Gethsemani, Kentucky. The most famous American Trappist, Thomas Merton, inspired a post–World War II vocation boom after he revealed the rhythmic beneficence of the order's life through his autobiography, *The Seven Storey Mountain*. In 1948, Our Lady of Guadalupe—sponsored by the Community of Valley Falls in Rhode Island and named for the patroness of Mexico—got its start in Pecos, New Mexico, where its sixteen founders purchased a dude ranch. In search of more promising farmland, in March 1955, the community of sixty sold their holdings to Benedictines and traveled to Oregon on a plane chartered by Mrs. Bob Hope.

The selection of Lafayette benefited a life of silence, inner discipline, and communion with God. The monks offer ten wooden kneelers in the sparse meditation room, which features a plank ceiling and an oversized glass window looking out on woodlands. Sitting in facing choir stalls, residents in hooded robes chant together and glance out at the yellow larches, Douglas firs, and red oaks filmed with Spanish moss.

To support themselves, Lafayette's monks originally handcrafted church pews. When the business folded in the 1960s, they developed a monograph and periodical bindery and book-repair service, labeled and warehoused pinot noirs and Rieslings for the Willamette Valley wine industry, and felled wood from their 900-acre, second-growth forest, after hiring an independent company to advise on environmental soundness. In the European religious tradition of fine foods, liqueurs, and herbs, they also baked and distributed ginger date-nut cake, honey-almond biscotti, and their distinctively dense, dark, sweet fruitcake. The steady income keeps them afloat while funding a local emergency shelter and food bank.

The fruitcake recipe, developed by Father Arnold with help from tasters and critics, contains glacéed pineapple and cherries, boiled raisins, honey, cinnamon, mace, pecans, and walnuts. It requires 165 minutes of baking at 275 degrees, followed by a baptism in 120-proof brandy. Directed by Brother Eugene Brodaczynski, a Korean War veteran, the stainless-steel bakery turns out 20,000 cakes annually at the rate of 80 a day for eight months. The one-, two-, and three-pounders rest for three months before the monks pack each in a holiday box. Telemarketer Brother Patrick Corkrean—nicknamed "The Happy Monk of the Happy Business Office"—presides over a toll-free phone line, VISA and MasterCard numbers, and computerized distri-

In the sylvan hill country of Yamhill County, Oregon, Our Lady of Guadalupe Trappist Abbey is home to an elderly brotherhood who follow a daily round of meditation, worship, and work. (Courtesy Our Lady of Guadalupe Trappist Abbey)

bution that make up a $100,000-a-year mail-order business.

Today, the thirty-seven monks do more than chop wood and make cakes. They rise at 3:30 A.M. to celebrate mass at 4:15. The four-hour workday begins at 8:15 A.M. After lunch, the men continue meditation and prayer. Since January 1999, the staff has launched a Web site to advertise its Guadalupe translations and such pamphlets as a golden-anniversary history, published in 1998. In addition, modern retreat houses receive guests for thirty days of solitude, spiritual regrouping, and weekday conferences with one of the monks. Retreat amenities include communal or separate meals, a lending library, hillside walks, and periods of work. The fee is whatever visitors can pay.

Sources: *Biography Resource Center* 1999; Bock 1997; Brinckmann 1998; Downey 1997; Gonzales 1998; Jackson, Kristin; "Our Lady of Guadalupe Trappist Abbey" 1999.

Painted Rock

Nature Conservancy Manager
P.O. Box 3087
California Valley, California 93453
805-475-2131

In California's San Joaquin Valley, a U-shaped sandstone outcrop known as Painted Rock—or La Piedra Pintada in Spanish—lies in the southwestern corner of the 180,000-acre Carrizo Plain Natural Area. In what is now San Luis Obispo County west of Bakersfield, the coastal California Chumash and their inland neighbors, the Yokut, settled the valley and established trade and religious rituals. The land, bounded by the Temblor and Caliente Mountains and permeated by the San Andreas Rift, forms a wildlife preserve rich in California jewel flowers, mallows, woolly threads, junipers, Sonoran shrubs, and blue oaks, a habitat for migratory birds and small animals.

A favorite feature is Painted Rock, a holy monolith honored by the Chumash, now located in the Santa Ynez Chumash Reservation. The rock itself stands 200 feet above the plain and stretches 1,000 feet in diameter. Through a natural opening on the eastern slope, researchers have excavated an oval amphitheatre, a natural bowl surmounted by a gallery. In red highlighted with black, white, yellow, and blue, the holy ones, decked in feathered ceremonial garb, inscribed a rock bowl with polychromatic pigment displaying dramatic scenes, grids and lines, and abstract maps of the heavens.

BELIEFS

Collected lore links Painted Rock to sacred art. In one account, the dreamer, or visionary, a priest of the feathered serpent, lectured on love, generosity, and the return of Quetzalcoatl, the Mesoamerican messiah who gave his life for the Aztec. According to another version, rancher Archibald McAlister learned the purpose of Painted Rock from his vaquero José Sequatero. José told of his mother, the wife of a Mojave chief, who fled across the Mojave Desert to rescue her illegitimate son, the issue of an extramarital affair. She searched for Painted Rock, a landmark known to her mother and grandmother.

Native lore linked the drawings to the arrival of conquistador Hernando de Cortez to Mexico and to the dreamer's prediction that white people would soon arrive. Recorded events noted the murder of Montezuma. When a young dreamer began his career, he established an earnest resolve to serve the truth by sacrificing his daughter before the congregation. He dedicated her blood to protect them from the advance of outsiders. He dipped his paint stick in blood and mixed pigments to outline his curse on invaders.

HISTORY

There is no detailed history of the early Chumash, Stone-Age hunter-gatherers who may have been the first aboriginal inhabitants of North America. For centuries, they lived along the Pacific shore from Estero Bay to Malibu Canyon and on the Channel Islands. They paddled along the shore in their redwood plank canoes, which had borne them down the coast from Northern California, a shore rich in shellfish, birds, and sea mammals.

Chumash animistic worship included day-long sings to accompany times of hunting and harvesting, for grinding acorn meal and making baskets, and for times of healing, welcoming the newly born, and war. For accompaniment to songs and festival dances, they shook turtle-shell rattles and deer-hoof clappers, beat elderberry rhythm strips, blew bird-bone and wood whistles and flutes, swung bull roarers, or ceremonial noisemakers, and sawed musical bows. They valued the Painted Rock area both for trading and ritual purposes. A similar site, Chumash Painted Cave, in the Santa Ynez Mountains near the coastal city of Santa Barbara, contains five feet of an original panel of rock art four times that large. One figure may be a drawing of a solar eclipse of November 24, 1677, an event that links the Chumash to recorded history.

The arrival of Spanish missionaries threatened the native population of California. There were 10,000 to 20,000 Chumash in the area when European missionaries arrived there in 1770. The Chumash, who were among those depleted in number, became virtually landless. Shortly, the Spanish *llaneros* (stockmen) brought their flocks to pasture. Undeterred by natural enemies, the livestock overgrazed, disturbing the delicate desert ecology and the social order of the Chumash. In 1876, the first photographers in California captured native petrography and piqued the interest of tourists, whose visits depleted the traditional grasslands. Scholarly interpretation of surviving Chumash rock art derives from Alfred Kroeber, Campbell Grant, Travis Hudson, and Georgia Lee. Overall, they surmised that the petrographs of Painted Rock and other sites express a shamanic vision of earth and the cosmos.

By 1885, homesteading had changed forever the aboriginal Chumash homeland. The rush to investigate Painted Rock brought vandals as well as viewers of Chumash rock paintings, which offer a tantalizing glimpse of this important California tribe. In 1977, Georgia Lee became the first researcher to reconstruct Chumash history from their own oral tradition. From these stories, she and later scholars determined that the polychrome mandalas, whales, swordfish, coyotes, deer, geometric forms and elaborate patterns, and fantastic birds and horned humans on Painted Rock related to mythological creatures, sacred cycles, and astronomical observation.

The creators of the drawings were Chumash dreamers. These spokespersons gained power through a dream helper—a hallucinogenic plant such as the white-blossomed datura, an animal such as a dolphin, turtle, snake, or eagle, or a natural force, such as wind, stars, or planets. Dreamers may have retreated to this sacred site to commune with supernatural phenomena and inscribe protective symbols and messages on the rock wall. Whether the result of trance, halluci-

nation, drug-primed vision, or altered consciousness resulting from vision quests, these magical creations transmit elements of Chumash life and purpose.

ACTIVITIES

Visitors favor Painted Rock, nearby Soda Lake, and its environs, which shelter golden eagles, sandhill cranes, condors, and red-tailed hawks. Near the end of the twentieth century, naturalists reintroduced the fox, pronghorn antelope, and tule elk, which once populated the Carrizo Plain. Much of the area's traffic centers on the centuries-old paintings, which suggest a ritual mural for the contemplation or edification of a regular native congregation, who once came to the Carrizo Plain to worship. Although art historians and researchers consider Painted Rock an element of antique sacred geography, the site remains sacred to the Chumash, who return for holy rituals.

Sources: Angel 1979; Cantor, George, 1993; "Carrizo Plain Natural Area"; Champagne 1994; "Chumash Indians"; Hyder and Lee 1994; Malinowski 1995; Milne 1995; "Painted Rock and Later Human History"; Parkman 1998; Patterson and Snodgrass 1994; Steen 1999; Steiger 1974; Walking Turtle 1993; "Who Are the Chumash?"; "Wishtoyo: The Home of the Chumash" 1999.

Palace of Gold

Dave Waterman, Manager
Road 1, NBU# 24
Moundsville, West Virginia 26041
304-843-1812
FAX 304-843-1853
palaceofgold@juno.com
www.palaceofgold.com

A vernal ashram on a winding road in the Blue Ridge Mountains outside of Wheeling, West Virginia, the Palace of Gold is both a retreat and a religious tourist attraction. Its devotees are conspicuous for their shaved heads and monochromatic robes of orange or white. Palace philosophy is a Western adaptation of conservative Hinduism known as the Hare Krishna movement. The introduction of the West to Krishna consciousness was the work of one elderly activist, Bhaktivedanta Swami Prabhupada.

BHAKTIVEDANTA SWAMI PRABHUPADA

Bhaktivedanta Swami Prabhupada, a Hindu religious teacher, gave North America its first substantial view of India's Krishna worship. Native to Calcutta, India, he was born Abhay Charan De into a religious family in 1896 and learned Krishna-centered activities in childhood. He enrolled at Scottish Churches' College and completed a B.A. in philosophy from the University of Calcutta at age twenty-four. His readiness for challenge came at the height of Gandhi's charismatic freedom movement. Dutifully, he married and sired one son but fought a strong urge to abandon family responsibility and preach the Bhagavadgita, the Hindu scripture.

At age twenty-six, Abhay joined the Gaudiya Vaisnava movement and passed through an initiation as a hermit and street beggar. He studied with Srila Bhaktisiddhanta Saraswati, who dispatched him to the West under the name Charanaravinda to spread the Krishna philosophy, transcendentalism, and Vedic scripture in English. In 1959, he added the title Swami after he joined a religious house. In acceptance of the spiritual order of *sannyasa* (renunciation), he deserted his wife, entered the ministry full time, and, in 1994, began publishing *Back to Godhead* in New Delhi with his own funds. In this phase of transformation, he adopted the name and title of A. C. Bhaktivedanta Swami and acquired free passage by steamer to the United States.

On arrival in New York City in 1965 after a difficult forty-day sea voyage, the Swami began distributing literature on the streets and founded the International Society for Krishna Consciousness (ISKCON) in July 1966. Three months later, his group performed their first public chanting in a city park. The alternative faith drew hippies to his Second Avenue storefront on the Lower East Side. By 1967, the movement spread to a Krishna center in San Francisco.

The swami forbade gambling, recreational sex, and stimulants, insisted on strict vegetarianism and the eating of *prasadam* (sanctified food) to purify the body, and taught followers the mahamantra: "Hare Krishna, Hare Krishna, Krishna Krishna, Hare Hare / Hare Rama, Hare Rama, Rama Rama, Hare Hare," a hypnotic chant that restored the mind to godliness. To assure right behavior, he insisted that each member associate only with Krishna-minded people, even if they had to dissociate themselves from friends and parents.

Without rest, the aged Swami produced eighty texts and numerous translations on religion, beginning with three volumes of commentary on *Srimad Bhagavatam*. Within twelve years, he initiated 4,000 adherents to Krishna worship. Many of his followers recruited others from lonely, alienated travelers clustered at bus stops and airports or wandering along roadsides or at parks and campuses. He structured a global missionary hierarchy to preach the faith and commanded disciples to build seven temples. At his death in 1977, he had opened centers in Boston, Buffalo, San Francisco, Los Angeles, Montreal, Hamburg, and London and had initiated Krishna worldwide.

HISTORY

From the beginning of Krishna consciousness in the United States, converts admired the break with standard faiths, which bored and alienated the young. The Swami's call for asceticism lured them to a new and unfamiliar set of ideals. The impetus for pilgrimage satisfied youthful wanderlust and sent devotees to the streets to swirl their long orange robes, sell pamphlets and incense, and aggressively panhandle pedestrians. A favorite spiritual destination was the Palace of Gold, a West Virginia sacred site jokingly called a religious Disneyland or America's Taj Mahal. Led by a guru, the palace housed male devotees. For worship, they shaved their heads, leaving a small ponytail at the nape, and danced at the altar before the statue of Krishna.

From the beginning, Krishna worship at the palace displayed misogyny. Women, whom the cult labeled as inferior and less capable of education, pulled their hair into plain ponytails, lived apart from men, and swayed on the perimeter during male-dominated worship. They lived humbly and submissively at the edge of Hindu society and received beatings for infractions. They married only with permission of the guru and procreated to rear Krishna children. Men fled unsuitable mates by entering the Order of Sannyasa, which freed them of earthly responsibility in order to follow God.

For urbanites, the palace's appeal was hill

country, grazing cattle, and an end to urbanism. In exchange for free room and board, pilgrims worked at farming and joined two hours of early morning worship ritual, which called for singing, chanting, whirling, and dancing. Each recitation of the mantra they uttered in their own style and speed and counted repetitions on a string of beads they carried in a pouch. During vegetarian meals, the assembly listened to reading from the scripture, which the guru Bhaktipad, the Swami's successor, intoned during a time of heightened receptivity. At *setsang* (assembly), disciples shared religious experiences and insights. At the end of the gathering, the guru tossed cookies as *prasadam* (a holy treat) to the crowd.

The Krishna movement began losing steam in the 1970s, when anticult deprogrammers stalked minors and reclaimed them from brainwashing. Decentralization of the Krishna movement began around 1985 as the strictures of Prabhupada receded in authority. In 1993, the idealized monastery stumbled after Swami Kirtanananda confessed to illicit seduction of minors. Devotees forced his resignation from the governing board and prohibited further deviant sexual practice. In an upsurge of purity, the faithful returned to standard chanting and temple dancing that Prabhupada had instituted.

ARCHITECTURE

At the forefront of the New Vrindaban complex stands the Palace of Gold, an anomaly in the West Virginia hill country. The effect is magical—a dazzling gilt shrine edged with concrete sunshades and topped with balusters, a central gold dome, and *chatras* (turrets) at each of the four corners. The walls of marble plate display rope-twist designs, gold columns, and brass handrails. Around the exterior, hand-wrought iron gates and railings are the work of residents.

Inside, artistry enhances the fantastic vision of a traditional Indian temple. Gold-tinged paintings cover vaulted ceilings; wood-framed stained-glass windows admit filtered light. Below are four altars and twenty *pujaris,* or worship sites. Beyond the palace lie tree-lined pathways that lead past thirty-foot statues of prancing acolytes, elephants, and sacred cows to the City of God. The piercing cry of peacocks disrupts the serenity of the grounds, where visitors occupy guest cabins.

ACTIVITIES

The Palace of Gold, led by Varsana Swami, is no longer a part of the International Society for Krishna Consciousness, but its acreage remains a religious site, theological education center, and popular religious tourist attraction open daily from 10:00 A.M. until dark. Visitors photograph the Radha-Vrindavana-Chandra Temple and take a thirty-five-minute guided tour of the palace. They can shop at a health-food store and gift shops, dine in vegetarian restaurants, peruse the library, and visit the elementary school and guest cabins. A highlight is the rose garden, which won awards in 1995 and 1996 from the American Rose Selections Committee. Many come specifically to ask questions about Nandagram School, the *bhakta* training center.

Devotees receive support, room and board, and counseling from trained leaders. At Rupanuga Vidypitha College, led by Danavir Goswami, students work toward a bachelor's degree in Vedic studies. Based on Prabhupada's texts, courses cover scripture, yoga, and Vedic literature. At the barns at Vraja Puja Farms, residents study agrarian life on fifty-seven acres set aside for hands-on learning and oxen training. They carry on the International Society for Cow Protection, an animal-rights campaign, by lovingly tending and milking the sacred herd by hand. The palace's cottage industry in dried arrangements of gourds, organic cookies and potpourri pies, candles and icons, herbal oils, and ghee, a staple Indian butter concentrate, puts residents to work earning funds to support the dairy. To spread Krishna consciousness, itinerant monks travel by van from the palace to mission sites, where they distribute thousands of religious texts written or translated by Swami Prabhupada.

Late in the twentieth century, palace residents began reestablishing links to the parent organization. To maintain the complex and turn it into a religious theme park, they solicited funds for a complete restoration, including refurbishment of gold leaf to the main dome, replacement of marble with granite, shoring up a leaky roof, and removal of crumbling sunshades. They built a pottery shop to recast molds to replace crumbling cement statuary and touched up ceiling paintings. To preserve the past, devotees are assembling 2,500 pieces of statuary for the grounds and a museum of memorabilia to express Prabhupada's biography and mission to the West.

Sources: *Biography Resource Center* 1999; *Encyclopedia of World Biography* 1998; Gentz 1973; Johnson 1984; "Krishna Today"; Lewis 1998; Muster 1997; "New Vrindavana As It Is Today"; "Palace of Gold" 1998; Shin 1987; Smith 1995.

Peace Chapel
See Chapel of Peace.

Pendle Hill
Daniel A. Seeger, Executive Secretary
Bobbi Kelly, Outreach Coordinator
338 Plush Mill Road
Wallingford, Pennsylvania 19086-6099
610-566-4507 ext. 137; 800-742-3150 ext. 142
pendlehill@pendlehill.org
www.pendlehill.org

Through myriad activities and periods of inner communion, Pendle Hill evidences the thriving American Quaker spirit. Although Quakerism is a minor Christian phenomenon in England and the United States, it survives from colonial times as a beacon of truth and affirmation of brotherhood, equality, and peace-loving community life. The Pendle Hill educational experiment in communal living, worship, study, and work draws people from many cultures and faiths to contemplate the ramifications of nonviolent faith as they apply to individual and world issues.

HISTORY
Quakerism is a democratic, deformalized sect without precedent in history. It began in 1652 with the public ministry of George Fox in northwest England. Since its passage aboard the *Woodhouse* on August 3, 1657, from Bridlington, England, to its first New World colony at Newport, Rhode Island, the American Society of Friends has prospered. From their founding, colonial Quakers accepted branding, flogging, exile, jail terms, and hanging for opposing obeisance to the monarchy and the Anglican Church

and challenging the sectarianism that requires oaths and pledges of tithes. After they settled colonial communities, Quaker missionaries spread their beliefs through Ireland, northern Europe, and the West Indies.

Historically, Quakers have quietly modeled a love of truth, equality, peace, simplicity, and community. In regular acts of love, mercy, and kindness, such spirited members as Elizabeth Fry, Isaac Penington, Margaret Fell, and Mary Dyer sought justice through charity, publication, and activism promoting prison reform, religious tolerance, and civil and human rights. They practiced their faith in daily relations with Native Americans and rebuked settlers who sold Indians alcohol and accused them of godlessness and savagery. In 1658, Puritans arrested Dyer and three others and hanged them all for violating orthodox Massachusetts law.

Quakers were active participants in the establishment of liberty. Led by Stephen Hopkins, they opposed the Stamp Act of 1765, demanded a Continental Congress in 1774, and supported the Declaration of Independence in 1776. Quakers and Mennonites, the nation's first abolitionists, rejected the 1783 Fugitive Slave Act and enabled the flight of slaves on the Underground Railroad, which profited from the direction of Isaac Hopper, Lucretia Mott, and Levi Coffin. During Reconstruction, Quakers boycotted Philadelphia's streetcars, which refused service to blacks. Friends meeting houses sprang up in Pennsylvania, Rhode Island, New York, Maryland, and North Carolina and gradually spread west. In the early twentieth century, Quaker suffragists Abby Kelley Foster, Susan B. Anthony, and Alice Paul demonstrated for women's rights and became one of the nation's first denominations to offer full participation to both sexes in church ministry and governance.

Espoused by Anna and Howard Brinton, Henry Cadbury, Hornell Hart, Gerald Heard, Rufus Jones, Douglas Steere, and Elton Trueblood, the Quaker pacifist stance is perhaps the sect's most enduring contribution to American life and thought. The Quaker pacifism depicted in folk artist Edward Hicks's *Peaceable Kingdom* helped shape conscientious objector status through the world wars and into the Vietnam War era, when volunteers staffed relief agencies

Through myriad activities and periods of inner communion, Pendle Hill in Wallingford, Pennsylvania, evidences the thriving American Quaker spirit. (Courtesy Pendle Hill)

open to both sides of the conflict. The strength of their conviction earned them the 1947 Nobel Peace Prize. That same year, an innovative champion of peace, history professor Gladdys Esther Muir, studied at Pendle Hill and composed a famous peace manifesto, "The Place of Brethren Colleges in Preparing Men and Women for Peace Leadership." The next year, she founded a peace studies program at Manchester College by focusing on war and peace, social change, nonviolent social activism, and conflict resolution. For a half century, the seminar, directed by Muir, defined issues, stimulated dissent, and readied peacemakers for national and international influence on the world climate.

BELIEFS

Quakers—also called Children of the Light—maintain that a divine spark flickers within each human spirit. By living free of frivolity, vanity, alcohol, drugs, and tobacco and by embracing charity, justice, fairness, and harmony with all humankind, they emulate the purity and selflessness of early Christians. The sect needs no clergy or doctrine; membership requires a re-

quest from an adult or automatic birthright of children born to members. Without sacraments, prayer books, hymns, or burdensome dogma, autonomous groups of Quakers join in silent worship to seek inner direction. Speech is spontaneous. When insight impels individuals to speak, they emphasize action against violence and social ills.

Pendle Hill devotes itself to transforming society through education that integrates intellectual, spiritual, and personal insight. The original purpose was to offer an adult educational experiment based on study, worship, work, and community life. Its tenets call for equality and respect for all, simplicity, inward harmony and service to others, and a communal search for spirit. Campus programs balance spiritual and mental training and discussion with entertainment, exercise, and creative fellowship. To achieve these aims, Pendle Hill accepts adult residents. To defray expenses, it offers loans, work grants, and eleven categories of scholarships for Quaker scholars and educators, foreign students, social activists, religious leaders, and active peacemakers.

FACILITIES

In a quiet suburban setting, Pendle Hill invites reverence and peace. The twenty-three-acre campus contains 140 species of trees and flowering shrubs. Its complex of sixteen buildings encompasses classrooms, meeting rooms, a shop, and the Spring House hermitage. A library of Quaker books complements the general collection of 12,000 volumes and varied newspapers and magazines. The art studio stocks looms, potter's wheels, and an electric kiln. A spacious playground fosters nonviolent play. The kitchen staff grows organic vegetables in the compound's garden. The bookstore specializes in such Quaker works as Elizabeth Watson's *Wisdom's Daughters,* Eileen Flanagan's *Listen with Your Heart: Seeking the Sacred in Romantic Love,* Hans Schmidt's *Quakers and Nazis,* Daniel Goleman's *Emotional Intelligence,* and *Worship in Song,* a Quaker hymnal.

Residents, called Sojourners, occupy simply furnished private rooms where smoking, drugs, and alcohol are prohibited. They share physical labor and communal meals in the dining hall or snacks in the dormitory kitchenette. In addition to classes in Quakerism, Bible, religious thought, literature and the arts, and social issues, the center offers time for personal retreat and renewal, solitude and contemplation, writing, research projects, worship, and fellowship. Sojourners may also read from the Peace Collection and Friends Historical Library at nearby Swarthmore College, walk the Swarthmore campus, and exercise at the gym or swimming pool.

ACTIVITIES

As an aid to personal exploration, Pendle Hill offers five-day courses, weekend conferences, sabbaticals, retreats, internships, and summer programs for young-adult leaders. The center invites the public to daily worship meeting, a half-hour of silence and spoken ministry. Other opportunities to await God's will occur before meals, in class, in prayer and healing sessions, and at the nightly epilogue. The staff reserves Wednesday afternoon for the practice of silent contemplation and offers one hour each week to individuals for one-on-one consultation on personal needs and interests.

The Pendle Hill Youth Camp explores Quakerism and alters lives through service and learning projects, worship, and community building.

DOUGLAS VAN STEERE

Prominent Quaker theologian and writer Douglas Steere and fellow Friends founded Pendle Hill, a center for study and contemplation twelve miles southwest of Philadelphia, in 1930 to serve those interested in the American Society of Friends. Steere, a lecturer and researcher fluent in French, German, and Scandinavian languages, believed that the true seeker of interfaith knowledge and understanding amplified core religious beliefs. Born August 31, 1901, in Harbor Beach, Michigan, he was educated at Michigan State University, Harvard University, and Oxford. A Rhodes Scholar and teacher, he chaired the philosophy department at Haverford College and was a visiting professor at Union Theological Seminary. Later, he lectured across the nation and in Tokyo, London, and Johannesburg. At the close of World War II, he organized the Quaker Relief Action group's donation of supplies to refugees in Poland, Norway, and Finland. As chairman of the Friends World Committee, he conducted missions in Europe, Africa, India, and Japan and served the Vatican Council as its Quaker delegate.

From 1954 to 1970, Steere chaired the Pendle Hill School of Religion and Social Studies. His publications range from a translation of Sören Kierkegaard's *Prayer and Worship* (1938) to articles and editorials for *Religion in Life* and a series of his own Quaker-centered writings—*Devotion* (1941), *On Beginning from Within,* (1943), *Doors into Life* (1948), *Time to Spare* (1948), *On Listening to Another* (1955), *Work and Contemplation* (1957), *Dimensions of Prayer* (1963), and, from 1965 to 1972, five pamphlets for Pendle Hill. At his death from Alzheimer's disease on February 6, 1995, he was working on a definitive text on the nature of contemplation, which he believed was the source of true communion with God. Haverford College honored Steere's memory with the Douglas Steere Contemplation Room.

The Weekend Workcamp program involves participants in low-income housing work, a visit to an African-American church, educational tours of Philadelphia, and a multifaceted survey of urban society. Groups discuss community, spirituality, social issues, and servant leadership and join in such crafts as bookmaking and printmaking, flower arranging, or collage. For fun, the staff hosts games, skits, music and storytelling, and campfire circles.

A resident study program consists of three ten-week terms annually. Daily fare includes Monday night lectures, seminars, and Web site information on such topics as prayer, Hildegard of Bingen, growing up Quaker, peace plans for Kosovo, the Gospels, modern peacemakers, holistic Bible reading, women's perspectives, the creative spirit, organic gardening, and discerning God's call to service. Pendle Hill Publications issues spiritual books and tracts on timely issues; the bookstore sells materials on religion and spirituality.

Recent additions to the Pendle Hill outreach have broadened its appeal. In 1997, residents continued the tradition of the Halloween Night walk up Pendle Hill. In December 1998, a campus meeting took action to lessen pollution and damage to the environment. The Pendle Hill On the Road (PHOR) program extends low-cost programs to such distant venues as Paullina, Iowa; Portland, Oregon; Nashville, Tennessee; and Houston, Texas. Topics allow participants to discuss mutual interests and problems of distant Quaker meetings, for example, "Strengthening Meeting Relationships," "Centering Prayer," "Aspects of Spirit," "Alternatives to Violence," and "Quaker Spiritual Formation."

Recent curriculum continues the tradition of examining current thought on important issues. In fall 1999, course titles ranged from "Learning from Schism" and "Living Ecological as if the Whole Earth Mattered" to "Healing after Violence," "An Introduction to Buddhist Meditation," and "The Brothers Karamazov: Must the Seed Die?" In 2000, staff scheduled courses on feminist perspectives on faith, Quaker journals, photography and the visual arts, and a holistic view of the Bible and an April celebration of Pendle Hill's seventieth anniversary. In addition, Pendle Hill initiated a series of science, technology, and religion forums, beginning with "Dialogue on Science and Religion" and "What Is Truth?" A panel of reconciliators, social activists, and relief workers encouraged nonviolence under the heading "Building a Culture of Peace: Reconciling the Past; Clarifying the Present; Imaging the Future."

Sources: Ahlstrom 1972; "America's First Peace Studies Program Celebrates Fifty Years"; *Biography Resource Center* 1999; Browne 1992; Buchanan 1999; *Eerdmans' Handbook to the World's Religions* 1982; Eller; "Inter-Faith Dialogue" 1997; *New Catholic Encyclopedia* 1967; O'Sullivan n. d.; "Pendle Hill"; "Quaker Electronic Archive and Meeting Place"; "Quaker Ideals"; Williams, Peter W., 1997.

Penitentes
See Hermanos Penitentes.

Pentecostals of Alexandria
Reverend G. Anthony Mangun
2817 Rapides Avenue
P.O. Box 8838
Alexandria, Louisiana 71306
318-487-8976
FAX 318-445-5406
wsbm777@aol.com
http://members.tripod.com/messiah_98/index.html

A phenomenon of rural religious fundamentalism, the Pentecostals of Alexandria charge the spirit with a vibrant style of worship that dates to America's revival movement. Pulsing and dramatic, the interaction of the preacher and the congregation moves from scripture to exhortation and gospel. One of the contributions of this vigorous faith to late-twentieth-century Christianity is a body of uplifting "heart music"— Dottie Rambo's "Behold the Lamb," Joel Hemphill's "He's Still Working on Me," Lanny Wolfe's "Greater Is He That Is in Me," Geron Davis's "Holy Ground," and Mark Carouthers's "Mercy Seat." These fresh praise songs with an Elvis beat buoy Alexandria's choir. Clad in teal and black robes, they sway to organ and drum, urging people in the pews to drop inhibitions. The clapping, shouting congregants express joy in a response their minister calls a baptism in the Holy Spirit. The conclusion is cathartic for suppliants, who weep and kneel to receive the laying on of hands.

BELIEFS

Like other Pentecostals and Assembly of God members, Alexandria's Pentecostals follow a time-honored pattern of worship. They adhere to informality and diminished liturgy and practice foot washing, charismatic healing, and glossolalia, or speaking in tongues, as evidence of the individual's receipt of sanctity. Religious ecstasy entered revivalism on January 1, 1901, during a service led by Holiness preacher Charles F. Parham in Topeka, Kansas, when Agnes Ozman, a student at Bethel Bible College, spoke in tongues. Worshippers interpreted the occurrence as a sign of God's touch. In subsequent sessions, Parham and others experienced the same effusive utterances. From 1905 to 1913, the phenomenon inspired the preaching of one of Parham's students, black evangelist William J. Seymour. His Azusa Street Revival at a warehouse in Los Angeles preceded an upsurge of the rural South's ecstatic worship, the beginning of Pentecostalism.

Doctrinal differences have isolated Alexandria's Pentecostals since 1916, when the main body of Pentecostalism labeled them heretics for their deviation from orthodox scriptural interpretation. Called the Oneness Pentecostals, they diverge from the parent denomination by rejecting the concept of a triune God and by embracing Jesus as the only deity. Their distinct shift away from bedrock Protestant tenets produced a new practice, the baptism of believers in the name of Jesus alone rather than Father, Son, and Holy Spirit.

The nation's 2.1 million Oneness Pentecostals further fragmented into separate organizations—the Assemblies of God, Church of the Foursquare Gospel, and Elim Missionary Assemblies, named for the desert oasis where the Children of Israel found twelve wells. Alexandria's church belongs to the United Pentecostal Church (UPC), a sect of 700,000 members organized around the denunciation of three-god theology. Their brash insistence on Jesus only implies that Christians baptized in the Trinity are unsaved and therefore doomed to perdition.

Critics label Oneness Pentecostals meanspirited, judgmental, and narrow-minded for an elitism that degrades all other believers as inferiors. One branch, the Oneness Apostolics, display extreme piety by banning jewelry and makeup, women's slacks and short hairstyles, membership in such secret orders as Masons, movie theaters, sports events, and television. Doctrinal differences keep the sect and its rivals in a constant state of contention, forcing members and leaders to abandon proud, rigid hard-liners in favor of peace.

HISTORY

One of the voices coaxing Pentecostals away from schism is the Reverend G. Anthony Mangun, an advocate of tolerance and reconciliation. The influential congregation he pastors dates to a Rapides Avenue storefront revival held in the late 1920s. After the itinerant evangelist completed the week's sessions, he left behind a handful of women who wanted to retain the revival spirit that earned spontaneously exuberant Pentecostals the derisive nickname of Holy Rollers. They formalized their intent by accepting the leadership of the Reverend L. L. Hall, who assembled worshippers in a building at Ninth and Madison Streets. After several moves, in 1931, the congregation of 17 built a small church home on Bertie Street.

The church's second decade brought growth and reaffirmation of the demonstrative Pentecostal faith. At a new building on Sixteenth and Day Streets, they hosted a ninety-day outdoor revival that brought their number to 50. Within five years, churchmen formed a construction crew to add a second story and basement levels to supply classrooms and an auditorium to accommodate 150. Mounting fervor prefaced a mission outreach in Bentley, Ball, Red Store, Tioga, and Belldeau.

The hiring of an energetic leader, the Reverend G. Anthony Mangun, in 1950 initiated a significant chapter in the life of the church that extended into the next millennium. Through his tent revivals, bus ministry, and radio broadcast, *Echoes of Faith,* the membership burgeoned to 400. Trustees razed the parsonage and church and erected a larger brick auditorium, two-story education wing, kitchen, and social room. The cycle of growth required another move in 1968, when the church sold its building and constructed a complex featuring a 1,300-seat auditorium.

A former pastor's son, the Reverend G. A. Mangun came from Plano, Texas, to pastor the Pentecostals of Alexandria in the late 1980s. On January 16, 1987, he dedicated the current facility, which serves over 2,700. Amid the controversy of creed and baptism, Mangun has survived a questionable link to President Bill Clinton, his close friend since Clinton's days as governor of Arkansas. The President's delight in fundamentalist music led to an invitation for Mangun's church choir to perform at both the 1993 and 1997 inaugural festivities, with Mickey Mangun, the minister's wife, directing "Lift up Holy Hands" and "He's Faithful." Clinton also attended performances of the *Messiah,* the church's annual Easter pageant coordinating 500 actors and singers in a dramatization of Christ's crucifixion and resurrection. In revelations of the 1997 scandal involving the use of the Lincoln bedroom for friends and campaign supporters, Mangun was one of many listed as overnight guests at the White House. He offered spiritual support to Clinton and once challenged politics by denouncing the 1996 policy allowing partial-birth abortions.

ACTIVITIES

The Pentecostals of Alexandria are active in the faith. Their music program includes youth and adult choirs and an orchestra. The Anchor outreach supports newcomers; Grace House shelters homeless men; a ministry to the deaf offers signing at services. In July 1996, the Reverend G. A. Mangun and his staff conducted a crusade in San Salvador, El Salvador, to an audience of 23,000. Other venues are singles and nursing home ministry, counseling, and compassionate care for the mentally handicapped. One of the church's innovations is a ministry to criminals. Volunteers offer substance-abuse classes, Bible study, and worship at Rapides Parish boot camp and jail, Bordelonville Women's and Winn correctional institutions, Beauregard and Cottonport prisons, and Rapides Parish Work Release. In addition, the staff maintains a multimedia Web site, missions hotline, White Steeple Books and Music, and radio broadcasts over KSYL.

Sources: Ahlstrom 1972; *Eerdmans' Handbook to the World's Religions* 1982; Gentz 1973; Grady 1997; Howell; "The Pentecostals of Alexandria"; Smith 1995; "Who Slept at the White House?" 1997; Wilson and Ferris 1989.

Pipestone National Monument

36 Reservation Avenue
Pipestone, Minnesota 56164
507-825-5464
FAX 507-825-5466

Keepers of the Sacred Tradition of Pipemakers
P.O. Box 24
Pipestone, Minnesota 56164
507-875-3734

Within tall prairie grasses sheltering Hiawatha Lake, Pipestone Creek, and Winnewissa Falls lies Pipestone National Monument, a fine-grained rock formation sacred to Native Americans since prehistory. Valued by multiple tribes are the quarries of pipestone, a soft, reddish argillite nearly concealed by grassy tufts along the west slope of a high plateau. The upland that separates the Mississippi and Missouri Rivers the French called Côteau des Prairies (Ridge of the Prairies). Nearly as famous as the pipestone deposits are the petroglyphs carved into the Sioux quartzite outcrops near the quarry pits. Of the 100,000 visitors to the site in Pipestone County annually, most come to study the geological formations that produced one of North America's most prized Native American resources.

Geologists account for pipestone as a natural formation resulting from deposits of sand and sediment that were compressed into sandstone. Beneath it, another layer of clay stone formed from red clay. A glacier scraped the topsoil away, revealing sandstone. The weight of the glacier and high temperatures transformed the stone into quartzite and the red clay sediment into pipestone. Up to twelve feet below the crust, two layers of quartzite trapped the pipestone vein.

Tribes dispatched groups to acquire pipestone for religious use. Dressed in ceremonial garb, a chosen leader would raise a boulder, swing it four times, and hurl it onto the quartzite that concealed the pipestone. Through sincere prayer, the leader obtained permission of the Great Spirit to burst through the quartzite layer and disclose the holy red substance below. From quarried materials, pipe makers shaped tubes, elbows, and bowls, which they often carved into animal and human shapes. The finished pipe carried human significance—four trailing ribbons

Native Americans quarrying rock at Pipestone, Minnesota (Minnesota Historical Society/Charles H. Bennett)

in black, white, red, and yellow represented the four directions, west, north, east, and south. The stem was a phallus and the bowl a female or earth form. Its ethereal smoke drifted upward to convey human concerns to God.

Over the past three millennia, Blackfoot, Cheyenne, Lakota Sioux, and Ojibway carved pipestone into sacred pipes or yard-long calumets, which their owners have borne over trade links more than 1,000 miles from the quarry. The quarry generated a law of nations: On holy turf, visitors suspended tribal animosities to share a pipe of sacred tobacco, or kinnikinnick, the Algonquin term for a mixed smoking material blended from red willow or dogwood inner bark, bearberry, dry sumac, and tobacco and used for purification. All departed in peace without using the approach to the hallowed site to military advantage.

The pipestone quarry bound a many-textured native population into one accord. The quarry's valued material produced pipes for reverencing the Great Spirit, whether he was identified as Wakan Tanka, Kitchi Manitou, or other terms for deity. Ritual smoking became the introit for prayer and meditation, blessing infants, welcoming

visitors, or honoring the deceased. To rally braves to war or to cement a trade of goods or hostages, pipe bearers offered a ceremonial smoke. During eras of conflict, the pipe symbolized a truce of safe conduct for tribe ambassadors signing a treaty or arriving in hostile territory on official business. From white observation of this single use, the pipe acquired the name of "peace pipe."

HISTORY

In the Lakota oral tradition, the stone was once the blood of victims of a catastrophic flood, which the Great Spirit sent to cleanse the earth. A Mississippi Sioux myth claims that the Great Spirit reddened the ledge with the buffalo he slew and ate and that he created the first human shape from the blood-red stone. This creation mythos links the stone to the very flesh and being of aborigines. According to a Minneconjou Lakota keeper of the Sioux Sacred Calf Pipe, White Buffalo Calf Woman delivered the first pipe to native peoples as a gift from the Great Spirit to preserve and unify humankind. From this lovely messenger, the pipe derived the name of "sacred calf pipe." (Steltenkamp 1982, 23) Ethnologist J. L. Smith surmised that the trans-

Within tall prairie grasses sheltering Hiawatha Lake, Pipestone Creek, and Winnewissa Falls, Minnesota, lies Pipestone National Monument, a fine-grained rock formation sacred to native Americans since prehistory. (Courtesy National Park Service)

mission was a real event and dated the sacred pipe and its wrappings to 1798.

As a symbol of earth, the stone bowl emits smoke messages into the heavens. Smoking ceremonies involve body decoration, prayers to the earth mother, and peaceful smoking before engaging in the seven sacred rites:

- Wacekiyapi—spirit-keeping, or reverence for deceased family members
- Tapa Wanka Yap—throwing the ball, an earth symbol
- Hunkapi—allying with relatives
- Ishna Ta Awi Cha Lowan—coming-of-age, or puberty, rites
- Wiwanyang Wacipi—Sun Dance
- Inikagapi—sweat lodge
- Hanbelachia—vision quest

Indians willingly traveled great distances to the Pipestone Quarries to acquire material for ritual items fundamental to worship. At the end of Lakota pipe-smoking rites, they acknowledged the interrelation of all living things.

George Catlin recorded a separate version of myth that pictured the Great Spirit in the shape of a great bird that perched on the wall of rock. The voice of God called all tribes to gather round. The bird broke free a sliver of red stone from a rock ledge. He molded it into a pipe, filled it with tobacco, and smoked it. He informed his hearers that pipestone symbolized human flesh, which he had created from the earth. To communicate with God, he commanded Indians to send messages through the pipes. He warned that pipestone was sacred and not to be used for mundane purposes and concluded with an injunction against fighting or even bringing war clubs and scalping knives onto the sacred red ledge. Before he dissolved into the clouds, he left two great ovens and two female guardians, Twomeccostee and Tsome-

GEORGE CATLIN, HENRY WADSWORTH LONGFELLOW, AND THE THREE MAIDENS PETROGLYPHS

An American artist who preserved on canvas the changing West, George Catlin lived at peace among Indian tribes across the United States. A native of Wilkes-Barre, Pennsylvania, he was born July 26, 1796, and studied law before establishing a career in art. He specialized in Native American ceremonies and daily life, particularly those of the Mandan of the Missouri Valley. He traveled on horseback to a fabled red-stone quarry, where natives stood back and tossed gifts of tobacco to the gods. Fearing he was a government spy, they attempted to scare him away with warnings that touching the hallowed rock would be a fearful sacrilege causing "a hole . . . in their flesh, and the blood could never be made to stop running." (Catlin 1989, 435)

Catlin ignored the warning and explored the area, which he described as belonging to the Sioux. He added that George Clark of the Lewis and Clark expedition thirty-three years earlier had reported "that every tribe on the Missouri told him they had been to this place, and that the Great Spirit kept the peace amongst his red children on that ground, where they had smoked with their enemies." (Catlin 1989, 436) In *North American Indians* (1839), Catlin extolled the beauty of the local rock, which "has a high polish on its surface, entirely beyond any results which could have been produced by diluvial action, being perfectly glazed as if by ignition." (Catlin 1989, 428)

In a conversation with a Mandan, Catlin learned that the Missouri tribe had visited Pipestone and made marks on the stones. The Mandan requested that Catlin speak to the Great Father, his name for the American president, to gain permission to return "to visit our medicines [for] our pipes are old and worn out." (Catlin 1989, 439) A Puncah chief of the upper Missouri had commented that he wanted to return to "the mountain of the red pipe" to restore intertribal peace.

He complained, "We have seen all nations smoking together at that place—but, my brother, it is not so now." (Catlin 1989, 439)

Catlin studied a column thirty-five feet high, where emerging braves tried to prove their mettle by climbing to the top without slipping to certain death on the crags below. He exulted in the breadth of emotion the quarry evoked and remarked, that the pipe

> has blown its fumes of peace and war to the remotest corners of the Continent; which has visited every warrior, and passed through its reddened stem the irrevocable oath of war and desolation. And here also, the peace-breathing calumet was born, and fringed with the eagle's quills, which has shed its thrilling fumes over the land, and soothed the fury of the relentless savage. (Catlin 1989, 429)

The sanctity of pipestone confirmed his belief that white Americans had misjudged natives as incapable of honor or long-lasting peace.

Carved in the quartzite bedrock that underlies a glacially deposited group of large granite boulders called the Three Maidens, Catlin saw a series of petroglyphs, which he referred to as tribal totems and weapons. In a sketch of Pipestone completed in 1836, he captured boulders known as the Three Maidens, which overlooked the quarries, a quartzite ledge, a creek, and a waterfall. In his journals, he noted that Indians considered the maidens as the quarries' guardian spirits, offered them ritual pinches of tobacco, and venerated the natural formation so much that they refrained from walking on grass in the area. He dispatched a sample of the red stone and sent it to Washington, D.C., for analysis. In his honor, geologists named the stone catlinite.

costecondee, whom medicine men consulted on the finer points of their art. After he dematerialized, the company found his footprints in the rock outcropping.

Another legend, recorded by James W. Lynd in 1860, states that a large company of Ehanktonwanna and Teetonwan Sioux gathered to work the quarry. Shortly before sunset, the skies clouded and thunder rolled. The workers were

fleeing to shelter when they spied a pillar of smoke above a huge boulder. It took the shape of a giant sitting on the rock with one arm extended to heaven. The other hand pointed to the giant's feet. After successive peals of thunder and lightning, the shape vanished. The next morning, the workers found images carved on the rock. Since that time, the Sioux have considered the spot *wakan* (sacred).

In the early nineteenth century, encroaching Europeans revealed the spot to the outside world. The first white observer, Philander Prescott, an agent for the North American Fur Company, documented in 1831 that Indians toiled with stones, hoes, axes, and even a six-pound cannonball to break through the quartzite and free the pipestone underneath. While working on a cartographic expedition for the U.S. government in the upper Mississippi area, a French scientist, Joseph N. Nicollet, traversed the quarry site in 1838. As proof of the visit, members of his party carved initials on the northern end of the quartzite ledge.

With the Indian Appropriations Bill of 1851, the U.S. government purchased the quarry as part of Sisseton and Wahpeton lands in southern Minnesota. Only the Yankton Sioux objected. In 1858, the government granted the Yankton unrestricted rights to the quarry on a 650-acre reservation after the tribe ceded 11 million acres of their land for settlement. Catlin's journals inspired poet Henry Wadsworth Longfellow to mention the sacred quarry in the Native American epic *The Song of Hiawatha* (1855). In the narration, the prophet Hiawatha follows the commands of Gitche Manito, another spelling of the name of the Great Spirit and master of life. Hiawatha visits Hereafter, a prairie land near the Pipestone quarry, where the God mounts a crag and summons all tribes to a gathering. The scenario evidences the sanctity of Pipestone, which Longfellow preserved in verse.

In 1859, W. O. Williams, who may have been part of a surveying party, copied the petroglyphs. By the 1870s, homesteader George A. Perley and Minnesota state geologists Newton H. Winchell and Warren Upham began mapping and cataloging the forty to fifty individual figures. In the 1880s, several years after whites opened a quartzite quarry operation and began building houses, Smithsonian Institution researchers Philetus Norris and Walter James Hoffman traced and recorded the carvings. In 1890, another viewer, German tourist Rudolph Cronau, published sketches of fourteen glyphs, which he drew before the citizens of Pipestone hired Leon H. Moore to slice them into thirty-six rock slabs around 1888 to protect them from vandalism. After their removal, Theodore H.

Lewis produced seventy-nine comprehensive sketches. The slabs went on exhibition at the 1904 Louisiana Purchase Exposition in St. Louis. In 1926, the petroglyph slabs passed to the care of the Pipestone County Historical Society, and twenty years later, to the National Park Service for exhibit at Pipestone National Monument, where they are secured in the visitor center.

In 1927, three Yankton Sioux elders stated their observation of the Three Maidens area, which they recognized as the holy ground of other tribes. Three witnesses—Many Dogs, Julia Conger, and Simon Antelope—testified to the long history of the place. Many Dogs recalled a visit in 1873, when he studied the petroglyphs. Julia Conger knew of them from her grandmother, who witnessed native worship involving sacrifices at the site and observed rock carvings of dogs, ponies, and other figures to denote a consecrated place. Simon Antelope, who visited in 1875, reported that vandals had defaced depictions of deer and Indian men and women. In an era that saw the dissolution of much aboriginal religion, these oral proofs of significance helped secure the monument's future.

As Native Americans agitated for autonomy, they began pressuring the government to relinquish rights to Pipestone National Monument. In 1987, a Yankton Sioux resolution initiated a series of demands to the Senate Select Committee on Indian Affairs and the U.S. Department of the Interior. To generate sympathy for their cause, they held the first of eight annual runs from Greenwood, South Dakota, to the quarries. In 1992, Keepers of the Treasures convened at Sioux Falls, South Dakota, to declare war on sacrilege debasing or abusing Sioux spirituality. They singled out the sale of sacred pipes at flea markets, unauthorized powwows, New-Age usurpation of aboriginal rites, and the use of sacred stone to make shot glasses, ashtrays, medallions, and trinkets.

In place of traditional significance, later viewers have established their own numinous interpretation, which some derive from listening to resident spirits. These visitors and local authorities surmise that there may be additional petroglyphs concealed through time by shifts in surface rock. In 1992, the maintenance chief discovered some faint petroglyphs of a bird, a turtle, two feet, three bird tracks, and six shape-less peckings previously undetected. In spring 1994, a visitor left an offering of tobacco tied to a bush. That same year, archeologists burned away grass from the acreage and discovered a bird track petroglyph on a quartzite ledge. In 1995, participants in the Pipestone Sun Dance requested use of the petroglyphs, which were calling to worshippers. Interviews in 1996 with Yankton Sioux, Flandreau-Santee Sioux, and Pipestone Dakota indicated that current tribes revere the quarries but have lost the original connection with the petroglyphs, which may have been spiritual guides, personal notations, directions or landmarks, or part of a winter count, a Native American census. Removal of the rock slabs from their original positions may have permanently obscured clues to the quarry's significance to native religion.

ACTIVITIES

Native Americans maintain the sanctity of Pipe-stone National Monument as a cultural, histori-cal and holy site. The creation of sacred pipes is traditionally a male-dominated ritual, accompa-nied by the making and guarding of the sacred pipe bundle, in which the pipe stays when not in service. To establish a link with nature, the pre-server of the pipe decorates the stem with an an-imal form and decorative marks. Holy men of-ten mark the bowl with symbols drawn from personal visions or from the tribe's symbolic leg-ends and myths. In early times, the user grasped the pipestem reverently and pointed it to the four directions, beginning with west and moving clockwise to the north, east, and south, and then up to the sky and down to earth. As the user dropped a pinch of tobbaco, sweet grass, or cedar into the bowl, he prayed over his offering and lifted the pipe to the heavenly powers.

Late-twentieth-century impetus to reclama-tion of the quarry came from the federal gov-ernment. On May 24, 1996, President Bill Clin-ton issued an executive order protecting and preserving Indian religions. On August 24, 1996, a handful of traditional pipe makers formed an extended stewardship: a spiritual church to pro-tect the site from exploitation or domination by one tribe or group, to pass along quarrying and pipe lore to youth, and to perpetuate free barter

among tribes and the sanctuary's neutrality as it had been for over a millennium. To launch the church, pipe makers entered a sweat lodge to seek divine guidance and assistance from the spirits and the sacred six directions. The confer-ence ended the next day with gifts to the creator and earth mother and a thanksgiving feast.

A Minnesota Red Lake Chippewa, Adam Fortunate Eagle, the Spiritual Leader of the Keepers of the Sacred Tradition of Pipemakers and author of *Alcatraz, Alcatraz: The Indian Occu-pation* (1992), sanctified the area by blessing Minnesota's quarries. His formal gesture ac-knowledged the importance of the pipe as a pri-mary tool of Indian ritual and token of pipe makers' sacred vows. The rededication of the pipe-making society revitalized an enduring faith and unites aboriginal nations in a binding trust. After purchasing a historical building as headquarters and assembly hall, Fortunate Eagle and his associates fostered state recognition of the spiritual organization and began compiling data on the importance of pipes to all tribes.

Current laws limit quarrying to that done by Native Americans. Over a period ranging up to six weeks after winter passes, diggers equipped with chisels, hammers, wedges, and shovels dig through the hard surface as their ancestors did. By forcing through crevices in the quartzite, they pry away surface stone to expose pipestone below and select the two-inch seam suited to pipe making. To pass the skill to the next gener-ation, members founded the Upper Midwest Indian Cultural Center at the monument office to demonstrate the craft and sell pipes to visi-tors. The Pipestone Historic District features buildings constructed of locally quarried Sioux quartzite.

An annual Hiawatha Pageant, begun in 1949, draws thousands to the natural amphitheater just north of the city at the quarry entrance to see local actors perform Henry Wadsworth Longfel-low's epic poem. A special performance marked the fiftieth anniversary of the pageant, which began from an Exchange Club project. Because the quarry had no electric power, viewers orig-inally lighted the first staging with car head-lights. Today, over 35,000 visitors see the pageant each summer. Current facilities offer a 5,000-seat amphitheater and lights and sound equipment to enhance the 1,500-foot stage. For verisimilitude, the 200 actors dress in authentic costumes purchased from the Indian Trading Post in Pawnee, Oklahoma.

Sources: Breeden 1976; Cantor, George, 1993; Carmody and Carmody 1993; Catlin 1989; Champagne 1994; Fode 1997; Hughes 1997; "Keepers of the Sacred Traditions of Pipemakers"; *Lakota: Seeking the Great Spirit* 1994; McCracken 1959; Milne 1995; Patterson and Snodgrass 1994; "Pipestone, Minnesota"; "Pipestone National Monument"; Rasmussen and Smith 1995; Ray 1994; Steiger 1974; Steltenkamp 1982; Thiessen 1999; Waldman 1990.

Plum Street Temple
Lewis H. Kamrass, Senior Rabbi
Richard M. Steinberg, Associate Rabbi
Plum Street
c/o 8329 Ridge Road
Cincinnati, Ohio 45236
513-579-9441; 513-793-2556
www.wisetemple.org

Cincinnati's grand "Alhambra Temple," the Plum Street synagogue survives as a result of a concerted rededication to a historic synagogue that dates to the American Civil War. Built in 1866 by Rabbi Isaac Mayer Wise, it began with 250 families and has grown to 1,300. In 1996, the congregation received an honor award from the National Trust for Historic Preservation for remaking a battered urban landmark into a viable temple.

HISTORY AND ARCHITECTURE
When Rabbi Isaac Mayer Wise imported the German concepts of Reform Judaism to the United States, he nurtured big plans. The congregation he eventually led began simply in 1840 with meetings at the Workum House on Third Street. By September 22, 1848, they had constructed a permanent worship center on Lodge Street. Upon his arrival in 1854, he planned the Temple of B'nai Yeshurun, a sanctuary in which 1,200 worshippers could enjoy a golden age and Cincinnati could serve the nation as the center of the reform movement.

Halfway through the Civil War, Rabbi Wise's followers pushed for completion of his goal. To

ISAAC MAYER WISE

A dynamic nineteenth-century religious leader and father of American Reform Jewry, Isaac Mayer Wise was a keen visionary who respected tradition and the tastes and needs of his adopted country. Born March 29, 1819, he was the son of teacher Leo and Regina Weiss (later changed to Wise) of Steingrub, Bohemia. He was home-schooled in Bible and Talmud before studying with his grandfather, a physician. Wise graduated from the universities of Prague and Vienna before earning the title of rabbi at age twenty-three.

The problems of leading a congregation and rearing a family of ten children forced Wise to immigrate to the United States in 1846 in search of freedom. While leading a congregation in Albany, New York, for four years, he initiated numerous innovations—the liturgical use of choral singing, confirmation instead of Bar Mitzvah, and an end to segregating women from men during worship. The speed of his changes dismayed congregants, who voted him out at Rosh Hashanah in 1850. A group of followers joined him in founding a reform synagogue, Anshe Emet (Men of Truth).

At age thirty-five, Wise moved west to Cincinnati to accept the rabbinate of Beth Eichim, where he remained to the end of his career. In 1856, he attempted to introduce a uniform prayer book, *Minhag America* (The Custom of America), and an American rabbinical college and to organize reform congregations nationwide but failed to counteract the disapproval of Orthodox rabbis. In 1873, he convened delegates from thirty-four reform congregations to establish the Union of American Hebrew Congregations. In two years, he led them in founding the Hebrew Union College, America's first Jewish seminary. He created and led the Central Conference of American Rabbis in 1889 and remained president and ethical and ritual authority over American Jews until his death on March 26, 1910. The conference adopted the *Union Prayer Book for Jewish Worship* and maintained unity among reformed Jews.

suit the lot on Eighth and Plum Streets, he chose a squared Byzantine-Moorish design with a deep-niched façade, a rose window, and twin minarets. Below the ornate roof railing, six pairs of stained-glass windows frame the upper story, with four smaller pairs on the first story. To the rear, gently rounded domes ennoble two side entrances. The temple was ready for occupancy in August 1866.

Cincinnati's Jews created a substantial worship center where the rabbi could emerge from behind the impressive red and gold ark through a passageway linked to his study. The American designer, James Keys Wilson, produced a Gothic basilica that preserved the conventions of clerestory, side aisles, transept, and rose window. He surrounded attendees with stained glass and installed an organ suited to the acoustics. Patterned arched ceilings matched the lacy edging that linked each bay to slender pillars and jeweled chandeliers suspended on chains. Above, the Ten Commandments bind the worship experience in unchanging law.

From its dedication on August 23, 1866, Plum Street Temple was an impressive, but deeply spiritual showplace. However, the dream of a unified reformed community held true only so long as Cincinnati Jews prospered downtown. As suburbia grew, the congregation built a satellite on the edge of town and enlarged to a third branch synagogue in Amberley. In 1902, members founded the Isaac M. Wise Center on Reading Road south of Ridgeway as a religious school. In 1925, it moved to a new site on North Crescent and Reading Road. In 1931, Plum Street's 650 members merged with Achim Sherith Israel's 258 congregants. A faithful group, the Friends of the Plum Street Temple, preserved its importance to the community and religious history. In 1975, the U.S. Department of the Interior added the temple to the National Register of Historic Places.

ACTIVITIES

Unlike religious spaces that become relics and museums, the temple is a working religious center. It remains open to the public; the temple sisterhood conducts guided tours. Out of respect for Rabbi Wise and his dream, members reserve the Plum Street Temple for Sabbath services, special ceremonies, and holy days.

In 1996, trustees completed a third renovation by enhancing the worship space with awe-inspiring artistry. They financed a new roof and wiring, remodeled the floor, and repaired paint and stenciling on pillars. They lighted the ark, where silver and red velvet embellish the Torah scrolls, and expressed the words of the psalmist David and prophet Isaiah in fourteen bands of gold calligraphy that encompass the architrave, the bottom segment of the entablature. In addition to use for a youth choir and sisterhood teas and breakfasts, current uses include a Safrai Gallery of Jerusalem Art Exhibit and Sale, Simchat Torah, Shavuot Sensation Service and Study Sessions, and Congregational Havdalah Service and New Millennium Event on January 1, 2000. The year's festivities continue with the Sisterhood Purim Pizza Dinner in costume, a Megillah Reading, Marriage Reconsecration Service, Congregational Seder, blessing of confirmands, Wise Center Day Camp, Selichot Dessert, and Sukkot Congregational Dinner and Family Service.

Sources: Ahlstrom 1972; Brody 1996; Grossman 1996; Lipman; Williams, Peter W., 1997.

Point Barrow

Arnold Brower, President
Bureau of Tribal Affairs
Point Barrow, Alaska 99723
907-852-4411

Native religion at Point Barrow, the northernmost promontory in the United States, links human subsistence to birds and sea life. A treeless tundra ice-bound in winter, the land demands respect. No less demanding is the sea, the source of raw material on an untillable landscape devoid of garden plots, firewood, and building material. In honor of centuries of survival, the Makah of Point Barrow pass to their offspring the 1,500-year Inupiat ritual sanctifying whaling as an indigenous way of life.

BELIEFS

According to mythologist Susan Feldman's story "Sedna, Mistress of the Underworld," drawn from Stith Thompson's *Tales of the North American Indians* (1929), whales connect directly to the icy peril of the deep and to frostbite that endangers the extremities. In the myth, a solitary Indian named Inung lived with his daughter

Sedna on the Alaskan shore. Seduced by a fulmar, a polar seabird, she flew away with him to the ice house of a deceitful lover. A year later, when Inung visited her, he slew the fulmar and retrieved Sedna in his boat. The birds set up a mournful keening for their fellow and stirred up the seas, which threatened Inung's frail craft.

To save himself, the father tossed Sedna overboard as a peace offering to undersea deities. Because she gripped the gunnels with her fingers, Inung chopped off her fingertips with a knife. When they fell into the sea, they changed into ten whales. His second chop at the bloody stumps produced ten seals, which swam away. The fulmars, believing the girl drowned, halted the storm. Her father pulled her back into the boat. From that day, she nourished a vicious hatred of him and taught her dogs to gnaw at his hands and feet.

Point Barrow's aborigines believed that the *tuungaq* (animal spirits) controlled the cosmos. To propitiate the spirits of land and sea, they respected the chants and curative magic formulas of the *angatqaq* (shaman). Likewise obedient to structured religion, Makah readied themselves for oceangoing expeditions with ancient ritual. In the waxing winter moon, Umiak crew members purified their bodies in frigid streams and lakes and then chafed their skin with hemlock twigs and nettles to toughen them for the spring hunt. The hardening process demanded abstinence from food and sex and required underwater swims to imitate the movements of *agvik*, the Umiak word for whales.

When the bowhead whales returned to the Arctic Ocean each March after migrating from the Bering Sea, the hunt began. The official start of the season was keyed to divine revelation—when a whaler first dreamed of the giant mammal. Parties of eight stocked their twenty-six-foot craft with two days' supply of water and food, hung charms from the mast, and paddled into the swells for an epic stalking of the whale. Essential to their search were bailers, sealskin floats, hand-wrapped sinew lines, and sixteen-foot harpoons tipped with sharpened mussel shell.

The hunt began quietly with prayer and watching. At the sign of fish fleeing a predator, the men anticipated the hump of a whale, a forward roll, and a waterspout from the blowhole.

To the animal's left, the seven oarsmen maneuvered close enough for the harpooner to stand and thrust his weapon. As the coil spooled out, the whalers dropped floats into the sea and prepared for the pull of a fifty-ton mammal towing them far from land.

The end of the hunt put man in contact with beast. As the whale pulled seaward in fog-bound waters, floats attached to the rope impeded his progress and forced him toward exhaustion and death from loss of blood. One heroic paddler leaped overboard to stitch the great lips shut to keep a bubble of air in the jaws so the carcass wouldn't sink. The others fought to keep the craft upright in the water and rescue any oarsman who fell overboard. When the crew pulled ashore, villagers, dancing and singing whalers' songs, converged on the whale and stuffed the blowhole with sacred eagle down. The beach reception marked a year of communal planning, ritual, storytelling, and blessing from the spirits of the deep.

HISTORY

The aborigines of Alaska have always been seafarers. According to one theory of aboriginal North America, Asiatic wanderers crossed the Beringia land bridge, which spanned the fifty-six-mile Bering Strait, and walked from Siberia to Alaska sometime before 10,000 B.C. Over centuries, the newcomers encompassed the coast into central and South America all the way to Tierra del Fuego. In 1964, researcher Louis Denbigh discovered paleoarctic flint tools at Cape Denbigh on Norton Sound that prove the settlement of a nonagrarian people in the Barrow region around 4000 B.C.

Asian-style pottery appeared 1,000 years later, followed by slate tools, oil lamps, and burins, sharp points used for etching. These early people lived in subterranean sod houses and balanced their existence between hunting caribou and, around 800 A.D., open-boat fishing with toggle-ended harpoons to secure the catch. Two centuries later, they evolved the classic Thule life way. No longer homebound, they ice-hunted, voyaged by two-person kayak and twenty-five-passenger umiak, traveled on land by dogsled, and settled into large villages. Whaling was ingrained in the social makeup and explains the good health of the Inupiat, who strengthened their hearts and tissues with nourishing fish oils.

The twentieth century saw an influx of outsiders among Alaska's northern maritime peoples. A jumping-off spot in circumpolar flight, Barrow was the point of departure for Sir George Hubert Wilkins, who flew over the North Pole in 1928, and the place where Wiley Post's plane went down in 1935, killing humorist Will Rogers. During World War II, the U.S. Navy established an Arctic research station at Barrow, which citizens formally incorporated in 1959. The area prospered from the sale of oil and natural gas deposits. Tourists thronged to the shores and boarded excursion craft for a glimpse of whales, Alaska's icon. In June 1977, natives held the first international Inuit Circumpolar Conference at Barrow.

The Inuit revamped their traditions in the late 1970s. Since the 1920s, their whalers had lived during turbulent times, when gray whales grew scarce and native hunters voluntarily ceased killing them. Because industrial whaling brought the big grays dangerously near extinction, in 1926, the International Whaling Commission had outlawed the slaughter of whales. In September 1977, the Inuit formed the Alaskan Commission to revoke the ban and to launch a scientific study of forces threatening the bowhead whale, which Alaska's legislators designated as the state mammal in October 1983. The fight against outsiders produced an immediate native unity, a bunker mentality that made a broad demarcation between "us" and "them."

ACTIVITIES

Championing the whale hunt has kept the tribe whole during years of neglected hunting tradition. In 1994, authorities removed the whale from the endangered species list, despite protests from the Sea Shepherd and save-the-whale groups. On October 23, 1997, the Makah of Seattle, Washington, brokered a deal with the thirty-nine-nation International Whaling Commission to allow them four gray whales annually in either spring or fall. Under an exemption of the Marine Mammal Protection Act, natives may harvest the animals for subsistence or noncommercial purposes. Ecologists were surprised that the Clinton-Gore administration kept promises made in an 1855 treaty allowing the Makah unlimited access to sea harvesting. The shift in policy made the Makah the only sanctioned whalers in the United States.

The Makah immediately advanced plans for a ceremonial hunt as the whales make their annual trip up the Pacific coast. Rejoicing, Wilson Arnold's great grandson, Greig Arnold, and great great grandson, also named Wilson Arnold, anticipated a return to traditional whaling to rejuvenate community nature beliefs and traditions, the backbone of the Makah social order. Dan Greene, director of Makah Fisheries, vowed to conserve the supply of whales to assure survival. A Weapons Improvement Program monitors the kill to spare unnecessary suffering. On May 22, 1999, a successful hunt made international news.

These aboriginal sea expeditions do more than resurrect ancient harpoons and canoes. A form of tribal identity, the return of whaling to the people of northern Alaska preserves both their lifestyle and their religion. According to tribesman Daves Sones, the tribe once more erects an old-time cedar longhouse for ritual, weddings, feasts, and holidays. They have restored the dying faith of elder whalers, who were children when the last whaling party left Point Barrow. Revitalization of the tribe has relieved the burden of seasonal unemployment and also reunited Indian villagers with other natives, whom they invite to harvest celebrations to share the meat. Such communal goals and decision making have rejuvenated spirituality and unity.

Point Barrow's whaling history accounts for a whole set of native values that local freelance writer Elise Patkotak calls the "virtue of cooperation." The task involves the whole town and builds a lasting camaraderie based on democratic principles and neighborliness. Included at the slaughter are prayers to spirits of dead whales to ensure successful hunting in the future and retrieval of bits of bone and tooth for the carving of amulets. The process is private, off limits to outsiders. Butchering customs allot flukes, blubber, *maktak* (or *muktuk*), baleen, and other delicacies to elders and widows and reward the crew for courage. The rare native nonparticipant receives nothing. Tribal officials reserve some whale parts for Thanksgiving, Christmas, the post-Christmas Messenger Feast, and Nalukataq (or Nalukatak), the spring whaling festival and blanket toss. The overall renaissance of northwestern Alaska has resulted in Inupiat Ilitqusiat (the Spirit Movement), a cultural rebirth through the celebration of heritage.

> **Sources:** Adams; "Archeology of the Tundra and Arctic Alaska"; Bock 1995; "The Bowhead Whale"; Breeden 1976; Carpenter 1992; Champagne 1994; Chance 1990; D'Oro and Hunter 1997; Feldman 1965; Huntington 1992; Mowat 1989; Patkotak 1996; Patterson and Snodgrass 1994; Ritter 1999; Rossiter 1997; "Science Improves When Archaeologists Work with Locals" 1997; Simon 1998; Westneat 1996, 1997; Williams, Brian, 1997.

Prayer Tower
Bill Shuler, Campus Pastor
Oral Roberts University
7777 South Tulsa Avenue
Tulsa, Oklahoma 74171
918-495-6807
FAX 918-495-6809
jerigler@oru.edu
www.oru.edu/

An unusual American shrine, the Prayer Tower of Oral Roberts University rises above the 500-acre campus of Oral Roberts University in Tulsa, Oklahoma, as a symbol and source of intercessory prayer. Like much of the creativity of the founder, the tower combines sincere faith in prayer with the razzle-dazzle of showmanship. Both a religious tourist attraction and a source of comfort to people in need, the tower focuses viewers on a carefully packaged representation of divine power.

ARCHITECTURE
According to KORU-FM, at the campus center, Oral Roberts's futuristic 200-foot tower, constructed from glass, steel, and plastic PVC pipes, projects perpetual prayer. Completed April 1, 1967, the giant vertical takes the form of a modernistic cross, highlighted by a multifacted Crown of Thorns observation deck, where the voice of Richard Roberts, Oral Roberts's son, declares, "No second-class buildings for God." Beneath a circlet of 1,000 reflector shields, the eternal gas flame represents the omnipresence of the Holy Spirit. The tower houses a welcome center that receives 5,000 visits per month and a six-room "Journey into Faith" sound and laser light show. The gift shop, open from 9:00 A.M. to 5:00 P.M. Monday through Saturday and from 1:00 to 5:00 P.M. on Sunday, stocks books, pamphlets, audio and video tapes, and mementos.

Central to the tower's function is the Abundant Life Prayer Group, a cadre of trained spiritual guides who located on the observation deck the day it opened. These men and women, called compassionate prayer partners, are available to pray with people by telephone twenty-four hours a day at 918-495-7777. Since the opening of the complex in 1967, the Prayer Tower has drawn millions of observers and seekers, who photograph the campus and the Ralph L. Reece Memorial sunken gardens below.

ACTIVITIES
The spiritual activities require coordination from campus pastor Bill Shuler, men's chaplain Earl McClellan, and women's chaplain Brenda Coomer. The trio organize the Spiritual Life Department, which transforms the university's 4,500 students into adherents of prayer on and off campus. In preparation, young missionaries attend Chapel services, Campus Church, communion, prayer, devotions, and retreats and take part in community outreach, missions, and a music ministry. Since 1976, the tradition of action has extended teams to healing and evangelism in 100 nations.

The seasonal events involve a Halloween Outreach to collect canned goods for Thanksgiving meals in the Tulsa area. Volunteers at the Irving development painted a church and cleaned homes and yards. Others mentored students, conducted inner-city evangelism, and counseled AIDS patients. Members of a 60-voice choir perform at all chapel and campus church services, record religious music on CD and audio cassette, and tour the nation and beyond each summer. In dormitories, 75 student chaplains staff each floor and supply at-large ministry to commuters through counseling, weekly devotion, and prayer.

Additional opportunities for service take students to the Children's Medical Center to aid abused children, to the Boy Scouts, and to Destination Discovery to be role models to poor

ORAL ROBERTS

One of America's most prominent televangelists, Granville Oral Roberts and his charismatic ministry have dominated evangelism in the last quarter of the twentieth century, particularly in the south central states. Born on January 24, 1918, in Pontotoc County, Oklahoma, he is the son of Ellia M. and Claudius Irwin Roberts, a Pentecostal preacher. To attend to a shifting mission field, the family moved frequently and lived on an erratic cash flow. Roberts's childhood difficulties with stuttering and tuberculosis preceded a miraculous healing in July 1935 in Ada, Oklahoma, by evangelist George Moncey. After delivering his first sermon in thanksgiving for the cure, Roberts followed his father into independent evangelicalism, wrote for the *Pentecostal Holiness Advocate,* and developed a compelling oratory.

Roberts's peripatetic career took him to largely rural audiences in Fuquay Springs, North Carolina; Shawnee, Oklahoma; Toccoa, Georgia; and Enid, Oklahoma. While enrolled at Phillips University, he heard God command him to heal people and added a weekly healing service to his calendar. He entered the ministry in 1947 as an ordained Pentecostal Holiness pastor, tent revivalist, and healer. By the 1950s, his revivals, sponsored by the Oral Roberts Evangelical Association, drew 12,500 per tent and spread energetic preaching through distribution of prayer cloths, over 200 radio stations, and by film and shortwave to much of the globe. He published a religious magazine, *Healing Waters,* an autobiography, *Oral Roberts' Life Story* (1952), and a bestseller, *If You Need Healing— Do These Things.*

Roberts earned criticism for commercialism after shifting his focus to building a sizeable empire, Oral Roberts University. He required full-scale fund-raising from sources he dubbed his "partners." With the aid of Dr. Billy Graham, he dedicated the campus and its business, theology, nursing, and education programs in 1967. Having established authority among spiritual leaders by attending the 1966 World Evangelistic Conference on Evangelism in Berlin, he broke with the Pentecostals in 1968 by giving up tent revivals and allying with Methodism, which retargeted his ministry from the working class to middle America. Inducted into the Oklahoma Hall of Fame in 1972, he earned notoriety for flamboyant appearances on talk shows and the idea of Christian enrichment on earth. He kept in the public eye through a television program, *Oral Roberts and You,* and optimistic slogans—"Expect a miracle," "Release your faith," and "Something good is going to happen to you."

During the 1970s, personal travails burdened Roberts. After the deaths of his daughter and son-in-law in a plane crash, the suicide of a son, the divorce of his designated heir Richard, and controversy over questionable ethics among his athletic staff, he determined to add to the university campus a visionary sixty-story City of Faith. Composed of a hospital, a clinic, medical and dental schools, a nurse training center, and a research center that Roberts predicted would find a cure for cancer, the eighty-acre complex foundered late in the century. A proposed law school also failed to live up to grandiose predictions.

Despite his grandstanding and castigation of mainstream secular culture, Roberts successfully manipulated the media and sustained his television program during disastrous scandals that felled televangelists Jim and Tammy Bakker and Jimmy Swaggart. Roberts continued to surprise followers with stout claims, such as the 1980 revelation from a 900-foot Christ that predicted Roberts would die if he didn't raise substantial funding for the City of Faith. In the 1990s, he continued writing, revising an autobiography, and appearing on Christian television broadcasts but turned over management of Oral Roberts University to son Richard Roberts.

children. They visit Tulsa County Correctional Center to befriend minimum-security prisoners with recreation and conversation, play basketball with troubled youth at the Lloyd Rader Recreation Center, and write letters for Prison Pen Pals. They also call on retirement centers, support adopt-a-grandparent programs, aid the homeless through Fishers of Men and troubled women through Mend Crisis Pregnancy Center, and share recreation with the mentally ill at Walker Hall and Shadow Mountain. To spread the faith, they evangelize Hispanic prospects through Vision de Felicidad, uplift children at the Cherokee Children's Mission in Tahlequah,

An unusual American shrine, the Prayer Tower of Oral Roberts University rises above the 500-acre campus of Oral Roberts University in Tulsa, Oklahoma, as a symbol and source of intercessory prayer. (Courtesy Public Relations, Oral Roberts University)

preach in the streets through Warriors For Christ and to teens through Concert Outreach, and reenact Bible scenes through the Chapel Drama and Character Mime Troupe.

Sources: Ahlstrom 1972; *American Decades* 1998; *Biography Resource Center* 1999; Bolling 1983; Brinkley 1986; Dobbin 1987; Fairlie 1987; McNichol 1987; "Oral Roberts Prayer Tower"; "Oral Roberts University"; *Religious Leaders in America* 1999; "Some Postcard Views of Oral Roberts University"; Williams, Peter W., 1997; Wilson and Ferris 1989.

Rainbow Bridge

Navajo Mountain, Utah
Glen Canyon National Recreation Area
Box 1507
Page, Arizona 86040
602-645-8200; 520-608-6404; 800-582-4351
(emergencies only)

One of the seven natural wonders and the world's largest natural span, Utah's petrified rainbow is sacred to the Navajo. It is situated at the rim of Lake Powell on the Colorado Plateau and is accessible daily free of charge by horseback, foot, or boat from Wahweap or Bullfrog. A monument of Four Corners, the convergence of Arizona, Colorado, New Mexico, and Utah, the uplift rose 3,000 feet as the earth warped and mountains pushed skyward. The graceful landform took shape from natural erosion 200 million years ago. Heavy rains called pluvials caused a watercourse from Navajo Mountain that curved around a jagged edge and forced its way through reddish-brown Kayenta and Navajo sandstone. The emerging bridge—a 275-foot span that is 42 feet thick and 33 feet wide at the crest of the arch—is fragile evidence of forces that will eventually undermine and destroy it.

HISTORY

From ancient times, indigenous peoples viewed the 290-foot-high stone bridge as a sacred site. The Anasazi appear to have sanctified nearby shrines before the coming of the San Juan Southern Paiute and their successors, the Navajo, who moved into the area in the nineteenth century. According to mythographer Karl Luckert, it was this latter group who sanctified the bridge. In the mid-1860s, when Colonel Christopher "Kit" Carson rounded up the Navajo and exiled them on the Bosque Redondo Reservation at Ft. Sumner, New Mexico, Hoskininni [or Hashke Neiniih] led sixteen Navajo and Paiute renegades into hiding south of Navajo Mountain, Utah. Along with ten refugees from Black Mesa, Arizona, the band hid out at the juncture of the Colorado and San Juan Rivers.

One of the group, Jayi Begay (or Jaa'f Biye), later called Sharkie, and the Paiute Nasja Begay were the first to view the bridge while trailing stray cattle into the canyon gorge. Sharkie probably named it Rock Rainbow and initiated bridge lore into Navajo religion as a hallowed rainbow capable of summoning rain. At his urging, Navajo singers, or medicine men, made pilgrimages to the site. Superstitious Navajo established the taboo forbidding traffic under the bridge without the protection of native prayers.

The bridge went unrecorded, even though Mormon pioneers, cowboys, trappers, or Spanish prospectors may have viewed it years before its official finding. Because of its isolation in rugged terrain, the white world didn't learn of the formation until 1909, after archeologist Dr. Byron Cummings and William Boone Douglass, surveyor for the General Land Office, joined southwestern explorer John Wetherill on an overland trek through San Juan County to locate it. According to varied tales, Wetherill's wife, Mary Louisa, learned of the bridge from Sharkie, who guided outsiders and traded at the Oljeto, Utah, outpost. Although Sharkie died before the expedition, the trio, aided by Ute guide Jim Mike and Paiute Nasja Begay, Sharkie's confidante, reached the site on August 14 and revealed the treasured span to adventurers. The *Deseret News* reported the sighting on September 3, setting off a stream of claims and counterclaims concerning the who, how, and when of discovery.

On May 30, 1910, President William Howard Taft proclaimed Rainbow Bridge a national monument. Among white outsiders to retrace the expedition were Theodore Roosevelt and Western writer Zane Grey, who described the setting in a novel, *The Rainbow Trail* (1915). A major change in accessibility arrived with the

One of the seven natural wonders and the world's largest natural span, Utah's petrified Rainbow Bridge is sacred to the Navajo. (Neil Rabinowitz/Corbis)

Glen Canyon Dam. In 1963, the rise of Lake Powell opened the way for thousands of tourists to visit Rainbow Bridge each year. The bridge remains in the headlines because of controversy over Lake Powell reservoir waters backing up to the foundation and from renewed interest from rock hounds, photographers, campers, and climbers.

Casual access to the bridge came under federal scrutiny in 1974, when the Navajo sued the U.S. secretary of the interior, the commissioner of the Bureau of Reclamation, and the director of the National Park Service. The purpose of this public complaint was the preservation of Navajo sacred geography from human violation. The court ruled that water storage superseded native concerns. In 1980, the Tenth District Court of Appeals ruled that reserving Rainbow Bridge for Navajo ceremony would violate public rights to the national park.

Thirteen years later, spokesperson Bonnie Brown and five other Navajo blockaded the natural stone bridge when they conducted sacred four-day cleansing ceremonies. In the nonviolent takeover of August 11, 1995, they staked a claim before the media to demand privacy, to protect thirteen endangered species on reservation land, and to remove desecration and defilement accumulated over a quarter century. A National Park Service management plan offered a compromise suggested by Hopi, Kaibab Paiute, Navajo, San Juan Southern Paiute, and White Mesa Ute. Among their restrictions was a prohibition of climbing, carving, or walking under the bridge to lessen human impact of 300,000 tourists per year and to preserve the dignity and holiness of the site.

ACTIVITIES

Today, visitors approach the bridge most often from Dangling Rope Marina. Hiking and backpacking permits are available from the Navajo Nation. Rangers patrol daily from Memorial Day through Labor Day and less frequently other times of the year. The most effective protector of the area are wild animals and reptiles as well as extreme summer and winter temperatures, ranging from 0 to 110°F, flash flooding, and the absence of roads, lodging, campsites, and natural cover.

According to historian Wally Brown, a Navajo tribesman of the Bitter Water Clan, there is a connection between the bridge and the modern legend of the Rainbow Bridge that links human animal lovers with their deceased pets. He surmises from sand paintings by the Anasazi and Towering Hand People that the bridge was a discovery during the Fremont Culture before 1200 A.D. The formation took precedence in healing ritual as a link between the earth and the hereafter. He connects the term "rainbow" to the beckoning white light that people report after brushes with death. Another aspect of the pet heaven is the Navajo belief that, at one time, humans spoke with animals, who were their earthly equals. The arrival of white culture diminished the native rapport with the creatures and compromised spiritual unity with the outdoors.

> **Sources:** Baum 1992; Campbell 1994; Donovan 1995; Feed 1999; "How Was Rainbow Bridge Formed?"; Jett 1992; Kelley and Francis 1994; McPherson 1992; "Native American Religious Freedom"; "Navajoland"; "Navajos Block Access to Rainbow Bridge" 1995; Nystedt 1997; "Rainbow Bridge"; "Rainbow Bridge National Monument," http://www.pagelakepowell, http://www.utahrec; Watkins 1997.

Rajneesh Foundation
See Osho Chidvilas.

Ramakrishna-Vivekananda Center of New York
17 East Ninety-Fourth Street
New York, New York 10128
212-534-9445
FAX 212-828-1618
VedantaSoc@aol.com

For over a century, the Ramakrishna-Vivekananda Center of New York has disseminated the religion of the Vedanta Society. Vedanta, or end knowledge, is the philosophy of complete understanding of the Vedas, India's most sacred texts. The center bases its philosophy on Vedantic precepts as manifested in the God-centered life of Sri Ramakrishna, a holy man who died in Calcutta in 1886, and his revered wife, Sri Sarada Devi. The center replicates the couple's dedication to contemplation and serenity and to the revelation of God in all ages, countries, or peoples. The society's deep spirituality avoids the dogma of cults and oppressive religions as it rewards faith through transforming power, universality, and love.

HISTORY
America received Swami Vivekananda as he began planning a city of God. Through public lectures in major American cities, he spread India's ancient religion and then established a permanent teaching platform—the Vedanta Society of New York, an accredited branch of the Ramakrishna Order of India. As the West's first auxiliary of Ramakrishna Math and Mission in Calcutta, the society began a world mission with small steps in April 1894, when Vivekananda held tentative parlor meetings at his residence on Fifth Avenue. As a guest of Helen Gould at her country estate of Lyndhurst at Irvington-on-Hudson and a protégé of prestigious insiders, he began to shape the Vedanta Society through contacts with the Union League Club. His initial lecture, "India and Hinduism," set in motion a fervid interest in the faith. He recruited Leon Landsberg as his first monastic disciple in the West.

In May, Vivekananda moved on to Boston and attended Greenacre Conference in Maine, where he acquired a valuable supporter, Dr. Lewis G. Janes, president of the Brooklyn Ethical Association. By November, the swami organized the Vedanta Society officially as a financial entity. To promote its mission, the Brooklyn Ethical Society fostered a series known as the Brooklyn Lectures, which introduced Vivekananda to sophisticated, enterprising people keenly interested in world religion. Assisted by Landsberg, he established headquarters in rented rooms; in January 1895, he began regular classes free of charge to three or four students.

Living the monk's simple existence, Vivekananda drew other disciples with discourse on jnana yoga, a philosophical enlightenment that seeks God through knowledge, as an

For over a century, the Ramakrishna-Vivekananda Center of New York has disseminated the religion of the Vedanta Society, an outreach based on the Vedas, India's most sacred texts. (Courtesy the Ramakrishna-Vivekananda Center of New York)

introduction to Vedantic philosophy. Valuing converts over a steady income, he survived on donations and the proceeds of secular lectures on India. By June, he welcomed a two-month rest at Elizabeth Dutcher's cottage at Thousand Island Park on the St. Lawrence River before carrying the mission to London.

When Vivekananda returned to headquarters in December, he found that Landsberg had assumed the title Swami Kripananda and the job of resident teacher. Vivekananda returned to regular classes on the four yogas—bhakti, jnana, kharma, and raja—and later published his popular *Raja Yoga* and other works on these interconnected approaches to enlightenment. Assured of a successful beginning in New York, he ended the American mission in spring 1896 and left the society with Swami Saradananda. Overflowing classes moved to the New Century Hall; another

disciple joined the staff. When Swami Abhedananda arrived, the society held the first birthday celebration of Sri Ramakrishna, founder of the Vedantic movement, and formally incorporated in 1898. Located in a permanent dwelling on Fifty-Eighth Street, the society lionized Vivekananda, who returned for a last visit before extending the mission to California. At his direction, the society adopted a permanent emblem of four yogis wrapped in eternity.

After Vivekananda's death in 1902, the society continued to grow with lectures attended by 600, classes for adults and children, and publication of books, pamphlets, and the *Vedanta Monthly Bulletin*. Staff purchased a permanent home at 135 West Eightieth Street and a 370-acre retreat at a farmhouse in Berkshire, Connecticut. Thus, New York became the Western world's established Vedantic center. During a de-

SWAMI VIVEKANANDA

A knowledgeable Orientalist, reformer, and inspired religious leader of the late nineteenth century, Swami Vivekenanda gained respect in India, America, and Great Britain for his charismatic teaching. American philosopher William James honored him as paragon of Vedantists. Born Narendranath Nath Datta to an attorney father and a deeply religious mother in Calcutta in 1863, he displayed a flair for scholarship, music, science, and language.

At age fifteen, despite skepticism toward organized religion, Vivekananda experienced a spiritual ecstasy, an exalted trance state. He allied with Brahmo Samaj (Association of God), a reformed branch of Hinduism, yet lacked the satisfaction of full commitment. He began a ministry after studying with Sri Ramakrishna, a revered priest of a Kali temple and Bengali saint who believed that God has appeared to humanity as the Divine Mother, Sita, Rama, Krishna, Muhammad, and Jesus Christ. At his mentor's death, Vivekananda took the title of swami (teacher), formed the Ramakrishna monastic order and, as senior monk, dedicated himself to world missions.

Throughout India, Vivekenanda became a source of pride in culture and tradition. He bore to the West the Hindu concept of panentheism, a belief that everything is an outgrowth of God, and an advocacy for human equality. His nascent ministry surged to international attention in 1893 at Chicago's Parliament of Religions of the World Colombian Exposition, where he represented Hinduism as India's spiritual ambassador. His idealism, eloquence, compassion, and scholarship in Eastern and Western culture appealed to socialites and Harvard intellectuals, who helped him introduce India's spiritual culture to the West and to enrich New-World religious consciousness.

dynamism, which permeates his collected writings, published in 1965. New York's Vedantists observed their first centenary in 1994.

BELIEFS

Vedanta draws on the Upanishads, the last of the Vedic books, mystical texts that outline Hindu ritual and doctrine. The Upanishads, literally "sessions with a teacher," accentuate knowledge of ascetic sages as a liberating force to end the cycle of birth, death, and rebirth that locks humans into a pattern of *samsara* (reincarnation). The Brhadaranyaka, one of the Vedas written before 500 B.C., stresses the cosmic connection to the self, which the seeker must identify through introspection. The attainment of self-knowledge produces a spiritual refuge from *samsara* and lasting peace.

Vedantism bases its outreach on four beliefs: that God is one, that all life is divine, that existence is a unified entity, and that all religion is a legitimate search for truth. According to Vedanta, every soul is perfectable and manifests its divinity through worship, meditation, unselfish service, and philosophical discrimination of universal truths. Vedantists identify a single God as the ultimate reality and attest to an all-pervading, self-manifesting spirit, the creative power of the universe. Out of respect for others, followers regard all cultural characterizations of God as valid and respect alternative methods of seeking union with the divine.

ACTIVITIES

Under the leadership of Swami Tathagatananda, resident spiritual leader, the Ramakrishna–Vivekananda Center stimulates innate spirituality through lectures, discussions, publications, and individual guidance. The center and twenty others across the United States tailor the long-term process of enlightenment and discipline to individual needs and temperaments. Training awakens seekers to the consciousness that animates all living beings and guides them toward virtue and right thinking. To suppress negative traits and desires and acquaint each with the godliness within, teachers pray, cite scripture, perform rituals, and serve others.

The center invites interested individuals to join the society. The staff holds services at 11:00 A.M.

cline in membership, Mary Morton enabled the society to buy property at its present site on West Seventy-First Street near Central Park, which accommodated an auditorium, a chapel, and America's first complete library of Hinduism and Vedanta. True to Vivekananda's mission, centers burgeoned in Boston, San Francisco, Chicago, Los Angeles, Seattle, St. Louis, and Portland. In 1962, the society celebrated his

on Sunday and at 8:00 P.M. on Tuesday and Friday. Evening classes include devotional singing
on Saturday and Sunday at 6:00 P.M. and study
of the gospel of Sri Ramakrishna and discussion
of the Bhagavad Gita. Members may consult in
private with the swami and read from the society's lending library. A bookstall at the rear of
the chapel sells books, pamphlets, and videos.
The center closes for the summer on June 30.

Sources: Ahlstrom 1972; *Biography Resource Center*
1999; Eck 1994; *Eerdmans' Handbook to the World's
Religions* 1982; *Encyclopedia of World Biography* 1998;
"Ramakrishna-Vivekananda Center of New York";
Religious Leaders of America 1999; Sircar n.d.; Smith
1958; "Vedanta, Ramakrishna, and Vivekananda."

Riverside Church

490 Riverside Drive
New York, New York 10027
212-870-6700
FAX 212-870-6800
www.theriversidechurchny.org

A miniature Peace Corps, Riverside Church is
a model of compassion and realistic commitment to alleviating human ills. Its interdenominational, interracial, and international congregation of 2,400 from forty identifiable social
groups suits a city blessed with a vigorous immigrant population. The church mission statement attests to a spirit of hospitality, a celebration of diversity, inclusion, and promotion of
peace and justice. Affiliated with both the
United Church of Christ and the American Baptists, Riverside witnesses to the possibilities derived from cooperation and open-
heartedness by taking an active role in community affairs.

HISTORY

Riverside's church history dates to a meeting
house in 1841. A progressive assembly, the congregation sought larger facilities and moved farther north in a series of churches known as
Norfolk Street Baptist, Stanton Street Church,
and Fifth Avenue Baptist Church, led by Dr.
Cornelius Woelfkin, a force for liberalism. In the
evolution of Riverside, parishioners had to settle the perennial Baptist battle over fundamen-

talism versus moderation and rule on the concept of biblical inerrancy. At the height of agita-
tion between rigid fundamentalists and a growing faction of modernists, famed American
preacher Dr. Harry Emerson Fosdick interposed
a sane and compassionate mediation.

Riverside took shape over a three-year period,
beginning in November 1927. At its dedication
on October 5, 1930, 6,000 crowded the entrance
to hear of a viable, ongoing experiment in interdenominationalism grounded in the spirit of
American freedom. Dr. Fosdick insisted that
newcomers, whatever their religious background,
affirm faith in Christ as the only requirement for
membership. The church treasury remained unal-
lied with rigid sectarianism. Rather, church
councils began a program of alms for the needy
in the community, nation, and world.

During the hardships of the Great Depression, the church established the Social Service
Department and set up women's sewing workshop. Additional outreach through the Riverside
Guild and Business and Professional Women's
Arts and Crafts moved the parish beyond the
time-worn missionary unions of the nineteenth
century. In the rebuilding era following World
War II, Dr. Fosdick advocated the Riverside
Fund to Build a Christian World. A Morningside Heights project united fourteen institutions
to improve life in New York's slums. Subsequent
activism brought church councils in confrontation with civil rights issues, the Vietnam War,
and urban crime and imprisonment.

Dr. Fosdick and his successor, Dr. Robert
James McCracken, set the standard for forceful,
thought-provoking pulpit performance. Subsequently, the church set a precedent for equality
by naming as senior minister the Reverend
James Forbes, Jr., the first black to pastor a large
predominately white church. Among dynamic
orators who have addressed worshippers are Dr.
Martin Luther King, Jr., who denounced the
Vietnam War, Marian Wright Edelman, who advocated children's healthcare, and Dr. Tony
Campolo, a champion of the poor. In recent
times, challenges to social injustice have been
the topics of guests speakers Jesse Jackson of the
Rainbow Coalition and Nelson Mandela, South
African freedom fighter and subsequent national
president.

A miniature Peace Corps, New York City's Riverside Church is a model of compassion and realistic commitment to alleviating human ills. (Photo by Bruce Auspach. Courtesy Communications Office, Riverside Church)

ARCHITECTURE

Modeled on the thirteenth-century Gothic design of Chartres Cathedral, Riverside was the work of architects Charles Collens and Henry C. Pelton. They combed Gothic edifices in western Europe to extract building concepts that best suited a contemporary urban church, such as the wrought-iron portals, six-pillared pulpit, carved stone reredos, multiwindowed apse, and vibrant mosaic mural in the Chapel of the Cross. Bordered by St. Luke's Hospital, Barnard College, Columbia University, Manhattan School of Music, Union Theological and Jewish Theological Seminaries, Grant's Tomb, and schools and residences of Harlem and Morningside Heights, the church sits on one of the city's highest points and occupies two blocks along 122nd Street and Riverside Drive overlooking the Hudson River.

The 100-foot church balances the 392-foot tower, a functional structure that allots twenty-four floors to church programs. The sanctuary interior, which seats 2,100, is a monument to human aspiration. The narthex features original Renaissance Flemish windows retrieved from a church destroyed by rioters during the French Revolution. Their colored-glass scenes illustrate events, miracles, and parables of Christ. The chancel floor labyrinth replicates a medieval design. The lacy carvings of the chancel screen honor learned scientists and thinkers—the Buddha, Socrates, Muhammad, Louis Pasteur, Andreas Vesalius, Joseph Lister, Rene Descartes, Robert Koch, Charles Darwin, Florence Nightingale, Johann Pestalozzi, and Albert Einstein. An inviting adjunct to the youth ministry is the Good Shepherd Chapel, tinged with stained-glass figures working, playing, and worshiping among familiar animal shapes.

HARRY EMERSON FOSDICK

A passionate speaker for mainline Protestantism in the pulpit, in print, and on the radio, Harry Emerson Fosdick helped ease Riverside Church through a painful growth to modernism. He was a native New Yorker and graduate of Colgate College, Columbia University, and Union Theological Seminary, located a block from Riverside Church. While teaching at the seminary from 1911 to 1946, he took the pulpit of a newly merged Presbyterian parish. In an autobiography, he wrote:

It was very attractive, I had had four years at large without a parish . . . the thought of having again my own congregation, with an opportunity for consecutive ministry and the chance to combine the two vocations I had always cared for most . . . I told the church that I knew nothing about Presbyterian law, that they must take full responsibility on that score, but that if such an arrangement as they suggested were permissible, I would accept. (Pultz 1996, n.p.)

He is best known for "Shall the Fundamentalists Win?," a controversial call for tolerance delivered May 21, 1922, and reprinted in *The Christian Century, The Baptist,* and *Christian Work.* His candor was refreshing. He exclaimed, "If they had their way, within the church, [fundamentalists] would set up in Protestantism a doctrinal tribunal more rigid than the Pope's." (Pultz 1996, n.p.)

Dr. Fosdick's conciliatory sermon rejected picayunish squabbles over virgin birth, scriptural inerrancy, and Christ's second coming. The uproar that followed brought cries of heresy from outraged reactionaries. A climate of political infighting and professional sabotage forced his resignation in March 1925. More opportunities came his way. He led Park Avenue Baptist Church and promoted a new inclusive church in Morningside Heights. The planning committee sold their old building and combined the proceeds with a donation from John D. Rockefeller, Sr., to build Riverside Church, where, until retirement at the end of World War II, Fosdick preached, published, and broadcast *The National Vespers Hour.*

The tower consists of meeting rooms and the Laura Spelman Rockefeller Memorial Carillon, a 1925 gift from the late John D. Rockefeller, Jr., to honor his mother. In 1955, a Dutch firm recast and retuned the bells and added two more. The full seventy-four-bell peal ranges in size from ten pounds to the twenty-ton Bourdon bell. Bell tolling is a Sunday tradition at 10:30 A.M. and 12:30 and 3:00 P.M. and is also performed for weddings and funerals and on Thanksgiving Day, Christmas Eve, and New Year's Eve.

The Riverside appeal rests on spirituality and beauty. The rose window expresses the apostles' lives through symbols. Christ Chapel, a Romanesque design patterned after the fortress church of St. Nazaire at Carcassonne, bears details from the early Middle Ages in a series of stained-glass teaching windows following Christ's life from the annunciation to his resurrection. Philanthropist John D. Rockefeller, Jr., enriched Riverside's art collection with three paintings by Heinrich Hofmann, including *Christ in Gethsemane,* which adorns the Gethsemane Chapel. A mid-Renaissance Flemish tapestry pictures ritual involving King Clovis I. A

late Renaissance tapestry depicts feasting at the return of the Prodigal Son.

ACTIVITIES

In addition to Sunday services, the staff offers Wednesday morning meditation, music, communion, worship, and healing. Additional prayer services, a contemplative walk of the labyrinth, a soup supper, and preaching bolster worshippers seeking a midweek uplift. To extend Riverside's outreach, the staff offers conferences, a theater, an Internet presence, advertising, and a media ministry through radio and television. Special events include an all-night, election-eve prayer vigil, a career day, a watchnight service, millennium studies, and a National Summit on Poverty. Staff counseling offers individual therapy, premarital counseling, couples and family therapy, divorce and bereavement counseling, and workshops on social and personal issues.

Riverside's music program coordinates the choir, chamber singers, inspirational choir, handbell choir, children's and cherub choirs, liturgical dance, and the Riverside Singers. Accompaniment from the two nave organs and instruments in Christ Chapel and the Chapel of the Cross offer flexibility in such programs as the Elijah Concert, African Nutcracker, Christmas at Riverside, Celebration Messiaen, and Handbell Festival. On sale in the visitors' center gift shop are choral and organ programs recorded at Riverside—*Behold the Star!, On a Summer's Evening, Comes Summer Time, Bells of Riverside,* and *Riverside Revisted.*

Church staff focuses on a broad-based education program bolstered by the Cloister Library, open Sunday through Thursday. Integral to adult Sunday morning Bible study are Riverside's discipleship curriculum and Kerygma, small covenant groups who follow creative learning styles. Ministry to elderly parishioners renews and empowers through exercise, fellowship, pastoral care, study, faith development, advocacy, volunteering, intergenerational activities, and educational and cultural opportunities. The children's and youth curriculum stresses faith, worship, and nurturance. Extending learning are children's worship services, held in the Chapel of the Cross. Staff schedules retreats, discussions on scripture, and cultural enrichment for young adults. The church school follows multicultural themes that parallel the ethnic, religious, and economic diversity of the student body. In addition to basic learning experiences, the church offers creative writing, conversational French, pottery, bowling, gymnastics, league softball, and basketball.

Riverside has made substantial advancements against poverty and social displacement. A conversational English course aids immigrant members in acclimating to their new country. A churchwide program addresses issues of job readiness, training, availability, and entitlements. The Job Center's volunteers maintain daily job postings, e-mail listings, and referrals in the Cloister Lounge on Claremont Avenue. An eight-week barber training course offers a specific life skill and advancement to apprenticeships.

To upgrade health and wellness, a ministry supports stress reduction, parenting, healing, holistic health, nutrition, fitness, advice on catastrophic illness, and support to caregivers. An antiracism task force promotes African American, Latino, and Native American appreciation and concerns through programs, peacemaking, and grants. The Maranatha ministry enriches spiritual community and fellowship within the lesbian, gay, and bisexual community. Specific strategies to combat social problems come from Riverside's prison minister, tutoring, girls' self-awareness program, men's club, emergency fund, thrift shop, clothing ministry and food pantry, Harlem Initiatives Together, and Handgun Litigation Project.

Sources: Ahlstrom 1972; *Almanac of Famous People* 1998; *American Decades* 1998; *Biography Resource Center* 1999; Broderick 1958; *Encyclopedia of World Biography* 1998; Pultz 1996; *Religious Leaders of America* 1999; "Review: 'Harry Emerson Fosdick: Preacher, Pastor, Prophet'" 1985; Rhem 1997; "The Riverside Church" 1999; Williams 1999; Wilson and Ferris 1989.

Rodef Shalom Congregation
Mark N. Staitman, Rabbi
4905 Fifth Avenue
Pittsburgh, Pennsylvania 15232
412-621-6566
FAX 412-621-5475
rshalom@pgh.net
http://trfn.clpgh.org/rodef

Led by Rabbi Mark N. Staitman, Rodef Shalom Congregation is a model urban Jewish community. With a staff of seven, including an organist and a music director, the temple offers a wide span of spiritual and fellowship activities, including a Web site and biweekly newsletter, *The Temple Bulletin.* Unique to the Pittsburgh congregation are its historic adaptation to American customs and continued growth in benevolence, education, and culture through an innovative biblical garden and an outreach to the gay, bisexual, and transgendered community.

HISTORY
Pittsburgh's Jews organized a synagogue in the 1840s. The largely middle-class residents from Germany, Lithuania, and the Polish-Prussian border shared livelihoods in the retailing of general merchandise, dry goods, and clothing. In 1847, they set up the Bes Almon (Mourner's House) and established a cemetery on Mount Troy. The next year, a kernel congregation known as the Shaare Shamayim (Gate of Heaven) rented space at Penn Avenue and Sixth

Unique in its outreach to the gay, bisexual, and transgendered community, Pittsburgh's Rodef Shalom Congregation is a model urban Jewish community. (Courtesy Glick Library, Rodef Shalom Congregation)

Street. By the 1850s, the growing congregation, enlarged by train service bringing newcomers to the city, had reached 60 families, most settling along the Allegheny River. In 1855, the Jewish community supported a Hebrew Ladies Aid Society to tend the sick and needy and a men's altruistic group known as the Hebrew Benevolent Society.

After several moves and a progression of lay Torah readers, the founders chartered Rodef Shalom. By 1859, they had launched a school and planned a permanent Orthodox worship center. The following year, architect Charles Bartberger initiated a building in the downtown area on Hancock Street. Completed March 20, 1862, the new structure sheltered 800 members in the only synagogue in western Pennsylvania. At the dedication, the Reverend William Armhold gave the welcoming speech in German, followed by a solo by prominent Pittsburgh vocalist Sigmund Apfelbaum. From the outset, Rodef Shalom pursued religious education and received Pittsburgh's first seven Jewish confirmands in 1862.

By 1863, the Jewish community had to resolve its commitment by making a choice—maintain orthodoxy or liberalize to reformed rituals. The spread of the American reformation of Judaism, begun in Charleston, had launched a shortened "Protestantized" service and vernacu-

lar prayers. Pittsburgh's community mulled over the shift from strict traditionalism. A majority vote opted for reform and selected the prayer book of Cincinnati reform leader Rabbi Isaac Mayer Wise, *Minhag America* (The Custom of America), over the orthodox *Minhag Ashkenaz* (German-Jewish Liturgy). The minority, primarily from Holland, Lithuania, and Poland, seceded and formed the Orthodox Tree of Life Synagogue.

Over the next decade, the Americanized Rodef Shalom congregation plunged into the Western Jewish reformation under the leadership of Rabbi Lippman Mayer, a proponent of reform and founder of the Jewish Chautauqua Society. The congregation shortened services, installed a pipe organ, and ended the custom of segregating worshippers by gender. In 1868, new blood typified the entrepreneurial growth of Pittsburgh: the German brothers Henry, Isaac, Jacob, and Morris Kaufmann opened a department store, the four Himmerlich brothers sold shoes, and an Alsatian pair, Emil and Jacques Adelsheimer, started an optical business. Second-generation members infused the immigrant community with an American outlook and a demand to replace German segments of liturgy with English. By 1874, the worshippers had dispensed with the yarmulke, established a strong choir program under the direction of Bertha

Benswanger, and joined the Union of American Hebrew Congregations, the umbrella organization uniting reform synagogues.

The Rodef Shalom Congregation took a significant stand at the 1885 conference of reformed rabbis, who issued the "Pittsburgh Platform," a liberalization of custom and belief that remained in force until 1937. The gathering declared that Judaism was a religion, not a nation, that keeping kosher was optional, and that the Bible was an ethical guide rather than an infallible instrument of God. The bold thrust into New-World thinking Americanized Pittsburgh Jews and eased them into community activities. One member, temple president Emanuel Wertheimer, pioneered service on the Allegheny council as one of its first Jews.

Pittsburgh's Jews established lasting social initiatives. In honor of the founders' early struggles, in 1894, 50 women organized the Columbian Council, later known as the National Council of Jewish Women, to feed dime lunches to poor female immigrants and to teach them English. In 1906, Mrs. Josiah Cohen organized the Sisterhood, a chapter of the Women of Reform Judaism, which launched the Glick Children's Library and Lippman Library. The emerging Columbian Settlement became Pittsburgh's first free night school. The Edgar Kaufmanns funded a new settlement, the Irene Kaufmann Settlement, named for their deceased daughter. Isaac Kaufmann donated a community medical clinic and underwrote the Camp Emma Farm.

The tradition of altruism and public service at Rodef Shalom strengthened Pittsburgh and beyond. Department store magnate Esther Gusky offered funds and land on Perrysville Avenue in Allegheny to build a three-story orphanage. Emanuel Wertheimer furnished the library; Paulina Frank, Isaac Lehman, Mrs. Moses Oppenheimer, and Rosalie Rauh paid for the dormitories. The congregation sheltered the orphans, one of whom, Louis Caplan, finished law school and served the Allegheny community. Likewise, Rodef Shalom members supported a coed YMHA and YWHA and Montefiore Hospital. Mrs. Edgar Kaufmann chaired the hospital board; Leon Falk added Falk Clinic to the hospital complex. The temple produced three judges, city council and school board members, and the Voter's League.

During the late 1930s and early 1940s, members rescued Jews from Nazi Germany and settled refugees in the United States. In 1948, the spirit of support aided the new state of Israel.

ARCHITECTURE

At the end of the nineteenth century, members moved from the Hill District to integrate Oakland, Shadyside, and East Liberty. Yet, the dominance of the Allegheny residents overrode a move to relocate the synagogue. To accommodate growth, the Rodef Shalom congregation chose to enlarge their building. A new structure on Eighth Street seated 800 on the ground floor and 200 in the balcony. The auction of pews in 1901 retired the mortgage by raising more than $122,000. Within four years, the popularity of Rabbi J. Leonard Levy tripled enrollment to 450 families. The vibrant, progressive congregation of Rodef Shalom dedicated themselves to civic responsibility, altruism, and cultural inclusion. The establishment of the University of Pittsburgh and the Syria Mosque gave further proof of the area's vigor. As Oakland and Shadyside blossomed into the city's cultural suburban center, the congregation chose to sell their temple to the Second Presbyterian Church.

With the aid of modernist architect Henry Hornbostel, the congregation built a new edifice in Shadyside at Morewood and Fifth Avenue near Montefiore Hospital, Andrew Carnegie's Museum of Art, and the Carnegie Institute of Technology, later named Carnegie-Mellon University. Hornbostel chose a subtle, distinctive blend of elegance and the exotic. He selected bricks of Pennsylvania clay and paired them with handmade tiles that echoed an ancient craft. His seating pattern held 900 on the first floor and 300 in the gallery; an additional auditorium increased seating capacity. He created a bas-relief for the façade and enhanced the structure with a ninety-foot double dome, the first of its size erected without structural steel. A stained-glass window built by the Willet Studio symbolized the eye of God and shed filtered light into the sanctuary.

At the persuasion of Rabbi Samuel H. Goldenson, the congregation fostered growth by relinquishing family-owned pews and inaugurating a system of unassigned seating. In 1921, a boost in membership brought a new staff member, assistant rabbi Dr. Solomon B. Freehof, prominent book reviewer and author of works on Judaic law and ritual. He upgraded the *Union Prayer Book for Jewish Worship;* his wife, Lillian Freehof, translated texts for the blind.

ACTIVITIES

The 1,600 families of Rodef Shalom compose a social and religious landmark and cultural catalyst for Pittsburgh. The Milton E. Harris Interfaith Institute promotes Jewish-Christian dialogue. Additional community involvement fuels the Self-Help Network, the Mother's Day Out program, the Pittsburgh New Music Ensemble, and chamber music concerts. The United Way trains volunteers at Rodef Shalom; five area food banks benefit from temple donations and ingathering. The Temple's Brotherhood, Sisterhood, and Junior Congregation chair the city's Israel Bond Drive. To the benefit of local Jews, Rodef Shalom, the leader of the reform movement in western Pennsylvania, promoted three fledgling congregations—Temple Sinai in Squirrel Hill, Temple Emanuel in the South Hills, and Temple David in Monroeville.

Significant to community outreach is the Rodef Shalom Biblical Botanical Garden, which attracts 6,000 students, botanists, and visitors annually during a fifteen-week season. The largest of its kind in North America and the only ongoing program of research and publication, the garden is located on one-third acre alongside Carnegie-Mellon University. It features 100 temperate and tropical plants as well as new seasonal plantings. The designer demonstrates the flora of Bible lands with typical topography—a waterfall, desert, and stream, which represents the Jordan River's path from Lake Kineret to the Dead Sea. Labeling, brochures, and an illustrated guidebook identify plants, which are paired with appropriate biblical verses. Scholarly inquiry and programs on new plants in Israel, herbs and medicinal plants, cosmetic substances, dyes, grains, papermaking, and Jewish costume involve visitors in the ongoing study of botany's importance to humankind.

In 1991, the Long Range Planning Committee surveyed leaders and members to review, assess, and map future direction in five areas—worship, ritual, education, membership, and administration. Essential to a plan of action was a balance of classical, traditional, and contemporary worship, maintaining quality religious education and youth services, developing family life education, formulating a strategy on the issue of intermarriage, and proposing a reform day school. At the heart of the congregation's vision is a nurturing connectedness with God and a meaningful identity with longstanding Jewish values. To acknowledge and embrace diversity, Rodef Shalom congregation celebrates sacred moments in family life and repatriates Jews who have strayed from the community. Current offerings include daily, Shabbat, and Shabbat eve services, Torah study, an art survey, volleyball, gift workshop, bookbinding, adult Hebrew classes, and introduction to Judaism.

Rodef Shalom prepares for the future by treasuring its young. Morning religious school educates children of the congregation in Hebraic heritage and values, prayer, Torah, and tradition. Students learn Hebrew, Israeli, and world history through formal lessons, holiday observances, art, cooking, and music. Like their elders, they move from the classroom into the community to practice the congregation's commitment to world betterment. Youth Hebrew classes on Tuesday and Thursday evening assemble at the synagogue and satellite locations. A Madrichim program for high school juniors and seniors introduces teens to teaching assistantships.

Adult programs answer specific congregational needs. The Brotherhood holds sports outings, pairs student interns with business mentors, distributes winter coats to the poor, hosts interfaith lectures and programs and breakfast speakers, sponsors musical concerts, supports organ donorship, and maintains a members' business directory. The Sisterhood staffs the Sewing Corner Workshop and contributes items to the Women's Shelter, Riverview Home for the Aged, and the temple Gift Corner. Multilayered committees superintend Lunch with the Rabbi, a Lunch and Learn Series, and a Wednesday Book Review Series. To strengthen contributions to the synagogue program, members hold an annual retreat and a women's Seder and beautify the building and grounds with handmade banners and Torah covers. The Rodef Shalom Family Center supports parents with First Friends, preschool, and extended-day enrichment programs and expands Jewish education for each generation. A Parent Lounge allows participants to relax, read, or visit while their children attend class.

To incorporate the gay community, in 1994, the congregation began sponsoring a Bet Tikvah (House of Hope) chapter. The organization began in Pittsburgh in 1988 to enrich spirituality and ease the difficulties experienced by Jewish homosexuals, transgenders, and bisexuals. Through monthly religious services, holiday observance, and social events such as a baby-naming ceremony for the adopted infant of two lesbian members and participation in the June Gay Pride Week, the group maintains inclusion of a minority often shunned by organized religion. Rabbi Andrew Bush, counselor and adviser to Bet Tikvah, considers the mission to the gay community an essential element of the synagogue's commitment to Jews.

> **Sources:** Ahlstrom 1972; Behr 1998; Biema 1999; Brody 1996; Gentz 1973; Klagsbrun 1996; "Rodef Shalom Congregation"; Sarna and Golden 1999.

Rothko Chapel
1409 Sul Ross at Yupon
Houston, Texas 77006
713-524-9839

An austere, provocative interfaith site, the Rothko Chapel draws the contemplative to experience an abstract alliance of space and architecture. The octagonal chapel honors the late freedom fighter Dr. Martin Luther King, Jr. Open daily from 10:00 A.M. to 6:00 P.M., the site features Mark Rothko's fourteen vast canvas panels that form three somber triptychs and five individual panels, ranging in hue from an intense plum to a matte ebony. Philanthropists Dominique and John de Menil commissioned the works in 1964, which Mark Rothko completed in 1966.

HISTORY
Originally, architect Philip Johnson designed the Rothko Chapel for the University of St. Thomas. Because of Rothko's objections to the plans, Johnson resigned from the project in 1967. The de Menils cancelled their initial offer and moved the project to downtown Houston.

Howard Barnstone and Eugene Aubrey revamped Johnson's blueprints by distributing natural light with a series of baffles. By 1970, trustees began construction.

Inaugurated in 1971, the ecumenical chapel fulfills Rothko's ambition to manipulate response to a series of interrelated paintings by controlling structure and lighting. The bland exterior is a mute impetus to reflection. The interior focuses natural light from skylights on Rothko's complex textured paintings, where the play of light on the noncommittal art series intrigues as it soothes. The viewer becomes an element in the interactive drama by moving about the white-walled space and perceiving the variables as an integrated whole. The chapel profits from a reflecting pool and forecourt, which juxtaposes Barnett Newman's *Broken Obelisk* (1967)—a stone lozenge upon a pyramid.

ACTIVITIES
Free of traditional religious symbolism, the Rothko chapel embraces individuals of all faiths and hosts a variety of commemorative, religious, political, and cultural events and educational symposia. It is a pluralistic meditation and prayer site that celebrates world holidays—Cinco de Mayo, Eid el-Adha, Eid el-Fitr, Good Friday, Now Ruz, Palm Sunday, Passover, Puja, Rosh Hashanah, and the United Nations' Universal Declaration of Human Rights. Each Sunday, one of Houston's ministers—selected from Quakers, Jews, Muslims, Baptists, Catholics, Episcopalians, Presbyterians, Hindus, Copts, and Greek Orthodox—hosts a time of prayer. In 1978, Whirling Dervishes from Konya, Turkey, presented a ritual Sufi ceremony. The following year, the Dalai Lama used the chapel as a gathering place for representatives of varied disciplines and religions.

The last two decades of the twentieth century saw increased activity. In 1981, the chapel was the site of Passover and Haggadah celebrations, Pandit Pran Nath's "Morning Ragas," and a Hebrew performance of American composer Steve Reich's *Tehillim*. In 1985, the Gyuto Tantric Monks of Tibet performed rare Tibetan Buddhist rituals, the Boys Choir of Harlem honored the birthday of Dr. Martin Luther King, Jr., and the Houston Interfaith Thanksgiving service welcomed Jews, Chris-

An austere, provocative interfaith site, Houston's Rothko Chapel draws the contemplative to experience an abstract alliance of space and architecture. (G.E. Kidder Smith/Corbis)

tians, and Muslims. The following year, the chapel saw the unveiling of the Carter-Menil Human Rights Prize and the Rothko Chapel Oscar Romero Award, which South African Archbishop Desmond M. Tutu presented to Bishop Proano of Ecuador. In 1987, composer Richard Landry performed *Mass for Pentecost*

Sunday, composed for the opening of the Menil Collection. A 1988 workshop on human-rights issues for young Americans and the 1989 celebration of the bicentennial of the French Declaration of the Rights of Man and the Citizen renewed the chapel's involvement in world freedom.

MARK ROTHKO

A twentieth-century genius and member of the New York School of Art, Mark Rothko dominated abstract American expressionism over five decades. Born Marcus Rothkowitz on September 26, 1903, in Dvinsk, Latvia, when he was age ten, he and his parents left Tsarist Russia and immigrated to Portland, Oregon. On scholarship, he followed a broad course of study for two years at Yale. Abandoning nebulous plans to study labor law or engineering, he moved to New York at age twenty to join the Art Students League and paint on canvas and Masonite. His early commissions included illustrations for Rabbi Lewis Browne's *The Graphic Bible* and some still lifes and solitary figures overwhelmed by urban settings.

The Great Depression forced Rothko to teach art classes and work at government projects to survive. His wife, Edith Schar, brought in a small income by designing jewelry. In the late 1940s, Rothko set out to redefine artistic idioms by abandoning identifiable shapes and conventional titles and differentiating his works by number. By the 1950s, his monumental mural for the Four Seasons restaurant in the Seagram Building had descended into brooding dark atmospheres dominated by red, maroon, brown, and black. In 1961, he accepted one of his greatest challenges, a series for the Holyoke Center of Harvard University, and received a retrospective at New York's Museum of Modern Art.

While working on the de Menil series from 1964 to 1967, Rothko absorbed himself in perceptual subtleties created by minute distinctions between shape and ground. The meditative qualities of black and violet canvases suited the impassive Houston chapel building and oblong pool. His refusal to analyze the work added to the mystique of an era of modernism that offered few tangible handholds to the average observer. In his honor, the de Menils named the building the Rothko Chapel.

Emotionally and physically unwell in his later years, Rothko suffered an aortic aneurysm in 1968. As his melancholia worsened, he wrangled with galleries over the way they grouped and displayed canvases. He retreated into gloom, painted in dim light, dropped tans and olives from his colorations, and worked from a grimly luminous palette of black, brown, and gray. He committed suicide on February 15, 1970.

The Houston Romanian and Hungarian communities gathered for the Reverend Laslo Tokes's 1990 memorial service for victims of the revolution against dictator Nicolai Ceausescu. The Dalai Lama returned in 1991 to pray for world peace. In 1994, the University of North Texas College of Music performed Morton Feldman's composition *The Rothko Chapel*. The following year, peace groups observed the fiftieth anniversary of the bombing of Hiroshima and Nagasaki. Two months later, Father Jon Cortina of the University of Central America led a series of programs detailing El Salvador's troubled past. During Women's History Month, Dr. Swanee Hunt honored women's contributions to democracy in Central and Eastern Europe. On the chapel's twenty-fifth anniversary, Andrew Young led an interfaith prayer service. At the end of the decade, Senator Javid Iqbal of Pakistan lectured on the lives of Islamic women.

Sources: *American Decades* 1998; *Biography Resource Center* 1999; Colpitt 1997; *Contemporary Artists* 1996; Eck 1994; *Encyclopedia of World Biography* 1998; Fox, Stephen; Lightman 1999; "Mark Rothko" 1999; "Outside the Rothko Chapel" 1998; Plagens 1998; Rosenblum 1998.

Russian Chapel

See Holy Trinity Chapel of Fort Ross.

San Juan Bautista Mission
Father Edward Fitz-Henry
Second and Mariposa Streets
P.O. Box 400
San Juan Bautista, California 95045-0400
831-623-2127
FAX 831-623-2433
www.dioceseofmonterey.org/parishes/
omsanjuan.htm

California's mission with the longest history of operation, San Juan Bautista is the fifteenth element in the mission string built by Franciscan evangelist Father Junípero Serra. Named for John the Baptist, the mission commemorates the forerunner and baptizer of Christ. The complex sits upon the San Andreas Fault at the foot of the Gavilon Mountains on El Camino Real (The King's Highway), a 650-mile intermission linkage system that still exists in fragments of dirt road. Nicknamed the Mission of Music, the church possesses precise acoustics that once echoed with strains of a Mission Indian choir. Currently, the church hosts a summer music festival and a Latin-American nativity play.

The mission is the heart of a small California Catholic community. On the mission grounds, Alfred Hitchcock filmed the conclusion of the film *Vertigo* with a dizzying confrontation at the bell tower. The mission complex abuts historic streets and buildings, one the former home of José Castro, military commander of Monterey, and also the home of the Patrick Breen family, survivors of the ill-fated Donner Party.

HISTORY

Built by Father Presidente Fermín Francisco de Lasuén, San Juan Bautista entered service on June 24, 1797. He chose the inland location be- cause it was a day's walk from missions at Santa Clara and Carmel. By Christmas, it had grown to an adobe church and monastery, barracks and a guardhouse for protective soldiers, a granary, and adobe houses for Mission Indians. In three years, the number of Indian converts grew to 500. After severe earthquake damage in October 1800, the padres enlarged the church and made repairs.

In 1808, Father Felipe Arroyo de la Cuesta, a skilled linguist and preacher in seven languages, drew up blueprints for a church with triple naves. At completion in 1812, the unique structure was the province's largest church. The population of 1,100 Indians had dropped by over half from deaths and desertions exacerbated because priests locked people in their rooms to separate males and females after work hours. To minimize the loss, Father Cuesta partitioned the extra naves to increase the intimacy and warmth of a small section.

In 1812, Father Estévan Tápis, gifted composer and acting father presidente of the missions, began developing an Indian music department. He organized a choir and invented and hand-lettered sheets of colored notes to teach singing. He taught people to play string, woodwind, brass, and percussion instruments, some handmade at the mission. Popular songs were "Alabado" (Song of Divine Praise), "Cántico del Alba" (Morning Song), and "Salve Regina" (Hail, Queen of Heaven). As described in diaries, he was a firm disciplinarian who applied shackles and the lash to men. He punished women by securing them in the stocks for up to three days. Runaway women required more severe chastisement with the lash, which the padre entrusted to another female. With the arrival of the Zacatecans in 1833, civil authorities decommissioned the church during a two-year secularization as San Juan Bautista changed into a frontier town. President James Buchanan restored the mission to church hands on November 19, 1859, shortly before construction of its wooden tower.

ARCHITECTURE

California's winsome Spanish mission San Juan Bautista rises modestly from a string of graceful arches and an inner corridor edging the padres' quarters. Beyond carved portals pierced by a cat door, red tile floors lead past ranks of hand-carved wood pews separated by arched walls. The eye halts at an elegant reredos. A local carpenter, Thomas Doak, a former sailor and California's first American citizen, painted the wood backdrop to resemble marble. At the altar is a fine folk painting of San Juan Bautista kneeling by a lamb at Christ's cross. The original statuary complements a large sandstone baptismal font where the first padre baptized Mission Indians.

Currently, the church maintains lighting from overhead chandeliers made from concentric rings of wrought iron and suspended among rough-hewn exposed beams. Additional lighting comes from candles in the six niches of the reredos. The twentieth-century restoration of historic elements brought about the removal of a concrete tower, repair of earthquake damage to the church and *campanario* (bell wall), and refurbishment of the Plaza Hotel and the stable, the jail, the smithy, and two adobe mansions, Castro House and Zanetta House. In October 1999, the staff removed the old confessional from the bell tower and placed it in service in the sacristy.

ACTIVITIES

Today, the mission is a popular religious tourist attraction. The property surrounding the mission and overlooking San Benito Valley is a state park open to picnickers. The mission museum contains two choral manuscripts, rawhide used in the original construction, part of a bass viol, a mortar for grinding medicines, and antique books. A favorite attraction is a three-cylinder barrel organ, a huge hurdy-gurdy made in London that Indians cranked for their amusement after its arrival in 1826. The organ's repertoire includes "Go to the Devil," "Spanish Waltz," "College Hornpipe," and "Lady Campbell's Reel."

At the mission church, Father Fitz-Henry holds daily mass with weekday services in the Guadalupe Chapel at 8:00 A.M., Saturday mass at 5:30 P.M. following confession, and Sunday services in English at 9:00 and 11:00 A.M. and in Spanish at 1:00 P.M. On holy days, he celebrates both morning and evening mass. In addition to weekly bilingual choir practice and Holy Hour on Friday at 8:30 A.M., the staff hosts three Al-

coholics Anonymous meetings weekly and weekend marriage encounters at the St. Francis Retreat House. In November 1999, the church honored the deceased in the Book of the Dead, held a candlelight All Saints' Day procession to San Juan Cemetery, hosted a Thanksgiving Day Feast, and organized a pilgrimage to view the Treasury of St. Francis of Assisi in San Francisco. The roomy, three-aisled church with its dark-stained reredos and six carvings is also a popular spot for weddings and baptisms.

A unique offering of the mission is the biennial pre-Christmas performance of Latino-American playwright Luis Miguel Valdez's spectacle *Pastorela* (The Shepherds' Play). The folk play, a centerpiece of the repertoire of a local company, El Teatro Campesino (The Farmworkers' Theater), arose from Cesar Chavez's United Farm Workers movement and raised money for the grape boycott. The presentation describes Jesus' birth from the point of view of shepherds who visit Bethlehem. Valdez, a former farmworker, founded his company in 1965 during the Delano Grape Strike to raise wages for migrant Latino harvesters. In 1999, Valdez directed the televised version of *Pastorela,* retold in verse, which featured Linda Ronstadt as the Archangel Michael.

> **See also** San Juan Capistrano Mission, San Luis Obispo de Tolosa.
> **Sources:** Ahlstrom 1972; Barratt 1996; "The Barrel Organ at Mission San Juan Bautista"; *Biography Resource Center* 1999; "California Mission History: San Juan Bautista"; Certini 1999; *Dictionary of Hispanic Biography* 1996; Drain 1994; Hanson 1997; Hughart 1998; "Luis Valdez"; Neuerburg 1995; "Pelican Network"; Protillo 1995; Summers 1997; Wright 1978.

San Juan Capistrano Mission
P.O. Box 697
San Juan Capistrano, California 92693
949-248-2048
www.missionsjc.com; www.sjc.net

A cherished religious site in California's mission chain, San Juan Capistrano, jewel of the state's original Spanish missions, has passed through a long history of service, cataclysm, and revitalization and into an era of artistic and historic prominence. Annually, a romantic celebration of migratory swallows revives church legend, drawing hundreds of photographers and artists. Strategically located in Orange County between Los Angeles and San Diego, it is a living monument to the vision of Father Junípero Serra, a notable Catholic pioneer of the U.S. Southwest.

HISTORY

The Mission Indians of central and southern California and the Baja peninsula formed a polyglot complex of 300 tribal bands—primarily the Cahuilla, Chumash, Costanoan, Diegueño, Fernandeño, Gabrielino, Juaneño, Luiseño, and Serrano, named in honor of Father Serra. They were coastal fishers and gatherers who subsisted on acorns and other nuts, mollusks, and fish. The addition of bulbs and roots to their diet earned them an unflattering pejorative, Digger Indians. After Franciscan friars corralled them in residences at Catholic missions, the Indians learned European customs, studied candle making and blacksmithing, tended gardens, and developed herd management.

The Westernization of coastal Indians was a violent, brutal process. Father Serra's mission string of nine units grew along the 532-mile stretch called El Camino Real (The King's Highway) with the addition of Santa Bárbara (1786), La Purísima Concepión (1787), Santa Cruz (1791), Nuestra Señora de Soledad (1791), San José de Guadalupe (1797), San Juan Bautista (1797), San Miguel Arcángel (1797), San Fernando Rey de España (1797), San Luis Rey (1798), Santa Inés (1804), San Rafael Arcángel (1817), and San Francisco Solano (1823). The friars controlled profits and held the people in a system of benign internment that eroded local customs, dialects, and religions. To assure obedience, priests isolated, imprisoned, lashed, branded, and executed those Indians who tried to escape or retaliate for unwanted confinement. Measles and venereal disease reduced the mission Indian population nearly 80 percent, from 70,000 to 15,000. In 1775, the Ipai and Tipai destroyed the San Diego Mission and killed its head priest. A decade later, Gabrielino seer Toypurina led an unsuccessful revolt at the San Gabriel Mission and suffered denunciation and deportation. In 1824, the rebel Pacomio's uprising of

A cherished religious site in California's mission chain, San Juan Capistrano, jewel of the state's original Hispanic missions, has passed through a long history of service, cataclysm, and revitalization. (North Wind Picture Archives)

2,000 Indians at La Purísima and Santa Barbara missions failed to end coercive treatment.

At the collapse of Spain's colony in 1822, Mexican General Figueroa ousted Spanish friars and seized and secularized the mission string in 1834. The Indians collected their share of the properties, but were inexperienced with land ownership. Rapidly, unprincipled usurpers cheated them of their lands. Under the pen name H. H., author Helen Hunt Jackson exposed the mistreatment of Mission Indians in a pro-Indian treatise, *A Century of Dishonor: A Sketch of the United States Government's Dealing with Some of the Indian Tribes* (1881). The Bureau of Indian Affairs located 30,000 Indians on thirty reservations. The community of San Juan Capistrano encircled the mission and became an incorporated city in the 1960s.

FATHER JUNÍPERO SERRA

A Spanish Franciscan evangelist, Father Junípero Serra, the Apostle of California, masterminded a string of twenty-one missions to headquarter a campaign for Christianizing California's aborigines known as the Mission Indians. Born on November 24, 1713, in Petra, Majorca, to farmer Antio Nadal and Margarita Rosa Ferrer Serra, he was named José Miguel Serra at birth. After study at the Lullian University of Palma, he altered his name upon entrance into the Franciscan order at age seventeen and became a priest at age twenty-five. At his alma mater, where he earned a Ph.D., he taught philosophy until, at his request, the order dispatched him to the Western Hemisphere to study at the Apostolic College of San Fernando in Mexico City. He traveled with Father Juan Crespi, Father Francisco Gomez, and a former pupil, historian Francisco Palóu, the father of California history, author of *Noticias de la Nueva California* (Observations on New California) (1774) and *Vida de Padre Junípero Serra* (Life of Father Junípero Serra) (1787).

On the way, Father Serra set to work by preaching at San Juan, Puerto Rico. Posted to Mexico's Sierra Gorda missions in 1750 to convert the Pamé Indians, he built the mission of Santiago de Jalpan and studied the Otomí dialect. For six years, he served the Inquisition as local commissioner until his appointment as head of Baja Californian missions. Although seriously lamed by leg ulcers and hampered by asthma, he tackled the mission fields of Mexico, Puebla, Oaxaca, Valladolid, and Guadalajara.

As the Spanish military extended farther north into Alta California and expelled the Jesuits, Father Serra followed expeditioner Gaspar de Portolá to San Diego and, in 1769, founded the first mission, San Diego de Alcala. Within twelve years he had established headquarters at Carmel in 1770 and built San Antonio de Padua and San Gabriel Arcángel outside Los Angeles the following year, San Luis Obispo de Tolosa in 1772, and Mission Dolores at San Francisco de Asís and San Juan Capistrano in 1776. He followed with Santa Clara de Asís in 1777 and San Buenaventura in 1782. His creation of mission forts and the publication of a treatise on strict mission conduct enabled the Spanish military to solidify their control of the Pacific coast.

Before his death on August 28, 1784, at Mission San Carlos Borromeo del Rio Carmelo in Monterey-Carmel, Father Serra developed a reputation for a worthy ministry to Indians, which he superintended via 10,000 miles of travel on land and sea. By 1790, San Juan Capistrano's native population reached 765. Critics declare that he enslaved and colonized unwilling indigenous peoples, whom he whipped into submission. More benign evaluations of mission work cite his defense of natives in an Indian Bill of Rights, the introduction of cattle and sheep herding and crafts, upgrading of sanitation and health, and the importation of Mexican grain and vegetable seeds, date palms, and other fruit stock. Overall, his first nine missions converted and baptized around 6,000 (some sources say 6,800) and confirmed 5,000. Among Father Serra's numerous honors are beatification by Pope John Paul II in 1985 and a statue in the Capitol Hall of Fame in Washington, D.C.

ARCHITECTURE

The San Juan Capistrano Mission, founded on November 1, 1776, bore the name of an Italian saint, John of Capistrano, a fifteenth-century Franciscan preacher and crusader. Initial construction halted after Indians attacked San Diego. The priests of San Juan buried the mission's bells and retreated to the safety of the San Diego presidio. When Father Serra reclaimed the mission site, he found its structure unharmed. He retrieved the bells and hung them in a tree until they could swing once more in a secure tower. Builder Isidor Aguilar completed the masonry of the church that became California's oldest surviving church.

Originally, Father Serra's church was a crude but functional frontier edifice that survived for six years before workers rebuilt it. At completion in 1806, its cruciform floor plan encompassed adobe, limestone, and sandstone hauled from arroyos and creek beds by oxcarts, carretas, burros, and Indian laborers. Its assembly and decoration departed from flat-roofed California mission architecture with the creation of seven domes. Extending 90 by 180 feet, the round-roofed building contains a 120-foot double-deck campanile and cross rising over the portal. In the quadrangle at left, a colonnade shades soap vats, wine barrels, brick kilns, a tannery pool and presses, soldiers' quarters, Indians' dormitories, and other utilitarian parts of the compound.

Because builders situated the complex over the Santa Barbara Channel tectonic fault, much of the original stonework, completed by unsupervised workers after stonemason Aguilar's death, collapsed in the 1812 earthquake. The cataclysm killed twenty-nine residents. The disheartened friars gave up reconstruction and carried on services in the original church. Vines overtook the collapsed roof; wild poinsettias grew at the portal. After decades of neglect, in 1865, President Abraham Lincoln returned San Juan Capistrano Mission to the management of the Catholic Church. In 1910, Father John O'Sullivan, a historian and restorer, revived the church, which had lapsed into limited use as a granary and storehouse. Archbishop Cantwell donated a golden altar. During repairs in 1994, researchers examined the original walls and determined that stonemasons used volcanic tuff rather than sandstone for much of the construction.

ACTIVITIES

The mission's second church, called Padre Serra's Chapel, survives in ruins alongside arches, a courtyard, and a garden. The chapel is still a hallowed site. The *campañario* holds the chime that currently announces mass. The gardens with their bougainvillea and other semitropical plants and Romanesque archways, fountain, and statues of Saint Francis d'Assisi and Father Serra embracing an Indian child perpetuate the aura of peace and sanctity. Nearby, California's oldest adobe house, built in 1794, exemplifies life in the Indian village. A mission library houses the era's most complete collection of religious texts; the museum displays a collection of vestments, relics, parchments, and paintings.

The complex excites the imagination of people worldwide for the swallows that nest there on their annual migration northward each Saint Joseph's Day, March 19. On schedule, the birds depart each Saint John's Day, October 23. Records indicate that they complete the route annually on time except for one season, when they encountered a storm at sea. The birds form nests out of saliva and mud and benefit the valley by feeding their young on local insects. Locals and visitors celebrate the swallow migration with festivals, a Swallows Day Parade, and, in late August, a two-act historical and religious pageant, *Capistrano.*

The chapel is open year-round from 8:00 A.M. to 5:00 P.M. Hours extend to 7:00 A.M. to 6:00 P.M. in summer. Baptisms and weddings are available in the adjacent parish church. Since 1995, the mission has sponsored a June flower and garden festival. On the last Saturday each month, the Mission Preservation Society hosts crafts, costumes, and reenactments during Living History Days. The mission courtyard is also the scene of concerts by the Capistrano Symphony Orchestra and other musical groups.

See also San Luis Obispo de Tolosa.
Sources: Alsberg 1949; Buchanan 1999; Champagne 1994; Drain 1994; Florin 1969; "Hidden Heritage Exploring the Valley's American Indian Past" 1993; Kanellos 1995, 1997; Ketchum 1957; Neuerburg 1995; Patterson and Snodgrass 1994; "Researcher Finds Surprises in Mission Walls" 1994; Snodgrass, *Encyclopedia of Frontier Literature,* 1997; Sullivan 1967; Waldman 1990; "Weekend Escape: Central California Mission Impossible" 1993; Wright 1978.

San Luis Obispo de Tolosa

Old Mission Parish
751 Palm Street
San Luis Obispo, California 93401
805-781-8220
FAX 805-781-8214
slogiftshop@thegrid.net
www.thegrid.net/slomission

The fifth in the mission string built by Father Junípero Serra, San Luis Obispo de Tolosa, near the confluence of Stenner and San Luis Creeks, is a thriving religious community with a history that dates to the early Hispanic settlement of California. The complex, near the base of the Santa Lucia Mountains, bears the name of a thirteenth-century Provençal saint, Louis Bishop of Toulouse, who renounced his royal title to serve the see of Toulouse. Pope John XXII canonized him in 1317. An unsigned painting, possibly by José de Páez, hangs in Mission San Carlos; a statue dated 1791 of San Luis's likeness is prized relic displayed beside the San Luis Obispo altar.

HISTORY

The mission lies in La Canada de Los Osos (The Valley of the Bears), named by Spanish expeditioner Gaspar de Portolá during his search for Monterey Bay in 1769, when he fed his party and local Indians on 4.5 tons of dried bear meat. With the aid of two priests, Juan Crespi and Francisco Gomez, Father Serra sent soldiers, muleteers, and pack animals loaded with supplies and established the site on September 1, 1772. Father José Cavalier, five soldiers, and two Chumash built palisades of boughs lashed together, chinked with brush, and plastered with mud. When the permanent structure stood complete two years later, its adobe foundations stretched sixty by twenty-four feet beneath walls of timbers and tule reeds. The complex combined storerooms, residences for single women, military barracks, and mills adjacent to arable land and pastures for livestock.

The mission suffered four successive threats to its stability. It survived an attack in 1774, when Indians ignited thatched tule roofs with fiery arrows. The event stirred friars to start a tile factory to mold fireproof terra-cotta slabs for roofing. On November 29, 1776, fire demolished most of the mission. In a dispatch to the viceroy of New Spain, Father Francisco Palóu, a noted biographer and historian, reported that the padres' residence was in flames along with the kitchen, furnishings, farm tools, and granary. Soldiers from the presidio awoke resident Indians and determined that they were not guilty of arson. When Father Junípero Serra investigated, he assigned reconstruction to Father Fermín Francisco de Lasuén, who was then chaplain of the presidio at Monterey. Father José Cavalier described a second fire on Christmas 1781, after an Indian from Baja discharged a gun, perhaps in celebration of midnight mass. Because of the throng of holiday worshippers, firefighters were able to control the blaze. The next November, the mission suffered a third, less severe blaze.

Building continued from 1794 to 1820 with additions to the quadrangle, upgrades, a weaving room, and more dormitories for Mission Indians. The number of native residents grew to 832. The friars recorded 2,074 baptisms and 1,091 deaths. In 1807, the mission became a retreat for priests. In 1810, support of the army during Mexico's revolt against the Spanish taxed the stores of Father Luis Antonio Martinez. Eight years later, he led a native company to San Juan Capistrano and Santa Barbara to ward off South American privateers. When two bells arrived in 1820 from Lima, Peru, the mission celebrated a short-lived success.

Within five years, the governor of California decommissioned the property, leaving it ripe for land speculators. Captain John Wilson and two partners purchased the mission and Laguna Rancho in 1845. When California entered the Union in 1848, the mission returned to the church. In 1856, the community incorporated as a town. In the 1880s, workers removed the portico, which an earthquake damaged in 1830.

When President Chester A. Arthur dispatched Helen Hunt Jackson, reformer and journalist for *Scribner's* magazine, to study the Mission Indians, she became obsessed with their plight. She first saw southern California in 1881, when she gathered materials for her report, which the government ignored, and for a novel, *Ramona* (1884), a classic historical romance about an ill-starred love between Alessandro, an Indian, and Ramona, of mixed Indian and Scot ancestry. Like Harriet Beecher Stowe's *Uncle Tom's Cabin,* Jackson's sad love story ignited the passion of mission enthusiasts, who visited the church, studied the life of Father Martinez, and revived the area as a sacred site. Among the fans of the old California mission system were writers Ina Coolbrith, Joaquin Miller, Charles Fletcher Lummis, George Wharton James, Gertrude Atherton, and Ambrose Bierce.

According to California historian Phil Brigandi, Jackson's fiction didn't relieve the plight of Mission Indians. Inadvertently, the best-selling novel invigorated tourism in southern California. The romance of the mission system appeared in verses, essays, columns, and novels and in the sketches of Henry Chapman Ford. The current pageant, *Ramona,* by Garnet Holme, held near Mount San Jacinto, and the Ramona Festival in Hemet, California, honor Hunt's enthusiasm for the past and her attempts to improve the outlook for Native Americans, which inspired active preservation drives.

During the twentieth century, the mission vision moved to extremes. Trustees modernized and protected the historic building by covering the colonnades, church, and residence with wood clapboard shingles and adding a New England-style belfry. In 1933, Father Harnett reversed the process by returning the mission to its original frontier mission style. By 1972, the mission and surrounding Mission Plaza had become the center of the city of San Luis Obispo.

ACTIVITIES

Mission San Luis Obispo de Tolosa currently thrives in San Luis Obispo, which bears the slogan "City with a Mission." Located on Monterey Street in Monterey Diocese, the mission centers a multiethnic community made up of Jews, Mormons, Muslims, and those of other faiths and students from two colleges. The downtown fountain, paths, and stained-glass windows nourish urban life.

The antique bells still call worshippers to services. As the headquarters of the parish, the mission is open daily from 9:00 A.M. to 5:00 P.M. Regular services, led by the Reverend Jerry Maher and the Reverend John Arul, include mass on weekdays at 7:00 A.M. and 12:10 P.M., Saturday at 7:00 A.M. and 5:30 P.M., and Sunday at 7:00, 9:00, and 10:30 A.M. and 7:00 P.M. in both English and Spanish and a Spanish mass on Thursday evening in the Old Mission. Worshippers visit the sanctuary to light candles and pray or to arrange weddings and baptisms.

In addition, the church outreach includes a children's and adult choir, pastoral counseling, marriage preparation, activities for youth and older members, public assistance through the St. Vincent de Paul society, a thrift store open Monday through Saturday, upkeep of the historic Old Mission Cemetery, and a gift shop and museum open daily by the front door of the mission. Principal Valerie Ratto operates the Old Mission School on Broad Street; the Reverend Charles J. Tilley heads the Mission College Preparatory school. Staff maintains a museum in the priests' former quarters to display photos, Father Serra's embroidered vestments, and memorabilia. Local religious-cultural events include the Madonnari Italian Street Painting Fest, the Easter egg hunt, a quilt show, the Obon and Mozart festivals, Christmas in the Plaza and a parade, a harvest festival, the Dia de los Muertos (Day of the Dead), the celebration of Women's Equality Day, the Blessing of the Animals, and aid to the elderly from items collected during Respect Life Week. In September 1997, the mission celebrated a 225th anniversary during the filming of *California's Gold,* a public broadcasting documentary in seven parts on California missions. Since 1998, the staff has maintained a bilingual Web site. In October 1999, the parish received visitors traveling through California on a pilgrimage to the state's missions. In August 2000, high school youth planned their own pilgrimage to Rome with visits to the shrines of Fátima in Portugal and Lourdes in France, and Assisi, Pisa, and Florence in Italy.

See also San Juan Capistrano Mission.
Sources: Alsberg 1949; *Biography Resource Center* 1999; Buchanan 1999; Champagne 1994; Drain 1994; *Encyclopedia of World Biography* 1998; Fish 1995; Florin 1969; *Historic World Leaders* 1994; Kanellos 1995; 1997; Ketchum 1957; Krieger 1996, 1997; Long 1999; Neuerburg 1995; Patterson and Snodgrass 1994; Sherr and Kazickas 1994; Snodgrass, *Encyclopedia of Frontier Literature,* 1997; Sullivan 1967; Waldman 1990; "Weekend Escape: Central California Mission Impossible" 1993; "Welcome to the Old Mission San Luis Obispo"; Wright 1978.

San Marga Iraivan Temple

Satguru Sivaya Subramuniyaswami
107 Kaholalele Road
Kapaa, Hawaii, 96746-9304
808-822-3012 ext. 237; 800-890-1008 ext. 222
FAX 808-822-4351
thondu@hindu.org
www.hindu.org/iraivan/;
www.saivasiddhanta.com/hawaii/

A silent citadel within a rainforest, Kauai's San Marga Iraivan Temple, the first traditional Hindu worship center constructed outside Asia, fulfills the three pillars of Saiva worship—*parampara* (tradition), scripture, and temple. Approached along San Marga (literally, "the path to oneness") and through the Rudraksha Meditation Forest, it lies at the core of the Kauai Aadheenam (monastery) temple complex 102 miles from Honolulu, Oahu, and a twenty-minute

An illustration of the San Marga Iraivan Temple, a traditional Hindu worship center located in the rainforest of Hawaii. (Courtesy of San Marga Iraivan Temple)

flight from Honolulu International Airport. The international administrative headquarters of the Saiva Siddhanta Church, this Polynesian ashram is situated in Wailua Homesteads five miles from the base of Mt. Waialeale, an extinct volcano. It overlooks the sacred Wailua River in a place ancient Hawaiians called the land Pihanakalani, meaning "where heaven touches earth."

The grounds of the San Marga Sanctuary encompass twenty-five shaded ponds and lakes, marshes, waterfalls, and ravines that shelter wildlife and birds as well as tropical and sacred plants. Walking trails extend to a 1,300-foot path covering the sixty-four *nayamars* (saints), San Marga Path, Rishi Valley, Pihanakalani Trail, and River Ridge Road. Hikers enjoy groves of plumeria, konrai forest hibiscus, fragrant lianas, lilikoi, and ferns, many donated by collectors of exotic flora. Authentic forestation requires the planting of rare palms, fruit trees, and traditional

sacred and medicinal trees from India and Sri Lanka—bilva, neem, curry leaf, rudraksha, cassia, betel, and areca nut. A vast collection of tropical flowers showcases 500 species of heliconia and ginger, 250 varieties of ti plants, and exotic orchids and bromiliads.

The temple structure is the creation of noted Hindu leader, the Satguru Suvaya Subramuniyaswami. It is not intended as a public sanctuary. Rather, it serves pilgrims seeking the height of religious attainment. These devotees begin a quest at home in fasting, prayer, and spiritual preparation for a divine destination. By letting go of the past and existing in the eternity of the moment, at San Marga, they reach beyond themselves for complete submergence in the God Siva.

BELIEFS

The San Marga Iraivan Temple preserves Hinduism's major tenets. First in importance is belief in Siva, a single, all-pervasive supreme being, an immanent and transcendent God who is both a creator and an invisible reality. Second, the temple testifies to divinity in unseen inner worlds, whom the devout seek through worship, ritual, sacrament, and personal devotion. Hindu philosophy maintains that all souls perpetually evolve toward union with God and ultimately find spiritual knowledge and liberation from the earthly cycle of life, death, and rebirth.

Central to Hindu faith is the belief that all life is sacred and worthy of love and reverence. Devotees, who celebrate both unity and diversity, believe that no one religion possesses the only way to salvation. Rather, all genuine religious faiths share commonalities and reach out to godly love and light. For this reason, Hindus respect and tolerate divergence in worship and anticipate a new age when religion will merge into a single quest bearing no name and no doctrines.

HISTORY

The San Marga Iraivan complex—which houses the theological seminary that trains religious leaders of the Saiva Siddhanta Church—has evolved from communion with God. Established in 1970 on fifty-one acres of tropical jungle on Kauai, Hawaii's mystical garden island, San Marga is a hallowed site benefiting pilgrims

SIVAYA SUBRAMUNIYASMI

To Hindus, Satguru Sivaya Subramuniyaswami is Sri Lanka's hereditary guru (teacher) of the island nation's 2.5 million followers of Lord Siva. They admire the guru for his peaceful presence, for inspiring the best in others, and for guiding lives toward truth and purity. On a more personal basis, he is their beloved "Gurudeva," a nickname for a right-thinking instructor in the ancient tradition of wisdom and awakening. As leader of the faith through a Tamil-based organization headquartered in Jaffna, Sri Lanka, he seeks to preserve, protect, and promote the Saivite Hindu religion and its religious codes of liturgy and temple ritual.

Born in Oakland, California, on January 5, 1927, Gurudeva grew up in the Lake Tahoe region and traveled to India and Sri Lanka in his youth. In 1949, under the influence of the enlightened holy man and mystic Jnaanaguru Yogaswami (master teacher) of Sri Lanka, he entered *sannyasa,* a holy life dedicated to religion. He learned hundreds of Yogaswami's epigrammatic songs and followed the divine path of dharma (cosmic order) and a realization of God within. Essential to the Yogaswami's philosophy were four great sayings: "Know thyself by thyself," "Siva is doing it all," "All is Siva," and the crucial admonition, "Be still."

Invigorated by his teacher's instruction, Gurudeva determined to join the late twentieth-century Hindu diaspora, the spread of the faithful from Asia into many lands. For the next five decades, as chief of the monastery of Kauai island, he modeled a contemplative life way and taught Hinduism to people of various faiths. For the good of all comers, he established a Siva temple to promote Sanatana Dharma (cosmic order) within the multicultural environment of Hawaii. His intent was to spread Hinduism via the functions of the Saiva Siddhanta Church, the Himalayan Academy, the Hindu Heritage Endowment, and a monthly international journal, *Hinduism Today,* in circulation since 1979 and advanced to a magazine in 1996. Through strict interpretation of Hindu tradition, he built a membership and dispatched missions to five continents, covering a branch monastery in Mauritius and fifty temples worldwide. The academy supplies books, courses, and travel and study programs to serious students of Hinduism. The Saiva Siddhanta Church congregation disciplines and supports a global fellowship of initiates, monks, and students who follow the *sadhana marga* (path of inner effort), yogic (enlightened) striving, and personal transformation.

The Gurudeva actively supervises the temple's outreach. He has published over thirty religious manuals on metaphysics, yoga, and mysticism. Under his direction, the temple's missionaries and teachers counsel and teach Saivism, or Siva worship, to children, youth, and adults. The monks issue *Hinduism Today* as a public service to strengthen Hindus by uplifting and informing them of the Sanatana Dharma everywhere. For classroom use, the Gurudeva offers a master course on Saivism and Hindu teachings of the Vedas, Hinduism's sacred writings. His Hindu Heritage Endowment, founded in 1995, provides a sound financial backing for the world's Hindu institutions.

In 1986, the World Religious Parliament in New Delhi honored the Gurudeva's international effort toward a Hindu renaissance by voting him one of five *jagadacharyas* (world teachers). Nine years later, the parliament conferred the title of Dharmachakra in honor of his effective publications. The Global Forum of Spiritual and Parliamentary Leaders for Human Survival chose him as its Hindu representative. He served in this capacity at Oxford, England, in 1988, Moscow in 1990, and Rio de Janeiro in 1992 by joining hundreds of the world's religious, political, and scientific leaders in a study of the future of human life on earth. At the 1993 Parliament of World Religions in Chicago, he accepted a copresidency along with Swami Chidananda Saraswati and Mata Amritanandamayi Ma.

The end of the twentieth century brought added responsibility. In 1997, the Gurudeva responded to President Bill Clinton's request for religious opinions on the ethics of cloning and headed the 125th anniversary of Satguru Yogaswami. In 1998, the Vishva Hindu Parishad of Kerala, India, recognized the Gurudeva as the Hindu Voice of the Century. In Hawaii, he currently serves Vision Kauai, a coterie of community heads composed of the mayor, past mayor, county council, and business and education leaders to plot the future of the island chain for the first two decades of the twenty-first century.

and religious students. The key factors in identifying outsiders as Hindus are reverence for the Vedas, recognition of diverse means to salvation, and realization that there are many gods. At the information center, a Nepalese Ganesha shrine features a traditional elephant carving in stone. Another stone monument marks the path to the Kadavul Hindu Temple, a traditional Siva temple enshrining a 200-year-old, six-foot bronze Siva Nataraja.

Iraivan, which embodies a 6,000-year-old Hindu tradition, occupies a sacred Hawaiian site of the ancient Ku temple, founded in 480 A.D. by Kuamo'o Mo'okini. The Hindu community profits from an affinity between Hinduism and indigenous Hawaiian religion, which the Gurudeva and his followers encourage to flourish once more among islanders. To both Hindus and native Hawaiians, God dwells everywhere in all things. The two faiths share a similar reverence and practice a prehistoric ritual worship expressed through the Hawaiian hula and Indian dance.

Significant to the Hindu community was a change in United States immigration policy. In previous decades, laws forbade the acceptance of Hindus as potential citizens. When attitudes changed during the administration of President John F. Kennedy, a swell of Hindus began establishing worship centers in a pluralistic society. To meet the needs of the faithful, the Gurudeva began planning the San Marga temple as a gift to the West. On February 15, 1975, he conceived a design from an early morning encounter with God. He perceived Lord Siva walking in the meadow alongside the Wailua River. In a triple image, the Gurudeva also envisioned Siva's face turned toward him, saw him seated on a boulder, and heard him say that the site would draw others to pray.

Laboring in time-honored style under the direction of Sri Tiruchy Mahaswamigal, Sri Balagangadaranatha Swami, and Sri Sivapuriswami, seventy-five *shilpi* (traditional sculptors) in Bangalore, India, reside with their families at an eleven-acre worksite donated by Sri Balagangadaranatha Swami. Daily, this guild of artisans carves stones with ancient hand tools and ships finished pieces to Hawaii to form the nation's first traditional Hindu temple. They intend the massive granite sanctuary to survive for 1,000 years. A source of *moksha* (release or deliverance), it symbolizes the end of *samsara,* a burdensome chain or cycle of existence, death, and rebirth that binds the soul to earth. A godly place, the temple is a *pujya tirtha* (sacred destination), which offers immediate oneness with the divine through emotional peace and mystical communion.

ARCHITECTURE

Built atop a black lava plinth out of 32 million pounds of white granite, the temple and its iconography form the West's most traditional tribute to the God Siva. Sri Vaidyanathan Ganapati Sthapati, India's foremost *sthapati* (temple architect and builder), began superintending the project in 1981. As head of the Government College of Architecture and Sculpture in Mahabalipuram, Tamil Nadu, for twenty-seven years, he led the renaissance of the ancient art of ritual stone carving. After retiring in 1988, he built temples and established the Vastu Vedic Research Foundation to learn the origins of ancient temple craft. A world-class builder, he constructed Hindu temples in India, Chicago, Washington, D.C., Kentucky, Boston, Baltimore, San Francisco, Great Britain, Singapore, Fiji, Malaysia, Mauritius, and the Seychelles and studied parallel styles of temple art among the Maya and Inca. At the San Marga foundation ceremony, he compared the building of a temple to the planting of a seed that would develop into the living body of God.

From the beginning, Sthapati followed the style of India's Chola empire, which flourished from the ninth to the thirteenth century. Using 108 cement trucks, he formed a 3-foot thick concrete foundation 188 by 82 feet on top of an expanse of lava to create a monolith capable of surviving well into the thirtieth century. The work, the largest single pour in the history of Hawaii, took twenty-four hours of continuous flow. The building, which is 118 by 82 by 35 feet, began in 1989 with donors contributing $5 per pound to purchase stone. Thus, the temple took shape gradually from a pay-as-you-go system requiring no bank loans.

The temple is a Deva/Mahadeva (soul) sanctuary where the spirit is free to roam in the safety and security of a consecrated atmosphere. Since 1987, the assembled stones have enshrined an inner sanctum that shelters the Sphatika Sivalinga, the world's largest single-point quartz crystal. The six-sided ice-colored jewel, a natural formation, weighs 700 pounds, and stands 39 inches high. To the faithful, it represents a sacred phallus, or fertility symbol, a source of Siva's creativity and godhood. In accordance with ancient scripture, the center channels and focuses spiritual power within the crystal to those who humble themselves and await its dawning.

The site allies beauty from a variety of sources. The pavilion rests on twenty-four 13-foot *bhadra* pillars. Outside the temple, gardens, groves, paths, and ponds reflect the serenity and sanctuary of a holy place. Sculpted panels picture temple history and the mystical philosophy of Siva's rule over a unified world. The ornate tower houses a stone bell. Etched in multiple languages is the motto "One God, One World." In 1997, the congregation commissioned portrait artist Sri Indra Sharma to paint Gurudeva standing life-size. The temple displays the finished 9-foot painting and sells autographed copies.

Although the temple draws thousands of visitors, it is more than a religious tourist attraction. Built at the center of a cloistered monastery, it serves as worship center for fellowship members and a shrine for the devout, who reverence an immanent and transcendent divinity. It is a sacred destination for seekers who pursue a single goal—to prepare themselves through fasting, meditation, and prayer to receive the *darshana* (philosophy) of Iraivan and to perform a daily *sadhana* (quest) at San Marga. These pilgrims receive access cards that allow continued access to the inner sanctum. The temple's vibrations obliterate subconscious *vasanas* (longings) and heal psychic wounds. The experience strips the pilgrim of burdens and releases the soul's inner purity. Departing under escort, seekers bear a new self-image and an understanding of the purpose of earthly life.

The San Marga complex gains respect as a monastery, the home of a *satguru,* and his staff of *sadhakas* (spiritual seekers), yogis (enlightened holy men), swamis (monks), and *acharyas* (religious teachers). Moreover, the monastery enrolls students worldwide at its theological seminary, which trains monks for the holy orders of *sannyasa,* a formal dedication to a sacred life at the Saiva Siddhanta Yoga Order. In a serene setting, the purified retreat within themselves through the practice of *raja yoga* (mastery of the mind).

ACTIVITIES

The temple serves some 100 members from Australia, England, Canada, Malaysia, Mauritius, Scotland, Singapore, Sri Lanka, and the United States and receives pilgrims from all parts of the globe. The monastery is open daily from 6:00 A.M. until noon, except on the half moon, full moon, and new moon, when the facility closes for a monks' retreat. At 9:00 A.M. the day before the retreat, the staff conducts a tour of the grounds and temple. They advise newcomers to dress for inclement weather for a visit to Hawaii's rainforest, the wettest spot on earth. Members observe a regular schedule of daily prayer, usually before dawn, annual pilgrimages, and weekly worship with their families at the temple. The faithful may wander the lake path and express joy in smiles and silent adoration of God. To achieve peace and union with the divine, they visit the building's shrines.

Hindus practice mantra yoga, a spoken and or intoned syllable or phrase that comforts, satisfies, and helps them achieve a balanced, serene spiritual state. The Eastern practitioner may choose the traditional *aum* or the syllables *so ham, om namah shivaya, hram,* or *hrim,* as a suitable utterance. The rhythmic repetition, called *japa,* requires strict control of thought and words. It may be voiced, whispered, or hummed, with or without prayer beads, or rosary, and with eyes open or shut. Situations vary for its practice:

- Daily *japa* to begin and end the day
- Circumstantial *japa* performed for religious festivals
- Penitential *japa* to overcome wrongdoing
- Moving *japa* throughout the day to maintain spiritual balance
- Uninterrupted *japa,* the reverential act of the dedicated religious

Control of thought, posture, concentration, breathing, and gesture empowers the practitioner to ignore extraneous distractions. Fuller worship involves a water offering, a devotional song, a ritual sacrifice, the lighting of incense or a lamp, reverence and contemplation of God, and *samadhi* (identification), the completed state of submergence into the divine and *bhakti* (love of God).

On April 4 and 5, 1995, at the two-day purification ceremony called Pancha Shila Nyasa (Touching the Earth with Five Sacred Stones), celebrants followed primeval rites recorded in Hindu scripture. Two eminent Hindu priests from India—Sivacharya Sambamurthi and Sivacharya Bhairava—conducted the ritual, during which they fasted, chanted, and observed sacred silence. A series of fire ceremonies cleansed the site and invoked the blessing of Siva, Hindu guardian spirits, and local Hawaiian deities. Joining 100 Hindus, composed of cloistered monks and adults and children of the church family, were special guests: island mayor Maryanne Kusaka, former mayor Joanne Yukimura, Polynesian priestess Leimomi Mo'okini Lum, Hawaiian *kahuna* (priest) Kahu Abraham Aua'ia Makiole, and Wendall Silva, Director of State Culture and Arts for Hawaii. Their part in the festivities began with a drummed processional to witness fire ceremonies.

The purpose of the gathering was the union of the temple with the Kauaian model of pluralism. Mayor Kusaka remarked on the holiness of the occasion, which inspired feelings of hospitality, peace, and humility. Priestess Lum offered two leis composed of varied flowers to represent cultural harmony within the island chain. The joint service concluded with offerings of water and salt, a Hawaiian chant, and invocations to Siva and Hawaiian gods to bless the venture. After three young women of the church performed a Bharata Natyam South Indian dance, the staff spread tables with a traditional South Indian vegetarian feast of rice and curried vegetables.

A private Hindu ceremony began the next morning at 5:30, at the end of which Subramuniyaswami displayed five sacred granite stones from India bearing inscriptions in Sanskrit, Tamil, and English. He placed them in the vault under the temple's northeast corner, the future location of the *sanctum sanctorum* (holy of holies). Eleven swamis presented trays of gemstones, gold, and silver donated by devotees worldwide. Additional contributions of sand, stones, and soil came from sacred sites in India, Europe, Russia, Australia, and North America and from Mayan and Incan holy sites in Central and South America. Over the stones, priests carrying gold ewers poured sacred water from the rivers of India and other countries and offered *vibhuti* (holy ash). The elder priest from Madras, India, Dr. Sambamurthi Sivachariya, president of the South India Priests Association, declared the site the true home of God.

> **Sources:** *Eerdmans' Handbook to the World's Religions* 1982; "Kauai Aadheenam" 1998; "A Photo Tour of Aadheenam"; "San Marga Iraivan Temple November Update" 1999; "Shiva Temple Constructed in Hawaii amid Protest" 1999; Skafte 1997; "Spirit Glossary" 1997; Subramuniyaswami 1999; "Who is a Hindu?" 1999; *World Religions* 1998.

San Miguel Mission

See Mission of San Miguel of Santa Fe.

Santa Fe Cathedral of St. Francis of Assisi

Marina Ochoa, Director of Archives
131 Cathedral Place
P.O. Box 2127
Santa Fe, New Mexico 87504-2127
505-982-5619
FAX 505-992-0341

The Santa Fe Cathedral of St. Francis of Assisi is a landmark sacred site in America's oldest capital city. It stands at the east end of San Francisco Street and embodies both the history and faith of the city's founders. The parish celebrated its first Episcopal, or bishop-led, mass in 1730, after Bishop Benito Crespo appointed as vicar Don Santiago Roybal, one of the nation's earliest native priests. Designed in French-Romanesque style, since 1825, the edifice carries the name of the diocese patron saint, Saint Francis of Assisi, the thirteenth-century Italian evangelist, poet, and founder of the Franciscans.

Santa Fe's Europeanized cathedral graces a city originally called La Villa Real de la Santa Fe de San Francisco de Assisi (The Royal City of

The Santa Fe Cathedral of St. Francis of Assisi is a landmark sacred site in America's oldest capital city. (David Muench/Corbis)

the Holy Faith of St. Francis of Assisi). Don Pedro de Peralta designated it in 1610 as the capital of the kingdom of New Mexico. The diocese once belonged to Durango in Chihuahua, Mexico, before it joined the American frontier. The church, named Our Lady of the Assumption, took shape above the remains of the ancient *parroquia* (parish church), probably built in 1625 by Father Alonso de Benavides, *custos* (superior) of the Indian Missions. During a rebellion of Pueblo in 1680, many settlers and twenty-one friars died; the parish burned, sending settlers fleeing to El Paso del Norte with their statue *La Conquistadora*. In 1693, General Don Diego de Vargas restored the city to its officials and the mission to the church in a formal ceremony.

ARCHITECTURE

Jean-Baptiste Lamy produced the progressive thrust that set Santa Fe on its way to greatness. At the terminus of the Santa Fe Trail that brought settlers from Franklin, Missouri, he erected the St. Francis Cathedral in sight of the Sangre de Cristo mountain range. To express his love for French architecture, he emulated the Auvergnat Cathedral and embellished a stolid, boxy Spanish hacienda style with the panache of Napoleon's Second Empire. A modest rose window over the double portals coordinates with stained-glass windows and the upper triangle pierced by an oculus. Overall, the cathedral's workmanship exalts Lamy's years of service to the American Southwest with the Romanesque grace of his native land.

An architectural treasure, the cathedral carries the name of the Order of Loretto, which converted much of the Southwest. After the laying of a cornerstone on July 14, 1867, a pair of French architect-builders, a father and son named Antoine and Projectus Moulay (or Molny), arrived from Volvic, Auvergne, drew plans and elevations, and initiated the structure

JEAN-BAPTISTE LAMY

The cathedral's medieval flavor derives from the vision of Bishop Jean-Baptiste Lamy, who employed Continental dignity and grandeur to portray the growth of Catholicism in the American Southwest. Born October 11, 1814, in Lempdes near Auvergne, France, he trained at Clermont-Ferrand and entered the priesthood at age twenty-four. After electing to carry Roman Catholicism to the Mississippi Valley, he left Europe in 1839. During this period of Americanization, when he retained close ties with France, he served for eleven years in Cincinnati, Ohio. Following his ministry in Ohio and Kentucky, he accepted the New Mexico diocese after Pope Pius IX separated it from the Durango see in 1849.

In 1851, Lamy arrived in Santa Fe to become the area's first bishop. As apostolic vicar to a hospitable community, he had to prove his mission to the Reverend John F. Ortiz, leader of local priests, by journeying to Durango to gain assurances from the Mexican bishop. After the preliminary shift of control, Lamy set up a regular calendar of mass and curtailed heavy pulpit charges for confirmations, weddings, and baptisms. The new diocese obtained full independence in 1853, when Lamy formally accepted the title of archbishop. With aid from the Vatican, he expanded the see to Arizona and Colorado and traveled to Rome to recruit priests to replace renegade fathers who denied his authority. Immediately, he brought six nuns of the Order of Loretto from Kentucky to teach English to Spanish-speaking parishioners. He also initiated a mission to Indians, a hospital, and an orphanage and furthered close relations with Protestants and Jews.

Lamy's choice of mansard roofs and towers on the cathedral and likewise on adobe schools, dormitories, hospitals, and convents leave his decidedly French mark on the predominantly Hispanic city, which glows with the earth tones of local building materials. Because the towers lack the three octagonal windowed stories and crosses on top depicted in drawings of the plans, the cathedral projects a human touch of work yet to be done.

The passage of the office of archbishop ended the influence of Lamy, who retired to his ranch in 1885 and died on February 13, 1888, when only the nave was complete. However, the original plans remained intact, honoring the first archbishop's vision. The second archbishop, John Baptist Salpointe, kept loose notes on church history, leaving some events unrecorded. The third, Placid Louis Chapelle, applied some of the style of his home church, St. Matthew's Cathedral in Washington, D.C., and simplified the transept to a square sanctuary so it would be complete by his installation in 1895.

Archbishop Lamy became a legend in Santa Fe. Three years after the territory gained statehood, Miguel Chaves donated a life-size statue of him, which William C. McDonald, the governor of New Mexico, and Archbishop John Baptist Pitaval unveiled on the front terrace on May 23, 1915. For the occasion, newspaper reporter Nestor Montoya, editor of the Albuquerque *La Bandera Americana,* read "En la Llageda," an appropriate verse by former priest and poet José Rómulo Ribera. The eight-stanza ode depicts Lamy as "the holy pastor," a vigorous, handsome hero entering the city in chivalric glory through *"arcos de triunfo"* (triumphal arches). A decade later, novelist Willa Cather began researching a fictionalized account of Lamy's accomplishments as the basis for a novel, *Death Comes for the Archbishop* (1927). A half century afterward, Paul Horgan authored a Pulitzer Prize-winning biography, *Lamy of Santa Fe: His Life and Times* (1975). To honor the founding father, the state of New Mexico named a liberty ship *Archbishop Lamy* during World War II. In 1950, the diocese celebrated a Lamy centennial, which concluded in the establishment of the Lamy memorial parish of St. John the Baptist.

in 1869 over foundations of the parish church, Our Lady of the Assumption, which they narrowed. Antoine Moulay suffered blindness in 1874 and returned to France, leaving the work for Projectus to complete. The cathedral parallels their creation of the Loretto Chapel on the Old Santa Fe Trail, which Projectus undertook during a halt in construction of the cathedral. In 1878, Lamy returned from France with additional funding and assistance. He acquired new plans from Francois Mallet of San Francisco, who designed the façade. The collaboration of Lamy with Mallet ended violently in September 1879, when Lamy's mentally unbalanced nephew shot and killed the architect for flirting with the young man's wife.

Under the direction of the firm of Monier and Machbeuf in 1882, local citizens carted away debris from the old church to ready the interior of the new cathedral. European artisans quarried and carved local stone from La Bajada Mesa west of town and imported additional material from Albuquerque to adorn the exterior. The clergy had to make do with a canvas and lumber false wall and a temporary altar. Stained glass in the rose window and the twelve nave windows picturing the apostles softened the pairing of stone with slate. The building was still incomplete after Lamy's retirement in 1885; artisans added a pair of 1,600-foot stone steeples as its last enhancement. The following March, staff blessed the cathedral bell.

Unlike other churches of the Southwest, the Santa Fe Cathedral is a model of European grace, featuring rounded polychrome Romanesque arches alternating red with white, twin steeples at the left and right corners, and Ionic capitals sculpted by Italian artisans. The portals open on a lofty lathe and plaster nave ceiling ringed by round arches supported by Corinthian columns and groin vaults of tufa, a volcanic stone. A St. Louis firm cast the corbels in iron. A clerestory and paired octagonal cylinders light the interior; brass sconces reflect on the pilasters of the side aisles. The rear balcony houses a pipe organ, set at an angle to the rose window. Steps lead from the wood floor up to the high altar, which Carlos Digneo carved from sandstone. Gothic pillars support a table slab sheltering a reclining Christ figure. The rear wall supports a crucifixion group.

During the tenure of Archbishop John Baptist Pitaval from 1909 to 1918, the cathedral interior acquired a coat of gray paint that was highlighted in gold leaf and warm tones. A substantial carved oak communion rail enclosed the sanctuary. A dignified turret topped the pulpit. Reproductions of Andrea del Sarto's *Madonna of the Harpies* and Raphael's *Madonna of the Chair* adorn the wall on opposite sides of the altar.

With a shift from French archbishops and the appointment of Albert Thomas Daeger, an American Franciscan, Santa Fe experienced a historical and religious revival. North of the city, a hilltop concrete cross honors Franciscan martyrs of 1680. The cathedral received a proper diocese insignia, designed by heraldry expert Chaignon de la Rose. Colored red and gold, it echoes the Franciscan emblem with an extended cross and the pierced hands of Saint Francis. At the upper left stands a Spanish castle. Over the design stands the bishop's miter. Under Archbishop Rudolph Aloysius Gerken, the tone of the exterior changed with the addition of aluminum paint on the roof, a flagstone terrace, and evergreens, spruces, and cedars. With the appointment of Archbishop Edwin Vincent Byrne, workers replaced the plain clerestory with stained-glass coats-of-arms of the eight archbishops.

Today, the cathedral entices religious tourists to see contrasting light and dark in ceiling, diagonal wooden flooring, and pillars. The bronze doors, sculpted by Donna Quasthoff and cast at the nearby Shidoni Foundry, display New Mexico's religious history in bas-relief within 16 cartouches. The story of Catholicism in the west begins in 1539 with the arrival of Fra Marcos de Niza among the Zuñi pueblos and concludes in 1986 with the building of the cathedral and its reredos. The Hebrew word "Yahweh" holds a prominent position at the top of the archway to commemorate support of local Jewish philanthropists. Decorative braid separates the segments and blends into a pair of imaginative door handles capped with lions' heads. A statue of Saint Francis with hands reaching out, palm up, blesses the congregation at the south transept portal.

A small structure on the northeast side, the Chapel of Our Lady of Peace (also, Chapel of Our Lady of the Rosary), in use since 1718, honors North America's oldest Madonna. A lacy wrought-iron screen separates worshippers from the altar. The *bulto* (sculpture), carved in Mexico City in the 1500s, was the first Marian statue in the country. In 1625, Brother Alonso de Benavides transported it to the site, where he built the original church. Because Governor Don Diego de Vargas and Hispanic settlers retook the area after twelve years of exile, the congregation originally named the statue *La Conquistadora* (Our Lady of the Conquest) in 1692 to signify the Virgin's protection of Hispanic settlers. The devout carry the Virgin's likeness in a June processional to mark the predominance of Catholicism in Santa Fe. Restored in 1954 in celebration of the Marian Year, the church represents colonial times with authentic early-eighteenth-century style.

The Blessed Sacrament Chapel features a modern glass partition separating it from the south transept and two stained-glass panels at the rear. John W. McHugh designed a reredos featuring woodwork by Robert Lavadie and Paul Martinez and set with Robert Lentz's paintings of fifteen American saints. The upper row situates Our Lady of Guadalupe with Saint Philip of Jesus and Saint Rose of Lima to the left and, to the right, Saint Martin de Porres and Saint Francis Solano. The center row places Saint Francis of Assisi at center, with Saint John Neuman and Saint Elizabeth Seton to the left and Saint Frances Cabrini and Saint Peter Calver at right. The bottom row features Blessed Kateri Tekakwitha, the first Native American saint, at center. To the left are Blessed Katherine Drexel and Saint Isaac Joques; to the right are Blessed Junípera Serra, creator of the California mission chain, and Saint Miguel Febres Cordero. The wooden frame rises to a three-dimensional sun that suggests primitive depictions of dawn.

ACTIVITIES

The cathedral is open from 6:00 A.M. to 6:00 P.M. In addition to weekday and Saturday mass at 7:00 A.M. and 5:15 P.M., there are four masses on Sunday—in the morning at 8:00 and 10:00, at noon, and in the evening at 5:15. Worshippers may seek confession on Saturday from 3:00 to 5:00 P.M. or by appointment and can arrange baptism and marriage in advance. Members extend worship through the Knights of Columbus, the parish rosary, the Franciscan Missionary Union, and choir and instrumental practice. As aids to families, staff offers marriage preparation, the Rite of Christian Initiation of Adults, classes in natural family planning, post abortion healing, education at the St. Francis Cathedral School, a Christian Maturity Retreat, and Respite for Caregivers. For Spanish-speaking members, the schedule includes Bible study in Spanish. Informal fellowship through a November pancake breakfast, a balloon breakfast on the Rio Grande, rosary rallies, the Catholic Network of Volunteer Services, Make-a-Difference Day, the Cristo Rey Arts and Crafts Fair, and concerts such as by the Russian Konevets Quartet center local lives around the cathedral.

See also Loretto Chapel.
Sources: Ahlstrom 1972; Beresky 1991; *Biography Resource Center* 1999; "Cathedral in Santa Fe"; Cather 1927; Chavez 1995; Lee 1989; Morgan 1994; *New Catholic Encyclopedia* 1967; Sheppard 1994; Snodgrass, *Encyclopedia of Frontier Literature,* 1997; Spritzer 1994.

El Santuário de Chimayó
Father Casimiro Roca
Route 76
Chimayo, New Mexico 87522
505-351-4889

A unique site in United States hallowed geography, New Mexico's El Sanctuário de Chimayó is a humble rural shrine that annually draws 300,000 pilgrims on an emotion-charged walk of the elderly and infirm to its healing sands. Located ten miles east of Española in the Sangre de Cristo (Blood of Christ) Mountains at Tsimajo'onwi, a Tewa healing shrine at least 600 years old, it was the site of an appearance of twin sun gods, who killed a villainous giant and forced a fiery geyser from the earth to create a *sipapu* (underworld link) of curative mud. In honor of its primordial holiness, the Tewa named it Tsimayopokwi (pool where large stones stand), a link to the underworld and to the birth canal of humanity.

Today, the shrine belongs secondhand to the Catholic mythos of the black Christ called Nuestro Señor de Esquípulas (Our Lord of Esquípulas). The syncretic figure is a complex convergence of beliefs. They began as a late-sixteenth-century cult conflating the legend of a Mayan chief with a holy city in eastern Guatemala where Chorti pilgrims honored a balsam carving of a black Christ at a healing spring long before the Spanish arrived in the New World. To encourage converts, the Southwest's missionary priests applied a process known as "baptizing the local customs" by deliberately overlaying the Central American Indian belief with Christian names and mysticism, thus fusing aboriginal practice with orthodox Catholic beliefs. By building a chapel over the Indian *sipapu,* newcomer priests established their claim to the region and its age-old sanctity.

The chapel stands at the upper end of a north-south highroad that was crucial to religious and commercial development in the Southwest. Like the Penitente Brotherhood of old, pilgrims and traders traveling from Mexico City to Santa Fe on El Camino Real (The King's Highway) passed a series of eight shrines on the way to Chimayó:

- The famed Nuestra Señora de Guadalupe (Our Lady of Guadalupe) in Mexico City
- Nuestra Señora de Talpa (Our lady of Talpa) in Talpa
- Guadalajara's Nuestra Señora de Zapopán
- Nuestra Señora de San Juan de los Lagos (Our Lady of the Lakes) in San Juan de los Lagos
- Zacatecas's Nuestra Señora de Patrocino (Our Lady of Protection)
- Santo Niño de Atocha (Holy Infant of Atocha) in Fresnillo
- Nuestro Señor de Mapimi in Cuencamé
- Parral's Nuestra Señora del Rayo (Our Lady of the Ray of Light) (Gutiérriez and Fabre 1995)

In the opposite direction from Mexico City, the traveler passed through a similar linkage of holy places through Central America to the Valley of Mexico, the Aztec heartland. Over the long trail, commerce and faith fed the culture that prefaced the arrival of white settlers.

Since 1594, the devout have carried away cakes of white clay, which they shaped into sacred images to rub on diseased parts of the body. Others ate the holy soil, formed it into a beneficent mud plaster, or mixed it into healing beverages to cure depression, cancer, rheumatism, and paralysis or to aid parturient women. By the 1790s, the followers of Christ of Esquípulas and geophagy, the consumption of holy dirt, spread through forty towns south from Mexico into Guatemala, Honduras, El Salvador, Nicaragua, and Costa Rica.

BELIEFS

Chimayó's wonder-working tradition derives from parallel lore. In Pueblo stories, a Picuris herder called Shamnoag discovered Chimayó's crucifix buried in the ground near his flock. He safeguarded it under his pillow, but when he awoke, the *santo* (holy object) had disappeared.

He found it in the original location. When he bore it across the mountains to his people, again it vanished and returned to the area around the standing rocks where he had discoverd it. The people of Picuris built a shed over the magic cross and named the shrine Shamno.

At Isleta, Tiwa speakers tell a variant tale about a shepherd who located an *escápula* (little carved head). Because the herder's wife ordered him to toss it in the fire, a sudden paralysis seized her. The couple experienced the same mysterious disappearance and recovery of the icon. Because they venerated San Escápulo, the woman's limbs healed spontaneously.

Among the Españoles Méxicanos (Spanish Mexicans), the Chimayó area, settled by the Spanish in 1692, has long been famous for weavers of fine woolen blankets and rugs. The Plaza of San Buenaventura, now called the Plaza del Cerro, dates to 1740, but the village, called San Buenaventura de Chimayó, remained an obscure backwater for another seventy years. In 1805, worship of Guatemala's black Christ reached the territory and fostered a movement and the building of an oratory. The name Esquípulas began appearing in baptismal records, proving that the Central American Christ group held credence among local people.

On Good Friday in 1810, while performing penance near the Santa Cruz River with fellow laymen of the Hermanidad de Nuestro Señor Jesus Nazareño (Brotherhood of Our Lord the Nazarene), a friar named Bernardo Abeyta experienced a vision of luminescence from a rise along the riverbank. When Don Abeyta brushed away soil, he disclosed a six-foot wood crucifix carved to represent Nuestro Señor de Esquípulas. One speculation on the mystical appearance of the Chimayó crucifix surmises that a Guatemalan missionary came to New Mexico to evangelize the Tewa, who slaughtered him and buried his corpse and the dark wooden crucifix near the river. Whatever its provenance, its mystic power took root in the local belief system in the same fashion as a reverence of magic earth in Etla and Tlacolula, Oaxaca. The brothers hurried to Santa Cruz to summon Father Sebastian Alvarez, who bore the holy symbol to the parish and enshrined it on the church altar. By morning, it had vanished. Searchers found it once more in its original spot in the soft dirt by the river.

Although the crucifix was removed two more times to Santa Cruz over that Easter weekend, it returned to the depression Don Abeyta dug by the river. It was not until 1813 that the crucifix found its current home on the altar of El Santuário de Nuestro Señor de Esquípulas (The Sanctuary of Our Lord of Esquípulas). The modest candlelit chapel took shape in El Portrero (The Horse Pasture) near the ancient Tewa site that had been revered for centuries for its healing geysers, hot springs, and therapeutic mud. Within three years, pilgrim traffic enlivened the crossroads and enriched its commerce.

In a variant story, Abeyta was a devotee of Esquípulas who petitioned the vicar general to permit the construction of a chapel honoring Christ on the cross. Illness struck Abeyta while he was tending sheep. Christ of Esquípulas appeared and healed him. Others seeking a cure knelt at the same place and recovered their health. To honor the place, Abeyta built El Santuário de Chimayó and became a wealthy merchant and village notable.

Today, pilgrims of many cultures value Chimayó's soil as Santa Madre Tierra (Holy Mother Earth), the source of blessing and cure. El Santuário de Chimayó is no longer an active parish church, but remains a religious shrine in Mexico and the American Southwest from word-of-mouth praise of its sanctity and a tradition of spiritual power. Artists capture its humble Spanish colonial mission design on photos, screen prints, sketches, and canvases. Since 1970, the shrine has claimed designation as a National Historic Landmark.

ARCHITECTURE

Heavy demands on the little chapel forced the local priest and parishioners to replace it with a sturdy twenty- by eighty-foot fortress-style mission made of hand-tooled timber with five-foot-thick adobe walls and exposed beams. Before becoming a popular locus for miracle seekers, it served the prosperous Abeyta family as a private chapel. In its evolution, the courtyard became both a garden and a burying ground. A symmetrical façade enhanced by twin bell tow-ers topped with a four-gabled roof and a simple Roman cross follows standard unarrayed architecture of the Hispanic frontier. The portal opens on a small narthex and directly into the nave. At the sanctuary behind the wood screen, worshippers may pray at the altar and move left through a small door into the adjacent Prayer Room, the sacristy that is half the length of the church. In the floor, an inexhaustible sand pit called El Pozito (The Little Well) has developed from the very hole that Don Abeyta dug.

In 1826, a churchman cleared the chapel of primitive folk art painted on hide and raw lumber. Until midcentury, area artists contributed *santos* (holy figures) to the reredos. The niche that shelters Don Abeyta's revered crucifix receives morning light from the clerestory overhead. Around it, *santeros* (makers of holy objects) José Aragón, Miguel Aragón, and Molleno grouped the Santísma Trinidad (Holy Trinity), the Virgen de los Dolores (Virgin of the Grieving), and Franciscan saints beneath the Franciscan seal. Each image poses within painted curtains as though appearing on a miniature stage. Additional *bultos* are carved in wood to represent Rafael the Archangel, whose wings are painted on the backdrop, and Santiago (Saint James), protected by a glass case to the right of the altar. Both are the work of unnamed folk artisans working in the New Mexican tradition. As researched for Willa Cather's *Death Comes for the Archbishop* (1927), the sanctuary's *santos* are a magnet to visitors, in particular, the Holy Infant of Atocha, protector of travelers, prisoners, and children. In its special niche near the holy sand, it stands on display dressed in sumptuous garments and shoes. Visitors offer it new baby shoes to replace those the child wears out from his local ministry.

Currently painted green and adorned with gold leaf, the Chimayan cross has found a permanent home but quickly lost out in importance to the earth itself and its healing powers. Each year, around 50,000 *peregrinos* (pilgrims) seeking cures at the American Lourdes make their trek during Semana Santa (Holy Week). They come, not to the crucifix at the altar, but to the curative earth in the Prayer Room, the small sacristy off the main chapel. Like Don Abeyta, they dig into it with their hands and carry it away in pockets and drawstring pouches.

Into the twentieth and twenty-first centuries, Chimayó's shrine has figured in local peace vigils. In spring 1945, Mexican-American soldiers from New Mexico's 200th Coast Artillery made a pilgrimage of thanksgiving after surviving the Bataan death march on Corregidor. Both physically and emotionally crippled in the last three years of World War II by one of the worst episodes of the Pacific theater, they kept their vows to venerate the Holy Child of Atocha if they survived Japanese torment. The next April, the Bataan survivors led 500 pilgrims for a thanksgiving mass at the shrine.

On the Saturday after Easter in 1982, an annual Prayer Pilgrimage for Peace made its first walk from Chimayó to Los Alamos, thirty-one miles west of the shrine in the Jimenez Mountains. Led by the Reverend John Leahigh, deacon of St. Charles Borromeo parish in Albuquerque, the dramatic gesture allied whites, Hispanics, and Native Americans in a public reminder of the area's historic part in the Manhattan Project at Los Alamos Laboratory, which produced the atomic bombs that, on August 6 and 9, 1945, annihilated the Japanese cities of Hiroshima and Nagasaki. In token of grassroots abhorrence of the bombing, during the first international Earth Run for Peace in 1986, runners ignited torches at the Chimayó shrine's eternal flame, a parallel to the ritual fires at the graves of President John F. Kennedy in Arlington Cemetery and of Dr. Martin Luther King, Jr., in Atlanta, Georgia. In 1991, during the Persian Gulf War, families posted yellow ribbons in the chapel in thanksgiving for soldiers who returned safely home.

ACTIVITIES

The little shrine remains open from 9:00 A.M. to 5:00 P.M. in summer and closes an hour earlier in winter. A priest celebrates mass each weekday at 7:00 A.M. and at noon on Sunday. On the last Sabbath in July, the shrine celebrates its annual feast. Pilgrims arrive at all hours in search of divine intervention against suffering. Seekers venerate the holy sand and rub it on twisted, aching bodies. Those who experience a cure leave donations and *ex-votos* (offerings) of *milagritos,* the silvered models of hands, eyes, and other parts of the body touched by a miracle, along with canes, braces, hospital bracelets, crutches, locks of hair, army dogtags, and written tributes to the wondrous shrine. The memorabilia of miracles cover the walls in testimony to individual cures.

Each year in the last week of Lent, pilgrims begin their walk to Chimayó. Some travel most of Holy Week, by day and night, bearing crosses along the interstate. Local hospitality offers bonfires, cool water, fruit, or a bowl of stew along the desert way. Pilgrims—many Hispanic or Native American—undergo treks that are a tradition of individual families and an integral part of native faith. Along the way, they sing the pilgrim's anthem "Bendito, Bendito" (Blessed, Blessed) and other sacred songs, pray in Spanish and English, and clasp Saint Christopher medals and rosaries. Individuals blend with a fellow stream of Christians, Jews, Muslims, Hindus, and New-Age seekers as they parallel the acequia and pass religious art and trinket peddlers on the way to the chapel.

Past flickering votive candles at a shrine of Our Lady of Guadalupe, along the adobe wall, and into the sagging, timber-framed front gate the pilgrims stream. In the hallowed grove, each cottonwood shelters one station of the cross set in stone and concrete. At center is a six-foot cross draped in rosaries and surrounded by more candles and photos and personal tokens denoting the people who have requested divine help. Father Casimiro Roca, a Catalonian priest, invites them inside to the raw wood pews and colorful Spanish colonial reredos for prayers. The pilgrims ask a little and a lot—a handful of soil to regenerate themselves or the suffering, dying people they love.

In 1999, two New Mexico natives—photographer Sam Howarth and bilingual oral historian Enrique R. Lamadrid—published *Pilgrimage to Chimayó: Contemporary Portrait of a Living Tradition*. As a gesture to one of the nation's prime holy locales, they recorded the traditional North American pilgrimage from as far south as Mexico through mountain villages and along major highways to the sacred shrine. Along the way, they interviewed pilgrims, residents, shopkeepers, tourists, and church officials—some on motorcycles, others in wheelchairs or pulling wagons. Most prayed ceaselessly that their long sojourn would bring a miracle.

Sources: Beresky 1991; Buchanan 1999; Canto 1994; Cather 1927; Drain 1994; Gallagher, *The Power of Place,* 1993; Gutiérriez and Fabre 1995; Howarth and Lamadrid 1999; Leahigh 1998; Martin 1969; McNelly 1997; Morgan 1994; *New Catholic Encyclopedia* 1967; Price 1989; Rodriguez and Gonzales 1997; "Sacred Sites of Northern New Mexico"; Silva 1995; Snodgrass, *Encyclopedia of Frontier Literature,* 1997; Spritzer 1994, Stark 1997; Sullivan 1967.

Second Baptist Church

Dr. Ed Young, Pastor
6400 Woodway
Houston, Texas 77057
713-465-3408
www.second.org/

Second Baptist Church in Houston is a Protestant phenomenon—the end-all, be-all southern congregation. The drive for accomplishment balances a spirit of challenge and daring for a program the staff proclaims a "Fellowship of Excitement." (Grossman 1991) Through vigorous religious marketing, the vivacious church manages a giant list of classes, services, and missions while designing more for coming generations of restless, transient Houstonites. Split on two campuses with a 1 to 145 ratio of staff to members, Second Baptist surpasses the old-style self-contained congregation with innovative methods of enrolling more people in the faith.

HISTORY

A Texas megachurch, Houston's Second Baptist claims a solid biblical foundation and commitment to the fundamentalist triad—ministry, Bible teaching, and missions. The congregation got its start in 1927 with a meeting at the old Taylor School with 121 people wanting to start a new church. They purchased a downtown facility, the former St. Paul's Methodist Church at Milam and McGowen Streets. The group prospered over the next seventeen years. In 1957, they resolved to build in the western part of the city to accommodate a 1,300-member congregation. At the corner of Voss and Woodway, the planning committee secured a 25-acre tract and constructed two education facilities and a gymnasium, which they inaugurated on October 1, 1961. Seven years later, they completed the current sanctuary and equipped it with with a grand pipe organ and six-story stained-glass windows.

In March 1977, Second Baptist celebrated a golden jubilee with addresses by past ministers. The next year, a pulpit committee hired Dr. Ed Young as the church's fifth pastor. Under his leadership, the church has flourished in commitment and outreach. Unprecedent growth required more construction. In 1986, the church met the challenge by dedicating a worship center and family life center.

Currently serving 24,000 members, with a weekly Bible study attendance of 6,000, the staff continues to baptize 1,000 newcomers annually and extends evangelism through a television program, *The Winning Walk,* an Angels of Light program, and mission projects in Mexico and Brazil. The addition of a west campus on 100 acres in October 1999 added worship space for 4,000. The complex consists of a multipurpose facility, education rooms, athletic fields, a racquetball court, and parking.

ACTIVITIES

Second Baptist Church follows the denomination's tradition of doing things in a big way. Staff accommodates varying age and lifestyle needs with different levels of Bible study, musical groups, and initiation classes for newcomers. Iron Men meet over coffee and pastries to discuss current issues. The Single Connection broadcasts in a talk-radio format Sunday evening on KKHT-FM. The church lending library shelves standard and large-print copies of religious works. On Monday night, upwards of 2,000 teens crowd into Metro Bible Study, a slick alternative worship blending sermons, prayer, tubs of popcorn, and pulsing rock music, with lyrics flashed above on two oversize screens. Derived from a similar singles ministry at Atlanta's Mt. Paran Church of God, the streetwise, pan-denominational approach suits youngsters turned off by adult doctrinal quibbles.

The church's interest in greater Houston is evident in a wide net of benevolence, including the Word at Work, a campaign to apply Christian principles to the workplace, and a mission trip to Ixtapa in November 1999. The church sponsors a blood drive, organ donation, a prison ministry, a school supply drive, and a twenty-four-hour prayer counseling to aid emergency situations. A feeding mission, the Star of Hope, offers three meals daily to the needy. A four-week video and lecture series, "Build Values for the Twenty-first Century," deals with thorny issues of witness and government. Annually, a tutorial program, Friends International, teaches English to 200 pupils from thirty-three countries. A career development and job support outreach lists jobs and resumes and coordinates efforts with employers. A crisis pregnancy center and postabortion class aids women facing difficult decisions. Other innovations in Christian life include a golf tournament, a weight workshop, mother/daughter and father/son retreats, birthing classes and single parent assistance, an adopt-a-student program, political action under Project Nehemiah, and a bookstore selling materials in English and Spanish and offering Christian music at listening stations. A singles ministry includes group meetings, weekly scriptural study, breakfasts and coffees, Saturday night and Sunday noon meals, mission projects, sports, chili cook-offs, day trips, bike rides and jogging, river tubing, movie nights, rodeo and Super Bowl parties, retreats, and marriage preparation.

Sources: Ahlstrom 1972; Corbett 1996; Grossman 1991; Hobert 1998; "Second Baptist Church, Houston" 1999.

Seton Shrine

333 South Seton Avenue
Emmitsburg, Maryland 21727
301-447-6606
FAX 301-447-6038
setonshrine@fwp.net
www.setonshrine.org.

The Basilica of the National Shrine of St. Elizabeth Ann Seton, commonly known as the Seton Shrine, honors the first U.S.-born saint. A popular pilgrimage site in Emmitsburg, Maryland, the shrine serves a dual purpose. As a memorial to early United States parochial educa-

A popular pilgrimage site in Emmitsburg, Maryland, the Seton Shrine honors St. Elizabeth Ann Seton, the first U.S. saint. (Courtesy Seton Shrine Center)

ELIZABETH ANN SETON

A proponent of Christian nursing cadres and founder of one of the largest orders of nuns, Elizabeth Anne Bayley Seton departed from wealth to a life of godly service constrained by vows of poverty and obedience. Although a stepsister of the Archbishop of Baltimore, she was a well-schooled, upper-class Episcopalian from New York City's Battery section. Her father, Dr. Richard Bayley, was the city's first health officer; his wife, Catherine Charlton Bayley, died in 1777 when Elizabeth was three years old.

Ironically, Seton earned the name Mother Seton after growing up motherless and living apart from her own children during much of their school years. She was the mother of two sons and three daughters in 1803, when her husband, importer William Magee Seton, died of consumption on a visit to Livorno in Tuscany, Italy. At age thirty, she faced the collapse of her family's wealth. A visit to Florence's La Santissima Annunziata (The Holiest Annunciation) Church in 1804 enticed her with the mysticism and divine pleasure of a religious vocation. A year later, she surprised her kin by converting to Catholicism.

For three years, Seton managed a New York boarding school for girls while her sons, William and Richard, attended a Jesuit boys' academy in Georgetown, Virginia. After she moved to Baltimore to manage a similar girls' school at St. Mary's College, she gained the support of the rector of St. Mary's Seminary. In December 1808, as Mother Seton, she enrolled seven pupils in the nation's first Catholic girls' parochial school, where a Sulpician priest, Father Pierre Babade, taught religion. Seton resettled the school in Emmitsburg in June 1809, when she founded the Sisters of St. Joseph and welcomed poor children to classes in academics, the arts, and religion.

Seton's vision advanced from teaching school to founding a women's religious order. On July 31, 1809, she organized the American Sisters of Charity, which grew to sixteen members in four years. She took holy vows in 1813. She, as mother superior, and her nuns functioned as public-health nurses and patterned their service after Saint Vincent de Paul and Louise de Marillac's French Sisters of Charity, organized in 1633 at Saint-Lazare in Paris. Mother Seton carried the ministry to St. Louis and established the nation's first Catholic hospital. Long after her death on January 4, 1821, two dozen sister communities, their members robed in gray-blue and capped in white cornettes, cared for lepers, the aged, deaf-mutes, and parturient women. Of particular note was their service during the Civil War at the Battle of Gettysburg.

Mother Seton's advancement to sainthood began in 1882 when James Cardinal Gibbons of Baltimore celebrated mass at her tomb. The paperwork passed through the Sacred Congregation of Rites in 1936; within four years, her cause moved to the formal level of research and documentation into miraculous cures of leukemia and meningitis. In 1959, Pope John XXIII declared her the Venerable Elizabeth Ann Seton and beatified her in 1963. Pope Paul VI canonized her in 1975.

tion and community nursing, it commemorates the work of the Sisters of Charity, whose service to the sick corresponds with periods of national need. As a monument to a Christian saint, the basilica hosts a stream of religious tourists and pilgrims who come to Emmitsburg out of love and adoration of a noble, dedicated teaching nun.

HISTORY
Built in 1965 a decade before the canonization of Saint Elizabeth Ann Seton, the shrine is a landmark in Emmitsburg, twenty-two miles north of Frederick, Maryland. The building combines multiple hues of marble, which give the effect of an Italian Renaissance temple. In 1968, the relics of Mother Seton were brought to the newly constructed Seton Shrine Chapel of St. Joseph's Provincial House of the Daughters of Charity and lie entombed under the altar.

Subsequent honors have brought the shrine much media attention. On September 14, 1975, before 1,000 nuns from the Americas, Italy, and missionary nations, Pope Paul VI proclaimed Seton, "the first daughter of the United States of America to be glorified with this incomparable attribute." ("St. Elizabeth Ann Seton" www.setonshrine.org) Her feast day is January 4. William D. Borders, Archbishop of Baltimore, dedicated the Seton Chapel on August 28, 1976. In 1991, Pope John Paul II elevated the chapel to a minor basilica, which Archbishop Agostino Cacciavilan, apostolic pro-nuncio to the United States, consecrated on August 4.

ACTIVITIES

The shrine, open daily from 10:00 A.M. to 4:30 P.M., features eucharistic liturgy on Saturday and Sunday at 9:00 A.M., offers daily novena prayers and novena masses on Mother's Day, the September 14 anniversary of Saint Elizabeth Ann Seton's canonization, and a Christmas novena from December 27 to January 4. The shrine is the setting of the annual October Pilgrimage for the Sea Services, honoring the U.S. Navy, Marine Corps, Coast Guard, and Merchant Marine, which includes a mass and reception.

The visitors center presents a twelve-minute historical video every half hour. In the museum, staff displays Seton's wedding ring, a lock of hair, and panels commemorating events in her life; the gift shop offers religious mementos, histories, and souvenirs. A self-guided tour includes the three-room Stone House, built in 1750, where the religious community began; the White House, or St. Joseph's House, where she founded her Catholic Parochial School System in 1810; and the cemetery where she was buried and an adjacent mortuary chapel that her sons built in her honor. The tour concludes at the basilica, where an authentic bone chip of Mother Seton adorns the altar cross. Three times a year, staff issues a shrine newletter, *The Seton Way.* Contributions maintain the shrine.

Sources: "The Basilica of the National Shrine of St. Elizabeth Ann Seton"; Bentley 1993; Brown 1997; Buchanan 1999; Bunson 1996; Butler 1997; "Catholic Online Saints" 1997; Dirvin 1975; Dolan 1968; Farmer 1992; Griffin and Griffin 1965; Jamieson and Sewall 1949; Kelly and Melville 1987; "Saint Elizabeth Ann Seton Pilgrimage"; Sherr and Kazickas 1994; Snodgrass 1999; "St. Elizabeth Ann Seton," http://www.catholic.org/, www.knight.org/, www.setonshrine.org; Yost 1947.

Shaker Meeting House, Sabbathday Lake, Maine

Shaker Museum
707 Shaker Road
New Gloucester, Maine 04260
207-926-4597; 800-533-9595

The only surviving active Shaker congregation, the Sabbathday Lake compound in Maine—1,800 acres located northwest of Portland and west of Lewiston and the Maine Turnpike—was originally the smallest of the eastern Shaker communities. It consists of eighteen buildings and encompasses the Dwelling House, the Shaker Museum, a store, a library, exhibits, a tree farm, an apple orchard, vegetable and herb gardens, hayfields, pastures, sheep, and other livestock. The congregation dates its founding to 1783 at Thompson's Pond Plantation, when Shaker missionaries assembled 200 worshippers.

The communitarian experiment thrived from an application of right spirit to productivity. A formal covenant on April 19, 1794, consecrated the group as a godly community, who raised a meeting house and, the next year, a dwelling house. By 1804, worshippers paid a heavy debt on a work complex containing a saw mill, linen weaving and carding mills, a tannery, a cooper's shop, barns, and a washhouse plus a main dwelling. By 1875, industrious Shakers were profiting from the manufacture of oak staves, which they exported to the West Indies for use in molasses barrels.

HISTORY

The United Society of Believers, which is a separatist offshoot of Quakerism and whose members worship through physical ecstasy, originated in Manchester, England in 1747. Under the leadership of James and Jane Wardley in the 1760s, they earned the name Shaking Quakers. The Wardleys preached a millennialist philosophy based on twelve virtues and four moral principles and foresaw the imminent return of Christ to earth in a female body. In 1770, member Ann Lee, an illiterate factory worker then thirty-four years old, assumed a central role. She was imprisoned for disrupting other congregations to spread the Shaker tenets of celibacy and purity. The seeming contradiction in her establishment

The only surviving active Shaker congregation, the Sabbathday Lake compound in Maine dates its founding to 1783. (Courtesy The Shaker Society, New Gloucester, Maine)

of a sexless faith made sense to believers who anticipated the immediate return of Christ and considered themselves the last earthly generation.

In 1774, a series of visions established Lee as leader under the name Mother Ann and also as Ann of the Word. The sect issued no formal creed or written statement of beliefs. An informal summation called the Three C's named community, celibacy, and confession of sin as the hallmarks of Shakerism. Mother Ann's motto expressed the simplicity of the faith: "To put our hands to work and hearts to God." For the sake of chastity, men and women dwelled apart in dormitories within self-contained communities. They remained unmarried and entered assemblies through separate doors. Worship was a spontaneous eruption of faith that mockers called a "Shaker high." In rapture with the spirit, segregated groups of men and women spoke in tongues, shook, spun, and leaped with joy in union with God.

In May 1774, Mother Ann led her followers—James Hocknell, Nancy Lee, William Lee, James Partington, Mary Partington, James Shep-

herd, and James Whitaker—from Manchester and Bolton, England, to New York aboard the *Mariah*. On August 6, they established themselves in two groups, in New York City and Niskayuna (now Watervliet) south of Albany, where they constructed a permanent complex. By 1776, Mother Ann's sect drew converts as well as persecution for refusing to support the American Revolution. Among those beaten, stoned, and imprisoned were three martyrs, Father William, Father James, and Mother Ann Lee.

The First Shaker Family at Watervliet near Albany, New York, originated American Shakerism. At its height in 1787, American converts Mother Lucy Wright and Father Joseph Meacham established the communal pattern that dominated the sect. Wright and Meacham led the Shaker congregation at New Lebanon, New York, which became the first organized Shaker community in 1788. It branched out to eighteen satellite groups in New York, Maine, New Hampshire, Massachusetts, Connecticut, Kentucky, Ohio, Indiana, Georgia, and Florida.

The interior of the Shaker Meeting House, Sabbathday Lake, Maine. (Courtesy The Shaker Society, New Gloucester, Maine)

By the 1860s, the faithful numbered 5,000. In New England, temporary adherents called Winter Shakers petitioned the congregation for succor and shelter until spring, but made no lasting commitment to the faith.

Shakers began publishing under the name of United Society of Believers in Christ's Second Appearing in 1790. In the 1840s, the chief historian, Elder Otis Sawyer of Portland, Maine, preserved the flavor of Shaker life in tunes and lyrics of songs and histories of Sabbathday Lake and the villages of Alfred and Gorham. He introduced the church family journal of activities and events in 1872, submitted articles and editorials to popular journals on sectarian views, and, in 1881, established and catalogued a comprehensive collection that now contains books, manuscripts, ephemera, periodicals, scrapbooks, photos, microfilm, audio and video tapes, indexes, and maps. In 1883, Brother Henry Green placed the archives in New Gloucester.

At the beginning of the Industrial Revolution, Sabbathday Lake declined at a slow rate during a period of rapid sect decline. In 1819,

the society absorbed the Gorham community. In 1931, the Alfred and Sabbathday Lake congregations merged, bringing archivist Sister R. Mildred Barker's collection at Alfred to the Shaker Library in New Gloucester. Staff stores the archives at the restored New Gloucester Shaker Schoolhouse, built in 1880 and adapted as a religious, genealogical, and historical research center. Under Brother Theodore E. Johnson, library director, Sister Barker maintained the collection under the Library of Congress system. The library, considered a sacred trust, opened to the public in 1960. In 1986, the sect installed a fireproof vault to house the most vulnerable print and archival materials.

BELIEFS

Shakerism is a joyous, dignified, but demanding faith. Followers emulate Jesus by living a daily example of faith and holiness. They acknowledge God as a pure, genderless spirit. This unity of being derives from the Judeo-Christian tradition that God created male and female yet possesses both qualities. Shakers believe that Jesus acquired godhood through baptism in the River Jordan. The descent of a dove symbolized God's spirit. Unlike other Christians, Shakers did not anticipate Jesus' return in human form. Rather, they sought the descent of the spirit of love and truth to the faithful. When Mother Ann Lee addressed followers, she denied divinity and claimed that she was subservient to Christ, who spoke through her. She identified Jesus' second appearance not as a woman but as the earthly church.

Shakers are practical idealists who embrace confession, spiritual authority, fervent worship, and the possibility of perfecting body and soul. They deny self by pooling resources and living in the moment rather than relying on storing up material things for the future. Their Christian poverty enforces a spirit of community, equality, and trust in God. They value all work as worship, cherish intellectual and artistic opportunities, support temperance and free speech, and reject slavery, debt, and competition. A bulwark of Shakerism is pacifism, which they demonstrate by refusing to bear arms, hold grudges, or seek revenge. Through acceptance of others, believers maintain a universal fellowship and equality that guides daily life. Embracing a mystical union with God, they pledge themselves to a hallowed oneness.

ARCHITECTURE

The Moses Johnson Lake Meeting House, erected in 1794 in the Dutch style by Nathan Merrill and Barnabas Briggs, is a sedate two-and-a-half-story clapboard building set behind a prim picket fence. Shaker crafters cut and planed the lumber and made nails, shingles, and brick for its construction. Stringently symmetrical, it features a gambrel roof decked with chimneys at each end and pierced by three shuttered dormer windows. Below, two doors and five shuttered windows mark the front, which preserves Shaker decorum by allowing male and female worshippers to enter separately.

The interior of the meeting house expresses the austerity and spirituality of Shakerism. Its colonial style creates an atmosphere of neatness and order through a simple Norway pine floor, twelve-beam ceiling, and blue painted walls. For congregational seating, two ranks of rows for women face two for men. At the sides, wood stoves connect to parallel chimneys. The sash windows are uncurtained and unadorned. Five upstairs rooms, which once served the ministry, currently house museum displays and arts and crafts.

ACTIVITIES

Shakerism is a dynamic faith that lacks outward sacraments and a formal, organized theology. Baptism in the faith is a visitation of the Holy Spirit. Daily meals form a communion in shared life and commitment. Revelation is an ongoing acceptance of spirituality through worship, prayer, and song. The afterlife offers a purified existence in a spirit world for believers and a separation from God for those who rejected him during their lives or who failed to keep divine commandments. Unlike fundamentalists, Shakers reject the inerrancy of scripture. They value biblical books as accounts composed by religious writers and scripts for Christlike actions.

Central to Shaker practice is the absence of embellishment. In place of frills, the devout practice simple, functional crafts—arranging and drying flowers, constructing wooden furniture and oval boxes, weaving ash baskets, blacksmithing, caning chairs, cooking with herbs, and turning fleece into woolen garments. Shaker inventions—the circular saw, the washing machine, the metal pen nib, the screw propeller, Babbitt metal, the rotary harrow, the automatic spring, the turbine waterwheel, the threshing machine, the clothespin, nested wooden storage boxes, handcut nails, the sash balance, and the flat broom—illustrate a progressive attitude toward labor saving. The cultivation of such handcrafts remained vigorous until the death of the last crafter, box maker Elder Delmer Wilson, in 1961. Beyond work, the faithful sing, dance, and worship vigorously and spontaneously.

Ann Lee's radical beliefs in celibacy and whirling dance no longer dominate the faith. As of the early twenty-first century, Shakers maintained their motto of "hands to work and hearts to God" while receiving outsiders and operating a library for scholarship and research. Currently, the congregation sustains itself through sale of tins of herbs, prints, woven goods, and manufactured woodenware, baskets, and fancy goods. Daily, members meet for breakfast at 7:30 A.M., pray and recite two psalms at 8:00, read the Bible, and sing a Shaker song. At 8:30, they start an eight-hour workday that breaks at 11:30 for prayer and the noon meal. Visitors attend Sunday Meeting and share a midday meal. Outsiders make pilgrimages to the village along with artists, writers, antiques dealers, collectors, and religious tourists. In spite of the modernity that colors these activities, the Sabbathday Lake Shakers remain committed to deliberate simplicity, humility, and equality of the sexes.

Sources: Ahlstrom 1972; Allen 1974; Barker 1978; Buchanan 1999; Grape 1998; Johnson 1969; Nartonis and Thompson 1998; *New Catholic Encyclopedia* 1967; Poppeliers 1974; "Sabbathday Lake;" Smith 1989; Sullivan 1997.

Sikh Center of San Francisco Bay
See Gurdwara Sahib El Sobrante.

Sisters of Benedict
Sister Marie Ballmann, Prioress
Red Plains Monastery
728 Richland Road S.W.
Piedmont, Oklahoma 73078-9324
405-373-4565
FAX 405-373-3392
osbokc@ionet.net
www.geocities.com/wellesley/6285

Relative newcomers among American Benedictine houses, Oklahoma's Sisters of Benedict have taken traditional hospitality to a higher level: In a spirit of respect, reverence, and nonviolence, they uplift as well as educate. By expanding retreats to a training program for spiritual counselors, the group has pioneered an in-depth method of preparing individuals to practice pastoral counseling. In a genealogy dating back through chapter houses in Iowa and Pennsylvania to a common eleventh-century mother house in Bavaria, this modern approach to clerical education and spiritual counseling derives from the medieval philosophy of the original patron, Saint Walburga.

SAINT WALBURGA

The first Christian nurse, Walburga—also called Walburgis of Heidenheim, Walpurga, and Walpurgis—was an eighth-century spiritual innovator and educational administrator of a co-educational religious house. As a sister of Saints Willibald and Winbald, at age ten, she followed their godly example by making an extensive pilgrimage. She trekked from Wessex, England, to Palestine and may have composed a Latin travelogue about the Holy Land. Enrolled as a novice at the monastery school at Wimborne, she learned medicine from Abbess Tetta and Abbess Lioba of Bischofsheim.

When Saint Boniface led a team of medical teachers to Swabia, Walburga joined the company of forty nuns. The first to ally the religious life with nursing, she treated plague victims at a six-bed hospice. At Hildersheim, she taught literature, music, classical language, math, and science and rose to an unprecedented post—the abbess of men and women at the double monastery. This liberalization of cloistering suggests the high regard that she earned for professionalism.

HISTORY
Red Plains Monastery began on August 15, 1968, with a group of sisters from St. Joseph Monastery in Tulsa, Oklahoma. The setting combines functional buildings on 21.5 acres of groomed lawn, oak, pine, maple, sycamore, willow, and prairie cottonwood. From 1981, the sisters have become contemporary pioneers by exploring inner sanctity through private days of recollection and individual and group retreats of one to ten days at the Benedictine Spirituality Center, opened in 1988. Located only thirty minutes from downtown Oklahoma City, the center offers seekers and visitors a chapel, meeting rooms, private bedrooms, an outdoor pool, and a gift shop. A mosaic of Saint Benedict, crafted by Ann Stuever and framed in redwood, hangs by the front door as a greeting to guests. The art barn is a separate craft building fitted with a potter's wheel and two kilns.

In 1998, the community, led by theologian Joanne Yankauskis, formed a complex by raising funds to purchase a house and 6.5 acres outside Piedmont. Adjacent to the Benedictine Spirituality Center and Lucy's Guest House, the new site unified the Sisters of Benedict and upgraded their property with the addition of a small chapel/prayer room, furniture, landscaping, and an endowment to fund maintenance. The oratory features the artistry of blacksmith Tom Joyce, a Tulsan who, in spring 1999, forged an adjustable metal ambo (lectern), a vessel of local clay nested in New Mexican stone, and a tabernacle and an oil lamp for the south niche forged from five metals. In token of plains agriculture, Joyce's tabernacle features an upward sprouting of metal shafts reminiscent of a shock of wheat. The portable tabernacle is a practical element that accommodates local mass as well as home service to the sick.

ACTIVITIES
Currently, the fourteen-member sisterhood follows a pattern of prayer, work, and communal living overlooking peaceful Eagle Lake and its bridge, a vegetable garden, a reflection footpath, and a prairie vista. Under the Rule of Saint Benedict and the guidance of Prioress Marie Ballmann, they host visitors and share a simple lifestyle of prayer at 7:30 A.M., noon, and 5:15 and 7:20 P.M. On Wednesday, they celebrate 7:30 A.M. communion at the neighboring Carmelite monastery. In addition to their duties as hostesses, good listeners, and vocation counselors at college campuses, the sisters offer Bethany Night for women intrigued by monastic life and they minister to the community, including nearby tornado victims.

The sisters maintain a peacemaker's touch in their ministry, in particular, in dispatching a Peace House volunteer, Nichole Tabor, to the Mexico Solidarity Network to protest terrorism and oppression of indigenous people in Chiapas, Mexico. In summer 1998, the nuns chose Sister Miriam Schnoebelen to represent them at the Hildegard Festival in St. Paul, Minnesota. The gathering honored a twelfth-century feminist, herbalist, medical professor, composer, and mystic. In winter 1998, former Cherokee chief Wilma Mankiller led a day conference on raising women's perspectives. Outings took the nuns to the Oklahoma governor's mansion in April 1999 for networking with nonreligious women at a benefit Spring Tasting Luncheon

and Style Show, where each guest received a Benedictine cookbook.

In their service to beginning spiritual counselors, the Sisters of Benedict foster quiet, relaxation, and enrichment through encounters with God. Residential retreats are available at a cost of $25 daily for room and board, or as a daily "at-home" prayer school, resulting from individual guided sessions of prayer and counseling tailored for lay persons, priests, and nuns. Another innovation of the sisterhood is a prayer card ministry, a form of religious journaling that records experiences of sorrow or celebration.

Unlike convents that limit themselves to day, weekend, and week-long solitude and study, each October, the Sisters of Benedict offer a seven-month study intensive. Based on the curriculum of Saint Ignatius of Loyola, founder of the Jesuits, the course calls for a rigorous schedule of daily prayer, group prayer once a month, and bimonthly guidance sessions. Beginning each fall, a more demanding Spiritual Direction Training course calls for a five-year commitment. Coursework opens with direction skills, spiritual classics from Saint Augustine to the present, and a two-year practicum. Over its first decade, the study intensive has trained forty people to master spiritual direction and pass their skills to others.

Sources: Ahlstrom 1972; Cooper 1996; Doyle 1948; Greenspan 1994; Herlihy 1990; Magner 1992; Nelson 1999; "The Order of St. Benedict"; Parry 1994; Ranft 1996; "Sisters of Benedict"; Snodgrass 1999; Theisen 1999.

Sitka National Historical Park
106 Metlakatla Street
P.O. Box 738
Sitka, Alaska 99835
907-747-6281
FAX 907-747-5938

Reverential art is a tradition among the Tlingit of Sitka, Alaska, the fabled Paris of the Pacific. The town bears an appropriate Tlingit name, which means "seaside haven." The aborigines—forebears of the Tlingit, Haida, Chilkat, and Tsimshian—date their arrival to Tongass Island during the glacial thaw around 8000 B.C., when they followed salmon streams to the south and fished for abundant sea life—halibut, black cod, sea mammals, and mollusks. Farther inland, they found berries and herbs as well as conifer forests, from which they fashioned rectangular plank houses and seaworthy canoes.

In the eighteenth century, the Haida, their lingual relatives, moved north from Queen Charlotte Sound to interact with the Tlingit. Both evolved a high degree of workmanship, particularly in wood. In boldly contoured totems, baskets, horn and copper jewelry and amulets, ceremonial regalia, and cedar bark and goat wool blankets, modern Tlingit artisans incorporate bold, bright geometric shapes to express a sense of oneness with the spirit world and the natural abundance of the Pacific coast.

BELIEFS

The Tlingit and Haida, the main totem carvers of the Pacific Northwest, share a mythic birth. In a legend retold in Brendan and Lauri Larson's *The Proud Chilkat* (1977), outsiders from the western Pacific—possibly Japan or coastal Asia—brought two sisters to Dall Island, Alaska. The girls married men from the Alaska river country. One couple established the Haida nation on the Queen Charlotte Islands. The pair immigrated to Prince of Wales Island to found the Tlingit nation, the Haidas' cousins.

According to folk beliefs, the Tlingit received a model of totem art from a mystic source. When a carved log beached itself on the shores of Shoe Alike, the local name for Sitka, local people studied its design. They determined that they could use lofty, erect red and yellow cedars to illustrate the gifts of the trickster raven, who blessed the world with sun, sea, and fish. The three-dimensional woodland and coastal figures represented owl, frog, beaver, serpent, snipe, eel, wolf, halibut, orca, and bear, the guardian spirits of the animal world. The Haida explanation of totemic creativity credits a master carver, who impressed his village with designs on the façade and lodge pole of his house. Out of generosity and regard for the tribe, he taught them how to shape poles and anchor them upright in the ground.

The shaman worked magic by furthering alliances with spirits. He was the only tribe member who dared climb the slopes of Mount St. Elias, a gathering ground for spirits. By propitiating these supernatural beings, the shaman could cure disease, recapture wandering souls, bless a hunt, protect fishers from foul weather and other dangers on the sea, and predict the future. Because of this great power over nature, the shaman lived apart from villagers, who feared and respected his trances, divination, and ritual songs. At chosen times on the calendar, he and his staff put on ceremonial headdresses and aprons to act out myths of death, reincarnation, and the mystic links between humankind and the animal and spirit worlds.

Totemism is a social institution that suits a preliterate people. It reached its height from 1800 to 1850 when carvers acquired sturdy tools. Often labeled idolatry, the practice is more appropriately identified as spiritual symbolism or reverence for ancestry. Totems record clan symbols, matrilineal genealogies, family crests, status, and legacies and land ownership during the period of prosperity that followed Alaska's rise to a Pacific trading mecca. In many-colored vertical abstracts, carvers developed totems into pictographic burial markers, heraldic steles, and historical records. The simplest serve as welcome markers and entrance posts. More complex carvings may ridicule a fallen dignitary, honor a hero, or note significant events.

More complex totems contain numerous figures placed in sequence to form a running pictorial narrative, like a vertical cartoon strip. When interpreted in story form, these three-dimensional pictographs commemorate Tlingit shamans' wrestling with the *kushtaka,* or land otter people, self-perpetuating humanoid otters who recovered people lost in the woods and turned them into *kushtaka.* The concept of the *kushtaka* explains the Tlingit reverence for animals, who share kinship with humankind. In the stories "The Woman Who Married a Bear" and "The Salmon Boy," native tellers, like totem carvers, express a reverence for shape shifting. In a less sophisticated style, the Haida renewed a relationship with nature through similar abstract animal forms carved in wood.

To dramatize their stories, such as Zot-kee and Th-tawk's battle with giant devilfish in 1600, the Tlingit and Haida evolved a highly stylized presentation by departing from realism to abstract and surreal modes. They presented split or fragmented glimpses of eyes, joints, fins, and feathers. Their bear or porcupine hair brushes delineated shapes with broad-form lines and colored surfaces with a waterproof paint mixed from mineral and plant substances, salmon roe, and spruce gum. For black pigment, artisans tinted the base with graphite and powdered hemlock bark. They achieved gold tones from yellow moss, brick red from hematite, and a unique aquamarine from corroded copper.

HISTORY

Located on Baranof Island on the southeastern panhandle, Sitka, the economic capital of colonial Alaska, is one of the state's most prosperous fishing communities. The town, a trading center by the beginning of the eighteenth century, depended on the Tlingit as intermediary agents to less sophisticated tribes. To protect their homeland, the Tlingit cleverly traded by canoe, paddling far from villages to conceal their prosperity. When red cedar grew scarce, they offered fish and skins for logs from their Haida allies.

The ruse worked until 1741, when Danish sailor Vitus Bering reported the commercial possibilities of the Alaskan coast to Tsar Ivan VI. Sitka's mystique as a Native American stronghold began on July 15, 1741, when Captain Alexei Chirikof led his party from the *St. Paul* inland into oblivion. No one established where he went or what happened to him and his men; however, the event marked the end of native dominance of the Alaska coast after outsiders learned of the area's wealth in timber, fish, and hides.

The Sitka National Monument honors another violent episode, when Tlingit warriors fought Russian traders at Fort St. Michael, a stronghold built in 1799 by Aleksandr Baranov to broaden commercial contacts for the Russian-American Fur Company. After three years of exploitation and abuse by whites, Chief Katlian's forces destroyed the fort, slaughtered the Russians, and recovered pelts that Baranov's Aleut hirelings took from Tlingit land. Two years later, Baranov returned to the Indian River delta at Sitka Sound with an unusual armada—120 Russians in four ships and 1,000 Aleut mercenaries in kayaks. They defeated the Tlingit in what is known as the Battle of Sitka. After the

Tlingit depleted their ammunition supply at their Kiksadi stockade, Baranov burned it. During the night, the Tlingit shaman prayed and chanted before leading survivors away in the dark. In what is called Old Sitka, Baranov founded Novo Arkhangelsk (New Archangel), named for the biblical angel Michael. In 1808, the trading village became the Russian-American capital of an empire that spread south to Fort Ross north of San Francisco.

The Russian presence remained tenuous into the nineteenth century. In 1818, continued Tlingit hostility forced the colonizers to establish a naval patrol. By 1821, the Tlingit had reinfiltrated their homeland. On October 18, 1867, the Russians opted to sell Alaska to the United States. U.S. Secretary of State William H. Seward negotiated with Tsar Nicholas I to pay $7,200,000 for land that American wags dubbed "Seward's Folly," a northern icebox. His foresight proved the wisdom of the purchase, which is virtually priceless for its mineral and oil deposits and value as a commercial center.

The use of the Tlingit totem declined from 1880 to 1950 after government officials banned the potlatch, a social giveaway of personal items. Unique ritual artistry survived mainly as Tlingit art history. Carvers exhibited their distinctive totem poles at the 1904 St. Louis World's Fair. At the 1939 San Francisco Exposition and later at a 1941 exhibit at the Museum of Modern Art in New York City, Tlingit pieces advanced from quaint examples of ethnology to folk art. In 1951, when authorities lifted the potlatch ban, totem art resurged among a new generation of native carvers. In 1972, the 106-acre Sitka National Historical Park became a state and national landmark. Its most valuable asset is a collection of totem poles made by the Haida of Prince of Wales Island. At the Southeast Alaska Indian Cultural Center, the Tlingit use traditional methods and such tools as the adz, stone ax, drill, and carving knife to design sacramental art and recarve valuable monuments lost to weather and decay.

ACTIVITIES

To the Tlingit and Haida, hunting and fishing are spiritual activities. Native devotion requires an appropriate spirit toward creatures killed for food. Because fishing is cyclical, villagers assemble for winter potlatch ceremonies, story performances, drumming, and dances. Celebrants dress in dance shirts and blankets, each decorated with mythic symbols. The shaman performs ritual steps and gestures to propitiate the spirit world and shower blessing on participants in the form of goose down. Today, troupes such as the Chilkat Dancers and Gei-Sun Dancers carry these ancient presentations to venues outside the community. Performer Elsie Meflott passes on folk ways of the Eagle clan that she learned from her parents. In childhood, she danced at the Alaska Native Brotherhood Hall in Haines, where a male played the part of the widow at a reenactment of her husband's funeral

Tlingit carvers continue to produce ceremonial and shamanic items—potlatch dishes and utensils, staffs, masks, boxes, and rattles. They imitate the proud carvings on canoe prows but are most famous for totem poles and house posts that relate a tale, event, or ancestral link to such totems as the bear, eagle, or orca, which may have saved the clan from famine or taught firemaking. In 1982, the Tlingit, Haida, and Tsimshian nations held their first combined cultural celebration. For such occasions, tribe members exhibit treasured art pieces and sing the songs and retell the stories of visual art as they replay the spiritual events of the past. By imitating ancestors, participants keep their memory alive.

Sources: Buchanan 1999; Cantor, George, 1993; "Central Council, Tlingit and Haida Tribes"; Cooday; Dauenhauer and Dauenhauer 1994; Jonaitis 1988; Milne 1995; Patterson and Snodgrass 1994; Reang 1998; "Sitka National Historic Park"; "Sitka Totem"; Snodgrass, *Encyclopedia of Frontier Literature,* 1997; Steiger 1974; "Tlingit Culture History"; "The Tlingit Nation"; "Totem Pole Art" 1998; Waldman 1990.

Sixteenth Street Baptist Church
Dr. Christopher M. Hamlin, Pastor
1530 Sixth Avenue North
Birmingham, Alabama 35203-1850
205-251-9402; 205-251-9811
www.16thstreet.org

A typical urban black church in the South, the Sixteenth Street Baptist Church has been the worship site, meeting and lecture hall, and social center of Birmingham's blacks for ninety years. It has hosted the nation's black notables—writer W. E. B. Dubois, educators Booker T. Washington and Mary McLeod Bethune, actor Paul Robeson, U.S. congressman Adam Clayton Powell, Jr., astronaut Mae Jemison, ethnographer Clarissa Pinkola Estes, and first lady Hillary Rodham Clinton. Since 1962, it began headquartering civil rights meetings and rallies that carried a high cost. The sanctuary entered United States history in 1963 when racists lobbed a bomb that killed four young worshippers. Undeterred, the local struggle for equality continued. Still integral to the city's self-image, the church remains in service as a symbol of survival and racial progress.

HISTORY
The Sixteenth Street Baptist Church got its start on September 1, 1873, as the First Colored Baptist Church of Birmingham. It served a city claiming the South's highest ratio of blacks, immigrants, and factory workers. Construction was a pinnacle in the lives of exslaves, who negotiated with the Elyton Land Company for donated land in "The Bottom." The emergent black working class obtained its understanding of Reconstruction, politics, and the future through the views of the church, which advanced from a tinner's shop on Fourth Avenue North and Twelfth Street to a rented building on Third Avenue North.

By July 1882, trustees bought the current site and adopted its name. Eight years after the church's formation, the Reverend Doctor William Reuben Pettiford organized community blacks to form the Alabama Penny Savings Bank, the state's first black savings institution. Over the next quarter century, the bank financed over 1,000 homes and churches. By 1909, the Sixteenth Avenue Baptist Church was ready for a permanent structure, designed by Tuskegee professor Wallace A. Rayfield and builder Cornelius Windham to seat 1,600. In modified Romanesque and Byzantine style, it features an expansive set of stairs leading to a triple-arched portal flanked by four-story towers. A cupola adorns the center of the roof.

The church produced a written record of staff and achievements by issuing a newsletter,

A typical urban black church in the South, the Sixteenth Street Baptist Church has been the worship site, meeting and lecture hall, and social center of Birmingham's blacks for 90 years. (Bettmann/Corbis)

The Evangel. Into the 1930s, congregants increased in number, chose the *Broadman Hymnal* for regular use, and started holiday traditions of Christmas and Easter cantatas performed by choirs and orchestra. In the 1950s, outspoken preacher Fred Lee Shuttlesworth recognized overt racism as the main obstacle to Birmingham blacks. On July 4, 1956, following Alabama's ban on the National Association for the Advancement of Colored People, he led a coalition of ministers to fight segregation. During hard times for black and Jewish citizens, the Ku Klux Klan marched and anonymous assailants bombed seven black homes. The city closed parks, playgrounds, and golf courses; police arrested the manager of the bus station for desegregating its lunch counter. In 1958, a bomb at Temple Beth-El failed to explode.

The assault on the former "Pittsburgh of the South" was the culmination of a civil rights campaign. Dr. Martin Luther King, Jr., the Reverend Ralph Abernathy, the Reverend F. L. Shuttlesworth, the Reverend Andrew Young, and the Southern Christian Leadership Conference inveighed against segregated transportation, public facilities, housing, and job opportunities. Their methods called for sit-ins, freedom walks, and boycotts. Blacks issued the "Birmingham Manifesto" on April 3, 1963, a polished treatise claiming that the city "segregated racially, exploited economically, and dominated politically." ("The Birmingham Manifesto" 1989, 160)

Police Commissioner Eugene "Bull" Connor closed parks and turned water cannons and attack dogs on resisters gathered at Kelly Ingram Park. Resultant turmoil filled television and print news. After the arrest of Dr. King and the Reverend Ralph Abernathy, on April 23, Dr. King issued "Letter from a Birmingham Jail," a brief, impassioned cry for nonviolent extremism. Governor George Corley Wallace made hate-filled speeches and gestures. He hid blatant racism under the code term "law and order." His regressive example produced more unrest and the bombing of protest headquarters at the A. G. Gaston Motel, which brought out 1,000 black marchers. When President John F. Kennedy threatened federal control by the Alabama National Guard, Wallace relented.

A court order and pre-school violence caused Kennedy to send in military units on September 10, 1963. Birmingham's Sixteenth Street Baptist Church broke into headlines with the bomb that exploded on September 15, at 10:22 A.M. on a Sunday morning as students departed basement church school rooms to don choir robes and participate in a Youth Day sermon on "The Love That Forgives." Racists hurled nineteen sticks of dynamite at exterior stairs, killing Cynthia Wesley, Carol Robertson, Addie Mae Collins, and Denise McNair, blinding Sarah Collins in one eye, injuring twenty-one others, and damaging the church's foundation and five cars. The concussion knocked the face of Christ from the rose window.

Global reaction was immediate. Civil rights attorney Charles Morgan, Jr., cited entrenched bias and hatred as the causes of violence. Welsh children in Cardiff began a penny campaign to replace the sanctuary's stained glass. National revulsion stimulated sympathy for President Lyndon Johnson's comprehensive Civil Rights Act of 1964 and the 1965 Voting Rights Act. Three decades later, on Spike Lee's CBS documentary *4 Little Girls* (1997), commentator Walter Cronkite reflected that the perverted act of bombing children forced white America to confront the true nature and result of festering hate.

When protesters assaulted the city's white police officers, two more black youths died in an exchange of blows from whips, clubs, knives, broken bottles, and rubble. In response, blacks renamed Birmingham the "Johannesburg of America." In 1964, the church reopened. Members mounted photos of the victims to the right of the pulpit and inscribed hopes that love and understanding would supplant bitterness and violence. The bombing remained unresolved until November 1977, when retired Birmingham employee and Ku Klux Klansman Robert E. "Dynamite Bob" Chambliss received a life sentence for first-degree murder.

Although trauma marred its progress, the church forged a future for its congregation that acknowledged violence in the past and hope for advancement and continued evangelism. In 1976, the Jefferson County Historical Commission formally recognized the church's role in local affairs; four years later, the U.S. Department of the Interior chose the church for the National Trust for Historic Preservation. To accommodate 90,000 visitors who annually view the facility and attend its functions, members shoulder a sizeable capital campaign to upgrade and preserve their church home.

ACTIVITIES

Open to the public Monday through Friday, 9:00 A.M. to 5:00 P.M., the Sixteenth Avenue Baptist Church remains a rallying point for activism. Staff offers tours by appointment. Docents point out the postbombing window, Welsh glass crafter John Petts's the *Wales Window for Alabama,* a protest-era view of the crucified Christ in purple, blue, and white. Beneath the panel is a simple citation, "You Do It to Me." The sanctuary invites visitors and pilgrims Wednesdays from noon to 4:00 to view the window and purchase postcards of it.

Statues, songs, and poems memorialized the four martyred girls: Richard Farina's poem "Birmingham Sunday" (1964), recorded by Joan Baez; Dudley Randall's poem "Ballad of Birmingham" (1965); Estella Conwill Majozo's "Steps to the City"; and verse by A. L. Walsh. Southwest sculptor John Henry Waddell erected a four-figure grouping facing north, south, east, and west. Entitled *That Which Might Have Been: Birmingham, 1963,* the figures are on display at the Unitarian Church of Phoenix in Paradise Valley, Arizona, where visitors reflect on the theme of lives cut short. At the First Baptist church of Englewood, New Jersey, the Chapel of the Four Children honors innocence and the struggle for freedom. In Chicago, the Carole Robertson Center for Learning dedicates its ministry of youth recreation, day care, family support, counseling, and child and family advocacy to the four Alabama martyrs.

In 1983, the *Birmingham News* set up a scholarship to educate deserving young citizens. In 1995, young-adult author Christopher Paul Curtis published *The Watsons Go to Birmingham—1963,* a multiple award-winning fictional account of a family's journey to visit a grandmother and their encounter with the bombing while they attend Sunday school at Sixteenth Avenue Baptist Church. In 1998, pastor Christopher M. Hamlin and Andrew Young published *Behind the Stained Glass: A History of the Sixteenth Street Baptist Church*. At Kelly Ingram Park, called "A Place of Revolution and Reconciliation" in the historic Civil Rights District, the public still gathers to trace Freedom Walk paths and to honor events that smashed the barriers of southern racism and discrimination. Sculpture depicts the jailing of children, attacks on protesters, and the strength of the clergy. A noble statue of Dr. Martin Luther King, Jr., faces the church.

A full schedule of events keeps Birmingham's Sixteenth Avenue Baptist Church in the cultural forefront. Since 1992, the congregation has supported Birmingham's Convention and Visitors Bureau, Landmark Tours, Jazz Hall of Fame, and Civil Rights Institute, located across the street from the sanctuary. Members have welcomed spiritual scholar and musical historian Jester Hairston, the Citadel Gospel Choir, and jazz great Wynton Marsalis's septet performing *In This House, On This Morning*. In 1996, the congregation hosted thousands of attendees at Atlanta's Summer Olympic Games.

> **Sources:** "The Birmingham Manifesto" 1989; Cantor 1991; Cohen and Jaeger 1995; Curtis 1995; Hamlin 1998; "Letter from a Birmingham Jail" 1989; Low and Clift 1981; Lumpkins 1993; Sherr and Kazickas 1994; "Southern Charm" 1996; Williams, Peter W., 1997; Wilson and Ferris 1989.

Sleeping Ute Mountain

Ute Mountain Ute Tribe
Towaoc, Colorado 81334
970-565-3751
www.dc.peachnet.edu/~janderso/physical/ute.htm

Sleeping Ute Mountain is a source of strength to the Weenuche band of seven groups that make up the Ute nation. Members of the Uto-Aztecan language family, they were originally hunters and relatives of the Bannock, Comanche, Chemehuevi, Goshute, Paiute, and Shoshone. Oral tradition records the Ute meeting with the area's aborigines, the Anasazi, also called the "ancient ones." Nearby is a holy relic of prehistory, the village of Mesa Verde in southwestern Colorado, which has preserved the way of life of an enduring people. In eroded sandstone above the Mesa Verde upland, the deserted community overlooks a vast valley floor. Its devotion to worship furthered the development of underground worship chambers called kivas, a form of Native American sanctuary still in use.

BELIEFS

The Ute continue to revere Sleeping Ute Mountain, a brooding rise southwest of Cortes and a source of legend. It is the source of creation, the beginning of Ute life on earth. In traditional stories, the mountain is the horizontal figure of a sleeping Indian, whose headdress inclines toward the north. With arms folded over his chest at the highest point, he flexes his knees and shanks to the south. Rock spires project from his feet like toes. At the base of Sleeping Ute Mountain lies the Mountain Ute Indian Reservation and the tribal town of Towaoc.

The stone figure was once a warrior God who helped Indians ward off evil. After a desperate battle, he found that his movements shoved mountains and valleys onto the flat plateau. To recover from combat, he stretched out, covered himself in fog and clouds, and fell into a permanent sleep. Animals came to drink his blood. Observers interpret rain clouds on the highest tor as the sleeping warrior God's approval of his people.

A seasonal legend is the origin of the Bear Dance. While a pair of brothers hunted in the mountains, they caught sight of a bear clawing and singing while cavorting around a tree. One brother continued the hunt. The brother who remained learned how to sing and dance. The bear rewarded him for respecting nature and dispatched him to teach the Ute the Bear Dance as a form of reverence for the bear's spiritual strength.

HISTORY

Nomads supplanted their early ancestors, the Anasazi, in 350 B.C., by migrating to southwest Colorado. In the wind-blown accumulations of soil blanketing Mesa Verde, these hunter-gatherers used simple digging sticks to plant corn, a

Colorado's Sleeping Ute Mountain is a source of strength to the Weenuche band of seven groups that make up the Ute nation. (North Wind Picture Archives)

staff of life. They cultivated garden plots in the spring, foraged and hunted during the summer, and returned to harvest cornfields in fall. In the snowy months of January through March, they planned for the new year and attended to home and hearth. Crafters among these early folk wove yucca baskets. To make them waterproof and keep out rodents and insects, they coated the insides with pitch from piñon trees.

Around 550 A.D., these prehistoric people built pit houses roofed in mud and logs. In place of a door, they used a ladder plunged through an opening in the roof that also served as ventilation and smoke vent. This method of entry offered privacy and safety from wandering animals and snakes. Two centuries later, the Navajo, like the Hopi and Zuñi, moved toward the pueblo life way and constructed the first stone dwellings above ground. Their lifestyle changed with the addition of beans to a grain and meat diet and the making of spears and atlatls, bows and arrows, rabbit fur and turkey feather blankets and capes, manos and metates for grinding corn, and

grayware pottery jars for storing seeds and water. They designed drills, stone-bladed knives, ladles, mugs, and bowls for food preparation and service and canteens for carrying water and food on journeys to the plateau.

By 1200, the mesa's golden age, the Anasazi had initiated cliff dwellings, a series of interlocking apartments attached to sheer rock walls. They positioned rooms to lie out of range of the hot sun and sheltered from wintry winds. Their clothing was minimal; sandals made possible rapid movement over rocky desert rife with scorpions and cactus. At the height of their civilization, they produced a unique pottery painted black and white. In front of the cliff at ground level, they constructed kivas for private worship, healing, and propitiation of nature gods for good weather and ample harvest. When a quarter-century drought struck, the Anasazi disappeared from history.

One proof of desert ingenuity was the construction of Mesa Verde, a flat-roofed stone and adobe apartment complex built around 1200 A.D.

by the nomadic San Juan Anasazi. The community was composed of 114 apartments and 8 kivas. Living in shady niches and alcoves among layered shale carved by plateau watercourses, they acclimated to a semiarid land. To supply their homes and gardens, they depended on springs and seeps for water. They heated and cooked over a juniper fire, hunted mule deer and small animals and birds, and gathered piñon nuts, juniper berries, and prickly pear cactus for complements to garden produce. For tools and construction, they preferred piñon pine.

The cliff dwellers made good use of their environment by conserving water for drinking and irrigation. Careful placement of the village offered free-flowing air currents to terraces, where they kept flocks of turkeys. For convenience, they used ladders, handholds, and steps to climb the vertical cliffside while bearing loads of gourds, corn, squash, melons, and beans. Instead of locking doors, they pulled up the ladders to halt invaders and predators. To preserve heat in winter, they constructed small entrances and covered them with sandstone slabs.

In the shady sacred rooms of the kivas, religious leaders, who were usually male, attended to ritual and seasonal planning, which required a close attention to the will of the gods. They also used the chambers as dens, workshops for weaving, and temporary getaways and visited from kiva to kiva through tunnels. To vent smoke and cool the kivas, they constructed vertical ventilation shafts. For historical and religious purpose, they painted the walls with geometric shapes. The importance of the kiva and dance plaza to worship suggests the significance of religion to the cliff dwellers' lives.

The cliff builders were gone when Ute Indians migrated to southwestern Colorado from the Great Basin farther to the southwest around 1400 A.D. They inhabited 225,000 square miles of mountains. Unlike the cliff dwellers, they built brush huts and wove garments of grass and rabbit skin. They also accommodated their life way to the desert by living in high country in summer and moving down the western slopes in winter. These migrations etched permanent trails on the land in Cochetopa Pass, Willow Creek Pass, Boreas Pass, and Georgia Pass.

When the Spanish conquistadors arrived in the sixteenth century, they chose the name Mesa Verde (Green Table) to describe the land. They taught the Ute about horses, which greatly altered aboriginal lifestyle. With greater mobility, formerly agrarian Indians were able to trek onto the plains to hunt buffalo. Plains style influenced them to construct tipis and wear skin garments. The Spanish also advanced trade, which opened the Ute knowledge of the world.

The 1848 Treaty of Guadalupe Hidalgo established the U.S. government claim to Ute territory and curtailed their autonomy. When whites built towns and a fort in the 1850s, Ute parties raided the newcomers. On December 25, 1854, marauders killed the residents of Fort Pueblo. Six cavalry companies led by Christopher "Kit" Carson hunted the Ute warriors through Cochetopa Pass until the Utes surrendered. Further disruption occurred after the Denver gold rush of 1859 and creation of the Colorado Territory two years later. Indian agents shifted Utes to the San Juan Mountain reservation. Additional strikes of precious metals forced a split into two bands. The Southern Ute settled on farms in southwestern Colorado; their other half, the Northern Ute, moved to Utah. After a fierce uprising against agent Nathan Meeker, only a small group of Southern Ute remained in Colorado.

ACTIVITIES

The Ute Mountain Utes, part of the Utes who have resided in southwestern Colorado for four centuries, have maintained a community in Towaoc on the western end of the old Southern Ute Reservation since 1895. With their cousins, the Southern Utes in Ignacio, they are Colorado's only native inhabitants. As indicated by goods traded from across the Southwest, the Mesa Verde area fosters interwoven religion systems revealed by Ute beadwork, Hopi kachinas, Papago and Apache baskets, New Mexico Pueblo pottery, and local Navajo rugs and sand paintings.

The Utes live comfortably in the twenty-first century while perpetuating traditional customs, in particular, veneration of Sleeping Ute Mountain. For a century, they have sponsored the mid-March Bear Dance, a four-day spring social honoring the grizzly. Utes believe that Sinawaf, the One-Above, created the bear to model strength, wisdom, and survival to the Ute. A beneficent creature, he was the alter ego of the Ute trickster, the mischievous Coyote.

In early times, the dance awakened the bear from his winter sleep to lead the Ute to roots, nuts, and berries. As part of the mating ritual, the dance enabled women to interact with likely mates and to pursue courtship and marriage. To prepare for the event, folk tellers revived animal lore around the campfire; singers dreamed of new songs to honor the bear. In early March, men prepared the corral while women made dance outfits. They approached the dance floor with plumes on their heads symbolizing personal troubles. On the last day of the festival, they cast off the plumes and hung them on a cedar tree.

The Ute hold their most spiritual rite at the annual Sun Dance, where they seek spiritual empowerment, purification, communion, or sanctification from the Great Spirit. The event begins with a dream, which compels the dancer to join the four-day ceremony, called *tagu-wuni* (standing thirsty) because it prohibits food and drink. The dancer represents family and clan in seeking and sharing divine power. The ritual requires mental and physical rigor. Participation affirms ancient bonds among the Ute, who reverence the midsummer tradition.

Sources: "Across the Great Divide: History"; Alsberg 1949; Buchanan 1999; Cantor, George, 1993; Champagne 1994; "Durango"; Gilpin 1968; James 1998; Johnson, Myke, 1995; Ketchum 1957; Milne 1995; Patterson and Snodgrass 1994; "Sleeping Ute Mountain"; Snider 1998; Sopronyi 1999; "The Southern Ute"; Steiger 1974; "Ute"; Waldman 1990; Wenger 1991; Wiget 1996.

Snoqualmie Falls

Snoqualmie Tribe
P.O. Box 280
Carnation, Washington 98014
206-333-6551

Snoqualmie Falls Preservation Project
419 Occidental Avenue South
Suite 201
Seattle, Washington 98104
206-625-9790

One of the borderline cases of government recognition, the Snoqualmie of Washington state, one of twenty-three indigenous tribes of the area, are an unrecognized tribe. Currently, they are fighting for fishing rights and for sacred ground, which powerful moneyed interests contest while seeking to install huge hydroelectric turbines on the Snoqualmie's holy river. This act of diminishing the flow and reducing the majesty of Snoqualmie Falls will desacralize an area that is a natural sanctuary, a tie to the divine.

The Snoqualmie Valley and the towns of Carnation, Fall City, Snoqualmie, and North Bend lie east of Seattle in rugged scenic terrain of the Cascade Mountains. Around 1.5 million vacationers and conventioneers come to the area for meetings, dining, hiking, skiing, mountain biking, fishing, water sports, golf, and camping. Snoqualmie Falls, a 268-foot cataract, occupies land coveted by tour developers and power and timber magnates. Unless the tribe receives formal acceptance as Native Americans, they have no means of protecting traditional lands that they hold sacred.

BELIEFS

According to Snoqualmie creation stories that Northwest Pacific mythologist Ella E. Clark collected from Herbert Hunt and Floyd Kaylor's *Washington West of the Cascades* (1917), the Snoqualmie earned the designation of People of the Moon from a creation myth. The moon, Snoqualm, supervised the heavens. He ordered Spider to connect earth and sky with a cedar bark rope. When Blue Jay and Fox descended to earth, Fox changed himself into Beaver. Snoqualm trapped Beaver and stretched his hide. Beaver reclaimed his hide, transformed himself once more into Fox, and created a pleasant earthly home for humankind. Snoqualm was so angry that he tried to descend the cedar bark rope but tumbled down to earth instead. His carcass formed Mount Si. His moon-shaped face remains on the rocky crags; the trees that Fox planted grew into the forest of the Cascade Mountains.

HISTORY

Even though the U.S. government discounts claims of continuous tribal existence and a distinctive geographic community, the Snoqualmie are a settled indigenous people who date their beginnings long before contact with Europeans

One of the borderline cases of government recognition, the Snoqualmie of Washington state are fighting for fishing rights and for sacred ground on the Snoqualmie's holy river. (Mike Zens/Corbis)

and the 1855 Treaty of Point Elliott, which recognized them as an organized tribe. When Washington bureaucrats forced native populations onto reservations, the Snoqualmie opted to remain an off-reservation tribe. They chose to stay at their *baxub* (sacred site) at Snoqualmie Falls in the shadow of Mount Si to care for a holy site that had been a gathering spot for centuries. The falls, with their shimmering mists and rainbows, are the focus of spirituality and culture and a traditional burying ground. In the philosophy of Ernie Barr, Jr., son of the late head chief Ernie Barr, the waters form the juncture of heaven and earth in creation mythology. As direct ties to divinity, the mists carry prayers, hopes, and dreams to the creator.

The Snoqualmie began encountering major difficulties in the mid-twentieth century. During the 1940s, the Tulalip Agency petitioned for a reservation for the tribe in the Tolt Valley and assisted members in negotiating hunting and fishing rights with the State of Washington. Around 1961, the Bureau of Indian Affairs (BIA) ruled that the landless tribe was voluntary rather than hereditary and that only 15 percent practiced the traditional religion. On these grounds, the BIA declared that the Snoqualmie had ceased being a distinct tribe from 1916 to 1979 and rescinded claims to tribal benefits. The designation of tribal sovereignty inhibited recognition with federal agencies and curtailed dispersal of funds for health, education, employment, and land use.

Most grievous to the Snoqualmie is the loss of the beloved falls. Since 1898, Puget Sound Power and Light has rechanneled 2,500 cubic feet of water away from the main channel to a generating facility by blasting behind and under the falls. A century later, the Snoqualmie entered a protracted fight against the Snoqualmie Falls Hydroelectric Project, a plan to renew the company's license for another forty years to divert more of the river—1,500 cubic feet—through dynamos to increase output of hydroelectric power. This violation of the water's natural path would starve the falls, a desecration sanctioned by the federal government. Through the Snoqualmie Falls Preservation Project, a coalition of the Snoqualmie Tribe, Church Council of Greater Seattle, and Washington Association of

Churches, Indians are defying the Federal Energy Regulatory Commission for discounting native religion and culture and for silencing a public hearing of sixty people by turning off electricity. The commission has ignored native oral traditions by forcing concerned parties to address their grievances in writing rather than in a public forum.

ACTIVITIES

The Snoqualmie Falls Preservation Project proposes a Spirit of the Falls Sanctuary Park, managed in part by the tribe. They also have pressed for freeing the holy water of human intervention. Federal authorities counter that decommissioning the hydrofacility and restoring the falls to full flow would increase tourism. The influx of more outsiders would diminish or deny privacy for worship. Under the 1993 American Indian Religious Freedom Act, the government has guaranteed tribes access to sacred geography unless there is a compelling interest to interfere. Snoqualmie members declare that the 1 percent of sales that Puget Power gets from the falls does not constitute that compelling interest. Additional federal policies—President Bill Clinton's 1994 regulation governing the environment around minority and low-income populations and the 1996 executive order protecting sacred sites—require agencies to establish environmental justice and to accommodate access to Indian religious practitioners and avoid harming the integrity of consecrated grounds.

The Snoqualmie profit from sympathetic reporting from the *Seattle Times,* which runs regular features, news articles, and editorials and posts them free through the archives of the newspaper Web site. An additional boost to Snoqualmie claims came in 1992 from anthropologist Ken Tollefson, who gained support from the State Advisory Council on Historic Preservation, which urged the National Park Service to place Snoqualmie Falls on the National Register of Historic Places. If the Snoqualmie gain historic recognition, they stand a chance of restoring the sacred falls to full flow and halting clear-cutting of forests at the base of the falls for a proposed residential development, commercial area, and golf course. The falls will become the state's first traditional cultural property. More important to Native Americans, the designation would set a precedent, since natural formations like cataracts are not usually listed for their cultural value.

> **Sources:** "As Fun as All Outdoors" 1999; "The City of Snoqualmie"; Clark 1953; Corsaletti 1999; DeWeese 1992; "Final Determination to Acknowledge the Snoqualmie Tribe Organization"; Grindeland 1999; Magnuson 1993; "Mount Baker—Snoqualmie National Forest"; "Native Rights Act Before Congress" 1992–1993; "Power Plant at Snoqualmie Falls, Sacred Site"; "Snoqualmie Falls Sacred Site."

Sonoma Yoga Center
See Aghor Ashram.

Spider Rock
See Canyon de Chelly.

St. Benedict Center
Father Thomas Leitner, Manager
P.O. Box 528
Schuyler, Nebraska 68661-0528
402-352-8819
FAX 402-352-8884
benedict.center@navix.net
www.megavision.com/benedict

A nonprofit restorative institute, St. Benedict Center combines the inviting, restful image of a modern inn with the hospitality for which the Benedictines are known. Located sixty miles from Lincoln on 160 acres near the intersection of Highways 15 and 30, the current brotherhood of nine monks welcomes all comers seeking spiritual enrichment. Grounded in traditions that date to the Middle Ages and the thrust of Vatican II, the center focuses on readjustment—balancing Catholic equilibrium, rechanneling the mind-set, and reaffirming the faith of lay and religious guests. The resulting calm uplifts and refuels flagging spirits through inward seeking, workshops, retreats, and seminars.

HISTORY
The prairie retreat grew from the outreach of the Missionary Benedictines of Christ the King

Priory in Schuyler, Nebraska. The mother house, founded by Andreas Amrhein in 1844, is the German Missionary Benedictine Congregation of St. Ottilien, who evangelized Tanzanians for six years. In flight from Nazi persecutors, the three founding monks—Father Haddelin Muller, Brother Placidus Husselein, and Brother Felix Meckel—came first to New York to evangelize German immigrants. The trio settled in Schuyler and affiliated with the Missionary Benedictine Sisters of Tutzing in Norfolk, Nebraska. Since 1935, they have supported missionaries in Togo, Zambia, Uganda, Kenya, India, Korea, the Philippines, and South America. Their priory, built in 1978, occupies sixteen acres of donated land fifteen miles north of town.

Father Prior Germar Neubert and his apostolate opened the retreat center in thanks to great-hearted Americans who have supported the monastery for over a half century. After a California benefactor endowed the center, the monks hired architect Ron Erickson to design it and broke ground across from the monastery on April 17, 1994. The plan, supervised by Sister Michele Lee, called for a pyramidal copper roof distinguished by an unadorned cross. Builders completed the retreat in 1997, creating a lake, bridge, and plaza to complement an expanse of prairie grass. In 1998, the center embraced Pope John Paul's "Year of the Spirit" as reorientation for a new millennium.

The center experience is part of a national movement to encourage a mystical union with divinity through departure from daily stress to rest in the Lord. The facility, a holy bed-and-breakfast, consists of Blessed Sacrament Chapel, meeting rooms accommodating 200, buffet-style dining halls seating 150, a solarium with a fireplace and library, a media room, an outdoor amphitheater, and a gift shop and lobby. At the entrance stands sculptor John Laiba's *Fountain of Life,* a grouping of rough-hewn South Dakota granite stelae raising a flowing chalice. Individual rooms parallel the sparse furnishings of a college dormitory with twin beds, a desk, two occasional chairs, and a wall crucifix.

The grounds extend the center's serenity with walks by the lake, where St. Louis sculptor Rudolph Torrini's bronze statue of Saint Benedict clad in an ankle-length habit reaches his arms to all. The priory cemetery, bordered by greenery and fencing, contains a modern cross formed of five vertical lines and four horizontals with uneven ends. A hillside pathway leads away from the plaza past conifers and deciduous trees to an altar and marked stations of the cross and the admonition to remember the grieving, troubled, abused, and dying.

ACTIVITIES

Nebraska's St. Benedict Center coordinates an array of visitors—ecumenical groups, parishes, schools, hospitals, twelve-step programs, non-profit organizations, couples, and individuals needing quiet withdrawal from routine to assess new directions and challenges. Up to thirty-six guests can choose solitude, in-depth reading, or sessions with a spiritual director and may join the monks in prayer at Christ the King Priory Chapel when bells toll at 5:45 and 6:10 A.M., noon, and 6:00 and 7:10 P.M. The Adoration Chapel remains open for private prayer and worship and contemplation of a series of stations of the cross, crafted in Peru. A lending library in the solarium stocks a variety of reading material. The media room augments education through audiovisual programs. The staff charges $39 to $46 a day per person for room and meals and suggests that donors earmark money for scholarships, center upkeep, or a needed item.

Into the twenty-first century, the center actively solicits residents through a Web site and newsletter, *Echo*. In 1999, special sessions on friendship, contemplative and personal prayer, Mary's role in the new millennium, midlife reflection, the death of a spouse, the practice of the *lectio divina* (divine office), and Christian symbolism combined with a piano concert by Father Ron Noecker accompanied by guitar, flute, and singers, a pre-Thanksgiving performance of the Omaha Symphony String Quartet, and an Advent celebration in mid-December with an exhibit of crêches and gift shop offerings of crafts, Christian art, and books.

Sources: "Benedictine Mission House and St. Benedict Center," "A Benedictine Monk Is One Called to Seek God" 1999; Doyle 1948; Nelson 1999; "The Order of St. Benedict," "St. Benedict Observes 'Year of the Spirit'" 1997; Theissen 1999.

St. Benedict's Abbey and Retreat Center

Abbot Leo Ryska
12605 224th Avenue
Benet Lake, Wisconsin 53102-0333
414-396-4311
FAX 414-396-4365
BenetLake1@aol.com
www.osb.org/osb/benlake/

Following St. Benedict of Nursia's sixth-century rules for monasteries, the monks of St. Benedict's Abbey and Retreat Center share the peace and sanctity of their abbey as though they were welcoming Christ. In the gently rolling hills of southeastern Wisconsin between Chicago and Milwaukee, the brothers of Benet Lake offer physical and spiritual replenishment to visitors. Whether visitors are short-timers or sabbaticals, individual seekers, families, or groups, the center welcomes people of all faiths or no faith. In the privacy of the woods and lake, all find a house of God and grounds for prayer.

BELIEFS

For over a half century, the Monks of Benet Lake have enjoyed the experience of shaping their lives through *ora et labora* (pray and work). They follow the Rule of Saint Benedict of Nursia, the spiritual touchstone of Western monasticism who developed from hermit to leader of Monte Cassino, Italy, a strong monastic community. In his words:

> Let all guests who arrive be received like Christ, for He is going to say, "I came as a guest, and you received Me." (Matthew 25:35)
>
> (St. Benedict's Abbey)

His instructions are clear on matters of hospitality. The abbot or brothers greet all upon arrival, pray together, and confer a kiss of peace. In humility and adoration of Christ, hosts commune with guests, treat them kindly, share their table, even during ritual fasts, and wash their feet. To the poor and pilgrims, monks are solicitous and respectful.

Benedict's directions call for a separate guest kitchen and cheerful attention to common domestic labors. He instructs the monastery's leader

The monks of St. Benedict's Abbey and Retreat Center in Benet Lake, Wisconsin, share the peace and sanctity of their abbey as though they were welcoming Christ. (Courtesy St. Benedict's Abbey)

to attend to a sacred calling and avoid idle chitchat with outsiders. Benedict's detailed rule outlines the fair and impartial assignment of monk's cowls and tunics, bedding, seasonal garments, and personal items, including writing tablets and pens. Anything extra should be distributed to the poor. Daily activities call each to prayer, work, and contemplation and include the making and sale of crafts reflecting God's glory.

HISTORY

St. Benedict's Abbey names as their founder Abbot Richard Felix of the mother house, Conception Abbey in Conception, Missouri, and the diocese of Kansas City–St. Joseph in 1870. The New World outreach dates to a grandmother house in Engelberg, Switzerland, founded by Blessed Conrad of Sellenbueren and monks from Muri in 1120. Upon arrival at Benet Lake on March 21, 1945, Father Felix set up quarters

in a cheerful three-story dwelling, where the brothers elected him their first abbot.

Abbot Felix's community was realistic about the spartan life and about their capabilities, both physical and financial. Despite the absence of amenities, early residents embraced community, prayer, and sacrifice and enjoyed an excitement and anticipation in what the abbey would become. During the post–World War II era, pioneering brothers and neighborhood volunteers worked at haymaking, wood chopping, and poultry farming: By 1952, they had constructed the first wing of a new monastery, which grew to a three-wing complex. That same year, the abbey became an independent house.

According to Abbot Felix's vision, the brethren focus on mission and hospitality. They have founded mission monasteries in the United States, Mexico, Belize, and Guatemala. Two of these—Our Lady of Guadalupe in Pecos, New Mexico, and Our Lady of Glastonbury in Hingham, Massachusetts—have developed into independent abbeys. Presently, St. Benedict's Abbey, under the direction of Abbot Leo Ryska, concentrates on the work of its retreat center and on nurturing numerous guests. The monks specialize in revitalizing faith in each through brief sojourns that restore and balance harried lives. In a relaxed, prayerful atmosphere, the brothers fine-tune the spirit.

ARCHITECTURE

St. Benedict's Abbey occupies 440 acres on the Wisconsin-Illinois border. The complex features three retreat facilities that accommodate up to 65 guests. The conference room holds 80; the refectory seats 100 for family-style meals. Seven private meeting rooms suit small group interaction. Nearby, the complex extends a lounge for snacks and coffee, a monastic library, and a chapel that offers an altar and seating for private devotions. Benet Hall guest center houses small groups and families in four rooms with private baths and with a kitchen, lounge, and dining room. Nearer to the lakeshore is the Cottage, a six-bedroom house intended for parish councils and groups requiring seclusion.

The abbey church is a modern facility featuring garnet carpeting and a central altar raised by a modest dais. The monks, who range in age from forty to eighty, occupy the choir behind the altar. Rows of chairs on the other three sides seat 220. On the wall behind the choir stand ranks of organ pipes. The upper reaches of the sanctuary expose beams and trusses and track lighting. Located in a prominent place is a thirty-nine-inch wood statue of a standing Madonna and child. A contemporary design, it features ivory skin tones beneath a muted head covering. The mild expression and gently blushing cheeks contrast a red tunic and gold robe edged in red and gold braid and lined in blue, the colors of traditional Mariology. The Christ child, lightly clasped in the Virgin's right hand, appears to reach toward worshipers.

ACTIVITIES

The abbey calls young men who wish to dedicate themselves to godliness in a close-knit monastic family. The abbey retreat center provides a flexible setting that suits programs to var-

---

STANLEY TIGERMAN

The abbey church was the work of architect Stanley Tigerman, author of *The Architecture of Exile* (1988). A giant of late-twentieth-century American architecture, he was born in Chicago on September 20, 1930, and studied at Massachusetts Institute of Technology and Yale University. Under the influence of modernist Mies van der Rohe, he and wife Margaret McCurry opened a joint practice in the 1960s but rebelled against the era's strictures with ventures in new directions. Faithful to the client rather than structural dogmatists, he designed the Illinois Regional Library for the Blind and Physically Handicapped and the Chicago Anti-Cruelty Society Adoption Center along with homes, churches, parking garages, restaurants, corporate offices, china and tableware, and furniture.

Tigerman taught design at Harvard, Yale, and the University of Illinois, where he directed the school of architecture. He joined Eva Maddox to found Chicago's Archeworks, a design workshop and school. A restless, pragmatic innovator, he has won awards from the *Chicago Tribune, Architectural Record, Metropolitan Home, Builder's Magazine, Progressive Architecture,* the Metropolitan Chicago Masonry Council, the Chicago and Illinois AIA, the Chicago Lighting Institute, the Chicago Building Congress, the Art Institute of Chicago, the American Wood Council, and international competitions and was nominated for National Professor of the Year and a National Book Award.

---

ied needs. Residents stroll the tree-lined shore of Benet Lake, walk the pine and spruce woods or apple orchard, and rest in the shade to read or contemplate. Annually, the brothers celebrate March 21 as the feast of Saint Benedict and the anniversary of his *transitus* (passing).

At the monastery jubilee on March 21, 1995, residents joined Right Reverend Marcel Rooney and well-wishers from the mother house to celebrate mass. According to the *Benet Lake News,* it was a day for greetings and reflection on the hidden beauties of faith and fidelity over fifty years of communal work toward a unified house and mission. An organ recital by Novice Arthur Rauh and two guest musicians performed the sacred compositions of Diderik Buxtehude, Johann Sebastian Bach, Marcel Dupré, and Christoph Schroeter. Violinist Ann Lemar performed contrasting pieces by Jean-Baptiste Senallié and Georg Friedrich Handel. The abbey's spring craft show organized twenty-six displays of wares that revitalized the tradition of handwork in the area.

Sources: "The Chicago School: Interview with Stanley Tigerman and Eva Maddox" 1998; *Contemporary Designers* 1999; Downey 1997; Doyle 1948; "The Order of St. Benedict"; "St. Benedict's Abbey"; Theisen 1999.

St. Fidelis Church
The Cathedral of the Plains
601 Tenth Street
Victoria, Kansas 67671
785-735-2777

Amid the tidy quilt squares of farms and urban development between Russel and Hays, Kansas, rise the twin spires of St. Fidelis Church. A fantasy structure in an agrarian land better known for silos and grain elevators, it attests to the faith of 250 pioneer families who wanted a special worship center to mark an ongoing relationship with the Almighty. A massive structure, it is one of the largest in the Midwest, a trans-Mississippi landmark to some 16,000 religious tourists annually. In typical rural style, it was built like a potluck church supper—out of 125,000 cubic feet of limestone, quarried in 8-foot slabs and hand-split, and 2,000 loads of sand hauled by mule- or horse-wagon, and donated to St. Fidelis Church at the rate of six loads of stone and four loads of sand per parish member.

HISTORY
The prairie town of Victoria, Kansas, was home to dissimilar factions—British gentleman-farmers and German-Russian immigrants, whom Catherine the Great had lured from Mainz-on-Rhine to southern Russia to farm the steppes. The two groups came in search of the area's prized possession, open land. On 69,000 acres owned by Scotsman George Grant and grazed by his herds of Aberdeen Angus, English blue bloods carved out estates. Simultaneously, poor European homesteaders fled tsarist taxation and conscription into the military in search of fairness, religious liberty, and an open landscape as similar to the Russian steppes as any in North America. On April 8, 1876, they ended their trek at Big Creek east of Fort Hay. It was a hard land, as shown by a cemetery marker erected by the Union Pacific Railway a quarter mile west of town over graves of six track builders slain by Cheyenne in October 1867. To survive the first year, Russian sodbusters hastily dug caves in the banks and concentrated on planting a limited supply of seeds.

The British influence provided a London city planner and, in 1873, the town name, derived from the English queen and empress of the British colonies; three years later, the farmers founded their own community, Herzog, named for a village on the Volga River. Their sod huts, which replaced the barbaric caves, symbolized a commitment to the land, a verdant, rooted union with the earth that supplied sustenance and a roof over their heads. For a worship site, they made do with a wooden cross around 15 feet high that they anchored in the soil. They postponed genuine celebrations of the mass, funerals, baptisms, and weddings until the next rotation of itinerant priests. Makeshift worship ended in 1878, when Capuchin friars settled in central Kansas.

By 1880, after the aristocrats tired of their experiment and moved on, the steady farm folk of Herzog had incorporated Victoria. With an eye toward hardy winter wheat, they judiciously plowed and planted the land. When time permitted, they worked toward a town church. Since 1877, their meeting place had been a rude shed nailed to one side of a residence. Two upgrades followed. The second, a stone church seating 600, they built in 1884 on 10 acres donated by the Union Pacific Railroad.

The community continued to grow and feel the need of a presentable church home at least twice the size of their last effort. Led by a Capuchin-Franciscan priest, Father Jerome Mueller, in 1907, the 1,700 citizens of Victoria tackled a mammoth undertaking—a stately, dignified edifice suited to their concept of God. Basing their theology on faith in God and a oneness with the prairie and sky, they assessed a

A fantasy structure in an agrarian land better known for silos and grain elevators, St. Fidelis Church attests to the faith of 250 pioneer families who wanted a special worship center to mark an ongoing relationship with the Almighty. (Courtesy St. Fidelis Church)

town, Pennsylvania—and by architect John Marshall of Topeka, Kansas, St. Fidelis took shape in 1908. Fourteen-man crews with eight-horse teams fetched pillars of Vermont granite from the depot. The crews of Topeka's E. F. A. Clark Construction Company worked in Bedford river sand and limestone. With hand drills and wedges, farmers quarried their share of donated stone along Big Creek in 50- to 100-pound blocks and hauled it by flatbed dray seven miles north to the city, where local masons dressed and fitted each piece. At first, workers moved finished blocks up ramps to the walls. When the church rose too high for wheelbarrows to reach, the site superintendent installed a horse-powered hoist to lift heavy slabs. By project's end, local workers had become skilled craftsmen.

At completion on August 27, 1911, the sturdy Romanesque church, facing west across the prairie, bore a customary Latin cross shape and replicated the cross at the top of each hip-roofed tower. Its four bells, cast by the H. Stuckstede Foundry of St. Louis and hand-tolled by trained bell ringers, range in size from 275 to 2,000 pounds. Since 1947, the bells have chimed at the command of an electronic timer.

Structural dimensions are 220 by 75 feet, with ceilings 44 feet high and transepts 110 feet wide. Set above a rose window honoring Saint Cecilia, patroness of Christian music, the stone figure of Saint Fidelis of Sigmaringen commemorates the Reformation-era Prussian attorney who offered his expertise in defense of the poor. After he took Capuchin vows, he set about converting Swiss Calvinists and died a gory death as Zwinglians shot and hacked into his skull in a roadway at Grisons in 1622. Inside the church, church members installed the gold-leaf reredos that a Chicago firm had crafted in 1893 for a previous altar. Around it, they painted the altar rail to resemble marble, a sign of heartland thrift and attention to detail.

Windows are a humanizing feature of St. Fidelis. On each side, a total of thirty colored windows and three rose windows display the craft of Munich glassworkers, handed down by ancestors since the Middle Ages. The lower story, pierced by nine windows to each side and three over the portal, honors the holy family, Saint John, Saint Francis of Assisi, and the prodigal

tithe of $45 from each of 250 families and constructed a church with spires reaching 141 feet into the heavens.

In 1912, populist presidential candidate William Jennings Bryan, the famed silver-tongued orator and Christian zealot, gave the church a permanent nickname. He saw St. Fidelis rising above the monotously flat prairie and dubbed it the Cathedral of the Plains, an erroneous title implying a bishop's church and administrative center of a diocese. The Kansas Historical Society has long valued the church as a state treasure. On May 14, 1971, it earned recognition from the National Register of Historic Places. On May 25, 1986, Bishop George Fitzsimons of Salina dedicated the church and its altar exclusively for worship.

ARCHITECTURE

Erected by John T. Comes of Pittsburgh, Pennsylvania—builder of the St. John the Baptist Catholic Church in Lawrenceville, Kansas, and St. Mary's Byzantine Catholic Church in Johnsson. Above, twenty-three windows display Christian emblems of the pelican, lamb, ox, lion, eagle, rose and lily, harp, trumpet, tower, sword, palm branch, keys, tiara, crosier, sword and chains, and wheat and grapes, symbols of the Eucharist. Paired north and south rose windows honor nine Franciscans and youthful saints.

St. Fidelis has weathered well. After eighty-three years, the finance council voted to restore the original structure while respecting the integrity of the original plan. The funds for repairs derived from tourist donations and a lump sum from the Rudy Wittman Memorial Trust. On advice from architect Wayne Brungardt of Hays, Kansas, trustees weatherproofed and upgraded acoustics, heating, and the electrical system.

Other detail work has ennobled Victoria's church. Under the supervision of Tim Linenberger of Salina, a great-grandson of the original painters, the council replastered and painted the interior in mauve and gold. Hand-stenciling echoes the hues of the stained glass. To accentuate the loft of the ceiling, Linenberger darkened the ribbing. To commemorate a diamond jubilee, in 1986, members installed an altar carved of Carrara and seated on sixteen columns of rossa antica marble, which parallel the marble artistry of a pulpit added in 1954.

ACTIVITIES
Open daily for mass and services, St. Fidelis is still Victoria's parish center. It offers traditional programs to 400 families, a festive Christmas Eve celebration, and guided tours for visitors. Newly married couples honor a church tradition of placing a rose at the shrine of the Virgin Mary, who holds out the infant Christ as a gift to humanity. At Christmas, a life-size nativity scene made in Oberammergau, Germany, in 1951, awes hundreds of pilgrims. Proof of the church's popularity emerges from simple mathematics: the town population has leveled out at 1,300, but Sunday masses serve a total of 1,600 worshippers, many from outlying towns.

The church bookstore features important historical works. In deference to the town and church, the staff stocks *Towers of Heavenly Recipes,* an anthology of German, Volga-German, and Russian cookery. For genealogists, *Die Herzoger* lists 120 years' worth of parishioners and their births, marriages, and deaths from 1876 to 1996. Other print materials include a book of daily prayers, a pictorial guide to St. Fidelis, and *Towers of Faith and Courage,* the 1976 centennial directory of the town of Victoria.

> **Sources:** Bentley 1993; Broderick 1958; Brown 1997; Buchanan 1999; Dary 1972; Farmer 1992; "Lawrenceville Historical Society"; "St. Fidelis Church, the Cathedral of the Plains" 1998; Tillman 1986; "Victoria" 1998.

St. John the Divine
See Cathedral Church of St. John the Divine.

St. John's Abbey
Father Francis Hoefgen, Guest Master
Order of Benedict, Inc.
Collegeville, Minnesota 56321
320-363-2573
FAX 320-363-2504
guestmaster@csbsju.edu

Built on a 2,480-acre tract ninety miles northwest of Minneapolis/St. Paul and twelve miles west of St. Cloud, St. John's Abbey and University occupies an inviting lake district that offers twelve miles of trails for hikers and naturalists. The natural preserve contains 1,500 acres of forest, covered with twenty-four types of hardwood trees and housing ninety species of birds plus squirrels, foxes, rabbits, deer, beavers, and mink. Standing out against sylvan beauty is St. John's Abbey Church and Bell Banner, the focus of a thriving campus that houses 210 monks, the largest Benedictine chapter house in the Western church. The abbey is committed to liturgical development and publication, pastoral ministry and missions, programs in religion and psychiatry, ecumenical scholarship, cultural preservation and promotion, and environmental conservation.

HISTORY
Father Louis Hennepin introduced Catholicism to Minnesota in 1680, when he discovered a cataract and named it St. Anthony Falls. Enriched by the fur trade and farming, the area flourished and joined the Northwest Territories

in 1787, shortly after the close of the American Revolution. In 1856, a party of five Benedictines obeyed a directive of the Reverend Franz Xavier Pierz by traveling from St. Vincent Abbey in Latrobe, Pennsylvania, to St. Cloud, Minnesota, to establish a branch of the Order of St. Benedict, an extension of the see of Baltimore under America's first bishop. The current abbey took shape in Collegeville. Monks framed log cabins for their immediate needs, carved out farms and outbuildings, and established a boys' school between Watab Creek and Lake Sagatagan. They loaded the curriculum with academics—mathematics, history, astronomy, rhetoric, classical language, German, and English. Two years after the monks' arrival, Minnesota joined the Union as the thirty-second state at the same time that St. John's Seminary obtained a charter.

The Benedictine ministry thrived with the nation. By 1860, itinerant monks dispatched from the East and their recruits were serving over fifty communities of German settlers in central Minnesota. At the end of the Civil War, the monastery advanced from priory to independent abbey, with Rupert Seidenbusch serving as the first abbot. Three years later, under the sanction of the state legislature, the school began issuing college and university degrees at Minnesota's oldest Catholic institution of higher learning. Missionary monks branched out to the north and south. In 1875, the abbot rose to bishop of the see of northern Minnesota and dispatched monks as parish fathers.

Under the far-reaching plan of Rupert's successor, Abbot Alexius Edelbrock, a son of pioneer German stock from St. Cloud, the complex grew from 52 to 136 priests, monks, and teachers; the student body rose to 350. While shepherding local progress, he advanced the chapter's mission commitments from 10 to 45. The quadrangle took shape, primarily from a deal with James J. Hill, whose Northern Railroad provided a year's free hauling. Monks augmented incoming freight with handmade clay brick. The surge in building faltered in 1889, when parish monks forced the abbot's resignation on grounds that he cared more for the campus than for pastoral ministry. After the brief administration of Bernard Locnikar, Abbot Peter Engel began a quarter century of progress, carrying the

monastery into the 1920s. In 1894, monk foresters established the state's first pine plantation; missionaries carried Catholicism to the Bahamas. St. John's extended its ministry to Ojibway and Sioux reservations in northern Minnesota and opened two frontier monasteries—St. Martin's Abbey in Olympia, Washington, and St. Peter's Abbey in Saskatchewan.

The heart of St. John's settlement was a sound educational program, composed of a high school, four-year college, and seminary. From 1921 to 1950, Abbot Alcuin Deutsch furthered mission to St. Maur's Priory, an interracial abbey in South Union, Kentucky, and foundations in Nassau, Bahamas; Humacao, Puerto Rico; Mexico City, Mexico; and Tokyo, Japan, and bolstered academics by naming Father Martin Schirber and Father Arno Gustin as progressive administrators of a burgeoning liturgical center. They achieved college accreditation in the liberal arts. Father Virgil Michel developed liturgical worship by founding a journal, *Orate Fratres,* later known as *Worship,* and issued *Sponsa Regis* magazine for convents, *The Bible Today,* and *American Benedictine Review.*

In midcentury during the post–World War II building boom, Abbot Baldwin Dworschak added a commodious monastic residence and four college dormitories, an abbey church, the Alcuin and Clemens Libraries, a science center, and the Institute for Ecumenical and Cultural Research. The firm of Hanson and Michaelson designed a college preparatory school complex, which currently accepts boys in grades seven through twelve and shares computer and library facilities with St. John's University and the College of St. Benedict. The complex also offers rural life and scriptural institutes, social amelioration of victims of sexual trauma, ecumenical dialogue, a divinity school, a college of arts and sciences, and a coeducational Graduate School of Theology to prepare serious students as parish liturgists, seminarians, directors of liturgical music, clergy, and in other aspects of worship.

ARCHITECTURE

The abbey church, begun in the late 1950s, displays the work of architect-furniture designer Marcel Breuer and his assistant, Hamilton Smith. Breuer was a modern technologist who designed the Whitney Museum in New York City, UNESCO headquarters in Paris, and St. John's University's Alcuin Library. A native of Pecs, Hungary, he trained at Allami Foreaiskola and at the Bauhaus in Weimar, Germany. Before opening an architectural practice in Berlin, he taught at the Bauhaus in Dessau for four years. After working for a year in London, he lectured at Harvard and worked with Walter Gropius. His New York practice functioned from 1946 until he retired thirty years later.

Breuer's splendid edifice contrasts the adjacent brick quadrangle, a model of sturdy frontier Gothic, and a wide expanse of blue water surrounded by the thick forest that impressed Minnesota's pioneers. Across from the modern honeycomb exterior stands the Bell Banner, a 112-foot cruciform monument made of steel reinforced by 2,500 tons of concrete. Its 15- by 8-foot white oak frame supports five bells, which replaced the original bells installed in 1897. Cast by Petit and Fritzen foundry in Aarle-Pixtel, Holland, and varying from 1,683 to 8,030 pounds, they entered service after dedication on Christmas 1989.

In token of entry to Christ through baptism, the portals open on the baptistery and a simple floor of terra-cotta tile. A silver lid covers a granite font carved from stone quarried at nearby Cold Spring. To the left of the baptismal square stands a statue of Saint John the Baptist, which Doris Caesar cast in bronze. Side stairs lead down to the crypt chapel of Our Lady of the Assumption, the parish church for members of the St. John the Baptist parish. Along the entrance wall are confessionals, a reconciliation room, and an organ gallery; at the back wall stands a shrine containing relics of saints.

Seating 2,000, the sanctuary encompasses a vast space and supports the weight of its great ceiling on accordian-fold panels of preformed concrete, which line the sides. Four sections of wooden pews and a freestanding cantilevered balcony provide an unobstructed view of the altar. To the right, a shrine to Our Lady displays a prized donation—a twelfth-century woodcarving of an austere Madonna with child seated on her lap. To the left, the aisle leads to the Blessed Sacrament Chapel.

Along the exterior shell, the architects set crosses formed of square blocks of gray granite, which hold candles each October 24 to mark the church's dedication. Standing 225 by 180 feet and rising to 65 feet, the chancel focuses attention at center on an abbot's chair, denoting his post as chancellor of the university, liturgical leader, and spiritual head of the monastery. Semicircular choir stalls seating 300 range out to each side. To the right, the Holtkamp organ masses sixty-four ranks of organ pipes concealed by a screen on the back wall. The white granite altar, the heart of abbey worship, faces the honeycombed stained-glass window, designed by Branislaw Bak, a member of the St. John's University art department, and constructed with the aid of monks and students. The design patterns elements of the liturgical year.

ACTIVITIES

The monks of St. John's Abbey follow the sixth-century Rule of Saint Benedict, a Christ-centered guide to monasticism that is the bedrock of Roman Catholic orders. The men work at a variety of jobs: teaching theology, science, music, art, history, literature, and language as well as fixing plumbing, building cabinets, writing and editing, maintaining a library, and gardening. Some become campus administrators of the university or prep school; others run Liturgical Press. Some are ordained priests, missionaries, and chaplains of hospitals and retirement homes. All serve God.

The St. John's Abbey code of hospitality respects Saint Benedict's admonition that residents receive guests as they would welcome Christ. Visitors often tour the buildings and study the abbey church architecture. Some make impromptu visits to talk with one of the brothers about spiritual matters or make a retreat for a weekend or several days of discussion on spiritual topics. Twelve single and double rooms with private baths are available at a nominal fee; meals in the guest dining hall include continental breakfast, lunch, and dinner, also at a reasonable cost.

Awaiting all comers are the sanctity of peace and harmony and an expanse of prairie, wetlands, forests, lakes, and designated trails. Private retreats allow seekers solitude for rest, reading, meditation, and prayer. The campus offers the Hill Monastic Manuscript Library, Ecumenical Center, Art Center, Museum of St. John's, and

St. John's University Bookstore. Oblates, or lay Benedictines, enrich Christian service by observing a modified rule and by attending oblate days at the home monastery for reflection or group retreat.

In the Abbey Church, the monastic community and their guests observe four prayer services daily—at 7:00 A.M., noon, and 5:00 P.M. mass and Eucharist and at evening prayers at 7:00 P.M. The community celebrates daily Eucharist at 5:00 P.M. and Sunday Eucharist at 10:30 A.M. A campus House of Prayer schedules a daily and weekend schedule of meditational retreats at varying levels of religious expectation. A Spiritual Life Program offers private retreats, for example, a 1994 program for law-enforcement officers and doctors integrating faith with the demands of their professions. Male guests considering the Benedictine order may follow the daily round of a monk's life through the Monastic Experience Program.

On the final Friday of each month since January 1996, the abbey has observed the Benedictine Day of Prayer. From 6:45 A.M. to 3:30 P.M., people of all faiths gather to pray with the monks, enjoy a communal breakfast, and partake of a spiritual conference that relates prayer to scripture. The morning develops styles of prayer with private reflection and an optional group prayer. After noon prayer and lunch, participants may again opt for reading and reflection or a group session.

In St. Joseph Hall, the abbey supports St. John's Pottery, an artistry integrating esthetic, scientific, humanistic, and moral attitudes toward living in nature. An intellectual and spiritual program, it successfully merges art in life and expresses the university's commitment to the environment, linking work with worship, and celebrating diverse cultures. Within the three-chambered, wood-burning Johanna kiln, named for Japonologist and art historian Johanna Becker, the university's first female professor, potters combine local clay and kaolin by an ancient Pacific Rim design method. Artist Richard Bresnahan, who trained at Nakazato Takashi Pottery in Japan, teaches interns, visiting crafters, and emerging artists in a learning environment formed of recycled materials in a nature-based system. The studio seal at the base of each piece allies the abbey church baldachin with the cross and altar.

In summer through Labor Day 1998, the Museum at Saint John's exhibited hallowed art in the Beuronese style, developed at the Archabbey of Beuron, Germany. The campus Beuronese artist, Brother Clement Frischauf, painted the apse of the Great Hall, featuring a grand Christ in medieval style with right hand uplifted in benediction. To his right side are the Greek initials iota sigma, the first and last letters of the Greek *Iesous;* at left are chi sigma, the first and last letters of the Greek *Christos.* In his left hand, an open book reads in Latin, "I am the way, the truth, and the life." The figure fills a golden semicircle above a line of lambs and a frieze of date palms, symbolizing resurrection in the desert, alternating with ten winged seraphs hiding their eyes. A running caption predicts the coming of the savior.

Sources: "Advent Day of Recollection" 1998; "A Benedictine Monk Is One Called to Seek God" 1999; Fry 1982; Kelly and Kelly 1992; "Liturgy in a Formative Environment"; *New Catholic Encyclopedia* 1967; "Sacred Art: Beuronese Art at St. John's" 1998; Sharp 1991; Sullivan 1967.

St. Louis Cathedral

Monsignor Ken Hedrick, Rector
615 Pére Antoine Alley
New Orleans, Louisiana 70116
504-525-9585
FAX 504-525-9583
www.saintlouiscathedral.org

The center of Louisiana Catholicism, New Orleans's St. Louis Cathedral in Jackson Square is one of the nation's most treasured and photographed metropolitan landmarks. On a pedestrian mall in the heart of the tourist center, its three majestic steeples crown an original *briqueté entre poteaux* (brickwork between posts) creation, a style that flourished into the mid-nineteenth century. A favorite sacred retreat, the cathedral is flanked by two antique treasures, the Cabildo and the Presbytère. The former, the municipal council hall where the Louisiana Purchase was signed, preserves museum exhibits that trace Louisiana history from exploration through Reconstruction. The Presbytère, designed as a residence for priests and sold to the city as a courthouse, displays memorabilia on state architecture, maritime and military history, portraits, and art.

Nearby stands a national landmark, the Lower Pontalba, an antebellum town home graced by lacy ironwork galleries that was once part of the parallel row houses built to the left and right of Jackson Square by Micaëla Leonarda Almonester, the Baroness Pontalba, whom the Ursuline nuns educated at their convent school two blocks from the cathedral. Other historic buildings include the state arsenal, built on the site of a Spanish prison, Creole House, and Jackson House. On the opposite green called Place d'Armes, sculptor Clark Mills's bronze equestrian statue of General Andrew Jackson symbolizes the Americanization of a cosmopolitan city. Hat in hand as his horse rears in salute, the figure overlooks a busy city street marked by the popular Café du Monde, artists at their easels, and horse-drawn carriages bearing visitors around the historic Vieux Carré.

HISTORY

The site dates to March 29, 1721, three years after Jean Baptiste Lemoyne, Sieur de Bienville, named the Mississippi Delta island La Nouvelle Orleans. The area merged strands of Choctaw, Chickasaw, African, French, and Spanish culture to create an infectiously winsome multiculturalism. French military engineer and city planner Adrien De Pauger, a Knight of St. Louis, selected the location as the center of the metropolitan diocese. He died some months short of seeing the building completed and was buried within the unfinished construction. Meanwhile, according to Jesuit historian François Xavier de Charlevoix, in 1722, the parish made do with a warehouse on Toulouse Street and a nearby tavern as temporary houses of worship. The next year, Father Raphael de Luxembourg, a Capuchin priest and founder of the first Louisiana school, lobbied for a permanent church for worshippers, who had moved services to a barracks on the corner of St. Peter and Chartres Streets.

By 1727, Louisiana's chief engineer LeBlond de la Tour had superintended construction of the Parish Church of St. Louis, a substantial cruciform building in *colombage* style capped by a modest bell tower and cross. To pegged timbers, contractor Michael Seringue added local brick between timber piers, a combination requiring no buttressing. Dedicated to Louis IX, medieval French monarch and saint, the cathedral became the worship site of French Governors Etienne de Périer, Jean Baptiste Lemoyne de Bienville, Pierre Rigaude de Vaudreuil, and Louis Billouart de Kerlerec and Spanish Governors Luis de Unzaga, Bernardo de Galvez, and Esteban Rodriguez Miro. Colonists and slaves alike brought children to be baptized at its font. Couples sought holy union at the altar; families bore deceased loved ones from the sanctuary to the St. Peter Street cemetery. Under the slate floor lay the remains of five commissioners, three Capuchin chaplains, a royal lieutenant and his wife, a trustee, and a parish priest. The colonial church became a gathering spot for citizens seeking news, which officials posted on the door.

In a year of triple calamities, New Orleans survived a flood, fire, and epidemic. The cathedral sustained serious damage on Good Friday, March 21, 1788, when a candle ignited lace altar draperies in the home of military treasurer Vincente José Nuñez on Chartres Street. The blaze that ruined 856 houses also charred the priests' residence and Casa Principal. A week later, the pastor, Capuchin priest Fra Antonio de Sedella, later known as Père Antoine, described a failed attempt to move church records to the residence of the tobacco director "two rifle shots" away (Huber and Wilson 1998, n.p.). In 1789, while the parish used makeshift quarters at the Almonester Chapel on the Ursuline property, workers carted away the blackened timbers and began reconstructing a larger edifice. A gift of Andalusian magnate Don Andrés Almonester y Roxas, the building was the design of Don Gilberto Guillemard.

With the blessing of Pope Pius VI, the flat-roofed church opened in December 1794 and survived another devastating blaze in the Quarter that same month. The building featured twin bell-topped hexagonal towers linked by a balustrade and plaster walls painted in faux marble, which echoed the marble floor and altar. Luis Peñalver y Cárdenas of Havana, the first bishop of the diocese of Louisiana and Florida, celebrated the first mass on Christmas Eve. In addition to squabbles between pastor and bishop, the setting witnessed the temporary replacement of Spain's flag with Napoleon's red, white, and blue on December 1, 1803, and the raising of the Stars and Stripes on December 21. Six months later, trustees installed a pair of bells cast in Havana and dubbed them St. Anthony and St. Joseph.

Local clockmaker Jean Delachaux acquired the first formal adornment in 1819, when he chose an ornate Parisian timepiece for the cathedral façade. To promote the site, the New Orleans City Council paid for the addition of a central tower, a masterwork that rose above the clock and housed a third bell. The tower's designer, diarist Benjamin Henry Latrobe, also built the U.S. Capitol and numerous churches, water systems, and civic buildings. Only months before his death from yellow fever, he described the placement of the bell in its cradle and Père Antoine's formal baptism of the bell as Victoire (Victory). Embossed between a pair of American eagles is a simple statement: *"Braves Louisianais, cette cloche dont le nom est Victoire a été fondue en mémoire de la glorieuse journée du 8 Janvier 1815"* (Worthy Louisianians, this bell named Victory was cast in memory of the glorious day of January 8, 1815). On the flange at the bottom is a second phrase, *"Fondue a Paris pour M. Jn. Delachaux de Nouvelle Orleans"* (Cast in Paris for Monsieur Jean Delachaux of New Orleans.) Latrobe died on September 3, 1820, before finishing the tower, which served the city as a watchpost.

Adornment continued in the 1820s. In 1823, French architect Antoine Leriche repaired walls and towers and whitewashed the discolored exterior. The next year, a decorated catafalque symbolized the death of Napoleon Bonaparte, whose funeral mass December 19 preceded a French oratorio and speech. In middecade, Italian painter Francisco Zapari decorated the nave and three altars. In 1829, the parish imported an organ. Père Antoine lived to see the emergence of the cathedral. After his death on January 22, 1829, at age eighty-one, citizens honored his four decades as parish priest with an imposing funeral mass. At the rectory, dignitaries and local mourners filed by his bier for three days before the formal ceremony, which began with cannon fire, a military procession, and a cortege of Masons, clergy, and dignitaries and concluded with interment under the shrine of Saint Francis of Assisi.

St. Louis Cathedral bears a direct link to the careers of Andrew Jackson and Zachary Taylor, seventh and twelfth U.S. presidents. A quarter century after his victory over the British, the white-haired Jackson returned to the square on January 8, 1840, to attend a declamation at the cathedral and to conduct a military review in the Place d'Armes, the park that contains his statue. On January 14, Bishop Antoine Blanc greeted Jackson, who installed the cornerstone of the central monument. Crowds attended the festivities and enjoyed a parade.

A parallel mililtary spectacle occurred seven years later, when General Zachary Taylor, hero of the Mexican War after capturing Monterey on September 24, 1846, arrived at the cathedral. His reception coincided with erection of façades around the square, suggested and bankrolled by Baroness Pontalba, who created a French atmosphere captured that year in the sketches of French artist-designer J. N. B. de Pouilly. Following a service, Taylor thrilled some 40,000 onlookers by riding his battle mount, Old Whitey, through the streets that lead to the St. Charles Hotel.

The church maintained its role in the beauty and appeal of New Orleans. In 1842, French clockmaker Stanislas Fournier dismantled the original clock and installed a trio of lighted clocks operated by a single shaft that extended from church tower and organ to a timepiece in the rear wall. In 1831, planners softened the building's exterior by closing part of Orleans Street and adding St. Anthony's Garden. The planting of oak, sycamore, and magnolia trees provided a pleasant retreat that remains popular with strolling visitors. Church officials took charge of St. Anthony's Garden in 1848 and bounded it with wrought iron.

The turf surrounds a white marble obelisk and funerary urn facing Royal Street, placed there by Vice-Consul Pierre Lacaze on Bastille Day in 1914. It honors 30 crewmen of the French corvette *Tonnerre* (Thunder) who died of yellow fever. Erected by Admiral Hamelin, naval minister to the Emperor Napoleon III, the memorial includes a statue of the Sacred Heart of Jesus and panels listing the sailors buried in the vault below. In 1941, Mrs. J. Cornelius Rathborne hired architect Richard Koch and landscape artist William S. Wiedorn to lay out paths edged in boxwood hedges as a gift to the cathedral. The gardeners updated the spot in September 1987 before the arrival of Pope John Paul II, who addressed over 1,000 priests and religious figures before leaving on a city tour and celebrating a shoreside mass at Lake Pontchartrain.

ARCHITECTURE

Trustees of St. Louis Cathedral kept pace with a period of expansion in New Orleans. The steady growth of the parish required the services of de Pouilly, designer of the Our Lady of Victory Church, Citizens' Bank of Louisiana, St. Louis Hotel, Olivier House, Dufilho Pharmacy, and imposing burial monument in St. Louis Cemetery No. 2, which was influenced by funerary art in Père Lachaise Cemetery in Paris. To complement the Cabildo and Presbytère, de Pouilly proposed lengthening the cathedral's front to accommodate four entrances and adding galleries. On March 12, 1849, parish agents contracted with Irish builder John Patrick Kirwan for the sizeable restoration. Excavation at the lateral walls proved the need to remove collapsing walls and replace the entire church. In 1850, the central tower crumbled, destroying the roof and walls. In view of the miscalculations of de Pouilly and Kirwan's shoddy work, trustees employed another architect-contractor, Alexander H. Sampson.

The building took shape in view of admiring citizens. Striking corner spires roofed with slate graced the mortar exterior. A central arch ornamented the grand exterior and produced an aura of sensible proportion enhanced by height and stability. Directed by Abbé Constantine Maenhaut, Belgian Louis Gille of Ghent constructed the baroque altars, which featured a carved white marble table and oversized reredos. He outlined the screen in Corinthian columns and classic entablature and sculpted life-size statues of Saints Peter and Paul and the symbolic female forms of faith, hope, and charity. Artist Alexandre Boule painted scrollery, paintings, and the figure of Saint Louis on the altar screen in

the act of handing his crown to the Virgin Mary. In 1850, the addition of a ceiling mural of Christ and the apostles between the clerestory windows emulated the artistry of Antonio Canova. The scene, set in an ornate medallion centered in the vaulted nave, completed the imposing thrust of columned upper galleries and braided outlines. Below, brilliant three-tiered chandeliers lighted the pews and central aisle. On the feast of Saint Barbara, December 7, 1851, despite a delayed arrival of the altars, Archbishop Blanc blessed New Orleans's cathedral as organ tones of "Ecce Sacerdos Magnus" (Behold the Great Priest) accompanied the procession through the rectangular sanctuary.

Remodeling in subsequent years required numerous artisans. In the 1870s, Alsatian painter Erasme Humbrecht retouched Boulet's murals, colonnades, and friezes and painted a grand depiction of Saint Louis launching the Seventh Crusade on the semicircle above the reredos and above a band recording Christ's words from John 14:6: "*Sum via et veritas et vita*" (I am the way and the truth and the life). Four decades later, philanthropist William Ratcliffe Irby underwrote a refurbishment that brought together fresco artist John Geiser and local painter Achille Peretti. In 1915, the diocese hired Swiss glass expert J. Julius Lips to repair the windows and contracted for a series of stained-glass scenarios from the life of Saint Louis, completed in 1929. The windows depict the French king's youth, coronation, marriage, building of Sainte Chapelle, departure on crusade, welcome to Damietta, ministry to lepers, sickness, return of his body, and canonization. Completed in chivalric style in bold shades of umber, olive, sky blue, ivory, and red, each window appears in a classic framework that mirrors ornate cartouches on the nave ceiling.

A rededication of St. Louis Cathedral on December 8, 1918, coincided with the investment of Archbishop John W. Shaw. Twenty years later, artist Valdemar Kjeldgaard retouched Humbrecht's work. The three-manual Möller pipe organ added in 1950 required restoration in 1975. Modernization through waterproofing, structural steel framing, and air conditioning maintained structural integrity into the twenty-first century.

ACTIVITIES

The appealing structure has intrigued a host of visitors, include General Charles de Gaulle, Ambassador Roberto Gaja, French President Valery Giscard d'Estaing and his wife, and the New Orleans Philharmonic, and hosted a showing of Vatican treasures during the 1984 Louisiana World's Fair. After the building's reclassification as a minor basilica in 1964, it rose in importance as the Metropolitan Church of the Archdiocese of New Orleans, a perpetually sacred worship center. Yet, for all its value as a tourist attraction and major Catholic enclave, St. Louis Cathedral remains an active church home to 300 families. The rectory shares space with the archives, which registers the sacraments of baptism, marriage, and deaths from colonial New Orleans to the present. The gradual shift from the Creole elite to less elegant working-class and immigrant families parallels the spread of the city from the Vieux Carré to the suburbs. In 1996, oblates of Mary Immaculate, the parish volunteer agency, ceased to function because of the decrease in members.

Today, the cathedral's ministry offers parish services ranging from hospital visits and service to the elderly to family and individual retreats and membership in the chancel choir and handbell choir. The seven steeple bells continue to ring the angelus and mark sacramental occasions. A cathedral school educates kindergarten through eighth grade; an after-school center cares for the children of working parents. A support group, Friends of St. Louis Cathedral, envisions the cathedral's future as an ongoing servant of the parish and community. The basilica continues to aid antiquarians and church historians with multiple volumes of parish records. The annual November 1 All Saints' Day celebration, called the New Orleans Memorial Day, brings throngs to deck the above-ground tombs of St. Louis Cemeteries with traditional chrysanthemum wreaths and bouquets.

Sources: *Biography Resource Center* 1999; Buchanan 1999; "Christmas New Orleans Style"; Gould and Nolan 1999; "The Governors of Louisiana"; "A Guide to New Orleans Architecture"; Harris 1977; "Historic Homes of New Orleans"; Huber and Wilson 1998; *New Catholic Encyclopedia* 1967; Sellers 1996; "St. Louis Cathedral"; "St. Louis Cathedral Slate Artwork"; Sturgis 1902; Sullivan 1967; Williams, Peter W., 1997.

St. Patrick's Cathedral

Edward M. Egan, Archbishop
460 Madison Avenue
New York, New York 10022
212-753-2261
FAX 212-755-4128
www.ny-archdiocese.org/pastoral/
cathedral_about.html

New York City's beloved St. Pat's is perhaps the nation's most famous, most treasured Catholic church. Situated on Madison Avenue between Fiftieth and Fifty-second Streets and regularly photographed from the front, the back, the sides, and above, it occupies a block bounded on the east by Madison Avenue. On prime land opposite Rockefeller Center's International Building and the Olympic Towers, it is the center of the New York see and a tourist imperative. Balancing its reputation for majesty is the St. Patrick's Day Parade, which courses by the portals on March 17 in honor of the energy and drive of the city's Irish Catholics.

HISTORY

Catholicism on Manhattan island dates to the work of hero missioner and martyr Saint Isaac Jogues, a Jesuit captive of the Iroquois whom Governor William Kieft ransomed. According to historian Francis Parkman, in 1643, Father Jogues received the blessing of Governor Kieft and the Dutch residents of Nieuw Amsterdam to convert the Mohawk. His outreach succeeded, but New York City produced no Catholic church home until the erection of St. Peter's in 1785.

The first St. Patrick's on Mulberry Street opened in 1815. Designed by Joseph Magnin, the Gothic Revival structure sported cast-iron columns shouldering a timber roof. The building burned in 1866. Following reconstruction in 1868, it was demoted to a less prestigious parish church after the new cathedral pushed it out of the running for diocese headquarters. The current St. Patrick's began with the purchase of land in 1810, originally intended for a college or burying ground. After four decades, trustees chose to build a cathedral.

Designer James Renwick began work in 1853. After five years of sketches and discussion,

New York City's beloved St. Pat's is perhaps the nation's most famous and most treasured Catholic church. (Michael S. Yamashita/Corbis)

planners accepted his Anglo–French Gothic design and laid the cornerstone in 1858. The Civil War intervened, delaying completion of the basic structure until May 25, 1879, when New York's second archbishop, John McCloskey (later Cardinal McCloskey), dedicated the building and appointed as archdiocese vicar William Quinn. The cathedral opened its school in 1882. Another six years were necessary for the building of the twin spires that rise from the sides of the façade, violating Renwick's original drawing of a single tower above the apse. Archbishop Michael Corrigan financed the work as well as the Lady Chapel, completed on the apse end in 1906 on a design by Charles T. Mathews. The church was consecrated in 1910.

ARCHITECTURE

Inspired by the cathedrals in Rheims, France, and Cologne, Germany, and facets of numerous continental European churches, St. Patrick's is an original. Its boldly proportioned totality sits on huge cubes of blue gneiss granite, lifting sharp foliated spires 330 feet, 24 feet more than the building's length. Lacking a stone ceiling, it required no flying buttresses and thus maintained a svelte exterior that suits the limited plot, which ensuing decades have walled in with modern skyscrapers. The builder chose walls of Dix Island granite quarried in Maine to support columns and attached a refined, genteel white marble surfacing transported from Pleasantville, New York. Renwick added seventeen side altars to different saints and created the white marble pulpit and high altar, under which New York's archbishops lie buried. Their *galeros,* or bishop's miters, hang from the ceiling over each tomb.

For its complementary artistic detail, the interior of the nation's most prominent Gothic structure has inspired high praise from the churched and unchurched alike. The stained glass came from the ateliers of Nicholas Lorin of Chartres and Henry Ely of Nantes and from the workshops of glass masters in Boston and Birmingham, England. Charles J. Connick supplied the famous rose window, the nave's most entrancing feature. Of his profession's subtle influence on the spirit, he predicted that radiant worship sites can regenerate the spirit. He remarked in 1931:

> Beauty can preach as very few men with
> bundles of words can preach. I want to
> make beautiful interiors for both churches
> and souls. I want men to hear my windows
> singing; to hear them singing of God; I
> want men to know that God is at the core
> of their own souls. ("The Symbolism of the
> Sanctuary" 1987)

In addition to colored glass, the cathedral delighted the eye with carving. Dutch sculptor Peter J. H. Cuypers carved the fourteen stations of the cross, which took first prize at the 1893 Chicago World's Fair. William O. Partridge contributed a massive Pietá and a statue of Saint Francis copied from an original by Giovanni Dupré at Assisi. Tiffany and Company designed the Saint Michael and Saint Louis altar; Paolo Medici of Rome, the Saint Elizabeth altar.

The cathedral has progressed in stages. It re-

JAMES RENWICK

When Archbishop John Hughes launched the construction of St. Patrick's Cathedral in 1853 to accommodate the influx of Irish and German immigrants, he entrusted the initial study and design to James Renwick, a prolific architect to the rich and powerful. Born in Bloomingdale, New York, on November 1, 1818, Renwick, son of a Columbia College engineering professor, emulated his father's career. Among his early works were the Erie Railroad and Croton reservoir and aqueduct. At age twenty-five, he diverted his professional interests to architecture, which he taught himself, and designed New York City's Grace Church, Calvary Church, Church of the Puritans, and St. Bartholomew's.

It seemed right and fitting that the thirty-eight-year-old architect tackle St. Patrick's Cathedral, a Gothic Revival design that Renwick had perfected in earlier applications. Working with associate William Rodriguez, he took two decades to complete the cathedral plus the archbishop's residence and parish house. In later years, Renwick established the neo-Romanesque turrets and gables of the Smithsonian Institution and built the Corcoran Gallery of Art, Vassar College, All Saints Church, and New York's Charity Hospital on Welfare Island. Well versed in French classics, he blended details for an eclectic finish unmistakable in its bold detail.

interior has accommodated regular worship, state occasions, society weddings, and sobering losses. In 1964, Pope Paul VI toured the structure; in October 1995, Pope John Paul climaxed a visit to New York City with a visit to St. Patrick's. Other historical events were the wakes of Governor Alfred E. Smith, Minister Jan Ignace Paderewski of Poland, and Senator Robert F. Kennedy. In 1989, the cathedral acquired modern amplification and lighting systems as well as a bas-relief shrine honoring New York's saint, Frances Cabrini. Popularly known as Mother Cabrini, an immigrant to New York from Lombardy, Italy, she founded Columbus Hospital and staffed it with Italian-speaking novices to tend refugees and immigrants.

Sources: *Almanac of Famous People* 1998; *Biography Resource Center* 1999; Broderick 1958; Cook 1979; *Encyclopedia of World Biography* 1998; Franz 1997; Goldberger 1979; Hamer 1997; Horsley; *New Catholic Encyclopedia* 1967; Sullivan 1967; "The Symbolism of the Sanctuary" 1987; Tauranac 1979; Williams, Peter W., 1997.

Subiaco Abbey

Abbot Jerome Kodell
405 North Subiaco Avenue
Subiaco, Arkansas 72865-4328
501-934-4295
subiaco@river-valley.net; jkodell@river-valley.net

ceived a pipe organ in 1931; the original underwent renovation and structural upgrading in 1921 and 1945. Francis Cardinal Spellman oversaw the completion of the stained-glass windows and installation of a new altar and bronze baldachin. Subsequent improvements to the bronze portals and rose window and addition of an elevator to the choir loft brought the church into the last half of the twentieth century.

ACTIVITIES

The seat of New York's archbishop, St. Patrick's Cathedral is the center of the city's Catholic life. Each year, more than 3 million people tour the building, which is open daily for prayer, meditation, and confession. Seating 2,400, the finished

A religious and historic landmark northeast of Mount Magazine, the stone bell tower of Subiaco Abbey, a self-sustaining mission institution, rings out the commitment of Catholic brothers ministering to Arkansas's coal mining district. For more than a century, the abbey has supplied staff to local parishes, prepared young men for college, launched new missions, and greeted visitors to Coury House, a retreat center. The church doubles as a parish church, where Subiaco Academy Student Choir supplies music and shares facilities with abbey monks.

HISTORY

On March 15, 1878, Father Wolfgang Schlumpf and two monks, Brother Casper Hildesheim and Brother Hilarin Benetz, arrived in Subiaco from St. Meinrad's Archabbey, which Benedictines

The stone bell tower of Subiaco Abbey, a self-sustaining mission institution, rings out the commitment of Catholic brothers ministering to Arkansas's coal mining district. (Courtesy Subiaco Abbey)

from Abbey Maria-Einsiedeln, Switzerland, founded in St. Meinrad, Indiana, in 1853. On a land grant from the Little Rock/Fort Smith branch of the Cairo and Fulton Railroad Company, the trio built St. Benedict's Priory at Creole, a hamlet five miles east of Paris in west-central Arkansas. Later named Subiaco Monastery, the brotherhood ministered to German-speaking Catholics of Logan County. In 1887, Brother Gall d'Aujourd'hui and eight novices arrived to lend a hand. Subiaco Abbey achieved abbey status in 1892, when Ignatius Conrad, a Swiss monk from the mother house, took the post of abbot and supervised the monks for thirty-three years.

The abbey established a coat of arms based on its history. Paired ravens parallel the Einsiedeln crest. Gold rose emblems on the birds' shoulders refer to Subiaco, Italy, Saint Benedict's hermitage where he hurled himself into a thorn

bush to dispel worldly thoughts. The emblem's cusped edge and black border represent the abbey's ties with Saint Meinrad. The crest omits the drama of a fire in 1927, which destroyed the original sanctuary.

To maintain the order, the abbey admits prospective monks from ages twenty-two to forty-five who profess a desire to join, love liturgy and prayer, maintain a community spirit, have no outside obligations, and possess fitness of body, mind, spirit, and character. Men who take holy vows at the abbey observe a pattern of activities that coordinate periods of prayer, reading, and reflection. The day begins at 5:45 A.M. with prayer and private study. After the Eucharist and breakfast, they work in the laundry, farm buildings, shops, classrooms, or offices. A break for noon prayer and lunch precedes afternoon work duties until prayer at 5:30 P.M., followed by dinner, vespers, evening recreation, and retirement to rooms at 9:00 P.M.

ARCHITECTURE

Trustees hired Father Michael McIverney, a monk and church designer at Belmont Abbey in North Carolina, to advise them on building Subiaco Abbey. The group rejected the plan, but accepted his recommendation of the Milwaukee firm of Brielmaier, Sherer, and Sherer as architects. The building that Joseph and Leo Brielmaier created perpetuates the modified Romanesque architecture that marked European cloisters of the Middle Ages. Opposite a modest landscaped forecourt, the complex features St. Benedict Abbey Church, built on the site of the burned church and dedicated on October 19, 1952, to Saint Benedict and Our Lady of Einsiedeln. Constructed by architect Bernard Kaelin, the church opened in 1959. The elegant native sandstone façade consists of two pairs of double doors and two side doors beneath an elongated stone cross and triple window. Before them stands a dramatic statue of Saint Benedict. To the right rear, a square bell tower rises above a parallel triple window to a red roof. The four bells honor Saints Cecilia, Gertrude, Mechtilde, and Hildegard.

Inside, the muted lighting casts soft shadows on rounded arches over a central aisle and two ranks of pews. Above the canopied altar, a balsa wood cross and poignant crucified Christ in olive wood center the reredos between two eighteen-foot Corinthian columns. Franz Mayer of Munich, Germany, designed the 182 stained-glass windows, which depict Saint Benedict's life, the mysteries of the rosary, and the lives of the Virgin Mary and Jesus. To the left, the Altar of the Blessed Sacrament and a rose window overlook worshippers at private prayer. Three paneled windows depict the holy family. A parallel rose window and panels above the baptismal font on the opposite side exalt Saint Benedict and the Trinity. Above the monks' choir, a three-manual organ designed by organ-liturgist Father Ermin Vitry and Martin Wicks of the Wicks Organ Company, Highland, Illinois, was ready for use in January 1959.

The abbey's inner court, lined by a colonnade, encloses four quadrants of green. Up the alleys that cross at center near neat beds of annuals, pedestrians arrive at the statue of Saint Benedict. In Jewett Memorial Hall on the east side of the square, a series of photos honors deceased monks. The monastery's tastefully appointed refectory features the brothers' carpentry in oak and cherry wood, a carved teak relief of the Last Supper, Beuronese murals, and a painting of Virgin and child by Arthur Spruggs. About the campus are Centenary, Wardlaw, Heard, and Alumni Halls, a fine arts building, shops, Villa Scholastica, a greenhouse, East Park, and the Abbey Cemetery.

ACTIVITIES

Two ministries attest to the success of the Benedictine mission—St. Benedict's Church and St. Scholastica Monastery, a convent for Benedictine women named after Benedict's twin sister. The first four nuns arrived in September 1878 and lived in the brothers' primitive dwelling until they could erect a log cabin for the sisters ten miles away on Shoal Creek. The women opened Logan County's first Catholic school. In addition to the farm and printshop, the monks built a seminary, St. Benedict's Church, and Subiaco Academy, a boys' college-prep high school founded in 1887 and serving a student body of 200. The academy has adopted a four-part aim:

- Service to God
- Respect for self and others
- Mutual support
- The value of work

Extracurricular scheduling offers tennis, football, soccer, basketball, baseball, and a school paper, the *Periscope*. Each summer, the Marion Glover/Subiaco Academy Football Camp for grades six through nine nurtures 160 board students and 50 commuters at a three-day intensive on sports fundamentals led by a staff of professional players and educators. The alumni sponsor Camp Subiaco in the Ouachita Mountains, a one-week experience offering archery, hiking, swimming, skiing, and riflery to boys from ages nine through thirteen.

The abbey museum displays sacred relics, specimens of taxidermy and minerals, and incunabula. Coury House Retreat Center welcomes 4,000 guests annually for meditation and spiritual replenishment. It lists as visitors the Arkansas Diocesan Council for Black Catholics, Arkansas Knights of Columbus, Catholic Women's Union, Christian Women Fellowship, and Cursillistas of Memphis, plus Protestant ministers, twelve step groups, and couples attending marriage encounters. At the invitation of Bishop Emmanuel Ledvina and Abbot Edward Burgert, Subiaco dispatched Brother Paul Nahlen to lead a party to the Southwest to establish Corpus Christi Abbey in Texas in 1959 on forty acres of donated land. A parallel mission to Central America in 1978 produced Santa Familia Monastery in Belize.

The abbey brotherhood communicates with the outside world through tours, publishing, and a Web site. Abbot Jerome Kodell published a limited-edition text, *Christ's Way: The Stations of the Cross,* containing photos by Francis Kirchner and meditations by Father David McKillin. Since 1997, Subiaco Abbey has been a stop on the tour for the annual Mount Magazine International Butterfly Festival.

Sources: Alsberg 1949; "Corpus Christi Abbey"; *New Catholic Encyclopedia* 1967; "St. Scholastica Monastery"; "Subiaco Abbey"; "Subiaco Academy" 1999; Sullivan 1967.

liefs that they must live in unity with the earth. Their daily existence depends on perpetual repairs, replastering, and bolstering of adobe walls. To recondition time-worn walls, women layer on mud and texturize it with sheepskin.

The internal workings of the pueblo suit its individuality. The people survive on farming, ranching, and offering horseback rides from Taos Indian Ranch to the canyon rim and an overlook of the Rio Grande Valley. Some work in the nearby town of Taos. Seasonal tourism supports food concessions, especially frybread and loaves and cookies baked outdoors in hive-shaped adobe ovens called *hornos,* which bakers fire with juniper. Artists at studios in the pueblo display sketches and paintings. Crafters offer mica- and gold-flecked pottery of tawny clay or black-on-black firing, willow baskets, beadwork, blankets, and smudge wands of sage, juniper, lavender, and sweet grass. Specialists produce taped ceremonial flute music, concha belts, fetishes and clay storyteller dolls representing mythic figures, Hopi kachina dolls, and shell or turquoise and silver jewelry. Favorites of children are doeskin moccasins, quivers, cradle-boards, and boots and cottonwood log drums covered in hides.

Under centralized management, pueblo dwellers perform a variety of internal occupations, including policing and sanitation. Most pueblo children attend a preschool and elementary school behind the south pueblo that is maintained by the Bureau of Indian Affairs. In addition to mostly native teachers, an education committee supervises curriculum and administers a scholarship program.

Taos Pueblo
P.O. Box 1846
Taos, New Mexico 87571
505-758-1028; 505-758-9593

Located two miles north of Taos, New Mexico, off state highway 68, the sacred sites of the Tiwa-speaking Taos Pueblo people are vital to the city, a native homeland and the largest of the nineteen multistoried Pueblo structures in the Southwest. As they have for ten centuries, these holy grounds represent a hallowed trust in the earth. The grounds are home to starlings and swallows, which nest in the walls. Certain segments of the elongated complex are spirit rooms, conduits to the afterlife. They accommodate rituals in six kivas, or underground sanctuaries, where elders teach and pray and spirits emerge from the *sipapu,* or spirit hole, in the center of the floor. Worshippers attend outdoor ceremonies at the dancer's plaza and Ma-whalo, or Blue Lake, a high mountain tarn fed by Rio Pueblo and overlooking the adobe community that is the tribe's origin and source of life. In the Taos cosmology, the lake gives birth to humanity and receives souls of the dead in the afterlife.

The tribe inhabits the nation's oldest active community, which is comparable in cultural significance to the Pyramid of Cheops, Taj Mahal, Acropolis, and Grand Canyon. The total population includes over 1,900 people. The pueblo houses 150 residents; some dwellers occupy apartments for ceremonies and then return to conventional homes. Others reside full time in summer homes and modern housing within the Pueblo land base of 95,000 acres. An aboriginal enclave that rejects piped-in water, sewer, and electricity, pueblo dwellers adhere to ancient be-

HISTORY
From ancient times, Blue Lake has been holy. The tribe keeps secret its detailed oral history, but other sources sketch in the pre-Columbian past. According to archeologists, area construction dates to the early eleventh century and continued to 1450. Legends tell of a great chief who established his people in the twelfth century at the foot of Mount Wheeler, the summit of the Sangre de Cristo (Blood of Christ)

Located two miles north of Taos, New Mexico, the sacred sites of the Tiwa-speaking Taos Pueblo natives are vital to the city and the Southwest. (North Wind Picture Archive)

Mountains. He chose the spot where an eagle dropped two feathers, one on each side of the stream. The people, perhaps a remnant of the Mesa Verde settlement, ended a migration north from arid land to the fertile valley but retained pottery, tools, pictographs, and petroglyphs that linked them to a primeval setting.

When Spanish explorer Francisco Vasquez de Coronado and his conquistadors arrived in 1540 in search of the golden cities of Cibola, they found the Hlauuma, or north house, and Hlauk-wima, or south house, already in use. Spanish and Mexican conquerors respected the Taos Pueblo's rights to Blue Lake but suppressed kachina dances and worship in underground kivas. After Spanish evangelists Christianized the indigenous people in the seventeenth century, the Taos Pueblo became a province of New Spain and ostensibly gave up animistic worship. In private, however, individuals maintained ancient beliefs and tribal rituals.

The Pueblo adopted both Spanish and English and converted overwhelmingly to Catholi-cism, the religion of 90 percent of the current community, but simultaneously practiced animism and worshiped in kivas. A minority honor the American peyote cult, which reveres the Sun Dance, sweat lodges, and vision quest. In 1619, Taos acquired its first church, named San Gerón-imo, or St. Jerome, in honor of the pueblo's patron saint. The symbiosis of white and native cultures generated grim forced-conversion stories of limbs hacked from elders, workers forced into slavery, children abducted from parents to be indoctrinated into Catholicism, and, in 1675, 47 native religious leaders executed or sold into bondage.

During the Spanish revolt of 1680, it is not surprising that Taos seethed with anarchy. During the ousting of Spaniards, rebels destroyed the chapel building. Rebuilt on the same foundation, the San Gerónimo Chapel survived until 1847—the year of the Taos Rebellion, a Hispanic and native uprising against the U.S. government that precipitated the Mexican War. Colonel Sterling Price retaliated by destroying the chapel a second time, killing 150 of 700 noncombatants who sheltered inside.

Out of respect for the tradition of natural decay, Taos natives left the remains of the old church for the earth to reabsorb. At the old cemetery, to hasten decay, they wrapped in blankets the martyred dead—members of the the Martinez, Aguilar, and Archuleta families—and nestled them close together. In 1850, the present two-story structure took shape, featuring a standard Spanish colonial balcony and twin bell towers. The governing structure consists of a tribal council of 50 male elders. A governor and his staff settle civil and business issues and manage relations with the outside world. The war chief and his staff protect the Indian lands beyond the pueblo.

In 1906, the U.S. government presented a dismaying challenge to Pueblo autonomy and sovereignty. President Theodore Roosevelt, an espoused conservationist, signed an order reclassifying the area as Taos National Forest, now Carson National Forest in honor of Colonel Christopher "Kit" Carson. Roosevelt made no effort to compensate the tribe for this parcel. His action deprived the tribe of 50,000 acres plus the mountain, lake, and its twenty-mile processional path, where worshippers annually ascend on a two-day horseback ride to hold private ceremonies at summer's end, immerse themselves in mystic ritual, and baptize believers in soul-strengthening waters. To lessen any backlash, the Indian Claims Commission offered $297,684.67 restitution. The Indians wisely rejected a cash settlement and offered their claims to the city of Taos in exchange for Blue Lake.

In 1933, Congress offered a fifty-year special use permit; the Bureau of Indian Affairs assured the Taos Pueblo that their sacred ground would survive intact for tribal use. Broken promises resulted in trout fishing, logging, road building, camping, grazing, and dumping and burning of trash on a revered shrine. At Blue Lake, tribe members found prayer sticks broken or stolen. Congress named the pueblo a National Historic Landmark in 1960 and, six years later, added it to the National Register of Historic Places. The World Council of Churches offered their support of Taos worship areas. In 1992, the United Nations admitted the pueblo to the World Heritage List, a testament to its uniqueness and cultural purity.

Ecology is central to the debate over sacred geography. The Taos Pueblo cherish Ma Wha Luna, or Red Willow Creek, the stream originating in the Blue Lake watershed that supplies the Pueblo village and its surroundings with water for irrigation, drinking, cooking, watering livestock, recreation, and bathing. In contrast to insurgent populations who continue to overlog, overgraze, and ranch to the detriment of the Taos area, indigenous people conserve and protect the stream as a source of renewal. Devout natives have requested that the military halt supersonic overflight and that airports at Angel Fire, Eagle's Nest, and Taos postpone noisy air traffic and aerial photography during pilgrimages.

To restore the wholeness of the area, which supplied healers with medicinal plants and wild asparagus and fostered sacred animals at its meadows and streams, native elders pressed suit over sixty-five years for Blue Lake. In 1970, Teresino Jiron, Al Lujan, Vincente Lujan, chairman Tony Reyna, Fred Romero, and Gilbert Suazo formed the committee that persuaded Congress to accept a compromise—relinquish Blue Lake and 48,000 adjacent acres to the Taos Pueblo, but retain the 2,000-acre Cu Tun Na (Where the Bears Live) and a segment of the pilgrimage trail. The next year, celebrants acknowledged the persistence of Taos governor Pa Chal Ma (Deer Catcher, or Paul Bernal) in demanding consecrated lands rather than cash. On August 14 and 15, 1971, celebrants prayed, sang and drummed, danced with bells tied to their feet, raised feathered lances, and held a buffalo feast. In joy, they tolled the mission bell to announce the return of Blue Lake, an assurance that the tribe would survive.

ARCHITECTURE

Pueblo architecture, which exemplifies the village aura of "a thousand years of tradition," perpetuates communion with the earth. The construction method, which involves no human-made fibers, requires sun-dried adobe bricks, or precast shapes made from earth mixed with straw and water. Roofs of the five-story complex rest on aged *vigas,* or timbers. Atop the timbers are aspen boughs and *latillas,* willow saplings cut into cross pieces that support the layered grass and packed earth above. There are no connecting doors or staircases in a pueblo. The original residents cut entrances in the roofs and climbed down piñon ladders, which they withdrew to keep out intruders.

The outer walls, which protect residents from extremes of temperature, require constant replastering; cleanliness necessitates additional whitewash on inner walls. The top floor serves as a storage closet for ceremonial items. The Spaniards called these flat-top adobe structures *pueblos,* a term that became the European designation for the tribe and for its strong-beamed apartment-style architecture, which formed a viable fortress in time of attack by marauding Comanche or Ute. At the corners, lookout posts and gates augmented safety, particularly during harvest, when Taoseños herded livestock into the plaza and guarded stores of grain and water. Today, peace prevails. The structures are a favorite with artists and photographers, who return to the area to capture the beauty and spiritual strength of the community.

The chapel of San Gerónimo complements the simplicity of the complex. Entered through an archway and double portal, it reveals darkened beams over a century and a half old. An austere style of woodcarving produced straight-backed pews and a pedestal offering holy water. Above the altar, a mural blends the saints and angels of traditional Catholic culture with native cornstalks. Statues of the Virgin Mary and two angels, surviving from the original edifice, wear seasonal dress: blue in summer, yellow for autumn, white for winter, and pale green in spring. In place of a crucifix, Pueblo Catholics prefer a coffin, which they drape in seasonal colors. The coffin is a mark of honor for Christ in that it deviates from blankets, the native burial covering.

ACTIVITIES

Tribal leaders have intensified education of youth to encourage appreciation and protection of Blue Lake and the traditional faith and oral lore, which members memorized to save it from misinterpretation or extinction. At the adobe pueblo complexes on opposite banks of Red Willow Creek, the small river that halves the plaza, ritual revives interest in native history and self-preservation. On roofs, housekeepers dry corn and plums. Hunters still stretch venison or hay on tall drying racks to preserve meat and grain for winter.

The month of December is a quiet time. Residents spend the period in contemplation of the traditional lifestyle, which bans cars and tourists as Taoseños return to handwork and community interdependence and entertain family from distant places. Spiritually restored from their meditations, each emerges in January with less stress and a stronger sense of oneness with nature, family, and tribe.

At the sacred dances, *koshare* clowns climb the pole. Signs request that visitors respect the privacy of tribe members at restricted areas, stay out of homes and ruins, and refrain from photographing the San Gerónimo Chapel interior or wading in the river. Taos pilgrims retreat to Blue Lake in late August to worship, pray, and admit members to the Taos Pueblo kiva societies, a preface to full participation in native religious life as well as secular political office. The *cacique,* or chief priest, superintends kiva chiefs, who preside over religious education and venerate the Corn Mother, Squash Maidens, and rain and hunting deities. The symbolism establishes the tribe's integrity, interdependence, and cohesion.

Using traditional techniques, native artists produce tanned buckskin moccasins, rawhide and cottonwood drums, rabbit skin rubs, woodcarvings and sculpture, painting, and jewelry. Local clay pottery and ceramics are both utilitarian and beautiful. Singers and dancers transcend time in frequent performances that perpetuate the Pueblo culture. Community authorities insist on respect from tourists and restrict photos and recording during ceremonies.

Holidays follow centuries-old motifs. Tribesmen perform the Turtle Dance on January 1; the Deer or Buffalo Dance takes place on January 6, with the Deer Maiden leading a herd of male deer. On May 3, Santa Cruz Feast Day, young people join the Corn Dance and take part in an annual sunrise footrace. Summer is rife with activities. June 13, San Antonio Feast Day, brings men and women together for a second Corn Dance; on June 24, the feast of San Juan calls all adults for a third Corn Dance. The second weekend in July brings intertribal dancers for the annual two-day powwow, which is both competition and fun for all. On July 25 and 26, Santa Ana Feast Day returns to the corn harvest theme for the selection of a queen and a traditional dance at Santiago.

The last quadrant of the year features uniquely Anglo-Indian festivities. Tribe members set aside September 29 for the San Gerónimo Eve Vespers and Sundown Dance, which is restricted to male performers. San Gerónimo Day, held annually on September 30, preserves the name of Saint Jerome, translator of the Bible into Latin. Coinciding with the fall trading festival, the holiday summons neighboring tribes to a major gathering and display of arts and crafts. An example of syncretic worship, the fusion of the native feast with a Catholic saint's day unites old with new. The day begins with relay races, which carry a spiritual meaning to runners. Friendly rivals from North House and South House compete along the course in front of the north building. The festival progresses to an all-day trade fair and intertribal dancing. A religious society of mummers, or acrobats, known as Black Eyes performs comic acts based on religious lore by climbing a fifty-foot white pole greased with buffalo tallow to capture mutton tied at the top. The pueblo ends the year with the torchlit Procession of the Virgin Mary after vespers along a path lit by flickering *farolitos*, ritual candles anchored in sand in a paper bag. Christmas eve culminates with mass in the chapel and luminaries, or bonfires, followed by the Christmas Day Deer Dance or Matachina Dance (in alternating years), featuring symbolic animal movement and the ancient Montezuma Dance.

> **Sources:** Beresky 1991; Carey 1993; Carmody and Carmody 1993; Collins 1991; Florin 1969; Guise 1997; Keegan 1991; "La Plaza, Taos Pueblo"; Morgan 1994; "Sacred Sites of Northern New Mexico"; Spritzer 1994; Steiger 1974; "Taos Pueblo"; "Taos Pueblo: A Thousand Years of Tradition"; Walking Turtle 1993.

Temple Beth Elohim
See Kahal Kadosh Beth Elohim.

Temple Emanu-El
Dr. Ronald B. Sobel, Senior Rabbi
1 East Sixty-fifth Street
New York, New York 10021
212-744-1400
FAX 212-570-0826
info@emanuelnyc.org
www.emanuelnyc.org

New York's prominent reform synagogue Temple Emanu-El presents a rugged, reassuring permanence in style, material, history, and philosophy. It is the largest of Judaism's liberal wing. The Hebrew name, meaning "God is with us," offers a clue to the congregation's strength. Their faith proved unshakeable in tenuous times, particularly the weeks following the dedication, which preceded the 1929 stock market crash and the onset of the Great Depression. For over a century and a half, this resilient body of worshippers has progressed from neophyte Americans to leaders of industry, politics, altruism, scholarship, the arts, and religion.

HISTORY

The original body of thirty-three German Jews, after meeting in a rented room on Grand and Clinton Streets on the Lower East Side in 1845, took more permanent quarters the next year in a Methodist Church on Chrystie Street. In 1854, they moved to a former Baptist Church on East Twelfth Street before constructing a sumptuous Moorish temple on Fifth Avenue fourteen years later. Acculturation as Americans came in part from the first rabbi, Dr. Gustave Gottheil of Manchester, England, author of the New World's first Jewish hymn book, who led services in English, not German. Additional departures from tradition occurred in 1874, when both rabbi and cantor abandoned head covering, added a Sunday lecture to the liturgy, and replaced bar-mitzvahs with confirmation for both boys and girls. In 1888, Emanu-El's staff hired Dr. Joseph Silverman, the city's first American-born rabbi and graduate of Hebrew Union College. On their golden anniversary, the congregation entered an era of social activism with the work of members Jacob Schiff, Adolph S. Ochs, and Solomon Loeb, who assisted nurse-social worker Lillian D. Wald in founding the Henry Street Settlement.

LILLIAN D. WALD

A pragmatic humanitarian, Lillian D. Wald determined to uplift the American underclass who crowded New York City's slums. At the Henry Street Settlement House, she improved the lives of Italians, Hungarians, and blacks. In a career crowded with innovations, she helped launch the Federal Children's Bureau and supported nonviolence, trade unions, feminism, education, and civil rights. A native of Cincinnati, Ohio, she was born March 10, 1867, to Jews who fled Europe, and she attended public school in Rochester, New York. After nurse's training at New York Hospital and experience on staff at the New York Juvenile Asylum, she furthered her training at the Women's Medical College. In 1893, she created her own job on New York's Lower East Side as a public-health nurse, a term she devised to describe the proactive aspects of good health.

With the gift of a house on Henry Street from Jacob Schiff, Wald initiated the nation's first community health service, which, by 1903, was treating 4,500 patients annually in eighteen districts. Her support for localized care for the poor led to the National Organization of Public Health Nurses, which taught home health principles. The Henry Street Settlement House grew with the addition of a convalescent center, summer field trips, a library, vocational training, insurance partnerships, and a savings bank. In 1909, it was the setting for a conference that grew into the National Association for the Advancement of Colored People.

Wald's immense contribution to social betterment covers a broad range of human attainment—the 1914 peace parade, investigation of exploitation of the poor in public-works projects, a State Bureau of Industries, woman's suffrage, and the Joint Board of Sanitary Control. For school children, she demanded lunch service, municipal playgrounds, special education for the handicapped, and public school nurses. In 1915, she issued *The House on Henry Street,* a testimonial to the value of supervised activities and attention to children's social and physical needs. During World War I, she extended the Henry Street Settlement House as wartime headquarters for the Red Cross and Food Council. In 1925, a second memoir, *Windows on Henry Street,* summarized a life committed to humanitarianism.

Other members of Temple Emanu-El, in addition to Lillian Wald, were at the forefront of progress in New York City.

- 1896—Member Adolph S. Ochs began publishing the *New York Times,* the nation's most respected media source.
- 1903—President Theodore Roosevelt appointed the nation's first Jewish cabinet member, Oscar S. Straus, as secretary of commerce and labor.
- 1906—Straus joined Jacob Schiff in founding the American Jewish Committee, a watchdog on Jewish rights worldwide.
- 1913—Louis Marshall's defense of Leo Frank preceded the creation of the Anti-Defamation League of B'nai B'rith.
- 1918—The congregation mourned 7 casualties among 229 members who served in World War I.

By 1925, the tripling of enrollment at Temple Emanu-El required new quarters. At this crucial point in temple history, congregants voted to merge with Temple Beth-El, with whom they worshiped at Fifth Avenue and Seventy-sixth Street for two years until the completion of a new Temple Emanu-El. On September 29, 1929, they inaugurated the present building with an unexpected event—the funeral of their brilliant, energetic president, Louis Marshall. In subsequent decades, Temple members continued to shine in United States history:

- In 1939, Irving Lehman, president of the congregation, was named Chief Justice of the New York Court of Appeals.
- From 1942 to 1945, over 1,350,000 soldiers passed through Isaac Mayer Wise Hall, which the congregation offered as a recreation canteen during World War II.
- In 1943, the women's auxiliary established a Red Cross unit, which produced 75,000 surgical bandages monthly.
- By war's end, 22 of the 591 members serving in the war had died in action.

At the end of its first century, Temple Emanu-El began Sabbath broadcasts on radio station WQXR and celebrated longevity with a seven-month series of conferences, lectures, concerts, and interfaith forums. In 1996, the temple made new headlines by broadcasting the first sound Internet religious service with the April 3 Passover Seder, followed in fall by live presentation of the Rosh Hashanah service. Endowed by Jeffrey S. Gould, the temple Web site also published vast Judaica resources, lectures, and concerts.

ARCHITECTURE

The current facility, completed in 1929 across from Central Park's East Green and zoo, makes as bold a Romanesque statement as the medieval cathedrals of Europe. Built of limestone, its arresting recessed arch accentuates five vertical columns and Oliver Smith's twelve-spoked wheel window, representing the twelve tribes of Israel. To the sides, lions top two semidetached columns to further the theme of God's protective might. Above three pairs of bronze portals, seven finger-shaped windows suggest a menorah.

The 147- by 77-foot interior, which seats 2,500, echoes the Magen David (Shield of David) in jewel-toned windows and mosaic tiles alongside stained-glass flowers and fruit, symbols of abundance. At the upper range of the 103-foot ceiling, light from the clerestory designed by the Nicola D'Ascenzo Studio of Philadelphia augments soft lamplight in illuminating a vast space freed of columns by the structural steel frame and a series of buttresses. Designers Clarence Stein, Robert D. Kohn, and Charles Butler selected master mason Rafael Guastavino to mount acoustical tile to buffer the sound echoed by the marble wainscoting. At the traditional eastern extreme, the ornate ark with support columns and tablets of the law of Moses draws attention beyond the bimah, or dais, which situates the rabbi's pulpit at the left and the cantor at the right.

Northward beyond the auditorium, the Byzantine Beth-El Chapel features twin domes and arches above pews seating 350. Above the steel arch doors is a Louis Comfort Tiffany window reclaimed from the Forty-third Street temple and reframed in marble. Downstairs, the

Isaac Mayer Wise Memorial Hall accommodates 1,500 for dining, social gatherings, and stage productions. The mainstay of the temple education program is a six-story religious school and community house built at Sixty-sixth Street and Fifth Avenue in 1959. At the fourth-floor conference room, lay scholars gather each Saturday for coffee and a stimulating discussion of the week's Torah reading.

ACTIVITIES

Under the direction of senior rabbi Dr. Donald B. Sobel, Temple Emanu-El schedules the kinds of religious, civic, and art experiences that suit a cultivated urban congregation. Beyond the traditional Saturday morning Torah study and Sabbath services, Saturday evening worship classes in Greenwald Hall initiate newcomers into such integral facets of worship as the prayers and verse of liturgy and traditions of High Holy Days. Staff encourages singles through Emanu-El League mixers, teaches a scholarly course in Hebrew, and closes each day with a lay reading of prayer, song, and kaddish, a ritual prayer for the dead. Helping Hands, a ministry to the homebound, attends to domestic needs and errands and escorts elderly or handicapped members to services. An adjunct, Dine Together, arranges meals and brunches to broaden acquaintances and friendships among members. The temple men's club also sponsors dinners, lectures, discussions of medical problems, assistance to students applying to college, and theater events. Another committee, Central Synagogue, supervises Torah study. A parents' organization enforces lessons of the religious school on Jewish identity. Other ministries include a Seder for the elderly, sign language interpreters, home delivery of Passover meals, and the Sunday Lunch Program, for which volunteers prepare and serve lunch to the poor and homeless. A full schedule of arts events offers gallery lectures, discussions on art films, studies in American Jewish history and Jewish identity, concerts by the Young Artists Series and the Ecumenical Choir, lectures on parenting and world events, and study of such authors as Jewish poet Emma Lazarus, author of "The New Colossus," which graces the Statue of Liberty.

Temple Emanu-El houses 500 pieces of Jewish art, ritual objects, and memorabilia dating from the fourteenth to the twentieth centuries. The core collection was the combined gift of Henry M. Toch and Judge Irving Lehman. Reva Godlove Kirschberg directs a three-room museum containing artifacts from France, Italy, North Africa, Holland, Russia, and Eastern Europe catalogued by Dr. Cissy Grossman. Among them are rare Torah ornaments, shields, pointers, a Hanukkah lamp, an ivory fan, a velvet prayer book, vases, a Sabbath tray and pitcher, spice boxes, and three Bloomingdale Torah crowns, which appear in Grossman's published overview, *A Temple Treasury: The Judaica Collection of Congregation Emanu-El of the City of New York* (1989).

Sources: Ahlstrom 1972; Biema 1999; Brainard 1922; Broderick 1958; Coss 1989; Daniels 1995; Fernandez; Guttman 1997; Hamerman 1996; Kraut 1994; "Lillian D. Wald," http://www.JWA.org/, http://www.netsrq.com/; McHenry 1980; Sherr and Kazickas 1994; Yost 1947.

Temple of Eck

Sri Harold Klemp, Pastor
Peter Skelskey, President
P.O. Box 27300
Minneapolis, Minnesota 55427
800-568-3463; 612-544-0066 department 151
info@eckankar.org
www.eckankar.org/

The Temple of Eck, an oasis of peaceful spirituality in the Eastern tradition, is a growing community of worshippers seeking individual rather than liturgical communion with God through self- and God-realization. A phenomenon of the last quarter of the twentieth century, Eck is a uniquely American faith based on the wisdom and other-worldliness of Indian and Tibetan mystics. It affirms that communion with the divine cannot be attained through ritual, ceremony, or adherence to a creed. Through simple liturgy and chant, Eckists seek to free their souls from the flesh to travel spiritual planes beyond time and to learn from mistakes in past lives how to rid themselves of worldly distractions.

HISTORY

In the New-Age syncretic spirit, the emerging Eckankar faith resounds with Hindu mood and appeal. Its founder, Kentucky-born theologian John Paul Twitchell, or Paulji, established the sect in 1965 and registered it as a nonprofit organization in 1970. After training under Sudar Singh in Paris and India and under Rebazar Tarzs, a Tibetan monk, Twitchell acted on a perception of God's presence he had experienced in 1956 during initiation into a mystical group, the Order of the Vairagi Masters. He gained additional enlightenment from a guru, Kirpal Singh, founder of the Ruhani Satsang movement, and published his experience with God in *The Tiger's Fang* (1969).

After six years of systematizing Eckankar theology in *Eckankar: The Key to Secret Worlds* (1969), *Drums of ECK* (1970), *Stranger by the River* (1970), *The Way of Dharma* (1971), *The Spiritual Notebook* (1971), *The Flute of God* (1971), *The Eckankar Dictionary* (1973), *Talons of Time* (1974), and other Eck texts, Twitchell died suddenly without realizing the dream of a temple he had planned for Charleston Peak outside Las Vegas, Nevada. His wife, Gail Twitchell, and directors of the church named Darwin Gross as *mahanta*, or Eck master. After marrying Gross, Gail Twitchell and he moved church headquarters from Minneapolis, Minnesota, to Menlo Park, California, where Harold Klemp became the third Eck master. Aided by Peter Skelsky, Klemp returned operations to Minnesota in January 1984 and established the world Temple of Eck at Chanhassen.

Eckists date the temple's beginning as May 22, 1989, the day the Chanhassen council okayed plans for construction. Dedicated on October 22, 1990, the temple offered a refuge to people who had tried mainstream religions and received rejection or were discontented. By the beginning of the twenty-first century, the faith claimed 50,000 members in 100 countries.

BELIEFS

Eckists refer to their faith as a religion of the light and sound of God. They consider Socrates, Plato, Jesus, Moses, Muhammad, Confucius, the Buddha, Krishna, Zoroaster, Martin Luther, Michelangelo, Nicholas Copernicus, William Shakespeare, Wolfgang Amadeus Mozart, Albert Einstein, Ralph Waldo Emerson, and others as former Eck masters who achieved earthly soul

The Temple of Eck was conceived as a way station, an earthly refuge on the journey to the soul's ultimate haven. (Courtesy of Temple of Eck)

journeys that enlightened and liberated them. They revere world scripture, including the Bible, Apocrypha, Torah, Cabala, Koran, Tao Te Ching, I Ching, Bhagavad Gita, and Book of Mormon.

Eck parallels the Radhasoami theology of India, a nineteenth-century Hindu movement that aids the soul or consciousness to transcend the physical body to higher spiritual realms by intoning a sound or connecting with a life current. Eck theology also incorporates glimmers of Rosicrucianism, a Catholic mysticism, and theosophy, an approach to God through spiritual insight. Eck practitioners experience the sight, sound, and taste of the divine, whom they call Sugmad. Through Eck, or the soul, worshippers channel a spiritual life force emanating from earth. To achieve oneness with God, they chant "Hu," a variant name for God, for twenty to thirty minutes daily. This sacrament removes layers of worldliness to reveal the divine through a voice or inner beacon within each follower, known as an Eckist or *ECK chela* (student).

According to Eckankar theology, the *tuza* (soul) is each person's repository of spirituality. Because the soul is eternal, it lives only the present but can discard earthly ties and journey out of the body to other levels of existence. This concept of soul travel explains how the individual can visit the five planes of material existence—physical, astral, causal, mental, etheric—and six upper levels. The negative aspect of humanity derives from karma and the five passions—anger, greed, lust, worldliness, and vanity. To pay the debt of evil in past lives and establish self-realization, a purified state that frees the soul at last from earthly attachment, each person must redeem the soul in subsequent lives. Other religions, including Christianity, may serve as the method of liberation.

Eckists do not seek converts or proselytize. Their moral beliefs and behavior are left to the individual, who pays $130 annually for a membership donation or $160 per family. Generally, Eckists avoid drugs, tobacco, and alcohol and involve themselves in community service. At worship, they hear readings from the twelve-volume *Shariyat-Ki-Sugmad,* chant, contemplate in silence, and discuss their faith. Individuals mark advances in understanding with five initiations, a series of private conferments occurring around twelve months apart. These steps culminate in a supreme status as *mahdis* (clergy). After achieving the second level, Eckists typically fast each Friday. Personal devotion calls for chanting God's name, meditating, singing, visualization, and trance. Each keeps a journal of dreams and interprets them as glimpses of upper worlds, prophecy, or elements of spiritual growth.

ARCHITECTURE
Chanhassen's Temple of Eck, the wisdom temple as well as community church, is an attractive, modern complex situated on a knoll between a terrace of white birch and Lake Ann, where members hike trails over the 174-acre site. The Eck master conceived it as a way station, an earthly refuge on the journey to the soul's ultimate haven. The temple's 50,000 square feet encompass a fellowship hall, a chapel, classrooms, a public reading room, and offices that issue the *Eckankar Journal* and a quarterly magazine, *Mystic World*. The two-story triplex consists of three octagonal areas—the temple, the lobby, and offices—built of a concrete and steel foundation and precast columns and planks.

Shaped like a Babylonian temple, the edifice rises on square pillars to a light gold anodized-aluminum ziggurat crown, an emblem of spiritual plateaus leading to a state of purity. The lobby contains a spiral staircase, illuminated by a skylight, leading to fellowship hall, the chapel, and the sanctuary. The hall serves large meetings, workshops, banquets, and receptions. The chapel accommodates 80 in upholstered seats. At a curtained curved wall beneath the three-tiered ceiling, staff conducts weddings, consecrations, receptions, and special events. In the airy second-floor sanctuary, a theater arrangement seats 800. The tranquil, light-toned decor of white, ecru, and blue combines soft lighting and whitewashed oak with accents of anodized aluminum.

ACTIVITIES
The Temple of Eck staff holds worship services from 10:00 to 11:00 A.M. the first Sunday of each month, followed by conversation and refreshments. The building is open Monday, Wednesday, and Friday from noon to 9:30 P.M. and on weekends from noon to 4:30 P.M. Visitors can access the reading room weekdays from 8:30 A.M. to 5:00 P.M. The temple closes for Christmas Eve, Christmas Day, and New Year's Eve. For children, the staff offers a parent-toddler room and religious education for ages three to thirteen. A relaxed environment, friendly conversation and refreshment, Friday night videos, and forty-five- to

sixty-minute tours of the complex help to dispel false views of Eckankar.

The temple calendar for 1999 listed an open house in late October, four-week *setsangs* (classes or seminars) in spiritual dreaming and past lives in October and November, a study of the healing chant of Hu in November, December lectures on secret teachings and reincarnation, a late winter forum of personal experiences with Eck, and New Year's gatherings. Staff posts a Web site, which contains sounds of chanting and an offer of free reading material. Additional information and sermons by Harold Klemp are available weekly on local television and through audio cassettes and videos.

Sources: Allen, 1994; Anderson 1995; *Biography Resource Center* 1999; Bristow 1998; "Eck Church Is Realizing Its Dream" 1999; "Eckankar," http://www.carm. org; "Eckenkar" 1997; "Eckenkar," http://www.religioustolerance; *Encyclopedia of Occultism and Parapsychology* 1996; Hexham and Poewe 1997; Klemp 1995; Lewis 1998; *Religious Leaders of America* 1999; Shard 1990; Waddington 1991; Zavoral 1997.

Thorncrown Chapel
Dell and Doug Reed, Administrators
12968 Highway 62 West
Eureka Springs, Arkansas 72632
501-253-7401
www.thorncrown.com

Constructed on a steep, rocky rise in the Ozark Mountains of northwest Arkansas, the dramatic Thorncrown Chapel blends with a woodsy path. Built according to Frank Lloyd Wright's principles of organic architecture, the ephemeral shape displays a vision of reverence in elemental, unpretentious metal and glass. The shrine, founded by the Reverend Jim Reed and inspired by the Gothic austerity of Sainte Chappelle in Paris, draws pilgrims—some every day—away from turmoil and rush into a uniquely comforting sacred space. The architect, E. Fay Jones, designed the entire facility, including furnishings and lighting, as a balm to the spirit.

HISTORY AND ACTIVITIES
Thorncrown Chapel is a phenomenon among the world's religious sites. Conceived, built, and

Constructed on a steep, rocky rise in the Ozark Mountains of northwest Arkansas, the dramatic Thorncrown Chapel blends with a woodsy path. (Timothy Hursley)

E. FAY JONES

Architect Euine Fay Jones, a native of Pine Bluff, Arkansas, designed the nondenominational Thorncrown Chapel to give wayfarers an oasis of quiet and rest. Born January 31, 1921, he was a tree-house builder in boyhood. He flew navy transports in the South Pacific in World War II and became one of the first graduates in architecture from the University of Arkansas. Further educated on fellowship at Rice University, in 1953, he entered the University of Arkansas faculty and rose to dean of the College of Architecture.

Before entering private practice, Jones studied with idol and mentor, Frank Lloyd Wright, at the Taliesin studio near Spring Green, Wisconsin, before building numerous residences and religious structures. In 1980, he undertook to harmonize nature as part of the decor of Thorncrown Chapel, a pinnacle of the era's art and artistry. For his masterwork, Jones won the 1980–1981 Rome Prize Fellowship, a distinguished professor award in 1985, and, in 1989, an American Institute of Architects gold medal.

After designing the Mildred B. Cooper Memorial Chapel in Bella Vista, Arkansas, Jones added the Thorncrown Worship Center in 1989 to relieve some of the demand for services and weddings in the chapel. He later built the Marty Leonard Community Chapel in Fort Worth, Texas; Pinecote Pavilion outside Picayune, Mississippi; and Pine Eagle Chapel at a Boy Scout camp outside Wiggins, Mississippi. In 1997, he received a commission for the Wallace All Faiths Chapel at Chapman University in California.

administered by amateurs, it reaches some unsatisfied spiritual need of city folk to retreat and regroup. Nearly two decades after Frank Lloyd Wright created the Wayfarers' Chapel in Palos Verdes, California, Jim Reed, a high school math teacher, conceived his sylvan chapel in summer 1977 as an antidote to littering outside the passion play performed nightly in Eureka Springs, Arkansas. By constructing a private worship site, he proposed to tap inner resources from visitors to live at one with nature rather than dirty it with trash. Someone suggested to Reed that Fay Jones was an architect imbued with spirituality and a gift for bringing nature and light into the worship experience.

To preserve the setting, Jones chose a framework and materials that could be carried into the woods without heavy equipment. For understatement, he blended indigenous stone and undressed Arkansas pine. A fantasy of criss-cross geometrics, the chapel stands among dogwood, maple, and hickory as an organic part of the clearing. The rhythms of sunrays reflected on glass generate a thick interlacing, a wholesome nest that has been called Ozark Gothic.

Only twenty-four by sixty feet on eight acres of rugged hillside, the chapel sits on a brick and fieldstone foundation, from which vertical beams rise like trunks to mesh beneath the gabled roof. Stained gray like natural stone and roofed in a rugged substance that mimics bark, the finished chapel suggests the rural sturdiness of a covered bridge, the everyday grace of shed, lean-to, and barn. The interior, with its flagstone floor, glass, and fir columns, accommodates 115 worshippers. The minimal walls admit an uplifting dazzle of light through interlocking trusses. Above, a sixty-foot gable rises to the tops of a stand of hickories. By night, lighting gives a lanternlike glow, as though lighting a beacon for travelers.

When Reed and Jones dedicated Thorncrown Chapel in summer 1980, they were overwhelmed by the response, which brought 40,000 visitors in a few months. A mix of architects, preachers, ecologists, and seekers find a gracious, reverent calm. For two decades the chapel has remained open daily for meditation and prayer. Since Reed's death in 1984, his wife Dell has administered the chapel. At age thirty-one, her son, Doug Reed, left his jail ministry in Waco, Texas, to pastor a quarter million itinerant chapel visitors annually and arrange nondenominational Sunday worship, special events, and weddings. A periodical, *Thorncrown Journal,* updates supporters on the chapel outreach.

See also Wayfarers' Chapel.

Sources: Barnes 1996; *Biography Resource Center* 1999; Dean 1991; *Encyclopedia of World Biography* 1998; Grossman 1993; Heyer 1997; Smith 1998; "Thorncrown Chapel"; "Thorncrown Chapel by E. Fay Jones"; Williams, Peter W., 1997; Wright 1989.

Touro Synagogue

85 Touro Street
Newport, Rhode Island 02840
401-847-4794
FAX 401-847-8121
office@tourosynagogue.org
www.tourosynagogue.org/index.htm

The oldest Jewish worship center to survive from pre-Revolutionary times and the first to be established in a British colony, Touro was the center of Rhode Island Hebraism. The building, which now serves 110 member families, was once home and haven to 15 Spanish-Portuguese families fleeing Catholic intolerance in Spain. For Rhode Islanders, the structure was more than a worship site: it was the setting for religious education for their children, a holiday feast hall, and the sacramental site of bar mitzvahs, weddings, and funeral memorials.

HISTORY

Touro Synagogue got its start from Yeshuat Israel (Salvation of Israel), a Sephardic assembly of highly cultivated Jews passing through Curaçao in the West Indies on their way to Newport in the American colonies. Lacking a temple and rabbi, their community life was limited to *minyanim* led by chanters and rented classrooms for their children. As they flourished in crafts, merchant sailing and imports, banking, and merchandising, their shops lined Bellevue Avenue. In 1677, they established a burial ground sanctified and limited to their sect. By the eighteenth century, their community was stable enough to welcome refugees from the Lisbon earthquake of 1755.

A century after the first Sephardic Jew arrived in Rhode Island, a newcomer brought the cross-cultural background of the Ashkenazim, the Jews who made their homes in northern Europe. After graduating from the Rabbinical Academy of Amsterdam, Holland, at age twenty, the Reverend Isaac de Abraham Touro rejuvenated the small community. To give them a worship center, he raised funds from numerous sources, in particular, New York's Shearith Israel congregation.

On June 30, 1759, Newport's Jews purchased land from Ebenezer Allen on Griffith Street for a synagogue and broke ground on August 1. Touro's followers chose New Haven's importer and skilled amateur architect Peter Harrison to construct a temple. Harrison admitted that he had no experience with Judaic religious architecture. After consulting books, he blended elements to produce a rich, but sedate Georgian original. Working gratis to the community from 1759 until December 2, 1763, he completed for Touro's 300 Jews a gem of classic geometric design.

The Revolutionary War sapped the strength and resources of coastal New England. Some of the original Touro congregation moved to Philadelphia and New York. In the absence of religious vigor, from 1781 to 1784, the Rhode Island General Assembly and state supreme court met in the synagogue. On August 17, 1790, during the nation's first presidential term, George Washington and Thomas Jefferson paid a social and political call on Newport and attended a town meeting at the local temple. Impressed by the words of synagogue warden Moses Seixas, President Washington promised to sanction no bigotry against a congregation he characterized as "the Children of the Stock of Abraham." ("The Historic Touro Synagogue") The presidential declaration was the first in the nation to acknowledge Jewish-Americans.

Seixas's speech and Washington's guarantee of freedom still stand on the west wall, but the president's beneficence failed to halt attrition of Touro. After the congregation formally ceased, they remanded title to the building and land to their benefactors in New York. The unused building weathered badly without regular care and use. The salvation of the deteriorating synagogue was a $20,000 bequest from two admirable benefactors, Isaac Touro's sons, Abraham and Judah, who launched a historic and preservation foundation. Preserved by this ample seed money, the building limped into the early nineteenth century, but sporadic use for holy days and receptions failed to revive it to former greatness.

In 1883, a new congregation, Jeshuat Israel, took shape under a respelling of the original name. Infused with Ashkenazi culture and energy, they adapted to Sephardic customs and rekindled a sense of community. Much admired by architects, historians, and tourists, Touro survived and entered the National Historic Site

The oldest Jewish worship center to survive from pre-Revolutionary times and the first to be established in a British colony, Touro was the center of Rhode Island Hebraism. (John T. Hopf)

SEPHARDIC JUDAISM

Sephardic Judaism refers to the Jews from Spain. In the Middle Ages, Hebraic communities thrived alongside Muslim enclaves as mutual interlopers in a largely Catholic milieu. The quick-witted learned Arabic, Spanish, and Latin in addition to Hebrew and the local Ladino dialect and adapted to a varied cultural expression in food, architecture, dress, and behavior. European history is filled with the wit and wisdom of Spain's Sephardic sages, notably Alfasi, a Moroccan rabbi who founded a school in Andalus; twelfth-century travel writer Benjamin of Tudela; poet and court physician Jehuda Halevi of Toledo; and Chasdai Crescas, reformer and freedom fighter from Saragossa. Cordoba alone produced four intellectual giants—physicians Hisdai and Moses Maimonides and Talmudic scholars Nachmanides of Gerona and Samuel ha-Nagid.

The progress of Jewish artisans, financiers, and doctors was two-edged. While success elevated them among the elite, their heightened prestige and wealth produced envy in the Catholic hierarchy, who, in 1480, appointed an inquisitor under the precepts laid down by Pope Gregory around 1240 to accuse, torture, and expel or execute the Iberian heretics. From 1481 to 1482, Catholic courts set up in Castile and Aragon directed their spite against Marranos, the Iberian Jews who continued to practice Judaism in secret after being forced to convert to Christianity.

As the noose tightened, Spanish ghettos were no longer safe. Desperate Jews emigrated to Palestine or North Africa or fled into hiding in Holland, France, England, Germany, and the eastern Mediterranean. The ones who stayed and embraced—or pretended to embrace—Catholicism, changed their names to rid themselves of the fatal taint of Jewry and links to Christ killers. The first party to seek religious freedom in the New World set sail in 1658 from Holland to Rhode Island, Roger Williams's nondenominational refuge.

---

listing in 1946. At the dedication on August 31, 1947, historian Carl Van Doren extolled U.S. citizens for honoring a shrine "consecrated to justice and holiness." (Broderick 1958, 22)

ARCHITECTURE

Constructed a decade after Harrison designed King's Chapel in Boston, the synagogue stands diagonally on the plot to align worshippers with the east and the holy city of Jerusalem. The brick cube bears a simplistic external styling that belies the ordered, symmetrical splendors of the interior. To the right, the arch and triangular pediment that completes Isaiah Rogers's wrought-iron gate echoes the gabled entrance, a second triangle-topped façade balanced on a pair of ionic columns and surrounded by steps on three sides. Similar arching in the leaded windows relieves straight lines and the regular dentate molding of the hipped roofline.

Inside the thirty- by forty-foot structure, a lofty domed ceiling enhances a heavily detailed molding, curved railings, and twelve columns—Corinthian upstairs and Ionic downstairs. These columns, made from whole trunks of twelve trees, symbolize the twelve tribes of Israel. They outline the first floor and three-sided upper gallery, which together seat 250. Louvered shutters suppress natural light from the plain-glass windows. The holy ark contains the continent's oldest hand-lettered Torah in the curtained holy of holies at the east end. Above it, a classic frame outlines the twin tablets of the Ten Commandments, painted by Newport artist Benjamin Howland. Illuminating the area is a suspended eternal light, emblem of the presence of Yahweh. An unexplained secret compartment under the teba (coffer) may have been a hiding place for runaway slaves on the Underground Railroad or may express a pervasive fear that Rhode Islanders would one day turn against Jews.

Over the centralized lectern on the ground floor, five low-slung brass candelabra—made by hand and donated from 1760 to 1770—light the bare floor and spindle-back settles. At center, the cantor occupies a railed bimah, where he chants liturgy and reads the scripture. A row of seats follows the wainscoting. Two raised seats at the north end elevate the congregational president and vice president. According to Orthodox tradition, the gallery serves female members, who sit apart from men. An adjacent two-story ell at left serves as a school.

ACTIVITIES

Since 1948, the nonsectarian Society of Friends of Touro Synagogue has dedicated itself to the building's upkeep and preservation and to the colonial Jewish cemetery, where Judah Touro is buried. The site was the subject of Henry Wadsworth Longfellow's poem "The Jewish Cemetery at Newport" (1890), which contrasts the serenity of the burying ground with the bustle of a harbor town:

> How strange it seems! These Hebrews in
>   their graves,
> Close by the street of this fair seaport town,
> Silent beside the never-silent waves,
> At rest in all this moving up and down!
> ("Henry Wadsworth Longfellow")

To honor religious freedom and the contributions of Jews to the nation's founding, the Friends built Patriot's Park next door and urged the U.S. Postal Service to design a commemorative stamp, issued in 1982 on George Washington's 250th birthday. Annually, the society schedules a reading of President Washington's letter and presents the Judge Alexander George Teitz Award to the person who exemplifies Washington's ideal of religious freedom. To assure a financial base for future restoration and expansion, in 1998, B. Schlessinger Ross, executive director of the Society of Friends of Touro Synagogue, and his group hired a professional fundraiser to raise $6 million, some of which financed a visitor's center.

Touro Synagogue holds services Saturday at 9:00 A.M. and on Friday ten months of the year at 7:30 P.M. The time shifts to fifteen minutes before sunset on Friday in July and August. Additional sessions offer adult and children's education and tefillin class, memorial services, and holy day observance. The congregation welcomes guests Sunday through Friday from 10:00 A.M. to 5:00 P.M. Visitors can tour the building mornings and afternoons from July until the first week in September, except for Jewish holidays. The staff stocks a gift shop and maintains a Web site with links to the Hebrew alphabet and language and information sources on Israel.

See also King's Chapel.

Sources: Ahlstrom 1972; Baer 1961; Berman; Bono; Broderick 1958; Brody 1996; Buchanan 1999; Chaliand and Rageau 1995; Deutsch 1998; Folberg 1995; Hastings 1951; "Henry Wadsworth Longfellow"; "The Historic Touro Synagogue"; "History of Jews in Spain"; Ketchum 1957; Klagsbrun 1996; Mutrux 1982; Perry 1987; Rose 1963; Roth and Wigoder 1977; Sinnott 1963; Smith 1989; Snodgrass 2000; "Touro Synagogue, America's Oldest Synagogue"; "200 Years of an Ethnic American Family"; Williams, Peter W., 1997.

Trappist Abbey

See Our Lady of Guadalupe Trappist Abbey.

Tri-County Assembly of God

Hugh H. Rosenberg, Founder
and Senior Pastor
7350 Dixie Highway
Fairfield, Ohio 45014
513-874-8575
assist@tcag.org
www.tcag.org/

In the spirit of fundamentalism, Tri-County Assembly of God likes to boast of expansion, souls saved, and pledges honored. Its history parallels the explosive growth of Pentecostalism in the second half of the twentieth century. Sprouting from 4 to 53.5 acres, the church lot is more than thirteen times its original size. The staff keeps an ongoing record of financial challenges to grow, add more rooms, and spread the Christian gospel to local people and prospective converts in other nations. The aggressive congregation foresees continued success as it attempts to Christianize the rest of the world's citizens.

BELIEFS

The Assemblies of God form the largest organized sect in the Pentecostal movement. It derives from the holiness wing of Methodism and the subsequent Apostolic Faith Movement, begun in Topeka, Kansas, in 1901. Members hold the singular belief that charismatic signs follow conversion and baptism. The second blessing to believers appears in episodes of healing and glossolalia, or speaking in tongues. Since 1914, the sect has taken on the elements of a formal denomination and follows standards of preaching and ministry, fellowship, and foreign missions.

In the spirit of fundamentalism, Tri-County Assembly of God in Fairfield, Ohio, likes to boast of expansion, souls saved, and pledges honored. (Courtesy Tri-County Assembly of God)

Organized Pentecostalism did not immediately coalesce into an orthodox faith. It suffered a shake-up in 1915 over doubts about the Trinity and requests for rebaptism in Jesus' name alone. Within a year, the majority silenced doubters of the triune God and initiated steady national growth and missions to South Africa and the Congo, Italy, Latin America, and the Philippines. Today, Assemblies of God doctrine maintains fundamental views on the need for repentance and redemption and widespread condemnation of jewelry and makeup, alcohol and drugs, and tobacco. Worship combines sermons and hymns with spontaneous demonstrations of praise and thanksgiving.

HISTORY

The organization of Tri-County Assembly of God began with one couple, Hugh and Joan Rosenberg, who had experience in Kansas and California before moving to Cincinnati. In August 1959, Hugh Rosenberg accepted a post as-

sisting the Reverend D. Leroy Sanders at First Christian Assembly and then felt a need to branch out to the suburbs. With funds from the parent organization and Mount Lookout Savings and Loan, he chose an unlikely setting for his church—a defunct box factory on a four-acre lot along Ohio State Route 4 north of Circle Freeway. Although the building was spartan, the location was fortuitous as traffic patterns funneled 100,000 people daily by the church door.

The ambitious new congregation of 27 adults and 11 children chose the name Tri-County Assembly of God from the nearby Tri-County Shopping Center. With volunteer labor, they built a functional one-story chapel and education center to accommodate 200. A group of 97 inaugurated the sanctuary on March 4, 1962, with familiar choruses of "How Great Thou Art" and "Blessed Assurance!" The Reverend D. Leroy Sanders of North Hollywood, California, delivered a dedicatory address on April 2, 1962, and read a congratulatory telegram from the mother church in Spring-field, Missouri.

Within a year, the congregation had out-grown its humble beginnings. Planners outlined a balcony and wing to the sanctuary to add 100 more seats and additional Sunday school space. In December 1964, they completed a triplex for staff housing and invited as dedication speaker the Reverend C. M. Ward from Revivaltime Media Ministries, the broadcast outreach of the Assemblies of God. In the second year, the staff increased with the hiring of an assistant pastor, the Reverend Earl W. Moore.

The church program flourished with more converts, additions to the Sunday school roll, and the Real Life Nursery School. To stem over-crowding, the congregation began a third build-ing phase aimed at a membership of 1,000 and purchased four adjoining acres. After completing the new sanctuary, members opened Tri-County Christian Schools in 1968 initially for first and second grades with plans for a full kindergarten through grade twelve parochial school with a gymnasium and kitchen, completed in 1970. By 1972, Tri-County had joined the top ten Assem-bly of God churches in the nation in size. Staff expanded the youth program with Cincinnati Teen Challenge and added a second morning service and a sports complex for the school. Within five years, the congregation had taken on a new venture, the Tri-County Girls Home.

The current sanctuary, begun in March 1978, doubled floor space to 116,000 square feet by adding a basement, offices, classrooms, a fellow-ship hall, and nurseries. The staff advanced its mission and financial undertakings with the Lay Leadership Institute, Home Cell Groups, and a fundraising campaign called Total Stewardship Aflame. They designed a church logo featuring three descending doves encircled by the words "Serving Family, Community, Country and World." The facility became the unofficial audi-torium for greater Cincinnati's religious rallies and concerts and hosted Christmas and Easter pageants that coordinated orchestras, choirs, ac-tors, and animals.

ACTIVITIES

In addition to an ample church calendar of wor-ship, Tri-County Assembly of God sponsors mis-sion couples in Belarus, El Salvador, the Fiji Is-lands, Portugal, Germany, and the Muslim world. Members attend such interchurch and parachurch events and conferences as Promise Keepers, Women's Ministries, Love Chapter Fel-lowships, Ladies Night Out, and 55 and Alive for senior adults. Light entertainment and fellow-ship from Gospel Sing Night, Lunch Box Social, and Birthday Bash creates a people-centered at-mosphere capable of fun as well as spirituality. Members maintain a shut-in ministry and Jireh House for needy families and send MKare Pack-ages filled with candy, toys, magazines, and books to children of foreign missionaries.

Tri-County Assembly of God schedules Sun-day services at 9:00 and 10:15 A.M. and 6:00 P.M. Junior High Delta Chi meets Tuesday evening; Missionettes for girls and Royal Rangers for boys meet Wednesday evening simultaneously with the adult choir and Bible study. Thursday is the meeting night for Senior High Delta Chi and men's Cross Trainers. The week concludes with Saturday evening prayer.

Sources: Ahlstrom 1972; "The Assemblies of God Online"; *Eerdmans' Handbook to the World's Religions* 1982; Gentz 1973; Grady 1997; "Revivaltime World Prayermeeting Announced"; "Tri-County Assembly of God"; Williams, Peter W., 1997; Wilson and Fer-ris 1989.

Trinity Church

Reverend Daniel Paul Matthews, Rector
Wall Street and Broadway
New York, New York 10006-2088
74 Trinity Place (office)
New York, New York 10006-2088
212-602-0800; 800-551-1220
congregational_office@ecunet.org
www.trinitywallstreet.org/

From the outset, Trinity, New York's oldest Epis-copal church, was a pacesetter in style, philan-thropy, and leadership. Located east of the Bat-tery in the southern tip of Manhattan Island, it enrolled worshippers of the caliber of George and Martha Washington; its steeple served as a landmark of New York Harbor. Among the dead in the burying ground lie prominent men of the Republic—publisher William Bradford, Commodore Silas Talbot, first commander of "Old Ironsides," Robert Fulton, inventor of the steamship *Clermont,* Declaration of Independence signer Francis Lewis, French Huguenot catechist Elisa Neau, New York University founder Albert Gallatin, and Alexander Hamilton, the nation's youngest framer of the Constitution and first secretary of the treasury, alongside sixteen officers of the Continental Army and Navy. A fine model of American neo-Gothic, the church entered the listings of the National Register of Historic Places.

In the twenty-first century, Trinity perpetuates a tradition of Christian stewardship from its 700 members. Church counseling expands social programs to the homeless, addicted, and mentally unfit; missions to Africa have entered a fourth century. Powered by volunteers from all five of New York's boroughs, the church is a force worldwide in the Episcopal commitment to nurture humanity, body and soul.

HISTORY

Founded in 1696, Trinity Parish received the approval of Governor Benjamin Fletcher to buy land for Manhattan's sole Church of England parish. On May 6, King William III chartered the project and set annual crown rent at one peppercorn. The notorious Atlantic pirate Captain Kidd lent builders a block and tackle to lay the stone foundation for the first wooden edifice, an unassuming gambrel-roofed church with a modest porch. Of the acreage that Queen Anne granted in 1705, the congregation divested much of their parcel of 215 acres to other institutions, including Columbia University, originally called King's College.

As New York's only church, Trinity was a center of activity. In 1709, the congregation founded Charity School, later named Trinity School, the city's oldest educational facility. By 1715, enrollment of needy children reached 650. In 1750, a fire that charred the steeple burned the school and parish records of baptisms, marriages, and burials to that point. Trinity Church remained the area's only church until the construction of St. George's in 1752 and St. Paul's in 1766.

Altruism became a congregational watchword. In 1767, Trinity members organized the

---

RICHARD UPJOHN

A meticulous taskmaster, Richard Upjohn set the tone for American Gothic architecture. A native of Shaftesbury, England, born January 22, 1802, he settled his family in New York in 1829 and opened a carpentry shop specializing in cabinetry. He moved to New Bedford, Massachusetts, in 1830 to work for a lumberman, where an eye for detail earned him a place among architects. Abandoning the faddish Greek Revival style he used for the Isaac Farrar home in Bangor, Maine, he built St. John's church, a Gothic structure that made his reputation.

In 1839, Upjohn took a commission to design Trinity Church, his masterwork. From a study of medieval style and philosophy, he pioneered a style that guided liturgical and civic architecture nationwide. He followed similar floor plans for New York's Church of the Ascension, Christ Church, and St. Thomas's; Grace Church in Providence, Rhode Island; Grace Church in Utica, New York; Albany's St. Peter's Church; and Boston's Central Congregational Church. He published sketches and photos in contemporary magazines and published *Rural Architecture* (1852). At peak performance in 1857, he organized and headed the American Institute of Architects. After his death on August 16, 1878, in Garrison, New York, his son and protégé, Richard M. Upjohn, succeeded him.

Society for the Relief of Widows and Orphans of Clergymen. The sanctuary was the site of the unassuming 1794 wedding between William Seton and Elizabeth Ann Bayley, who embraced Catholicism in widowhood, founded a school and the Sisters of Charity, and became the nation's first saint, canonized in 1975 by Pope Paul VI. The church also sponsored the Protestant Episcopal Society for Promoting Religion and Learning in the State of New York in 1802; six years later, it opened the African Episcopal Catechetical Institution.

Although the clergy honored the English monarchy, Trinity led a groundswell toward abandoning English and Anglican ties, forming the Continental Congress, and furthering a homegrown denomination, the Protestant Episcopal Church of America. The prominent building hosted a visit from General George Washington but did not survive the American Revolution because of a disastrous fire on September 21, 1776, occurring five days after his unsuccessful match-up against Redcoat General William Howe at the Battle of Harlem Heights. The church and school collapsed in ruin when flames devoured 500 houses and left thousands homeless.

While the congregation pondered the physical church, vestrymen also tackled matters of principle. By 1784, the question of loyalties ended with the hiring of a Whig rector, the Reverend Dr. Samuel Provoost, and formal separation from crown loyalties. Within three years, Dr. Provoost became New York's bishop. The newly inaugurated President Washington and first lady Martha Washington made Trinity their church home. The staff's importance to city history is evident in streets named Rector, Vesey, Barclay, Moore, and Charlton after pastors and church wardens.

A second Trinity entered construction in 1788. Until the replacement opened on March 25, 1790, the congregation had to share facilities at St. Paul's Chapel, New York City's oldest public building still in use. The tower of the second Trinity received bells transported from England aboard the *Favorite* in 1797. The sanctuary remained in use over four decades. When heavy snows threatened its safety in 1839, the congregation opted to dismantle it and build the third Trinity. During construction, they established Trinity Cemetery in 1842 on 23 acres along Riverside Drive, a parcel once owned by naturalist John James Audubon.

The present edifice at Wall Street and Broadway is the third Trinity built on the original plot. Designer Richard Upjohn applied scholarship and creativity in making it a noble feature of the city's landscape. Dedicated on Ascension Day, May 21, 1846, it housed period art and craft and a resonant peal of ten bells that once signaled fire companies.

Charity continued to rank high in Trinity's priorities. In 1857, the congregation began ministering to the poor of the Bowery during an economic downturn that left 40,000 jobless. In 1863, Rector Morgan Dix, a champion of ecumenism and inclusion, summoned federal troops

to protect black students when rioters plotted an attack on St. John's Chapel. Months after the close of the Civil War, Trinity opened the parish's first free chapel, St. Chrysostom's, named for the late-fourth-century reformer and orator known as the "golden-tongued." (Snodgrass 1999) In 1879, the church established a mission house to superintend a girls' vocational school, a home for elderly women, home economics classes for immigrant women, a workingmen's club, and a relief bureau to aid the sick and unemployed. The outreach grew rapidly, requiring a new facility in 1888 and enlargement in 1896.

In the spirit of Morgan Dix, in 1910, Rector William T. Manning spread ecumenism; nine years later, he abolished the elitist practice of selling pew space. Trinity began broadcasting services by radio on December 24, 1922, when a Christmas Eve observance reached as far south as Cuba. In 1927, a program of interfaith cooperation and unity produced the World Conference on Faith and Order, forerunner of the World Council of Churches. During the Great Depression, church buildings housed soup kitchens and sheltered New York's homeless.

Trinity's rental proceeds from 6 million square feet of office space in twenty-seven prime urban locations made it one of the city's largest commercial landlords. During World War II, the congregation used profits to transform Trinity Mission House into a center producing bandages and surgical dressings. Eighty-four of its members served in the military. The staff initiated New Year's Day prayer services, beginning three weeks after Japan's attack on Pearl Harbor with a throng of 1,000 worshippers. Generous members held intercessory prayer meetings and collected offerings for war chaplains. Hourly thanksgiving services on V-E Day concluded a signal era of patriotism and support for the war effort.

Like the rest of the nation, Trinity entered a growth phase in 1946, when it purchased 470 acres in West Cornwall, Connecticut, for a camp and retreat on the Housatonic River. The Trinity Conference Center currently schedules summer programs and meetings, which offer group and individual relaxation through yoga and meditation, nature walks, throught-provoking film, sacred song, and liturgical dance. In the 1950s, the sizeable ministry added youth programs to the Lower East Side and a quarterly Episcopal magazine, *Trinity News.* In 1967, the church sponsored Trinity Institute, a continuing-education program currently led by the Reverend Dr. Frederic B. Burnham to renew clergy and laity.

ARCHITECTURE

Built in a New World version of English perpendicular, the present Trinity Church combines sandstone and stained glass in a revolutionary high church American neo-Gothic. Resplendent in a dramatic upthrust reminiscent of medieval European cathedrals, it lifts a Gothic cross 281 feet above a square tower at the top of a hexagonal spire that was once the city's highest point. Unlike simpler Puritan edifices, the building glories in pointed arches and a strong vertical presentation devoid of flying buttresses. Twenty turrets line the upper story, separating each element of the clerestory; a similar alignment of turrets and windows enhances the roofline of the first story. In recent years, a thorough wash removed urban grime to uncover a pink luster that must have delighted its original church family.

Through heavy bronze portals created by Viennese artist Karl Bitter, Trinity displays icons and grandeur consistent with its English origins. Below interlaced vault ribbing, worshippers occupy two ranks of carved pews to each side of a wide central aisle. Surrounding stained glass culminates in a chancel window—one of the largest stained-glass expanses in the United States. It portrays Jesus and Saints Peter, Matthew, Mark, Luke, John, and Paul alongside symbols of the Trinity and Eucharist. Behind the carved marble altar adorned with glass mosaics and semiprecious stones, the ornate reredos designed by architect Frederick Clark Withers emphasizes religious figures and a series of uptilted triangles crowned by a central oval. The north and south doors are the work of Scottish artist J. Massey Rhind and Cincinnati native Charles Henry Nieuhaus, sculptor of the Library of Congress.

Medieval touches like the cenotaphs of the Right Reverend Benjamin T. Onderdonk and the Reverend Dr. Morgan Dix summon the austere piety and formalism of such Anglican shrines as Canterbury Cathedral. To the left of the sanctuary, a museum displays a charter signed by William II of England and silver presented by four English monarchs—William and Mary, Queen Anne, and George III. The Chapel of All Saints to the right of the altar displays the artistry of Thomas Nash. In the adjacent room lies the foundation stone from the second Trinity Church and some headstone fragments from the original churchyard. The burying ground features New York City's oldest carved gravestone, dated 1681, a Soldiers' Memorial Monument to unmarked graves of soldiers and sailors, and the Astor Cross, sculpted by Thomas Nash in 1914. In the Trinity Church Cemetery, the newest burial ground, lie naturalist John James Audubon, poet Clement Moore, philanthropist John Jacob Astor, and Alfred, son of novelist Charles Dickens.

ACTIVITIES

Led by the Reverend Daniel Paul Andrews, the flow of missions and worthy projects moved seamlessly from Trinity's colonial past into the last decades of the twentieth century. In 1968, the membership founded Trinity Institute to stimulate inquiry into the interdependence of the church and society. It has welcomed Maya Angelou, Archbishop Desmond Tutu, and the Archbishop of Canterbury to its lectern. The Trinity Grants program, begun in 1971, underwrites varied city and world projects that foster spiritual and community development. Since 1982, St. Paul's Shelter on Broadway and Fulton Street offers transitional shelter and training for up to 14 male residents. A larger mission, St. Margaret's House on Fulton Street, provides shelter, meals, and social services for 250 elderly, disabled, and poor men and women. In 1988, an additional ministry, John Heuss House several blocks southeast at 42 Beaver Street, opened a twenty-four-hour service of support, food, clothing, and showers to homeless and mentally ill street dwellers.

Into the twenty-first century, the church maintains leadership in Christian media and education. Trinity Music schedules cultural arts, concerts, opera, and contemporary music for nursing homes, hospitals, homeless shelters, and treatment facilities. Trinity Parish Preschool and Nursery, opened at 68 Trinity Place in 1979, offers childcare to 75 nursery and preschool children. The church's Hudson Square Noontime Concert and Beethoven Summer Music Festival continue to draw visitors to the Wall Street community. A full-service Christian bookshop, Trinity Bookstore, began stocking religious works in 1983 and caters to the financial district. Since 1985, church media services have enlarged church influence through videotaping and editing for Trinity Television, winner of Emmy and Gabriel Awards, a Religious Public Relations Council citation, and a CINE Golden Eagle for a biography, *Faithful Defiance: A Portrait of Desmond Tutu* (1989). The Episcopal Cathedral Teleconferencing Network began satellite broadcasting in 1992 to beam interactive, live religious programs across North America.

In a tradition developed over three centuries, Trinity Church maintains a standard schedule of worship and holy sacraments. Children's programs enrich learning with creative play, music, and drama. A family choir, organized in 1977, presents four programs each season and one monthly church service. At Saturday rehearsals, the director trains in sight-reading, vocal production, and liturgical procession. In addition to regular worship, the staff leads morning and evening prayer at All Saints' Chapel, communion and healing services, a Discovery Program for youth, premarital counseling, a library resource center, a Friday night film series, and pastoral care. Priests celebrate the Eucharist for homebound members and those in hospitals and nursing homes. Timely outreaches include collections for Kosovan refugees, Alpha evangelism, an AIDS task force, and support of the citywide AIDSWALK. Twelve-step programs benefit those addicted to alcohol, drugs, overeating, and gambling. The Counseling and Human Development Center networks with pastoral psychotherapists at ten city locations to assist victims of emotional illness and addiction.

Sources: Ahlstrom 1972; *Almanac of Famous People* 1998; *Biography Resource Center* 1999; Broderick 1958; Buchanan 1999; *Encyclopedia of World Biography* 1998; Fitch 1973; Ketchum 1957; "Looking Back, Moving Ahead," Pace 1997; "Richard Upjohn"; Snodgrass 1999; "Trinity Church" 1995; Williams, Peter W., 1997; Williams 1999.

Trinity Episcopal Church

Samuel Thames Lloyd III, Rector
Copley Square
Clarendon and Boylston Streets
Boston, Massachusetts 02116
617-536-0944
FAX 617-536-8916
gbadeau@trinitychurchboston.org
www.trinitychurchboston.org/

Boston's historic house of worship Trinity Episcopal Church dominates the cityscape with an energy and mystique uncommon in American architecture. Named one of the ten greatest public buildings in the nation by the American Institute of Architects, Trinity manifests a Franco-Spanish design by Henry Hobson Richardson. Inside, myriad treasures of religious art greet the eye.

HISTORY

Trinity's membership dates to October 17, 1733, and its first church home to 1734, when the congregation sought quarters on Summer Street and Bishop's Alley. In 1829, planners built a first permanent structure in stone Gothic Revival. At the urging of Rector Phillips Brooks—ninth rector of Trinity, sixth Episcopal bishop of Massachusetts, and the composer of "O Little Town of Bethlehem" (1867)—a building committee purchased land at Copley Square in January 1872. The decision was prophetic, for, eight months later, the Boston Fire of November 8 and 9 decimated the original sanctuary.

Trinity folk were lucky in their timing. Unlike others who had no place to turn, the congregation was well into the building process at the time of the disaster and moved temporarily into Huntington Hall, a lecture auditorium at Massachusetts Institute of Technology. On May 20, 1875, when Rector Brooks laid the cornerstone, trustees began supervising an astonishingly rapid construction schedule. Erected on 4,500 piles steadying it on reclaimed land in a Back Bay landfill, the current edifice was ready for occupancy on February 9, 1877. It was the culmination of a competition among six leading architectural firms. For a winning design, the building committee offered a flat $300 in exchange for full rights to the plan.

After Richardson's death, a competitor, Richard Morris Hunt, and Charles McKim oversaw additions and alterations to the original blueprint. In 1897, the firm of Shepley, Rutan, and Coolidge supplied a west porch based on a sketch by Stanford White, designer of the library rotunda of the University of Virginia. The choice of an altar remained unsettled until 1914, when a temporary baldachin and altar replaced a mundane wooden Lord's Table.

A new pulpit replacing the one made by Rector Brooks in 1916 displays carvings of Brooks and four historic preachers—Saint Paul, Saint Chrysostom, Martin Luther, and Bishop Hugh Latimer, martyred at the stake in Oxford in 1555. Another addition, the chancel and refurbished altar, dedicated on December 18, 1938, was the work of Charles D. Maginnis, designer of Boston College's Gasson Hall. A restoration in 1957 retouched delicate tones in the interior art.

ARCHITECTURE

For all its French Romanesque impact, Trinity Church exemplifies unity, proportion, and consistency. The central square lantern tower, weighing 11 million pounds and supported on 2,000 pilings, rises from a modified Greek cross shape to a multisided, red-tiled roof. Its four turreted piers stand on massive granite blocks. An exterior frieze features bas-reliefs of the biblical patriarch Abraham and the prophet Isaiah. Two lesser towers anchor the triple-arched grand portal. At center, modest filigree links four pairs of Corinthian columns in a heavily shadowed entranceway completed in 1897. Ranging out from the square are greenways dotted with trees and modern streetlights, forming an inviting oasis amid Boston skyscrapers.

Unlike that of any other church of its time, the nave grasps the attention with an exuberant grandeur, much of it supplied from the ateliers of France and Great Britain. Seating 1,500 and reaching upward 103 feet, it incorporates carved black walnut beams, wide columns, exposed trusses, and brocaded bands in wine and gilt encircling the rich interior under the clerestory. Depicting scenes of David and Solomon, the holy family, Christ and his parables, the apostles, and Saint Luke are elaborate stenciling and mu-

HENRY HOBSON RICHARDSON

During an era of inconstant tastes, Henry Hobson Richardson developed from experimenter to one of American architecture's pacesetters. Born on September 29, 1838, in St. James, Louisiana, he completed an engineering degree at Harvard. At age twenty-one, he toured the United Kingdom and then became the second American to study at école des Beaux-Arts in Paris before apprenticing with Jules Louis André. Under the direction of Théodore Labrouste, in 1862, Richardson worked on the Hospice d'Ivry outside Paris during the period when a Union blockade prohibited his return to the port of New Orleans.

At war's end, Richardson applied a flair for high Victorian Gothic to city hall in Brookline, Massachusetts, and Chicago's American Merchants' Union Express Company Building. Subsequent construction of the Hampden County Courthouse, North Congregational Church, and Church of Unity in Springfield, Massachusetts; Grace Church in West Medford, Massachusetts; and the Brattle Square Church in Boston preceded the triumph of avant-garde romanticism for Trinity Church. He won the commission by designing a centralized Byzantine Greek cross adapted from his personal touchstone, St. Mark's Cathedral in Venice. He embellished the basic plan with texture and detail from Spain's Salamanca Cathedral, French Auvergne style, and the Provençal churches of Saint-Gilles-du-Gard and St. Trophime at Arles. When he died on April 27, 1886, Richardson was a financial failure, but he had achieved a Romanesque individuality that set American civic and church architecture on its own course.

rals on the tower walls, over arches and lancet windows, and in the nave and west vestibule. The list of artists is impressive—John La Farge; Henry Holiday; Eugene Oudinot of Paris, Cottier and Company, and Heaton, Butler, and Bayne of England; and London artists Clayton and Bell, and Burlison and Grills. The stained-glass windows come from Boston artist Margaret Redmond and the collaboration of England's pre-Raphaelite masters, William Morris and Edward Burne-Jones, who produced exquisite images of David and Solomon for the baptistery window. In the gallery, an organ built in 1926 by the Skinner Organ Company pairs with a new chancel organ by Aeolian Skinner company, which Sir William McKie dedicated on November 17, 1963. A three-manual console behind the rector's stall controls the total sound system of 6,898 pipes, which vary from an inch to 32 feet high.

The artistry augments a design that is remarkably suited to enhancement. Bas-relief under the apse windows presents images ot Saint Paul before Agrippa, Saint Athanasius at the Council of Nicaea, Saint Augustine, Saint Francis and the beggar, John Wycliffe, John Wesley, and Phillips Brooks. In the baptistery stands Daniel Chester French's bust of Brooks. Augustus Saint-Gaudens designed a second statue of Brooks, which stands outside the north transept.

ACTIVITIES

Under the leadership of Rector Samuel Thames Lloyd III, Trinity offers a full Sabbath schedule, beginning at 7:45 A.M. with communion and a homily and continuing with services at 9:00 and 11:00 A.M. and 6:00 P.M. The Parish and Trinity choirs and Canterbury Singers lead the music program, which also welcomes visiting choirs and musicians. A beloved Christmas tradition, the Trinity candlelight service, takes place the Sunday preceding Christmas. Free organ recitals welcome walk-in visitors on Friday at 12:15 P.M. Volunteers host tours at noon on Sunday.

Trinity looms large on the city scene. Stewardship reaches out to public schools, shelters, and soup kitchens. Through partnering with other social welfare agencies, Trinitarians support Habitat for Humanity, rehabilitation of young males incarcerated for major crimes, and a monthly evening of pizza, popcorn, and movies for the homeless. In cooperation with the Greater Boston Interfaith Organization, members sponsor housing for the needy. A grants committee offers stipends from $1,000 to $5,000 for worthy altruistic endeavors.

Sources: *Almanac of Famous People* 1998; *Biography Resource Center* 1999; Boulton 1992; *Encyclopedia of World Biography* 1998; Falk 1985; Mutrux 1982; O'Gorman 1997; Pettys 1985; Smith 1989; "Trinity Church in the City of Boston"; Williams, Peter W., 1997; Williams 1999.

Triumph Church and New Life Christian Fellowship

Dan and Sue Landry, Co-Pastors
P.O. Box 821271
Vicksburg, Mississippi 39182
4305 I-20 Frontage Road
Vicksburg, Mississippi 39180
601-636-5282
triumph@vicksburg.com
www.vicksburg.com/~triumph

Renowned for southern hospitality, acceptance, and forgiveness to the community, Triumph Church and New Life Christian Fellowship models a charismatic self-confidence in Vicksburg, a Mississippi River city once torn by civil war. Hosting Pastor Dan Landry's compassion and care from "the crack house to the penthouse," the church is a nondenominational, multicultural spiritual center that accepts as a mission all the people in a sixty-mile radius of the city. (church brochure, n.d.) Located near the Vicksburg National Military Park only blocks from the Mississippi River, the congregation offers a church home to all, regardless of previous religious experience, denomination, worship style, race, or socioeconomic background.

The staff refuses to alter aims to comply with the pressures of a neo-Nazi group, which damaged the integrated New Life Christian Fellowship on Mount Alban Road on a Saturday night spree on March 19, 1995. The anonymous vandals smashed the sanctuary's glass front and left racist and swastika-waving literature in the parking lot, at a school and Sav-A-Center grocery, and throughout a residential section. Their motive appears to have been outrage that 30 percent of Triumph members are nonwhite. A month later, the perpetrators slashed a cat's throat at the ministers' doorstep. With only a mailing address of NSDAP, a Nazi organization in Lincoln, Nebraska, as evidence, police questioned suspects from hate groups distributing "prowhite" literature, but found no direct links to the Vicksburg incident.

Terrorism made no inroads toward suppressing Triumph Church. In a letter from the church office, secretary Carol Anne Marble declared,

There is much social persecution suffered by black and white members from their families and other associates, but the fruit of the labor is well worth it. But we know that the Lord sent the Landrys and others here for a work, and He has encouraged us by sending hungry souls and granting salvation to hundreds of souls during these last five years. We also have multitudes of testimonies of people receiving financial blessings, physical healings, and miracles of many kinds. (letter, December 7, 1999)

The church's stance received the backing of its religious neighbors: Mormon, Catholic, Methodist, Presbyterian, Baptist, Episcopalian, Christian, Greek Orthodox, and Jewish. Pastor Dan Landry wrote a letter to the *Vicksburg Post* acknowledging the outpouring of support that enabled "God's Church to stand united." (letter, undated)

BELIEFS

In charismatic tradition, Triumph Church offers energetic "revival-style" preaching, strengthened by testimony, compassion, and intercessory gifts of the Holy Spirit. The network of love and support for the hurting, lost, and underprivileged enfolds an array of seekers—workers on Mississippi gambling boats, gang members, and women hardened by profligacy and loss of self-respect. To remove the pain of the past, the pastors stress Christian salvation through belief in Jesus Christ. To manifest a change of heart, newcomers accept repentance, confession, baptism in water and in the Holy Spirit, and a life of obedience, faith, and fellowship with other Christians.

Typical of worship at Triumph Church are the actions of spirit-moved worshippers—the raising of hands in prayer, singing and clapping, speaking in tongues, dancing and playing musical instruments, and physical response to God. Those seized by emotion experience a state of weeping and collapse known as "slain in the spirit." To generate healing, members pray for the sick and perform a dynamic "laying on of hands," a personal application of faith's curative power.

ACTIVITIES

Triumph follows the usual Protestant schedule of church school and Sunday morning worship from 10:00 A.M. to noon and an Old South tradition of Sunday evening worship from 6:00 to 8:00 P.M. Adjunct services consist of Ladies' Lunch Hour Prayer and choir rehearsal along with junior and ladies' dance practice on Tuesday and prayer meeting Wednesday from 6:15 to 8:30 P.M., which begins with informal prayer and meditation, followed by group intercessionary prayer and healing. Adults attend the midweek Life Application School of the Bible for lectures on marital growth, financial maturity, biblical interpretation, and health and spiritual topics. A parallel Eternity Youth Service involves teens in upbeat praise and topical messages; the youngest children attend entertaining and educational programs, skits, and shows.

Members conduct missions at home and around the globe. For the community's hungry, they extend the Feed My Sheep Program, which distributes food at 9:00 A.M. on the third Tuesday of each month. Sponsored by the Mississippi Food Network, the bags contain free staples from USDA pantries. The Watchmen program, another community mission, divides members into groups of twenty families and individuals to monitor attendance, promote spiritual growth and well-being, and render Christian assistance to the needy and prisoners. An asset to the church's spiritual armory is Triumph Bookstore, which stocks works by Christian authors for sale a half hour before and after each service. Beyond the church walls, Gene Johnson and other members support River City Rescue Mission, which has harbored families, offered vocational training and financial assistance, countered substance abuse, and housed men since 1991 and which serves 1,400 meals per month to any who ask for food.

Services led by the pastors concentrate on healing, help, praise, and worship and gird the faithful for spiritual and personal challenge through down-to-earth, family-centered programs. Marriage encounter sessions foster healthy home life by encouraging postive change:

- Improved communication between husband and wife
- Right attitudes toward marriage and individual aims
- Forgiveness that moves past hurts
- Exposure of manipulation to promote honest relationships
- Leaving childhood baggage behind

• Understanding and meeting each other's needs

Children meet twice a month for Sonshine Kids Club; Triumphant Teens gather for activities, Bible study, and personal and group counseling. For male members, a leadership builder, Men of Wisdom, meets the first Saturday of the month for fellowship. A fourth program, Crown Ministry Financial Planning, demonstrates a growing movement toward Christian money management. Additional activities, such as the Christmas performance of *In His Presence,* provide an outlet for creativity and individual enthusiasm. Signers for the deaf aid the hearing impaired; a bus ministry brings youth from several outlying neighborhoods to regular services and special events. To enhance gospel teachings, an interpretive dance and drama team acts out the spirit of scripture. A hospitality team offers visitors refreshments and friendship. Groups design fabric banners encouraging worship and praise during worship services. Old-fashioned dinner on the ground brings the church body together for a picnic and fellowship.

Sources: Ahlstrom 1972; Gallaspy 1995; "Neo-Nazi Ideology 1998"; Stockstill February 26, 1995, March 1995; "Triumph Church."

Tsubaki America Shrine

Reverend Doctor Yukitaka Yamamoto,
High Priest
1545 West Alpine
Stockton, California 95204
209-466-5323
FAX 209-463-1826
tsubakiamerica@bigplanet.com
www.kannagara.org/GujiSan.htm

One of America's peaceful, reassuring religious sites is the Tsubaki shrine. It is named the Tsubaki America Shrine to distinguish it from the parent site, the Tsubaki Grand Shrine in Mie, Japan. As a part of everyday society, the California shrine offers participatory polytheistic ritual to make contact with spirits of the animate and inanimate world, offer thanks, and ask forgiveness. In traditional Asian style, the site opens on a *torii,* a double-linteled ceremonial gate through

which visitors enter a hallowed enclosure. After walking the *sando,* or approach pathway, to the shrine itself, worshippers attend ceremonies led by priests, who offer food and flowers at the shrine of the *kami,* Japanese nature gods.

HISTORY AND BELIEFS

Shinto, or "the God way," is a theanthropic religion—a merger of the mystic and the concrete. Its doctrine is a primal awareness of the self and the world. Through age-old festivals, rituals, and symbols, it evidences a mind-set that is the essence of Japan but also applies to other people and places. At the heart of worship are the *kami,* divine beings and protectors who inspire wonder and gratitude, and Daishizen, a concept of the cosmos. Pursuit of the divine way and a balanced life in the cosmos is known as *kannagara,* an outlook marked by harmony, peace, and fulfillment. Achievement of a sense of completion and purity does not derive from preaching, creeds, scripture, or dogma. Instead, priests perform ancient rituals of thanksgiving and purification that become a nonverbal foundation for life.

The Shinto purification ceremony precedes religious functions and events. As honor to the ancestral *kami,* it restores a heavenly state by removing sins and earthly contaminants. At the Tsubaki Grand Shrine in Japan, priests stand under the sacred waterfall as a form of ascetic cleansing; worshippers stop by an ablution basin to wash their hands and mouth. For followers to emulate deity, they must return to a childlike state. The ideal is a rigorous self-discipline that promotes righteousness, tolerance, and right thinking that seeks prosperity for all creation.

Another custom associated with Shintoism is the ceremonial tea. Around 1000 A.D., the Japanese imported the Chinese custom of refreshing themselves with tea. The highly mannered tea ceremony cultivates good feelings by harmonizing human relations. The *wabi,* or spirit of the tea ceremony, reduces aggression and stress by centering the mind on calm and mutual respect. In the sixteenth century, Sen-no-Rikyu formalized the ceremony, which became a Japanese tradition, but not a religion.

To further a beneficial encounter between national groups and religions and to promote and understanding of Shinto and its goal of

One of America's peaceful, reassuring religious sites is the Tsubaki America Shrine in Stockton, California. (Courtesy Tsubaki Grand Shrine of America)

world peace, the Reverend Doctor Yukitaka Yamamoto, former high priest of the Tsubaki Grand Shrine, brought Shintoism to the United States. In 1979, he founded a nonprofit American *jinja* (shrine) for the state of California. He wrote *The Way of the Kami* (1999) to relieve American suspicion of unfamiliar Japanese customs, which critics during World War II maligned as nationalistic fanaticism.

In 1987, the Reverend Doctor Yamamoto's consortium purchased property in Stockton, California, and built an outdoor shrine and Tsubaki House, a culture center joining American and Japanese customs. Exalted in the garden are the *kami* of pioneering and guidance; Sarutahiko, the sun *kami;* Amaterasu Ohmikami, the harmony *kami;* Ame No Uzume No Mikoto, the *kami* of the land of America; and Ukanomitamano-kami, the *kami* of the life source. Since the opening of the American shrine, four priests and their families have served the California project.

ACTIVITIES

The staff of the Tsubaki American Shrine observes a ritual calendar of events. On January 1,

they conduct Saitan-sai welcoming the New Year. On February 3, they honor the arrival of spring with Setsubun-sai, Mamemaki-Shinji, and a bean-throwing festival. Later in the month at Kinen-sai, they pray that the unsown rice will net a good harvest. Also in February are Yakuyoke-taisai rituals for men aged twenty-five to forty-two and women aged nineteen to thirty-three. The spring ritual, Shunki-taisai, precedes the May celebration of Chinza-taisai, the anniversary of the founding of the American shrine. At the end of June, staff conducts the great purification at Nagoshi-no-Oharai. The fall ceremony, Syuki-taisai, occurs early in October, five weeks before the November Hichi-Go-san-sai, a "Five, Seven, and Three Festival" honoring boys aged three and five and girls aged three and seven. December 4 brings two rituals—the Oharai-siki purification ceremony and Mochi-tsuki, the ritual making of rice cakes.

In spring and fall, the staff invite visitors to the Oharai ceremony, a re-creation of the ablutions of the ancestral *kami,* Izanagi-no-Mikoto (He Who Invites). According to Shinto scripture, Kojiki (Record of Ancient Matters), com-

piled from oral tradition in 712, the *kami* purified themselves in divine waters to remove
worldly impurities. The shrine's Web site pictorial explanation clarifies the following parts of
the rite:

- *Shubatu* (purification)—priests cleanse offerings and participants.
- *Ippai* (ritual bow)—the priest bows to the
  kami, honoring the beneficent powers of
  nature.
- *Kaihi*—the priest performs a ritual opening of the shrine door.
- *Kensen* (presentation)—the kami presents
  sacred food items from the sea, river, plain,
  mountain, and human gardens, such as
  rice, sake, salt, water, fruit, and vegetables.
- *Nurito-sojo* (prayer)—Priests recite a
  norito, a statement of ritual significance and
  a plea for peace, happiness, and prosperity
  for spectators.
- *Tamagushi-hairei* (formal worship)—The
  presenter holds a branch in both hands,
  bows, rotates it clockwise with leaves toward the spectators, bows twice, claps
  twice, and bows again.
- *Tessen* (removal)—Priests remove the food
  offering.

- *Heihi* (closure)—Priests close the portal.
- *Ippai* (ritual bow)—Priests make formal
  obeisance to the *kami.*

At the end of the Oharai, spectators enter the
house to greet priests and each other.

In addition to ceremonies, the staff conducts
public education by mailing a monthly Japanese
newsletter, *Tsubaki Shinbun,* and the quarterly
Tsubaki America News. Priests meet monthly
with Japanese religious leaders, host visits of
public school and university students, and engage in interfaith ceremonies, workshops, publications, videos, and visitations. In summer 1999,
the Reverend Doctor Yamamoto represented
Tsubaki America at the Congress of International Association for Religious Freedom in
Vancouver, British Columbia. After conducting
a Shinto workshop, he conducted rites at a
portable shrine.

See also Kannagara Jinja.

Sources: Bowker 1997; "Center for Shinto Studies
and Japanese Culture" 1998; Eck 1994; *Eerdmans'
Handbook to the World's Religions* 1982; Piggott 1973;
Sonoda n.d.; Tsumuro 1988; *World Religions* 1998;
Yamamoto, 1999.

religious tolerance. His description of the church is the third stage in human life on earth, a restorative era following creation and the fall of humankind into depravity and rootlessness. Central to his vision of world peace is a rejuvenation of the family through the union of sincere couples dedicated to marriage and a stable home and the end to widespread adultery, abandonment, separation, and divorce. To achieve these expansive goals, the church centers activity on mass weddings, recruitment, fund-raising, and promulgation of the claim that the Reverend Moon is the anticipated messiah.

Unification Church

4 West Forty-third Street
New York, New York 10036
212-997-0050 ext. 213
pr@hsanahq.org
www.unification.org

Listed officially as the Holy Spirit Association for the Unification of World Christianity, the church created by the Reverend Sun Myung Moon is one of the nation's richest and most controversial new religions. Known in Asia as the Tong Il Movement and in the Americas as Moonies or the Unified Family, it has taken as its goal the worldwide alliance of all denominations by ridding them of any variances from basic Christianity. The ultimate end is theocracy, a supreme religion ruling the world.

From the beginning, the serene exterior of the Reverend Moon's organization has produced dissimilar interpretations of his rapidly growing faith. Some see it as a syncretic religion that combines Korean Confucianism with Christian principles to generate a "Kingdom of Sky on Earth." Those who fear the Reverend Moon's power over large groups of young disciples aged eighteen to thirty describe the church at best as exploitive of the unwary and at worst as a dictatorial cult.

BELIEFS

The Reverend Moon sees himself as the Lord of the Second Advent, an incarnation of prophecy on earth to complete the work begun by Jesus and tragically cut short by his crucifixion. According to Moon's principles, as stated in Young Oon Kim's *The Divine Principles* (1956), the Unification Church intends to promote understanding, appreciate religious diversity, and foster

ACTIVITIES

The Unification Church lost face in the world in the late 1990s from multiple obstacles but continued the mass nuptials followed by forty days of sexual abstinence that are the Reverend Moon's trademark. On June 13, 1998, he united 7,000 couples at New York City's Madison Square Garden. His public pursuit of more nuptials offset damaging rumors of a sumptuous lifestyle and of impropriety and estrangement in his own marriage. He weathered a virulent separation from daughters Un Jin and Sun Jin and daughter-in-law Nansook Hong, who left home and repudiated arranged marriages. Nansook Hong published *In the Shadow of the Moons* (1998), a gossipy excoriation of family and church tyranny. More difficulties plagued the church in the late 1990s, beginning with expulsion from Venezuela and banning of the church in 1997. In December 1998, five Asian companies of Tong Il, the Reverend Moon's eleven-member conglomerate, declared bankruptcy. Complaints of overly aggressive recruitment on the University of Maryland's campus brought additional negative publicity.

At the end of the twentieth century, the Reverend Moon worked energetically toward family ethics and world peace by uniting 40,000 in marriage at a February mass wedding in 1999 and by calling for a United Nations-based global coalition to end war through religious, educational, and cultural means. Within the church's Family Federation for World Peace and Unifica-

REVEREND SUN MYUNG MOON

A charismatic evangelist and visionary, the Reverend Sun Myung Moon bases his theology on the belief that impiety on earth is delaying Christ's promised second coming to reclaim humankind. Born to a Presbyterian family on January 6, 1920, in Kwangju Sangsa Ri, North Korea, Moon experienced a vision of Jesus on Easter 1936 and subsequent encounters with Moses, the Buddha, and God. He began molding his career as an evangelist while enrolled in engineering courses at Watseka University. For six months, he studied with a Korean messiah, Paik Moon Kim, at a Christian monastery. Moon left the Korean Presbyterian faith in 1948 and led an independent mission to North Korea. He survived persecution and torture by Communists, who deny the existence of a divine power. During the Korean War, a United Nations force released him from two and a half years at hard labor.

In 1954, the Reverend Sun Myung Moon founded his religion in Pusan, South Korea, and quickly gained a hold in Japan. In 1960, his marriage to Hak Ja Han and the establishment of a family of twelve children presented the image of the true family that his faith extols. Despite repeated arrests, he spread the Unification ministry in the 1960s by dispatching disciple Young Oon Kim to begin recruitment in Eugene, Oregon, and throughout the world. The Reverend Sun Myung Moon reached his first triumph in the United States through the 1971–1972 "Day of Hope" tour, which energized the movement. Young people began joining in large numbers. After he emigrated to the United States in 1972, he ran ads in major newspapers and organized his famous Moonies to sell candy, candles, potted plants, and cut flowers to raise funds for his campaign. He announced that his disciples numbered 30,000 within four years and his treasury topped $20 million.

The Reverend Sun Myung Moon bought a twenty-acre manor in New York as his home and headquarters. From there, he ran a theological seminary, fishing and ginseng companies, the New Yorker Hotel and other investment properties, the Little Angels dance troupe, the Go World Brass Band, newspapers in New York and Washington, D.C., and such benevolences as Church and Social Action and Project Volunteer. In the press, he appeared among powerful members of Congress, President Richard Nixon, General Alexander Haig, and President George Bush but came under attack for directing a huge volunteer staff of neat, pink-cheeked, middle-class disciples. The July 1983 issue of *New Republic* quotes Moon's tentative self-identification as the real messiah.

Stiff opposition to the Reverend Sun Myung Moon's clout derived from the South Korean Intelligence Agency, which suspected him of stockpiling weapons for world takeover, and from anticult and deprogramming groups, in particular, the Watchman Fellowship, Trancenet on Unificationism, and disgruntled individuals who had left the church to denounce it and seek its downfall. Responding to the complaints of parents concerned for youth involved in the Unification Church, the U.S. government launched investigations, which culminated in the Reverend Sun Myung Moon's conviction of tax evasion and a thirteen-month prison term in Danbury, Connecticut, ending in with his release in 1985. He immediately resumed a series of lectures and globetrotting, publications, broadcasts, and Internet sites.

tion, staff debated social problems, in particular, shifts in family structure and stability and a lapse in individual purity and righteousness. To carry this theme onto the stage, programmers scheduled songs by the Little Angels of Korea chorus. In spring 1999, the Reverend Sun Myung Moon and his wife held a large blessing of couples in Seoul, Korea, and telecast the ritual over satellite communications and the Internet. In May, he continued the Unification world campaign by addressing groups in Uruguay and Chile.

Sources: Appel 1983; Barker 1984, 1996; Beverly 1998; *Biography Resource Center* 1999; Collins 1999; Dorsey 1999; *Encyclopedia of Occultism and Parapsychology* 1996; *Encyclopedia of World Biography* 1998; Johnson 1984; Laver and Kaihla 1995; Lewis 1998; MacHarg 1997; Melton 1992; "Moon Struck" 1998; *Religious Leaders of America* 1999; Rice 1982; Singer and Lalich 1995; "South Korean Business: The Eclipse of the Moon, Inc." 1998; Talbot 1997; "The Unification Church," http:// cti.itc.virginia.edu/ 1999; "The Unification Church," http://www.unification.org 1999; Waldrep 1996; *World Religions* 1998; Zeinert 1997.

Listed officially as the Holy Spirit Association for the Unification of World Christianity, the church created by the Reverend Sun Myung Moon is one of the nation's richest and most controversial new religions. (Corbis-Bettmann)

Universal Peace Buddha Temple of New York

Venerable Sayadaw Ashin Indaka
619 Bergen Street
Brooklyn, New York 11238

Mahasi Retreat Center
63 Gordan's Corner Road
Manaplan, New Jersey 07726
732-792-1484
FAX 732-792-1484

The Universal Peace Buddha Temple of New York, like newly introduced sects of the past, got its start as a storefront operation serving an immigrant population two blocks from the Bergen Street subway station. The temple was the project of the Venerable Sayadaw Ashin Indaka, an experienced monk, scholarly writer, and teacher. To serve the growing Asian community of New York City, he follows the teaching of the Buddha to do no evil, cultivate good, and purify the mind.

HISTORY

Borne by missionaries from India around the fifth century A.D., Burma's branch of Buddhism developed from Hinayana or Theravada beliefs. Because of the abuses of priests of the Tantric branch of Buddhism, Hinayana quickly took precedence. In 1044, King Anawrahta unified the Burmese, converted to ascetic Hinayana Buddhism, and adopted it as a state religion. His reign produced temples and a state supervisory. The faith lost its strict organization over centuries of political disorder and then returned to a former height in 1472 under Dammazedi, who dispatched monks to Sri Lanka to renew ties with Southeast Asian orthodoxy.

Buddhism remained at the forefront of Burmese life until 1885, when the British colonized Upper Burma and disbanded the state religious hierarchy as a discouragement of strong nationalism. When Burma gained independence in 1948, Buddhism returned to preeminence among 90 percent of the people. From 1961 to 1971, the faith gained a respected proponent in diplomat U Thant, secretary general of the United Nations.

When the faith advanced to New York City, in August 19, 1981, the American Burma Buddhist Association adopted a simple aim of preserving culture among Burmese immigrants to

SAYADAW ASHIN INDAKA

The Venerable Sayadaw Ashin Indaka, born in Burma on August 11, 1940, joined the Buddhist order at age twenty. He completed a monastic education at Pajjotarama Pali University and mastered language and Buddhism. At the outset of his career, he taught *dhamma,* the Buddhist concept of cosmic order. In 1973, he opened a meditation center at Tachileik in eastern Burma and excelled at the theory and practice of meditation according to Theravada beliefs, the fundamentals taught by the Buddha himself. After twenty years as a monk, he entered twelve weeks of intense training in Vipassana, or Thai meditation, with the Most Venerable Mahasi Sayadaw, the great rejuvenator of Hinayana Buddhism, a southern branch of the faith that promotes detachment from self.

Fortified by experience and training, in 1982, Indaka accepted a post in the United States as resident monk and meditation instruction at the Buddhist Temple of Tennessee. The next year, he accepted an invitation from the Burmese community in New York City to supervise worship in Brooklyn. As founder of the temple and creator of the Mahasi Meditation Center, he offers courses on Sutra and Abhidhamma, the thematic arrangement of Buddhist scripture, to Burmese and American members and instructs them in insight meditation. In addition to education, he publishes articles on Buddhism.

the United States. Staff established the Universal Peace Buddha Temple in an unassuming four-story brick building. On the top floor, planners created an atmosphere of worship and meditation by installing a four-foot brass statue of the Burmese Buddha on a lacquered and gilded throne of teakwood. The sacred site receives offerings of flowers and food as well as incense. Staff has launched a fund drive to construct a pagoda and meditation *dhamma* hall at the Mahasi Meditation Retreat Center, a frame farmhouse in rural Manaplan, New Jersey.

ACTIVITIES

The annual calendar schedules a January New Year ceremony, a prayer and meditation ritual that cultivates loving kindness toward all creation, and a March Htamane Pye Daw, a social event marked by the making and eating of a seasonal dish formed of sticky rice, oil, sesame seeds, peanuts, and coconut. Spring brings Buddha Day to commemorate the Buddha's birth, enlightenment, and *parinibbana,* the release into enlightenment, and Thingyan, or Burmese New Year festival, in May, a time for performing meritorious deeds and sprinkling fellow celebrants with Thingyan water. The last half of the year brings Wazo in July to offer robes to monks for a three-month temple rainy season retreat, and the Kathina ritual in November, which also bestows robes and other essentials on monks.

To maintain communication with worshippers, the American Burma Buddhist Association meets the first Sunday of each month to plan activities. Staff maintains congregation interest through news and announcements in the *Lokachamtha,* the association newsletter, issued quarterly in Burmese and English. On the second Sunday of each month, monks conduct *dhamma* talks based on Buddhist philosophy and practice. On Saturdays, as a means of transmitting Burmese traditions and culture, monks hold classes for children in Burmese language and Buddhist principles.

In addition to its temple and lectures, the American Burma Buddhist Association maintains the Mahasi Retreat Center for religious and social activities. The spacious rural setting suits the practice of Vipassana, or Thai meditation, an insightful reflection led by temple monks. On Saturdays, shrine officials coordinate a Buddhist service and sitting meditation at 5:00 A.M. and 6:00 P.M. These sessions are open to the public.

Sources: *Biography Resource Center* 1999; *Eerdmans' Handbook to the World's Religions* 1982; *Encyclopedia of World Biography* 1998; Epstein; Herbrechtsmeier 1993; Ling 1972; *New Catholic Encyclopedia* 1967; Smith 1995; "Theravada Buddhism;" *World Religions* 1998.

Ursuline Convent

Alice Cangelosi, Archivist
1100 Chartres Street
New Orleans, Louisiana 70116
504-529-3040

One of many American religious sites that have undergone a transformation, the Ursuline Convent on State Street in New Orleans, a registered National Historic Landmark, has passed through various stages on its way to the twenty-first century. It owes ongoing joyful service and spiritual uplift to the Ursuline sisters. Honoring the name of Saint Ursula, patron of women's education, the convent served the territory's first community of female religious, who escorted prospective French brides to Louisiana and chaperoned them until they found husbands. The oldest building in the Mississippi Valley and the only structure to survive from French colonial times, the convent is a quarter century older than the United States and 200 years older than the women's movement. A woman-centered endeavor, the convent pioneered a series of national firsts benefiting women and children:

- First orphanage and day nursery
- First free school for slaves and Indian girls
- First women's shelter
- First headquarters for a Sodality of Our Lady for Catholic Women

Like the Christian religious houses of Europe, which sheltered the poor and succored fallen crusaders in the early Middle Ages, the convent was a reception center for wounded British soldiers and way station for poor Acadians and dispossessed Indians and blacks, who sought food, clothing, and refuge. To prestigious visitors of New Orleans, a call at the convent was an essential part of a New World tour. For this reason, the nuns welcomed Louis Philippe, Duc d'Orlèans and later king of France; Aaron Burr, U.S. vice president; President James Madison; Mother Philippine Rose Duchesne, founder of America's Society of the Sacred Heart; Mother Cornelia Peacock Connelly, founder of the Society of the Holy Child Jesus; the poet-missionary Abbé Adrien Emmanuel Rouquette; Confederate poet and editor Father Abram Ryan; Father Isaac Thomas Hecker, founder of the Paulist Fathers; Mother Frances Xavier Cabrini, the first American saint; French President Giscard d'Estaing and his wife, Anne-Aymone; as well as Henriette Delille, New Orleans's own saint-in-the-making.

The complex consists of the original hall, a kitchen and laundry, bishops' service building, porter's lodge, and warehouse plus the remains of a seminary and garden. Adjacent to the convent is St. Mary's Church, a national shrine and active nonparochial worship site. The chain of worshippers initiated by the nuns progressed from French pioneers through Spanish, Creole, Irish, German, Slavonian, and Italian settlers as well as Native Americans and black slaves. At present, the property is open to all neighbors and visitors. As the shrine of Our Lady of Prompt Succor, the church houses the patroness of both the city of New Orleans and the state of Louisiana.

HISTORY

Established in the old French colonial capital of New Orleans, the convent merged a military installation with a godly mission. Newly arrived from Rouen, France, aboard *La Gironde* on August 7, 1727, to staff a hospital and educate and catechize Catholic girls, twelve Ursuline sisters began their service to New Orleans at Kolly Townhouse, bringing with them a French clock that is still on display. One of the coterie, Sister Francis Xavier, became the first female pharmacist in the Western Hemisphere; another, Sister Saint Stanislaus, originally Marie-Madeleine Hachard, the state's first female author, published *Relation du Voyage des Dames Ursulines de Rouen a la N'lle Orleans* (Recounting the Voyage of the Ursuline Nuns from Rouen to New Orleans) (1727).

To house the newcomers properly, Père Nicolas Ignace de Beaubois bought temporary quarters on Bienville and Chartres Streets. At Easter 1729, the women initiated hospital work. Constructed next to the hospital by royal charter in July 1734, a second building on Decatur Street flourished from 1734 to 1752. Led by Governor Jean Baptiste Lemoyne de Bienville and other dignitaries, the sisters progressed from their old house down Chartres Street to the parish church before moving on to the new

MOTHER HENRIETTE DELILLE

Integral to the history of the Ursuline Convent is the work of evangelist Henriette Delille, *une femme de couleur libre* (a free-born woman of color), social worker, and educator who took holy vows in 1836 and dedicated herself to helping slaves. Born in 1812 to Jean Baptiste Delille-Sarpy and Marie Josephe Diaz (alternatively given as Pouponne Dias), a free-born quadroon, she came from a long line of strong women. Her great great grandmother, Marianne Nanette Piquery, was the slave mistress of Etienne Dubreuil, planter and royal engineer who designed local canals and levees. On October 16, 1763, for 2,800 livres, Nanette bought the freedom of her daughter, Cecile Dubreuil, and two grandchildren, Henriette Laveau and Narciso, from Dubreuil's son Claude Joseph Villars. Trained in herbalism and nursing, Delille followed the family tradition of baptizing slave children and standing as their godmother. At age seventeen, she followed the example of Sister Saint Marthe Fontier and chose a celibate life.

A rebel against class and color, Delille joined Cuban missionary Juliette Gaudin, Josephine Charles, and Susanne Navarre in a biracial mission to catechize and succor New Orleans slaves and free-born blacks. On November 21, 1842, Delille founded the Sisters of the Holy Family, a confraternity of black female parish aides to the destitute black population of New Orleans, with herself as mother superior. A branch of the sisters recruited free blacks in a society that operated a girls' school. After Mother Delille's death in 1862, the community flourished as mother house to schools, orphanages, and retirement homes in Louisiana, Texas, California, Washington, D.C., and Belize, Central America.

In the second half of the twentieth century, Sister Audrey Marie Detiege researched the life of Henriette Delille. She published a preliminary monograph, *Henriette Delille: Free Woman of Color* (1976), but died without completing a definitive biography. One purpose of Detiege's investigation was the furtherance of Delille's canonization, which began in 1989. She became the first native-born black American nominated for sainthood in the Catholic Church.

convent, which fronted on the thriving Mississippi Delta.

The new building projected a grand image in *briqueté entre poteaux* (brickwork between posts), erected by French colonial chief engineer Ignace François Broutin and his army staff. A multipurpose three-story hall beneath a central turret and two chimneys, it featured an orphans' infirmary, classrooms, a dining hall, and a dormitory on the ground floor, where the sisters mothered thirty orphaned children surviving a Natchez Indian massacre at Fort Rosalie. The staff operated a parallel school for the city's elite, the daughters of moneyed planters, as well as black and Indian girls, who learned the art of turning silkworm cocoons into silk. Among the privileged learning music, manners, literature, and homemaking was Micaëla Leonarda Almonester, future Baroness Pontalba, New Orleans philanthropist and builder of row houses along Jackson Square.

Central to historical significance is a graciously curved cypress staircase, a surviving element of a building erected in 1727, which led to the nuns' quarters, library, sewing room, head nurse's station, and nuns' sick room. The building opened directly into the hospital on the east side for ease of access to sick and injured soldiers, whose number had risen from 30 to 120 because of the sisters' reputation for beauty, tender hearts, and quality bedside care.

Because the first permanent convent crumbled from humidity and weather, a replacement cloister took shape at right angles to its predecessor in 1752 and remained in service until 1824. Built by Broutin's corps, it featured more substantial stuccoed brick walls. On Good Friday, March 21, 1788, when a candle ignited lace altar draperies in the home of military treasurer Vincente José Nunez on Chartres Street, the spreading conflagration leveled 856 homes and the Church of St. Louis and threatened the convent. Père Antoine formed a slave-manned bucket brigade to save the Royal Hospital, barracks, and Ursuline chapter house.

Less reassuring to the community was the tenuous state of the French regime after Napoleon's rise. In May 1803, twenty-seven nuns split into two cells: fifteen sisters and the mother superior boarded a ship for Cuba; the remaining eleven stayed in New Orleans. When the territory passed to the United States in December, the city faction received a handwritten letter of encouragement, friendship, and respect from President Thomas Jefferson, who asked the convent to continue service as teachers of young women. Throughout these alterations, the Ursuline Convent witnessed significant moments in southern and United States History. One such moment was the night of prayer in 1815, when General Andrew "Old Hickory" Jackson triumphed over the British in a lopsided victory at the Battle of New Orleans. The general thanked the nuns in person for their intercessory vigil.

By 1820, when the city voted to extend Chartres and Hospital Streets, bisecting the original plot, the Ursulines at first fought the city council and then opted to resettle at a new location two miles downriver at the former Duplessis Plantation. They completed the move in 1824. The former convent became the see's first permanent archbishop's residence, which also housed a vicar general, two priests, visitors, and servants. In a turnabout from the river to the opposite direction, Bishop Louis du Bourg reestablished the entrance from Decatur to Ursulines Street and rented the ground floor to a private school. In 1827, the building became a public school; from 1831 to 1834, it hosted Louisiana state legislators. In 1936, the Vieux Carré Commission promoted reclamation of buidlings like the Ursuline Convent, which retained the flavor and purpose of the original colonies. With a grant from the National Park Service and the assistance of Myldred Masson Costa and other alumnae of the girls' school, who named themselves the Old Ursuline Convent Guild, the buildings entered a new era.

ARCHITECTURE

During the migration of Ursuline sisters from building to building, their chapel passed through its own incarnations. The first structure, named L'Ancienne Eglise (The Ancient Church)—formally Our Lady of Victories—was a small building opened around 1749 at the corner of Decatur and Ursulines Streets and in service until the 1830s. In 1786, the Almonester Chapel, donated by Don Andrés Almonester, adjoined the second convent building and featured Gothic windows set with colored glass and a pitched roof supported by columns. An unpretentious parish church, it became the temporary St. Louis Church, or bishop's church, after fire destroyed the original structure. The chapel later served as a seminary and school for Italian immigrant children, taught by Scalabrini fathers. In 1810, Mother Michel Gensoul installed a statue, *Our Lady of Prompt Succor;* in 1828, Bishop Rosati enlarged the original floor plan. Its plain façade displays classical elements selected by French architect-designer J. N. B. de Pouilly, company architect and city planner for the New Orleans Improvement Company. He was the original designer of St. Louis Cathedral as well as the St. Louis Hotel, Citizens' Bank of Louisiana, Olivier House, Dufilho Pharmacy, and tomb sculpture in St. Louis Cemetery No. 2, which bears the influence of funerary art in Père Lachaise Cemetery in Paris.

The final worship center, which Bishop Antoine Blanc built on Chartres Street in 1845, replaced the Almonester Chapel, which fell into decline and vanished from history. Among the six buildings on the Ursuline site, the new church, which served Creole and German families, possesses Louisiana-style panache. Its pine and cypress ceiling features a gold medallion encasing the Holy Spirit with unfurled wings and ranks of *fleurs de lis* that fill out the cartouche. At the side aisles, six crystal chandeliers light the pews. Across the arch at the front of the nave, a scroll bears the request, *"Saint Marie, Notre Dame des Victoires, Priez pour Nous"* (Holy Mary, Our Lady of Victories, Pray for Us). Medallions containing a shamrock and Celtic cross bear witness to Irish influence among parishioners. Bavarian stained glass dramatizes the annunciation and assumption, paired scenes from the life of the Virgin Mary. Architectural detail focuses on a grand reredos, rich with gold mosaic and Corinthian columns, which shelter a contrite, demure image of the Virgin. To each side, angels hoist flambeaux. A smaller pair at the top blow trumpets.

Through wrought-iron gates and past an enameled Maltese cross, an adjacent shrine honoring the Order of St. Lazarus of Jerusalem once served the nuns as their office and workroom. After its remodeling, it reopened on November 29, 1980, before a royal guest, Prince Francisco

Enrique de Borbon y de Borbon of Spain. The room's tasteful collection of shields and flags of the four U.S. commanderies and the Texas delegation links the New World to chivalric orders dating to the eleventh century and extols the piety and philanthropy of Louis XV, former grand master of the Hospitallers of St. Lazare. Beneath a ceiling medallion, the slender altar balances on a stylized shell, a standard token received by pilgrims to Palestine. New Orleans sculptor Charles H. Reinike III created a bas-relief of Christ beckoning to Lazarus. The scene captures a dramatic moment in Christian history as four witnesses hover at the top of the stair. Mary and Martha flank Christ and marvel at the burial bands unfurling from Lazarus's miraculously revived form. Currently, the shrine offers worshippers a private chapel that also serves the city's bishops and archbishops.

Originally called Sainte Marie de Archevêché (St. Mary of the Archbishopric, shortened to L'Evêché) (1845), the chapel has borne several names—Holy Trinity for the Germans (1851), St. Mary, St. Mary's Italian Church (1924), and Our Lady of Victory Church, Chapel of the Archbishops, an imposing title chosen in 1976 to commemorate ties with a chapel in Rouen, France. In 1994, Archbishop Francis B. Schulte chose the current and less grandiose designation of St. Mary's Church. On May 18, 1997, he dedicated a battle scene created by Italian mosaicist Sergio Papucci on the site of the Almonester Chapel, where Ursuline sisters prayed before the statue of *Our Lady of Prompt Succor.*

ACTIVITIES

Still serving the community and visitors, the inviting village chapel ties past to present. It survived the hurricane of 1915, which destroyed the bell tower, and, in 1977, underwent restoration under the direction of Monsignor Earl Woods. The organ pipes, which serve no console, remain a symbol of a past worship phase. Another link to history is the annual January 8 thanksgiving commemorating the Battle of New Orleans. By extension, the parish continues to call on Our Lady of Prompt Succor during hurricane season through novenas and private supplication and depend on her intercession to protect levees, dams, and floodwalls. The chapel maintains a perpetual novena and mass on Saturday afternoon and receives pilgrims.

Sources: *Biography Resource Center* 1999; Bruns and Woods 1982; Gould and Nolan 1999; "A Guide to New Orleans Architecture"; Harris 1977; Huber and Wilson 1998; "Louisiana Authors"; *New Catholic Encyclopedia* 1967; "The Old Ursuline Convent"; "The Old Ursuline Convent in the French Quarter" 1996; Reynolds 1991; Sellers 1996; Sturgis 1902; Sullivan 1967; Whittington 1996; Wilhelm 1966.

ment. False information from anthropologists, writers, and filmmakers has exaggerated such fearful versions of voodoo as gruesome torture of animals, entrapment of unwary souls, and creation of robotic zombies.

In reality, voodooists worship an omnipresent creator of the universe. To reach divinity, they supplicate the *loa,* or *orisha,* intermediaries like saints. *Loa* function as messengers between earth and God and as agents of spiritual balance and communicate with living beings through dreams. The purpose of voodoo is to direct and manifest knowledge and energy through spells or hexes, manipulations of positive and negative forces, such as the summoning of ancestral spirits to predict the future and guard a household. Rituals reach emotional heights in music and chanting, drumming, ecstatic gesturing and dancing, trance, and a spiritual possession by *loa* that parallels the frenetic ecstasy of Pentacostalism. The most prominent of New Orleans practitioners, Marie Laveau, became so famous in the mid-1800s for her connections with divine powers that people continue to visit her grave to seek intervention.

V

Voodoo Spiritual Temple

Miriam and Oswan Chamani, Priests
828 North Rampart Street
New Orleans, Louisiana 70116
504-522-9627
voodoo@gnofn.org
home.gnofn.org

In the twenty-first century, Priests Miriam and Oswan Chamani, practitioners at the Voodoo Spiritual Temple, combat the Hollywood version of an ancient pagan belief. Priestess Miriam entered practice in 1975. She studied spiritualism and the occult in Chicago and sought ordination as a bishop at the Angel All Nations Spiritual Church. Her husband and partner, Priest Oswan Chamani, a native of Belize, is skilled in Central American obeah, a form of sorcery that he learned from African diviners. He specializes in trees, roots, plants and shrubs as well as snake handling and the cure of snakebite and disease.

BELIEFS

Voodoo—alternatively spelled voudou, voudon, vodom, vodou, vodon, and hoodoo—derived from the Fon term *vodu,* meaning spirit or deity. An animistic folk practice that was once the national religion of Haiti, it derives from the Fon of Dahomey, Yoruba of Nigeria, and Kongo of Zaire and Angola. Traditionally, voodoo allies the powers of an invisible creator. When black Dahomian slaves reached the West Indies, New Orleans, and other parts of the Western Hemisphere, they carried with them definitive beliefs and rituals. Because white masters forced them to accept baptism and Catholic ritual, they practiced their ancestral beliefs and customs in private, gradually fusing them with elements of Catholicism. The need to hide pagan worship infused voodoo with a sinister, menacing ele-

ACTIVITIES

The Voodoo Spiritual Temple issues a truthful image of ancient African beliefs through lectures and tours of New Orleans cemeteries. To seekers, the staff offers consultations about world events, spiritualism, love, knowledge, religion, finance, and ancestry. Officials are proficient in individual bone readings and divination through cards and palmistry. They also perform voodoo weddings, the *damballah* healing ritual, the *erzulie* love ritual, and the snake dance. Priests/priestesses can personalize potions—juju for protection and mojo or gris-gris for sexual or financial success. The temple encourages volunteers who want to serve others, issues a newsletter, *Voodoo Realist,* and distributes Priest Oswan Chamani's book *Belizean Herbs: Their Uses and Applications.*

Sources: Bowker 1997; "Briggs First Dictionary of Occult Terminology"; Cavendish 1970; Eck 1994; Scales; "Voodoo Spiritual Temple"; *World Religions* 1998; Zeinert 1997.

W

Waldensian Presbyterian Church

Reverend T. Field Russell
10 Rodoret Street SE
P.O. Box 216
Valdese, North Carolina 28690
828-874-2531
waldensian@hci.net
www.hci.net/~waldensian

The Waldensian Presbyterians of Valdese in North Carolina's Blue Ridge Mountains come from a long line of survivors. To honor faith and history, local families remain clannish, follow European traditions, speak an Italo-French patois, and revisit their cultural past annually in a summer outdoor drama. A late-summer street festival and regularly scheduled services carry cadences that remind ancestral Waldenses of persecution, the heroism of founder Peter Valdes, and sources of community pride.

HISTORY

The radical Waldenses prefigured the Reformation in their rejection of orthodox Catholicism. The Waldensian Presbyterian Church serves a community whose ancestors survived religious terrorism and attempts at extermination. By immigrating to North America, the first 29 pioneers preserved language and folk and religious customs of central and southern Europe. They arrived in Valdese, North Carolina, from Italy's Cottian Alps in May 1893 to settle on the Catawba River. In the New World's largest Waldensian colony, they attempted to farm rocky soil before investing church coffers in manufacturing, including the Waldensian Bakery and Alba-Waldensian knitting mill.

The Waldensian Church is the world's oldest evangelical church. In 1897, two years after its 220 members allied with Southern Presbyterians, Valdese settlers broke ground for a Romanesque sanctuary resembling those found in Italy. Dedicated on July 4, 1899, it embraced both a European heritage and American Independence Day. Members adopted an Americanized service in which ushers passed a collection plate rather than stood at the door to receive offerings from departing members. Altar communion gave place to pew service. Males and females mingled rather than separated to opposite sides of the sanctuary. Women no longer wore white lace collars, aprons, shawls, and a white *coiffe* to cover their hair. English began replacing French in liturgy and church minutes. Mission teachers stressed memorizing passages of scripture to preserve sanctity among the young.

Waldensian prosperity was the subject of a centennial celebration in 1993, when members dedicated Centennial Park and Fountain on Main Street. The old ways flourish in western North Carolina in the Waldensian winery and bakery, grist mill, museum, and outdoor drama, *From This Day Forward*. The Waldensian emblem is an ornate symbolism of hard times and hope: a blue sky centers the oval shield below the Latin motto *"Lux Lucet in Tenebris"* (Let Light Shine in the Shadows), a reminder of the intent of medieval forebears.

ARCHITECTURE

The Waldensian Presbyterian Church features a modified Gothic façade in gray stone, steep gables, and a square tower at right of the front entrance. The current structure grew from a simple sanctuary to an esthetically unified complex featuring Tron Hall's choir room, Pioneer Hall classrooms, a stage, and a kitchen. Stained-glass windows, designed by P. J. Reeves and Company of Philadelphia, Pennsylvania, in 1947, symbolize the spread of the denomination to thirteen nations and preserve important historical events. Choir stalls seat chancel and youth choirs behind paired pulpits for the senior and the associate pastor. On the left side of the property, a stone-walled circular garden and

PETER VALDES

Peter Valdes—also identified as Gualdensis, Peter Valdo, Peter Waldo, Valdenius, and Valdesius—promoted religious and personal liberty. He succeeded in mercantilism in late-twelfth-century Lyons, France. He turned from business to charismatic evangelism and founded the Waldenses (also Vaudois, Valdenses, or Waldensians). His impetus was a combination of scriptural interpretation and the example of Saint Alexis, the Cathari, and rebel priest Pierre de Bruys. After Valdes dispatched his wife and daughters to convents in 1175, he spent his savings on feeding the hungry before becoming a recluse and wandering preacher. He led a humble sect who patterned their lives after that of Christ.

Valdes angered the established church by choosing to study scripture directly rather than read church teachings and by advocating freedom of conscience and education free of clericalism. For challenging the priests who controlled sacraments and doctrine, he brought down on his sect the wrath of Pope Innocent III and widespread persecution by Cistercian monks under the pope's successors, Gregory IX, Alexander III, and Lucius III, who excommunicated the Waldenses for heresy. During the witch hunts of 1211, fanatics burned eighty Waldenses from Strasbourg. Survivors fled to the Piedmont, Lombardy, Provence, and the Rhine Valley and formed small communities in Austria, Bohemia, and northern Spain. Waldensianism survives in the Italian hill country and western North Carolina.

fountain connects to the sidewalk, inviting pedestrians to enjoy its benches and view of the mountains.

ACTIVITIES

The church follows Sunday school at 9:30 A.M. with a standard worship service at 11:00 A.M. and schedules prayer groups, ecumenical worship, and an annual Christmas cantata. The music program features adult and youth handbell choirs and French hymns. For the elderly, the staff supplies large-print bulletins, hearing aids, and services on tape. A church library and festivals educate modern Waldensians on their history; short-term courses and preconfirmation study

extend religious education at individual levels of competence. Waldensians host an August festival, The Celebration of the Glorious Return, which offers a street fair, an art show, craft booths, traditional food, and games of boccie (bowling) on the lawn.

Children are a sect focus. Staff leads Youth Clubsports teams, scouting, and Vacation Bible School and sends local groups to Montreat Youth Conference and Camp Grier Presbyterian Summer Camp. For adults, marriage-enrichment sessions, Men of the Church, Presbyterian Women, Inquirers Class, and Golden Years Travelers maintain interest during different life phases. In addition to pastoral care and counseling, the church aids the community through a food pantry, the Agape Retirement Home, the Habitat for Humanity, the Burke County United Christian Ministries, the Grandfather Home for Children, the Good Samaritan Medical Clinic, partnerships with a Guatemalan Presbyterian congregation and the Waldensian Methodist Church of Italy, and world hunger relief campaigns.

The Waldensian Museum, organized in 1955, displays mannequins in historic costumes and catalogues thousands of pioneer items, including clothing, tools, furniture, toys, books, pictures, and household items. On Sundays from 3:00 to 5:00 P.M. and in summer on Thursday through Sunday evenings from 5:00 to 8:00, volunteer docents inform tour groups and visitors and sell dolls, songbooks, and volumes on history, genealogy, and the Waldensian faith. From mid-July through mid-August, local players stage annual productions of Fred Cranford's *From This Day Forward,* one of the state's popular outdoor dramas. The production re-creates life in Europe and the struggle to make a new home in North Carolina.

Sources: Clifton 1992; Cooper 1996; Cranford 1969; "Destination: Valdese" 1998; Emmory 1997; Everts 1986; Harpur 1995; Hastings 1951; *History and Heritage of the Waldensian Presbyterian Church* 1993; Hodges 1999; McCallum; "Medieval Sourcebook: The Conversion of Peter Waldo"; "Preface to the Reader" 1996; Ranft 1996; "Town of Valdese"; "Waldensian Confessions of Faith"; "Waldensians and the Waldensian Church"; Walker 1996; Watts 1965; *World Religions* 1998.

Washington Islamic Mosque and Cultural Center

2551 Massachusetts Avenue N.W.
Washington, D.C. 20008
202-332-8343; 202-234-5035

A bright relief from typically American architecture, the Washington Islamic Mosque and Cultural Center stands in white-walled splendor at the corner of Belmont Road and Massachusetts Avenue beside Rock Creek Park. The crenellated structure, which stretches over 30,000 square feet, is the worship locus for area Muslims and a religious and social welcome center to Islamic dignitaries who come to Washington on business. A home on Embassy Row to one of the nation's fastest-growing faiths, it expresses the desire of Muslims to blend into the national culture and take a rightful place among the enduring buildings of the nation's capital.

BELIEFS

Islam, a monotheistic faith founded in Arabia in the seventh century A.D., derives from the Arabic word for "submission to God." It follows the teachings of a holy book, the Qur'an, or Koran, and honors as prophets Adam, Abraham, Moses, David, Solomon, Jonah, and the rest of the Old Testament patriarchs and Jesus as well. The five pillars of Islam govern Muslim lives:

- *Shahadah*—Accept Allah as the supreme deity and honor Muhammad, his prophet or apostle.
- *Salat*—Cleanse the body before prayer five times daily:
  Fajr at dawn
  Juma'a at noon
  Asr at midafternoon
  Maghrib at dusk
  Isha at evening.
- *Sawm*—Fast from dawn until sunset each day during Ramadan, a moveable feast during the ninth month in the Islamic lunar year, when devout adults forego food, water, sex, and cigarettes during daylight hours.
- *Zakat*—Perform acts of charity for the poor, orphans, travelers, slaves, prisoners, and relatives.
- *Hadj,* or *hajj*—Make a pilgrimage to Mecca once in a lifetime. A person who has completed this requirement earns the title of Hadji or Hajji.

A sixth unwritten pillar is *jihad,* a holy war against sedition by the ungodly or any major threat to Islam.

Muslim conservatism bans alcohol and drugs, affirms marriage within the faith, and differentiates gender roles and behavior. Islam condones polygamy up to four wives, but Islamic men rarely take more than one wife. Conversely, the faith opposes anything that threatens the home and childbearing—premarital sex, abortion, divorce, and homosexuality. Many support school prayer; fewer reject dating and dancing. The most devout women follow *hijab,* modest dress without makeup, and wear ankle-length skirts, long sleeves, and head scarfs that cover the neck and extend to the hairline. Veiling is primarily an Eastern custom. Only the rare Muslim immigrant to America dons the complete black covering known as a *chador* or *burka.*

Islam in the United States is skewed to nonwhite populations who follow the Sunni majority rather than the Shii minority. The two branches differ over the question of succession to Muhammad. The Sunnites, who account for 85 percent of Muslims, follow a caliph, or political defender of the faith; the other 15 percent, the Shi'ites, rally to an imam, a religio-political leader. Of American Muslims, black converts account for 42 percent. At least 50 percent are immigrants from Muslim nations. Half of those are from India or Pakistan. Since 1960, the number of U.S. mosques has grown from 160 to 1,200, concentrated in California, New York, Illinois, and New Jersey.

HISTORY

Conceived in 1945 from the Islamic imperative to build an Islamic cultural and religious headquarters in the United States, the Washington Islamic Mosque and Cultural Center derives from a consortium of Islamics and diplomats from Muslim nations worldwide. Construction began four years later on a design by the Egyptian Ministry and American architect Irvin S. Porter. American Muslim builder A. J. Howar oversaw the project, which Egyptian artisans aided with hand-painting on the walls and ceiling.

In summer 1956, dignitaries passed through flags of Islamic nations and down the fenced entry to gather at the mosque's dedication. Built of Alabama limestone, it sits at an oblique angle to face Mecca. Above, a graceful minaret rising at center from a square tower and an upper-level observation platform establish eastern Mediterranean influence. A symmetrical arrangement of windows pierces the left and right wings, which house administrative offices and a library. Entry through the five-arched portico and double row of columns leads to the inset *mehrab,* a prayer niche directed toward Mecca's sacred Kaaba and decorated with Arabic script. Unlike Christian and Jewish decor, the filigreed designs are strictly esthetic and bear no religious symbolism.

Inside, color weaves complex matrices dating back to early Middle Eastern civilization. Calligraphied scripture draws the attention of worshippers to the walls and ceilings with aphorisms, verses, and adoration of Allah by his many names—merciful and compassionate, the truth, sustainer, seer, and the wise. Decorators arranged blue, turquoise, and gold tiles from the Samerbank Yildez Porcelain Factory in Turkey above overlapping Iranian carpets used five times daily when women and men kneel in separate areas to pray and Vermont marble beneath the Egyptian light fixtures and pulpit. Other gifts of Islamic countries adorn the walls to enhance the spiritual and esthetic impact of the center. On the ground floor, an auditorium seating 300 welcomes attendees to lectures on Muslim literature, culture, arts, philosophy, and religion. The gift shop sells religious and educational items. The mosque is open to visitors daily from 10:00 A.M. to 5:00 P.M. except Friday, when it receives only Muslims.

Sources: Bowker 1997; Broderick 1958; Gentz 1973; Sharma 1987; Sharn 1996; Smith 1995; Stone 1994; Wang; Williams, Peter W., 1997; *World Religions* 1998.

Washington National Cathedral

Massachusetts and Washington Avenues N.W.
Washington, D.C. 20016-5098
202-537-6207; 800-319-7073
FAX 202-364-6611
tours@cathedral.org

http://muspin.gsfc.nasa.gov/Prime/
dctour/washcath

One of the splendors of Washington, D.C., the Washington National Cathedral is an architectural treasure that uplifts eye and heart with its magnificence. Properly named the Cathedral Church of St. Peter and St. Paul, it is the last model of the pure English Gothic building techniques that began in Chaucer's time. It began serving the nation as a state church long before completion in 1990 and hosts a million visitors annually. An Episcopal structure, it compares with the best of medieval Catholic sanctuaries, including St. Paul's in London, Notre Dame in Paris, and Chartres Cathedral. Although the structure derived its design from a consortium of engineers and specialists, it owes continuity to architect Philip Frohman.

HISTORY
Erected on fifty-three acres at the crest of Mount St. Alban in Cleveland Park, the Washington National Cathedral, the world's sixth largest cathedral, has earned the title of "sermon in stone." (Montgomery 1990, 3) It was conceived before the American Revolution, but the building evolved over the republic's first two centuries. Planning began in 1791 as part of city planner Pierre L'Enfant's vision of a national capital, which called for "a great church for national purposes." (Montgomery 1990, 1) It could not be funded by the government, so it was not built at that time. The Episcopal diocese of Virginia, founded in 1785, took the lead a century later. During an era of peace and prosperity, Washingtonians met with Charles C. Glover to make concrete advances. In 1893, the steering committee formed the Protestant Episcopal Cathedral Foundation. Congress chartered the group as the Cathedral Foundation.

Founders drew strength from the first Washington bishop, Henry Yates Satterlee, who declared that the cathedral should be "forever free and open" to all. (Montgomery 1990, 1) Five years later, the founders raised private funds to purchase the site for $245,000. Their reliance on English Gothic Revivalist Dr. George Bodley and Boston architect Henry Vaughan as designers ended within months following Dr. Bodley's

One of the splendors of Washington, D.C., the Washington National Cathedral is an architectural treasure that uplifts eye and heart with its magnificence. (Kelly-Mooney Photography/Corbis)

death. The loss did not deter the ambitious Episcopalians, who simultaneously established the National Cathedral School for Girls and the St. Albans School for Boys while working toward a grand cathedral.

The project received federal recognition on September 29, 1907, when President Theodore Roosevelt attended the laying of the rectangular foundation stone and proclaimed, "Godspeed the work begun this day." ("Washington National Cathedral") He tapped the same gavel that George Washington had wielded to lay the foundation stone for the U.S. Capitol. Growing from east to west, the cathedral took shape in Indiana limestone. It opened in 1912 after builders completed the Bethlehem Chapel, a ground-level sanctuary at the apse end of the church.

After architect Philip Frohman began work, within fifteen years, he completed the south transept's Chapel of St. Joseph of Arimathea and Resurrection Chapel and moved on to St. Mary's Chapel on the main floor. By 1929, he spread a roof over the Great Choir and advanced steadily into the north and south transepts during the Great Depression. World War II halted construction until 1948. Another lapse between 1957 and 1960 delayed completion. The upper reaches began their rise in 1960. By 1970, visitors could see the outlines of the west façade's great portals. Shortly after Frohman's death in 1972, construction ended briefly because of a shortfall of funds. The task of touring the country to raise an additional $10 million fell to an able speaker, John Thomas Walker, Washington's first black bishop.

Sculptor Frederick Hart, famous for executing *Three Soldiers,* a bronze statue alongside the Vietnam Veterans Memorial, added a focal detail to the portals. In 1974, he won an international competition to fill a bare triangle above the western façade. By 1987, he had amalgamated elements of world religion in a bas-relief entitled *Ex Nihilo* [From Nothing], *the Creation of Mankind out of Nothing, as Narrated in the Book of Genesis.* A swirling panoply of life from chaos, it depicts male and female forms arising from waves. When artisans set the bronze gates and gargoyles in place in 1987, only three years of detail work remained until the cathedral stood whole. President George Bush addressed on-lookers on September 29, 1990, when workers wedged the final stone into the southwest tower.

ARCHITECTURE

Designed without structural steel in fourteenth-century English Gothic style, the cathedral materialized in medieval fashion, stone on stone, and stretched 514 feet in length. Coordinated iconography expresses biblical history from creation at the west end to Christ's resurrection and ascension to the east. Externally, the building features architectural and artistic appointments usually limited to European churches—filigreed stone pinnacles, gargoyles and angels, over 200 stained-glass windows, flying buttresses, bosses sculpted by Granville Barker and Theodore Barbarossa, and vaults. The ground floor stretches east to west from the Bethlehem Chapel to the St. Joseph of Arimathea Chapel at the crossing and the Resurrection Chapel in the south transept to a museum shop stocked with a tasteful selection of historical, architectural, and liturgical items ranging from children's books to CDs, posters, jewelry, art books, and iconography.

The appointments of the sanctuary preserve a quiet dignity that balances opulence and artistry. The nave soars from the geometric mosaic floor upward 100 feet to a ceiling tiled in Catalan style by master mason Rafael Guastavino and his son, Rafael, Jr. On the main floor, the high altar at the extreme apse end leads to the great choir and pulpit. To the left, St. Mary's chapel and Holy Spirit Chapel, and to the right, St. John's Chapel, the scaled-down Children's Chapel, and the War Memorial Chapel expand the religious amenities for small services. In the north end stands a cathedra formed of stone from Glastonbury Abbey, the legendary burial place of King Arthur and Queen Guinevere of Camelot. In the crypt of the Chapel of Joseph of Arimathea lies a distinguished nurse, Mabel Boardman, the second president of the American Red Cross. The Cathedral Columbarium houses the ashes of two American pioneers, Helen Keller and her mentor, Anne Sullivan Macy. Also interred in the complex are Andrew Mellon, cathedral founder Bishop Henry Yates Satterlee, Secretary of State Cordell Hull, first lady Edith Galt Wilson, and President Woodrow Wilson, whose ornate monument reprises the tombs of medieval knights.

PHILIP FROHMAN

A voice of the new century, Philip Hubert Frohman supplied the Washington National Cathedral with the vigor and enthusiasm of the 1900s. Born in New York City on November 16, 1887, he studied at Throop Polytechnic Institute and Throop College of Engineering and developed skill as well as dedication to authenticity. With a specialty in church architectural engineering, at age twenty-one, he opened a practice in Pasadena, California, and designed Trinity Episcopal Church in Santa Barbara before returning to the East Coast. After a year in Boston, in 1920, he became one of the triad of Frohman, Robb, and Little, where he remained until 1934.

Foremost of Frohman's projects were Trinity College Chapel in Hartford, Connecticut, and the Episcopal Cathedral in Baltimore, Maryland, both completed in 1932. The last thirty-six years of his life, he worked alone in Washington, D.C., where he died on October 30, 1972. He oversaw the erection of Trinity Episcopal Church in Morgantown, West Virginia, in 1952, but, for a half century as Architect of the Cathedral, devoted most of his energies to the Washington project. He and his predecessor, Henry Vaughan, lie buried in the cathedral crypt.

Ervin Bossanyi's jewel-toned glass windows honor Wilson's efforts for world peace.

Music parallels architectural elegance. From the carved wood choir stall tinged by fading afternoon light, the boys of the Cathedral Choir of Boys and Men perform for evensong. The source of the cathedral's substantial music program is a 185-rank Skinner organ. The towers lift the cathedral heavenward in the style of the medieval cathedral towers of Europe. On the west end facing Wisconsin Avenue, the towers of St. Peter and St. Paul combine loft with function by housing conference rooms, offices, and equipment storage. They are linked by a gallery seven stories above the nave above the west rose window. At 676 feet, the cathedral's Gloria in Excelsis Central Tower—built above the crossing and supervised by Dean Francis B. Sayre, Woodrow Wilson's grandson—is the highest point in Washington. It houses the Kibbey Car-

illon and a peal of bells rung by hand. Bell practice draws many visitors, as do Rodney Winfield's *Space Window,* a braille visitor station, and the "history kneelers" in St. John's Chapel.

ACTIVITIES

Although the edifice took shape slowly, as a national church, it received every United States president elected after its commission. Dr. Martin Luther King, Jr., preached his final sermon from the cathedral pulpit. The staff has welcomed Queen Elizabeth II, Charles de Gaulle, and Indira Gandhi and has organized services for many denominations and for ecumenical and interfaith programs and national events, including the funerals of President Dwight Eisenhower and Ron Brown, a cabinet member from the Clinton administration, memorial ceremonies honoring victims of the 1998 bombing of U.S. embassies in Tanzania and Kenya, representation by South Africa's Bishop Desmond Tutu at the Peace Cross Centenary, and a Smithsonian jazz performance celebrating the centennial of Duke Ellington. As the chief mission church of the Episcopal Diocese of Washington, the Washington National Cathedral houses the Episcopal bishop of Washington, the Right Reverend Ronald H. Haines, and its administrative dean, the Very Reverend Nathan D. Baxter, as well as the presiding bishop of the Episcopal Church U.S.A., the Most Reverend Frank T. Griswold III.

Except for services, religious holidays, and special events, such as D.C. Day on June 27, the Cathedral remains open daily from 10:00 A.M. to 4:30 P.M. The nave receives the public week nights until 9:00 P.M. from May 1 through Labor Day. The gardens are open until dusk. For private prayer, worshippers use the Good Shepherd Chapel from 6:00 A.M. to 10:00 P.M. daily. Visitors access site diagrams in English, French, German, Spanish, Italian, Russian, and Japanese. For a donation of $3 for adults and $1 for children, docent-led tours are available from Monday through Saturday from 10:00 to 11:30 A.M. and 12:45 to 3:15 P.M. and Sunday from 12:30 to 2:45 P.M.

Regular services conform to the Book of Common Prayer and offer worship and communion. The cathedral is one of two U.S. cathedrals perpetuating the English tradition of a male chancel choir. Since 1909, the cathedral has hosted the Boy Choristers, who join the adult men as the church's principal liturgical singers. The boys received scholarships to attend St. Albans, a cathedral boys' school, and weekly practice eighteen hours of singing in addition to a full academic program.

Special events include performances of the 200-voice Cathedral Choral Society, which Dr. Paul Callaway formed in 1941 as a resident symphonic chorus presenting works from the Renaissance to contemporary composition. He introduced a forty-four-year stint as the choir's director with a rendering of the *Verdi Requiem*. Since 1985, J. Reilly Lewis, a graduate of the Juilliard School of Music, has led the choral society in frequent concerts featuring the National Symphony Orchestra. The society, accompanied by London native Nicholas White, has premiered twenty works and showcases young vocalists who became professional musicians. Outside the cathedral, the society performs at Constitution Hall and the Kennedy Center as well as on national radio and television broadcasts. Assisting the music programs is choirmaster and organist Dr. Douglas Major, who joined the staff in 1974. He directs the all-professional Cathedral Choir of Men and Boys and annually plays for over 250 musical services.

The cathedral staff takes pride in individual artistry in fine woodcarving, needlework, wrought iron, and calligraphy. It offers a medieval workshop to introduce children to Gothic art and architecture. In 1996, staff sponsored a first juried calligraphy exhibition on the theme of Visions of the Spirit and reprises the competition at the millennial celebration, Jubilee 2000: Proclaiming God's Reconciling Love in a New Era. Other special events range from an iconography workshop, a Quiet Day to explore mysticism, and an ensemble honoring Hildegard of Bingen to greenhouse lectures on cooking with herbs, a lock-in for youth to explore the sanctuary, and a Help the Homeless service. As personal stewardship, standing committees tend the altar, ring bells, assist at communion, usher, and make altar cloths.

The grounds feature the Bishop's Garden and the Herb Cottage, a source of potted plants and herbs. Located in one of the oldest buildings in the cathedral close, it once was the baptistery.

The gardening staff sells dried herbs, foods, and such gift items as china, scented oils and soaps, jams and jellies, specialty teas, cards, calendars, and seasonal goods. The cathedral archives maintains historical records, service registers, leaflets, scrapbooks, and news items dating from 1894 to 1985. In addition, the staff preserves records of iconography and furnishings, architectural and construction data, and the quarterly magazine *Cathedral Age* dating from 1925 along with facts on cathedral artists and photos of national events

The cathedral's schedule requires four canons, seventeen volunteer chaplains, staff associates, docents, and friends of the cathedral. The combined staff manages 1,700 annual liturgies, which include four Sunday Eucharist services spaced from 8:00 to 11:00 A.M., a 4:00 P.M. evensong, and a 6:30 P.M. laying on of hands. Daily, scheduling calls for a 7:30 A.M. and noon Eucharist, intercessory prayers at 2:30 P.M., a 4:00 P.M. evensong Monday through Friday, and Saturday evening prayer at 4:00 P.M.

Sources: "Blind Can Get Feel for Size of Cathedral" 1998; Broderick 1958; Burchard 1998; "Clinton Honors Embassy Bomb Victims" 1998; Graves; Hamer 1997; Montgomery 1990; Mutrux 1982; Sherr and Kazickas 1994; "Warner, Robb to Read at Service" 1998; "Washington National Cathedral"; Williams, Peter W., 1997.

Wat Carolina Buddhajakra Vanaram

Somdej Phra Nyanasamvara, Supreme Patriarch
Buddhist Association of North Carolina
1610 Midway Road
Bolivia, North Carolina 28422
910-253-4526
FAX 910-253-6618
debby@webtrawler.com
www.wisecom.com/wat

On an inland road from Wilmington, North Carolina, southwest to Bolivia lies hallowed ground, the high-gabled Wat Carolina Buddhajakra Vanaram. The monastery's brothers follow the tradition of ancient elders, the least altered form of Buddhism. By definition, the temple and its altar to the Buddha are the source of enlightenment and long- and short-term education to those who would follow the great teacher. Relaxed among coastal pines that dot the sandy plains, beginners learn Vipassana meditation, the Thai form of meditation evolved at Wat Nong Pa Pong, the seat of Thailand's forest monasteries.

Buddhism is an integral part of Southeast Asian life. Over three quarters of Thailand's males enter religious service, have their heads shaved, and wear the draped garb of monastic disciples. Monks in Theravada Buddhism—based on the original, unadulterated teachings of Gautama Buddha—follow strict codes of conduct and discipline that date to the third century B.C. According to the Buddha, the holy life follows the Eightfold Path and requires an attitude of prayerful restraint, respect for all living things, and no contact with money, commerce, weapons, games, or women. Once daily after noon, monks eat in private from their alms bowls. They never cook for themselves or consume alcohol. They attend no festive occasions, entertainments, or ceremonies. Discipline in piety and morality aids concentration, the basis for insight and wisdom.

HISTORY

For over a decade, Wat Carolina Buddhajakra Vanaram has served as the Carolinas' center of Theravada Buddhism. The monastery's abbot, Phrakru Buddhamonpricha, monitors the physical and spiritual development of the community. He guides monks in the 2,500-year tradition ordained by a reform movement known as the Dhammayut Nikaya. Since war with Burma in 1767 destroyed the former Thai capital of Ayutthaya and forced the people into the forests, the restructuring of conduct under King Rama IV (Phra Maha Mongkut) and the reform movement led his son, King Rama V (Chulalongkorn), to a strict interpretation of the Vinaya, the opening chapter of Pali scripture that established order and discipline. Under the Dhammayut Nikaya, reformed monks follow Theravada Buddhist principles, the purest form of the religion, which rejects idols and ritual and focuses on enlightenment of the self.

Today, Theravada Buddhists honor as their benefactor King Bhumibol Adulyadej, also known as Rama IX of the Chakri dynasty of Thailand. An American born to Prince Mahidol of Songkhla in Cambridge, Massachusetts, on December 5, 1927, he has held the throne of Thailand since age nineteen. A defender of national independence in the tradition of his grandfather, Chulalongkorn, who ended Siam's slave system, Bhumibol was studying in Switzerland when his brother died unexpectedly from the attack of an unknown assailant. After marrying Queen Sirikit, Bhumibol continued graduate work in political science and law until a national crisis forced his return to Bangkok's Chitralada Palace. Among his benefits to Thai subjects are the curtailment of the opium trade, modernization of travel and communications, and educational advancement.

As "soul of the Thai kingdom" and a patron of Buddhism, Bhumibol supports the traditional faith as a stimulus to religious tolerance. (*Biography Resource Center* 1999) He promoted establishment of the Headquarters of the World Fellowship of Buddhism in Thailand and models the Buddha's concepts of piety and benevolence through public obeisance to the Emerald Buddha, a two-foot-tall green jasper icon displayed in Bangkok's Wat Phra Keo. Since the inception of Wat Carolina, members have advocated the building of a temple to honor Bhumibol's birthplace.

Incorporated on June 10, 1988, as a nonprofit organization and service to area Buddhists, the complex is still under construction. Supervised by association president Sounthone Hemvong, its nucleus is the devotion of Phrakru Buddhamnpricha, the first resident monk, a veteran of the Thai army and degreed education major who prepared twelve years for his ascetic life, and Pra Thong Chai, a former architect and owner of an import-export business. To welcome the men and support their vocation, Raleigh Buddhists presented a crepe paper money tree decked with contributions for the building fund. In August 1988 at nearby Antioch Baptist Church, the Reverend Dee Froeber invited the monks to address the congregation and explain their work as an introduction to an alternative religious viewpoint.

ARCHITECTURE

At the center of a 20.9-acre wooded tract fronting Midway Road, the red-roofed temple is a single-story frame structure perched on stilts in the swampy drainage of Lockwood Folly River.

The temple's high-gabled entrance and central dome with spire balance an extended roofline and railed decks that offer views of the glade. Inside, worshippers leave pairs of shoes at the door and kneel on an Oriental rug before a statue of the Buddha. The chief abbot sits nearby on a low platform to bless visitors with holy water. The only decorations are flowers, candles, and incense.

In the 500-volume lending library, completed in 1995, staff and members welcomed visitors from as far away as California and Oklahoma to a 1996 New Year's ritual. Plans for the complex call for erecting a 10,700-square-foot meditation hall on a concrete foundation already poured. In addition, planners anticipate a pagoda, a large residential unit for monks, a separate kitchen and dining hall, a single-story retirement center, an entrance gate and ample parking, and three shelters on landscaped parks and a wildlife refuge.

ACTIVITIES

At Wat Carolina Buddhajakra Vanaram, ten to fifteen members follow the teachings of monks and nuns who express *dhamma* (or *dharma*), the concept of cosmic order that the Buddha discovered intuitively. The focus of wat (temple) teachings to young Buddhists cover five moral injunctions:

- Never kill any beings, even insects.
- Never take the belongings of others.
- Never misuse the body.
- Never lie.
- Never drink alcohol or take illicit drugs.

Along with these five prohibitions is the one positive law—to be kind and loving, happy and grateful.

The staff welcomes all to regular Vipassana meditation services each Sunday from 2:00 to 3:00 P.M., when followers discuss and practice seated meditation. Central to the staff's principles is the pure thought advocated in the Dhammapada, the scriptural essence of Theravada Buddhism. Annual holy days reveal many facets of the Theravadan faith:

- Magha Puja, or Sangha Day, celebrated with chanting

- The May observance of Visakha Puga, or Buddha Day, which commemorates the Buddha's birth in 623 B.C., awakening in 594 B.C., and Parinibbana, his release from life into blessedness, in 543 B.C.
- The July Asalha Puda, or Dhamma Day, which acknowledges the Buddha's first lecture and his activation of the wheel of Dhamma
- Pavarana Day in October, a monastery retreat when the monks focus on meditation
- Kathin at the end of October, an annual celebration, chanting, and feast concluding the Buddhist Lent
- Anapanasati Day, a November commemoration of the Buddha's instruction on breathing.

Among the aims of Wat Carolina are to further charitable institutions that support Buddhist ideals and to promote cultural understanding and interaction between Americans and Southeast Asians.

Sources: *Biography Resource Center 1999; Eerdmans' Handbook to the World's Religions 1982; Encyclopedia of World Biography 1998; Essen 1988; Ling 1972; "Local Baptists Are Not Bigots about Buddhists" 1988; Minchin 1996; Nash 1996; Smith 1995; Usher 1988; "Wat Carolina Buddhajakra Vanaram"; World Religions 1998.*

Wat Lao Buddhavong

3043 Catlett Road
Catlett, Virginia 20119
540-788-9201; 540-788-4968
FAX 540-788-1219
webmaster@watlao.org
http://watlao.org;
http://watlaobuddhavong.org

Located off highway I-66 southwest of Washington, D.C., in the state of Virginia, Wat Lao Buddhavong is a traditional Laotian Buddhist community. Led by the Reverend Bounmy Kittithammavanno, members support Buddhists through the Washington metropolitan area. The temple serves as a conduit of religious faith and Southeast Asian culture. The staff welcomes all who want to learn or practice Laotian Buddhism at the area's only temple. In addition to services in the *sala,* or worship hall, the temple contains a library and offers instruction in meditation, Lao language, and traditional arts to enhance the education of Lao youth in their native heritage.

Arranged on fifty-eight acres, the temple is the design of Lao architect Oudarone Sombath of Falls Church, Virginia. The complex consists of the main worship hall for religious activities and a *sim,* or chapel, a smaller service center decorated with traditional Buddhist ornamentation and used for the ordination of monks. In addition, the *kooti,* or monk's living quarters, compose two stories of a brick building at the front of the grounds.

HISTORY AND ACTIVITIES

Wat Lao Buddhavong is the outgrowth of demand for a space where Laotians in the greater Washington area could express their faith and national customs. In 1980, the community began discussing how to foster strength and cohesion, especially for its youth. After attending services at other Buddhist facilities and renting dormitory space for monks, the Lao Buddhist Association bought a house on an acre lot at 5248 Clifton Street, Alexandria, Virginia. Buddhist services on this property caused congestion that violated zoning regulations. In December 1985, the Reverend Bounmy Kittithammavanno and three members purchased the present site, brick house, and barn in Catlett and retired the debt in five years.

Wat Lao Buddhavong supports an inclusive calendar of activities, including a Mother's Day banquet and Fourth of July celebration. The height of the year, Boun Pimai Lao, or Lao New Year, brings together prayers with traditional three-day festivities. Small sand *stupas,* or dome-shaped shrines, sport streamers as symbolic requests for health and happiness over the next twelve months. Members sing traditional Lao folk songs and join in the *ramwong* (circle dance), a Thai group dance popularized in the early twentieth century as a joyous conclusion to a gathering.

As part of the temple education program, on April 17, 1999, the staff organized a four-hour Asian health fair sponsored by the Indochinese Community Center, Asian Pacific Islander American Health Forum, and Arlington County Health Department. In addition to disseminating information about wellness, professionals monitored cholesterol, blood pressure and glucose levels, glaucoma and general vision, and nutrition. Specialists from the American Cancer Society, the Whitman-Walker Clinic, the Northern Virginia Alliance on Smoking and Health, Positive Choices, and the Piedmont Coalition against Tobacco offered diet counseling, training in home breast exams, and advice on HIV, AIDS, and other sexually transmitted diseases.

The congregation participated in a regional Boun Awk Phun Sah ceremony at Wat Lao in Manassas, Virginia, which convened 500 people from around the country for two days of fellowship. The ritual ended a ninety-day fasting period known as Kaou Cham Sinh, when monks stay indoors and limit their diet to vegetables and rice. Highlights of the event are Loia Kathong, the floating of lighted candles to bear participants' wishes, and Boun Souang Heua, traditional Lao boat races. Celebrants enjoyed Lao foods, cultural music, dancing, chanting, and blessing from the monks.

The wat has published a film, *Too Much Air to Breathe: Lao Buddhist Community and Healing,* a twenty-eight-minute discourse on Lao Buddhist culture narrated at the wat by the Reverend Bounmi and some members. The text explores religious principles and practice among Southeast Asian-Americans. Visual imagery interweaves the tension between the culture in the homeland and compromises with American lifestyles. Among the segments are a merit-making ceremony, women with shaved heads offering sweet rice enfolded in banana leaves, and a young monk's confession of his misspent youth.

Sources: "Audio-Visual Collection"; *Eerdmans' Handbook to the World's Religions* 1982; "July 4th Events" 1999; Nash 1996; "Old Chiang Mai Culture Center" 1998; Smith 1995; "Virginia Wat Lao Buddhavong" 1997; "Welcome to Wat Lao Buddhavong."

Wayfarers' Chapel

Reverend Harvey A. Tafel
5755 Palos Verdes Drive South
Rancho Palos Verdes, California 90275
310-541-1967; 310-377-1650
FAX 310-541-1435
Harveyt@wayfarerschapel.org
www.wayfarerschapel.org

The Wayfarers' Chapel, a petite Swedenborgian sanctuary on the shore of the Palos Verdes Peninsula, retains the magic communion with nature that once gladdened early worshippers at gatherings in glades and woods. A crystal structure open to nature, the chapel is a favorite baptism, blessing, and wedding site and the wayfarer's welcome respite overlooking the Pacific Ocean. Designed by American architect Lloyd Wright, son of Frank Lloyd Wright, and completed in 1949, it glorifies God while honoring Emanuel Swedenborg, eighteenth-century mystic, scientist, and theologian who founded a transcendental Christian faith known as Swedenborgianism.

BELIEFS

Swedenborgians based their unconventional mysticism and neoplatonic philosophy on a supreme being who is the equivalent of the loving life force. They characterize humankind as a part of God and exalt the creative energy that empowers and sustains living things. The devout worship Christ as an earthly incarnation of God. In imitation of divine love, they share uncompromising affection, kindness, and caring through self-expression, family relationships, friendship, hospitality, and protection of the universe.

Because Swedenborgians believe that God's love is eternal, they conclude that human life extends forever. After the physical body's death, the true self survives intact in a spiritual world, which surrounds and permeates the material world. They acknowledge creative people—artists, poets, and musicians—as communicants with the spiritual realm. For all poeple, the opportunity to grow and authenticate the spirit comes from service, community, and recreation. The most positive form of spiritual generation is work in harmony with divine providence, which bestows blessing and wisdom to all who seek union with God.

HISTORY AND ARCHITECTURE

The first conception of a forest church and national memorial to Swedenborg came from a follower, Elizabeth Schellenberg, in 1928. After repeated petitions to the Church of the New Jerusalem, she found a supporter in Narcissa Cox Vanderlip, a Swedenborgian who donated

The Wayfarers' Chapel, a petite Swedenborgian sanctuary on the shore of the Palos Verdes Peninsula, retains the magic communion with nature that once gladdened early outdoor worshippers. (G.E. Kidder Smith/Corbis)

acreage in Palos Verdes in open farmland on a gravel road. After Ralph Juster drew initial plans for a mission type structure, the Great Depression and World War II slowed execution of the design. By war's end, he was no longer satisfied with his initial drawings.

At Juster's insistence, Narcissa Vanderlip's son, Kelvin Vanderlip, headed the building committee and, in 1946, selected Lloyd Wright, designer of the Hollywood Bowl, to redraw a chapel reflecting the progressive philosophy of Emanual Swedenborg. On July 16, 1949, the group laid the cornerstone, a natural boulder marked with a cross, the year, and the Greek letters alpha and omega, symbols of Christ's importance to the world. Wright and his son, assistant architect Eric Lloyd Wright, oversaw completion on Mother's Day, May 13, 1951, when the Reverend Leonard Tafel and the president of the General Convention of Swedenborgian Churches officiated at the dedication.

To harmonize hallowed space through human genius, Wright merged architecture with the living environment. He united at thirty- and sixty-degree angles panes of clear glass edged in coastal redwood above a basis of earthquake-proof concrete, steel, and local fieldstone. Within a pleasant grove on 3.5 acres overlooking the sea, the harmony of physical and mental elements converge in a unique glass structure often called the Tree Chapel. Inside, sword ferns, cymbidium orchids, and grape ivy soften the aisles, walls, and natural baptismal font hollowed into the stone; a toyon tree climbs to the commanding glass circle above the altar, a symbol of wholeness and oneness with God in eternity.

The finished structure, which seats 100, serves members and visiting worshippers each Sunday from 11:00 A.M. to 2:00 P.M. The altar introduces the opening phrase of the Lord's Prayer. At the base, three stone steps bear additional inscriptions from the prayer. Inviting paths lead individuals through dappled shade past memorial gardens and a reflecting pool and modest fountain. Three years after completion of the original complex, Lloyd Wright added the Hallelujah Tower, a slender stone column strengthened with steel-reinforced concrete and housing sixteen bells. Beneath a modest cross, the tower lights the way for sailors entering the Catalina Channel. Their delight in the structure resulted in a new name, God's Candle. Visitors walking from the stele through the blue tile-roofed colonnade arrive at a hillside stream and terraced turf sheltering an amphitheater, which overlooks Abalone Cove and Catalina Island.

EMANUEL SWEDENBORG

Emanuel Swedenborg (originally Svedberg or Swedberg) was a troubled genius and devout student of the Christian faith. A native of Stockholm, he was born on January 29, 1688, to Sara Behm and Jesper Swedberg, a professor of theology and Lutheran bishop. Swedenborg mastered metallurgy along with war strategy, astronomy and cosmology, anatomy, politics and finance, and the Bible. After extensive travels through northern Europe and Britain, he dedicated himself to mathematics and physics before taking a post as assessor of the Royal College of Mines. At age forty-six, he published *Prodomus Philosophie Ratiocinantrio de Infinite* (We Proceed by the Rational Philosophy of the Infinite) (1734), containing his musings on the relationship between infinity and humanity.

After resigning his position to serve God, Swedenborg spent the remainder of his life interpreting scripture, analyzing true Christian faith, and furthering spiritual enlightenment through love and wisdom. Although he claimed to be in contact with angels and divinities via daily trances, detractors diagnosed his odd behavior as chronic paranoia. After his death in London on March 29, 1772, publication of his collected writings, *Treatise on Four Doctrines,* prompted followers to establish the Church of the New Jerusalem, which reached the United States in 1792 with a threefold gospel of the divinity of Christ, the sacredness of the Bible, and the function of charity.

ACTIVITIES

Within green lawns, gardens, stone paths, and tall trees, the Wayfarers' Chapel produces a startling convergence of light captured within a human-made structure open daily from 9:00 A.M. to 4:00 P.M. Services follow a pattern similar to a Unitarian fellowship—welcome, lighting the Angels' Candle, song, presenting congregational concerns, discussion, song, prayer and blessing, meditation, song, and extinguishing the candle. When not in use for Sunday worship or vespers, the chapel is a favorite Pacific coast site for Christmas Eve candlelight and Easter sunrise services, Christmas and Palm Sunday pageants, reenactment of the Last Supper, New Year's rededication and renewal, me-

morials, baptisms, anniversaries, and weddings and renewal of vows, its most frequent uses. In 1976, Loyd Wright addressed the congregation at the quarter century celebration; at his death two years later, the chapel held a memorial service for him. The careful scheduling of marriages approaches 2,000 per year, including those of celebrities Gary Burghoff, Dennis Hopper, Brian Wilson, and Jayne Mansfield to Mickey Hargitay. The staff allows music, photography, limousine service, decorations, outside wedding directors and clergy of all faiths, and rehearsals and provides prenuptial counseling and dressing area.

In addition to formal gatherings, regular attendees, known as Wayfarers, have chosen benevolences suited to their unusual chapel. They offer the building free for community fundraisers and as a space for workshops, lectures, concerts, art shows, and musical events. Alliance with San Pedro's Interfaith Shelter provides a food pantry for the homeless and a nearby refurbished barracks for stays of up to ninety days. Two recent features of the annual calendar are a blessing of the animals, which brings people and pets into a sanctified space, and celebration of the chapel's golden anniversary on June 20, 1999. By the end of the twentieth century, staff raised funds for a visitor center to replace a structure destroyed in 1982 following hill slippage. A series of reflective discussions on life rhythms, joy, and healing began in September 1999 and continued through late spring 2000.

> Sources: *Almanac of Famous People* 1998; *American Decades* 1998; *Biography Resource Center* 1999; *Business Leader Profiles for Students* 1999; *Contemporary Heroes and Heroines* 1998; *Encyclopedia of Occultism and Parapsychology* 1996; *Encyclopedia of World Biography* 1998; Martin 1988; Rado 1999; Sandefur 1999; "A Southern California Wedding at the Wayfarers' Chapel"; "The Wayfarers' Chapel"; "Wayfarers' Chapel"; Williams, Peter W. 1997; Zacharias n.d.

Wellspring Church and Christian Center
George and Sharon Stover, Co-Pastors
1401 North Decatur, Suite 14
Las Vegas, Nevada 89108
702-631-5027
FAX 702-631-4221
wellspring@unidial.com
www.wellspringministries.com

A member of the Full Gospel Fellowship located at a shopping center in Las Vegas, Nevada, the Wellspring Church and Christian Center takes pride in its newness and spontaneity. As cited in church publications and on Web pages, it is post-denominational and multiracial. Its passion is a ministry of reconciliation and the establishment of David's tabernacle to unite all tribes, tongues, and language groups under the tenets of Christianity and to welcome all to an international house of prayer. Through kinetic services of physical praise and witness, believers display oneness with a divine power that lifts them out of their seats and into Pentecostal rapture.

BELIEFS
As affiliates of the Full Gospel Fellowship of Churches and Ministers and of the International Charismatic Bible Ministries of Oral Roberts University, Wellspring Church follows a full gospel creed that is dynamic, charismatic, and binding. The scriptures form the final authority for matters of faith and practice of Pentecostalism. Like Christ's disciples, they wait for the supernatural experience that indicates oneness with God. The steps toward salvation from sin are clear objectives:

- Baptism and acceptance of the Holy Spirit
- Identification with a body of Christian believers
- Remaining steadfast in Bible beliefs
- Developing a personal relationship with the divine through prayer

From readings of the book of Revelation, Full Gospel believers anticipate the immediate return of Christ to earth and on-the-spot rescue from perdition through grace. They undergo baptism by immersion and commemorate the Lord's Supper. From experience with earthly temptation, they respect the powers and allure of Satan, the counterdeity of hell. Full Gospel faith falls into a black versus white polarity: adherents anticipate eternal life for themselves and eternal damnation for unbelievers. In group sessions, members await dramatic evidence of Christ's intervention in human life. In addition to emotional and spiritual renewal, followers believe in miracles and faith healing, fireballs bursting from the evangelist's hands, signs and wonders from the sky, and being "slain in the spirit," a fainting or collapse or outburst of "holy laughter" that indicates the working of the Holy Ghost.

HISTORY AND ACTIVITIES
Copastors George and Sharon Stover are evidence of the evangelical revival of the late 1960s. Since their founding of a joint ministry, they have dedicated their lives to preaching, saving non-Christians, and equipping their ministries. Both grew up in southern California in

unchurched families and became high school sweethearts in 1957. George Stover served in the military; Sharon studied nursing. After their marriage in 1962 at Fort Huachuca in Tombstone Territory, Arizona, they moved to Las Vegas to mount a mission campaign to proselytize Mormons, Masons, Jehovah's Witnesses, and non-Christians. Church programming includes correspondence courses and encouragement of tithing a tenth of all income to missions and warnings against interracial marriage and against belief in evolution.

The Wellspring Church and Christian Center schedules Sunday morning Bible study at 9:45, followed at 10:30 with worship in English and Spanish, and a 6:00 P.M. Miracle Service. Additional programming offers a praise gathering on Thursdays at 7:00 P.M. Staff conducts a 5:00 P.M. prayer hour, drama team practice at 6:00, and Life Care Group home Bible study at 7:00 each Tuesday. On Wednesday, members can participate in Daughters of Zion women's Bible ministry and Victorious Christian Living. Thursday's program features the Midweek Miracle and Praise Service. The week ends with seminars, youth events, and P.O.W.E.R. Night prayer hour on Friday and men's Bible study and fellowship breakfast, Adopt-A-Block, Resurrection Choir Practice, and Reach-a-Kid for Christ puppet ministry on Saturday.

Pastor George Stover publishes sermons via audio and video cassette through the church book store and airs messages over television on *Streams in the Desert,* a series available twice on Wednesday and once on Friday, Saturday, and Sunday. In late November 1999, the congregation attended a revival, the Second Annual Greater Anointings Conference, and celebrated their faith at a Y2K Celebration on New Year's Eve 1999 that hosted a communion potluck dinner, worship and testimony, a movie, fellowship, games, and midnight communion. In February 2000, they began the millennium with Congress 200 on Prayer and Intercession. A concert series coordinated violinist Maurice Sklar, Miracle on 26th Street, and the Miracle City Choir.

Church ministry includes the Wellspring Victorious Christian Living Discipleship Center, the Wellspring Bible and Book Store, and the Wellspring Food Distribution Center. A global outreach spreads the Stovers' evangelism to Hong Kong, China, the Philippines, Mexico, Jamaica, and Romania. Plans for twenty-first-century outreach target Ghana, Indonesia, Great Britain, Nigeria, and South Africa. The staff issues two texts in Spanish, *Lenguas Porque y Quando* (Tongues: When and Why) and *Fortalezas en la Mente* (Strongholds in the Mind). A three-year course at the Wellspring Bible Institute toward certification prepares the serious English- or Spanish-speaking evangelist for ministry and leadership in Christian education, ministerial theology, and advanced theology.

Sources: Ahlstrom 1972; "Full Gospel Associated Churches"; "Full Gospel Television"; Smith 1995; "Wellspring Church and Christian Center."

West Parish Meetinghouse
2049 Meetinghouse Road
P.O. Box 219
West Barnstable, Massachusetts 02668
508-362-4445
westpar@capecod.net

America's oldest Congregational sanctuary, West Parish Meetinghouse is a thriving period piece surviving from the time of colonial meeting houses. More than a museum, it is a citadel of the founders' spirit, the force that united worshippers against the corruption and authoritarianism of England's Anglican church. Over 380 years after a bold stand against two kings and a state religion, members retain a commitment to a democratic religious structure that respects the individual conscience.

HISTORY
The American Congregational tradition got an unpromising start from a small circle of godly men praying together in Southwark outside London in 1616. Their decision was momentous—to wrench themselves from the Church of England, an institutional giant that refused them autonomy as stringently as it rejected internal reform. With Henry Jacob as their minister, the nonconformists elected to follow an independent path and gave themselves the name Congregationalists, a title that deliberately shifted emphasis from authority figures to pew-

level worship. For eighteen years, some sixty Southwark rebels worshiped secretly and survived official silencing, persecution, and imprisonment by King James I before their exile to the New World.

Meanwhile, other disgruntled British subjects migrated to the colonies. In 1620, England's Reformed Protestantism arrived in the Western Hemisphere aboard the *Mayflower*, bearer of a band of newcomers who established a religious outlook and practice that prevailed for several centuries. In the primitive Atlantic shore environment, Pilgrims and Puritans belabored by English Anglicans made a fresh start as the Massachusetts Bay Colony. They bore the stern principles and scriptural commitment of two Swiss reformers—Ulrich Zwingli of Zurich and John Calvin from Geneva. These freedom lovers rejected papist tyranny and England's state religion, opting to pledge allegiance to Christ alone. Through God-centered lives, they intended the New England experiment to enlighten and liberate the world.

Led by the Reverend John Lothrop, Congregationalists departed England for Massachusetts in 1634 and lived in the coastal town of Scituate for five years before settling on donated land in Cape Cod at Barnstable. In October 1639, worshippers free of interference from King Charles I celebrated communion with their beloved pewter vessels at a spot later named Sacrament Rock. Seven years later, Lothrop's followers erected a church home on Cobb Hill a half mile away.

By 1717, the congregation was sturdy enough to split into sibling parishes, East and West. East Parish chose the liberal drift to Unitarianism. Still devoutly Congregationalist, West Parish stuck with its original tenets. To meet community needs, on Thanksgiving Day 1719, they completed a new meeting house. As was the colonial custom, it doubled as the local academy. The top floor served as the classroom of patriots James Otis and Mercy Otis Warren. When the congregation outgrew the building, they divided it in the middle and connected the ends to an eighteen-foot extender. A bequest from a renowned patriot, Colonel James Otis, Sr., underwrote the church's half-ton bell, which the Revere foundry in Boston cast under the direc-

tion of Paul Revere's grandson. West parishioners installed the bell in 1808 in one of New England's first bell towers.

Massachusetts shed its authoritarian colonial church in 1833, when Congregationalism separated from state government. Still the state's largest Protestant denomination, it supports restoration and reclamation of historic church homes and the perpetuation of a faith that came of age along with liberty and the Constitution. Allied with the Massachusetts Conference of the United Church of Christ in Framingham since 1957, it is a product of the merger of Christian, Congregational, evangelical, and reformed denominations.

BELIEFS

Since the seventeenth century, Congregationalists, like other Christian sects, have followed God as revealed in Christ. They profess a witness in worship and ministry through sacred gatherings, acknowledge salvation through God's grace, and obey no ecclesiastical or political authority beyond their own congregation. The church governs itself openly and democratically through an elected council. They observe holy communion and infant baptism as their only two sacraments and practice ritual marriage and confirmation.

Congregational worship is a combined service of praise, thanksgiving, confession of shortcomings, plea for mercy, blessing, reading of scripture, and biblical interpretation from the pulpit but omits the chants common in England. In 1959, the sect adopted the United Church of Christ confession of faith and maintained the original intent to follow God's will. Congregants also join in the standard Protestant liturgy of the Lord's Prayer, group and responsive reading, and hymn singing.

The church bases its organization on a covenant with God. Adult members vote for deacons, who superintend spiritual affairs, and elect trustees to oversee the building, property, organ, and equipment. The ruling body names pulpit committees to interview prospective ministers, who must deliver a test sermon before awaiting the vote of the congregation. Beyond the local level, the conference sets the moral and ecclesiastical tone and wrestles with pervasive issues, such as admitting gay members, disciplining ministers for controversial opinions, or hiring female and nonwhite ministers.

ARCHITECTURE

The meeting house earns its title of the Rooster Church for the oversized fowl gripping a gold ball that crowns the steeple. The original ornament arrived in 1723 from England with its gold ball brim full with communion wine. A New Testament symbol of Peter's repentence for denying Christ, the five-foot cock decks the bell tower as its most distinctive exterior feature. The simplicity of the tall wooden column and four windows marking the rising stories culminates in a double gallery.

A restored masterwork of colonial Massachusetts, the structure thrusts upward in a proud pose of early American piety and thrift. It owes its longevity to Elizabeth Crocker Jenkins, who, in 1954, headed the West Parish Memorial Foundation's restoration process and personally walked the upper-story beams to inspect for structural soundness. The group preserved the integrity, warmth, and intimacy of Tudor architecture. Seating 350, the sanctuary organizes worshippers in box pews and a balcony on three sides of a rectangle. At center is a wood-capped pedestal lectern below exposed beams. The gabled side entrance of West Parish Meetinghouse is open to summer visitors daily from 9:00 A.M. to 5:00 P.M. The staff holds Sunday services at 10:00 A.M.

Sources: Ahlstrom 1972; Lynch 1999; Mutrux 1982; *New Catholic Encyclopedia* 1967; Smith 1989; "West Parish of Barnstable."

Wisteria Campground
See Circle Sanctuary Nature Preserve.

Yellowstone

National Park Service Information Office
P.O. Box 168
Yellowstone National Park, Wyoming 82190
307-344-7381
www.nps.gov/yell/

The oldest and most prized U.S. national park since 1872, Yellowstone sprawls over acreage in northwestern Wyoming, southern Montana, and eastern Idaho. From 1886 to 1916, the U.S. Army administered the site until it passed to the National Park Service. In 1972, the 80-mile stretch known as the John D. Rockefeller, Jr., Memorial Parkway linked Yellowstone to the Grand Teton National Park; six years later, Yellowstone became one of UNESCO's 630 World Heritage Properties. Vacationers escape city life to swim, fish, and boat, walk the stirring gorges, and photograph majestic cataracts and colorful effects of seasonal change. Campers, hikers, and bikers enjoy 500 miles of roads and 1,000 miles of trails.

Yellowstone's sanctity derives from the world's most spectacular display of geothermal phenomena and from free-roaming herds of American bison, or buffalo. Like corn to the Hopi and tobacco to the Sioux, the buffalo was a staple of plains culture. Because plains Indians venerated it with sacred dance and dressed in buffalo hides for ceremonies, they respected Yellowstone as an edenic homeland granted to their ancestors by the Great Spirit. In consecrated confines, seekers gazed upward at the Milky Way, the world's backbone, and awaited communion with a *puha,* a divine spirit or guardian in animal form. With reverence, individuals performed simple rituals of thanksgiving, rites of passage, and healing.

BELIEFS

Yellowstone occupies a prime position in native creation lore. In one story, the adventures of a snake account for the area's native inhabitants, who lived within the natural bulwark of snow-topped mountains. In the lengthy narrative, the wandering snake received the kindness of these Indians. While enjoying hospitality with a chief, the snake fell in love with the chief's daughter. He was so heartsick that he collapsed by the fire and prepared to die. An aged medicine man heard the snake's longing for a human wife and worked magic at the fireside to make its elongated body into a man. From the union of snake-man and Indian princess came a new tribe—the Pe-sik-na-ta-pe, or Snake.

In a Shoshone story, Taivotsi dreamed that he should seek the petrographs of Willow Creek to acquire spiritual power. He performed a ritual cleansing in the sacred waters and slumped on the ground in a trance to await a visit of a procession of *puhas,* which took the ritual number four. He lay still at the approach of the owl, deer, and coyote, but retreated from the fourth, a rattlesnake. Had he maintained his pose, he would have received the snake's supernatural medicine. Because Taivotsi fled, he suffered a mysterious leg paralysis that reduced him to walking with crutches.

In a somber Cheyenne myth, the Great Spirit promised perpetual prosperity if the Indians promised to revere the buffalo and kill them only out of need. When early people disobeyed, the Great Spirit dispersed them with smoke and downpours. On a tall crag, they gathered around Spotted Bear, the medicine man, to hear again the sermon on preserving the way of the buffalo. He helped them spread a hallowed white buffalo hide across the valley. The gesture ended their punishment. Bright sunshine sparkled across the hide in white, blue, and red. When it shrank, it formed a rainbow overhead, blessing the whole Yellowstone Valley.

HISTORY

Aborigines living in the area named the region for the towering yellow crags. The Minnetaree

Yellowstone's sanctity derives from the world's most spectacular display of geothermal phenomena and from free-roaming herds of American bison or buffalo. (National Park Service)

called the Yellowstone River Mi-tsi-a-da-zi (Rock Yellow River), which French trappers translated as Yellow Stone. Early European explorers mistook native reverence for Yellowstone as avoidance or fear of its hydrothermal wonders. Later investigation proved that aborigines had a long history of pilgrimages to the land and that one band, the Tukuarika, or Sheepeater, Shoshone, lived there after fleeing south from the vengeful Blackfoot. Likewise, the Bannock, Crow, Flathead, and Nez Percé valued the land and mined its black obsidian, a volcanic glass, widely traded for use in blades, arrowheads, choppers, scrapers, mirrors, and jewelry.

In 1804, President Thomas Jefferson commissioned captains Meriwether Lewis and William Clark to undertake a grueling surveying mission. On their way to the Pacific Ocean, they paddled down the Yellowstone River. The first popular report on Yellowstone resulted in 1806 from the homeward journey of Clark. The following year, Indian agent and trader Manuel Lisa hired trapper and guide John Colter for a surveying mission to Montana. In addition to setting up Fort Manuel, the area's first trading post, these frontier partners became the first Europeans to view the geysers and establish ongoing trade with the Crow.

The 3,468-square-mile park entered history after the 1870 expedition of Nathaniel P. Langford and Henry D. Washburn, who investigated wild rumors of geologic beauty and underground hot springs and geysers. The men were so impressed by Yellowstone that they resolved to protect it for public use. On March 1, 1872, Congress agreed and, with the concurrence of President Ulysses S. Grant, set aside the Yellowstone National Park from sale or settlement. The act conserved a national treasure: Grand Canyon, Yellowstone River, volcanic plateaus, fossil forests, basalt lava flows, burbling paint pots, 10,000 hot springs, and geysers and steam vents. Tribe names and historical terms survive in the Shoshone, Snake, and Yellowstone Lakes; the Absaroka, Beartooth, Gallatin, Snowy, and Teton Mountains; and the Beaverhead, Custer, Gallatin, Shoshone, Targhee, and Teton National Forests.

Misunderstanding about Indian visits to Yellowstone perpetuated fallacies into the last half of the nineteenth century. In 1850, Father Pierre Jean de Smet wrote in his diary that Indians bypassed geysers in silence because "they regard them as the abode of underground spirits always at war with one another, and continually at the anvil forging their weapons." (Janetski 1987, 78) Although he had never visited the site, he attested that passing Indians left offerings to the subterranean mystery. In a report to the U.S. secretary of the interior in 1878, park superintendent P. W. Norris erroneously assured him that "pagan Indians" were too superstitious even to enter Yellowstone. (Janetski 1987, 77)

In 1879, events began clarifying Indian reverence for Yellowstone. Native dwellers influenced Philetus Norris to name the Sheepeater Cliffs after a minor band of Shoshone, who lived in relative isolation in the confines of Yellowstone. Another section, Absaroka Range, designated in 1885 by a team of U.S. government geologists, preserves the native name for the Crow Nation. From the late 1950s into the 1960s, archeological digs financed by the University of Montana identified some 500 prehistoric sites in the park and left more for later investigation.

ACTIVITIES

The myriad beauties of Yellowstone are obvious sources of Native American reverence for nature and for the creator. Integral to worship is a spontaneous thanksgiving for medicinal plants and vines and groves of lodgepole pine, aspen, and cottonwood, all important to the native life way. The abundance of waterfowl, trout, small game, bison, elk, bighorn sheep, pronghorn deer, moose, bear, and coyote supplied tribes for centuries with food and the raw materials for housing, clothing, weapons, and tools. The Shoshone, who revere the anthropomorphized wolf as the supreme father, support the reestablishment of the wolf on national park land. They return to the primeval religious sites to propitiate the *puha* as figures of ceremonial animism. In a dream state called *navushieip,* the Shoshone humble themselves before the divine and await a dream or vision from God. In sight of the Tetons, they refrain from pointing to the peaks or mentioning the range's true name, which is "black standing up."

The serenity of Yellowstone suffered two late-twentieth-century cataclysms. In summer 1988, carelessness and unusually dry conditions precipitated eight fires over 1.4 million acres of undeveloped land. Severe heat left 1,400 acres barren and deprived game of winter grazing. A greater threat arose between whites and Indians in February 1999, when Indians protested Montana cattle ranchers' slaughter of bison that strayed from the park. Joseph Chasing Horse, a spiritual leader and ambassador to the United Nations for the Lakota Sioux Nations, and 100 representatives of American Indian tribes stressed their ancient belief that Native Americans share a divine kinship with buffalo.

From prehistory, buffalo hide and bones provided valuable raw material for tools, clothing, and bedding; the flesh offered partakers a form of holy Eucharist. According to Crow spokeswoman Yor Yellowtail Toineeta's monograph *Absarog-Issawua* (1970), plains Indians wasted no part of the buffalo. Dried droppings served as fuel; the hooves became clappers for doorbells; and matted shag lined cradles and became the first disposable diapers. The early-twentieth-century Crow chief Plenty Coups mourned the loss of the sacred beast with sad words: "When the buffalo went away the hearts of my people fell to the ground, and they could not lift them up again. After this nothing happened. There was little singing anywhere." (Heinerman 1989, 112)

To emphasize the symbiosis between Indians and the buffalo, an entourage of Algonquin, Apache, Assiniboine, Blackfoot, Cheyenne, Crow, Navajo, Nez Percé, Tuscarora, and Ute traveled 500 miles on foot and horseback in a nonviolent spiritual pilgrimage from Rapid City in the sacred Black Hills of South Dakota to the Yellowstone's north entrance to reverence American bison as a source of life and prosperity to the plains Indian. To the Sioux, the animal is Tatanka Oyate (He who owns us), a term capturing the vital importance of the buffalo to tribal culture. Chasing Horse asserted an ancestral belief that the extinction of the buffalo will spell a similar fate for the Indian.

The stalemate between whites and Indians derived from Chasing Horse's claim that slaughter of buffalo perpetuated the racist policies of the previous century, when the U.S. government deliberately subjugated Indians by depriving them of buffalo. The confrontation ended in a compromise: health officials agreed to isolate maverick buffalo and slaughter only those that test positive to brucellosis, a disease that could spread to cattle. One dissenter, Gloria Norlin, director of One People One Nation, stated that she supplied buffalo meat to Indian reservations and had mailed seven bison skulls to federal prisons, where Indian inmates used them to perform spiritual ceremonies.

Sources: "Distribution of Bison Meat Causing Some Divisions among Indians" 1999; Haggart; Heinerman 1989; Hultkrantz 1987; "Indians Plan March to Yellowstone to Boost Awareness of Bison Killing" 1999; Iwanski 1999; Janetski 1987; Johnson 1996; "Joseph Chasing Horse, Lakota Spiritual Leader"; Patterson and Snodgrass 1994; "Sheepeater Campaign of 1879"; "The Snake with Big Feet" 1998; Snodgrass, *Encyclopedia of Frontier Literature*, 1997; Steiger 1974; "The Total Yellowstone History Page"; Walking Turtle 1993.

ington, D.C. began gathering informally for religious celebration and social interaction. Through newspaper advertisement, Sam Bhathena summoned 20 fellow Zoroastrians to list others sharing the faith. The successful organization, led by Mobeds Adi Unwalla, Noshir Karanjia, and Sam Patel, focused on ritual activities and functions in members' homes. To extend the sect's influence, members invited Zoroastrian immigrants and attended theological congresses and meetings in Chicago and New York City.

Zoroastrian Association of Metropolitan Washington (ZAMWI)

Kersi Bhikhaji Shroff, President
2347 Hunter Mill Road
Vienna, Virginia 22181
kshr@loc.gov
www.nicom.com/~zamwi

Serving Washington D.C., suburban Maryland, and Northern Virginia, the Zoroastrian Association of Metropolitan Washington exemplifies a cohesive religious and social body. From its inception, it has preserved an ancient Eastern faith along with the languages and cultures that are part of eastern Mediterranean and Indian subcontinental history. Like most orthodox religions, sect aims call for religious observance at annual festivals and for the bringing up of families in a traditional form of Iranian and Indian monotheism.

Zoroastrians are born into the faith and dedicate themselves to goodness in thought, word, and deed. They base their theology on scripture contained in the Avesta and abstract verse in the Gathas. Their creed calls for worship of the supreme god Ahura Mazda and recognition of his immortal attendants, the Amesha Spentas, and of Angra Mainya, the repository of evil, violence, and death. The faithful reverence *asha* (righteous law), recognize the judgment of the soul before it is consigned to heaven or hell, and anticipate the birth of a savior and an apocalyptic battle between good and evil prefacing the end of time. At worship, the devout pray and observe symbolic ritual before a sacred fire, the ineffable symbol of God.

HISTORY

During an upsurge of religion in the mid-1970s, Zoroastrians living in and around Wash-

After adopting a constitution in 1978, on April 30, 1979, the 32 Washington founders formalized a nonprofit religious association, which they dubbed ZAMWI Inspired by the urgings of Khojeste Mistree to study the faith and its history, they pursued a set of principles:

- Promoting cohesion
- Perpetuating the faith
- Teaching prayers and tenets to the young
- Developing leadership
- Advancing knowledge in adult members
- Studying Zoroastrian scholarship
- Building a learning center and fire temple

Additional aims include embracing nonbelieving spouses and children of members, admitting associate members, and increasing awareness of the faith to outsiders.

Because the association's founding coincided with the Islamic Revolution in Iran, trustees aided several Iranian Zoroastrians in gaining political asylum through the U.S. Department of State. The mounting diaspora soon doubled the membership by adding Iranian Zoroastrians to the original Parsis. The group accepted the challenge of a combined culture and began presenting lectures and publishing a newsletter and annual reports in Farsi, Iran's dominant language. The Vandsar Committee acquired donated land in Vienna, Virginia, near Dulles International Airport. They held activities in a small house on the property and converted a separate building into a prayer room. In 1996, trustees began developing the site and raising funds for a permanent edifice.

During this growth period, members accepted honorary *mobed* (priest) services from Adi Unwalla and Noshir Karanjia, who came from New Jersey to conduct funerals until local volunteer Ervad Behram Panthaki accepted the responsibility. The availability of a priest invigorated the membership. In 1994, ZAMWI received around 100 worshippers for a Muktad ceremony celebrating the end of the year and initiated religious classes for youth. Simultaneously, founding president Adi Davar developed a scholarly course of study for adults on Zoroastrianism. Another contributor, James Lovelace, lectured on comparative religions. Young members formed the Zoroastrian Youth Club to foster activities and a class on the early scriptural hymns of the *Gathas* and to raise funds for poverty relief in Iran and India.

ACTIVITIES

In 1998, the ZAMWI calendar offered a gathering in Silver Springs for a children's program, a procession of Amesha Spentas (beneficent immortals), prayers, recitation from the *Epic of Shahnameh Ferdowsi,* and a bonfire followed by dinner. Late in March, members celebrated Norouz, the thirteenth day of New Year's festivities, with Iranian dance, comic skits, and a buffet and honored the birthday of Asho Zarathushtra, the Persian sage and founder of the faith who died around 551 B.C. In late August, observance of Pateti called for prayers for the dead and floral offerings. Fall extended involvement of the faithful with an October Mehrgan celebration, which marked the season with dinner, dance, and a door prize.

Activities in 1999 brought some variety with a children's play, *Norooz* [New Day] *Around the World,* a stick dance by the association's Golden Girls, the formation of Dari classes, a slide show on Iran, a community fire-lighting and prayer classes, monthly family prayer meetings, and a Diva Dance at the Pateti celebration. To attend to internal matters, planners scheduled a May clean-up day and a survey of member satisfaction. Continued interest in world faiths called for support for the Zoroastrian Olympics in Los Angeles, hospitality to visitors attending the Federation of Zoroastrian Association of North America, attendance at the International Avesta Conference in Calgary and a Parliament of World Religions in South Africa, and plans for the World Zoroastrian Congress in Houston in December 2000.

Sources: Bowker 1997; *Eerdmans' Handbook to the World's Religions* 1982; *Encyclopedia Britannica;* Gentz 1973; Smith 1995; "Stanford University Zoroastrian Group" 1997; *World Religions* 1998; "ZAMWI"; "Zoroastrianism"; "Zoroastrianism Page."

A TIME LINE OF AMERICAN
RELIGIOUS PLURALISM

5000 B.C.	Evidence indicates that Texas Indians practice peyotism.
	Native worshippers lay the central cairn at Medicine Wheel, Wyoming.
1500 B.C.	Natives complete the worship site at Medicine Wheel, Wyoming.
1054	The Anasazi follow the supernova of the Crab Nebula to Oraibi, Arizona.
ca. 1100	The Acoma establish Acoma Pueblo, one of the oldest continuously inhabited communities in North America.
1125	The Pueblo occupy the Oraibi complex.
1200	The San Juan Anasazi build Mesa Verde and worship in underground kivas.
1356	America's oldest bell, the San José Bell, is cast in Spain.
1536	Mennonites adopt their name from the baptism of Menno Simons, a converted Dutch Catholic priest.
1540	Conquistador Francisco Vasquez de Coronado visits Acoma Pueblo.
September 16, 1541	Spanish conquistador Hernando de Soto arrives at Hot Springs, Arkansas, where natives reverence healing.
1593	Moravians become the first Protestant Church to publish a

	modern-language Bible based on original Hebrew, Aramaic, and Greek texts.
1594	Pilgrims begin visiting El Sanctuário de Chimayó, New Mexico, in search of miraculous healing.
January 21, 1599	Vincente de Zaldivar burns and pillages Acoma Pueblo.
1600	Roman Catholic priests proselytize the Acoma.
1612	Santa Fe workers build San Miguel Mission, the nation's oldest mission church, in the Barrio de Analco, the oldest Hispanic neighborhood in North America.
1619	Taos Pueblo acquires its first church, San Gerónimo, named for Saint Jerome, translator of the Vulgate Bible.
1620	Reformed Protestants arrive in the Western Hemisphere aboard the *Mayflower* to found the Massachusetts Bay Colony.
1629	Father Juan Ramirez builds the church of San Esteven del Rey at the Acoma Pueblo.
	Franciscan friars operate the San Francisco Mission in Arizona.
1634	English Congregationalists settle in Barnstable, Massachusetts.
May 28, 1638	Swedish Lutherans arrive in the colonies and erect Fort Christina near Wilmington, Delaware.

1639	Roger Williams launches the American Baptist community of Providence, Rhode Island.	1692	Guadalupe del Paso subdues the Acoma.
1655	Dutch invaders halt attempts of Swedish colonists to build a Lutheran church.	1693	General Don Diego de Vargas restores the Santa Fe mission to the church.
August 3, 1657	Quaker immigrants arrive at Newport, Rhode Island.	1709	Trinity Church founds Trinity School, New York City's oldest educational facility.
1658	Puritans hang Quakers for violating Massachusetts law.	1710	Marquis de Peñuela rebuilds San Miguel Mission.
1660	Founders establish the Bruton Parish Episcopal Church at Middle Plantation in Williamsburg, Virginia.	1720	Pueblo and Navajo migrate into Anasazi stone strongholds in Chaco Canyon, New Mexico.
June 25, 1673	Missionaries Jacques Marquette and Louis Joliet arrive in St. Louis, Missouri.	1722	Congregationalists seek entrance into the Church of England.
November 24, 1677	Chumash Painted Cave, in the Santa Ynez Mountains, Santa Barbara, California, records a solar eclipse.	August 7, 1727	Ursuline nuns arrive in New Orleans to educate young girls.
1680	Father Louis Hennepin introduces Catholicism to Minnesota.	1736	John Wesley begins mission work in Savannah, Georgia, that is the beginning of American Methodism.
August	Popé of San Juan Pueblo ousts Spanish rulers and priests from New Mexico and burns San Miguel Mission.	1740	Workers build Santa Fe's Loretto Chapel from puddled adobe.
1681	Huguenots fleeing France arrive at Charles Town, South Carolina.	1748	America's first architect, Peter Harrison, erects Boston's King's Chapel, the nation's first major stone structure.
1685	Sephardic Jews seek religious freedom in Rhode Island, Roger Williams's nondenominational refuge.	1749	Kahal Kadosh Beth Elohim unites Sephardic Jewish pioneers in Charleston, South Carolina, including Moses Lindo, the colonies' first indigo cultivator, and Joseph Levy, possibly North America's first Jewish military officer.
1686	On Boston Common, colonists establish King's Chapel, the first colonial Anglican church.		
1688	Abolitionists sign the Germantown Mennonite Resolution against Slavery.	1753	Moravians establish the Bethabara Moravian theocratic commune in Winston-Salem, North Carolina.
	Anglicans build their first New England sanctuary in Boston.	1765	Quakers oppose the Stamp Act.
1690	Immigrants form the Germantown Mennonite Church, the nation's oldest living congregation, in Germantown, Pennsylvania.	1767	New York City's Trinity Church organizes the Society for the Relief of Widows and Orphans of Clergymen.
		1768	America's first native-born musician, William Billings,

composes a liturgical round, "When Jesus Wept."

1769   Father Junípero Serra, the Apostle of California, founds his first mission, San Diego de Alcala.

1770   John Murray organizes American Universalism.

William Billings collects original liturgical music in *The New England Psalm Singer.*

September 1, 1772   Father José Cavalier, five soldiers, and two Chumash build the palisades of San Luis Obispo de Tolosa Mission.

1774   Quakers demand a Continental Congress.

May   Mother Ann Lee begins leading English Shakers to New York.

1775   Sweet Medicine receives a medicine bundle and teaches the Sun Dance to the Cheyenne.

The Ipai and Tipai destroy the San Diego Mission and kill its head priest.

April 18   Paul Revere hangs two lanterns in the steeple of Old North Church as a signal to patriots to prepare for invasion.

1776   Quakers support the Declaration of Independence in 1776.

August 1   Francis Salvador becomes the first Jew to die for the American cause when Indians murder him.

September 21   New York City's Trinity Church burns as a result of the Battle of Harlem Heights.

November 1   The San Juan Capistrano Mission opens over the Santa Barbara Channel tectonic fault.

1777   Old Swedes Church in Wilmington, Delaware, serves as temporary quarters for the Redcoats after the Battle of the Brandywine.

1781   At the Battle of Yorktown, the Bruton Parish Episcopal Church of Williamsburg, Virginia, serves as a military storehouse and dressing station.

October 19   Boston's Old North Church bells ring out Cornwallis's surrender at Yorktown.

1782   Circling Raven foresees the coming of Jesuit missionaries to Idaho.

1783   Quakers and Mennonites, the nation's first abolitionists, reject the Fugitive Slave Act.

1784   John Wesley issues a prayer book, *The Sunday Service of the Methodists in North America,* which incorporates the revision of the Church of England's *Thirty-Nine Articles of Religion.*

New York City's Trinity Church formally separates from the Church of England.

December 24   Sixty American Methodist lay ministers organize Methodist Episcopalism at Baltimore's Lovely Lane Church, the source of American Methodism.

1785   Gabrielino seer Toypurina leads an unsuccessful revolt at the San Gabriel Mission.

James Freeman directs the revision of the Book of Common Prayer to exclude references to the Trinity.

St. Peter's Church becomes New York City's first Catholic church.

Timothy Dwight composes an American epic, *The Conquest of Canaan.*

1787   Richard Allen founds the African Methodist Episcopal Church.

1788   The Shaker congregation at New Lebanon, New York, becomes the first organized Shaker community in the New World.

March 21	New Orleans's cathedral burns.		a vision of the Chimayó crucifix near Santa Cruz, New Mexico.
1789	Methodist Publishing House begins printing religious works in Nashville, Tennessee.	1814	Robert Mills, the nation's first Native American architect, completes the First Unitarian Church of Philadelphia.
August 17, 1790	George Washington promises religious freedom to Jews in Newport, Rhode Island.	1815	General Andrew "Old Hickory" Jackson thanks the Ursuline nuns of New Orleans for praying that he triumph over the British at the Battle of New Orleans.
1791	Pierre L'Enfant calls for the building of a great national church in Washington, D.C.		
	The Emanuel African Methodist Episcopal Church forms the Free African Society.	1816	Harvard opens the nation's first unaffiliated graduate divinity school.
1792	Swedenborgianism reaches the United States.	1818	Timothy Dwight issues a five-volume masterwork, *Theology Explained and Defended*.
April 19, 1794	The Shakers found Sabbathday Lake commune.	1824	Carpenters at Fort Ross, California, construct Holy Trinity Chapel for Russian Orthodox worship.
August 21, 1796	Non-Trinitarians adopt the name Unitarian in Philadelphia.		
June 24, 1797	San Juan Bautista enters the California mission chain.		Kahal Kadosh Beth Elohim requests an abridged Sephardic Orthodox liturgy.
1798	White Buffalo Calf Woman delivers the first pipe to native peoples as a gift from the Great Spirit to preserve and unify humankind.	1831	The Flathead dispatch a delegation to St. Louis to learn about European religion and about combating disease.
1803	Urban Guillet leads Trappist monks to Baltimore, Maryland, in search of a refuge.	September 9, 1832	Pulpit orator and essayist Ralph Waldo Emerson delivers "The Last Supper," a farewell sermon that ends his ministry.
1805	The worship of Guatemala's black Christ reaches New Mexico.	1834	Mexican general Figueroa secularizes the California mission string.
	Lieutenant Antonio Narbona massacres 115 Navajo in Canyon de Chelly.		
1808	Congregationalists institute a seminary at Andover, Maryland.	August 24, 1835	Wesleyan Grove tenting grounds opens on Martha's Vineyard, Massachusetts.
	Harlem's Abyssinian Baptist Church begins two centuries of civil-rights activism.	1838	Missouri governor Lillburn W. Boggs launches an extermination drive against local Mormons.
July 31, 1809	Seton organizes the American Sisters of Charity.	October 30	A raid of the state militia against Mormons at Haun's Mill, Missouri, kills seventeen.
1810	Elizabeth Seton establishes the first Catholic parochial school system.		
Good Friday	Friar Bernardo Abeyta experiences	1839	Richard Upjohn designs Trinity

Church, New York's oldest Episcopal church.

George Catlin describes sacred pipestone in *North American Indians*.

1840   Father Pierre Jean de Smet ministers to the Flathead of Idaho.

1841   The Russian American Company initiates Orthodox religious observances in Kenai, Alaska.

July 29   Father Pierre Jean de Smet celebrates Idaho's first mass with the state's first Catholics.

1842   German Lutherans immigrate to the United States and form the Amana communes.

1844   B. F. White and E. J. King publish popular American hymns in *The Sacred Harp*.

1845   Organizers of the Society of St. Vincent de Paul convene at the Cathedral Basilica of St. Louis for their first conference.

German Jews form Temple Emmanu-El on New York City's Lower East Side.

1846   Father Boniface Wimmer founds St. Vincent's Archabbey and College in Latrobe, Pennsylvania.

Rabbi Isaac Mayer Wise immigrates to Albany, New York, from Bohemia.

1847   Big Bethel African Methodist Episcopal Church becomes Georgia's first AME church.

Bishop Jean Baptiste Lamy systematically obliterates Hispanic customs in New Mexico.

Mormons depart Missouri to found an empire in Utah.

Philadelphia's Jews set up the Bes Almon and establish a cemetery on Mount Troy.

April 26   A Chicago consortium of

ministers from fifteen congregations organizes Missouri Lutheranism.

July 24   Brigham Young leads 148 Mormon refugees to the Wasatch Mountains to escape lethal vigilantism and murder in Missouri and Illinois.

July 28   With the tip of his cane, Young chooses a spot for the Mormon temple block.

August 22   The Mormon Tabernacle Choir delivers its first performance.

December 21, 1848   Trappist monks from Melleray, France, buy a farm near Bardstown, Kentucky.

1850   Dr. Rob Morris founds the Order of the Eastern Star.

Totemism reaches its height in Sitka, Alaska.

1850s   Peyotism spreads across the Rio Grande Valley to tribes of the Great Basin.

1851   Through the Indian Appropriations Bill of 1851, the U.S. government purchases the pipestone quarry as part of Sisseton and Wahpeton lands in southern Minnesota.

1852   The first Benedictine nuns arrive in the United States from Bavaria.

September   The Sisters of Loretto, pioneer teaching nuns, arrive in Santa Fe, New Mexico.

1853   James Renwick begins building New York City's St. Patrick's Cathedral.

Jean Baptiste Lamy becomes the Southwest's first Roman Catholic bishop.

1854   America's oldest bell arrives at Santa Fe by oxcart from Mexico City.

1855   Philadelphia's Jews support a Hebrew Ladies Aid Society and the men's Hebrew Benevolent Society.

Poet Henry Wadsworth Longfellow mentions the sacred pipestone quarry in his Native-American epic, *The Song of Hiawatha*.

A U.S. treaty with the Makah allows unlimited access to sea harvesting, the only sanctioned whaling in the United States.

Treaties reserve Enola Hill, Oregon, for native use.

1856 Jewish poet Penina Moise authors *Hymns Written for the Use of Hebrew Congregations*.

Rabbi Isaac Mayer Wise introduces a uniform prayer book, *Minhag America*.

1857 William Savage Pitts composes "The Church in the Wildwood."

1858 The government grants the Yankton Sioux unrestricted rights to the pipestone quarry.

1862 At the Battle of Williamsburg, Virginia, Union doctors treat soldiers from both sides at the Bruton Parish Episcopal Church.

1863 The Abraham Lincoln Cane confers sovereignty on the Acoma.

The nation's first female minister, Olympia Brown, is ordained.

January 1 The Emancipation Proclamation frees slaves.

1864 Colonel Christopher "Kit" Carson decimates the Navajo at Canyon de Chelly.

Amanites settle near Cedar Rapids, Iowa.

May Father Thomas O'Reilly, the only Catholic chaplain in the Civil War, threatens General William T. Sherman with mutiny of Catholic soldiers if the army harms Atlanta's churches.

December 19 The citizens of Bradford, Iowa, open a Congregational church called the Little Brown Church in the Vale.

1866 Isaac Leeser mourns damage to South Carolina's synagogues in his newspaper, the *Occident*.

1867 The original Mormon Tabernacle opens in Salt Lake City.

1868 Episcopalians found the University of the South.

The U.S. government cedes the Black Hills to the Sioux.

November 27 General George Armstrong Custer leads a massacre of Cheyenne at the Washita River in Oklahoma.

1869 The San Carlos Apache Reservation takes possession of Mount Graham, Arizona.

1872 A federal survey team gives right of way over the Black Hills to the Northern Pacific Railroad.

Yellowstone becomes the nation's oldest and most prized national park.

1873 Rabbi Isaac Mayer Wise establishes the Union of American Hebrew Congregations.

1875 Archbishop Lamy furthers close relations with New Mexico's Protestants and Jews.

Mary Baker Eddy issues the Christian Science textbook *Science and Health with Key to the Scriptures*.

The Union of American Hebrew Congregations founds the Hebrew Union College, America's first Jewish seminary.

April 23 An executive order forces the Yavapai from the Camp Verde Reserve on the March of Tears.

1876 Monks from Pennsylvania found St. Bernard Abbey in Alabama.

June 25	Sioux and Cheyenne defeat General George Armstrong Custer at the Battle of the Little Bighorn.
1877	The U.S. government resettles the Coeur d'Alene away from Old Mission and the tribal cemetery.
September 5	A Sioux prison guard assassinates Crazy Horse, an influential holy man and leader.
1879	Mary Baker Eddy charters Christian Science headquarters in Boston.
	Red Cloud signs over the Black Hills to federal agents.
July 16	The Methodist Tabernacle opens in Oak Bluffs, Massachusetts.
1881	Helen Hunt Jackson exposes the mistreatment of Mission Indians in *A Century of Dishonor: A Sketch of the United States Government's Dealing with Some of the Indian Tribes.*
1884	Jackson publishes *Ramona,* now an annual pageant held near Mount San Jacinto, California.
	U.S. government agents halt the Sun Dance.
ca. 1885	The death of wild buffalo curtails the religion of plains Indians.
1885	The "Pittsburgh Platform" liberalizes Jewish custom and belief.
1887	The Kiowa celebrate their last Sun Dance on the Washita River.
1888	John Muir champions the preservation of Mount Shasta, California.
	King David Kalakaua anthologizes *The Legends and Myths of Hawaii.*
	Temple Emanu-El hires Dr. Joseph Silverman, the city's first American-born rabbi and graduate of Hebrew Union College.
1889	Rabbi Isaac Mayer Wise leads the Central Conference of American Rabbis.
February 23	Five nuns build Holy Name Convent and Academy in San Antonio, Florida.
1890	Henry Wadsworth Longfellow's poem "The Jewish Cemetery at Newport" honors the Jews of Newport, Rhode Island.
November	The Paiute prophet Wovoka leads a native revival and introduces the Ghost Dance.
December 28	The Seventh Cavalry massacres 250 noncombatants at Wounded Knee, South Dakota.
1890s	John Wilson of the Caddo and Quanah Parker of the Comanche formalize peyote ceremonies.
1893	President Grover Cleveland makes Crater Lake, Oregon, a part of the Cascade Range Forest Reserve.
	The Episcopal diocese plans the Washington National Cathedral, the world's sixth largest cathedral.
	The first Bahá'i reach the United States.
	Swami Vivekenanda represents Hinduism at Chicago's Parliament of Religions of the World Colombian Exposition.
May	Waldensians arrive in Valdese, North Carolina, from Italy's Cottian Alps and form the New World's largest Waldensian colony.
1894	Fifty Pittsburgh women organize the National Council of Jewish Women.
April	The Ramakrishna Order of India begins a world mission headquartered in New York City.
November	Swami Vivekenanda organizes the Vedanta Society in New York City.
1895	Tewa-Hopi potter Nampeyo revives ancient Navajo symbolism.

	The Blackfoot Confederacy of Siksika, Kainah, and Piegan tribes signs away ownership of Badger–Two Medicine Area in Heart Butte, Montana.
	The Reverend Anna Howard Shaw, a frontier orator and suffragist, speaks at the Mormon Tabernacle on the emancipation of women.
1901	The Apostolic Faith Movement begins in Topeka, Kansas.
January 1	Agnes Ozman launches glossolalia at a revival in Topeka, Kansas.
1902	Beacon House Publishing opens in Boston.
1903	A. J. Tomlinson founds the Church of God.
	With the gift of a house on Henry Street from Jacob Schiff, nurse Lillian Wald begins treating 4,500 patients annually in eighteen districts.
1906	The African-American Church of God originates from the Azusa Street Revival of William Seymour, father of American Pentecostalism.
September	The Hopi of Oraibi split over the issue of appeasing whites.
September 24	Congress names Devils Tower, Wyoming, the nation's first national monument.
1907	The U.S. Parks Commission establishes Chaco Culture National Historical Park in New Mexico.
September 29	President Theodore Roosevelt attends the formal founding of the Washington National Cathedral.
1908	Mary Baker Eddy founds the *Christian Science Monitor*.
	The Reverend Dr. Adam Clayton Powell, Sr., joins the staff of the Abyssinian Baptist Church of

	Harlem.
1909	A conference at the Henry Street Settlement House grows into the National Association for the Advancement of Colored People.
May 30, 1910	President William Howard Taft proclaims Rainbow Bridge, Utah, a national monument.
1912	Father Paul Dobberstein begins work on the Grotto of the Redemption in West Bend, Iowa.
	William Jennings Bryan dubs St. Fidelis Church of Victoria, Kansas, the "Cathedral of the Plains."
	Brother Joseph Zoettl begins building the Ave Maria Grotto in Cullman, Alabama.
1913	Archeologist John F. G. Stokes identifies a shrine at Kamohio Bay, Kaho'Olawe, Hawaii.
	Temple Emmanu-El member Louis Marshall initiates the Anti-Defamation League of B'nai B'rith.
1914	Lillian Wald and Jews from Temple Emmanu-El launch a pre–World War I peace parade.
1915	Mark Levy introduces messianic Judaism in New York City.
April	Messianic Jews found the Hebrew Christian Alliance.
1916	A schism among Pentecostals results in the Oneness Pentecostals, who reject the Trinity and embrace Jesus as the only deity.
1917	Lillian Wald extends the Henry Street Settlement House as wartime headquarters for the Red Cross and Food Council.
October 1918	The Firstborn Church of Christ, forerunner of the Native American Church, incorporates in Oklahoma.

1919	Peyotism becomes the belief system of 75 percent of the Shoshone.
1920	The U.S. military chooses Kaho'Olawe, Hawaii, for ordnance training and an artillery range.
1921	Bahá'is host a Race Amity conference in Springfield, Massachusetts.
May 21, 1922	Dr. Harry Emerson Fosdick delivers the sermon "Shall the Fundamentalists Win?," a controversial call for tolerance.
1925	Lillian Wald's memoir, *Windows on Henry Street,* summarizes a life committed to humanitarianism.
1926	A Montana judge upholds a 1923 antipeyote ordinance.
	The International Whaling Commission outlaws the slaughter of whales.
1927	Willa Cather publishes *Death Comes for the Archbishop.*
	In Houston, Texas, 121 people begin a church that grows into Second Baptist, a megachurch serving 24,000 members.
December 5	King Bhumibol, head of Burmese Buddhism, is born in Cambridge, Massachusetts.
1928	Elizabeth Schellenberg plans the Wayfarers' Chapel of Rancho Palos Verdes, California, as a tribute to Emanuel Swedenborg.
	Horticulturist Dr. Henry Moore of Islington, Ontario, designs the International Peace Garden to be built on the North Dakota border with Canada.
June 9, 1929	Adah Robinson completes construction of the Boston Avenue Methodist Church in Tulsa, Oklahoma.
November	Lula Jones and Nellie Davis write *Heaven Bound,* an allegorical

	morality play, for presentation at Atlanta's Big Bethel AME Church.
1930	Douglas Steere founds a peace center at Pendle Hill, Pennsylvania.
	W. Fard Muhammad declares that Allah appeared to him.
October 5	Riverside Church of New York City launches an experiment in interdenominationalism grounded in the spirit of American freedom.
1931	Antelope Canyon, Arizona, becomes a public landmark.
	Archivist Sister R. Mildred Barker places her collection at the Shaker Library in New Gloucester, Massachusetts.
	W. Fard Muhammad establishes the Nation of Islam in Detroit.
June 1, 1932	Amanites dismantle their Iowa commune and replace it with the Amana Church Society.
1936	The Reverend Adam Clayton Powell, Jr., succeeds his father as pastor of the Abyssinian Baptist Church of Harlem.
1937	The Wheelwright Museum of the American Indian in Santa Fe preserves Anasazi sacred ritual.
1938	The Reverend Dr. Adam Clayton Powell, Sr., publishes *Against the Tide.*
1939	Tlingit carvers exhibit totems at the San Francisco Exposition.
1940	Chief Henry Standing Bear hires Korczak Ziolkowski to begin sculpting the Crazy Horse Monument.
1941	Citizens of Hot Springs, Arkansas, initiate a pageant, Saga of the Waters.
	Tlingit carvers exhibit religious art at the Museum of Modern Art in New York City.

1942   Temple Emmanu-El's Isaac Mayer Wise Hall launches a military canteen.

1945   The Reverend Adam Clayton Powell, Jr., enters the U.S. Congress and launches a drive for racial equality.

              The Reverend Dr. Adam Clayton Powell, Sr., publishes *Riots and Ruins.*

              The Washington Islamic Mosque and Cultural Center derives from a consortium of Islamics and diplomats from Muslim nations worldwide.

1946   Miguel Archibeque organizes El Concilio Supremo Arzobispal to legitimize village chapters of the Hermanos Penitentes.

1947   Calvary Church in Charlotte, North Carolina, launches an unaffiliated evangelical outreach.

              Quaker Gladdys Esther Muir issues a peace manifesto, "The Place of Brethren Colleges in Preparing Men and Women for Peace Leadership."

              Quakers receive the Nobel Peace Prize.

1948   George Harrison designs and installs the organ at the Mormon Tabernacle.

              Gladdys Muir founds a peace studies program at Manchester College.

              Monks establish Our Lady of Guadalupe in Pecos, New Mexico.

              Trappist monk Thomas Merton publishes *The Seven Storey Mountain.*

February 25   Ebenezer Baptist Church in Atlanta ordains Dr. Martin Luther King, Jr.

1949   Imam Mohamad Jawad Chirri hosts *Islam in Focus* on Detroit radio.

              A chapel in Prague, Oklahoma, receives a papal designation as the National Shrine of the Infant Jesus of Prague.

              Actors perform the first annual Hiawatha Pageant in Pipestone, Minnesota.

              Mepkin Abbey opens on a former rice plantation in South Carolina.

1950   Baron Hirsch Synagogue, the nation's largest Orthodox Jewish temple, opens in Memphis, Tennessee.

              Dr. Billy Graham initiates a popular radio show, *Hour of Decision.*

              The Sioux revive the Sun Dance.

1951   U.S. authorities lift the potlatch ban in the Pacific Northwest. Gerald Gardner revives the Wiccan coven.

1952   Elizabeth Chapin Patterson establishes the Meher Baba Center at Myrtle Beach, South Carolina.

May 3, 1953   The Bahá'i temple opens in Wilmette, Illinois.

1954   Gerald Gardner publishes *Witchcraft Today,* a Wiccan handbook.

              L. Ron Hubbard founds the Church of Scientology.

April 1   Congress sanctions the building of an Air Force Academy.

1955   Dan Katchongvu informs Congress that the Hopi anticipate a messiah.

              Eero Saarinen applies modern techniques in his design for the Chapel of Massachusetts Institute of Technology.

              Louis Farrakhan joins the Nation of Islam as a disciple.

              The Reverend Adam Clayton Powell, Jr., urges President

Dwight D. Eisenhower to end colonialism.

July 4, 1956   Members of Birmingham's Sixteenth Street Baptist Church fight Alabama's ban on the National Association for the Advancement of Colored People

1957   Dr. Billy Graham pioneers the televised religious crusade.

1958   A bomb at Birmingham's Temple Beth-El fails to explode.

1959   After dissidents flee Cuban dictator Fidel Castro, Santería spreads across the Americas.

1960   At the end of a civil-rights campaign in Montgomery, Alabama, Dr. Martin Luther King, Jr., joins his father's pastorate at Ebenezer Baptist Church in Atlanta.

Dr. Billy Graham convenes the first conference on world evangelism in Montreux, Switzerland.

L. Ron Hubbard publishes *Dianetics: The Modern Science of Mental Health.*

Arthur M. Brazier begins pastoring the Apostolic Church of God in Chicago.

August 14   Ronald S. Ligon opens Christus Gardens, a Christian theme park, in Gatlinburg, Tennessee.

1960s   Young Oon Kim begins recruiting Moonies in Eugene, Oregon.

1961   The Bureau of Indian Affairs removes tribal status from the Snoqualmie.

To ally non-Christians, Christians, and nontheists, Unitarians join Universalists as Unitarian Universalists.

1962   Birmingham's Sixteenth Street Baptist Church begins headquartering civil-rights

meetings and rallies.

A judge in Needles, California, sanctions consumption of peyote for legitimate religious ritual.

1963   The Air Force Academy Chapel opens.

April 3   Blacks issue the "Birmingham Manifesto" to protest racial segregation.

April 23   Dr. Martin Luther King, Jr., pens his "Letter from a Birmingham Jail," championing nonviolent extremism.

August 28   Dr. Martin Luther King, Jr., leads a march on Washington.

September 15   Racists lob a bomb that kills four young worshippers at Birmingham's Sixteenth Street Baptist Church.

1964   Mark Rothko accepts a commission to create canvases that adorn the ecumenical Rothko Chapel in Houston, Texas.

1965   Bhaktivedanta Swami Prabhupada gives North America its first view of Krishna worship.

Dr. Billy Graham publishes a bestseller, *World Aflame.*

John Paul Twitchell establishes Eck.

Dr. Martin Luther King, Jr., leads a voting rights march in Selma and Montgomery, Alabama.

February 21   Black assassins gun down Malcolm X as he delivers a speech in Harlem.

1967   Dr. Billy Graham helps dedicate Oral Roberts University in Tulsa, Oklahoma.

The Krishna movement spreads to San Francisco.

Urgyen Sangharakshita forms the Friends of the Western Buddhist Order.

April 1   Oral Roberts dedicates the Prayer
           Tower at the center of the Oral
           Roberts University campus.

1968   Laura Gilpin publishes details of
           native religion in *The Enduring
           Navaho.*

           The Reverend Troy D. Perry
           founds the Metropolitan
           Community Church of Los
           Angeles to minister to gay
           Christians.

April 4   A lone gunman assassinates Dr.
           Martin Luther King, Jr.

1969   John Paul Twitchell systematizes
           Eckankar theology in *Eckankar:
           The Key to Secret Worlds.*

           N. Scott Momaday publishes a
           monumental Kiowa memoir, *The
           Way to Rainy Mountain.*

1970   San Marga Iraivan Temple, the first
           traditional Hindu worship center
           constructed outside Asia, opens on
           Kauai, Hawaii.

           The American Indian Movement
           protests the film *A Man Called
           Horse* for sacrilege.

           The Native American Church
           becomes the largest and most
           influential Indian religious body.

           Yor Yellowtail Toineeta's
           monograph *Absarog-Issawua*
           clarifies the native attitude toward
           the sacred buffalo.

1971   Ram Dass's bestseller *Be Here Now*
           introduces Hinduism to
           Americans.

           The Reverend Sun Myung Moon
           launches his "Day of Hope" tour.

           Victor Christ-Janer applies post-
           and-lintel styling to the
           modernistic Charterhouse of the
           Transfiguration in Arlington,
           Vermont.

August 14–15 Residents of Taos Pueblo celebrate
           the return of Blue Lake for

religious ceremonies.

1972   Atlanta's Big Bethel AME Church
           opens Bethel Towers, a 182-unit
           apartment complex for low-
           income elderly.

           Investor Robert Johnson builds
           Holy Land USA, a religious
           theme park in Bedford, Virginia.

           Tri-County Assembly of God in
           Fairfield, Ohio, grows to be one of
           the top ten Assembly of God
           churches in the nation.

           Oral Roberts enters the
           Oklahoma Hall of Fame.

1973   Dr. Billy Graham founds the
           World Emergency Fund.

1974   Ram Dass offers lectures and
           workshops through the Hanuman
           Foundation.

           The Navajo sue the U.S. secretary
           of the interior, commissioner of
           the Bureau of Reclamation, and
           director of the National Park
           Service to preserve Navajo sacred
           geography from human violation.

           Zen expert Daisetz Teitaro
           Suzuki issues *An Introduction to
           Zen Buddhism.*

1975   Jan Hai completes *The History of
           Hinayana Buddhism.*

           Pope Paul VI proclaims Elizabeth
           Seton the first U.S. saint.

           Priests Miriam and Oswan
           Chamani open the Voodoo
           Spiritual Temple in New Orleans.

           I. M. Pei modernizes the Christian
           Science Center in Boston.

1976   Native Hawaiians make their first
           legal visit to Kaho'Olawe.

1977   Circle Sanctuary publishes *Circle
           Magic Songs,* a miscellany of songs,
           articles, chants, and illustrations,
           and initiates a Pan Pagan Festival.

           Coretta Scott King inters her

husband's remains in a memorial tomb at the Center for Non-Violent Social Change in Atlanta.

Georgia Lee reconstructs Chumash history from oral tradition.

Tirupatiah Tella, president of Telugu Association of Greater Chicago, organizes plans for the Hindu Temple of Greater Chicago.

Urgyen Sangharakshita of the Aryaloka Buddhist Retreat Center of Newmarket, New Hampshire, defends homosexuals.

March 7 Martyrs George Helm and Kimo Mitchell drown while visiting Kaho'Olawe, Hawaii.

June Natives hold the first international Inuit Circumpolar Conference at Barrow, Alaska.

September Inuit form the Alaskan Commission to revoke the ban on ritual whaling.

November Robert E. "Dynamite Bob" Chambliss receives a life sentence for the bombing of Birmingham's Sixteenth Street Baptist Church.

1978 Washington, D.C., Zoroastrians found "ZAMWI," a local support group.

Congress passes the American Indian Religious Freedom Act.

Jan Hai and Wing Sing establish the Texas Buddhist Association and build the Buddha Light Temple.

Louis Kaplan launches the *Jewish TV Broadcast,* the nation's first messianic Jewish series.

Luther Standing Bear describes the sanctity of Enchanted Rock in *Land of the Spotted Eagle.*

Selena Fox founds the Church of Circle Wicca.

1979 Appalachian Bishops issue a pastoral letter, *This Land Is Home to Me.*

Bhagwan Shree Rajneesh declares that Rajneeshism can rescue humankind from destruction.

Margot Adler launches American Wiccans with *Drawing Down the Moon: Witches, Druids, Goddess-Worshippers, and Other Pagans in America Today.*

Satguru Sivaya Subramuniyaswami founds a monthly international journal, *Hinduism Today.*

The Reverend Doctor Yukitaka Yamamoto introduces Shintoism in the United States.

1980 Courts rule that reserving Rainbow Bridge for Navajo ceremonies would violate public rights.

E. Fay Jones undertakes a commission to build Thorncrown Chapel in Eureka Springs, Arkansas.

Oral Roberts declares that a 900-foot Christ predicts that Roberts will die if he doesn't raise funding for the City of Faith.

1981 Bhagwan Rajneesh establishes the Rajneesh Foundation in Montclair, New Jersey.

Chevron and Belgian Petrofina drill for oil in Badger–Two Medicine Area, Heart Butte, Montana.

The A. R. Mitchell Memorial Museum of Western Art begins a collection of Hispanic religious folk art.

August 19 The American Burma Buddhist Association aims to preserve the culture of Burmese immigrants.

1982 Evangelist Greg Laurie launches Harvest Ministries, Inc.®, in Riverside, California.

The Tlingit, Haida, and Tsimshian nations hold their first combined cultural celebration.

1983 The Venerable Sayadaw Ashin Indaka begins supervising Burmese Buddhists in Brooklyn, New York.

Dr. Billy Graham issues a controversial jeremiad, *Approaching Hoofbeats: The Four Horsemen of the Apocalypse.*

1984 Father Aelred charters the Monastery of Christ in the Desert outside Abiquiu, New Mexico.

January John Paul Twitchell establishes the world Temple of Eck at Chanhassen, Minnesota.

1985 Dr. Robert Schuller publishes *The Power of Being Debt Free.*

Louis Farrakhan packs New York City's Madison Square Garden for a speech advocating pride, atonement, and self-reliance.

Pope John Paul II beatifies Father Junípero Serra.

January 25 Sthapathi Ganapathi, the retired principal of the only College of Temple Architecture near Madras, India, completes the Hindu Temple of Greater Chicago.

October The Rajneesh Foundation abandons its ashram in Antelope, Oregon.

1986 The Wiping of Tears/Mending the Sacred Hoop Ride preserves the prophetic dreams of Black Elk.

1987 Mennonites establish a policy of admitting only celibate gays to membership.

The Billy Graham Training Center at the Cove opens in Asheville, North Carolina.

May 21 The Acoma demonstrate against the establishment of El Malpais National Monument and

Conservation Area.

June 1 The American Indian Religious Freedom Act passes the U.S. House unanimously.

December 17 The Senate unanimously approves El Malpais National Monument and Conservation Area.

1988 The University of Arizona selects Mount Graham as the location for seven telescopes.

June 10 Wat Carolina Buddhajakra Vanaram establishes Burmese Buddhism in the Carolinas.

1989 Dr. Cissy Grossman issues *A Temple Treasury: The Judaica Collection of Congregation Emanu-El of the City of New York.*

Laguna poet Paula Gunn Allen anthologizes Navajo myths in *Spider Woman's Granddaughters: Traditional Tales and Contemporary Writing by Native American Women.*

1990 President George Bush ends military target practice on Kaho'Olawe and ponders returning the island to citizen control.

The Supreme Court rules that peyote carries religious diversity from a right to a luxury.

September 29 President George Bush addresses onlookers at the completion of the Washington National Cathedral.

1991 David Yonngi Cho, pastor of the Korean Assemblies of God in Seoul, envisions a spiritual tumult in the United States.

Ram Dass and Mirabai Bush compose *Compassion in Action: Setting Out on the Path of Service,* a treatise on volunteerism.

Shri Acharya Abhidhyanananda founds the Abhidhyan Yoga Institute, Inc.

The American Buddhist Congress forms a statewide association to enrich Buddhism in Texas.

The Dalai Lama prays for world peace at the Rothko Chapel in Houston, Texas.

July
Joseph Cardinal Bernardin establishes the Monastery of the Holy Cross in metropolitan Chicago.

1992
Adam Fortunate Eagle, the Spiritual Leader of the Keepers of the Sacred Tradition of Pipemakers, issues *Alcatraz, Alcatraz: The Indian Occupation.*

Earth First! protests logging on Enola Hill in Portland, Oregon.

Keepers of the Treasures convene at Sioux Falls, South Dakota, to declare war on sacrilege against Sioux spirituality.

Restorers of Kaho'Olawe construct a platform honoring ancestors.

The United Nations admits Taos Pueblo to the "World Heritage List."

Walter Speedis, Cascades Klickitat elder, testifies to the sanctity of Enola Hill in Portland, Oregon.

September
Lien Hoa Buddhist Temple in Olympia, Washington, honors the founding of the Unified Vietnamese Buddhist Congregation in the United States.

1993
Rabbi Rafael G. Grossman publishes *Binah: The Modern Quest for Torah Understanding.*

Evangelist Greg Laurie publishes *On Fire.*

The first Unity Ride unites the Sioux.

The Wintun force the U.S. Forest Service to study Panther

Meadows, California, as a sacred medicine site.

Jerry Flute of the Medicine Wheel Coalition, demands a halt to traffic at Medicine Wheel, Wyoming.

Satguru Sivaya Subramuniyaswami cochairs the Parliament of the World's Religions in Chicago.

June
The U.S. Supreme Court declares that Lukumi ritual sacrifice is both humane and constitutionally sanctioned.

October
Navajo Leroy Jackson, activist for Diné CARE, is found dead in his van.

1994
Bhaktivedanta Swami Prabhupada publishes *Back to Godhead.*

Hawaiian natives begin repatriating the island of Kaho'Olawe.

The second Sioux Unity Ride doubles the route.

April 29
Bill Clinton meets with 200 Indian leaders and promises to protect native rights to practice aboriginal faith.

August
The birth of a white female buffalo calf signifies to plains Indians that the world is ready for peace and harmony.

October 6
President Bill Clinton legitimizes use of peyote as part of traditional Indian worship services.

December
Nation of Islam members purchase Muhammad Farms in Terrell County, Georgia.

1995
Arthur M. Brazier co-initiates the Woodlawn Organization to protest the dismantling of Chicago's Jackson Park El.

The Blackfoot launch Aamskapi-Pikuni Radio to preserve the Pikuni language.

Dr. Arvol Looking Horse asserts that Wakan Tanka, the Great Spirit, created all nature.

George Johnson describes the Hermanos Penitentes in *Fire in the Mind*.

Kate Penfield anthologizes eleven addresses by Baptists in *Into a New Day: Exploring a Baptist Journey of Division, Diversity, and Dialogue*.

Nelson Foster publishes a pictorial tribute, *Kaho'olawe:Na Leo o Kanaloa*.

Satguru Sivaya Subramuniyaswami founds the Hindu Heritage Endowment to back the world's Hindu institutions.

The Abyssinian Baptist Church welcomes Fidel Castro to Harlem.

The third Unity Ride makes a 450-mile trek ending in Prince Alberta, Saskatchewan.

March 19 — Neo-Nazis deface Triumph Church and New Life Christian Fellowship, a multicultural congregation in Vicksburg, Mississippi.

April 4–5 — One hundred Hindus join dignitaries from the Hawaiian Islands in a model of pluralistic celebration.

June 18 — The Brownsville Revival begins on Father's Day in Pensacola, Florida.

August 11 — Bonnie Brown and five other Navajo blockade Rainbow Bridge during four-day cleansing ceremonies.

October 16 — At the Washington, D.C., Mall, Louis Farrakhan leads black males in the first Holy Day of Atonement and Reconciliation, the largest U.S. audience ever commanded by a black speaker.

1996 — Aghor Ashram of Sonoma, California, funds a mobile clinic in Varanasi, India.

Navajo storyteller Geri Keams publishes coyote lore on an audiotape, *Sacred Twins and Spider Woman*.

The Reverend G. Anthony Mangun of the Pentecostals of Alexandria, Louisiana, denounces President Bill Clinton's policy allowing partial-birth abortions.

The Reverend Peter J. Gomes publishes *The Good Book: Reading the Bible with Mind and Heart*, which calls for Christians to halt the persecution and marginalization of women and gays.

March 24 — Nonsectarian Christians form the Crossroads Community Church of Hyde Park in Cincinnati, Ohio.

April 3 — New York City's Temple Emmanu-El broadcasts the first sound Internet religious service.

April 5 — Indians issue a formal claim on Enola Hill, Oregon.

April 14 — The world's largest organ recital takes place at the Mormon Tabernacle in Salt Lake City, Utah.

May 3 — A fifty-day Unity Ride passes through the Bighorn Medicine Wheel and Devils Tower, Wyoming.

May 24 — President Bill Clinton issues an executive order protecting and preserving Indian religions.

June 21 — Arvol Looking Horse leads the world prayer day at the Black Hills.

August 24 — Traditional pipe makers form a spiritual church to protect the Pipestone National Monument from exploitation or domination by one tribe or group.

October–November — Messianic Jews mingle with fundamentalist Christians during four weeks of interchurch evangelism and renewal.

1997 — Aghor Ashram of Sonoma, California, funds a clinic and elementary school in Madhya Pradesh, India.

Dr. Robert Schuller publishes *If It's Going to Be, It's up to Me.*

Harvard's Board of Ministry sanctions gay marriages.

In Spike Lee's CBS documentary *4 Little Girls,* commentator Walter Cronkite reflects on a bombing that forced white America to confront racism.

August 12 — Flooding closes Lower Antelope Canyon, Arizona.

October 14 — The Franconia Mennonite Conference expels Germantown, Pennsylvania's Mennonite Church for admitting gay members.

October 23 — The Makah of Seattle, Washington, negotiate the right to hunt four gray whales during annual rituals.

1998 — After suffering a stroke, Ram Dass writes *Conscious Aging.*

Dianne Aprile publishes *The Abbey of Gethsemani: Place of Peace and Paradox.*

Nansook Hong's *In the Shadow of the Moons* exposes family faults and tyranny of the Unification Church.

Rattlesnake Productions produces *Backbone of the World: The Blackfeet.*

Satguru Sivaya Subramuniyaswami earns the title of Hindu Voice of the Century.

The Sacred Land Film Project produces *In the Light of Reverence.*

February 6 — Lower Antelope Canyon reopens.

June 13 — The Reverend Sun Myung Moon unites 7,000 couples at New York City's Madison Square Garden.

July — 41,000 men attend a rally of Promise Keepers in Philadelphia.

August — The Reverend Calvin O. Butts recommends that Americans forgive President Bill Clinton for sexual improprieties.

winter — Former Cherokee chief Wilma Mankiller leads a day conference on raising women's perspectives at the St. Benedict Center in Schuyler, Nebraska.

December — Ben Long revives fresco art for the Chapel of the Prodigal at Montreat-Anderson College in North Carolina.

1999 — Evangelist Greg Laurie publishes *The Upside Down Church* and *Discipleship: The Next Step in Following Jesus.*

Luis Miguel Valdez directs a television version of his folk spectacle *Pastorela.*

Sedona, Arizona, presents Crossing Worlds, a multicultural experience in sacred landscape, myth and legends, history, and earth wisdom.

The Reverend Doctor Yukitaka Yamamoto composes *The Way of the Kami* to introduce Americans to Japanese customs.

January — The Abyssinian Baptist Church of Harlem calls for an end to suspicion and distrust between blacks and Jews.

February — Indians protest Montana cattle ranchers' slaughter of bison.

February 15 — The Abyssinian Baptist Church of Harlem leads a rally and prayer to end police brutality.

May 22 — The Makah make international news by successfully hunting a whale as a form of tribal identity.

June — Koichi Larry Barrish, the only American Shinto priest, presents a workshop at the General Assembly of the Unitarian Universalist

Association in Salt Lake City, Utah.

June The Lama Foundation, *Last Straw* Journal, and Perma-culture Drylands Institute cosponsor a week-long Natural Building Permaculture Convergence.

July The Lakota bless wild horses as symbols of freedom.

August Koichi Larry Barrish and Dr. Yukitaka Yamamoto conduct a

Shinto seminar at the Congress of International Association for Religious Freedom in Vancouver.

2000 A French film crew makes a documentary of the French Huguenot Church's annual French liturgy.

January 27 Bethabara Moravian community celebrates the historic union with the Lutheran church.

RELIGIOUS SITES BY STATE

Alabama
Ave Maria Grotto, Cullman
Sixteenth Street Baptist Church, Birmingham
Alaska
Holy Assumption of the Virgin Mary Church,
  Kenai
Point Barrow
Sitka National Historical Park, Sitka
Arizona
Antelope Canyon, Page
Canyon de Chelly, Chinle
Cathedral Rock, Sedona
Chuska Mountains, Tsaile
Mount Graham, San Carlos
Oraibi, Kykotsmovi
Osho Chidvilas, Tucson
Arkansas
Hot Springs Mountain, Hot Springs
Subiaco Abbey, Subiaco
Thorncrown Chapel, Eureka Springs
California
Abhidhyan Yoga Institute, Nevada City
Aghor Ashram, Sonoma
Church of Scientology Los Angeles, Los Angeles
Crystal Cathedral, Garden Grove
Gurdwara Sahib El Sobrante, El Sobrante
Harvest Ministries, Inc.®, Riverside
Holy Trinity Chapel of Fort Ross, Jenner
Mount Shasta, Mt. Shasta
Painted Rock, California Valley
San Juan Bautista Mission, San Juan Bautista
San Juan Capistrano Mission, San Juan Capistrano
San Luis Obispo de Tolosa, San Luis Obispo
Tsubaki America Shrine, Stockton
Wayfarers' Chapel, Rancho Palos Verdes
Colorado
Air Force Academy Chapel, Colorado Springs
Holy Cross Abbey, Cañon City
Native American Church, Boulder

Sleeping Ute Mountain, Towaoc
Connecticut
Cathedral of St. Joseph, Hartford
Dwight Chapel, New Haven
First Presbyterian Church, Stamford
Delaware
Christ Lutheran Church, Seaford
Old Swedes Church, Wilmington
Florida
Brownsville Assembly of God, Pensacola
Church of Lukumi Babalu Aye, Hialeah
Holy Name Monastery, St. Leo
Georgia
Big Bethel African Methodist Episcopal Church,
  Atlanta
Catholic Shrine of the Immaculate Conception,
  Atlanta
Ebenezer Baptist Church, Atlanta
Hawaii
Kaho'Olawe, Honolulu
San Marga Iraivan Temple, Kapaa
Idaho
Old Mission of the Sacred Heart, Cataldo
Illinois
Apostolic Church of God, Chicago
Bahá'i House of Worship, Wilmette
Hindu Temple of Greater Chicago, Lemont
Monastery of the Holy Cross, Chicago
Mosque Maryam, Chicago
Indiana
Nappanee Missionary Church, Nappanee
Iowa
Amana Church Society, Middle Amana
Grotto of the Redemption, West Bend
Little Brown Church in the Vale, Nashua
Kansas
St. Fidelis Church, Victoria
Kentucky
Abbey of Gethsemani, Trappist

Mount Tabor Retreat Center, Martin

Louisiana

Pentecostals of Alexandria, Alexandria

St. Louis Cathedral, New Orleans

Ursuline Convent, New Orleans

Voodoo Spiritual Temple, New Orleans

Maine

Shaker Meeting House, Sabbathday Lake, New
  Gloucester

Maryland

Lovely Lane Methodist Church, Baltimore

Seton Shrine, Emmitsburg

Massachusetts

Chapel of Massachusetts Institute of Technology,
  Cambridge

Church of the Blessed Sacrament, Holyoke

First Church of Christ, Scientist, Boston

King's Chapel, Boston

Memorial Church of Harvard University,
  Cambridge

Methodist Tabernacle, Oak Bluffs

Old North Church, Boston

Trinity Episcopal Church, Boston

West Parish Meetinghouse, West Barnstable

Michigan

Detroit Zen Center, Hamtramck

Islamic Center of America, Detroit

Minnesota

Pipestone National Monument, Pipestone

St. John's Abbey, Collegeville

Temple of Eck, Chanhassen

Mississippi

Triumph Church and New Life Christian
  Fellowship, Vicksburg

Missouri

Cathedral Basilica of St. Louis, St. Louis

Diana's Grove, Salem

Montana

Badger–Two Medicine Area, Heart Butte

Nebraska

St. Benedict Center, Schuyler

Nevada

Wellspring Church and Christian Center, Las
  Vegas

New Hampshire

Aryaloka Buddhist Retreat Center, Newmarket

New Jersey

Cathedral Basilica of the Sacred Heart, Newark

New Mexico

Acoma Pueblo, Acomita

Chaco Canyon, Nageezi

Hermanos Penitentes, Truchas

Lama Foundation, San Cristobal

Loretto Chapel, Santa Fe

Mission of San Miguel of Santa Fe, Santa Fe

Monastery of Christ in the Desert, Abiquiu

Santa Fe Cathedral of St. Francis of Assisi, Santa
  Fe

El Santuário de Chimayó, Chimayo

Taos Pueblo, Taos

New York

Abyssinian Baptist Church, New York

Cathedral Church of St. John the Divine, New
  York

Ramakrishna-Vivekananda Center of New York,
  New York

Riverside Church, New York

St. Patrick's Cathedral, New York

Temple Emanu-El, New York

Trinity Church, New York

Unification Church, New York

Universal Peace Buddha Temple of New York,
  Brooklyn

North Carolina

Bethabara Moravian Church, Winston-Salem

Billy Graham Training Center at the Cove,
  Asheville

Calvary Church, Charlotte

Chapel of the Prodigal, Montreat

Waldensian Presbyterian Church, Valdese

Wat Carolina Buddhajakra Vanaram, Bolivia

North Dakota

Chapel of Peace, Dunseith

Ohio

Crossroads Community Church of Hyde Park,
  Cincinnati

Plum Street Temple, Cincinnati

Tri-County Assembly of God, Fairfield

Oklahoma

Boston Avenue Methodist Church, Tulsa

National Shrine of the Infant Jesus of Prague,
  Prague

Prayer Tower, Tulsa

Sisters of Benedict, Piedmont

Oregon

Crater Lake

Enola Hill, Portland

Our Lady of Guadalupe Trappist Abbey, Lafayette

Pennsylvania

Congregation Beth Yeshua, Philadelphia

First Unitarian Church of Philadelphia,
  Philadelphia

Germantown Mennonite Church, Philadelphia

Pendle Hill, Wallingford

Rodef Shalom Congregation, Pittsburgh
Rhode Island
First Baptist Church of America, Providence
Touro Synagogue, Newport
South Carolina
Emanuel African Methodist Episcopal Church,
    Charleston
French Huguenot Church, Charleston
Kahal Kadosh Beth Elohim, Charleston
Meher Spiritual Center, Myrtle Beach
Mepkin Abbey, Moncks Corner
South Dakota
Black Hills
Tennessee
All Saints' Chapel, Sewanee
Baron Hirsch Synagogue, Memphis
Christus Gardens, Gatlinburg
Texas
Cathedral of Hope, Dallas
Enchanted Rock, Fredericksburg
Jade Buddha Temple, Houston
Rothko Chapel, Houston
Second Baptist Church, Houston
Utah
Echo Canyon, Kanab
Mormon Tabernacle, Salt Lake City
Rainbow Bridge, Navajo Mountain

Vermont
Charterhouse of the Transfiguration, Arlington
Virginia
Bruton Parish Church, Williamsburg
Holy Land USA, Bedford
Wat Lao Buddhavong, Catlett
Zoroastrian Association of Metropolitan
    Washington, Vienna
Washington
Kannagara Jinja, Granite Falls
Lien Hoa Buddhist Temple, Olympia
Snoqualmie Falls, Carnation
Washington, D.C.
Center for Dao-Confucianism
Washington Islamic Mosque and Cultural Center
Washington National Cathedral
West Virginia
Palace of Gold, Moundsville
Wisconsin
Circle Sanctuary Nature Preserve, Mt. Horeb
St. Benedict's Abbey and Retreat Center, Benet
    Lake
Wyoming
Devils Tower National Monument, Devils Tower
Medicine Wheel, Lovell
Yellowstone, Yellowstone National Park

GLOSSARY

a cappella [ah · cah · pehl´ lah] singing without musical accompaniment, the style of the Amana Church Society and the Monastery of Christ in the Desert.

aadheenam [ahd · hee´ nahm] a Hindu monastery.

Aarti [ahr´ tee] the ceremonial conclusion to daily prayers in Hindu ritual.

abbey [ab´ bee] a community of monks or nuns in a sanctified monastery or convent governed by an abbot or abbess.

acharya [ah · chahr´ yah] a religious teacher of Hinduism.

agape [uh · gah´ pay] the Greek term for unconditional love that is the equivalent of Christian love.

aghor [ah´ gohr] a Hindu concept of simple, natural consciousness.

alpha and omega [al´ fah oh · may´ gah] the first and last letters of the Greek alphabet, which the book of Revelation names as symbols of the beginning and ending of time (1:8, 11).

ambulatory [am´ byoo · luh · toh · ree] a passage or covered walkway behind the high altar and around the altar in the apse, or altar end, of a church.

amud [ah´ mood] a lectern used by a cantor during a Jewish religious service.

animism [a´ nih · mihzm] in hunting cultures, a mystic relationship between animals and hunters that requires prayers of thanksgiving and regret for taking the lives of their kill.

apse [aps] the projecting semicircular niche facing the main seating area of a church and containing the high altar and pulpit.

architrave [ahr´ kih · trayv] the basis, or lowest segment, of formal entablature.

Ashkenazi [ahsh · keh · nah´ zee] adj. **Ashkenazic** the German strand of European Judaism, as opposed to the Sephardic, or Iberian, strand.

ashram [ash´ ram] a spiritual retreat center.

Ave Maria [ah´ vay mah · ree´ ah] Latin for "Hail, Mary," the first two words of a favorite Catholic prayer.

bab [bab] literally, "the gate," the formal title of a divine messenger of Allah.

babalawo [bah · bah · lah´ woh] a priest in the Santerían faith.

Bahá'i [buh · hy´] an offshoot of the Persian Babi movement.

baldachin or **baldachino** [bahl´ duh · kihn, bahl · duh · kee´ noh] a fixed ornamental canopy sheltering a religious figure or sacred object, such as an altar; the ciborium.

baptismal font [bap · tihz´ muhl fahnt] a pedestal and basin to hold water for Christian baptismal services and naming ceremonies.

bas-relief [bah´ ree · leef] a sculptured effect on

445

a two-dimensional wall or mural suggesting the third dimension.

bhakti [bahk´ tee] the Sanskrit term for loving devotion to God.

bhakti yoga [bahk´ tee yoh´ gah] enlightenment through good cheer and love.

biblical inerrancy [in · ehr´ rahn · see] the fundamentalist belief that the Bible is the complete, infallible word of God.

bimah [bee´ mah] the dais where a cantor chants liturgy and reads the scripture for Jewish worship services.

B'nai B'rith [b'nay brihth] a Jewish educational and philanthropic organization whose name is Hebrew for "sons of the covenant."

box pew an enclosed, high-backed bench purchased by a family for regular use.

brothers members of a male religious community who have not taken holy orders and who voluntary live in a religious community with no aspiration other than to devote themselves to holy work.

Buddha Day [boo´ dah] a May religious festival commemorating Buddha's birth, enlightenment, and parinibbana, the release into enlightenment. *See also* **parinibbana.**

bulto [bool´ toh] a primitive statue carved from wood.

buttress [buht´ trehs] a pier that supports or strengthens a wall, often by countering the thrust of an inner arch.

caliph [cah · leef´] the political leader and defender of the faith among Sunni Muslims.

calumet [ka · loo · may´] a peace pipe, a ritual pipe circulated among Indians and guests as a gesture of friendship and hospitality.

campanario [kahm · pah · nah´ ryoh] a bell wall.

campanile [kahm · pah · neel´] a bell tower.

canon [ka´ nuhn] the title of a priest who serves on staff at a cathedral.

canonical hour [ka · nah´ nih · kahl] one of the divisions of the day appointed for observation of devotion. The hours begin with lauds at matins, followed by prime, terce, sext, none, vespers, and compline.

cantilever [kan´ tih · lee · vuhr] a projecting beam or bracket that supports a balcony or other architectural detail.

carillon [kah´ rihl · lahn] a set of bells arranged in a scale and played like a keyboard instrument.

cartouche [kahr · toosh´] an oval frame containing an emblem or symbol.

cathedra [kah · thee´ drah] the formal bishop's chair in a cathedral.

cenobite [sih´ noh · byt] a monk or nun living in a religious community.

cenotaph [sih´ noh · taf] an unoccupied ceremonial tomb or monument honoring a person whose remains are buried elsewhere.

chador [chah´ dohr] the head-to-foot black covering that Iranian women must wear to conform to local Islamic custom. The most extreme *chador* covers the face with a black mesh to prohibit even a glimpse of the face or hair.

chalice [cha´ lihs] a ritual cup that holds wine for the two-part act of holy communion observed by Christians.

chancel [chan´ sihl] the section of a church facing the audience and containing the altar, choir, and pulpit.

chaplain [chap´lihn] a member of the clergy associated with a chapel, branch of the military, institution, school, family, or court.

Charanamrit [chah · rah · nahm´ reet] holy water used in daily Hindu ritual.

charismatic [ka · rihz · ma´ tihk] a style of preaching or evangelism that derives its compelling charm from the persuasiveness, personality, and magnetic force of the speaker.

chrism [krihzm] oil that is blessed for application during anointing, baptism, confirmation, and ordination.

Chrismon [krihs´ mahn] a Christmas ornament reflecting a religious symbol, particularly various types of crosses and emblems associated with saints and apostles.

chuppah [hoo´ puh] a ritual canopy under which a rabbi performs a Jewish wedding.

clerestory [kleer´ stoh · ree] an upper level or band of windows that illuminates the galleries of a lofty building.

cloister [kloy´ stuhr] a courtyard or enclosure bounded by covered walks or a colonnade.

colombage [koh · lohm · bazh´] half-timber construction, employing patterned timber framing and filling with masonry or stonework, which is covered with plaster or stucco.

columbarium [kah · loom · bah´ ryoom] a burial structure formed of connected vaults and niches.

compline [kahm´ plihn] the seventh and last canonical hour.

Corinthian [koh · rihn´ thyuhn] a classic Greek decorative style incorporating capitals ringed with acanthus leaves.

corpus [kohr´ puhs] pl. **corpora** the three-dimensional figure of Christ that adorns a crucifix.

croning [kroh´ nihng] the Wiccan ritual celebrating menopause.

cubiculum [kyoo · bih´ kyoo · luhm] the main living quarters of the cell occupied by a Carthusian monk.

daily text a guided devotional reading founded among Moravians by Count Nicholaus von Zinzendorf in 1731 and now available in twenty-seven languages. The forerunner of published devotional daybooks, this text, known as a watch-word, specifies paired scripture from the Old and New Testament along with a prayer and hymn stanza.

darshana [dahr · sha´ nah] Hindu philosophy or philosophical concepts.

dhamma or **dharma** [dah´ mah or dahr´ mah] the Hindu concept of cosmic order.

Dhammapada [dah · mah · pah´ dah] the essence of Theravada Buddhist scripture advocating right thinking as a pathway to cosmic order.

diaspora [dy · as´ poh · rah] the intentional or forced spread of a culture or religious group from their native land into new territory.

Diwali or **Divali** [dee · wah´ lee] the Hindu New Year and light festival, when celebrants honor Lakshmi, the Goddess of good luck who calls on each house lit by a lamp.

dolmen [dohl´ mihn] a prehistoric burial monument formed by a massive horizontal stone supported on several smaller stones.

donate [doh´ nayt] a resident of a Carthusian monastery who promises to observe obedience and chastity without giving up personal possessions.

Doric [doh´ rihk] a classic Greek decorative style incorporating simply curved capitals.

Du'a Kumail or **Kumayl** [doo · ah´ koo · mayl´] a traditional Islamic profession of faith comprised of a heartfelt invocation to Allah and summary of his goodness.

ecumenism [eh · kyoo´ mih · nihzm] the promotion of unity and cooperation among denominations.

eremitic [eh · rih · mih´ tihk] reclusive, solitary.

Eucharist [yoo´ kuh · rihst] communion, the ritual consumption of bread and wine in commemoration of Christ's crucifixion.

exemplum [ek · zehm´ ploom] pl. **exempla** a

parable or illustrative story told for its educational or moral value.

façade [fuh · sahd´] the front or face of a structure, sometimes added as an adornment to the underlying wall.

faceted glass [fa´ sih · tihd] chipped or chunk glass that is unusually dense.

Feast of the Assumption [as · suhmp´ shuhn] an annual Catholic celebration of the ascendance of the Virgin Mary into heaven.

fléche [flehsh] an arrowlike spire that tops a cathedral above the transept.

fresco [frehs´ koh] artfully applied plaster that is mixed with paint and applied wet to create a design or picture.

Gathas [gah´ thaz] the early Zoroastrian scriptural hymns.

gazebo [guh · zee´ boh] an open pavilion constructed as an observation point; a belvedere.

Gemeinhaus [geh · myn´ hows] German for community house or congregation house, the Moravian gathering hall and worship space.

Georgian [johr´ juhn] stately English architecture characteristic of George I, George II, and George III.

gingerbread scrolled wood or minutely detailed fretwork.

glossolalia [glahs · soh · lay´ lyuh] an ecstatic, unintelligible utterance erupting spontaneously during the emotional and spiritual transport common to Pentecostal worship.

Gothic [gah´ thik] a European architectural style common in the late Middle Ages and marked by dark interiors, massive stone walls, pointed arches, flying buttresses, and ribbed vaults.

***Gottesacker* (God's Acre)** [gaht · tuh · sa´ kuhr] German term for a Moravian burial ground, where interment under uniform white stones is chronological by gender rather than in family plots.

Granth or ***Guru Granth*** [goo´ roo granth] the Sikh book of scripture.

Great Spirit the Native American concept of a supreme deity.

Greek cross a religious symbol or church floor plan composed of four perpendicular arms equal in length like a plus sign.

groin [groyn] the connecting point where ceiling vaults come together.

guji [goo · jee´] a chief priest at a Shinto shrine.

gurdwara [goord · wah´ rah] literally "the guru's door," a temple or holy place where Sikhs gather and read scripture.

guru [goo´ roo] a Hindu teacher.

hadj or ***hajj*** an obligatory pilgrimage to Mecca required once in a lifetime of all adherents to Islam. After the journey, the pilgrim may take the title of Hadji or Hajji.

handfasting in the Wiccan tradition, a ritual betrothal, mating, or commitment ceremony.

hatha yoga [hah´ thah yoh´ gah] a rigorous physical regimen accompanying meditation that arouses dormant energy.

heiau [hay · ow´] a Hawaiian family chapel or temple complex, a walled enclosure made of stone and capped with coral or rock to be used for worship, education, or healing.

hermitage [huhr´ mih · tihj] a private retreat or secluded residence.

hijab [hee´ jahb] the modest dress code of Islamic women, which advocates no makeup, ankle-length skirts, and head scarfs that extend to the hairline.

Hinayana Buddhism [hee · nah · yah´ nah boo´ dihzm] the Southern Buddhism of Sri Lanka and Southeast Asia, which focuses on detachment from self.

hip roof a roof formed of four planes intersecting at a horizontal ridge.

holy of holies a curtained niche in a synagogue that conceals the most sacred chamber and contains the Torah; also, an inner sanctum at any sacred site.

Hu [hyoo] in the Eck faith, the name of the most high, which worshippers chant to achieve an elevated state.

icon [ey´ kahn] a picture of a saint or sacred scene venerated by the faithful through prayers and liturgy.

iconostasis [ey´ kah · nahs´ tuh · sihs] an icon screen at the altar of a Russian Orthodox church.

IHS an abbreviation of Iesous, the Greek word for Jesus.

ileke [ee · lay´ kay] a necklace strung with beads representing each deity of the Santería faith and bestowed on an infant or newly baptized member.

illumination [ihl · loo · mih · nay´ shuhn] a symbolic or illustrative page decoration on a text.

imam [ee´ mahm] a leader of Muslims.

Ionic [ey · ah´ nihk] a classic Greek decorative style incorporating a single horizontal scroll above fluted columns.

jagadacharya [jah · gah´ dah · chahr · yah] a world teacher of Hinduism.

japa [jah´ pah] the Hindu worshipper's rhythmic repetition of a focal sound or phrase as an introit to a reverential mental state.

jnana yoga [juh · nah´ nuh yoh´ gah] philosophical enlightenment that seeks God through knowledge.

Kaaba [kah · ah´ bah] the worship site that Allah ordered Abraham and his son Ishmael to build in Mecca.

kachina [kuh · chee´ nuh] one of over 250 benevolent ancestral spirits of the Hopi and Pueblo.

kaddish [kah´ dihsh] a traditional Hebrew doxology or prayer for peace recited at burials and memorial services and on subsequent anniversaries of the death.

kahuna [kah · hoo´ nah] a native Hawaiian priest or sage.

kami [kah´ mee] the beneficent powers of nature venerated at a Shinto shrine.

kannagara [kahn · nah · gah´ rah] in the Shinto faith, the pursuit of God's way and a balanced life in the cosmos that results in harmony, peace, and fulfillment.

karma [kahr´ mah] the determination of a life based on actions in a previous existence.

karma yoga [kahr´ mah yoh´ gah] enlightenment through solitude, silence, and restraint.

Kathina [kah · thee´ nah] in Buddhism, the upbeat, festive November cloth ceremony bestowing robes, candles, soap, tea, notebooks, and other essentials on monks.

kerygma [keh · rihg´ mah] proclaiming or preaching the Gospels.

khalsa [kahl´ sah] the Sikh belief in a chosen race of soldier-saints who live ascetically, devote themselves to prayer, and fight for righteousness.

kiddush [kih´ duhsh] a ritual blessing delivered over wine or bread during a Jewish holy day.

kippa or **kippot** [keep´ pah] a ritual head-covering worn by Jews during worship; a yarmulke.

kirtan [keer´ tahn] the singing of praise to Vahiguru and Vahiguru's loved ones as a form of ritual prayer for Sikhs.

kiva [kee´ vah] an underground worship chamber of the Southwest Anasazi and Pueblo tribes where tribesmen stored sacred implements, conducted traditional ritual, and taught the young their sacred responsibilities.

koan [koh´ ahn] an ancient Chinese adage or proverb—a brain teaser that has either no correct answer or a surprising answer derived from unusual methods of viewing a problem.

kooti [koo´ tee] the living quarters for monks at a Lao Buddhist temple.

kupuna [koo · poo´ nah] a native Hawaiian elder and spiritual counselor.

lampada [lam´ pah · dah] in the Russian Orthodox faith, a ceremonial lamp lighted and placed before a sacred icon.

Latin cross a religious symbol or church floor plan composed of four arms, with the vertical set longer than the horizontal.

lauds [lawds] a solemn praise to God delivered at a postmidnight worship service during the first canonical hour.

lectio divina [lehk´ tee · oh dee · vee´ nah] Latin for "divine office," the phrase refers to the lectionary, the fixed cycle of public readings of scripture as an adjunct to ritual.

lintel [lihn´ t'l] a horizontal structure propped on beams at either end.

loa [loh´ ah] in voodoo, intermediaries like saints who function as messengers between earth and God and as agents of spiritual balance.

love feast a nonsacramental fellowship meal of the early Christian church revived in Moravian churches on August 13, 1727.

Magen David [mah´ gihn] literally, the "Shield of David," the symbol is a six-pointed star formed of two overlapping triangles.

mahanta [mah · hahn´ tah] a master of the Eck faith.

mahdis [mah´ dees] an Eck minister, who has attained the fifth initiation or level of understanding.

Makahiki [mah · kah · hee´ kee] in native Hawaiian worship, a four-month season of thanksgiving and propitiation of the land god Lono for continued good harvests.

mandala [man´ duh · luh] a graphic symbol, often in the form of a circle separated into quadrants.

mantra [man´ trah] a spoken and or intoned syllable, sacred name, word, or phrase that comforts, satisfies, and invokes a balanced, serene spiritual state during meditation.

Marranos [mahr · rah´ nohs] the Iberian Jews forced to convert to Christianity who continued to practice Judaism in secret.

math [mahth] a Hindu convent of celibate mendicants.

matins [ma´ tihns] morning prayer service.

medicine man a spiritual agent empowered by magic, prayer, and symbol to interpret phenomena, administer ritual, and perform ceremony.

mehrab [may · rahb´] a prayer niche or inset in the front wall of a mosque.

menorah [mih · noh´ rah] a seven- or nine-branch candelabrum used in Jewish ritual as a reminder of the exploits of Judah Maccabaeus, a Hebrew patriot and bold military leader.

mezuzah [meh · zoo´ zuh] or **mezzuzah** a doorpost bracket that houses a strip of parchment inscribed with two verses from the Torah—Deuteronomy 6:4–9 and 11:13–21.

milagrito [mee · lah · gree´ to] a silvered model of a hand, eye, heart, and or other body part miraculously cured.

minaret [mih · nah · reht´] a slender tower on a mosque from the balcony of which a muezzin calls Muslims to prayer.

minyanim [mihn · yuh · neem´] s. *minyan* worship gatherings consisting of at least ten Jews.

misogi [mih · soh´ gee] the Shinto ablution, or water purification, ritual.

moat [moht] a trench surrounding a building or wall as a deterrent to invaders.

mobed [moh´ behd] a Zoroastrian priest.

moksha or *moksa* [mohk´ shah] the Hindu and Sikh concept of release, liberation, or deliverance from a cycle of reincarnation, as taught by Krishna in the *Bhagavad Gita*.

monastery [mah´ nih · steh · ree] the building in which monks live, work, and conduct a religious life.

monism [moh´ nyzm] an Oshoan belief that God and matter are one.

monk [muhnk] a member of a community of men who live apart from the world under vows of poverty, chastity, and obedience according to some rule of religious order.

Muktad or **Mukhtad** [mook´ tahd] a Zoroastrian ceremony of repentance and forgiveness marking the end of the year.

mutualism [myoo´ choo · uh · lihzm] the practice of pure communism through group work and life in a strictly defined closed society like the Amana colony.

narthex [nahr´ thehks] the vestibule or lobby of a church.

nave [nayv] the portion of a church in which spectators sit.

navushieip [nah · voo · sheep´] the Shoshone dream state that begins with a humble pose before the divine to await a dream or vision.

nayamar [nah · yah´ mahr] a Hindu saint.

nirvana [nuhr · vah´ nah] in Buddhist philosophy, an ideal mental state of full enlightenment.

none [nohn] the fifth canonical hour.

noosphere [noh´ oh · sfeer] a web of human consciousness that encircles the earth and all human activity and thought.

Norouz or **Norooz** or **Nowruz** [noh´ rooz] the thirteenth day of Zoroastrian New Year's festivities.

novice [nah´ vihs] title of a monastic resident during the two years that precede the taking of vows.

obeah [oh´ bay · ah] a Haitian form of voodoo.

obelisk [ah´ bih · lihsk] a slender pillar or stele that tapers to a pyramid on top.

oblate [ohb´ layt] a voluntary or lay resident of a monastic community living under modified rule to join in the religious experience or stewardship outreach.

oculus [ah´ kyoo · luhs] a circular opening, skylight, or window at the peak of a gable or top of a dome.

oratory [ohr´ uh · toh · ree] the Benedictine term for chapel.

orisha [oh · ree´ shah] *See loa.*

panentheism [pan · ihn´ thee · izm] a belief that everything is an outgrowth of God.

parampara [pah·· rahm´ pah · rah] the Hindu tradition.

parinibbana [pah · rih · nihb · bah´ nah] the release of the Buddha from life into blessedness, in 543 B.C.

paten [pa´ t'n] a ceremonial plate used to serve bread or wafers during a Christian communion service.

patristic writings [pah · trihs´ tihk] compositions of the fathers of the Catholic church.

pediment [peh´ dih · mihnt] a triangular section of the façade below a roofed gable.

Pentecost [pehn´ tih · kahst] in Judaism, the presentation of the Ten Commandments to Moses on Mount Sinai; in Christianity, the descent of the Holy Spirit on Christ's apostles.

Pesach [pay´ sak] the Jewish Passover.

peyotism [pay · yoh´ tihzm] Native American religion based on the ingestion or smoking of peyote.

pier [peer] an upright that supports part of a wall.

pluvial [ploo´ vyuhl] a ceremonial cloak or vestment worn by a Catholic priest.

pohaku [poh · hah´ koo] a ceremonial stone in the ancient Hawaiian religion.

Pooja and Archana [poo´ jah ahr · kah´ nah] ritual prayers performed daily by Hindus, beginning with praise of the deities.

portico [pohr´ tih · koh] an entranceway or porch.

postulant [pahs´ tyoo · luhnt] a probationary member of a religious order.

prasad or *prasadam* or *prashadam* [prah´ sahd, prah´ sah · dahm] food blessed by a holy person of the Hindu faith and distributed during meals or at the end of daily worship.

préau [pray´ oh] the courtyard of a monastery.

presidio [preh · see´ dyoh] the military compound in a frontier mission fort.

priest [preest] in Catholicism, the sanctified minister of divine worship who has the power of offering sacrifice, blessing, and absolution and who preaches, celebrates mass, and forgives sins.

prime [prym] the second canonical hour.

pueblo [pwehb´ loh] a concentrated Indian commune or settlement formed of interlinking buildings and flat-roofed chambers made of adobe.

puha [poo´ hah] in Shoshone ceremonial animism, any animal imbued with a spirit or spark of divinity.

puja or *pujya tirtha* [poo´ jah teer´ thah] a sacred Hindu sanctuary or destination welcoming pilgrims to oneness with God.

pujari [poo · jah´ ree] Hindu worship site.

Qibla [keeb´ lah] the direction of prayers toward the Islamic holy of holies in Mecca.

raja yoga [rah´ jah yoh´ gah] the mastery of the mind through meditation and oneness with God.

Ramanavami [rah · mah · nah · vah´ mee] the Hindu festival honoring the Rama's birth.

reredos [reh´ reh · dohs] an ornamental altar screen, a feature of cathedral architecture that separates the pulpit from the choir.

retablos [ray · tah´ blohs] a series of saints painted on wooden panels behind a church altar.

riza [ree´ zah] the engraved metal shield around an icon.

rochet or **rocheta** [roh · keht´] a surplice or decorative smock worn by a Catholic bishop or abbot.

roshi [roh´ shee] a teacher of Zen Buddhism who leads the novice to enlightenment.

sacrament [sak´ rah · mehnt] a holy act ordained by scripture. In the Catholic faith, seven rites are sacraments—baptism, confirmation, Eucharist, penance, holy orders, matrimony, and last rites.

sacristy [sak´ rih · stee] a closet or room for robing or storing sacred vessels and linens.

sadhaka [sah · dah´ kah] a spiritual seeker of the Hindu faith.

sadhana [sah · dah´ nah] the Sanskrit term for a quest.

sadhana marga [sah · dah´ nah mahr´ gah] the Hindu path of inner effort.

sadhu [sah´doo] a wandering Hindu seeker.

sala [sah´ lah] the large worship hall of a Laotian Buddhist temple.

samadhi [sah´ mah · dee] the Hindu concept of identification with God or submergence into the divine.

samsara [sahm · sah´ rah] the Hindu concept of reincarnation, a burdensome chain or cycle of existence, death, and rebirth that binds the soul to earth.

sanctuary the main worship area of a church and the location of a principal altar.

sanctum sanctorum [sahnk´ toom sahnk · toh´

room] a Latin phrase denoting the holy of holies, the most sacred part of a shrine, altar, or sanctuary.

sando [sahn´ doh] the approach pathway that leads from the *torii*, or entrance gate, of a Shinto shrine to the purification font and buildings.

sangha [sahn · gah´] a Buddhist assembly.

Sangha Day [sahn · gah´] a Buddhist harvest festival and celebration of the spiritual community, often honoring a local ordination. The event begins with a procession. After the ordinand's initiation, others celebrate with outdoor entertainments and feasting.

sannyasa [sahn · yah´ sah] the holy life of a monk formally trained and dedicated to Hinduism and the worship of the God Siva (or Shiva).

sannyasi [sahn · yah´ see] a Hindu monk who has renounced a secular life and entered a holy order.

santero [sahn · tay´ roh] a maker of holy figures or carved icons.

santo [sahn´ toh] a holy object, image, or icon.

satguru [saht · goo´ roo] a spiritual master of Hinduism.

satori [sah · toh´ ree] the Zen Buddhist concept of enlightenment.

scry [skry] to perform divination by gazing into water, fire, or a crystal ball.

see a region or jurisdiction where a bishop rules over the faithful and controls the actions of lesser religious officials.

setsang [seht´ sahng] an assembly or seminar of Hindus for the sharing of religious experiences.

seva [see´ vah] the Hindu concept of selfless service to the community.

sext [sehkst] the fourth canonical hour.

sexton [sehks´ tuhn] a church property manager.

shakti [shahk´ tee] the Hindu concept of spiritual energy.

shaman [shah´ muhn] a practitioner of magical religion who enters ecstatic trance states to contact benevolent spirits.

shamanism [shah´ muh · nihzm] practice of interconnected ritual, beliefs, and oral traditions to restore health or well-being of a person or tribe.

Shi'i or **Shi'ites** [shee´ ee; shee´ eyts] the branch of Islam followed by 15 percent of Muslims, who rally around an imam, a religio-political leader.

shilpi or *silpi* [sheel´ pee] sculptors or artisans working in tightly organized guilds to produce stone carvings in the Hindu tradition.

Sh'ma or **Shema** [shuh · mah´] the Jewish confession of faith in one God: "Hear, O Israel, the Lord our God is the Sole Eternal Being" (Deuteronomy 6:4).

Sikh [seek] a disciple or follower of a monotheistic faith that began in India with an alliance of Hinduism with Islam.

sim [sihm] the chapel of a Laotian Buddhist temple.

Simchat Torah an October Jewish festival that ends the annual reading of the Torah and initiates the next year's reading. Festivities include singing, dancing, and a procession about the synagogue with Torah scrolls.

sipapu [see · pah´ poo] in Hopi and Navajo worship, a small hole, wellspring, or sacred hollow in the floor of a kiva to symbolize the birth of humankind from the underworld.

speaking in tongues *See* **glossolalia.**

spire the tapered crown of a steeple or tower.

stake a diocese center of Mormon worship.

stele [stee´ lee] a pillar or slab carved with ritual words and symbols.

sthapati [sthah · pah´ tee] a traditional Hindu temple architect, designer, and builder.

stupa [stoo´ pah] a dome-shaped Buddhist shrine.

Sufi [soo´ fee] a Muslim mystic also known as a whirling dervish.

Sugmad [soog´ mahd] In the Eck faith, a sacred name for God.

Sun Dance among plains tribes (Arapaho, Assiniboin, Cheyenne, Cree, Crow, Dakota, Kiowa, Mandan, Omaha, Pawnee, Ponca, Shoshone, Sioux, Ute), a most holy rejuvenation ceremony calling for commitment of self to the creator through dance, chant, prayer, fasting, and, in some cases, piercing of the chest.

Sun-do [suhn´ doo] in Zen Buddhism practice, a series of prostrations that calm the mind and promote health.

Sunni or **Sunnites** [soon´ nee; soon´ nyts] the branch of Islam followed by 85 percent of Muslims, who follow a caliph or political defender of the faith. *See also* **Shi'i**.

Sutra [soot´ rah] a summary of Vedic teaching.

suttee [soo · tee´] the ritual immolation on a deceased husband's funeral pyre once required of Hindu widows.

swami [swah´ mee] a Hindu monk.

sweat lodge a domed lodge, or *inipi,* formed of woven willow branches covered with skins, carpet, blankets, or tarp. At a hole in the ground below, the lodge dwellers, whether Native Americans or pagan worshippers, sprinkle herbed water on hot stones and inhale cleansing steam. They remain in the lodge to commune with divinities or spirits.

tallit [tahl´ liht] a traditional Jewish fringed prayer shawl.

Tantric [tan´ trihk] a therapeutic liberation of the spirit through Hindu meditation, visualization of divinity, self-purification, and yoga, or enlightenment.

teba [tee´ buh] or **tebah** or **teva** a chest or coffer placed on the platform of a synagogue or incorporated in a central column supporting the roof.

tefillin [tee · fihl´ lun] phylacteries worn on the left arm and head of pious Jews and containing scriptural passages on slips of paper.

terce [tuhrs] the third canonical hour.

tessera [tehs´ suh · rye] pl. **tesserae** individual tiles, stones, or pieces that make up a mosaic.

Theravada [thay · rah · vah´ dah] literally, "ancient teachings," the earliest form of Buddhism based on Gautama's original teachings.

Thingyan [theeng´ yahn] Burmese New Year festival, a May festival calling for meritorious deeds and sprinkling fellow celebrants with Thingyan water.

tintinnabulum [tihn · tihn · na´ byoo · luhm] pl. **tintinnabula** a small bell used in celebration of a Catholic mass.

torii [tohr´ ee · ee] a ceremonial gate or colonnade of gates that precede a Shinto shrine to indicate that the space inside is holy.

totem [toh´ tuhm] a heraldic pole revered by Northwest Indians to celebrate acquisition of a title or name, commemorate a ritual occasion, or preserve and honor the remains of the dead.

transept [tran´ sehpt] a lateral arm of a cross-shaped church.

triptych [trihp´ tihk] an altar picture or mural divided into three poses or scenarios.

Vajrayana Buddhism [vahj · rah · yah´ nah] a mystical form of Mahayana Buddhism known as the "diamond path," a Tibetan philosophy that incorporates more scripture than the narrowly orthodox Theravada Buddhism and offers more variety in popular devotion methods.

vasana [vah · sah´ nah] the Sanskrit term for human longing, an earthly diversion from union with God.

Vatican II a council of Roman Catholic authorities and led by Pope John XXII from 1962 to 1965 to modernize the relationship between the church and practitioners of the faith.

vault [vawlt] a lofty ceiling roofed by arched plaster or masonry.

Vedanta [vay · dahn´ tah] Hindu philosophy derived from the sacred Upanishads, which are the final part of the ancient Vedas.

Vedas [vay´ dahs] Hinduism's sacred writings.

vespers [vehs´ puhrs] the sixth canonical hour.

vibhuti [vih · boo´ tee] the Sanskrit term for holy ash.

Vinaya [vih · nah´ yah] the oldest Buddhist scripture, which contains the code of conduct for monks and priests.

Vipissana meditation [vy · pees · sah´ nah] the Thai form of meditation evolved at Wat Nong Pa Pong, the seat of Thailand's forest monasteries.

vision quest a spiritual quest for a guardian spirit among plains Indians. As a preparation for adulthood, teenagers journeyed to the Great Spirit through solitude, fasting, and purification in sweat lodges.

vocation [voh · kay´ shuhn] a personal inclination or divine call to a religious life.

wa'a'auhau [wah´ ah · ow · how] a ceremonial canoe of gifts that Hawaiians set adrift as a ritual gesture to Tahiti, the motherland.

wabi [wah´ bee] the spirit of the Shinto tea ceremony, which reduces violence and stress by centering the mind on calm and mutual respect.

Wakan Tanka [wah´ kahn tahn´ kah] the Sioux name for the Great Spirit or Great Mystery, God of all creation.

wat [vaht] the Southeast Asian term for temple, as in Angkor Wat.

Wazo [wah´ zoh] in Burmese Buddhism, a July religious occasion when monks receive robes for their three-month temple rainy season retreat.

Wesak [way´ sahk] the annual festival of the Buddha on the full moon of Taurus, the year's holiest day and the high point of earth's receipt of incoming spiritual energy.

whirling dervish *See* **Sufi.**

yeshivah [yeh · shee´ vah] a Jewish Torah school.

Yeshua [yeh´ shoo · ah] the Hebrew spelling of the Greek name of Jesus.

yoga [yoh´ gah] the Hindu concept of enlightenment.

yogaswami [yoh´ gah · swah · mee] a master teacher of the Hindu faith.

yogi [yoh´ gee] an enlightened Hindu holy man.

ziggurat [zihg´ guh · raht] a stepped pyramidal roof.

BIBLIOGRAPHY

Abbott, William. "Tickling the Sleeping Volcanoes." http://www.acme-outfitters.com/travel/shasta.html.

Abel, Heather. "Mt. Graham Telescope Rides through Congress." *High Country News* (Paonia, Colo.) (May 13, 1996).

"Abhidhyan Yoga Institute." http://www.abhidhyan.org.

"About Kenai." http://www.alaskaone.com/kvcb/AboutKenai/aboutkenai.htm.

"Abyssinian Baptist Church." http://www.harlemlive.org/wharlem/abyssin.html.

"Academy Chapel Booked As New Graduates Marry." *The Gazette.* (May 21, 1998).

"ACOA at African Church Meeting." *Religious Action Network News.* (winter 1997).

"Acoma Pueblo." http://www.indianpueblo.org/acoma.html.

"Across the Great Divide: History." http://best4x4.landrover.com/adventures/greatdivide/history/indian.html.

"Adam Clayton Powell, Jr." http://www.usbol.com/ctjournal/ACPowellbio.html.

Adams, Jacob. "Office of the President." http://arcticcircle.uconn.edu/ArcticCircle/ANWR/asrcadams.html.

Adamson, Stephen, managing ed. *Mother Earth, Father Sky: Native American Myth.* London: Duncan Baird Publishers, 1997.

Adler, Margot. *Drawing Down the Moon: Witches, Druids, Goddess-Worshippers, and Other Pagans in America Today.* New York: Viking Press, 1979.

"Advent Day of Recollection." *The Oblate.* (November–December 1998).

"Aghor Ashram." http://www.aghor.org/ashram.html.

Ahlstrom, Sydney E. *A Religious History of the American People.* New Haven: Yale University Press, 1972.

Aiken, Wayne. "American Atheists Picket Promise Keepers Founder 'Coach' Bill McCartney." http://www.americanatheist.org/supplement/chpicket2.html.

Albach, Carl R.. "Miracle or a Wonder of Construction?" *Consulting Engineer.* (December 1965).

Albanese, Catherine L. *Nature Religion in America: From the Algonkian Indians to the New Age.* Chicago: University of Chicago Press, 1990.

"All Saints' Chapel." http://smith2.sewanee.edu/gsmith/MapServe/AllSaints/History.

"All US Tribes." http://indy4.fdl.cc.mn.us/~isk/maps/usmapindex.html.

Allen, James B. *The Company Town in the American West.* Norman: University of Oklahoma Press, 1966.

Allen, M. Catharine. *The American Shakers, a Celibate, Religious Community.* Sabbathday Lake, Maine: The Unived Society, 1974.

Allen, Martha Sawyer. "Gathering of Souls." *Minneapolis-St. Paul Star-Tribune.* (July 3, 1994).

Allman, John W. "Brownsville Revival's Crusade to Change Financial Procedures." *Pensacola News Journal* (March 5, 1998).

Almanac of Famous People. Detroit: Gale Research, 1998.

Alsberg, Henry G., ed. *The American Guide.* New York: Hastings House, 1949.

Amana Church Society Newsletter. (April 1999).

Ambrosino, Jonathan. "Trinity Church on the Green." http://infopuq.uquebec.ca/~uss1010/orgues/etatsunis/nhaventc.html (1997).

American Decades (CD-ROM). Detroit: Gale Research, 1998.

"American Natives and the Environment." http://conbio.rice.edu/NAE/forestry.html.

"American Swedish Historical Museum." http://www.libertynet.org/ashm/.

"America's First Peace Studies Program Celebrates Fifty Years." http://www.communinet.org/ news_journal/9.2front.html.

Anderson, Dana. "Eckankar." *Minnesota Daily News*. (February 27, 1995).

Anderson, Edward F. *Peyote: The Divine Cactus*. Tucson: University of Arizona Press, 1996.

Anderson, Erika. "Shrine Celebrates 150 Years." *Georgia Bulletin*. (September 28, 1999).

Anderson, Hilda. "Sun-Drenched Lakes of Northern Idaho Perfect for Autumn Excursions." *Seattle Post-Intelligencer*. (September 9, 1999).

Andre, Brother. "Carthusian Way of Life" (pamphlet). Burlington, Vt.: The Carthusian Order, 1987.

Angel, Myron. *The Painted Rock of California*. Los Angeles: Padre Productions, 1979.

"Annual Report" (flyer). Nappanee, Ind.: Nappanee Missionary Church, 1998.

"Apache Survival Coalition." http://planet-peace. org/mt_graham/asc_background.html (1996).

Appel, Willa. *Cults in America: Programmed for Paradise*. New York: Holt, Rinehart & Winston, 1983.

Aprile, Dianne. *The Abbey of Gethsemani: Place of Peace and Paradox*. Louisville, Ky.: Trout Lily Press, 1998.

"Archbishop to Lead Pilgrimage to National Shrines." *Georgia Bulletin*. (July 2, 1998).

"Archeology at Colonial Williamsburg." http:// www.history.org/cwf/argy/argycexc.htm.

"Archeology of the Tundra and Arctic Alaska." http://www.nps.gov/akso/akarc/arctic.htm.

"Architect Frank Furness." http://brookemansion. com/furness.html.

"Architecture." http://www.intellex.com/ ~baw53/ Tulsa/architec.htm.

Armstrong, Karen. *The Battle for God*. New York: Alfred A. Knopf, 2000.

Armstrong-Ingram, R. Jackson. "Jean-Baptiste Louis Bourgeois." http://h-net2.msu.edu/ ~bahai/notes/bourgeoi.htm.

"Artist Takes Creations to a Higher Level." *Chicago Tribune*. (August 15, 1997).

"An Artistic Treasure." *Reflection*. (summer 1999): 8–9.

Artola, Juan Plazaola. "The Sacred." *UNESCO Courier*. (November 1990): 10–14.

"Aryaloka Retreat Center." http://www.ziplink. net/~vajramat/aryaloka.

"As Fun as All Outdoors." *Seattle Times*. (June 18, 1999).

"The Assemblies of God Online." http://home.ag. org/mirror/index.html.

Atencio, Ernie. "After a Heavy Harvest and a Death, Navajo Forestry Realigns with Culture." *High Country News* (Paonia, Colo.) (October 31, 1994).

"Atlanta History Center." http://www.atlhist.org.

"Atlanta Lucky but Wary." http://web.cln.com/ newsstand/070696/M_CHURCH.HTM (1996).

Atwal, Sandy. "Defending the Faith—Scientology, Dianetics, and the Church of L. Ron Hubbard." *Imprint*. (February 21, 1997).

"Audio-Visual Collection." http://www.asu.edu/ clas/asian/sea/avlist.html.

"Ave Maria Grotto." http://www.roadside america.com/attract/ALCULave.html.

"Backbone of the World." http://conbio.rice. edu/nae/docs/backbone.html (1999).

"Badger-Two Medicine Area." http://users.aol. com/wildmt/badger.htm.

Baer, Yitzhak. *A History of the Jews in Christian Spain*. Philadelphia: The Jewish Publication Society of America, 1961.

"The Bahá'i Faith." http://www.us.bahai.org.

"The Bahá'i House of Worship in Wilmette." http://bounty.bcca.org/~cvoogt/images/ wilmette.html.

"The Bahá'is" (pamphlet). Oakham, Leicestershire: Bahá'i Publishing Trust of the United Kingdom, 1992.

Ball, Ann. *A Handbook of Catholic Sacramentals*. Manassas, Va.: Trinity Communications, 1994.

Baly, Monica E. *Nursing and Social Change* New York: Routledge, 1995.

Barbato, Robert. "In the Land of the Pioneer: A History of the Capuchin Franciscan Friars in the Western United States." http://www. beafriar.com/pioneer.html.

Barker, Eileen. "Joseph Fichter and the New Religions." *Sociology of Religion* (winter 1996): 373–377.

———. *The Making of a Moonie: Choice or Brainwashing*. New York: Basil Blackwell, 1984.

Barker, R. Mildred. *The Sabbathday Lake Shakers: An Introduction to the Shaker Heritage*. Sabbathday Lake, Maine: Shaker Press, 1978.

Barlow, Bernyce. *Sacred Sites of the West*. St. Paul, Minn.: Llewellyn Publications, 1997.

Barnes, Steve. "Thorncrown Chapel." *Active Years.* (August 1996).

Baron, Dan. "Woodlawn Groups Fight for El and against Gentrification." *Community Media Workshop Newstips.* (October 26, 1995).

"Baron Hirsch Synagogue." http://www. baronhirsch.org.

Barra, Paul. "Mepkin Kicks off Concert Season with 'Messiah.'" *The New Catholic Miscellany.* (1999).

Barratt, Elizabeth. "Visit the Past at Mission San Juan Bautista." *Miracle Miles.* (January 31, 1996).

"The Barrel Organ at Mission San Juan Bautista." http://www.sirius.com/~ststones/sanjuan. html.

"The Basilica of the National Shrine of St. Elizabeth Ann Seton." http://www.setonshrine. org/Shrine.htm.

Bates-Rudd, Rhonda. "In Search of Serenity." *Chicago Tribune.* (January 16, 1997).

"Battle of Wounded Me." *New York Times.* (July 10, 1994).

Bauer, Deborah. "Yale students, Dwight Neighbors Spar over New Building Addition." *Yale Daily News.* (April 24, 1998).

Baum, Dan. "Sacred Places." *Mother Jones.* (March–April 1992): 32–38, 75.

Bawer, Bruce. *Stealing Jesus: How Fundamentalism Betrays Christianity.* New York: Crown Publishers, Inc., 1997.

Becker, Nancy. "Protecting International Sacred Sites." (spring 1993).

Behr, John. "Orthodoxy." (lecture delivered at the University of North Carolina) (March 23, 1998).

Bellafante, G. "Broken Peace." *Time.* (July 31, 1995): 62.

"Bells Ring out for Commencement." *Harvard University Gazette.* (June 4, 1998).

"Bells to Ring on Commencement Day." *Harvard University Gazette.* (May 28, 1998).

"Beloved Community of Memory and Hope." *The Congregationalist.* 159, no. 1 (1998–1999).

"Benedictine Mission House and St. Benedict Center." http://www.megavision.net/benedict/.

"A Benedictine Monk Is One Called to Seek God." http://www.osb.org/osb/sja/vocatns1. html (1999).

Bennett, Ross, ed. *America's Wonderlands: Our National Parks.* Washington, D.C.: National Geographic, 1975.

Bentley, James. *A Calendar of Saints.* London: Little, Brown & Co., 1993.

Beresky, Andrew E. *Fodor's New Mexico.* New York: Fodor's Travel Publications, 1991.

Berman, Rivka Chaya. "Touro Synagogue, R. I." *Images.,* http://www.imageusa.com/ARTICLES/history.htm

Bernal, Roy W. "All Indian Pueblo Council." http://www.senate.gov/~scia/1998hrgs/0407_ rb. htm.

"Bethabara Moravian Church." http://www. bethabara.org.

Beverly, James A. "Moon Struck." *Christianity Today.* (November 16, 1998): 20–21.

Beyer, Dominique. "The Proud Tower." *UNESCO Courier.* (November 1990): 18–20.

"Bhagwan Shree Rajneesh—Guru in the Western Wild." *U.S. News & World Report.* (October 14, 1985): 15.

Biema, David Van. "Back to the Yarmulke." *Time.* (June 7, 1999): 65.

Bierhorst, John, ed. *The Red Swan: Myths and Tales of the American Indians.* New York: Farrar, Straus & Giroux, 1976.

———. *The Way of the Earth: Native America and the Environment.* New York: William Morrow & Co., 1994.

"Big Bethel AME Church." http://www.bigbethelame.org (1999).

Big Bethel AME Church: A Century of Progress and Christian Service. Atlanta: privately published, 1968.

"Billy Graham Training Center at the Cove." http://www.odell.com/billy.htm.

"Billy Graham's Illness Forces Him to Postpone Harvard Events." *Charlotte Observer.* (February 10, 1999).

"Biogeographic Regions of Arizona." http:// dana. ucc.nau.edu/~are-p/road_map/eco/ colplat. html.

"Biography of Guadalupe Lupita Gallego." http://lcweb2.loc.gov/wpa/19140407.html (1938).

Biography Resource Center (database). http:// galenet.com (1999).

"The Birmingham Manifesto." *The Negro Almanac.* Harry A. Ploski and James Williams, eds. Detroit: Gale Research, 1989.

Bishop, Peter, and Michael Darton. *The Encyclope-*

dia of World Faiths: An Illustrated Survey of the World's Living Religions. London: MacDonald & Co., 1987.

Biskupic, Joan Biskupic. "Court Says Ban On Ritual Sacrifice Violates Free Exercise of Religion." *Washington Post.* (June 12, 1993).

Black, Alan W. "Is Scientology a Religion?" http://bible.ca/scientology-is-a-religion-black.htm (1996).

"Black Hills Sight to See—Devils Tower." http://www.americanparknetwork.com/parkinfo/ru/sights/devil.html.

"Black Mesa Area." http://www-atm.ucdavis.edu/~wxauto/fos/fpus/zones/AZZ039.

"Blessed Sacrament: The Dream of Its People Remembered" (brochure). Holyoke, Mass.: privately published, 1988.

"Blessed Sacrament School." http://www.excell.net/blessed2.

"Blind Can Get Feel for Size of Cathedral." *Milwaukee Journal Sentinel.* (October 4, 1998).

Blow, Michael. *The American Heritage History of the Thirteen Colonies.* New York: American Heritage Publishing, 1967.

Bock, Paula. "Caring: This Is the Gift." *Seattle Times Magazine.* (December 21, 1997): 8–13, 22.

———. "A Whaling People: The Makah Hunt for Tradition and Memories of Whaling." *Seattle Times.* (November 26, 1995).

Bolling, Landrum R. "Oral Roberts' 'Impossible' Dream." *Saturday Evening Post.* (September 1983).

Bono, Dianne. "Honor, Virtue and Dignity as an Impetus for Reform among Late-Medieval and Renaissance Humanists in Italy and in Spain." http://www.duke.edu/~rwitt/diannes-text.html.

Boon, Donald J. "Hermanos Penitentes." *Catholic Encyclopedia.* New York: Robert Appleton Co., 1911.

"Boston Avenue Methodist Church." http://www.bostonavenueumc.org/historyframe.html.

Boulton, Alexander O. "Fortress America." *American Heritage.* (December 1992): 108–116.

"The Bowhead Whale." http://www.geobop.com/Eco/AK6.htm.

Bowker, John, ed. *The Oxford Dictionary of World Religions.* Oxford: Oxford University Press, 1997.

Boyle, Daniel C. "History of Holyoke's St.

Patrick's Day Parade." http://www.ci.holyoke.ma.us/PattiesDay/HistoryPage.htm.

Brackett, Elizabeth. "A New Partnership." *PBS News.* (October 8, 1997).

Brainard, Annie M. *The Evolution of Public Health Nursing.* Philadelphia: W. B. Saunders Co., 1922.

"A Brand New National Monument." http://www.wilderness.org/ccc/fourcorners/grand-staircase.htm.

Braswell, Lynn. "Popular Evangelist to Deliver Message During Hickory Crusade." *Hickory (NC) Daily Record.* (September 28, 1999).

Breeden, Robert L., ed. *Clues to America's Past.* Washington, D.C.: National Geographic, 1976.

"A Brief History of Mennonites." http://www2.southwind.net/~gcmc/gi.html#history.

"Briefing." *The Gazette.* (October 7, 1999).

"Briggs First Dictionary of Occult Terminology." http://users.visi.net/~robinson/shadows/b1d/b1dv.html.

Brinckmann, Jonathan. "Many Shun 'Feel-Good' Approach in Timber." *(Portland) Oregonian.* (April 26, 1998).

Brinkley, Alan. "Review of 'Oral Roberts: An American Life.'" *New Republic.* (September 29, 1986): 28–33.

Brinkley-Rogers, Paul. "Guilty Plea over Sacred Hopi Mask." *(Phoenix) Arizona Republic.* (June 27, 1995).

Bristow, Ginger. "Old Approach to Spiritual Trip." *Albany Times Union.* (September 12, 1998).

Brock, Kathy. "Helilogging Work Lifts Columbia's Fortunes." *Portland Business Journal.* (July 22, 1996).

Broderick, Robert C., ed. *The Catholic Encyclopedia.* Nashville, Tenn.: Thomas Nelson Publishers, 1987.

———. *Historic Churches of the United States.* New York: Wilfred Funk, 1958.

Brody, Seymour. *Jewish Heroes and Heroines of America.* Hollywood, Fla.: Lifetime Books, 1996.

Brown, Alban. *Lives of the Saints.* New York: Barnes & Noble, 1997.

Brown, Dee. *Bury My Heart at Wounded Knee.* New York: Henry Holt & Co., 1970.

Browne, Gordon. "Introducing Quakers" (leaflet), Wallingford, Pa.: Pendle Hill, 1992.

"The Brownsville Revival." http://www.brownsville-revival.org.

Brozan, Nadine. "For Blacks and Jews, Hopes for

Renewed Link." *New York Times.* (January 18, 1999).

Bruns, J. Edgar, and Earl C. Woods. *Archbishop Antoine Blanc Memorial.* New Orleans: Laborde Printing Co., 1982.

"Bruton Parish Church." http://www.bruton-parish.org/history.htm.

"Bruton Parish Church."http://www.history.org/places/hb/hbbruch.htm.

"Bruton Parish Church." http://www.wm.edu/SO/canterbury/bruton.html.

"Bruton Parish Church, Williamsburg, Virginia." http://www.silverchat.com/~id/bruton.html.

"Bruton Parish Episcopal Church." http://www.geocities.com/CollegePark/Campus/brupc.html.

Buchanan, Bill. "High-Rise Answers Big Bethel's Prayer." *Atlanta Journal & Constitution.* (October 10, 1972).

———. "Pearly Gates' Swing Open for Church Musical Here." *Atlanta Journal & Constitution.* (November 7, 1971).

Buchanan, Paul D. *Historic Places of Worship.* Jefferson, N.C.: McFarland & Co., 1999.

"Buddhist Leader Outed for Gay Relationship." *Seattle Gay News.* (February 21, 1999).

Buehner, Kristin. "Hail Mary." *Globe-Gazette.* (June 28, 1998).

Bullard, George. "Muslims Raise $3 Million for Mosque." *Detroit News.* (March 8, 1999).

———. "New Mosque Will Bridge Past, Future." *Detroit News.* (June 28, 1999).

———. "Sacred Places: Islamic Center Looks to Expand in New Mosque for 10,000 Faithful." *Detroit News.* (December 12, 1998).

Bunson, Margaret, and Matthew Bunson. *Lives of the Saints You Should Know.* Huntington, Ind.: Our Sunday Visitor, Inc., 1996.

Bunting, Madelaine. "The Dark Side of Enlightenment." *London Guardian.* (January 4, 1998).

Burchard, "Center Keeps Blind Visitors in Touch with National Cathedral." *Fort Worth Star-Telegram.* (September 27, 1998).

Burns, Paul. "Villages Classified: The Old North Church." http://www.villagesclassified.com/article_church.html (February 2, 1997).

Business Leader Profiles for Students. Detroit: Gale Research, 1999.

Bustamante, Adrian H. "San Miguel Chapel in the History of Santa Fe" (pamphlet). Santa Fe, N.Mex.: St. Michael's College, 1993.

Butler, Alban. *Lives of the Saints.* New York: Barnes & Noble, 1997.

"Byodo-In Temple." http://www.geocities.com/TheTropics/Shores/5731/temple.html.

"Calendar of Events." *Yale Bulletin and Calendar.* (April 5–12, 1999).

Calian, Carnegie Samuel. "Redeeming the Wasteland." *Christianity Today.* (October 2, 1995): 92.

"California Mission History: San Juan Bautista." http://www.californiamissions.com/morehistory/sjbautista.html.

Campbell, David. "Navajo Mountain—Rainbow Bridge." http://www.angeles.sierraclub.org/dps/archives/dps00343.htm (1994).

Campbell, Elizabeth. "Tar Heel Towns." *State Magazine.* (September 1997): 12–14.

Canto, Minerva. "Chimayo Walk Reaffirms Faith." *Albuquerque Journal North.* (April 2, 1994).

Cantor, George. *Historic Landmarks of Black America.* Detroit: Gale Research, 1991.

———. *North American Indian Landmarks: A Travelers Guide.* Detroit: Gale Research, 1993.

Cantor, Norman F., ed. *The Civilization of the Middle Ages.* New York: Harper Perennial, 1993.

"Canyon de Chelly." http://www.svn.net/jcorman/spiderw.html.

"Canyon de Chelly National Monument." http://www.llbean.com/parksearch/parks/htm5519gd.htm.

Capps, Michael A. "Architect with a Vision." http://www.cambio.net/Eerobio.html.

Carey, Henry. "The Rooted Meet the Transient at Taos Pueblo." *High Country News* (Paonia, Colo.) (March 8, 1993).

Carmody, Denise Lardner, and John Tully Carmody. *Native American Religions: An Introduction.* New York: Paulist Press, 1993.

Carpenter, Gilbert C., Sr., and Gilbert C. Carpenter, Jr. *Mary Baker Eddy: Her Spiritual Footsteps.* Santa Clarita, Calif.: Pasadena Press, 1985.

Carpenter, Les. "Inuvialuit Bowhead Harvest." *Inuit Whaling.* Inuit Circumpolar Conference, Greenland, June 1992.

"Carrizo Plain Natural Area." http://www.sierraclub.org/chapters/santalucia/carrizo.html.

Carroll, Jackson W. "Horizontal Religion: Congregating." *Christian Century.* (October 13, 1993).

Carter, Tom. "The Road to Atlanta." *(Lexington, Kentucky) Herald-Leader*. (1996).

"Carthusian Monks and Carthusian Nuns." http://www.chartreux.org/index_us.html.

"The Carthusian Way of Life" (brochure), Arlington, Vt.: Charterhouse of the Transfiguration, 1987.

Cassidy, Sallie A. "Spiritual Renewal Stirs Greater Philadelphia Area." *Christian Life.* http://www.charismamag.com (1996).

Castro, Fidel. "Excerpt from Fidel Castro's Address to Abyssinian Baptist Church in Harlem." *Progressive News and Views.* (October 26, 1995).

"Cathedral in Santa Fe." http://jan.ucc.nau.edu/~ec23/cathedral.html.

"Cathedral of Hope." http://www.cohmcc.org/index.htm.

"The Cathedral of St. Joseph" (brochure). Hartford, Conn.: privately printed, 1962.

"The Cathedral of St. Louis." http://www.cathedralstl.org (1999).

Cather, Willa. *Death Comes for the Archbishop.* New York: Alfred A. Knopf, 1927.

"Catholic Committee of Appalachia." http://www.cathcomappalachia.org/index.htm.

"The Catholic Encyclopedia." http://www.csn.net/advent/cathen/12493a.htm (1997).

"Catholic Online Saints." http://www.catholiconline.com/saints.html (1997).

Catlin, George. *North American Indians.* New York: Viking-Penguin, 1989.

Cavendish, Richard, ed. *Man, Myth, and Magic.* New York: Marshall Cavendish Corp., 1970.

"Center for Shinto Studies and Japanese Culture." http://uts.cc.utexas.edu/~kaze/shinto/ (1998).

"Central Council, Tlingit and Haida Tribes." http://www.tlingit-haida.org.

Certini, Rose. "Path of the Padres: Indians Were First, but Europeans Left Their Lasting Mark." *Merced (California) Sun-Star.* (March 12, 1999).

"Chaco Canyon." http://www.rt66.com/~wanchek/chaco.htm.

"Chaco Canyon National Historical Park." http://www.cr.nps.gov/worldheritage/chaco.htm.

"Chaco Culture." http://www.nps.gov/chcu (1998).

Chaliand, Gérard, and Jean-Pierre Rageau. *The Penguin Atlas of Diasporas.* New York: Viking, 1995.

Champagne, Duane, ed. *Chronology of Native North American History.* Detroit: Gale Research, 1994.

———. *Native North American Almanac.* Detroit: Gale Research, 1998.

Chance, Norman A. *The Inupiat and Arctic Alaska.* New York: Harcourt Brace, 1990.

"Chapel, Air Force Academy." http://www.colorado-mall.com/HTML/EDUCATIONAL/COLLEGES/AFA/CHAPEL/CHAPEL.HTML.

Charles, Eleanor. "Seasonal Songs of Many Faiths." *New York Times.* (December 12, 1999).

"Charlotte Churches." http://www.citytravelers.com/churches.htm.

"Charlotte's Best." http://www.charlottesbest.com/Issue/Features/Yearbook/Review.htm.

"Les Chartreuses dans le Monde." http://chartreux.org/maisons/maisons.htm#Transfiguration.

Chavez, Fray Angelico. *The Santa Fe Cathedral.* Santa Fe, N.Mex.: Schifani Brothers Printing, 1995.

Chevalier, Jean, and Alain Gheerbrant. *The Penguin Dictionary of Symbols.* London: Penguin Books, 1996.

"The Chicago School: Interview with Stanley Tigerman and Eva Maddox." *Architecture.* (April 1998): 53–54.

Chirri, Mohamad Jawad. "The Battle of Uhud." http://www.al-islam.org/history/history/ohod.html (1988).

———. "Inquiries about Islam." http://www.al-islam.org/inquiries/intro.html (1986).

"Christ Chapel/Old North Church." http://www.iboston.org/buildings/building_index.html.

"Christ Lutheran Church." http://www.capps-assoc.com/church.html.

"Christmas New Orleans Style." http://www.new orleansonline.com/xmas98/07gospel.html.

"Christus Gardens." http://www.christusgardens.com/

"Chronological History of Idaho." http://www2.state.id.us/gov/1803-47.htm.

"Chronology of California History." http://www.notfrisco.com/almanac/timeline/goldrush.html.

"Chumash Indians." http://www.calpoly.edu/~mstiles/chumash.html.

Chupa, Anna Maria. "Ave Maria Grotto." http://

www.erc.msstate.edu/~achupa/am/am3.html (1998).

"The Church of Scientology." http://www.scientology.org.

"Church of the Lukumi Babalu Aye." http://home.earthlink.net/~clba/tableof.htm (1999).

Church, Sandra. "The Peaceful People." http://press-gopher.uchicago.edu:70/CGI/cgi-bin/hfs.cgi/99/new_mexico/92003702.ctl (1995).

"Chuska Mountains." http://www.cnetco.com/~dinecare/forestry.html.

"The City of Snoqualmie." http://www.edc-sea.org/cities/profiles/snoqualmie.html.

"Clare Booth Luce." http://clerkweb.house.gov/womenbio/Bio/luce.htm.

Clark, Ella E. *Indian Legends of the Pacific Northwest*. Berkeley: University of California Press, 1953.

"Classes." http://www.shamanic.org/classes.htm.

Clevenger, Allan. "Now Lama Foundation has a Home in Taos." *Lama Newsletter*. (spring/summer 1998).

Clifton, Chas S. *Encyclopedia of Heresies and Heretics*. Santa Barbara, Calif.: ABC-Clio, 1992.

"Clinton Honors Embassy Bomb Victims." *AP Online*. http://www.mediainfo.com (September 11, 1998).

Coates, Karen J. "Stairway to Heaven." *Sierra*. (November–December 1996): 27–28.

Cobb, Ahad. "Moving Forward." *Lama Newsletter*. (spring/summer 1998).

Cody, Edmund R. *History of the Coeur d'Alene Mission of the Sacred Heart*. Cataldo, Idaho: Old Mission, 1930.

"Coeur d'Alene Indians." http://www.coeurdalene.com/history/indians.html.

Coffins, Joel. "Asian Immigrants Bring Attention to Buddhism." *The (Olympia, Washington) Olympian*. (March 14, 1999).

Cohen, Debra Nussbaum. "Jews Back away from Jubilee Being Promoted by Messianics." *Jewish Bulletin of Northern California*. (March 6, 1998).

Cohen, Diane, and A. Robert Jaeger. "Affirming Our Collective Stake in Safeguarding Sacred Places." *Historic Preservation News*. (February–March 1995).

Cohn, Bob, and David A. Kaplan. *Religious Cults in America*. New York: H. W. Wilson & Co., 1994.

Cohn-Sherbok, Lavinia. *Who's Who in Christianity*. Chicago: Routledge, 1998.

Cole, Juan R. I. "The Bahá'i Faith in America as Panopticon, 1963–1997." *Journal for the Scientific Study of Religion*. (June 1998): 134–198.

Collins, Donna. "Growing up with the Moonies." *Good Housekeeping* (December 1999): 134–137.

Collins, John James. *Native American Religions: A Geographical Survey*. Lewiston, Dyfed, Wales: Edwin Mellen Press, 1991.

"Color and Light." *Sewanee Magazine*. (fall 1997): 9–11.

Colpitt, Frances. "Outtakes from the Chapel." *Art in America*. (June 1997): 98–99.

Confucius. *The Analects of Confucius*. New York: HarperCollins, 1992.

"Congregation Beth Yeshua." http://www.cby.org/(1999).

"Congregations under Censure." http://www.geocities.com/HotSprings/Spa/1042/shame.html (1999).

Contemporary Artists. Detroit: St. James Press, 1996.

Contemporary Black Biography. Detroit: Gale Group, 1999.

Contemporary Designers. Detroit: St. James Press, 1999.

Contemporary Heroes and Heroines. Detroit: Gale Research, 1998.

Contemporary Photographers. Detroit: St. James Press, 1996.

Cooday, Jesse. "Tlingit History." http://alaska.alaskan.com/docs/tlingithistory.html.

Cook, Leland A. *St. Patrick's Cathedral*. New York: Quick Fox, 1979.

Cooper, J. C., ed. *Dictionary of Christianity*. Chicago: Fitzroy Dearborn, 1996.

Copeland, Larry. "Old Church Where King Preached Gets Modern Sanctuary." *Charlotte Observer*. (March 8, 1999).

Corbett, Christopher. "Second Baptist Houston Counters Charge of Politics." http://www.fni.com/heritage/may96/SecBapt.html (1996).

"Corpus Christi Abbey." http://www.rc.net/corpuschristi/cca/history.html.

Corsaletti, Louis T. "Farmland to Be Preserved as Passive Recreational Area." *Seattle Times*. (February 8, 1999).

Coss, Clare. *Lillian Wald: Progressive Activist*. New York: Feminist Press, 1989.

Costella, Matt. "The Brownsville/Pensacola Outpouring: Revival or Pandemonium?" *Foundation*. (March–April 1997).

"The Costner Brothers and the Black Hills." http://users.skynet.be/kola/costner.htm.

"The Cove." http://www.thecove.org.

Covington, Dennis. *Salvation on Sand Mountain.* Reading, Mass.: Addison-Wesley, 1995.

Cranford, Fred B. *The Waldenses of Burke County* (monograph). Valdese, N.C.: Burke County Cultural Heritage Project, Title III, ESEA, 1969

Cranford, Steve. "Table Talk." *Business Journal of Charlotte.* (November 11, 1996).

Crann, Alice. "A Year of Saving Souls." *Pensacola News Journal.* (June 1996). http://www.netastic.com/oflare/Pensacola/revival_1year.html.

"Crater Lake National Park." http://www.areaparks.com/craterlake/crater_lake_national_park.htm.

"Crater Lake National Park History." http://www.nps.gov/crla/clnp-his.htm.

"Crater Lake, Oregon." http://vulcan.wr.usgs.gov/Volcanoes/CraterLake/Locale/framework.html.

"Creating a Medicine Wheel." http://www.sd.com.au/db/medicine.htm.

"Creation Myths from around the World." http://www.dc.peachnet.edu/~shale/humanities/literature/religion/creation.html.

Crespi, M. "Saving Sacred Places." *National Parks.* (July–August 1991): 18–19.

Crispen, Ellen Furlong. "A Cow Creek Legend." http://www.cowcreek.com/story/x05myths/index.html (1999).

Crockett, David R. "Sunday August 29–Saturday, September 4, 1847." http://www.lds-gems.com/archive/150/aug2947.html (1997).

———. "Sunday September 17–Saturday, September 23, 1848." http://www.81.cyberhost.net/ldsgems/archive/150/sept1748.html (1997).

Cross, Jai. "Land Restoration's Final Year." *Lama Newsletter.* (spring/summer 1998).

"Crossing Worlds." http://www.crossingworlds.com (1999).

"Crossroads Community Church of Hyde Park." http://www.crossroadshp.org/.

Crumm, David. "Leaders Debate the Changes That Religious Diversity Brings to the Millennium." *Fort Worth Star-Telegram.* (November 14, 1999).

Cuevas, Lou. *Apache Legends: Songs of the Wind Dancer.* Happy Camp, Calif.: Naturegraph Publishers, Inc., 1991.

Cummings, Patricia J. "Preserving Sacred Sites." *Earth Island Journal.* (spring 1993): 28.

Cunningham, Lawrence S. "Preferred Providers: How the Church Chooses Its Doctors." *U.S. Catholic.* (April 1998): 17–23.

Curtis, Christopher Paul. *The Watsons Go to Birmingham—1963.* New York: Dell Publishing 1995.

Curtis, Edward S. *Chiefs and Warriors.* Boston: Bulfinch, 1996.

———. *Native Family.* Boston: Bulfinch, 1996.

———. *The North American Indian.* Boston,: Bulfinch, 1997.

"Czech Bible of Kralice." http://www.fee.vutbr.cz/UIVT/homes/michal/kr/ (1998).

Dakin, Edwin F. *Mrs. Eddy: The Biography of a Virginal Mind.* Magnolia, Mass.: Peter Smith, 1990.

Daley, Yvonne. "Carthusians Lead Lives of Solitude." *Rutland (Vermont) Daily Herald.* (August 24, 1990).

"Damaged Kodiak Archives Open Window for Ex-professor." *Anchorage Daily News.* (July 6, 1998).

Daniels, Doris Groshen. *Always a Sister: The Feminism of Lillian D. Wald.* New York: Feminist Press, 1995.

Dark, Alx "Rednecks for Wilderness." http://www.emeraldnet.net/~alxdark/ma_title. html (1993).

Darley, Alex M. *The Penitentes of New Mexico.* New York: Ayer Co., 1974.

Dary, David. "The Cathedral of the Plains." *Kansas City Star, Sunday Magazine.* (December 17, 1972): 7–10.

Dauenhauer, Nora Marks, and Richard Dauenhauer, eds. *Haa Kusteeyí, Our Culture: Tlingit Life Stories.* Seattle: University of Washington Press, 1994.

Daugherty, John. "Making a Mountain into a Starbase. *High Country News* (Paonia, Colo.) (July 24, 1995).

Davie, Dennis. "Forest Networking a Project of Ecological Enterprises." http://forests.lic.wisc.edu/gopher/america/calidemi.txt (1996).

Dean, Andrea Oppenheimer. "The Cathedral Builder Born 500 Years Too Late." *Smithsonian.* (August 1991): 102–110.

"Delaware (Lenape) Indians." http://www.cowboy.net/native/lenape/index.html.

"Delaware Swedish Colonial Society." http://members.aol.com/sakerthing/sr-dscs.htm.

Deloria, Vine, Jr. *The Metaphysics of Modern Existence.* New York: Harper & Row, 1979.

Descamps-Lequime, Sophie. "A Sense of Awe." *UNESCO Courier.* (November 1990): 21–23.

"Destination: Valdese." *Charlotte Observer.* (February 15, 1998).

Deutsch, Claudia H. "Raising More Than the Church Roof." *New York Times.* (November 18, 1998).

"Devils Tower, Wyoming." http://volcano.und. nodak.edu/vwdocs/volc_images/north_amer- ica/devils_tower.html.

DeWeese, Geoffrey S. "Prof. Aids in Asking Falls Become a Cultural Site." *(Fresno, California) Falcon News.* (March 4, 1992).

DeWitt, Jim, and J. Lee Grady. "Pensacola Out- pouring Continues to Draw Huge Crowds." http://www.strang.com/cm/stories/cn196106 .htm (1996).

"Diana's Grove." http://www.dianasgrove.com (1999).

Dictionary of Hispanic Biography. Detroit: Gale Re- search, 1996.

"A Digital Archive of American Architecture." http://infoeagle.bc.edu/bc_org/avp/cas/fnart/ fa267/egyptrev.html.

Dimmitt, Travis. "Pietism." http://www.nwmis- souri.edu/nwcourses/History155/religion/ midtermprojects/travisdimmitt/index.html (1998).

"Dine CARE," http://www.cnetco.com/ ~dinecare/.

"Diocese of Boise." *Catholic Encyclopedia.* http:// www.newadvent.org/cathen/02623b.htm.

"The Diocese of Missouri." http://webusers. anet-stl.com/~rsmorley/11.htm.

"Directory of Latin Masses." http://www. erols. com/lein/lla/double.html.

Dirvin, Joseph I. *Mrs. Seton: Foundress of the Ameri- can Sisters of Charity.* New York: Farrar, Straus & Giroux, 1975.

"Discovery Park." http://www.discoverypark.com (1999).

"Distribution of Bison Meat Causing Some Divi- sions among Indians." *Billings Gazette.* (January 16, 1999).

"Diversity in New Mexico Reflects National Trend." *Hickory* (NC) *Daily Record.* (October 2, 1999).

Dixon, John Morris. "Both Symbolically and Functionally, a New Jewish Center Combines a Sense of Community with Openness to the World." *Architectural Record.* (July 1998): 96ff.

Dobbin, Muriel. "What Will Oral Roberts Do Next?" *U.S. News & World Report.* (March 9, 1987): 25.

"Dogs Aid Search for Flood Victims." *Washington Post.* (August 23, 1997).

Dolan, Josephine A., *History of Nursing.* Philadel- phia: W. B. Saunders Co., 1968.

Donovan, Bill. "Rainbow Bridge Open after Four-Day Closure." *(Window Rock, Arizona) Navajo Times.* (August 7,1995).

D'Oro, Rachel, and Don Hunter. "Rescuers Lift 142 Whalers off Ice." *Anchorage Daily News.* (May 19, 1997).

Dorsey, Gary. "Unification Church Group Sues State over Task Force; Investigation of Cults Called Unconstitutional." *Baltimore Sun.* (Au- gust 26, 1999).

Dougherty, John. "Making a Mountain into a Starbase: The Long and Bitter Battle over Mt. Graham." *High Country News.* (July 24, 1995).

Dowling, Claudia Glenn. "A Light in the Desert." http://pathfinder.com/Life/monks/monastery. html.

Downey, Michael. *Trappist: Living in the Land of Desire.* New York: Paulist Press, 1997.

Doyle, Leonard J., trans. *The Rule of St. Benedict.* Collegeville, Minn.: Order of St. Benedict, Inc., 1948.

"Dr. Billy Graham." http://denig.com/chris- tian/graham.html (1990).

Drain, Thomas A. *A Sense of Mission: Historic Churches of the Southwest.* San Francisco: Chronicle Books, 1994.

Dunlop, Beth. "Ten Years after the Original Church Was Built, the Same Architect Designs a New Parish Hall and Courtyard." *Architectural Record.* (July 1998): 92ff.

"Durango." http://durangonow.com/history/ute- history.html.

Durham, Michael. "Landmarks on the Rim." *American Heritage.* (April 1967): 136–137.

Durkin, Mary Cabrini. "A Short Tour of the Cathedral Basilica of the Sacred Heart" (bro- chure). Newark, N.J.: privately published, n.d.

"The Dwelling Place." http://www.geocities. com/Athens/9871/ (1997).

"Ebenezer Baptist Church." http://www. ebenezer.org/began.html.

"Ebenezer Baptist Prepares for a Big Move."

http://www.accessatlanta.com/news/1998/
12/06/ebenezer.html (December 6, 1998).

"Eck Church Is Realizing Its Dream." *Chicago Tribune.* (July 16, 1999).

Eck, Diana L. *On Common Ground: Columbia University Press* (CD-ROM). New York: Columbia University Press, 1994.

"Eckankar." http://www.carm.org/c_eckankar.htm.

"ECKANKAR." http://www.eckankar.org/home. html (1997).

"ECKANKAR." http://www.religioustolerance.org/eck.htm.

Eerdmans' Handbook to the World's Religions. Grand Rapids, Mich.: William B. Eerdmans Publishing Co., 1982.

Ehrlich, Eugene, and Gordon Carruth. *The Oxford Illustrated Literary Guide to the United States.* New York: Oxford University Press, 1982.

Ekstrom, Reynolds R. *The New Concise Catholic Dictionary.* Mystic, Conn.: Twenty-Third Publications, 1995.

"Eleven Killed in Canyon Flash Flood." http://www.deserthighlights.com/news/antelope.htm (1997).

Eliade, Mircea, ed. *The Encyclopedia of Religion.* New York: Macmillan, 1987.

Eller, Vernand. "Where Is True Christianity to Be Found?" http://www.wco.com/~hdrake/eller2/ part2.html.

Emerson, Ralph Waldo. "The Last Supper." http://www.rain.org/~elw/emerson/uncoll.txt (1832).

Emmory, Donna. "Visit Burke County—Discover Valdese." *AAA Carolinas Newsletter.* (May–June 1997): 16.

"Enchanted Rock Archives." http://www.texfiles.com/erarchives/index.htm.

"Enchanted Rock State Natural Area." http://www.tpwd.state.tx.us/park/enchantd/en-chantd.htm.

Encyclopedia Americana (CD-ROM). Danbury, Conn.: Grolier, 1999.

Encyclopedia Britannica, http://www.eb.com.

Encyclopedia of Occultism and Parapsychology. 4th ed. Detroit: Gale Research, 1996.

Encyclopedia of World Biography. Detroit: Gale Research, 1998.

Engelbrecht, P. J. "Pa. Mennonite Congregation Ousted for Accepting Gays." *Outlines.* (October 28, 1997).

"Enola Hill Timber Sale." http://www.planetpeace.org/environmental/enola.html (1996).

Enomoto, Catherine Kekoa. "My Turn," *Honolulu Star-Bulletin.* (March 18, 1997).

"Environmental Movement Fights Clinton's Ecology Double-Talk." *EarthWINS.* (April 9, 1997).

Epstein, Ron. "Comments on Buddhism." http://online.sfsu.edu/~rone/COMMENTS%20ON%20BUDDHISM.htm.

Epstein, Ronald. "In the Chinese Consciousness-Only School According to the Cheng Wei-Shi Lun." *Vajra Bodhi Sea.* (January–March 1985).

Erlande-Brandenburg, Alain. "A Real of Light." *UNESCO Courier.* (November 1990): 39–42.

Essen, Jennifer. "Bolivia Church Learns about Buddhist Faith." *Wilmington (NC) Morning Star.* (August 29, 1988).

Everts, W. W. "The Church in the Wilderness." http://users.aol.com/libcfl2/wilder.htm (1986).

Evolution of a Nation." http://www-dept.stanford.edu/group/Thinker/v2/v2n3/Saudi.html.

"An Evolving Church Is Expressed by Rigid Forms Set within Chaos." *Architectural Record.* (July 1998): 94.

Faherty, William Barnaby. "The Great Saint Louis Cathedral" (brochure). St. Louis: Cathedral of St. Louis, 1988.

Fairlie, Henry. "Evangelists in Babylon: The Wages of Sin." *New Republic.* (April 27, 1987) 22–24.

Falk, Peter Hastings, ed. *Who Was Who in American Art.* Madison, Conn.: Sound View Press, 1985.

Fanselow, Julie. "Lined in Silver." http://www.homeandawaymagazine.com/silver.html.

Farley, Christopher John. "Book of Black Architects Lays a Cultural Foundation." *USA Today.* (February 17, 1992).

Farmer, David Hugh. *The Oxford Dictionary of Saints.* New York: Oxford University Press, 1992.

"Farrakhan Addresses Philadelphia Rally on Racial Healing." *Jet.* (May 5, 1997): 16–17.

Farrakhan, Louis. "Second Opinion." http://users.aol.com/camkem/eyeview/mmonman.num.

Feed, Walton. "An Introduction to Navajo Culture." http://www.waltonfeed.com/peoples/navajo/culture.html (1999).

Feldman, Susan, ed. *The Storytelling Stone.* New York: Laurel Books, 1965.

Fernandez, Gerard. "Temple Emanu-El." http://

www.fordham.edu/halsall/medny/fernandez.
html.

Fields, Valerie. "Soul Searching: Ministries Work
with Christians Struggling with Homosexuality." *Arlington (Texas) Morning News.* (August 8,
1998).

"Final Determination to Acknowledge the Snoqualmie Tribe Organization." http://www.
doi.gov/bia/snoqtech.htm.

Fingarette, Herbert. "Who Is Confucius."
http://www.wam.umd.edu/~tkangwho.html.

"Firewatch." http://140.190.128.190/merton/
merton.html.

"First Baptist Church, Providence, Rhode Island."
http://libraries.mit.edu/rvc/kidder/RI19.
html.

"The First Church of Christ, Scientist." http://
www.tfccs.com/GV/TMC/TMCMain.html
(1999).

"First Pilgrimage to Fort Ross." http://www.
holy-trinity.org/history/1925/07.17.Fort-
Ross.html.

"First Presbyterian Church, Stamford, Connecticut." http://www.fishchurch.org.

Fish, Peter. "Romance Meets Reality in Hemet."
Sunset. (April 1995): 18.

Fitch, James Marston. *American Building: The Historical Forces That Shaped It.* New York:
Schocken Books, 1973.

Fixler, David A. "Boston's Best Buildings: A Personal View" (lecture). http://www.perrydean.
com/files/bostbest.htm. (1996).

"Flocking to Pageant's 'Pearly Gates.'" *New York
Times.* (November 10, 1985).

Florian, Sister M. "The Inexplicable Stairs." *St.
Joseph Magazine.* (April 1960).

Florin, Lambert. *Historic Western Churches.* Seattle:
Superior Publishing, 1969.

Fode, Mark. "Inkpadutaís Bloody Path in 1856
Went Through Quarries." *Pipestone County
(Minnesota) Star.* (April 10, 1997).

Folberg, Neil, "And I Shall Dwell Among Them."
Aperture, New York. (1995).

Ford, Gary D. "From Whom All Blessings
Flow." *Southern Living.* (December 1998):
104–109.

"Former King Congregation Moves." http://
deltasigmatheta.com/news28.htm (1999).

"Fort Ross State Historical Park." http://www.
mcn.org/1/rrparks/parks/fortr.htm.

Foster, Nelson. *Kaho'olawe: Na Leo o Kanaloa.*
Honolulu: Ai Pohaku Press, 1995.

Fox, Selena. "Circle Sanctuary's Stone Circle."
Circle. (spring 1998).

———. "Sacred Fire, Sacred Flames at the Pagan
Spirit Gathering." *Circle.* (spring 1999).

Fox, Stephen. "The Rothko Chapel."
http://houston.sidewalk.com/detail/31116.

Francione, Gary L., and Anna E. Charlton. "Santeria and Animal Sacrifice." http://www.ani-
mal-law.org/sacrifice/.

Franz, Marcus. "St. Patrick's Cathedral." http://
www.fordham.edu/halsall/medny/stpat1.html
(1997).

Franzwa, Gregory M. *The Old Cathedral.* St.
Louis: Basilica of St. Louis, the King, 1965.

Fraser, Frances. *The Bear Who Stole the Chinook.*
Vancouver: Douglas & McIntyre, 1968.

Freeman, Linda. "Native Tribes of Siskiyou
County." http://www.snowcrest.net/freemanl/
atlas/native.html (1997).

French, Howard W. "Oahu, beyond Pearl Harbor
and Waikiki." *New York Times.* (1999).

"Friends of the Western Buddhist Order." http://
balrog.joensuu.fi/~jlavi/buddhism/FWBO.
html.

"Friends of the Western Buddhist Order." http://
www.fwbo.org/index.html.

Fries, Adelaide. *The Moravians in Georgia, 1735–
1740.* Baltimore: Genealogical Publishing Co.,
1967.

Fry, Rev. Timothy, "Saint John's Abbey: A Tradition in the Service of God." Atchison, Kans.:
St. Benedict's Abbey, 1982.

"Full Gospel Associated Churches." http://fgac.
trinitytemplefgc.org/.

"Full Gospel Television." http://www.fgtv.org/.

Funk, Tim. "World Wide Web of Worship." *Charlotte Observer.* (July 10, 1999).

"Fur Traders and Missionaries." http://members.
aol.com/spokanetr/index3.html.

Gabriel, Peggy. "Journalists Take a Fresh Look at
Appalachia." *Catholic Journalist.* (December
1998).

Gallagher, Winifred. *The Power of Place.* New York:
Poseidon Press, 1993.

———. "Sacred Places." *Psychology Today.* (January–February 1993): 62–66.

Gallaspy, Beth. "Rescue Mission Gets New
Name, Board." *Vicksburg Post.* (March 1995).

Garfield, Ken. "Hallelujah, Calvary!" *Charlotte
Observer.* (May 24, 1999).

———. "Preaching Harmony Between the Races."
Charlotte Observer. (November 22, 1999).

Gaskie, Margaret. "To Gather Together." *Architectural Record*. (January 1990): 123–135.

"Gatlinburg Christmas Manger Light Display Wins Award." *(Oak Ridge, Tennessee) Oak Ridger*. (December 31, 1998).

"Gay Buddhist Controversy Rocks Western Buddhist Order." *Seattle Gay News*. (February 26, 1999).

"Gay Congregation Passes $6.2 Million Milestone for New Cathedral." *Out! Magazine* (New Zealand). (January 21, 1998).

Gentz, William H., general ed. *The Dictionary of Bible and Religion*. Nashville, Tenn.: Abingdon Press, 1973.

Geroy, Amanda. "The Effects of Spiritual Practice." *Lama Newsletter*. (spring/summer 1998).

Gibson, Clare. *Sacred Symbols*. Rowayton, Conn.: Saraband, Inc., 1998.

Gibson, Stan. "An Uncelebrated Anniversary." http://www.dickshovel.com/parts.html.

———, and Jack Hayne. "Witnesses to Carnage." http://www.dickshovel.com/parts2.html.

Giès, Jacques. "Heavenward Steps." *UNESCO Courier*. (November 1990), 26–29.

Giese, Paula. "Stone Wheels and Dawn Stars Rising." http://indy4.fdl.cc.mn.us/~isk/stars/starkno7.html (1996).

Gillespie, Leila. "Honors Student Seizes Chance." *Spouters*. (fall 1994).

Gilpin, Laura. *The Enduring Navaho*. Austin: University of Texas Press, 1968.

"*Glaubensbekentniss* or Profession of Faith." Middle Amana, Iowa: Amana Church Society, 1988.

Glover, Sherry. "On the Nature of Compassion." http://www.cs.uh.edu/~tihuang/tba-page/cmpssion.htm. (1997).

Goeringer, Conrad. "Sun, Sand, Water—The Ecstasy of the Beach." *American Atheist*. (July 1998).

Goldberger, Paul. *The City Observed, New York: A Guide to The Architecture of Manhattan*. New York: Vintage Books, 1979.

Golvin, Jean-Claude. "Precincts of Eternity." *UNESCO Courier*. (November 1990): 5–17.

Gomes, Andrew. "Protection of Archeological Sites Lies in Hands of Cultural Surveys." *(Honolulu) Pacific Business News*. (September 22, 1997).

Gonzales, Cristine. "Marketing: Word-of-mouth Recipe Sells Abbey Fruitcakes." *(Portland) Oregonian*. (November 18, 1998).

"The Good Book: Discovering the Bible's Place in Our Lives." *Publishers Weekly*. (September 16, 1996): 66.

Gorder, Steven F. "International Peace Garden." http://www.peacegarden.com/ (1996).

Gould, Stephen Jay. "Review: 'Fire in the Mind.'" *New York Times*. (October 16, 1995).

Gould, Virginia Meacham, and Charles E. Nolan. *Henriette Delille: Servant of Slaves*. New Orleans: Laborde Printers, 1999.

"The Governors of Louisiana." http://www.sec.state.la.us.

Grady, J. Lee. "The Other Pentecostals." *Charisma*. (June 1997).

Grafstein, Laurence. "Messianic Capitalism: The Invisible Hand That Feeds the Cults." *New Republic*. (February 20, 1984): 14–16.

Graham, Billy. "Billy Graham Evangelistic Association and Affiliated Organizations." Minneapolis, Minn., 1999.

Grape, Nancy. "Seeking the Shakers." *Blethen Maine Newspapers Inc.* http://www.mainetoday.com. (March 22, 1998).

Graves, Denyce. "A Cathedral Christmas." http://www.denycegraves.com/bios.html.

"Great Day for the Monks." *Louisville Times*. (June 3, 1901).

Greenspan, Karen. *The Timetables of Women's History*. New York: Touchstone, 1994.

Griffin, Gerald Joseph, and H. Joann King Griffin. *Jensen's History and Trends of Professional Nursing*. St. Louis: C. V. Mosby Co., 1965.

Grimes, Barbara F., ed. *Ethnologue*. 13th ed. Dallas, Tex.: Summer Institute of Linguistics, Inc., 1996.

Grindeland, Sherry. "Bringing the Past into the Present." *Seattle Times*. (February 1, 1999).

Grinnell, George Bird. *Cheyenne Campfire*. Lincoln: University of Nebraska Press, 1971.

Grossman, Cathy. "The Medium is the Mission at Second Baptist Church." *USA Today*. (August 6, 1991).

———. "Sanctuaries of Worship Are Standouts by Design." *USA Today*. (July 22, 1993).

Grossman, Cathy Lynn. "Congregations Rebuild Their Foundations of Faith." *USA Today*. (December 9, 1996).

Grossman, Kate N. "Black Megachurches: Changing Spiritual Needs Fuel Growth." *Arlington (Texas) Morning News* (October 11, 1999).

"Grotto of the Redemption." http:// www.nwcybermall.com/grotto.htm, 1999.

"Grotto of the Redemption." http://www.road-sideamerica.com/attract/IAWESgrot.html

"Group's List of Endangered Wild Lands Focuses on the West." *Billings Gazette.* (July 1, 1998).

Gubernat, Michael. "History of the Cathedral Basilica of the Sacred Heart." http://www.rcan.org/RCAN/cathist2.htm (1996).

"A Guide to New Orleans Architecture." http://neworleansonline.com/arc-vc.htm.

Guillory, Todd A. "1900 Storm." http://www.utmb.edu/galveston/history/1900storm.html (1995).

Guise, Paul. "Pueblos: Masonry and Adobe Communal Houses." http://indy4.fdl.cc.mn.us/~isk/maps/houses/pueblo.htm (1997).

Gutiérriez, Ramón A., and Geneviève Fabre. *Feasts and Celebrations in North American Ethnic Communities.* Albuquerque: University of New Mexico Press, 1995.

Guttman, Melinda Given. "The Treasure of Congregation Temple Emanu-El." http://www.ny-museums.com/Emanu-el.htm (1997).

Haggart, Steven. "Early History of Yellowstone National Park." http://www.nezperce.com/yelpark9.html.

Hague, Harlan. "California's Russian Connection." http://www.softadventurenet/cal-russian.htm.

"Haida Indians" http://alaska.alaskan.com/akencinfo/haida.html.

"Haida Myths." http://www.uwgb.edu/~galta/mrr/haida/myth.htm.

Hall, C. G., sponsor. *Arkansas: A Guide to the State.* New York: Hastings House, 1941.

Hallam, Elizabeth, general ed. *Saints: Who They Are and How They Help You.* New York: Simon & Schuster, 1994.

Hamer, Linnea. "The Old World Builds the New: The Guastavino Company and the Technology of the Catalan Vault." http://users.aimnet.com/~tcolson/pages/ announc/octagon/octagon.htm (1997).

Hamerman, Don. "Our Place in History." http://www.emanuelnyc.org/history/timeline/timeline.html (1996).

Hamilton, Candy. "One Man's Rock Is Another's Holy Site." *Christian Science Monitor.* (June 12, 1996).

Hamlin, Christopher M. *Behind the Stained Glass.* Birmingham, Ala.: Crane Hill Publishers, 1998.

Hanson, Pat. "The Incomparable Luis Valdez, Leader of a Teledramatic Revolution." *Hispanic Outlook in Higher Education.* (May 30, 1997): 9.

Hargrave, Thomas P. "Tom's Harley-Davidson and Sidecar Page." http://ro.com/~thargrav/local.htm (August 13, 1999).

Haring, Scott. "Ave Maria Grotto." http://www.io.com/~sdharing/Grotto.html.

Harpur, James. *Revelations: The Medieval World.* New York: Henry Holt & Co., 1995.

Harris, Cyril M., ed. *Historic Architecture Sourcebook.* New York: McGraw-Hill, 1977.

Harris, Hamil R., and Valerie Strausas. "Farrakhan May Leave Hospital This Week." *Washington Post,* (April 4, 1999).

Harrod, Howard. *Renewing the World: Plains Indian Religion and Morality.* Albuquerque: University of Arizona Press, 1987.

"Harry Bertoia" http://interstyle.net/istyle1classic02bertoia.htm.

"Harvest Online." http://www.harvest.org/.

Harvey, Steve. "Big Bethel Church Pushes Community Service Programs." *Atlanta Journal & Constitution.* (July 4, 1987).

Hastings, James, ed. *Encyclopedia of Religion and Ethics.* New York: Charles Scribner's Sons, 1951.

Hatch, James V. *Black Images on the American Stage.* New York: DBS Publications, Inc., 1970.

Hauser, Beth. "Moody Bible President Speaks at Calvary." *Charlotte Christian News.* (April 13, 1999).

"Hawaiian Sacred Sites and Power Spots." http://www.psience.net/sites (1999).

Hayes, V. Dion. "Indians Sue Mining Companies to Clean up Idaho's Polluted Waterways." http://www.newstimes.com/archive96/dec2696/nation.htm.

"Heaven Bound." *Life.* (May 17, 1943): 27.

"Heaven Bound" (program), Atlanta: privately published, 1998.

"Heaven Bound: Big Bethel African Methodist Choir." http://newdeal.feri.org/library/ e81b.htm.

Heinerman, John. *Spiritual Wisdom of the Native Americans.* San Rafael, Calif.: Cassandra Press, 1989.

Helbig, Jack. "Review of 'We're Heaven Bound.'" *Booklist.* (November 15, 1994).

Henderson, Alice Corbin. *Brothers of Light: The Penitentes of the Southwest.* Las Cruces, N.Mex.: Yucca Tree Press, 1998.

Hennes, Robin. "Amana Colonies: Most Frequently Asked Questions." http://lucy.uwec.edu/academic/geography/Ivogeler/w188/articles/amana.htm (1997).

"Henry Wadsworth Longfellow." http://library.utoronto.ca/www/utel/rp/poems/longfe15.html.

Herbrechtsmeier, Williams. "Buddhism and the Definition of Religion: One More Time." *Journal for the Scientific Study of Religion.* (May 1993).

Herlihy, David. *Opera Muliebria: Women and Work in Medieval Europe.* New York: McGraw-Hill, 1990.

Hexham, Irving, and Karla Poewe. "UFO Religion: A Science Fiction Tradition." *The Christian Century.* (May 7, 1997): 439–440.

Heyer, Paul. *American Architecture: Ideas and Ideologies in the Late Twentieth Century.* New York: John Wiley & Sons, 1997.

"Hidden Canyons of the Southwest." http://www.mysteriousplaces.com/canyons/antelope.html.

"Hidden Heritage Exploring the Valley's American Indian Past." *Los Angeles Times,* Valley Edition (October 13 1993).

Hindmarsh, D. Bruce. "The Moravian Church in England, 1728–1760," *Church History.* (June 1, 1999): 471.

"Hindu Temple in Illinois." http://www.ssvt.org.

"Hindu Temple of Greater Chicago." http://www.ramatemple.org/hisrevp1.html.

"Hinduism in America." http://www.brown.edu/Departments/AmCiv/Studentprojects/apurva/index.htm.

Hinnells, John R. *The Penguin Dictionary of Religions.* London: Penguin Books, 1984.

Hirsch, Arthur H. *The Huguenots of Colonial South Carolina.* Columbia: University of South Carolina Press, 1998.

"Historic Church Gets HUD Grant." *Atlanta Journal & Constitution.* (February 25, 1980).

"Historic Homes of New Orleans." http://neworleansonline.com/hisho-lsm.htm.

"Historic Old Salem." http://cgibin1.erols.com/fmoran/hist.html.

"The Historic Touro Synagogue." http://www.gen.com/tayas/.

Historic World Leaders. Detroit: Gale Research, 1994.

History and Heritage of the Waldensian Presbyterian Church. Valdese, N.C.: privately published, 1993.

"History of Acoma." http://www.enchantedvisions.com/acomahis.html.

"History of Amana Colonies." http://www.amanacolonies.com/history.htm.

"A History of Circle Sanctuary." http://www.circlesanctuary.org/aboutcircle/circlehistory.html.

"History of Harvest Christian Fellowship and the Calvary Chapel Movement." http://www.baylor.edu/~Ryan_Darling/history.html.

"History of Jews in Spain." http://www.geocities.com/Athens/Academy/8636/History.html.

"History of Kenai." http://alaskan.com/docs/kenaihistory.html.

"History of the Church Maria and St. Antony of Padua—Infant Jesus of Prague." http://www.karmel.at/prag-jesu/english/eng/historen.htm

"History of the Cistercian Order." http://tvland.maxinet.com/trappist/History.html.

"History of 'The Little Brown Church in the Vale.'" http://www.marshallco.net/axtell/st-bridget/song.html.

"The History of Wicca." http://www.witchcraft.simplenet.com/wiccahistory.html.

Hobert, Rowland. "Smells Like Holy Spirit." *Houston Press.* (February 19, 1998).

Hodges, Miles. "Philosophers, Scientists, and Theologians of the Middle Ages." http://www2.cybernex.net/~mhodges/reference/middleages.htm (1999).

Hogan, Moreland. "Looking Around and Up." *Cityscape.* (June 2, 1998).

Hollister, C. Warren. *Medieval Europe: A Short History.* New York: McGraw-Hill, 1994.

Holmes, Cecile S. "Buddhist Temple Meets Changing Needs in Texas." *Charlotte Observer.* (March 18, 2000).

Holmes, George, ed. *The Oxford Illustrated History of Medieval Europe.* Oxford: Oxford University Press, 1988.

Holt, Tim. "Mt. Shasta." *The Jefferson Monthly.* http://www.jeffnet.org/jpr/feature1.html.

"Holy Assumption of the Virgin Mary Church." http://www.oca.org (1999).

"Holy Cross Abbey." http://www.holycross-abbey.org/whatisit.htm (1999).

"Holy Land USA." http://www.holyland.pleasevisit.com/index.html.

"Holy Name Monastery." http://monet.saintleo.edu (1998).

"Holy Trinity Chapel." http://www.oca.org/OCA/pim/oca-we-ftrhtc.html (1999).

"Home in the City." *Chicago Tribune*. (December 31, 1993).

"Homosexual Denomination Building Cathedral in Texas." http://www.whidbey.net/~dcloud/fbns/homosexualdenomination.htm (1998).

"The Hopi." http://gemini.tntech.edu/~kosburn/hopi.html.

"Hopi." http://www.humboldt.edu/~rwj1/hop.html.

"The Hopi Prophecy Rock." http://www.powersource.com/powersource/gallery/places/azna.html.

Hoppe, Emilie. *Seasons of Plenty: Amana Communal Cooking*. Ames: Iowa State University Press, 1998.

Horsley, Carter B. "The Midtown Book: St. Patrick's Cathedral." http://www.thecityreview.com/stpats.html.

Hoss, Carl. "Old North Church." http://www.oldnorth.com/main.htm (1999).

"Hot Springs National Park." http://www.hsnp.com/index.good.one.html.

Houtte, Melissa. "Utah's National Parks" (brochure). San Francisco: American Park Network, 1999.

"How the Canyons Were Made." http://www.insiders.com/utah/legend-recreation.htm.

"How Was Rainbow Bridge Formed?" http://www.nps.gov/rabr/rabrfrm.htm.

Howarth, Sam, and Enrique R. Lamadrid. *Pilgrimage to Chimayó*. Santa Fe: Museum of New Mexico Press, 1999.

Howell, B. A. "Over Four Thousand People Receive the Holy Ghost in El Salvador." http://www.apostolic-voice.org/salvador.htm.

Hoyt, Charles K.. "Newly Resurrected, the Historic Building Continues Its Active Association with Baltimore's African-American Community." *Architectural Record*. (February 1997): 112 ff.

Huang, T. Mark. "Texas Buddhist Council." http://www.cs.uh.edu/~tihuang/tbc/mission.htm (1997).

Huber, Leonard V., and Samuel Wilson, Jr. *The Basilica on Jackson Square: The History of the St. Louis Cathedral and Its Predecessors, 1727–1998*. New Orleans: Laborde Printing Co., 1998.

Hughart, Kathy. *Woman and Power in Alta California: 1790–1835*. http://www.acusd.edu/~khughart/women/1Title.html (1998).

Hughes, Bill. "Experience the Monastic Life at Mepkin Abbey Site" http://www.thestate.com/webwatch/w1.htm.

Hughes, David T. *Perceptions of the Sacred: A Review of Selected Native American Groups and Their Relationships with the Catlinite Quarries*. Wichita, Kans.: Wichita State University, 1997.

"The Huguenot Church." http://www.huguenotsociety.org/church.htm.

"The Huguenot Society of South Carolina." http://www.huguenotsociety.org/.

Hultkrantz, Ake. *Native Religions of North America: The Power of Visions and Fertility*. Prospect Heights, Ill.: Waveland Press, 1987.

"The Humaniversity." http://www.humaniversity.nl/.

Huntington, Henry, "Alaska Eskimo Whaling." *Inuit Whaling*. Inuit Circumpolar Conference, June 1992.

Hurley, Timothy. "Environmental Restoration of Kaho'Olawe to Proceed." *Maui News*. (June 20, 1997).

Hyder, William D., and Georgia Lee. "The Shamanic Tradition in Chumash Art." http://zzyx.ucsc.edu/Comp/Bill/shamtrad.html. (1994).

"Idaho Indian Reservations." http://www.rootsweb.com/~idreserv/.

Iler, David. "Sedona: New Age Portal or Paradise Lost?" *Cyberwest Magazine*. http://www.cyberwest.com/v5adwst1.html (December 1, 1995).

"Images from Enchanted Rock State Natural Area." http://uts.cc.utexas.edu/~rmr/er.html.

"Imam W.D. Muhammad Joins Farrakhan Followers at Saviours' Day," *Final Call*. (February 27, 1999).

"Immaculate Conception, Atlanta." http://www.archatl.com/icatl01.jpg.

"The Impact of Proposed Amendments to the American Indian Religious Freedom Act on Other Uses of Public Lands." http://www. yvwiiusdinvnohii.net/govlaw/AIRFAamend.htm (1993).

"Indians Plan March to Yellowstone to Boost Awareness of Bison Killing." *Billings Gazette*. (January 31, 1999).

"In Search of a Spiritual Path." *Detroit News*. (December 21, 1995).

"In Search of Serenity." *Chicago Tribune* (January 26, 1997).

"Institute of Sacred Music." http://www.yale.edu/ism/before.ISM.html.

"Inter-Faith Dialogue." http://www.web.net/~cym/interfth.html (1997).

"International Peace Garden." http://town.-boissevain.mb.ca/attract/pgarden.htm.

"International Peace Garden." http://www.whispersonthewind.org/_states/peaceupp.html.

"International Spirit Gathering." http://www.circlesanctuary.org/psg/.

"Interview with Charlie Maxwell." *Pacific Connections.* (September–October 1996).

"Introduction to Gateway." http://www.passionplayusa.com/gate.html.

Irwin, Julie. "Churches Follow Flocks to Suburbia." *Cincinnati Enquirer.* (June 29, 1998).

———. "Religion Suddenly Rocks." *Cincinnati Enquirer.* (October 17, 1998).

Isay, David. "There Isn't Any Redemption without a Little Bit of Blood." *Culturefront.* (fall 1998).

"Islamic Center of America." http://www.icofa.com (1999).

"Islamic References." http://www.sijpa.org/references.htm.

Istomin, Alexei A. "The Indians at the Ross Settlement" (pamphlet). Fort Ross, Calif.: Fort Ross Interpretive Association, Inc., 1992.

"It's Not Just Another Boring Religion." *The (Olympia, Washington) Olympian.* (March 14, 1999).

Iwanski, Len. "Indians Protest Buffalo Killings near Yellowstone with Pilgrimage." *Nando Times* (Raleigh, NC). (February 27, 1999).

Jackson, Kristin. "Monks Offer Food and Rest for the Soul." *Seattle Times* (n.d.).

Jackson, Samuel Macauley. *The New Schaff-Herzog Encyclopedia of Religious Knowledge.* Grand Rapids, Mich.: Baker Book House, 1969.

Jacoby, Susan. "Beyond Charm in Charleston." *New York Times.* (May 2, 1999).

"Jade Buddha Temple." http://www.jadebuddha.org/English/index.htm.

James, George. "Places of the Heart." *New York Times.* (March 28, 1999).

James, Harry C. *Pages from Hopi History.* Albuquerque: University of Arizona Press, 1974.

James, Kathleen. "Kiva." http://nardac.mip.berkeley.edu (1998).

Jamieson, Elizabeth, and Mary F. Sewall. *Trends in Nursing History.* London: W. B. Saunders Co., 1949.

Jamison, Suzanne. "Evolution of Leadership in a

Traditional Fraternity." http://swanet.org/frater.html.

Janetski, Joel C. *The Indians of Yellowstone Park.* Salt Lake City: University of Utah Press, 1987.

Jarvis, Thea. "Atlanta Youth Groups Greet Visitors." *(Atlanta) Georgia Bulletin.* (July 18, 1996).

Jett, Stephen C. "The Great 'Race' to 'Discover' Rainbow Natural Bridge in 1909." *Kiva Magazine.* 58, no. r1, 1992.

"John Wesley." http://www.coastalgeorgia.com/jw.html.

Johnson, Allen, and Dumas Malone, eds. *Dictionary of American Biography.* New York: Charles Scribner's Sons, 1930.

Johnson, George. "Fire in the Mind." http://www.santafe.edu/~johnson/fire.preface.html (1995).

Johnson, Joan. *The Cult Movement.* New York: Franklin Watts, 1984.

Johnson, Myke. "Wanting to Be an Indian: When Spiritual Teaching Turns into Cultural Theft" (pamphlet). Boston: Respect, Inc., 1995.

Johnson, Shelli. "Early History of Man and Yellowstone." *Yellowstone Journal.* (May–June 1996).

Johnson, Theodore E. *Life in the Christ Spirit.* Sabbathday Lake, Maine: The United Society, 1969.

Johnson, Virginia. "Hermano Juan Sandoval Penitente." *San Miguel Parish News.* (March 29–30, 1997).

Jonaitis, Aldona. *From the Land of the Totem Poles.* Seattle: University of Washington Press, 1988.

Jones, Geri. "Religious Revival." *Hickory (NC) Daily Record.* (October 2, 1999).

Jones, Lisa. "Sound-Bite Slogans Distort a Complicated Reality." *High Country News* (Paonia, Colo.). (July 24, 1995).

"Joseph Chasing Horse, Lakota Spiritual Leader." http://www.enetis.net/~wolfsong/Joe.html.

Joseph, Frank, ed. *Sacred Sites of the West: A Guide to Mystical Centers.* Surrey, B.C.: Hancock House, 1997.

Josephson, Russell. "Salt Lake Mormon Tabernacle Choir Discography." http://www.geocities.com/SunsetStrip/ 7158/ mtchist.htm (1999).

Joyce, Robert F. "The Carthusian Foundation in America" (brochure). Burlington, Vt.: privately published, 1963.

"Judaism." http://www.religioustolerance.org.

"July 4th Events." *Washington Post.* (July 1, 1999).

Kaczor, Bill. "Going Strong: Long-Running Revival Still Has Strong Hold." *Hickory (NC) Daily Record.* (July 3, 1999).

"Kahal Kadosh Beth Elohim." http://www.awod.com/gallery/probono/kkbe/.

"Kaho'Olawe Mahakiki Overview." http://www.brouhaha.net/ohana/makahiki.html.

Kalakaua, David. *The Legends and Myths of Hawaii.* Rutland, Vt.: Charles E. Tuttle Co., 1972.

Kalani, Lyn, Lynn Rudy, and John Sperry, general eds. *Fort Ross.* Fort Ross, Calif.: Fort Ross Interpretive Association, 1998.

"Kalmar Nyckel." http://www.kalnyc.org/.

Kanellos, Nicolás. *Chronology of Hispanic-American History from Pre-Columbian Times to the Present.* Detroit: Gale Research, 1995.

———. *Hispanic Firsts: 500 Years of Extraordinary Achievement.* Detroit: Visible Ink Press, 1997.

Kang, Dr. Thomas Hosuck. "Confucianism." http://www.wam.umd.edu/~tkang/ (1999).

"Kannagara Jinja." http://www.kannagara.org (1998).

Kasindorf, Martin. "Babbitt: Save the Land or Step Aside." *USA Today.* (December 13, 1999).

"Kauai Aadheenam." *Hinduism Today.* (August 19, 1998).

Kaye, Ron, and Connie Schmidt. "Buddha Me Happy." *Houston Sidewalk.* (June 26, 1999).

Keegan, Marcia. *Taos Pueblo and Its Sacred Blue Lake.* Santa Fe, N. Mex.: Clear Light Publishers, 1991.

Keen, Lisa, and Suzanne B. Goldberg. *Strangers to the Law: Gay People on Trial.* Ann Arbor: University of Michigan Press, 1998.

Keenan, Hugh T. " 'Heaven Bound' at the Crossroads: A Sketch of a Religious Pageant." *Journal of American Culture.* (fall 1988): 39–45.

"Keepers of the Sacred Traditions of Pipemakers." http://www.bnd.net/pipemakers/.

Kelleher, Ray. "Rejoice and Be Glad." *Seattle Times.* (November 10, 1996).

Kelley, Klara Bonsack, and Harris Francis. *Navajo Sacred Places.* Bloomington: Indiana University Press, 1994.

Kelly, Ellen, and Annabelle Melville. *Elizabeth Seton: Selected Writings.* New York: Paulist Press, 1987.

Kelly, Jack, and Marcia Kelly. *Sanctuaries: The Complete United States.* New York: Bell Tower Books, 1992.

Kelly, Michael. "Banality and Evil." *New Republic.* (May 5, 1997): 6.

Kennedy, Ira. "Visitor's Guide to the Center of the World." http://llanotexas.com/ersna/index. htm (1998).

Kennedy, John S. "What Is a Cathedral?" *Hartford Courant.* (June 24, 1962).

Kenworthy, Tom. "Intersection of Mountains, Plains at 'a Crossroads.'" *Washington Post.* (August 25, 1997).

Ketchum, Richard M. *The American Heritage Book of Great Historic Places.* New York: American Heritage Publishing Co., 1957.

"The Kidder Smith Images Project." http://libraries.mit.edu/rvc/kidder/CT34.html.

Kiefer, James E. "Biographical Sketches of Memorable Christians of the Past." http://justus.anglican.org/resources/bio.

Kimball, Stanley. "The Mormon Trail in Utah." http://www.media.utah.edu/medsol/UCME/m/MORMONTRAIL.html.

King, Serge Kahili. "Kahuna and Hawaiians." *Aloha International.* http://www.huna.org/html/hunahaw.html.

"Kirtan and Katha." http://www.sikhi.demon.co.uk/kirtan.htm.

"Kit Carson Historic Museums." http://www.laplaza.com/a_l/art/kitcarson/sites.htm.

Klagsbrun, Francine. *Jewish Days.* New York: Farrar, Straus & Giroux, 1996.

"Klamath Tribes History." http://www.klamathtribes.org/history.html.

Klein, Anne C. "Buddhism in Houston." http://rodin.cs.uh.edu/~tihuang/bud_hou.htm (1999).

Klemp, Joan, Anthony Moore, and Mary Carroll Moore, eds. *Eckankar: Ancient Wisdom for Today.* Minneapolis, Minn.: Eckankar, 1995.

Knudsen, Andreas. "Blackfeet: Land and Language Is the Heritage." *Indigenous Affairs.* (January–March 1996).

Kraker, Daniel, "Soul Attractions." *Utne Reader.* (July–August 1997): 76–77.

Kraut, Alan. *Silent Travelers: Germs, Genes, and the "Immigrant Menace."* New York: BasicBooks, 1994.

Krieger, Dan. "Readers Were Spellbound by Mission Lore." *San Luis Obispo Telegram-Tribune.* (July 13, 1996).

———. "Tall Tales about Tiles Aren't True." *San Luis Obispo Telegram-Tribune.* (August 16, 1997).

"Krishna Today." http://www.trancenet.org/krishna/.

Krodel, Beth. "Muslims' Growth Spurs Building

of $15-million Mosque." *Detroit Free Press.* (June 23, 1999).

Kubany, Elizabeth. "A Congregation's Desire to House Classrooms and Worship Space Together Was the Starting Point for a New Synagogue." *Architectural Record.* (July 1998): 88ff.

Kubota, Gary T. "Kaho'Olawe Going Back to Native Foliage." *Honolulu Star-Bulletin.* (July 3, 1997).

———. "Kaho'Olawe Planners Vote for Fishing Ban." *Honolulu Star-Bulletin.* (May 23, 1997).

Lacour, Greg. "Prodigal Pilgrimage." *Charlotte Observer.* (October 2, 1999).

LaDuke, Winona. "Dilemma of Indian Forestry." *Earth Island Journal.* (summer, 1994).

Laird, Michael. "The Calvary Organ." http://theatreorgans.com/laird/calvary/index.html.

Lakota: Seeking the Great Spirit. London: Labyrinth Publishing, 1994.

"Lama Foundation." http://www.taosnet.com/lama/index.html.

"The Lama Foundation Fire." http://www. ic. org/pnp/lamafire.html.

Lamar, Harold. "Making Sweet Auburn Sweet Again." *Atlanta Tribune.* (June 1999).

Lamm, N. "Lunar New Year Ushers in Year of the Ox." *The (Olympia, Washington) Olympian.* (February 6, 1997).

Lampis, Anna Rosa. "Large Binocular Telescope." http://medusa.as.arizona.edu/lbttx.html (1999).

"Landmarks at Harvard." http://www.news. harvard.edu/hno.subpages/intro_harvard/visiting/landmarks.html.

Lane, Bilden C.. "Fierce Landscapes and the Indifference of God." *Christian Century.* (October 11, 1989): 907–910.

Lapahie, Harrison. "The Navajo Creation Story." http://www.lapahie.com/Creation.html.

"La Plaza, Taos Pueblo." http://www.laplaza. org/comm/about_taos/about_taos_pueblo. html.

"The Last Word." *The Sounding Board.* (spring 1999): 16.

"Latin Chant Is New Wave." *Chicago Tribune.* (March 29, 1996).

Latkin, Carl A. "Feelings after the Fall: Former Rajneeshpuram Commune Members' Perceptions of and Affiliation with the Rajneeshee Movement." *Sociology of Religion.* (March 22, 1994): 65–73.

———, Richard A. Hagan, Richard A. Littman, and Norman D. Sundberg. "Who Lives in Utopia? A Brief Report on the Rajneeshpuram Research Project." *Sociological Analysis.* (1987): 73–81.

Lattin, Don. "Chronicle Religion: Ram Dass." *San Francisco Examiner.* (May 26, 1997).

Laver, Ross, and Paul Kaihla. "Sun Myung Moon Embraces the High and Mighty." *Maclean's.* (October 23, 1995): 46.

"Lawrenceville Historical Society." http://trfn. clpgh.org/lhs/stjohns.html.

Leahigh, John. "An Experience of Eucharistic Ecclesiology." *Emmanuel Magazine.* (July–August 1998).

Leahy, Donna. *Wisdom of the Plain Folk.* New York: Penguin Studio, 1997.

LeBaron, Gaye. "A Future Saint's Observations of Our Russian Fort." *Press Democrat.* (August 8, 1999).

Lee, Hermione. *Willa Cather: A Life Saved Up.* London: Virago Press, 1989.

Leeming, David Adams. *The World of Myth.* Oxford: Oxford University Press, 1992.

Lehn, Cornelia. *Peace Be with You.* Newton, Kans.: Faith and Life Press, 1980.

Lenz, Thomas J. "Building a Force for the Common Good." *Shelterforce Online.* (September–October, 1998). http://www.nhi.org/online/issues/101/lenz.html.

"Letter from a Birmingham Jail." *The Negro Almanac.* Harry A. Ploski and James Williams, eds. Detroit: Gale Research, 1989.

"Letters." *High Country News* (Paonia, Colo.). (June 24, 1996).

Lewis, David Rich. "Native Americans and the Environment: A Survey of Twentieth-Century Issues." *American Indian Quarterly.* (summer 1995): 423–451.

Lewis, James R. *Cults in America.* Santa Barbara, Calif.: ABC-Clio, 1998.

Lewis, Roger. "Review of 'Fire in the Mind.'" *Los Angeles Times Book Review.* (October 1, 1995).

"Life in the English Colonies." http://www2. tltc.ttu.edu/Harper/2300/WebLinks/Pre1800/Colonialto1776.

"The Life of St. Innocent of Alaska." http:// www. oca.org/Feasts-and-Saints/OCA/Life-of-St-Innocent-MP.html.

Lightman, Victoria Hodge. "Rothko Chapel." http://houston.sidewalk.com/detail/442 (1999).

"Lillian D. Wald." http://www.JWA.org/exhib98/wald/lwbio.htm.

"Lillian D. Wald." http://www.netsrq.com/~dbois/wald.html.

Lilly, Edward G., ed. *Historic Churches of Charleston*. Charleston, S.C.: Legerton & Co., 1966.

Ling, T. O. *A Dictionary of Buddhism*. New York: Charles Scribner's Sons, 1972.

Linn, Charles. "Places of Worship: Where We Seek the Light." *Architectural Record*. (July 1998, 87).

Linscheid, John. "Germantown Mennonite Church." http://www.seas.upenn.edu/~linsch/GMChtml (1998).

Linthicum, Leslie. "Chaco Canyon Endangered." *Albuquerque Journal*. (April 21, 1999).

Lipman, David E. "Gates to Jewish Heritage." http://www.jewishgates.org/personalities/wise.stm.

"The Little Brown Church." http://www.drake.edu/journalism/brides96/dm/mag/features/church/church.html (1996).

"The Little Brown Church in the Vale." http://www.littlebrownchurch.org (1997).

Little, Jon. "Borough Might Return Village to Tribe." *Anchorage Daily News*. (August 7, 1998).

———. "Kenai Tribe Fights for Subsistence." *Anchorage Daily News*. (May 7, 1999).

"Liturgy in a Formative Environment." http://www.litpress.org/life.html.

"Local Baptists Are Not Bigots about Buddhists." *Wilmington (NC) Star-News*. (September 11, 1988).

"Local History and Attractions in Charlotte." http://www.cms.k12.nc.us/allschools/elizabeth/cyberfair.htm.

Loeffler, Jan. "The Seventh Abbot." http://ourworld.compuserve.com/homepages/Jan_Loeffler/jal205.htm (1996).

Loftin, John D. *Religion and Hopi Life in the Twentieth Century*. Bloomington: Indiana University Press, 1991.

Loftus, Margaret. "The Fight for Devils Tower." *U.S. News & World Report*. (June 16, 1997): 12.

Long, Magon. "Mission Culture Provides Area's Religious Roots." *San Luis Obispo County Telegram-Tribune*. (1999).

Longfellow, Henry Wadsworth. "Paul Revere's Ride." http://english-www.hss.cmu.edu/poetry/paul-revere.html.

Loofbourow, Leon L. *Steeples among the Sage*. San Francisco: Historical Society of the California-Nevada Annual Conference of the Methodist Church, 1964.

"Looking Back, Moving Ahead." http://www.trinitywallstreet.org/looking.html.

Loomis, Sylvia. "Interview with Mrs. Gene Kloss." http://sirismm.si.edu/aaa/transnda/KLOSSGEN.TXT (1965).

Lopez, Robert S. *The Birth of Europe*. New York: M. Evans & Co., 1967.

"Loretto Chapel." http://www.lorettochapel.com.

Lorie, Peter, and Julie Foakes. *The Buddhist Directory: United States of America and Canada*. Boston: Charles E. Tuttle Co., 1997.

Louden-Sundahl, Tamara. "1998 Round-Up: Mitchell Portrayed Image of Cowboys." *Trinidad Plus*. (September 1, 1998).

"Louis Farrakhan." http://www.forerunner.com/forerunner/X0065_Nation_of_Islam.html.

"Louisiana Authors." http://indigo.lib.lsu.edu/la/h.html.

"Lovely Lane United Methodist Church." http://www.gbgm-umc.org/lovelylaneumc/.

Low, W. Augustus, and Virgil A. Clift. *Encyclopedia of Black America*. New York: Da Capo, 1981.

"Luis Valdez." http://spider.invsn.com/fotpl/valley4e.htm.

Lummis, Charles F. *Pueblo Indian Folk-Stories*. Lincoln: University of Nebraska Press, 1992.

Lumpkins, Barbranda. "Unsung Landmarks to Black Achievement." *USA Today*. (February 4, 1993).

Lynch, Brad. "Lawyer-Turned-Pastor Tries W. Parish Pulpit." *Barnstable (Massachusetts) Patriot*. (January 28, 1999).

Lyon, Mack. *Atlanta Architecture: The Victorian Heritage*. Atlanta: Atlanta Historical Society, 1976.

MacDonald, Darvesha. "The Mystery of Renewal." *Lama Newsletter*. (spring–summer 1998).

MacDonald, Margaret Read, ed. *The Folklore of World Holidays*. Detroit: Gale Research, 1992.

MacHarg, Kenneth D. "Venezuela Restricts Unification Church." *Christianity Today*. (November 17, 1997) 76.

Mack, Stephen R. "John Muir, William Gladstone Steele, and the Creation of Yosemite and Crater Lake National Parks." http://www.nps.gov/crla/steel.htm.

Magdalena, Amari. "The Medicine Wheel: The Circle of Life." http://www.sonoranshaman.com/medicinewheel.htm (1996).

Magner, Lois N. *A History of Medicine.* New York: Marcel Dekker, 1992.

Magnuson, Jon. "The Mending of Creation." *Christian Century.* (April 21, 1993): 420–422.

Malinowski, Sharon, ed. *Notable Native Americans.* Detroit: Gale Group, 1995.

Mallia, Joseph. "Inside the Church of Scientology: Powerful Church Targets Fortunes, Souls of Recruits." *Boston Herald.* (March 1, 1998).

"The Malpais."http://hanksville.phast.umass.edu/geology/malpais.html.

Maneck, Susan S., "Women in the Bahá'i Faith." *Religion and Women.* Albany: State University of New York Press, 1994.

Mano, D. Keith. "Dinner on Rajneesh." *National Review.* (April 7, 1989): 56–58.

Marable, Manning. "Black Fundamentalism: Farrakhan and Conservative Black Nationalism." *Race and Class.* (April 15, 1998): 1–23.

"Mark Rothko." http://www.nga.gov/feature/rothko (1999).

Marlowe, Kimberly B.. "Santa Fe, Cool." *Seattle Times.* (May 17, 1998).

Marriott, Alice, and Carol K. Rachlin. *Plains Indian Mythology.* New York: Meridian Books, 1975.

Martin, Bob. "Sanctuário de Chimayó," *New Mexico Magazine.* (April 1969).

Martin, Douglas. "Spirits Are Willing, but Buildings Are Weak." *New York Times.* (August 11, 1996).

Martin, Ernest O. *Lloyd Wright, Architect and Designer of the Wayfarers Chapel* (pamphlet). Palos Verdes, Calif.: Wayfarers Chapel, 1988.

"Martin Luther King, Jr., National Historic Site." http://www.thomson.com/gale/avs/ga.html.

Mathes, Matt. "USDA Forest Service Decides Against New Ski Area at Mt. Shasta." http://www.r5.fs.fed.us/forestmanagement/html/no_ski_area.html (1998).

Maynor, Malinda, and Toby McLeod. "America's First People Still Seek Religious Freedom." *Earth Island Journal.* (summer 1999).

Mazza, Patricia. "Indigenous Voices." http://www.tnews.com (1995).

McAllister, J. Gilbert. *Archaeology of Kahoolawe* (monograph). New York: Kraus Reprint Co., 1973.

McCallum, Dennis. "The Waldensian Movement from Waldo to Reformation IV." http://www.xenos.org/essays/waldo5.htm.

McCracken, Harold. *George Catlin and the Old Frontier.* New York: Dial Press, 1959.

McCullen, Kevin. "Forest Service Bows to Indians' Wishes on Religious Site." *(Denver) Rocky Mountain News.* (July 26, 1992).

McDougall, Connie. "Take a Deep Breath and Let Yoga Soothe Season's Stress." *Seattle Times.* (December 11, 1998).

McGowan, James C. "Going Indian." *Whole Earth Review.* (winter 1993): 106–109.

McGrath, Bernadette. "Sermons: Biblical Wisdom for Daily Living." *Library Journal.* (May 1, 1998): 106.

McGrath, Beth. "In Search of Morality." *Library Journal.* (October 1, 1997): 90.

McHenry, Robert, ed. *Liberty's Women.* Springfield, Mass.: G. C. Merriam Co., 1980.

McKee, John. "Second Ascent of Shasta Butte." *San Francisco Daily Herald.* (October 9, 1854).

McKown, Robin. *Heroic Nurses.* New York: G. P. Putnam's Sons, 1966.

McMillan, Alex Frew. "Mansion in the Sky." *Business North Carolina.* (December 1998): 40–53.

McMorrough, Jordan. "Priests of the Diocese Gather for Sacred Chrism Mass." *The Catholic Miscellany.* (1997–1998).

McNamee, Gregory. "The Future of a Sacred Past." *Desert USA.* (April 1999).

McNelly, N. A. F. "The Dust That Heals." http://halfmoon.org/story/chimdust.html (1997).

McNichol, Tom. "False Profits: Merger Mania Hits the Televangelists." *New Republic.* (April 13, 1987): 11–12.

McPherson, Robert S. *Sacred Land, Sacred View: Navajo Perceptions of the Four Corners.* Salt Lake City: Signature Books, 1992.

"Medieval Sourcebook: The Conversion of Peter Waldo." http://www.fordham.edu/halsall/source/waldo1.html.

"Meher Baba." http://www.cybertrails.com/babadas/MeherBaba.html.

"Meher Baba Spiritual Center." http://www.avatarmeherbaba.org/mscenter.html.

"Meher Baba Web Sites." http://indians.australians.com/meherbaba/links.htm.

Mellskog, Pam. "House of Salvation." *Vital Ministry.* (September–October 1999).

Melton, J. Gordon. *Encyclopedic Handbook of Cults in America.* New York: Garland, 1992.

"Memorial Church." http://www.memorialchurch.harvard.edu.

"Memorial Church Welcomes Gay Commitment Rites." *Harvard Magazine*. (September–October 1997).

"The Mennonite Church and Homosexuality." http://www.religioustolerance.org/hom_men.htm.

"Mennonite Church Expelled for Accepting Gays." *CNN News*. http://cnn.com/US/9711/05/gay.mennonite (November 4, 1997).

"Mepkin Abbey." http://www.mepkinabbey.org.

"Mid-American Buddhist Association." http://www.econ.uiuc.edu/~wee/MABA/html/sangha.html (1999).

Miller, Corki, and Mary Ellen Snodgrass. *Storytellers*. Jefferson, N.C.: McFarland & Co., 1998.

Miller, Joaquin. "Mt. Shasta Grizzly Legend." http://www.whitestareagle.com/natlit/mt-shasta.htm (1998).

Miller, Roger L. "The Mormon Tabernacle Choir." http://eddy.media.utah.edu/medsol/UCME/m/MORMONTABCHOIR.html.

Milne, Courtney. *Sacred Places in North America: A Journey into the Medicine Wheel*. New York: Stewart, Tabori & Chang, 1995.

Milstein, Michael. "Medicine Wheel Remains Unprotected." *High Country News* (Paonia, Colo.) (May 3, 1993).

———. "Sawmill Suit Threatens Medicine Wheel Plan." *Wyoming Gazette*. (March 26, 1999).

Minchin, Marty. "Buddhists Welcome New Year." *Wilmington* (NC) *Morning Star*. (January 1, 1996).

Minzesheimer, Bob. "In New York City, Castro Is Man of Hour." *USA Today*. (October 24, 1995).

Mirsky, Jennette. *Houses of God*. New York: Viking Press, 1965.

"Mission of San Miguel of Santa Fe." http://www.nmohwy.com/m/misamisf.htm.

Moberg, David. "New City-Suburban Coalition Tackles Shared Social Problems." *North Shore Magazine*. (January 1998).

Momaday, N. Scott. *The Way to Rainy Mountain*. Albuquerque: University of New Mexico Press, 1969.

"Monasterio de la Nuestra Senora Soledad." http://www.users.csbsju.edu/~wrkshop3/kele/project.html.

"The Monastery of Christ in the Desert." http://www.christdesert.org/noframes/tour/brief.html.

"The Monastery Sustainability Project." http://www.denmansantafe.com/monastery.htm.

Monroe, Elvira. *A Guide to Places of Worship in and around San Francisco*. San Carlos, Calif.: Wide World Publishing, 1984.

Montgomery, Nancy S., ed. "The Washington National Cathedral" (brochure). Washington, D.C.: Washington National Cathedral, 1990.

"Montreat College." http://www.montreat.edu (1999).

"Moon Struck." *People Weekly*. (September 21, 1998): 89.

"The Moravian Church." http://cti.itc.virginia.edu/~jkh8x/soc257/nrms/Moravian.html.

"The Moravian Church." http://www.moravian.org.

"Moravian Church Genealogy." http://www.enter.net/~smschlack.

"Moravians, Lutherans Align Faith." *Greensboro* (NC) *News and Record*. (January 29, 2000).

"The Moravian Museum." http://www.atlantik.cz/mzm/index.html.en.

"More about Ram Dass." http://www.more-about.com/spirit/ram-dass.htm.

"More Than 41,000 Flock to Veterans Stadium" http://www.promisekeepers.org/pkpress/98conf-phily-pub.htm (1998).

Morgan, Brandt. *The Santa Fe and Taos Book*. Stockbridge, Mass.: Berkshire House, 1994.

"The Mormon Tabernacle Organs." http://theatreorgans.com/mormon/.

"Morris Brown College History." http://www.morrisbrown.edu/History/default.htm.

Moses, Alexandra R. "Local Muslim Leaders Decry Bombing of Iraq on Eve of Ramadan." *Detroit News*. (December 19, 1998).

Moses, Daniel David, and Terry Goldie, eds. *An Anthology of Canadian Native Literature in English*. Toronto: Oxford University Press, 1992.

"Mount Baker—Snoqualmie National Forest." http://www.fs.fed.us/r6/mbs/forestfacts.htm.

"The Mount Graham Case." http://users.skynet.be/Kola/mtgrah.htm (1999).

"Mount Graham Time Line." *High Country News*. (Paonia, Colo.) (July 24, 1995).

"Mount Mazama Volcano and Crater Lake." http://vulcan.wr.usgs.gov/Volcanoes/CraterLake/description_crater_lake.html.

"Mount Shasta Eruptive History." http://vulcan.wr.usgs.gov/Volcanoes/Shasta/EruptiveHistory/framework.html

Mowat, Farley. *The Polar Passion: The Quest for the*

North Pole. Toronto: McClellan & Stewart, 1989.

"Mt. Hood Wilderness." http://web4.integraonline.com/~swamp/wmthood.html.

"Mt. Shasta Ski Area Becomes Past History." *The Nordic Voice.* (June 1998).

Muhammad, Dionne. "Muslim Students Hold 2nd Annual Conference." *Final Call.* (September 22, 1998).

Mulligan, Hugh A. "12 Holy Men Pass Another Silent Year on Equinox Mountain." *Rutland (Vermont) Daily Herald.* (December 29, 1980).

"Muralists Index." http://www.lamurals.org/MCLA/Muralists.html.

Murray, Barbara. "Interpreting the Atonement: Race." *U.S. News & World Report.* (October 27, 1997): 44.

Murray, Peter, and Linda Murray. *The Oxford Companion to Christian Art and Architecture.* London: Oxford University Press, 1996.

Muschamp, Herbert. "When the Cathedral Turned Black." *New Republic.* (April 23, 1990): 28–33.

Muster, Nori J. *Betrayal of the Spirit: My Life behind the Headlines of the Hare Krishna Movement.* Champaign: University of Illinois Press, 1997.

Mutrux, Robert. *Great New England Churches: 65 Houses of Worship That Changed Our Lives.* Chester, Conn.: Globe Pequot Press, 1982.

Myren, Robert. "The Little Brown Church in Story and in Song" (pamphlet). Mason City, Iowa: Stoyles Graphic Services, n.d.

Naffah, Christiane. "Hub of the Islamic Community." *UNESCO Courier.* (November 1990): 34–38.

"Nappanee Missionary Church." http://www.nmc1.org/.

Nartonis, David K, and Bryan Thompson. "Seeking God in a Harried Life." *Christian Science Monitor.* (February 26, 1998).

Nash, Michael L. "The Thai Monarchy." *Contemporary Review.* (August 1996): 66–69.

"The Nation of Islam." http://cti.itc.virginia.edu/~jkh8x/soc257/nrms/Nofislam.html.

"Nation of Islam Leader Minister Louis Farrakhan Takes Four-Month Sabbatical for Health Reasons." *Jet.* (April 5, 1999): 10.

"National Landmarks." *National Park Service Morning Report.* (February 24, 1999).

"Native American Religion." http://cti.itc.virginia.edu/~jkh8x/soc257/nrms/naspirit.html.

"Native American Religious Freedom." http://hanksville.phast.umass.edu/misc/religiousfreedom.html.

"Native Americans for Enola vs. the United States Forest Service." http://www.achp.gov/book/case131.html (1995).

"Native Rights Act before Congress." *Earth Island Journal.* (winter 1992–1993).

"Nature Notes from Crater Lake." *Nature Notes,* Crater Lake, Oregon: Crater Lake History Association, 1995.

"Navajo Rugs." http://www.cia-g.com/~gathplac/Navajo_rugs.htm.

"Navajoland." http://www.navajoland.com/.

"Navajos Block Access to Rainbow Bridge." *Tucson Citizen.* (August 12, 1995).

Nelson, Robert, "Advancing Retreats." *Omaha World Herald.* (March 13, 1999).

"Neo-Nazi Ideology 1998." http://www.africa2000.com/XNDX/xneonazi.html.

Neuerburg, Norman. *Saints of the California Missions.* Santa Barbara, Calif.: Bellerophon Books, 1995.

New Catholic Encyclopedia. Washington, D.C.: Catholic University of America Press, 1967.

"New Mexico State Timeline." http://hobbspublib.leaco.net/nmtimeln.htm.

"New Vrindavana As It Is Today." http://www.hkw.iskcon.net/15.6/newv.htm.

"Newcomer's Guide to New Haven Churches." http://www.yale.edu/ygcf/various/newcomer.html.

Newman, Andy. "Prayer in New York, Protest in Washington." *New York Times.* (February 16, 1999).

"Newyorkcarver.Com." http://www.newyorkcarver.com (1999).

"Nez Perce National Historical Park." http://www.halcyon.com/rdpayne/npnhpjoseph.html.

"North Idaho." http://www.visitid.org/regions/north_idaho/region1_98.html (1998).

Niebuhr, Gustav (a). "Lutheran Group Approves Link to Episcopalians." *New York Times.* (August 20, 1999).

——— (b). "Witches Cast as Neo-Pagans Next Door." *New York Times.* (October 31, 1999).

———, and Laurie Goodstein. "A New Generation of Evangelists Is Vying for a National Pulpit." *New York Times.* (January 1, 1999).

Niles, Susan A. "Grottos of the American Midwest." http://www.lafayette.edu/niless/awst-home. htm (1995).

"1999–2000 Dissertation Fellowship Grant Abstracts." http://www.louisville-institute.org/grdissabs.html (1997).

"1997 Landmarks at Risk Report." http://www2. cr.nps.gov/nhl/at_risk97/Section8_Intro.html (1997).

"1997 NHL Endangered List." http://www2. cr.nps.gov/nhl/at_risk97/Section8_Intro. html.

Noel, Peter. "In the Shadow of Death." *Village Voice.* (March 17, 1999).

Norbert, Bob. "Mystery Man of Fort Ross Skeleton Found Outside Cemetery." *(San Francisco) Press Democrat.* (September 7, 1999).

———. "Russian Legacy Lives on in Coastal Faces, Places." *(San Francisco) Press Democrat.* (July 24, 1997).

"North American Scene." *Christianity Today.* (January 12, 1998).

"North Iowa Attractions." http://www. globegazette.com/sitepages/community/attractionspages/Wesley.htm.

Norton, Henry Franklin. *A History of Martha's Vineyard.* Henry Franklin Norton and Robert Emmett Pyne, Publishers: 1923.

Notable Asian Americans. Detroit: Gale Research, 1995.

"NOTcoffeeHouse Poetry and Performance Series." http://www.notcoffeehouse.org.

Nystedt, Annette. "The Navajo Nation Natural Heritage Program." http://www.heritage.tnc. org/nhp/us/navajo (1997).

"Oak Bluffs." http://www.mvrental.com/html/body_ob_town_info.html.

"Oak Bluffs Town Government." http://mvy. com/obinfo.html (1999).

O'Connor, Michael J. "Soul Food." *Architecture.* (November 1998): 51.

"Official Response of the Japanese Church to the Lineamenta." http://www.02.so-net.ne.jp/~catholic/EDOC/Linea.htm (1997).

O'Gorman, James F. *Living Architecture: A Biography of H. H. Richardson.* New York: Simon & Schuster, 1997.

"Old Chiang Mai Culture Center." http://www. infothai.com/cmculture/ (1998).

"Old Mission State Park." http://www. idoc.state. id.us/IRTI/Site/1spOld.html (1996).

"Old North Church." http://www.marblehead. com/tour/oldnorth/.

"Old Salem Online." http://www.mesda.org/oldsalemonline/briefhistory.html.

"Old Swedes Church." http://www.oldswedes. org/index.htm.

"The Old Ursuline Convent." http://www.accesscom.net/ursuline/page2.htm.

"The Old Ursuline Convent in the French Quarter." http://www.yatcom.com/neworl/feature/old/1996/feature_0603.html (1996).

Oldziey, Pepper, Dennis Smith, and Ed Phillips. "Uniting the Human Family" (pamphlet). Regional Baha'i Council of the Southern States, 1998.

Olson, Sheri. "A New Rose Window, by Olson Sundberg Architects, Creates a Magical Play of Reflected Light." *Architectural Record.* (July 1998): 102ff.

Olswanger, Anna, and Rafael Grossman. "Helping Children Grieve." *Jewish Family & Life.* http://www.Jewishfamily.com (1996).

Omandam, Pat. "Fallen Warriors." *Honolulu Star-Bulletin.* (August 11, 1998).

O'Neil, Peggy. "Antelope Canyon—Spectacular Slot Canyons." http://www.blackrabbit.com/antelope.htm (1999).

"Online Kirtan." http://members.tripod.com/raghbir/sound.html.

"Oral Roberts Prayer Tower." http://www.roadsideamerica.com/map/ok.html.

"Oral Roberts University." http://www.oru. edu/.

"The Order of St. Benedict." http://www.osb. org/osb/gen/bendct.html.

"Order of the Eastern Star." http://pws. prserv.net/papadon/star.htm.

"Osho." http://www.religioustolerance.org/rajneesh.htm.

"Osho: Never Born, Never Died." http://www.sannyas.net/osho02.htm.

O'Sullivan, William. "Spiritual R&R: Pendle Hill, a Retreat Center, Is a Quiet Place to Relax, Reflect, and Read to Your Heart's Content." *Washingtonian.* (n. d): 104–105.

"Our Lady of Guadalupe Trappist Abbey." http://www.trappistabbey.org/ (1999).

"Outpouring of Repentance." *Renewed Network.* (April 21, 1997).

"Outside the Rothko Chapel." http://www.infocalypse.demon.co.uk/outside.html (1998).

Pace, Gregory. "Trinity Church." http://www. fordham.edu/halsall/medny/trinity1.html (1997).

"Padmasambhava." http://www.aroter.org/images/drawings/padma.htm.

Paige, H. W. "Sacred Places." *America*. (January 21, 1989): 34–35.

"Painted Rock and Later Human History." http://www.ca.blm.gov/bakersfield/carrizo/human.html.

"The Paiute Story of Creation." http://www.pcsedu.com/pcs/archlgy/legend.htm.

"Palace of Gold." http://www.palaceofgold.com (1998).

Palm, Kristin. "Real Enlightenment: How Americans Are Discovering the Road to the Dharma." *(Detroit) Metro Times.* (February 25, 1998).

Palmer, Susan J. "Charisma and Abdication: A Study of the Leadership of Bhagwan Shree Rajneesh." *Sociological Analysis.* (1988): 119–135.

Pappis, Nick. "Campus Revivals of the Past." http://www.forerunner.com/forerunner/X0586_Campus_Revivals_Past.html.

Parish, Otis. "The First People." http://www.mcn.org/ed/ross/Referenc/kashaya/firstp.htm.

Parker, Laura. "Sunday Sermons Look at Clinton's Confession." *USA Today.* (August 24, 1998).

Parkman, E. Breck. "The Fort Ross Global Village Project." http://www. mcn.org/ed/ross/paper.htm (1997).

———. "Rock Art Stories." *California Indian Storytelling Time.* (1998).

Parrinder, Geoffrey. *Religions of the Modern World, from Primitive Beliefs to Modern Faiths.* New York: Hamlyn Publishing, 1971.

Parry, Melanie, ed. *Larousse Dictionary of Women.* New York: Larousse Kingfisher Chambers, 1994.

Patkotak, Elise. "Fall Whaling Main Attraction in This Community." *Heartland.* (September 29, 1996).

Patterson, Lotsee, and Mary Ellen Snodgrass. *Indian Terms of the Americas.* Englewood, Colo.: Libraries Unlimited, 1994.

Pederson, Rena. "Opinion: in Search of Beauty." *Dallas Morning News.* (March 21, 1999).

"Pelican Network." http://www.pelicannetwork.net/sanjuanbautista.htm.

Pelikan, Jaroslav. *On Searching the Scriptures—Your Own or Someone Else's.* New York: Quality Paperback Club, 1992.

"Pendle Hill." http://www.pendlehill.org.

"The Pentecostals of Alexandria." http://members.tripod.com/messiah_98/index.html.

Perk, Jeff. "Exploring the Islands: Martha's Vineyard and Nantucket." *Massachusetts Handbook.* Moon Travel Handbooks, 1999.

Perkerson, Medora Field. "Heaven Bound." *Atlanta Journal Magazine.* (August 29, 1937) 9.

Perry, T. A. *The Moral Proverbs of Santob de Carrión: Jewish Wisdom in Christian Spain.* Princeton, N.J.: Princeton University Press, 1987.

Perry, Wayne. "College of the Siskiyous." http;//cos.siskiyous.edu (1998).

Pettys, Chris. *Dictionary of Women Artists.* Boston: G. K. Hall, 1985.

"Peyote Bill Signed." http://www.ndsn.org/NOV94/PEYOTE.html (November 1994).

"The Peyote Religion." http://web.jet.es/zaratrusta/rel.html.

"Peyote Shortage Strikes Native American Church." *New York Times.* (March 21, 1995).

"A Photo Tour of Aadheenam." http://www.hinduismtoday.kauai.hi.us/ashram/Saiva SiddhantaChurch/MonasticLife/tour.htm.

Pickford, Tom. "Ashram Camp Held in the Redwood Country." *Sri Sarveshwari Times.* (September 1999).

Pierce, James Smith. *From Abacus to Zeus: A Handbook of Art History.* Englewood Cliffs, N.J.: Prentice Hall, 1991.

"Pietro Annigoni." http://www.gandynet.com/art/Artists/Annigoni/tour7.htm.

Piggott, Juliet. *Japanese Mythology.* London: Paul Hamlyn Publishing, 1973.

Pille, Roger. "Lost Sheep." *Cincinnati CityBeat.* (December 19–January 1, 1996).

Pina, Michael L.. "Winston-Salem." *American Visions.* (1995): 10–14.

"Pipestone, Minnesota." http://www.pipestone.mn.us.

"Pipestone National Monument." http://www.nps. zgov/pipe.

Plagens, Peter. "Darkness into Light." *Newsweek.* (June 1, 1998): 68.

Ploski, Harry A., and James Williams, eds. *The Negro Almanac.* Detroit: Gale Research, 1989.

Plotkin, Wendy. "1960s Organizing in an African-American Community." http://uac.rdp.utoledo.edu/comm-org/papers96/alinsky/woodlawn.html.

Podell, Janet, ed. *Religion in American Life.* New York: H. W. Wilson, 1987.

Poppeliers, John, ed. *Shaker Built.* Washington, D.C.: U.S. Department of the Interior, 1974.

"Positive Voices." http://www.positivevoices. com/.

Powell, Adam Clayton. *Keep the Faith, Baby!* New York: Trident Press, 1967.

Powell, Lyman P. *Mary Baker Eddy: A Life Size Portrait.* Boston: Christian Science Publishing Society, 1950.

Powell, Peter. *Sweet Medicine: The Continuing Role of the Sacred Arrow, the Sun Dance, and the Sacred Buffalo Hat in Northern Cheyenne History.* Norman: University of Oklahoma Press, 1969.

"Power Plant at Snoqualmie Falls, Sacred Site." http://www.yvwiiusdinvnohii.net/news/snoqtrib.htm.

"Prayers to God the Son." http://www.immaculateheart.com/Mary/htm.

"Preacher Gets Try-Out at Calvary Church." *WBTV-News.* (May 18, 1997).

"Preface to the Reader." http://www.cs.utk.edu/~mclennan/OM/BA/AV/praefatio.htm (1996).

Price, Jess. "On the Road to Chimayo." *New Mexico Magazine.* (March 1989).

Pristin, Terry. "Harlem Minister Urges Boycott to Protest Racism." *New York Times.* (March 20, 1999).

"Protect the Rocky Mountain Front from Mineral Development." http://nativeforest.org/alerts alert10.html (1997).

Protillo, Ernesto B. "La Pastorela Lives on at San Juan Bautista Mission." *Tucson Citizen.* (December 20, 1995).

Pulido, Alberto. "Genealogy and Los Hermanos Penitentes." *New Mexico Genealogist.* (September 1999).

Pultz, David. "The Preaching of 'Shall the Fundamentalists Win?'" http://firstpresnyc.org/fosdick.htm (1996).

"Quaker Electronic Archive and Meeting Place." http://www.qis.net/~daruma/index.html.

"Quaker Ideals." http://www.georgefox.edu/nonfox/fahe/Support/qideals.htm.

Raby, F. J. E., ed. *A History of Christian-Latin Poetry.* Oxford: Clarendon Press, 1953.

Radin, Paul. *The Story of the American Indian.* Garden City, N.Y.: Garden City Publishing, 1927.

———. *The Trickster: A Study in American Indian Mythology.* New York: Schocken Books, 1972.

Rado, Jessie. "Wayfarers Chapel Fiftieth Anniversary" (pamphlet). Palos Verdes, Calif.: privately published, 1999.

Rahim, Husein A. "Du'a Kumayl." http://www.al-islam.org/kumayl/english.htm.

"Rainbow Bridge." http://www.infowest.com/Utah/canyonlands/ rainbow.html.

"Rainbow Bridge National Monument." http://www.pagelakepowell.com/rabr.htm.

"Rainbow Bridge National Monument." http://www.utahrec.com/natmonu/rainbowb.htm.

Rainville, Brian. "Celebrate the Year of the Dog." *The (Olympia, Washington) Olympian.* (February 9, 1994).

"Ram Dass." http://www.openmindopenheart.org/UnityArden/RamDass.html/.

"Ramakrishna-Vivekananda Center of New York." http://www.ramakrishna.org.

Rambler, Sandra. "Former Councilmember Cited by UA Officers for Praying on Sacred Apache Mountain, Mt. Graham." http://www.alphacdc.com/ien/apache.html (1997).

Ramirez, Anthony. "Another Hit Could Give Witches a Bad Name." *New York Times.* (August 22, 1999).

Ramirez, Deborah. "Santeria Moves to Cyberspace." *(Fort Lauderdale) South Florida Sun-Sentinel.* (January 7, 2000).

Ranft, Patricia. *Women and the Religious Life in Premodern Europe.* New York: St. Martin's Press, 1996.

Rasmussen, Karen, and Craig R. Smith. "The Case for a 'Re-Vision' of the First Amendment." http://www.csulb.edu/~research/Cent/Amendindian.html (1995)

Ray, Lisa M. "Pipestone." *Minnesota Calls.* (March–April 1994).

Raymond, John. "Novena Prayer to the Miraculous Infant of Prague." http://www.monksofadoration.org/53.html.

Reang, Putsata. "Writing the Story, Saving the Past." *Seattle Times.* (March 5, 1998).

Reeve, Kevin. "The Music of One." *Imprint.* (winter 1997).

"Reformation Nailed as No. 1." *USA Today.* (December 8, 1999).

Reini, Roger. "The Bahá'i House of Worship." http://fp-www.wwnet.net/~rreini/personal_bahai/houseofworship.htm (1999).

Religious Leaders of America. Farmington Hills, Mich.: Gale Group, 1999.

"Researcher Finds Surprises in Mission Walls." *Los Angeles Times,* Home Edition. (July 30 1994).

"Review: 'Harry Emerson Fosdick: Preacher, Pastor, Prophet.'" *New Republic.* (May 6, 1985): 36–38.

"Review: 'Ritual and Devotion in Buddhism.'" *Publishers Weekly*. (April 22, 1996): 65.

"Review: 'We're Heaven Bound.'" *Book News*. (June 1, 1995).

"Revival Briefs." *Christian Daily News*. (November 25, 1998).

"Revivaltime World Prayermeeting Announced." http://home.ag.org/mirror/info/wnn-wni/archived/9506/0695-06.htm.

Reynolds, Jenneke. "Ursuline Academy, New Orleans, Louisiana." http://www.gnofn.org/~ursuline (1991).

Reynolds, William J. "History of Hymns: The Little Brown Church in the Vale." http://www.umr.org/SFvale.htm (1996).

Rhem, Richard. "Meeting God Again for the First Time." http://www.novagate.com/~christcommunity/sermons/092197sermon.htm (1997).

Rice, Edward. *American Saints and Seers: American-Born Religions and the Genius behind Them*. New York: Four Winds Press, 1982.

"Richard Upjohn." http://www.tulane.edu/lester/text/19thCentury/Neo.Gothic/Neo.Gothic7.html.

Rigali, Justin. "Great Impact and Long Lasting Significance." *St. Louis Review*. (February 5, 1999).

Ritter, John. "Mormons' Property Buy Challenged." *USA Today*. (November 23, 1999).

———. "Way of Life Could Fade with Whale Population" *USA Today*. (October 4, 1999).

"The Riverside Church." http://www.theriversidechurchny.org (1999).

Rives, Lucy Lee. "The Little World of Brother Joe." *Dinkler-AMA*. (December 1962): 28–30.

Robertson, Gary D. "Religious Organizations Aren't Leaving Y2K to Faith." *Bakersfield Californian*. (April 5, 1999).

"Rodef Shalom Congregation." http://trfn.clpgh.org/rodef/garden.htm.

Rodriguez, Roberto, and Patricia Gonzales. "Pilgrims, Not Cultists, Come to Chimayo." http://www.latinolink.com/opinion/opinion97/0411ospe.htm (1997).

Rogers, Jay. "In the Media Spotlight: Furor over Homosexuality Continues at Harvard." *Forerunner*. (April 1992).

Rooke, Marti. "Religion Set to Rock in Hickory." *Charlotte Observer*. (September 26, 1999).

Rose, Harold Wickliffe. *The Colonial Houses of Worship in America*. New York: Hastings House, 1963.

Rosen, M. "At Odds in the Black Hills." *People*. (February 27, 1995): 47–48.

Rosenblum, Robert. "Isn't It Romantic?" *Artforum*. (May 1998).

Rossiter, William. "The Makah Whaling Dance." *Whales Alive!* Georgetown, Conn.: Cetacean Society International, January 1997.

Roth, Cecil, and Geoffrey Wigoder, eds. *The New Standard Jewish Encyclopedia*. 5th ed. Garden City, N.Y.: Doubleday & Co., 1977.

Rothacker, Jennifer. "Meher Baba's Retreat Is a Quiet Spot for the Soul." *Charlotte Observer*. (July 3, 1999).

Rouse, J. K. *Colonial Churches in North Carolina*. Kannapolis, N.C.: privately printed, 1961.

Ruby, R. H., and J. A. Brown. *The Spokane Indian—Children of the Sun*. Norman: University of Oklahoma Press, 1970.

Rudin, Marcia. "What Parents Need to Know about Cults." *PTA Today*. (November 1989).

Rudner, Ruth. "Sacred Geographies." *Wilderness*. (fall 1994): 10–27.

Rudoff, Hyman. "Chaco Canyon." *(Delmar, Maryland) Shore Journal*. (September 7, 1997).

"Sabbathday Lake." http://www.shakerworkshops.com/sdl.htm.

"Sacrament in the Mormon Tabernacle." *Harper's Weekly*. (September 30, 1871).

"The Sacred Arrow Renewal." http://www.uwgb.edu/~galta/mrr/cheyenne/arrowcr.htm.

"Sacred Art: Beuronese Art at St. John's." http://www.users.csbsju.edu/~museum/beuron/index.html (1998).

"Sacred Harp Singing." http://www.mcsr.olemiss.edu/~mudws/harp.html.

"Sacred Mountains as Geographical Markers." http://xroads.virginia.edu/g/MA97/dinetah/geo.html.

"Sacred Places." *UNESCO Courier*. (November 1990): 10–42.

"Sacred Sites of Northern New Mexico." http://www.unm.edu/~nomalia/index.html.

"Saint Elizabeth Ann Seton Pilgrimage." http://www.elizabeth-seton.pvt.k12.md.us/alum/pilgrim.html.

"Same-Sex Ceremonies to Be Available to University Members at Memorial Church." *Harvard University Gazette*. (August 7, 1997).

"San Marga Iraivan Temple November Update." *Hinduism Today*. (November 1999): 20–21.

Sandefur, Tim. "Frank Lloyd Wright's Humanism." *The Humanist*. (May 1, 1999): 40.

"Sangharakshita." http://www.fwbo.org/sangharakshita.html.

"Santa Fe." http://www.nmtraveler.com/santafe.html (1997).

"Santeria." http://www.themystica.com/mystica/articles/s/santeria.html.

"Santeria, La Regla Lucumi, Lakumi." http://www.religioustolerance.org/santeri.htm.

Sappell, Joel, and Robert W. Welkos. "The Scientology Story" (series). *Los Angeles Times*. (June 24–29, 1990).

Sarna, Jonathan, and Jonathan Golden. "The American Jewish Experience through the Nineteenth Century: Immigration and Acculturation." http://www.nhc.rtp.nc.us:8080/tserve/nineteen/nkeyinfo/judaism.htm (1999).

Sawyer, Gene. *Celebrations: Asia and the Pacific*. Honolulu: Friends of the East-West Center, 1978.

Scales, Mausiki. "Weathering the Storm: An Africanism in America." *Behind the Veil*. http://cds.aas.duke.edu/cds/btv/images/weathering_the_storm.htm.

Schlosser, Jim. "Moravian Church Owns Up to Slave-Owning Past." *Los Angeles Sentinel*. (November 27, 1997).

"Schola Cantorum of St. Peter the Apostle." http://www.thirdcoast.net/scholasp.

Schuller, Robert, "Crystal Cathedral Album" (brochure), Garden Grove, Calif: Robert Schuller Ministries, 1997.

Schwartz, Benjamin I. *The World of Thought in Ancient China*. Cambridge, Mass.: Harvard University Press, 1985.

"Science Improves When Archaeologists Work with Locals." *Frontiers*. (January 1997).

"Scientology in Your Community." http://www.scientologi.no/outreach/intro.htm.

Scully, Francis J. *Hot Springs, Arkansas and Hot Springs National Park*. Little Rock, Ark.: Pioneer Press, 1966.

Searle, Bonita Cox. "A Brief History of the Amana Society." http://www.ipfw.edu/ipfwhist/home/searle.htm.

"Seattle Aikido History." http://www.wuji.com/seattleaikido.htm (1998).

"Second Baptist Church, Houston." http://www.second.org (1999).

Sellers, Charles. *St. Louis IX, King of France,*

Through Ten Stained Glass Windows. New Orleans: Laborde Printing, 1996.

"Settlement Clears the Way for Church's Program to Be Televised." *(Abilene) Texas News*. (March 14, 1999).

"Seventh Generation Fund—Threatened Sacred Sites." http://www.honorearth.com/sgf/site thrt.html.

Shard, Randel. "A Few Words of Enlightenment from the Living Pamphlet." *(Minneapolis) Minnesota Daily News*. (May 8, 1990).

Sharma, Arvind, ed. *Women in World Religions*. Albany: State University of New York Press, 1987.

Sharn, Lori. "FBI Investigating Threats to Mosques." *USA Today*. (May 8, 1996).

Sharp, Dennis. *The Illustrated Encyclopedia of Architects and Architecture*. New York: Quatro Publishing, 1991.

Sharples, Roberta. "The Way of the Circle." *Lama Newsletter*. (spring–summer 1998).

"Sheepeater Campaign of 1879." http://gorp.com/gorp/resource/us_river/id/she_midd.htm.

"Shelters of the Lord." *Economist*. (March 24, 1990).

Sheppard, Carl. *The Archbishop's Cathedral*. Santa Fe, N.Mex.: Cimarron Press, 1994.

Sherr, Lynn, and Jurate Kazickas. *Susan B. Anthony Slept Here: A Guide to American Women's Landmarks*. New York: Times Books, 1994.

"Shi'ites Under Attack." http://www.al-islam.org/underattack.

Shin, Larry D. *The Dark Lord: Cult Images and the Hare Krishnas in America*. Philadelphia: Westminster Press, 1987.

Shireman, Laura. "A Vision Becomes Tradition: The Coeur d'Alene Tribe Celebrates Its Conversion to Catholic Faith." *Spokane Spokesman-Review*. (August 15, 1999).

"Shiva Temple Constructed in Hawaii amid Protest." *News India Times*. (April 15, 1999).

"Shrine of the Infant of Prague." http://niwg.op.org/niwg/inffal96.htm.

Sibley, Celestine. "'Heaven Bound' Tradition to Be Sorely Missed." *Atlanta Journal & Constitution*. (November 22, 1995).

Siegel, Nina. "Can Harlem's Heritage Be Saved?" *New York Times*. (February 7, 1999).

Sigal, Laurence. "The Once and Future City." *UNESCO Courier*. (November 1990): 33.

Sigelman, Nelson. "Interest in Camping Surprising Prospects for Oak Bluffs Campground Unclear." *Martha's Vineyard Times*. (April 16, 1998).

"Silence in the City." http://www.chicagomonk. org/.

Silva, Richard. "Column." *Albuquerque Tribune*. (July 15, 1995).

Simon, Jim. "Whale Hunt Throws Tribe into Risky Waters." *Seattle Times*. (March 13, 1998).

"Sims Flat History Trail." http://www. r5.fs.fed.us/heritage/112.HTM.

Singer, Christopher M., and Rhonda Bates-Rudd. "Islam Uses Logic to Improve Society." *Detroit News*. (April 12, 1998).

Singer, Margaret Thaler, and Janja Lalich. *Cults in Our Midst*. San Francisco: Jossey-Bass Publishers, 1995.

Singing the Living Tradition. Boston: Unitarian Universalist Association, 1993.

Sinnott, Edmund W. *Meetinghouse and Church in Early New England*. New York: McGraw-Hill, 1963.

Sircar, Jayanta L. "The Vedanta Society of New York: A Review of the First Century." *Bulletin of the Sri Ramakrishna Institute of Culture*. Calcutta. (n.d.).

"Sisters of Benedict." http://www.geocities.com/ Wellesley/6285.

"Sitka National Historic Park." http://www. nps.gov/akso/gis/sitk/sitk.htm.

"Sitka Totem." http://ag.arizona.edu/~brussell/ ak/11.html.

Skafte, Dianne. *Listening to the Oracle*. San Francisco: Harper, 1997.

"Sleeping Ute Mountain." http://www.dc.peach-net.edu/~janderso/physical/ute.htm.

Smaus, Jewel Spangler. *Mary Baker Eddy: The Golden Days*. Boston: Christian Science Publishing Society, 1966.

Smith, G. E. Kidder. *The Beacon Guide to New England Houses of Worship*. Boston: Beacon Press, 1989.

Smith, Gerald L. "Episcopal Things." http://www.andrew.ang-md.org/episc.dict. html (1994).

Smith, Huston. *The Illustrated World's Religions*. San Francisco: HarperCollins, 1994.

———. *The Religions of Man*. New York: Harper & Row, 1958.

———, and Reuben Snake. *One Nation under God: The Triumph of the Native American Church*. Santa Fe, N. Mex.: Clear Light Publishers, 1996.

Smith, Jane I. *Islam in America*. New York: Columbia University Press, 1999.

Smith, Jonathan Z., general ed. *The HarperCollins Dictionary of Religion*. San Francisco: Harper San Francisco, 1995.

Smith, Tracy A. "Fay Jones at Laura Russo." *Art in America*. (May 1998): 135–136.

Smothers, Ronald. "Stolen French Relics Recovered in Newark." *New York Times*. (April 9, 1998).

"The Snake with Big Feet." http://www.waking-dove.com/councilf/lsp/snake_feet.htm (1998).

Snider, Elizabeth "Anasazi Sacred Sites." http://www.arthistory.sbc.edu/sacredplaces/an asazi.html (1998).

Snodgrass, Mary Ellen. *Crossing Barriers: People Who Overcame*. Englewood, Colo.: Libraries Unlimited, 1993.

———. *The Encyclopedia of Frontier Literature*. Santa Barbara, Calif.: ABC-Clio, 1997.

———. *The Encyclopedia of Southern Literature*. Santa Barbara, Calif.: ABC-Clio, 1997.

———. *The Encyclopedia of Utopian Literature*. Santa Barbara, Calif.: ABC-Clio, 1995.

———. *Historical Encyclopedia of Nursing*. Santa Barbara, Calif.: ABC-Clio, 1999.

———. *Signs of the Zodiac: A Reference Guide to Historical, Mythological, and Cultural Associations*. Westport, Conn.: Greenwood Press, 1997.

———. *Who's Who in the Middle Ages*. Jefferson, N.C.: McFarland & Co., 2000.

"Snoqualmie Falls Sacred Site." http://conbio. rice.edu/nae/docs/snoqualmie.html.

Solibakke, Eric. "Avatar Meher Baba." http://home.sol.no/~erics/bababiog.html.

"Some Postcard Views of Oral Roberts University." http://hpserv.keh.utulsa.edu/~arnoldb/ oruviews.html.

Sonoda, Minoru, "The Paradigm of Matsuri" (brochure). Tokyo: Jinja-Honcho, n.d.

Sopronyi, Judith P. "Colorado's Mesa Verde Mystery of the Ancient Ones." *Historic Traveler*. (April 22, 1999).

"Soup Kitchen Cantata." http://www.cathchari-tiesffldcty.com/PRCanta.html (January 1998).

"South Korean Business: The Eclipse of the Moon, Inc.," *Economist*. (December 5, 1998): 72.

"A Southern California Wedding at the Wayfarers' Chapel." http://www.wedstar.com/ Wayfarers Chapel/.

"Southern Charm." *Coast-to-Coast*. (June 1996).

"The Southern Ute." http://members.aol.com/Donh523/navapage/sute.htm.

Spaugh, Herbert. "A Short Introduction to the History, Customs and Practices of the Moravian Church." *Everyday Counselor.* Winston-Salem, N.C.: New Philadelphia Moravian Church, 1999.

"Spider Rock." http://www.ilhawaii.net/~stony/lore38.html (1996).

"Spirit Glossary." http://www.au.spiritweb.org/Spirit/glossary.html (1997).

"Spirit of Spider Woman: Tradition and Trade in Navajo Arts." http://denver.sidewalk.com/detail/36390.

"The Spiritual Test." *Sunday London Times.* (August 16, 1998).

Spritzer, Lois, executive ed. *Birnbaum's Santa Fe and Taos.* New York: HarperPerennial, 1994.

"Sri Siva Vishnu Temple." http://www.ssvt.org (1997).

"Sri Venkateswara Temple." http://www.indiareview.com/htcsnj/index.htm.

"St. Benedict Observes 'Year of the Spirit.'" *Schuyler (Nebraska) Sun.* (July 10, 1997).

"St. Benedict's Abbey." http://www.osb.org/osb/benlake.

"St. Elizabeth Ann Seton." http://www.catholic.org/saints/saints/elizabethannseton.html.

"St. Elizabeth Ann Seton." http://www.knight.org/advent/cathen/137391a.htm.

"St. Elizabeth Ann Seton." http://www.setonshrine.org/Index.htm#top.

"St. Fidelis Church, the Cathedral of the Plains." http://www.dailynews.net/org/stfidelis (1998).

"St. John the Divine." http://www.stjohndivine.org/toursevents/exhibits.html.

"St. Joseph's Staircase." http://www.escape.ca/~cpnchris/staircase.html.

"St. Louis Cathedral." http://saintlouiscathedral.org/current.htm.

"St. Louis Cathedral Slate Artwork." http://www.usacitylink.com/mardigr/98121.html.

"St. Scholastica Monastery." http://www.catholic-church.org/scholastica/history.htm.

"St. Vincent de Paul." http://www.catholic.org/saints/saints/vincentdepaul.html.

"Stanford University Zoroastrian Group." http://www.stanford.edu/group/zoroastrians/ (1997).

Stark, Robert. "News from the Pilgrimage." *Newsletter of the Congregation of the Blessed Sacrament.* (summer 1997).

"State Will Restore Old Greek Chapel." *San Francisco Examiner.* (October 23, 1915).

"A Statement from Dr. Arvol Looking Horse." http://www.wintercount.org/people/lakota.web.

Steele, Joanne. "Mount Shasta's Healing Waters." http://www.kidsart.com/waters.html (1997).

Steen, Francis F. "Local California History." http://cogweb.english.ucsb.edu/steen/Chumash/index.html (1999).

Steiger, Brad. *Medicine Power.* Garden City, N.Y.: Doubleday & Co., 1974.

Steltenkamp, Michael F. *The Sacred Vision: Native American Religion and Its Practice Today.* New York: Paulist Press, 1982.

Stern, Richard L. "Bhagwan Washington?" *Forbes.* (June 24, 1991): 16–17.

"Stockade and Chapel at Fort Ross." http://geogweb.berkeley.edu/GeoImages/QTVR/Sonoma/FortRossL.html.

Stockman, Robert H., "The American Bahá'i Community in the Nineties." *America's Alternative Religions.* Albany: State University of New York Press, 1995.

Stockstill, E. H. "Churches, Grocery Hit by Hate Vandals." *Vicksburg Post.* (March 1995).

———. "Reaching out: Triumph Church Takes Ministry Straight to Needs of Community." *Vicksburg Post.* (February 26, 1995).

Stoddard, Maynard Good. "If It's Going to Be, It's Up to Me." *Saturday Evening Post.* (July–August 1997): 32.

Stone, Andrea. "Allah Beckons." *USA Today.* (January 27, 1994).

"The Story of Kahal Kadosh Beth Elohim." http://www.ccpl.org/ccl/kkbetour.html.

Strom, Karen. "Acoma Opposition to the El Malpais National Monument." http://hanksville.phast.umass.edu/geology/acoma_malpais.html (1994).

Sturgis, Russell. *A Dictionary of Architecture and Building.* New York: Macmillan, 1902.

"Subiaco Abbey." http://www.butterflyfestival.com/history3.htm.

"Subiaco Academy." http://www.catholic-church.org/subiaco/academy.html (1999).

Subramuniyaswami, Satguru Sivaya. "Is Your House a Home or a Hotel Room?" *Hinduism Today.* (November 1999): 10–11.

Sugg, Redding S., Jr. "Heaven Bound." *Southern Folklore Quarterly.* (December 1963): 249.

Suggs, Charlene. "Where I Live During the Summer Solstice." *Circle*. (spring 1999).

Sullivan, Kay. *The Catholic Tourist Guide*. New York: Meredith Press, 1967.

Sullivan, Michael. "Robert Newton Peck and Shaker Beliefs: A Day the Truth Would Die." *ALAN Review*. (fall 1997).

"Summer Listings." *National Catholic Reporter*. (April 19, 1996) 22–47.

Summers, William John. "California Mission Music." *California Mission Studies Association*. (1997).

Sutphen, Dick. *Sedona: Psychic Energy Vortexes*. Malibu, Calif.: Valley of the Sun Publishing, 1988.

Suzuki, Daisetz Teitaro. *An Introduction to Zen Buddhism*. New York: Causeway, 1974.

Swan, J. A. "An Adventurer's Baedeker." *American Health*. (November 1989): 54–55.

Swanton, John R. *The Indians of the Southeastern United States*. Grosse Pointe, Mich.: Scholarly Press, 1969.

"Sweet Auburn." www.sweetauburn.com (1999).

"The Symbolism of the Sanctuary." http://www.geocities.com/CapitolHill/1864/sanctuary.html (1987).

Talbot, Margaret. "Married in a Mob." *New Republic*. (December 22, 1997): 14.

Tanasychuk, John. "Varied Houses of Worship." *Detroit Free Press*. (November 10, 1997).

"Taos Pueblo." http://www.indianpueblo.org/taos.html.

"Taos Pueblo: A Thousand Years of Tradition" (leaflet). Taos, N. Mex.: Tribal Tourism Office, n.d.

Tapia, Andrés T. "Soul Searching—How Is the Black Church Responding to the Urban Crisis?" http://www.loritapia.com/andrestapia/HTML/race/blk_church_ct.htm.

Tauranac, John. *Essential New York*. New York: Holt, Rinehart & Winston, 1979.

Taylor, Bill. "Salvage Rider Will Destroy Sacred Sites." *High Country News* (Paonia, Colo.) (May 27, 1996).

Taylor, M. Jane. "Internet Bomb Threat Aimed at MCC in Texas." *Washington (D.C.) Blade*. (April 17, 1998).

Teish, Luisah. "Big Mommas and Golden Apples." *Ms*. (October–November 1999): 64–65.

"Temple Square." *The Utah Encyclopedia*. http://eddy.media.utah.edu/ucme/t/TEMPLESQUARE.html.

Theisen, Jerome. "The Benedictines: An Introduction." http://www.osb.org/osb/gen/bend-ctns.html (1999).

"Theravada Buddhism." http://www.buddhanet.net/burma.htm.

"There's a Church in the Valley by the Wildwood." http://www.rootsweb.com/~iachicka/lbc.htm.

Thiessen, Thomas D. "Pipestone Petroglyphs." http://www.pclink.com/cbailey/pipestone.html (1999).

Thomas, Gary. "The Lord Is Gathering His People." *Charisma*. (1996).

———. "The Return of the Jewish Church." *Christianity Today*. (September 7, 1998): 62.

Thompson, Clay. "Charity, Not Zealotry: ASU Professor Sets Record Straight on New Mexico Catholic Order." *(Phoenix) Arizona Republic*. (August 29, 1998).

Thompson, Courtney. "Native Americans Are Taking a More Prominent Role in Managing Northwest Public Lands and Resources." *Seattle Times*, editorial page. (June 27, 1999).

Thompson, Nick. "The Danger of Bipolarization." *Stanford (California) Daily*. (April 3, 1996).

"Thorncrown Chapel." http://www.johnco.cc.ks.us/~jjackson/modarc.html.

"Thorncrown Chapel by E. Fay Jones." http://www.arch.cuhk.edu.hk/people/stud94_95-96cheung.sf/TChapel.htm.

Tickle, Phyllis A. *God-Talk in America*. New York: Crossroad Publishing, 1997.

Tillman, Gilmary. "Cathedral of the Plains" (brochure). Victoria, Kans.: St. Fidelis, 1986.

Titone, Julie. "Religious Roots: Tribe's Observance of Catholic Feast Puts Spotlight on State's Oldest Building." *Spokane Spokesman-Review*. (August 16, 1997).

"Tlingit Culture History." http://members.aol.com/waya94/tlingan2.htm.

"The Tlingit Nation." http://kafka.uvic.ca/~maltwood/nwcp/tlingit/intro.html.

"To Gather Together." *Architectural Record*. (January 1990): 123–135.

"To the Peoples of the World" (pamphlet). Thornhill, Ontario: Bahá'i Peace Council of Canada, 1986.

"The Tonkawa Indians." http://www.ci.round-rock.tx.us/planning/hispres/rrcollection/early-history.

Torres, Nohea. "Kaho'Olawe." http://gohawaii. miningco.com/gi/dynamic/offsite.htm?site=ht tp://leahi.kcc.hawaii.edu/~dennisk/

Torrez, Robert J. "A Cuarto Centennial History of New Mexico." http://nmgs.org/ artcuar3.htm (1998).

"The Total Yellowstone History Page." http://www.yellowstone-natl-park.com/his-tory.html.

"Totem Pole Art." *Trails West*. (December 6, 1998).

"Touro Synagogue, America's Oldest Synagogue." http://www.tourosynagogue.org/index.htm.

"Towards a Dictionary of Communitarian Soci-eties." http://home.att.net/~tnovae/diction. htm.

"Town of Valdese." http://www.ci.valdese.nc.us/ index.htm.

"Training Center Is Now Graham's Legacy." *Houston Chronicle*. (December 12, 1995).

"Transportation Dilemma." *Mt. Tabor News*. (sum-mer 1999): 2.

"Trappist." http://www.paulist.org/trappist.

Travis, Jack, ed. *African-American Architects in Cur-rent Practice*. New York: Princeton Architectural Press, 1991.

"Tri-County Assembly of God." http://www. tcag.org/.

"Trinity Church" (brochure). New York: Ruder-Finn Design, 1995.

"Trinity Church in the City of Boston." http:// www.trinitychurchboston.org/.

"Triumph Church." http://www.vicksburg.com/ ~triumph.

Tsumuro, Yukihiko. "Purpose of Tsubaki Amer-ica." http://www.csuchico.edu/~georgew/tsa/ purpose.html (1988).

"Tulsa Area Libraries." http://www.tulsa.ouhsc. edu/new/library/liblinks.htm.

"Tunica County, Mississippi." http://www.allred-net.com/mscounty/counties/tunica.htm.

"200 Years of an Ethnic American Family." http://www.eyesofglory.com/familyhist.htm.

"Two Hundredth Anniversary of Russian-Ameri-can Company." http://ns.vologda.ru/~avo/ Eng/Events/FortRoss.htm.

Tyner, Jarvis. "Fidel Castro Cheered at Harlem Meeting." *People's Weekly World*. (October 23, 1995).

Ulibarri, Sabine R. *Mi Abuela Fumaba Puros*. Skokie, Ill.: Distribooks, Inc., 1994.

"The Unification Church." http://cti.itc.

virginia.edu/~jkh8x/soc257/nrms/Unification. html (1999).

"The Unification Church." http://www.unifica-tion.org (1999).

"Unitarian Universalist Association." http://www. religioustolerance.org/u-u.htm.

"United Methodist Church." http://www. marinersbethel.com/newpage1.htm.

"Unity Ride." http://carbon.cudenver.edu/ ~ccambrid/unity1.html (1996).

"Updating Monastic Tradition." *Chicago Tribune*. (March 17, 1995).

"U.S. Air Force Academy Cadet Chapel." http://www.usafa.af.mil/hc.

Usher, Susan. "Buddhists Find Peaceful Haven." *Brunswick (NC) Beacon*. (July 7, 1988).

"Ute." http://www.ausbcomp.com/redman/ ute.htm.

"Vedanta, Ramakrishna, and Vivekananda." http:// www.silcom.com/~origin/sbcr/sbcr084.

"Victoria." http://www.ellisco.org/victoria.htm (1998).

"Vincent de Paul and Louise de Marillac, Com-passionate Servants and Saints." http://www. cptryon.org/vdp/vdp-ldm/index.html.

"Virginia Wat Lao Buddhavong." http://www.asi-acom.com/html/events.html (1997).

"The Vision of Race Unity: America's Most Challenging Issue" (pamphlet). Wilmette, Ill.: Bahá'í Publishing Trust, 1991.

"Visit Bethlehem Now, Then." *(Murfreesboro, Ten-nessee) Daily News Journal*. (December 25, 1998).

Vogel, Howard J. "Bear Butte, Black Hills." http://web.hamline.edu/law/lawrelign/sa-cred/bearb.html (1998).

Vollers, M. "Costner's Last Stand." *Esquire*. (June 1996): 100–107.

"Voodoo Spiritual Temple." http://home.gnofn. org.

Vosburgh, Frederick C., ed. *The Civil War*. Wash-ington, D.C.: National Geographic, 1969.

Voyat, Gilbert. *Cognitive Development among Sioux Children*. New York: Plenum Press, 1983.

Vu, Harriet. "Foundations of Mahayana Bud-dhism." http://www.geocities.com/Athens/ 8916/index2.html.

Waddington, Chris. "Gathering Is a Mix of Re-treat, Reunion, Christmas Party." *Minneapolis-St. Paul Star-Tribune*. (October 29, 1991).

"Wagon Train Now in Henefer after Passing

through Echo Canyon." http://www. ksl. com/dump/tv/stories/Jul97/file17104833. htm (1997).

Wakley, Darrel La Mar. *Downey and Beyond.* http://www.ida.net/users/lamar/titelof book.html (1998).

"Waldensian Confessions of Faith." http://www. pb.org/articles/walden.html.

"Waldensians and the Waldensian Church." http://www.arpnet.it./~valdese/english.htm.

Waldman, Carl. *Who Was Who in Native American History: Indians and Non-Indians from Early Contacts through 1900.* New York: Facts on File, 1990.

Waldrep, Bob. "Unification Church Influence in America." *Watchman Expositor.* (1996) 8.

Waley, Arthur, trans. *Confucianism: The Analects of Confucius.* New York: Continuum, 1986.

Walker, Barbara G. *The Woman's Encyclopedia of Myths and Secrets.* Edison, N.J.: Castle Books, 1996.

Walker, Glenn, "Shasta Literature." http://www. whitestareagle.com/natlit/shasta.htm (1998).

Walking Turtle, Eagle. *Indian America.* 3rd ed. Santa Fe, N.Mex.: John Muir Publications, 1993.

Walsh, Bruce. "The Mt. Graham Red Squirrel." http://medusa.as.arizona.edu/graham/envir.ht ml (2000).

Wang, Sean. "Mosques around the World." http://info.uah.edu/msa/mosques.html.

"Warner, Robb to Read at Service." *Richmond (Virginia) Times-Dispatch.* (August 22,1998).

Wartzman, Rick. "A Houston Clergyman Pushes Civic Projects along with Prayers." *Wall Street Journal.* (February 20, 1996).

Washburn, Gary. "CTA Board Backs Demolition of Green Line Woodlawn Leg." *Chicago Tribune.* (June 6, 1996).

"Washington National Cathedral." http:// muspin.gsfc.nasa.gov/Prime/dctour/ washcath_photo.html.

"Wat Carolina Buddhajakra Vanaram." http:// www.wisecom.com/wat/.

Waters, Frank. *Book of the Hopi.* New York: Penguin, 1963.

Watkins, Maryann. "Rainbow Bridge—The Navajo Connection." http://www.erinet.com/ ghost/navajo.htm (1997).

Watts, George B. *The Waldenses of Valdese.* Valdese, N.C.: privately published, 1965.

"The Wayfarers' Chapel." http://www.math.ucla. edu/~liuli/wedding/chapel2.html.

"Wayfarers' Chapel." http://www.seeingstars. com/Churches/Wayfarers.shtml.

Webster, Douglas O. "The Good Book: Reading the Bible with Mind and Heart." *Christianity Today.* (April 7, 1997): 42–45.

Weddell, James R. "The Black Hills Are Not for Sale." http://users.skynet.be/kola/bhills.htm.

"Weekend Escape: Central California Mission Impossible." *Los Angeles Times*, Home Edition. (November 7, 1993).

Weiss, Jeffrey,. "Giving Thanks: Man Bequeaths over $4 Million to Cathedral of Hope." *Dallas Morning News.* (September 23, 1999).

"Welcome to El Sobrante Gurdwara Sahib." http://www.angelfire.com/ak/satguru (1999).

"Welcome to the First Unitarian Church of Philadelphia." http://www.firstuu-philly.org/ welcome.htm.

"Welcome to the Old Mission San Luis Obispo." http://www.thegrid.net/slomission/.

"Welcome to the University of the South." http://www.sewanee.edu/Theology/theol.html.

"Welcome to UFMCC World Center." http://www.ufmcc.com/.

"Welcome to Wat Lao Buddhavong." http:// listings-wizards-r-us.com/dcwatlao/watlaodc. htm.

Welker, Glenn. "Origin of the Clans." http:// www.indians.org/welker/theclans.htm (1998).

"Wellspring Church and Christian Center." http://www.wellspringministries.com/firstpg2. htm.

Wenger, Gilbert R. *The Story of Mesa Verde National Park.* Mesa Verde, Colo.: Mesa Verde Museum Association, 1991.

"West Parish of Barnstable." http://www. vsi. cape.com/~barnucc/church/wbarnstable.html.

Westneat, Danny. "Makah Whaling OK'd." *Seattle Times.* (October 23, 1997).

———. "Whales Die, a Culture Lives." *Seattle Times.* (October 13, 1996).

"WFRN Ministry Links." http://wfrn.com/Ministry.stm.

Wharton, Tom. "Cliffs to Caves to Coves: These Sites Are Utah Pleasures, National Treasures." *Salt Lake Tribune.* (September 19, 1996).

"What Do Lutherans Believe?" *A Week in the Life of the Lutheran Church—Missouri Synod.* St. Louis: Concordia Publishing House, 1996.

"What Is Unitarian Universalism?" http://www. libertynet.org/firstuu/uupg3.html.

Whitall, Susan. "Power of Worship Drives the

Lives of Metro Detroiters." *Detroit News*. (April 12, 1998).

Whittington, Paul. "Mother Henriette Delille: A Woman of Vision," (essay). St. Louis: Aquinas Institute of Theology, 1996.

"Who Are Lien-Hoa?" http://www.geocities. com/Athens/7483/lhchapter.html (1997).

"Who Are the Chumash?" http://www. rain.org/eagle/chumash1.htm.

"Who Are Moravians?" *The Lutheran*. (August 1, 1999): 43.

"Who is a Hindu?" *Hinduism Today*. (October 1999): 8.

"Who Slept at the White House?" *The Daily Republican*. (February 25, 1997).

Wiget, Andrew. *Handbook of Native American Literature*. New York: Garland. 1996.

Wilgoren, Jodie. "Under One Roof, Prayers for Diallo and a Hug for Giuliani." *New York Times*. (April 21, 1999).

Wilhelm, Robert Bela. "Our Lady of Prompt Succor." http://www.storyfest.com/prompt-succor.html (1966).

Williams, Brian. "Should the Makah Tribe Be Allowed to Resume the Hunting of Grey Whales?" *MSNBC News Forum*. (January 1997).

Williams, Peter W. *Houses of God: Region, Religion, and Architecture in the United States*. Urbana: University of Illinois Press, 1997.

———. "The Iconography of the American City: or, A Gothic Tale of Modern Times." *Church History*. (June 1999): 373–398.

Wilson, Charles Reagan, and William Ferris, eds. *Encyclopedia of Southern Culture*. Chapel Hill: University of North Carolina Press, 1989.

Wilson, Leslie Perrin. "New England Transcendentalism." *Concord Magazine*. (November 1998).

Winner, Lauren. "Review: 'Houses of God: Region, Religion, and Architecture in the United States.'" *Journal of Southern Religion* 1, no. 1, (1998).

"Wishtoyo: The Home of the Chumash." http://www.wishtoyo.org (1999).

"A Woman in a Monastery." *Cleveland Press*. (June 2, 1901).

"Woman's Civil Rights Lawsuit against Nation of Islam Is Thrown Out." *Jet*. (August 30, 1999) 31.

Woodward, Kenneth L. "From the Glass House to the White House." *Newsweek*. (March 3, 1997): 62.

World Religions. New York: Macmillan Reference USA, 1998.

"Worship and Prayer." http://www.orthodox. clara.net/worship.htm.

Wright, Ralph B. *California's Missions*. Arroyo Grande, Calif.: Hubert A. Lowman, 1978.

Wright, Sylvia Hart. *Sourcebook of Contemporary North American Architecture: From Postwar to Postmodern*. New York: Van Nostrand Reinhold, 1989.

"Yale through the Seasons." http://pantheon.cis. yale.edu/~ykchou/yaleEx.html.

"Yale University." http://www.cis.yale.edu/.

Yamamoto, Yukitaka. *The Way of the Kami*. Stockton, Calif.: Tsubaki America Publications, 1999.

"Yavapai-Apache Web Site." http://www.yavapai-apache-nation.com/index.html.

Yost, Edna. *American Women of Nursing*. Philadelphia: J. B. Lippincott Co., 1947.

Young, Simon, ed., *Texas Buddhist Association 20th Anniversary*. Houston, Tex., Buddhist Association, June 6, 1999.

Zacharias, Paul B. "Swedenborgians See It This Way" (brochure). Newton, Mass.: J. Appleseed & Co., n.d.

"ZAMWI." http://www.nicom.com/~zamwi/.

Zavoral, Nolan, "Eckankar's Soul Travel Opens Roads to Insight," *Minneapolis–St. Paul Star-Tribune*. (October 25, 1997).

Zehr, Mary Ann. "Guardians of the Faith." *Education Week*. (January 20, 1999).

Zeinert, Karen. *Cults*. Springfield, N.J.: Enslow Publishers, 1997.

Zielbauer, Paul. "Parents Fly Back to Africa with Body of Son Killed by Police." *New York Times*. (February 15, 1999).

"Zoroastrianism." http://www.religioustolerance.org/zoroastr.htm.

"Zoroastrianism Page." http://coulomb.ecn.purdue.edu/~bulsara/ZOROASTRIAN/zoroastrian.html.

Zweig, Stefan. *Mental Healers: Franz Anton Mesmer, Mary Baker Eddy, Sigmund Freud*. New York: Frederick Ungar, 1990.

Bibliography

INDEX

Note: Major entries are marked in boldface. Brackets indicate illustrations or capsule definitions or biographies.

A. R. Mitchell Memorial Museum of Western Art, 162
Aamskapi-Pikuni Radio, 29
Abbate, Peter Paul, 100
Abbey of Gethsemani, **1–4**, [3], 216
The Abbey of Gethsemani: Place of Peace and Paradox, 3
Abbey of Melleray, 1, 216
Abdu'l-Bahá, 32
Abernathy, Ralph, 334
Abeyta, 320
Abhidhyan Yoga Institute, **4–5**
Abhidhyanananda, Acharya, 4
Abhignana Shakuntalam, 163
abolitionism, 148. See *also* slavery
abortion, 272
Abraham Lincoln Cane, 9, 10
Absarog-Issawua, 420
Abundant Life Prayer Group, 282
abuse, 305, 362
Abyssinian Baptist Church, **5–7**, [6]
Achumawi, 235
Acoma, 7–10
Acoma Pueblo, **7–10,** [8]
Adams, John, 147
Adams, Samuel, 252
Addams, Jane, 148
Adi Granth, 157
Adler, Margot, 104
adobe, 363–364. See *also* mission style
Affiliated Tribes of the Northwest Indians, 136–137
Africa, 96, 97, 397
African Episcopal Catechetical Institution, 379
African Methodist Episcopal (AME), 39–41
African-American Church of God, 22–23
Against the Tide, 5
Agee Fire, 111

Aghor Ashram, **10–11**
agnosticism, 149
agrarianism, 19, 20, 153, 198, 216–217, 227, 231, 237, 248, 256, 265–266, 344, 347, 361–365, [362]
Aguilar, Isidor, 306
Ahura Mazda, 421
Ai'ai, 190
AIDS memorial, 73, 74
AIDS task force, 382
AIDSWALK, 382
Air Force Academy Chapel, **11–15,** [12]
Akshaya, 164–165
Alabama, 25–27, 333–336, [334]
Alan, Jim, 104
Alaska, 165–167, [166], 279–282, 330–333
Alcatraz, Alcatraz: The Indian Occupation, 277
Aleut, 171–175, [172]
Algonquin, 420
All Faiths Peace Chapel. See Chapel of Peace
All Saints' Chapel, University of the South, **15–17,** [16]
All-America City, 165–167, [166]
allegory, 40
Allen, Paula Gunn, 62
Allen, Richard, 40, 132, 205
altruism, 297, 379
'Altsé Hastiin and 'Altsé 'Asdzáá, 101
Aluli, Noa Emmett, 192
Ama No Murakumo Kukisamuhara Ryu O Haya Takemusu OhKami, 193
Amana Church Society, **17–20,** [18]
Amana Society, Inc., 19
Amanism, 17–20
Amaterasu Ohmikami, 387
Ame No Uzume No Mikoto, 193, 387
American Baptist Church, 293–295, [293], [294]
American Bible Society, 22

American Bicentennial, 229
American Buddhist congress, 183
American Burma Buddhist Association, 391–392, [392]
American Cassinese Congregation, 167–168
American Civil Liberties Union, 96–97
American folk architecture, 155–157, [156]
American Folklore Society, 41
American Guild of Organists, 229
American Indian Movement (AIM), 47, 233–234
American Indian Religious Freedom Act, 9–10, 48, 102, 135, 233, 234, 245, 341
American Institute of Architects, 382
American Jewish Committee, 366
American Muslim Mission, 231
American Needlepoint Guild, 253
American Pentecostalism, 22
American Red Cross, 20, 26, 99, 148, 366, 404
American Revolution, 187, 250–254, 326, 348–349, 373, 380, 402
American Sisters of Charity. See Sisters of Charity
American Unitarian Association, 147
American Universalism, 147
America's Society of the Sacred Heart, 393
Amesha Spentas, 422
Amish, 153
Amritras Radio, 158
Anabaptists, 153
Analects, 81
Ananda, Bhante Siyabalagoda, 199–200
Anasazi, 21, 59–61, 81–84, [82], 129–130, 257, 287, 289, 336
San Juan Anasazi, 337–338
Anderson, Dallas, 115
Anderson, Ned, 234
Angel, Milton, 35
Angel Moroni, 228

Anglicanism, 53–55, [54], 195, [207], 250, 267, 378–379, 413–414
animism, 102–106, [103], 149, 206
Annebras, 181
Annigoni, Pietro, 90
Antelope Canyon, **20–23,** [21]
Antelope, Simon, 276
Anthony, Susan B., 148, 267
anticultism, 390
Anti-Defamation League of B'nai B'rith, 366
antifundamentalism, 149
antiracism, 295
Antonio, Santana, 10
Apache, 9, 29, 134, 244, 257, 338, 420
Apache Mohave, 76
    Mescalero Apache, 61
    San Carlos Apache, 232–234, [233], 235
    Yavapai-Apache, 76–78
Apache Survival Coalition, 233, 234
apartheid, 6
apocalypse, 107
Apostolic Church of God, **22–23**
Approaching Hoofbeats: The Four Horsemen of the Apocalypse, 42
Ara Orun, 96
Aragón, José, 320
Aragón, Miguel, 320
Arapaho, 119, 209
Archibeque, Miguel, 161
The Architecture of Exile, 345
Arikara, 44, 210
Arizona, 20–23, 59–63, [60], 76–78, 101–102, 232–234, [233], 255–259, 259–261, [260], 287–289, [288]
Arkansas, 175–177, [176], 357–360, [358], 370–372, [371], [372]
Armstrong, Gerald, 98
Arthur, Chester A., 257, 308
Aryaloka Buddhist Retreat Center, **23–25**
Asbury, Francis, 205, 220
Asceticism, 90–93, [92], 157, 391, 406–408
Asian Indians in America, 163
Assembly of God, 50–53, 270, 376–378, [377]
Assenza, Enzo, 75
Assiniboine, 420
astrology, 102–106, [103], 121–123
astronomy, 119, 190, 209. *See also* equinox, solstice
Atlanta, 39–41, 127–129, [128]
Audubon Society, 233–234, 236
Augsburg Lutheran Church, 38
Austin, Henry, 123–125
Austin, Sharon G., 129
Authoritarianism, 206
Ave Maria Grotto, **25–27,** [26]
Avesta, 421

Awake America, 52
Aztec, 244–245, 263
Azusa Street Revival, 22, 271
Azzahra Islamic Center of Orange County, 181

The Bab, 33
Baba, Meher, 211–213
Babalz Ayi, 96
Babbitt, Bruce, 29, 120
Babbitt, Charles J., 233–234
Babylonian style, 370
Back to Godhead, 265
Backbone of the World: The Blackfeet, 30
Badger–Two Medicine Area, **29–30**
Baez, Joan, 335
Bahá'i House of Worship, **30–33,** [31]
Bahá'i News
Baháism, 30–33
Bahá'u'llah, 32, **33,** 34
Baker Massacre, 30
Bakker, Jim, 57, 283
Bakker, Tammy, 283
"Ballad of Birmingham," 335
Band on the Hand, 96
Bandung Conference, 7
Bannock, 419
Bantu, 96
Baptists, 5–7, 42, 127–129, [128], 139–141, [140], 220, 333–336, [334], 385, 408
    American Baptists, 139–141, [140], 214
    Northern, 141
    Southern, 141
Barbarossa, Theodore, 100, 404
Barboncito, 61
Bardolph, Richard, 93
Barillet, Jean, 75
Barker, Granville, 404
Barnbaum, Bruce, 21
Barnes, Henry, 79
Barnett, George D., 63–65, [64]
Baron Hirsch Synagogue, **34–35**
Barr, Ernie, 341
Barrish, Koichi Larry, 193–195
Bartberger, Charles, 296
Barton, Clara, 148
Basket Makers, 129–130
Be Here Now, 197
Beacon House Publishing, 149
Bear Butte, 44, 46, 48
beauty way, 78, 82–83
Begay, Jayi, 287
Begay, Nasja, 287
Begaye, Adella, 102
Behind the Stained Glass: A History Of the Sixteenth Street Baptist Church, 336
Behold, 129
Belizean Herbs: Their Uses and Applications, 397

bell-ringing, 215
Benedictines, 25–27, 67, 167–168, 170–171, [171], 223–225, [224], 225–227, [226], [329], 329–330, 342–343, 348–351, 357–360, [358]
Berditschevsky, Michelle, 236
Bering, Vitus, 332
Bernal, Paul, 363
Bernice Pauahi Bishop Museum, 191
Bertoia, Harry, 85
Besançon, Hugues, 151
Bet Tikvah, 299
Bethabara Moravian Church, **35–39,** [36]
Bethune, Mary McLeod, 333
Beuronese style, 351
Bhagavad Gita, 164, 292
Bharatanatyam, 163
Bhumibol Adulyadej, 407
Big Bethel African Methodist Episcopal Church, **39–41,** [40]
Bigfoot, 210
Bilingualism, 69, 97, 113, 150–152, 159, 171–175, [172], 183–185, [184], [185], 193–195, [194], 199, 296, 304, 309, 362, 365, 375, 399–400, [400], 408–410, 421–422
Bill of Rights, 96–97
Billings, William, 196
Billy Graham Evangelistic Association, 42, 160
Billy Graham Training Center at the Cove, **41–44,** [42], 159
Binah: The Modern Quest for Torah Understanding, 35
"Birmingham Manifesto," 334
Birmingham News, 335
"Birmingham Sunday," 335
Birth of the Vacation, 222
Bitter, Karl, 381
Black Elk, 210
Black Elk, Wallace, 47
Black Eyes, 365
Black Fathers, 167
Black, Galen, 245
Black Hills, **44–48,** [45], [47]
Black, Lydia, 165
Black Mesa, 101, 102, 255, 287
Black Muslims, 229–232, [230], [231]
Blackfoot, 29–30, 209, 273, 419, 420
"Blessing Song," 101
blessing way, 82–83, 102
The Blitz, 146
Blue Lake, 361–365
Boardman, Mabel, 404
Bodhi Chinese School, 184
Bodhidharma, 117
Boggs, Lillburn W., 227

bombing, church, 333–336, [334]
Book of Architecture, 139
Book of Common Prayer, 55, 195, 405
Book of Songs, 81
Bossanyi, Ervin, 404–405
Boston, [141], [142], [143], 141–144, 147, 195–196, [196], 221, [250], [251], 250–254, 382–384, [383]
Boston Avenue Methodist Church, **48–50,** [49]
Boston Freedom Trail, 195, 253
Boston Tea Party, 139
Bourgeois, Jean-Baptiste Louis, [31], 32–33
Bradford, William, 378–379
Bradley, Jared J., 237
Brahmanism, 157
Brave Dogs Society, 29
Brazier, Arthur M., 22–23
Breuer, Marcel, 349–350
Brigham, Charles, 141
Broadman Hymnal, 334
Broken Obelisk, 299, **[300]**
Broutin, Ignace François, 394
Brown, Bonnie, 288
Brown, Joseph, 139–141, [140]
Brown, Morris, 132
Brown, Nicholas, 139
Brown, Olympia, 148
Brown, Ron, 405
Brown, Wally, 289
Brown University, 139, 140
Brownsville Assembly of God, **50–53**
Bruno, St., **92**
Bruton Parish Church, **53–55, [54]**
Buchanan, James, 303
Buckskin, Floyd, 235
Buddha's Light, 185
Buddhism, 4, 23–25, 149, 183–185, [184], [185], 199–200
  Burmese, 391–392, [392]
  Hinayanan, 185, 391–392, [392]
  Laotian, 408–410
  Mahayana, 4–5
  Theravadan, 5, 24, 391–392, [392], 406–408
  Tibetan, 299
  Vajrayana, 4
  Zen, 117–118, 124
Buddhist Association of Olympia and Neighboring Communities, 199
Buffalo, 364, 417, 418
Bulfinch, Charles, 250–251
Bunker Hill, Battle of, 252
Bunyan, John, 40
Bureau of Indian Affairs (BIA), 101–102, 235, 341, 361
Burne-Jones, Edward, 383–384
Burr, Aaron, 393
Bush, George, 42, 229, 390, 404
Bush, Mirabai, 197
Butts, Calvin O. III, 5–7

Byzantine architecture, 33, 63–65, [64], 367
  Byzantine-Moorish, 278–279

Caddo, 175, 176, 245
Cahuilla, 305
Calapooia, 235
California, 4–5, 10–11, 97–99, [98], 113–115, [157], 157–158, 159–160, [160], 171–175, [172], 234–236, 263–264, 303–304, 304–307, [305], [306], 307–309, 386–388, [387], 401, [410], 410–412, [411]
Calling Youth to Christ, 42
Calvary Church, **57–59,** [58]
Calvin, John, 147, 151, 414
Calvinism, 141, 347
Camino Real, El, 305, 319
Campbell, Joseph, 59–60, [60]
Canada, 86–87
Canadian and American Unity Rides, 210
Candomble, 97
Canova, Antonio, 354
Canterbury Cathedral, 146
Canyon de Chelly, **59–63,** [60]
Cao Dai, 199
Captain Jack, 235
Capuchins, 346, 352
Careless, George, 228
Carey, George L., 17
carillon, 88, 146, 294
Carole Robertson Center for Learning, 335
Carpelan, Mary, 236
Carruthers, Garrey, 9
Carson, Christopher "Kit," 61, 287, 338, 363
Carter, Jimmy, 42
Carter-Menil Human Rights Prize, 300
Carthusians, 90–93, [92]
Carvalho, Solomon N., 189
Casavant Frères, 16
Cassutta, Araldo, 143
caste system, 157
Castro, Fidel, 6, 95
Catalan style, 404
Cataldo, Joseph, 248
Cathari, 400
Cathedral Age, 406
Cathedral Basilica of St. Louis, [63], **63–65,** [64]
Cathedral Basilica of the Sacred Heart, **67–70, [68]**
Cathedral Church of Saint Peter and Saint Paul. *See* Washington National Cathedral
Cathedral Church of St. John the Divine, **70–73,** [71], 228
Cathedral of Hope, **73–74**

Cathedral of St. Joseph, **75–76**
Cathedral Rock, **76–78**
Cather, Willa, 316, 320
Catholic Shrine of the Immaculate Conception, **78–80**
Catholicism, Roman, 1–4, [3], 9–10, 11–15, 25–27, 36, [63], 63–65, [64], 67–70, [68], 75–76, 78–80, 95–97, [96], [97], 99–101, [100], 160–162, 167–168, 170–171, [171], 199, 202, 203–205, [204], 222–223, 237–238, [238], 240–244, [242], 247–250, 259, 261–262, [262], 303–304, 304–307, [305], [306], 307–309, [323], 323–325, [324], [329], 329–330, 342–343, 343–346, 346–348, [347], 351–355, 355–[357], [356], 357–360, [358], 362, 379, 385, [394], 394–396, 397. *See also* Russian Orthodoxy
Catlin, George, 274–276, [275]
Cayuse, 136–137
Cedar Man, 246
Celibacy, 325–326, 328, 394. *See also* monasticism
Celtic tradition, 102–106, [103]
Centennial Prayer, 87
Center for Dao-Confucianism, **80–81**
Central America, 318–319
Central Conference of American Rabbis, 278
A Century of Dishonor: A Sketch of the United States Government's Dealing with Some of the Indian Tribes, 305
Cernera, Phil, 249
Chaco Canyon, **81–84,** [82]
Chamani, Miriam and Oswan, 397
Chambliss, Robert E., 335
Ch'an, 117
Changing Woman, 83, 101
Channing, William Ellery, 147, 148
chant, 168, 185, 190, 197, 265, 368–370, [369], 373, 409, 414
Chapel of Massachusetts Institute of Technology, [84], **84–86,** [85]
Chapel of Peace, **86–87**
Chapel of St. James the Fisherman, 85
Chapel of the Prodigal, **88–90,** [89], [90]
Charterhouse of the Transfiguration, **90–93,** [92]
Chasing Horse, Joseph, 420
Chávez, César, 304
Chernoff, David, 108
Chernoff, Joel, 107–108
Chernoff, Martin and Yohanna, 107
Cherokee, 136, 283–284
Cherokee War, 187

Cheyenne, 44, 46, 118–121, [119], 209, 273, 417, 420
  Northern Cheyenne, 209
  Southern Cheyenne, 246
Chicago, 22–23, 30–33, 162–165, 225–227, [226], 229–232, [230], [231]
Chickasaw, 352
Child-Born-of-Water, 101
Children of the American Revolution, 253
Childs, John, 251
Chilkat, 330–333
China, 117, 143, 185
Chinese American Relief Association, 184
Chippewa, 210, 277
Chirri, Mohammad Jawad, 179
Cho, David Yonngi, 52
Choctaw, 352
Chouteau, Auguste, 63
Chrismon tree, 207
Christ Chapel, Boston. *See* Old North Church
Christ in Gethsemane, 294
Christ Lutheran Church, **93–94**
Christ the Good Shepherd, 114
"Christ the Lord is Risen Today," 206
Christian Church, 385
Christian Science, 19
Christian Science Journal, 142
Christian Science Monitor, 142
Christian Science Quarterly, 144
Christianity, 30, 48, 118, 148, 159, 206, 239–240, 259, 389. *See also* Catholicism, Mormons, Protestantism, Shakers
Christianity Today, 42
Christ-Janer, Victor, 91–93, [92]
Christ's Way: The Stations of the Cross, 360
Christus Gardens, **94–95,** [95]
Chrysostom, Saint John, 66
Chugach, 173
Chulalongkorn, 407
Chumash, 263–264, 305
Church of Circle Wicca, 104
Church of England, 206, 251, 413
Church of God, 22–23
Church of Lukumi Babalu Aye, **95–97,** [96], [97]
Church of Scientology Los Angeles, **97–99,** [98]
Church of the Blessed Sacrament, **99–101,** [100]
Church of the Foursquare Gospel, 271
Church of the Living God, 22
Chuska Mountains, **101–102**
Circle Coven, 104
Circle Magic Songs, 104
Circle Network News, 103, 104

Circle Sanctuary Nature Preserve, **102–106,** [103]
Circling Raven, 247
Cistercians, 1–4, [3], 215–219, [216], [217], 261–262, [262]
civil disobedience, 7, 93, 192–193
"Civil Disobedience and the American Constitutional Order," 93
Civil Rights, 5–7, 127–129, [128], 131–133, 149, 267, 333–336, [334]
Civil Rights Act, 335
Civil Rights District, 336. *See also* Voting Rights Act
Civil War, 19, 39, 46, 48, 54, 61, 78–80, 127, 131–133, 142, 151, 187–188, 200–201, 278–279, 349, 356, 380
Civilian Conservation Corps (CCC), 86–87
Clark, Ella A., 109–110, 135–136, 235, 339
Clark, Randy, 108
Clemens, Donella, 154
Cleveland, Grover, 110–111
Clinton, Bill, 6, 33, 42, 131, 136–137, 245, 271–272, 277, 311, 341
Clinton, Hillary Rodham, 333
Close Encounters of the Third Kind, 120
Coeur d'Alene, 247–250
Coffin, Levi, 267
Cognitive Development among Sioux Children, 44
Coke, Thomas, 205
Coleman, Gregory D., 41
Coletti, Joseph Arthur, 213–214
College of William and Mary, 53
Collens, Charles, 293
Colonial period, 187, 194, 250–254, 326, 348–349, 373, 380, 402, 413–414, 415
colonial style, 213–214, [214]
Colorado, 11–15, 167–168, 244–246, 336–339, [337]
Colter, Jane, 61
Colter, John, 419
Comanche, 61, 133, 245
Comenius, John Amos, 36
Comes, John T., 347
"Coming of the Black Robes," 249–250
commercialism, 136, 211, 283
communes, 259–260
Compassion in Action: Setting Out on the Path of Service, 197
El Concilio Supremo Arzobispal, 161
Confessio Bohemica, 36
Confucianism, 80–81. *See also* Korean Confucianism
Conger, Julia, 276
Congregation Beth Yeshua, **106–108**

Congregationalism, 124, 147, 195, 200–203, [201], [202], 251, 413–415
Congress of International Association for Religious Freedom, 194, 388
Connecticut, 75–76, 123–125, [124], 144–146, [145], 326
Connelly, Cornelia Peacock, 393
Connick, Charles J., 356
The Conquest of Canaan, 124
Conquistadora, La, 315
Conscious Aging, 198
conservatism, 23, 42, 93–94, 153, 206
Contemplation in a World of Action, 2
Continental Army and Navy, 378–379
The Continental Harmony, 196
Cook, Loretta Afraid-of-Bear, 246
Corn Mother, 364
Cornwallis, Charles, 252
Coronado, Francisco Vasquez de, 9, 257, 362
Cortez, Hernando de, 263
Costanoan, 305
Couche, La, 64
The Cove. *See* Billy Graham Training Center at the Cove
Coyote, 59, 130, 235, 338–339
Coyote Boy, 256
crafts, 225, 328–329, 337, 351, 361, 364
Cram, Ralph Adams, 15, 70–71, 72
Crater Lake, **108–111,** [109]
Crazy Horse Memorial, 44–48, [45]
Creighton, Elsie, 135
Creole culture, 171–175, [172], 351–355
Crispen, Ellen Furlong, 235
Crossroads Community Church of Hyde Park, **111–113**
Crow, 44, 119, 209, 419, 420
Crow Dog, Leonard, 47
Crystal Cathedral, 74, **113–115**
Cuba, 95, 97
Cultural Conservancy, 236
Cumberland, Francisco, 224
Curtis, Christopher Paul, 335–336
Curtis, Edward S., 44–45, 109
Custer, George Armstrong, 46
Cutler, Timothy, 250, [251]
Cuypers, Peter J. H., 356
Cyrillus a Matre Dei, 241
Czechoslovakia, 240–244, [242]

Dade Community College, 96
Daily, Truman, 246
Dalin, Cyrus E., 228
Les Dames de Charité, 65
dance, 83, 96, 106, 163, 190, 200, 249, 258, 266, 409
  Basket Dance, 258–259
  Bean Dance, 258
  Bear Dance, 336, 338–339

Buffalo Dance, 364
Chilkat Dancers, 333
Contra Dance, 207
Corn Dance, 364–365
Deer Dance, 364, 365
English country dance, 207
Fire Dance, 62
Flute Dance, 258
Gei-Sun Dancers, 333
Ghost Dance, 46–47
Home Dance, 258
hula, 193
Kado, 120
Matachina Dance, 365
Sacred Arrow Bundle Dance, 46
Snake Dance, 83, 257, 258
square dance, 207
stick dance, 422
Sun Dance, 30, 46, **47**, 121, 274, 277, 339
Sundown Dance, 365
Turtle Dance, 364
Wuwuchim, 258
Yei-Bei-Chei dance, 62
Dao-Confucianism, 80–81
Dass, Ram, 197–199, [198]
David, Christian, 36
Davidson, Dr. J. G., 90–91
Davis, Nellie Lindley, 40
Davis, Ola Cassadore, 232, 234
Dawes, Henry, 257
Dawes, William "Billy," 252
"Day of Hope," 390
Daynes, Joseph J., 228
de Andreis, Felix, 63
de Espejo, Antonio, 76–77
de Gaulle, Charles, 405
de la Cuesta, Felipe Arroyo, 303
De La Salle Christian Brothers, 223
de la Tour, LeBlond, 352
de Lara, Maria Manriquez, 241
de Lasuén, Fermín Francisco, 303, 308
de Marillac, Louise, [65], 324
de Menil, Dominique and John, 299
de Páez, José, 307
de Paul, Vincent, 64–65, [65], 324
de Pouilly, J. N. B., 353, 354
de Rosas, Luis, 222
de Smet, Pierre Jean, 63, 247–248, 419
de Soto, Hernando, 175
de Továr, Pedro, 257
de Vaca, Cabeza, 76
Death Comes for the Archbishop, 316, 320
Declaration of Independence, 378–379
Delachaux, Jean, 353
Delano Grape Strike, 304
Delaware, 37, 93–94, 254–255
Delaware Swedish Colonial Society, 255

Delille, Henriette, 393–394, [394]
Deliverance Evangelistic Church, 108
Deloria, Vine, 121
Dena'ina Athabascan, 165
Denver Gold Rush, 338
deprogramming, 390
Derujinsky, Gleb, 75
d'Estaing, Giscard and Anne-Aymone, 393
Detroit Zen Center, **117–118**
Dev, Guru Nanak, 157
Devi, 162–164
Devi, Sarada, 289
Devils Tower National Monument, **118–121**, [119]
Dewdney, Edward, 47
DeWolf, Ronald, 98
Dhamma, 92
Dhammapada, 408
Dharma, 185
Dharma Life, 25
Diallo, Amadou, 6–7
Diana's Grove, **121–123**, [122]
Dianetics, 98
Dianetics: The Modern Science of Mental Health, 98
Diegueños, 305
Digger Indians. *See* Paiute
Digneo, Carlos, 317
Diné. *See* Navajo
Diné Citizens Against Ruining Our Environment (Diné CARE), 102
diorama, 94–95, [95]
Ditmars, Isaac, 67
The Divine Principles, 389
Dix, Dorothea, 148
Diyinii, 101
Dobberstein, Paul, 155–157, [156]
Domenici, Pete, 9–10
Dominion of God Incorporated, 22
Donnellon, David, 180
drama, 39–41, 114, 285, 386
folk drama, 304
outdoor drama, 399–400, [400]. *See also koshare*, mime, mumming
Drawing Down the Moon: Witches, Druids, Goddess-Worshippers, and Other Pagans in America Today, 104
dream catchers, 62
dream interpretation, 369–370, 419
Dream People, 244
Drowne, Shem, 253
drug rehabilitation, 98–99
drumming, 83, 96, 102, 104, 106, 123, 136, 233–234, 246, 249, 258, 270, 332–333
bata drums, 96, 97
Dubois, W. E. B., 333

DuBourg, Louis W., 63
Duchesne, Philippine Rose, 63, 66, 393
Dull Knife, 46
Durga, 163, 164
Dutch style, 325–328, [326], [327]
Dwelling Place Monastery, 237
Dwight Chapel, **123–125**, [124]
Dwight, Timothy, 123–125, **[124]**
Dyer, Mary, 267

Eagle Elk, 45
Eagle Shirt, 248–249
Earley, John J., 32
Earth Day, 105
Earth First!, 136, 232
Earth Healer, 218
Earth Run for Peace, 321
Ebenezer Baptist Church, **127–129**, [128]
Ebenezer Credit Union, 129
Ebenezer Society, 19
Echo Canyon, **129–131**, [130]
Echoes of Faith, 271
Eck, 368–370, [369]
Eckankar Journal, 370
Eckankar: The Key to Secret Worlds, 368
ecology, 197–199, [198]. *See also* Audubon Society, Earth First!, National Environmental Policy Act, National Geographic Society, National Historic Landmarks, National Historic Site, National Natural Landmark, National Park Service, National Register of Historic Places, National Trust for Historic Places, National Trust for Historic Preservation, Natural Resource Damage Assessment, panentheism, Sierra Club, whaling, Wicca, World Heritage List
eco-village design, 198
ecumenism, 2, 15–17, 100, 127, 148, 299, 380
Eddy, Mary Baker, [141], 141–144, [142]
Edelman, Marian Wright, 292
Edict of Nantes, 151
Edwards, Jonathan, 124, 220
Eisenhower, Dwight D., 7, 11, 192, 405
Ekaku, Hakuin, 117
El-Amin, Abdullah, 179–180
Eleggua, 96
Elim Missionary Assemblies, 271
Elizabeth II, 405
Ellington, Duke, 405
Emancipation Proclamation, 131–132

Emanuel African Methodist Episcopal
    Church, **131–133**
Embury, Philip, 205
Emerson, Ralph Waldo, 148
Enchanted Rock, **133–135**, [134]
Endangered Species Act, 232
The Enduring Navaho, 62
enemy way, 82–83
Enola Hill, **135–137**
Environmental Protection Agency,
    249
Epic of Shahnameh Ferdowsi, 422
Episcopalianism, 15–17, 70–73, [71],
    [250], 250–254, [251], 324,
    378–382, [379], 382–384, [383],
    385, 402–406, [403]. *See also*
    African-Methodist Episcopal
equinox, 34, 105, 123
Erdrich, Louise, 62
Estes, Clarissa Pinkola, 333
ethnocentrism, 244
Eurocentrism, 190, 305, 314–318,
    [315], [316]
Evangelical Council for Financial
    Accountability, 52–53
evangelicalism, 41–44, 50–53, 57–59,
    239–240, 282–285, [283], [284],
    399–400, [400], 414
evangelism, [42], 159–157, [157],
    219–222, [220], 270–272, 282-
    –285, [283], [284], 319,
    322–323, 335, 389–391, [390],
    [391]
Evans, Anne, 194
Ex Nihilo, 404

The Faith of Islam, 179
*Faithful Defiance: A Portrait of Desmond
    Tutu*, 382
Family Federation for World Peace
    and Unification, 389–390
Fanning the Flame, 240
Farina, Richard, 335
Farrakhan, Louis, 57, 229–232, **[230]**,
    [231]
fascism, 149
Favrile glass, 149
Feast of Fire, 52–53
Federal Aviation Agency, 91
Federal Children's Bureau, 366
Federal Energy Regulatory
    Commission, 341
Federal Theatre Project, 41
Fell, Margaret, 267
female clergy, 148, 149
feminism, 150, 270, 330, 366
Fernandeño, 305
Festival of Churches, 151
The Final Call, 231
Fire Baptized Holiness Church of
    God of the Americas, 22
Fire in the Mind, 160

First Amendment, 48, 135
First Baptist Church, Englewood,
    New Jersey, 335
First Baptist Church, Manhattan, 5
First Baptist Church of America,
    139–141, [140]
First Church of Christ, Scientist,
    [141], 141–144, [142], [143],
    228
First Mennonite Church of San
    Francisco, 154
First Presbyterian Church, Stamford,
    Connecticut, **144–146**, [145]
First Unitarian Church of
    Philadelphia, **147–150**, [148]
Firstborn Church of Christ, 245
Fisk, Charles B., 213
The Five Daily Prayers, 179
Flaming Arrow's People, 8
Flathead, 247, 419
Florida, 50–53, 95–97, [96], [97],
    170–171, [171], 326
Florida Endowment for the
    Humanities, 95–96
Florida Folklife Festival, 96
Flute, Jerry, 210
folk art, 32. *See also* American folk
    architecture, crafts, dance
folk society, 160–162
Folsom, William H., 228
Ford, Gerald, 42, 253
Ford, Henry Chapman, 308
Ford, Tennessee Ernie, 202
Fore, William F., 38
Foreman, Dave, 232
Fort Ross Chapel. *See* Holy Trinity
    Chapel at Fort Ross
Fortalezas En La Mente, 413
Fortunate Eagle, Adam, 277
Fosdick, Harry Emerson, 292, **[294]**
Foss, Samuel, 201
Foster, Abby Kelley, 267
Foster, Nelson, 192
Fountain of Life, 342
Fournier, Stanislas, 353
Fox, Selena, 104, 105
Fox, Virgil, 114
Franciscans, 2, 9, 161, 257, 304–307,
    [305], [306], 346
Franco, Mark, 235
Franconia Mennonite Conference,
    154
Frank, Leo, 366
Franklin, Benjamin, 147
Free African Society, 132
Freeman, James, 195
Frei, Emil, 65–66
Fremont Culture, 289
French and Indian War, 37, 251,
    252
French, Daniel Chester, 384

French Declaration of the Rights of
    Man and the Citizen, 300
French Huguenot Church, **150–152,**
    [151]
French Revolution, 151, 216, 261
fresco, 88–90, [89], [90]
Frischauf, Clement, 351
Frohman, Philip Hubert, 404–405,
    [405]
*From Milk to Meat: Primer for Christian
    Living*, 22–23
From This Day Forward, 399–400,
    [400]
Fry, Elizabeth, 267
Fuller, Margaret, 148
fundamentalism, 22–23, 42, 97–98,
    239–240, 270–272, 292,
    376–378, [377]. *See also*
    antifundamentalism, evangelicalism,
    evangelism
Fugitive Slave Act, 267
Fuqua, J. B., 114
Furlow, Henry J., 40
Furness, Frank, 147, 149

Gabrielino, 305
Gage, Thomas, 252
Gallagher, Misha, 62
Ganapathi, Sthpathi, 163
Gandhi, 265
Gandhi, Indira, 405
Ganesha, 164, 312
Gap, Eva, 246
Gardner, Gerald, 103–104
Gathas, 421
Gathering of the Dervish Healing
    Order, 198
Gaucher, Peter, 247
Geiser, John, 354
Genesee Abbey, 1
gen-X, 112, 159
geophagy, 319
Georgia, 39–41, 78–80, 127–129,
    [128], 326
Georgian style, 196, [250], 250–254
Germantown Mennonite Church,
    153–155, [154]
Germantown Mennonite Resolution
    against Slavery, 153
Geronimo, 232
Gethsemani Abbey. *See* Abbey of
    Gethsemani
Gibault, Pierre, 63
Gibbs, Sir James, 139–141, **[140],**
    196
Gilpin, Laura, 62
Ginsberg, Allen, 198
Gitche Manito, 276
Giuliani, Rudolph, 6, 7
Glennon, John J., 63, 65
The Glory of Christmas, 114
The Glory of Easter, 114

glossolalia, 22, 51, 271, 385
goddess worship, 102–106, [103], 121–123, [122]
God's Trombones, 41
Gomes, Gloria, 236
Gomes, Peter John, 213–215
Gonzaga College, 248
The Good Book: Reading the Bible with Mind and Heart, 214
Gothic, 5, 15–17, [16], 48–50, [49], 75–76, 203, [293], 370, 399–400, [400], 406
    Anglo-French, 355–356
    English Gothic Revival, 402–404, [403]
    French Gothic, 67–73, [68], [71]
    Gothic Revival, 149, 150, 187–189, [188], 355, 357, 382–384
    medieval Gothic, 150
    neo-Gothic, 123–125, [124], 379, 381
    Ozark Gothic, 372
Grace, Daddy, 22
Graham, Billy, 41–44, [42], 52–53, 57, 59, 88, 159, 214, 220, 240, 283
Graham, Franklin, 42, 59, 88
Graham, Ruth Bell, 88
Grant, Campbell, 264
Grant, Julia Dent, 221
Grant, Ulysses S., 221, 419
The Graphic Bible, 301
Great American Smokeout, 74
Great Awakening, 124, 220
Great Depression, 7, 19, 40–41, 49, 228, 292, 365, 380, 410
Great Society, 7
Great Spirit, 45–46, 119, 175, 210, 248, 258, 273, 274, 276, 417
Greek Orthodox, 15, 231, 385
Greek Revival, 148
Greene, Dan, 281
Greving, Louis, 155–157, [156]
Grey, Zane, 287
Grossman, Cissy, 368
Grossman, Rafael G., 34–35
Grotto of the Redemption, **155–157,** [156]
Grow, Henry, 228
Growth or Death, 74
Grube, Bernard Adam, 37
Gruber, Johann A., 18
Gruchy, Thomas James, 251
Grue, Jack, 35
Guastavino, Rafael, and Rafael, Jr., 68, 70, 367, 404
Guatemala, 319
Guillemard, Gilberto, 352
Guillet, Urban, 216
Gully, Ben, 113
Gurdwara Sahib El Sobrante, [157], **157–158**

Habitat for Humanity, 3, 17, 20, 35–36, 50, 58–59, 384
Hachard, Marie-Madeleine, 393
Hai, Jan, 183–185, [184], **[185]**
Haida, 330–333
Hale, Albert, 22
Hallelujah Tower, 411
hallucinogens, 244–246, 264
Halsey, William, 189
Ham, Mordecai F., 42, 57
Hamilton, Alexander, 151, 378–379
Hamlin, Christopher M., 336
Hammarstrom, Olav, 85
Hancock, John, 252
Hanuman, 162–164
Hanuman Foundation, 198
Hare Krishna, 264–267, [265]
Haring, Keith, 73
"Hark the Herald Angels Sing," 206
Harlem, 5–7
Harlem Heights, Battle of, 380
Harrison, George Donald, **228**
Harrison, Peter, 195–196, **[196],** 373–375, [374], [375]
Harrison, Wallace Kirkman, 144–145
Hart, Frederick, 404
Harvard, John, 213
Harvard Memorial Church. *See* Memorial Church of Harvard University
Harvard University, 147, 148, 195, 198, 213–215, [214], 251
Harvest Ministries, Inc.®, **159–160,** [160]
Haverford College, 269
Hawaii, 173, 189–193, [191], 309–314, [310], [311]
Hawthorne, Nathaniel, 195
healing, 62, 77, 102, 135, [141], 141–144, [142], [143], 192, 235, 263, 283, 294, 318–322, 417
    damballah, 397
    faith healing, 142
    health fair, 409
    hydrotherapy, 175–177, [176]
    ki healing, 194
    self-healing, 81
    spiritual healing, 143, 198
Healing Waters, 283
Heaven Bound, 39–41
Heaven's Child, 59
Heavy Runner, Floyd, 30
Hebrew Benevolent Society, 187, 296
Hebrew Christian Alliance (HCA), 107
Hebrew Ladies Aid Society, 296
Hebrew Orphan Society, 187
Hebrew Union College, 278
Heck, Barbara, 205
Hedge, Frederic Henry, 148
Heinemann, Barbara, 18–19
Heinerman, John, 47

Heinz, George L., 70–71, [71]
Helm, George, 190, 192
Henig, Ron, 35
Henley, Richard, 88–90, [89], [90]
Henriette Delille: Free Woman of Color, 394
Henry Street Settlement, 365–366
herbalism, 104, 105
Heritage USA, 57
Hermanidad de Nuestro Señor Jesus Nazareño, 319–320
Hermanos Penitentes, **160–162,** 319
Heston, Charlton, 86
Heuduck, Arno, 66
Heuduck, Paul, 65–66
Hiawatha Pageant, 277
Hicks, Edward, 267–268
Hidatsa, 210
hijab, 401
Hill, Steve, 52
Hillman, John Wesley, 110
Hindu Temple of Greater Chicago, 162–165
Hinduism, 4, 10–11, 30, 148, 149, 157, 162–165, 197–199, [198], 264–267, [265], 289–292, [290], [291], 309–314, [310], [311], 368
    Samkhya, 10
    Vedanta, 289–292, [290], [291]
Hinduism Today, 311
Hirsch, Willard, 189
The History of Hinayana Buddhism, 185
Hoa Hao, 199
Hoffman, Malvina, 213–214
Hofmann, Heinrich, 294
Hogan, Linda, 62
Hohokam, 76, 257
Holiday, Henry, 383–384
Hollerith, Herman IV
Holley, Horace Hotchkiss, 32
Holocaust, 13, 35, 100
Holtkamp, Walter, 14
Holy Assumption of the Virgin Mary Church, **165–167, [166]**
Holy Cross Abbey, **167–168**
Holy Homosexuals: The Truth about Being Gay or Lesbian & Christian, 74
Holy Land USA, **168–170, [169]**
Holy Name Monastery, **170–171, [171]**
Holy Rock, Johnson, 48, 120
Holy Spirit Abbey, 1
Holy Trinity Abbey, 1
Holy Trinity Chapel of Fort Ross, **171–175, [172]**
Holy Trinity Episcopal Church. *See* Old Swedes Church
holy way, 82–83
homosexuality, 24, 73, 73–74, 149, 153–155, [154], 198, 213–215, 231, 295, 295, 299

Hook, Dorothy, 167
Hopi, 8, 9, 59, 61–62, 255–259, 288, 337, 417
Hopkins, Stephen, 267
Hopper, Isaac, 267
Horgan, Paul, 316
Hornbostel, Henry, 297
Hosier, Harry, 205
Hoskininni, 287
Hot Springs Mountain, **175–177, [176]**
Hour of Decision, 42
The Hour of Prayer, 113, 115
House of Navajo Religion, 83
The House on Henry Street, 366
Housing and Urban Development (HUD), 40
Howar, A. J., 401–402
Howarth, Sam, 321–322
Howe, Julia Ward, 148
Howe, Leanne, 62
Howland, Benjamin, 375
Hubbard, L. Ron, 97–99, [98]
Hudson Bay Company, 235, 247
Hudson, Travis, 264
Huet, Charles, 248
Huguenots, 150–152, 379, [151]
Huichol, 244–245
humanism, 30–33, 80–81, 259
  secular humanism, 149
Humbrecht, Erasme, 354
Hunt, Richard Morris, 383
Hurung Whuti, 256
Huss, John, 36
Huxley, Aldous, 198
Huybrechts, Brother, 248
Hymns Written for the Use of Hebrew Congregations, 187
hypnotism, 142

I Ching, 81
ICHTHUS, 144–146, [145]
iconography, 62, 70, 90, 226, 404
Idaho, 247–250, 417
idealism, 239–240
idolatry, 157
If It's Going to Be, It's Up to Me, 114
Illinois, 22–23, 30–33, 162–165, 225–227, [226], 229–232, [230], [231], 401
The Illustrated Biography of Buddha's Life, 185
immigration, 95–97, [96], [97], 150–152, [151], 162–165, 171–175, [172], 175–177, [176], 183–185. [184], [185], 189–193, [191], 199–200, 253, 254–255, [278], 278–279, 295–296, 297, 326, 342–343, 346–348, [347], 357, 373–376, [374], [375], 380, 391–392, [392], 398, 399–400, [400], 421–422

In His Presence, 386
In the Light of Reverence, 137
In the Shadow of the Moons, 389
In This House, On This Morning, 336
Inca, 314
Indaka, Sayadaw Ashin, 391–392, **[392]**
India, 10, 11, 289, [290]
Indian Appropriations Bill of 1851, 276
Indian Bill of Rights, 306
Indian War of 1858, 248
Indiana, 239–240, 326
Indians Claims Commission, 363
Industrial Revolution, 151, 327
Infant Jesus of Prague, 240–244, **[242]**
infanticide, 157
Inquiries about Islam, 179
Inquisition, 222, 375
Inspirationism, 18–19
Institutes of the Christian Religion, 151
integration, 7
interdenominationalism, 111–113
International Alliance of Messianic Congregations and Synagogues, 108
International Covenant on Civil and Political Rights, 48
International Hebrew Christian Alliance, 107
International Society for Krishna Consciousness, 266
International Thomas Merton Society, 2
International Whaling Commission, 281
Internet, 367
Into a New Day: Exploring a Baptist Journey of Division, Diversity, and Dialogue 140–141
An Introduction to Zen Buddhism, 117
Inuit, 32
Inupiat, 280–281
Iowa, 17–20, 155–157, [156], 200–203, [201], [202]
Ipai, 305
Isaiah, Metropolitan, 15
Islam, 15, 30, 33, 118, 157, 175–[176]–177, 229–232, [230], [231], 401–402
Islam in Focus, 179
Islamic Center of America, **179– 181,** [180], [181]
Israel, 108
Italian Renaissance style, [323], 323–325, [324]
Izanagi-no-Mikoto, 387

Jackson, Andrew, 176, 351–355, 395
Jackson, Helen Hunt, 305, 308
Jackson, Jesse, 292
Jackson, Leroy, 102

Jackson Square, 351–355
Jade Buddha Temple, **183–185,** [184], [185]
Jamestown, 54
Jankowski, Michael, 168
Japan, 193–195, [194], 386–388, [387]
Jarrett, Dale, 160
Jayesh, Prem, 259
Jefferson, Thomas, 147, 148, 175, 373, 419
Jehovah's Witnesses, 413
Jemison, Mae, 333
Jeshuat Israel, 373
Jesse Owens Humanitarian Award, 22–23
Jesuits, 247–250, 306
Jesus Movement, 159
"The Jewish Cemetery at Newport," 376
Jewish Chautauqua Society, 296
Jewish Press, 35
Jewish TV Broadcast, 107
Jews for Jesus, 107–108
Jim Crow, 7
John Paul II, Pope, 67, 306
John XXIII, Pope, 75, 99, 324
Johnson, George, 160
Johnson, James Weldon, 41
Johnson, Lyndon, 7, 229, 335
Johnson, Niels, 228
Johnson, Philip, 74, 299
Johnson, Robert, 169
Jones, Cynthia, 121
Jones, Daniel, 222
Jones, E. Fay, 16–17, 370–372, [371], [372]
Jones, Lula Byrd, 40
Jones, William, 252
Joset, Joseph, 248
Juaneño, 305
Judaism, 11–15, 30, 118, 149, 259, 385
  Ashkenazic Judaism, 373
  messianic Jews, 106–108
  Orthodox Judaism, 34–35, 278, 295–299, [296]
  protestantized Jews, 296
  Reformed Judaism, 187–189, [188], [278], 278–279, 296, 365–368, [366]
  Sephardic Judaism, 187, 373–376, [374], **[375]**
Judge Alexander George Teitz Award, 376
Jung, Karl, 59–60, [60]
Just As I Am, 42
Juster, Ralph, 410–411

Kabotie, Fred, 61
kachina, 8, 256–258, 338
Kacmarcik, Frank, 218
Kado, 120. See also dance

Kahal Kadosh Beth Elohim, **187–189,** [188]
Kaho'Olawe, **189–193,** [191]
Kaho'olawe: Na Leo o Kanaloa, 192
Kainah, 29
Kalakaua, David, 190
Kalinga style, 163–164
Kalmar Nyckel, 254, 255
Kamalapukwia, 77
kami, 193–195, [194], 386–388, [387]
Kane, 190
Kang, Thomas Hosuck, **80–81**
kannagara, 386
Kannagara Jinja, **193–195, [194]**
Kansas, 346–348, [347]
Kaplan, Louis, 107
Kartikeya, 164
Karuk, 234, 236
Kashaya Pomo, 171–175, [172]
Katchongvu, Dan, 258
Kaufman, Frieda, 153
Keams, Geri, 62
Keeley, P. C., 75
Keepers of the Treasures, 276
Keller, Helen, 404
Kenaitze, 165–167, [166]
Kennedy, Ira, 133
Kennedy, John F., 101, 229, 312, 321, 335
Kenton, Harold, 234
Kentucky, 1–4, [3], 237–238, [238], 326
Keres, 8
Kierkegaard, Sören, 269
Kilpatrick, John A., 2
Kim, Paik Moon, 390
Kim, Young Oon, 389
King, Bruce, 9
King, Coretta Scott, 129
King, E. J., 196
King, Martin Luther, Jr., 6, 7, 127–129, [128], 292, 299, 321, 334, 336, 405
King, Martin Luther, Sr., 5, 7, 127–129, [128]
King's Chapel, Boston, 147, **195–196,** [196], 250, 375
Kinya'a, 83
Kiowa, 44, 46, 61, 119
Kirschberg, Reva Godlove, 368
Kirwan, John Patrick, 354
Kitab-i-Aqdas, 33
Kitcheyan, Buck, 234
Kitchi Manitou, 273
kiva, 61, 83, 256–258, 338, 361, 362, 364
Klah, Hosteen, 83
Klamath, 108–111, [109], 234, 235
Klauder, Charles, 124
Klickitat, 136
Knights of Columbus, 76, 79, 244, 249, 318

koans, 117
Koch, Richard, 354
Kodiak, 173
Kohemalamalama 'o Kanaloa, 190
Kojiki, 387–388
Korean Confucianism, 389
Korean Presbyterianism, 390
Korean War, 213, 380
koshare, 259, 364
Kresge Chapel. *See* Chapel of Massachusetts Institute of Technology
Krishna, 164
Kroeber, Alfred, 264
Ku, 190, 312
Ku Klux Klan, 334, 335
Kuamo'o Mo'okini, 312
Kusav, 130
Kwakiutl, 135
Kwan-Yin, 183

La Farge, C. Grant, 70–73, [71], 383–384
La Farge, John, 149
La Mousse, Ignace, 247
labyrinth, 106, 121, 123
Laclède-Liguest, Pierre, 63
Ladies of Charity, 65
Lady Liberty League, 103
Laguna, 62
Laiba, John, 342
Lakota. *See* Sioux
Lakshmana, 162–164
Lama, Dalai, 117, 118, 301
Lama Foundation, **197–199, [198]**
Lamadrid, Enrique R., 321–322
Lamb, 107–108
Lame Deer, 119
Lame Deer, John, 47
Lamy, Jean-Baptiste, 161, 203, 314–318, [315], **[316]**
Lamy of Santa Fe: His Life and Times, 316
Landry, Richard, 300
Landsburg, Leon, 289
Lane, Jeanne, 72
The Language of Truth, 185
Lanier, Charles, 150
Lanier, Sidney, 151
Lao Buddhist Association, 409
Last Straw, 198
"The Last Supper," 148
Latiku, 8
Latino, 304
Latrobe, Benjamin H., 148, 353
Latter Day Saints. *See* Mormons
Laurie, Greg, 159–160, [160]
Laveau, Marie, 397
Lazarus, Emma, 367
Leary, Timothy, 198
Lee, Ann, 325–326, 328
Lee, Georgia, 264

Lee, Robert E., 151
Lee, Spike, 335
The Legends and Myths of Hawaii, 190
Lehman, Irving, 366
Lenape, 37
L'Enfant, Pierre, 402
Lenguas Porque y Quando, 413
Lenni Lenape, 254
Lentz, Robert, 318
Leonori, Aristide, 66
Leriche, Antoine, 353
"Letter from a Birmingham Jail," 334
Levy, Joseph, 187
Levy, Mark, 107
Lewis and Clark expedition, 275, 419
Lewis and Clark National Forest, 29–30
Lewis, J. Reilly, 406
liberalism, 57–59, 99–100, 148, 292, 296
Lichty, Richard, 154
Lien Hoa Buddhist Temple, **199–200**
Ligon, Ronald S., 94–95, [95]
Lincoln, Abraham, 9, 131–132
Lindo, Moses, 187
Lisa, Manuel, 419
Little Big Horn, Battle of the 45
Little Brown Church in the Vale **200–203, [201], [202]**
"The Little Brown Church in the Vale," 200–203, [201], **[202]**
Llao, Chief 109–110
loa 397
Loire, Gabriel 75, 144
Lololoma 257
Lone Wolf, Rip, 137
Long, Ben, 88–90, [89], [90]
Long Walk, 61
Longfellow, Henry Wadsworth, 151, 250–252, 276, 277, 376
Lono, 190
Looking Horse, Arvol, 48, 120, 121, 210–211
Lopez, David, 188–189
Loretto Academy of Our Lady of Light, 203
Loretto Chapel, **203–205,** [204], 222, 316
Lotus Realm, 25
Lotz, Anne Graham, 42
Louisiana, 270–272, 351–355, [394], 394–396, 397
love feast, 37, 38–39
Love Without Condemnation, 115
Lovely Lane Methodist Church, **205–207, [206]**
Love-Stanley, Ivenue, 129
Lowell, James Russell, 214
Luce, Clare Booth, 217
Luckert, Karl, 287
Luiseño, 305
Luther, Martin, 93, 153

Lutheran Confessions, 93
Lutheran, German, 17–20
Lutheranism, 38, 93–94
Luther's Small Catechism, 93
Lynch, James, 39

Madison, James, 393
Magee, Vishu, 198
The Magic Circle Show, 104
Magical Journeys, 104
Maginnis, Charles D., 383
Magnin, 355
Mahalakshmi, 164
Mahaprabhu, Aghoreshwar, 10–11
Mahasi Retreat Center, 391–392, [392]
Maine, 325–328, [326], [327]
Majozo, Estella Conwill, 335
Makah, 279–282
makali'i, 192
Maklak, 109
Mal, Arjan, 157
Malcolm X, 230
male-centered worship, 160–162, 277
Mallet, Francois, 316–317
Malpais National Monument and Conservation Area, El, 9–10
Manchester College, 268
Mandan, 210, 275
Mandela, Nelson, 292
Mangun, G. Anthony, 271
Manhattan Project, 321
Manitou, 46. *See also* Great Spirit
Mankiller, Wilma, 330
Manuelito, 61
Many Dogs, 276
March of Tears, 77
Marchionni, Jean-Claude, 71
Maricopa, 62
Marine Mammal Protection Act, 281
Marquette, Jacques, 63
Marquez, Alfredo, 234
marriage encounter, 385–386
Marsalis, Wynton, 336
Marshall, Louis, 366
Martello, Leo, 104
Martha's Vineyard Campmeeting Association, 221
Martin Luther King Jr. Historical District, 39
Martin Luther King National Historic Site, 127
Maryland, 205–207, [206], [207], 267, [323], 323–325, [324]
Masons, 86, 87, 413
Mass, 249
    Latin Gregorian Mass, 93
Mass for Pentecost Sunday, 300
Massachusetts, [84], 84–86, [85], 99–101, [100], [141], 141–144, [142], [143], 195–196, [196], 213–215, [214], 219–222, [220],

250–254, [250], [251], 267, 326, 382–384, [383], 413–415
Massachusetts Bay Colony, 195
Massachusetts Committee of Correspondence, 252
Massachusetts Foundation for the Humanities, 222
Massachusetts Metaphysical College, 142
Massacre Cave, 61
Matchabelli, Norina, 212
Mather, Cotton, Increase, and Samuel, 250
Maxwell, Charlie, 190
Maxwell Museum of Anthropology, 83
Maya, 314
Mayflower, 195, 414
McConnell, Les, 136
McDaniel, Allen, 32–33
McHugh, John W., 318
McIverney, Michael, 359
McKim, Charles, 383
Meacham, Joseph, 326
Meals on Wheels, 66
Medici, Paolo, 356
medicine man. *See* shamanism
medicine wheel, 72, 76, 77–78
Medicine Wheel, **209–211**
meditation, 4–5, 11, 23–25, 78, 80–81, 183–185, [184], [185], 197, 211–213, 259, 260, 294, 392, 409
    Chinkon Gyo Ho, 194
    insight meditation, 392
    Rudraksha Meditation Forest, 309–310
    Thai meditation, 392
    Vipassana, 198, 392, 407
Meditation in Sahehain, 181
Meflott, Elsie, 333
megachurch, 22–23, 159–160, 322–323
Meher Spiritual Center, **211–213**
Memorial Church of Harvard University, **213–215,** [214]
Mennonites, 153–155, [154], 267
Mepkin Abbey, 1, **215–219,** [216], [217]
Merton, Thomas, 1, **2,** 17, 217, 224, 261
Mesa Verde, 336–339, [337], 362
Messner, Roe, 57
metaphysics, 142, 311
Methodism, 48–50, 205–207, [206], 219–222, [220], 283, 385
Methodist Publishing House, 207
Methodist Tabernacle, **219–222,** [220]
Metropolitan Community Church (MCC), 73–74
Metz, Christian, 18–19
Meusebach, John O., 133

Mexica, 244–245
Mexican War, 353, 362–363
Mexico, 203, 244–245, 305, 306, 315, 318–322
Michigan, 117–118, 175–177, [176]
Midsummer ritual, 47
Militov, Igumen Nikolai, 165
Million Man March, 57, 231
Mills, Clark, 352
Mills, Robert, 147–148, **[148]**
Mills, Willis, 144
Mime, 285. *See also* mumming
Minhag America, 178, 296
Minnesota, 271–278, [273], [274], [275], 348–351, 368–370, [369]
Minnetaree, 417–419
Misogi Shu Ho, 194
misogyny, 265
Mission Indians, 303–304, 304–307, [305], [306] 307–309
Mission of San Miguel of Santa Fe, **222–223**
mission style, 81, 203–205, [204], 222–223, 303–304, 304–307, [305], [306], 307–309, 318–322, 410–411
mission work, 11, 50, 58–59, 63, 67, 69–70, 73, 79, 80–81, 93, 113–115, 129, 159–160, [160], 183–185, [184], [185], 206–207, 218, 238, 243, 265, 267, 272, 283–284, 289–292, [290], [291], 304–307, [305], [306], 307–309, 314–318, [315], [316], 318–322, 322–323, 349, 360, 376–378, [377], 380, 381, 385, [394], 394–396, 400, 412–413
Mississippi, 384–386
Missouri, [63], 63–65, [64], 121–123, [122]
Missouri Lutheranism, 93–94
Mitchell, Harry Kunihi, 190
Mitchell, Kimo, 192
Miwok, 173
Moa'ulanui, 190
modernism, [12], 12–15, 57–59, [58], [84], 84–86, [85], 144–146, [145], 187, 292, 294, 299–301
Modoc, 234, 235
Mohawk, 355
Moise, Penina, 187
Moja Arts Festival, 132–133
Mojave, 263
Molala, 109
Molleno, 320
Momaday, N. Scott, 120
Monasterio de Nuestra Señora de la Soledad, 224
Monastery of Christ in the Desert, **223–225,** [224]
Monastery of the Holy Cross, **225–227,** [226]

monasticism, 2, 3, 4, 215–219, [216], [217], 223–225, [224], 225–227, [226], 237–238, [238], [329], 329–330, 343–346, [344], [345], 357–360, [358], 406–408, 408–410

monotheism, 32, 149, 157, 401

Monster Slayer, 101

Montana, 29–30, 417, 419, 420

Montana Wilderness Society, 30

Montezuma, 263

Montezuma Well, 77

Monticello, 148

Montreat-Anderson College, 88–90, [89], [90]

Moody, Dwight Lyman, 220

Moon, Sun Myung, 389–391, **[390]**, [391]

Moore, Henry, 86

Moorish architecture, [31], 31–33, 365

moral relativism, 111

Moral Society of Yale College, 124

morality play, 39–41

Moravianism, 35–39, 206

Morenon, Ernest E., 100

Morgan, Charles, 335

Morgan, J. P., 70

Mormon Pioneer National Historic Trail, 131

Mormon Tabernacle, [227], **227–229,** [228]

Mormon Tabernacle Choir, 202, 228

Mormon War, 228

Mormons, 131, [227], 227–229, [228], 232, 257, 385, 413

Morris, William, 383–384

Morris Brown AME Church, 132

Morris Brown College, 39

Mosaic, 65, 75

Mosie, Wendsler, 234

Mosque Maryam, **229–232, [230],** **[231]**

Mott, Lucretia, 267

Moulay, Antoine and Projectus, 203, 315–316

Mount Carmel Guild, 67

Mount Graham, **232–234,** [233]

Mount Shasta, **234–236**

Mount Tabor Retreat Center, **237–238,** [238]

Mount Zion AME Church, 132

Mourning to Morning, 74

Muhammad, Elijah, 230, 231

Muhammad, Siyyid Ali. *See* The Bab

Muhammad University of Islam, 231

Muhammad, W. Fard, 230

Muhammad, Wallace D., 231

Muir, Gladdys Esther, 268

Muir, John, 235–236

multiculturalism, 30–33, 103, 259–261, [260], 384–386

multiracialism, 30–33, 98–99, 384–386

mumming, 365

mural, 50, 66, 189

Murillo, Bartolomé Esteban, 78

Music and the Spoken Word, 229

Muslim American Youth Academy, 179–180

"My Answer," 42

mysticism, 149, 199, 209–211, 311, 369, 419

nature mysticism, 102–106, [103]

Mythmakers: Gospel, Culture, and the Media, 38

Nakashima, George, 225

Nampeyo, 61

Nancy Bryan Luce Gardens, 218

Napoleon Bonaparte, 353

Nappanee Missionary Church, **239–240**

Narbona, Antonio, 61

Narragansett Indians, 139

Nash, Thomas, 381

Natchez Indians, 394

Natchez Trace, 175

Nation of Islam (NOI), 229–232, [230], [231]

Nation of Islam Student Association, 231

National AIDS Memorial Book of Remembrance, 73

National Association for the Advancement of Colored People (NAACP), 32, 366

National Association of Gardeners of the United States, 86

National Cathedral. *See* Washington National Cathedral

National Council of Jewish Women, 297

National Environmental Policy Act, 232

National Geographic Society, 83

National Historic Landmarks, 7–8, 17, 48, 166, 167, 187, 209, 236, 249, 253

National Historic Site, 373–375

National Natural Landmark, 133

National Organization of Public Health Nurses, 366

National Park Service, 87, 131, 249, 276, 288, 395, 417

National Register of Historic Places, 33, 79, 127, 133, 136, 168, 192, 195, 236, 279, 341–342, 363, 379

National Shrine of the Infant Jesus of Prague, **240–244,** [242]

National Spiritual Assembly of the Bahá'is of the United States, 32

National Trust for Historic Places, 136

National Trust for Historic Preservation, 278, 335

The National Vespers Hour, 294

National Wilderness Preservation System, 236

Native American Church, **244–246**

Native Families, 44–45

Native Forest Products Industry (NFPI), 101–102

Natural Resource Damage Assessment, 249

Navajo, 9, 20–23, 32, 59–63, [60], 83–84, 101–102, 257, 287–289, [288], 337, 420

Navigator's Chair, 190

navushieip, 419

Nazism, 342. *See also* neo-Nazism

Nebraska, 244, 342–343

neo-Buddhism, 199

neoclassicism, 149

neo-evangelicalism, 42

neo-Nazism, 384–386

neopaganism, 149

neo-Sufi, 211

Neubert, Germar, 342

Neutra, Richard, 113

Nevada, 412–413

New Age, 120, 236, 244, 258, 276, 321, 368–370, [369]

New Beginning, A, 159

New Clairvaux Abbey, 1

"The New Colossus," 367

The New England Psalm Singer, 196

New Hampshire, 23–25, 326

New Horizon Sanctuary, 129

New Jersey, 67–70, [68], 391–392, [392], 401

New Mexico, 7–10, 81–84, [82], 160–162, 197–199, [198], 203–205, [204], 222–223, 223–225, [224], 257, 261, 314–318, [315], [316], 318–322, 361–365, [362]

New York, 5–7, 70–73, [71], 220, 221, 267, 278, 289–292, [290], [291], 293–295, [293], [294], 326, 355–357, [356], [357], 365–368, [366], 378–382, [379], 389–391, [390], [391], 391–392, [392], 401

New York Times, 366

New York University, 378–379

Newman, Barnett, 299

Newman, Robert, 252

Nez Percé, 135, 137, 248, 419, 420

Nicholas I, 332

Nicollet, Joseph N., 276

Nieuhaus, Charles Henry, 381

Nigeria, 96

night way, 82–83

Nixon, Richard, 42, 229, 390

Nobel Peace Prize, 268
non-denominational, 57–59, 73–74,
    84–86, [84], [85], 86–87, 94–95,
    [95], 211–213, 213–215, [214],
    299–301, [300], [301], 373. *See
    also* interdenominationalism
nontheism, 149
Norlin, Gloria, 420
North American Fur Company, 276
North American Indians, 275
North Carolina, 35–39, 41–44, 57–59,
    [58], 88–90, [89], [90], 267,
    399–400, [400], 406–408
North Dakota, 86–87
Noticias de la Nueva California, 306
Nuestra Señora Arcángel Mission,
    305
Nuestra Señora de Patrocino, 319
Nuestra Señora de San Juan de los
    Lagos, 319
Nuestra Señora de Talpa, 319
Nuestra Señora de Zapopán, 319
Nuestro Señor de Esquípulas,
    318–320
Nuestro Señor del Rayo, 319
numerology, 157
nursing, 324, 329, 366, 394, 404
Nye, Chauncy, 110

Obatala, 96
obeah, 97, 397
Occident, 188
Ochs, Adolph S., 366
Oduduwa, 96
Office of Ethnic and Cultural Affairs,
    98–99
Ogden, Peter Skene, 235
Oggzn, 96
Oglala, 44–48, [45]
Ohio, 111–113, [278], 278–279, 326,
    376–378, [377]
Ojibway, 210, 273, 349
O'Keeffe, Georgia, 225
Oklahoma, 48–50, 240–244, [242],
    282–285, [283], [284], [329],
    329–330
Old Mission of the Sacred Heart,
    247–250
Old North Church, [250], **250–254,**
    [251]
Old Salem, 38–39
Old Swedes Church, **254–255**
Olney, Ray, 135
On The Errors of the Trinity, 147
Oñate, Juan de, 9
One People One Nation, 420
Oneness Pentecostals, 271
Operation Christmas Child, 42, 59
Oraibi, **255–259**
Oral Roberts University, 282–285,
    [283], [284]
Order of the Eastern Star, 86, 87

Oregon, 108–111, [109], 135–137,
    261–262, [262]
O'Reilly, Thomas, 78–80
organ, 196
    Aeolian-Skinner, 72, 114, 141, 228,
        383–384, 405
    Allen Renaissance, 88, 150
    American Classic, 229
    Austin, 75, 188, 207, 229, 255
    barrel, 304
    Green, 54
    Henry Erben tracker, 150, 187, 188
    Isham, 213
    Kimball, 229
    Möller, 14, 39, 50, 58, 354
    Ontko and Young, 188
    Rodgers Cambridge, 168
    Ruffatti, 114
    Schantz, 67
    Visser-Rowland, 145
    Wicks, 359
    Zimmer, 218
orisha, 95, 96, 97, 397
O'Rourke, Jeremiah, 67
Orthodox Tree of Life Synagogue,
    296
Ortiz, José Antonio, 223
Osadca, Apollinaire, 75
Osho Chidvilas, **259–261,** [260]
*OSHO Chidvilas—Flowering of
    Consciousness*, 260
Osho Times International, 260
Oshzn, 96
Otoe-Missouri, 246
Otomí, 306
Oudinot, Eugene, 383
Our Lady of Guadalupe, 318, 319,
    321
Our Lady of Guadalupe Trappist
    Abbey, **261–262,** [262]
Our Lady of Prompt Succor, 395, 396
Our Lady of Victories, 395
Ozanam, Frederic, 65
Ozman, Agnes, 271

Pacem in Terris, 100
Pacheco, Manuel, 233
pacifism, 2, 267–268, 328, 366, 387,
    389–390, 404–405
Pacomio, 305
paganism, 102–106, [103], 121–123,
    [122], 257, 397, 419
paho, 256
Paine, Thomas, 147
Painted Rock, **263–264**
Paiute, 46, 130–131, 287
    Kaibab Paiute, 288
    San Juan Southern Paiute, 288
Palace of Gold, **264–267, [265]**
Palóu, Francisco, 306, 308
Pamé, 306
Pan Pagan Festival, 104

pantheism, 102–106, [103], 291
Papago, 338
Papucci, Sergio, 396
Parents and Friends of Lesbians and
    Gays (PFLAG), 74
Parham, Charles F., 271
Parker, Quanah, 245
Parker, Theodore, 148
Parliament of World Religions, 311
parochial school, 19, 37, 38, 51, 63,
    76, 93, 99–101, [100], 153, 158,
    168, 170–171, [171], 175–177,
    [176], 183–185, [184], [185],
    187, 199, 203, 222, 237–238,
    [238], 248, 249, 257, 296, 309,
    318, [323], 323–325, [324],
    351–355, 359, [394], 394–396,
    404. *See also* yeshivahs
Parsis, 421
Partridge, William O., 356
Parvati, 164
Pastorela, 304
Patel, Sheela Ambalal, 260
Patkotak, Elise, 281
Patterson, Elizabeth Chapin, 211–213
Paul, Alice, 267
"Paul Revere's Ride," 250–252
Paulist Fathers, 393
Paytiamo, James, 8
Pawnee, 222
peace pipe, 273
Peaceable Kingdom, 267
Pearl Harbor, 191
Peccini, Tommaso, 75
Pei, Ieoh Ming, **143**
Peirz, Franz Xavier
Pelton, Henry C., 293
Pend d'Oreille, 248
Pendle Hill, **267–270, [268], [269]**
Pendley, William Perry, 120
Penfield, Kate, 140–141
Penington, Isaac, 267
Penniman, James, 252
Pennsylvania, 106–108, 147–150,
    [148], 153–155, [154], 267–270,
    [268], [269], 267, 295–299, [296]
Pentecostal Holiness Advocate, 283
pentecostalism, 22–23, 50–53, 108,
    270–272, 376–378, [377],
    412–413
Pentecostals of Alexandria, **270–272**
People's Voice, 7
Peretti, Achille, 354
Perlman, Susan, 107–108
Permaculture Drylands Institute,
    198
Perry, Troy D., 73
Petefish, Andy, 120
Peters, Chris, 234, 235
petroglyphs, 82, 190, 272, 275,
    276–277, 417
Petts, John, 335

peyotism, 244–246

Philadelphia, 147–150, [148], 153–155, [154], 220, 269

Piazza, Michael S., 74

Piccolo Spoleto, 132–133, 151–152

Pichardo, Ernesto, 96–97

pictographs, 59

Piegan, 29

pietism, 37, 270–272, 381

pilgrimage, 249–250, 309, 310–312, 318–322, [323], 323–325, [324], 329

Pilgrimage to Chimayó: Contemporary Portrait of a Living Tradition, 321–322

Pilgrim's Progress, 40

Pinchot, Gifford, 236

pipe, sacred, 47, 48, 120, 210, 271–278, [273], [274], [275]

Pipestone National Monument, **271–278,** [273], [274], [275]

Pitcairn, Robert, 252

Pitts, William Savage, 200–203, [201], [202]

"The Place of Brethren Colleges in Preparing Men and Women for Peace Leadership," 268

Plenty Coups, 420

Plum Street Temple, [278], **278–279**

pluralism, 107–108, 111, 117–118, 148

Pohlik-Lah/Karuk, 234, 235

Point, Nicholas, 248

Point Barrow, **279–282**

Polynesians, 189–193, [191], 312, 314

Pomo, 171–175, [172]

Popé, 222

Pope, John Russell, 124

post-and-lintel, 91–93, [92]

potlatch, 333

Powell, Adam Clayton, Jr., 5–7, **[6],** 333

Powell, Dr. Adam Clayton, Sr., 5, 6

The Power of Being Debt Free, 114

powwow, 249, 364–365

Prabhupada, Bhaktivedanta, 264–267, **[265]**

pragmatism, 195

prayer, 299

prayer chain, 244

prayer circle, 136

prayer niche, 402

Prayer Pilgrimage for Peace, 321

prayer room, 320

prayer school, 330

prayer shrine, 209

prayer stick, 256, 363

Prayer Tower, **282–285,** [283]-[284]
  vernacular prayer, 296
  pre-Raphaelite style, 149, 383–384

Presbyterianism, 57–59, 88–90, [89], [90], 150–152, [151], 220, 385,

390

Southern Presbyterians, 399–400, [400]. *See also* Korean Presbyterianism

primitivism, 91–93, [92]

prison reform, 267

Prodomus Philosophie Ratiocinantrio de Infinite, 411

Professional Grounds Management Society, 86

Promise Keepers, 57, 59, 108, 378

Prophecy Rock, 258

The Prophet Mohammad: The Ethical Prospect, 181

proselytism, 239–240, 412–413

Protect Kaho'Olawe 'Ohana, 190

Protestant Episcopal Church, 151, 379–380

Protestant Episcopal Foundation, 402–404

Protestantism, 11–15, 150, 254–255, [294], 322. *See also* African Methodist Episcopal, Amanism, Anglicanism, antifundamental-ism, Assembly of God, Baptist, Calvinism, Christian Church, Christian Science, Church of God, Congregationalism, Episcopalianism, evangelicalism, fundamentalism, Inspirationism, German Lutheranism, Huguenots, Lutheranism, Mennonites, Methodism, Metropolitan Community Church, Missouri Lutheranism, Moravianism, non-denominational, Pentacostalism, Presbyterianism, Puritanism, Quakerism, Reformed Church in America, revivalism, Shakers, Swedish Lutheranism, Waldensians

Pueblo, 83, 222, 257, 315, 319, 338, 361–365, [362]

Pueblo Bonito, 81–84, [82]

Puncah, 275

purification, 35, 193–195, [194], 386–388, [387]

Purísma Concepción Mission, 305

Puritan-Congregationalism, 200

Puritanism, 124, 142, 147, 148, 195, 267, 381

Pu'u Moiwi, 191

Qazwini, Hassan, 175–177, **[176]**

Qibla, 181

Quaker Relief Action, 269

Quakerism, 267–270, [268], [269], 325

Quasthoff, Donna, 317

Quetzalcoatl, 263

Quimby, Phineas Parkhurst, 142

Quiver, Elaine, 120

Rabbani, Shoghi Effendi, 32

Rabinowitz, Joseph, 107

Race Amity, 32

racism, 333–336, [334], 420

Radha, 164

Radhasoami theology, 369

Raggi, Gonippo, 67

Rainbow Bridge, **287–289,** [288]

Rainbow Coalition, 292

Rainbow Family Values, 74

Rain-in-the-Face, 46

Rajagopalan, Hema, 163

Rajneesh, Bhagwan Shree, 259–261, **[260]**

Rajneesh Foundation, 259–261, [260]

Rajneesh Times, 259

Raker, John E., 235–236

Rama, 162–164

Ramakrishna Math and Mission, 289

Ramakrishna-Vivekananda Center of New York, 213–214, **289–292, [290], [291]**

Ramayana, 163

Ramirez, Juan, 9

Ramji, Baba Harihar, 11

Ramona, 308

Randall, Dudley, 335

Ravalli, Antonio, 248

Rayfield, Wallace A., 333–334

Read the Word, 50

Reagan, Ronald, 10, 42, 143, 229

Reardon, Mary, 66

Reconstruction, 267

Red Cloud, 46

Redbird, Ida, 62

Redhouse, Ervin, 101, 102

Redmond, Margaret, 383–384

Reformation, Protestant, 36, 150

Reformed Church in America, 113

Reformed Society of Israelites, 187

La Regla Lucumi. *See* Santería

Reich, Steve, 299

Reilly, Paul, 67

reincarnation, 157, 291

Reinike, Charles H. III, 396

Relation du Voyage des Dames Ursulines de Rouen a la N'lle Orleans, 393

Religious Life at Harvard, 214

religious tolerance, 267, 294, 310

Religious Zionists of America, 34–35

Renaissance-Byzantine, 63–65, [64], 141, 143

Renewed Unitas Fratrum, 36

Renwick, James, 355–357, [356], **[357]**

retreats, 3–4, 23–25, 215–219, [216], [217], 237–238, [238], 343–346, [344], [345], 370–372, [371], [372], 391–392, [392]

"The Return of the Prodigal," 88–90, [89], [90]
Revere, Paul, 195, [250], 250–254, 414
revivalism, 42, 50–53, 219–222, **[220]**, 270–272, 384–385
Revivaltime Media Ministries, 378
Rhind, J. Massey, 381
Rhoads, Ross, 57
Rhode Island, 139–141, [140], 267, 373–376, [374], [375]
Richardson, Henry Hobson, 382–383, **[383]**
Richelieu, Cardinal Armand, 151
Ridges, Joseph H., 228
Riots and Ruins, 5
Riverside Church, 228, **293–295,** [293], [294]
Roberts, Oral, 282–285, **[283]**, [284]
Roberts, Richard, 283
Robertson, Jerry, 76
Robeson, Paul, 333
Robinson, Adah, 49
Rockefeller, John D., Sr., 140, 294
Rodef Shalom Biblical Botanical Garden, 298
Rodef Shalom Congregation, **295–299,** [296]
Roman Catholic Web Ring, 226
Romanelli, Giovanni Francesco, 72
Romanesque, 33, 39–40, [40], 63–65, [64], 70–73, [71], 206, 317, 347, 359
French Romanesque, 383
romanticism, 147–148
Roosevelt, Franklin D., 71
Roosevelt, Theodore, 111, 120, 287, 363, 366, 404
Rosati, Joseph, 63, 65
Rosen, Moishe, 107–108
Rosenberg, Hugh H., and Joan, 376–378, [377]
Rosicrucianism, 369
Roszak, Theodore, 85
Rothko, Mark, 299–301
Rothko Chapel, **299–301,** [300], [301]
The Rothko Chapel, 301
Rothko Chapel Oscar Romero Award, 300
Rouquette, Adrien Emmanuel, 393
Royal Canadian Mounted Police, 87
Roybal, Santiago, 314
Rule of Saint Benedict, 167–168, 170, 217, 224, 237–238, [238]
Rumi, 212
runes, 102–106, [103]
Rupanuga Vidypitha College, 266
Russell, Patricia Mousetrail, 246
Russian American Trading Company, 165, 171–175, [172]
Russian Chapel. *See* Holy Trinity Chapel of Fort Ross

Russian Orthodoxy, 165–167, [166], 171–175, [172]
Russian-American Fur Company, 32
Ruth, Larry, 80

Saarinen, Eero, [84], [85], 85–86
Saarinen, Gottlieb Eliel, 85
Sacred Buffalo Calf Pipe. *See* pipe, sacred
sacred circle, 209–211. *See also* medicine wheel
Sacred Earth Coalition, 135, 136
The Sacred Harp, 196
Sacred Land Film Project, 137
Sacred Twins and Spider Woman, 62
"Saga of the Waters," 176
Saint Bartholomew's Day Massacre, 151
Saint-Gaudens, Augustus, 384
Saiva Siddhanta Church, 309–314, [310], [311]
Sakarakaamche, 77
Salem College, 37
Salish, 209, 247
Salvador, Francis, 187
Samooh Relief Fund, 11
Sampson, Alexander H., 354
San Antonio de Padua Mission, 306
San Buenaventura Mission, 306
San Diego de Alcala Mission, 305, 306
San Estevan del Rey de España Mission, 9
San Fernando Rey Mission, 305
San Francisco Solano Mission, 305
San Gabriel Arcángel Mission, 305
San Gerónimo Church, 362, 364
San José de Guadalupe Mission, 305
San Juan Bautista Mission, **303–304,** 305
San Juan Capistrano Mission, **304–307,** [305], [306], 308
San Luis Obispo de Tolosa, 306, **307–309**
San Luis Rey Mission, 305
San Marga Iraivan Temple, **309–314,** [310], [311]
San Miguel Arcángel Mission, 305
San Miguel Mission. *See* Mission of San Miguel de Santa Fe
San Rafael Arcángel Mission, 305
sand painting, 62, 289, 338
Sangharakshita, Urgyen, 23–25, **[24]**
Sansom Street Church, 148
Santa Barbara Mission, 305, 308
Santa Clara de Asís, 306
Santa Cruz Mission, 305
Santa Fe Cathedral of St. Francis of Assisi, **314–318,** [315], [316]
Santa Inés Mission, 305
Santería, 95–97, [96], [97]

Santiago de Jalpan Mission, 306
Santo Niño de Atocha, 319, 320, 321
Santos, Susana, 136
El Santuário de Chimayó, 162, **318–322**
Sarutahiko, 387
Sarutahiko No OhKami, 193
satori, 117
Sawyer, Otis, 327
Saybrooke Confession of Faith, 251
Scalabrini Fathers, 395
Scanlan, Dolorosa, 170
The Scarlet Letter, 195
Schellenberg, Elizabeth, 410
Schiff, Jacob, 366
School of Evangelism, 42
Schuller, Robert, 113–115
Science and Health with Key to the Scriptures, 142, 144
Scientology, 97–99, [98]
Scientology Handbook, 99
scrying, 105
Sears, Vicki, 62
Seattle Times, 341
Second Baptist Church, **322–323**
Second Empire style, [315]
Second Great Awakening, 124, 220
Second Vatican Council, 217
sectarianism, 195
Sedna, 279–280
segregation, 7
Seixas, Moses, 373
seminary, 310, 390
Sen-no-Rikyu, 386
Seneca, 19
Sequatero, José, 263
Serra, Junípero, 303–304, 304–307, [305], **[306],** 318
Serrano, 305
Servetus, Michael, 147
Seton Hall University, 67
Seton Shrine, **323–325,** [323], [324]
seva, 197, 198
Seven Circuit Labyrinth, 106
"Seven Habits of Highly Biblical Churches," 111
The Seven Storey Mountain, 2, 261
Sewanee Review, 15
Seward, William H., 332
sexual revolution, 239
Seymour, William, 22, 271
Shaker Meeting House, **325–328,** [326], [327]
Shakers, 325–328, [326], [327]
"Shall the Fundamentalists Win?," 294
shamanism, 102–106, [103], 133–135, [134], 209–211, 222, 234, 236, 244–246, 247, 274–275, 277, 279–282, 287, 330–333, 417
Shamnoag, 319
Shango, 96
Shao-lin boxing, 117

Shariyat-Ki-Sugmad, 369
Sharkie, 287
Sharma, Indra, 313
Shasta, 234, 235
Shaw, Alfred, 32–33
Shaw, Anna Howard, 228–229
Shearit Israel, 187–188
Shih, Hung-I, 183
Shi'ites, 401
shilpi, 312
Shinob, 130
Shintoism, 193–195, [194], 386–388, [387]
Shiva, 165
Sh'ma, 188
Shoshone, 130, 209, 245, 417
    Sheepeater Shoshone, 419
Shuswap, 247
Shuttlesworth, Fred Lee, 333–334
Sierra Club, 120, 233, 235–236
Sierra Gorda missions, 306
signing
    for Native Americans, 249
    for the deaf, 203, 386
SiJohn, Henry, 249
Sikh Center of San Francisco Bay. *See* Gurdwara Sahib El Sobrante
Sikhism, **[157]**, 157–158
Siksika, 29
The Silent Life, 217
Silko, Leslie Marmon, 62
Silverman, Dr. Joseph, 365–366
Siminekem, 248–249
Simmons, B. J., 94
Simons, Menno, 153
Sinagua, 76
Sinawaf, 338–339
Sing, Wing, 183, 185
The Singing Master's Assistant, 196
Sioux, 32, 44–48, [45], 119, 120, 209, 273, 349, 417, 420
    Cheyenne River Sioux, 121
    Ehanktonwanna Sioux, 275
    Flandreau-Santee Sioux, 277
    Lakota, 29, 44–48, [45], 118–121, [119], 133–135, [134], 246, 273, 420
    Minneconjou Lakota, 273
    Teton Sioux, 46–47
    Teetonwan Sioux, 275
    Yankton Sioux, 46–47, 276, 277
sipapu, 61, 83, 258, 318, 361
Sisk-Franco, Caleen, 236
Sisseton, 276
Sisters of Benedict, **[329], 329–330**
Sisters of Charity, 67, [323], [324], 323–325, 379
Sisters of Charity of St. Vincent de Paul, 63, 65
Sisters of Loretto, 1, 203–205, [204], 316
Sisters of Mercy, 75, 76

Sisters of St. Joseph, 248
Sisters of St. Joseph of Carondelet, 63
Sisters of the Holy Family, 394
Sita, 164
Sitka, Battle of, 332
Sitka National Historical Park, **330–333**
Sitting Bull, 46, 210–211
Sityatki Revival Movement, 61
Siva, 312
Six-Day War, 107
Sixteenth Street Baptist Church, **333–336,** [334]
Skell, Chief, 109–110
slavery, 32, 40, 96, 127–129, 140, 142, 153, 222, 352, 362, 375, 394. *See also* Richard Allen, Emancipation Proclamation, Denmark Vesey, Fugitive Slave Act
Sleeping Ute Mountain, **336–339,** [337]
Smith, Alfred, 245
Smith, Chuck, 159
Smith, J. L., 273–274
Smith, Joseph, 227
Smithsonian Astrophysical Observatory, 232
Smithsonian Institution, 61, 85
Snake, Reuben, 244
Snake Indians, 417
Snoqualm, 339
Snoqualmie Falls, **339–342,** [340]
Snoqualmie Falls Preservation Project, 341
So, Huynh Phu, 199
Sobel, Ronald B.
Society for the Relief of Widows and Orphans of Clergymen, 379
Society of St. Vincent de Paul, 63, 65, 76
Society of the Holy Child Jesus, 393
Socinianism, 147
solstice, 102, 104, 123, 209, 210, 211, 255, 339
Sombath, Oudarone,
Sones, Daves, 281
The Song of Hiawatha, 276
Songs in the Night, 42
Sonoma Yoga Center. *See* Aghor Ashram
Sons of Liberty, 251–252
South Carolina, 131–133, 150–152, [151], 187–189, [188], 211–213, 215–219, [216], [217]
South Dakota, 44–48
Southern Christian Leadership Conference, 127, 334
Spain, 373, 375
Spangenberg, Augustus Gottlieb, 37
Spanish baroque, 78
Speedis, Walter, 136

Spider Rock, 59–60
Spider Woman, 59–60, 62–63, 83
Spider Woman's Granddaughters: Traditional Tales and Contemporary Writing by Native American Women, 62
The Spiral Dance by Starhawk, 104
Spiritual Wisdom of the Native Americans, 47
Spotswood, Alexander, 53
Spotted Bear, 417
Spotted Elk, Abraham, 245
Sprague, Lynn, 236
Squash Maidens, 364
Sri Sarveshwari Times, 11
Sri Siva Vishnu Temple, 163
Srimad Bhagavatam, 265
St. Alberic, 215
St. Benedict Center, **342–343**
St. Benedict of Nursia, 1, 170, **217,** 225–227, [226], 329, 342, 358
St. Benedict's Abbey and Retreat Center, **343–346,** [344], [345]
St. Bernard Abbey, 25–27
St. Elizabeth Anne Seton, 66, 318, 379
St. Fidelis Church, **346–348,** [347]
St. Francis of Assisi, 314–318, [315], [316], 356
St. Frances Xavier Cabrini, 66, 318, 357, 393
St. Ignatius of Loyola, 330
St. Innocent, 174
St. Isaac Jogues, 66, 318, 355
St. John of Capistrano, 306
St. John the Divine. *See* Cathedral Church of St. John the Divine
St. John's Abbey, **348–351**
St. John's Pottery, 351
St. Joseph, 205
St. Leo College, 171
St. Louis Cathedral, **351–355**
St. Lucia, 254, 255
St. Matthew's Church, Washington, D. C., 316
St. Miguel Febres Cordero, 318
St. Patrick's Cathedral, 216, **355–357,** [356], [357]
St. Robert of Molesme, 215
St. Stephen Harding, 215
St. Ursula, 393
St. Vincent's Archabbey and College, 167
St. Walburga, [329]
Stamp Act, 267
Standing Bear, Henry, 47–48
Standing Bear, Luther, 133
Stanley, William J. III, 129
Status, Carol, 120
Steel, William Gladstone, 110–111
Steere, Douglas Van, **269**
Stensgar, Ernie, 249–250
"Steps to the City," 335

Stevenson, James, 61
Sthapati, Vaidyanathan Ganapati, 312
Stokes, John F. G., 190–191
Stone Woman, 131
Storm, Patricia, 121
storytelling, 30, 77, 103, 119, 123, 249, 333, 361
Stover, George and Sharon, 412–413
Straus, Oscar S., 366
Strawbridge, Robert, 205
Streams in the Desert, 413
Strong, Ted, 244
Subiaco Abbey, **357–360,** [358]
Subramuniyaswami, Sivaya, 309–314, [310], **[311]**
suburbanism, 279, 377
The Suffolk Harmony, 196
suffragism, 228–229
Sufism, 198, 212
Suggs, Charlene, 104
Sugmad, 369
Sumner, James, 139
Sunday, Billy, 220
The Sunday Service of the Methodists in North America, 206
Sun-do, 118
Sunim, Sahn Bul, 118
Sunnites, 401
surrealism, 90, 331–332
suttee, 157
Sutton, Jim, 110
Suzuki, Daisetz Teitaro, 117
Swaggart, Jimmy, 283
Swarthmore College, 269
sweat lodge, 45, 101, 137, 274
Swedenborg, Emanuel, 410–411, **[411]**
Swedenborgianism, 409–412, [410], [411]
Swedish Lutheranism, 254–255
Swedish Missionary Society, 254
Sweet Auburn, 39–41, 127–129, [128]
Sweet Medicine, 46
syncretism, 30–33, 96, 118, 148, 260, 361–365, [362], 368–370, [369], 389–391, [390], [391]. See also Eck, non-denominationalism, Swedenborgianism, transdenominationalism, Unitarianism
Syria Mosque, 297

Taft, William Howard, 258, 287
Taivotsi, 417
Takelma, 109
Tall Bull, Bill, 210
Tall House People, 83
Tall Mountain, Mary, 62
Tamanous, 235
Tanaina, 173
The Tantrik Path, 4
Taoism, 102–106, [103], 117. See also Dao-Confucianism

Taos Pueblo, 361–365, [362]
Taos Rebellion, 362–363
Tápis, Estévan, 303
tarot, 102–106, [103], 121, 260
Taste of Amana, A, 20
Tawa, 61
taxation, 97–99
Taylor, Zachary, 353
tea ceremony, 198, 386
Teatro Campesino, El, 304
Tehillim, 299
Tekakwitha, Kateri, 318
Televangelism, 284, 322, 378, 382
Telugu Association of Greater Chicago, 162
Temple Beth El, Birmingham, 334
Temple Beth Elohim. See Kahal Kadosh Beth Elohim
Temple Emanu-El, **365–368,** [366]
Temple of Eck, 368–370, [369]
A Temple Treasury: The Judaica Collection of Congregation Emanu-El of the City of New York, 368
"Ten Vital Tenets, a Formal Statement of the Re-awakening in the New Community," 18
Tennessee, 15–17, [16], 34–35, 94–95, [95]
Terrorism, 384–386
Tewa, 8, 61, 318, 319
Tewaquaptewa, 257
Texas, 73–74, 133–135, [134], 183–185, [184], [185], 299–301, [300], [301], 322–323
Texas Buddhist Association, 183–185, [184], [185]
Texas Buddhist College, 184
Thant, U, 391
"That Which Might Have Been: Birmingham, 1963," 335
Theology Explained and Defended, 124
"Thinking Aloud," 35
third-world religion, 95–97, [96], [97]
Afro-Caribbean religion, 95–96, [97]. See also Africa, Central America
"30 Days of Gathering Around Jesus," 108
Thirty-Nine Articles of Religion, 206
This Land Is Home to Me, 237
Thom, Charlie, 236
Thomas Merton Center, 2
Thorncrown Chapel, **370–372,** [371], [372]
Thurmond, Strom, 42
Tiffany, Louis Comfort, 149
Tiffany glass, 33
Tigerman, Stanley, **[345]**
The Tiger's Fang, 368
Tipai, 305
Tiwa, 8, 319, 361–365, [362]

Tlaxcala, 222
Tlingit, 173, 330–333
To Build a Church, 80
Together in the Harvest, 52–53
Toineeta, Yor Yellowtail, 420
Tollefson, Ken, 341
Tomlinson, A. J., 22
Tong Il Movement, 389
Tonkawa, 134
Too Much Air To Breathe: Lao Buddhist Community and Healing, 409
Torkillus, Reorus, 254
Torrini, Rudolph, 342–343
totemism, 330–333
tourism, religious, 25–27, [16], 44–48, [45], [47], 59–63, [60], 76–78, 81–84, [82], 94–95, [95], 118–120, [119], 129–131, [130], 133–135, [134], 135–137, 155–157, [156], 168–170, [169], 175–177, [176], 203–205, [204], 209–211, 219–222, [220], 287–289, [288], 304–307, [305], [306], 307–309, 330–333, 361–365, [362], 370–372, [371], [372], 410–412, 417–420, [418]
Touro, Abraham and Judah, 373
Touro, Isaac de Abraham, 373–376
Touro Synagogue, 196, 373–376, [374], [375]
Tower of Hope, 113
Towering Hand People, 289
Towers of Heavenly Recipes, 348
Town, Ithiel, 228
Toypurina, 305
Tracenet on Unificationism, 390
traditionalism, 187
trance, 123, 264
transdenominationalism, 108
Trappist Abbey. See Our Lady of Guadalupe Trappist Abbey
Trappists, 1–4, [3], 215–219, [216], [217], 224, 261–262, [262]
Treatise on Four Doctrines, 411
Treaty of Guadalupe Hidalgo, 227, 257, 338
Treaty of Point Elliott, 340–341
Tri-County Assembly of God, **376–378,** [377]
Trinity Church, 149, **378–382,** [379]
Trinity Episcopal Church, **382–384,** [383]
Trinity News, 381
Triumph Church and New Life Christian Fellowship, **384–386**
Trouillard, Philip, 150
True Solitude, 2
Tsimshian, 330–333
Tsistsista, 48
Tsosie, Sue, 21
Tsubaki America News, 388

Tsubaki America Shrine, 193, **386–388,** [387]
Tsubaki Grand Shrine, 194, 386
Tudor style, 415
Tulley, Earl, 101
Tunica-Biloxi, 175, 176
Tuscarora, 420
Tutu, Desmond, 382, 405
Twenty-Four Rules of True Godliness, 18
Twisted Earth, 247–248
Twitchell, John Paul, 368

Ukanomita-mano-kami, 3878
Umatilla, 135, 136–137
Umpqua, 109, 234, 235
Uncegila, 44
Underground Railroad, 267, 375
Unification Church, **389–391, [390], [391]**
Union of American Hebrew Congregations, 188, 278
Union Prayer Book for Jewish Worship, 87, 278, 298
Unitarian Universalists, 149, 194
Unitarianism, 30, 147–150, [148], 195–196, [196], 414
New World Unitarianism, 147
United Church of Christ, 293–295, [293], [294], 414
United Farm Workers, 304
United House of Prayer, 22
United Nations, 6
United Pentecostal Church, 271
United Society of Believers in Christ's Second Appearing, 325–328, [326], [327]
United States Commission on International Religious Freedom, 33
United States Supreme Court, 96–97, 245
United Way, 298
Unity Rides, 210
Universal Declaration of Human Rights, 48
Universal Peace Buddha Temple of New York, **391–392,** [392]
Universalist Church, 32
University of Arizona, 232–234, [233]
University of Pittsburgh, 297
University of the South, 15–17
University of Toronto, 234
University of Vermont, 91
Unspeakable: Buddhism and the Gay News, 24
Upanishads, 291
Upjohn, Richard, 380
urbanism, 220, 278–279, [278], 293–295, 295–299, [296]
Ursa Major, 119
Ursuline Convent, **394–396,** [394]
Ursulines, 352, [394], 394–396

Utah, 129–131, [130], [227] , 227–229, [228], 287–289, [288]
Ute, 61, 130, 167, 257, 336–339, [337], 420
Mountain Ute, 338
Southern Ute, 338
Uto-Aztecan, 257, 336
Weenuche, 336, [337]
White Mesa Ute, 288
utopianism, 17–20, 81, 227–228

Valdes, Peter, 399–400, **[400]**
Valdez, Luis Miguel, 304
Valenzuela, Diana, 233–234
Vanderlip, Narcissa Cox, 410
Vargas, Diego de, 315, 317
Vatican II, 87, 99–100, [100], 342
Vaughan, Henry, 72
Vedanta Society, 289–292, [290], [291]
Vedas, 289–292, 311
vegetarianism, 24, 199, 219, 409
Veniaminov, Father Ioann, 73
Venkateshwara, 164
Verity, Simon, 71
Vermont, 90–93, [92]
vernacular architecture, 25–27
Vesey, Denmark, 132–133
Victorian style, 149
Vida de Padre Junípero Serra, 306
Vietnam, 199–200
Vietnam War, 200, 213, 245, 267–268, 292
Vietnamese Buddhist Youth Association in the United States, 200
Vinayaka, 162–164
Vincentians, 65
Vinegar Bible, 253
Vineyard Christian Fellowship, 108
Viollet-le-Duc, 203
Virginia, 53–55, [54], 168–170, [169], 408–410, 421–422
Vishnu, 163–164
vision quest, 29–30, 45, 106, 135, 137, 274
Vivekenanda, Swami, 289–292, [290], **[291]**
von Wicht, John, 66
Voodoo. *See* obeah
Voodoo Realist, 397
Voodoo Spiritual Temple, **397**
Voting Rights Act, 335
A Vow to Cherish, 240
Voyat, Gilbert, 44
Vulgate Bible, 93

Waddell, John Henry, 335
Wagner, E. Glenn, 57
Wahpeton, 276
Wakan Tanka. *See* Great Spirit
Wakinyan, 44
Wald, Lillian D., 365–336, **[366]**

Waldensian Presbyterian Church, **399–400, [400]**
Waldensians, 253, 399–400, [400]
"The Wales Window for Alabama," 335
Wall, Aelred, 224
Wallace, George Corley, 334–335
Walsh, A. L., 335
Walsh, Emmett Michael, 217
Walsh, Thomas J., 67
Walters, Anna Lee, 62
Walulatuma, Sylvia, 136
Ward, C. M., 378
Ward, E. C., 51
Wardley, James and Jane, 325
Ware, Henry, 147, 195
Warm Springs Indians, 135, 136–137
Warner, C. L., 188–189
Warren, Joseph, 252
Washington, Booker T., 333
Washington, George, 147, 151, 253, 373, 376, 378, 379–380, 404
Washington, Martha, 151, 378
Washington, D.C., 80–81, 401–402, 402–406, [403]
Washington Islamic Mosque and Cultural Center, **401–402**
Washington National Cathedral, **402–406,** [403]
Washington state, 193–195, [194], 199–200, 339–342, [340]
Washita River massacre, 46, 120
Wat Carolina Buddhajakra Vanaram, **406–408**
Wat Lao Buddhavong, **408–410**
Watchman Fellowship, 390
The Waters of Siloe, 2
The Watsons Go to Birmingham—1963, 335–336
The Way of the Kami, 387
Way of the Saints, 96
The Way to Rainy Mountain, 120
Wayfarers' Chapel, [410], **409–412,** [411]
Weatherwax Brothers Quartet, 202
Webb, Thomas, 205
Weddell, James R., 48
Weissner, Andrew, 236
Welch, Franklin, 141
Welch, Todd, 120
Wellspring Church & Christian Center, **412–413**
We're Heaven Bound!: Portrait of a Black Sacred Drama, 41
Wesley, Charles, 37, 205–207, [206], [207], 252
Wesley, John, 22, 37, 205–207, **[206]**
West Parish Meetinghouse, **413–415**
West Virginia, 264–267, [265]
whaling, 279–282
"What Do the Muslims Want?," 230
Wheelwright, Mary Cabot, 83

"When Jesus Wept," 196
White, B. F., 196
White Buffalo Calf Woman, 120, 210, 273, 420
White Cloud, Johnny, 245
White, Edward B., 150
White, Stanford, 383
Whitefield, George, 220
Wicca, 102–106, [103], 149
Wiedorn, William S., 354
Wijiji, 83
Williams, Alfred Daniel, 127
Williams, Roger, 139
Williamsburg, 53–55, [54]
Williamsburg, Battle of, 54
Wilson, Edith Galt, 404–405
Wilson, Henry, 72
Wilson, James Keys, 279
Wilson, John, 245
Wilson, Woodrow, 404–405
Wimmer, Boniface, 167
Windham, Cornelius, 333–334
Windows on Henry Street, 366
Windrom, Tom, 94
Winnebago, 244
The Winning Walk, 322
Winter, Lumen Martin, 13, 14
Winthrop, John, 195
Winthrop, Robert, 136
Wintun, 29, 234, 236
Wiping of Tears/Mending the Sacred Hoop Ride, 210
Wisconsin, 102–106, [103], 343–346, [344], [345]
Wise, Isaac Mayer, [278], 278–279, 296, 366
Wisteria Campground. *See* Circle Sanctuary
witch hunts, 400
Witchcraft Today, 103–104
Withers, Frederick Clark, 381
Witzeman, Bob, 234
Wizard Island, 108–111, [109]

Wolf, Henry Van, 114
Wolpert, Ludwig Y., 13
women's rights, 199. *See also* civil rights, feminism, male-centered worship
Woodcock, S. S., 221
Woodhouse, 267
Wopila Ride, 210
World Aflame, 42
World Conference on Faith and Order, 380
World Council of Churches, 363, 380
World Ecumenical Conference, 41
World Emergency Fund, 42
World Evangelistic Conference, 283
World Fellowship of Buddhism, 407
World Gospel Feast, 22
World Heritage List, 363
World War I, 26, 93, 213, 366
World War II, 7, 71, 146, 179, 191, 214, 229, 281, 292, 316, 320, 344, 349, 366, 380, 387, 410
Wounded Knee massacre, 46–47, 210
Wovoka, 46–47
Wren, Christopher, 250
Wright, Charles F., 99–100
Wright, Frank Lloyd, 372, 410, 411, 412
Wright, Lloyd, 409–412, [410], [411]
Wright, Lucy, 326
Wyatt, Greg, 72
Wyden, Ron, 135, 137
Wyoming, 118–121, [119], 209–211, 245, 417–420, [418]
Wysocki, Matthew, 144–145

Xavier, Francis, 393

Yakima, 135, 136, 244
Yakut, 173
Yale University, 123–125, [124]
Yamamoto, Yukitaka, 193–195, [194], 386–388, [387]

Yei, 82–83
Yellowstone, 417–420, [418]
yeshivahs, 108
Yeshua, 107–108
yoga, 10–11, 23–25, 311, 313
  abhidhyan yoga, 4
  bhakti yoga, 290
  hatha yoga, 198
  jnana yoga, 290
  kharma yoga, 198, 290
  mantra yoga,
  nonmeditational yoga, 4–5
  raja yoga, 290
  tantric yoga, 4–5
Yorktown, Battle of, 56
Yoruba, 96
Youkioma, 257–258
Young, Andrew, 301, 334, 336
Young, Brigham, 227, 228
Young, Theodore, 75
Youth for Christ, 42
Yureerachen, 247

Zah, Peterson, 102
Zaldivar, Juan de, 9
Zaldivar, Vincente de, 9
Zarathustra, Asho, 422
Zen. *See* Buddhism
Zephier, Mitchell, 48
Zettler, Franz, 69
Ziolkowski, Korczak, 47–48
Zion Canyon, 131
zionism, 35
Zoettl, Joseph, 25–27
Zoroastrian Association of Metropolitan Washington, **421–422**
Zoroastrianism, 211, 421–422
Zuñi, 8, 9, 317, 337
Zuñi-Acoma Trail, 8
Zwingli, Ulrich, 414